Analysis of Investments

AND

Management of Portfolios

9TH EDITION

Analysis of Investments

· · · A N D · · ·

Management of Portfolios

9TH EDITION

Keith C. Brown

UNIVERSITY OF TEXAS AT AUSTIN

Frank K. Reilly

UNIVERSITY OF NOTRE DAME

SOUTH-WESTERN
CENGAGE Learning™

Australia · Brazil · Japan · Korea · Mexico · Singapore · Spain · United Kingdom · United States

SOUTH-WESTERN
CENGAGE Learning™

**Analysis of Investments and
Management of Portfolios, Ninth Edition**

Keith C. Brown and Frank K. Reilly

Editorial Director: Jack W. Calhoun

Editor-in-Chief: Alex von Rosenberg

Executive Editor: Mike Reynolds

Developmental Editor: Margaret Kubale

Marketing Coordinator: Suellen Ruttkay

Marketing Manager: Nathan Anderson

Content Project Manager:
   Jacquelyn K Featherly

Media Editor: Scott Fidler

Manufacturing Coordinator: Kevin Kluck

Senior Editorial Assistant: Adele Scholtz

Production House/Compositor: Cadmus/KGL

Senior Art Director: Michelle Kunkler

Cover Images: © Steve Digital Vision/
   Getty Images

For product information and technology assistance, contact us at
Cengage Learning Customer & Sales Support, 1-800-354-9706
For permission to use material from this text or product,
submit all requests online at **www.cengage.com/permissions**
Further permissions questions can be emailed to
permissionrequest@cengage.com

ExamView® and ExamView Pro® are registered trademarks of FSCreations, Inc. Windows is a registered trademark of the Microsoft Corporation used herein under license. Macintosh and Power Macintosh are registered trademarks of Apple Computer, Inc. used herein under license.

Library of Congress Control Number: 2008934727

Student Edition ISBN 13: 978-0-324-65842-2

Student Edition ISBN 10: 0-324-65842-7

Cengage Learning International Offices

Asia
cengageasia.com
tel: (65) 6410 1200

Australia/New Zealand
cengage.com.au
tel: (61) 3 9685 4111

Brazil
cengage.com.br
tel: (011) 3665 9900

India
cengage.co.in
tel: (91) 11 30484837/38

Latin America
cengage.com.mx
tel: +52 (55) 1500 6000

UK/Europe/Middle East/Africa
cengage.co.uk
tel: (44) 207 067 2500

Represented in Canada by Nelson Education, Ltd.
nelson.com
tel: (416) 752 9100/(800) 668 0671

For product information: **international.cengage.com**
Visit your local office: **international.cengage.com/regions**
Visit our corporate website: **cengage.com**

Printed in Canada
1 2 3 4 5 6 7 12 11 10 09 08

To Sheryl, Alexander, and Andrew
who make it all worthwhile

K.C.B.

To my best friend & wife,
Therese,
and the greatest gifts and
sources of our happiness,
Frank K. III, Charlotte, and Lauren
Clarence R., II, Michelle, Sophie, and Cara
Therese B., and Denise
Edgar B., Lisa, Kayleigh, Madison J. T., and Francesca

F.K.R.

···· BRIEF CONTENTS ····

Part 1: The Investment Background, 1
1   The Investment Setting, 3
2   The Asset Allocation Decision, 31
3   Selecting Investments in a Global Market, 61
4   Organization and Functioning of Securities Markets, 91
5   Security-Market Indexes, 127

Part 2: Developments in Investment Theory, 149
6   Efficient Capital Markets, 151
7   An Introduction to Portfolio Management, 181
8   An Introduction to Asset Pricing Models, 205
9   Multifactor Models of Risk and Return, 237

Part 3: Valuation Principles and Practices, 263
10   Analysis of Financial Statements, 265
11   An Introduction to Security Valuation, 317

Part 4: Analysis and Management of Common Stocks, 355
12   Macroanalysis and Microvaluation of the Stock Market, 357
13   Industry Analysis, 407
14   Company Analysis and Stock Valuation, 453
15   Technical Analysis, 517
16   Equity Portfolio Management Strategies, 539

Part 5: Analysis and Management of Bonds, 577
17   Bond Fundamentals, 579
18   The Analysis and Valuation of Bonds, 609
19   Bond Portfolio Management Strategies, 677

Part 6: Derivative Security Analysis, 725
20   An Introduction to Derivative Markets and Securities, 727
21   Forward and Futures Contracts, 763
22   Option Contracts, 801
23   Swap Contracts, Convertible Securities, and Other Embedded Derivatives, 847

Part 7: Specification and Evaluation of Asset Management, 889
24   Professional Money Management, Alternative Assets, and Industry Ethics, 891
25   Evaluation of Portfolio Performance, 937

Appendixes A–D, 985

Comprehensive References List, 995

Glossary, 1013

Index, 1029

· · · · CONTENTS · · · ·

PART 1: THE INVESTMENT BACKGROUND 1

Chapter 1: The Investment Setting 3

What Is an Investment? 3

Investment Defined 4

Measures of Return and Risk 5

*Measures of Historical Rates of Return 5,
Computing Mean Historical Returns 7,
Calculating Expected Rates of Return 9,
Measuring the Risk of Expected Rates of Return
12, Risk Measures for Historical Returns 13*

Determinants of Required Rates of Return 14

*The Real Risk-Free Rate 15, Factors Influencing
the Nominal Risk-Free Rate (NRFR) 15, Risk
Premium 17, Risk Premium and Portfolio
Theory 19, Fundamental Risk versus Systematic
Risk 20, Summary of Required Rate of Return 20*

Relationship between Risk and Return 20

*Movements along the SML 21, Changes in the
Slope of the SML 21, Changes in Capital Market
Conditions or Expected Inflation 23, Summary
of Changes in the Required Rate of Return 23*

Chapter 1 Appendix: Computation of Variance
and Standard Deviation 28

Chapter 2: The Asset Allocation Decision 31

Individual Investor Life Cycle 32

*The Preliminaries 32, Investment Strategies Over
an Investor's Lifetime 32, Life Cycle Investment
Goals 34*

The Portfolio Management Process 35

The Need For a Policy Statement 36

*Understand and Articulate Realistic Investor
Goals 36, Standards for Evaluating Portfolio
Performance 37, Other Benefits 38*

Input to the Policy Statement 38

*Investment Objectives 39, Investment
Constraints 42*

Constructing the Policy Statement 47

*General Guidelines 47, Some Common
Mistakes 47*

The Importance of Asset Allocation 48

*Investment Returns after Taxes and Inflation 50,
Returns and Risks of Different Asset Classes 51,
Asset Allocation Summary 52*

Chapter 2 Appendix: Objectives and Constraints
of Institutional Investors 56

Chapter 3: Selecting Investments in a Global Market 61

The Case for Global Investments 62

*Relative Size of U.S. Financial Markets 63, Rates
of Return on U.S. and Foreign Securities 64, Risk
of Combined Country Investments 64*

Global Investment Choices 69

*Fixed-Income Investments 69, International
Bond Investing 73, Equity Instruments 73,
Special Equity Instruments: Options 75, Futures
Contracts 76, Investment Companies 76, Real
Estate 78, Low-Liquidity Investments 79*

Historical Risk–Returns on Alternative Investments 80

*World Portfolio Performance 80, Art and
Antiques 82, Real Estate 84*

Chapter 3 Appendix: Covariance 89

Chapter 4: Organization and Functioning of Securities Markets 91

What Is a Market? 92

*Characteristics of a Good Market 92, Decimal
Pricing 93, Organization of the Securities
Market 93*

Primary Capital Markets 94

*Government Bond Issues 94, Municipal Bond
Issues 94, Corporate Bond Issues 94, Corporate
Stock Issues 95, Private Placements and Rule
144A 96,*

Secondary Financial Markets 97

*Why Secondary Markets Are Important 97,
Secondary Bond Markets 97, Financial Futures
98, Secondary Equity Markets 98*

Classification of U.S. Secondary Equity Markets 101

*Primary Listing Markets 101, Regional
Stock Exchanges 107, The Third Market 107,
Alternative Trading Systems (ATSs) 107*

Detailed Analysis of Exchange Markets 108

Exchange Membership 108, Types of Orders 108, Exchange Market Makers 113, New Trading Systems 115, Innovations for Competition 116, Future Trading Techniques and Exchange Mergers 117

Chapter 4 Appendix: Characteristics of Developed and Developing Markets around the World   121

Chapter 5: Security-Market Indexes   127

Uses of Security-Market Indexes   128

Differentiating Factors in Constructing Market Indexes   128

The Sample 128, Weighting Sample Members 129, Computational Procedure 129

Stock-Market Indexes   129

Price-Weighted Index 129, Value-Weighted Index 131, Unweighted Index 131, Style Indexes 133, Global Equity Indexes 133

Bond-Market Indexes   137

U.S. Investment-Grade Bond Indexes 139, High-Yield Bond Indexes 139, Global Government Bond Indexes 139

Composite Stock-Bond Indexes   139

Comparison of Indexes over Time   142

Correlations between Monthly Equity Price Changes 142, Correlations between Monthly Bond Indexes 142, Mean Annual Security Returns and Risk 143

Chapter 5 Appendix: Stock-Market Indexes   146

PART 2: DEVELOPMENTS IN INVESTMENT THEORY   149

Chapter 6: Efficient Capital Markets   151

Why Should Capital Markets Be Efficient?   152

Alternative Efficient Market Hypotheses   153

Weak-Form Efficient Market Hypothesis 153, Semistrong-Form Efficient Market Hypothesis 153, Strong-Form Efficient Market Hypothesis 153

Tests and Results of Efficient Market Hypotheses   154

Weak-Form Hypothesis: Tests and Results 154, Semistrong-Form Hypothesis: Tests and Results 156, Strong-Form Hypothesis: Tests and Results 166

Behavioral Finance   170

Explaining Biases 170, Fusion Investing 171

Implications of Efficient Capital Markets   172

Efficient Markets and Technical Analysis 172, Efficient Markets and Fundamental Analysis 172, Efficient Markets and Portfolio Management 174

Chapter 7: An Introduction to Portfolio Management   181

Some Background Assumptions   181

Risk Aversion 182, Definition of Risk 182

Markowitz Portfolio Theory   182

Alternative Measures of Risk 183, Expected Rates of Return 183, Variance (Standard Deviation) of Returns for an Individual Investment 184, Variance (Standard Deviation) of Returns for a Portfolio 185, Standard Deviation of a Portfolio 189, A Three-Asset Portfolio 196, Estimation Issues 197, The Efficient Frontier 197, The Efficient Frontier and Investor Utility 199

Chapter 7 Appendix:

A. Proof That Minimum Portfolio Variance Occurs with Equal Weights When Securities Have Equal Variance   203

B. Derivation of Weights That Will Give Zero Variance When Correlation Equals –1.00   204

Chapter 8: An Introduction to Asset Pricing Models   205

Capital Market Theory: An Overview   205

Background for Capital Market Theory 206, Developing the Capital Market Line 207, Risk, Diversification, and the Market Portfolio 210, Investing with the CML: An Example 213

The Capital Asset Pricing Model   214

A Conceptual Development of the CAPM 215, The Security Market Line 216

Relaxing the Assumptions   222

Differential Borrowing and Lending Rates 222, Zero-Beta Model 223, Transaction Costs 224, Heterogeneous Expectations and Planning Periods 225, Taxes 225

Additional Empirical Tests of the CAPM   226

Stability of Beta 226, Relationship between Systematic Risk and Return 226, Summary of CAPM Risk–Return Empirical Results 228

The Market Portfolio: Theory versus Practice   228

Chapter 9: Multifactor Models of Risk and Return   237

Arbitrage Pricing Theory   238

Using the APT 240, Security Valuation with the APT: An Example 241, Empirical Tests of the APT 243

Multifactor Models and Risk Estimation   246

Multifactor Models in Practice 247, Estimating Risk in a Multifactor Setting: Examples 251

PART 3: VALUATION PRINCIPLES AND PRACTICES   263

Chapter 10: Analysis of Financial Statements   265

Major Financial Statements   266

Generally Accepted Accounting Principles 266, Balance Sheet 266, Income Statement 267, Statement of Cash Flows 267, Measures of Cash Flow 269, Purpose of Financial Statement Analysis 271

Analysis of Financial Ratios   271

Importance of Relative Financial Ratios 271

Computation of Financial Ratios   272

Common Size Statements 273

Evaluating Internal Liquidity   275

Internal Liquidity Ratios 275, Inventory Turnover 277

Evaluating Operating Performance   278

Operating Efficiency Ratios 278, Operating Profitability Ratios 280

Risk Analysis   286

Business Risk 286, Financial Risk 288, Proportion of Debt (Balance Sheet) Ratios 291, Earnings and Cash Flow Coverage Ratios 293, Cash Flow–Outstanding Debt Ratios 295, External Market Liquidity Risk 296

Analysis of Growth Potential   297

Importance of Growth Analysis 297, Determinants of Growth 297

Comparative Analysis of Ratios   299

Internal Liquidity 299, Operating Performance 299, Risk Analysis 301, Growth Analysis 301

Analysis of Non-U.S. Financial Statements   301

The Quality of Financial Statements   301

Balance Sheet 302, Income Statement 302, Footnotes 302

The Value of Financial Statement Analysis   302

Specific Uses of Financial Ratios   303

Stock Valuation Models 303, Estimating the Ratings on Bonds 304, Predicting Insolvency (Bankruptcy) 305, Limitations of Financial Ratios 305

Chapter 11: An Introduction to Security Valuation   317

An Overview of the Valuation Process   318

Why a Three-Step Valuation Process?   319

General Economic Influences 319, Industry Influences 321, Company Analysis 321, Does the Three-Step Process Work? 322

Theory of Valuation   322

Stream of Expected Returns (Cash Flows) 323, Required Rate of Return 323, Investment Decision Process: A Comparison of Estimated Values and Market Prices 323

Valuation of Alternative Investments   324

Valuation of Bonds 324, Valuation of Preferred Stock 325, Approaches to the Valuation of Common Stock 326, Why and When to Use the Discounted Cash Flow Valuation Approach 327, Why and When to Use the Relative Valuation Techniques 327, Discounted Cash Flow Valuation Techniques 328, Infinite Period DDM and Growth Companies 332, Valuation with Temporary Supernormal Growth 333, Present Value of Operating Free Cash Flows 335, Present Value of Free Cash Flows to Equity 336

Relative Valuation Techniques   336

Earnings Multiplier Model 336, The Price/Cash Flow Ratio 339, The Price/Book Value Ratio 339, The Price/Sales Ratio 340, Implementing the Relative Valuation Technique 340

Estimating the Inputs: The Required Rate of Return and the Expected Growth Rate of Valuation Variables   341

Required Rate of Return (k) 341, Estimating the Required Return for Foreign Securities 343, Expected Growth Rates 345, Estimating Dividend Growth for Foreign Stocks 348

Chapter 11 Appendix: Derivation of Constant Growth Dividend Discount Model (DDM)   352

PART 4: ANALYSIS AND MANAGEMENT OF COMMON STOCKS   355

Chapter 12: Macroanalysis and Microvaluation of the Stock Market   357

The Components of Market Analysis   357

Macromarket Analysis 358, Economic Activity and Security Markets 358, Economic Series and Stock Prices 359, The Cyclical Indicator Approach 359, Monetary Variables, the Economy, and Stock Prices 363, Money Supply and the Economy 363, Money Supply and Stock Prices 364, Monetary Policy and Stock Returns 364, Inflation, Interest Rates, and Security Prices 364, Analysis of World Security Markets 367

Microvaluation Analysis   367

Applying the DDM Valuation Model to the Market 368, Market Valuation Using the Free Cash Flow to Equity (FCFE) Model 374

Valuation Using the Earnings Multiplier Approach 377

Two-Part Valuation Procedure 377, Importance of Both Components of Value 377

Estimating Expected Earnings per Share 378

Estimating Gross Domestic Product 380, Estimating Sales per Share for a Market Series 380, Alternative Estimates of Corporate Net Profits 382, Estimating Aggregate Operating Profit Margin 382, Estimating Depreciation Expense 386, Estimating Interest Expense 388, Estimating the Tax Rate 389, Calculating Earnings per Share: An Example 389

Estimating the Stock Market Earnings Multiplier 392

*Determinants of the Earnings Multiplier 393, Estimating the Required Rate of Return (**k**) 393, Estimating the Growth Rate of Dividends (**g**) 393, Estimating the Dividend-Payout Ratio (**D**$_1$/**E**$_1$) 394, Estimating an Earnings Multiplier: An Example 395, Calculating an Estimate of the Value for the Market Series 398, Using Other Relative Valuation Ratios 398*

Microvaluation of World Markets 401

Chapter 13: Industry Analysis **407**

Why Do Industry Analysis? 408

Cross-Sectional Industry Performance 408, Industry Performance over Time 409, Performance of the Companies within an Industry 409, Differences in Industry Risk 410, Summary of Research on Industry Analysis 410, Industry Analysis Process 410

The Business Cycle and Industry Sectors 411

Inflation 412, Interest Rates 413, International Economics 413, Consumer Sentiment 413

Structural Economic Changes and Alternative Industries 413

Demographics 413, Lifestyles 414, Technology 414, Politics and Regulations 414

Evaluating the Industry Life Cycle 415

Analysis of Industry Competition 416

Competition and Expected Industry Returns 417

Estimating Industry Rates of Return 418

Valuation Using the Reduced Form DDM 419, Industry Valuation Using the Free Cash Flow to Equity (FCFE) Model 426

Industry Analysis Using the Relative Valuation Approach 428

The Earnings Multiple Technique 428

Other Relative Valuation Ratios 440

The Price/Book Value Ratio 440, The Price/ Cash Flow Ratio 440, The Price/Sales Ratio 443, Summary of Industry/Market Ratios 443

Global Industry Analysis 444

Chapter 13 Appendix:

A. Preparing an Industry Analysis: What Is an Industry? 450

Characteristics to Study 450, Factors in Industry Analysis 450, Sources of Industry Information 451

B. Insights on Analyzing Industry ROAs 451

Insights on Industry ROAs 451

Chapter 14: Company Analysis and Stock Valuation **453**

Company Analysis versus Stock Valuation 454

Growth Companies and Growth Stocks 454, Defensive Companies and Stocks 455, Cyclical Companies and Stocks 455, Speculative Companies and Stocks 455, Value versus Growth Investing 456

Economic, Industry, and Structural Links to Company Analysis 456

Economic and Industry Influences 456, Structural Influences 456

Company Analysis 457

Firm Competitive Strategies 457, Focusing a Strategy 458, SWOT Analysis 459, Some Lessons from Lynch 460, Tenets of Warren Buffett 460

Estimating Intrinsic Value 461

Present Value of Dividends 461, Present Value of Dividends Model (DDM) 465, Present Value of Free Cash Flow to Equity 466, Present Value of Operating Free Cash Flow 467, Relative Valuation Ratio Techniques 470

Estimating Company Earnings per Share 470

Company Sales Forecast 473, Estimating the Company Profit Margin 475

Walgreen Co.'s Competitive Strategies 475

The Internal Performance 476, Importance of Quarterly Estimates 478

Estimating Company Earnings Multipliers 478

Macroanalysis of the Earnings Multiple 480, Microanalysis of the Earnings Multiplier 480, Making the Investment Decision 486

Additional Measures of Relative Value 487

*Price/Book Value (**P/BV**) Ratio 487, Price/Cash Flow (**P/CF**) Ratio 487, Price/Sales (**P/S**) Ratio 488, Summary of Relative Valuation Ratios 490*

Analysis of Growth Companies 491

Growth Company Defined 491, Actual Returns above Required Returns 491, Growth Companies and Growth Stocks 492, Alternative Growth Models 492, No-Growth Firm 492, Long-Run Growth Models 493, The Real World 495

Measures of Value Added 496

Economic Value Added (EVA) 496, Market Value Added (MVA) 498, Relationships between EVA and MVA 498, The Franchise Factor 498, Growth Duration Model 499

Site Visits and the Art of the Interview 503

When to Sell 503

Influences on Analysts 504

Efficient Markets 504, Paralysis of Analysis 504, Analyst Conflicts of Interest 505

Global Company and Stock Analysis 505

Availability of Data 505, Differential Accounting Conventions 505, Currency Differences (Exchange Rate Risk) 506, Political (Country) Risk 506, Transaction Costs and Liquidity 506, Valuation Differences 506, Summary 506

Chapter 15: Technical Analysis **517**

Underlying Assumptions of Technical Analysis .. 518

Advantages of Technical Analysis 519

Challenges to Technical Analysis 520

Challenges to Technical Analysis Assumptions 520, Challenges to Technical Trading Rules 521

Technical Trading Rules and Indicators 521

Contrary-Opinion Rules 522, Follow the Smart Money 524, Momentum Indicators 525, Stock Price and Volume Techniques 526

Technical Analysis of Foreign Markets 533

Foreign Stock Market Indexes 533, Technical Analysis of Foreign Exchange Rates 533

Technical Analysis of Bond Markets 534

Chapter 16: Equity Portfolio Management Strategies **539**

Passive versus Active Management 540

An Overview of Passive Equity Portfolio Management Strategies 541

Index Portfolio Construction Techniques 542, Tracking Error and Index Portfolio Construction 543, Methods of Index Portfolio Investing 545

An Overview of Active Equity Portfolio Management Strategies 548

Fundamental Strategies 549, Technical Strategies 552, Anomalies and Attributes 553, Forming Momentum-Based Stock Portfolios: Two Examples 556, Tax Efficiency and Active Equity Management 558

Value versus Growth Investing: A Closer Look ... 559

An Overview of Style Analysis 562

Asset Allocation Strategies 568

Integrated Asset Allocation 568, Strategic Asset Allocation 570, Tactical Asset Allocation 570, Insured Asset Allocation 572, Selecting an Active Allocation Method 572

PART 5: ANALYSIS AND MANAGEMENT OF BONDS **577**

Chapter 17: Bond Fundamentals **579**

Basic Features of a Bond 579

Bond Characteristics 580, Rates of Return on Bonds 582, The Global Bond Market Structure 582, Participating Issuers 583, Participating Investors 585, Bond Ratings 585

Alternative Bond Issues 587

Domestic Government Bonds 587, Government Agency Issues 589, Municipal Bonds 592, Corporate Bonds 593, International Bonds 601

Obtaining Information on Bond Prices 601

Interpreting Bond Quotes 602

Chapter 18: The Analysis and Valuation of Bonds **609**

The Fundamentals of Bond Valuation 610

The Present Value Model 610, The Yield Model 612

Computing Bond Yields 613

Nominal Yield 613, Current Yield 613, Promised Yield to Maturity 614, Promised Yield to Call 616, Realized (Horizon) Yield 617

Calculating Future Bond Prices 618

Realized (Horizon) Yield with Differential Reinvestment Rates 619, Price and Yield Determination on Noninterest Dates 620, Yield Adjustments for Tax-Exempt Bonds 621, Bond Yield Books 621

Bond Valuation Using Spot Rates 622

What Determines Interest Rates? 623

Forecasting Interest Rates 624, Fundamental Determinants of Interest Rates 625, The Term Structure of Interest Rates 628

Calculating Forward Rates from the Spot Rate Curve 633

Term-Structure Theories 635

Expectations Hypothesis 635, Liquidity Preference (Term Premium) Hypothesis 637, Segmented

Market Hypothesis 638, Trading Implications of the Term Structure 638, Yield Spreads 639

What Determines the Price Volatility for Bonds? 640

Trading Strategies 642, Duration Measures 642, Modified Duration and Bond Price Volatility 646, Bond Convexity 647, Duration and Convexity for Callable Bonds 652, Limitations of Macaulay and Modified Duration 655

Yield Spreads with Embedded Options 663

Static Yield Spreads 663

Option-Adjusted Spread 664

Chapter 19: Bond Portfolio Management Strategies **677**

Bond Portfolio Performance, Style, and Strategy 677

Passive Management Strategies 680

Buy-and-Hold Strategy 680, Indexing Strategy 681, Bond Indexing in Practice: An Example 681

Active Management Strategies 682

Interest Rate Anticipation 683, Valuation Analysis 685, Credit Analysis 685, Yield Spread Analysis 689, Implementing an Active Bond Transaction 690, Active Global Bond Investing: An Example 693

Core-Plus Management Strategies 695

Matched-Funding Management Strategies 697

Dedicated Portfolios 698, Immunization Strategies 699, Horizon Matching 707

Contingent and Structured Management Strategies 708

Contingent Immunization 708

Chapter 19 Appendix: Bond Immunization and Portfolio Rebalancing 722

PART 6: DERIVATIVE SECURITY ANALYSIS **725**

Chapter 20: An Introduction to Derivative Markets and Securities **727**

Overview of Derivative Markets 728

The Language and Structure of Forward and Futures Markets 729, Interpreting Futures Price Quotations: An Example 730, The Language and Structure of Option Markets 732, Interpreting Option Price Quotations: An Example 734

Investing with Derivative Securities 735

The Basic Nature of Derivative Investing 736, Basic Payoff and Profit Diagrams for Forward Contracts 738, Basic Payoff and Profit Diagrams for Call and Put Options 740, Option Profit Diagrams: An Example 743

The Relationship between Forward and Option Contracts 745

Put-Call-Spot Parity 745, Put-Call Parity: An Example 747, Creating Synthetic Securities Using Put-Call Parity 748, Adjusting Put-Call-Spot Parity for Dividends 749, Put-Call-Forward Parity 750

An Introduction to the Use of Derivatives in Portfolio Management 751

Restructuring Asset Portfolios with Forward Contracts 752, Protecting Portfolio Value with Put Options 753, An Alternative Way to Pay for a Protective Put 755

Chapter 21: Forward and Futures Contracts **763**

An Overview of Forward and Futures Trading 764

Futures Contract Mechanics 765, Comparing Forward and Futures Contracts 767

Hedging with Forwards and Futures 767

Hedging and the Basis 767, Understanding Basis Risk 768, Calculating the Optimal Hedge Ratio 769

Forward and Futures Contracts: Basic Valuation Concepts 770

Valuing Forwards and Futures 770, The Relationship between Spot and Forward Prices 771

Financial Forwards and Futures: Applications and Strategies 773

Interest Rate Forwards and Futures 773, Long-Term Interest Rate Futures 773, Short-Term Interest Rate Futures 778, Stock Index Futures 781, Currency Forwards and Futures 787

Chapter 21 Appendix:

A. A Closed-Form Equation for Calculating Duration 798

B. Calculating Money Market Implied Forward Rates 800

Chapter 22: Option Contracts **801**

An Overview of Option Markets and Contracts 802

Option Market Conventions 802, Price Quotations for Exchange-Traded Options 803

The Fundamentals of Option Valuation 809

The Basic Approach 809, Improving Forecast Accuracy 810, The Binomial Option Pricing Model 815, The Black-Scholes Valuation Model 817, Estimating Volatility 821, Problems with Black-Scholes Valuation 822

Option Valuation: Extensions and Advanced Topics 823

Valuing European-Style Put Options 823, Valuing Options on Dividend-Bearing Securities 824, Valuing American-Style Options 825, Other Extensions of the Black-Scholes Model 826

Option Trading Strategies   828

*Protective Put Options 829, Covered Call Options
831, Straddles, Strips, and Straps 831, Strangles 833,
Chooser Options 834, Spreads 835, Range
Forwards 837*

Chapter 23: Swap Contracts, Convertible Securities, and Other Embedded Derivatives 847

OTC Interest Rate Agreements   848

*Forward-Based Interest Rate Contracts 848,
Option-Based Interest Rate Contracts 855*

Swap Contracting Extensions   858

*Equity Index-Linked Swaps 858, Credit-Related
Swaps 860*

Warrants and Convertible Securities   863

*Warrants 863, Convertible Securities 865,
Convertible Preferred Stock 866, Convertible
Bonds 866*

Other Embedded Derivatives   870

*Dual Currency Bonds 871, Equity-Index Linked
Notes 872, Commodity-Linked Bull and Bear
Bonds 875, Swap-Linked Notes 877*

Valuing Flexibility: An Introduction to Real Options   878

Company Valuation with Real Options 879

PART 7: SPECIFICATION AND EVALUATION OF ASSET MANAGEMENT 889

Chapter 24: Professional Money Management, Alternative Assets, and Industry Ethics 891

The Asset Management Industry: Structure and
Evolution   892

Private Management and Advisory Firms   894

*Investment Strategy at a Private Money
Management Firm 896*

Organization and Management of Investment
Companies   897

*Valuing Investment Company Shares 898,
Closed-End Versus Open-End Investment
Companies 898, Fund Management Fees 902,
Investment Company Portfolio Objectives 902,
Breakdown by Fund Characteristics 904, Global
Investment Companies 905, Mutual Fund
Organization and Strategy: An Example 905*

Investing in Alternative Asset Classes   906

*Hedge Funds 910, Characteristics of a Hedge Fund
911, Hedge Fund Strategies 912, Risk Arbitrage
Investing: A Closer Look 914, Hedge Fund
Performance 916, Private Equity 918*

Ethics and Regulation in the Professional Asset
Management Industry   924

*Regulation in the Asset Management Industry
924, Standards for Ethical Behavior 926,
Examples of Ethical Conflicts 928*

What Do You Want from a Professional
Asset Manager?   929

Chapter 25: Evaluation of Portfolio Performance 937

What Is Required of a Portfolio Manager?   938

Early Performance Measurement Techniques   939

*Portfolio Evaluation before 1960 939, Peer Group
Comparisons 939*

Composite Portfolio Performance Measures   939

*Treynor Portfolio Performance Measure 941, Sharpe
Portfolio Performance Measure 943, Jensen Portfolio
Performance Measure 944, The Information
Ratio Performance Measure 946, Comparing the
Composite Performance Measures 947*

Application of Portfolio Performance Measures   950

Portfolio Performance Evaluation: Some Extensions   955

*Components of Investment Performance 956,
Performance Measurement with Downside Risk
957, Holdings-Based Performance Measurement
959, Performance Attribution Analysis 963,
Measuring Market Timing Skills 966*

Factors That Affect Use of Performance Measures   967

*Demonstration of the Global Benchmark Problem
968, Implications of the Benchmark Problems 969,
Required Characteristics of Benchmarks 969*

Evaluation of Bond Portfolio Performance   970

*Returns-Based Bond Performance Measurement
970, Bond Performance Attribution 971*

Reporting Investment Performance   973

*Time-Weighted and Dollar-Weighted Returns
974, Performance Presentation Standards 975*

APPENDIX A: How to Become a CFA® Charterholder 985

APPENDIX B: Code of Ethics and Standards of Professional Conduct 987

APPENDIX C: Interest Tables 989

APPENDIX D: Standard Normal Probabilities 993

Comprehensive References List 995

Glossary 1013

Index 1029

···· PREFACE ····

The pleasure of authoring a textbook comes from writing about a subject that you enjoy and find exciting. As an author, you hope that you can pass on to the reader not only knowledge but also the excitement that you feel for the subject. In addition, writing about investments brings an added stimulant because the subject can affect the reader during his or her entire business career and beyond. We hope what readers derive from this course will help them enjoy better lives through managing their financial resources properly.

The purpose of this book is to help you learn how to manage your money so that you will derive the maximum benefit from what you earn. To accomplish this purpose, you need to learn about the investment alternatives that are available today and, what is more important, to develop a way of analyzing and thinking about investments that will remain with you in the years ahead when new and different investment opportunities become available.

Because of its dual purpose, the book mixes description and theory. The descriptive material discusses available investment instruments and considers the purpose and operation of capital markets in the United States and around the world. The theoretical portion details how you should evaluate current investments and future opportunities to develop a portfolio of investments that will satisfy your risk–return objectives.

Preparing this ninth edition has been challenging for two reasons. First, many changes have occurred in the securities markets during the last few years in terms of theory, new financial instruments, trading practices, and a significant credit/liquidity disruption. Second, as mentioned in prior editions, capital markets continue to become very global in nature. Consequently, early in the book we present the compelling case for global investing. Subsequently, to ensure that you are prepared to function in a global environment, almost every chapter discusses how investment practice or theory is influenced by the globalization of investments and capital markets. This completely integrated treatment is to ensure that you develop a broad mindset on investments that will serve you well in the 21st century.

Intended Market

This text is addressed to both graduate and advanced undergraduate students who are looking for an in-depth discussion of investments and portfolio management. The presentation of the material is intended to be rigorous and empirical, without being overly quantitative. A proper discussion of the modern developments in investments and portfolio theory must be rigorous. The discussion of numerous empirical studies reflects the belief that it is essential for alternative investment theories to be exposed to the real world and be judged on the basis of how well they help us understand and explain reality.

Key Features of the Ninth Edition

When planning the ninth edition of *Analysis of Investments and Management of Portfolios* we wanted to retain its traditional strengths and capitalize on new developments in the investments area to make it the most comprehensive investments textbook available.

First, the current edition maintains its unparalleled international coverage. Investing knows no borders, and although the total integration of domestic and global investment opportunities may seem to contradict the need for separate discussions of international issues, it in fact makes the need for specific information on non-U.S. markets, instruments, conventions, and techniques even more compelling.

Second, today's investing environment includes derivative securities not as exotic anomalies but as standard investment instruments. We felt that *Analysis of Investments and Management of Portfolios* must reflect that reality. Consequently, our four chapters on derivatives are written to provide the reader with an intuitive, clear discussion of the different instruments, their markets, valuation, trading strategies, and general use as risk management/return enhancement tools.

Third, Chapter 24, "Professional Money Management," has been significantly revised to include an extensive discussion of the hedge fund and private equity industries. In a very short period of time, these forms of "alternative" assets have emerged as some of the most important vehicles for attracting investment capital throughout the world. We provide a discussion of how these industries are structured and have evolved over the past decade, as well as a breakdown of the myriad portfolio strategies that hedge fund and private equity managers employ. We also contrast the salient characteristics of these funds with more traditional professional money management products, such as mutual funds.

Fourth, we have added many new questions and problems to the end-of-chapter material, including a significant number of CFA exercises, to provide more student practice on executing computations concerned with more sophisticated investment problems. These are designated by the CFA icon.

Fifth, we have updated and enhanced the collection of Thomson ONE: Business School Edition exercises in several end-of-chapter problem sets. Thomson ONE: BSE is a professional analytical package used by professionals world-wide. Our text allows one-year access for students to Thomson ONE: BSE, which contains information on firms, including financial statement comparisons with competitors, stock price information, and indexes for comparing firm performance against the market or sector. Thomson ONE: BSE is a great package for hands-on learning which rivals or exceeds those offered by other textbook publishers.

Major Content Changes in the Ninth Edition

The text has been thoroughly updated for currency. In addition to these time-related revisions, we have also made the following specific changes to individual chapters:

Chapter 2 In this asset allocation chapter there is an extended discussion of the importance of the policy statement and its components. We discuss several tax changes and how they impact the asset allocation decision, and provide an example of a risk tolerance questionnaire and examples of asset allocations across risk tolerances. We also demonstrate the importance of investing early and regularly. We emphasize not only what should be done, but also some common mistakes by investors. Finally, we consider in detail how the asset allocation decision affects long-run risk-return results, and how asset allocation differs among foreign countries and is changing.

Chapter 3 The updated evidence of returns (especially 2004–2007) continues to support the notion of global diversification, and a new study of global assets supports the use of a global measure of systematic risk to explain asset returns. Also, there is a consideration of new investment instruments available for global investors, including global index funds and, notably, exchange-traded funds (ETFs) for numerous countries that trade continuously.

Chapter 4 Because of the significant growth in trading volume experienced by the electronic communication networks (ECNs), this chapter was heavily rewritten to reflect the new and rapidly evolving secondary market for stocks. This includes a fairly detailed discussion of the significant changes on the NYSE during 2006–2008. We also consider the rationale for the continuing consolidation of global exchanges across asset classes of stocks, bonds, and derivatives.

In addition, we note that the corporate bond market also experienced major changes in how and when trades are reported and the number of bond issues involved. We demonstrate that global markets and exchanges continue to consolidate.

Chapter 5 Contains an expanded discussion of growth and value style stock indexes and an updated analysis of the relationship among indexes.

Chapter 6 Considers new studies that both support the efficient market hypothesis but also provide new evidence of anomalies. The section that describes *behavioral finance* and discusses how it explains many of the anomalies has been expanded to consider additional insights and updated to include recent studies. There is an expanded discussion of the practical implications of the recent findings and how they relate to the efficient market hypothesis for analysts, portfolio managers, and individual investors.

Chapter 8 This chapter has been substantially revised to present the important transition between modern portfolio theory and the Capital Asset Pricing Model (CAPM) in a more intuitive way. The discussion also contains several examples of how the CAPM is measured and used in practice, both in the United States and global markets.

Chapter 9 The discussion of the theory and practice using multifactor models of risk and expected return has been updated and expanded. The connection between the Arbitrage Pricing Theory (APT) and empirical implementations of the APT continues to be stressed, both conceptually and with several new examples.

Chapter 10 Contains a detailed comparison of alternative cash flow specifications and how they are used in valuation models and credit analysis. There is also a discussion of how to analyze operating leases and a demonstration of how the capitalization of these leases and the implied interest dramatically impacts the financial risk ratios for retail firms like Walgreens that use this tool. We also demonstrate how to measure operating leverage related to business risk.

Chapter 11 Emphasizes the two alternative approaches to valuation (present value of cash flows and relative valuation). We discuss how and when they should be implemented and consider the estimation of the variables that are relevant for all valuation models.

Chapter 12 This chapter considers both the macroeconomic variables that affect capital markets and demonstrates the microvaluation of these markets using the valuation concepts and models considered in Chapter 11.

Chapter 13 We reorganized the industry analysis presentation to increase the emphasis on the macroanalysis of an industry and concentrated this analysis in the early part of the chapter. This macroanalysis has a large impact on the subsequent microanalysis (valuation) of the industry.

Chapter 14 Following a unique discussion of a growth company and a growth stock, we provide an updated valuation of the Walgreens stock using the alternative techniques. We consistently emphasize a key point that an outstanding company like Walgreens can have a fully valued or overvalued stock. There is also an expanded discussion dealing with the importance of quarterly earnings estimates. We conclude the chapter with a consideration of several models that can be used to value true growth companies.

Chapter 16 Contains an expanded discussion of the relative merits of passive versus active management techniques for equity portfolio focusing on the important role of tracking error. New material on measuring the tax efficiency of an equity portfolio has been introduced, along with an enhanced analysis of equity portfolio investment strategies, including fundamental and technical approaches, as well as a detailed description of equity style analysis.

Chapter 17 Because of the major credit-liquidity problems encountered in the U.S. bond market during 2007–2008 (that impacted security markets around the world), several discussions in the chapter have been added or adjusted. This includes government sponsored entities (GSEs—specifically, Fannie Mae and Freddie Mac), municipal bond insurance (and bond insurance in general), collateralized debt obligations (CDOs), and auction-rate securities.

Chapter 18 Contains a discussion of the calculation and use of empirical duration. We also consider the relationship between static yield spreads and option-adjusted spreads (OAS) and what variables affect the option-adjusted spreads.

Chapter 19 This chapter on bond portfolio management strategies has been enhanced and revised to include an extended discussion comparing active and passive fixed-income strategies, as well as new and updated examples of how the bond immunization process functions. New material on how the investment style of a fixed-income portfolio is defined and measured in practice has also been included.

Chapter 20 Enhanced discussions of the "fundamentals" associated with using derivative securities (e.g., interpreting price quotations, basic payoff diagrams, basic strategies). We also provide updated examples of both basic and intermediate risk management applications using derivative positions.

Chapter 21 Updated examples and applications are provided throughout the chapter, emphasizing the role that forward and futures contracts play in managing exposures to equity, fixed-income, and foreign exchange risk.

Chapter 22 Presents a revised discussion linking valuation and applications of call and put options in the context of investment management. The chapter contains both new and updated examples designed to illustrate how investors use options in practice.

Chapter 23 Includes a revised discussion of several advanced derivative applications (e.g., swap contracting, convertible securities, structured notes, real options), as well as updated examples and applications of each of these applications. An extensive discussion of how credit default derivatives are used in practice has also been included.

Chapter 24 Contains a significantly revised and updated discussion of the organization and participants in the professional asset management industry. Of particular note is an extensive update of the structure and strategies employed by hedge funds as well as new analysis of how private equity funds function. The discussion of ethics and regulation in the asset management industry that concludes the chapter has also been expanded considerably.

Chapter 25 Provides an updated and considerably expanded application of the performance measurement techniques that are introduced throughout the chapter. The discussion has been expanded to include a new section on how the concept of "downside" risk can be incorporated into the performance measurement process and the examination of techniques that focus on the security holdings of a manager's portfolio, rather than the returns the portfolio generates.

Supplement Package

The preparation of the ninth edition provided the opportunity to enhance the supplement products offered to instructors and students who use *Analysis of Investments and Management of Portfolios.* The result of this examination is a greatly improved package that provides more than just basic answers and solutions. We are indebted to the supplement writers who devoted their time, energy, and creativity to making this supplement package the best it has ever been.

STOCK-TRAK® Thousands of students every year use STOCK-TRAK® to practice investment strategies, test theories, practice day trading, and learn about the various markets. A coupon for a price reduction for this optional stock simulation is included with the text.

The Instructor's Manual is available on international.cengage.com. The *Instructor's Manual*, written by Narendar Rao at Northeastern Illinois University, contains a brief outline of each chapter's key concepts and equations that can be easily copied and distributed to students as a reference tool.

Test Bank The *Test Bank,* written by Brian Boscaljon at Penn State University-Erie, includes an extensive set of new questions and problems and complete solutions to the testing material. The *Test Bank* is available on international.cengage.com. For instructors who would like to prepare their exams electronically, the *ExamView* version contains all the test questions found in the printed version. It is available on international.cengage.com.

The Solutions Manual This contains all the answers to the end-of-chapter questions and solutions to end-of-chapter problems. Edgar A. Norton at Illinois State University was ever diligent in the preparation of these materials, ensuring the most error-free solutions possible. It is available on international.cengage.com.

Lecture Presentation Software A comprehensive set of PowerPoint slides created by Yulong Ma at California State University Long Beach is available on international.cengage.com. Each chapter has a self-contained presentation that covers all the key concepts, equations, and examples within the chapter. The files can be used as is for an innovative, interactive class presentation. Instructors who have access to Microsoft PowerPoint can modify the slides in any way they wish, adding or deleting materials to match their needs.

Web Site The text's *Web Site* can be accessed through international.cengage.com and includes up-to-date teaching and learning aids for instructors and students. The *Instructor's Manual, Test Bank,* and PowerPoint slides are available to instructors for download.

· · · · ACKNOWLEDGMENTS · · · ·

So many people have helped us in so many ways that we hesitate to list them, fearing that we may miss someone. Accepting this risk, we will begin with the University of Notre Dame and the University of Texas at Austin because of their direct support. Reviewers for this edition were:

Bolong Cao
University of California San Diego

Donald L. Davis
Golden Gate University

Dragon Tang
University of Hong Kong

Eleanor Xu
Seton Hall University

Yexiao Xu
The University of Texas at Dallas

We were fortunate to have the following excellent reviewers for earlier editions:

John Alexander
Clemson University

Robert Angell
East Carolina University

George Aragon
Boston College

Brian Belt
University of Missouri–Kansas City

Omar M. Benkato
Ball State University

Arand Bhattacharya
University of Cincinnati

Carol Billingham
Central Michigan University

Susan Block
University of California–Santa Barbara

Gerald A. Blum
Babson College

Paul Bolster
Northeastern University

Robert E. Brooks
University of Alabama

Robert J. Brown
Harrisburg, Pennsylvania

Charles Q. Cao
Pennsylvania State University

Atreya Chakraborty
Brandeis University

Hsiu-lang Chen
University of Illinois at Chicago

Dosoung Choi
University of Tennessee

Robert Clark
University of Vermont

John Clinebell
University of Northern Colorado

James D'Mello
Western Michigan University

Eugene F. Drzycimski
University of Wisconsin–Oshkosh

William Dukes
Texas Tech University

John Dunkelberg
Wake Forest University

Eric Emory
Sacred Heart University

Thomas Eyssell
University of Missouri–St. Louis

Heber Farnsworth
Washington University, St. Louis

James Feller
Middle Tennessee State University

Eurico Ferreira
Clemson University

Michael Ferri
John Carroll University

Greg Filbeck
University of Toledo

Joseph E. Finnerty
University of Illinois

Harry Friedman
New York University

R. H. Gilmer
University of Mississippi

Steven Goldstein
University of South Carolina

Steven Goldstein
Robinson-Humphrey/American Express

Keshav Gupta
Oklahoma State University

Sally A. Hamilton
Santa Clara University

Eric Higgins
Drexel University

Ronald Hoffmeister
Arizona State University

Shelly Howton
Villanova University

Ron Hutchins
Eastern Michigan University

A. James Ifflander
Arizona State University

Stan Jacobs
Central Washington University

Kwang Jun
Michigan State University

Jaroslaw Komarynsky
Northern Illinois University

Malek Lashgari
University of Hartford

Danny Litt
Century Software Systems/UCLA

Miles Livingston
University of Florida

Christopher Ma
Texas Tech University

Ananth Madhaven
University of Southern California

Davinder Malhotra
Philadelphia College of Textiles and Science

Stephen Mann
University of South Carolina

Iqbal Mansur
Widener University

Linda Martin
Arizona State University

George Mason
University of Hartford

John Matthys
DePaul University

Michael McBain
Marquette University

Dennis McConnell
University of Maine

Jeanette Medewitz
University of Nebraska–Omaha

Jacob Michaelsen
University of California–Santa Cruz

Nicholas Michas
Northern Illinois University

Thomas W. Miller Jr.
University of Missouri–Columbia

Lalatendu Misra
University of Texas–San Antonio

Michael Murray
LaCrosse, Wisconsin

Jonathan Ohn
Wagner College

Henry Oppenheimer
University of Rhode Island

John Peavy
Southern Methodist University

George Philippatos
University of Tennessee

George Pinches
University of Kansas

Rose Prasad
Central Michigan University

Laurie Prather
University of Tennessee at Chattanooga

George A. Racette
University of Oregon

Murli Rajan
University of Scranton

Narendar V. Rao
Northeastern Illinois University

Steve Rich
Baylor University

Bruce Robin
Old Dominion University

James Rosenfeld
Emory University

Stanley D. Ryals
Investment Counsel, Inc.

Jimmy Senteza
Drake University

Katrina F. Sherrerd
CFA Institute

Shekar Shetty
University of South Dakota

Frederic Shipley
DePaul University

Douglas Southard
Virginia Polytechnic Institute

Harold Stevenson
Arizona State University

Lawrence S. Tai
Loyola Marymount College

Kishore Tandon
The City University of New York–Baruch College

Donald Thompson
Georgia State University

David E. Upton
Virginia Commonwealth University

E. Theodore Veit
Rollins College

Premal Vora
King's College

Bruce Wardrep
East Carolina University

Richard S. Warr
North Carolina State University

Robert Weigand
University of South Florida

Russell R. Wermers
University of Maryland

Rolf Wubbels
New York University

Sheng-Ping Yang
Wayland Baptist University

Valuable comments and data support has come from my frequent co-author David Wright, University of Wisconsin—Parkside. Once more, we were blessed with bright, dedicated research assistants when we needed them the most. These include Adam Ashley and Jon Keehn, who were extremely careful, dependable, and creative.

Current colleagues have been very helpful: Yu-Chi Chang, Rob Batallio, Mike Hemler, Jerry Langley, and Paul Schultz, University of Notre Dame. As always, some of the best insights and most stimulating comments continue to come during too-infrequent walks with a very good friend, Jim Gentry of the University of Illinois.

We are convinced that professors who want to write a book that is academically respectable and relevant, as well as realistic, require help from the "real world." We have been fortunate to develop relationships with a number of individuals (including a growing number of former students) whom we consider our contacts with reality.

The following individuals have graciously provided important insights and material:

Sharon Athey
Brown Brothers Harriman

Joseph Bencivenga
Bankers Trust

David G. Booth
Dimensional Fund Advisors, Inc.

Gary Brinson
GP Investments

David Chapman
Boston College

Dwight D. Churchill
Fidelity Investments

Abby Joseph Cohen
Goldman, Sachs and Company

Robert Conway
Goldman, Sachs and Company

Robert J. Davis
Crimson Capital Company

Philip Delaney Jr.
Northern Trust Bank

Sam Eisenstadt
Value Line

Frank J. Fabozzi
Journal of Portfolio Management

Kenneth Fisher
Forbes

John J. Flanagan Jr.
Lawrence, O'Donnell, Marcus and Company

H. Gifford Fong
Gifford Fong Associates

Martin S. Fridson
Fridson Vision, LLC

M. Christopher Garman
Merrill, Lynch, Pierce, Fenner & Smith

Khalid Ghayur
Morgan Stanley

William J. Hank
Moore Financial Corporation

Rick Hans
Walgreens Corporation

Lea B. Hansen
Greenwich Associates

W. Van Harlow
Fidelity Investments

Craig Hester
Hester Capital Management

Joanne Hill
Goldman, Sachs and Company

John W. Jordan II
The Jordan Company

Andrew Kalotay
Kalotay Associates

Luke Knecht
Dresdner RCM Capital Management

Warren N. Koontz Jr.
Loomis, Sayles and Company

Mark Kritzman
Windham Capital Management

Sandy Leeds
University of Texas

Martin Leibowitz
Morgan Stanley

Douglas R. Lempereur
Templeton Investment Counsel, Inc.

Robert Levine
Nomura Securities

Amy Lipton
Bankers Trust

George W. Long
Long Investment Management Ltd.

Scott Lummer
Lummer Investment Consulting

John Maginn
Maginn Associates

Scott Malpass
University of Notre Dame

Jack Malvey
Lehman Brothers

Andras Marosi
University of Alberta

Dominic Marshall
Scott Creek Investment Management

Frank Martin
Martin Capital Management

Todd Martin
Martin Capital Management

Joseph McAlinden
Morgan Stanley

Richard McCabe
Merrill, Lynch, Pierce, Fenner & Smith

Michael McCowin
State of Wisconsin Investment Board

Terrence J. McGlinn
McGlinn Capital Markets

Kenneth Meyer
Lincoln Capital Management

Janet T. Miller
Rowland and Company

Brian Moore
U.S. Gypsum Corp.

Salvator Muoio
SM Investors, LP

David Nelms
Discover Financial Services

George Noyes
Standish Mellon Asset Management

Ian Rossa O'Reilly
Wood Gundy, Inc.

Robert Parrino
University of Texas

Philip J. Purcell III
PJP Investments

Jack Pycik
Consultant

John C. Rudolf
Summit Capital Management

Guy Rutherford
Morgan Stanley

Ron Ryan
Asset Liability Management

Mark Rypzinski
Henry & Co.

Robert F. Semmens Jr.
Semmens Private Investments

Brian Singer
UBS Global Asset Management

Clay Singleton
Rollins College

Donald J. Smith
Boston University

Fred H. Speece Jr.
Speece, Thorson Capital Group

Laura Starks
University of Texas

William M. Stephens
Husic Capital Management

James Stork
Uitermarkt & Associates

Lawrence S. Tai
Loyola Marymount College

Kevin Terhaar
UBS Global Asset Management

William M. Wadden
LongShip Capital Management

William Way
University of Texas

Ken Wiles
Fulcrum Financial Group

Robert Wilmouth
National Futures Association

Richard S. Wilson
Consultant

Hong Yan
University of South Carolina

We continue to benefit from the help and consideration of the dedicated people who are or have been associated with the CFA Institute: Tom Bowman, Whit Broome, Jeff Diermeier, Bob Johnson, Bob Luck, Sue Martin, Katie Sherrerd, and Donald Tuttle.

Professor Reilly would like to thank his assistant, Rachel Karnafel, who had the unenviable task of keeping his office and his life in some sort of order during this project.

As always, our greatest gratitude is to our families—past, present, and future. Our parents gave us life and helped us understand love and how to give it. Most important are our wives who provide love, understanding, and support throughout the day and night. We thank God for our children and grandchildren who ensure that our lives are full of love, laughs, and excitement.

Keith C. Brown
Austin, Texas
Frank K. Reilly
Notre Dame, Indiana
September 2008

Keith C. Brown holds the position of University Distinguished Teaching Professor of Finance and Fayez Sarofim Fellow at the McCombs School of Business, University of Texas. He received his B.A. in Economics from San Diego State University, where he was a member of the Phi Beta Kappa, Phi Kappa Phi, and Omicron Delta Epsilon honor societies. He received his M.S. and Ph.D. in Financial Economics from the Krannert Graduate School of Management at Purdue University. Since leaving school in 1981, he has specialized in teaching Investment Management, Portfolio Management and Security Analysis, Capital Markets, and Derivatives courses at the undergraduate, MBA, and Ph.D. levels and has received numerous awards for teaching innovation and excellence, including election to the University's prestigious Academy of Distinguished Teachers. In addition to his academic responsibilities, he has also served as President and Chief Executive Officer of The MBA Investment Fund, L.L.C., a privately funded investment company managed by graduate students at the University of Texas.

Professor Brown has published more than 40 articles, monographs, chapters, and papers on topics ranging from asset pricing and investment strategy to financial risk management. His publications have appeared in such journals as *Journal of Finance, Journal of Financial Economics, Review of Financial Studies, Journal of Financial and Quantitative Analysis, Review of Economics and Statistics, Financial Analysts Journal, Financial Management, Journal of Investment Management, Advances in Futures and Options Research, Journal of Fixed Income, Journal of Applied Corporate Finance,* and *Journal of Portfolio Management.* In addition to his contributions to *Analysis of Investments and Management of Portfolios, Ninth Edition,* he is a co-author of *Interest Rate and Currency Swaps: A Tutorial,* a textbook published in 1995 through the Association for Investment Management and Research (AIMR). He received a Graham and Dodd Award from the Financial Analysts Federation as an author of one of the best articles published by *Financial Analysts Journal* in 1990, and a Smith-Breeden Prize from the *Journal of Finance* in 1996.

In August 1988, Professor Brown received his charter from the Institute of Chartered Financial Analysts (ICFA). He has served as a member of AIMR's CFA Candidate Curriculum Committee and Education Committee, and on the CFA Examination Grading staff. For five years, he was the research director of the Research Foundation of the ICFA, from which position he guided the development of the research portion of the organization's worldwide educational mission. For several years, he was also associate editor for *Financial Analysts Journal* and currently holds that position for *Journal of Investment Management* and *Journal of Behavioral Finance.* In other professional service, Professor Brown has been a regional director for the Financial Management Association and has served as the applied research track chairman for that organization's annual conference.

Professor Brown is the co-founder and senior partner of Fulcrum Financial Group, a portfolio management and investment advisory firm located in Austin, Texas, and Las Vegas, Nevada, that currently oversees portfolios holding a total of $60 million in fixed-income securities. From May 1987 to August 1988 he was based in New York as a senior consultant to the Corporate Professional Development Department at Manufacturers Hanover Trust Company. He has lectured extensively throughout the world on investment and risk management topics in the executive development programs for such companies as Fidelity Investments, JP Morgan Chase, BMO Nesbitt Burns, Merrill Lynch, Chase Manhattan Bank, Chemical Bank, Lehman Brothers, Union Bank of Switzerland, Shearson, Chase Bank of Texas, The Beacon Group, Motorola, and Halliburton. He is an Advisor to the Boards of the Texas Teachers Retirement

System and the University of Texas Investment Management Company and serves on the Investment Committee of LBJ Asset Management Partners.

Frank K. Reilly is the Bernard J. Hank Professor of Finance and former dean of the Mendoza College of Business at the University of Notre Dame. Holding degrees from the University of Notre Dame (B.B.A.), Northwestern University (M.B.A.), and the University of Chicago (Ph.D.), Professor Reilly has taught at the University of Illinois, the University of Kansas, and the University of Wyoming in addition to the University of Notre Dame. He has several years of experience as a senior securities analyst, as well as experience in stock and bond trading. A Chartered Financial Analyst (CFA), he has been a member of the Council of Examiners, the Council on Education and Research, the grading committee, and was Chairman of the Board of Trustees of the Institute of Charted Financial Analysts and Chairman of the Board of the Association of Investment Management and Research (AIMR) (now the CFA Institute). Professor Reilly has been president of the Financial Management Association, the Midwest Business Administration Association, the Eastern Finance Association, the Academy of Financial Services, and the Midwest Finance Association. He is or has been on the board of directors of the First Interstate Bank of Wisconsin, Norwest Bank of Indiana, the Investment Analysts Society of Chicago, UBS Global Funds (Chairman), Fort Dearborn Income Securities (Chairman), Discover Bank, NIBCO, Inc., International Board of Certified Financial Planners, Battery Park High Yield Bond Fund, Inc., Morgan Stanley Trust FSB, the CFA Institute Research Foundation (Chairman), the Financial Analysts Seminar, the Board of Certified Safety Professionals, and The University Club at the University of Notre Dame.

As the author of more than 100 articles, monographs, and papers, his work has appeared in numerous publications including *Journal of Finance, Journal of Financial and Quantitative Analysis, Journal of Accounting Research, Financial Management, Financial Analysts Journal, Journal of Fixed Income,* and *Journal of Portfolio Management.* In addition to *Analysis of Investments and Management of Portfolios, Ninth Edition,* Professor Reilly is the co-author of another textbook, *Investments, Seventh Edition* (South-Western, 2006) with Edgar A. Norton. He is editor of *Readings and Issues in Investments, Ethics and the Investment Industry,* and *High Yield Bonds: Analysis and Risk Assessment.*

Professor Reilly was named on the list of *Outstanding Educators in America* and has received the University of Illinois Alumni Association Graduate Teaching Award, the Outstanding Educator Award from the M.B.A. class at the University of Illinois, and the Outstanding Teacher Award from the M.B.A. class and the Senior Class at Notre Dame. He also received from the CFA Institute both the C. Stewart Sheppard Award for his contribution to the educational mission of the Association and the Daniel J. Forrestal III Leadership Award for Professional Ethics and Standards of Investment Practice. He was part of the inaugural group selected as a Fellow of the Financial Management Association International. He is or has been a member of the editorial boards of *Financial Management, The Financial Review, International Review of Economics and Finance, Journal of Financial Education, Quarterly Review of Economics and Finance,* and the *European Journal of Finance.* He is included in the *Who's Who in Finance and Industry, Who's Who in America, Who's Who in American Education,* and *Who's Who in the World.*

PART 1
The Investment Background

CHAPTER 1
The Investment Setting

CHAPTER 2
The Asset Allocation Decision

CHAPTER 3
Selecting Investments in a Global Market

CHAPTER 4
Organization and Functioning of Securities Markets

CHAPTER 5
Security-Market Indexes

The chapters in this section will provide a background for your study of investments by answering the following questions:

- *Why do people invest?*
- *How do you measure the returns and risks for alternative investments?*
- *What factors should you consider when you make asset allocation decisions?*
- *What investments are available?*
- *How do securities markets function?*
- *How and why are securities markets in the United States and around the world changing?*
- *What are the major uses of security-market indexes?*
- *How can you evaluate the market behavior of common stocks and bonds?*
- *What factors cause differences among stock- and bond-market indexes?*

In the first chapter, we consider why an individual would invest, how to measure the rates of return and risk for alternative investments, and what factors determine an investor's required rate of return on an investment. The latter point will be important in subsequent analyses when we work to understand investor behavior, the markets for alternative securities, and the valuation of various investments.

Because the ultimate decision facing an investor is the makeup of his or her portfolio, Chapter 2 deals with the all-important asset allocation decision. This includes specific steps in the portfolio management process and factors that influence the makeup of an investor's portfolio over his or her life cycle.

To minimize risk, investment theory asserts the need to diversify. Chapter 3 begins our exploration of investments available to investors by making an overpowering case for investing globally rather than limiting choices to only U.S. securities. Building on this premise, we discuss several investment instruments found in global markets. We conclude the chapter with a review of the historical rates of return and measures of risk for a number of alternative asset groups.

In Chapter 4, we examine how markets work in general, and then specifically focus on the purpose and function of primary and secondary bond and stock markets. During the last 15 years, significant changes have occurred in the operation of the securities market, including a trend toward a global market, electronic trading markets, and substantial worldwide consolidation. After discussing these changes and the rapid development of new capital markets around the world, we speculate about how global markets will continue to consolidate and increase available investment alternatives.

Investors, market analysts, and financial theorists generally gauge the behavior of securities markets by evaluating the return and risk implied by various market indexes and evaluate portfolio performance by comparing a portfolio's results to an appropriate benchmark. Because these indexes are used to make asset allocation decisions and then to evaluate portfolio performance, it is important to have a deep understanding of how they are constructed and the numerous alternatives available. Therefore, in Chapter 5, we examine and compare a number of stock-market and bond-market indexes available for the domestic and global markets.

This initial section provides the framework for you to understand various securities, how to allocate among alternative asset classes, the markets where they are bought and sold, the indexes that reflect their performance, and how you might manage a collection of investments in a portfolio. Specific portfolio management techniques are described in later chapters.

CHAPTER 1

The Investment Setting

After you read this chapter, you should be able to answer the following questions:

- Why do individuals invest?
- What is an investment?
- How do investors measure the rate of return on an investment?
- How do investors measure the risk related to alternative investments?
- What factors contribute to the rates of return that investors require on alternative investments?
- What macroeconomic and microeconomic factors contribute to changes in the required rates of return for investments?

This initial chapter discusses several topics basic to the subsequent chapters. We begin by defining the term *investment* and discussing the returns and risks related to investments. This leads to a presentation of how to measure the expected and historical rates of returns for an individual asset or a portfolio of assets. In addition, we consider how to measure risk not only for an individual investment but also for an investment that is part of a portfolio.

The third section of the chapter discusses the factors that determine the required rate of return for an individual investment. The factors discussed are those that contribute to an asset's *total* risk. Because most investors have a portfolio of investments, it is necessary to consider how to measure the risk of an asset when it is a part of a large portfolio of assets. The risk that prevails when an asset is part of a diversified portfolio is referred to as its *systematic risk*.

The final section deals with what causes *changes* in an asset's required rate of return over time. Notably, changes occur because of both macroeconomic events that affect all investment assets and microeconomic events that affect the specific asset.

1.1 What Is an Investment?

For most of your life, you will be earning and spending money. Rarely, though, will your current money income exactly balance with your consumption desires. Sometimes, you may have more money than you want to spend; at other times, you may want to purchase more than you can afford based on your current income. These imbalances will lead you either to borrow or to save to maximize the long-run benefits from your income.

When current income exceeds current consumption desires, people tend to save the excess. They can do any of several things with these savings. One possibility is to put the money under a mattress or bury it in the backyard until some future time when consumption desires exceed current income. When they retrieve their savings from the mattress or backyard, they have the same amount they saved.

Another possibility is that they can give up the immediate possession of these savings for a future larger amount of money that will be available for future consumption. This trade-off of *present* consumption for a higher level of *future* consumption is the reason for saving. What you do with the savings to make them increase over time is *investment*.[1]

Those who give up immediate possession of savings (that is, defer consumption) expect to receive in the future a greater amount than they gave up. Conversely, those who consume more than their current income (that is, borrow) must be willing to pay back in the future more than they borrowed.

The rate of exchange between *future consumption* (future dollars) and *current consumption* (current dollars) is the *pure rate of interest*. Both people's willingness to pay this difference for borrowed funds and their desire to receive a surplus on their savings give rise to an interest rate referred to as the *pure time value of money*. This interest rate is established in the capital market by a comparison of the supply of excess income available (savings) to be invested and the demand for excess consumption (borrowing) at a given time. If you can exchange $100 of certain income today for $104 of certain income one year from today, then the pure rate of exchange on a risk-free investment (that is, the time value of money) is said to be 4 percent (104/100 – 1).

The investor who gives up $100 today expects to consume $104 of goods and services in the future. This assumes that the general price level in the economy stays the same. This price stability has rarely been the case during the past several decades when inflation rates have varied from 1.1 percent in 1986 to as much as 13.3 percent in 1979, with an average of about 5.0 percent a year from 1970 to 2007. If investors expect a change in prices, they will require a higher rate of return to compensate for it. For example, if an investor expects a rise in prices (that is, he or she expects inflation) at the rate of 2 percent during the period of investment, he or she will increase the required interest rate by 2 percent. In our example, the investor would require $106 in the future to defer the $100 of consumption during an inflationary period (a 6 percent nominal, risk-free interest rate will be required instead of 4 percent).

Further, if the future payment from the investment is not certain, the investor will demand an interest rate that exceeds the nominal risk-free interest rate. The uncertainty of the payments from an investment is the *investment risk*. The additional return added to the nominal, risk-free interest rate is called a *risk premium*. In our previous example, the investor would require more than $106 one year from today to compensate for the uncertainty. As an example, if the required amount were $110, $4 (4 percent) would be considered a risk premium.

1.1.1 Investment Defined

From our discussion, we can specify a formal definition of investment. Specifically, an **investment** is the current commitment of dollars for a period of time in order to derive future payments that will compensate the investor for (1) the time the funds are committed, (2) the expected rate of inflation, and (3) the uncertainty of the future payments. The "investor" can be an individual, a government, a pension fund, or a corporation. Similarly, this definition includes all types of investments, including investments by corporations in plant and equipment and investments by individuals in stocks, bonds, commodities, or real estate. This text emphasizes investments by individual investors. In all cases, the investor is trading a *known* dollar amount today for some *expected* future stream of payments that will be greater than the current outlay.

At this point, we have answered the questions about why people invest and what they want from their investments. They invest to earn a return from savings due to their deferred consumption. They want a rate of return that compensates them for the time, the expected rate of inflation, and the uncertainty of the return. This return, the investor's **required rate of return**, is discussed throughout this book. A central question of this book is how investors select investments that will give them their required rates of return.

---

[1] In contrast, when current income is less than current consumption desires, people borrow to make up the difference. Although we will discuss borrowing on several occasions, the major emphasis of this text is how to invest savings.

The next section of this chapter describes how to measure the expected or historical rate of return on an investment and also how to quantify the uncertainty of expected returns. You need to understand these techniques for measuring the rate of return and the uncertainty of these returns to evaluate the suitability of a particular investment. Although our emphasis will be on financial assets, such as bonds and stocks, we will refer to other assets, such as art and antiques. Chapter 3 discusses the range of financial assets and also considers some nonfinancial assets.

. . . .
1.2 Measures of Return and Risk

The purpose of this book is to help you understand how to choose among alternative investment assets. This selection process requires that you estimate and evaluate the expected risk-return trade-offs for the alternative investments available. Therefore, you must understand how to measure the rate of return and the risk involved in an investment accurately. To meet this need, in this section we examine ways to quantify return and risk. The presentation will consider how to measure both *historical* and *expected* rates of return and risk.

We consider historical measures of return and risk because this book and other publications provide numerous examples of historical average rates of return and risk measures for various assets, and understanding these presentations is important. In addition, these historical results are often used by investors when attempting to estimate the *expected* rates of return and risk for an asset class.

The first measure is the historical rate of return on an individual investment over the time period the investment is held (that is, its holding period). Next, we consider how to measure the *average* historical rate of return for an individual investment over a number of time periods. The third subsection considers the average rate of return for a *portfolio* of investments.

Given the measures of historical rates of return, we will present the traditional measures of risk for a historical time series of returns (that is, the variance and standard deviation).

Following the presentation of measures of historical rates of return and risk, we turn to estimating the *expected* rate of return for an investment. Obviously, such an estimate contains a great deal of uncertainty, and we present measures of this uncertainty or risk.

1.2.1 Measures of Historical Rates of Return

When you are evaluating alternative investments for inclusion in your portfolio, you will often be comparing investments with widely different prices or lives. As an example, you might want to compare a $10 stock that pays no dividends to a stock selling for $150 that pays dividends of $5 a year. To properly evaluate these two investments, you must accurately compare their historical rates of returns. A proper measurement of the rates of return is the purpose of this section.

When we invest, we defer current consumption in order to add to our wealth so that we can consume more in the future. Therefore, when we talk about a return on an investment, we are concerned with the *change in wealth* resulting from this investment. This change in wealth can be either due to cash inflows, such as interest or dividends, or caused by a change in the price of the asset (positive or negative).

If you commit $200 to an investment at the beginning of the year and you get back $220 at the end of the year, what is your return for the period? The period during which you own an investment is called its *holding period*, and the return for that period is the **holding period return (HPR)**. In this example, the HPR is 1.10, calculated as follows:

$$\text{HPR} = \frac{\text{Ending Value of Investment}}{\text{Beginning Value of Investment}} \qquad 1.1$$

$$= \frac{\$220}{\$200} = 1.10$$

This value will always be zero or greater—that is, it can never be a negative value. A value greater than 1.0 reflects an increase in your wealth, which means that you received a positive rate of return during the period. A value less than 1.0 means that you suffered a decline in wealth, which indicates that you had a negative return during the period. An HPR of zero indicates that you lost all your money.

Although HPR helps us express the change in value of an investment, investors generally evaluate returns in *percentage terms on an annual basis*. This conversion to annual percentage rates makes it easier to directly compare alternative investments that have markedly different characteristics. The first step in converting an HPR to an annual percentage rate is to derive a percentage return, referred to as the **holding period yield (HPY)**. The HPY is equal to the HPR minus 1.

1.2
$$HPY = HPR - 1$$

In our example:

$$HPY = 1.10 - 1 = 0.10$$
$$= 10\%$$

To derive an *annual* HPY, you compute an *annual* HPR and subtract 1. Annual HPR is found by:

1.3
$$\text{Annual HPR} = HPR^{1/n}$$

where:

n = number of years the investment is held

Consider an investment that cost $250 and is worth $350 after being held for two years:

$$HPR = \frac{\text{Ending Value of Investment}}{\text{Beginning Value of Investment}} = \frac{\$350}{\$250}$$
$$= 1.40$$
$$\text{Annual HPR} = 1.40^{1/n}$$
$$= 1.40^{1/2}$$
$$= 1.1832$$
$$\text{Annual HPY} = 1.1832 - 1 = 0.1832$$
$$= 18.32\%$$

If you experience a decline in your wealth value, the computation is as follows:

$$HPR = \frac{\text{Ending Value}}{\text{Beginning Value}} = \frac{\$400}{\$500} = 0.80$$
$$HPY = 0.80 - 1.00 = -0.20 = -20\%$$

A multiple-year loss over two years would be computed as follows:

$$HPR = \frac{\text{Ending Value}}{\text{Beginning Value}} = \frac{\$750}{\$1,000} = 0.75$$
$$\text{Annual HPR} = (0.75)^{1/n} = 0.75^{1/2}$$
$$= 0.866$$
$$\text{Annual HPY} = 0.866 - 1.00 = -0.134 = -13.4\%$$

In contrast, consider an investment of $100 held for only six months that earned a return of $12:

$$HPR = \frac{\$112}{100} = 1.12(n = 0.5)$$
$$\text{Annual HPR} = 1.12^{1/.5}$$

$$= 1.12^2$$
$$= 1.2544$$
$$\text{Annual HPY} = 1.2544 - 1 = 0.2544$$
$$= 25.44\%$$

Note that we made some implicit assumptions when converting the HPY to an annual basis. This annualized holding period yield computation assumes a constant annual yield for each year. In the two-year investment, we assumed an 18.32 percent rate of return each year, compounded. In the partial year HPR that was annualized, we assumed that the return is compounded for the whole year. That is, we assumed that the rate of return earned during the first half of the year is likewise earned on the value at the end of the first six months. The 12 percent rate of return for the initial six months compounds to 25.44 percent for the full year.[2] Because of the uncertainty of being able to earn the same return in the future six months, institutions will typically not compound partial year results.

Remember one final point: The ending value of the investment can be the result of a positive or negative change in price for the investment alone (for example, a stock going from $20 a share to $22 a share), income from the investment alone, or a combination of price change and income. Ending value includes the value of everything related to the investment.

1.2.2 Computing Mean Historical Returns

Now that we have calculated the HPY for a single investment for a single year, we want to consider **mean rates of return** for a single investment and for a portfolio of investments. Over a number of years, a single investment will likely give high rates of return during some years and low rates of return, or possibly negative rates of return, during others. Your analysis should consider each of these returns, but you also want a summary figure that indicates this investment's typical experience, or the rate of return you should expect to receive if you owned this investment over an extended period of time. You can derive such a summary figure by computing the mean annual rate of return for this investment over some period of time.

Alternatively, you might want to evaluate a portfolio of investments that might include similar investments (for example, all stocks or all bonds) or a combination of investments (for example, stocks, bonds, and real estate). In this instance, you would calculate the mean rate of return for this portfolio of investments for an individual year or for a number of years.

Single Investment Given a set of annual rates of return (HPYs) for an individual investment, there are two summary measures of return performance. The first is the arithmetic mean return, the second is the geometric mean return. To find the **arithmetic mean** (AM), the sum (Σ) of annual HPYs is divided by the number of years (n) as follows:

$$AM = \Sigma HPY / n \qquad\qquad \textbf{1.4}$$

where:

ΣHPY = the sum of annual holding period yields

An alternative computation, the **geometric mean (GM)**, is the nth root of the product of the HPRs for n years.

$$GM = [\pi HPR]^{1/n} - 1 \qquad\qquad \textbf{1.5}$$

where:

π = the product of the annual holding period returns as follows:

$$(HPR_1) \times (HPR_2) \cdots (HPR_n)$$

---

[2] To check that you understand the calculations, determine the annual HPY for a three-year HPR of 1.50. (Answer: 14.47 percent.) Compute the annual HPY for a three-month HPR of 1.06. (Answer: 26.25 percent.)

To illustrate these alternatives, consider an investment with the following data:

Year	Beginning Value	Ending Value	HPR	HPY
1	100.0	115.0	1.15	0.15
2	115.0	138.0	1.20	0.20
3	138.0	110.4	0.80	−0.20

$$
\begin{aligned}
AM &= [(0.15) + (0.20) + (-0.20)]/3 \\
&= 0.15/3 \\
&= 0.05 = 5\% \\
GM &= [(1.15) \times (1.20) \times (0.80)]^{1/3} - 1 \\
&= (1.104)^{1/3} - 1 \\
&= 1.03353 - 1 \\
&= 0.03353 = 3.353\%
\end{aligned}
$$

Investors are typically concerned with long-term performance when comparing alternative investments. GM is considered a superior measure of the long-term mean rate of return because it indicates the compound annual rate of return based on the ending value of the investment versus its beginning value.[3] Specifically, using the prior example, if we compounded 3.353 percent for three years, $(1.03353)^3$, we would get an ending wealth value of 1.104.

Although the arithmetic average provides a good indication of the expected rate of return for an investment during a future individual year, it is biased upward if you are attempting to measure an asset's long-term performance. This is obvious for a volatile security. Consider, for example, a security that increases in price from \$50 to \$100 during year 1 and drops back to \$50 during year 2. The annual HPYs would be:

Year	Beginning Value	Ending Value	HPR	HPY
1	50	100	2.00	1.00
2	100	50	0.50	−0.50

This would give an AM rate of return of:

$$
\begin{aligned}
[(1.00) + (-0.50)]/2 &= .50/2 \\
&= 0.25 = 25\%
\end{aligned}
$$

This investment brought no change in wealth and therefore no return, yet the AM rate of return is computed to be 25 percent.

The GM rate of return would be:

$$
\begin{aligned}
(2.00 \times 0.50)^{1/2} - 1 &= (1.00)^{1/2} - 1 \\
&= 1.00 - 1 = 0\%
\end{aligned}
$$

This answer of a 0 percent rate of return accurately measures the fact that there was no change in wealth from this investment over the two-year period.

When rates of return are the same for all years, the GM will be equal to the AM. If the rates of return vary over the years, the GM will always be lower than the AM. The difference between the two mean values will depend on the year-to-year changes in the rates of return. Larger annual changes in the rates of return—that is, more volatility—will result in a greater difference between the alternative mean values.

---

[3] Note that the GM is the same whether you compute the geometric mean of the individual annual holding period yields or the annual HPY for a three-year period, comparing the ending value to the beginning value, as discussed earlier under annual HPY for a multiperiod case.

An awareness of both methods of computing mean rates of return is important because most published accounts of long-run investment performance or descriptions of financial research will use both the AM and the GM as measures of average historical returns. We will also use both throughout this book with the understanding that the AM is best used as an expected value for an individual year, while the GM is the best measure of long-term performance since it measures the compound annual rate of return for the asset being measured.

A Portfolio of Investments   The mean historical rate of return (HPY) for a portfolio of investments is measured as the weighted average of the HPYs for the individual investments in the portfolio, or the overall change in value of the original portfolio. The weights used in computing the averages are the relative *beginning* market values for each investment; this is referred to as *dollar-weighted* or *value-weighted* mean rate of return. This technique is demonstrated by the examples in Exhibit 1.1. As shown, the HPY is the same (9.5 percent) whether you compute the weighted average return using the beginning market value weights or if you compute the overall change in the total value of the portfolio.

Although the analysis of historical performance is useful, selecting investments for your portfolio requires you to predict the rates of return you *expect* to prevail. The next section discusses how you would derive such estimates of expected rates of return. We recognize the great uncertainty regarding these future expectations, and we will discuss how one measures this uncertainty, which is referred to as the risk of an investment.

1.2.3 Calculating Expected Rates of Return

Risk is the uncertainty that an investment will earn its expected rate of return. In the examples in the prior section, we examined *realized* historical rates of return. In contrast, an investor who is evaluating a future investment alternative expects or anticipates a certain rate of return. The investor might say that he or she *expects* the investment will provide a rate of return of 10 percent, but this is actually the investor's most likely estimate, also referred to as a *point estimate*. Pressed further, the investor would probably acknowledge the uncertainty of this point estimate return and admit the possibility that, under certain conditions, the annual rate of return on this investment might go as low as −10 percent or as high as 25 percent. The point is, the specification of a larger range of *possible* returns from an investment reflects the investor's uncertainty regarding what the *actual* return will be. Therefore, a larger range of possible returns makes the investment riskier.

An investor determines how certain the expected rate of return on an investment is by analyzing estimates of possible returns. To do this, the investor assigns probability values to

---

Exhibit 1.1 Computation of Holding Period Yield for a Portfolio

Investment	Number of Shares	Beginning Price	Beginning Market Value	Ending Price	Ending Market Value	HPR	HPY	Market Weight[a]	Weighted HPY
A	100,000	$10	$1,000,000	$12	$1,200,000	1.20	20%	0.05	0.01
B	200,000	20	4,000,000	21	4,200,000	1.05	5	0.20	0.01
C	500,000	30	15,000,000	33	16,500,000	1.10	10	0.75	0.075
Total			$20,000,000		$21,900,000				0.095

$$HPR = \frac{21,900,000}{20,000,000} = 1.095$$

$$HPY = 1.095 - 1 = 0.095$$

$$= 9.5\%$$

[a]**Weights** are based on beginning values.

all *possible* returns. These probability values range from zero, which means no chance of the return, to one, which indicates complete certainty that the investment will provide the specified rate of return. These probabilities are typically subjective estimates based on the historical performance of the investment or similar investments modified by the investor's expectations for the future. As an example, an investor may know that about 30 percent of the time the rate of return on this particular investment was 10 percent. Using this information along with future expectations regarding the economy, one can derive an estimate of what might happen in the future.

The *expected* return from an investment is defined as:

$$\text{Expected Return} = \sum_{i=1}^{n}(\text{Probability of Return}) \times (\text{Possible Return})$$

1.6
$$E(R_i) = [(P_1)(R_1) + (P_2)(R_2) + (P_3)(R_3) + \cdots + (P_nR_n)]$$

$$E(R_i) = \sum_{i=1}^{n}(P_i)(R_i)$$

Let us begin our analysis of the effect of risk with an example of perfect certainty wherein the investor is absolutely certain of a return of 5 percent. Exhibit 1.2 illustrates this situation.

Perfect certainty allows only one possible return, and the probability of receiving that return is 1.0. Few investments provide certain returns and would be considered risk-free investments. In the case of perfect certainty, there is only one value for P_iR_i:

$$E(R_i) = (1.0)(0.05) = 0.05$$

In an alternative scenario, suppose an investor believed an investment could provide several different rates of return depending on different possible economic conditions. As an example, in a strong economic environment with high corporate profits and little or no inflation, the investor might expect the rate of return on common stocks during the next year to reach as high as 20 percent. In contrast, if there is an economic decline with a higher-than-average rate of inflation, the investor might expect the rate of return on common stocks during the next year to be −20 percent. Finally, with no major change in the economic environment, the rate of return during the next year would probably approach the long-run average of 10 percent.

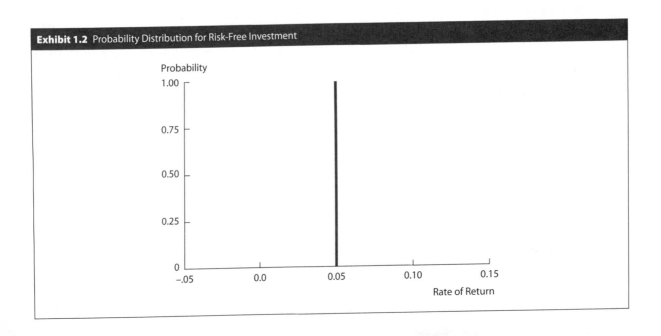

Exhibit 1.2 Probability Distribution for Risk-Free Investment

The investor might estimate probabilities for each of these economic scenarios based on past experience and the current outlook as follows:

Economic Conditions	Probability	Rate of Return
Strong economy, no inflation	0.15	0.20
Weak economy, above-average inflation	0.15	−0.20
No major change in economy	0.70	0.10

This set of potential outcomes can be visualized as shown in Exhibit 1.3.

The computation of the expected rate of return $[E(R_i)]$ is as follows:

$$E(R_i) = [(0.15)(0.20)] + [(0.15)(-0.20)] + [(0.70)(0.10)]$$
$$= 0.07$$

Obviously, the investor is less certain about the expected return from this investment than about the return from the prior investment with its single possible return.

A third example is an investment with 10 possible outcomes ranging from −40 percent to 50 percent with the same probability for each rate of return. A graph of this set of expectations would appear as shown in Exhibit 1.4.

In this case, there are numerous outcomes from a wide range of possibilities. The expected rate of return $[E(R_i)]$ for this investment would be:

$$E(R_i) = (0.10)(-0.40) + (0.10)(-0.30) + (0.10)(-0.20) + (0.10)(-0.10) + (0.10)(0.0)$$
$$+ (0.10)(0.10) + (0.10)(0.20) + (0.10)(0.30) + (0.10)(0.40) + (0.10)(0.50)$$
$$= (-0.04) + (-0.03) + (-0.02) + (-0.01) + (0.00) + (0.01) + (0.02) + (0.03)$$
$$+ (0.04) + (0.05)$$
$$= 0.05$$

The *expected* rate of return for this investment is the same as the certain return discussed in the first example; but, in this case, the investor is highly uncertain about the *actual* rate of return. This would be considered a risky investment because of that uncertainty. We would anticipate that an investor faced with the choice between this risky investment and the certain (risk-free) case would select the certain alternative. This expectation is based on the belief that most investors are **risk averse**, which means that if everything else is the same, they will select the investment that offers greater certainty (i.e., less risk).

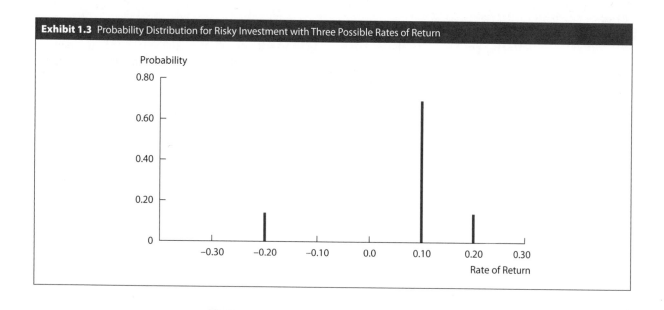

Exhibit 1.3 Probability Distribution for Risky Investment with Three Possible Rates of Return

Exhibit 1.4 Probability Distribution for Risky Investment with 10 Possible Rates of Return

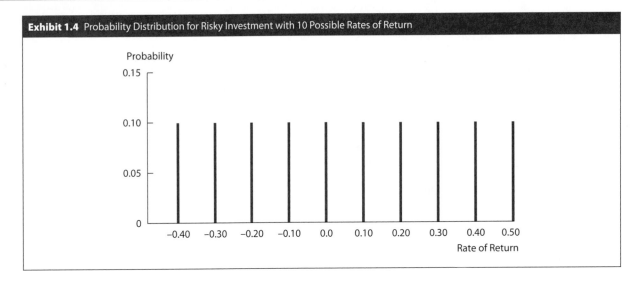

1.2.4 Measuring the Risk of Expected Rates of Return

We have shown that we can calculate the expected rate of return and evaluate the uncertainty, or risk, of an investment by identifying the range of possible returns from that investment and assigning each possible return a weight based on the probability that it will occur. Although the graphs help us visualize the dispersion of possible returns, most investors want to quantify this dispersion using statistical techniques. These statistical measures allow you to compare the return and risk measures for alternative investments directly. Two possible measures of risk (uncertainty) have received support in theoretical work on portfolio theory: the *variance* and the *standard deviation* of the estimated distribution of expected returns.

In this section, we demonstrate how variance and standard deviation measure the dispersion of possible rates of return around the expected rate of return. We will work with the examples discussed earlier. The formula for variance is as follows:

1.7
$$\text{Variance } (\sigma^2) = \sum_{i=1}^{n} (\text{Probability}) \times \left(\begin{array}{c} \text{Possible} \\ \text{Return} \end{array} - \begin{array}{c} \text{Expected} \\ \text{Return} \end{array} \right)^2$$

$$= \sum_{i=1}^{n} (P_i)[R_i - E(R_i)]^2$$

Variance The larger the **variance** for an expected rate of return, the greater the dispersion of expected returns and the greater the uncertainty, or risk, of the investment. The variance for the perfect-certainty (risk-free) example would be:

$$(\sigma^2) = \sum_{i=1}^{n} P_i[R_i - E(R_i)]^2$$

$$= 1.0(0.05 - 0.05)^2 = 1.0(0.0) = 0$$

Note that, in perfect certainty, there is *no variance of return* because there is no deviation from expectations and, therefore, *no risk* or *uncertainty*. The variance for the second example would be:

$$(\sigma^2) = \sum_{i=1}^{n} P_i[R_i - E(R_i)]^2$$

$$= [(0.15)(0.20 - 0.07)^2 + (0.15)(-0.20 - 0.07)^2 + (0.70)(0.10 - 0.07)^2]$$

$$= [0.010935 + 0.002535 + 0.00063]$$

$$= 0.0141$$

Standard Deviation The **standard deviation** is the square root of the variance:

$$\text{Standard Deviation} = \sqrt{\sum_{i=1}^{n} P_i [R_i - E(R_i)]^2} \qquad \textbf{1.8}$$

For the second example, the standard deviation would be:

$$\sigma = \sqrt{0.0141}$$
$$= 0.11874 = 11.874\%$$

Therefore, when describing this investment example, you would contend that you expect a return of 7 percent, but the standard deviation of your expectations is 11.87 percent.

A Relative Measure of Risk In some cases, an unadjusted variance or standard deviation can be misleading. If conditions for two or more investment alternatives are not similar—that is, if there are major differences in the expected rates of return—it is necessary to use a measure of *relative variability* to indicate risk per unit of expected return. A widely used relative measure of risk is the **coefficient of variation (CV)**, calculated as follows:

$$\begin{aligned} \text{Coefficient of} \\ \text{Variation (CV)} \end{aligned} = \frac{\text{Standard Deviation of Returns}}{\text{Expected Rate of Return}} \qquad \textbf{1.9}$$

$$= \frac{\sigma_i}{E(R)}$$

The *CV* for the preceding example would be:

$$CV = \frac{0.11874}{0.07000}$$

$$= 1.696$$

This measure of relative variability and risk is used by financial analysts to compare alternative investments with widely different rates of return and standard deviations of returns. As an illustration, consider the following two investments:

	Investment A	Investment B
Expected return	0.07	0.12
Standard deviation	0.05	0.07

Comparing absolute measures of risk, investment B appears to be riskier because it has a standard deviation of 7 percent versus 5 percent for investment A. In contrast, the *CV* figures show that investment B has less *relative* variability or lower risk per unit of expected return because it has a substantially higher expected rate of return:

$$CV_A = \frac{0.05}{0.07} = 0.714$$

$$CV_B = \frac{0.07}{0.12} = 0.583$$

1.2.5 Risk Measures for Historical Returns

To measure the risk for a series of historical rates of returns, we use the same measures as for expected returns (variance and standard deviation) except that we consider the historical holding period yields (HPYs) as follows:

$$\sigma^2 = \left[\sum_{i=1}^{n} [\text{HPY}_i - E(\text{HPY})]^2 \right] \Big/ n \qquad \textbf{1.10}$$

where:

$$\sigma^2 = \text{the variance of the series}$$
$$\text{HPY}_i = \text{the holding period yield during period } i$$
$$E(\text{HPY}) = \text{the expected value of the holding period yield that is equal to the arithmetic}$$
$$\text{mean (AM) of the series}$$
$$n = \text{the number of observations}$$

The standard deviation is the square root of the variance. Both measures indicate how much the individual HPYs over time deviated from the expected value of the series. An example computation is contained in the appendix to this chapter. As is shown in subsequent chapters where we present historical rates of return for alternative asset classes, presenting the standard deviation as a measure of risk (uncertainty) for the series or asset class is fairly common.

1.3 Determinants of Required Rates of Return

In this section, we continue our consideration of factors that you must consider when selecting securities for an investment portfolio. You will recall that this selection process involves finding securities that provide a rate of return that compensates you for: (1) the time value of money during the period of investment, (2) the expected rate of inflation during the period, and (3) the risk involved.

The summation of these three components is called the *required rate of return*. This is the minimum rate of return that you should accept from an investment to compensate you for deferring consumption. Because of the importance of the required rate of return to the total investment selection process, this section contains a discussion of the three components and what influences each of them.

The analysis and estimation of the required rate of return are complicated by the behavior of market rates over time. First, a wide range of rates is available for alternative investments at any time. Second, the rates of return on specific assets change dramatically over time. Third, the difference between the rates available (that is, the spread) on different assets changes over time.

The yield data in Exhibit 1.5 for alternative bonds demonstrate these three characteristics. First, even though all these securities have promised returns based upon bond contracts, the promised annual yields during any year differ substantially. As an example, during 2002 the average yields on alternative assets ranged from 1.61 percent on T-bills to 7.80 percent for Baa corporate bonds. Second, the changes in yields for a specific asset are shown by the three-month Treasury bill rate that went from 1.37 percent in 2004 to 3.16 percent in 2005. Third, an example of a change in the difference between yields over time (referred to as a spread) is shown by the Baa–Aaa spread.[4] The yield spread in 2002 was 131 basis points (7.80–6.49), but the spread in 2004 was only 76 basis points (6.39–5.63). (A basis point is 0.01 percent.)

Exhibit 1.5 Promised Yields on Alternative Bonds

Type of Bond	2001	2002	2003	2004	2005	2006	2007
U.S. government 3-month Treasury bills	3.40%	1.61%	1.01%	1.37%	3.16%	4.73%	4.48%
U.S. government 10-year bonds	4.09	3.10	2.10	2.79	3.93	4.77	4.94
Aaa corporate bonds	7.08	6.49	5.66	5.63	5.24	5.59	5.56
Baa corporate bonds	7.95	7.80	6.76	6.39	6.06	6.48	6.47

Source: *Federal Reserve Bulletin*, various issues.

[4] Bonds are rated by rating agencies based upon the credit risk of the securities, that is, the probability of default. Aaa is the top rating Moody's (a prominent rating service) gives to bonds with almost no probability of default. (Only U.S. Treasury bonds are considered to be of higher quality.) Baa is a lower rating Moody's gives to bonds of generally high quality that have some possibility of default under adverse economic conditions.

Because differences in yields result from the riskiness of each investment, you must understand the risk factors that affect the required rates of return and include them in your assessment of investment opportunities. Because the required returns on all investments change over time, and because large differences separate individual investments, you need to be aware of the several components that determine the required rate of return, starting with the risk-free rate. The discussion in this chapter considers the three components of the required rate of return and briefly discusses what affects these components. The presentation in Chapter 11 on valuation theory will discuss the factors that affect these components in greater detail.

1.3.1 The Real Risk-Free Rate

The **real risk-free rate (RRFR)** is the basic interest rate, assuming no inflation and no uncertainty about future flows. An investor in an inflation-free economy who knew with certainty what cash flows he or she would receive at what time would demand the RRFR on an investment. Earlier, we called this the *pure time value of money*, because the only sacrifice the investor made was deferring the use of the money for a period of time. This RRFR of interest is the price charged for the risk-free exchange between current goods and future goods.

Two factors, one subjective and one objective, influence this exchange price. The subjective factor is the time preference of individuals for the consumption of income. When individuals give up $100 of consumption this year, how much consumption do they want a year from now to compensate for that sacrifice? The strength of the human desire for current consumption influences the rate of compensation required. Time preferences vary among individuals, and the market creates a composite rate that includes the preferences of all investors. This composite rate changes gradually over time because it is influenced by all the investors in the economy, whose changes in preferences may offset one another.

The objective factor that influences the RRFR is the set of investment opportunities available in the economy. The investment opportunities are determined in turn by the *long-run real growth rate of the economy*. A rapidly growing economy produces more and better opportunities to invest funds and experience positive rates of return. A change in the economy's long-run real growth rate causes a change in all investment opportunities and a change in the required rates of return on all investments. Just as investors supplying capital should demand a higher rate of return when growth is higher, those looking for funds to invest should be willing and able to pay a higher rate of return to use the funds for investment because of the higher growth rate. Thus, a *positive* relationship exists between the real growth rate in the economy and the RRFR.

1.3.2 Factors Influencing the Nominal Risk-Free Rate (NRFR)

Earlier, we observed that an investor would be willing to forgo current consumption in order to increase future consumption at a rate of exchange called the *risk-free rate of interest*. This rate of exchange was measured in real terms because the investor wanted to increase the consumption of actual goods and services rather than consuming the same amount that had come to cost more money. Therefore, when we discuss rates of interest, we need to differentiate between *real* rates of interest that adjust for changes in the general price level, as opposed to *nominal* rates of interest that are stated in money terms. That is, nominal rates of interest that prevail in the market are determined by real rates of interest, plus factors that will affect the nominal rate of interest, such as the expected rate of inflation and the monetary environment. It is important to understand these factors.

As noted earlier, the variables that determine the RRFR change only gradually over the long term. Therefore, you might expect the required rate on a risk-free investment to be quite stable over time. As discussed in connection with Exhibit 1.5, rates on three-month T-bills were *not* stable over the period from 2001 to 2007. This is demonstrated with additional observations in Exhibit 1.6, which contains yields on T-bills for the period 1986 to 2007.

Investors view T-bills as a prime example of a default-free investment because the government has unlimited ability to derive income from taxes or to create money from which to

Exhibit 1.6   Three-Month Treasury Bill Yields and Rates of Inflation

Year	3-Month T-bills	Rate of Inflation	Year	3-Month T-bills	Rate of Inflation
1986	5.98%	1.10%	1997	5.06%	1.70%
1987	5.78	4.40	1998	4.78	1.61
1988	6.67	4.40	1999	4.64	2.70
1989	8.11	4.65	2000	5.82	3.40
1990	7.50	6.11	2001	3.40	1.55
1991	5.38	3.06	2002	1.61	2.49
1992	3.43	2.90	2003	1.01	1.87
1993	3.33	2.75	2004	1.37	3.26
1994	4.25	2.67	2005	3.16	3.42
1995	5.49	2.54	2006	4.73	2.54
1996	5.01	3.32	2007	4.48	4.08

Source: *Federal Reserve Bulletin*, various issues; *Economic Report of the President*, various issues.

pay interest. Therefore, one could expect that rates on T-bills should change only gradually. In fact, the data show a highly erratic pattern. Specifically, there was an increase in yields from 4.64 percent in 1999 to 5.82 percent in 2000 before declining by over 80 percent in three years to 1.01 percent in 2003. Clearly, the nominal rate of interest on a default-free investment is *not* stable in the long run or the short run, even though the underlying determinants of the RRFR are quite stable. The point is, two other factors influence the *nominal risk-free rate (NRFR)*: (1) the relative ease or tightness in the capital markets, and (2) the expected rate of inflation.

Conditions in the Capital Market   You will recall from prior courses in economics and finance that the purpose of capital markets is to bring together investors who want to invest savings with companies or governments who need capital to expand or to finance budget deficits. The cost of funds at any time (the interest rate) is the price that equates the current supply and demand for capital. A change in the relative ease or tightness in the capital market is a short-run phenomenon caused by a temporary disequilibrium in the supply and demand of capital.

As an example, disequilibrium could be caused by an unexpected change in monetary policy (for example, a change in the growth rate of the money supply) or fiscal policy (for example, a change in the federal deficit). Such a change in monetary policy or fiscal policy will produce a change in the NRFR of interest, but the change should be short-lived because, in the longer run, the higher or lower interest rates will affect capital supply and demand. As an example, an increase in the federal deficit caused by an increase in government spending (easy fiscal policy) will increase the demand for capital and increase interest rates. In turn, this increase in interest rates (for example, the price of money) will cause an increase in savings and a decrease in the demand for capital by corporations or individuals. These changes in market conditions will bring rates back to the long-run equilibrium, which is based on the long-run growth rate of the economy.

Expected Rate of Inflation   Previously, it was noted that if investors expected the price level to increase during the investment period, they would require the rate of return to include compensation for the expected rate of inflation. Assume that you require a 4 percent real rate of return on a risk-free investment but you expect prices to increase by 3 percent during the investment period. In this case, you should increase your required rate of return by this expected rate of inflation to about 7 percent $[(1.04 \times 1.03) - 1]$. If you do not increase your required return, the $104 you receive at the end of the year will represent a real return of about 1 percent, not 4 percent. Because prices have increased by 3 percent during the year, what previously cost $100 now costs $103, so you can consume only about 1 percent more at the end of the year [($104/103) − 1]. If you had required a 7.12 percent nominal return, your real consumption could have increased by 4 percent [($107.12/103) − 1]. Therefore, an investor's nominal required rate of return on a risk-free investment should be:

$$\text{NRFR} = (1 + \text{RRFR}) \times (1 + \text{Expected Rate of Inflation}) - 1 \qquad \textbf{1.11}$$

Rearranging the formula, you can calculate the RRFR of return on an investment as follows:

$$\text{RRFR} = \left[\frac{(1 + \text{NRFR of Return})}{(1 + \text{Rate of Inflation})} \right] - 1 \qquad \textbf{1.12}$$

To see how this works, assume that the nominal return on U.S. government T-bills was 9 percent during a given year, when the rate of inflation was 5 percent. In this instance, the RRFR of return on these T-bills was 3.8 percent, as follows:

$$\begin{aligned}
\text{RRFR} &= [(1 + 0.09)/(1 + 0.05)] - 1 \\
&= 1.038 - 1 \\
&= 0.038 = 3.8\%
\end{aligned}$$

This discussion makes it clear that the nominal rate of interest on a risk-free investment is not a good estimate of the RRFR, because the nominal rate can change dramatically in the short run in reaction to temporary ease or tightness in the capital market or because of changes in the expected rate of inflation. As indicated by the data in Exhibit 1.6, the significant changes in the average yield on T-bills typically were related to large changes in the rates of inflation.

The Common Effect All the factors discussed thus far regarding the required rate of return affect all investments equally. Whether the investment is in stocks, bonds, real estate, or machine tools, if the expected rate of inflation increases from 2 percent to 6 percent, the investor's required rate of return for *all* investments should increase by 4 percent. Similarly, if a decline in the expected real growth rate of the economy causes a decline in the RRFR of 1 percent, the required return on all investments should decline by 1 percent.

1.3.3 Risk Premium

A risk-free investment was defined as one for which the investor is certain of the amount and timing of the expected returns. The returns from most investments do not fit this pattern. An investor typically is not completely certain of the income to be received or when it will be received. Investments can range in uncertainty from basically risk-free securities, such as T-bills, to highly speculative investments, such as the common stock of small companies engaged in high-risk enterprises.

Most investors require higher rates of return on investments if they perceive that there is any uncertainty about the expected rate of return. This increase in the required rate of return over the NRFR is the **risk premium (RP)**. Although the required risk premium represents a composite of all uncertainty, it is possible to consider several fundamental sources of uncertainty. In this section, we identify and discuss briefly the major sources of uncertainty, including: (1) business risk, (2) financial risk (leverage), (3) liquidity risk, (4) exchange rate risk, and (5) country (political) risk.

Business risk is the uncertainty of income flows caused by the nature of a firm's business. The less certain the income flows of the firm, the less certain the income flows to the investor. Therefore, the investor will demand a risk premium that is based on the uncertainty caused by the basic business of the firm. As an example, a retail food company would typically experience stable sales and earnings growth over time and would have low business risk compared to a firm in the auto industry, where sales and earnings fluctuate substantially over the business cycle, implying high business risk.

Financial risk is the uncertainty introduced by the method by which the firm finances its investments. If a firm uses only common stock to finance investments, it incurs only business risk. If a firm borrows money to finance investments, it must pay fixed financing charges (in the form of interest to creditors) prior to providing income to the common stockholders, so the uncertainty of returns to the equity investor increases. This increase in uncertainty because of fixed-cost financing is called *financial risk* or *financial leverage* and causes an increase in the stock's risk premium. For an extended discussion on this, see Brigham (2007).

Liquidity risk is the uncertainty introduced by the secondary market for an investment. When an investor acquires an asset, he or she expects that the investment will mature (as with a bond) or that it will be salable to someone else. In either case, the investor expects to be able to convert the security into cash and use the proceeds for current consumption or other investments. The more difficult it is to make this conversion to cash, the greater the liquidity risk. An investor must consider two questions when assessing the liquidity risk of an investment: (1) How long will it take to convert the investment into cash? (2) How certain is the price to be received? Similar uncertainty faces an investor who wants to acquire an asset: How long will it take to acquire the asset? How uncertain is the price to be paid?[5]

Uncertainty regarding how fast an investment can be bought or sold, or the existence of uncertainty about its price, increases liquidity risk. A U.S. government Treasury bill has almost no liquidity risk because it can be bought or sold in minutes at a price almost identical to the quoted price. In contrast, examples of illiquid investments include a work of art, an antique, or a parcel of real estate in a remote area. For such investments, it may require a long time to find a buyer and the selling prices could vary substantially from expectations. Investors will increase their required rates of return to compensate for this uncertainty regarding timing and price. Liquidity risk can be a significant consideration when investing in foreign securities depending on the country and the liquidity of its stock and bond markets.

Exchange rate risk is the uncertainty of returns to an investor who acquires securities denominated in a currency different from his or her own. The likelihood of incurring this risk is becoming greater as investors buy and sell assets around the world, as opposed to only assets within their own countries. A U.S. investor who buys Japanese stock denominated in yen must consider not only the uncertainty of the return in yen but also any change in the exchange value of the yen relative to the U.S. dollar. That is, in addition to the foreign firm's business and financial risk and the security's liquidity risk, the investor must consider the additional uncertainty of the return on this Japanese stock when it is converted from yen to U.S. dollars.

As an example of exchange rate risk, assume that you buy 100 shares of Mitsubishi Electric at 1,050 yen when the exchange rate is 115 yen to the dollar. The dollar cost of this investment would be about $9.13 per share (1,050/115). A year later you sell the 100 shares at 1,200 yen when the exchange rate is 130 yen to the dollar. When you calculate the HPY in yen, you find the stock has increased in value by about 14 percent (1,200/1,050) − 1, but this is the HPY for a Japanese investor. A U.S. investor receives a much lower rate of return, because during this period the yen has weakened relative to the dollar by about 13 percent (that is, it requires more yen to buy a dollar—130 versus 115). At the new exchange rate, the stock is worth $9.23 per share (1,200/130). Therefore, the return to you as a U.S. investor would be only about 1 percent ($9.23/$9.13) versus 14 percent for the Japanese investor. The difference in return for the Japanese investor and U.S. investor is caused by exchange rate risk—that is, the decline in the value of the yen relative to the dollar. Clearly, the exchange rate could have gone in the other direction, the dollar weakening against the yen. In this case, as a U.S. investor, you would have experienced the 14 percent return measured in yen, as well as a gain from the exchange rate change.

[5] You will recall from prior courses that the overall capital market is composed of the primary market and the secondary market. Securities are initially sold in the primary market, and all subsequent transactions take place in the secondary market. These concepts are discussed in Chapter 4.

The more volatile the exchange rate between two countries, the less certain you would be regarding the exchange rate, the greater the exchange rate risk, and the larger the exchange rate risk premium you would require. For an analysis of pricing this risk, see Jorion (1991).

There can also be exchange rate risk for a U.S. firm that is extensively multinational in terms of sales and components (costs). In this case, the firm's foreign earnings can be affected by changes in the exchange rate. As will be discussed, this risk can generally be hedged at a cost.

Country risk, also called *political risk*, is the uncertainty of returns caused by the possibility of a major change in the political or economic environment of a country. The United States is acknowledged to have the smallest country risk in the world because its political and economic systems are the most stable. During the spring and summer of 2008 examples of countries with high country risk would be: Pakistan where Taliban terrorists are attempting to block an attempt at democracy; China where clashes with Tibet is overshadowing the 2008 Olympics; Venezuela where Chavez is attempting to nationalize oil operations owned by Exxon and other U.S. firms; and, India where food riots are threatening political stability. Individuals who invest in countries that have unstable political or economic systems must add a country risk premium when determining their required rates of return.

When investing globally (which is emphasized throughout the book), investors must consider these additional uncertainties. How liquid are the secondary markets for stocks and bonds in the country? Are any of the country's securities traded on major stock exchanges in the United States, London, Tokyo, or Germany? What will happen to exchange rates during the investment period? What is the probability of a political or economic change that will adversely affect your rate of return? Exchange rate risk and country risk differ among countries. A good measure of exchange rate risk would be the absolute variability of the exchange rate relative to a composite exchange rate. The analysis of country risk is much more subjective and must be based on the history and current political environment of the country.

This discussion of risk components can be considered a security's *fundamental risk* because it deals with the intrinsic factors that should affect a security's volatility of returns over time. In subsequent discussion, the standard deviation of returns is referred to as a measure of the security's *total risk*, which considers the individual stock by itself—that is, the stock is not considered as part of a portfolio.

Risk Premium = f (Business Risk, Financial Risk, Liquidity Risk, Exchange Rate Risk, Country Risk)

1.3.4 Risk Premium and Portfolio Theory

An alternative view of risk has been derived from extensive work in portfolio theory and capital market theory by Markowitz (1952, 1959) and Sharpe (1964). These theories are dealt with in greater detail in Chapter 7 and Chapter 8 but their impact on a stock's risk premium should be mentioned briefly at this point. These prior works by Markowitz and Sharpe indicated that investors should use an *external market* measure of risk. Under a specified set of assumptions, all rational, profit-maximizing investors want to hold a completely diversified market portfolio of risky assets, and they borrow or lend to arrive at a risk level that is consistent with their risk preferences. Under these conditions, they showed that the relevant risk measure for an individual asset is its *comovement with the market portfolio*. This comovement, which is measured by an asset's covariance with the market portfolio, is referred to as an asset's **systematic risk,** the portion of an individual asset's total variance that is attributable to the variability of the total market portfolio. In addition, individual assets have variance that is unrelated to the market portfolio (the asset's nonmarket variance) that is due to the asset's unique features. This nonmarket variance is called *unsystematic risk*, and it is generally considered unimportant because it is eliminated in a large, diversified portfolio. Therefore, under these assumptions, *the risk premium for an individual earning asset is a function of the asset's systematic risk with the aggregate market portfolio of risky assets*. The measure of an asset's systematic risk is referred to as its *beta*:

Risk Premium = f (Systematic Market Risk)

1.3.5 Fundamental Risk versus Systematic Risk

Some might expect a conflict between the market measure of risk (systematic risk) and the fundamental determinants of risk (business risk, and so on). A number of studies have examined the relationship between the market measure of risk (systematic risk) and accounting variables used to measure the fundamental risk factors, such as business risk, financial risk, and liquidity risk. The authors of these studies (especially Thompson, 1976) have generally concluded that *a significant relationship exists between the market measure of risk and the fundamental measures of risk.* Therefore, the two measures of risk can be complementary. This consistency seems reasonable because, one might expect the market measure of risk to reflect the fundamental risk characteristics of the asset. For example, you might expect a firm that has high business risk and financial risk to have an above-average beta. At the same time, as we discuss in Chapter 8, a firm that has a high level of fundamental risk and a large standard deviation of return on stock can have a lower level of systematic risk simply because the variability of its earnings and its stock price is not related to the aggregate economy or the aggregate market. Therefore, one can specify the risk premium for an asset as either:

$$\text{Risk Premium} = f(\text{Business Risk, Financial Risk, Liquidity Risk, Exchange Rate Risk, Country Risk})$$

or

$$\text{Risk Premium} = f(\text{Systematic Market Risk})$$

1.3.6 Summary of Required Rate of Return

The overall required rate of return on alternative investments is determined by three variables: (1) the economy's RRFR, which is influenced by the investment opportunities in the economy (that is, the long-run real growth rate); (2) variables that influence the NRFR, which include short-run ease or tightness in the capital market and the expected rate of inflation (notably, these variables, which determine the NRFR, are the same for all investments); and (3) the risk premium on the investment. In turn, this risk premium can be related to fundamental factors, including business risk, financial risk, liquidity risk, exchange rate risk, and country risk, or it can be a function of an asset's systematic market risk (beta).

Measures and Sources of Risk In this chapter, we have examined both measures and sources of risk arising from an investment. The *measures* of risk for an investment are:

- Variance of rates of return
- Standard deviation of rates of return
- Coefficient of variation of rates of return (standard deviation/means)
- Covariance of returns with the market portfolio (beta)

The *sources* of risk are:

- Business risk
- Financial risk
- Liquidity risk
- Exchange rate risk
- Country risk

1.4 Relationship between Risk and Return

Previously, we showed how to measure the risk and rates of return for alternative investments and we discussed what determines the rates of return that investors require. This section discusses the risk-return combinations that might be available at a point in time and illustrates the factors that cause *changes* in these combinations.

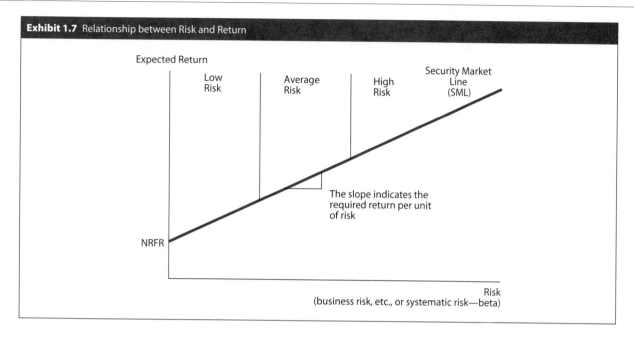

Exhibit 1.7 Relationship between Risk and Return

Exhibit 1.7 graphs the expected relationship between risk and return. It shows that investors increase their required rates of return as perceived risk (uncertainty) increases. The line that reflects the combination of risk and return available on alternative investments is referred to as the **security market line (SML)**. The SML reflects the risk-return combinations available for all risky assets in the capital market at a given time. Investors would select investments that are consistent with their risk preferences; some would consider only low-risk investments, whereas others welcome high-risk investments.

Beginning with an initial SML, three changes can occur. First, individual investments can change positions on the SML because of changes in the perceived risk of the investments. Second, the slope of the SML can change because of a change in the attitudes of investors toward risk; that is, investors can change the returns they require per unit of risk. Third, the SML can experience a parallel shift due to a change in the RRFR or the expected rate of inflation—that is, a change in the NRFR. These three possibilities are discussed in this section.

1.4.1 Movements along the SML

Investors place alternative investments somewhere along the SML based on their perceptions of the risk of the investment. Obviously, if an investment's risk changes due to a change in one of its risk sources (business risk, and such), it will move along the SML. For example, if a firm increases its financial risk by selling a large bond issue that increases its financial leverage, investors will perceive its common stock as riskier and the stock will move up the SML to a higher risk position. Investors will then require a higher rate of return. As the common stock becomes riskier, it changes its position on the SML. Any change in an asset that affects its fundamental risk factors or its market risk (that is, its beta) will cause the asset to move *along* the SML as shown in Exhibit 1.8. Note that the SML does not change, only the position of specific assets on the SML.

1.4.2 Changes in the Slope of the SML

The slope of the SML indicates the return per unit of risk required by all investors. Assuming a straight line, it is possible to select any point on the SML and compute a risk premium (RP) for an asset through the equation:

$$RP_i = E(R_i) - NRFR \qquad \text{1.13}$$

Exhibit 1.8 Changes in the Required Rate of Return Due to Movements along the SML

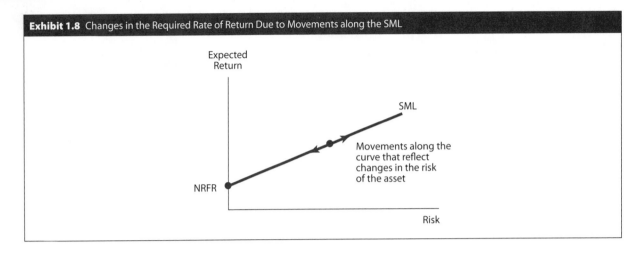

where:

RP_i = risk premium for asset i
$E(R_i)$ = the expected return for asset i
NRFR = the nominal return on a risk-free asset

If a point on the SML is identified as the portfolio that contains all the risky assets in the market (referred to as the *market portfolio*), it is possible to compute a market RP as follows:

1.14
$$RP_m = E(R_m) - NRFR$$

where:

RP_m = the risk premium on the market portfolio
$E(R_m)$ = the expected return on the market portfolio
NRFR = the nominal return on a risk-free asset

This market RP is *not constant* because the slope of the SML changes over time. Although we do not understand completely what causes these changes in the slope, we do know that there are changes in the *yield* differences between assets with different levels of risk even though the inherent risk differences are relatively constant.

These differences in yields are referred to as **yield spreads**, and these yield spreads change over time. As an example, if the yield on a portfolio of Aaa-rated bonds is 7.50 percent and the yield on a portfolio of Baa-rated bonds is 9.00 percent, we would say that the yield spread is 1.50 percent. This 1.50 percent is referred to as a credit risk premium because the Baa-rated bond is considered to have higher credit risk—that is, it has a higher probability of default. This Baa–Aaa yield spread is *not* constant over time, as shown by the substantial volatility in the yield spreads shown in Exhibit 1.9.

Although the underlying risk factors for the portfolio of bonds in the Aaa-rated bond index and the Baa-rated bond index would probably not change dramatically over time, it is clear from the time-series plot in Exhibit 1.9 that the difference in yields (i.e., the yield spread) has experienced changes of more than 100 basis points (1 percent) in a short period of time (for example, see the yield spread increase in 1974 to 1975 and the dramatic declines in yield spread during 1983–84 and 2003–04). Such a significant change in the yield spread during a period where there is no major change in the fundamental risk characteristics of Baa bonds relative to Aaa bonds would imply a change in the market RP. Specifically, although the

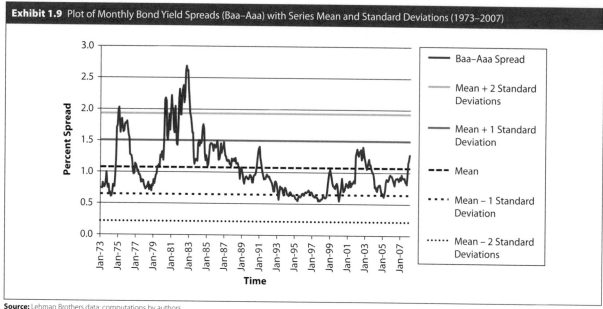

Exhibit 1.9 Plot of Monthly Bond Yield Spreads (Baa–Aaa) with Series Mean and Standard Deviations (1973–2007)

Source: Lehman Brothers data; computations by authors.

intrinsic financial risk characteristics of the bonds remain relatively constant, investors have changed the yield spreads they demand to accept this relatively constant difference in financial risk.

This change in the RP implies a change in the slope of the SML. Such a change is shown in Exhibit 1.10. The exhibit assumes an increase in the market risk premium, which means an increase in the slope of the market line. Such a change in the slope of the SML (the market risk premium) will affect the required rate of return for all risky assets. Irrespective of where an investment is on the original SML, its required rate of return will increase, although its individual risk characteristics remain unchanged.

1.4.3 Changes in Capital Market Conditions or Expected Inflation

The graph in Exhibit 1.11 shows what happens to the SML when there are changes in one of the following factors: (1) expected real growth in the economy, (2) capital market conditions, or (3) the expected rate of inflation. For example, an increase in expected real growth, temporary tightness in the capital market, or an increase in the expected rate of inflation will cause the SML to experience a parallel shift upward as shown in Exhibit 1.11. The parallel shift occurs because changes in expected real growth or in capital market conditions or a change in the expected rate of inflation affect the economy's nominal risk-free rate (NRFR) that impacts all investments, no matter what their levels of risk are.

1.4.4 Summary of Changes in the Required Rate of Return

The relationship between risk and the required rate of return for an investment can change in three ways:

1. A movement *along* the SML demonstrates a change in the risk characteristics of a specific investment, such as a change in its business risk, its financial risk, or its systematic risk (its beta). This change affects only the individual investment.

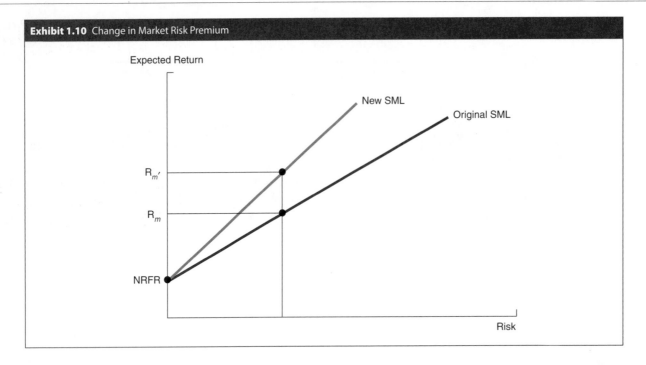

Exhibit 1.10 Change in Market Risk Premium

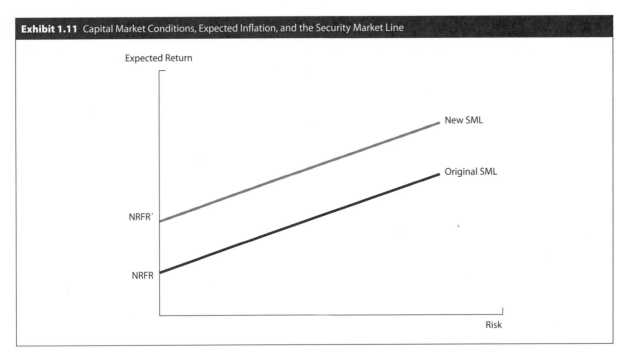

Exhibit 1.11 Capital Market Conditions, Expected Inflation, and the Security Market Line

2. A change in the *slope* of the SML occurs in response to a change in the attitudes of investors toward risk. Such a change demonstrates that investors want either higher or lower rates of return for the same risk. This is also described as a change in the market risk premium (R_m − NRFR). A change in the market risk premium will affect all risky investments.
3. A *shift* in the SML reflects a change in expected real growth, a change in market conditions (such as ease or tightness of money), or a change in the expected rate of inflation. Again, such a change will affect all investments.

• • • • SUMMARY • • • •

The purpose of this chapter is to provide background that can be used in subsequent chapters. To achieve that goal, we covered several topics:

- We discussed why individuals save part of their income and why they decide to invest their savings. We defined *investment* as the current commitment of these savings for a period of time to derive a rate of return that compensates for the time involved, the expected rate of inflation, and the uncertainty.
- We examined ways to quantify historical return and risk to help analyze alternative investment opportunities. We considered two measures of mean return (arithmetic and geometric) and applied these to a historical series for an individual investment and to a portfolio of investments during a period of time.
- We considered the concept of uncertainty and alternative measures of risk (the variance, standard deviation, and a relative measure of risk—the coefficient of variation).
- Before discussing the determinants of the required rate of return for an investment, we noted that the estimation of the required rate of return is complicated because the rates on individual investments change over time, because there is a wide range of rates of return available on alternative investments, and because the differences between required

returns on alternative investments (for example, the yield spreads) likewise change over time.

- We examined the specific factors that determine the required rate of return: (1) the real risk-free rate, which is based on the real rate of growth in the economy, (2) the nominal risk-free rate, which is influenced by capital market conditions and the expected rate of inflation, and (3) a risk premium, which is a function of fundamental factors, such as business risk, or the systematic risk of the asset relative to the market portfolio (that is, its beta).
- We discussed the risk-return combinations available on alternative investments at a point in time (illustrated by the SML) and the three factors that can cause changes in this relationship. First, a change in the inherent risk of an investment (that is, its fundamental risk or market risk) will cause a movement along the SML. Second, a change in investors' attitudes toward risk will cause a change in the required return per unit of risk—that is, a change in the market risk premium. Such a change will cause a change in the slope of the SML. Finally, a change in expected real growth, in capital market conditions, or in the expected rate of inflation will cause a parallel shift of the SML.

Based on this understanding of the investment environment, you are prepared to consider the asset allocation decision, which is discussed in Chapter 2.

• • • • SUGGESTED READINGS • • • •

Fama, Eugene F., and Merton H. Miller. *The Theory of Finance.* New York: Holt, Rinehart and Winston, 1972.

Fisher, Irving. *The Theory of Interest.* New York: Macmillan, 1930, reprinted by Augustus M. Kelley, 1961.

• • • • QUESTIONS • • • •

1. Discuss the overall purpose people have for investing. Define investment.
2. As a student, are you saving or borrowing? Why?
3. Divide a person's life from ages 20 to 70 into 10-year segments and discuss the likely saving or borrowing patterns during each period.
4. Discuss why you would expect the saving-borrowing pattern to differ by occupation (for example, for a doctor versus a plumber).
5. *The Wall Street Journal* reported that the yield on common stocks is about 2 percent, whereas a study at the University of Chicago contends that the annual rate of return on common stocks since 1926 has averaged about 12 percent. Reconcile these statements.
6. Some financial theorists consider the variance of the distribution of expected rates of return to be a good measure of uncertainty. Discuss the reasoning behind this measure of risk and its purpose.
7. Discuss the three components of an investor's required rate of return on an investment.
8. Discuss the two major factors that determine the market nominal risk-free rate (NRFR). Explain which of these factors would be more volatile over the business cycle.
9. Briefly discuss the five fundamental factors that influence the risk premium of an investment.
10. You own stock in the Gentry Company, and you read in the financial press that a recent bond offering has raised the firm's debt/equity ratio from 35 percent to 55 percent. Discuss the effect of this change on the variability of the firm's net income stream, other factors being constant. Discuss how this change would affect your required rate of return on the common stock of the Gentry Company.

11. Draw a properly labeled graph of the security market line (SML) and indicate where you would expect the following investments to fall along that line. Discuss your reasoning.
    a. Common stock of large firms
    b. U.S. government bonds
    c. U.K. government bonds
    d. Low-grade corporate bonds
    e. Common stock of a Japanese firm

12. Explain why you would change your nominal required rate of return if you expected the rate of inflation to go from 0 (no inflation) to 4 percent. Give an example of what would happen if you did not change your required rate of return under these conditions.

13. Assume the long-run growth rate of the economy increased by 1 percent and the expected rate of inflation increased by 4 percent. What would happen to the required rates of return on government bonds and common stocks? Show graphically how the effects of these changes would differ between these alternative investments.

14. You see in *The Wall Street Journal* that the yield spread between Baa corporate bonds and Aaa corporate bonds has gone from 350 basis points (3.5 percent) to 200 basis points (2 percent). Show graphically the effect of this change in yield spread on the SML and discuss its effect on the required rate of return for common stocks.

15. Give an example of a liquid investment and an illiquid investment. Discuss why you consider each of them to be liquid or illiquid.

• • • • PROBLEMS • • • •

1. At the beginning of last year, you invested $4,000 in 80 shares of the Chang Corporation. During the year, Chang paid dividends of $5 per share. At the end of the year, you sold the 80 shares for $59 a share. Compute your total HPY on these shares and indicate how much was due to the price change and how much was due to the dividend income.

2. On February 1, you bought 100 shares of stock in the Francesca Corporation for $34 a share and a year later you sold it for $39 a share. During the year, you received a cash dividend of $1.50 a share. Compute your HPR and HPY on this Francesca stock investment.

3. On August 15, you purchased 100 shares of stock in the Cara Cotton Company at $65 a share and a year later you sold it for $61 a share. During the year, you received dividends of $3 a share. Compute your HPR and HPY on your investment in Cara Cotton.

4. The rates of return computed in Problems 1, 2, and 3 are nominal rates of return. Assuming that the rate of inflation during the year was 4 percent, compute the real rates of return on these investments. Compute the real rates of return if the rate of inflation was 8 percent.

5. You are considering acquiring shares of common stock in the Madison Beer Corporation. Your rate of return expectations are as follows:

MADISON BEER CORP.

Possible Rate of Return	Probability
−0.10	0.30
0.00	0.10
0.10	0.30
0.25	0.30

Compute the expected return $[E(R_i)]$ on your investment in Madison Beer.

6. A stockbroker calls you and suggests that you invest in the Lauren Computer Company. After analyzing the firm's annual report and other material, you believe that the distribution of expected rates of return is as follows:

LAUREN COMPUTER CO.

Possible Rate of Return	Probability
−0.60	0.05
−0.30	0.20
−0.10	0.10
0.20	0.30
0.40	0.20
0.80	0.15

Compute the expected return $[E(R_i)]$ on Lauren Computer stock.

7. Without any formal computations, do you consider Madison Beer in Problem 6 or Lauren Computer in Problem 7 to present greater risk? Discuss your reasoning.

8. During the past five years, you owned two stocks that had the following annual rates of return:

Year	Stock T	Stock B
1	0.19	0.08
2	0.08	0.03
3	−0.12	−0.09
4	−0.03	0.02
5	0.15	0.04

   a. Compute the arithmetic mean annual rate of return for each stock. Which stock is most desirable by this measure?
   b. Compute the standard deviation of the annual rate of return for each stock. (Use Chapter 1 Appendix if necessary.) By this measure, which is the preferable stock?
   c. Compute the coefficient of variation for each stock. (Use the Chapter 1 Appendix if necessary.) By this relative measure of risk, which stock is preferable?
   d. Compute the geometric mean rate of return for each stock. Discuss the difference between the arithmetic mean return and the geometric mean return for each stock. Discuss the differences in the mean returns relative to the standard deviation of the return for each stock.

9. You read in *BusinessWeek* that a panel of economists has estimated that the long-run real growth rate of the U.S. economy over the next five-year period will average 3 percent. In addition, a bank newsletter estimates that the average annual rate of inflation during this five-year period will be about 4 percent. What nominal rate of return would you expect on U.S. government T-bills during this period?

10. What would your required rate of return be on common stocks if you wanted a 5 percent risk premium to own common stocks given what you know from Problem 10? If common stock investors became more risk averse, what would happen to the required rate of return on common stocks? What would be the impact on stock prices?

11. Assume that the consensus required rate of return on common stocks is 14 percent. In addition, you read in *Fortune* that the expected rate of inflation is 5 percent and the estimated long-term real growth rate of the economy is 3 percent. What interest rate would you expect on U.S. government T-bills? What is the approximate risk premium for common stocks implied by these data?

12. During the past year, you had a portfolio that contained U.S. government T-bills, long-term government bonds, and common stocks. The rates of return on each of them were as follows:

U.S. government T-bills	5.50%
U.S. government long-term bonds	7.50
U.S. common stocks	11.60

During the year, the consumer price index, which measures the rate of inflation, went from 160 to 172 (1982 − 1984 = 100). Compute the rate of inflation during this year. Compute the real rates of return on each of the investments in your portfolio based on the inflation rate.

THOMSON ONE | Business School Edition

1. Read *A Guide to Using Thomson One: Business School Edition* by Rosemary Carlson, which was shrink-wrapped with your text. Thomson One: Business School Edition is a special version of a powerful data and analytical package used by many investment professionals. It will be useful to you in this and other classes you are taking this semester.

2. Follow the directions in section III "How do I find general overview information for a firm?" for Walgreens (stock symbol: WAG) and Wal-Mart (WMT), two firms in the retail industry (or try two firms in an industry of your choice). On what stock markets are the firms traded? How do their growth rates in sales and earnings compare? How have their stocks performed over the past few months? Are stock analysts recommending investors buy or sell each of the two firm's stocks?

Computation of Variance and Standard Deviation

Variance and standard deviation are measures of how actual values differ from the expected values (arithmetic mean) for a given series of values. In this case, we want to measure how rates of return differ from the arithmetic mean value of a series. There are other measures of dispersion, but variance and standard deviation are the best known because they are used in statistics and probability theory. Variance is defined as:

$$\text{Variance } (\sigma^2) = \sum_{i=1}^{n} (\text{Probability})(\text{Possible Return} - \text{Expected Return})^2$$

$$= \sum_{i=1}^{n} (P_i)[R_i - E(R_i)]^2$$

Consider the following example, as discussed in the chapter:

Probability of Possible Return (P_i)	Possible Return (R_i)	P_iR_i
0.15	0.20	0.03
0.15	−0.20	−0.03
0.70	0.10	0.07
		$\Sigma = 0.07$

This gives an expected return $[E(R_i)]$ of 7 percent. The dispersion of this distribution as measured by variance is:

Probability (P_i)	Return (R_i)	$R_i - E(R_i)$	$[R_i - E(R_i)]^2$	$P_i[R_i - E(R_i)]^2$
0.15	0.20	0.13	0.0169	0.002535
0.15	−0.20	−0.27	0.0729	0.010935
0.70	0.10	0.03	0.0009	0.000630
				$\Sigma = 0.014100$

The variance (σ^2) is equal to 0.0141. The standard deviation is equal to the square root of the variance:

$$\text{Standard Deviation } (\sigma^2) = \sqrt{\sum_{i=1}^{n} P_i[R_i - E(R_i)]^2}$$

Consequently, the standard deviation for the preceding example would be:

$$\sigma_i = \sqrt{0.0141} = 0.11874$$

In this example, the standard deviation is approximately 11.87 percent. Therefore, you could describe this distribution as having an expected value of 7 percent and a standard deviation of 11.87 percent.

In many instances, you might want to compute the variance or standard deviation for a historical series in order to evaluate the past performance of the investment. Assume that you are given the following information on annual rates of return (HPY) for common stocks listed on the New York Stock Exchange (NYSE):

Year	Annual Rate of Return
2009	0.07
2010	0.11
2011	−0.04
2012	0.12
2013	−0.06

In this case, we are not examining expected rates of return but actual returns. Therefore, we assume equal probabilities, and the expected value (in this case the mean value, R) of the series is the sum of the individual observations in the series divided by the number of observations, or 0.04 (0.20/5). The variances and standard deviations are:

Year	R_i	$R_i - \bar{R}$	$(R_i - \bar{R})^2$	
2009	0.07	0.03	0.0009	$\sigma^2 = 0.0286/5$
2010	0.11	0.07	0.0049	$= 0.00572$
2011	−0.04	−0.08	0.0064	
2012	0.12	0.08	0.0064	$\sigma = \sqrt{0.00572}$
2013	−0.06	−0.10	0.0110	$= 0.0756$
			$\Sigma = 0.0286$	

We can interpret the performance of NYSE common stocks during this period of time by saying that the average rate of return was 4 percent and the standard deviation of annual rates of return was 7.56 percent.

Coefficient of Variation

In some instances, you might want to compare the dispersion of two different series. The variance and standard deviation are *absolute* measures of dispersion. That is, they can be influenced by the magnitude of the original numbers. To compare series with greatly different values, you need a *relative* measure of dispersion. A measure of relative dispersion is the coefficient of variation, which is defined as:

$$\text{Coefficient of Variation } (CV) = \frac{\text{Standard Deviation of Returns}}{\text{Expected Rate of Return}}$$

A larger value indicates greater dispersion relative to the arithmetic mean of the series. For the previous example, the CV would be:

$$CV_1 = \frac{0.0756}{0.0400} = 1.89$$

It is possible to compare this value to a similar figure having a markedly different distribution. As an example, assume you wanted to compare this investment to another investment that had an average rate of return of 10 percent and a standard deviation of 9 percent. The standard deviations alone tells you that the second series has greater dispersion (9 percent versus 7.56 percent) and might be considered to have higher risk. In fact, the relative dispersion for this second investment is much less.

$$CV_1 = \frac{0.0756}{0.0400} = 1.89$$

$$CV_2 = \frac{0.0900}{0.1000} = 0.90$$

Considering the relative dispersion and the total distribution, most investors would probably prefer the second investment.

Problems

1. Your rate of return expectations for the common stock of Gray Disc Company during the next year are:

GRAY DISC CO.

Possible Rate of Return	Probability
−0.10	0.25
0.00	0.15
0.10	0.35
0.25	0.25

a. Compute the expected return $[E(R_i)]$ on this investment, the variance of this return (σ^2), and its standard deviation (σ).

b. Under what conditions can the standard deviation be used to measure the relative risk of two investments?

c. Under what conditions must the coefficient of variation be used to measure the relative risk of two investments?

2. Your rate of return expectations for the stock of Kayleigh Computer Company during the next year are:

KAYLEIGH COMPUTER CO.

Possible Rate of Return	Probability
−0.60	0.15
−0.30	0.10
−0.10	0.05
0.20	0.40
0.40	0.20
0.80	0.10

a. Compute the expected return $[E(R_i)]$ on this stock, the variance (σ^2) of this return, and its standard deviation (σ).
b. On the basis of expected return $[E(R_i)]$ alone, discuss whether Gray Disc or Kayleigh Computer is preferable.
c. On the basis of standard deviation (σ) alone, discuss whether Gray Disc or Kayleigh Computer is preferable.
d. Compute the coefficients of variation (CVs) for Gray Disc and Kayleigh Computer and discuss which stock return series has the greater relative dispersion.

3. The following are annual rates of return for U.S. government T-bills and U.K. common stocks.

Year	U.S. Government T-Bills	U.K. Common Stock
2009	0.063	0.150
2010	0.081	0.043
2011	0.076	0.374
2012	0.090	0.192
2013	0.085	0.106

a. Compute the arithmetic mean rate of return and standard deviation of rates of return for the two series.
b. Discuss these two alternative investments in terms of their arithmetic average rates of return, their absolute risk, and their relative risk.
c. Compute the geometric mean rate of return for each of these investments. Compare the arithmetic mean return and geometric mean return for each investment and discuss this difference between mean returns as related to the standard deviation of each series.

CHAPTER 2

The Asset Allocation Decision*

After you read this chapter, you should be able to answer the following questions:

- What is involved in the asset allocation process?
- What are the four steps in the portfolio management process?
- What is the role of asset allocation in investment planning?
- Why is a policy statement important to the planning process?
- What objectives and constraints should be detailed in a policy statement?
- How and why do investment goals change over a person's lifetime?
- Why do asset allocation strategies differ across national boundaries?

The previous chapter informed us that *risk drives return*. Therefore, the practice of investing funds and managing portfolios should focus primarily on managing risk rather than on managing returns.

This chapter examines some of the practical implications of risk management in the context of asset allocation. **Asset allocation** is the process of deciding how to distribute an investor's wealth among different countries and asset classes for investment purposes. An **asset class** is comprised of securities that have similar characteristics, attributes, and risk/return relationships. A broad asset class, such as "bonds," can be divided into smaller asset classes, such as Treasury bonds, corporate bonds, and high-yield bonds. We will see that, in the long run, the highest compounded returns will most likely accrue to those investors with larger exposures to risky assets. We will also see that although there are no shortcuts or guarantees to investment success, maintaining a reasonable and disciplined approach to investing will increase the likelihood of investment success over time.

The asset allocation decision is not an isolated choice; rather, it is a component of a structured four-step portfolio management process that we present in this chapter. As we will see, the first step in the process is to develop an investment policy statement, or plan, that will guide all future decisions. Much of an asset allocation strategy depends on the investor's policy statement, which includes the investor's goals or objectives, constraints, and investment guidelines.

What we mean by an "investor" can range from an individual to trustees overseeing a corporation's multibillion-dollar pension fund, a university endowment, or invested premiums for an insurance company. Regardless of who the investor is or how simple or complex the investment needs, he or she should develop a policy statement before making long-term investment decisions. Although most of our examples will be in the context of an individual investor, the concepts we introduce here—investment objectives, constraints, benchmarks, and so on—apply to any investor, individual or institution. We'll review historical data to show the importance of the asset allocation decision and discuss the need for investor education, an important issue for companies who offer retirement or savings plans to their employees. The chapter concludes by examining asset allocation strategies across national borders to

*The authors acknowledge the collaboration of Professor Edgar Norton of Illinois State University on this chapter.

show the effect of regulations, market environment, and culture on investing patterns; what is appropriate for a U.S.-based investor is not necessarily appropriate for a non-U.S.-based investor.

2.1 Individual Investor Life Cycle

Financial plans and investment needs are as different as each individual. Investment needs change over a person's life cycle. How individuals structure their financial plan should be related to their age, financial status, future plans, risk aversion characteristics, and needs.

2.1.1 The Preliminaries

Before embarking on an investment program, we need to make sure other needs are satisfied. No serious investment plan should be started until a potential investor has adequate income to cover living expenses and has a safety net should the unexpected occur.

Insurance Life insurance should be a component of any financial plan. Life insurance protects loved ones against financial hardship should death occur before our financial goals are met. The death benefit paid by the insurance company can help pay medical bills and funeral expenses and provide cash that family members can use to maintain their lifestyle, retire debt, or invest for future needs (for example, children's education, spouse retirement). Therefore, one of the first steps in developing a financial plan is to purchase adequate life insurance coverage.

Insurance can also serve more immediate purposes, including being a means to meet long-term goals, such as retirement planning. On reaching retirement age, you can receive the cash or surrender value of your life insurance policy and use the proceeds to supplement your retirement lifestyle or for estate planning purposes.

Insurance coverage also provides protection against other uncertainties. *Health* insurance helps to pay medical bills. *Disability* insurance provides continuing income should you become unable to work. *Automobile and home* (or rental) insurances provide protection against accidents and damage to cars or residences.

Although nobody ever expects to use his or her insurance coverage, a first step in a sound financial plan is to have adequate coverage "just in case." Lack of insurance coverage can ruin the best-planned investment program.

Cash Reserve Emergencies, job layoffs, and unforeseen expenses happen, and good investment opportunities emerge. It is important to have a cash reserve to help meet these occasions. In addition to providing a safety cushion, a cash reserve reduces the likelihood of being forced to sell investments at inopportune times to cover unexpected expenses. Most experts recommend a cash reserve equal to about six months' living expenses. Calling it a "cash" reserve does not mean the funds should be in cash; rather, the funds should be in investments you can easily convert to cash with little chance of a loss in value. Money market or short-term bond mutual funds and bank accounts are appropriate vehicles for the cash reserve.

Similar to the financial plan, an investor's insurance and cash reserve needs will change over his or her life. The need for disability insurance declines when a person retires. In contrast, other insurance, such as supplemental Medicare coverage or long-term-care insurance, may become more important.

2.1.2 Investment Strategies Over an Investor's Lifetime

Assuming the basic insurance and cash reserve needs are met, individuals can start a serious investment program with their savings. Because of changes in their net worth and risk tolerance, individuals' investment strategies will change over their lifetime. In the following sections, we review various phases in the investment life cycle. Although each individual's needs and preferences are different, some general traits affect most investors over the life cycle.

Exhibit 2.1 Rise and Fall of Personal Net Worth over a Lifetime

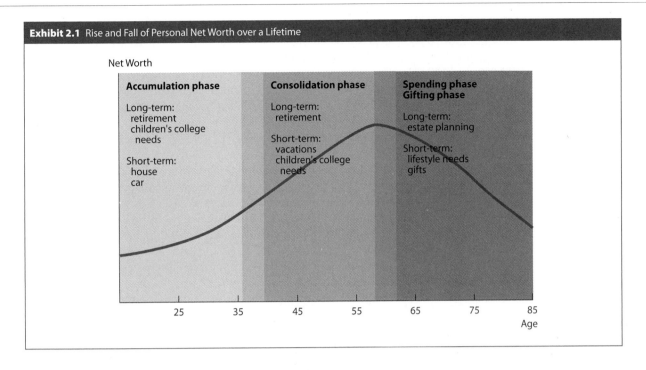

The four life-cycle phases are shown in Exhibit 2.1 (the third and fourth phases—spending and gifting—are shown as concurrent) and described here.

Accumulation Phase Individuals in the early-to-middle years of their working careers are in the **accumulation phase**. As the name implies, these individuals are attempting to accumulate assets to satisfy fairly immediate needs (for example, a down payment for a house) or longer-term goals (children's college education, retirement). Typically, their net worth is small, and debt from car loans or their own past college loans may be heavy. As a result of their typically long investment time horizon and their future earning ability, individuals in the accumulation phase are willing to make relatively high-risk investments in the hopes of making above-average nominal returns over time.

Here we must emphasize the wisdom of investing early and regularly in one's life. Funds invested in early life-cycle phases, with returns compounding over time, will reap significant financial benefits during later phases. Exhibit 2.2 shows growth from an initial $10,000 investment over 20, 30, and 40 years at assumed annual returns of 7 and 8 percent. The middle-aged

Exhibit 2.2 Benefits of Investing Early

		The Future Value of an Initial $10,000 Investment	The Future Value of Investing $2,000 Annually	The Future Value of the Initial Investment Plus the Annual Investment
Interest rate	7.0%			
20 years		$38,696.84	$81,990.98	$120,687.83
30 years		$76,122.55	$188,921.57	$265,044.12
40 years		$149,744.58	$399,270.22	$549,014.80
Interest rate	8.0%			
20 years		$46,609.57	$91,523.93	$138,133.50
30 years		$100,626.57	$226,566.42	$327,192.99
40 years		$217,245.21	$518,113.04	$735,358.25

Source: Calculations by authors.

person who invests $10,000 "when he or she can afford it" will only reap the benefits of compounding for 20 years or so before retirement. The person who begins saving at a younger age will reap the much higher benefits of funds invested for 30 or 40 years. Regularly investing $2,000 a year reaps large benefits over time, as well. As shown in Exhibit 2.2, a person who has invested a total of $90,000—an initial $10,000 investment followed by $2,000 annual investments over 40 years—will have over half a million dollars accumulated assuming the 7 percent return. If the funds are invested more aggressively and earn the 8 percent return, the accumulation will be nearly three-quarters of a million dollars.

Consolidation Phase Individuals in the **consolidation phase** are typically past the midpoint of their careers, have paid off much or all of their outstanding debts, and perhaps have paid, or have the assets to pay, their children's college bills. Earnings exceed expenses, so the excess can be invested to provide for future retirement or estate planning needs. The typical investment horizon for this phase is still long (20 to 30 years), so moderately high risk investments are attractive. At the same time, because individuals in this phase are concerned about capital preservation, they do not want to take very large risks that may put their current nest egg in jeopardy.

Spending Phase The **spending phase** typically begins when individuals retire. Living expenses are covered by social security income and income from prior investments, including employer pension plans. Because their earning years have concluded (although some retirees take part-time positions or do consulting work), they seek greater protection of their capital. At the same time, they must balance their desire to preserve the nominal value of their savings with the need to protect themselves against a decline in the *real* value of their savings due to inflation. The average 65-year-old person in the United States has a life expectancy of about 20 years. Thus, although their overall portfolio may be less risky than in the consolidation phase, they still need some risky growth investments, such as common stocks, for inflation (purchasing power) protection.

The transition into the spending phase requires a sometimes difficult change in mindset; throughout our working life we are trying to save; suddenly we can spend. We tend to think that if we spend less, say 4 percent of our accumulated funds annually instead of 5, 6, or 7 percent, our wealth will last far longer. Although this is correct, a bear market early in our retirement can greatly reduce our accumulated funds. Fortunately, there are planning tools that can give a realistic view of what can happen to our retirement funds should markets fall early in our retirement years; this insight can assist in budgeting and planning to minimize the chance of spending (or losing) all the saved retirement funds. Annuities, which transfer risk from the individual to the annuity firm (most likely an insurance company), are another possibility. With an annuity, the recipient receives a guaranteed, lifelong stream of income. Options can allow for the annuity to continue until both a husband and wife die.

Gifting Phase The **gifting phase** is similar to, and may be concurrent with, the spending phase. In this stage, individuals may believe they have sufficient income and assets to cover their current and future expenses while maintaining a reserve for uncertainties. Excess assets can be used to provide financial assistance to relatives or friends, to establish charitable trusts, or to fund trusts as an estate planning tool to minimize estate taxes.

2.1.3 Life Cycle Investment Goals

During an individual's investment life cycle, he or she will have a variety of financial goals. **Near-term, high-priority goals** are shorter-term financial objectives that individuals set to fund purchases that are personally important to them, such as accumulating funds to make a house down payment, buy a new car, or take a trip. Parents with teenage children may have a near-term, high-priority goal to accumulate funds to help pay college expenses. Because of the emotional importance of these goals and their short time horizon, high-risk investments are not usually considered suitable for achieving them.

Long-term, high-priority goals typically include some form of financial independence, such as the ability to retire at a certain age. Because of their long-term nature, higher-risk investments can be used to help meet these objectives.

Lower-priority goals are just that—it might be nice to meet these objectives, but it is not critical. Examples include the ability to purchase a new car every few years, redecorate the home with expensive furnishings, or take a long, luxurious vacation. A well-developed policy statement considers these diverse goals over an investor's lifetime. The following sections detail the process for constructing an investment policy, creating a portfolio that is consistent with the policy and the environment, managing the portfolio, and monitoring its performance relative to its goals and objectives over time.

2.2 The Portfolio Management Process*

The process of managing an investment portfolio never stops. Once the funds are initially invested according to the plan, the real work begins in evaluating the portfolio's performance and updating the portfolio based on changes in the environment and the investor's needs.

The first step in the portfolio management process, as seen in Exhibit 2.3, is for the investor, either alone or with the assistance of an investment advisor, to construct a **policy statement**. The policy statement is a road map; in it, investors specify the types of risks they are willing to take and their investment goals and constraints. All investment decisions are based on the policy statement to ensure they are appropriate for the investor. We examine the process of constructing a policy statement in the following section. Because investor needs change over time, the policy statement must be periodically reviewed and updated.

The process of investing seeks to peer into the future and determine strategies that offer the best possibility of meeting the policy statement guidelines. In the second step of the portfolio management process, the portfolio manager should study current financial and economic conditions and forecast future trends. The investor's needs, as reflected in the policy statement,

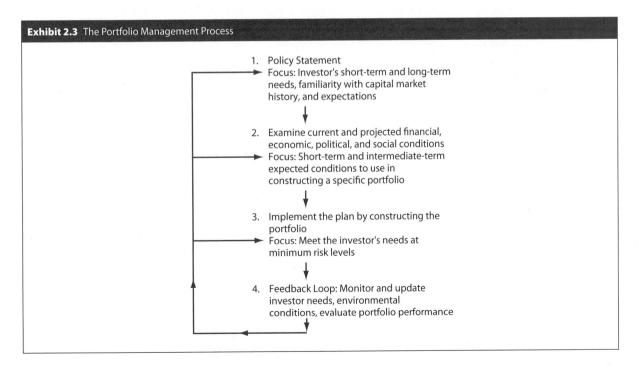

Exhibit 2.3 The Portfolio Management Process

1. Policy Statement
   Focus: Investor's short-term and long-term needs, familiarity with capital market history, and expectations

2. Examine current and projected financial, economic, political, and social conditions
   Focus: Short-term and intermediate-term expected conditions to use in constructing a specific portfolio

3. Implement the plan by constructing the portfolio
   Focus: Meet the investor's needs at minimum risk levels

4. Feedback Loop: Monitor and update investor needs, environmental conditions, evaluate portfolio performance

*This section and the one that follows benefited from insights contained in Maginn, Tuttle, Pinto, and McLeavey (2007), especially Chapters 1 and 2.

and financial market expectations will jointly determine **investment strategy**. Economies are dynamic; they are affected by numerous industry struggles, politics, and changing demographics and social attitudes. Thus, the portfolio will require constant monitoring and updating to reflect changes in financial market expectations. We examine the process of evaluating and forecasting economic trends in Chapter 12.

The third step of the portfolio management process is to **construct the portfolio**. With the investor's policy statement and financial market forecasts as input, the advisors implement the investment strategy and determine how to allocate available funds across different countries, asset classes, and securities. This involves constructing a portfolio that will minimize the investor's risks while meeting the needs specified in the policy statement. Financial theory frequently assists portfolio construction, as is discussed in this book's Part 2. Some of the practical aspects of selecting investments for inclusion in a portfolio are discussed in Part 4 and Part 5.

The fourth step in the portfolio management process is the **continual monitoring** of the investor's needs and capital market conditions and, when necessary, updating the policy statement. Based upon all of this, the investment strategy is modified accordingly. An important component of the monitoring process is to evaluate a portfolio's performance and compare the relative results to the expectations and the requirements listed in the policy statement. The evaluation of portfolio performance is discussed in Chapter 25. Once you have completed the four steps, it is important to recognize that this is a continuous process—it is essential to revisit all the steps to ensure that the policy statement is still valid, that the economic outlook has not changed, etc.

2.3 The Need For a Policy Statement

As noted in the previous section, a policy statement is a road map that guides the investment process. Constructing a policy statement is an invaluable planning tool that will help the investor understand his or her needs better as well as assist an advisor or portfolio manager in managing a client's funds. While it does not guarantee investment success, a policy statement will provide discipline for the investment process and reduce the possibility of making hasty, inappropriate decisions. There are two important reasons for constructing a policy statement: First, it helps the investor decide on realistic investment goals after learning about the financial markets and the risks of investing. Second, it creates a standard by which to judge the performance of the portfolio manager.

2.3.1 Understand and Articulate Realistic Investor Goals

When asked about their investment goal, people often say, "to make a lot of money," or some similar response. Such a goal has two drawbacks: First, it may not be appropriate for the investor, and second, it is too open-ended to provide guidance for specific investments and time frames. Such an objective is well suited for someone going to the racetrack or buying lottery tickets, but it is inappropriate for someone investing funds in financial and real assets for the long term.

An important purpose of writing a policy statement is to help investors understand their own needs, objectives, and investment constraints. As part of this, investors need to learn about financial markets and the risks of investing. This background will help prevent them from making inappropriate investment decisions in the future based on unrealistic expectations and increase the possibility that they will satisfy their specific, measurable financial goals.

Thus, the policy statement helps the investor to specify realistic goals and become more informed about the risks and costs of investing. Market values of assets, whether they be stocks, bonds, or real estate, can fluctuate dramatically. For example, during the October 1987 crash, the Dow Jones Industrial Average (DJIA) fell more than 20 percent in one day; in October 1997, the Dow fell "only" 7 percent. A review of market history shows that it is not unusual for asset prices to decline by 10 percent to 20 percent over several months—for example, the months following the market peak in March 2000, and the major decline when the market reopened after September 11, 2001. The problem is, investors typically focus on a single statistic, such as an 11 percent average annual rate of return on stocks, and expect the market to rise 11 percent every year. Such thinking ignores the risk of stock investing. Part of the process of developing a policy statement is for the investor to become familiar with the risks of investing, because we know that a strong positive relationship exists between risk and return.

One expert in the field recommends that investors should think about the following set of questions and explain their answers as part of the process of constructing a policy statement:

1. What are the real risks of an adverse financial outcome, especially in the short run?
2. What probable emotional reactions will I have to an adverse financial outcome?
3. How knowledgeable am I about investments and financial markets?
4. What other capital or income sources do I have? How important is this particular portfolio to my overall financial position?
5. What, if any, legal restrictions may affect my investment needs?
6. How would any unanticipated consequences of fluctuations in portfolio value affect my investment policy?

Adapted from Charles D. Ellis, *Investment Policy: How to Win the Loser's Game* (Homewood, IL: Dow Jones–Irwin, 1985), 25–26. Reproduced with permission of the McGraw-Hill Companies.

In summary, constructing a policy statement is mainly the investor's responsibility. It is a process whereby investors articulate their realistic needs and goals and become familiar with financial markets and investing risks. Without this information, investors cannot adequately communicate their needs to the portfolio manager. Without this input from investors, the portfolio manager cannot construct a portfolio that will satisfy clients' needs. The result of bypassing this step will most likely be future aggravation, dissatisfaction, and disappointment.

2.3.2 Standards for Evaluating Portfolio Performance

The policy statement also assists in judging the performance of the portfolio manager. Performance cannot be judged without an objective standard; the policy statement provides that objective standard. The portfolio's performance should be compared to guidelines specified in the policy statement, not on the portfolio's overall return. For example, if an investor has a low tolerance for risky investments, the portfolio manager should not be fired simply because the portfolio does not perform as well as the risky S&P 500 stock index. Because risk drives returns, the investor's lower-risk investments, as specified in the investor's policy statement, will probably earn lower returns than if all the investor's funds were placed in the stock market.

The policy statement will typically include a **benchmark portfolio**, or comparison standard. The risk of the benchmark, and the assets included in the benchmark, should agree with the client's risk preferences and investment needs. Notably, both the client and the portfolio manager must agree that the benchmark portfolio reflects the risk preferences and appropriate return requirements of the client. In turn, the investment performance of the portfolio manager should be compared to this benchmark portfolio. For example, an investor who specifies low-risk investments in the policy statement should compare the portfolio manager's performance against a low-risk benchmark portfolio. Likewise, an investor seeking high-risk, high-return investments should compare the portfolio's performance against a high-risk benchmark portfolio.

Because it sets an objective performance standard, the policy statement acts as a starting point for periodic portfolio review and client communication with managers. Questions concerning portfolio performance or the manager's faithfulness to the policy can be addressed in the context of the written policy guidelines. Managers should mainly be judged by whether they consistently followed the client's policy guidelines. The portfolio manager who makes unilateral deviations from policy is not working in the best interests of the client. Therefore, even significant deviations that result in higher portfolio returns can and should be grounds for the manager's dismissal.

Thus, we see the importance of the client constructing the policy statement: The client must first understand his or her own needs before communicating them to the portfolio manager. In turn, the portfolio manager must implement the client's desires by following the investment guidelines. As long as policy is followed, shortfalls in performance should not be a major concern. Remember that the policy statement is designed to impose an investment discipline on the client and portfolio manager. The less knowledgeable they are, the more likely clients are to inappropriately judge the performance of the portfolio manager.

2.3.3 Other Benefits

A sound policy statement helps to protect the client against a portfolio manager's inappropriate investments or unethical behavior. Without clear, written guidance, some managers may consider investing in high-risk investments, hoping to earn a quick return. Such actions are probably counter to the investor's specified needs and risk preferences. Though legal recourse is a possibility against such action, writing a clear and unambiguous policy statement should reduce the possibility of such inappropriate manager behavior.

Just because one specific manager currently manages your account does not mean that person will always manage your funds. As with other positions, your portfolio manager may be promoted or dismissed or take a better job. Therefore, after a while, your funds may come under the management of an individual you do not know and who does not know you. To prevent costly delays during this transition, you can ensure that the new manager "hits the ground running" with a clearly written policy statement. A policy statement should prevent delays in monitoring and rebalancing your portfolio and will help create a seamless transition from one money manager to another.

To sum up, a clearly written policy statement helps avoid future potential problems. When the client clearly specifies his or her needs and desires, the portfolio manager can more effectively construct an appropriate portfolio. The policy statement provides an objective measure for evaluating portfolio performance, helps guard against ethical lapses by the portfolio manager, and aids in the transition between money managers. Therefore, the first step before beginning any investment program, whether it is for an individual or a multibillion-dollar pension fund, is to construct a policy statement.

An appropriate policy statement should satisfactorily answer the following questions:

1. Is the policy carefully designed to meet the specific needs and objectives of this particular investor? (Cookie-cutter or one-size-fits-all policy statements are generally inappropriate.)
2. Is the policy written so clearly and explicitly that a competent stranger could use it to manage the portfolio in conformance with the client's needs? In case of a manager transition, could the new manager use this policy statement to handle your portfolio in accordance with your needs?
3. Would the client have been able to remain committed to the policies during the capital market experiences of the past 60 to 70 years? That is, does the client fully understand investment risks and the need for a disciplined approach to the investment process?
4. Would the portfolio manager have been able to maintain the policies specified over the same period? (Discipline is a two-way street; we do not want the portfolio manager to change strategies because of a disappointing market.)
5. Would the policy, if implemented, have achieved the client's objectives? (Bottom line: Would the policy have worked to meet the client's needs?)

Adapted from Charles D. Ellis, *Investment Policy: How to Win the Loser's Game* (Homewood, IL: Dow Jones–Irwin, 1985), 62. Reproduced with permission of the McGraw-Hill Companies.

2.4 Input to the Policy Statement

Before an investor and advisor can construct a policy statement, they need to have an open and frank exchange of information, ideas, fears, and goals. To build a framework for this information-gathering process, the client and advisor need to discuss the client's investment objectives and constraints. To illustrate this framework, we discuss the investment objectives and constraints that may confront "typical" 25-year-old and 65-year-old investors.

2.4.1 Investment Objectives

The investor's **objectives** are his or her investment goals expressed in terms of both risk and returns. The relationship between risk and returns requires that goals not be expressed only in terms of returns. Expressing goals only in terms of returns can lead to inappropriate investment practices by the portfolio manager, such as the use of high-risk investment strategies or account "churning," which involves moving quickly in and out of investments in an attempt to buy low and sell high.

For example, a person may have a stated return goal such as "double my investment in five years." Before such a statement becomes part of the policy statement, the client must become fully informed of investment risks associated with such a goal, including the possibility of loss. *A careful analysis of the client's risk tolerance should precede any discussion of return objectives.* It makes little sense for a person who is risk averse to have his/her funds invested in high-risk assets. Investment firms survey clients to gauge their risk tolerance. Sometimes investment magazines or books contain tests that individuals can take to help them evaluate their risk tolerance (see Exhibit 2.4). Subsequently, an advisor will use the results of this evaluation to categorize a client's risk tolerance and suggest an initial asset allocation such as those contained in Exhibit 2.5.

Risk tolerance is more than a function of an individual's psychological makeup; it is affected by other factors, including a person's current insurance coverage and cash reserves. Risk tolerance is also affected by an individual's family situation (for example, marital status and the number and ages of children) and by his or her age. We know that older persons generally have shorter investment time frames within which to make up any losses; they also have years of experience, including living through various market gyrations and "corrections" (a euphemism for downtrends or crashes) that younger people have not experienced or whose effect they do not fully appreciate. Risk tolerance is also influenced by one's current net worth and income expectations. All else being equal, individuals with higher incomes have a greater propensity to undertake risk because their incomes can help cover any shortfall. Likewise, individuals with larger net worths can afford to place some assets in risky investments while the remaining assets provide a cushion against losses.

A person's return objective may be stated in terms of an absolute or a relative percentage return, but it may also be stated in terms of a general goal, such as capital preservation, current income, capital appreciation, or total return.

Capital preservation means that investors want to minimize their risk of loss, usually in real terms: They seek to maintain the purchasing power of their investment. In other words, the return needs to be no less than the rate of inflation. Generally, this is a strategy for strongly risk-averse investors or for funds needed in the short-run, such as for next year's tuition payment or a down payment on a house.

Capital appreciation is an appropriate objective when the investors want the portfolio to grow in real terms over time to meet some future need. Under this strategy, growth mainly occurs through capital gains. This is an aggressive strategy for investors willing to take on risk to meet their objective. Generally, longer-term investors seeking to build a retirement or college education fund may have this goal.

When **current income** is the return objective, the investors want the portfolio to concentrate on generating income rather than capital gains. This strategy sometimes suits investors who want to supplement their earnings with income generated by their portfolio to meet their living expenses. Retirees may favor this objective for part of their portfolio to help generate spendable funds.

The objective for the **total return** strategy is similar to that of capital appreciation; namely, the investors want the portfolio to grow over time to meet a future need. Whereas the capital

---

Exhibit 2.4 How Much Risk Is Right for You?

You've heard the expression "no pain, no gain"? In the investment world, the comparable phrase would be "no risk, no reward."

How you feel about risking your money will drive many of your investment decisions. The risk-comfort scale extends from very conservative (you don't want to risk losing a penny regardless of how little your money earns) to very aggressive (you're willing to risk much of your money for the possibility that it will grow tremendously). As you might guess, most investors' tolerance for risk falls somewhere in between.

If you're unsure of what your level of risk tolerance is, this quiz should help.

1. You win $300 in an office football pool. You: (a) spend it on groceries, (b) purchase lottery tickets, (c) put it in a money market account, (d) buy some stock.
2. Two weeks after buying 100 shares of a $20 stock, the price jumps to over $30. You decide to: (a) buy more stock; it's obviously a winner, (b) sell it and take your profits, (c) sell half to recoup some costs and hold the rest, (d) sit tight and wait for it to advance even more.
3. On days when the stock market jumps way up, you: (a) wish you had invested more, (b) call your financial advisor and ask for recommendations, (c) feel glad you're not in the market because it fluctuates too much, (d) pay little attention.
4. You're planning a vacation trip and can either lock in a fixed room-and-meals rate of $150 per day or book standby and pay anywhere from $100 to $300 per day. You: (a) take the fixed-rate deal, (b) talk to people who have been there about the availability of last-minute accommodations, (c) book standby and also arrange vacation insurance because you're leery of the tour operator, (d) take your chances with standby.
5. The owner of your apartment building is converting the units to condominiums. You can buy your unit for $75,000 or an option on a unit for $15,000. (Units have recently sold for close to $100,000, and prices seem to be going up.) For financing, you'll have to borrow the down payment and pay mortgage and condo fees higher than your present rent. You: (a) buy your unit, (b) buy your unit and look for another to buy, (c) sell the option and arrange to rent the unit yourself, (d) sell the option and move out because you think the conversion will attract couples with small children.
6. You have been working three years for a rapidly growing company. As an executive, you are offered the option of buying up to 2% of company stock: 2,000 shares at $10 a share. Although the company is privately owned (its stock does not trade on the open market), its majority owner has made handsome profits selling three other businesses and intends to sell this one eventually. You: (a) purchase all the shares you can and tell the owner you would invest more if allowed, (b) purchase all the shares, (c) purchase half the shares, (d) purchase a small amount of shares.
7. You go to a casino for the first time. You choose to play: (a) quarter slot machines, (b) $5 minimum-bet roulette, (c) dollar slot machines, (d) $25 minimum-bet blackjack.
8. You want to take someone out for a special dinner in a city that's new to you. How do you pick a place? (a) read restaurant reviews in the local newspaper, (b) ask coworkers if they know of a suitable place, (c) call the only other person you know in this city, who eats out a lot but only recently moved there, (d) visit the city sometime before your dinner to check out the restaurants yourself.
9. The expression that best describes your lifestyle is: (a) no guts, no glory, (b) just do it!, (c) look before you leap, (d) all good things come to those who wait.
10. Your attitude toward money is best described as: (a) a dollar saved is a dollar earned, (b) you've got to spend money to make money, (c) cash and carry only, (d) whenever possible, use other people's money.

SCORING SYSTEM: Score your answers this way: (1) a-1, b-4, c-2, d-3 (2) a-4, b-1, c-3, d-2 (3) a-3, b-4, c-2, d-1 (4) a-2, b-3, c-1, d-4 (5) a-3, b-4, c-2, d-1 (6) a-4, b-3, c-2, d-1 (7) a-1, b-3, c-2, d-4 (8) a-2, b-3, c-4, d-1 (9) a-4, b-3, c-2, d-1 (10) a-2, b-3, c-1, d-4.

What your total score indicates:

- 10–17: You're not willing to take chances with your money, even though it means you can't make big gains.
- 18–25: You're semi-conservative, willing to take a small chance with enough information.

- 26–32: You're semi-aggressive, willing to take chances if you think the odds of earning more are in your favor.
- 33–40: You're aggressive, looking for every opportunity to make your money grow, even though in some cases the odds may be quite long. You view money as a tool to make more money.

---

appreciation strategy seeks to do this primarily through capital gains, the total return strategy seeks to increase portfolio value by both capital gains and reinvesting current income. Because the total return strategy has both income and capital gains components, its risk exposure lies between that of the current income and capital appreciation strategies.

Investment Objective: 25-Year-Old What is an appropriate investment objective for our typical 25-year-old investor? Assume he holds a steady job, is a valued employee, has adequate insurance coverage, and has enough money in the bank to provide a cash reserve. Let's also assume that his current long-term, high-priority investment goal is to build a retirement fund. Depending on his risk preferences, he can select a strategy carrying moderate to high amounts of risk because the income stream from his job will probably grow over time. Further,

Exhibit 2.5 Initial Risk and Investment Goal Categories and Asset Allocations Suggested by Investment Firms

FIDELITY INVESTMENTS SUGGESTED ASSET ALLOCATIONS:

	Cash/Short-Term	Bonds	Domestic Equities	Foreign Equities
Short-term	100%	0%	0%	0%
Conservative	30	50	20	0
Balanced	10	40	45	5
Growth	5	25	60	10
Aggressive growth	0	15	70	15
Most aggressive	0	0	80	20

VANGUARD INVESTMENTS SUGGESTED ASSET ALLOCATIONS:

Overall Objective	Risk Level	Cash/Short-Term	Bonds	Stocks
Income-oriented	Conservative	0%	100%	0%
	Moderate	0	80%	20%
	Aggresive	0	70%	30%
Balanced	Conservative	0%	60%	40%
	Moderate	0	50%	50%
	Aggresive	0	40%	60%
Growth	Conservative	0%	30%	70%
	Moderate	0	20%	80%
	Aggresive	0	0%	100%

T. ROWE PRICE MATRIX

Non-retirement-goals Matrix

Your Time Horizon

Your Risk Tolerance		3–5 years	6–10 years	11+ years
	Higher	**Strategy 2** 20% cash 40% bonds 40% stocks	**Strategy 3** 10% cash 30% bonds 60% stocks	**Strategy 5** 100% stocks
	Moderate	**Strategy 1** 30% cash 50% bonds 20% stocks	**Strategy 2** 20% cash 40% bonds 40% stocks	**Strategy 4** 20% bonds 80% stocks
	Lower	**All Cash** 100% cash	**Strategy 1** 30% cash 50% bonds 20% stocks	**Strategy 3** 10% cash 30% bonds 60% stocks

Source: Based on data sampled from Personal.Fidelity.com, Vanguard.com, and TRowePrice.com.

given his young age and income growth potential, a low-risk strategy, such as capital preservation or current income, is inappropriate for his retirement fund goal; a total return or capital appreciation objective would be most appropriate. Here's a possible objective statement:

> *Invest funds in a variety of moderate- to higher-risk investments. The average risk of the equity portfolio should exceed that of a broad stock market index, such as the NYSE stock index. Foreign and domestic equity exposure should range from 80 percent to 95 percent of the total portfolio. Remaining funds should be invested in short- and intermediate-term notes and bonds.*

Investment Objective: 65-Year-Old Assume our typical 65-year-old investor likewise has adequate insurance coverage and a cash reserve. Let's also assume she is retiring this year. This individual will want less risk exposure than the 25-year-old investor, because her earning power from employment will soon be ending; she will not be able to recover any investment losses by saving more out of her paycheck. Depending on her income from social security and a pension plan, she may need some current income from her retirement portfolio to meet living expenses. Given that she can be expected to live an average of another 20 years, she will need protection against inflation. A risk-averse investor will choose a combination of current income and capital preservation strategy; a more risk-tolerant investor will choose a combination of current income and total return in an attempt to have principal growth outpace inflation. Here's an example of such an objective statement:

> *Invest in stock and bond investments to meet income needs (from bond income and stock dividends) and to provide for real growth (from equities). Fixed-income securities should comprise 55–65 percent of the total portfolio; of this, 5–15 percent should be invested in short-term securities for extra liquidity and safety. The remaining 35–45 percent of the portfolio should be invested in high-quality stocks whose risk is similar to the S&P 500 index.*

More detailed analyses for our 25-year-old and our 65-year-old would make more specific assumptions about the risk tolerance of each, as well as clearly enumerate their investment goals, return objectives, the funds they have to invest at the present, the funds they expect to invest over time, and the benchmark portfolio that will be used to evaluate performance.

2.4.2 Investment Constraints

In addition to the investment objective that sets limits on risk and return, certain other constraints also affect the investment plan. Investment constraints include liquidity needs, an investment time horizon, tax factors, legal and regulatory constraints, and unique needs and preferences.

Liquidity Needs An asset is **liquid** if it can be quickly converted to cash at a price close to fair market value. Generally, assets are more liquid if many traders are interested in a fairly standardized product. Treasury bills are a highly liquid security; real estate and venture capital are not.

Investors may have liquidity needs that the investment plan must consider. For example, although an investor may have a primary long-term goal, several near-term goals may require available funds. Wealthy individuals with sizable tax obligations need adequate liquidity to pay their taxes without upsetting their investment plan. Some retirement plans may need funds for shorter-term purposes, such as buying a car or a house or making college tuition payments.

Our typical 25-year-old investor probably has little need for liquidity as he focuses on his long-term retirement fund goal. This constraint may change, however, should he face a period of unemployment or should near-term goals, such as honeymoon expenses or a house down payment, enter the picture. Should any changes occur, the investor needs to revise his policy statement and financial plans accordingly.

Our soon-to-be-retired 65-year-old investor has a greater need for liquidity. Although she may receive regular checks from her pension plan and social security, it is not likely that they will equal her working paycheck. She will want some of her portfolio in liquid securities to meet unexpected expenses, bills, or special needs such as trips or cruises.

Time Horizon Time horizon as an investment constraint briefly entered our earlier discussion of near-term and long-term high-priority goals. A close (but not perfect) relationship exists between an investor's time horizon, liquidity needs, and ability to handle risk. Investors with long investment horizons generally require less liquidity and can tolerate greater portfolio risk: less liquidity because the funds are not usually needed for many years; greater risk tolerance because any shortfalls or losses can be overcome by earnings and returns in subsequent years.

Investors with shorter time horizons generally favor more liquid and less risky investments because losses are harder to overcome during a short time frame.

Because of life expectancies, our 25-year-old investor has a longer investment time horizon than our 65-year-old investor. But, as discussed earlier, this does not mean the 65-year-old should place all her money in short-term CDs; she needs the inflation protection that long-term investments such as common stock can provide. Still, because of the time horizon constraint, the 25-year-old can have a greater proportion of his portfolio in equities—including stocks in small firms, as well as international and emerging market firms—than the 65-year-old.

Tax Concerns Investment planning is complicated by the tax code; taxes complicate the situation even more if international investments are part of the portfolio. Taxable income from interest, dividends, or rents is taxable at the investor's marginal tax rate. The marginal tax rate is the proportion of the next one dollar in income paid as taxes. Exhibit 2.6 shows the marginal tax rates for different levels of taxable income. As of 2007, the top federal marginal tax rate was 35 percent.

Capital gains or losses arise from asset price changes. They are taxed differently than income. Income is taxed when it is received; capital gains or losses are taxed only when an asset is sold and the gain or loss, relative to its initial cost or **basis**, is realized. **Unrealized capital gains** (or *losses*) reflect the price change in currently held assets that have *not* been sold; the tax liability on unrealized capital gains can be deferred indefinitely. If appreciated assets are passed on to an heir upon the investor's death, the basis of the assets is considered to be their value on the date of the holder's death. The heirs can then sell the assets and pay lower capital gains taxes if they wish. **Realized capital gains** occur when an appreciated asset is sold; taxes are due on the realized capital gains only. As of 2007, the maximum tax rate on stock dividends and long-term capital gains is 15 percent.

Some find the difference between average and marginal income tax rates confusing. The **marginal tax rate** is the part of each additional dollar in income that is paid as tax. Thus, a married person, filing jointly, with an income of $50,000 will have a marginal tax rate of 15 percent. The 15 percent marginal tax rate should be used to determine after-tax returns on investments.

The **average tax rate** is simply a person's total tax payment divided by their total income. It represents the average tax paid on each dollar the person earned. From Exhibit 2.6, a married person, filing jointly, will pay $6,717.50 in tax on a $50,000 income [$1,565 + 0.15($50,000 − $15,650)]. This average tax rate is $6,717.50/$50,000 or 13.4 percent. Note that the average tax rate is a weighted average of the person's marginal tax rates paid on each dollar of income. The first $15,650 of income has a 10 percent marginal tax rate; the next $34,350 has a 15 percent marginal tax rate:

$$\frac{\$15,650}{\$50,000} \times 0.10 + \frac{\$34,350}{\$50,000} \times 0.15 = 0.134, \text{ or the average tax rate of 13.4 percent}$$

Another tax factor is that some sources of investment income are exempt from federal and state taxes. For example, interest on federal securities, such as Treasury bills, notes, and bonds, is exempt from state taxes. Interest on municipal bonds (bonds issued by a state or other local governing body) is exempt from federal taxes. Further, if investors purchase municipal bonds issued by a local governing body of the state in which they live, the interest is exempt from

Exhibit 2.6 Individual Marginal Tax Rates, 2007

For updates, go to the IRS Web site, *http://www.irs.gov.*

| | IF TAXABLE INCOME | | THE TAX IS | | |
| | | | THEN | | |
	Is Over	**But Not Over**	**This Amount**	**Plus This %**	**Of the Excess Over**
Single	$0	$7,825	$0.00	10%	$0
	$7,825	$31,850	$782.50	15%	$7,825
	$31,850	$77,100	$4,386.25	25%	$31,850
	$77,100	$160,850	$15,698.75	28%	$77,100
	$160,850	$349,700	$39,148.75	33%	$160,850
	$349,700	—	$101,469.25	35%	$349,700
Married Filing Jointly	$0	$15,650	$0.00	10%	$0
	$15,650	$63,700	$1,565.00	15%	$15,650
	$63,700	$128,500	$8,772.50	25%	$63,700
	$128,500	$195,850	$24,972.50	28%	$128,500
	$195,850	$349,700	$43,830.50	33%	$195,850
	$349,700	—	$94,601.00	35%	$349,700

both state and federal income tax. Thus, high-income individuals have an incentive to purchase municipal bonds to reduce their tax liabilities.

The after-tax return on taxable investment income is

$$\text{After-Tax Income Return} = \text{Pre-Tax Income Return} \times (1 - \text{Marginal Tax Rate})$$

Thus, the after-tax return on a taxable bond investment should be compared to that of municipals before deciding which security a tax-paying investor should purchase.[1] Alternatively, we could compute a municipal's equivalent taxable yield, which is what a taxable bond investment would have to offer to produce the same after-tax return as the municipal. It is given by

$$\text{Equivalent Taxable Yield} = \frac{(\text{Municipal Yield})}{(1 - \text{Marginal Tax Rate})}$$

To illustrate, if an investor is in the 28 percent marginal tax bracket, a taxable investment yield of 8 percent has an after-tax yield of 8 percent $\times$ (1 – 0.28) or 5.76 percent; an equivalent-risk municipal security offering a yield greater than 5.76 percent offers the investor greater after-tax returns. On the other hand, a municipal bond yielding 6 percent has an equivalent taxable yield of: 6 percent/(1 – 0.28) = 8.33 percent; to earn more money after taxes, an equivalent-risk taxable investment has to offer a return greater than 8.33 percent.

There are other means of reducing investment tax liabilities. Contributions to an IRA (individual retirement account) may qualify as a tax deduction if certain income limits are met. Even without that deduction, taxes on any investment returns of an IRA, including any income, are deferred until the funds are withdrawn from the account. Any funds withdrawn from an IRA are taxable as current income, regardless of whether growth in the IRA occurs as a result of capital gains, income, or both. For this reason, to minimize taxes advisors recommend investing in stocks in taxable accounts and bonds in tax-deferred accounts such as IRAs. When funds are withdrawn from a tax-deferred account such as a regular IRA, assets are taxed (at most) at a 35 percent income tax rate (Exhibit 2.6)—even if the source of the stock return is primarily capital gains. In a taxable account, capital gains are taxed at the maximum 15 percent capital gains rate.

---

[1] Realized captial gains on municipal securities are taxed, as are all other capital gains; similarly for capital losses. Only the income from municipals is exempt from federal income tax.

The benefits of deferring taxes can dramatically compound over time, as we saw in Chapter 1. For example, $1,000 invested in an IRA at a tax-deferred rate of 8 percent grows to $10,062.66 over thirty years; in a taxable account (assuming a 28 percent marginal (federal + state) tax rate), the funds would grow to only $5,365.91. After thirty years, the value of the tax-deferred investment has grown to be nearly twice as large as the taxable investment.

With various stipulations, as of 2008, tax-deductible contributions of up to $5,000 can be made to a traditional IRA. A Roth IRA contribution is *not* tax deductible and contribution limits mirror those of the traditional IRA. The returns in a Roth IRA will grow on a tax-deferred basis and can be withdrawn, tax-free, if the funds are invested for at least five years and are withdrawn after the investor reaches age $59\frac{1}{2}$.[2]

For money you intend to invest in some type of IRA, the advantage of the Roth IRA's tax-free withdrawals will outweigh the tax-deduction benefit from the regular IRA—unless you expect your tax rate when the funds are withdrawn to be substantially less than when you initially invest the funds. Let's illustrate this with a hypothetical example.

Suppose you are considering investing $2,000 in either a regular or Roth IRA. Let's assume for simplicity that your combined federal and state marginal tax rate is 28 percent and that, over your 20-year time horizon, your $2,000 investment will grow to $20,000, tax-deferred in either account; this represents an average annual return of 12.2 percent.

In a Roth IRA, no tax is deducted when the $2,000 is invested; in a regular IRA, the $2,000 investment is tax-deductible and will lower your tax bill by $560 (0.28 × $2,000). Thus, in a Roth IRA, only $2,000 is assumed to be invested; for a regular IRA, both the $2,000 and the $560 tax savings are assumed to be invested. We will assume the $560 is invested at an after-tax rate of [12.2% × (1 – 0.28) = 8.8 percent]. After 20 years, this amount will grow to $3,025. The calculations in Exhibit 2.7 show that at the end of the 20-year time horizon the Roth IRA will give you more after-tax dollars unless you believe your tax bracket will be lower then *and you invest the regular IRA tax savings*.

Another tax-deferred investment is the cash value of life insurance contracts; these accumulate tax-free until the funds are withdrawn. Also, employers may offer 401(k) or 403(b) plans, which allow the employee to reduce taxable income by making tax-deferred investments. Many times employee contributions are matched by employer donations (up to a specified limit), thus allowing the employees to double their investment with little risk.

At times investors face a trade-off between taxes and diversification needs. If entrepreneurs concentrate much of their wealth in equity holdings of their firm, or if employees purchase substantial amounts of their employer's stock through payroll deduction plans during their working life, their portfolios may contain a large amount of unrealized capital gains. In addition, the risk position of such a portfolio may be quite high because it is concentrated in a single company. The decision to sell some of the company stock in order to diversify the portfolio's risk by reinvesting the proceeds in other assets must be balanced against the resulting tax liability.

Our typical 25-year-old investor probably is in a fairly low tax bracket, so detailed tax planning and tax-exempt income, such as that available from municipals, will not be major concerns. Nonetheless, he should still invest as much as possible into such tax-deferred plans as IRAs or 401(k)s for the retirement portion of his portfolio. If other funds are available for investment, they should be allocated based on his shorter- and longer-term investment goals.

Our 65-year-old investor may face a different situation. If she had been in a high tax bracket prior to retiring—and therefore has sought tax-exempt income and tax-deferred investments—her situation may change shortly after retirement. After her retirement, without large regular paychecks, the need for tax-deferred investments or tax-exempt income becomes

---

[2] Earlier tax-free withdrawals are possible if the funds are to be used for educational purposes or first-time home purchases.

Exhibit 2.7 Comparing the Regular versus Roth IRA Returns

	Regular IRA	Roth IRA
Invested funds:	$2,000 + $560 tax savings on the tax-deductible IRA investment	$2,000 (no tax deduction)
Time horizon:	20 years	20 years
Rate of return assumption:	12.2 percent tax-deferred on the IRA investment; 8.8 percent on invested tax savings (represents the after-tax return on 12.2 percent)	12.2 percent tax-deferred on the IRA investment
Funds available after 20 years (taxes ignored)	$20,000 (pre-tax) from IRA investment; $3,025 (after-tax) from invested tax savings	$20,000 from IRA investment
Funds available after 20 years, 15 percent marginal tax rate at retirement	$20,000 less tax (0.15 × $20,000) plus $3,025 from invested tax savings equals **$20,025**	**$20,000**
Funds available after 20 years, 28 percent marginal tax rate at retirement	$20,000 less tax (0.28 × $20,000) plus $3,025 from invested tax savings equals **$17,425**	**$20,000**
Funds available after 20 years, 40 percent marginal tax rate at retirement	$20,000 less tax (0.40 × $20,000) plus $3,025 from invested tax savings equals **$15,025**	**$20,000**

---

less. Taxable investments may then offer higher after-tax yields than tax-exempt municipals if her tax bracket is lower. If her employer's stock is a large component of her retirement account, she must make careful decisions regarding the need to diversify versus the cost of realizing large capital gains (in her lower tax bracket).

Legal and Regulatory Factors Both the investment process and the financial markets are highly regulated and subject to numerous laws. At times, these legal and regulatory factors constrain the investment strategies of individuals and institutions.

For example, funds removed from a regular IRA, Roth IRA, or 401(k) plan before age $59\frac{1}{2}$ are taxable and subject to an additional 10 percent withdrawal penalty. You may also be familiar with the tag line in many bank CD advertisements—"substantial interest penalty upon early withdrawal." Regulations and rules such as these may make such investments unattractive for investors with substantial liquidity needs in their portfolios.

Regulations can also constrain the investment choices available to someone in a fiduciary role. A *fiduciary,* or trustee, supervises an investment portfolio of a third party, such as a trust account or discretionary account.[3] The fiduciary must make investment decisions in accordance with the owner's wishes; a properly written policy statement assists this process. In addition, trustees of a trust account must meet the prudent-man standard, which means that they must invest and manage the funds as a prudent person would manage his or her own affairs. Notably, the prudent-man standard is based on the composition of the entire portfolio, not each individual asset.[4]

All investors must respect certain laws, such as insider trading prohibitions against the purchase and sale of securities on the basis of important information that is not publicly known. Typically, the people possessing such private, or insider, information are the firm's managers, who have a fiduciary duty to their shareholders. Security transactions based on access to insider information violates the fiduciary trust the shareholders have placed with management because the managers seek personal financial gain from their privileged position as agents for the shareholders.

---

[3] A discretionary account is one in which the fiduciary, many times a financial planner or stockbroker, has the authority to purchase and sell assets in the owner's portfolio without first receiving the owner's approval.

[4] As we will discuss in Chapter 7, it is sometimes wise to hold assets that are individually risky in the context of a well-diversified portfolio, even if the investor is strongly risk averse.

For our typical 25-year-old investor, legal and regulatory matters will be of little concern, with the possible exception of insider trading laws and the penalties associated with early withdrawal of funds from tax-deferred retirement accounts. Should he seek a financial advisor to assist him in constructing a financial plan, that advisor would have to obey the regulations pertinent to a client–advisor relationship. Similar concerns confront our 65-year-old investor. In addition, as a retiree, if she wants to do estate planning and set up trust accounts, she should seek legal and tax advice to ensure her plans are properly implemented.

Unique Needs and Preferences   This category covers the individual and sometimes idiosyncratic concerns of each investor. Some investors may want to exclude certain investments from their portfolio solely on the basis of personal preference or for social consciousness reasons. For example, they may request that no firms that manufacture or sell tobacco, alcohol, pornography, or environmentally harmful products be included in their portfolio. Some mutual funds screen according to this type of social responsibility criterion.

Another example of a personal constraint is the time and expertise a person has for managing his or her portfolio. Busy executives may prefer to relax during nonworking hours and let a trusted advisor manage their investments. Retirees, on the other hand, may have the time but believe they lack the expertise to choose and monitor investments, so they also may seek professional advice.

In addition, a business owner with a large portion of her wealth—and emotion—tied up in her firm's stock may be reluctant to sell even when it may be financially prudent to do so and then reinvest the proceeds for diversification purposes. Further, if the stock holdings are in a private company, it may be difficult to find a buyer unless shares are sold at a discount from their fair market value. Because each investor is unique, the implications of this final constraint differ for each person; there is no "typical" 25-year-old or 65-year-old investor. Each individual will have to decide on—and then communicate specific goals in a well-constructed policy statement.

· ·

2.5 Constructing the Policy Statement

As we have seen, the policy statement allows the investor to communicate his or her objectives (risk and return) and constraints (liquidity, time horizon, tax, legal and regulatory, and unique needs and preferences). This communication gives the advisor a better chance of implementing an investment strategy that will satisfy the investor. Even if an advisor is not used, each investor needs to take this first important step of the investment process and develop a financial plan to guide the investment strategy. To do without a plan or to plan poorly is to place the success of the financial plan in jeopardy.

2.5.1 General Guidelines

Constructing a policy statement is the investor's responsibility, but investment advisors often assist in the process. Here, for both the investor and the advisor, are guidelines for good policy statement construction.

In the process of constructing a policy statement, investors should think about the set of questions suggested previously on page 37.

When working with an investor to create a policy statement, an advisor should ensure that the policy statement satisfactorily answers the questions suggested previously on page 38.

2.5.2 Some Common Mistakes

When constructing their policy statements, participants in employer-sponsored retirement plans need to realize that through such plans 30–40 percent of their retirement funds may be invested in their employer's stock. Having so much money invested in one asset violates diversification principles and could be costly. To put this in context, most mutual funds are limited by law to having no more than 5 percent of their assets in any one company's stock; a firm's pension plan can invest no more than 10 percent of their funds in its own stock. As noted by Schulz (1996), individuals are unfortunately doing what government regulations prevent many institutional investors from doing. In addition, some studies point out that the average stock allocation in retirement plans is lower than it should be to allow for growth of principal over time—i.e., investors tend to be too conservative.

Another consideration is the issue of stock trading. A number of studies by Barber and Odean (1999, 2000, 2001) and Odean (1998, 1999) have shown that individual investors typically trade stocks too often (driving up commissions), sell stocks with gains too early (prior to further price increases), and hold onto losers too long (as the price continues to fall). These costly mistakes are especially true for men and online traders.

Investors, in general, seem to neglect that important first step to achieve financial success: They do not plan for the future. Studies of retirement plans discussed by Ruffenach (2001) and Clements (1997a, b, c) show that Americans are not saving enough to finance their retirement years and they are not planning sufficiently for what will happen to their savings after they retire. Around 25 percent of workers have saved less than $50,000 for their retirement. Finally, about 60 percent of workers surveyed confessed they were "behind schedule" in planning and saving for retirement.

2.6 The Importance of Asset Allocation

A major reason why investors develop policy statements is to provide guidance for an overall investment strategy. Though a policy statement does not indicate which specific securities to purchase and when they should be sold, it should provide guidelines as to the asset classes to include and a range of percents of the investor's funds to invest in each class. How the investor divides funds into different asset classes is the process of asset allocation. Rather than provide strict percentages, asset allocation is usually expressed in ranges. This allows the investment manager some freedom, based on his or her reading of capital market trends, to invest toward the upper or lower end of the ranges. For example, suppose a policy statement requires that common stocks be 60 percent to 80 percent of the value of the portfolio and that bonds should be 20 percent to 40 percent of the portfolio's value. If a manager is particularly bullish about stocks, she will increase the allocation of stocks toward the 80 percent upper end of the equity range and decrease bonds toward the 20 percent lower end of the bond range. Should she be optimistic about bonds or bearish on stocks, that manager may shift the allocation closer to 40 percent invested in bonds with the remainder in equities.

A review of historical data and empirical studies provides strong support for the contention that the asset allocation decision is a critical component of the portfolio management process. In general, there are four decisions involved in constructing an investment strategy:

- What asset classes should be considered for investment?
- What policy weights should be assigned to each eligible asset class?
- What are the allowable allocation ranges based on policy weights?
- What specific securities or funds should be purchased for the portfolio?

The asset allocation decision involves the first three points. How important is the asset allocation decision to an investor? In a word, *very.* Several studies by Ibbotson and Kaplan (2000); Brinson, Hood, and Beebower (1986); and Brinson, Singer, and Beebower (1991) have examined the effect of the normal policy weights on investment performance, using data from both pension funds and mutual funds, during time periods extending from the early 1970s to the late 1990s. The studies all found similar results: About 90 percent of a fund's returns over time can be explained by its target asset allocation policy. Exhibit 2.8 shows the relationship between returns on the target or policy portfolio allocation and actual returns on a sample mutual fund.

Exhibit 2.8 Time-Series Regression of Monthly Fund Return versus Fund Policy Return: One Mutual Fund, April 1988–March 1998

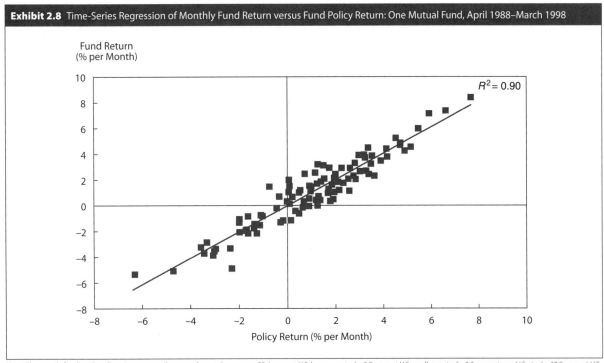

Note: The sample fund's policy allocations among the general asset classes were 52.4 percent U.S. large-cap stocks, 9.8 percent U.S. small-cap stocks, 3.2 percent non-U.S. stocks, 20.9 percent U.S. bonds, and 13.7 percent cash.

Source: Copyright © 2000, Association for Investment Management and Research. Reproduced and republished from "Does Asset Allocation Policy Explain 40, 90 or 100 Percent of Performance?" in the *Financial Analysts Journal,* January/February 2000, with permission from the CFA Institute. All Rights Reserved.

Rather than looking at just one fund and how the target asset allocation determines its returns, some studies have looked at how much the asset allocation policy affects returns on a variety of funds with different target weights. For example, Ibbotson and Kaplan (2000) found that, across a sample of funds, about 40 percent of the difference in fund returns is explained by differences in asset allocation policy. And what does asset allocation tell us about the *level* of a particular fund's returns? The studies by Brinson and colleagues (1986, 1991) and Ibbotson and Kaplan (2000) answered that question as well. They divided the policy return (what the fund return would have been had it been invested in indexes at the policy weights) by the actual fund return (which includes the effects of varying from the policy weights and security selection). Thus, a fund that was passively invested at the target weights would have a ratio value of 1.0, or 100 percent. A fund managed by someone with skill in market timing (for moving in and out of asset classes) and security selection would have a ratio less than 1.0 (or less than 100 percent); the manager's skill would result in a policy return less than the actual fund return. The studies showed the opposite: The policy-return/actual-return ratio averaged over 1.0, showing that asset allocation explains slightly more than 100 percent of the level of a fund's returns. Because of market efficiency, fund managers practicing market timing and security selection, on average, have difficulty surpassing passively invested index returns, after taking into account the expenses and fees of investing.

Thus, asset allocation is a very important decision. Across all funds, the asset allocation decision explains an average of 40 percent of the variation in fund returns. For a single fund, asset allocation explains 90 percent of the fund's variation in returns over time and slightly more than 100 percent of the average fund's level of return.

Good investment managers may add some value to portfolio performance, but the major source of investment return—and risk—over time is the asset allocation decision (Brown, 2000).

2.6.1 Investment Returns after Taxes and Inflation

Exhibit 2.9 provides additional historical perspectives on returns. It indicates how an investment of $1 would have grown over the 1981–2007 period and, using fairly conservative assumptions, examines how investment returns are affected by taxes and inflation.

Focusing first on stocks, funds invested in 1981 in the Dow Jones Wilshire 5000 stocks would have averaged a 9.41 percent annual return through 2007. Unfortunately, this return is unrealistic because if the funds were invested over time, taxes would have to be paid and inflation would erode the real purchasing power of the invested funds.

Except for tax-exempt investors and tax-deferred accounts, annual tax payments reduce investment returns. Incorporating taxes into the analysis lowers the after-tax average annual return of a stock investment to 6.78 percent.

But the major reduction in the value of our investment is caused by inflation. The real after-tax average annual return on a stock over this time frame was only 3.68 percent, which is quite a bit less than our initial unadjusted 9.41 percent return!

This example shows the long-run impact of taxes and inflation on the real value of a stock portfolio. For bonds and bills, however, the results in Exhibit 2.9 show something even more

---

Exhibit 2.9 The Effect of Taxes and Inflation on Investment Returns: 1981–2007

	Before Taxes and Inflation	After Taxes	After Taxes and Inflation	After Inflation (Only)
Common stocks (Wilshire 5000)	9.41%	6.78%	3.68%	6.31%
Long-term government bonds (10 year constant maturity)	7.33%	5.28%	2.18%	4.23%
Treasury bills (3 month constant maturity)	5.55%	3.99%	0.89%	2.45%
Municipal bonds (est.)	6.88%	6.88%	3.78%	3.78%

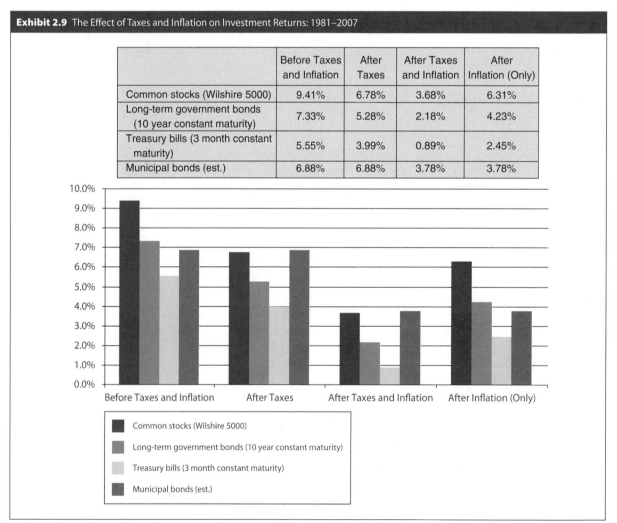

Assumptions: 28 percent tax rate on income; 20 percent on price change. Compound inflation rate was 3.1 percent for full period.

Source: Computations by authors, using data indicated.

surprising. After adjusting for taxes, long-term bonds maintained their purchasing power; T-bills barely provided value in real terms. One dollar invested in long-term government bonds in 1981 gave the investor an annual average after-tax real return of 2.18 percent. An investment in Treasury bills earned an average rate of only 0.89 percent after taxes and inflation. Municipal bonds, because of the protection they offer from taxes, earned an average annual real return of almost 4.00 percent during this time.

This historical analysis demonstrates that, for taxable investments, a reasonable way to maintain purchasing power over long time periods when investing in financial assets is to invest in common stocks. Put another way, an asset allocation decision for a taxable portfolio that does not include a substantial commitment to common stocks makes it difficult for the portfolio to maintain real value over time.[5]

Notably, the fourth column, labeled "After inflation (only)," is more encouraging since it refers to results for a tax-free retirement account that is only impacted by inflation. These results should encourage investors to take advantage of tax-free opportunities.

2.6.2 Returns and Risks of Different Asset Classes

By focusing on returns, we have ignored its partner—risk. Assets with higher long-term returns have these returns to compensate for their risk. Exhibit 2.10 illustrates returns (unadjusted for costs and taxes) for several asset classes over time. As expected, the higher returns available from equities (both large cap and small cap) come at the cost of higher risk. This is precisely why investors need a policy statement and why the investor and manager must understand the capital markets and have a disciplined approach to investing. Safe Treasury bills will sometimes outperform equities, and, because of their higher risk, common stocks sometimes lose significant value. These are times when undisciplined and uneducated investors become frustrated, sell their stocks at a loss, and vow never to invest in equities again. In contrast, these are times when disciplined investors stick to their investment plan and position their portfolios for the next bull market.[6] By holding on to their stocks and continuing to purchasing more at depressed prices, the equity portion of the portfolio will experience a substantial increase in the future.

The asset allocation decision determines to a great extent both the returns and the volatility of the portfolio. Exhibit 2.10 indicates that stocks are riskier than bonds or T-bills. Exhibit 2.11 shows that stocks have sometimes experienced returns lower than those of T-bills for extended

Exhibit 2.10 Summary Statistics of Annual Returns, 2003–2007, U.S. Securities

	Geometric Mean (%)	Arithmetic Mean (%)	Standard Deviation (%)
Large company stocks (S&P 500)	12.83%	13.15%	9.75%
Small company stocks (Russell 2000)	14.87%	15.99%	18.55%
Government bonds (Lehman Brothers)	4.10%	4.12%	2.58%
Corporate bonds (Lehman Brothers)	4.81%	4.83%	2.36%
Intermediate-term government bonds (Lehman Brothers)	3.69%	3.72%	2.77%
Intermediate-term corporate bonds (Lehman Brothers)	4.52%	4.54%	2.21%
30-day Treasury bill (Federal Reserves)	2.92%	2.93%	1.81%
U.S. inflation (Federal Reserves)	3.03%	3.04%	0.85%

Source: Calculations by authors, using data noted.

[5] Of course other equity-oriented investments, such as venture capital or real estate, may also provide inflation protection after adjusting for portfolio costs and taxes. Future studies of the performance of Treasury inflation-protected securities (TIPs) will likely show their usefulness in protecting investors from inflation as well.
[6] Newton's law of gravity seems to work two ways in financial markets. What goes up must come down; it also appears over time that what goes down may come back up. Contrarian investors and some "value" investors use this concept of reversion to the mean to try to outperform the indexes over time.

Exhibit 2.11 Higher Returns Offered by Equities over Long Time Periods Time Frame: 1934–2003

Length of Holding Period (calendar years)	Percentage of Periods That Stock Returns Trailed T-Bill Returns*
1	35.7%
5	18.2
10	11.5
20	0.0
30	0.0

*Price change plus reinvested income
Source: Author calculations.

periods of time. Still, the long-term results in Exhibit 2.10 show that sticking with an investment policy through difficult times provides attractive long-term rates of return.[7]

One popular way to measure risk is to examine the variability of returns over time by computing a standard deviation or variance of annual rates of return for an asset class. This measure, which is used in Exhibit 2.10, indicates that stocks are risky and T-bills are relatively safe. Another intriguing measure of risk is the probability of *not* meeting your investment return objective. From this perspective, the results in Exhibit 2.11 show that if the investor has a long time horizon (i.e., approaching 20 years), the risk of equities is small and that of T-bills is large because of their differences in long-term expected returns.

2.6.3 Asset Allocation Summary

A carefully constructed policy statement determines the types of assets that should be included in a portfolio. The asset allocation decision, not the selection of specific stocks and bonds, determines most of the portfolio's returns over time. Although seemingly risky, investors seeking capital appreciation, income, or even capital preservation over long time periods should stipulate a sizable allocation to the equity portion in their portfolio. As noted in this section, a strategy's risk depends on the investor's goals and time horizon. As demonstrated, investing in T-bills may actually be a riskier strategy than investing in common stocks due to the risk of not meeting long-term investment return goals after considering the impact of inflation and taxes.

Asset Allocation and Cultural Differences Thus far, our analysis has focused on U.S. investors. Non-U.S. investors make their asset allocation decisions in much the same manner; but because they face different social, economic, political, and tax environments, their allocation decisions differ from those of U.S. investors. Exhibit 2.12 shows the equity allocations of pension funds in several countries. As shown, the equity allocations vary dramatically from 79 percent in Hong Kong to 37 percent in Japan and only 8 percent in Germany.

National demographic and economic differences can explain much of the divergent portfolio strategies. Of these six nations, the average age of the population is highest in Germany and Japan and lowest in the United States and the United Kingdom, which helps explain the greater use of equities in the U.S. and U.K. Government privatization programs during the 1980s in the United Kingdom encouraged equity ownership among individual and institutional investors. In Germany, regulations prevent insurance firms from having more than 20 percent of their assets in equities. Both Germany and Japan have banking sectors that invest privately in firms and whose officers sit on corporate boards. Since 1980, the cost of living in the United Kingdom has increased at a rate about two times that of Germany and this inflationary

[7] The added benefits of diversification—combining different asset classes in the portfolio—may reduce overall portfolio risk without harming potential return. The topic of diversification is discussed in Chapter 7.

Exhibit 2.12 Equity Allocations in Pension Fund Portfolios

Country	Percentage in Equities
Hong Kong	79
United Kingdom	78
Ireland	68
United States	58
Japan	37
Germany	8

Exhibit 2.13 Asset Allocation and Inflation for Different Countries' Equity Allocation as of December 1997; Average Inflation Measured Over 1980–1997

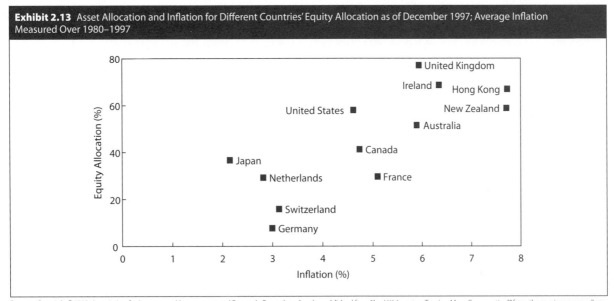

bias in the U.K. economy favors higher equity allocations. Exhibit 2.13 shows the positive relationship between the level of inflation in a country and its pension fund allocation to equity. These results indicate that the general economic environment and its demographics have an effect on the asset allocation in a country.

The need to invest in equities for portfolio growth is less in Germany because workers receive generous state pensions. Germans show a cultural aversion to the stock market because they are more risk averse and consider stock investing a form of gambling. Although this attitude is changing, the German stock market is relatively illiquid, and Gumbel (1995) noted that only a handful of stocks account for 50 percent of total stock trading volume. New legislation that encourages 401(k)-like plans in Germany may encourage an increase in equity investments.

Other Organization for Economic Cooperation and Development (OECD) countries place regulatory restrictions on institutional investors. As noted by Witschi (1998) and Chernoff (1996), pension funds in Austria must have at least 50 percent of their assets in bank deposits or schilling-denominated bonds. Belgium requires pension funds to invest a minimum of 15 percent in government bonds. Finland places a 5 percent limit on investments outside its borders by pension funds, and French pension funds must invest a minimum of 34 percent in public debt instruments.

Asset allocation policy and strategy are determined in the context of an investor's objectives and constraints. Among the factors that explain differences in investor behavior across countries, however, are their demographics, as well as the political and economic environments.

• • • • SUMMARY • • • •

- In this chapter, we saw that investors need to prudently manage risk within the context of their investment goals and preferences. Income, spending, and investing behavior will change over a person's lifetime.
- We reviewed the importance of developing an investment policy statement before implementing an investment plan. By forcing investors to examine their needs, risk tolerance, and familiarity with the capital markets, policy statements help investors correctly identify appropriate objectives and

constraints. In addition, the policy statement provides a standard by which to evaluate the performance of the portfolio manager.

- We also reviewed the importance of the asset allocation decision in determining long-run portfolio investment returns and risks. Because the asset allocation decision follows setting the objectives and constraints, it is clear that the success of the investment program depends on the first step, the construction of the policy statement.

• • • • SUGGESTED READINGS • • • •

Ibbotson, R. S., M. A. Milevsky, P. Chen, and K. X. Zhu. *Lifetime Financial Advice: Human Capital Asset Allocation and Insurance.* Charlottesville, VA: The Research Foundation of the CFA Institute, 2007.

Milevsky, Mosha A., and Chris Robinson. "A Sustainable Spending Rate without Simulation," *Financial Analysts Journal* 61, no. 6 (November–December, 2005).

Miller, Janet T., ed. *Investment Counseling for Private Clients, III.* Charlottesville, VA: AIMR, 2001.

Mitchell, Roger S., ed. *Investment Counseling for Private Clients, II.* Charlottesville, VA: AIMR, 2000.

Thaler, Richard, and Schlomo Benartzi. "Save More Tomorrow; Using Behavioral Economics to Increase Employee Savings," *Journal of Political Economy*, 112, no. 1 (February 2004).

• • • • QUESTIONS • • • •

1. "Young people with little wealth should not invest money in risky assets such as the stock market, because they can't afford to lose what little money they have." Do you agree or disagree with this statement? Why?

2. Your healthy 63-year-old neighbor is about to retire and comes to you for advice. From talking with her, you find out she was planning on taking all the money out of her company's retirement plan and investing it in bond mutual funds and money market funds. What advice should you give her?

3. Discuss how an individual's investment strategy may change as he or she goes through the accumulation, consolidation, spending, and gifting phases of life.

4. Why is a policy statement important?

5. Use the questionnaire "How much risk is right for you?" (Exhibit 2.4) to determine your risk tolerance. Use this information to help write a policy statement for yourself.

6. Your 45-year-old uncle is 20 years away from retirement; your 35-year-old older sister is about 30 years away from retirement. How might their investment policy statements differ?

7. What information is necessary before a financial planner can assist a person in constructing an investment policy statement?

8. Use the Internet to find the home pages for some financial-planning firms. What strategies do they emphasize? What do they say about their asset allocation strategy? What are their firms' emphases—for example, value investing, international diversification, principal preservation, retirement and estate planning?

 9. **CFA EXAMINATION LEVEL III** Mr. Franklin is 70 years of age, is in excellent health, pursues a simple but active lifestyle, and has no children. He has interest in a private company for $90 million and has decided that a medical research foundation will receive half the proceeds now and will be the primary

beneficiary of his estate upon his death. Mr. Franklin is committed to the foundation's well-being because he believes strongly that, through it, a cure will be found for the disease that killed his wife. He now realizes that an appropriate investment policy and asset allocations are required if his goals are to be met through investment of his considerable assets. Currently, the following assets are available for use in building an appropriate portfolio:

$45.0 million cash (from sale of the private company interest, net of pending
$45 million gift to the foundation)
10.0 million stocks and bonds ($5 million each)
9.0 million warehouse property (now fully leased)
1.0 million Franklin residence
_____
$65.0 million total available assets

a. Formulate and justify an investment policy statement setting forth the appropriate guidelines within which future investment actions should take place. Your policy statement must encompass all relevant objective and constraint considerations.

b. Recommend and justify a long-term asset allocation that is consistent with the investment policy statement you created in Part a. Briefly explain the key assumptions you made in generating your allocation.

· · · · **PROBLEMS** · · · ·

1. Assume that the rate of inflation during all these periods was 3 percent a year. Compute the real value of the two tax-deferred portfolios in problems 4a and 5a.

2. What is the marginal tax rate for a single individual if her taxable income is $20,000? $40,000? 60,000? What is her tax bill for each of these income levels? What is her average tax rate for each of these income levels?

3. a. Someone in the 15 percent tax bracket can earn 10 percent on his investments in a tax-exempt IRA account. What will be the value of a $10,000 investment in 5 years? 10 years? 20 years?
   b. Suppose the preceding 10 percent return is taxable rather than tax-deferred. What will be the after-tax value of his $10,000 investment after 5, 10, and 20 years?

4. What is the marginal tax rate for a couple, filing jointly, if their taxable income is $20,000? $40,000? $60,000? What is their tax bill for each of these income levels? What is the average tax rate for each of these income levels?

5. a. Someone in the 36 percent tax bracket can earn 9 percent annually on her investments in a tax-exempt IRA account. What will be the value of a one-time $10,000 investment in 5 years? 10 years? 20 years?
   b. Suppose the preceding 9 percent return is taxable rather than tax-deferred and the taxes are paid annually. What will be the after-tax value of her $10,000 investment after 5, 10, and 20 years?

6. Suppose your first job pays you $28,000 annually. What percentage should your cash reserve contain? How much life insurance should you carry if you are unmarried? How much if you are married with two young children?

· · · · · APPENDIX: CHAPTER 2 · · · ·

Objectives and Constraints of Institutional Investors

Institutional investors manage large amounts of funds in the course of their business. They include mutual funds, pension funds, insurance firms, endowments, and banks. In this appendix, we review the characteristics of various institutional investors and discuss their typical investment objectives and constraints.

Mutual Funds

A mutual fund pools sums of money from investors, which are then invested in financial assets. Each mutual fund has its own investment objective, such as capital appreciation, high current income, or money market income. A mutual fund will state its investment objective, and investors choose the funds in which to invest. Two basic constraints face mutual funds: those created by law to protect mutual fund investors and those that represent choices made by the mutual fund's managers. Some of these constraints will be discussed in the mutual fund's prospectus, which must be given to all prospective investors before they purchase shares in a mutual fund. Mutual funds are discussed in more detail in Chapter 24.

Pension Funds

Pension funds are a major component of retirement planning for individuals. As of 2007, U.S. pension assets were nearly $17 trillion. Basically, a firm's pension fund receives contributions from the firm, its employees, or both. The funds are invested with the purpose of giving workers either a lump-sum payment or the promise of an income stream after their retirement. **Defined benefit pension plans** promise to pay retirees a specific income stream after retirement. The size of the benefit is usually based on factors that include the worker's salary, or time of service, or both. The company contributes a certain amount each year to the pension plan; the size of the contribution depends on assumptions concerning future salary increases and the rate of return to be earned on the plan's assets. Under a defined benefit plan, the company carries the risk of paying the future pension benefit to retirees; should investment performance be poor, or should the company be unable to make adequate contributions to the plan, the shortfall must be made up in future years. "Poor" investment performance means the actual return on the plan's assets fell below the assumed **actuarial rate of return**. The actuarial rate is the discount rate used to find the present value of the plan's future obligations and thus this rate determines the size of the firm's annual contribution to the pension plan.

    Defined contribution pension plans do not promise set benefits but only specified contributions to the plan. As a result, employees' benefits depend on the size of the contributions made to the pension fund and the returns earned on the fund's investments. Thus, the plan's risk related to the rates of return on investments is borne by the employee. Unlike a defined benefit plan, employees' retirement income is not an obligation of the firm.

    A pension plan's objectives and constraints depend on whether the plan is a *defined benefit plan* or a *defined contribution plan*. We review each separately below.

Defined Benefit The plan's risk tolerance depends on the plan's funding status and its actuarial rate. For **underfunded plans** (where the present value of the fund's liabilities to employees exceeds the value of the fund's assets), a more conservative approach toward risk is taken to ensure that the funding gap is closed over time. This may entail a strategy whereby the firm makes larger plan contributions and assumes a lower actuarial rate. **Overfunded plans** (where the present value of the pension liabilities is less than the plan's assets) allow a more aggressive investment strategy, which implies a higher actuarial rate. This allows the firm to reduce its contributions and increases the risk exposure of the plan. The return objective is to meet the plan's actuarial rate of return, which is set by actuaries who estimate future pension obligations based on assumptions about future salary increases, current salaries, retirement patterns, worker life expectancies, and the firm's benefit formula. Obviously, the actuarial rate helps determine the size of the firm's plan contributions over time.

The liquidity constraint on defined benefit funds is mainly a function of the average age of employees. A younger employee base means less liquidity is needed; an older employee base generally means more liquidity is needed to pay current pension obligations to retirees. The time horizon constraint is also affected by the average age of employees, although some experts recommend using a 5- to 10-year horizon for planning purposes. Taxes are not a major concern to the plan, because pension plans are exempt from paying tax on investment returns. The major legal constraint is that the plan must be run in accordance with the Employee Retirement and Income Security Act (ERISA), and investments must satisfy the "prudent-expert" standard when evaluated in the context of the overall pension plan's portfolio.

Defined Contribution   Notably, the individual employee decides how his or her contributions to the plan are to be invested. As a result, the objectives and constraints for defined contribution plans depend on the individual. Because the employee carries the risk of inadequate retirement funding rather than the firm, defined contribution plans are generally more conservatively invested (the majority of research indicates that employees tend to be too conservative). If, however, the plan is considered part of an estate planning tool for a wealthy founder or officer of the firm, a higher risk tolerance and return objective are appropriate because most of the plan's assets will ultimately be owned by the individual's heirs.

The liquidity and time horizon needs for the plan differ depending on the average age of the individual employees and the degree of employee turnover within the firm. Similar to defined benefit plans, defined contribution plans are tax-exempt and are governed by the provisions of ERISA.

Endowment Funds

Endowment funds arise from contributions made to charitable or educational institutions. Rather than immediately spending the funds, the organization invests the money for the purpose of providing a future stream of income to the organization. The investment policy of an endowment fund is the result of a "tension" between the organization's need for current income and the desire for a growing future stream of income to protect against inflation.

To meet the institution's operating budget needs, the fund's return objective is often set by adding the spending rate (the amount taken out of the funds each year) and the expected inflation rate. Funds that have more risk-tolerant trustees may have a higher spending rate than those overseen by more risk-averse trustees. Because a total return approach usually serves to meet the return objective over time, the organization is generally withdrawing both income and capital gain returns to meet budgeted needs. The risk tolerance of an endowment fund is largely affected by the collective risk tolerance of the organization's trustees.

Due to the fund's long-term time horizon, liquidity requirements are minor except for the need to spend part of the endowment each year and maintain a cash reserve for emergencies. Many endowments are tax-exempt, although income from some private foundations can be taxed at either a 1 percent or 2 percent rate. Short-term capital gains are taxable, but long-term capital gains are not. Regulatory and legal constraints arise on the state level, where most endowments are regulated. Unique needs and preferences may affect investment strategies, especially among college or religious endowments, which may have strong preferences about social investing issues.

Insurance Companies

The investment objectives and constraints for an insurance company depend on whether it is a life insurance company or a nonlife (such as a property and casualty) insurance firm.

Life Insurance Companies   Except for firms dealing only in term life insurance, life insurance firms collect premiums during a person's lifetime that must be invested until a death benefit is paid to the insurance contract's beneficiaries. At any time, the insured can turn in her policy and receive its cash surrender value. Discussing investment policy for an insurance firm is also complicated by the insurance industry's proliferation of insurance and quasi-investment products.

Basically, an insurance company wants to earn a positive "spread," which is the difference between the rate of return on investment minus the rate of return it credits its various policyholders. This concept is similar to a defined benefit pension fund that tries to earn a rate of return in excess of its actuarial rate. If the spread is positive, the insurance firm's surplus reserve account rises; if not, the surplus account declines by an amount reflecting the negative spread. A growing surplus is an important competitive tool for life insurance companies. Attractive investment returns allow the company to advertise better policy returns than those of its competitors. A growing surplus also allows the firm to offer new products and expand insurance volume.

Because life insurance companies are quasi-trust funds for savings, fiduciary principles limit the risk tolerance of the invested funds. The National Association of Insurance Commissioners (NAIC) establishes risk categories for bonds and stocks; companies with excessive investments in higher-risk categories must set aside extra funds in a mandatory securities valuation reserve (MSVR) to protect policyholders against losses.

Insurance companies' liquidity needs have increased over the years due to increases in policy surrenders and product-mix changes. A company's time horizon depends upon its specific product mix. Life insurance policies require longer-term investments, whereas guaranteed insurance contracts (GICs) and shorter-term annuities require shorter investment time horizons.

Tax rules changed considerably for insurance firms in the 1980s. For tax purposes, investment returns are divided into two components: first, the policyholder's share, which is the return portion covering the actuarially assumed rate of return needed to fund reserves; and second, the balance that is transferred to reserves. Unlike pensions and endowments, life insurance firms pay income and capital gains taxes at the corporate tax rates on the returns transferred to reserves.

Except for the NAIC, most insurance regulation is on the state level. Regulators oversee the eligible asset classes and the reserves (MSVR) necessary for each asset class and enforce the "prudent-expert" investment standard. Audits ensure that various accounting rules and investment regulations are followed.

Nonlife Insurance Companies Cash outflows are somewhat predictable for life insurance firms, based on their mortality tables. In contrast, the cash flows required by major accidents, disasters, and lawsuit settlements are not as predictable for nonlife insurance firms.

Due to their fiduciary responsibility to claimants, risk exposures are low to moderate. Depending on the specific company and competitive pressures, premiums may be affected by both the probability of a claim and the investment returns earned by the firm. Typically, casualty insurance firms invest their insurance reserves in relatively safe bonds to provide needed income to pay claims; capital and surplus funds are invested in equities for their growth potential. As with life insurers, property and casualty firms have a stronger competitive position when their surplus accounts are larger than those of their competitors. Many insurers now focus on a total return objective as a means to increase their surplus accounts over time.

Because of uncertain claim patterns, liquidity is a concern for property and casualty insurers who also want liquidity so they can switch between taxable and tax-exempt investments as their underwriting activities generate losses and profits. The time horizon for investments is typically shorter than that of life insurers, although many invest in long-term bonds to earn the higher yields available on these instruments. Investing strategy for the firm's surplus account focuses on long-term growth.

Regulation of property and casualty firms is more permissive than for life insurers. Similar to life companies, states regulate classes and quality of investments for a certain percentage of the firm's assets. Beyond this restriction, insurers can invest in many different types and qualities of instruments, although some states limit the proportion that can be invested in real estate assets.

Banks

Pension funds, endowments, and insurance firms obtain virtually free funds for investment purposes. Not so with banks. To have funds to lend, they must attract investors in a competitive interest rate environment. They compete against other banks and also against companies that offer other investment vehicles, from bonds to common stocks. A bank's success relies primarily on its ability to generate returns in excess of its funding costs.

A bank tries to maintain a positive difference between its cost of funds and its returns on assets. If banks anticipate falling interest rates, they will try to invest in longer-term assets to lock in the returns while seeking short-term deposits, whose interest cost is expected to fall over time. When banks expect rising rates, they will try to lock in longer-term deposits with fixed-interest costs, while investing funds short term to capture rising interest rates. The risk of such strategies is that losses may occur should a bank incorrectly forecast the direction of interest rates. The aggressiveness of a bank's strategy will be related to the size of its capital ratio and the oversight of regulators.

Banks need substantial liquidity to meet withdrawals and loan demand. A bank has two forms of liquidity. *Internal liquidity* is provided by a bank's investment portfolio that includes highly liquid assets. A bank has *external liquidity* if it can borrow funds in the federal funds markets (where banks lend reserves to other banks), from the Federal Reserve Bank's discount window, or if it can sell certificates of deposit at attractive rates.

Banks have a short time horizon for several reasons. First, they have a strong need for liquidity. Second, because they want to maintain an adequate interest revenue–interest expense spread, they generally focus on shorter-term investments to avoid interest rate risk and to avoid getting "locked in" to a long-term revenue source. Third, because banks typically offer short-term deposit accounts (demand deposits, NOW accounts, and such) they need to match the maturity of their assets and liabilities to avoid taking undue risks.[8] This desire to match the maturity of assets and liabilities is shared by virtually all financial institutions.

Banks are heavily regulated by numerous state and federal agencies. The Federal Reserve Board, the Comptroller of the Currency, and the Federal Deposit Insurance Corporation all oversee various components of bank operations. The Glass-Steagall Act restricts the equity investments that banks can make. Unique situations that affect each bank's investment policy depend on their size, market, and management skills in matching asset and liability sensitivity to interest rates. For example, a bank in a small community may have many customers who deposit their money with it for the sake of convenience. A bank in a more populated area will find its deposit flows are more sensitive to interest rates and competition from nearby banks.

Institutional Investment Summary

Among the great variety of institutions, each institution has its "typical" investment objectives and constraints. This discussion has indicated the differences that exist among types of institutions and some of the major issues confronting them. Notably, just as with individual investors, "cookie-cutter" policy statements are inappropriate for institutional investors. The specific objectives, constraints, and investment strategies must be determined on a case-by-case basis.

---

[8] An asset/liability mismatch caused the ultimate downfall of savings and loan associations. They attracted short-term liabilities (deposit accounts) and invested in long-term assets (mortgages). When interest rates became more volatile in the early 1980s and short-term rates increased dramatically, S&Ls experienced negative spreads and suffered significant losses.

CHAPTER 3
Selecting Investments in a Global Market*

After you read this chapter, you should be able to answer the following questions:

- Why should investors have a global perspective regarding their investments?
- What has happened to the relative size of U.S. and foreign stock and bond markets?
- What are the differences in the rates of return on U.S. and foreign securities markets?
- How can changes in currency exchange rates affect the returns that U.S. investors experience on foreign securities?
- Is there additional advantage to diversifying in international markets beyond the benefits of domestic diversification?
- What alternative securities are available? What are their cash flow and risk properties?
- What are the historical return and risk characteristics of the major investment instruments?
- What is the relationship among the returns for foreign and domestic investment instruments? What is the implication of these relationships for portfolio diversification?

Individuals are willing to defer current consumption for many reasons. Some save for their children's college tuition or their own; others wish to accumulate down payments for a home, car, or boat; others want to amass adequate retirement funds for the future. Whatever the reasons for an investment program, the techniques we used in Chapter 1 to measure risk and return will help you evaluate alternative investments.

But what are those alternatives? Thus far, we have said little about the investment opportunities available in financial markets. In this chapter, we address this issue by surveying investment alternatives. This is essential background for making the asset allocation decision discussed in Chapter 2 and for later chapters where we analyze several individual investments, such as bonds, common stock, and other securities. It is also important when we consider how to construct and evaluate portfolios of investments.

As an investor in the 21st century, you have an array of investment choices unavailable a few decades ago. As discussed by Miller (1991), a combination of dynamic financial markets, technological advances, and new regulations have resulted in numerous new investment instruments and expanded trading opportunities. Improvements in communications and relaxation of international regulations have made it easier for investors to trade in both domestic and global markets. Telecommunications networks enable U.S. brokers to reach security exchanges in London, Tokyo, and other European and Asian cities as easily as those in New York, Chicago, and other U.S. cities. The competitive environment in the brokerage industry and the deregulation of the banking sector have made it possible for more financial institutions to compete for investor dollars. This has spawned investment vehicles with a variety of maturities, risk–return characteristics, and cash flow patterns. In this chapter, we examine some of these choices.

As an investor, you need to understand the differences among investments so you can build a properly diversified **portfolio** that conforms to your objectives. That is, you should

* The authors acknowledge data collection help on this chapter from Edgar Norton of Illinois State University and David J. Wright from the University of Wisconsin—Parkside.

seek to acquire a group of investments with different patterns of returns over time. If chosen carefully, such portfolios minimize risk for a given level of return because low or negative rates of return on some investments during a period of time are offset by above-average returns on others. Your goal should be to build a balanced portfolio of investments with relatively stable overall rates of return. A major goal of this text is to help you understand and evaluate the risk–return characteristics of investment portfolios. An appreciation of alternative security types is the starting point for this analysis.

This chapter is divided into three main sections. Because investors can choose securities from around the world, we initially look at a combination of reasons why investors *should* include foreign as well as domestic securities in their portfolios. Taken together, these reasons provide a compelling case for global investing.

In the second section of this chapter, we discuss securities in domestic and global markets, describing their main features and cash flow patterns. You will see that the varying risk–return characteristics of alternative investments suit the preferences of different investors.

The third and final section contains the historical risk and return performance of several investment instruments from around the world and examines the relationship among the returns for many of these securities. These results provide strong empirical support for global investing.

3.1 The Case for Global Investments

Twenty years ago, the bulk of investments available to individual investors consisted of U.S. stocks and bonds. Now, however, a call to your broker gives you access to a wide range of securities sold throughout the world. Currently, you can purchase stock in General Motors or Toyota, U.S. Treasury bonds or Japanese government bonds, a mutual fund that invests in U.S. biotechnology companies, a global growth stock fund or a German stock fund, or options on a U.S. stock index.

Several changes have caused this explosion of investment opportunities. For one, the growth and development of numerous foreign financial markets, such as those in Japan, the United Kingdom, and Germany, as well as emerging markets, such as China and India, have made these markets accessible and viable for investors around the world. U.S. investment firms have recognized this opportunity and established facilities in these countries aided by advances in telecommunications technology that allows constant contact with offices and financial markets around the world. In addition to the efforts by U.S. firms, foreign firms and investors undertook counterbalancing initiatives, including significant mergers of firms and security exchanges. As a result, as described by Pardee (1987), investors and investment firms can easily trade securities in markets around the world.

Three interrelated reasons U.S. investors should think of constructing global investment portfolios can be summarized as follows:

1. When investors compare the absolute and relative sizes of U.S. and foreign markets for stocks and bonds, they see that ignoring foreign markets reduces their choices to less than 50 percent of available investment opportunities. Because more opportunities broaden your range of risk–return choices, it makes sense to evaluate foreign securities when selecting investments and building a portfolio.
2. The rates of return available on non-U.S. securities often have substantially exceeded those for U.S.-only securities. The higher returns on non-U.S. *equities* can be justified by the higher growth rates for the countries where they are issued.
3. A major tenet of investment theory is that investors should diversify their portfolios. Because the relevant factor when diversifying a portfolio is low correlation between asset returns over time, diversification with foreign securities that have very low correlation with U.S. securities can substantially reduce portfolio risk.

In this section, we analyze these reasons to demonstrate the advantages to a growing role of foreign financial markets for U.S. investors and to assess the benefits and risks of trading in these markets. Notably, the reasons that global investing is appropriate for U.S. investors are generally even more compelling for non-U.S. investors.

3.1.1 Relative Size of U.S. Financial Markets

Prior to 1970, the securities traded in the U.S. stock and bond markets comprised about 65 percent of all the securities available in world capital markets. Therefore, a U.S. investor selecting securities strictly from U.S. markets had a fairly complete set of investments available. Under these conditions, most U.S. investors probably believed that it was not worth the time and effort to expand their investment universe to include the limited investments available in foreign markets. That situation has changed dramatically over the past 38 years. Currently, investors who ignore foreign stock and bond markets limit their investment choices substantially.

Exhibit 3.1 shows the breakdown of securities available in world capital markets in 1969 and 2006. Not only has the overall value of all securities increased dramatically (from $2.3 trillion to $103 trillion), but the composition has also changed. Concentrating on proportions of bond and equity investments, the exhibit shows that in 1969 U.S. dollar bonds and U.S. equity securities made up 53 percent of the total value of all securities versus 28.4 percent for the total of nondollar bonds and equity. By 2006, U.S. bonds and equities accounted for 41.0 percent of the total securities market versus 47.4 percent for nondollar bonds and stocks. These data indicate that if you consider only the U.S. proportion of this combined stock and bond market, it has declined from 65 percent of the total in 1969 to about 46 percent in 2006.

The point is, the U.S. security markets now include a smaller proportion of the total world capital market, and this trend will almost certainly continue. The faster economic growth of many other countries compared to the United States will require foreign governments and individual companies to issue debt and equity securities to finance this growth. Therefore, U.S. investors should consider investing in foreign securities because of the growing importance of these foreign securities in world capital markets. Put another way, not investing in foreign stocks and bonds means you are ignoring over 50 percent of the securities that are available to you. This approximate 50-50 breakdown is about the same for bonds alone, while U.S. stocks are only about 42 percent of global stocks.

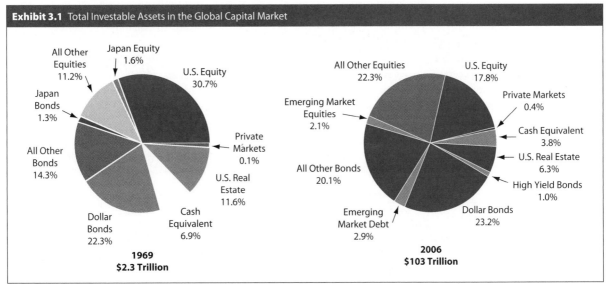

Exhibit 3.1 Total Investable Assets in the Global Capital Market

Source: UBS Global Asset Management.

3.1.2 Rates of Return on U.S. and Foreign Securities

An examination of the rates of return on U.S. and foreign securities not only demonstrates that many non-U.S. securities provide superior rates of return but also shows the impact of the exchange rate risk discussed in Chapter 1.

Global Bond-Market Returns Exhibit 3.2 reports annual rates of return for several major international bond markets for 1999–2007. The returns have been converted to U.S. dollar returns, so the exhibit shows mean annual returns and standard deviations that a U.S.-based investor would receive. An analysis of the returns in Exhibit 3.2 indicates that the return performance of the U.S. bond market ranked fifth out of the six countries. Part of the reason for the better performance in dollar terms of the non-U.S. markets is that the dollar generally weakened during this time frame, giving U.S. investors a boost to their foreign returns. Put another way, U.S. investors who invested in these foreign bonds received the return on the bonds equal to that of local investors but also received a return for holding the currency that appreciated relative to the U.S. dollar.

Global Equity-Market Returns Exhibit 3.3 shows the annual returns in U.S. dollars for 34 major equity markets yearly from 2003 through 2006. The United States' average rank in U.S. dollar returns in 2003–2006 was 29.5 out of 34 countries (and it was never in the top 25). Its performance was well behind the returns of numerous stock markets in these years.

These results for equity and bond markets around the world indicate that investors who limit themselves to the U.S. market may well experience rates of return below those in many other countries.

3.1.3 Risk of Combined Country Investments

Thus far, we have discussed the risk and return results for individual countries. In Chapter 1, we considered the idea of combining a number of assets into a portfolio and noted that investors should create diversified portfolios to reduce the variability of the returns over time. We discussed how proper diversification reduces the variability (our measure of risk) of the portfolio because alternative investments have different patterns of returns over time. Specifically, when the rates of return on some investments are negative or below average, other investments in the portfolio will be experiencing above-average rates of return. Therefore, if a portfolio is properly diversified, it should provide a more stable rate of return for the total portfolio (that is, it will have a lower standard deviation and therefore less risk). Although we will discuss and demonstrate portfolio theory in detail in Chapter 7, we need to consider the concept at this point to fully understand the benefits of global investing.

The way to measure whether two investments will contribute to diversifying a portfolio is to compute the correlation coefficient between their rates of return over time. Correlation coefficients can range from +1.00 to −1.00. A correlation of +1.00 means that the rates of return for these two investments move exactly together. Combining investments that move

Exhibit 3.2 Long-Term Government Bond Annual Rates of Return in U.S. Dollars: 1999–2007

	Geometric Mean (%)	Arithmetic Mean (%)	Standard Deviation (%)
Canada	12.29	12.77	11.09
France	7.51	8.69	16.62
Germany	7.69	8.9	16.79
Japan	3.57	4.19	12.15
United Kingdom	6.48	6.84	9.39
United States	6.44	6.75	8.59

Exhibit 3.3 Annual Returns in U.S. Dollar Terms

| | Performance of Dow Jones Global Indexes | | | | | | | |
| | 2006 | | 2005 | | 2004 | | 2003 | |
	U.S. Dollar Returns	Rank	U.S. Dollar Returns	Rank	U.S. Dollar Returns	Rank	U.S. Dollar Returns	Rank
U.S.	13.80%	31	4.50%	26	10.16%	30	28.44%	31
Australia	28.30%	24	11.30%	15	28.69%	14	45.95%	15
Austria	38.20%	12	20.90%	11	67.96%	1	58.26%	9
Belgium	32.40%	19	3.30%	28	43.07%	5	40.78%	18
Brazil	42.00%	9	48.00%	2	36.22%	8	131.40%	2
Canada	16.40%	29	25.50%	5	21.98%	19	51.54%	11
Chile	30.50%	21	10.90%	17	25.59%	17	83.53%	4
Denmark	34.20%	16	21.90%	9	28.75%	13	49.35%	14
Finland	28.40%	23	13.70%	14	5.84%	32	17.33%	34
France	34.00%	17	9.10%	19	17.07%	23	39.11%	20
Germany	35.20%	14	8.50%	21	14.29%	26	61.33%	7
Greece	34.80%	15	14.00%	13	40.02%	6	65.08%	6
Hong Kong	38.20%	12	6.90%	23	17.99%	22	38.69%	21
Indonesia	62.00%	2	8.90%	20	31.84%	10	65.95%	5
Ireland	42.40%	7	−0.10%	30	37.91%	7	44.26%	16
Italy	31.40%	20	−2.00%	32	27.59%	15	38.35%	23
Japan	1.80%	34	25.30%	7	16.62%	25	37.61%	24
Malaysia	33.00%	18	−1.00%	31	11.11%	29	26.19%	32
Mexico	39.20%	10	40.00%	3	46.53%	3	31.46%	28
Netherlands	30.00%	22	10.80%	18	11.84%	28	25.27%	33
New Zealand	13.40%	32	−3.30%	33	30.03%	12	50.85%	12
Norway	43.10%	6	21.00%	10	46.47%	4	40.62%	19
Philippines	49.50%	3	26.80%	4	30.09%	11	49.62%	13
Portugal	42.20%	8	25.50%	5	21.24%	20	38.53%	22
Singapore	38.70%	11	11.10%	16	19.09%	21	36.27%	26
South Africa	18.20%	28	23.50%	8	52.17%	2	41.78%	17
South Korea	15.40%	30	58.40%	1	23.99%	18	31.45%	29
Spain	46.80%	4	3.20%	29	26.07%	16	55.59%	10
Sweden	43.50%	5	8.40%	22	33.50%	9	60.06%	8
Switzerland	27.50%	26	14.90%	12	14.18%	27	33.14%	27
Taiwan	20.90%	27	3.90%	27	10.03%	31	36.63%	25
Thailand	6.10%	33	5.10%	24	−8.77%	33	138.70%	1
U.K.	28.20%	25	5.00%	25	16.93%	24	28.54%	30
Venezuela	63.00%	1	−19.30%	34	−18.83%	34	119.88%	3

Source: *The Wall Street Journal*, various issues, and author calculations.

together in a portfolio would not help diversify the portfolio because they have identical rate-of-return patterns over time. In contrast, a correlation coefficient of −1.00 means that the rates of return for two investments move exactly opposite to each other. When one investment is experiencing above-average rates of return, the other is suffering through similar below-average rates of return. Combining two investments with large negative correlation in a portfolio would be ideal for diversification because it would stabilize the rates of return over time, reducing the standard deviation of the portfolio rates of return and hence the risk of the portfolio. Therefore, if you want to diversify your portfolio and reduce your risk, you want an investment that has either *low positive* correlation, *zero* correlation, or, ideally, *negative correlation* with the other investments in your portfolio. With this in mind, the following discussion considers the correlations of returns among U.S. bonds and stocks with the returns on foreign bonds and stocks.

Global Bond Portfolio Risk Exhibit 3.4 lists the correlation coefficients between rates of return for bonds in the United States and bonds in major foreign markets in U.S. dollar terms

Exhibit 3.4 Correlation Coefficients between U.S. Dollar Rates of Return on Bonds in the United States and Major Foreign Markets: 1988–2006 (Monthly Data)

	Correlation Coefficient
Canada	0.74
France	0.65
Germany	0.65
Japan	0.38
United Kingdom	0.73
Average	0.63

Source: Data from MSCI.

from 1988 to 2006. For a U.S. investor, the important correlations are between the rates of return in U.S. dollars, and these correlations averaged less than 0.65.

These relatively low positive correlations among returns in U.S. dollars mean that U.S. investors have substantial opportunities for risk reduction through global diversification of bond portfolios. A U.S. investor who bought bonds in these markets would substantially reduce the standard deviation of a well-diversified U.S. bond portfolio.

Why do these correlation coefficients for returns between U.S. bonds and those of various foreign countries differ? That is, why is the U.S.–Canada correlation 0.74, whereas the U.S.–Japan correlation is only 0.38? The answer is because the international trade patterns, economic growth, fiscal policies, and monetary policies of the countries differ. We do not have an integrated world economy but, rather, a collection of economies that are related to one another in different ways. As an example, the U.S. and Canadian economies are closely related because of these countries' geographic proximity, similar domestic economic policies, and the extensive trade between them. Each is the other's largest trading partner. In contrast, the United States has less trade with Japan and the fiscal and monetary policies of the two countries differ dramatically. For example, the U.S. economy was growing during much of the 1990s while the Japanese economy experienced a prolonged recession.

The point is, macroeconomic differences cause the correlation of bond returns between the United States and each country to likewise differ. These differing correlations make it worthwhile to diversify with foreign bonds, and the different correlations indicate which countries will provide the greatest reduction in the standard deviation (risk) of bond portfolio returns for a U.S. investor.

Also, *the correlation of returns between a single pair of countries changes over time* because the factors influencing the correlations, such as international trade, economic growth, fiscal policy, and monetary policy, change over time. A change in any of these variables will produce a change in how the economies are related and in the relationship between returns on bonds. For example, the correlation in U.S. dollar returns between U.S. and Japanese bonds was 0.07 in the late 1960s and 1970s; it was 0.35 in the 1980s and 0.15 in the 1990s but only about 0.10 in the 1995–2006 time frame.

Exhibit 3.5 shows what happens to the risk–return trade-off when we combine U.S. and foreign bonds. A comparison of a completely non-U.S. portfolio (100 percent foreign) and a 100 percent U.S. portfolio indicates that the non-U.S. portfolio has both a higher rate of return and a higher standard deviation of returns than the U.S. portfolio. Combining the two portfolios in different proportions provides an interesting set of points.

As we will discuss in Chapter 7, the expected rate of return is a weighted average of the two portfolios. In contrast, the risk (standard deviation) of the combination is *not* a weighted average but also depends on the correlation between the two portfolios. In this example, the risk levels of the combined portfolios decline below those of the individual portfolios. Therefore, by adding foreign bonds that have low correlation with a portfolio of U.S. bonds, a U.S. investor

Exhibit 3.5 Risk–Return Trade-Off for International Bond Portfolios

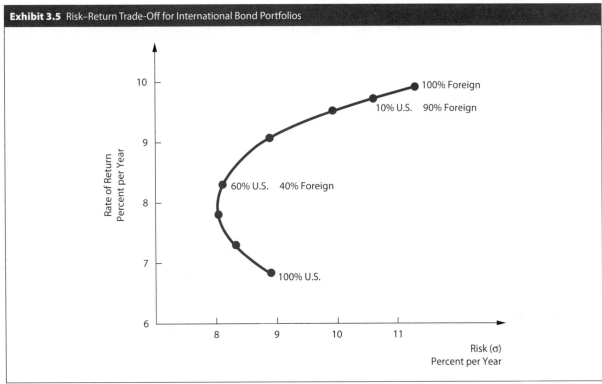

Source: Kenneth Cholerton, Pierre Piergerits, and Bruno Solnik, "Why Invest in Foreign Currency Bonds?" *Journal of Portfolio Management* 12, no. 4 (Summer 1986): 4–8. This copyrighted material is reprinted with permission from *Journal of Portfolio Management*, a publication of Institutional Investor, Inc.

is able to not only increase the expected rate of return but also reduce the risk compared to a total U.S. bond portfolio.

Global Equity Portfolio Risk The correlation of world equity markets resembles that for bonds. Exhibit 3.6 lists the correlation coefficients between monthly equity returns in U.S. dollars of each country and the U.S. market for the period from 1988 to 2006. Only 2 of the 11 correlations between U.S. dollar returns were over 0.60, and the average correlation was only 0.55.

These relatively small positive correlations between U.S. stocks and foreign stocks have similar implications to those derived for bonds. Investors can reduce the overall risk of their stock portfolios by including foreign stocks.

Exhibit 3.7 demonstrates the impact of international equity diversification. These curves demonstrate that, as you increase the number of randomly selected securities in a portfolio, the standard deviation will decline due to the benefits of diversification *within your own country*. This is referred to as *domestic diversification*. After a certain number of securities (40 to 50), the curve will flatten out at a risk level that reflects the basic market risk for the domestic economy [see Campbell, Lettau, Malkiel, and Xu (2001)]. The lower curve illustrates the benefits of international diversification. This curve demonstrates that adding foreign securities to a U.S. portfolio to create a global portfolio enables an investor to experience lower overall risk because the non-U.S. securities are not correlated with our economy or our stock market, allowing the investor to eliminate some of the basic market risks of the U.S. economy.

To see how this works, consider, for example, the effect of inflation and interest rates on all U.S. securities. As discussed in Chapter 1, all U.S. securities will be affected by these variables. In contrast, a Japanese stock is mainly affected by what happens in the Japanese economy and will typically not be affected by changes in U.S. variables. Thus, adding Japanese, Australian, and Italian stocks to a U.S. stock portfolio reduces the portfolio risk of the global portfolio to a level that reflects only worldwide systematic factors.

Exhibit 3.6 Correlation Coefficients between U.S. Dollar Rates of Return on Common Stocks in the United States and Major Foreign Stock Markets: 1988–2006

	Correlation Coefficient
Australia	0.49
Canada	0.73
France	0.60
Germany	0.60
Italy	0.39
Japan	0.34
Netherlands	0.66
Spain	0.57
Sweden	0.62
Switzerland	0.53
United Kingdom	0.64
Average	0.56

Source: Correlation table computed by the authors using monthly data from MSCI.

Exhibit 3.7 Risk Reduction through National and International Diversification

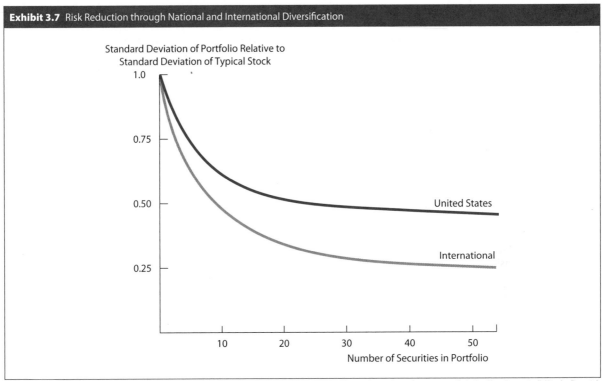

Source: Copyright 1974, Association for Investment Management and Research. Reproduced and republished from "Why Not Diversify Internationally Rather Than Domestically?" in the *Financial Analysts Journal*, July/August 1974, with permission from the Association for Investment Management and Research. All Rights Reserved. For a more recent analysis of this phenomenon, see Campbell, Lettau, Malkiel, and Xu (2001).

Summary on Global Investing At this point, we have considered the relative size of the market for non-U.S. bonds and stocks and found that it has grown in size and importance, becoming too big to ignore. We have also examined the rates of return for foreign bond and stock investments and determined that, when considering results, their rates of return were often superior to those in the U.S. market. Finally, we discussed constructing a portfolio of investments and the importance of diversification in reducing the variability of returns over time, which reduces the risk of the portfolio. As noted, to have successful diversification, an investor should combine investments with low positive or negative correlations between rates of return. An analysis of the correlation between rates of return on U.S. and foreign bonds and stocks indicated a consistent pattern of relatively low positive correlations. Therefore, the existence of similar rates of return on foreign securities combined with low correlation coefficients indicates that adding foreign stocks and bonds to a U.S. portfolio *will almost certainly reduce the risk of the portfolio and can possibly increase its average return.*

As promised, several rather compelling reasons exist for adding foreign securities to a U.S. portfolio. Therefore, developing a global investment perspective is important because such an approach has been shown to be justified, and this current trend in the investment world is expected to continue. Implementing this new global investment perspective will not be easy because it requires an understanding of new terms, instruments (such as Eurobonds), and institutions (such as non-U.S. stock and bond markets). Still, the effort is justified because you are developing a set of skills and a way of thinking that will enhance your long-term investing results.

The next section presents an overview of investment alternatives from around the world, beginning with fixed-income investments and progressing through numerous alternatives.

3.2 Global Investment Choices

This section provides an important foundation for subsequent chapters in which we describe techniques to value individual investments and combine alternative investments into properly diversified portfolios that conform to your risk–return objectives. In this section, we briefly describe the numerous investment alternatives available. The purpose of this survey is to introduce each of these investment alternatives so you can appreciate the full spectrum of opportunities. Most of these assets will be described in greater detail in subsequent chapters.

The investments are divided by asset classes. First, we describe fixed-income investments, including bonds and preferred stocks. In the second subsection, we discuss equity investments, and the third subsection contains a discussion of special equity instruments, such as warrants and options, which have characteristics of both fixed-income and equity instruments. In subsection four, we consider futures contracts that allow for a wide range of return–risk profiles. The fifth subsection considers investment companies.

All these investments are called *financial assets* because their payoffs are in money. In contrast, *real assets*, such as real estate, are discussed in the sixth subsection. We conclude with assets that are considered *low liquidity investments* because of the relative difficulty in buying and selling them. This includes art, antiques, coins, stamps, and precious gems.

The final section of the chapter describes the historical return and risk patterns for many individual investment alternatives and the correlations among the returns for these investments. This additional background and perspective will help you evaluate individual investments in order to build a properly diversified portfolio of global investments.

3.2.1 Fixed-Income Investments

Fixed-income investments have a contractually mandated payment schedule. Their investment contracts promise specific payments at predetermined times, although the legal force behind the promise varies and this affects their risks and required returns. At one extreme, if the issuing firm does not make its payment at the appointed time, creditors can declare the issuing firm in default. In other cases (for example, income bonds), the issuing firm must make payments only if it earns profits. In yet other instances (for example, preferred stock), the issuing firm does not have to make payments unless its board of directors votes to do so.

Investors who acquire fixed-income securities (except preferred stock) are really lenders to the issuers. Specifically, you lend some amount of money, the *principal*, to the borrower. In return, the borrower typically promises to make periodic interest payments and to pay back the principal at the maturity of the loan.

Savings Accounts You might not think of savings accounts as fixed-income investments, yet an individual who deposits funds in a savings account at a financial institution is really lending money to the institution and, as a result, earning a fixed payment. These investments are considered to be convenient, liquid, and low risk because almost all are insured. Consequently, their rates of return are generally low compared with other alternatives. Several versions of these accounts have been developed to appeal to investors with differing objectives.

Passbook savings accounts have no minimum balance, and funds may be withdrawn at any time with little loss of interest. Due to their flexibility, the promised interest on passbook accounts is relatively low.

For investors with larger amounts of funds who are willing to give up liquidity, financial institutions developed **certificates of deposit (CDs)**, which require minimum deposits (typically $500) and have fixed durations (usually three months, six months, one year, two years). The promised rates on CDs are higher than those for passbook savings accounts, and the rate increases with the size and the duration of the deposit. An investor who wants to cash in a CD prior to its stated expiration date must pay a heavy penalty in the form of a much lower interest rate.

Investors with large sums of money ($10,000 or more) can invest in Treasury bills (T-bills)—short-term obligations (maturing in 3 to 12 months) of the U.S. government. To compete against T-bills, banks issue money market certificates, which require minimum investments of $10,000 and have minimum maturities of six months. The promised rate on these certificates fluctuates at some premium over the weekly rate on six-month T-bills. Investors can redeem these certificates only at the bank of issue, and they incur penalties if they withdraw their funds before maturity.

Capital Market Instruments **Capital market instruments** are fixed-income obligations that trade in the secondary market, which means you can buy and sell them to other individuals or institutions. Capital market instruments fall into four categories: (1) U.S. Treasury securities, (2) U.S. government agency securities, (3) municipal bonds, and (4) corporate bonds.

U.S. Treasury Securities All government securities issued by the U.S. Treasury are fixed-income instruments. They may be bills, notes, or bonds depending on their times to maturity. Specifically, bills mature in one year or less, notes in over one to 10 years, and bonds in more than 10 years from time of issue. U.S. government obligations are essentially free of credit risk because there is little chance of default and they are highly liquid.

U.S. Government Agency Securities Agency securities are sold by various agencies of the government to support specific programs, but they are not direct obligations of the Treasury. Examples of agencies that issue these bonds include the Federal National Mortgage Association (FNMA or Fannie Mae), which sells bonds and uses the proceeds to purchase mortgages from insurance companies or savings and loans; and the Federal Home Loan Bank (FHLB), which sells bonds and loans the money to its 12 banks, which in turn provide credit to savings and loans and other mortgage-granting institutions. Other agencies are the Government National Mortgage Association (GNMA or Ginnie Mae), Banks for Cooperatives, Federal Land Banks (FLBs), and the Federal Housing Administration (FHA).

Although the securities issued by federal agencies are not direct obligations of the government, they are considered default-free because it is believed that the government would not allow them to default. Also, they are fairly liquid. Still, because they are not officially guaranteed by the Treasury, they are not considered riskless and because they are not as liquid as Treasury bonds, they typically provide slightly higher returns than Treasury issues.

Municipal Bonds Municipal bonds are issued by local government entities as either general obligation or revenue bonds. General obligation bonds (GOs) are backed by the full taxing power of the municipality, whereas revenue bonds pay the interest from revenue generated by specific projects (e.g., the revenue to pay the interest on sewer bonds comes from water taxes).

Municipal bonds differ from other fixed-income securities because they are tax-exempt. The interest earned from them is exempt from taxation by the federal government and historically by the state that issued the bond, provided the investor is a resident of that state. For this reason, municipal bonds are popular with investors in high tax brackets. For an investor having a marginal tax rate of 35 percent, a regular bond with an interest rate of 8 percent yields a net return after taxes of only 5.20 percent $[0.08 \times (1 - 0.35)]$. Such an investor would prefer a tax-free bond of equal risk with a 6 percent yield. This allows municipal bonds to offer yields that are generally 20 to 30 percent lower than yields on comparable taxable bonds.

Corporate Bonds Corporate bonds are fixed-income securities issued by industrial corporations, public utility corporations, or railroads to raise funds to invest in plant, equipment, or working capital. They can be broken down by issuer (industrial or utility), in terms of credit quality (measured by the ratings assigned by an agency on the basis of probability of default), in terms of maturity (short term, intermediate term, or long term), or based on some component of the indenture (sinking fund or call feature). Historically, corporate bonds have been substantially less liquid than Treasury or agency bonds. While they are still less liquid, the difference has declined due to real-time quotes for about 6,000 bonds on the NYSE and improved acquisition alternatives, described by Kim (2007).

All bonds include an **indenture**, which is the legal agreement that lists the obligations of the issuer to the bondholder, including the payment schedule and features such as call provisions and sinking funds. **Call provisions** specify when a firm can issue a call for the bonds prior to their maturity, at which time current bondholders must submit the bonds to the issuing firm, which redeems them (that is, pays back the principal and a small premium). A **sinking fund** provision specifies payments the issuer must make to redeem a given percentage of the outstanding issue prior to maturity.

Corporate bonds fall into various categories based on their contractual promises to investors. They will be discussed in order of their seniority.

Secured bonds are the most senior bonds in a firm's capital structure and have the lowest risk of distress or default. They include various secured issues that differ based on the assets that are pledged. **Mortgage bonds** are backed by liens on specific assets, such as land and buildings. In the case of default, the proceeds from the sale of these assets are used to pay off the mortgage bondholders. **Collateral trust bonds** are a form of mortgage bond except that the assets backing the bonds are financial assets, such as stocks, notes, and other high-quality bonds. Finally, **equipment trust certificates** are mortgage bonds that are secured by specific pieces of transportation equipment, such as locomotives and boxcars for a railroad and airplanes for an airline.

Debentures are promises to pay interest and principal, but they pledge no specific assets (referred to as *collateral*) in case the firm does not fulfill its promise. This means that the bondholder depends on the success of the borrower to make the promised payment. Debenture owners usually have first call on the firm's earnings and any assets that are not already pledged by the firm as backing for senior secured bonds. If the issuer does not make an interest payment, the debenture owners can declare the firm bankrupt and claim any unpledged assets to pay off the bonds.

Subordinated bonds are similar to debentures, but, in the case of default, subordinated bondholders have claim to the assets of the firm only after the firm has satisfied the claims of all senior secured and debenture bondholders. That is, the claims of subordinated bondholders are secondary to those of other bondholders. Within this general category of subordinated issues, you can find senior subordinated, subordinated, and junior subordinated bonds. Junior subordinated bonds have the weakest claim of all bondholders.

Income bonds stipulate interest payment schedules, but the interest is due and payable only if the issuers earn the income to make the payment by stipulated dates. If the company does not earn the required amount, it does not have to make the interest payment and it cannot be declared in default. Instead, the interest payment is considered in arrears and, if subsequently earned, it must be paid off. Because the issuing firm is not legally bound to make its interest payments except when the firm earns it, an income bond is not considered as safe as a debenture or a mortgage bond, so income bonds offer higher returns to compensate investors for the added risk. There are a limited number of corporate income bonds. In contrast, income bonds are fairly popular with municipalities because municipal revenue bonds are basically income bonds.

Convertible bonds have the interest and principal characteristics of other bonds, with the added feature that the bondholder has the option to turn them back to the firm in exchange for its common stock. For example, a firm could issue a $1,000 face-value bond and stipulate that owners of the bond could turn the bond in to the issuing corporation and convert it into 40 shares of the firm's common stock. These bonds appeal to investors because they combine the features of a fixed-income security with the option of conversion into the common stock of the firm, should the firm prosper.

Because of their desirable conversion option, convertible bonds generally pay lower interest rates than nonconvertible debentures of comparable risk. The difference in the required interest rate increases with the growth potential of the company because this increases the value of the option to convert the bonds into common stock. These bonds are almost always subordinated to the nonconvertible debt of the firm, so they are considered to have higher credit risk and receive a lower credit rating from the bond rating firms.

An alternative to convertible bonds is a debenture with warrants attached. The **warrant** is likewise an option that allows the bondholder to purchase the firm's common stock from the firm at a specified price for a given time period. The specified purchase price for the stock set in the warrant is typically above the price of the stock at the time the firm issues the bond but below the expected future stock price. The warrant makes the debenture more desirable, which lowers its required yield. The warrant also provides the firm with future common stock capital when the holder exercises the warrant and buys the stock from the firm.

Unlike the typical bond that pays interest every six months and its face value at maturity, a **zero coupon bond** promises no interest payments during the life of the bond but only the payment of the principal at maturity. Therefore, the purchase price of the bond is the present value of the principal payment at the required rate of return. For example, the price of a zero coupon bond that promises to pay $10,000 in five years with a required rate of return of 8 percent is $6,756. To find this, assuming semiannual compounding (which is the norm), use the present value factor for 10 periods at 4 percent, which is 0.6756.

Preferred Stock **Preferred stock** is classified as a fixed-income security because its yearly payment is stipulated as either a coupon (for example, 5 percent of the face value) or a stated dollar amount (for example, $5 preferred). Preferred stock differs from bonds because its payment is a dividend and therefore not legally binding. For each period, the firm's board of directors must vote to pay it, similar to a common stock dividend. Even if the firm earned enough money to pay the preferred stock dividend, the board of directors could theoretically vote to withhold it. Because most preferred stock is cumulative, the unpaid dividends would accumulate to be paid in full at a later time.

Although preferred dividends are not legally binding, as are the interest payments on a bond, they are considered *practically* binding because of the credit implications of a missed dividend. Because corporations can exclude 80 percent of intercompany dividends from taxable income, preferred stocks have become attractive investments for financial corporations. For example, a corporation that owns preferred stock of another firm and receives $100 in dividends can exclude 80 percent of this amount and pay taxes on only 20 percent of it ($20).

Assuming a 40 percent tax rate, the tax would only be $8 or 8 percent versus 40 percent on other investment income. Due to this tax benefit, the yield on high-grade preferred stock is typically lower than that on high-grade bonds.

3.2.2 International Bond Investing

As noted earlier, more than half of all fixed-income securities available to U.S. investors are issued by firms in countries outside the United States. Investors identify these securities in different ways: by the country or city of the issuer (for example, United States, United Kingdom, Japan); by the location of the primary trading market (for example, United States, London); by the home country of the major buyers; and by the currency in which the securities are denominated (for example, dollars, yen, euros). We identify foreign bonds by their country of origin and include these other differences in each description.

A **Eurobond** is an international bond denominated in a currency not native to the country where it is issued. Specific kinds of Eurobonds include Eurodollar bonds, Euroyen bonds, and Eurosterling bonds. A Eurodollar bond is denominated in U.S. dollars and sold outside the United States to non-U.S. investors. A specific example would be a U.S. dollar bond issued by General Electric and sold in London. Eurobonds are typically issued in Europe, with the major concentration in London.

Eurobonds can also be denominated in yen. For example, Nippon Steel can issue Euroyen bonds for sale in London. Also, if it appears that investors are looking for foreign currency bonds, a U.S. corporation can issue a Euroyen bond in London.

Yankee bonds are sold in the United States, denominated in U.S. dollars, but issued by foreign corporations or governments. This allows a U.S. citizen to buy the bond of a foreign firm or government but receive all payments in U.S. dollars, eliminating exchange rate risk.

An example would be a U.S. dollar–denominated bond issued by British Airways. Similar bonds are issued in other countries, including the Bulldog Market, which involves British sterling–denominated bonds issued in the United Kingdom by non-British firms, or the Samurai Market, which involves yen-denominated bonds issued in Japan by non-Japanese firms.

International domestic bonds are sold by an issuer within its own country in that country's currency. An example would be a bond sold by Nippon Steel in Japan denominated in yen. A U.S. investor acquiring such a bond would receive maximum diversification but would incur exchange rate risk.

3.2.3 Equity Instruments

This section describes several equity instruments, which differ from fixed-income securities because their returns are not contractual. As a result, you can receive returns that are much better or much worse than what you would receive on a bond. We begin with common stock, the most popular equity instrument and probably the most popular investment instrument.

Common stock represents *ownership* of a firm. Owners of the common stock of a firm share in the company's successes and problems. If—like Wal-Mart, Zimmer Holdings, Google, or Apple—the company prospers, the investor receives high rates of return and can become wealthy. In contrast, the investor can lose money if the firm does not do well or even goes bankrupt, as the once formidable K-Mart, Enron, W. T. Grant, and several U.S. airlines all did. In these instances, the firm may be forced to liquidate its assets and pay off all its creditors. Notably, the firm's preferred stockholders and common stock owners receive what is left, which is usually little or nothing. Investing in common stock entails all the advantages and disadvantages of ownership and is a relatively risky investment compared with fixed-income securities.

Common Stock Classifications When considering an investment in common stock, people tend to divide the vast universe of stocks into categories based on general business lines and by industry within these business lines. The division includes broad classifications for industrial firms, utilities, transportation firms, and financial institutions. Within each of these broad classes are industries. The industrial group, which is very diverse, includes such industries as automobiles, industrial machinery, chemicals, and beverages. Utilities include electrical power companies, gas suppliers, and the water industry. Transportation includes airlines, trucking firms, and railroads. Financial institutions include commercial banks, savings and loans, insurance companies, and investment firms.

An alternative classification scheme might separate domestic (U.S.) and foreign common stocks. We avoid this division because the business line–industry breakdown is more appropriate and useful when constructing a diversified portfolio of global common stock investments. With a global capital market, the focus of analysis should include all the companies in an industry viewed in a global setting. The point is, it is not relevant whether a major chemical firm is located in the United States or Germany, just as it is not relevent whether a computer firm is located in Michigan or California. Therefore, when considering the automobile industry, it is necessary to go beyond pure U.S. auto firms like General Motors and Ford and consider auto firms from throughout the world, such as Honda Motors, Porsche, Daimler, Nissan, Toyota, and Fiat.

Acquiring Foreign Equities

We begin our discussion on foreign equities by considering how you buy and sell these securities because this procedural information has often been a major impediment. Many investors may recognize the desirability of investing in foreign common stock because of the risk and return characteristics, but they may be intimidated by the logistics of the transaction. The purpose of this section is to alleviate this concern by explaining the alternatives available. Currently, there are several ways to acquire foreign common stock:

1. Purchase or sale of American Depository Receipts (ADRs)
2. Purchase or sale of American shares
3. Direct purchase or sale of foreign shares listed on a U.S. or foreign stock exchange
4. Purchase or sale of international or global mutual funds or exchange-traded funds (ETFs)

Purchase or Sale of American Depository Receipts The easiest way to acquire foreign shares directly is through **American Depository Receipts (ADRs)**. These are certificates of ownership issued by a U.S. bank that represent indirect ownership of a certain number of shares of a specific foreign firm on deposit in a bank in the firm's home country. ADRs are a convenient way to own foreign shares because the investor buys and sells them in U.S. dollars and receives all dividends in U.S. dollars. Therefore, the price and returns reflect both the domestic returns for the stock and the exchange rate effect. Also, the price of an ADR can reflect the fact that it represents multiple shares—for example, an ADR can be for 5 or 10 shares of the foreign stock. ADRs can be issued at the discretion of a bank based on the demand for the stock. The shareholder absorbs the additional handling costs of an ADR through higher transfer expenses, which are deducted from dividend payments.

ADRs are quite popular in the United States because of their diversification benefits, as documented by Wahab and Khandwala (1993). By the end of 2006, 462 foreign companies had stocks listed on the New York Stock Exchange (NYSE) and 356 of these were available through ADRs, including all the stock listed from Japan, the United Kingdom, Australia, Mexico, and the Netherlands.

Purchase or Sale of American Shares American shares are securities issued in the United States by a transfer agent acting on behalf of a foreign firm. Because of the added effort and expense incurred by the foreign firm, a limited number of American shares are available.

Direct Purchase or Sale of Foreign Shares The most difficult and complicated foreign equity transaction takes place in the country where the firm is located because it must be carried out in the foreign currency and the shares must then be transferred to the United States. This routine can be cumbersome. A second alternative is a transaction on a foreign stock exchange outside the country where the securities originated. For example, if you acquired shares of a French auto company listed on the London Stock Exchange (LSE), the shares would be denominated in pounds and the transfer would be swift, assuming your broker has a membership on the LSE.

Finally, you could purchase foreign stocks listed on the NYSE or NASDAQ. This is similar to buying a U.S. stock, but only a limited number of foreign firms qualify for—and are willing to accept—the cost of listing. Still, this number is growing. At the end of 2006, more than 107 foreign firms (mostly Canadian) were directly listed on the NYSE, in addition to the firms that were available through ADRs. Also, many foreign firms are traded on the NASDAQ market.

Purchase or Sale of Global Mutual Funds or ETFs   Numerous mutual funds or exchange-traded funds (ETFs) make it possible for investors to indirectly acquire the stocks of firms from outside the United States. The alternatives range from *global funds,* which invest in both U.S. stocks and foreign stocks, to *international funds,* which invest almost wholly outside the United States. In turn, international funds can (1) diversify across many countries, (2) concentrate in a segment of the world (for example, Europe, South America, the Pacific basin), (3) concentrate in a specific country (for example, the Japan Fund, the Germany Fund, the Italy Fund, or the Korea Fund), or (4) concentrate in types of markets (for example, emerging markets, which would include stocks from countries such as Thailand, Indonesia, India, and China). A mutual fund is a convenient path to global investing, particularly for a small investor, because the purchase or sale of one of these funds is similar to a transaction for a comparable U.S. mutual fund.

A recent innovation in the world of index products are exchange-traded funds (ETFs) that are depository receipts for a portfolio of securities deposited at a financial institution in a unit trust that issues a certificate of ownership for the portfolio of stocks (similar to ADRs discussed earlier). The stocks in a portfolio are those in an index like the S&P 500 or the Russell 3000 and dozens of country or specific-industry indexes. As of early 2008 the *Wall Street Journal* had a separate listing of "Exchange Traded Portfolios" that contained over 600 different portfolios to consider. A significant advantage is that ETFs can be bought and sold (including short sales) continuously on an exchange like common stock. Another advantage is that they do not have management fees, but there is the typical transaction cost for the purchase or sale of ETF shares.[1]

3.2.4 Special Equity Instruments: Options

In addition to common stock investments, it is also possible to invest in equity-derivative securities, which are securities that have a claim on the common stock of a firm. This would include **options**—rights to buy or sell common stock at a specified price for a stated period of time. The two kinds of option instruments are (1) warrants and (2) puts and calls.

Warrants   As mentioned earlier, a warrant is an option issued by a corporation that gives the holder the right to acquire a firm's common stock from the company at a specified price within a designated time period. The warrant does not constitute ownership of the stock, only the option to buy the stock.

Puts and Calls   A **call option** is similar to a warrant because it is an option to buy the common stock of a company within a certain period at a specified price called the *striking price.* A call option differs from a warrant because it is not issued by the company but by another investor who is willing to assume the other side of the transaction. Options also are typically valid for a shorter time period than warrants. Call options are generally valid for less than a year, whereas warrants often extend more than five years. The holder of a **put option** has the right to sell a given stock at a specified price during a designated time period. Puts are useful

---

[1] Mutual funds and ETFs are discussed further in the next section and in Chapters 16 and 25.

to investors who expect a stock price to decline during the specified period or to investors who own the stock and want hedge protection from a price decline.

3.2.5 Futures Contracts

Another instrument that provides an alternative to the purchase of an investment is a **futures contract**. This agreement provides for the future exchange of a particular asset at a specified delivery date (usually within nine months) in exchange for a specified payment at the time of delivery. Although the full payment is not made until the delivery date, a good-faith deposit, the **margin**, is made to protect the seller. This is typically about 10 percent of the value of the contract.

The bulk of trading on the commodity exchanges is in futures contracts. The current price of the futures contract is determined by the participants' beliefs about the future for the commodity. For example, in July of a given year, a trader could speculate on the Chicago Board of Trade for wheat in September, December, March, and May of the next year. If the investor expected the price of a commodity to rise, he or she could buy a futures contract on one of the commodity exchanges for later sale. If the investor expected the price to fall, he or she could sell a futures contract on an exchange with the expectation of buying similar contracts later when the price had (hopefully) declined to cover the sale.

Several differences exist between investing in an asset through a futures contract and investing in the asset itself. One is the use of a small good-faith deposit, which increases the volatility of returns. Because an investor puts up only a small portion of the total value of the futures contract (10 to 15 percent), when the price of the commodity changes, the change in the total value of the contract (up or down) is large compared to the amount invested. Another unique aspect is the term of the investment: Although stocks can have infinite maturities, futures contracts typically expire in less than a year.

Financial Futures In addition to futures contracts on commodities, there also has been the development of futures contracts on financial instruments, such as T-bills, Treasury bonds, and Eurobonds. For example, it is possible to buy or sell a futures contract that promises future delivery of $100,000 of Treasury bonds at a set price and yield. The major exchanges for financial futures are the Chicago Mercantile Exchange (CME) and the Chicago Board of Trade (CBOT).[2] These futures contracts allow individual investors, bond portfolio managers, and corporate financial managers to protect themselves against volatile interest rates. Certain currency futures allow individual investors or portfolio managers to speculate on or to protect against changes in currency exchange rates. Finally, there are futures contracts on various stock market series, such as the S&P (Standard & Poor's) 500, the *Value Line* Index, and the Nikkei Average on the Tokyo Stock Exchange.

3.2.6 Investment Companies

The investment alternatives described so far are individual securities that can be acquired from a government entity, a corporation, or another individual. However, rather than directly buying an individual stock or bond issued by one of these sources, you may choose to acquire these investments indirectly by buying shares in an investment company, also called a **mutual fund**, that owns a portfolio of individual stocks, bonds, or a combination of the two. Specifically, an **investment company** sells shares in itself and uses the proceeds of this sale to acquire bonds, stocks, or other investment instruments. As a result, an investor who acquires shares in an investment company is a partial owner of the investment company's portfolio of stocks or bonds. We will distinguish between investment companies by the types of investment instruments they acquire.

Money Market Funds **Money market funds** are investment companies that acquire high-quality, short-term investments (referred to as *money market* instruments), such as T-bills,

---

[2] These two exchanges merged in early 2008.

high-grade commercial paper (public short-term loans) from various corporations, and large CDs from the major money center banks. The yields on the money market portfolios always surpass those on normal bank CDs because the investment by the money market fund is larger and the fund can commit to longer maturities than the typical individual. In addition, the returns on commercial paper are above the prime rate. The typical minimum initial investment in a money market fund is $1,000, it charges no sales commission, and minimum additions are $250 to $500. You can always withdraw funds from your money market fund without penalty (typically by writing a check on the account), and you receive interest to the day of withdrawal.

Individuals tend to use money market funds as alternatives to bank savings accounts because they are generally quite safe (although they are not insured, they typically limit their investments to high-quality, short-term investments), they provide yields above what is available on most savings accounts, and the funds are readily available. Therefore, you might use one of these funds to accumulate funds to pay tuition or for a down payment on a car. Because of relatively high yields and extreme flexibility and liquidity, the total value of these funds reached more than $2.5 trillion in 2007.

Bond Funds Bond funds generally invest in various long-term government, corporate, or municipal bonds. They differ by the type and quality of the bonds included in the portfolio as assessed by various rating services. Specifically, the bond funds range from those that invest only in risk-free government bonds and high-grade corporate bonds to those that concentrate in lower-rated corporate or municipal bonds, called **high-yield bonds** or *junk bonds*. The expected rate of return from various bond funds will differ, with the low-risk government bond funds paying the lowest returns and the high-yield bond funds expected to provide the highest returns.

Common Stock Funds Numerous common stock funds invest to achieve stated investment objectives, which can include aggressive growth, income, precious metal investments, and international stocks. Such funds offer smaller investors the benefits of diversification and professional management. They include different investment styles, such as growth or value, and concentrate in alternative-sized firms, including small-cap, mid-cap, and large-capitalization stocks. To meet the diverse needs of investors, numerous funds have been created that concentrate in one industry or sector of the economy, such as chemicals, electric utilities, health, housing, and technology. These funds are diversified within a sector or an industry, but are not diversified across the total market. Investors who participate in a sector or an industry fund bear more risk than investors in a total market fund because the sector funds will tend to fluctuate more than an aggregate market fund that is diversified across all sectors. Also, international funds that invest outside the United States and global funds that invest in the United States and in other countries offer opportunities for global diversification by individual investors, as documented by Bailey and Lim (1992).

Balanced Funds **Balanced funds** invest in a combination of bonds and stocks of various sorts depending on their stated objectives.

Index Funds Index funds are mutual funds created to equal (track) the performance of a market index like the S&P 500. Such funds appeal to *passive* investors who want to simply experience returns equal to some market index either because they do not want to try to "beat the market" or they believe in efficient markets and do not think it is possible to do better than the market in the long run. Given the popularity of these funds, they have been created to emulate numerous stock indexes including very broad indexes like the Dow Jones Wilshire 5000 and broad foreign indexes like the EAFE index. In addition, numerous nonstock indexes including various bond indexes have been created for those who want passive bond investing.[3]

---

[3] Stock and bond indexes are discussed in Chapter 5.

Exchange-Traded Funds (ETFs)   A problem with mutual funds in general and index funds in particular is that they are only priced daily at the close of the market and all transactions take place at that price. As a result, if you are aware of changes taking place for the aggregate market due to some economic event during the day and want to buy or sell to take advantage of this, you can put in an order for a mutual fund, but it will not be executed until the end of the day at closing prices. In response to this problem, the AMEX in 1993 created an indexed fund tied to the S&P 500—that is, an exchange-traded fund, ETF—that could be traded continuously because the prices for the 500 stocks are updated continuously so it is possible to buy and sell this ETF like a share of stock, as noted previously. This concept of an ETF has been applied to numerous foreign and domestic indexes including the Morgan Stanley Capital International (MSCI) indexes. Barclay's Global Investors (BGI) have created "i shares," using the MSCI indexes for numerous individual countries, that have been analyzed by Khorana, Nelling, and Trester (1998).

3.2.7 Real Estate

Like commodities, most investors view real estate as an interesting and profitable investment alternative but believe that it is only available to a small group of experts with a lot of capital to invest. In reality, some feasible real estate investments require no detailed expertise or large capital commitments. We will begin by considering low-capital alternatives.

Real Estate Investment Trusts (REITS)   A **real estate investment trust** is an investment fund designed to invest in various real estate properties. It is similar to a stock or bond mutual fund, except that the money provided by the investors is invested in property and buildings rather than in stocks and bonds. There are several types of REITs.

 Construction and development trusts lend the money required by builders during the initial construction of a building. *Mortgage trusts* provide the long-term financing for properties. Specifically, they acquire long-term mortgages on properties once construction is completed. *Equity trusts* own various income-producing properties, such as office buildings, shopping centers, or apartment houses. Therefore, an investor who buys shares in an equity real estate investment trust is buying part of a portfolio of income-producing properties.

 REITs have experienced periods of great popularity and significant depression in line with changes in the aggregate economy and the money market. Although they are subject to cyclical risks depending on the economic environment, they offer small investors a way to participate in real estate investments, as described by Hardy (1995), Kuhn (1996), and Myer and Webb (1993).

Direct Real Estate Investment   The most common type of direct real estate investment is the purchase of a home, which is the largest investment most people ever make. Today, according to the Federal Home Loan Bank, the average cost of a single family house exceeds $140,000. The purchase of a home is considered an investment because the buyer pays a sum of money either all at once or over a number of years through a mortgage. For most people, those unable to pay cash for a house, the financial commitment includes a down payment (typically 10–20 percent of the purchase price) and specific mortgage payments over a 20- to 30-year period that amortize both the loan's principal and interest due on the outstanding balance. Subsequently, a homeowner hopes to sell the house for its cost plus a gain.

Raw Land   Another direct real estate investment is the purchase of raw land with the intention of selling it in the future at a profit. During the time you own the land, you have negative cash flows caused by mortgage payments, property maintenance, and taxes. An obvious risk is the possible difficulty of selling it for an uncertain price. Raw land generally has low liquidity compared to most stocks and bonds. An alternative to buying and selling the raw land is the development of the land.

Land Development   Land development can involve buying raw land, dividing it into individual lots, and building houses on it. Alternatively, buying land and building a shopping mall would also be considered land development. This is a feasible form of investment but requires a substantial commitment of capital, time, and expertise. Although the risks can be high because of the commitment of time and capital, the rates of return from a successful housing or commercial development can be significant, as shown in studies by Goetzmann and Ibbotson (1990) and Ross and Zisler (1991). Diversification benefits are documented in Hudson-Wilson and Elbaum (1995).

Rental Property Many investors with an interest in real estate investing acquire apartment buildings or houses with low down payments, with the intention of deriving enough income from the rents to pay the expenses of the structure, including the mortgage payments. For the first few years following the purchase, the investor generally has no reported income from the building because of tax-deductible expenses, including the interest component of the mortgage payment and depreciation on the structure. Subsequently, rental property provides a cash flow and an opportunity to profit from the sale of the property, as discussed by Harris (1984).

3.2.8 Low-Liquidity Investments

Most of the investment alternatives we have described thus far are traded on securities markets and except for real estate, have good liquidity. In contrast, the investments we discuss in this section have very poor liquidity and financial institutions do not typically acquire them because of the illiquidity and high transaction costs compared to stocks and bonds. Many of these assets are sold at auctions, causing expected prices to vary substantially. In addition, transaction costs are high because there is generally no national market for these investments, so local dealers must be compensated for the added carrying costs and the cost of searching for buyers or sellers. Therefore, many financial theorists view the following low-liquidity investments more as hobbies than investments, even though studies have indicated that some of these assets have experienced substantial rates of return.

Antiques The greatest returns from antiques are earned by dealers who acquire them at estate sales or auctions to refurbish and sell at a profit. If we gauge the value of antiques based on prices established at large public auctions, it appears that many serious collectors enjoy substantial rates of return. In contrast, the average investor who owns a few pieces to decorate his or her home finds such returns elusive. The high transaction costs and illiquidity of antiques may erode any profit that the individual may expect to earn when selling these pieces.

Art The entertainment sections of newspapers or the personal finance sections of magazines often carry stories of the results of major art auctions, such as when Van Gogh's *Irises* and *Sunflowers* sold for $59 million and $36 million, respectively.

Obviously, these examples and others indicate that some paintings have increased significantly in value and thereby generated large rates of return for their owners. However, investing in art typically requires substantial knowledge of art and the art world, a large amount of capital to acquire the work of well-known artists, patience, and an ability to absorb high transaction costs. For investors who enjoy fine art and have the resources, these can be satisfying investments; but, for most small investors, it is difficult to get returns that compensate for the uncertainty, illiquidity, and high transaction costs.

Coins and Stamps Many individuals enjoy collecting coins or stamps as a hobby and as an investment. The market for coins and stamps is fragmented compared to the stock market, but it is more liquid than the market for art and antiques as indicated by the publication of weekly and monthly price lists.[4] An investor can get a widely recognized grading specification on a

---

[4] A weekly publication for coins is *Coin World*, published by Amos Press, Inc., 911 Vandermark Rd., Sidney, OH 45367. There are several monthly coin magazines, including *Coinage*, published by Miller Magazines, Ventura, CA. Amos Press also publishes several stamp magazines, including *Linn's Stamp News* and *Scott Stamp Monthly*. These magazines provide current prices for coins and stamps.

coin or stamp, and, once graded, a coin or stamp can usually be sold quickly through a dealer, as described by Henriques (1989) and Bradford (1989). It is important to recognize that the percentage difference between the bid price the dealer will pay to buy the stamp or coin and the asking or selling price the investor must pay the dealer is going to be substantially larger than the bid-ask spread on stocks and bonds.

Diamonds   Diamonds can be and have been good investments during many periods. Still, investors who purchase diamonds must realize that (1) diamonds can be highly illiquid, (2) the grading process that determines their quality is quite subjective, (3) most investment-grade gems require substantial capital, and (4) they generate no positive cash flow during the holding period until the stone is sold. In fact, during the holding period, the investor must cover costs of insurance and storage and there are appraisal costs before selling.

In this section, we have briefly described the most common investment alternatives. We will discuss many of these in more detail when we consider how you evaluate them for investment purposes.

In our final section, we will present data on historical rates of return and risk measures, as well as correlations among several of these investments. This should give you some insights into future expected returns and risk characteristics for these investment alternatives.

· ·

3.3 Historical Risk–Returns on Alternative Investments

How do investors weigh the costs and benefits of owning investments and make decisions to build portfolios that will provide the best risk–return combinations? To help individual or institutional investors answer this question, financial theorists have examined extensive data to provide information on the return and risk characteristics of various investments.

There have been numerous studies of the historical rates of return on common stocks (both large-capitalization stocks in terms of aggregate market value and small-capitalization stocks).[5] In addition, there has been a growing interest in bonds. Because inflation has been so pervasive, many studies include both nominal and real rates of return on investments. Still other investigators have examined the performance of such assets as real estate, foreign stocks, art, antiques, and commodities. The subsequent review of these results should help you to make decisions on building your investment portfolio and on the allocation to the various asset classes.

3.3.1 World Portfolio Performance

A study by Reilly and Wright (2004) examined the performance of numerous assets, not only in the United States, but around the world. Specifically, for the period from 1980 to 2001, they examined the performance of stocks, bonds, cash (the equivalent of U.S. T-bills), real estate, and commodities from the United States, Canada, Europe, Japan, and the emerging markets. They computed annual returns, risk measures, and correlations among the returns for alternative assets. Exhibit 3.8 shows the geometric and arithmetic average annual rates of return, the standard deviations of returns, and the systematic risk (beta) for the 22-year period.

Asset Return and Total Risk   The results in Exhibit 3.8 generally confirm the expected relationship between annual rates of return and the total risk (standard deviation) of these securities. The riskier assets—those that had higher standard deviations—experienced higher returns. For example, the U.S. stock indexes had relatively high returns (10 to 15 percent) and

---

[5] Small-capitalization stocks were broken out as a separate class of asset because several studies have shown that firms with relatively small capitalization (stock with low market value) have experienced rates of return and risk significantly different from those of stocks in general. Therefore, they were considered a unique asset class. We will discuss these studies in Chapter 6, which deals with the efficient markets hypothesis. The large-company stock returns are based upon the S&P Composite Index of 500 stocks—the S&P 500 (described in Chapter 5).

Exhibit 3.8 Summary Risk–Return Results for Alternative Capital Market Assets: 1980–2001

Index	Arithmetic Mean Return	Geometric Mean Return	Standard Deviation Annual Return	Beta With SP500	Beta With Brinson
S&P 500	15.94	14.96	15.12	1.00	1.35
Wilshire 5000	14.96	13.89	15.66	1.01	1.41
Russell 1000	15.38	14.37	15.32	1.01	1.37
Russell 1000 Value	15.71	14.94	13.45	0.82	1.10
Russell 1000 Growth	15.23	13.51	19.71	1.15	1.58
Russell 2000	13.58	12.33	17.06	1.01	1.52
Russell 2000 Value	16.16	14.93	16.68	0.77	1.12
Russell 2000 Growth	11.69	9.78	21.31	1.07	1.61
Russell 3000	15.15	14.16	15.12	1.01	1.38
Russell 3000 Value	15.68	14.92	13.32	0.82	1.10
Russell 3000 Growth	14.95	13.29	19.37	1.00	1.39
IFC Emerging Markets	9.81	6.09	29.72	0.56	0.86
MSCI EAFE	13.50	11.38	22.74	0.61	1.23
Toronto Stock Exchange 300	7.64	6.69	14.65	0.85	1.29
Financial Times All-Share	12.39	11.51	13.83	0.71	1.07
Frankfurt (FAZ) Index	11.75	9.27	24.43	0.68	1.01
Nikkei Index	4.66	2.17	22.67	0.55	1.03
Tokyo Stock Exchange Index	6.41	3.71	24.20	0.43	0.84
M-S World Index	13.52	11.62	21.45	0.67	1.28
Brinson GSMI	12.67	12.13	11.04	0.62	1.00
LB Government Bond	9.98	9.76	7.24	0.09	0.20
LB Corporate Bond	10.86	10.47	9.69	0.16	0.31
LB Aggregate Bond	10.25	9.98	7.96	0.11	0.24
LB High Yield Bond	11.88	11.23	12.64	0.24	0.43
ML World Government Bond	8.59	8.31	8.12	0.03	0.18
ML World Government Bond without U.S.	9.64	8.96	12.81	0.00	0.23
Wilshire Real Estate	11.62	10.31	16.25	0.56	0.87
GS Commodities Index	9.20	6.64	23.29	0.06	0.11
GS Energy Commodities Sub-Index	17.55	9.84	43.25	−0.09	−0.13
GS Non-Energy Commodities Sub-Index	4.71	3.83	13.65	0.15	0.25
GS Industrial Metals Commodities Sub-Index	10.57	5.15	42.06	0.24	0.45
GS Precious Metals Commodities Sub-Index	−2.39	−3.38	13.88	0.11	0.29
GS Agriculture Commodities Sub-Index	1.33	−0.25	18.09	0.16	0.23
GS Livestock Commodities Sub-Index	10.00	8.45	18.81	0.10	0.18
Treasury Bill–30 Day	6.74	6.70	2.90	0.00	0.00
Treasury Bill–6 Month	7.38	7.33	3.37	0.00	0.01
Treasury Note–2 Year	8.43	8.35	4.36	0.04	0.08
Inflation	3.89	3.86	2.54	−0.01	−0.02

Statistics for Treasury Bill–6 month and Treasury Note–2 year are based on 1981–2001 data only.

Statistics for ML World Government Bond indexes are based on 1986–2001 data only.

Statistics for GS Commodities Sub-Index are based on 1983–2001 data only.

Source: Frank K. Reilly and David J. Wright, "An Analysis of Risk-Adjusted Performance for Global Market Assets," *Journal of Portfolio Management* 30, no. 3 (Spring 2004): 63–77. This copyrighted material is reprinted with permission from *Journal of Portfolio Management*, a publication of Institutional Investor, Inc.

large standard deviations (13 to 21 percent). It is not a surprise that the highest-risk asset class (without commodities) was emerging market stock with a standard deviation of 29.72 percent, whereas risk-free U.S. cash equivalents (30-day T-bills) had low returns (6.70 percent) and the smallest standard deviation (2.90 percent).

Return and Systematic Risk As shown in Exhibit 3.8, in addition to total risk (standard deviation), the authors also considered systematic risk, which is the volatility of an asset relative to a market portfolio of risky assets (this was discussed briefly in Chapter 1). One of the conclusions of Reilly and Wright's (2004) study was that the systematic risk measure (beta) did a better job of explaining the returns during the period than the total risk measure. In addition, the beta risk measure that used the Brinson index as a market proxy was somewhat better

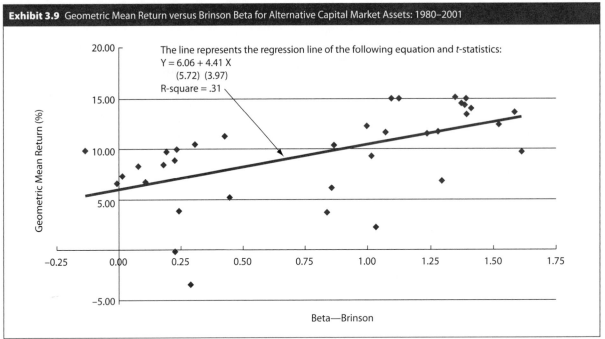

Exhibit 3.9 Geometric Mean Return versus Brinson Beta for Alternative Capital Market Assets: 1980–2001

The line represents the regression line of the following equation and *t*-statistics:
Y = 6.06 + 4.41 X
  (5.72) (3.97)
R-square = .31

Geometric Mean Return (%)

Beta—Brinson

Source: Frank K. Reilly and David J. Wright, "An Analysis of Risk-Adjusted Performance for Global Market Assets," *Journal of Portfolio Management* 30, no. 3 (Spring 2004): 63–77. This copyrighted material is reprinted with permission from *Journal of Portfolio Management*, a publication of Institutional Investor, Inc.

than the beta that used the S&P 500 Index. Thus, Exhibit 3.9 which contains the scatter plot of geometric mean rate of return and systematic risk indicates the expected positive risk–return relationship.

Correlations between Asset Returns Exhibit 3.10 is a correlation matrix of selected U.S. and world assets. The first column shows that U.S. equities (as represented by the broad Wilshire 5000 Index) have a reasonably high correlation with Canadian and U.K. stocks (0.793 and 0.672) but low correlation with emerging market stocks and Japanese stocks (0.441 and 0.335). Also, U.S. equities show almost zero correlation with world government bonds, except U.S. bonds (−0.013). Recall from our earlier discussion that you can use this information to build a diversified portfolio by combining those assets with low positive or negative correlations.

The correlation of returns with inflation has implications regarding the ability of an asset class to be an inflation hedge—a good hedge should have a strong positive correlation with inflation. As shown, most assets (including common stocks) have negative correlations, which implies that they are poor inflation hedges. The exceptions appear to be some commodities and short-term government bonds (especially 30-day Treasury bills).

3.3.2 Art and Antiques

Unlike financial securities, where the results of transactions are reported daily, art and antique markets are fragmented and lack any formal transaction reporting system. This makes it difficult to gather data. The best-known series that attempted to provide information about the changing value of art and antiques were developed by Sotheby's, a major art auction firm. These value indexes covered 13 areas of art and antiques and a weighted aggregate series that combined the 13 areas.

Reilly (1992) examined these series for the period from 1976 to 1991 and computed rates of return, measures of risk, and the correlations among the various art and antique series and compared them to stocks, bonds, and the rate of inflation.

Exhibit 3.10 Correlations among Global Capital Market Asset Monthly Returns: 1980–2001

Index	Dow-Jones Wilshire 5000	IFC Emerging Market Stock	MSCI EAFE	M-S World Stock	Brinson GSMI	Inflation
S&P 500	0.983	0.392	0.538	0.604	0.915	−0.115
Wilshire 5000	1.000	0.414	0.545	0.607	0.926	−0.116
Russell 1000	0.991	0.396	0.536	0.602	0.922	−0.121
Russell 1000 Value	0.851	0.339	0.458	0.518	0.801	−0.108
Russell 1000 Growth	0.968	0.378	0.524	0.586	0.897	−0.116
Russell 2000	0.877	0.401	0.470	0.513	0.811	−0.132
Russell 2000 Value	0.778	0.329	0.409	0.452	0.729	−0.138
Russell 2000 Growth	0.750	0.305	0.399	0.432	0.700	−0.113
Russell 3000	0.995	0.402	0.538	0.603	0.925	−0.123
Russell 3000 Value	0.858	0.344	0.462	0.521	0.807	−0.112
Russell 3000 Growth	0.828	0.283	0.449	0.489	0.781	−0.126
IFC Emerging Market	0.414	1.000	0.386	0.395	0.411	−0.002
MSCI EAFE	0.545	0.386	1.000	0.982	0.744	−0.155
Toronto Stock Exchange 300	0.793	0.451	0.547	0.604	0.780	−0.105
Financial Times All Share	0.672	0.443	0.581	0.597	0.685	−0.090
Frankfurt (FAZ) Index	0.537	0.433	0.486	0.499	0.545	−0.127
Nikkei Index	0.431	0.388	0.722	0.712	0.531	−0.057
Tokyo Stock Exchange Index	0.335	0.321	0.681	0.667	0.439	−0.061
M-S World Index	0.607	0.395	0.982	1.000	0.785	−0.157
Brinson GSMI	0.926	0.411	0.744	0.785	1.000	−0.161
LB Government Bond	0.209	−0.136	0.167	0.164	0.352	−0.097
LB Corporate Bond	0.298	−0.051	0.203	0.210	0.426	−0.139
LB Aggregate Bond	0.250	−0.092	0.188	0.188	0.389	−0.113
LB High Yield Bond	0.488	0.213	0.357	0.370	0.551	−0.151
ML World Government Bond	0.046	−0.187	0.423	0.400	0.280	−0.065
ML World Government Bond except U.S.	−0.013	−0.157	0.474	0.448	0.232	−0.049
Wilshire Real Estate	0.624	0.278	0.370	0.410	0.617	−0.167
Goldman Commodities Index	0.077	0.033	0.106	0.113	0.071	0.043
Goldman Energy Commodities Sub-Index	−0.032	−0.002	0.014	0.016	−0.042	0.161
Goldman Non-Energy Commodities Sub-Index	0.232	0.124	0.262	0.271	0.241	−0.054
Goldman Industrial Metals Commodities Sub-Index	0.173	−0.022	0.165	0.181	0.196	−0.076
Goldman Precious Metals Commodities Sub-Index	0.121	0.032	0.191	0.223	0.163	−0.011
Goldman Agriculture Commodities Sub-Index	0.178	0.087	0.158	0.171	0.160	−0.049
Goldman Livestock Commodities Sub-Index	0.106	0.055	0.152	0.148	0.130	−0.016
Treasury Bill–30 day	−0.064	−0.086	−0.035	−0.054	−0.037	0.529
Treasury Bill–6 Month	0.054	−0.116	0.014	0.008	0.125	0.277
Treasury Note–2 Year	0.178	−0.118	0.122	0.123	0.299	−0.028
Inflation	−0.116	−0.002	−0.155	−0.157	−0.161	1.000

ML World Government Bond indexes based on 1986–2001 data only.

GS Commodities Sub-Index based on 1983–2001 data only.

Treasury Bill–6 Month and Treasury Note–2 year based on 1981–2001 data only.

Source: Frank K. Reilly and David J. Wright, "An Analysis of Risk-Adjusted Performance for Global Market Assets," *Journal of Portfolio Management* 30, no. 3 (Spring 2004): 63–77. This copyrighted material is reprinted with permission from *Journal of Portfolio Management*, a publication of Institutional Investor, Inc.

Although there was a wide range of mean returns and risk, a risk–return plot indicated a fairly consistent relationship between risk and return during this 16-year period. Comparing the art and antique results to bond and stock indexes indicated that stocks and bonds experienced results that were very consistent with the art and antique series.

Analysis of the correlations among these assets using annual rates of return revealed several important relationships. First, the correlations among alternative antique and art categories vary substantially from above 0.90 to negative correlations. Second, the correlations between art/antiques and bonds were generally negative. Third, the correlations of art/antiques with stocks were typically small positive values. Finally, the correlation of art and antiques with the rate of inflation indicates that several of the categories were fairly good inflation hedges since they were positively correlated with inflation. Notably, they were clearly superior inflation hedges compared to long-term bonds and common stocks as documented in Fama (1991) and Jaffe and Mandelker (1976). The reader should recall our earlier observation that most art and antiques are quite illiquid and the transaction costs are fairly high compared to financial assets.

3.3.3 Real Estate

Somewhat similar to art and antiques, returns on real estate are difficult to derive because of the limited number of transactions and the lack of a national source of data for the transactions that allows one to accurately compute rates of return. In the study by Goetzmann and Ibbotson (1990), the authors gathered data on commercial real estate through REITs and Commingled Real Estate Funds (CREFs) and estimated returns on residential real estate from a series created by Case and Shiller (1987). The summary of the real estate returns compared to various stock, bond, and an inflation series is contained in Exhibit 3.11. As shown, the two commercial real estate series reflected strikingly different results. The CREFs had lower returns and low volatility, while the REIT index had higher returns and risk. Notably, the REIT returns were higher than those of common stocks, but the risk measure for real estate was lower (there was a small difference in the time period). The residential real estate series reflected lower returns and low risk. The longer-term results indicate that all the real estate series experienced lower returns and lower risk than common stock.

The correlations in Exhibit 3.12 among annual returns for the various asset groups indicate a relatively low positive correlation between commercial real estate and stocks. In contrast, there was negative correlation between stocks and residential and farm real estate. This negative relationship with real estate was also true for 20-year government bonds. Studies by Eichholtz (1996), Mull and Socnen (1997), and Quan and Titman (1997) that considered international commercial real estate and REITs indicated that the returns were correlated with stock prices but they still provided significant diversification benefits.

Exhibit 3.11 Summary Statistics of Commercial and Residential Real Estate Series Compared to Stocks, Bonds, T-bills, and Inflation

Series	Date	Geometric Mean	Arithmetic Mean	Standard Deviation
Annual Returns 1969–1987				
CREF (Comm.)	1969–87	10.8%	10.9%	2.6%
REIT (Comm.)	1972–87	14.2	15.7	15.4
C&S (Res.)	1970–86	8.5	8.6	3.0
S&P (Stocks)	1969–87	9.2	10.5	18.2
LTG (Bonds)	1969–87	7.7	8.4	13.2
TBILL (Bills)	1969–87	7.6	7.6	1.4
CPI (Infl.)	1969–87	6.4	6.4	1.8
Annual Returns over the Long Term				
I&S (Comm.)	1960–87	8.9%	9.1%	5.0%
CPIHOME (Res.)	1947–86	8.1	8.2	5.2
USDA (Farm)	1947–87	9.6	9.9	8.2
S&P (Stocks)	1947–87	11.4	12.6	16.3
LTG (Bonds)	1947–87	4.2	4.6	9.8
TBILL (Bills)	1947–87	4.9	4.7	3.3
CPI (Infl.)	1947–87	4.5	4.6	3.9

Source: William N. Goetzmann and Roger G. Ibbotson, "The Performance of Real Estate as an Asset Class," *Journal of Applied Corporate Finance* 3, no. 1 (Spring 1990): 65–76. Reprinted with permission.

Exhibit 3.12 Correlations of Annual Real Estate Returns with the Returns on Other Asset Classes

	I&S	CREF	CPI Home	C&S	Farm	S&P	20-Yr. Gvt.	1-Yr. Gvt.	Infl.
I&S	1								
CREF	0.79	1							
CPI Home	0.52	0.12	1						
C&S	0.26	0.16	0.82	1					
Farm	0.06	−0.06	0.51	0.49	1				
S&P	0.16	0.25	−0.13	−0.20	−0.10	1			
20-Yr. Gvt.	−0.04	0.01	−0.22	−0.54	−0.44	0.11	1		
1-Yr. Gvt.	0.53	0.42	0.13	−0.56	−0.32	−0.07	0.48	1	
Infl.	0.70	0.35	0.77	0.56	0.49	−0.02	−0.17	0.26	1

Note: Correlation coefficient for each pair of asset classes uses the maximum number of observations, that is, the minimum length of the two series in the pair.

Source: William N. Goetzmann and Roger G. Ibbotson, "The Performance of Real Estate as an Asset Class," *Journal of Applied Corporate Finance* 3, no. 1 (Spring 1990): 65–76. Reprinted with permission.

These results imply that returns on real estate are equal to or slightly lower than returns on common stocks, but real estate possesses favorable risk results. Specifically, real estate had much lower standard deviations as unique assets and either low positive or negative correlations with other asset classes in a portfolio context.

• • • • SUMMARY • • • •

- Investors who want the broadest range of choices in investments must consider foreign stocks and bonds in addition to domestic financial assets. Many foreign securities offer investors higher risk-adjusted returns than do domestic securities. In addition, the low positive or negative correlations between foreign and U.S. securities make them ideal for building a diversified portfolio.

- Exhibit 3.13 summarizes the risk and return characteristics of the investment alternatives described in this chapter. Some of the differences are due to unique factors that we discussed. Foreign bonds are considered riskier than domestic bonds because of the unavoidable uncertainty due to exchange rate risk and country risk. The same is true for foreign and domestic common stocks. Such investments as art, antiques, coins, and stamps require heavy liquidity risk premiums. You should divide consideration of real estate investments between your personal home, on which you do not expect as high a return because of nonmonetary factors, and commercial real estate, which requires a much higher rate of return due to cash flow uncertainty and illiquidity.

- Studies on the historical rates of return for investment alternatives such as the excellent book by Ibbotson and Brinson (1993) (including bonds, commodities, real estate, foreign securities, and art and antiques) point toward two generalizations:
  1. A positive relationship typically holds between the rate of return earned on an asset and the variability of its historical rate of return or its systematic risk (beta). This is expected in a world of risk-averse investors who require higher rates of return to compensate for more uncertainty.
  2. The correlation among rates of return for selected alternative investments is typically quite low, especially for U.S. and foreign stocks and bonds and between these financial assets and real assets, as represented by art, antiques, and real estate. This confirms the advantage of diversification among investments from different asset classes and from around the world.

- In addition to describing many direct investments, such as stocks and bonds, we also discussed investment companies that allow investors to buy investments indirectly. These can be important to investors who want to take advantage of professional management but also want instant diversification with a limited amount of funds. With $10,000, you may not be able to buy many individual stocks or bonds, but you could acquire shares in a mutual fund or an ETF, which would give you a share of a diversified portfolio that might contain 100 to 150 different U.S. and international stocks or bonds.

- Now that we know the range of domestic and foreign investment alternatives, our next task is to learn about the markets in which they are bought and sold. That is the objective of the following chapter.

Exhibit 3.13 Alternative Investment Risk and Return Characteristics

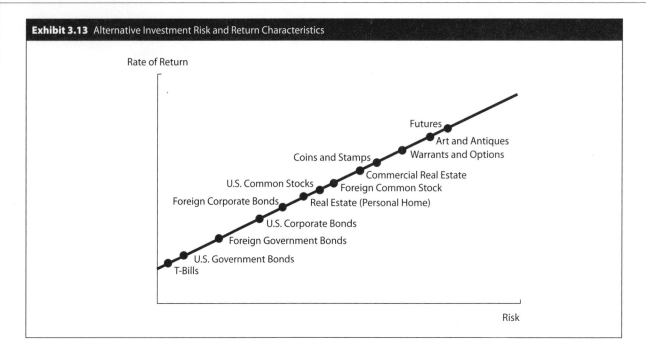

· · · · **SUGGESTED READINGS** · · · ·

Grabbe, J. Orlin. *International Financial Markets.* New York: Elsevier Science Publishing, 1986.

Hamao, Yasushi. "Japanese Stocks, Bonds, Inflation, 1973–1987." *Journal of Portfolio Management* 16, no. 2 (Winter 1989).

Lessard, Donald R. "International Diversification." In *The Financial Analyst's Handbook,* 2d ed., ed. Sumner N. Levine. Homewood, IL: Dow Jones–Irwin, 1988.

Malvey, Jack. "Global Corporate Bond Portfolio Management." In *The Handbook of Fixed-Income Securities,* 7th ed., ed. Frank J. Fabozzi. New York: McGraw-Hill, 2005.

Rosenberg, Michael R. "International Fixed-Income Investing: Theory and Practice." In *The Handbook of Fixed-Income Securities,* 7th ed., ed. Frank J. Fabozzi. New York: McGraw-Hill, 2005.

Siegel, Laurence B., and Paul D. Kaplan. "Stocks, Bonds, Bills, and Inflation Around the World." In *Managing Institutional Assets,* ed. Frank J. Fabozzi. New York: Harper & Row, 1990.

Solnik, Bruno, and Dennis McLeavey. *International Investments,* 5th ed. Reading, MA: Addison-Wesley, 2004.

Steward, Christopher. "International Bond Markets and Instruments." In *The Handbook of Fixed-Income Securities,* 7th ed., ed. Frank J. Fabozzi. New York: McGraw-Hill, 2005.

· · · · **QUESTIONS** · · · ·

1. What are the advantages of investing in the common stock rather than the corporate bonds of a company? Compare the certainty of returns for a bond with those for a common stock. Draw a line graph to demonstrate the pattern of returns you would envision for each of these assets over time.

2. Discuss three factors that cause U.S. investors to consider including various global securities in their portfolios.

3. Discuss why international diversification reduces portfolio risk. Specifically, why would you expect low correlation in the rates of return for domestic and foreign securities?

4. Discuss why you would expect a *difference* in the correlation of returns between securities from the United States and from alternative countries (for example, Japan, Canada, South Africa).

5. Discuss whether you would expect any *change* in the correlations between U.S. stocks and the stocks for different countries. For example, discuss whether you would expect the correlation between U.S. and Japanese stock returns to change over time. If so, why?

6. When you invest in Japanese or German bonds, what major additional risks must you consider besides yield changes within the country?

7. Some investors believe that international investing introduces additional risks. Discuss these risks and how they can affect your return. Give an example.

8. What alternatives to direct investment in foreign stocks are available to investors?

9. You are a wealthy individual in a high tax bracket. Why might you consider investing in a municipal bond rather than a straight corporate bond, even though the promised yield on the municipal bond is lower?

10. You can acquire convertible bonds from a rapidly growing company or from a utility. Speculate on which convertible bond would have the lower yield and discuss the reason for this difference.

11. Compare the liquidity of an investment in raw land with that of an investment in common stock. Be specific as to why and how the liquidity differs. (Hint: Begin by defining *liquidity*.)

12. What are stock warrants and call options? How do they differ?

13. Discuss why financial analysts consider antiques and art to be illiquid investments. Why do they consider coins and stamps to be more liquid than antiques and art? What must an investor typically do to sell a collection of art and antiques? Briefly contrast this procedure to the sale of a portfolio of stocks listed on the New York Stock Exchange.

14. You have a fairly large portfolio of U.S. stocks and bonds. You meet a financial planner at a social gathering who suggests that you diversify your portfolio by investing in emerging market stocks. Discuss whether the correlation results in Exhibit 3.10 support this suggestion.

15. **CFA EXAMINATION LEVEL I** Chris Smith of XYZ Pension Plan has historically invested in the stocks of only U.S.-domiciled companies. Recently, he has decided to add international exposure to the plan portfolio.
   a. Identify and briefly discuss *three* potential problems that Smith may confront in selecting international stocks that he did not face in choosing U.S. stocks.

16. **CFA EXAMINATION LEVEL III** TMP has been experiencing increasing demand from its institutional clients for information and assistance related to international investment management. Recognizing that this is an area of growing importance, the firm has hired an experienced analyst/portfolio manager specializing in international equities and market strategy. His first assignment is to represent TMP before a client company's investment committee to discuss the possibility of changing their present "U.S. securities only" investment approach to one including international investments. He is told that the committee wants a presentation that fully and objectively examines the basic, substantive considerations on which the committee should focus its attention, including both theory and evidence. The company's pension plan has no legal or other barriers to adoption of an international approach; no non-U.S. pension liabilities currently exist.
   a. Identify and briefly discuss *three* reasons for adding international securities to the pension portfolio and *three* problems associated with such an approach.
   b. Assume that the committee has adopted a policy to include international securities in its pension portfolio. Identify and briefly discuss *three* additional *policy-level* investment decisions the committee must make *before* management selection and actual implementation can begin.

• • • • PROBLEMS • • • •

1. Using published sources (for example, the *Wall Street Journal, Barron's, Federal Reserve Bulletin*), look up the exchange rate for U.S. dollars with Japanese yen for each of the past 10 years (you can use an average for the year or a specific time period each year). Based on these exchange rates, compute and discuss the yearly exchange rate effect on an investment in Japanese stocks by a U.S. investor. Discuss the impact of this exchange rate effect on the risk of Japanese stocks for a U.S. investor.

2. **CFA EXAMINATION LEVEL I** (Adapted) The following information is available concerning the historical risk and return relationships in the U.S. capital markets:

U.S. Capital Markets Total Annual Returns, 1960–1984

Investment Category	Arithmetic Mean	Geometric Mean	Standard Deviation of Return[a]
Common stocks	10.28%	8.81%	16.9%
Treasury bills	6.54	6.49	3.2
Long-term government bonds	6.10	5.91	6.4
Long-term corporate bonds	5.75	5.35	9.6
Real estate	9.49	9.44	3.5

[a]Based on arithmetic mean.

Source: Adapted from R. G. Ibbotson, Laurence B. Siegel, and Kathryn S. Love, "World Wealth: Market Values and Returns," *Journal of Portfolio Management* 12, no. 1 (Fall 1985): 4–23. Copyright *Journal of Portfolio Management*, a publication of Institutional Investor, Inc. Used with permission.

    a. Explain why the geometric and arithmetic mean returns are not equal and whether one or the other may be more useful for investment decision making. [5 minutes]

    b. For the time period indicated, rank these investments on a risk-adjusted basis from most to least desirable. Explain your rationale. [6 minutes]

    c. Assume the returns in these series are normally distributed.

        (1) Calculate the range of returns that an investor would have expected to achieve 95 percent of the time from holding common stocks. [4 minutes]

        (2) Suppose an investor holds real estate for this time period. Determine the probability of at least breaking even on this investment. [5 minutes]

    d. Assume you are holding a portfolio composed entirely of real estate. Discuss the justification, if any, for adopting a mixed asset portfolio by adding long-term government bonds. [5 minutes]

3. Using a recent edition of *Barron's,* examine the weekly percentage change in the stock price indexes for Japan, Germany, United Kingdom, and the United States. For each of three weeks, which foreign series moved most closely with the U.S. series? Which series diverged most from the U.S. series? Discuss these results as they relate to international diversification.

4. You are given the following long-run annual rates of return for alternative investment instruments:

U.S. Government T-bills	3.50%
Large-cap common stock	11.75
Long-term corporate bonds	5.50
Long-term government bonds	4.90
Small-capitalization common stock	13.10

The annual rate of inflation during this period was 3 percent. Compute the real rate of return on these investment alternatives.

5. Using a source of international statistics, compare the percentage change in the following economic data for Japan, Germany, Canada, and the United States for a recent year. What were the differences, and which country or countries differed most from the United States?

    a. Aggregate output (GDP)

    b. Inflation

    c. Money supply growth

THOMSON ONE | Business School Edition

1. Compare the performance of several country markets. Using the "index" tab, do a search on FTSE. You will obtain a list of many FTSE indexes. Select at least three from different countries or regions (such as Eurobloc, Americas, and Japan). How have their stock markets been performing of late?

2. Some indexes are presented in both U.S. dollar terms and in terms of other currencies. Compare the performance of the DJ Euro STOXX index in terms of euros and the U.S. dollar. Find one other index that will allow a comparison between two different currencies and discuss their relative performance.

3. Using daily stock prices for indexes from the United States, Japan, Canada, and a composite of emerging markets (or China, India, and Indonesia), compute daily percent changes for 25 trading days. Compute the correlations among these indexes. Rank the correlations from high to low.

Covariance

Because most students have been exposed to the concepts of covariance and correlation, the following discussion is set forth in intuitive terms with examples. A detailed, rigorous treatment is contained in DeFusco, McLeavey, Pinto, and Runkle (2004).

Covariance is an absolute measure of the extent to which two sets of numbers move together over time, that is, how often they move up or down together. In this regard, *move together* means they are generally above their means or below their means at the same time. Covariance between i and j is defined as

$$\text{COV}_{ij} = \frac{\sum (i - \bar{i})(j - \bar{j})}{n}$$

If we define $(i - \bar{i})$ as i' and $(j - \bar{j})$ as j', then

$$\text{COV}_{ij} = \frac{\sum i'j'}{n}$$

Obviously, if both numbers are consistently above or below their individual means at the same time, their products will be positive, and the average will be a large positive value. In contrast, if the i value is below its mean when the j value is above its mean or vice versa, their products will be large negative values, giving negative covariance.

Exhibit 3A.1 should make this clear. In this example, the two series generally moved together, so they showed positive covariance. As noted, this is an *absolute* measure of their relationship and, therefore, can range from $+\infty$ to $-\infty$. Note that the covariance of a variable with itself is its *variance*.

Correlation

To obtain a relative measure of a given relationship, we use the **correlation coefficient** (r_{ij}), which is a measure of the relationship:

$$r_{ij} = \frac{\text{COV}_{ij}}{\sigma_i \sigma_j}$$

You will recall from your introductory statistics course that

$$\sigma_i = \sqrt{\frac{\sum (i - \bar{i})^2}{N}}$$

Exhibit 3A.1 Calculation of Covariance

Observation	i	j	$i - \bar{i}$	$j - \bar{j}$	$i'j'$
1	3	8	−4	−4	16
2	6	10	−1	−2	2
3	8	14	+1	+2	2
4	5	12	−2	0	0
5	9	13	+2	+1	2
6	11	15	+4	+3	12
Σ	42	72			34
Mean	7	12			

$$\text{COV}_{ij} = \frac{34}{6} = +5.67$$

Exhibit 3A.2 Calculation of Correlation Coefficient

Observation	$i - \bar{i}^a$	$(i - \bar{i})^2$	$j - \bar{j}^a$	$(j - \bar{j})^2$
1	−4	16	−4	16
2	−1	1	−2	4
3	+4	1	+2	4
4	−2	4	0	0
5	+2	4	+1	1
6	+4	16	+3	9
		42		34

$$\sigma_i^2 = 42/6 = 7.00 \qquad\qquad \sigma_j^2 = 34/6 = 5.67$$

$$\sigma_i = \sqrt{7.00} = 2.65 \qquad\qquad \sigma_j = \sqrt{5.67} = 2.38$$

$$r_{ij} = COV_{ij}/\sigma_i\sigma_j = \frac{5.67}{(2.65)(2.38)} = \frac{5.67}{6.31} = 0.898$$

If the two series move completely together, then the covariance would equal $\sigma_i\sigma_j$ and

$$\frac{COV_{ij}}{\sigma_i\sigma_j} = 1.0$$

The correlation coefficient would equal unity in this case, and we would say the two series are perfectly correlated. Because we know that

$$r_{ij} = \frac{COV_{ij}}{\sigma_i\sigma_j}$$

we also know that $COV_{ij} = r_{ij}\sigma_i\sigma_j$. This relationship may be useful when computing the standard deviation of a portfolio, because in many instances the relationship between two securities is stated in terms of the correlation coefficient rather than the covariance.

Continuing the example given in Exhibit 3A.1, the standard deviations are computed in Exhibit 3A.2, as is the correlation between i and j. As shown, the two standard deviations are rather large and similar but not exactly the same. Finally, when the positive covariance is normalized by the product of the two standard deviations, the results indicate a correlation coefficient of 0.898, which is obviously quite large and close to 1.00. This implies that these two series are highly related.

Problems

1. As a new analyst, you have calculated the following annual rates of return for the stocks of both Lauren Corporation and Kayleigh Industries.

Year	Lauren's Rate of Return	Kayleigh's Rate of Return
2004	5	5
2005	12	15
2006	−11	5
2007	10	7
2008	12	−10

Your manager suggests that because these companies produce similar products, you should continue your analysis by computing their covariance. Show all calculations.

2. You decide to go an extra step by calculating the coefficient of correlation using the data provided in Problem 1. Prepare a table showing your calculations and explain how to interpret the results. Would the combination of the common stock of Lauren and Kayleigh be good for diversification?

CHAPTER 4

Organization and Functioning of Securities Markets*

After you read this chapter, you should be able to answer the following questions:

- What is the purpose and function of a market?
- What characteristics determine the quality of a market?
- What is the difference between a primary and secondary capital market and how do these two markets support each other?
- What are Rules 415 and 144A and how do they affect corporate security underwriting?
- For secondary equity markets, what are the two basic trading systems?
- How are call markets typically used in U.S. markets?
- How are national exchanges around the world linked and what is meant by "passing the book"?
- What are Electronic Communication Networks (ECNs) and alternative trading systems (ATSs) and how do they differ from the primary listing markets?
- What are the major types of orders available to investors and market makers?
- What new trading systems on the NYSE and on NASDAQ have made it possible to handle the growth in U.S. trading volume?
- What are the three recent innovations that contribute to competition within the U.S. equity market?
- What are Rule 390 and the trade-through rule and what is their effect regarding competition on the U.S. equity market?
- What are the factors causing a global consolidation of stock, bond, and derivative exchanges? What will this global marketplace look like?

The stock market, the Dow Jones Industrials, and the bond market are part of our everyday experience. Each evening on television news broadcasts we find out how stocks and bonds fared; each morning we read in our daily newspapers about expectations for a market rally or decline. Yet most people have an imperfect understanding of how domestic and world capital markets actually function. To be a successful investor in a global environment, you must know what financial markets are available around the world and how they operate.

In this chapter we take a broad view of securities markets and provide a detailed discussion of how major stock markets function. We also consider how global securities markets have changed during recent years and conclude with a discussion of how they will change in the future.

We begin with a discussion of securities markets and the characteristics of a good market. We describe two components of the capital markets: primary and secondary. Our main emphasis is on the secondary stock market including the national stock exchanges around the world and how these markets, separated by geography and by time zones, are becoming linked into a 24-hour market. We also consider regional stock markets and the NASDAQ

* The authors acknowledge helpful comments on this chapter from Robert Battalio and Paul Schultz of the University of Notre Dame.

market and provide a detailed analysis of how alternative exchange markets operate, including the Electronic Communication Networks (ECNs). In the final section we consider numerous recent changes in financial markets, including significant mergers, and future changes expected. These numerous changes in our securities markets will have a profound effect on what investments are available from around the world and how we buy and sell them.

4.1 What Is a Market?

A **market** is the means through which buyers and sellers are brought together to aid in the transfer of goods and/or services. Several aspects of this general definition seem worthy of emphasis. First, a market need not have a physical location. It is only necessary that the buyers and sellers can communicate regarding the relevant aspects of the transaction.

Second, the market does not necessarily own the goods or services involved. For a good market, ownership is not involved; the important criterion is the smooth, cheap transfer of goods and services. In most financial markets, those who establish and administer the market do not own the assets but simply provide a physical location or an electronic system that allows potential buyers and sellers to interact. They help the market function by providing information and facilities to aid in the transfer of ownership.

Finally, a market can deal in any variety of goods and services. For any commodity or service with a diverse clientele, a market should evolve to aid in the transfer of that commodity or service. Both buyers and sellers benefit from the existence of a market.

4.1.1 Characteristics of a Good Market

Throughout this book, we will discuss markets for different investments such as stocks, bonds, options, and futures in the United States and throughout the world. We will refer to these markets using various terms of quality such as *strong, active, liquid,* or *illiquid.* There are many financial markets, but they are not all equal—some are active and liquid, others are relatively illiquid and inefficient in their operations. To appreciate these discussions, you should be aware of the following characteristics that investors look for when evaluating the quality of a market.

One enters a market to buy or sell a good or service quickly at a price justified by the prevailing supply and demand. To determine the appropriate price, participants must have timely and accurate information on the volume and prices of past transactions and all currently outstanding bids and offers. Therefore, one attribute of a good market is **timely and accurate information** on past transactions and prevailing buy and sell orders.

Another prime requirement is **liquidity**, the ability to buy or sell an asset quickly and at a known price—that is, a price not substantially different from the prices for prior transactions, assuming no new information is available. An asset's likelihood of being sold quickly, sometimes referred to as its *marketability,* is a necessary, but not a sufficient, condition for liquidity. The expected price should also be fairly certain, based on the recent history of transaction prices and current bid–ask quotes. For a formal discussion of liquidity, see Handa and Schwartz (1996) and AIMR's articles on *Best Execution and Portfolio Performance* (Jost, 2001).

A component of liquidity is **price continuity**, which means that prices do not change much from one transaction to the next unless substantial new information becomes available. Suppose no new information is forthcoming, and the last transaction was at a price of $20; if the next trade were at $20.10, the market would be considered reasonably continuous.[1] A continuous market without large price changes between trades is a characteristic of a liquid market.

---

[1] You should be aware that common stocks are currently sold in decimals (dollars and cents), which is a significant change from the pre-2000 period when they were priced in eighths and sixteenths. This change to decimals is discussed in the following subsection.

A market with price continuity requires *depth,* which means that there are numerous potential buyers and sellers willing to trade at prices above and below the current market price. These buyers and sellers enter the market in response to changes in supply, demand, or both and thereby prevent drastic price changes. In summary, liquidity requires marketability and price continuity, which, in turn, requires depth.

Another factor contributing to a good market is the **transaction cost**. Lower costs (as a percent of the value of the trade) make for a more efficient market. An individual comparing the cost of a transaction between markets would choose a market that charges 2 percent of the value of the trade compared with one that charges 5 percent. Most microeconomic textbooks define an efficient market as one in which the cost of the transaction is minimal. This attribute is referred to as *internal efficiency.*

Finally, a buyer or seller wants the prevailing market price to adequately reflect all the information available regarding supply and demand factors in the market. If such conditions change as a result of new information, the price should change accordingly. Therefore, participants want prices to adjust quickly to new information regarding supply or demand, which means that prevailing market prices reflect all available information about the asset. This attribute is referred to as **external**, or **informational**, **efficiency**. We discuss this attribute extensively in Chapter 6.

In summary, a good market for goods and services has the following characteristics:

1. Timely and accurate information on the price and volume of past transactions.
2. Liquidity, meaning an asset can be bought or sold quickly at a price close to the prices for previous transactions (has price continuity), assuming no new information has been received. In turn, price continuity requires depth.
3. Low transaction costs, including the cost of reaching the market, the actual brokerage costs, and the cost of transferring the asset.
4. Prices that rapidly adjust to new information, so the prevailing price is fair since it reflects all available information regarding the asset.

4.1.2 Decimal Pricing

Prior to the initiation of changes in late 2000 that were completed in early 2001, common stocks in the United States were always quoted in fractions. Specifically, prior to 1997 they were quoted in eighths (e.g., $\frac{1}{8}, \frac{2}{8}, \ldots, \frac{7}{8}$), with each eighth equal to $0.125. This was modified in 1997 when the fractions for most stocks went to sixteenths (e.g., $\frac{1}{16}, \frac{2}{16}, \ldots, \frac{15}{16}$), equal to $0.0625. Now U.S. equities are priced in decimals (cents), so the minimum spread can be in cents (e.g., $30.10–$30.12).

The espoused reasons for the change to decimal pricing are threefold. First, is the ease with which investors can understand the prices and compare them. Second, decimal pricing should save investors money since it reduces the size of the bid–ask spread from a minimum of 6.25 cents (when prices are quoted in sixteenths) to 1 cent (when prices are in decimals). Notably this reduced spread is also why many brokers and investment firms were against the change—the spread is the price of liquidity for the investor and the compensation to the dealer. Third, the change should make U.S. markets more competitive on a global basis since other countries price on a comparable basis. Thus, transaction costs should be lower.

The effect of decimalization has been substantial. Because it reduced spread size, there has been a decline in transaction costs. This has led to a decline in transaction size and a corresponding increase in the number of transactions—for example, the number of transactions on the NYSE went from a daily average of 877,000 in 2000 to 7,813,000 during the first half of 2007, while the average trade size went from 1,187 shares in 2000 to 334 shares in the first half of 2007.

4.1.3 Organization of the Securities Market

Before we discuss the specific operation of the securities market, we need to understand its overall organization. The principal distinction is between **primary markets**, where new securities are sold, and **secondary markets**, where outstanding securities are bought and sold. Each of these markets is further divided based on the economic unit that issued the security. We will consider each of these major segments of the securities market, with an emphasis on the individuals involved and the functions they perform.

4.2 Primary Capital Markets

The primary market is where new issues of bonds, preferred stock, or common stock are sold by government units, municipalities, or companies to acquire new capital. For a review of studies on the primary market, see Jensen and Smith (1986).

4.2.1 Government Bond Issues

U.S. government bond issues are subdivided into three segments based on their original maturities. **Treasury bills** are negotiable, non-interest-bearing securities with original maturities of one year or less. **Treasury notes** have original maturities of 2 to 10 years. Finally, **Treasury bonds** have original maturities of more than 10 years.

To sell bills, notes, and bonds, the Treasury relies on Federal Reserve System auctions. (The bidding process and pricing are discussed in Chapter 17.)

4.2.2 Municipal Bond Issues

New municipal bond issues are sold by one of three methods: competitive bid, negotiation, or private placement. **Competitive bid** sales typically involve sealed bids. The bond issue is sold to the bidding syndicate of underwriters that submits the bid with the lowest interest cost in accordance with the stipulations set forth by the issuer. **Negotiated sales** involve contractual arrangements between underwriters and issuers wherein the underwriter helps the issuer prepare the bond issue and set the price and has the exclusive right to sell the issue. **Private placements** involve the sale of a bond issue by the issuer directly to an investor or a small group of investors (usually institutions).

Note that two of the three methods require an *underwriting* function. Specifically, in a competitive bid or a negotiated transaction, the investment banker typically underwrites the issue, which means the investment firm purchases the entire issue at a specified price, relieving the issuer from the risk and responsibility of selling and distributing the bonds. Subsequently, the underwriter sells the issue to the investing public. For municipal bonds, this underwriting function is performed by both investment banking firms and commercial banks.

The underwriting function can involve three services: origination, risk-bearing, and distribution. Origination involves the design of the bond issue and initial planning. To fulfill the risk-bearing function, the underwriter acquires the total issue at a price dictated by the competitive bid or through negotiation and accepts the responsibility and risk of reselling it for more than the purchase price. Distribution means selling it to investors, typically with the help of a selling syndicate that includes other investment banking firms and/or commercial banks.

In a negotiated bid, the underwriter will carry out all three services. In a competitive bid, the issuer specifies the amount, maturities, coupons, and call features of the issue and the competing syndicates submit a bid for the entire issue that reflects the yields they estimate for the bonds. The issuer may have received advice from an investment firm on the desirable characteristics for a forthcoming issue, but this advice would have been on a fee basis and would not necessarily involve the ultimate underwriter who is responsible for risk-bearing and distribution. Finally, a private placement involves no risk-bearing, but an investment banker would typically assist in locating potential buyers and negotiating the characteristics of the issue.

4.2.3 Corporate Bond Issues

Corporate bond issues are almost always sold through a negotiated arrangement with an investment banking firm that maintains a relationship with the issuing firm. In a global capital market that involves an explosion of new instruments, the origination function, which involves the design of the security in terms of characteristics and currency, is becoming more important because the corporate chief financial officer (CFO) will probably not be completely familiar with the availability and issuing requirements of many new instruments and the alternative capital markets around the world. Investment banking firms compete for underwriting business by creating new instruments that appeal to existing investors and by advising issuers regarding desirable countries and currencies. As a result, the expertise of the investment banker can help reduce the issuer's cost of new capital.

Once a stock or bond issue is specified, the underwriter will put together an underwriting syndicate of other major underwriters and a selling group of smaller firms for its distribution, as shown in Exhibit 4.1.

4.2.4 Corporate Stock Issues

In addition to the ability to issue fixed-income securities to get new capital, corporations can also issue equity securities—generally common stock. For corporations, new stock issues are typically divided into two groups: (1) seasoned equity issues and (2) initial public offerings (IPOs).

Seasoned equity issues are new shares offered by firms that already have stock outstanding. An example would be General Electric, which is a large, well-regarded firm that has had public stock trading on the NYSE for longer than 50 years. If General Electric needed additional capital, it could sell additional shares of its common stock to the public at a price very close to the current market price of the firm's stock.

Initial public offerings (IPOs) involve a firm selling its common stock to the public for the first time. At the time of an IPO, there is no existing public market for the stock; that is, the company has been closely held. An example was an IPO by Polo Ralph Lauren at $26 per share. The company is a leading manufacturer and distributor of men's clothing. The purpose of the offering was to get additional capital to expand its operations.

New issues (seasoned or IPOs) are typically underwritten by investment bankers, who acquire the total issue from the company and sell the securities to interested investors. The underwriter gives advice to the corporation on the general characteristics of the issue, its

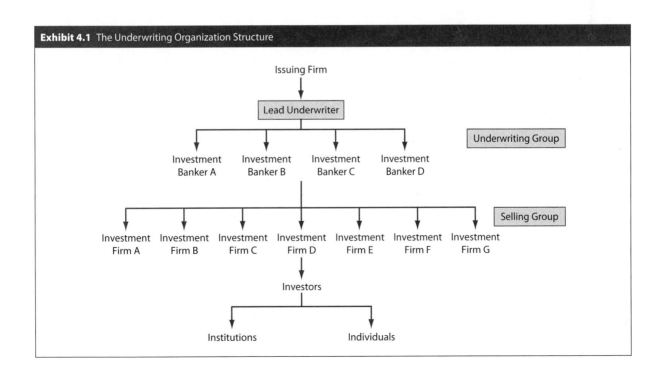

Exhibit 4.1 The Underwriting Organization Structure

pricing, and the timing of the offering. The underwriter also accepts the risk of selling the new issue after acquiring it from the corporation. For further discussion, see Brealey and Myers (2004, Chapter 15).

Relationships with Investment Bankers   The underwriting of corporate issues typically takes one of three forms: negotiated, competitive bids, or best-efforts arrangements. As noted, negotiated underwritings are the most common, and the procedure is the same as for municipal issues.

A corporation may also specify the type of securities to be offered (common stock, preferred stock, or bonds) and then solicit competitive bids from investment banking firms. This is rare for industrial firms but is typical for utilities, which may be required by law to sell the issue via a competitive bid. Although a competitive bid typically reduces the cost of an issue, it also means that the investment banker gives less advice but still accepts the risk-bearing function by underwriting the issue and fulfills the distribution function.

Alternatively, an investment banker can agree to sell an issue on a *best-efforts basis*. This is usually done with speculative new issues. In this arrangement, the investment banker does not underwrite the issue because it does not buy any securities. The stock is owned by the company, and the investment banker acts as a *broker* to sell whatever it can at a stipulated price. Because it bears no risk, the investment banker earns a lower commission on such an issue than on an underwritten issue.

Introduction of Rule 415   The typical practice of negotiated arrangements involving numerous investment banking firms in syndicates and selling groups has changed with the introduction of Rule 415, which allows large firms to register security issues and sell them piecemeal during the following two years. These issues are referred to as *shelf registrations* because, after they are registered, the issues lie on the shelf and can be taken down and sold on short notice whenever it suits the issuing firm. As an example, Apple Computer could register an issue of 5 million shares of common stock during 2009 and sell a million shares in early 2009, another million shares in late 2009, 2 million shares in early 2010, and the rest in late 2010.

Each offering can be made with little notice or paperwork by one underwriter or several. In fact, because relatively few shares may be involved, the lead underwriter often handles the whole deal without a syndicate or uses only one or two other firms. This arrangement has benefited large corporations because it provides great flexibility, reduces registration fees and expenses, and allows firms issuing securities to request competitive bids from several investment banking firms.

On the other hand, some observers fear that shelf registrations do not allow investors enough time to examine the current status of the firm issuing the securities. Also, the follow-up offerings reduce the participation of small underwriters because the underwriting syndicates are smaller and selling groups are almost nonexistent. Shelf registrations have typically been used for the sale of straight debentures rather than common stock or convertible issues. For further discussion of Rule 415, see Rogowski and Sorensen (1985).

4.2.5 Private Placements and Rule 144A

Rather than a public sale using one of these arrangements, primary offerings can be sold privately. In such an arrangement, referred to as a *private placement,* the firm designs an issue with the assistance of an investment banker and sells it to a small group of institutions. The firm enjoys lower issuing costs because it does not need to prepare the extensive registration statement required for a public offering. The institution that buys the issue typically benefits because the issuing firm passes some of these cost savings on to the investor as a higher return. In fact, the institution should require a higher return because of the absence of any secondary market for these securities, which implies higher liquidity risk.

The private placement market changed dramatically when Rule 144A was introduced by the SEC. This rule allows corporations—including non-U.S. firms—to place securities privately with large, sophisticated institutional investors without extensive registration documents. A major innovation is that these securities can subsequently be traded among these large sophisticated investors (those with assets in excess of $100 million). The SEC intends to provide more financing alternatives for U.S. and non-U.S. firms and possibly increase the number, size, and liquidity of private placements, as discussed by Milligan (1990) and Hanks (1990). Presently, more than 85 percent of high-yield bonds are issued as 144A issues.

4.3 Secondary Financial Markets

In this section we first consider the purpose and importance of secondary markets and provide an overview of the secondary markets for bonds, financial futures, and stocks. Next, we consider national stock markets around the world. Finally, we discuss other primary listing markets, regional exchanges, third markets, and the rapidly growing electronic communication networks (ECNs) and provide a detailed presentation on the functioning of stock exchanges.

Secondary markets permit trading in outstanding issues; that is, stocks or bonds already sold to the public are traded between current and potential owners. The proceeds from a sale in the secondary market do not go to the issuing unit (the government, municipality, or company), but rather to the current owner of the security.

4.3.1 Why Secondary Markets Are Important

Before discussing the various segments of the secondary market, we must consider its overall importance. Because the secondary market involves the trading of securities initially sold in the primary market, *it provides liquidity to the individuals who acquired these securities.* After acquiring securities in the primary market, investors may want to sell them again to acquire other securities, buy a house, or go on a vacation. The primary market benefits greatly from the liquidity provided by the secondary market because investors would hesitate to acquire securities in the primary market if they thought they could not subsequently sell them in the secondary market. That is, without an active secondary market, potential issuers of stocks or bonds in the primary market would have to provide a much higher rate of return to compensate investors for the substantial liquidity risk.

Secondary markets are also important to those selling seasoned securities because the prevailing market price of the securities (*price discovery*) is determined by transactions in the secondary market. New issues of outstanding stocks or bonds to be sold in the primary market are based on prices and yields in the secondary market. Notably, the secondary market also has an effect on market efficiency and price volatility, as discussed by Foster and Viswanathan (1993) and Jones, Kaul, and Lipson (1994). Even forthcoming IPOs are priced based on the prices and values of comparable stocks or bonds in the public secondary market.

4.3.2 Secondary Bond Markets

The secondary market for bonds distinguishes among those issued by the federal government, municipalities, or corporations.

Secondary Markets for U.S. Government and Municipal Bonds U.S. government bonds are traded by bond dealers that specialize in either Treasury bonds or agency bonds. Treasury issues are bought or sold through a set of 35 primary dealers, including large banks in New York and Chicago and some of the large investment banking firms (for example, Merrill Lynch, Goldman Sachs, Morgan Stanley). These institutions and other firms also make markets for government agency issues, but there is no formal set of dealers for agency securities.

The major market makers in the secondary municipal bond market are banks and investment firms. Banks are active in municipal bond trading and underwriting of general obligation issues since they invest heavily in these securities. Also, many large investment firms have municipal bond departments that underwrite and trade these issues.

Secondary Corporate Bond Markets   Currently, all corporate bonds are traded over the counter by dealers who buy and sell for their own accounts. The major bond dealers are the large investment banking firms that underwrite the issues: firms such as Merrill Lynch, Goldman Sachs, J.P. Morgan, Lehman Brothers, and Morgan Stanley. Because of the limited trading in corporate bonds compared to the fairly active trading in government bonds, corporate bond dealers do not carry extensive inventories of specific issues. Instead, they hold a limited number of bonds desired by their clients, and when someone wants to do a trade, they work more like brokers than dealers.

Notably, there is a movement toward a widespread transaction-reporting service as with stocks, especially for large, actively traded bond issues. As discussed in Chapter 17, starting in July 2005, dealers have been required to report trades within 15 minutes of the transaction on 17,000 corporate bonds. As shown in Exhibit 4.2, the *Wall Street Journal* carries a daily table that provides benchmark data for a large set of secondary bond series.

4.3.4 Financial Futures

In addition to the market for the bonds, a market has developed for futures contracts related to these bonds. These contracts allow the holder to buy or sell a specified amount of a given bond issue at a stipulated price. The two major futures exchanges are the Chicago Board of Trade (CBOT) and the Chicago Mercantile Exchange (CME) that merged during 2007. We discuss these futures contracts and the futures market in Chapter 19.

4.3.5 Secondary Equity Markets

Before 2000, the secondary equity markets in the United States and around the world were divided into three segments: national stock exchanges, regional stock exchanges, and over-the-counter (OTC) markets for stocks not on an exchange. Because of numerous changes over the past decade, a better classification has been suggested by Harris (2003), as presented in Exhibit 4.3. Following our background discussions on alternative trading systems and call versus continuous markets, we will describe the market types listed in Exhibit 4.3 and discuss how they complement and compete against each other to provide price discovery and liquidity to individual and institutional investors.

Basic Trading Systems   Although stock exchanges are similar in that only qualified stocks can be traded by individuals who are members of the exchange, they can differ in their *trading systems.* There are two major trading systems, and an exchange can use one or a combination of them. One is a *pure auction market* (also referred to as an *order-driven market*), in which interested buyers and sellers submit bid-and-ask prices (buy and sell orders) for a given stock to a central location where the orders are matched by a broker who does not own the stock but acts as a facilitating agent. Participants also refer to this system as *price-driven* because shares of stock are sold to the investor with the highest bid price and bought from the seller with the lowest offering price. Advocates of an auction market argue for a very centralized market that ideally will include all the buyers and sellers of the stock.

The other major trading system is a *dealer market* (also referred to as a *quote-driven* market) where individual dealers provide liquidity for investors by buying and selling the shares of stock for themselves. Ideally, with this system there will be numerous dealers who will compete against each other to provide the highest bid prices when you are selling and the lowest asking price when you are buying stock. Clearly, this is a very decentralized system that derives its benefit from the competition among the dealers to provide the best price for the buyer and seller. When we discuss the various equity markets, we will indicate the trading system used.

Exhibit 4.2 Bond Benchmarks

Tracking Bond Benchmarks

Return on investment and spreads over Treasurys and/or yields paid to investors compared with 52-week highs and lows for different types of bonds

Total return close	YTD total return (%)	Index	Latest	Low 0	YIELD (%), 52-WEEK RANGE ○ Latest 3 6 9 12 15	High
1270.59	6.1%	**Broad market** Lehamn Aggregate	4.960	4.960		5.850
1576.61	4.7	**U.S. Corporate** Lehman Brothers	5.590	5.390		6.200
1602.07	5.3	Intermediate	5.310	5.210		6.010
1803.77	3.1	Long term	6.370	5.290		6.730
333.33	4.4	Double-A-rated	5.220	5.071		5.920
339.98	4.9	Triple-B-rated	6.000	5.700		6.460
191.34	1.0	**High Yield Constrained** Merrill Lynch	9.455	7.380		9.455
170.05	−0.7%	Triple-C-rated	12.689	9.243		12.689
1568.36	1.6	High Yield 100	8.631	6.865		8.639
167.91	0.6	Global High Yield Constrained	9.375	7.239		9.375
136.89	−3.0	Europe High Yield Constrained	9.111	6.036		9.111
1197.15	6.6	**U.S. Agency** Lehamn	4.360	4.360		5.560
1105.93	6.6	10-20 years	4.270	4.270		5.520
1773.04	6.6	20-plus years	5.210	5.021		5.970
1311.83	5.6	**Mortgage-Backed** Lehman	5.560	5.400		6.190
1298.70	6.2	Ginnie Mae (GNMA)	5.480	5.433		6.210
754.48	5.6	Fannie Mae (FNMA)	5.550	5.385		6.180
1178.51	5.5	Freddie Mae (FHLMC)	5.580	5.406		6.200
343.87	3.3	**Muni Master** Merrill Lynch	3.894	3.730		4.294
228.04	4.0	7-12 year	3.791	3.670		4.256
245.74	2.6	12-22 year	4.337	3.940		4.733
236.03	0.3	22-plus year	4.886	4.119		5.154
1530.69	6.7	**Yankee** Lehman	4.950	4.950		5.890
376.72	4.2	**Global Government** J.P. Morgan	3.390	3.343		4.050
518.25	4.0	Canada	4.090	3.901		4.680
233.32	2.7	EMU	4.270	3.780		4.790
438.77	2.7	France	4.190	3.707		4.730
329.81	3.0	Germany	4.110	3.699		4.700
229.52	2.7	Japan	1.440	1.440		1.870
352.47	2.9	Netherlands	4.180	3.694		4.730
511.27	4.4	U.K.	4.450	4.226		5.160
401.94	4.5	Emerging Markets**	6.760	6.336		7.235

*Constrained indexes limit individual issuer concentrations to 2% the High yield 100 are the 100 largest bonds   In U.S. dollar terms Euro-zone bonds

**EMBI Global Index   Sources: Dow Jones Indexes; Merrill Lynch; Lehman Brothers; J.P.Morgan

Source: *Wall Street Journal*, November 23, 2007, C11.

Call versus Continuous Markets Beyond the different trading systems for equities, the operation of exchanges can differ in terms of when and how the stocks are traded.

In **call markets**, the intent is to gather all the bids and asks for the stock at a point in time and attempt to arrive at a single price where the quantity demanded is as close as possible to the quantity supplied. Call markets are generally used during the early stages of development of an exchange when there are few stocks listed or a small number of active investors–traders. For an exchange that is strictly a call market with a few listed stocks and traders, a designated market maker would call the roll of stocks and ask for interest in one stock at a time. After determining the available buy and sell orders, exchange officials specify a single price that will satisfy *most* of the orders, and all orders are transacted at this price.

Notably, call markets also are used at the opening for stocks on a large exchange if there is an overnight buildup of buy and/or sell orders, in which case the opening price can differ

Exhibit 4.3 U.S. Secondary Equity Markets: Classification and Examples

Market Type	Examples
Primary listing markets	New York Stock Exchange American Stock Exchange NASDAQ National Market System (NMS) NASDAQ Small-Cap Market (SCM) NASDAQ OTC Electronic Bulletin Board National Quotation Bureau (NQB) Pink Sheets
Regional markets	Boston Stock Exchange Chicago Stock Exchange Cincinnati Stock Exchange Pacific Exchange Philadelphia Stock Exchange
Third-market dealers/brokers	Madoff Investment Securities Knight Trading Group Jefferies Group ITG NASDAQ InterMarket

Alternative Trading Systems (ATSs)
  Electronic Communications
  Networks (ECNs)
	Archipelago
	BRUT
	Instinet
	Island
	REDIBook

Electronic Crossing Systems (ECSs)	POSIT Global Instinet Crossing Arizona Stock Exchange

Source: Adapted from Larry Harris, *Trading and Exchanges* (New York: Oxford University Press, 2003), p. 49.

from the prior day's closing price. Also, a call market process is used if trading is suspended during the day because of some significant new information. In either case, the specialist or market maker would attempt to derive a new equilibrium price using a call-market approach that would reflect the imbalance and take care of most of the orders. For example, assume a stock has been trading at about $42 per share and some significant, new, positive information was released overnight or during the day. If it happened overnight it would affect the opening price; if it happened during the day, trading would be temporarily suspended and a call-market process would be used to determine a new equilibrium price that reflects the supply and demand due to the new information. If the buy orders were three or four times as numerous as the sell orders, the new price based on the call market might be $44. For an analysis of price movements surrounding trading halts, see Hopewell and Schwartz (1978) and Fabozzi and Ma (1988). Several studies have shown that using the call-market mechanism contributes to a more orderly market and less volatility at openings and following trading halts.

In a **continuous market**, trades occur at any time the market is open wherein stocks are priced either by auction or by dealers. In a dealer market, dealers make a market in the stock, which means that they are willing to buy or sell for their own account at a specified bid-and-ask price. In an auction market, enough buyers and sellers are trading to allow the market to be continuous; that is, when one investor comes to buy stock, there is another investor available and willing to sell stock. A compromise between a pure dealer market and a pure auction market is a combination structure wherein the market trading system is basically an auction market, but there exists an intermediary who is willing to act as a dealer if the pure auction market does not have enough activity. These intermediaries who act as both brokers and dealers provide temporary liquidity to ensure the market will be liquid and continuous.

The two tables in the chapter appendix list the characteristics of stock exchanges around the world and indicate whether the exchange provides a continuous market, a call-market mechanism, or a mixture of the two. Notably, many continuous auction market exchanges employ a call-market mechanism on specific occasions at the open and during trading suspensions. The NYSE is such a market.

4.4 Classification of U.S. Secondary Equity Markets

In this section we consider the different secondary equity markets that currently exist in the United States, as listed in Exhibit 4.3.

4.4.1 Primary Listing Markets

Primary listing markets are formal exchanges or markets where a corporate stock is primarily or formally listed. This category includes the two traditional national exchanges (New York Stock Exchange and American Stock Exchange) and the NASDAQ markets that previously were considered over-the-counter markets but are now recognized as equity markets that simply differ in how they trade securities (as will be discussed).

New York Stock Exchange (NYSE) The New York Stock Exchange (NYSE), the largest organized securities market in the United States, was established in 1817 as the New York Stock and Exchange Board. The Exchange dates its founding to when the famous Buttonwood Agreement was signed in May 1792 by 24 brokers.[2] The name was changed to the New York Stock Exchange in 1863.

At the end of 2007, approximately 2,850 companies had their stock listed on the NYSE, for a total of about 3,000 stock issues (common and preferred) with a total market value of more than $14 trillion. The specific listing requirements for the NYSE appear in Exhibit 4.4.

The average number of shares traded daily on the NYSE has increased steadily and substantially, as shown in Exhibit 4.5. Prior to the 1960s, the daily share trading volume averaged less than 3 million shares, compared with the 2007 average daily volume of about 2.55 billion shares.

The NYSE has dominated the other exchanges in the United States in trading volume. Given its stringent listing requirements and its prestige, most of the largest and best known U.S. companies are listed on the NYSE. Historically, about 55 percent of the trading volume for these stocks takes place on the NYSE.

The volume of trading and relative stature of the NYSE is reflected in the price of a membership on the exchange (referred to as a *seat*). As shown in Exhibit 4.6, prior to going

---

Exhibit 4.4 Listing Requirements for Stocks on the NYSE

Aggregate pretax income over the last three years	10,000,000
Pretax income in each of the last two years	2,000,000
Shares publicly held	1,100,000
Market value of publicly held shares[a]	100,000,000
Minimum number of holders of round lots (100 shares or more)	2,200

[a] This minimum required market value is $60 million for spin-offs, carve-outs, or IPOs and it varies over time, depending on the value of the NYSE Common Stock Index. For specifics, see the *2007 NYSE Fact Book*, 37.
Source: *NYSE Fact Book* (New York: NYSE, 2007): 37.

---

[2] The NYSE considers the signing of this agreement the birth of the Exchange and celebrated its 200th birthday during 1992.

Exhibit 4.5 Average Daily Reported Share Volume Traded on Selected Stock Markets (× 1,000)

Year	NYSE*	NASDAQ	Year	NYSE*	NASDAQ
1955	2,578	N.A.	1996	411,953	543,700
1960	3,042	N.A.	1997	526,925	650,324
1965	6,176	N.A.	1998	673,590	801,747
1970	11,564	N.A.	1999	809,183	1,077,500
1975	18,551	5,500	2000	1,041,578	1,759,900
1980	44,871	26,500	2001	1,239,957	1,900,068
1985	109,169	82,100	2002	1,441,015	1,752,643
1990	156,777	131,900	2003	1,398,400	1,449,000
1995	346,101	401,400	2004	1,871,760	1,259,000
			2005	1,900,000	NA
			2006	2,352,500	NA
			2007	2,550,000(e)	NA

* Changed to NYSE Group in January 2004.
N.A. = not available.
Sources: *NYSE Fact Book* (various issues); Nasdaq Research Department.

Exhibit 4.6 Membership Prices on the NYSE ($000)

Year	High	Low	Year	High	Low
1925	$150	$99	1996	$1,450	$1,225
1935	140	65	1997	1,750	1,175
1945	95	49	1998	2,000	1,225
1955	90	49	1999	2,650	2,000
1960	162	135	2000	2,000	1,650
1965	250	190	2001	2,300	2,000
1970	320	130	2002	2,550	2,000
1975	138	55	2003	2,000	1,500
1980	275	175	2004	1,515	1,030
1985	480	310	2005	3,250	975
1990	430	250			
1995	1,050	785			

Source: *NYSE Fact Book* (New York: NYSE, 2005): 110. Reprinted by permission of the New York Stock Exchange.

public in 2006, the price of membership fluctuated in line with trading volume and other factors that influence the profitability of membership, see Ip (1998a).

American Stock Exchange (AMEX) The American Stock Exchange (AMEX) was begun by a group who traded unlisted shares at the corner of Wall and Hanover Streets in New York. It was originally called the Outdoor Curb Market. In 1910, it established formal trading rules and changed its name to the New York Curb Market Association. The members moved inside a building in 1921 and continued to trade mainly in unlisted stocks (stocks not listed on one of the registered exchanges) until 1946, when its volume in listed stocks finally outnumbered that in unlisted stocks. The current name was adopted in 1953.

The AMEX is a national exchange, distinct from the NYSE because, except for a short period in the late 1970s, no stocks have been listed on both the NYSE and AMEX at the same time. Historically, the AMEX emphasized foreign securities and warrants.

The AMEX became a major stock options exchange in January 1975 and subsequently has added options on interest rates and stock indexes. In addition, a large number of exchange-traded funds (ETFs) that have grown in number and popularity (as discussed in Chapter 3) are listed on the AMEX.

The AMEX and the NASDAQ merged in 1998, but in 2005 NASDAQ sold the AMEX back to its members (see Horowirtz and Kelly, 2005). The AMEX was finally acquired by the NYSE in 2007.

Global Stock Exchanges The equity-market environment outside the United States is similar in that each country typically will have one relatively large exchange that dominates the market. Examples include the Tokyo Stock Exchange, the London Stock Exchange, the Frankfurt Stock Exchange, and the Paris Bourse. Exhibit 4A.1 in the chapter appendix lists the exchanges in developed economies, along with some descriptive characteristics of these exchanges.

In a few instances there may also be regional exchanges, but these are rare. Notably, even in small or emerging economies, stock exchanges have been created because of the liquidity that secondary equity markets provide, as discussed earlier. Exhibit 4A.2 lists and describes many of the emerging-market exchanges.

Three points about these international exchanges: first, there has been a trend toward consolidations or affiliations that will provide more liquidity and greater economies of scale to support the technology required by investors. Second, many of the larger companies in these countries that can qualify for listing on a U.S. exchange become dual-listed. As a result, about 20 percent of the stocks listed on the NYSE are non-U.S. firms. Third, the existence of these strong international exchanges has made possible a global equity market wherein stocks that have a global constituency can be traded around the world continuously, as discussed in the following section. There is intense competition between the various exchanges, as discussed by Ewing and Ascarelli (2000) and Cherney and Beal (2000), as well as a trend toward consolidation as discussed at the end of this chapter.

The Global 24-Hour Market Our discussion of the global securities market will emphasize the markets in New York, London, and Tokyo because of their relative size and importance, and because they represent the major segments of a worldwide 24-hour stock market. You will often hear about a continuous market where investment firms "pass the book" around the world. This means the major active market in securities moves around the globe as trading hours for these three markets begin and end.

Consider the individual trading hours for each of the three exchanges, translated into a 24-hour eastern standard time (EST) clock:

	Local Time (24-hr. notations)	24-Hour EST
New York Stock Exchange (NYSE)	0930–1600	0930–1600
Tokyo Stock Exchange (TSE)	0900–1100	2300–0100
	1300–1500	0300–0500
London Stock Exchange (LSE)	0815–1615	0215–1015

Imagine trading starting in New York at 0930 and going until 1600 in the afternoon, being picked up by Tokyo late in the evening and going until 0500 in the morning, and continuing in London (with some overlap) until it begins in New York again (with some overlap) at 0930. Alternatively, it is possible to envision trading as beginning in Tokyo at 2300 hours and continuing until 0500, when it moves to London, then ends the day in New York. This latter model seems the most relevant, because the first question a London trader asks in the morning is, "What happened in Tokyo?" The U.S. trader asks, "What happened in Tokyo and what *is* happening in London?" The point is, the markets operate almost continuously and are related in their response to economic events. Therefore, investors are not dealing with three separate and distinct exchanges, but with one interrelated world market. Clearly, this interrelationship is growing daily because of numerous multiple listings where stocks are listed on several exchanges around the world (such as the NYSE and TSE) and the availability of sophisticated telecommunications. Examples of stocks that are part of this global market are General Electric, Pfizer, Johnson & Johnson, and McDonald's.

The NASDAQ Market[3] This market system was historically known as the over-the-counter (OTC) market, which included stocks not formally listed on the two major exchanges (NYSE and AMEX). This description has changed since it was recognized that this is an equity market similar to the major exchanges with several minor differences. The first difference is that it is a dealer market, in contrast to a broker/dealer (specialists) market as is the NYSE. Second, trading on NASDAQ takes place electronically rather than on a trading floor as in the other exchanges. Notably, as will be discussed, the NYSE has adopted electronic trading and it is growing rapidly. What the NASDAQ has in common with the other exchanges is a set of requirements for a stock to be traded on the NASDAQ National Market System (NMS). Also while NASDAQ dealers do not have to pay for a seat (membership) on the exchange, they are required to be members of the National Association of Security Dealers (NASD) and abide by its rules.

The NASDAQ market is the largest U.S. secondary market in terms of the number of issues traded. As noted earlier, there are about 3,000 issues traded on the NYSE. In contrast, more than 2,800 issues are actively traded on the NASDAQ NMS and almost 700 on the NASDAQ Small-Cap Market (SCM). The NASDAQ market is also the most diverse secondary market component in terms of quality because it has multiple minimum requirements. Stocks that trade on the NASDAQ market (NMS and SCM) range from those of small, unprofitable companies to large, extremely profitable firms such as Microsoft and Intel.

NASDAQ's growth in average daily trading is shown in Exhibit 4.5 relative to that of the NYSE. At the end of 2007 an estimated 650 issues of NASDAQ were either foreign stocks or American Depository Receipts (ADRs), representing over 8 percent of total NASDAQ share volume. About 300 of these issues trade on both NASDAQ and a foreign exchange such as Toronto. NASDAQ has developed a link with the Singapore Stock Exchange that allows 24-hour trading from NASDAQ in New York to Singapore to a NASDAQ/London link and back to New York.

Although the NASDAQ market has the greatest number of issues, the NYSE has a larger total value of trading. In 2007 the approximate value of average daily equity trading on the NYSE was about $52 billion and on NASDAQ was about $31 billion.

Operation of the NASDAQ Market As noted, stocks can be traded on the NASDAQ market as long as there are dealers willing to make a market by buying or selling for their own account.[4]

The NASDAQ Quotation System The *National Association of Securities Dealers Automated Quotation (NASDAQ) system* is an automated, electronic quotation system. Any number of dealers can elect to make markets in a NASDAQ stock. The actual number depends on the activity in the stock. In 2007, the average number of market makers for all stocks on the NASDAQ NMS was about eight.

NASDAQ makes all dealer quotes available immediately. The broker can check the quotation machine and call the dealer with the best market, verify that the quote has not changed, and make the sale or purchase. The NASDAQ quotation system has three levels to serve firms with different needs and interests.

Level 1 provides a single median representative quote for the stocks on NASDAQ. This quotation system is for firms that want current quotes on NASDAQ stocks but do not consistently buy or sell these stocks for their customers and are not market makers. This representative quote changes constantly to adjust for any changes by individual market makers.

Level 2 provides instantaneous current quotations on NASDAQ stocks by all market makers in a stock. This quotation system is for firms that consistently trade NASDAQ stocks. Given an order to buy or sell, brokers check the quotation machine, call the market maker with the

---

[3] NASDAQ is an acronym for National Association of Securities Dealers Automated Quotations. The system is discussed in detail in a later section. To be traded on the NMS, a firm must have a certain size and trading activity and at least four market makers. A specification of requirements for various components of the NASDAQ system is contained in Exhibit 4.7.

[4] *Dealer* and *market maker* are synonymous.

best market for their purposes (highest bid if they are selling, lowest offer if buying), and consummate the deal.

Level 3 is for NASDAQ market makers. Such firms want Level 2, but they also need the capability to change their own quotations, which Level 3 provides.

Listing Requirements for NASDAQ Quotes and trading volume for the NASDAQ market are reported in two lists: a National Market System (NMS) list and a regular NASDAQ list. Exhibit 4.7 contains the alternative standards for initial listing and continued listing on the NASDAQ NMS as of late 2007. A company must meet all of the requirements under at least one of the three listing standards for initial listing and then meet at least one continued listing standard to maintain its listing on the NMS. For stocks on this system, reports include up-to-the-minute volume and last-sale information for the competing market makers as well as end-of-the-day information on total volume and high, low, and closing prices.

A Sample Trade Assume you are considering the purchase of 100 shares of Intel. Although Intel is large enough and profitable enough to be listed on the NYSE, the company has never applied for listing because it enjoys an active market on NASDAQ. (It is one of the volume

Exhibit 4.7 NASDAQ National Market Listing Requirements

A company must meet all of the requirements under at least one of three listing standards for initial listing on The NASDAQ National Market®. A company must continue to meet at least one continued listing standard to maintain its listing.

Requirements	INITIAL LISTING			CONTINUED LISTING	
	Standard 1 Marketplace Rule 4420(a)	Standard 2 Marketplace Rule 4420(b)	Standard 3 Marketplace Rule 4420(c)	Standard 1 Marketplace Rule 4450(a)	Standard 2 Marketplace Rule 4450(b)
Stockholders' equity	$15 million	$30 million	N/A	$10 million	N/A
Market value of listed securities	N/A	$550 million	$850 million[1,2]	N/A	$50 million
or			or		or
Total assets			$75 million		$50 million
and			and		and
Total revenue	N/A	$110 million	$90 million		$50 million
Income from continuing operations before income taxes (in latest fiscal year or 2 of last 3 fiscal years)	$2.2 million	N/A	N/A	N/A	N/A
Publicly held shares[3]	1.1 million	1.1 million	1.1 million	750,000	1.1 million
Market value of publicly held shares	$8 million	$18 million	$20 million	$5 million	$15 million
Minimum bid price	$5	$5	$5[2]	$1	$1
Shareholders (round lot holders)[4]	450	450	450	400	400
Market makers[5]	3	3	3	2	4
Operating history	N/A	2 years	N/A	N/A	N/A
Corporate governance[6]	Yes	Yes	Yes	Yes	Yes

[1]For initial listing under Standard 3, a company must satisfy one of the following: the market value of listed securities requirement or the total assets and the total revenue requirement. Under Marketplace Rule 4200(a)(20), listed securities is defined as "securities quoted on NASDAQ or listed on a national securities exchange."
[2]Seasoned companies (those companies already listed or quoted on another market place) qualifying only under the market value of listed securities requirement of Standard 3 must meet the market value of listed securities and the bid price requirements for 90 consecutive trading days prior to applying for listing.
[3]Publicly held shares is defined as total shares outstanding less any shares held by officers, directors, or beneficial owners of 10 percent or more.
[4]Round lot holders are shareholders of 100 shares or more.
[5]An Electronic Communications Network (ECN) is not considered a market maker for the purpose of these rules.
[6]Marketplace Rules 4350 and 4351.

Source: http://www.Nasdaq.com (accessed September 2007).

leaders, with daily volume typically above 25 million shares and often in excess of 50 million shares.) When you contact your broker, she will consult the NASDAQ quotation machine to determine the current dealer quotations for INTC, the trading symbol for Intel.[5] The quote machine will show that about 35 dealers are making a market in INTC. An example of differing quotations might be as follows:

Dealer	Bid	Ask
1	30.60	30.75
2	30.55	30.65
3	30.50	30.65
4	30.55	30.70

Assuming these are the best markets available from the total group, your broker would call either dealer 2 or dealer 3 because they have the lowest offering prices. After verifying the quote, your broker would give one of these dealers an order to buy 100 shares of INTC at $30.65 a share. Because your firm was not a market maker in the stock, the firm would act as a broker and charge you $3,065 plus a commission for the trade. If your firm had been a market maker in INTC, with an asking price of $30.65 the firm would have sold the stock to you at $30.65 net (without commission). If you had been interested in selling 100 shares of Intel instead of buying, the broker would have contacted dealer 1, who made the highest bid ($30.60).

Changing Dealer Inventory Let's consider the price quotations by a NASDAQ dealer who wants to change his inventory on a given stock. For example, assume dealer 4, with a current quote of 30.55 bid–30.70 ask, decides to increase his holdings of INTC. The NASDAQ quotes indicate that the highest bid is currently 30.60. Increasing the bid to 30.60 would bring some of the business currently going to dealer 1. Taking a more aggressive action, dealer 4 might raise the bid to 30.63 and buy all the stock offered, because he has the highest bid. In this example, the dealer raises the bid price but does not change the ask price, which was above those of dealers 2 and 3. This dealer will buy stock but probably will not sell any. A dealer who had excess stock would keep the bid below the market (lower than 30.60) and reduce the ask price to 30.65 or less. Dealers constantly change their bid-and-ask prices, depending on their current inventories or changes in the outlook based on new information for the stock.

Other NASDAQ Market Segments Now that we are familiar with the NASDAQ system and its operation, we can easily describe the other segments of this market since the major differences relate to the size and liquidity of the stocks involved.

- **The NASDAQ Small-Cap Market (SCM)** has initial listing requirements that consider the same factors as the NMS but are generally about one-half to one-third of the values required for the NMS. As of late 2007 there were about 700 stocks listed in the NASDAQ small-cap segment. This compares to about 600 stocks listed in the section entitled "NASDAQ NM Issues Under $100 Million Market Cap" and about 2,200 in the section entitled "NASDAQ National Market Issues." In total, the NASDAQ NMS contained 2,860 issues as of late 2007. Therefore, the total NASDAQ market includes almost 3,600 issues (2,860 NMS and about 700 issues on the SCM).
- **The NASDAQ** *OTC Electronic Bulletin Board (OTCBB)* reports indications for smaller stocks sponsored by NASD dealers. As of late 2007 there were about 3,400 stocks included on the OTCBB.
- **The National Quotation Bureau (NQB) Pink Sheets** report order indications for the smallest publicly traded stocks in the United States. Pre-1970, these pink sheets (actually

---

[5] Trading symbols are one- to four-letter codes used to designate stocks. Whenever a trade is reported on a stock ticker, the trading symbol appears with the figures. Many symbols are obvious, such as GM (General Motors), F (Ford Motors), GE (General Electric), GS (Goldman Sachs), HD (Home Depot), AMGN (Amgen), and DELL (Dell).

printed on pink sheets of paper) were the primary daily source of OTC stock quotes. With the creation of the NASDAQ electronic quotation system, the sheets were superseded. Currently, the NQB publishes a weekly edition on paper and distributes a daily edition electronically with these small-stock quotes.

4.4.2 Regional Stock Exchanges

The second category in Harris's classfication of U.S. secondary markets (Exhibit 4.3) is the regional market. Regional exchanges typically have the same operating procedures as national exchanges in the same countries, but they differ in their listing requirements. Regional stock exchanges exist for two main reasons: First, they provide trading facilities for local companies not large enough to qualify for listing on a national exchange. Their listing requirements are typically less stringent than for national exchanges.

Second, regional exchanges in some countries list firms that also list on one of the national exchanges to give local brokers access to these securities. As an example, Wal-Mart and General Motors are listed on both the NYSE and several regional exchanges. This dual listing allows a local brokerage firm that is not a member of the NYSE to buy and sell shares of the dual-listed stock without going through the NYSE. In addition, regional exchanges can trade some stocks on the NASDAQ market under *unlisted trading privileges* (UTP) granted by the SEC. The majority of trading on regional exchanges is due to dual-listed and UTP stocks.

The regional exchanges in the United States as of 2004 are shown in Exhibit 4.3. The Chicago, Pacific, and PBW exchanges accounted for about 90 percent of the volume on all U.S. regional exchanges. A discussion at the end of the chapter will consider regional exchange mergers.

4.4.3 The Third Market

Harris's third category is called the third market. The term **third market** involves dealers and brokers who trade shares that are listed on an exchange away from the exchange. Although most transactions in listed stocks take place on an exchange, an investment firm that is not a member of an exchange can make a market in a listed stock away from the exchange. Most third market trading is in well-known stocks such as General Electric, Coca-Cola, and Johnson & Johnson. The success or failure of the third market depends on whether the non–exchange market in these stocks is as good as the exchange market and whether the relative cost of the transaction compares favorably with the cost on the exchange. This market is critical during the relatively few periods when trading is not available on the NYSE either because trading is suspended or the exchange is closed. This market has also grown because of the quality and cost factors mentioned. Third market dealers typically display their quotes on the *NASDAQ InterMarket* system. For articles that discuss the impact of third market trading and the practice of purchasing order flow, see Battalio (1997); Battalio, Greene, and Jennings (1997); and Easley, Kiefer, and O'Hara (1996).

4.4.4 Alternative Trading Systems (ATSs)

The final category in Exhibit 4.3 is alternative trading systems where the biggest changes have occurred during the last decade. *Alternative trading systems (ATSs)* are nontraditional, computerized trading systems that compete with or supplement dealer markets and traditional exchanges. These trading systems facilitate the exchange of millions of shares every day through electronic means. Notably, they do not provide listing services. The most well-known ATSs are the Electronic Communication Networks (ECNs) and the Electronic Crossing Systems (ECSs).

- *Electronic Communication Networks (ECNs)* are electronic facilities that match buy and sell orders directly via computer, mainly for retail and small institutional trading. ECNs do *not* buy or sell from their own account but act as very cheap, efficient electronic brokers. As shown in Exhibit 4.2, the major ECNs are Archipelago, BRUT, Instinet, Island, and REDIBook.

- *Electronic Crossing Systems (ECSs)* are electronic facilities that act as brokers to match *large* buy and sell orders. The most well-known ECSs are POSIT, Global Instinet Crossing, and Arizona Stock Exchange.

The trading of exchange-listed stocks using one of these ATSs has become the *fourth market.*

4.5 Detailed Analysis of Exchange Markets

The importance of listed exchange markets requires that we discuss them at some length. In this section, we discuss alternative members on the exchanges, the major types of orders, and exchange market makers—a critical component of a good exchange market.

4.5.1 Exchange Membership

Stock exchanges typically have four major categories of membership: (1) specialist, (2) commission broker, (3) floor broker, and (4) registered trader. We will discuss specialists (or exchange market makers), who constitute about 25 percent of the total membership on exchanges, after our description of types of orders.

Commission brokers are employees of a member firm who buy or sell for the customers of the firm. When an investment firm receives an order to buy or sell a stock, it transmits it to a commission broker, who takes it to the appropriate trading post on the floor and completes the transaction.

Floor brokers are independent members of an exchange who act as brokers for other members. As an example, when commission brokers for Merrill Lynch become too busy to handle all of their orders, they will ask one of the floor brokers to help them. For a discussion of unwanted notoriety for these brokers, read Starkman and McGeehan (1998) and McGee (1998).

Registered traders use their memberships to buy and sell for their own accounts. While they save commissions on their trading, observers believe they provide the market with added liquidity, even though regulations limit how they trade and how many registered traders can be in a trading crowd around a specialist's booth at any time. Today they often are called **registered competitive market makers (RCMMs)** and have specific trading obligations set by the exchange. Their activity is reported as part of the specialist group.[6]

4.5.2 Types of Orders

It is important to understand the different types of orders available to investors and the specialist as a dealer.

Market Orders The most frequent type of order is a **market order**, an order to buy or sell a stock at the best current price. An investor who enters a market sell order indicates a willingness to sell immediately at the highest bid available at the time the order reaches a specialist on an exchange, a NASDAQ dealer, or an ECN. A market buy order indicates the investor is willing to pay the lowest offering price available at the time on the exchange, the NASDAQ, or an ECN. Market orders provide immediate liquidity for an investor willing to accept the prevailing market price.

Assume you are interested in General Electric (GE) and you call your broker to find out the current "market" on the stock. The quotation machine indicates that the prevailing market is 40 bid–40.10 ask. This means that the highest current bid on the books of the specialist is 40;

---

[6] Prior to the 1980s, there also were odd-lot dealers who bought and sold to individuals with orders for less than round lots (usually 100 shares). Currently, this function is handled by either the specialist or some large brokerage firm.

that is, $40 is the most that anyone has offered to pay for GE. The lowest offer is 40.10; that is, this is the lowest price anyone is willing to accept to sell the stock. If you placed a market buy order for 100 shares, you would buy 100 shares at $40.10 a share (the lowest ask price) for a total cost of $4,010 plus commission. If you submitted a market sell order for 100 shares, you would sell the shares at $40 each and receive $4,000 less commission.

Limit Orders   The individual placing a **limit order** specifies the buy or sell price. You might submit a limit-order bid to purchase 100 shares of Coca-Cola (KO) stock at $50 a share when the current market is 55 bid–55.10 ask, with the expectation that the stock will decline to $50 in the near future.

You must also indicate how long the limit order will be outstanding. Alternative time specifications are basically boundless. A limit order can be instantaneous ("fill or kill," meaning fill the order instantly or cancel it). It can also be good for part of a day, a full day, several days, a week, or a month. It can also be open-ended, or good until canceled (GTC).

Rather than wait for a given price on a stock, because KO is listed on the NYSE your broker will give the limit order to the specialist, who will put it in a limit-order book and act as the broker's representative. When and if the market price for KO reaches the limit-order price, the specialist will execute the order and inform your broker. The specialist receives a small part of the commission for rendering this service.

Special Orders   In addition to these general orders, there are several special types of orders. A *stop loss order* is a conditional market order whereby the investor directs the sale of a stock if it drops to a given price. Assume you buy a stock at 50 and expect it to go up. If you are wrong, you want to limit your losses. To protect yourself, you could put in a stop loss order at 45. In this case, if the stock dropped to 45, your stop loss order would become a market sell order, and the stock would be sold at the prevailing market price. The stop loss order does not guarantee that you will get the $45; you can get a little bit more or a little bit less. Because of the possibility of market disruption caused by a large number of stop loss orders, exchanges have, on occasion, canceled all such orders on certain stocks and not allowed brokers to accept further stop loss orders on those issues.

A related stop loss tactic for an investor who has entered into a short sale is a *stop buy order*. Such an investor who wants to minimize loss if the stock begins to increase in value would enter this conditional buy order at a price above the short-sale price. Assume you sold a stock short at 50, expecting it to decline to 40. To protect yourself from an increase, you could put in a stop buy order to purchase the stock using a market buy order if it reached a price of 55. This conditional buy order would hopefully limit any loss on the short sale to approximately $5 a share.

Margin Transactions   When investors buy stock, they can pay for the stock with cash or borrow part of the cost, leveraging the transaction. Leverage is accomplished by buying on margin, which means the investor pays for the stock with some cash and borrows the rest through the broker, putting up the stock for collateral.

As shown in Exhibit 4.8, the dollar amount of margin credit extended by NYSE members increased consistently since 1993, hitting a peak in early 2000 followed by a decline into 2003 and a subsequent increase in dollar terms but not as a percent of market capitalization. The interest rate charged on these loans by the investment firms is typically 1.50 percent above the rate charged by the bank making the loan. The bank rate, referred to as the *call money rate,* is generally about 1 percent below the prime rate. For example, in July 2008 the prime rate was 5.00 percent, and the call money rate was 3.75 percent.

Federal Reserve Board Regulations T and U determine the maximum proportion of any transaction that can be borrowed. This *margin requirement* (the proportion of total transaction value that must be paid in cash) has varied over time from 40 percent (allowing loans of 60 percent of the value) to 100 percent (allowing no borrowing). As of July 2008, the initial margin

Exhibit 4.8 NYSE Member Firm Customers' Margin Debt in Dollars and as a Percentage of U.S. Market Capitalization: 1993–2004

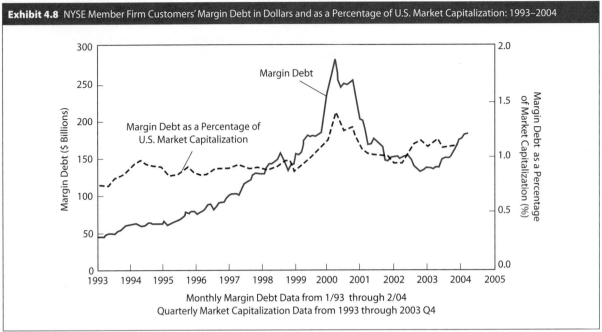

Monthly Margin Debt Data from 1/93 through 2/04
Quarterly Market Capitalization Data from 1993 through 2003 Q4

Sources: Federal Reserve Board; New York Stock Exchange; Goldman Sachs Portfolio Strategy.

requirement specified by the Federal Reserve was 50 percent, although individual investment firms can require higher percents.

After the initial purchase, changes in the market price of the stock will cause changes in the *investor's equity,* which is equal to the market value of the collateral stock minus the amount borrowed. Obviously, if the stock price increases, the investor's equity as a proportion of the total market value of the stock increases, that is, the investor's margin will exceed the initial margin requirement.

Assume you acquired 200 shares of a $50 stock for a total cost of $10,000. A 50 percent initial margin requirement allowed you to borrow $5,000, making your initial equity $5,000. If the stock price increases by 20 percent to $60 a share, the total market value of your position is $12,000, and your equity is now $7,000 ($12,000–$5,000), or 58 percent ($7,000/$12,000). In contrast, if the stock price declines by 20 percent to $40 a share, the total market value would be $8,000, and investor's equity would be $3,000 ($8,000–$5,000), or 37.5 percent ($3,000/$8,000).

This example demonstrates that buying on margin provides all the advantages and the disadvantages of leverage. Lower margin requirements allow you to borrow more, increasing the percentage of gain or loss on your investment when the stock price increases or decreases. The leverage factor equals 1/percent margin. Thus, as in the example, if the margin is 50 percent, the leverage factor is 2, that is, 1/0.50. Therefore, when the rate of return on the stock is plus or minus 10 percent, the return on your equity is plus or minus 20 percent. If the margin requirement declines to 33 percent, you can borrow more (67 percent), and the leverage factor is 3(1/0.33). As discussed by Ip (2000), when you acquire stock or other investments on margin, you are increasing the financial risk of the investment beyond the risk inherent in the security itself. You should increase your required rate of return accordingly.

The following example shows how borrowing by using margin affects the distribution of your returns *before commissions and interest* on the loan. If the stock increased by 20 percent, your return on the investment would be as follows:

1. The market value of the stock is $12,000, which leaves you with $7,000 after you pay off the loan.

2. The return on your $5,000 investment is

$$\frac{7,000}{5,000} - 1 = 1.40 - 1$$

$$= 0.40 = 40\%$$

In contrast, if the stock declined by 20 percent to $40 a share, your return would be as follows:

1. The market value of the stock is $8,000, which leaves you with $3,000 after you pay off the loan.
2. The negative return on your $5,000 investment is

$$\frac{3,000}{5,000} - 1 = 0.60 - 1$$

$$= -0.40 = -40\%$$

Notably, this symmetrical increase in gains and losses is only true prior to commissions and interest. Obviously, if we assume a 7 percent interest on the borrowed funds (which would be $5,000 × 0.07 = $350) and a $100 commission on the transaction, the results would indicate a lower positive return and a larger negative return as follows:

$$\text{20\% increase:} \quad \frac{\$12,000 - \$5,000 - \$350 - \$100}{5,000} - 1 = \frac{6,550}{5,000} - 1 = 0.31 = 31\%$$

$$\text{20\% decline:} \quad \frac{\$8,000 - \$5,000 - \$350 - \$100}{5,000} - 1 = \frac{2,550}{5,000} - 1 = -0.49 = -49\%$$

In addition to the initial margin requirement, another important concept is the **maintenance margin**, which is the required proportion of your equity to the total value of the stock after the initial transaction; the maintenance margin protects the broker if the stock price declines. At present, the minimum maintenance margin specified by the Federal Reserve is 25 percent, but, again, individual brokerage firms can dictate higher margins for their customers. If the stock price declines to the point where your investor's equity drops below 25 percent of the total value of the position, the account is considered undermargined, and you will receive a **margin call** to provide more equity. If you do not respond with the required funds in time, the stock will be sold to pay off the loan. The time allowed to meet a margin call varies between investment firms and is affected by market conditions. Under volatile conditions, the time allowed to respond to a margin call can be shortened drastically.

Given a maintenance margin of 25 percent, when you buy on margin you must consider how far the stock price can fall before you receive a margin call. The computation for our example is as follows: If the price of the stock is P and you own 200 shares, the value of the position is 200P and the equity in the account is (200P − $5,000). The percentage margin is (200P − 5,000)/200P. To determine the price, P, that is equal to 25 percent (0.25), we use the following equation:

$$\frac{200P - 5,000}{200P} = 0.25$$

$$200P - \$5,000 = 50P$$

$$150P = \$5,000$$

$$P = \$33.33$$

Therefore, when the stock is at $33.33, the equity value is exactly 25 percent; so if the stock declines from $50 to below $33.33, you will receive a margin call.

To continue the previous example, if the stock declines to $30 a share, its total market value would be $6,000 and your equity would be $1,000, which is only about 17 percent of the total value ($1,000/$6,000). You would receive a margin call for approximately $667, which would give you equity of $1,667, or 25 percent of the total value of the account ($1,667/$6,667). If the stock declined further, you would receive additional margin calls.

Short Sales Most investors purchase stock ("go long") expecting to derive their return from an increase in value. If you believe that a stock is overpriced, however, and want to take advantage of an expected decline in the price, you can sell the stock short. A **short sale** is the sale of stock that you do not own with the intent of purchasing it back later at a lower price. Specifically, you would *borrow* the stock from another investor through your broker and sell it in the market. Subsequently you would replace it at (you hope) a price lower than the price at which you sold it (this is referred to as *covering your short position*). Although a short sale has no time limit, the lender of the shares can decide to sell the shares, in which case your broker must find another investor willing to lend the shares. For discussions of both good and bad experiences with short-selling, see Power (1993), Loomis (1996), Weiss (1996), Beard (2001), and McKay (2005).

Two technical points affect short sales.[7] The first technical point concerns dividends. The short seller must pay any dividends due to the investor who lent the stock. The purchaser of the short-sale receives the dividend from the corporation, so the short seller must pay a similar dividend to the person who lent the stock.

Secondly, short sellers must post the same margin as an investor who had acquired stock. This margin can be in cash or any unrestricted securities owned by the short seller.

To illustrate this technique and demonstrate these technical points, consider the following example using Cara Corporation stock that is currently selling for $80 a share. You believe that the stock is overpriced and decide to sell 1,000 shares short at $80. Your broker borrows the Cara Corporation stock on your behalf, and sells it at $80 and deposits the $80,000 (less commissions that we will ignore in this example) in your account. Although the $80,000 is in your account, you cannot withdraw it. In addition, you must post 50 percent margin ($40,000) as collateral. Your percent margin equals:

$$\text{Percent Margin} = \frac{\text{Value of Equity}}{\text{Value of Stock Owed}}$$

The value of your equity equals: the cash from the sale of stock ($80,000), plus the required margin deposited ($40,000), minus the value of the stock owed (1,000p). Therefore, the percent margin at the initiation is

$$\text{Percent Margin} = \frac{\$80,000 + \$40,000 - \$80,000}{\$80,000}$$

$$= \frac{\$40,000}{\$80,000} = 0.50$$

Similar to the discussion under margin transactions, it is necessary to continue to compare the percent margin over time to the maintenance margin (assumed to be 25 percent). Notably, in the case of a short sale, a price decline is a postive event related to the percent margin. For

[7] Prior to June 2007 there was a rule that short sales of individual stocks could only be made on "upticks" meaning the price of the short sale had to be higher than the last trade price. As discussed in Jakab (2007), this rule was eliminated in 2007 by the SEC.

example, if we assume that the price of Cara Corporation stock declines to $70, the percent margin would increase as follows:

$$\frac{\text{Equity}}{\text{Value of Stock Owed}} = \frac{\$80,000 + \$40,000 - \$70,000}{\$70,000}$$

$$= \frac{\$50,000}{\$70,000} = 0.71$$

Alternatively, if the stock price increases to $90 a share, the percent margin would experience a decline as follows:

$$\frac{\text{Equity}}{\text{Value of Stock Owed}} = \frac{\$80,000 + \$40,000 - \$90,000}{\$90,000}$$

$$= \frac{\$30,000}{\$90,000} = 0.33$$

As before, it is important to determine the stock price that would trigger a margin call, which is computed as follows:

$$\frac{\text{Equity}}{\text{Value of Stock Owed}} = \frac{\$120,000 - 1,000\,P}{1,000\,P} = 0.25$$

$$= \$120,000 - 1,000\,P = 250\,P$$

$$= 1,250\,P = 120,000$$

$$P = \$96$$

Therefore, if the stock price moves against your short sale and increases above $96, you will receive a margin call. Given this unlimited upside potential (which is a negative event for the short seller), it is easy to understand why many short-sellers consistently enter stop-gain orders along with selling a stock short to limit this loss and possibly avoid a margin call—that is, put in a stop-gain order at some price below 96.

4.5.3 Exchange Market Makers

Now that we have discussed the overall structure of the exchange markets and the orders that are used to buy and sell stocks, we can discuss the role and function of the market makers on the exchange. These people and the role they play differ among exchanges. For example, on U.S. exchanges these people were historically called specialists. In late 2007, it was proposed that they be referred to as designated market makers (DMM), as discussed in Lucchetti (2007). Most exchanges do not have a single market maker but have competing dealers. On exchanges that have designated market makers, these individuals are critical to the smooth and efficient functioning of these markets.

As noted, a major requirement for a good market is liquidity, which depends on how the market makers do their job. Our initial discussion centers on the DMMs' role in U.S. markets, followed by a consideration of comparable roles on exchanges in other countries.

U.S. Markets The specialist (DMM) is a member of the exchange who applies to the exchange to be assigned stocks to handle. The typical specialist will handle 10 to 15 stocks. The minimum capital requirement for specialists is currently $1 million or the value of 15,000 shares of each stock assigned, whichever is greater.

Functions of the Specialist (DMM)*[8] Specialists (DMMs) have two major functions. First, they serve as *brokers* to match buy and sell orders and to handle special limit orders placed with member brokers. As noted earlier, an individual broker who receives a limit order (or stop loss or stop buy order) leaves it with the specialist (DMM) who executes it when the specified price occurs.

The second major function of a specialist is to act as a *dealer* to maintain a fair and orderly market by providing liquidity when the normal flow of orders is not adequate. As a dealer, the specialist must buy and sell for his or her own account (like a NASDAQ dealer) when public supply or demand is insufficient to provide a continuous, liquid market.

Consider the following example. If a stock is currently selling for about $40 per share, assume that the current bid and ask in an auction market (without the intervention of the specialist) was 40 bid–41 ask. Under such conditions, random market buy and sell orders might cause the stock price to fluctuate between 40 and 41 constantly—a movement of 2.5 percent between trades. Most investors would probably consider such a price pattern too volatile; the market would not be considered liquid. Under such conditions, the specialist is expected to provide "bridge liquidity" by entering alternative bids and asks or both to narrow the spread and improve the stock's price continuity. In this example, the specialist could enter a bid of 40.40 or 40.50 or an ask of 40.50 or 40.60 to narrow the spread to 10 cents.

Specialists can enter either side of the market, depending on several factors, including the trend of the market. Notably, they are expected to buy or sell against the market when prices are clearly moving in one direction. Specifically, they are required to buy stock for their own inventories when there is a clear excess of sell orders and the market is definitely declining. Alternatively, they must sell stock from their inventories or sell it short (i.e., borrow shares) to accommodate an excess of buy orders when the market is rising. Specialists are not expected to prevent prices from rising or declining, but only to ensure that *prices change in an orderly fashion* (that is, to maintain price continuity). Evidence that they have fulfilled this requirement is that during recent years NYSE stocks traded unchanged from, or within 10 cents of, the price of the previous trade about 95 percent of the time.

Assuming that there is not a clear trend in the market, several factors will affect how specialists close the bid–ask spread. One factor is their current inventory position in the stock. For example, if they have large inventories of a given stock, all other factors being equal, they would probably enter on the ask (sell) side to reduce these heavy inventories. In contrast, specialists who have little or no inventory of shares because they had been selling from their inventories, or selling short, would tend toward the bid (buy) side of the market to rebuild their inventories or close out their short positions.

Second, the position of the limit-order book will influence how they narrow the spread. Numerous limit buy orders (bids) close to the current market and few limit sell orders (asks) might indicate a tendency toward higher prices because demand is apparently heavy and supply is limited. Under such conditions, a specialist who is not bound by one of the other factors would probably opt to accumulate stock in anticipation of a price increase.

Specialist Income The specialist derives income from the broker and dealer functions. The actual breakdown between the two sources depends on the specific stock. In an actively traded stock such as IBM or GE, a specialist has little need to act as a dealer because the substantial public interest in the stock creates a tight market (that is, a narrow bid–ask spread). In such a case, the main source of income would come from maintaining the limit orders for the stock. The broker income derived from high-volume stocks such as Microsoft, and Proctor & Gamble, and GE, is substantial and without risk.

---

[8] The discussion in this section describes the functions of the specialist prior to 2008. In a subsequent section we will discuss the significant changes that are occuring and how these changes impact these duties and what has happened to the specialist community on the NYSE.

In contrast, a stock with low trading volume and substantial price volatility would probably have a fairly wide bid–ask spread, and the specialist would have to be an active dealer. The specialist's income from such a stock would depend on his or her ability to trade it profitably. Theoretically, specialists should have a major advantage when trading because of their limit-order books. Officially, only specialists are supposed to see the limit-order book, which would contain important information regarding the current supply and demand for a stock. The fact is, most specialists routinely share the limit-order book with other brokers, so it is not a competitive advantage.

Most specialists attempt to balance their portfolios between strong broker stocks that provide steady, riskless income and stocks that require active dealer roles. It has been noted that an increase in dealer activity has been matched with an increase in return on capital for specialists. For further analysis of specialists, see Madhaven and Sofianos (1998) and Benveniste, Marcus, and Wilhelm (1992).

4.5.4 New Trading Systems

As daily trading volume has gone from about 5 million shares to more than a billion shares on both the NYSE and NASDAQ, it has become necessary to introduce new technology into the trading process. Following are some technological innovations that assist in the trading process.

On the NYSE:

- **Super Dot.** Super Dot is an electronic order-routing system through which member firms transmit market and limit orders in NYSE-listed securities directly to the posts where securities are traded or to the member firm's booth. After the order has been executed, a report of execution is returned directly to the member firm office over the same electronic circuit, and the execution is submitted directly to the comparison systems. Member firms can enter market orders up to 2,099 shares and limit orders in round or odd lots up to 30,099 shares. An estimated 85 percent of all market orders enter the NYSE through the Super Dot system.
- **The Display Book.** The Display Book is an electronic workstation that keeps track of all limit orders and incoming market orders. This includes incoming Super Dot limit orders.
- **Opening Automated Report Service (OARS).** OARS, the opening feature of the Super Dot system, accepts member firms' preopening market orders up to 30,099 shares. OARS automatically and continuously pairs buy and sell orders and presents the imbalance to the specialist prior to the opening of a stock. This system helps the specialist determine the opening price and the potential need for a preopening call market, as discussed earlier.
- **Market-Order Processing.** Super Dot's postopening market-order system is designed to accept member firms' postopening market orders up to 30,099 shares. The system provides rapid execution and reporting of market orders. During 2007, 94.5 percent of market orders were executed and reported in less than 30 seconds.
- **Limit-Order Processing.** The limit-order processing system electronically files orders to be executed when and if a specific price is reached. The system accepts limit orders up to 99,999 shares and electronically updates the Specialists' Display Book. Good-until-canceled orders that are not executed on the day of submission are automatically stored until executed or canceled.

On the NASDAQ:

- **Small-Order Execution System (SOES).** Market makers receiving SOES orders must honor their bids for automatic executions up to 1,000 shares. SOES was introduced in 1984 and became compulsory following the October 1987 crash.
- **SelectNet.** SelectNet is an order-routing and execution service for institutional investors that allows brokers and dealers to communicate through NASDAQ terminals instead of the phone. Once two parties agree to a trade on SelectNet, the execution is automatic.

4.5.5 Innovations for Competition

By this time you should realize that the U.S. secondary equity market is being served by two competing models. As mentioned early in this chapter, the first is the *order-driven* stock exchange market where buy and sell orders interact directly with the specialist market maker acting as both a broker and a dealer when necessary. This model is ideal for a secondary market when there is a concentration of participants and all orders come to one central location (either physically or electronically).

The second model is a *quote-driven* market, also referred to as a dealer market, where numerous dealers compete against each other by providing bid–ask quotations and commit to buy and sell given securities at these quoted prices. Generally, in this model buy and sell orders never interact directly, but the best prices are derived due to the competition among dealers who are independent and separated—it is a fragmented market.

Given these two models, the Securities and Exchange Commission has encouraged competition between the two market models by encouraging three innovations: the CQS, the ITS, and the CAES.

The *Consolidated Quotation System (CQS)* is an electronic service that provides quotations on issues listed on the NYSE, the AMEX, and regional exchanges, and issues traded by market makers in the NASDAQ InterMarket (the third market). Provided to subscribers by the Composite Quotation Service, the CQS makes it possible for subscribers to see all competing dealer and exchange quotes for a stock listed on any exchange. The volume of trading for stocks on the consolidated tape has grown dramatically and is now over 400 billion shares annually.

The *Intermarket Trading System (ITS)* is a centralized quotation and routing system developed by the American, Boston, Chicago, New York, Pacific, and Philadelphia Stock Exchanges and the NASD. ITS consists of a central computer facility with interconnected terminals in the participating market centers. As shown in Exhibit 4.9, the number of issues included, the volume of trading, and the size of trades have all grown substantially. There were more than 5,000 issues included on the system in 2004.

With ITS, brokers and market makers in each market center indicate specific buying and selling commitments through a composite quotation display that shows the current quotes for each stock in every market center. A broker is expected to go to the best market to execute a customer's order by sending a message committing to a buy or sell at the price quoted. When this commitment is accepted, a message reports the transaction. The following example illustrates how ITS works.

A broker on the NYSE has a market order to sell 100 shares of Wal-Mart Stores (WMT) stock. Assuming the quotation display at the NYSE shows that the best current bid for WMT is on the Pacific Stock Exchange (PSE), the broker will enter an order to sell 100 shares at the bid

Exhibit 4.9 Intermarket Trading System (ITS) Activity

		DAILY AVERAGE		
Year	Issues Eligible	Share Volume	Executed Trades	Average Size of Trade
1980	884	1,565,900	2,868	546
1985	1,288	5,669,400	5,867	966
1990	2,126	9,387,114	8,744	1,075
1995	3,542	12,185,064	10,911	1,117
1996	4,001	12,721,968	11,426	1,113
1997	4,535	15,429,377	14,057	1,098
1998	4,844	18,136,472	17,056	1,063
1999	5,056	21,617,723	19,315	1,119
2000	4,664	28,176,178	23,972	1,175
2001	4,575	34,029,513	29,728	1,145
2002	4,718	50,036,437	37,694	1,327
2003	4,808	64,077,468	46,582	1,376
2004	5,041	70,924,190	53,331	1,330

Source: *NYSE Fact Book* (New York: NYSE, 2005): 28. Reprinted by permission of the New York Stock Exchange.

on the PSE. Within seconds, the commitment flashes on the computer screen and is printed out at the PSE specialist's post, where it is executed against the PSE bid. The transaction is reported back to New York and on the consolidated tape. Both brokers receive immediate confirmation and the results are transmitted at the end of each day. Thereafter, each broker completes his or her own clearance and settlement procedure.

The ITS system currently provides centralized quotations for stocks listed on the NYSE and specifies whether a bid or ask *away* from the NYSE market is superior to that *on* the NYSE. Note, however, that the system lacks several characteristics. It does not automatically execute at the best market. Instead, an investor must contact the market maker and indicate that he wants to buy or sell, at which time the bid or ask may be withdrawn. Also, it is not mandatory that a broker go to the best market. Although the best price may be at another market center, a broker might consider it inconvenient to trade on that exchange if the price difference is not substantial. Still, even with these shortcomings, substantial technical and operational progress has occurred through this central quotation and routing system.

The *Computer-Assisted Execution System (CAES)* is a service created by NASDAQ that automates order routing and transaction execution for securities listed on domestic exchanges that are part of the ITS. This system makes it possible for market makers who are involved with ITS to execute trades with specialists on the exchanges using CAES.

4.5.6 Future Trading Techniques and Exchange Mergers

One cannot help but be struck by the significant changes that have taken place in both the U.S. and global equity markets during the new millennium. The technological advances and the decimalization of prices have contributed to significant reductions in trading costs for institutional and retail investors. Although we have two different trading models (order-driven and quote-driven), it appears that they can survive together. But both are challenged by the ECNs that can match orders electronically and provide faster, cheaper transactions. Based on the percent of NASDAQ transactions completed on the ECNs (about 30 to 35 percent), it appears that the ECNs are very good at finding, matching, and executing trades for dealer stocks (as brokers) and when they cannot broker the trade they send the orders to the NASDAQ market. The unknown factor with ECNs is "best price."

Trading Regulations In response to challenges from the ECNs, the order-driven exchanges (mainly the NYSE) have attempted regulations to protect the exchange from competition. To protect its centralized auction market, the NYSE introduced Rule 390, which required members to obtain the exchange's permission to carry out a transaction in a listed stock off the exchange. The NYSE argued that without such a rule, the market would become fragmented and many orders would be internalized (members would match orders between customers) rather than exposed to the public. After several years of debate, the SEC ruled that this regulation was clearly anticompetitive and Rule 390 was rescinded in May 2000.

The second regulation that constrains the ECNs from competing with the NYSE is the *trade-through rule,* which dictates that markets *not* ignore superior prices that are available in competing markets. Put another way, traders are not allowed to "trade through" superior prices—for example, if the best bid is at $30, a dealer cannot fill the order at $29.95. This rule worked to the advantage of the NYSE because the bulk of trading in listed stocks (historically about 70 to 80 percent) is done on the exchange, so one would expect it to have the best price. The problem is that the search for the best price and the ensuing order transfer can slow the trade by about 30 seconds, which is a long time on the exchange, and prices can change in the interim. Thus the debate is over *speed of execution* versus *best price.* Discussions on the controversy included Solomon and Kelly (2003), Kelly (2004a, b), Craig and Kelly (2004), and Kelly and Solomon (2004).

The speed-of-execution contingent (ECNs and other ATSs) want some flexibility on the price: either allow the customer to specify a price range of one to three cents a share from the best price or have a general band whereby the order can be consummated if the electronic price is within one or two cents of the best price. The NYSE is considering such price bands but contend that block traders need to have the benefit of specialists who can ensure the best price for the total block. There is also a greater need for specialists for very small illiquid shares. The point is, relatively small transactions (e.g., under 5,000 shares) for large, liquid stocks (e.g., GE, IBM, 3M, and Johnson and Johnson) can be handled quickly and at very low cost via electronic trading and will typically be at the best price. But very large block trades for liquid stocks and most trades for very small illiquid stocks usually need human intervention.

So, where *do* we go from here? Most likely, further technological advances and the Internet will greatly influence the answer. But it is also likely that human financial experts will always be needed to exercise judgment in the investment process. Coincident with the debate on how stocks should be traded is a related question on the basic future of the NYSE as a public entity, as discussed in Der Hovanesian (2004), Anderson (2005), and Ascarelli and McKay (2005).

Changes to the NYSE[9] While there have been numerous changes across the security markets, the most significant impact has been on the NYSE with the introduction of the "hybrid market" that combined the traditional specialist system with the electronic market following the acquisition of Archipelago in April 2006 (which is referred to as NYSE Arca). The major impact has been on the specialist portion of the exchange wherein the volume of trading by specialists has declined dramatically. The most significant effect is that as of November 2007 about 85 percent of the orders of the NYSE are filled electronically, but the specialists are still trading some large transactions that encompass about 1.5 billion shares a day. The full impact of the changes include competition on the NYSE between Arca and the NYSE specialist. Specifically, since the acquisition of Arca, its market share of NYSE-listed stocks has increased from 5 to 12 percent, while the NYSE specialist share has declined from 76 percent to 44 percent. This implies that the total proportion of trading of NYSE listed stocks by the two NYSE components (Arca and specialist) has declined rapidly from 76 percent in late 2006, to 66 percent in January 2007, and only 56 percent in September 2007. While the Arca component is very similar to the NASDAQ system, the Arca share of trading NASDAQ stocks has declined from 21 percent in May 2006 to 14 percent in September 2007. There has also been an impact on block trading on the NYSE because of low-cost rapid electronic trading of less than blocks (which are trades of 10,000 shares or more). In contrast to the year 2004, when shares sold in blocks constituted almost 49 percent of total volume on the NYSE, this proportion declined to 20 percent in September 2006 and to 12 percent in September 2007.

Given these reductions in relative trading volume, it is not a surprise that the quality of trading has suffered. Three major measures of trading quality are: (1) the frequency when the NYSE sets the national best bid or offer (NBBO), (2) the percent of orders when price was improved, and (3) the percent of price improvement. A study by the NYSE showed that the NYSE had the NBBO 67 percent of the time in late 2006 but only 55 percent during the second quarter of 2007. Similarly, the percent of NYSE orders with price improvement went from 1.47 percent to 0.03 percent. Finally, the size of price improvement went from 10.66 percent in July 2006 to 1.39 percent in July 2007.

Because of this decline in volume of trading, several specialist firms suffered significant losses and there has been a major wave of consolidations. Specifically, the total number of specialist firms declined from more than 40 in the early 1990s to seven in October 2007— and to only five in November 2007 when two additional firms decided to leave the business (Vander Moolen Specialists and SIG Specialists, Inc.) (see Dowell, 2007). Besides the consolidaion of firms, the specific number of specialist traders who work on the floor of the NYSE declined from about 400 in October 2006 to 220 in November 2007 (see Luccetti, 2007). Given that the number of stocks listed on the exchange has not changed very much, the number of stocks assigned to each of the remaining specialists almost doubled during 2007, which has

---

[9] This subsection benefited from the very thorough discussion in an article by Chapman (2007) that chronicled the numerous changes on the exchange that were being engineered by the new leaders of the NYSE—Duncan Niederauer and Larry Leibowitz.

likely contributed to the decline in trading quality. Another reflection of the ongoing change is the decline in space allocated to trading on the NYSE that has gone from five rooms in the NYSE building prior to October 2006 to four rooms in November 2006 and only two rooms in November 2007 (see Bergstrom, 2007).

Global Consolidation of Security Exchanges.   One of the most significant changes in security markets over the past decade has been the substantial consolidation of exchanges around the world. This global consolidation of stock, bond and derivative exchanges has been driven by two factors. First is the rapid globalization of the markets wherein investors and investment firms are interested in trading continuously around the clock anywhere in the world in virtually any asset class and communication technology makes this possible. Second is the need for the latest and best technology that will allow an exchange to compete in this global market. Notably, this technology is very expensive to develop and maintain and, therefore, it is imperative to take full advantage of the significant economies of scale available in this sector. In turn, this means exchanges need to be dominant in a country and geographic region. The result is consolidation across borders and asset classes. A primary example is the NYSE acquiring Archipelago (an ECN) and then buying the Eurex Exchange which included several international stock and derivative exchanges. Similarly, in the U.S., virtually all the regional exchanges that existed in 2004 have since merged or been acquired. The long-term outlook is for a relatively few full service exchanges that will trade all the major asset classes.

• • • • SUMMARY • • • •

- The securities market is divided into primary and secondary markets. While primary markets are important sources of new capital for the issuers of securities, the secondary markets provide the liquidity that is critical to the primary markets.

- The composition of the secondary bond market has experienced small changes over the past 20 years. In sharp contrast, the secondary equity market has experienced significant change and is continuing to evolve due to new technology and consolidation. In addition to several primary listing markets that include exchanges and several NASDAQ components, the secondary market includes several robust regional exchanges, a viable third market, and most recently, the creation, growth, and consolidation of numerous alternative trading systems that provide automatic electronic transactions for stocks on both exchanges and dealer markets.

- The components of a good exchange market include several types of membership as well as various types of orders. In addition, market makers play a critical role in maintaining the liquidity of the market.

- It appears that changes, especially those due to these technological innovations, have only just begun. Therefore, it is important for investors who will be involved in this market to understand how this market has evolved, what is its current structure, and how it can develop in the future. As an investor, you will need to understand how to analyze securities to find the best securities for your portfolio, but also you need to know the best way to buy/sell the security, that is, how and where to complete the transaction. Our discussion in this chapter should provide the background you need to make that trading decision.

• • • • SUGGESTED READINGS • • • •

Barclay, Michael, Terrence Hendershott, and D. Timothy McCormick. "Competition among Trading Venues: Information and Trading on Electronic Communications Networks." *Journal of Finance* 58, no. 6 (December 2003).

Huang, Roger. "The Quality of ECN and Nasdaq Market-Maker Quotes." *Journal of Finance* 57, no. 3 (June 2002).

• • • • QUESTIONS • • • •

1. Define *market* and briefly discuss the characteristics of a good market.
2. You own 100 shares of General Electric stock and you want to sell it because you need the money to make a down payment on a car. Assume there is absolutely no secondary market system in common stocks. How would you go about selling the stock? Discuss what you would have to do to find a buyer, how long it might take, and the price you might receive.
3. Define *liquidity* and discuss the factors that contribute to it. Give examples of a liquid asset and an illiquid asset, and discuss why they are considered liquid and illiquid.
4. Define a primary and secondary market for securities and discuss how they differ. Discuss how the primary market is dependent on the secondary market.
5. Give an example of an initial public offering (IPO) in the primary market. Give an example of a seasoned equity issue in the primary market. Discuss which would involve greater risk to the buyer.
6. Find an advertisement for a recent primary offering in the *Wall Street Journal.* Based on the information in the ad, indicate the characteristics of the security sold and the major underwriters. How much new capital did the firm derive from the offering before paying commissions?
7. Briefly explain the difference between a competitive-bid underwriting and a negotiated underwriting.
8. The figures in Exhibit 4.6 reveal a major change over time in the price paid for a membership (seat) on the NYSE. What has caused this change over time?
9. What are the major reasons for the existence of regional stock exchanges? Discuss how they differ from the national exchanges.
10. Which segment of the secondary stock market (listed exchanges or NASDAQ) is larger in terms of the number of issues? Which is larger in terms of the value of the issues traded?
11. Discuss the three levels of NASDAQ in terms of what each provides and who would subscribe to each.
12. a. Define the third market. Give an example of a third-market stock.
    b. Define the fourth market. Discuss why a financial institution would use the fourth market.
13. Briefly define each of the following terms and give an example.
    a. *Market order*
    b. *Limit order*
    c. *Short sale*
    d. *Stop loss order*
14. Briefly discuss the two major functions and sources of income for the NYSE specialist.

• • • • PROBLEMS • • • •

1. Suppose you buy a round lot of Francesca Industries stock on 55 percent margin when the stock is selling at $20 a share. The broker charges a 10 percent annual interest rate, and commissions are 3 percent of the stock value on the purchase and sale. A year later you receive a $0.50 per share dividend and sell the stock for 27. What is your rate of return on Francesca Industries?
2. The stock of the Madison Travel Co. is selling for $28 a share. You put in a limit buy order at $24 for one month. During the month, the stock price declines to $20, then jumps to $36. Ignoring commissions, what would have been your rate of return on this investment? What would be your rate of return if you had put in a market order? What if your limit order was at $18?
3. You decide to sell short 100 shares of Charlotte Horse Farms when it is selling at its yearly high of $56. Your broker tells you that your margin requirement is 45 percent and that the commission on the purchase is $155. While you are short the stock, Charlotte pays a $2.50 per share dividend. At the end of one year, you buy 100 shares of Charlotte at $45 to close out your position and are charged a commission of $145 and 8 percent interest on the money borrowed. What is your rate of return on the investment?
4. Two years ago, you bought 300 shares of Kayleigh Milk Co. for $30 a share with a margin of 60 percent. Currently, the Kayleigh stock is selling for $45 a share. Assuming no dividends and ignoring commissions, compute (a) the annualized rate of return on this investment if you had paid cash, and (b) your rate of return with the margin purchase.

5. Lauren has a margin account and deposits $50,000. Assume the prevailing margin requirement is 40 percent, commissions are ignored, and the Gentry Shoe Corporation is selling at $35 per share.
   a. How many shares can Lauren purchase using the maximum allowable margin?
   b. What is Lauren's profit (loss) if the price of Gentry's stock
      i.   rises to $45?
      ii. falls to $25?
   c. If the maintenance margin is 30 percent, to what price can Gentry Shoe fall before Lauren will receive a margin call?

6. You own 200 shares of Shamrock Enterprises that you bought at $25 a share. The stock is now selling for $45 a share.
   a. You put in a stop loss order at $40. Discuss your reasoning for this action.
   b. If the stock eventually declines in price to $30 a share, what would be your rate of return with and without the stop loss order?

7. You have $40,000 to invest in Sophie Shoes, a stock selling for $80 a share. The initial margin requirement is 60 percent. Ignoring taxes and commissions, show in detail the impact on your rate of return if the stock rises to $100 a share and if it declines to $40 a share assuming: (a) you pay cash for the stock, and (b) you buy it using maximum leverage.

THOMSON ONE | Business School Edition

1. On which stock markets are the following firms traded: Abbott Labs, Apple Computer, ExxonMobil, Intel, Johnson and Johnson, Microsoft?
2. Suppose you purchased Microsoft stock on January 15, 2008, and sold it two months later on March 15, 2008. What would your percentage price return be? What would the percentage return be if you had used 75 percent margin? 50 percent margin?
3. Redo exercise 2 but this time assume you purchased Microsoft on March 15, 2008, and sold it two months later on May 15, 2008. What would the annualized returns be if you bought the stock with cash? If you used 75 percent margin? 50 percent margin?

• • • APPENDIX: CHAPTER 4 • • • •

Characteristics of Developed and Developing Markets around the World

(Exhibits 4A.1 and 4A.2 on the following pages)

A P P E N D I X

Exhibit 4A.1 Developed Markets around the World

Country	Principal Exchange	Other Exchanges	Total Market Capitalization ($ billions)	Available Market Capitalization ($ billions)	Trading Volume ($ billions)	Domestic Issues Listed	Total Issues Listed	Auction Mechanism	Official Specialists	Options/ Futures Trading	Price Limits	Principal Market Indexes
Australia	Sydney	5	82.3	53.5	39.3	N.A.	1,496	Continuous	No	Yes	None	All Ordinaries— 324 issues
Austria	Vienna	—	18.7	8.3	37.2	125	176	Call	Yes	No	5%	GZ Aktienindex— 25 issues
Belgium	Brussels	3	48.5	26.2	6.8	186	337	Mixed	No	Few	10%	Brussels Stock Exchange Index— 186 issues
Canada	Toronto	4	186.8	124.5	71.3	N.A.	1,208	Continuous	Yes	Yes	None	TSE 300 Composite Index
Denmark	Copenhagen	—	29.7	22.2	11.1	N.A.	284	Mixed	No	No	None	Copenhagen Stock Exchange Index— 38 issues
Finland	Helsinki	—	9.9	1.7	5.2	N.A.	125	Mixed	N.A.	N.A.	N.A.	KOP (Kansallis-Osake-Pannki) Price Index
France	Paris	6	256.5	137.2	129.0	463	663	Mixed	Yes	Yes	4%	CAC General Index—240 issues
Germany	Frankfurt	7	297.7	197.9	1,003.7	N.A.	355	Continuous	Yes	Options	None	DAX; FAZ (Frankfurter Allgemeine Zeitung)
Hong Kong	Hong Kong	—	67.7	37.1	34.6	N.A.	479	Continuous	No	Futures	None	Hang Seng Index— 33 issues
Ireland	Dublin	—	8.4	6.4	5.5	N.A.	N.A.	Continuous	No	No	None	J&E Davy Total Market index

Country	City							Trading				Index
Italy	Milan	9	137.0	73.2	42.6	N.A.	317	Mixed	No	No	10–20%	Banca Commerciale—209 issues
Japan	Tokyo	7	2,754.6	1,483.5	1,602.4	N.A.	1,576	Continuous	Yes	No	10% down	TOPIX—1,097 issues; TSE II—423 issues; Nikkei 225
Luxembourg	Luxembourg	—	1.5	0.9	0.1	61	247	Continuous	N.A.	N.A.	N.A.	Domestic Share Price Index—9 issues
Malaysia	Kuala Lumpur	—	199.3	95.0	126.4	430	478	Continuous	No	No	None	Kuala Lumpur Composite Index—83 issues
The Netherlands	Amsterdam	—	112.1	92.4	80.4	279	569	Continuous	Yes	Options	Variable	ANP—CBS General Index—51 issues
New Zealand	Wellington	—	6.7	5.3	2.0	295	451	Continuous	No	Futures	None	Barclay's International Price Index—40 issues
Norway	Oslo	9	18.4	7.9	14.1	N.A.	128	Call	No	No	None	Oslo Bors Stock Index—50 issues
Singapore	Singapore	—	28.6	15.6	8.2	N.A.	324	Continuous	No	No	None	Straits Times Index—30 issues; SES—32 issues
South Africa	Johannesburg	—	72.7	N.A.	8.2	N.A.	N.A.	Continuous	No	Options	None	JSE Actuaries Index—141 issues

(*continued*)

Exhibit 4A.1 *(continued)*

Country	Principal Exchange	Other Exchanges	Total Market Capitalization ($ billions)	Available Market Capitalization ($ billions)	Trading Volume ($ billions)	Domestic Issues Listed	Total Issues Listed	Auction Mechanism	Official Specialists	Options/ Futures Trading	Price Limits	Principal Market Indexes
Spain	Madrid	3	86.6	46.8	41.0	N.A.	368	Mixed	No	No	10%	Madrid Stock Exchange Index—72 issues
Sweden	Stockholm	—	59.0	24.6	15.8	N.A.	151	Mixed	No	Yes	None	Jacobson & Ponsbach—30 issues
Switzerland	Zurich	6	128.5	75.4	376.6	161	380	Mixed	No	Yes	5%	Société de Banque Suisse—90 issues
United Kingdom	London	5	756.2	671.1	280.7	1,911	2,577	Continuous	No	Yes	None	Financial Times—(FT) Ordinaries—750 issues; FTSE 100; FT 33
United States	New York	6	9,431.1	8,950.3	5,778.7	N.A.	3,358	Continuous	Yes	Yes	None	S&P 500; Dow Jones Industrial Average; Wilshire 5000; Russell 3000

Notes: Market capitalizations (both total and available) are as of December 31, 1990, except for South African market capitalization, which is from 1988. Available differs from total market capitalization by subtracting cross holdings, closely held and government-owned shares, and takes into account restrictions on foreign ownership. Number of issues listed are from 1988 except for Malaysia, which is from 1994. Trading volume data are from 1990 except for Switzerland, which are from 1988. Trading institutions data are from 1987. Market capitalizations (both total and available) for all countries except the United States and South Africa are from the Salomon-Russell Global Equity Indices. U.S. market capitalization (both total and available) is from the Frank Russell Company. All trading volume information (except for Switzerland) and Malaysian total issues listed are from the *Emerging Stock Markets Factbook: 1991*, International Finance Corp., 1991. Trading institutions information is from Richard Roll, "The International Crash of 1987," *Financial Analysts Journal*, September/October 1988. South African market capitalization, number of issues listed for all countries (except Malaysia), and Swiss trading volume are reproduced courtesy of Euromoney Books, extracted from *The G.T. Guide to World Equity Markets: 1989, 1988.*

Source: From *Global Investing: The Professional Guide to the World Capital Markets* by Roger G. Ibbotson and Gary P. Brinson, pp. 109–111. Copyright © 1993. Reprinted by permission of The McGraw-Hill Companies, Inc.

Exhibit 4A.2 Emerging Markets around the World

Country	Principal Exchange	Other Exchanges	Market Capitalization ($ billions)	Trading Volume ($ billions)	Total Issues Listed	Auction Mechanism	Principal Market Indexes
Argentina	Buenos Aires	4	36.9	11.4	156	N.A.	Buenos Aires Stock Exchange Index
Brazil	São Paulo	9	189.2	109.5	544	Continuous	BOVESPA Share Price Index—83 issues
Chile	Santiago	—	68.2	5.3	279	Mixed	IGPA Index—180 issues
China	Shanghai	1	43.5	97.5	291	Continuous	Shanghai Composite Index
Colombia	Bogotá	1	14.0	2.2	90	N.A.	Bogotá General Composite Index
Greece	Athens	—	14.9	5.1	216	Continuous	Athens Stock Exchange Industrial Price Index
India	Bombay	14	127.5	27.3	4,413	Continuous	Economic Times Index—72 issues
Indonesia	Jakarta	—	47.2	11.8	216	Mixed	Jakarta Stock Exchange Index
Israel	Tel Aviv	—	10.6	5.5	267	Call	General Share Index—all listed issues
Jordan	Amman	—	4.6	0.6	95	N.A.	Amman Financial Market Index
Mexico	Mexico City	—	130.2	83.0	206	Continuous	Bolsa de Valores Index—49 issues
Nigeria	Lagos	—	2.7	N.A.	177	Call	Nigerian Stock Exchange General Index
Pakistan	Karachi	—	12.2	3.2	724	Continuous	State Bank of Pakistan Index
Philippines	Makati	1	55.5	13.9	189	N.A.	Manila Commercial & Industrial Index—25 issues
Portugal	Lisbon	1	16.2	5.2	195	Call	Banco Totta e Acores Share Index—50 issues
South Korea	Seoul	—	191.8	286.0	699	Continuous	Korea Composite Stock Price Index
Taiwan	Taipei	—	247.3	711.0	313	Continuous	Taiwan Stock Exchange Index
Thailand	Bangkok	—	131.4	80.2	389	Continuous	Securities Exchange of Thailand Price Index
Turkey	Istanbul	—	21.6	21.7	176	Continuous	Istanbul Stock Exchange Index—50 issues
Venezuela	Caracas	1	4.1	0.9	90	Continuous	Indice de Capitalization de la BVC
Zimbabwe	N.A.	—	1.8	0.2	64	N.A.	Zimbabwe S.E. Industrial Index

Notes: Market capitalizations, trading volume, and total issues listed are as of 1994. Market capitalization, trading volume, and total issues listed for Brazil and São Paulo only. Trading volume for the Philippines is for both Manila and Makati. Total issues listed for India is Bombay only. Trading institutions information is from 1987 and 1988. Market capitalizations, trading volume, and total issues listed are from the *Emerging Stock Markets Factbook: 1995*, International Finance Corp., 1995. Trading institutions information is from Richard Roll, "The International Crash of 1987," *Financial Analysts Journal*, September/October 1988.

Source: From *Global Investing: The Professional Guide to the World Capital Markets* by Roger G. Ibbotson and Gary P. Brinson, pp. 125–126. Copyright © 1993. Reprinted by permission of The McGraw-Hill Companies, Inc.

CHAPTER 5
Security-Market Indexes

After you read this chapter, you should be able to answer the following questions:

- What are some major uses of security-market indexes?
- What major characteristics cause alternative indexes to differ?
- What are the major stock-market indexes in the United States and globally, and what are their characteristics?
- Why are bond indexes more difficult to create and maintain than stock indexes?
- What are the major bond-market indexes for the United States and the world?
- What are some of the composite stock–bond market indexes?
- Where can you get historical and current data for all these indexes?
- What is the relationship among many of these indexes in the short run (monthly)?

A fair statement regarding **security-market indexes**—especially those outside the United States—is that everybody talks about them but few people understand them. Even those investors familiar with widely publicized stock-market series, such as the Dow Jones Industrial Average (DJIA), usually know little about indexes for the U.S. bond market or for non-U.S. stock markets such as Tokyo or London.

Although portfolios are obviously composed of many different individual stocks, investors typically ask, "What happened to the market today?" The reason for this question is that if an investor owns more than a few stocks or bonds, it is cumbersome to follow each stock or bond individually to determine the composite performance of the portfolio. Also, there is an intuitive notion that most individual stocks or bonds move with the aggregate market. Therefore, if the overall market rose, an individual's portfolio probably also increased in value. To supply investors with a composite report on market performance, some financial publications or investment firms have created and maintain stock-market and bond-market indexes.

In the initial section of this chapter we discuss several ways that investors use security-market indexes. An awareness of these significant functions should provide an incentive for becoming familiar with these indexes and indicates why we present a full chapter on this topic. In the second section we consider what characteristics cause various indexes to differ. Investors need to understand these differences and why one index is preferable for a given task because of its characteristics. In the third section we present the most well-known U.S. and global stock-market indexes, separated into groups based on the weighting scheme used. In section four we consider bond-market indexes—a relatively new topic because the creation and maintenance of total return bond indexes are relatively new. Again, we consider international bond indexes following the domestic indexes. In the fifth section we consider composite stock market–bond market series. In our final section we examine how alternative indexes relate to each other over monthly intervals. This comparison demonstrates the important factors that cause high or low correlation among series. With this background, you should be able to make an intelligent choice of the index that is best for you based on how you want to use it.

5.1 Uses of Security-Market Indexes

Security-market indexes have at least five specific uses. A primary application is to use the index values to compute total returns and risk measures for an aggregate market or some component of a market over a specified time period and use the computed return-risk results as a *benchmark* to judge the performance of individual portfolios. A basic assumption when evaluating portfolio performance is that any investor should be able to experience a risk-adjusted rate of return comparable to the market by randomly selecting a large number of stocks or bonds from the total market; hence, a superior portfolio manager should consistently do better than the market. Therefore, *an aggregate stock- or bond-market index can be used as a benchmark to judge the performance of professional money managers.*

An obvious use of indexes is to develop an index portfolio. As we have discussed, it is difficult for most money managers to consistently outperform specified market indexes on a risk-adjusted basis over time.[1] If this is true, an obvious alternative is to invest in a portfolio that will emulate this market portfolio. This notion led to the creation of *index funds* and *exchange-traded funds* (ETFs), whose purpose is to track the performance of the specified market series (index) over time. The original index funds were common-stock funds as discussed in Malkiel (2004), Chapter 14, and Mossavar-Rahmani (2005). The development of comprehensive, well-specified bond-market indexes and the inability of most bond-portfolio managers to outperform these indexes have led to a similar phenomenon in the fixed-income area (bond-index funds), as noted by Hawthorne (1986) and Dialynas (2001).

Securities analysts, portfolio managers, and academicians doing research use security-market indexes to examine the factors that influence aggregate security price movements (that is, the indexes are used to measure aggregate market movements) and to compare the risk-adjusted performance of alternative asset classes (e.g., stocks versus bonds versus real estate).

Another group interested in an aggregate market index is composed of "technicians," who believe past price changes can be used to predict future price movements. For example, to project future stock price movements, technicians would plot and analyze price and volume changes for a stock-market series like the Dow Jones Industrial Average.

Finally, work in portfolio and capital market theory has implied that the relevant risk for an individual risky asset is its *systematic risk,* which is the relationship between the rates of return for a risky asset and the rates of return for a market portfolio of risky assets.[2] Therefore, an aggregate market index is used as a proxy for the market portfolio of risky assets.

5.2 Differentiating Factors in Constructing Market Indexes

Because the indexes are intended to reflect the overall movements of a group of securities, we need to consider three factors that are important when constructing an index intended to represent a total population.

5.2.1 The Sample

The first factor is the sample used to construct an index. The size, the breadth, and the source of the sample are all important.

A small percentage of the total population will provide valid indications of the behavior of the total population *if* the sample is properly selected. In some cases, because of the economics of computers, virtually all the stocks on an exchange or market are included, with a few deletions of unusual securities. The sample should be *representative* of the total population;

---

[1]Throughout this chapter and the book, we will use *indicator series* and *indexes* interchangeably, although *indicator series* is the more correct specification because it refers to a broad class of series; one popular type of series is an index, but there can be other types and many different indexes.

[2]This concept and its justification are discussed in Chapter 7 and Chapter 8. Subsequently, in Chapter 25, we consider the difficulty of finding an index that is an appropriate proxy for the theoretical market portfolio of risky assets.

otherwise, its size will be meaningless. A large biased sample is no better than a small biased sample. The sample can be generated by completely random selection or by a nonrandom selection technique designed to incorporate the important characteristics of the desired population. Finally, the *source* of the sample is important if there are any differences between segments of the population, in which case samples from each segment are required.

5.2.2 Weighting Sample Members

The second factor is the weight given to each member in the sample. Three principal weighting schemes are used for security-market indexes: (1) a price-weighted index, (2) a market-value-weighted index, and (3) an unweighted index, or what would be described as an equal-weighted index. We will discuss each of these in detail and consider examples of them.

5.2.3 Computational Procedure

The final consideration is the computational procedure used. One alternative is to take a simple arithmetic mean of the various members in the index. Another is to compute an index and have all changes, whether in price or value, reported in terms of the basic index. Finally, some prefer using a geometric mean of the components rather than an arithmetic mean.

5.3 Stock-Market Indexes

As mentioned previously, we hear a lot about what happens to the Dow Jones Industrial Average (DJIA) each day. You might also hear about other stock indexes, such as the S&P 500 index, the NASDAQ composite, or even the Nikkei Average. If you listen carefully, you will realize that these indexes experience different percentage changes (which is the way that the changes should be reported). Reasons for some differences are obvious, such as the DJIA versus the Nikkei Average, but others are not. In this section we briefly review how the major series differ in terms of the characteristics discussed in the prior section, which will help you understand why the percent changes over time for alternative stock indexes *should* differ.

We have organized the discussion of the indexes by the weighting of the sample of stocks. We begin with the price-weighted index because some of the most popular indexes are in this category. The next group is the value-weighted index, which is the technique currently used for most indexes. Finally, we will examine the unweighted indexes.

5.3.1 Price-Weighted Index

A **price-weighted index** is an arithmetic mean of current stock prices, which means that index movements are influenced by the differential prices of the components.

Dow Jones Industrial Averge The best-known price-weighted index is also the oldest and certainly the most popular stock-market index, the Dow Jones Industrial Average (DJIA). The DJIA is a price-weighted average of 30 large, well-known industrial stocks that are generally the leaders in their industry (blue chips). The DJIA is computed by totaling the current prices of the 30 stocks and dividing the sum by a divisor that has been adjusted to take account of stock splits and changes in the sample over time.[3] The divisor is adjusted so the index value will be the same before and after the split. An adjustment of the divisor is demonstrated in Exhibit 5.1. The equation for the index is

$$\text{DJIA}_t = \sum_{i=1}^{30} \frac{P_{it}}{D_{adj}}$$

[3]A complete list of all events that have caused a change in the divisor since the DJIA went to 30 stocks on October 1, 1928, is contained in Phyllis S. Pierce, ed., *The Business One Irwin Investor's Handbook* (Burr Ridge, IL: Dow Jones Books, annual).

Exhibit 5.1 Example of Change in DJIA Divisor When a Sample Stock Splits

Stock	Before Split	After Three-for-One Split by Stock A
	Prices	Prices
A	30	10
B	20	20
C	10	10
	$60 \div 3 = 20$	$40 \div X = 20$ $X = 2$
		(New Divisor)

where:

$$\text{DJIA}_t = \text{the value of the DJIA on day } t$$
$$P_{it} = \text{the closing price of stock } i \text{ on day } t$$
$$D_{adj} = \text{the adjusted divisor on day } t$$

In Exhibit 5.1, we employ three stocks to demonstrate the procedure used to derive a new divisor for the DJIA when a stock splits. When stocks split, the divisor becomes smaller, as shown. The cumulative effect of splits can be derived from the fact that the divisor was originally 30.0, but as of May 23, 2008, it was 0.122820114.

The adjusted divisor ensures that the new value for the index is the same as it would have been without the split. In this case, the presplit index value was 20. Therefore, after the split, given the new sum of prices, the divisor is adjusted downward to maintain this value of 20. The divisor is also changed when there is a change in the sample makeup of the index.

Because the index is price weighted, a high-priced stock carries more weight than a low-priced stock. As shown in Exhibit 5.2, a 10 percent change in a $100 stock ($10) will cause a larger change in the index than a 10 percent change in a $30 stock ($3). For Case A, when the $100 stock increases by 10 percent, the average rises by 5.5 percent; for Case B, when the $30 stock increases by 10 percent, the average rises by only 1.7 percent.

The DJIA has been criticized on several counts. First, the sample used for the index is limited to 30 nonrandomly selected blue-chip stocks that cannot be representative of the thousands of U.S. stocks. Further, the stocks included are large, mature, blue-chip firms rather than typical companies. Several studies have shown that the DJIA has not been as volatile as other market indexes, and its long-run returns are not comparable to other NYSE stock indexes.

In addition, because the DJIA is price weighted, when companies have a stock split, their prices decline and therefore their weight in the DJIA is reduced—even though they may be large and important. Therefore, the weighting scheme causes a downward bias in the DJIA

Exhibit 5.2 Demonstration of the Impact of Differently Priced Shares on a Price-Weighted Index

Stock	Period T	PERIOD T + 1	
		Case A	Case B
A	100	110	100
B	50	50	50
C	30	30	33
Sum	180	190	183
Divisor	3	3	3
Average	60	63.3	61
Percentage change		5.5	1.7

because high-growth stocks will have higher prices and because such stocks tend to split, they will consistently lose weight within the index. For a discussion of specific differences between indexes, see Ip (1998b). Dow Jones also publishes a price-weighted index of 20 stocks in the transportation industry and 15 utility stocks. Detailed reports of the averages are contained daily in the *Wall Street Journal* and weekly in *Barron's,* including hourly figures.

Nikkei–Dow Jones Average Also referred to as the Nikkei Stock Average Index, the Nikkei–Dow Jones Average is an arithmetic mean of prices for 225 stocks on the First Section of the Tokyo Stock Exchange (TSE). This best-known series in Japan shows stock price trends since the reopening of the TSE. Notably, it was formulated by Dow Jones and Company, and, similar to the DJIA, it is a price-weighted index. It is also criticized because the 225 stocks only comprise about 15 percent of all stocks on the First Section. It is reported daily in the *Wall Street Journal* and the *Financial Times* and weekly in *Barron's.*

5.3.2 Value-Weighted Index

A **value-weighted index** is generated by deriving the initial total market value of all stocks used in the index (Market Value = Number of Shares Outstanding (or freely floating shares) × Current Market Price). Prior to 2004, the tradition was to consider all outstanding shares. In mid-2004, Standard & Poor's began only considering "freely floating shares" that exclude shares held by insiders. This initial figure is typically established as the base and assigned an index value (the most popular beginning index value is 100, but it can vary—say, 10, 50). Subsequently, a new market value is computed for all securities in the index, and the current market value is compared to the initial "base" market value to determine the percentage of change, which in turn is applied to the beginning index value.

$$\text{Index}_t = \frac{\sum P_t Q_t}{\sum P_b Q_b} \times \text{Beginning Index Value}$$

where:
$\quad$ Index_t = index value on day t
$\quad\quad$ P_t = ending prices for stocks on day t
$\quad\quad$ Q_t = number of outstanding or freely floating shares on day t
$\quad\quad$ P_b = ending price for stocks on base day
$\quad\quad$ Q_b = number of outstanding or freely floating shares on base day

A simple example for a three-stock index in Exhibit 5.3 indicates that there is an *automatic adjustment* for stock splits and other capital changes with a value-weighted index because the decrease in the stock price is offset by an increase in the number of shares outstanding. In a value-weighted index, the importance of individual stocks in the sample depends on the market value of the stocks. Therefore, a specified percentage change in the value of a large company has a greater impact than a comparable percentage change for a small company. As shown in Exhibit 5.4, if we assume that the only change is a 20 percent increase in the value of stock A, which has a beginning value of $10 million, the ending index value would be $202 million, or an index of 101. In contrast, if only stock C increases by 20 percent from $100 million, the ending value will be $220 million or an index value of 110. The point is, price changes for the large market value stocks in a value-weighted index will dominate changes in the index value over time. Therefore, it is important to be aware of the large-value stocks in the index.

5.3.3 Unweighted Index

In an **unweighted index**, all stocks carry equal weight regardless of their price or market value. A $20 stock is as important as a $40 stock, and the total market value of the company is unimportant. Such an index can be used by individuals who randomly select stock for their portfolio and invest the same dollar amount in each stock. One way to visualize an unweighted index is

---

Exhibit 5.3 Example of a Computation of a Value-Weighted Index

Stock	Share Price	Number of Shares	Market Value
December 31, 2008			
A	$10.00	1,000,000	$ 10,000,000
B	15.00	6,000,000	90,000,000
C	20.00	5,000,000	100,000,000
Total			$200,000,000
			Base Value Equal to an Index of 100
December 31, 2009			
A	$12.00	1,000,000	$ 12,000,000
B	10.00	12,000,000[a]	120,000,000
C	20.00	5,500,000[b]	110,000,000
Total			$242,000,000

$$\text{New Index Value} = \frac{\text{Current Market Value}}{\text{Base Value}} \times \text{Beginning Index Value}$$

$$= \frac{\$242,000,000}{\$200,000,000} \times 100$$

$$= 1.21 \times 100$$

$$= 121$$

[a]Stock split two-for-one during the year.
[b]Company paid a 10 percent stock dividend during the year.

to assume that equal dollar amounts are invested in each stock in the portfolio (for example, an equal $1,000 investment in each stock would work out to 50 shares of a $20 stock, 100 shares of a $10 stock, and 10 shares of a $100 stock). In fact, the actual movements in the index are typically based on *the arithmetic mean of the percent changes in price or value for the stocks in the index.* The use of percentage price changes means that the price level or the market value of the stock does not make a difference—each percentage change has equal weight. This arithmetic mean of percent changes procedure is being used in academic studies when the authors specify equal weighting.

In contrast to computing an arithmetic mean of percentage changes, both Value Line and the *Financial Times* Ordinary Share Index compute a *geometric* mean of the holding period returns and derive the holding period yield from this calculation. Exhibit 5.5, which contains an example of an arithmetic and a geometric mean, demonstrates the downward bias of the geometric calculation. Specifically, the geometric mean of holding period yields (HPY) shows an average change of only 5.3 percent versus the actual change in wealth of 6 percent.

Exhibit 5.4 Demonstration of the Impact of Different Values on a Market-Value-Weighted Stock Index

	DECEMBER 31, 2008			DECEMBER 31, 2009			
				Case A		Case B	
Stock	Number of Shares	Price	Value	Price	Value	Price	Value
A	1,000,000	$10.00	$ 10,000,000	$12.00	$ 12,000,000	$10.00	$ 10,000,000
B	6,000,000	15.00	90,000,000	15.00	90,000,000	15.00	90,000,000
C	5,000,000	20.00	100,000,000	20.00	100,000,000	24.00	120,000,000
			$200,000,000		$202,000,000		$220,000,000
Index Value			100.00		101.00		110.00

Exhibit 5.5 Example of an Arithmetic and Geometric Mean of Percentage Changes

	SHARE PRICE			
Stock	T	T + 1	HPR	HPY
X	10	12	1.20	0.20
Y	22	20	0.91	−0.09
Z	44	47	1.07	0.07

$$\Pi = 1.20 \times 0.91 \times 1.07 \qquad \Sigma = 0.18$$
$$= 1.168 \qquad 0.18/3 = 0.06$$
$$1.168^{1/3} = 1.0531 \qquad = 6\%$$
$$\text{Index Value (T)} \times 1.0531 = \text{Index Value (T + 1)}$$
$$\text{Index Value (T)} \times 1.06 = \text{Index Value (T + 1)}$$

5.3.4 Style Indexes

Financial service firms such as Dow Jones, Moody's, Standard & Poor's, Russell, and Wilshire Associates are generally very fast in responding to changes in investment practices. One example is the growth in popularity of small-cap stocks following academic research in the 1980s that suggested that over long-term periods, small-cap stocks outperformed large-cap stocks on a risk-adjusted basis. In response to this, Ibbotson Associates created the first small-cap stock index, and this was followed by small-cap indexes by Frank Russell Associates (the Russell 2000 index), the Standard & Poor's 600, the Wilshire 1750, and the Dow Jones Small-Cap Index. For a comparative analysis of these indexes, see Reilly and Wright (2002). This led to sets of size indexes, including large-cap, midcap, small-cap, and microcap. These new size indexes were used to evaluate the performance of money managers who concentrated in those size sectors.

The next innovation was for money managers to concentrate in *types* of stocks—that is, *growth* stocks or *value* stocks. We included a designation of these stocks in Chapter 2 in terms of what they are and how they are identified. As this money management innovation evolved, the financial services firms again responded by creating indexes of growth stocks and value stocks based on relative P/E, price–book value, price–cash flow ratios, and other metrics such as return on equity (ROE) and revenue growth rates.

Eventually, these two factors (size and type) were combined into six major style categories:

Small-cap growth   Small-cap value
Midcap growth   Midcap value
Large-cap growth   Large-cap value

Currently, most money managers identify their investment style as one of these, and consultants generally use these categories to identify money managers.

The most recent addition to style indexes are those created to track ethical funds referred to as *socially responsible investment* (SRI) funds. These SRI indexes are further broken down by country and include a global ethical stock index.

The best source for style stock indexes (both size and type of stock) is *Barron's*.

Exhibit 5.6 shows the stock market indexes from the *Wall Street Journal,* which contains values for many of the U.S. stock indexes we have discussed. Exhibit 5.7 shows a table for numerous international stock indexes contained in the *Wall Street Journal.*

5.3.5 Global Equity Indexes

As shown in Exhibits 5.7 and 5A.2 (the latter is in this chapter's appendix), there are stock-market indexes available for most individual foreign markets. While these local indexes are closely followed within each country, a problem arises in comparing the results implied by these indexes to one another because of a lack of consistency among them in sample selection,

Exhibit 5.6 U.S. Stock Market Indexes

Major U.S. Stock Market Indexes

	High	Low	Close	Net chg	% chg	Low	Close (●)	High	% chg	YTD	3–yr. ann.
Dow Jones											
Industrial Average	12622.07	12196.87	12216.40	−144.92	−1.17	11740.15		14164.53	−1.1	−7.9	5.2
Transportation Avg	4932.57	4707.17	4754.10	46.45	0.99	4140.29		5446.49	−1.2	4.0	8.3
Utility Average	483.19	472.24	473.43	−4.29	−0.90	473.43		552.74	−5.3	−11.1	10.1
Wishire 5000	13665.15	13232.07	13225.14	−81.28	−0.61	12822.54		15806.69	−8.0	−10.6	4.6
Barron's 400	286.25	275.71	277.58	1.87	0.68	268.14		350.95	−11.1	−12.0	5.7
Nasdaq Stock Market											
Nasdaq Composite	2346.78	2256.87	2261.18	3.07	0.14	2169.34		2859.12	−6.6	−14.7	4.3
Nasdaq 100	1831.98	1760.14	1767.57	15.58	0.89	1673.03		2238.98	−0.3	−15.2	6.3
Standard & Poor's											
500 Index	1359.68	1312.95	1315.22	−14.29	−1.07	1273.37		1565.15	−7.4	−10.4	3.9
MidCap 400	797.34	769.84	772.48	2.63	0.34	744.89		926.23	−9.0	−10.0	5.6
SmallCap 600	374.59	361.53	361.96	−0.33	−0.09	344.69		445.19	−12.1	−8.4	4.0
Other Indexes											
Russell 2000	705.99	682.48	683.18	1.76	0.26	643.97		855.77	−14.7	−10.8	3.6
NYSE Composite	8958.16	8717.54	8762.12	44.56	0.51	8489.38		10311.61	−5.4	−10.0	7.1
Value Line	401.74	387.19	387.62	0.14	0.04	372.77		508.42	−17.8	−12.0	0.2
Amex Biotech	741.05	695.65	719.19	23.54	3.38	667.21		849.84	−5.9	−8.6	12.9
Amex Pharmaceutical	301.93	297.25	297.66	−0.90	−0.30	289.54		372.37	−13.0	−12.1	−1.8
KBW Bank	89.54	78.52	78.66	−7.19	−8.38	75.31		118.17	−30.9	−11.2	−6.3
PHLX§ Gold/Silver	184.98	170.75	180.27	8.26	4.80	125.64		206.37	31.6	4.0	24.9
PHLX§ Oil Service	283.19	258.66	−276.50	17.76		214.63		312.20	28.8	−8.3	26.3
PHLX§ Semiconductor	356.55	338.79	339.28	−0.61	−0.18	334.93		546.59	−27.1	−16.9	−6.5
CBOE Volatility	27.04	24.75	25.71	−0.91	−3.42	11.98		32.24	75.6	14.3	23.2

Header spans: LATEST WEEK (High, Low, Close, Net chg, % chg); 52-WEEK RANGE (Low, Close ●, High, % chg); % CHG (YTD, 3–yr. ann.)

§Philadelphia Stock Exchange

Source: From the *Wall Street Journal*, March 31, 2008, p. C4. Copyright 2008 DOW JONES & Co., Inc.

weighting, or computational procedure. To solve these comparability problems, several investment data firms have computed a set of consistent country stock indexes. As a result, these indexes can be directly compared and combined to create various regional indexes (for example, Pacific Basin). We will describe the three major sets of global equity indexes.

FT/S&P-Actuaries World Indexes The FT/S&P-Actuaries World Indexes are jointly compiled by the Financial Times Limited, Goldman Sachs & Company, and Standard & Poor's (the "compilers") in conjunction with the Institute of Actuaries and the Faculty of Actuaries. Approximately 2,500 equity securities in 30 countries are measured, covering at least 70 percent of the total value of all listed companies in each country. All securities included must allow direct holdings of shares by foreign nationals.

The indexes are market value weighted and have a base date of December 31, 1986 = 100. The index results are typically reported in U.S. dollars, but, on occasion, have been reported in U.K. pound sterling, Japanese yen, euros, and the local currency of the country. In addition to the individual countries and the world index, there are several geographic subgroups, subgroups by market value, and by industry sectors as shown in Exhibit 5.8.

Morgan Stanley Capital International (MSCI) Indexes The Morgan Stanley Capital International Indexes consist of three international, 22 national, and 38 international industry indexes. The indexes consider some 1,673 companies listed on stock exchanges in 22 countries, with a combined market capitalization that represents approximately 60 percent of the aggregate market value of the stock exchanges of these countries. All the indexes are market

Exhibit 5.7 International Stock Market Indexes

International Stock Indexes

Region/Country	Index	Close (LATEST WEEK)	% chg	Low (52-WEEK RANGE)	Close (●)	High	YTD % chg
World	**DJ World Index**	272.83	2.36	261.44	▪▪▪▪▪▪	320.33	−9.3
	DJ World ex U.S.	248.69	4.74	231.73	▪▪▪▪▪▪	291.11	−8.5
	MSCI EAFE*	2045.44	4.75	1913.54	▪▪▪▪▪▪	2388.74	−9.2
DJ Wilshire	**Global**	2796.36	2.58	2676.75	▪▪▪▪▪▪	3295.00	−9.8
	Global ex U.S.	2505.26	4.91	2353.27	▪▪▪▪▪▪	2948.89	−9.4
	Global Dev. ex U.S.	2388.58	4.75	2228.75	▪▪▪▪▪▪	2807.20	−8.7
	Global Small-Cap	3204.22	3.34	3031.44	▪▪▪▪▪▪	3867.76	−9.7
	Global Large-Cap	2720.55	2.49	2603.93	▪▪▪▪▪▪	3193.26	−9.8
Americas	**DJ Americas**	340.11	−0.15	330.40	▪▪▪▪▪▪	399.86	−9.8
Brazil	Sao Paulo Bovespa	60452.12	2.48	45597.48	▪▪▪▪▪▪	65790.80	−5.4
Canada	S&P/TSX Comp	13233.79	3.59	12132.13	▪▪▪▪▪▪	14625.76	−4.3
Mexico	IPC All-Share	30089.90	3.50	25284.88	▪▪▪▪▪▪	32836.12	1.9
Venezuela	Caracas General	35260.63	−0.11	34172.43	▪▪▪▪▪▪	50333.34	−7.0
Europe	**DJ Stoxx 600**	306.69	3.32	290.06	▪▪▪▪▪▪	400.31	−15.9
	DJ Stoxx 50	3029.86	3.01	2873.33	▪▪▪▪▪▪	3998.93	−17.8
Euro zone	DJ Euro Stoxx	347.74	4.02	328.12	▪▪▪▪▪▪	442.87	−16.2
	DJ Euro Stoxx 50	3641.05	3.85	3431.82	▪▪▪▪▪▪	4557.57	−17.2
Belgium	Bel-20	3700.41	2.14	3460.00	▪▪▪▪▪▪	4756.82	−10.3
France	CAC 40	4695.92	3.58	4431.04	▪▪▪▪▪▪	6168.15	−16.4
Germany	DAX	6559.90	3.80	6182.30	▪▪▪▪▪▪	8106	−18.7
Israel	Tel Aviv	1022.99	3.00	964.38	▪▪▪▪▪▪	1237.13	−15.9
Italy	S&P/MIB	31696	4.36	30371	▪▪▪▪▪▪	44364	−17.8
Netherlands	AEX	440.99	3.57	415.92	▪▪▪▪▪▪	561.90	−14.5
Russia	DJ Russia Titans 10	6549.33	3.44	6035.72	▪▪▪▪▪▪	7920.96	−14.6
Spain	IBEX 35	13442.4	3.69	12254.6	▪▪▪▪▪▪	15945.7	−11.5
Sweden	SX All Share	312.49		293.53	▪▪▪▪▪▪	427.24	−11.2
Switzerland	Swiss Market	7239.35	3.27	6774.26	▪▪▪▪▪▪	9531.46	−14.7
U.K.	FTSE 100	5692.9	3.60	5414.4	▪▪▪▪▪▪	6732.4	−11.8
Asia-Pacific	**DJ Asia-Pacific**	145.42	3.51	133.78	▪▪▪▪▪▪	172.49	−8.0
Australia	S&P/ASX 200	5351.1	4.36	5086.1	▪▪▪▪▪▪	6828.7	−15.6
China	DJ CBN China 600	30995.33	−3.13	22152.43	▪▪▪▪▪▪	44631.83	−25.2
Hong Kong	Hang Seng	25285.95		19800.93	▪▪▪▪▪▪	31638.22	−16.3
India	Bombay Sensex	16371.29		12455.37	▪▪▪▪▪▪	20873.33	−19.3
Japan	Nikkei Stock Avg	12820.47	2.71	11787.51	▪▪▪▪▪▪	18261.98	−16.2
Singapore	Straits Times	3031.90		2792.75	▪▪▪▪▪▪	3831.19	−12.5
South Korea	Kospi	1701.83	3.41	1452.55	▪▪▪▪▪▪	2064.85	−10.3
Taiwan	Weighted	8623.48	1.16	7408.40	▪▪▪▪▪▪	9809.88	1.4

*Europe, Australia, Far East, U.S.-dollar terms

Source: WSJ Market Data Group

Source: From the *Wall Street Journal*, March 31, 2008, p. C4. Copyright 2008 by DOW JONES & Co., Inc.

value weighted. Exhibit 5.9 contains the countries included, the percent weights based on GDP, the number of stocks, the market values for stocks, and the market value weights in the EAFE and world indexes.

In addition, the following relative valuation information is available: (1) price-to-book value (P/BV) ratio, (2) price-to-cash earnings (earnings plus depreciation) (P/CE) ratio, (3) price-to-earnings (P/E) ratio, and (4) dividend yield (YLD). These ratios help in analyzing different valuation levels among countries and over time for specific countries.

Notably, the Morgan Stanley group index for Europe, Australia, and the Far East (EAFE) is the basis for futures and options contracts on the Chicago Mercantile Exchange and the Chicago Board Options Exchange.

Exhibit 5.8 Financial Taxes Global Equity Index Series

FTSE GLOBAL EQUITY INDEX SERIES

Mar 17

Countries & regions	No of Stock	US $ Index	Day %	Mth %	YTD %	Total retn	YTD %	Gross Div Yield
FTSE Global All-Cap	7852	381.63	−2.4	−4.8	−13.6	426.22	−13.2	2.7
FTSE Global Large Cap	1224	355.10	−2.3	−4.6	−13.7	399.82	−13.2	2.8
FTSE Global Mid Cap	1636	451.33	−2.6	−5.1	−13.3	495.67	−13.0	2.3
FTSE Global Small Cap	4992	459.01	−2.7	−5.4	−13.6	499.92	−13.4	2.0
FTSE All-World Large/Mid (Cap)	2860	227.80	−2.4	−4.7	−13.6	266.59	−13.2	2.7
FTSE World (Large/Mid/Cap)	2437	398.79	−2.2	−4.4	−13.2	626.30	−12.8	2.8
FTSE Global All Cap ex-UK	7395	383.54	−2.1	−4.8	−13.4	425.33	−13.1	2.5
FTSE Global All Cap ex USA	5495	473.81	−3.3	−4.0	−13.9	540.61	−13.5	3.1
FTSE Global All Cap ex JAPAN	6532	385.94	−2.6	−4.8	−13.9	433.24	−13.5	2.7
FTSE Global All Cap ex Eurobloc	7010	366.94	−2.3	−5.5	−13.5	406.93	−13.1	2.5
FTSE All-World Developed	1995	353.25	−2.1	−4.4	−13.4	395.38	−13.0	2.8
FTSE Developed All-Cap	6124	362.51	−2.2	−4.4	−13.3	404.33	−12.9	2.7
FTSE Developed Large Cap	836	335.54	−2.1	−4.3	−13.5	377.48	−13.1	2.9
FTSE Developed Europe Large Cap	229	405.41	−3.5	−1.8	−14.4	476.25	−13.9	4.0
FTSE Developed Europe Mid Cap	289	522.14	−3.5	−1.4	−11.7	593.93	−11.5	3.0
FTSE Dev Europe. Small Cap	1094	614.16	−3	−0.9	−10.6	693.77	−10.4	2.7
FTSE All-World Developed Europe	518	264.37	−3.5	−1.7	−14.0	327.42	−13.6	3.8
FTSE North America Large Cap	306	291.04	−1	−5.4	−12.6	321.11	−13.2	2.2
FTSE North America Mid Cap	419	385.21	−2.1	−6.8	−13.8	414.77	−13.0	1.8
FTSE North America Small Cap	1879	388.54	−2.4	−6.8	−13.4	415.23	−13.4	1.5
FTSE All-World North America	725	190.35	−1.2	−5.4	−12.8	216.78	−13.2	2.2
FTSE All-World Dev ex North Am	1270	250.41	−3.1	−3.3	−14.0	302.51	−12.8	3.5
FTSE Japan Large Cap	170	327.09	−0.7	−5.4	−11.0	346.01	−11.0	1.9
FTSE Japan Mid Cap	304	372.85	0.3	−1.7	−8.0	393.09	−8.0	1.7
FTSE Japan Small Cap	849	377.92	0.9	−0.6	−8.6	402.80	−8.5	1.9
FTSE Japan (Large/Mid/Cap)	471	128.70	0.5	−4.7	−10.5	153.91	−10.4	1.8
FTSE Asia Pacific Large Cap ex Japan	352	549.29	−4.4	−11.7	−20.4	644.94	−19.8	3.2
FTSE Asia Pacific Large Cap ex Japan	450	659.12	−4.3	−10.8	−19.3	762.48	−18.9	2.8
FTSE Asia Pacific Small Cap ex Japan	1000	581.25	−5	−11.8	−23.5	666.68	−23.2	2.7
FTSE All-World Asia Pacific Ex Japan	802	425.78	−4.4	−11.6	−20.2	532.99	−19.7	3.1
FTSE All Emerging All-Cap	1728	731.65	−4.3	−7.5	−16.0	836.54	−15.6	2.3
FTSE All Emerging Large Cap	388	735.82	−4.2	−7.1	−15.1	842.59	−14.7	2.3
FTSE All Emerging Mid Cap	477	731.54	−4	−7.9	−16.4	839.44	−16.1	2.8
FTSE All Emerging Small Cap	863	697.17	−4.8	−10.0	−21.3	785.70	−21.1	1.8
FTSE All-World All Emerging Europe	67	721.96	−3.6	−1.8	−15.2	834.64	−15.2	1.9
FTSE Latin Americas All-Cap	200	1358.07	−3.3	−0.5	−3.6	1594.48	−3.3	2.2
FTSE Middle East Africa All-Cap	193	666.18	−5	−1.9	−11.8	778.38	−11.4	3.0
FTSE UK All Cap	457	−362.27	−5.1	−4.5	−15.2	432.56	−14.3	4.0
FTSE USA All Cap	2357	304.91	−1.2	−5.9	−13.2	333.59	−12.8	2.1
FTSE Europe All Cap	1733	450.68	−3.5	−1.6	−13.7	523.88	−13.3	3.6
FTSE Euronloc All Cap	842	487.87	−2.7	−0.8	−14.1	564.94	−13.9	3.7
FTSE All-World Sector Indices								
Oil & Gas	126	499.09	−3.4	−1.1	−11.2	604.67	−10.8	2.2
Oil & Gas Producers	98	458.09	−3.3	−1.1	−11.1	557.94	−10.7	2.4
Oil Equipment & Services	28	473.61	−4	−1.0	−12.1	558.74	−11.9	0.9

Countries & regions	No of Stock	US $ Index	Day %	Mth %	YTD %	Total retn	YTD %	Gross Div Yield
Basic Materials	2.57	615.39	−3.7	−0.6	−4.9	738.92	−4.6	2.1
Chemicals	105	473.77	−1.8	−1.5	−8.4	566.72	−8.2	2.2
Forestry & Paper	20	238.47	−.5	−5.9	−17.8	299.26	−17.5	4.3
Industrial Metals	85	899.54	−3.5	−1.9	−4.4	1080.62	−4.0	2.7
Mining	47	1364.05	−5.8	−1.1	−0.5	1635.11	0.0	1.1
Industrials	483	249.77	−2.3	−4.5	−12.7	287.28	−12.4	2.3
Construction & Materials	104	485.62	−3.3	−5.6	−16.3	575.85	−16.0	2.4
Aerospace & Defence	24	316.17	−1.4	−4.5	−10.5	363.39	−10.6	1.8
General Industrials	50	197.58	−0.2	−2.5	−10.2	234.97	−9.6	3.0
Electronic & Electrical Equipment	75	216.16	−5.5	−8.1	−21.6	240.66	−21.1	1.8
Industrial Engineering	82	529.82	−2.3	−1.5	−12.9	609.91	−12.7	2.0
Industrial Transportation	88	392.71	−1.7	−6.4	−7.0	450.23	−6.8	2.3
Support Services	59	191.60	−2.2	−4.2	−8.5	213.33	−8.3	2.1
Consumer Goods	353	273.59	−1.6	−2.1	−10.4	317.84	−10.0	2.4
Automobiles & Parts	77	263.33	−1.5	−6.3	−14.6	306.15	−14.5	2.4
Beverages	40	306.09	−0.2	−2.3	−7.9	359.70	−7.4	2.3
Food Producers	84	386.89	−1.7	2.9	−5.9	459.47	−5.7	2.4
Household Goods	49	262.90	−1.1	−2.9	−11.5	303.01	−11.5	2.3
Leisure Goods	30	242.45	−2	−2.8	−15.4	270.25	−15.3	1.5
Personal Goods	60	334.15	−2	−1.2	−10.4	383.36	−10.5	2.1
Tobacco	13	628.19	−2.8	−2.9	−8.5	877.17	−7.3	3.6
Health Care	139	217.53	−0.8	−6.3	−12.0	251.10	−11.3	2.3
Health Care Equipment & Services	59	299.62	−1.6	−11.5	−16.4	315.79	−16.3	0.6
Pharmaceuticals & Biotechnology	80	166.71	−0.3	−4.4	−10.4	193.36	−9.5	2.9
Consumer Services	369	202.79	−1.8	−6.4	−12.2	224.26	−12.0	2.1
Food & Drug Retailers	44	206.46	−2	−4.4	−13.3	231.62	−13.1	1.8
General Retailers	110	240.10	−1.6	−5.6	−11.4	263.01	−11.1	2.0
Media	100	142.06	−1.7	−7.2	−12.4	156.49	−12.2	2.1
Travel & Leisure	109	219.02	−2.2	−7.0	−12.4	244.68	−12.0	2.3
Telecommunications	115	170.14	−1.3	−7.7	−16.7	207.13	−16.4	4.0
Fixed Line Telecommunications	69	156.97	−0.4	−5.8	−14.3	195.08	−14.0	4.9
Mobile Telecommunications	46	162.95	−2.7	−10.8	−20.3	194.05	−20.2	2.1
Utilities	145	341.84	−1	−2.6	−9.2	447.33	−8.9	3.2
Electricity	98	355.22	−0.9	−3.1	−8.9	466.95	−8.4	3.2
Gas, Water & Multiutilities	47	392.22	−1.2	−1.7	−9.8	510.30	−9.6	3.3
Financials	666	228.32	−3.5	−8.3	−19.3	279.81	−18.8	4.3
Banks	271	246.80	−3.5	−7.9	−18.7	315.93	−17.9	5.3
Nonlife Insurance	69	185.24	−2.3	−5.3	−16.2	209.26	−16.0	2.8
Life Insurance	41	218.54	−3.3	−3.7	−19.2	264.54	−19.0	3.5
Real Estate	130	345.63	−3.1	−10.2	−17.6	447.32	−17.1	3.8
General Financial	148	187.84	−5	−13.7	−25.2	211.85	−24.9	2.6
Equity Investment Instruments	7	280.78	−3.3	−7.4	−13.4	351.62	−12.4	4.7
Technology	207	96.10	−1.2	−3.5	−16.7	101.38	−16.6	1.3
Software & Computer Services	66	137.35	−1	−4.4	−16.8	143.75	−16.6	0.9
Technology Hardware & Equipment	141	82.63	−1.3	−3.2	−16.7	87.52	−16.5	1.5

The FTSE Global Equity Index Series, launched in 2003, contains the FTSE Global Small Cap Indices and broader FTSE Global All Cap Indices (Large/Mid/Small cap) as, well as the enhanced FTSE All-World Index Series (large/mid cap) - please see www.ftse.com/gels. As of January 2nd 2006, FTSE is basing its sector indices on the industrial Classification Benchmark - please see www.ftse.com/icb. For constituent changes and other information about FTSE, please see www.ftse.com. © FTSE International Limited 2008, All rights reserved. "FTSE", "FT-SE" and "Footsie" are trade marks of the London Stock Exchange and The Financial Times and are used by FTSE International under license.

Source: From the *Financial Times*, March 19, 2008, p. 23.

Dow Jones World Stock Index

In January 1993, Dow Jones introduced its World Stock Index. Composed of more than 2,200 companies worldwide and organized into 120 industry groups, the index includes 32 countries representing more than 80 percent of the combined capitalization of these countries. In addition to the 32 individual countries shown in Exhibit 5.10, the countries are grouped into five regions: Americas, Europe, South Africa, Pacific, and Nordic. Finally, each country's index is calculated in its own currency as well as in U.S. dollars. The index for the individual countries is reported daily in the *Wall Street Journal* (domestic) and in the *Wall Street Journal Europe.* It is published weekly in *Barron's.*

Comparison of World Stock Indexes

As shown in Exhibit 5.11, the correlations between the three series since December 31, 1991, when the DJ series became available, indicate that the results with the various world stock indexes are quite comparable.

A summary of the characteristics of the major price-weighted, market-value-weighted, and equal-weighted stock price indexes for the United States and major foreign countries is contained in Exhibit 5A.1 in the chapter appendix. As shown, the major differences are the number of stocks in alternative indexes, but more important is the *source* of the sample (e.g.,

Exhibit 5.9 Market Coverage of Morgan Stanley Capital International Indexes as of November 30, 2004

| | GDP WEIGHTS[a] | | | WEIGHT AS PERCENT OF INDEX | |
	Percent EAFE	Companies in Index	Market Cap. U.S. $ Billion	EAFE	World
Austria	1.8	13	69.6	0.3	0.1
Belgium	2.3	20	239.5	1.3	0.5
Denmark	3.4	20	137.8	0.8	0.3
Finland	2.0	19	198.2	1.8	0.6
France	10.7	57	1,412.7	9.4	3.9
Germany	14.8	47	1,056.1	6.8	2.8
Greece	1.1	20	109.9	0.5	0.2
Ireland	1.0	15	93.9	0.8	0.3
Italy	9.6	41	606.7	4.0	1.6
The Netherlands	3.2	26	508.9	4.8	1.9
Norway	1.6	14	133.0	0.6	0.2
Portugal	0.9	10	67.2	0.4	0.1
Spain	5.3	31	774.7	3.8	1.5
Sweden	1.9	44	353.6	2.5	1.0
Switzerland	1.8	35	707.0	6.9	2.8
United Kingdom	10.8	121	2,560.0	25.2	10.3
Europe	69.1	563	9,118.0	69.5	28.5
Australia	3.5	72	675.0	5.4	2.2
Hong Kong	1.0	37	402.5	1.7	0.7
Japan	25.4	344	3,492.2	22.3	9.1
New Zealand	0.5	16	25.8	0.2	0.1
Singapore	0.6	35	169.0	0.6	0.3
Pacific	30.9	504	4,764.4	30.5	12.5
Pacific ex Japan	5.6	160	1,272.2	6.2	3.4
EAFE	100.0	1,067	13,002.4	100.0	40.9
Canada	—	90	1,083.7	—	2.9
United States	—	51.6	14,816.4	—	51.3
The World Index	—	1,673	29,782.5	—	100.0
EMU	51.5	299	5,217.8	—	13.6
Europe ex UK	58.2	412	6,549.2	—	18.1
Far East	27.0	416	4,062.7	24.8	10.2
North America	—	606	15,900.1	—	54.1
Kokusai Index (World ex Japan)	—	1,329	29,453.7	—	90.9

[a]GDP weight figures represent the initial weights applicable for the first month. They are used exclusively in the MSCI "GDP weighted" indexes.
Source: MSCI. Reprinted with permission.

stocks from the NYSE, NASDAQ, all U.S. stocks, or stocks from a foreign country such as the United Kingdom or Japan).

5.4 Bond-Market Indexes[4]

Investors know little about the growing number of bond-market indexes currently available because these indexes are relatively new and not widely published. Knowledge regarding these indexes is important because of the growth of fixed-income money managers and mutual funds and the consequent need to have a reliable set of benchmarks to use in evaluating their performance. Also, because the performance of many fixed-income money managers has been unable to match that of the aggregate bond market, interest has been growing in bond-index funds, which requires the development of an index to emulate as discussed by Dialynas (2001) and Volpert (2005).

[4]The discussion in this section draws heavily from Reilly and Wright (2005).

Exhibit 5.10 Dow Jones Global Indexes

DOW JONES GLOBAL INDEXES										
Region/ Country	DJ Global Indexes, Local Curr. 02/29/08	Wkly % Chg.		DJ Global Indexes, U.S. $ 02/29/08	Wkly % Chg.		DJ Global Indexes, U.S. $ on 12/31/07	Pont Chg. From 12/31/07		% Chg. From 12/31/07
Americas				**346.74**	—	**1.14**	**376.93**	—	**30.19**	— **8.01**
Brazil	8011287.02	—	1.08	1875.73	+	0.25	1826.35	+	49.38	+ 2.70
Canada	452.34	—	1.11	533.56	—	0.36	541.71	—	8.15	— 1.50
Chile	602.20	—	2.31	495.92	—	0.17	484.00	+	11.93	+ 2.46
Mexico	1958.05	—	2.24	560.38	—	1.64	555.82	+	4.56	+ 0.82
U.S.	324.53	—	1.64	324.53	—	1.64	357.48	—	32.95	— 9.22
Latin America				**821.59**	—	**0.30**	**804.38**	+	**17.22**	+ **2.14**
Europe				**350.74**	+	**2.14**	**385.74**	—	**35.00**	— **9.07**
Austria	357.48	—	0.66	422.70	+	1.79	469.46	—	46.76	— 9.96
Belguim	362.68	+	1.63	429.07	+	4.14	449.48	—	20.41	— 4.54
Denmark	481.89	—	0.44	580.99	+	2.10	607.52	—	26.53	— 4.37
Finland	1521.24	—	0.77	1608.79	+	1.68	1691.70	—	82.91	— 4.90
France	303.06	—	0.58	363.22	+	1.88	406.94	—	43.72	— 10.74
Germany	294.93	—	1.00	347.64	+	1.45	398.19	—	50.55	— 12.70
Greece	358.74	—	5.13	313.11	—	2.78	381.50	—	68.39	— 17.93
Ireland	437.99	+	0.03	505.94	+	2.51	532.05	—	26.10	— 4.91
Italy	265.53	+	0.40	257.96	+	2.88	286.20	—	28.24	— 9.87
Netherlands	343.85	—	0.14	405.52	+	2.33	448.92	—	43.40	— 9.67
Norway	409.18	+	0.37	469.15	+	2.45	521.31	—	52.16	— 10.01
Portugal	284.61	+	0.37	292.18	+	2.85	338.31	—	43.13	— 13.64
Spain	502.29	+	1.15	446.42	+	3.65	497.01	—	50.59	— 10.18
Sweden	523.63	+	2.03	500.56	+	4.11	526.68	—	26.12	— 4.96
Switzerland	450.28	+	0.90	585.14	+	4.99	606.25	—	21.11	— 3.48
United Kingdom	249.03	—	0.03	264.97	+	1.11	290.11	—	25.14	— 8.67
South Africa				**323.49**	+	**3.38**	**359.46**	—	**35.97**	+ **10.01**
Pacific Region				**149.90**	+	**2.73**	**158.10**	—	**8.20**	— **5.19**
Australia	378.77	+	0.26	466.18	+	1.99	500.10	—	33.92	— 6.78
Hong Kong	475.94	+	3.02	475.73	+	3.25	546.49	+	70.75	— 12.95
Indonesia	841.59	—	0.87	184.94	+	0.31	179.43	+	5.51	+ 3.07
Japan	87.46	+	0.16	104.84	+	2.90	108.94	—	4.10	— 3.76
Malaysia	261.23	—	0.52	222.51	+	0.18	229.71	—	7.20	— 3.14
New Zealand	160.70	—	1.35	238.28	—	1.82	261.90	—	23.62	— 9.02
Philippines	299.71	+	1.54	192.38	+	1.99	218.92	—	26.54	— 12.13
Singapore	248.59	—	1.16	288.90	—	0.31	318.97	—	30.07	— 9.43
South Korea	358.08	+	1.51	289.10	+	2.54	322.13	—	33.03	+ 10.25
Taiwan	207.38	+	3.58	172.89	+	4.92	165.93	+	6.96	+ 4.20
Thailand	159.38	+	2.29	119.43	+	4.97	112.92	+	6.52	+ 5.77
Euro Zone				**368.67**	+	**2.09**	**412.42**	—	**43.74**	— **10.61**
Europe (ex. U.K.)				**400.87**	+	**2.61**	**441.77**	—	**40.89**	— **9.26**
Nordic Region				**636.76**	+	**2.74**	**678.26**	—	**41.44**	— **6.11**
Pacific Region (ex. Japan)				**368.06**	+	**2.54**	**394.34**	—	**26.28**	— **6.66**
World (ex. U.S.)				**253.41**	+	**2.31**	**271.84**	—	**18.43**	— **6.78**
DOW JONES WORLD STOCK INDEX				**277.38**	+	**0.63**	**300.88**	—	**23.50**	— **7.81**

Indexes based on 12/31/91 = 100

Source: From *Barron's* March 3, 2008, p. M43. Copyright 2008 by DOW JONES & Co., Inc.

Notably, it is more difficult to create and compute a bond-market index than a stock-market index for several reasons. First, the universe of bonds is much broader than that of stocks, ranging from U.S. Treasury securities to bonds in default. Second, the universe of bonds is changing constantly because of new issues, bond maturities, calls, and bond sinking funds. Third, the volatility of prices for individual bonds and bond portfolios changes because bond price volatility is affected by duration, which is likewise changing constantly because of changes in maturity, coupon, and market yield (see Chapter 17). Finally, significant problems can arise in correctly pricing the individual bond issues in an index (especially corporate and mortgage

Exhibit 5.11 Correlations of Percentage Price Changes of Alternative World Stock Indexes 12/31/91–12/31/07

	U.S. Dollars
Financial Times/S&P-Morgan Stanley Capital International	.996
Financial Times/S&P-Dow Jones	.995
Morgan Stanley Capital International-Dow Jones	.993

bonds) compared to the current and continuous transactions prices available for most stocks used in stock indexes.

Our subsequent discussion is divided into the following three subsections: (1) U.S. investment-grade bond indexes, including Treasuries; (2) U.S. high-yield bond indexes; and (3) global government bond indexes. All of these indexes indicate total rates of return for the portfolio of bonds and are market value weighted. Exhibit 5.12 is a summary of the characteristics for the indexes available for these three segments of the bond market.

5.4.1 U.S. Investment-Grade Bond Indexes

As shown in Exhibit 5.12, four investment firms have created and maintain indexes for Treasury bonds and other bonds considered investment grade, that is, the bonds are rated Bbb or higher. As demonstrated in a subsequent section, the relationship among the returns for these investment-grade bonds is strong (that is, correlations average about 0.95), regardless of the segment of the market.

5.4.2 High-Yield Bond Indexes

One of the fastest-growing segments of the U.S. bond market during the past 25 years has been the high-yield bond market, which includes bonds that are not investment grade—that is, they are rated Bb, B, Ccc, Cc, and C. Because of this growth, four investment firms created indexes related to this market. A summary of the characteristics for these indexes is included in Exhibit 5.13. For an analysis of the alternative high-yield bond benchmarks, see Reilly and Wright (1994); for an overall analysis of this market, see Reilly and Wright (2001).

5.4.3 Global Government Bond Indexes

The global bond market has experienced significant growth in size and importance during the past 15 years. Notably, this global bond segment is completely dominated by government bonds because few non-U.S. countries have a viable corporate bond market. Once again, several major investment firms have created indexes that reflect the performance for the global bond market. As shown in Exhibit 5.12, although the various indexes have similar computational characteristics, the total sample sizes and the numbers of countries included differ.

5.5 Composite Stock-Bond Indexes

Beyond separate stock indexes and bond indexes for individual countries, a natural step is the development of a composite index that measures the performance of all securities in a given country. With a composite index investors can examine the benefits of diversifying with a combination of asset classes such as stocks and bonds in addition to diversifying within the asset classes of stocks or bonds. There are two such indexes available.

First, a market-value-weighted index called Merrill Lynch–Wilshire Capital Markets Index (ML–WCMI) measures the total return performance of the combined U.S. taxable

Exhibit 5.12 Summary of Bond-Market Indexes

Name of Index	Number of Issues	Maturity	Size of Issues	Weighting	Pricing	Reinvestment Assumption	Subindexes Available
U.S. Investment-Grade Bond Indexes							
Lehman Brothers	5,000+	Over 1 year	Over $100 million	Market value	Trader priced and model priced	No	Government, gov./corp., corporate mortgage-backed, asset-backed
Merrill Lynch	5,000+	Over 1 year	Over $50 million	Market value	Trader priced and model priced	In specific bonds	Government, gov./corp., corporate, mortgage
Ryan Treasury	300+	Over 1 year	All Treasury	Market value and equal	Market priced	In specific bonds	Treasury
Smith Barney	5,000+	Over 1 year	Over $50 million	Market value	Trader priced	In one-month T-bill	Treas.-agency, broad inv. grade, corporate, mortgage
U.S. High-Yield Bond Indexes							
C. S. First Boston	423	All maturities	Over $75 million	Market value	Trader priced	Yes	Composite and by rating
Lehman Brothers	624	Over 1 year	Over $100 million	Market value	Trader priced	No	Composite and by rating
Merrill Lynch	735	Over 1 year	Over $25 million	Market value	Trader priced	Yes	Composite and by rating
Smith Barney	299	Over 7 years	Over $50 million	Market value	Trader priced	Yes	Composite and by rating

(continued)

Exhibit 5.12 (continued)

Global Government Bond Indexes

Lehman Brothers	800	Over 1 year	Over $200 million	Market value	Trader priced	Yes	Composite and 13 countries, local and U.S. dollars
Merrill Lynch	9,736	Over 1 year	Over $50 million	Market value	Trader priced	Yes	Composite and 9 countries, local and U.S. dollars
J. P. Morgan	445	Over 1 year	Over $100 million	Market value	Trader priced	Yes in index	Composite and 11 countries, local and U.S. dollars
Smith Barney	400	Over 1 year	Over $250 million	Market value	Trader priced	Yes at local short-term rate	Composite and 14 countries, local and U.S. dollars

Source: Frank K. Reilly, Wenchi Kao, and David J. Wright, "Alternative Bond Market Indexes," *Financial Analysts Journal* 48, no. 3 (May–June, 1992): 14–58; Frank K. Reilly and David J. Wright, "An Analysis of High-Yield Bond Benchmarks," *Journal of Fixed Income* 3, no. 4 (March 1994): 6–24; and Frank K. Reilly and David J. Wright, "Global Bond Markets: Alternative Benchmarks and Risk-Return Performance," presented at Midwest Finance Association Meeting, Chicago, IL, March 2000.

fixed-income and equity markets. It is basically a combination of the Merrill Lynch fixed-income indexes and the Dow Jones Wilshire 5000 common-stock index. As such, it tracks more than 10,000 U.S. stocks and bonds and, as of March 2008, the relative weights are about 40 percent bonds and 60 percent stocks.

The second composite index is the Brinson Partner Global Security Market Index (GSMI), which contains U.S. stocks and bonds as well as non-U.S. equities and nondollar bonds along with an allocation to cash. The specific breakdown as of February 2008 was U.S. equities, 40 percent; non-U.S. equities, 25 percent; U.S. bonds, 24 percent; and non-U.S. bonds, 11 percent.

Although related to the relative market values of these asset classes, the weights specified were derived using optimization techniques to identify the portfolio mix of available global asset classes that matches the risk level of a typical U.S. pension plan. The index is balanced to the policy weights monthly.

Because the GSMI contains both U.S. and international stocks and bonds, it is clearly the most diversified benchmark available with a weighting scheme that approaches market values. As such, it is closest to the theoretically specified "market portfolio of risky assets" referred to in the CAPM literature. It is used in Reilly and Akhtar (1995) to demonstrate the impact of alternative benchmarks when evaluating global portfolio performance.

5.6 Comparison of Indexes over Time

We now look at price movements in the different indexes for monthly intervals.

5.6.1 Correlations between Monthly Equity Price Changes

Exhibit 5.13 contains a listing of the correlation coefficients of the monthly percentage of price changes for a set of U.S. and non-U.S. equity-market indexes with the S&P 500 index during the 22-year period from 1980 to 2001. Most of the correlation differences are attributable to the different sample of firms listed on the different stock exchanges. Most of the major indexes—except the Nikkei Stock Average—are market-value-weighted indexes that include a large number of stocks. Therefore, the computational procedure is generally similar and the sample sizes are large or all-encompassing. Thus, the major difference between the indexes is that the sample of stocks are from different segments of the U.S. stock market or from different countries.

There is a high positive correlation (0.98–0.99) between the S&P 500 and the several comprehensive U.S. equity indexes, Wilshire, NYSE, and Russell 3000. In contrast, there are lower correlations between these comprehensive indexes and various style indexes such as the Russell Large-Cap 1000 (0.886) or the Russell 2000 Small-Cap index (0.783).

The correlations between the S&P 500 and indexes from Canada, the United Kingdom, Germany, and Japan support the case for global investing. Specifically, the U.S.–Toronto correlation was about 0.75, the U.S.–*Financial Times* correlation was about 0.67, and the U.S.–Japan correlations (the Nikkei and the Tokyo S.E.) averaged about 0.38. These diversification results were confirmed with the composite international series—with the MSCI EAFE and the IFC Emerging Market the correlations were about 0.54 and 0.39, respectively. These results confirm the benefits of global diversification because, as discussed in Chapter 7, such low correlations would definitely reduce the variance of a pure U.S. stock portfolio.

5.6.2 Correlations between Monthly Bond Indexes

The correlations with the monthly Lehman Bros. Govt. bond return index in Exhibit 5.13 consider a variety of bond indexes. The correlations between the longer-term U.S. investment-grade bond indexes ranged from about 0.94 to 0.98, confirming that although the *level* of interest rates differs due to the risk premium, the overriding factors that determine the rates of return for investment-grade bonds over time are *systematic* interest rate variables.

The correlations among investment-grade bonds and high-yield bonds indicate significantly lower correlations (about 0.49) caused by definite equity characteristics of high-yield

Exhibit 5.13 Correlation Coefficients between Monthly Percentage Price Changes in Various Stock and Bond Indexes, 1980–2001

Stock Indexes	S&P 500	Bond Indexes	Lehman Brothers Govt. Bonds
Wilshire 5000	0.983	LB Aggregate Bonds	0.981
NYSE Composite	0.993	LB Corporate Bonds	0.945
Russell 3000	0.992	LB High-Yield Bonds	0.489
Russell 1000	0.886	ML World Govt Bonds[a]	0.596
Russell 2000	0.783	ML World Govt Bonds	0.345
MSCI EAFE	0.538	w/o U.S.[a]	
Toronto S.E. 300	0.753	Treasury Bill—30-day	0.186
Financial Times	0.667	Treasury Bill—6-month[b]	0.561
All-Share		Treasury Bill—2-year[b]	0.917
Frankfurt (FAZ) Index	0.536		
Nikkei Index	0.418		
Tokyo S.E. Index	0.328		
IFC Emerging Mkt.	0.392		
M.S. World Index	0.604		
Brinson GSMI	0.915		

[a]Based on 1986–2001 data only
[b]Based on 1981–2001 data only
Source: Frank K. Reilly and David J. Wright, "An Analysis of Risk-Adjusted Performance for Global Market Assets," *Journal of Portfolio Management* 30, no. 3 (Spring, 2004), pp. 63–77. This copy-righted material is reprinted with permission from *Journal of Portfolio Management,* a publication of Institutional Investor, Inc.

bonds as shown in Reilly and Wright (2001). Finally, the low and diverse relationships among U.S. investment-grade bonds and world government bonds without the United States (about 0.35) reflect different interest rate movements and exchange rate effects (these non-U.S. government results are presented as U.S. dollar returns). Again, these results support the benefits of global diversification of bond portfolios.

5.6.3 Mean Annual Security Returns and Risk

The use of security indexes to measure returns and risk was demonstrated in Exhibit 3.14, which showed the average annual price change, or rate of return, and risk measure for a large set of asset indexes. As one would expect, there were clear differences between the indexes due to the different asset classes (e.g., stocks versus bonds) and the different samples within asset classes (e.g., the results for NYSE stocks versus NASDAQ stocks). Equally important, the results were generally consistent with what one should expect in a risk-averse world—that is, there was a positive relationship between the average rate of return for an asset and its measure of risk (e.g., the return-risk results for T-Bills versus the results for the S&P 500 stocks).

• • • • SUMMARY • • • •

- Given the several uses of security-market indexes, it is important to know how they are constructed and the differences between them. To use one of the many indexes to determine how the market is doing, you need to be aware of what market you are dealing with so you can select the appropriate index. As an example, are you only interested in the NYSE or do you also want to consider NASDAQ? Beyond the U.S. market, are you interested in Japanese or U.K. stocks, or do you want to examine the total world market? This choice is discussed in Merjos (1990).

- Indexes are also used as benchmarks to evaluate portfolio performance.[5] In this case, you must be sure the index (benchmark) is consistent with your investing universe. If you are investing worldwide, you should not judge your performance relative to the DJIA, which is limited to 30 U.S. blue-chip stocks. For a bond portfolio, the index should match your investment philosophy. Finally, if your portfolio contains both stocks and bonds, you must evaluate your performance against an appropriate combination of indexes.

[5]Chapter 25 includes an extensive discussion of the purpose and construction of benchmarks and considers the use of benchmarks in the evaluation of portfolio performance.

- Investors need to examine numerous market indexes to evaluate the performance of their investments. The selection of the appropriate indexes for information or evaluation will depend on how knowledgeable you are about the various indexes. The background from this chapter should help you understand what to look for and how to make the right decision in this area.

• • • • SUGGESTED READINGS • • • •

- Fisher, Lawrence, and James H. Lorie. *A Half Century of Returns on Stocks and Bonds.* Chicago: University of Chicago Graduate School of Business, 1977.

- Ibbotson Associates. *Stocks, Bonds, Bills, and Inflation.* Chicago: Ibbotson Associates, annual.

• • • • QUESTIONS • • • •

1. Discuss briefly several uses of security-market indexes.
2. What major factors must be considered when constructing a market index? Put another way, what characteristics differentiate indexes?
3. Explain how a market index is price weighted. In such a case, would you expect a $100 stock to be more important than a $25 stock? Give an example.
4. Explain how to compute a value-weighted index.
5. Explain how a price-weighted index and a value-weighted index adjust for stock splits.
6. Describe an unweighted price index and describe how you would construct such an index. Assume a 20 percent price change in GM ($40/share; 50 million shares outstanding) and Coors Brewing ($25/share and 15 million shares outstanding). Explain which stock's change will have the greater impact on this index.
7. If you correlated percentage changes in the Wilshire 5000 equity index with percentage changes in the NYSE composite and the NASDAQ composite index, would you expect a difference in the correlations? Why or why not?
8. There are high correlations between the monthly percentage price changes for the alternative NYSE indexes. Discuss the reason for this similarity: is it size of sample, source of sample, or method of computation?
9. Assume a correlation of 0.82 between the Nikkei and the TSE Composite Index. Examine the correlation between the TSE and the S&P 500 index in Exhibit 5.13. Explain why these relationships differ.
10. You learn that the Wilshire 5000 market-value-weighted index increased by 16 percent during a specified period, whereas a Wilshire 5000 equal-weighted index increased by 23 percent during the same period. Discuss what this difference in results implies.
11. Why is it contended that bond-market indexes are more difficult to construct and maintain than stock-market indexes?
12. Suppose the Wilshire 5000 market-value-weighted index increased by 5 percent, whereas the Merrill Lynch–Wilshire Capital Markets Index increased by 15 percent during the same period. What does this difference in results imply?
13. Suppose the Russell 1000 increased by 8 percent during the past year, whereas the Russell 2000 increased by 15 percent. Discuss the implication of these results.
14. Based on what you know about the *Financial Times* (FT) World Index, the Morgan Stanley Capital International World Index, and the Dow Jones World Stock Index, what level of correlation would you expect between monthly rates of return? Discuss the reasons for your answer based on the factors that affect indexes.
15. How would you explain that the ML High-Yield Bond Index was more highly correlated with the NYSE composite stock index than the ML Aggregate Bond Index?
16. Assuming that the mandate to a portfolio manager was to invest in a broadly diversified portfolio of U.S. stocks, which two or three indexes should be considered as an appropriate benchmark? Why?

• • • • PROBLEMS • • • •

1.

	PRICE			SHARES		
Company	A	B	C	A	B	C
Day 1	12	23	52	500	350	250
Day 2	10	22	55	500	350	250
Day 3	14	46	52	500	175[a]	250
Day 4	13	47	25	500	175	500[b]
Day 5	12	45	26	500	175	500

[a]Split at close of Day 2.
[b]Split at close of Day 3.

   a. Calculate a Dow Jones Industrial Average for days 1 through 5.
   b. What effects have the splits had in determining the next day's index? (Hint: think of the relative weighting of each stock.)
   c. From a copy of the *Wall Street Journal,* find the divisor that is currently being used in calculating the DJIA. (Normally this value can be found on pages C2 and C3.)

2. Utilizing the price and volume data in Problem 1,
   a. Calculate a Standard & Poor's Index for days 1 through 5 using a beginning index value of 10.
   b. Identify what effects the splits had in determining the next day's index. (Hint: think of the relative weighting of each stock.)

3. Based on the following stock price and shares outstanding information, compute the beginning and ending values for a price-weighted index and a market-value-weighted index.

	DECEMBER 31, 2008		DECEMBER 31, 2009	
	Price	Shares Outstanding	Price	Shares Outstanding
Stock K	20	100,000,000	32	100,000,000
Stock M	80	2,000,000	45	4,000,000[a]
Stock R	40	25,000,000	42	25,000,000

[a]Stock split two-for-one during the year.

   a. Compute the percentage change in the value of each index during the year.
   b. Explain the difference in results between the two indexes.
   c. Compute the percentage change for an unweighted index and discuss why these results differ from those of the other indexes.

4. For the past five trading days, on the basis of figures in the *Wall Street Journal,* compute the daily percentage price changes for the following stock indexes.
   a. DJIA
   b. S&P 500
   c. NASDAQ Composite Index
   d. FT-100 Share Index
   e. Nikkei 225 Stock Price Average
   f. Discuss the difference in results for Parts a and b, a and c, a and d, a and e, and d and e. What do these differences imply regarding diversifying within the United States versus diversifying between countries?

5. You are given the following information regarding prices for a sample of stocks.

		PRICE	
Stock	Number of Shares	T	T +1
A	1,000,000	60	80
B	10,000,000	20	35
C	30,000,000	18	25

   a. Construct a *price-weighted* index for these three stocks, and compute the percentage change in the index for the period from T to T + 1.
   b. Construct a *value-weighted* index for these three stocks, and compute the percentage change in the index for the period from T to T + 1.
   c. Briefly discuss the difference in the results for the two indexes.

6. a. Given the data in Problem 1, construct an equal-weighted index by assuming $1,000 is invested in each stock. What is the percentage change in wealth for this portfolio?

b. Compute the percentage of price change for each of the stocks in Problem 5. Compute the arithmetic mean of these percentage changes. Discuss how this answer compares to the answer in Part a.

c. Compute the geometric mean of the percentage changes in Part b. Discuss how this result compares to the answer in Part b.

THOMSON ONE | Business School Edition

1. Collect price and number of outstanding share data from the past 10 days on the following firms: Amazon (AMZN), Family Dollar (FDO), J.C. Penney (JCP), Target (TGT), and Wal-Mart (WMT). Using this data, create a "retail sales stock index" by computing a value-weighted index. What is the overall percent change of the index over the 10 days?

2. Using the market values for each stock on day l, compute the relative weight for each of the five stocks. Which stock has the largest weight and which stock has the smallest weight?

3. Using the data from above, compute a price-weighted and unweighted stock index. What is the overall percent change on each index? How do the behaviors of the value-weighted, price-weighted, and unweighted indexes compare over the 10 days?

4. Compare the performance during the 10-day time frame of (a) the price-weighted retail sales stock index with the Dow Jones Industrial Average and (b) the value-weighted retail sales stock index with the S&P 500.

· · · · · APPENDIX: CHAPTER 5 · · · · ·

Stock-Market Indexes

Exhibit 5A.1 Summary of Stock-Market Indexes

Name of Index	Weighting	Number of Stocks	Source of Stocks
Dow Jones Industrial Average	Price	30	NYSE, NASDAQ
Nikkei–Dow Jones Average	Price	225	TSE
S&P 400 Industrial	Market value	400	NYSE, NASDAQ
S&P Transportation	Market value	20	NYSE, NASDAQ
S&P Utilities	Market value	40	NYSE, NASDAQ
S&P Financials	Market value	40	NYSE, NASDAQ
S&P 500 Composite	Market value	500	NYSE, NASDAQ
NYSE			
Industrial	Market value	1,601	NYSE
Utility	Market value	253	NYSE
Transportation	Market value	55	NYSE
Financial	Market value	909	NYSE
Composite	Market value	2,818	NYSE
NASDAQ			
Composite	Market value	5,575	NASDAQ
Industrial	Market value	3,394	NASDAQ
Banks	Market value	375	NASDAQ
Insurance	Market value	103	NASDAQ
Other finance	Market value	610	NASDAQ
Transportation	Market value	104	NASDAQ
Telecommunications	Market value	183	NASDAQ
Computer	Market value	685	NASDAQ
Biotech	Market value	121	NASDAQ
AMEX Market Value	Market value	900	AMEX
Dow Jones Equity Market Index	Market value	2,300	NYSE, AMEX, NASDAQ
Wilshire 5000 Equity Value	Market value	5,000	NYSE, AMEX, NASDAQ
Russell Indexes			
3000	Market value	3,000 largest in U.S.	NYSE, AMEX, NASDAQ

Exhibit 5A.1 Summary of Stock-Market Indexes (continued)

Name of Index	Weighting	Number of Stocks	Source of Stocks
1000	Market value	1,000 largest of 3,000	NYSE, AMEX, NASDAQ
2000	Market value	2,000 smallest of 3,000	NYSE, AMEX, NASDAQ
Financial Times Actuaries Index			
All Share	Market value	700	LSE
FT100	Market value	100 largest	LSE
Small-Cap	Market value	250	LSE
Midcap	Market value	250	LSE
Combined	Market value	350	LSE
Tokyo Stock Exchange Price Index (TOPIX)	Market value	1,800	TSE
Value Line Averages			
Industrials	Equal (geometric mean)	1,499	NYSE, AMEX, NASDAQ
Utilities	Equal	177	NYSE, AMEX, NASDAQ
Rails	Equal	19	NYSE, AMEX, NASDAQ
Composite	Equal	1,695	NYSE, AMEX, NASDAQ
Financial Times Ordinary Share Index	Equal (geometric mean)	30	LSE
FT-Actuaries World Indexes	Market value	2,275	24 countries, 3 regions (returns in $, £, ¥, DM, and local currency)
Morgan Stanley Capital International (MSCI) Indexes	Market value	1,375	19 countries, 3 international, 38 international industries (returns in $ and local currency)
Dow Jones World Stock Index	Market value	2,200	13 countries, 3 regions, 120 industry groups (returns in $, £, ¥, DM, and local currency)
Euromoney—First Boston Global Stock Index	Market value	—	17 countries (returns in $ and local currency)
Salomon-Russell World Equity Index	Market value	Russell 1000 and S-R PMI of 600 non-U.S. stocks	22 countries (returns in $ and local currency)

Source: Compiled by authors.

Exhibit 5A.2 Foreign Stock-Market Indexes

Name of Index	Weighting	Number of Stocks	History of Index
ATX-index (Vienna)	Market value	All listed stocks	Base year 1967, 1991 began including all stocks (Value = 100)
Swiss Market Index	Market value	18	Base year 1988, stocks selected from the Basle, Geneva, and Zurich Exchanges (Value = 1500)
Stockholm General Index	Market value	All listed stocks	Base year 1979, continuously updated (Value = 100)
Copenhagen Stock Exchange Share Price Index	Market value	All traded stocks	Share price is based on average price of the day
Oslo SE Composite Index (Sweden)	Market value	25	Base year 1972 (Value = 100)
Johannesburg Stock Exchange Actuaries Index	Market value	146	Base year 1959 (Value = 100)

Exhibit 5A.2 (continued)

Name of Index	Weighting	Number of Stocks	History of Index
Mexican Market Index	Market value	Variable number, based on capitalization and liquidity	Base year 1978, high dollar returns in recent years
Milan Stock Exchange MIB	Market value	Variable number, based on capitalization and liquidity	Change base at beginning of each year (Value = 1000)
Belgium BEL-20 Stock Index	Market value	20	Base year 1991 (Value = 1000)
Madrid General Stock Index	Market value	92	Change base at beginning of each year
Hang Seng Index (Hong Kong)	Market value	33	Started in 1969, accounts for 75 percent of total market
FT-Actuaries World Indexes	Market value	2, 275	Base year 1986
FT-SE 100 Index (London)	Market value	100	Base year 1983 (Value = 1000)
CAC General Share Index (French)	Market value	212	Base year 1981 (Value = 100)
Morgan Stanley World Index	Market value	1,482	Base year 1970 (Value = 100)
Singapore Straits Times Industrial Index	Unweighted	30	
German Stock Market Index (DAX)	Market value	30	Base year 1987 (Value = 1000)
Frankfurter Allgemeine Zeitung Index (FAZ) (German)	Market value	100	Base year 1958 (Value = 100)
Australian Stock Exchange Share Price Indexes	Market value	250	Introduced in 1979
Dublin ISEQ Index	Market value	All stocks traded	Base year 1988 (Value = 1000)
HEX Index (Helsinki)	Market value	Varies with different indexes	Base changes every day
Jakarta Stock Exchange	Market value	All listed shares	Base year 1982 (Value = 100)
Taiwan Stock Exchange Index	Market value	All listed stocks	Base year 1966 (Value = 100)
TSE 300 Composite Index (Toronto)	Market value	300	Base year 1975 (Value = 1000)
KOSPI (Korean Composite Stock Price Index)	Market value (adjusted for cross-holdings)	All listed stocks	Base year 1980 (Value = 100)

Source: Compiled by authors.

PART 2
Developments in Investment Theory

CHAPTER 6
Efficient Capital Markets

CHAPTER 7
An Introduction to Portfolio Management

CHAPTER 8
An Introduction to Asset Pricing Models

CHAPTER 9
Multifactor Models of Risk and Return

The chapters in Part 1 provided background on why individuals invest their funds and what they expect to derive from this activity. We also argued very strongly for a global investment program, described the major instruments and capital markets in a global investment environment, and showed the relationship among these instruments and markets.

We now are ready to discuss how to analyze and value the various investment instruments available. In turn, valuation requires the estimation of expected returns (cash flows) and a determination of the risk involved in the securities. Before we can begin the analysis, we need to understand several major developments in investment theory that have influenced how we specify and measure risk in the valuation process. The purpose of the four chapters in Part 2 is to provide this background on risk and asset valuation.

Chapter 6 describes the concept of efficient capital markets, which hypothesizes that security prices reflect the effect of all information. This chapter considers why markets should be efficient, discusses how one goes about testing this hypothesis, describes the results of numerous tests that both support the hypotheses and indicate the existence of anomalies that are inconsistent with the hypotheses. There is also a consideration of behavioral finance, which has experienced a growth in reputation because it provides a rationale for some of the results. We conclude the chapter with an extensive discussion of the implications of the results for those engaged in technical and fundamental analysis as well as portfolio management.

Chapter 7 provides an introduction to portfolio theory, which was developed by Harry Markowitz. This theory provided the first rigorous measure of risk for investors and showed how one selects alternative assets to diversify and reduce the risk of a portfolio. Markowitz also derived a risk measure for individual securities within the context of an efficient portfolio.

Following the development of the Markowitz portfolio model, William Sharpe and several other academicians extended the Markowitz model into a general equilibrium asset pricing model that included an alternative risk measure for all risky assets. Chapter 8 contains a detailed description of these developments and an explanation of the relevant risk measure implied by this valuation model, referred to as the *capital asset pricing model* (CAPM). We introduce the CAPM at this early point in the book because the risk measure implied by this model has been used extensively in various valuation models. Although the CAPM has long been the preeminent theoretical explanation in finance for the connection between risk and expected return, the past several decades have seen the rise of several competing models.

Chapter 9 is devoted to exploring several of these alternative asset pricing models, which differ from the CAPM primarily by specifying multiple risk factors in lieu of a single market portfolio-based variable. The chapter begins with an examination of the *arbitrage pricing theory* (APT), which is the conceptual foundation for virtually all of the subsequent multifactor asset pricing models. The APT, which was developed by Steve Ross in response to criticisms of the CAPM, suggests a linear relationship between a stock's expected return and many systematic risk factors.

One severe challenge for investors attempting to use the APT in practice is that it offers no theoretical guidance as to either the number or the identity of the risk factors. To overcome this problem, researchers have developed several *multifactor models,* which attempt to link a stock's realized returns to market data on a collection of pre-specified variables that are believed to proxy for the APT risk factors. In specifying these variables, both macroeconomic and microeconomic approaches and risk factors have been adopted. After explaining these various approaches, we demonstrate how they are used by investors to both evaluate individual companies and assess the investment styles of money managers and mutual funds.

CHAPTER 6
Efficient Capital Markets

After you read this chapter, you should be able to answer the following questions:

- What does it mean to say that capital markets are efficient?
- Why *should* capital markets be efficient?
- What factors contribute to an efficient market?
- Given the overall efficient market hypothesis (EMH), what are the three subhypotheses and what are the implications of each of them?
- How do you test the three efficient market subhypotheses and what are the results of the tests?
- For each set of tests, which results support the EMH and which results indicate an anomaly related to the hypothesis?
- What is behavioral finance and how does it relate to the EMH?
- What are some of the major findings of behavioral finance and what are the implications of these findings for the EMH?
- What are the implications of the efficient market hypothesis test results for the following?
  - Technical analysis
  - Fundamental analysis
  - Portfolio managers with superior analysts
  - Portfolio managers with inferior analysts

An **efficient capital market** is one in which security prices adjust rapidly to the arrival of new information and, therefore, the current prices of securities reflect all information about the security. Some of the most interesting and important academic research during the past 30 years has analyzed whether our capital markets are efficient. This extensive research is important because its results have significant real-world implications for investors and portfolio managers. In addition, the question of whether capital markets are efficient is one of the most controversial areas in investment research. A new dimension has been added to the controversy because of the rapidly expanding research in behavioral finance that has major implications regarding the concept of efficient capital markets and has been providing some intriguing insights on reasons for many of the anomalies identified.

Because of its importance and controversy, you need to understand the meaning of the terms *efficient capital markets* and the *efficient market hypothesis (EMH)*. You should understand the analysis performed to test the EMH and the results of studies that either support or contradict the hypothesis. Finally, you should be aware of the implications of these results when you analyze alternative investments and work to construct a portfolio.

We are considering the topic of efficient capital markets at this point for two reasons. First, the prior discussion indicated how the capital markets function, so now it seems natural to consider the efficiency of these markets in terms of how security prices react to new information. Second, the overall evidence on capital market efficiency is best described as mixed; some studies support the hypothesis, and others do not. The implications of these diverse results are important for you as an investor involved in analyzing securities and building a portfolio.

This chapter contains five major sections. The first discusses why we would expect capital markets to be efficient and the factors that contribute to an efficient market where the prices of securities reflect available information.

The efficient market hypothesis has been divided into three subhypotheses to facilitate testing. The second section describes these three subhypotheses and the implications of each of them.

The third section is the largest section because it contains a discussion of the results of numerous studies. This review of the research reveals that a large body of evidence supports the EMH, but a growing number of other studies do not support the hypotheses.

In the fourth section, we discuss the concept of behavioral finance, the studies that have been done in this area related to efficient markets, and the conclusions as they relate to the EMH.

The final section discusses what these results imply for an investor who uses either technical analysis or fundamental analysis or what they mean for a portfolio manager who has access to superior or inferior analysts. We conclude with a brief discussion of the evidence for markets in foreign countries.

6.1 Why Should Capital Markets Be Efficient?

As noted earlier, in an efficient capital market, security prices adjust rapidly to the infusion of new information, and, therefore, current security prices fully reflect all available information. To be absolutely correct, this is referred to as an **informationally efficient market**. Although the idea of an efficient capital market is relatively straightforward, we often fail to consider *why* capital markets *should* be efficient. What set of assumptions imply an efficient capital market?

An initial and important premise of an efficient market requires that *a large number of profit-maximizing participants analyze and value securities,* each independently of the others.

A second assumption is that *new information regarding securities comes to the market in a random fashion,* and the timing of one announcement is generally independent of others.[1]

The third assumption is especially crucial: *the buy and sell decisions of all those profit-maximizing investors who adjust security prices rapidly to reflect the effect of new information.* Although the price adjustment may be imperfect, it is unbiased. This means that sometimes the market will overadjust and other times it will underadjust, but you cannot predict which will occur at any given time. Security prices adjust rapidly because of the many profit-maximizing investors competing against one another to profit from the new information.

The combined effect of (1) information coming in a random, independent, unpredictable fashion and (2) numerous competing investors adjusting stock prices rapidly to reflect this new information means that one would expect price changes to be independent and random. You can see that the adjustment process requires a large number of investors following the movements of the security, analyzing the impact of new information on its value, and buying or selling the security until its price adjusts to reflect the new information. This scenario implies that informationally efficient markets require some minimum amount of trading and that more trading by numerous competing investors should cause a faster price adjustment, making the market more efficient. We will return to this need for trading and investor attention when we discuss some anomalies of the EMH.

Finally, because security prices adjust to all new information, these security prices should reflect all information that is publicly available at any point in time. Therefore, the security prices that prevail at any time should be an unbiased reflection of all currently available information, including the risk involved in owning the security. Therefore, in an efficient market, *the expected returns implicit in the current price of the security should reflect its risk,* which

---

[1] New information, by definition, must be information that was not known before, and is not predictable. If it were predictable, it would have been impounded in the security price.

means that investors who buy at these informationally efficient prices should receive a rate of return that is consistent with the perceived risk of the stock. Put another way, in terms of the CAPM that is discussed in Chapter 8, all stocks should lie on the SML such that their expected rates of return are consistent with their perceived risk.

6.2 Alternative Efficient Market Hypotheses

Most of the early work related to efficient capital markets was based on the *random walk hypothesis,* which contended that changes in stock prices occurred randomly. This early academic work contained extensive empirical analysis without much theory behind it. An article by Fama (1970) attempted to formalize the theory and organize the growing empirical evidence. Fama presented the efficient market theory in terms of a *fair game model,* contending that investors can be confident that a current market price fully reflects all available information about a security and, therefore, the expected return based upon this price is consistent with its risk.

In his original article, Fama divided the overall efficient market hypothesis (EMH) and the empirical tests of the hypothesis into three subhypotheses depending on the information set involved: (1) weak-form EMH, (2) semistrong-form EMH, and (3) strong-form EMH.

In a subsequent review article, Fama (1991a) again divided the empirical results into three groups but shifted empirical results between the prior categories. Therefore, the following discussion uses the original categories, noted above, but organizes the presentation of results using the new categories.

In the remainder of this section, we describe the three subhypotheses and the implications of each of them. As noted, the three subhypotheses are based on alternative information sets. In the following section, we briefly describe how researchers have tested these hypotheses and summarize the results of these tests.

6.2.1 Weak-Form Efficient Market Hypothesis

The **weak-form EMH** assumes that current stock prices fully reflect *all security market information,* including the historical sequence of prices, rates of return, trading volume data, and other market-generated information, such as odd-lot transactions, block trades, and transactions by exchange specialists. Because it assumes that current market prices already reflect all past returns and any other security market information, this hypothesis implies that past rates of return and other historical market data should have no relationship with future rates of return (that is, rates of return should be independent). Therefore, this hypothesis contends that you should gain little from using any trading rule that decides whether to buy or sell a security based on past rates of return or any other past security market data.

6.2.2 Semistrong-Form Efficient Market Hypothesis

The **semistrong-form EMH** asserts that security prices adjust rapidly to the release of *all public information;* that is, current security prices fully reflect all public information. The semistrong hypothesis encompasses the weak-form hypothesis, because all the market information considered by the weak-form hypothesis, such as stock prices, rates of return, and trading volume, is public. Notably, public information also includes all nonmarket information, such as earnings and dividend announcements, price-to-earnings (P/E) ratios, dividend-yield (D/P) ratios, price-book value (P/BV) ratios, stock splits, news about the economy, and political news. This hypothesis implies that investors who base their decisions on any important new information *after it is public* should not derive above-average risk-adjusted profits from their transactions, considering the cost of trading because the security price already reflects all such new public information.

6.2.3 Strong-Form Efficient Market Hypothesis

The **strong-form EMH** contends that stock prices fully reflect *all information from public and private sources.* This means that no group of investors has monopolistic access to information relevant to the formation of prices. Therefore, this hypothesis contends that no group of investors should be able to consistently derive above-average risk-adjusted rates of return. The strong-form EMH encompasses both the weak-form and the semistrong-form EMH. Further, the strong-form EMH extends the assumption of efficient markets, in which prices adjust rapidly to the release of new public information, to assume perfect markets, in which all information is cost-free and available to everyone at the same time.

6.3 Tests and Results of Efficient Market Hypotheses

Now that you understand the three components of the EMH and what each of them implies regarding the effect on security prices of different sets of information, we can consider the tests used to see whether the data support the hypotheses. Therefore, in this section we discuss the specific tests and summarize the results of these tests.

Like most hypotheses in finance and economics, the evidence on the EMH is mixed. Some studies have supported the hypotheses and indicate that capital markets are efficient. Results of other studies have revealed some **anomalies** related to these hypotheses, indicating results that do not support the hypotheses.

6.3.1 Weak-Form Hypothesis: Tests and Results

Researchers have formulated two groups of tests of the weak-form EMH. The first category involves statistical tests of independence between rates of return. The second set of tests entails a comparison of risk–return results for trading rules that make investment decisions based on past market information relative to the results from a simple buy-and-hold policy, which assumes that you buy stock at the beginning of a test period and hold it to the end.

Statistical Tests of Independence As discussed earlier, the EMH contends that security returns over time should be independent of one another because new information comes to the market in a random, independent fashion and security prices adjust rapidly to this new information. Two major statistical tests have been employed to verify this independence.

First, **autocorrelation tests** of independence measure the significance of positive or negative correlation in returns over time. Does the rate of return on day t correlate with the rate of return on day $t - 1$, $t - 2$, or $t - 3$?[2] Those who believe that capital markets are efficient would expect insignificant correlations for all such combinations.

Several researchers have examined the serial correlations among stock returns for several relatively short time horizons including 1 day, 4 days, 9 days, and 16 days. The results typically indicated insignificant correlation in stock returns over time. Some recent studies that considered portfolios of stocks of different market size have indicated that the autocorrelation is stronger for portfolios of small market size stocks. Therefore, although the older results tend to support the hypothesis, the more recent studies cast doubt on it for portfolios of small firms, although these results could be offset by the higher transaction costs of small-cap stocks and nonsynchronous trading for small-cap stocks.

The second statistical test of independence as discussed by DeFusco et al. (2004), is the **runs test**. Given a series of price changes, each price change is either designated a plus $(+)$ if it is an increase in price or a minus $(–)$ if it is a decrease in price. The result is a set of pluses and minuses as follows: $+ + + - + - - + + - - + +$. A run occurs when two consecutive changes are the same; two or more consecutive positive or negative price changes constitute one run. When the price changes in a different direction, such as when a negative price change is followed by a positive price change, the run ends and a new run may begin. To test for independence, you would compare the number of runs for a given series to the number in a table of expected values for the number of runs that should occur in a random series.

---

[2] For a discussion of tests of time-series independence, see DeFusco, McLeavey, Pinto, and Runkle (2004), Chapter 10.

Studies that have examined stock price runs have confirmed the independence of stock price changes over time. The actual number of runs for stock price series consistently fell into the range expected for a random series. Therefore, these statistical tests of stocks on the NYSE and on the NASDAQ market have likewise confirmed the independence of stock price changes over time.

Although short-horizon stock returns have generally supported the weak-form EMH, several studies that examined price changes for individual *transactions* on the NYSE found significant serial correlations. Notably, none of these studies attempted to show that the dependence of transaction price movements could be used to earn above-average risk-adjusted returns after considering the trading rule's substantial transaction costs.

Tests of Trading Rules The second group of tests of the weak-form EMH were developed in response to the assertion that the prior statistical tests of independence were too rigid to identify the intricate price patterns examined by technical analysts. As we will discuss in Chapter 15, technical analysts do not expect a set number of positive or negative price changes as a signal of a move to a new equilibrium in the market. They typically look for a general consistency in the price trends over time. Such a trend might include both positive and negative changes. For this reason, technical analysts believed that their trading rules were too sophisticated and complicated to be properly tested by rigid statistical tests.

In response to this objection, investigators attempted to examine alternative technical trading rules through simulation. Advocates of an efficient market hypothesized that investors could not derive abnormal profits above a buy-and-hold policy using any trading rule that depended solely on past market information.

The trading rule studies compared the risk–return results derived from trading-rule simulations, including transaction costs, to the results from a simple buy-and-hold policy. Three major pitfalls can negate the results of a trading-rule study:

1. The investigator should *use only publicly available data* when implementing the trading rule. As an example, the trading activities of specialists as of December 31 may not be publicly available until February 1, so you should not factor in information about specialist trading activity until the information is public.
2. When computing the returns from a trading rule, you should *include all transaction costs* involved in implementing the trading strategy because most trading rules involve many more transactions than a simple buy-and-hold policy.
3. You must *adjust the results for risk* because a trading rule might simply select a portfolio of high-risk securities that should experience higher returns.

Researchers have encountered two operational problems in carrying out these tests of specific trading rules. First, some trading rules require too much subjective interpretation of data to simulate mechanically. Second, the almost infinite number of potential trading rules makes it impossible to test all of them. As a result, only the better-known technical trading rules have been examined.

Another factor that should be recognized is that the simulation studies have typically been restricted to relatively simple trading rules, which many technicians contend are rather naïve. In addition, many of these studies employed readily available data from the NYSE, which is biased toward well-known, heavily traded stocks that certainly should trade in efficient markets. Recall that markets should be more efficient when there are numerous aggressive, profit-maximizing investors attempting to adjust stock prices to reflect new information, so market efficiency will be related to trading volume. Specifically, *more trading in a security should promote market efficiency.* Alternatively, for securities with relatively few stockholders and little trading activity, the market could be inefficient simply because fewer investors would be analyzing the effect of new information, and this limited interest would result in insufficient trading activity to move the price of the security quickly to a new equilibrium value that reflects the new information. Therefore, using only active, heavily traded stocks when testing a trading rule could bias the results toward finding efficiency.

Results of Simulations of Specific Trading Rules In the most popular trading technique, filter rule, an investor trades a stock when the price change exceeds a filter value set for it. As an example, an investor using a 5 percent filter would envision a positive breakout if the stock were to rise 5 percent from some base, suggesting that the stock price would continue to rise. A technician would acquire the stock to take advantage of the expected continued rise. In contrast, a 5 percent decline from some peak price would be considered a breakout on the downside, and the technician would expect a further price decline and would sell any holdings of the stock and possibly even sell the stock short.

Studies of this trading rule have used a range of filters from 0.5 percent to 50 percent. The results indicated that small filters would yield above-average profits *before* taking account of trading commissions. However, small filters generate numerous trades and, therefore, substantial trading costs. When these trading costs were considered, all the trading profits turned to losses. Alternatively, trading using larger filters did not yield returns above those of a simple buy-and-hold policy.

Researchers have simulated other trading rules that used past market data other than stock prices. Trading rules have been devised that consider advanced-decline ratios, short sales, short positions, and specialist activities.[3] These simulation tests have generated mixed results. Most of the early studies suggested that these trading rules generally would not outperform a buy-and-hold policy on a risk-adjusted basis after commissions, although several recent studies have indicated support for specific trading rules. Therefore, most evidence from simulations of specific trading rules indicates that most trading rules tested have not been able to beat a buy-and-hold policy. Therefore, these test results generally support the weak-form EMH, but the results are not unanimous.

6.3.2 Semistrong-Form Hypothesis: Tests and Results

Recall that the semistrong-form EMH asserts that security prices adjust rapidly to the release of all public information; that is, security prices fully reflect all public information. Studies that have tested the semistrong-form EMH can be divided into the following sets of studies:

1. *Studies to predict future rates of return using available public information beyond pure market information such as prices and trading volume considered in the weak-form tests.* These studies can involve either *time-series analysis* of returns or the *cross-section distribution* of returns for individual stocks. Advocates of the EMH contend that it would not be possible to predict *future* returns using past returns or to predict the distribution of future returns (e.g., the top quartile or decile of returns) using public information.
2. *Event studies that examine how fast stock prices adjust to specific significant economic events.* A corollary approach would be to test whether it is possible to invest in a security after the public announcement of a significant event (e.g., earnings, stock splits, major economic data) and experience significant abnormal rates of return. Again, advocates of the EMH would expect security prices to adjust rapidly, such that it would not be possible for investors to experience superior risk-adjusted returns by investing after the public announcement and paying normal transaction costs.

Adjustment for Market Effects For any of these tests, you need to adjust the security's rates of return for the rates of return of the overall market during the period considered. The point is, a 5 percent return in a stock during the period surrounding an announcement is meaningless until you know what the aggregate stock market did during the same period and how this stock normally acts under such conditions. If the market had experienced a 10 percent

---

[3] Many of these trading rules are discussed in Chapter 15, which deals with technical analysis.

return during this announcement period, the 5 percent return for the stock may be lower than expected.

Authors of pre-1970 studies generally recognized the need to make such adjustments for market movements. They typically assumed that the individual stocks should experience returns equal to the aggregate stock market. Thus, the market-adjustment process simply entailed subtracting the market return from the return for the individual security to derive its **abnormal rate of return**, as follows:

6.1
$$AR_{it} = R_{it} - R_{mt}$$

where:

AR_{it} = abnormal rate of return on security i during period t
R_{it} = rate of return on security i during period t
R_{mt} = rate of return on a market index during period t

In the example where the stock experienced a 5 percent increase while the market increased 10 percent, the stock's abnormal return would be minus 5 percent.

Since the 1970s, many authors have adjusted the rates of return for securities by an amount different from the market rate of return because they recognize that, based on work with the CAPM, all stocks do not change by the same amount as the market. That is, as will be discussed in Chapter 8, some stocks are more volatile than the market, and some are less volatile. These possibilities mean that you must determine an **expected rate of return** for the stock based on the market rate of return *and* the stock's relationship with the market (its beta). As an example, suppose a stock is generally 20 percent more volatile than the market (that is, it has a beta of 1.20). In such a case, if the market experiences a 10 percent rate of return, you would expect this stock to experience a 12 percent rate of return. Therefore, you would determine the abnormal rate of return by computing the difference between the stock's actual rate of return and its *expected rate of return* as follows:

6.2
$$AR_{it} = R_{it} - E(R_{it})$$

where:

$E(R_{it})$ = the expected rate of return for stock i during period t based on the market rate of return and the stock's normal relationship with the market (its beta)

Continuing with the example, if the stock that was expected to have a 12 percent return (based on a market return of 10 percent and a stock beta of 1.20) had only a 5 percent return, its abnormal rate of return during the period would be minus 7 percent. Over the normal long-run period, you would expect the abnormal returns for a stock to sum to zero. Specifically, during one period the returns may exceed expectations and the next period they may fall short of expectations.

To summarize, there are two sets of tests of the semistrong-form EMH. The first set of studies are referred to as **return prediction studies**. For this set of studies, investigators attempt to predict the time series of future rates of return for individual stocks or the aggregate market using public information. For example, is it possible to predict abnormal returns over time for the market based on public information such as specified values or changes in the aggregate dividend yield or the risk premium spread for bonds? Another example would be **event studies** that examine abnormal rates of return for a period immediately after an announcement of a significant economic event, such as a stock split, a proposed merger, or a stock or bond issue, to determine whether an investor can derive above-average risk-adjusted rates of return by investing after the release of public information.

The second set of studies are those that predict cross-sectional returns. In these studies, investigators look for public information regarding individual stocks that will allow them to predict the cross-sectional distribution of future risk-adjusted rates of return. For example, they test whether it is possible to use variables such as the price-earnings ratio, market value size, the price/book-value ratio, the P/E/growth rate (PEG) ratio, or the dividend yield to predict which stocks will experience above-average (e.g., top quartile) or below-average risk-adjusted rates of return in the future.

In both sets of tests, the emphasis is on the analysis of abnormal rates of return that deviate from long-term expectations or returns that are adjusted for a stock's specific risk characteristics and overall market rates of return during the period.

Results of Return Prediction Studies The **time-series analysis** assumes that in an efficient market the best estimate of *future* rates of return will be the long-run *historical* rates of return. The point of the tests is to determine whether any public information will provide superior estimates of returns for a short-run horizon (one to six months) or a long-run horizon (one to five years).

Risk Premium Proxies The results of these studies have indicated limited success in predicting short-horizon returns, but the analysis of long-horizon returns has been quite successful. A prime example is dividend yield studies. After postulating that the aggregate dividend yield (D/P) was a proxy for the risk premium on stocks, they found a positive relationship between the D/P and future long-run stock market returns.

In addition, several studies have considered two variables related to the term structure of interest rates: (1) a *default spread,* which is the difference between the yields on lower-grade and Aaa-rated long-term corporate bonds (this spread has been used in earlier chapters of this book as a proxy for a market risk premium), and (2) the *term structure spread,* which is the difference between the long-term Treasury bond yield and the yield on one-month Treasury bills. These variables have been used to predict stock returns and bond returns. Similar variables in foreign countries have also been useful for predicting returns for foreign common stocks.

The reasoning for these empirical results is as follows: When the two most significant variables—the dividend yield (D/P) and the bond default spread—are high, it implies that investors are expecting or requiring a high return on stocks and bonds. Notably, this occurs during poor economic environments, as reflected in the growth rate of output. A poor economic environment also implies a low-wealth environment wherein investors perceive higher risk for investments. As a result, for investors to invest and shift consumption from the present to the future, they will require a high rate of return (i.e., a high risk premium). It is suggested that, if you invest during this risk-averse period, your subsequent returns will be above normal. In contrast, when these values are small, it implies that investors have reduced their risk premium and required rates of return and, therefore, their future returns will be below normal. The results of these studies that support this expectation would be evidence against the EMH because they indicate you can use public information to predict future abnormal returns.

Quarterly Earnings Reports Studies that address quarterly reports are considered part of the times-series analysis. Specifically, these studies question whether it is possible to predict future returns for a stock based on publicly available quarterly earnings reports. The typical test examined firms that experienced changes in quarterly earnings that differed from expectations.

The results generally indicated abnormal returns during the 13 or 26 weeks *following* the announcement of a large *unanticipated* earnings change—referred to as an **earnings surprise**. These results suggest that an earnings surprise is *not* instantaneously reflected in security prices.

An extensive analysis by Rendleman, Jones, and Latané (1982) and a follow-up by Jones, Rendleman, and Latané (1985) using a large sample and daily data from 20 days before a quarterly earnings announcement to 90 days after the announcement indicated that 31 percent of the total response in stock returns came before the earnings announcement, 18 percent on the day of the announcement, and 51 percent *afterward.*

Several studies examined reasons for the earnings drift following earnings announcements and found that unexpected earnings explained more than 80 percent of the subsequent stock price drift for the total time period. Authors who reviewed the prior studies such as Benesh and Peterson (1986), Bernard and Thomas (1989), and Baruch (1989), contended that the reason for the stock price drift was the *earnings revisions* that followed the earnings surprises and contributed to the positive correlations of prices.

In summary, these results indicate that the market has not adjusted stock prices to reflect the release of quarterly earnings surprises as fast as expected by the semistrong EMH, which implies that earnings surprises and earnings revisions can be used to predict returns for individual stocks. These results are evidence against the EMH.[4]

The final set of calendar studies questioned whether some regularities in the rates of return during the calendar year would allow investors to predict returns on stocks. These studies include numerous studies on "the January anomaly" and studies that consider a variety of other daily and weekly regularities.

The January Anomaly   Several years ago, Branch (1977) and Branch and Chang (1985) proposed a unique trading rule for those interested in taking advantage of tax selling. Investors (including institutions) tend to engage in tax selling toward the end of the year to establish losses on stocks that have declined. After the new year, the tendency is to reacquire these stocks or to buy similar stocks that look attractive. This scenario would produce downward pressure on stock prices in late November and December and positive pressure in early January. Such a seasonal pattern is inconsistent with the EMH since it should be eliminated by arbitrageurs who would buy in December and sell in early January.

A supporter of the hypothesis found that December trading volume was abnormally high for stocks that had declined during the previous year and that significant abnormal returns occurred during January for stocks that had experienced losses during the prior year. It was concluded that, because of transaction costs, arbitrageurs must not be eliminating the January tax-selling anomaly. Subsequent analysis showed that most of the January effect was concentrated in the first week of trading, particularly on the first day of the year.

Several studies provided support for a January effect inconsistent with the tax-selling hypothesis by examining what happened in foreign countries that did not have our tax laws or a December year-end. They found abnormal returns in January, but the results could not be explained by tax laws. It has also been shown that the classic relationship between risk and return is strongest during January and there is a year-end trading volume bulge in late December–early January.

As pointed out by Keim (1986), despite numerous studies, the January anomaly poses as many questions as it answers.

Other Calendar Effects   Several other "calendar" effects have been examined, including a monthly effect, a weekend/day-of-the-week effect, and an intraday effect. One study found a significant monthly effect wherein all the market's cumulative advance occurred during the first half of trading months.

An analysis of the weekend effect found that the mean return for Monday was significantly negative during five-year subperiods and a total period. In contrast, the average return for the other four days was positive.

A study decomposed the Monday effect that is typically measured from Friday close to Monday close into a *weekend effect* (from Friday close to Monday open), and a pure *Monday trading effect* (from Monday open to the Monday close). It was shown that the negative Monday effect found in prior studies actually occurs from the Friday close to the Monday open (it is

---

[4] Academic studies such as these, which have indicated the importance of earnings surprises, have led the *Wall Street Journal* to publish a section on earnings surprises in connection with regular quarterly earnings reports.

really a weekend effect). After adjusting for the weekend effect, the pure Monday trading effect was positive. Subsequently, it was shown that the Monday effect was on average positive in January and negative for all other months.

Finally, for *large firms,* the negative Monday effect occurred before the market opened (it was a weekend effect), whereas for *smaller firms* most of the negative Monday effect occurred during the day on Monday (it was a Monday trading effect).

Predicting Cross-Sectional Returns Assuming an efficient market, *all securities should have equal risk-adjusted returns* because security prices should reflect all public information that would influence the security's risk. Therefore, studies in this category attempt to determine if you can use public information to predict what stocks will enjoy above-average or below-average risk-adjusted returns.

These studies typically examine the usefulness of alternative measures of size or quality to rank stocks in terms of risk-adjusted returns. Keep in mind that all of these tests involve *a joint hypothesis* because they not only consider the efficiency of the market but also are dependent on the asset pricing model that provides the measure of risk used in the test. Specifically, if a test determines that it is possible to predict risk-adjusted returns, these results could occur because the market is not efficient, *or* they could be because the measure of risk is faulty and, therefore, the measures of risk-adjusted returns are wrong.

Price-Earnings Ratios Several studies beginning with Basu (1977) have examined the relationship between the historical **price-earnings (P/E) ratios** for stocks and the returns on the stocks. Some have suggested that low P/E stocks will outperform high P/E stocks because growth companies enjoy high P/E ratios, but the market tends to overestimate the growth potential and thus overvalues these growth companies, while undervaluing low-growth firms with low P/E ratios. A relationship between the historical P/E ratios and subsequent risk-adjusted market performance would constitute evidence against the semistrong EMH, because it would imply that investors could use publicly available information regarding P/E ratios to predict future abnormal returns.

Performance measures that consider both return and risk indicated that low P/E ratio stocks experienced superior risk-adjusted results relative to the market, whereas high P/E ratio stocks had significantly inferior risk-adjusted results.[5] Subsequent analysis concluded that publicly available P/E ratios possess valuable information regarding future returns, which is inconsistent with semistrong efficiency.

Peavy and Goodman (1983) examined P/E ratios with adjustments for firm size, industry effects, and infrequent trading and likewise found that the risk-adjusted returns for stocks in the lowest P/E ratio quintile were superior to those in the highest P/E ratio quintile.

Price-Earnings/Growth Rate (PEG) Ratios During the past decade, there has been a significant increase in the use of the ratio of a stock's price-earnings ratio divided by the firm's expected growth rate of earnings (referred to as the PEG ratio) as a relative valuation tool, especially for stocks of growth companies that have P/E ratios substantially above average. Advocates of the PEG ratio hypothesize an inverse relationship between the PEG ratio and subsequent rates of return—that is, they expect that stocks with relatively low PEG ratios (i.e., less than one) will experience above-average rates of return while stocks with relatively high PEG ratios (i.e., in excess of three or four) will have below-average rates of return. A study by Peters (1991) using quarterly rebalancing supported the hypothesis of an inverse relationship. These results would constitute an anomaly and would not support the EMH. A subsequent study by Reilly and Marshall (1999) assumed annual rebalancing and divided the sample on the basis of a risk measure (beta), market value size, and by expected growth rate. Except for stocks with low

---

[5] Composite performance measures are discussed in Chapter 25.

betas and very low expected growth rates, the results were not consistent with the hypothesis of an inverse relationship between the PEG ratio and subsequent rates of return.

In summary, the results related to using the PEG ratio to select stocks are mixed—several studies that assume either monthly or quarterly rebalancing indicate an anomaly because the authors use public information and derive above-average rates of return. In contrast, a study with more realistic annual rebalancing indicated that no consistent relationship exists between the PEG ratio and subsequent rates of return.

The Size Effect Banz (1981) examined the impact of size (measured by total market value) on the risk-adjusted rates of return. The risk-adjusted returns for extended periods (20 to 35 years) indicated that the small firms consistently experienced significantly larger risk-adjusted returns than the larger firms. Reinganum (1981) contended that it was the size, not the P/E ratio, that caused the results discussed in the prior subsection, but this contention was disputed by Basu (1983).

Recall that abnormal returns may occur because the markets are inefficient or because the market model provides incorrect estimates of risk and expected returns.

It was suggested that the riskiness of the small firms was improperly measured because small firms are traded less frequently. An alternative risk measure technique confirmed that the small firms had much higher risk, but the consideration of the higher betas did not account for the large difference in rates of return.

A study by Stoll and Whaley (1983) that examined the impact of transaction costs confirmed the size effect but also found that firms with small market value generally have low stock prices. Because transaction costs vary inversely with price per share, these costs must be considered when examining the small-firm effect. It was shown that there was a significant difference in the percentage total transaction cost for large firms (2.71 percent) versus small firms (6.77 percent). This differential in transaction costs, assuming frequent trading, can have a significant impact on the results. Assuming daily transactions, the original small-firm effects are reversed. The point is, size-effect studies must consider realistic transaction costs and specify holding period assumptions. A study by Reinganum (1983) that considered both factors over long periods demonstrated that infrequent rebalancing (about once a year) is almost ideal—the results beat long-run buy-and-hold and avoids frequent rebalancing that causes excess costs. In summary, small firms outperformed large firms after considering higher risk and realistic transaction costs, assuming annual rebalancing.

Most studies on the size effect employed large databases and long time periods (over 50 years) to show that this phenomenon has existed for many years. In contrast, a study that examined the performance over various intervals of time concluded that *the small-firm effect is not stable.* During most periods investigators found the negative relationship between size and return; but, during selected periods (such as 1967 to 1975), they found that large firms outperformed the small firms. Notably, this positive relationship held during the following recent periods: 1984–1987; 1989–1990; and 1995–1998. Reinganum (1992) acknowledges this instability but contends that the small-firm effect is still a long-run phenomenon.

In summary, firm size is a major efficient market anomaly. The two strongest explanations are higher risk measurements due to infrequent trading and the higher transaction costs. Depending on the frequency of trading, these two factors may account for much of the differential. Keim (1983) also related it to seasonality. These results indicate that the size effect must be considered in any event study that considers long time periods and contains a sample of firms with significantly different market values.

Neglected Firms and Trading Activity Arbel and Strebel (1983) considered an additional influence beyond size—attention or neglect. They measured attention in terms of the number of analysts who regularly follow a stock and divided the stocks into three groups: (1) highly followed, (2) moderately followed, and (3) neglected. They confirmed the small-firm effect but also found a neglected-firm effect caused by the lack of information and limited institutional interest. The neglected-firm concept applied across size classes. Contrary results are reported by Beard and Sias (1997) who found no evidence of a neglected firm premium after controlling for capitalization.

James and Edmister (1983) examined the impact of trading volume by considering the relationship between returns, market value, and trading activity. The results confirmed the relationship between size and rates of return, but the results indicated no significant difference between the mean returns of the highest and lowest trading activity portfolios. A subsequent study hypothesized that firms with less information require higher returns. Using the period of listing as a proxy for information, they found a negative relationship between returns and the period of listing after adjusting for firm size and the January effect.

Book Value–Market Value Ratio   This ratio relates the book value (BV) of a firm's equity to the market value (MV) of its equity. Rosenberg, Reid, and Lanstein (1985) found a significant positive relationship between current values for this ratio and future stock returns and contended that such a relationship between available public information on the BV/MV ratio and future returns was evidence against the EMH.[6]

Strong support for this ratio was provided by Fama and French (1992) who evaluated the joint effects of market beta, size, E/P ratio, leverage, and the BV/MV ratio (referred to as BE/ME) on a cross section of average returns. They analyzed the hypothesized positive relationship between beta and expected returns and found that this positive relationship held pre-1969 but disappeared during the period 1963 to 1990. In contrast, the negative relationship between size and average return was significant by itself and significant after inclusion of other variables.

In addition, they found a significant positive relationship between the BV/MV ratio and average return that persisted even when other variables are included. Most importantly, *both* size and the BV/MV ratio are significant when included together and they dominate other ratios. Specifically, although leverage and the E/P ratio were significant by themselves or with size, they become insignificant when *both* size and the BV/MV ratio are considered.

The results in Exhibit 6.1 show the separate and combined effect of the two variables. As shown, going across the Small-ME (small size) row, BV/MV captures strong variation in average returns (0.70 to 1.92 percent). Alternatively, controlling for the BV/MV ratio leaves a size effect in average returns (the high BV/MV results decline from 1.92 to 1.18 percent when going from small to large). These positive results for the BV/MV ratio were replicated for returns on Japanese stocks.

In summary, studies that have used publicly available ratios to predict the cross-section of expected returns for stocks have provided substantial evidence in conflict with the semistrong-form EMH. Significant results were found for P/E ratios, market value size, and BV/MV ratios. Although the research by Fama and French indicated that the optimal combination appears to be size and the BV/MV ratio, a study by Jensen, Johnson, and Mercer (1997) indicates that this combination only works during periods of expansive monetary policy.

Results of Event Studies   Recall that the intent of event studies is to examine abnormal rates of return surrounding significant economic information. Those who advocate the EMH would expect returns to adjust quickly to announcements of new information such that investors cannot experience positive abnormal rates of return by acting after the announcement. Because of space constraints, we can only summarize the results for some of the more popular events considered.

The discussion of results is organized by event or item of public information. Specifically, we will examine the price movements and profit potential surrounding stock splits, the sale of initial public offerings, exchange listings, unexpected world or economic events, and the

---

[6] Many studies define this ratio as "book-to-market value" (BV/MV) because it implies a positive relationship, but most practitioners refer to it as the "price-to-book value" (P/B) ratio. Obviously the concept is the same, but the sign changes.

Exhibit 6.1 Average Monthly Returns on Portfolios Formed on Size and Book-to-Market Equity; Stocks Sorted by ME (Down) and Then BE/ME (Across); July 1963 to December 1990

In June of each year *t,* the NYSE, AMEX, and NASDAQ stocks that meet the CRSP-COMPUSTAT data requirements are allocated to 10 size portfolios using the NYSE size (ME) breakpoints. The NYSE, AMEX, and NASDAQ stocks in each size decile are then sorted into 10 BE/ME portfolios using the book-to-market ratios for year *t* – 1. BE/ME is the book value of common equity plus balance-sheet deferred taxes for fiscal year *t* – 1, over market equity for December of year *t* – 1. The equal-weighted monthly portfolio returns are then calculated for July of year *t* to June of year *t* + 1.

Average monthly return is the time-series average of the monthly equal-weighted portfolio returns (in percent).

The All column shows average returns for equal-weighted size decile portfolios. The All row shows average returns for equal-weighted portfolios of the stocks in each BE/ME group.

BOOK-TO-MARKET PORTFOLIOS

	All	Low	2	3	4	5	6	7	8	9	High
All	1.23	0.64	0.98	1.06	1.17	1.24	1.26	1.39	1.40	1.50	1.63
Small-ME	1.47	0.70	1.14	1.20	1.43	1.56	1.51	1.70	1.71	1.82	1.92
ME-2	1.22	0.43	1.05	0.96	1.19	1.33	1.19	1.58	1.28	1.43	1.79
ME-3	1.22	0.56	0.88	1.23	0.95	1.36	1.30	1.30	1.40	1.54	1.60
ME-4	1.19	0.39	0.72	1.06	1.36	1.13	1.21	1.34	1.59	1.51	1.47
ME-5	1.24	0.88	0.65	1.08	1.47	1.13	1.43	1.44	1.26	1.52	1.49
ME-6	1.15	0.70	0.98	1.14	1.23	0.94	1.27	1.19	1.19	1.24	1.50
ME-7	1.07	0.95	1.00	0.99	0.83	0.99	1.13	0.99	1.16	1.10	1.47
ME-8	1.08	0.66	1.13	0.91	0.95	0.99	1.01	1.15	1.05	1.29	1.55
ME-9	0.95	0.44	0.89	0.92	1.00	1.05	0.93	0.82	1.11	1.04	1.22
Large-ME	0.89	0.93	0.88	0.84	0.71	0.79	0.83	0.81	0.96	0.97	1.18

Source: Eugene F. Fama and Kenneth French, "The Cross Section of Expected Stock Returns," *Journal of Finance* 47, no. 2 (June 1992): 446. Reprinted with permission of Blackwell Publishing.

announcements of significant accounting changes. Notably, the results for most of these studies have supported the semistrong-form EMH.

Stock Split Studies Many investors believe that the prices of stocks that split will increase in value because the shares are priced lower, which increases demand for them. In contrast, advocates of efficient markets would not expect a change in value because the firm has simply issued additional stock and nothing fundamentally affecting the value of the firm has occurred.

The classic study by Fama, Fisher, Jensen, and Roll (1969), referred to hereafter as FFJR, hypothesized no significant price change following a stock split, because any relevant information (such as earnings growth) that caused the split would have already been discounted. The FFJR study analyzed abnormal price movements surrounding the time of the split and divided the stock split sample into those stocks that did or did not raise their dividends. Both groups experienced positive abnormal price changes prior to the split. Stocks that split but did *not* increase their dividend experienced abnormal price *declines* following the split and within 12 months lost all their accumulated abnormal gains. In contrast, stocks that split and increased their dividend experienced no abnormal returns after the split.

These results support the semistrong EMH because they indicate that investors cannot gain from the information on a stock split after the public announcement. These results were confirmed by most (but not all) subsequent studies. In summary, most studies found no short-run or long-run positive impact on security returns because of a stock split, although the results are not unanimous.

Initial Public Offerings (IPOs) During the past 20 years, a number of closely held companies have gone public by selling some of their common stock. Because of uncertainty about the appropriate offering price and the risk involved in underwriting such issues, it has been hypothesized that the underwriters would tend to underprice these new issues.

Given this general expectation of underpricing, the studies in this area have generally considered three sets of questions: (1) How great is the underpricing on average? Does the underpricing vary over time? If so, why? (2) What factors cause different amounts of underpricing for alternative issues? (3) How fast does the market adjust the price for the underpricing?

The answer to the first question is an average underpricing of about 17 percent, but it varies over time as shown by the results in Exhibit 6.2 for the total period 1975–2007 and for various subperiods. The major variables that cause differential underpricing seem to be various risk measures, the size of the firm, the prestige of the underwriter, and the status of the firm's accounting firm. On the question of direct interest to the EMH, results in Miller and Reilly (1987) and Ibbotson, Sindelar, and Ritter (1994) indicate that the price adjustment to the underpricing takes place within one day after the offering. Therefore, it appears that some underpricing occurs based on the original offering price, but the ones who benefit from this underpricing are basically the investors who receive allocations of the original issue.

Exhibit 6.2 Number of Offerings, Average First-Day Returns, and Gross Proceeds of Initial Public Offerings in 1975–2007

Year	Number of Offerings[1]	Average First-Day Return %[2]	Gross Proceeds, $ Millions[3]
1975	12	−1.5	262
1976	26	1.9	214
1977	15	3.6	127
1978	20	11.2	209
1979	39	8.5	312
1980	75	13.9	934
1981	197	6.2	2,367
1982	81	10.7	1,016
1983	521	9.0	11,225
1984	222	2.5	2,841
1985	216	6.2	5,492
1986	480	5.9	15,816
1987	341	5.6	12,911
1988	128	5.4	4,125
1989	119	7.9	5,155
1990	112	10.5	4,225
1991	287	11.7	15,398
1992	395	10.1	21,777
1993	505	12.7	28,899
1994	412	9.8	17,784
1995	461	21.1	28,745
1996	687	17.0	42,572
1997	483	13.9	32,478
1998	317	20.1	34,585
1999	487	69.6	65,069
2000	385	55.4	65,627
2001	81	13.7	34,368
2002	70	8.6	22,136
2003	68	12.4	10,122
2004	186	12.2	32,380
2005	169	9.8	28,677
2006	164	11.3	30,686
2007	160	13.5	35,197
1975–1979	112	5.7	1,124
1980–1989	2,380	6.8	61,880
1990–1999	4,146	21.1	291,531
2000–2007	1283	24.8	259,193
1975–2007	**7,921**	**17.2**	**613,728**

[1] The number of offerings excludes IPOs with an offer price of less than $5.00, ADRs, best efforts, units, and Regulation A offers (small issues, raising less than $1.5 million during the 1980s), real estate investment trusts (REITs), partnerships, and closed-end funds. Banks and S&Ls and non-CRSP-listed IPOs are included.

[2] First-day returns are computed as the percentage return from the offering price to the first closing market price.

[3] Gross proceeds data are from Securities Data Co., and exclude overallotment options but include the international tranche, if any. No adjustments for inflation have been made.

Source: Jay R. Ritter, "Summary Statistics on 1975–2007 Initial Public Offerings with an Offer Price of $5.00 or More" (University of Florida, January 2008).

More specifically, institutional investors captured most (70 percent) of the short-term profits. This rapid adjustment of the initial underpricing would support the semistrong EMH. Finally, studies by Ritter (1991); Carter, Dark, and Singh (1998); and Loughran and Ritter (1995) that examined the long-run returns on IPOs indicate that investors who acquire the stock after the initial adjustment do *not* experience positive long-run abnormal returns.

Exchange Listing A significant economic event for a firm is listing its stock on a national exchange, especially the NYSE. Such a listing is expected to increase the market liquidity of the stock and add to its prestige. An important question is, can an investor derive abnormal returns from investing in the stock when a new listing is announced or around the time of the actual listing? The results regarding abnormal returns from such investing were mixed. All the studies agreed that (1) the stocks' prices increased before any listing announcements, and (2) stock prices consistently declined after the actual listing. The crucial question is, What happens between the announcement of the application for listing and the actual listing (a period of four to six weeks)? A study by McConnell and Sanger (1989) points toward profit opportunities immediately after the announcement that a firm is applying for listing and there is the possibility of excess returns from price declines after the actual listing. Finally, studies that have examined the impact of listing on the risk of the securities found no significant change in systematic risk or the firm's cost of equity.

In summary, listing studies that provide evidence of short-run profit opportunities for investors using public information would not support the semistrong-form EMH.

Unexpected World Events and Economic News The results of several studies that examined the response of security prices to world or economic news have supported the semistrong-form EMH. An analysis of the reaction of stock prices to unexpected world events, such as the Eisenhower heart attack, the Kennedy assassination, and military events, found that prices adjusted to the news before the market opened or before it reopened after the announcement (generally, as with the World Trade Center attack, the Exchanges are closed immediately for various time periods—e.g., one to four days). A study by Pierce and Roley (1985) that examined the response to announcements about money supply, inflation, real economic activity, and the discount rate found an impact that did not persist beyond the announcement day. Finally, Jain (1988) did an analysis of hourly stock returns and trading volume response to surprise announcements and found that unexpected information about money supply impacted stock prices within one hour. For a review of studies that considered the impact of news on individual stocks, see Chan (2003).

Announcements of Accounting Changes Numerous studies have analyzed the impact of announcements of accounting changes on stock prices. In efficient markets, security prices should react quickly and predictably to announcements of accounting changes. An announcement of an accounting change that affects the economic value of the firm should cause a rapid change in stock prices. An accounting change that affects reported earnings but has no economic significance should not affect stock prices. For example, when a firm changes its depreciation accounting method for reporting purposes from accelerated to straight line, the firm should experience an increase in reported earnings, but there is no economic consequence. An analysis of stock price movements surrounding this accounting change supported the EMH because there were no positive price changes following the change, and there were some negative price changes because firms making such an accounting change are typically performing poorly.

During periods of high inflation, many firms will change their inventory method from first-in, first-out (FIFO) to last-in, first-out (LIFO), which causes a decline in reported earnings but benefits the firm because it reduces its taxable earnings and, therefore, tax expenses. Advocates of efficient markets would expect positive price changes because of the tax savings, and study results confirmed this expectation.

Therefore, studies such as those by Bernard and Thomas (1990) and Ou and Penman (1989) indicate that the securities markets react quite rapidly to accounting changes and adjust security prices as expected on the basis of changes in true value (that is, analysts pierce the accounting veil and value securities on the basis of economic events).

Corporate Events Corporate finance events such as mergers and acquisitions, spin-offs, reorganization, and various security offerings (common stock, straight bonds, convertible bonds) have been examined, relative to two general questions: (1) What is the market impact of these alternative events? (2) How fast does the market adjust the security prices?

Regarding the reaction to corporate events, the answer is very consistent—stock prices react as one would expect based on the underlying economic impact of the action. For example, the reaction to mergers is that the stock of the firm being acquired increases in line with the premium offered by the acquiring firm, whereas the stock of the acquiring firm typically declines because of the concern that they overpaid for the firm. On the question of speed of reaction, the evidence indicates fairly rapid adjustment—that is, the adjustment period declines as shorter interval data are analyzed (using daily data, most studies find that the price adjustment is completed in about three days). Studies related to financing decisions are reviewed by Smith (1986). Studies on corporate control that consider mergers and reorganizations are reviewed by Jensen and Warner (1988). Numerous corporate spin-offs have generated interesting stock performance as shown by Desai and Jain (1999) and Chemmanur and Yan (2004).

Summary on the Semistrong-Form EMH Clearly, the evidence from tests of the semistrong EMH is mixed. The hypothesis receives almost unanimous support from the numerous event studies on a range of events including stock splits, initial public offerings, world events and economic news, accounting changes, and a variety of corporate finance events. About the only mixed results come from exchange listing studies.

In sharp contrast, the numerous studies on predicting rates of return over time or for a cross section of stocks presented evidence counter to semistrong efficiency. This included time-series studies on risk premiums, calender patterns, and quarterly earnings surprises. Similarly, the results for cross-sectional predictors such as size, the BV/MV ratio (when there is expansive monetary policy), and P/E ratios indicated nonefficiencies.

6.3.3 Strong-Form Hypothesis: Tests and Results

The strong-form EMH contends that stock prices fully reflect *all information,* public and private. This implies that no group of investors has access to *private information* that will allow them to consistently experience above-average profits. This extremely rigid hypothesis requires not only that stock prices must adjust rapidly to new public information but also that no group has access to private information.

Tests of the strong-form EMH have analyzed returns over time for different identifiable investment groups to determine whether any group consistently received above-average risk-adjusted returns. Such a group must have access to and act upon important private information or an ability to act on public information before other investors, which would indicate that security prices were not adjusting rapidly to *all* new information.

Investigators have tested this form of the EMH by analyzing the performance of the following four major groups of investors: (1) *corporate insiders,* (2) *stock exchange specialists,* (3) *security analysts* at Value Line and elsewhere, and (4) *professional money managers.*

Corporate Insider Trading Corporate insiders are required to report monthly to the SEC on their transactions (purchases or sales) in the stock of the firm for which they are insiders. Insiders include major corporate officers, members of the board of directors, and owners of 10 percent or more of any equity class of securities. About six weeks after the reporting period, this insider trading information is made public by the SEC. These insider trading data have been used to identify how corporate insiders have traded and determine whether they bought on balance before abnormally good price movements and sold on balance before poor market periods for their stock. The results of studies including Chowdhury, Howe, and Lin (1993) and Pettit and Venkatesh (1995) have generally indicated that corporate insiders consistently enjoyed above-average profits, heavily dependent on selling prior to low returns and not selling before strong returns. This implies that many insiders had private information from which they derived above-average returns on their company stock.

In addition, an earlier study found that *public* investors who consistently traded with the insiders based on announced insider transactions would have enjoyed excess risk-adjusted returns (after commissions), although a subsequent study concluded that the market had eliminated this inefficiency after considering total transaction costs.

Overall, these results provide mixed support for the EMH because several studies indicate that insiders experience abnormal profits, while subsequent studies indicate it is no longer possible for noninsiders to use this information to generate excess returns. Notably, because of investor interest in these data as a result of academic research, the *Wall Street Journal* currently publishes a monthly column entitled "Inside Track" that discusses the largest insider transactions.

Stock Exchange Specialists Several studies have determined that specialists have monopolistic access to certain important information about unfilled limit orders, and they should be able to derive above-average returns from this information. This expectation is generally supported by the data. First, specialists generally make money because they typically sell shares at higher prices than their purchased price. Also, they apparently make money when they buy or sell after unexpected announcements and when they trade in large blocks of stock. An article by Ip (2001b) supported this belief; it contended that specialists are doing more trading as dealers and the return on their capital was in excess of 20 percent.

Security Analysts Several tests have considered whether it is possible to identify a set of analysts who have the ability to select undervalued stocks. The analysis involves determining whether, after a stock selection by an analyst is made known, a significant abnormal return is available to those who follow these recommendations. These studies and those that discuss performance by money managers are more realistic and relevant than those that considered corporate insiders and stock exchange specialists because these analysts and money managers are full-time investment professionals with no obvious advantage except emphasis and training. If anyone should be able to select undervalued stocks, it should be these "pros." We initially examine Value Line rankings and then analyze the usefulness of recommendations by individual analysts.

The Value Line Enigma Value Line (VL) is a large well-known advisory service that publishes financial information on approximately 1,700 stocks. Included in its report is a timing rank, which indicates Value Line's expectation regarding a firm's common stock performance over the coming 12 months. A rank of 1 is the most favorable performance and 5 is the worst. This ranking system, initiated in April 1965, assigns numbers based on four factors:

1. An earnings and price rank of each security relative to all others
2. A price momentum factor
3. Year-to-year relative changes in quarterly earnings
4. A quarterly earnings "surprise" factor (actual quarterly earnings compared with VL estimated earnings)

The firms are ranked based on a composite score for each firm. The top and bottom 100 are ranked 1 and 5, respectively; the next 300 from the top and bottom are ranked 2 and 4; and the rest (approximately 900) are ranked 3. Rankings are assigned every week based on the latest data. Notably, all the data used to derive the four factors are public information.

Several years after the ranking was started, Value Line contended that the stocks rated 1 substantially outperformed the market and the stocks rated 5 seriously underperformed the market (the performance figures did not include dividend income but also did not charge commissions).

Early studies on the Value Line enigma indicated that there was information in the VL rankings (especially either rank 1 or 5) and in changes in the rankings (especially going from 2 to 1). Recent evidence indicates that the market is fairly efficient, because the abnormal adjustments appear to be complete by Day + 2. An analysis of study results over time indicates a faster adjustment to the rankings during recent years. Also, despite statistically significant price changes, mounting evidence indicates that it is not possible to derive abnormal returns from these announcements after considering realistic transaction costs. The strongest evidence regarding not being able to use this information is that Value Line's Centurion Fund, which concentrates on investing in rank-1 stocks, has consistently underperformed the market over the past decade.

Analysts' Recommendations There is evidence in favor of the existence of superior analysts who apparently possess private information. A study by Womack (1996) found that analysts appear to have both market timing and stock-picking ability, especially in connection with relatively rare sell recommendations. Jegadeesh et al. (2004) found that consensus recommendations do not contain incremental information for most stocks beyond other available signals (momentum and volume), but *changes* in consensus recommendations are useful. Alternatively, research by Ivkovic and Jegadeesh (2004) indicated that the most useful information consisted of upward earning revisions in the week prior to earnings announcements. A recent study by Goff, Hulbart, Keasler, and Walsh (2008) examined the information content of analyst recommendations after the passage of Regulation Fair Disclosure (REGFD) and concluded that recommendation changes continue to be informative.

Performance of Professional Money Managers The studies of professional money managers are more realistic and widely applicable than the analysis of insiders and specialists because money managers typically do not have monopolistic access to important new information but are highly trained professionals who work full time at investment management. Therefore, if any "normal" set of investors should be able to derive above-average profits, it should be this group. Also, if any noninsider should be able to derive inside information, professional money managers should, because they conduct extensive management interviews.

Most studies on the performance of money managers have examined mutual funds because performance data are readily available for them. Recently, data have become available for bank trust departments, insurance companies, and investment advisers. The original mutual fund studies indicated that most funds did not match the performance of a buy-and-hold policy.[7] When risk-adjusted returns were examined *without* considering commission costs, slightly more than half of the money managers did better than the overall market. When commission costs, load fees, and management costs were considered, approximately two-thirds of the mutual funds did *not* match aggregate market performance. It was also found that successful funds during individual years were inconsistent in their performance over time.

Now that it is possible to get performance data for pension plans and endowment funds, several studies have documented that the performances of pension plans did not match that of the aggregate market. The performance by endowments is interesting. Specifically, the results for a large sample of endowments confirm the inability to outperform the market. In contrast, the largest endowments in terms of size experienced superior risk-adjusted performance because of their ability and willingness to consider a wide variety of asset classes such as venture capital, unique hedge funds, real estate, and commondities on a global basis.

---

[7] These studies and others on this topic are reviewed in Chapter 24.

Exhibit 6.3 Annualized Rates of Return for Mellon Analytical Solutions U.S. Equity Universes for Benchmark Indexes during Alternative Periods Ending December 31, 2007

	1 Year	2 Years	3 Years	4 Years	5 Years	8 Years	10 Years
U.S. Equity Universe Medians							
Equity Accounts	6.72	10.84	9.75	10.44	14.27	4.58	7.89
Equity Oriented Accounts	6.87	10.83	9.70	10.49	14.28	4.31	7.89
Equity Pooled	5.27	10.78	9.40	10.12	13.98	4.66	7.69
Special Equity Pooled	−1.27	7.15	7.49	10.41	16.68	10.95	9.93
Value Equity Accounts	2.53	10.58	9.79	11.34	15.10	8.82	8.79
Market Oriented Accounts	6.52	10.88	9.43	10.23	13.89	3.83	7.15
Midcap Equity Accounts	9.56	11.52	11.35	13.09	17.70	10.52	11.22
Growth Equity Accounts	14.86	11.35	10.65	10.49	14.57	1.02	7.16
Small Cap Accounts	2.00	8.69	8.79	10.92	17.29	11.65	10.48
Mutual Fund Universe—Medians							
Balanced Mutual Funds	18.51	21.87	17.63	18.78	24.10	13.11	13.12
Equity Mutual Funds	6.35	9.81	8.65	9.56	13.94	4.26	6.85
Benchmark Indexes							
Russell 1000 Growth Index	11.81	10.43	8.68	8.08	12.11	−2.93	3.83
Russell 1000 Index	5.77	10.51	9.08	9.65	13.43	2.17	6.20
Russell 1000 Value Index	−0.17	10.47	9.32	11.07	14.63	6.77	7.68
Russell 2000 Growth Index	7.05	10.15	8.11	9.63	16.50	0.65	4.32
Russell 2000 Index	−1.57	7.94	6.80	9.57	16.25	6.68	7.08
Russell 2000 Value Index	−9.78	5.55	5.27	9.28	15.80	12.60	9.06
Russell 2500 Index	1.38	8.52	8.38	10.78	16.99	8.36	9.01
Russell 3000 Index	5.14	10.30	8.89	9.65	13.63	2.49	6.22
Russell Midcap Index	5.60	10.32	11.09	13.31	18.21	8.89	9.91

Source: Mellon Analytical Solutions, Tacoma, WA. Reprinted by permission.

The figures in Exhibit 6.3 provide a rough demonstration of rate of return results for recent periods. These data are collected by Mellon Analytical Services as part of its performance evaluation service. Exhibit 6.3 contains the median rates of return for several investment groups compared to a set of Russell indexes, including the very broad Russell 3000 index.[8] These results show that five of the nine equity universes beat the Russell 3000 universe in all periods and two were superior in all but one period. Likewise, the Russell 3000 index only beat one of the mutual fund universes during three of the seven periods. A comparison of style accounts (growth and value) indicated similar results. Therefore, for these periods, most of the money manager rate of return results (not risk-adjusted) were inconsistent with the strong-form EMH.

Conclusions Regarding the Strong-Form EMH
The tests of the strong-form EMH have generated mixed results. The result for two unique groups of investors (corporate insiders and stock exchange specialists) did not support the hypothesis because both groups apparently have monopolistic access to important information and use it to derive above-average returns.

Tests to determine whether there are any analysts with private information concentrated on the Value Line rankings and publications of analysts' recommendations. The results for Value Line rankings have changed over time and currently tend toward support for the EMH. Specifically, the adjustment to rankings and ranking changes is fairly rapid, and it appears that trading is not profitable after transaction costs. Alternatively, individual analysts' recommendations and overall consensus changes seem to contain significant information.

Finally, recent performance by professional money managers provided mixed support for the strong-form EMH. Most money manager performance studies before 2002 have indicated

[8] The results for these individual accounts have an upward bias because they consider only accounts retained (for example, if a firm or bank does a poor job on an account and the client leaves, those results would not be included).

that these highly trained, full-time investors could not consistently outperform a simple buy-and-hold policy on a risk-adjusted basis. In contrast, the recent results shown in Exhibit 6.3 (that are not risk-adjusted) show that about half the non-mutual fund universe beat the broad Russell 3000 index, while the equity mutual fund results supported the EMH for long-term periods. Because money managers are similar to most investors who do not have access to inside information, these latter results are more relevant to the hypothesis. Therefore, there is mixed support for the strong-form EMH as applied to most investors.

· ·

6.4 Behavioral Finance[9]

Our discussion up to this point has dealt with standard finance theory and how to test within this theoretical context whether capital markets are informationally efficient. However, in the 1990s, a new branch of financial economics was added to the mix. **Behavioral finance** considers how various psychological traits affect how individuals or groups act as investors, analysts, and portfolio managers. As noted by Olsen (1998), behavioral finance advocates recognize that the standard finance model of rational behavior and profit maximization can be true within specific boundaries' but they assert that it is an *incomplete* model since it does not consider individual behavior. It is argued that some financial phenomena can be better explained using models where it is recognized that some investors are *not* fully rational or realize that it is *not* possible for arbitrageurs to offset all instances of mispricing (Barberis and Thaler, 2003). Specifically, according to Olsen (1998), behavioral finance

> *seeks to understand and predict systematic financial market implications of psychological decisions processes . . . behavioral finance is focused on the implication of psychological and economic principles for the improvement of financial decision-making. (p. 11)*

While it is acknowledged that currently there is no unified theory of behavioral finance, the emphasis has been on identifying portfolio anomalies that can be explained by various psychological traits in individuals or groups or pinpointing instances when it is possible to experience above-normal rates of return by exploiting the biases of investors, analysts, or portfolio managers.

6.4.1 Explaining Biases

Over time it has been noted that investors have a number of biases that negatively affect their investment performance. Advocates of behavioral finance have been able to explain a number of these biases based on psychological characteristics. One major bias documented by Scott, Stumpp, and Xu (1999) is the propensity of investors to hold on to "losers" too long and sell "winners" too soon. Apparently, investors fear losses much more than they value gains—a tendency toward loss aversion. This is explained by *prospect theory,* which contends that utility depends on deviations from moving reference points rather than absolute wealth.

There are two related biases that seriously impact analysis and investment decisions. The first is *belief perseverance,* which means that once people have formed an opinion (on a company or stock) they cling to it too tightly and for too long. As a result, they are reluctant to search for contradictory beliefs and even when they find such evidence, they are very skeptical about it or even misinterpret such information. A related bias is *anchoring,* wherein individuals who are asked to estimate something, start with an initial arbitrary (casual) value, and then adjust away from it. The problem is that the adjustment is often insufficient. Therefore, if your initial estimate is low, you may raise it with information, but it is likely you will not raise it enough and thus will end up below the "best estimates."

Another bias documented by Solt and Statman (1989) and Shefrin and Statman (1996) for growth companies is *overconfidence* in forecasts, which causes analysts to overestimate

---

[9] The discussion in this section was enhanced by two outstanding survey articles by Barberis and Thaler (2003) and by Hirschleifer (2001), as well as presentations at the CFA Research Foundation Workshop in Vancouver (May 2008).

growth rates for growth companies and overemphasize good news and ignore negative news for these firms. Analysts and many investors also suffer from *representativeness*, which causes them to believe that the stocks of growth companies will be "good" stocks. This bias is also referred to as *confirmation bias*, whereby investors look for information that supports prior opinions and decisions they have made. They also experience sample size neglect wherein they are prone to extrapolate the high growth results from a few past years (e.g., 4–6 years) for long-term periods. As a result, they will misvalue the stocks of these generally popular companies. Overconfidence is also related to *self-attribution bias* where people have a tendency to ascribe any success to their own talents while blaming any failure on "bad luck," which causes them to overestimate their talent (Gervais and Odean, 2001). Overconfidence is also nurtured by *hindsight bias*, which is a tendency after an event for an individual to believe that he or she predicted it, which causes people to think that they can predict better than they can.

A study by Brown (1999) examined the effect of *noise traders* (nonprofessionals with no special information) on the volatility of closed-end mutual funds. When there is a shift in sentiment, these traders move together, which increases the prices and the volatility of these securities during trading hours. Also, Clark and Statman (1998) find that noise traders tend to follow newsletter writers, who in turn tend to "follow the herd." These writers and "the herd" are almost always wrong, which contributes to excess volatility.

Shefrin (2001) describes *escalation bias,* which causes investors to put more money into a failure that they feel responsible for rather than into a success. This leads to the relatively popular investor practice of "averaging down" on an investment that has declined in value since the initial purchase rather than consider selling the stock if it was a mistake. The thinking is that if it was a buy at $40, it is a screaming bargain at $30. Obviously, an alternative solution is to reevaluate the stock to see if some important bad news was missed in the initial valuation (therefore, sell it and accept the loss), or to confirm the initial valuation and acquire more of the "bargain." The difficult psychological factor noted by Shefrin (1999) is that you must seriously look for the bad news and consider the negative effects of this news on the valuation.

6.4.2 Fusion Investing

According to Charles M. C. Lee (2003), *fusion investing* is the integration of two elements of investment valuation—fundamental value and investor sentiment. In Robert Shiller's (1984) formal model, the market price of securities is the expected dividends discounted to infinity (its fundamental value) plus a term that indicates the demand from noise traders who reflect investor sentiment. It is contended that when noise traders are bullish, stock prices will be higher than normal or higher than what is justified by fundamentals. Under this combination pricing model of fusion investing, investors will engage in fundamental analysis but also should consider investor sentiment in terms of fads and fashions. During some periods, investor sentiment is rather muted and noise traders are inactive, so that fundamental valuation dominates market returns. In other periods, when investor sentiment is strong, noise traders are very active and market returns are more heavily impacted by investor sentiments. Both investors and analysts should be cognizant of these dual effects on the aggregate market, various economic sectors, and individual stocks.

Beyond advocating awareness of the dual components of fusion investing, results from other studies have documented that fundamental valuation may be the dominant factor but it takes much longer to assert itself—about three years. To derive some estimate of changing investor sentiment, Lee proposes several measures of investor sentiment, most notably analysts' recommendations, price momentum, and high trading turnover. Significant changes in these variables for a stock will indicate a movement from a glamour stock to a neglected stock or vice versa. The market price of a glamour stock will exceed its intrinsic value.

· ·
6.5 Implications of Efficient Capital Markets

Having reviewed the results of numerous studies related to different facets of the EMH, the important question is, What does this mean to individual investors, financial analysts, portfolio managers, and institutions? Overall, the results of many studies indicate that the capital markets are efficient as related to numerous sets of information. At the same time, research has uncovered a substantial number of instances where the market fails to adjust prices rapidly to public information. Given these mixed results regarding the existence of efficient capital markets, it is important to consider the implications of this contrasting evidence of market efficiency.

The following discussion considers the implications of both sets of evidence. Specifically given results that support the EMH, we consider what techniques will not work and what you should do if you cannot beat the market. In contrast, because of the evidence that fails to support the EMH, we discuss what information and psychological biases should be considered when attempting to derive superior investment results through active security valuation and portfolio management.

6.5.1 Efficient Markets and Technical Analysis

The assumptions of technical analysis directly oppose the notion of efficient markets. A basic premise of technical analysis is that stock prices move in trends that persist.[10] Technicians believe that when new information comes to the market, it is not immediately available to everyone but is typically disseminated from the informed professional to the aggressive investing public and then to the great bulk of investors. Also, technicians contend that investors do not analyze information and act immediately. This process takes time. Therefore, they hypothesize that stock prices move to a new equilibrium after the release of new information in a gradual manner, which causes trends in stock price movements that persist.

Technical analysts believe that nimble traders can develop systems to detect the beginning of a movement to a new equilibrium (called a "breakout"). Hence, they hope to buy or sell the stock immediately after its breakout to take advantage of the subsequent, gradual price adjustment.

The belief in this pattern of price adjustment directly contradicts advocates of the EMH who believe that security prices adjust to new information very rapidly. These EMH advocates do not contend, however, that prices adjust perfectly, which implies a chance of overadjustment or underadjustment. Still, because it is uncertain whether the market will over- or underadjust at any time, you cannot derive abnormal profits from adjustment errors.

If the capital market is weak-form efficient as indicated by most of the results, then prices fully reflect all relevant market information so technical trading systems that depend only on past trading data *cannot* have any value. By the time the information is public, the price adjustment has taken place. Therefore, a purchase or sale using a technical trading rule should not generate abnormal returns after taking account of risk and transaction costs.

6.5.2 Efficient Markets and Fundamental Analysis

As you know from our prior discussion, fundamental analysts believe that, at any time, there is a basic intrinsic value for the aggregate stock market, various industries, or individual securities and that these values depend on underlying economic factors. Therefore, investors should determine the intrinsic value of an investment asset at a point in time by examining the variables that determine value such as future earnings or cash flows, interest rates, and risk variables. If the prevailing market price differs from the estimated intrinsic value by enough to cover transaction costs, you should take appropriate action: You buy if the market price is substantially below intrinsic value and do not buy, or you sell, if the market price is above the intrinsic value. Investors who are engaged in fundamental analysis believe that, occasionally, market price and intrinsic value differ but eventually investors recognize the discrepancy and correct it.

---

[10] Chapter 15 contains an extensive discussion of technical analysis.

An investor who can do a superior job of *estimating* intrinsic value can consistently make superior market timing (asset allocation) decisions or acquire undervalued securities and generate above-average returns. Fundamental analysis involves aggregate market analysis, industry analysis, company analysis, and portfolio management. The divergent results from the EMH research have important implications for all of these components.

Aggregate Market Analysis with Efficient Capital Markets Chapter 11 makes a strong case that intrinsic value analysis should begin with aggregate market analysis. Still, the EMH implies that if you examine only *past* economic events, it is unlikely that you will outperform a buy-and-hold policy because the market rapidly adjusts to known economic events. Evidence suggests that the market experiences long-run price movements; but, to take advantage of these movements in an efficient market, you must do a superior job of *estimating* the relevant variables that cause these long-run movements. Put another way, if you only use *historical* data to estimate future values and invest on the basis of these "old news" estimates, you will *not* experience superior, risk-adjusted returns.

Industry and Company Analysis with Efficient Capital Markets As we discuss in Chapter 13, the wide distribution of returns from different industries and companies clearly justifies industry and company analysis. Again, the EMH does not contradict the potential value of such analysis but implies that you need to (1) understand the relevant variables that affect rates of return and (2) do a superior job of *estimating future* values for these relevant valuation variables. To demonstrate this, Malkiel and Cragg (1970) developed a model that did an excellent job of explaining past stock price movements using historical data. When this valuation model was employed to project *future* stock price changes using *past* company data, however, the results were consistently inferior to a buy-and-hold policy. This implies that, even with a good valuation model, you *cannot* select stocks that will provide superior future returns using only past data as inputs. The point is, most analysts are aware of the several well-specified valuation models, so the factor that differentiates superior from inferior analysts is the ability to *provide more accurate estimates* of the critical inputs to the valuation models.

A study by Benesh and Peterson (1986) showed that the crucial difference between the stocks that enjoyed the best and worst price performance during a given year was the relationship between expected earnings of professional analysts and actual earnings (that is, it was *earnings surprises*). Specifically, stock prices increased if actual earnings substantially exceeded expected earnings and stock prices fell if actual earnings were below expected levels. As suggested by Fogler (1993), if you can do a superior job of projecting earnings and your expectations *differ from the consensus* (i.e., you project earnings surprises), you will have a superior stock selection record. To summarize this discussion, there are two factors that are required to be a superior analyst: (1) you must be *correct* in your estimates, and (2) you must be *different* from the consensus. Remember, if you are only correct and not different, that assumes you were predicting the consensus and the consensus was correct, which implies no surprise and no abnormal price movement.

The quest to be a superior analyst holds some good news and some suggestions. The good news is related to the strong-form tests that indicated the likely existence of superior analysts. It was shown that the rankings by Value Line contained information value, even though it might not be possible to profit from the work of these analysts after transaction costs. Also, the price adjustments to the publication of analyst recommendations also point to the existence of superior analysts. The point is, there are some superior analysts, but only a limited number, and it is *not* an easy task to be among this select group. Most notably, to be a superior analyst you must do a superior job of *estimating* the relevant valuation variables and *predicting earnings surprises* because you differ from the consensus.

The suggestions for those involved in fundamental analysis are based on the studies that considered the cross section of future returns. As noted, these studies indicated that P/E ratios, size, and the BV/MV ratios were able to differentiate future return patterns with size and the BV/MV ratio appearing to be the optimal combination. Therefore, these factors should be considered when selecting a universe or analyzing firms. In addition, the evidence suggests that neglected firms should be given extra consideration. Although these ratios and characteristics have been shown to be useful in isolating superior stocks from a large sample, it is our suggestion that they are best used to derive a viable sample to analyze from the total universe (e.g., select 200 stocks to analyze from a universe of 3,000). Then the 200 stocks should be rigorously valued using the techniques discussed in subsequent chapters.

How to Evaluate Analysts or Investors If you want to determine if an individual is a superior analyst or investor, you should examine the performance of numerous securities that this analyst or investor recommends over time in relation to the performance of a set of randomly selected stocks of the same risk class. The stock selections of a superior analyst or investor should *consistently* outperform the randomly selected stocks. The consistency requirement is crucial because you would expect a portfolio developed by random selection to outperform the market about half the time.

Conclusions about Fundamental Analysis A text on investments can indicate the relevant variables that you should analyze and describe the important analysis techniques, but actually estimating the relevant variables is as much an art and a product of hard work as it is a science. If the estimates could be done on the basis of some mechanical formula, you could program a computer to do it, and there would be no need for analysts. Therefore, the superior analyst or successful investor must understand what variables are relevant to the valuation process and have the ability and work ethic to do a superior job of *estimating* values for these important valuation variables. Alternatively, one can be superior if he or she has the ability to interpret the impact or estimate the effect of some public information better than others.

6.5.3 Efficient Markets and Portfolio Management

As noted, studies have indicated that the majority of professional money managers cannot beat a buy-and-hold policy on a risk-adjusted basis. One explanation for this generally inferior performance is that there are no superior analysts and the cost of research and trading forces the results of merely adequate analysis into the inferior category. Another explanation, which is favored by the authors and has some empirical support from the Value Line and analyst recommendation results, is that money management firms employ both superior and inferior analysts and the gains from the recommendations by the few superior analysts are offset by the costs and the poor results derived from the recommendations of the inferior analysts.

This raises the question, Should a portfolio be managed actively or passively? The following discussion indicates that the decision of how to manage the portfolio (actively or passively) depends on whether the manager (or an investor) has access to superior analysts. A portfolio manager with superior analysts or an investor who believes that he or she has the time and expertise to be a superior investor can manage a portfolio actively by looking for undervalued or overvalued securities and trading accordingly. In contrast, without access to superior analysts or the time and ability to be a superior investor, you should manage passively and assume that all securities are properly priced based on their levels of risk.

Portfolio Management with Superior Analysts A portfolio manager with access to superior analysts who have unique insights and analytical ability should follow their recommendations. The superior analysts should make investment recommendations for a certain proportion of the portfolio, and the portfolio manager should ensure that the risk preferences of the client are maintained.

Also, the superior analysts should be encouraged to concentrate their efforts in mid-cap and small-cap stocks that possess the liquidity required by institutional portfolio managers. But because these stocks typically do not receive the attention given the top-tier stocks, the markets for these neglected stocks may be less efficient than the market for large well-known stocks that are being analyzed by numerous analysts.

Recall that capital markets are expected to be efficient because many investors receive new information and analyze its effect on security values. If the number of analysts following a stock differ, one could conceive of differences in the efficiency of the markets. New information on top-tier stocks is well publicized and rigorously analyzed so the price of these securities should adjust rapidly to reflect the new information. In contrast, mid-cap and small-cap stocks receive less publicity and fewer analysts follow these firms, so prices are expected to adjust less rapidly to new information. Therefore, the possibility of finding temporarily undervalued securities among these neglected stocks is greater. Again, in line with the cross-section study results, these superior analysts should pay particular attention to the BV/MV ratio, to the size of stocks being analyzed, and to the monetary policy environment.

Portfolio Management without Superior Analysts   A portfolio manager (or investor) who does not have access to superior analysts should proceed as follows. First, he or she should *measure the risk preferences* of his or her clients, then build a portfolio to match this risk level by investing a certain proportion of the portfolio in risky assets and the rest in a risk-free asset, as discussed in Chapter 8.

The risky asset portfolio must be *completely diversified* on a global basis so it moves consistently with the world market. In this context, proper diversification means eliminating all unsystematic (unique) variability. In our prior discussion, it was estimated that it required about 20 securities to gain most of the benefits (more than 90 percent) of a completely diversified portfolio. More than 100 stocks are required for complete diversification. To decide how many securities to actually include in your global portfolio, you must balance the added benefits of complete worldwide diversification against the costs of research for the additional stocks.

Finally, you should *minimize transaction costs.* Assuming that the portfolio is completely diversified and is structured for the desired risk level, excessive transaction costs that do not generate added returns will detract from your expected rate of return. Three factors are involved in minimizing total transaction costs:

1. *Minimize taxes.* Methods of accomplishing this objective vary, but it should receive prime consideration.
2. *Reduce trading turnover.* Trade only to liquidate part of the portfolio or to maintain a given risk level.
3. *When you trade, minimize liquidity costs by trading relatively liquid stocks.* To accomplish this, submit limit orders to buy or sell several stocks at prices that approximate the specialist's quote. That is, you would put in limit orders to buy stock at the bid price or sell at the ask price. The stock bought or sold first is the most liquid one; all other orders should be withdrawn.

In summary, if you lack access to superior analysts, you should do the following:

1. Determine and quantify your risk preferences.
2. Construct the appropriate risk portfolio by dividing the total portfolio between risk-free assets and a risky asset portfolio.
3. Diversify completely on a global basis to eliminate all unsystematic risk.
4. Maintain the specified risk level by rebalancing when necessary.
5. Minimize total transaction costs.

The Rationale and Use of Index Funds and Exchange-Traded Funds As discussed, efficient capital markets and a lack of superior analysts imply that many portfolios should be managed *passively* to match the performance of the aggregate market, minimizing the costs of research and trading. In response to this demand, several institutions have introduced *index funds,* which are security portfolios designed to duplicate the composition, and performance, of a selected market index series.

Notably, this concept of stock-market index funds has been extended to other areas of investments and, as discussed by Gastineau (2001) and Kostovetsky (2003), has been enhanced by the introduction of exchange-traded funds (ETFs). Index bond funds attempt to emulate the bond-market indexes discussed in Chapter 5. Also, some index funds focus on specific segments of the market such as international bond-index funds, international stock-index funds that target specific countries, and index funds that target small-cap stocks in the United States and Japan. When financial planners want a given asset class in their portfolios, they often use index funds or ETFs to fulfill this need. Index funds or ETFs are less costly in terms of research and commissions, and, they generally provide the same or better performance than the majority of active portfolio managers. A recent innovation suggested by Arnott, Hsu, and West (2008) in this area is to weight the stocks in an index fund based on fundamentals such as earnings, cash flow, and/or dividends rather than market values.

Insights from Behavioral Finance As noted earlier, the major contributions of behavioral finance researchers are explanations for some of the anomalies discovered by prior academic research. They also suggest opportunities to derive abnormal rates of return by acting on some of the deeply ingrained biases of investors. For some further analysis, see Barbaris, Schliefer, and Vishney (1998). Clearly, their findings support the notion that the stocks of growth companies typically will not be growth stocks because analysts become overconfident in their ability to predict future growth rates and eventually derive valuations that either fully value or overvalue future growth. Behavioral finance research also supports the notion of contrary investing, confirming the notion of the herd mentality of analysts in stock recommendations or quarterly earning estimates and the recommendations by newsletter writers. Also, it is important to recall the loss aversion and escalation bias that causes investors to ignore bad news and hold losers too long and in some cases acquire additional shares of losers to average down the cost. Before averaging down, be sure you reevaluate the stock and consider all the potential bad news we tend to ignore. Finally, recognize that market prices are a combination of fundamental value and investor sentiment.

• • • • SUMMARY • • • •

- The efficiency of capital markets has implications for the investment analysis and management of your portfolio. Capital markets should be efficient because numerous rational, profit-maximizing investors react quickly to the release of new information. Assuming prices reflect new information, they are unbiased estimates of the securities' true, intrinsic value, and there should be a consistent relationship between the return on an investment and its risk.
- The voluminous research on the EMH has been divided into three segments that have been tested separately. The weak-form EMH states that stock prices fully reflect all market information, so any trading rule that uses past market data to predict future returns should have no value. The results of most studies consistently supported this hypothesis.

- The semistrong-form EMH asserts that security prices adjust rapidly to the release of all public information. The tests of this hypothesis either examine the opportunities to predict future rates of return (either a time series or a cross section) or they involve event studies in which investigators analyzed whether investors could derive above-average returns from trading on the basis of public information. The test results for this hypothesis were clearly mixed. On the one hand, the results for almost all the event studies related to economic events such as stock splits, initial public offerings, and accounting changes consistently supported the semistrong hypothesis. In contrast, several studies that examined the ability to predict rates of return on the basis of unexpected quarterly earnings, P/E ratios, size, neglected stocks, and the BV/MV ratio, as well as several calendar effects, generally did not support the hypothesis.

- The strong-form EMH states that security prices reflect all information. This implies that nobody has private information, so no group should be able to derive above-average returns consistently. Studies that examined the results for corporate insiders and stock exchange specialists do not support the strong-form hypothesis. An analysis of individual analysts as represented by Value Line or by recommendations published in the *Wall Street Journal* give mixed results. The results indicated that the Value Line rankings have significant information but it may not be possible to profit from it, whereas the recommendations by analysts indicated the existence of private information. In contrast, the performance by professional money managers supported the EMH because their risk-adjusted investment performance (whether mutual funds or pension funds) was typically inferior to results achieved with buy-and-hold policies.

- During the past decade, there has been significant research in behavioral finance by investigators who contend that the standard finance theory model is incomplete since it does not consider implications of psychological decisions made by individuals that both help explain many anomalies and note the existence of several biases and provide opportunities for excess returns. It is important to be aware of a number of biases for two reasons: first, they can lead to inferior performance as an analyst and portfolio manager; second, it is possible to exploit them for excess returns.

- Given the mixed results, it is important to consider the implications of all of this for technical or fundamental analysts and for portfolio managers. The EMH indicates that technical analysis should be of no value. All forms of fundamental analysis are useful, but they are difficult to implement because they require the ability *to estimate future values* for relevant economic variables. Superior analysis is possible but difficult because it requires superior projections. Those who manage portfolios should constantly evaluate investment advice to determine whether it is superior.

- Without access to superior analytical advice, you should run your portfolio like an index fund or an ETF. In contrast, those with superior analytical ability should be allowed to make decisions, but they should concentrate their efforts on mid-cap firms and neglected firms where there is a higher probability of discovering misvalued stocks. The analysis should be particularly concerned with a firm's BV/MV ratio, its size, and the monetary environment.

- This chapter contains some good news and some bad news. The good news is that the practice of investment analysis and portfolio management is not an art that has been lost to the great computer in the sky. Viable professions still await those willing to extend the effort and able to accept the pressures. The bad news is that many bright, hardworking people with extensive resources make the game tough. In fact, those competitors have created a fairly efficient capital market in which it is extremely difficult for most analysts and portfolio managers to achieve superior results.

• • • • SUGGESTED READINGS • • • •

Ariely, Dan, *Predictably Irrational: The Hidden Forces that Shape Our Decisions*, New York: Harper Collins, 2008.

Arnott, Robert D., Jason C. Hsu, and John M. West, *The Fundamental Index* New York: Wiley, 2008.

Ball, Ray. "The Theory of Stock Market Efficiency: Accomplishments and Limitations." *Journal of Applied Corporate Finance* 8, no. 1 (Spring 1995).

Barberis, Nicholas, and Richard Thalen. "A Survey of Behavioral Finance." *Handbook of the Economics of Finance,* ed. G.M. Constantianides, M. Harris, and Rene Stulz. New York: Elsevier Science, 2003.

Berkowitz, Stephen A., Louis D. Finey, and Dennis Logue. *The Investment Performance of Corporate Pension Plans.* New York: Quorum Books, 1988.

Bernard, Victor. "Capital Markets Research in Accounting During the 1980s: A Critical Review," in *The State of Accounting Research as We Enter the 1990s*, ed. Thomas J. Frecka. Urbana: University of Illinois Press, 1989.

Fama, Eugene. "Market Efficiency, Long-Term Returns, and Behavioral Finance." *Journal of Financial Economics* 49, no. 3 (September 1998): 283–306.

Gervais, S., and T. Odean, "Learning to be Overconfident," *Review of Financial Studies* 14, no. 1 (2001): 1–27.

Hartford, Tim, *The Logic of Life*, New York: Random House, 2008.

Hirschleifer, David. "Investor Psychology and Asset Pricing." *Journal of Finance* 56, no. 4 (August 2001): 1533–1597.

Keim, Donald B., and Robert F. Stambaugh. "Predicting Returns in Stock and Bond Markets." *Journal of Financial Economics* 17, no. 2 (December 1986).

Koller, Tim, Marc Goedhart, and David Wessels. *Valuation: Measuring and Managing the Value of Companies,* 4th ed. New York: Wiley, 2005.

Shefrin, Hersh, and Meir Statman. "Behavioral Capital Asset Pricing Theory." *Journal of Financial and Quantitative Analysis* 30, no. 3 (September 1995a).

Shefrin, Hersh. *A Behavioral Approach to Asset Pricing Theory.* Amsterdam: Elsevier-North Holland, 2005.

Shermer, Michael, *The Mind of the Market*, New York: Times Books, 2008.

Wood, Arnold S., ed. *Behavioral Finance and Decision Theory in Investment Management.* Charlottesville, VA: AIMR, 1995.

• • • • QUESTIONS • • • •

1. Discuss the rationale for expecting an efficient capital market. What factor would you look for to differentiate the market efficiency for two alternative stocks?
2. Define and discuss the weak-form EMH. Describe the two sets of tests used to examine the weak-form EMH.
3. Define and discuss the semistrong-form EMH. Describe the two sets of tests used to examine the semistrong-form EMH.
4. What is meant by the term *abnormal rate of return?*
5. Describe how you would compute the abnormal rate of return for a stock for a period surrounding an economic event. Give a brief example for a stock with a beta of 1.40.
6. Assume you want to test the EMH by comparing alternative trading rules to a buy-and-hold policy. Discuss the three common mistakes that can bias the results against the EMH.
7. Describe the results of a study that supported the semistrong-form EMH. Discuss the nature of the test and specifically why the results support the hypothesis.
8. Describe the results of a study that did *not* support the semistrong-form EMH. Discuss the nature of the test and specifically why the results did not support the hypothesis.
9. For many of the EMH tests, it is really a test of a "joint hypothesis." Discuss what is meant by this concept. What are the joint hypotheses being tested?
10. Define and discuss the strong-form EMH. Why do some observers contend that the strong-form hypothesis really requires a perfect market in addition to an efficient market? Be specific.
11. Discuss how you would test the strong-form EMH. Why are these tests relevant? Give a brief example.
12. Describe the results of a study that did *not* support the strong-form EMH. Discuss the test involved and specifically why the results reported did not support the hypothesis.
13. Describe the results of a study that *did* support the strong-form EMH. Discuss the test involved and specifically why these results support the hypothesis.
14. Describe the general goal of behavioral finance.
15. Why do the advocates of behavioral finance contend that the standard finance theory is incomplete?
16. What does the EMH imply for the use of technical analysis?
17. What does the EMH imply for fundamental analysis? Discuss specifically what it does not imply.
18. In a world of efficient capital markets, what do you have to do to be a superior analyst? How would you test whether an analyst was superior?
19. What advice would you give to your superior analysts in terms of the set of firms to analyze and variables that should be considered in the analysis? Discuss your reasoning for this advice.
20. How should a portfolio manager without any superior analysts run his or her portfolio?
21. Describe the goals of an index fund. Discuss the contention that index funds are the ultimate answer in a world with efficient capital markets.
22. At a social gathering, you meet the portfolio manager for the trust department of a local bank. He confides to you that he has been following the recommendations of the department's six analysts for an extended period and has found that two are superior, two are average, and two are clearly inferior. What would you recommend that he do to run his portfolio?
23. **CFA EXAMINATION LEVEL I**
    a. List and briefly define the *three* forms of the efficient market hypothesis. [6 minutes]
    b. Discuss the role of a portfolio manager in a perfectly efficient market. [9 minutes]
24. **CFA EXAMINATION LEVEL II** Tom Max, TMP's quantitative analyst, has developed a portfolio construction model about which he is excited. To create the model, Max made a list of the stocks currently in the S&P 500 Stock Index and obtained annual operating cash flow, price, and total return data for each issue for the past five years. As of each year-end, this universe was divided into five equal-weighted portfolios of 100 issues each, with selection based solely on the price/cash flow rankings of the individual stocks. Each portfolio's average annual return was then calculated.

    During this five-year period, the linked returns from the portfolios with the lowest price/cash flow ratio generated an annualized total return of 19.0 percent, or 3.1 percentage points better than the 15.9 percent return on the S&P 500 Stock Index. Max also noted that the lowest price–cash-flow portfolio had a below-market beta of 0.91 over this same time span.
    a. Briefly comment on Max's use of the beta measure as an indicator of portfolio risk in light of recent academic tests of its explanatory power with respect to stock returns. [5 minutes]

b. You are familiar with the literature on market anomalies and inefficiencies. Against this background, discuss Max's use of a single-factor model (price–cash flow) in his research. [8 minutes]

c. Identify and briefly describe *four* specific concerns about Max's test procedures and model design. (The issues already discussed in your answers to Parts a and b may *not* be used in answering Part c.) [12 minutes]

25. **CFA EXAMINATION LEVEL III**

a. Briefly explain the concept of the *efficient market hypothesis* (EMH) and each of its three forms— *weak, semistrong, and strong*—and briefly discuss the degree to which existing empirical evidence supports each of the three forms of the EMH. [8 minutes]

b. Briefly discuss the implications of the efficient market hypothesis for investment policy as it applies to:
  (i) technical analysis in the form of charting, and
  (ii) fundamental analysis. [4 minutes]

c. Briefly explain *two* major roles or responsibilities of portfolio managers in an efficient market environment. [4 minutes]

d. Briefly discuss whether active asset allocation among countries could consistently outperform a world market index. Include a discussion of the implications of *integration versus segmentation* of international financial markets as it pertains to portfolio diversification, but ignore the issue of stock selection. [6 minutes]

· · · · **PROBLEMS** · · · ·

1. Look up the daily trading volume for the following stocks during a recent five-day period:
   • Merck
   • Anheuser Busch
   • Intel
   • McDonald's
   • General Electric

   Randomly select five stocks from the NYSE and examine their daily trading volume for the same five days.

   a. What are the average volumes for the two samples?

   b. Would you expect this difference to have an impact on the efficiency of the markets for the two samples? Why or why not?

2. Compute the abnormal rates of return for the following stocks during period t (ignore differential systematic risk):

Stock	R_{it}	R_{mt}
B	11.5%	4.0%
F	10.0	8.5
T	14.0	9.6
C	12.0	15.3
E	15.9	12.4

   R_{it} = return for stock i during period t
   R_{mt} = return for the aggregate market during period t

3. Compute the abnormal rates of return for the five stocks in Problem 1 assuming the following systematic risk measures (betas):

Stock	β_i
B	0.95
F	1.25
T	1.45
C	0.70
E	−0.30

4. Compare the abnormal returns in Problems 2 and 3 and discuss the reason for the difference in each case.

CHAPTER 7

An Introduction to Portfolio Management

After you read this chapter, you should be able to answer the following questions:

- What do we mean by *risk aversion*, and what evidence indicates that investors are generally risk averse?
- What are the basic assumptions behind the Markowitz portfolio theory?
- What do we mean by *risk*, and what are some measures of risk used in investments?
- How do we compute the expected rate of return for an individual risky asset or a portfolio of assets?
- How do we compute the standard deviation of rates of return for an individual risky asset?
- What do we mean by the *covariance* between rates of return, and how is it computed?
- What is the relationship between covariance and correlation?
- What is the formula for the standard deviation for a *portfolio* of risky assets, and how does it differ from the standard deviation of an individual risky asset?
- Given the formula for the standard deviation of a portfolio, how do we diversify a portfolio?
- What happens to the standard deviation of a portfolio when we change the correlation between the assets in the portfolio?
- What is the risk–return efficient frontier of risky assets?
- Would you expect different investors to select different portfolios from the set of portfolios on the efficient frontier?
- What determines which portfolio on the efficient frontier is selected by an individual investor?

One of the major advances in the investment field during the past few decades has been the recognition that you cannot create an optimum investment portfolio by simply combining numerous individual securities that have desirable risk–return characteristics. Specifically, it has been shown that an investor must consider the relationship *among* the investments to build an optimum portfolio that will meet investment objectives. The recognition of how to create an optimum portfolio was demonstrated in the derivation of portfolio theory.

In this chapter we explain portfolio theory step by step. We introduce the basic portfolio risk formula for combining different assets. Once you understand this formula and its implications, you will understand *why* you should diversify your porfolio and also *how* you should diversify.

7.1 Some Background Assumptions

Before presenting portfolio theory, we need to clarify some general assumptions of the theory. This includes not only what we mean by an *optimum portfolio* but also what we mean by the terms *risk aversion* and *risk.*

One basic assumption of portfolio theory is that investors want to maximize the returns from your total set of investments for a given level of risk. To adequately deal with such an assumption requires certain ground rules. First, your portfolio should *include all of your assets and liabilities*, not only your marketable securities but also your car, house, and less marketable investments such as coins, stamps, art, antiques, and furniture. The full spectrum of investments must be considered because the returns from all these investments interact, and *this relationship among the returns for assets in the portfolio is important.* Hence, a good portfolio is not simply a collection of individually good investments.

7.1.1 Risk Aversion

Portfolio theory also assumes that investors are basically **risk averse**, meaning that, given a choice between two assets with equal rates of return, they will select the asset with the lower level of risk. Evidence that most investors are risk averse is that they purchase various types of insurance, including life insurance, car insurance, and health insurance. Buying insurance basically involves an outlay of a given known amount to guard against an uncertain, possibly larger, outlay in the future. Further evidence of risk aversion is the difference in promised yield (the required rate of return) for different grades of bonds with different degrees of credit risk. Specifically, the promised yield on corporate bonds increases from AAA (the lowest risk class) to AA to A, and so on, indicating that investors require a higher rate of return to accept higher risk.

This does not imply that everybody is risk averse, or that investors are completely risk averse regarding all financial commitments. The fact is, not everybody buys insurance for everything. Some people have no insurance against anything, either by choice or because they cannot afford it. In addition, some individuals buy insurance related to some risks such as auto accidents or illness, but they also buy lottery tickets and gamble at race tracks or in casinos, where it is known that the expected returns are negative (which means that participants are willing to pay for the excitement of the risk involved). This combination of risk preference and risk aversion can be explained by an attitude toward risk that depends on the amount of money involved. Researchers such as Friedman and Savage (1948) speculate that this is the case for people who like to gamble for small amounts (in lotteries or slot machines) but buy insurance to protect themselves against large losses such as fire or accidents.

While recognizing such attitudes, we assume that most investors with a large investment portfolio are risk averse. Therefore, we expect a positive relationship between expected return and expected risk, which is consistent with historical results as shown in Chapter 3.

7.1.2 Definition of Risk

Although there is a difference in the specific definitions of *risk* and *uncertainty*, for our purposes and in most financial literature the two terms are used interchangeably. For most investors, *risk* means *the uncertainty of future outcomes.* An alternative definition might be *the probability of an adverse outcome.* In our subsequent discussion of portfolio theory, we consider several measures of risk that are used when developing and applying the theory.

7.2 Markowitz Portfolio Theory

In the early 1960s, the investment community talked about risk, but there was no specific measure for the term. To build a portfolio model, however, investors had to quantify their risk variable. The basic portfolio model was developed by Harry Markowitz (1952, 1959), who derived the expected rate of return for a portfolio of assets and an expected risk measure. Markowitz showed that the variance of the rate of return was a meaningful measure of portfolio risk under a reasonable set of assumptions. More important, he derived the formula for computing the variance of a portfolio. This portfolio variance formula not only indicated the importance of diversifying investments to reduce the total risk of a portfolio but also showed *how* to effectively diversify. The Markowitz model is based on several assumptions regarding investor behavior:

1. Investors consider each investment alternative as being represented by a probability distribution of expected returns over some holding period.
2. Investors maximize one-period expected utility, and their utility curves demonstrate diminishing marginal utility of wealth.

3. Investors estimate the risk of the portfolio on the basis of the variability of expected returns.
4. Investors base decisions solely on expected return and risk, so their utility curves are a function of expected return and the expected variance (or standard deviation) of returns only.
5. For a given risk level, investors prefer higher returns to lower returns. Similarly, for a given level of expected return, investors prefer less risk to more risk.

Under these assumptions, *a single asset or portfolio of assets is considered to be efficient if no other asset or portfolio of assets offers higher expected return with the same (or lower) risk or lower risk with the same (or higher) expected return.*

7.2.1 Alternative Measures of Risk

One of the best-known measures of risk is the *variance,* or *standard deviation of expected returns.*[1] It is a statistical measure of the dispersion of returns around the expected value whereby a larger variance or standard deviation indicates greater dispersion. The idea is that the more disperse the expected returns, the greater the uncertainty of future returns.

Another measure of risk is the *range of returns.* It is assumed that a larger range of expected returns, from the lowest to the highest, means greater uncertainty regarding future expected returns.

Instead of using measures that analyze all deviations from expectations, some observers believe that investors should be concerned only with returns below expectations, which means only deviations below the mean value. A measure that only considers deviations below the mean is the *semivariance.* An extension of the semivariance measure only computes expected returns *below zero* (that is, negative returns), or returns below the returns of some specific asset such as T-bills, the rate of inflation, or a benchmark. These measures of risk implicitly assume that investors want to *minimize the damage* (regret) from returns less than some target rate. Assuming that investors would welcome returns above some target rate, the returns above such a target rate are not considered when measuring risk.

Although there are numerous potential measures of risk, we will use the variance or standard deviation of returns because (1) this measure is somewhat intuitive, (2) it is a correct and widely recognized risk measure, and (3) it has been used in most of the theoretical asset pricing models.

7.2.2 Expected Rates of Return

We compute the expected rate of return for an *individual investment* as shown in Exhibit 7.1. The expected return for an individual risky asset with the set of potential returns and an assumption of the different probabilities used in the example would be 10.3 percent.

The expected rate of return for a *portfolio* of investments is simply the weighted average of the expected rates of return for the individual investments in the portfolio. The weights are the proportion of total value for the individual investment.

Exhibit 7.1 Computation of the Expected Return for an Individual Asset

Probability	Possible Rate of Return (percent)	Expected Security Return (percent)
0.35	0.08	0.0280
0.30	0.10	0.0300
0.20	0.12	0.0240
0.15	0.14	0.0210
		$E(R_i) = 0.1030$

[1]We consider the variance and standard deviation as one measure of risk because the standard deviation is the square root of the variance.

Exhibit 7.2 Computation of the Expected Return for a Portfolio of Risky Assets

Weight (w$_i$) (percent of portfolio)	Expected Security Return (R$_i$)	Expected Portfolio Return (w$_i$ × R$_i$)
0.20	0.10	0.0200
0.30	0.11	0.0330
0.30	0.12	0.0360
0.20	0.13	0.0260
		E(R$_{port}$) = 0.1150

The expected rate of return for a hypothetical portfolio with four risky assets is shown in Exhibit 7.2. The expected return for this portfolio of investments would be 11.5 percent. The effect of adding or dropping any investment from the portfolio would be easy to determine; we would use the new weights based on value and the expected returns for each of the investments. We can generalize this computation of the expected return for the portfolio E(R$_{port}$) as follows:

7.1
$$E(R_{port}) = \sum_{i=1}^{n} w_i R_i$$

where:

w$_i$ = the weight of an individual asset in the portfolio, or the percent of the portfolio in Asset i

R$_i$ = the expected rate of return for Asset i

7.2.3 Variance (Standard Deviation) of Returns for an Individual Investment

As noted, we will be using the variance or the standard deviation of returns as the measure of risk. Therefore, at this point we demonstrate how to compute the standard deviation of returns for an individual investment. Subsequently, after discussing some other statistical concepts, we will consider the determination of the standard deviation for a *portfolio* of investments.

The variance, or standard deviation, is a measure of the variation of possible rates of return R$_i$ from the expected rate of return E(R$_i$) as follows:

7.2
$$\text{Variance} = \sigma^2 = \sum_{i=1}^{n} [R_i - E(R_i)]^2 P_i$$

where:

P$_i$ = probability of the possible rate of return R$_i$

7.3
$$\text{Standard Deviation} = \sigma = \sqrt{\sum_{i=1}^{n} [R_i - E(R_i)]^2 P_i}$$

The computation of the variance and standard deviation of returns for the individual risky asset in Exhibit 7.1 is set forth in Exhibit 7.3.

Exhibit 7.3 Computation of the Variance for an Individual Risky Asset

Possible Rate of Return (R$_i$)	Expected Security Return E(R$_i$)	R$_i$ − E(R$_i$)	[R$_i$ − E(R$_i$)]^2	P$_i$	[R$_i$ − E(R$_i$)]^{2}P$_i$
0.08	0.103	−0.023	0.0005	0.35	0.000185
0.10	0.103	−0.003	0.0000	0.30	0.000003
0.12	0.103	0.017	0.0003	0.20	0.000058
0.14	0.103	0.037	0.0014	0.15	0.000205
					0.000451

Variance = σ^2 = 0.000451

Standard Deviation = σ = 0.021237

7.2.4 Variance (Standard Deviation) of Returns for a Portfolio

Two basic concepts in statistics, covariance and correlation, must be understood before we discuss the formula for the variance of the rate of return for a portfolio.

Covariance of Returns   In this subsection we discuss what the covariance of returns is intended to measure, give the formula for computing it, and present an example of its computation. **Covariance** is a measure of the degree to which two variables move together relative to their individual mean values over time. In portfolio analysis, we usually are concerned with the covariance of *rates of return* rather than prices or some other variable.[2] A positive covariance means that the rates of return for two investments tend to move in the same direction relative to their individual means during the same time period. In contrast, a negative covariance indicates that the rates of return for two investments tend to move in different directions relative to their means during specified time intervals over time. The *magnitude* of the covariance depends on the variances of the individual return series, as well as on the relationship between the series.

Exhibit 7.4 contains the monthly rates of return values for U.S. stocks (measued using the Wilshire 5000 index) and bonds (measured by the Lehman Brothers Treasury Bond Index). Both indexes are total return indexes—that is, the stock index includes dividends paid and the bond index includes accrued interest, as discussed in Chapter 5. Using end-of-month values for each index, we compute the percentage change in the index each month, which equals its monthly rates of return during 2007. Exhibits 7.5 and 7.6 contain a time-series plot of these monthly rates of return. Although the rates of return for the two assets moved together during some months, in other months they moved in opposite directions. The covariance statistic provides an *absolute* measure of how they moved together over time.

For two assets, *i* and *j*, we define the covariance of rates of return as

7.4
$$\text{Cov}_{ij} = E\left\{[R_i - E(R_i)][R_j - E(R_j)]\right\}$$

Exhibit 7.4 Listing of Monthly Rates of Return for U.S. Stocks and Bonds during 2007

2007	Wilshire 5000 Stock Index Monthly Rate of Return (%)	Lehman Brothers Treasury Bonds Index Monthly Rate of Return (%)
Jan	−1.51	−0.16
Feb	0.96	1.66
Mar	3.77	−0.05
Apr	3.33	0.52
May	−1.55	−0.90
Jun	−3.47	−0.04
Jul	1.12	1.66
Aug	3.46	1.57
Sep	2.03	0.54
Oct	−4.73	0.79
Nov	−0.76	3.07
Dec	−6.23	0.08
Mean	−0.30	0.73

Sources: Wilshire Associates and Lehman Brothers.

[2]Returns, of course, can be measured in a variety of ways, depending on the type of asset. You will recall that we defined returns (Ri) in Chapter 1 as:

$$R_i = \frac{EV - BV + CF}{BV}$$

where EV is ending value, BV is beginning value, and CF is the cash flow during the period.

Exhibit 7.5 Time-Series Plot of the Monthly Returns for Wilshire 5000 Stock Index, 2007

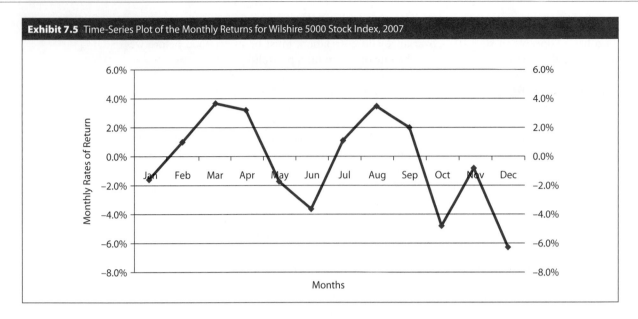

When we apply this formula to the monthly rates of return for the Wilshire 5000 stock and the Treasury bond indexes during 2007, it becomes

$$\frac{1}{11}\sum_{i=1}^{12}[R_i - \overline{R}_i][R_j - \overline{R}_j]$$

Note that when we apply formula 7.4 to actual sample data, we use the sample mean ($\overline{R}$) as an estimate of the expected return and divide the values by ($n - 1$) rather than by n to avoid statistical bias.

As can be seen, if the rates of return for one asset are above (below) its mean rate of return ($\overline{R}$) during a given period and the returns for the other asset are likewise above (below) its mean rate of return during this same period, then the *product* of these deviations from the mean is positive. If this happens consistently, the covariance of returns between these two assets will be some large positive value. If, however, the rate of return for one of the securities is above its mean return, while the return on the other security is below its mean return, the product will

Exhibit 7.6 Time-Series Plot of the Monthly Returns for Lehman Brothers Treasury Bond Index, 2007

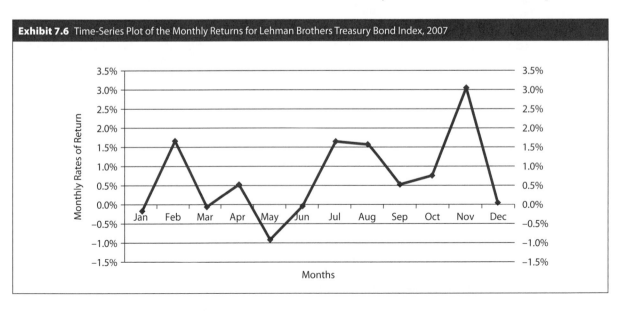

be negative. If this contrary movement happens consistently, the covariance between the rates of return for the two assets will be a large negative value.

Exhibit 7.7 includes the monthly rates of return during 2007 contained in Exhibit 7.4. One might expect returns for the two asset indexes to have reasonably low covariance because of the differences in the nature of these assets. The arithmetic means of the monthly returns were

$$(\overline{R}_i) = \frac{1}{11}\sum_{i=1}^{12} R_{it} = -0.30 \text{ (stocks)}$$

and

$$(\overline{R}_j) = \frac{1}{11}\sum_{j=1}^{12} R_{jt} = 0.73 \text{ (bonds)}$$

We rounded all figures to the nearest hundredth of 1 percent, so there may be small rounding errors. The average monthly return was –0.30 percent for the Wilshire 5000 stock index and 0.73 percent for the Treasury bond index. The results in Exhibit 7.7 show that the covariance between the rates of return for these two assets was

$$Cov_{ij} = \frac{1}{11} \times 9.35$$

$$= 0.85$$

Interpretation of a number such as 0.85 is difficult; is it high or low for covariance? We know the relationship between the two assets is generally positive, but it is not possible to be more specific. Exhibit 7.8 contains a scatterplot with paired values of R_{it} and R_{jt} plotted against each other. This plot demonstrates the linear nature and strength of the relationship. It is not surprising that the relationship during 2007 was not very strong, since during five months the two assets moved counter to each other. As a result, the overall covariance was a small positive value.

Covariance and Correlation Covariance is affected by the variability of the two individual return indexes. Therefore, a number such as the 0.85 in our example might indicate a weak positive relationship if the two individual indexes were volatile, but would reflect a strong positive relationship if the two indexes were stable. Obviously, we want to standardize this

Exhibit 7.7 Computation of Covariance of Returns for the Wilshire 5000 Stock Index and Lehman Brothers Treasury Bond Index, 2007

	Wilshire 5000 Stock Index (R_i)	Lehman Brothers Treasury Bonds (R_j)	Wilshire 5000 Stock Index ($R_i - \overline{R}_i$)	Lehman Brothers Treasury Bonds $R_j - \overline{R}_j$)	Wilshire 5000 Stock Index ($R_i - \overline{R}_i$) × Lehman Brothers Treasury Bonds ($R_j - \overline{R}_j$)
Jan	−1.51	−0.16	−1.21	−0.89	1.07
Feb	0.96	1.66	1.26	0.93	1.17
Mar	3.77	−0.05	4.07	−0.78	−3.15
Apr	3.33	0.52	3.62	−0.21	−0.77
May	−1.55	−0.90	−1.25	−1.63	2.03
Jun	−3.47	−0.04	−3.17	−0.77	2.45
Jul	1.12	1.66	1.42	0.93	1.32
Aug	3.46	1.57	3.76	0.84	3.16
Sep	2.03	0.54	2.32	−0.19	−0.44
Oct	−4.73	0.79	−4.43	0.06	−0.26
Nov	−0.76	3.07	−0.46	2.34	−1.08
Dec	−6.23	0.08	−5.93	−0.65	3.84
Mean	−0.30	0.73			sum = 9.35

cov ij = 9.35 / 11 = 0.85

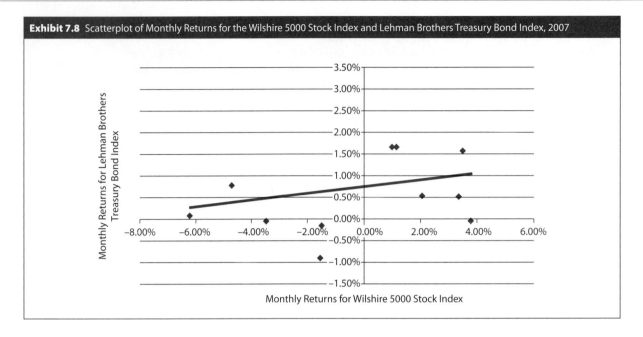

Exhibit 7.8 Scatterplot of Monthly Returns for the Wilshire 5000 Stock Index and Lehman Brothers Treasury Bond Index, 2007

covariance measure. We do so by taking into consideration the variability of the two individual return indexes, as follows:

7.5
$$r_{ij} = \frac{\text{Cov}_{ij}}{\sigma_i \sigma_j}$$

where:

r_{ij} = the correlation coefficient of returns
σ_i = the standard deviation of R_{it}
σ_j = the standard deviation of R_{jt}

Standardizing the covariance by the product of the individual standard deviations yields the **correlation coefficient** r_{ij}, which can vary only in the range −1 to +1. A value of +1 indicates a perfect positive linear relationship between R_i and R_j, meaning the returns for the two assets move together in a completely linear manner. A value of −1 indicates a perfect negative relationship between the two return indexes, so that when one asset's rate of return is above its mean, the other asset's rate of return will be below its mean by a comparable amount.

To calculate this standardized measure of the relationship, we need to compute the standard deviation for the two individual return indexes. We already have the values for $(R_{it} - \overline{R}_i)$ and $(R_{jt} - \overline{R}_j)$ in Exhibit 7.7. We can square each of these values and sum them as shown in Exhibit 7.9 to calculate the variance of each return series; again, we divide by $(n - 1)$ to avoid statistical bias.

$$\sigma_i^2 = \frac{1}{11} \, 120.91 = 10.99$$

and

$$\sigma_j^2 = \frac{1}{11} \, 13.05 = 1.19$$

The standard deviation for each index is the square root of the variance for each, as follows:

$$\sigma_i = \sqrt{10.99} = 3.32$$

$$\sigma_j = \sqrt{1.19} = 1.09$$

Exhibit 7.9 Computation of Standard Deviation of Monthly Returns for the Wilshire 5000 Stock Index and Lehman Brothers Treasury Bond Index, 2007

2007	Wilshire 5000 Stock Index		Lehman Brothers Treasury Bond Index	
	$(R_i - \bar{R}_i)$	$(R_i - \bar{R}_i)^2$	$(R_j - \bar{R}_j)$	$(R_j - \bar{R}_j)^2$
Jan	−1.21	1.46	−0.89	0.79
Feb	1.26	1.59	0.93	0.87
Mar	4.07	16.52	−0.78	0.60
Apr	3.62	13.13	−0.21	0.04
May	−1.25	1.56	−1.63	2.64
Jun	−3.17	10.08	−0.77	0.59
Jul	1.42	2.02	0.93	0.87
Aug	3.76	14.14	0.84	0.71
Sep	2.32	5.40	−0.19	0.04
Oct	−4.43	19.62	0.06	0.00
Nov	−0.46	0.21	2.34	5.48
Dec	−5.93	35.18	−0.65	0.42
		sum = 120.91		sum = 13.05
	variance$_i$ = 120.91 / 11 =	10.99	variance$_j$ = 13.05 / 11 =	1.19
	Standard Deviation$_i$ = $(10.99)^{1/2}$= 3.32		Standard Deviation$_j$ = $(1.19)^{1/2}$= 1.09	

Thus, based on the covariance between the two indexes and the individual standard deviations, we can calculate the correlation coefficient between returns for common stocks and Treasury bonds during 2007:

$$r_{ij} = \frac{\text{Cov}_{ij}}{\sigma_i \sigma_j} = \frac{0.85}{(3.32)(1.09)} = \frac{0.85}{3.62} = 0.235$$

Obviously, this formula also implies that

$$\text{Cov}_{ij} = r_{ij} \sigma_i \sigma_j = (0.235)(3.32)(1.09) = 0.85$$

7.2.5 Standard Deviation of a Portfolio

As noted, a correlation of +1.0 indicates perfect positive correlation, and a value of –1.0 means that the returns moved in completely opposite directions. A value of zero means that the returns had no linear relationship, that is, they were uncorrelated statistically. That does *not* mean that they are independent. The value of r_{ij} = 0.235 is not significantly different from zero. This insignificant positive correlation is not unusual for stocks versus bonds during a short time period such as one year.

Portfolio Standard Deviation Formula Now that we have discussed the concepts of covariance and correlation, we can consider the formula for computing the standard deviation of returns for a *portfolio* of assets, our measure of risk for a portfolio. In Exhibit 7.2, we showed that the expected rate of return of the portfolio was the weighted average of the expected returns for the individual assets in the portfolio; the weights were the percentage of value of the portfolio. One might assume it is possible to derive the standard deviation of the portfolio in the same manner, that is, by computing the weighted average of the standard deviations for the individual assets. This would be a mistake. Markowitz (1959) derived the general formula for the standard deviation of a portfolio as follows:

7.6

$$\sigma_{\text{port}} = \sqrt{\sum_{i=1}^{n} w_i^2 \sigma_i^2 + \sum_{i=1}^{n} \sum_{\substack{j=1 \\ i \neq j}}^{n} w_i w_j \text{Cov}_{ij}}$$

where

σ_{port} = the standard deviation of the portfolio

w_i = the weights of an individual asset in the portfolio, where weights are determined by the proportion of value in the portfolio

σ_i^2 = the variance of rates of return for asset i

Cov_{ij} = the covariance between the rates of return for assets i and j, where $Cov_{ij} = r_{ij}\sigma_i\sigma_j$

This formula indicates that the standard deviation for a portfolio of assets is a function of the weighted average of the individual variances (where the weights are squared), *plus* the weighted covariances between all the assets in the portfolio. The very important point is that the standard deviation for a portfolio of assets encompasses not only the variances of the individual assets but *also* includes the covariances between all the pairs of individual assets in the portfolio. Further, it can be shown that, in a portfolio with a large number of securities, this formula reduces to the sum of the weighted covariances.

Impact of a New Security in a Portfolio Although in most of the following discussion we will consider portfolios with only two assets (because it is possible to show the effect in two dimensions), we will also demonstrate the computations for a three-asset portfolio. Still, it is important at this point to consider what happens in a large portfolio with many assets. Specifically, what happens to the portfolio's standard deviation when we add a new security to such a portfolio? As shown by the formula, we see two effects. The first is the asset's own variance of returns, and the second is the covariance between the returns of this new asset and the returns of *every other asset that is already in the portfolio*. The relative weight of these numerous covariances is substantially greater than the asset's unique variance; the more assets in the portfolio, the more this is true. This means that the important factor to consider when adding an investment to a portfolio that contains a number of other investments is *not* the new security's own variance but the *average covariance of this asset with all other investments in the portfolio*.

Portfolio Standard Deviation Calculation

Because of the assumptions used in developing the Markowitz portfolio model, any asset or portfolio of assets can be described by two characteristics: the expected rate of return and the expected standard deviation of returns. Therefore, the following demonstrations can be applied to two *individual* assets, two *portfolios* of assets, or two *asset classes* with the indicated rate of return–standard deviation characteristics and correlation coefficients.

Equal Risk and Return—Changing Correlations Consider first the case in which both assets have the same expected return and expected standard deviation of return. As an example, let's assume

$$E(R_1) = 0.20, \quad E(\sigma_1) = 0.10$$

$$E(R_2) = 0.20, \quad E(\sigma_2) = 0.10$$

To show the effect of different covariances, we assume different levels of correlation between the two assets. We also assume that the two assets have equal weights in the portfolio ($w_1 = 0.50$; $w_2 = 0.50$). Therefore, the only value that changes in each example is the correlation between the returns for the two assets.

Now consider the following five correlation coefficients and the covariances they yield. Since $Cov_{ij} = r_{ij}\sigma_i\sigma_j$, the covariance will be equal to $r_{1,2}$ (0.10)(0.10) because the standard deviation of both assets is 0.10.

a. For $r_{1,2} = 1.00$, $Cov_{1,2} = (1.00)(0.10)(0.10) = 0.01$

b. For $r_{1,2} = 0.50$, $Cov_{1,2} = (0.50)(0.10)(0.10) = 0.005$

c. For $r_{1,2} = 0.00$, $Cov_{1,2} = (0.00)(0.10)(0.10) = 0.000$

d. For $r_{1,2} = -0.50$, $\text{Cov}_{1,2} = (-0.50)(0.10)(0.10) = -0.005$
e. For $r_{1,2} = -1.00$, $\text{Cov}_{1,2} = (-1.00)(0.10)(0.10) = -0.01$

Now let's see what happens to the standard deviation of the portfolio under these five conditions.

When we apply the general portfolio formula from Equation 7.6 to a two-asset portfolio, it is

7.7
$$\sigma_{\text{port}} = \sqrt{w_1^2\sigma_1^2 + w_2^2\sigma_2^2 + 2w_1w_2r_{1,2}\sigma_1\sigma_2}$$

or

$$\sigma_{\text{port}} = \sqrt{w_1^2\sigma_1^2 + w_2^2\sigma_2^2 + 2w_1w_2\text{Cov}_{1,2}}$$

Thus, in Case a:

$$\sigma_{\text{port(a)}} = \sqrt{(0.5)^2(0.10)^2 + (0.5)^2(0.10)^2 + 2(0.5)(0.5)(0.01)}$$
$$= \sqrt{(0.25)(0.01) + (0.25)(0.01) + 2(0.25)(0.01)}$$
$$= \sqrt{0.01}$$
$$= 0.10$$

In this case, where the returns for the two assets are perfectly positively correlated, the standard deviation for the portfolio is, in fact, the weighted average of the individual standard deviations. The important point is that we get no real benefit from combining two assets that are perfectly correlated; they are like one asset already because their returns move together.

Now consider Case b, where $r_{1,2}$ equals 0.50.

$$\sigma_{\text{port(b)}} = \sqrt{(0.5)^2(0.10)^2 + (0.5)^2(0.10)^2 + 2(0.5)(0.5)(0.005)}$$
$$= \sqrt{(0.0025) + (0.0025) + 2(0.25)(0.005)}$$
$$= \sqrt{0.0075}$$
$$= 0.0866$$

The only term that changed from Case a is the last term, $\text{Cov}_{1,2}$, which changed from 0.01 to 0.005. As a result, the standard deviation of the portfolio declined by about 13 percent, from 0.10 to 0.0866. Note that *the expected return of the portfolio did not change* because it is simply the weighted average of the individual expected returns; it is equal to 0.20 in both cases.

You should be able to confirm through your own calculations that the standard deviations for Portfolios c and d are as follows:

c. 0.0707

d. 0.05

The final case, where the correlation between the two assets is -1.00, indicates the ultimate benefits of diversification.

$$\sigma_{\text{port(e)}} = \sqrt{(0.5)^2(0.10)^2 + (0.5)^2(0.10)^2 + 2(0.5)(0.5)(-0.01)}$$
$$= \sqrt{(0.0050) + (-0.0050)}$$
$$= \sqrt{0}$$
$$= 0$$

Here, the negative covariance term exactly offsets the individual variance terms, leaving an overall standard deviation of the portfolio of zero. *This would be a risk-free portfolio.*

Exhibit 7.10 illustrates a graph of such a pattern. Perfect negative correlation gives a mean combined return for the two securities over time equal to the mean for each of them, so the returns for the portfolio show no variability. Any returns above and below the mean for each of the assets are *completely offset* by the return for the other asset, so there is *no variability* in total returns—that is, *no risk*—for the portfolio. Thus, a pair of completely negatively correlated assets provides the maximum benefits of diversification by completely eliminating risk.

The graph in Exhibit 7.11 shows the difference in the risk–return posture for our five cases. As noted, the only effect of the change in correlation is the change in the standard deviation of this two-asset portfolio. Combining assets that are not perfectly correlated does *not* affect the expected return of the portfolio, but it *does* reduce the risk of the portfolio (as measured by its standard deviation). When we eventually reach the ultimate combination of perfect negative correlation, risk is eliminated.

Combining Stocks with Different Returns and Risk   We have seen what happens when only the correlation coefficient (covariance) differs between the assets. We now consider two assets (or portfolios) with different expected rates of return and individual standard deviations.[3] We will show what happens when we vary the correlations between them. We will assume two assets with the following characteristics.

Asset	$E(R_i)$	w_i	σ_i^2	σ_i
1	0.10	0.50	0.0049	0.07
2	0.20	0.50	0.0100	0.10

We will use the previous set of correlation coefficients, but we must recalculate the covariances because this time the standard deviations of the assets are different. The results are shown in this table.

Case	Correlation Coefficient ($r_{1,2}$)	Covariance ($r_{1,2}\sigma_1\sigma_2$)
a	+1.00	0.0070
b	+0.50	0.0035
c	0.00	0.0000
d	−0.50	−0.0035
e	−1.00	−0.0070

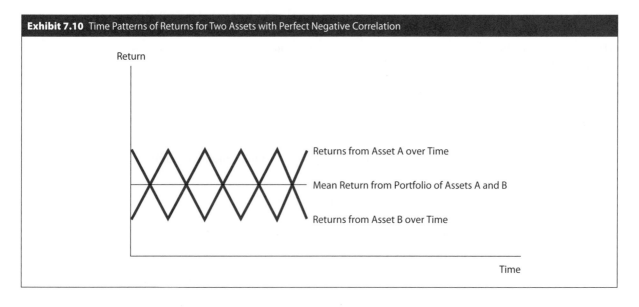

Exhibit 7.10 · Time Patterns of Returns for Two Assets with Perfect Negative Correlation

Return

Returns from Asset A over Time

Mean Return from Portfolio of Assets A and B

Returns from Asset B over Time

Time

[3]As noted, these could be two asset classes. For example, Asset 1 could be low risk–low return bonds and Asset 2 could be higher return–higher risk stocks.

Exhibit 7.11 Risk–Return Plot for Portfolios with Equal Returns and Standard Deviations but Different Correlations

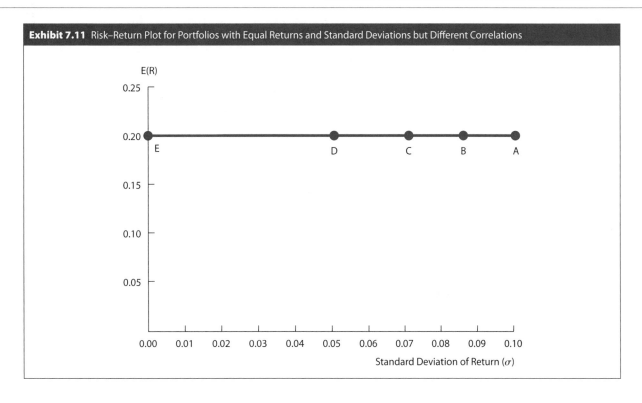

Because we are assuming the same weights in all cases (0.50 – 0.50), the expected return in every instance will be

$$E(R_{port}) = 0.50\,(0.10) + 0.50\,(0.20)$$
$$= 0.15$$

The portfolio standard deviation for Case a will be

$$\sigma_{port(a)} = \sqrt{(0.5)^2(0.07)^2 + (0.5)^2(0.10)^2 + 2(0.5)(0.5)(0.0070)}$$
$$= \sqrt{0.007225}$$
$$= 0.085$$

Again, with perfect positive correlation, the portfolio standard deviation is the weighted average of the standard deviations of the individual assets:

$$(0.5)\,(0.07) + (0.5)\,(0.10) = 0.085$$

As you might envision, changing the weights with perfect positive correlation causes the portfolio standard deviation to change in a linear fashion. This will be an important point to remember when we discuss the capital asset pricing model (CAPM) in the next chapter.

For Cases b, c, d, and e, the portfolio standard deviations are as follows[4]:

$$\sigma_{port(b)} = \sqrt{(0.001225) + (0.0025) + (0.5)(0.0035)}$$
$$= \sqrt{0.005475}$$
$$= 0.07399$$

$$\sigma_{port(c)} = \sqrt{(0.001225) + (0.0025) + (0.5)(0.00)}$$
$$= 0.0610$$

---

[4]In all the following examples, we will skip some steps because you are now aware that only the last term changes. You are encouraged to work out the individual steps to ensure that you understand the computational procedure.

$$\sigma_{\text{port(d)}} = \sqrt{(0.001225) + (0.0025) + (0.5)(-0.0035)}$$

$$= 0.0444$$

$$\sigma_{\text{port(e)}} = \sqrt{(0.003725) + (0.5)(-0.0070)}$$

$$= 0.015$$

Note that, in this example, with perfect negative correlation the portfolio standard deviation is not zero. This is because the different examples have equal weights, but the asset standard deviations are not equal.[5]

Exhibit 7.12 shows the results for the two individual assets and the portfolio of the two assets assuming the correlation coefficients vary as set forth in Cases a through e. As before, the expected return does not change because the proportions are always set at 0.50–0.50, so all the portfolios lie along the horizontal line at the return, R = 0.15.

Constant Correlation with Changing Weights   If we changed the weights of the two assets while holding the correlation coefficient constant, we would derive a set of combinations that trace an ellipse starting at Asset 2, going through the 0.50–0.50 point, and ending at Asset 1. We can demonstrate this with Case c, in which the correlation coefficient of zero eases the computations. We begin with 100 percent in Asset 2 (Case f) and change the weights as follows, ending with 100 percent in Asset 1 (Case l):

Case	w_1	w_2	$E(R_i)$
f	0.00	1.00	0.20
g	0.20	0.80	0.18
h	0.40	0.60	0.16
i	0.50	0.50	0.15
j	0.60	0.40	0.14
k	0.80	0.20	0.12
l	1.00	0.00	0.10

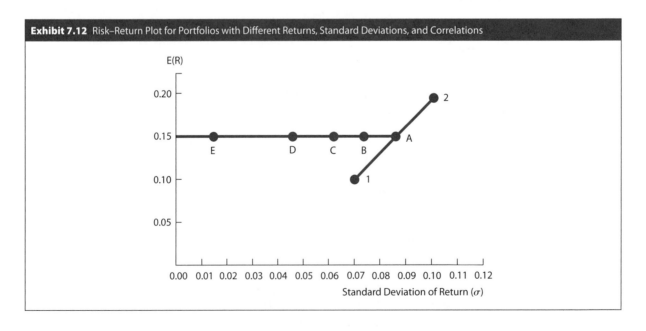

Exhibit 7.12   Risk–Return Plot for Portfolios with Different Returns, Standard Deviations, and Correlations

[5]The two appendixes to this chapter show proofs for equal weights with equal variances and solve for the appropriate weights to get zero standard deviation when standard deviations are not equal.

We already know the standard deviations (σ) for portfolios f and l (only one asset) and portfolio (i). In Cases g, h, j, and k, the standard deviations are[6]

$$\sigma_{\text{port(g)}} = \sqrt{(0.20)^2(0.07)^2 + (0.80)^2(0.10)^2 + 2(0.20)(0.80)(0.00)}$$
$$= \sqrt{(0.04)(0.0049) + (0.64)(0.01) + (0)}$$
$$= \sqrt{0.006596}$$
$$= 0.0812$$

$$\sigma_{\text{port(h)}} = \sqrt{(0.40)^2(0.07)^2 + (0.60)^2(0.10)^2 + 2(0.40)(0.60)(0.00)}$$
$$= \sqrt{0.004384}$$
$$= 0.0662$$

$$\sigma_{\text{port(j)}} = \sqrt{(0.60)^2(0.07)^2 + (0.40)^2(0.10)^2 + 2(0.60)(0.40)(0.00)}$$
$$= \sqrt{0.003364}$$
$$= 0.0580$$

$$\sigma_{\text{port(k)}} = \sqrt{(0.80)^2(0.07)^2 + (0.20)^2(0.10)^2 + 2(0.80)(0.20)(0.00)}$$
$$= \sqrt{0.003536}$$
$$= 0.0595$$

The various weights with a constant correlation yield the following risk–return combinations.

Case	w_1	w_2	$E(R_i)$	$E(\sigma_{\text{port}})$
f	0.00	1.00	0.20	0.1000
g	0.20	0.80	0.18	0.0812
h	0.40	0.60	0.16	0.0662
i	0.50	0.50	0.15	0.0610
j	0.60	0.40	0.14	0.0580
k	0.80	0.20	0.12	0.0595
l	1.00	0.00	0.10	0.0700

A graph of these combinations appears in Exhibit 7.13. We could derive a complete curve by simply varying the weighting by smaller increments.

A notable result is that with low, zero, or negative correlations, it is possible to derive portfolios that have *lower risk than either single asset*. In our set of examples where $r_{ij} = 0.00$, this occurs in Cases h, i, j, and k. This ability to reduce risk is the essence of diversification.

As shown in Exhibit 7.13, assuming the normal risk–return relationship where assets with higher risk (larger standard deviation of returns) provide high rates of return, it is possible for a conservative investor to experience *both* lower risk *and* higher return by diversifying into a higher risk–higher return asset, assuming that the correlation between the two assets is fairly low. Exhibit 7.13 shows that, in the case where we used the correlation of zero (0.00), the low-risk investor at Point 1—who would receive a return of 10 percent and risk of 7 percent—could, by investing in portfolio j, *increase* the return to 14 percent *and* experience a *decline* in risk to 5.8 percent by investing (diversifying) 40 percent of the portfolio in riskier Asset 2. As noted, the benefits of diversification are critically dependent on the correlation between assets. The exhibit shows that there is even some benefit when the correlation is 0.50 rather than zero.

Exhibit 7.13 also shows that the curvature in the graph depends on the correlation between the two assets or portfolios. With $r_{ij} = +1.00$, the combinations lie along a straight line between the two assets. When $r_{ij} = 0.50$, the curve is to the right of the $r_{ij} = 0.00$ curve; when $r_{ij} = -0.50$, it is to the left. Finally, when $r_{ij} = -1.00$, the graph would be two straight lines that would touch

[6]Again, you are encouraged to fill in the steps we skipped in the computations.

Exhibit 7.13 Portfolio Risk–Return Plots for Different Weights When $r_{i,j} = +1.00; +0.50; 0.00; -0.50; -1.00$

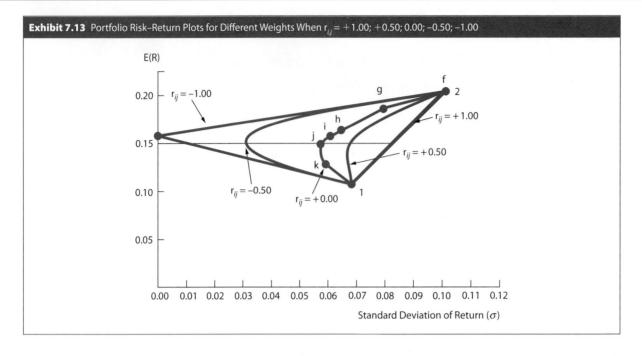

at the vertical line (zero risk) with some combination. As shown in Appendix 7B, it is possible to solve for the specified set of weights that would give a portfolio with zero risk. In this case, it is $w_1 = 0.412$ and $w_2 = 0.588$, which implies an E(R) of 0.1588.

7.2.6 A Three-Asset Portfolio

A demonstration of what occurs with a three-asset portfolio is useful because it shows the dynamics of the portfolio process when assets are added. It also shows the rapid growth in the computations required, which is why we will stop at three!

In this example, we will combine three asset classes we have been discussing: stocks, bonds, and cash equivalents.[7] We will assume the following characteristics:

Asset Classes	E(R$_i$)	E(σ_i)	w$_i$
Stocks (S)	0.12	0.20	0.60
Bonds (B)	0.08	0.10	0.30
Cash equivalent (C)	0.04	0.03	0.10

The correlations are

$$r_{S,B} = 0.25; \ r_{S,C} = -0.08; \ r_{B,C} = 0.15$$

Given the weights specified, the $E(R_{port})$ is

$$E(R_{port}) = (0.60)(0.12) + (0.30)(0.08) + (0.10)(0.04)$$

$$= (0.072 + 0.024 + 0.004) = 0.100 = 10.00\%$$

When we apply the generalized formula from Equation 7.6 to the expected standard deviation of a three-asset portfolio, it is

7.8

$$\sigma_{port}^2 = (w_S^2\sigma_S^2 + w_B^2\sigma_B^2 + w_C^2\sigma_C^2)$$

$$+ (2w_Sw_B\sigma_S\sigma_B\sigma_{S,B} + 2w_Sw_C\sigma_S\sigma_C\sigma_{S,C} + 2w_Bw_C\sigma_B\sigma_C\sigma_{B,C})$$

[7]The asset allocation articles regularly contained in the *Wall Street Journal* generally refer to these three asset classes.

From the characteristics specified, the standard deviation of this three-asset-class portfolio (σ_{port}) would be

$$\sigma^2_{port} = [(0.6)^2(0.20)^2 + (0.3)^2(0.10)^2 + (0.1)^2(0.03)^2]$$

$$+ \{[2(0.6)(0.3)(0.20)(0.10)(0.25)] + [2(0.6)(0.1)(0.20)(0.03)(-0.08)]$$

$$+ [2(0.3)(0.1)(0.10)(0.03)(0.15)]\}$$

$$= [0.015309 + (0.0018) + (-0.0000576) + (0.000027)]$$

$$= 0.0170784$$

$$\sigma_{port} = (0.0170784)^{1/2} = 0.1306 = 13.06\%$$

7.2.7 Estimation Issues

It is important to keep in mind that the results of this portfolio asset allocation depend on the accuracy of the statistical inputs. In the current instance, this means that for every asset (or asset class) being considered for inclusion in the portfolio, we must estimate its expected returns and standard deviation. We must also estimate the correlation coefficient among the entire set of assets. The number of correlation estimates can be significant—for example, for a portfolio of 100 securities, the number is 4,950 (that is, 99 + 98 + 97 +…). The potential source of error that arises from these approximations is referred to as *estimation risk.*

We can reduce the number of correlation coefficients that must be estimated by assuming that stock returns can be described by the relationship of each stock to a market index—that is, a single index market model, as follows:

7.9
$$R_i = a_i + b_iR_m + \varepsilon_i$$

where:

b_i = the slope coefficient that relates the returns for Security i to the returns for the aggregate stock market

R_m = the returns for the aggregate stock market

If all the securities are similarly related to the market and a slope coefficient b_i is derived for each one, it can be shown that the correlation coefficient between two securities i and j is

7.10
$$r_{ij} = b_ib_j\frac{\sigma^2_m}{\sigma_i\sigma_j}$$

where:

σ^2_m = the variance of returns for the aggregate stock market

This reduces the number of estimates from 4,950 to 100—that is, once we have derived a slope estimate b_i for each security, we can compute the correlation estimates. Notably, this assumes that the single index market model provides a good estimate of security returns.

7.2.8 The Efficient Frontier

If we examined different two-asset combinations and derived the curves assuming all the possible weights, we would have a graph like that in Exhibit 7.14. The envelope curve that contains the best of all these possible combinations is referred to as the **efficient frontier**. Specifically, the efficient frontier represents that set of portfolios that has the maximum rate of return for every given level of risk or the minimum risk for every level of return. An example of such a frontier is shown in Exhibit 7.15. Every portfolio that lies on the efficient frontier has either a higher rate of return for equal risk or lower risk for an equal rate of return than some portfolio beneath the frontier. Thus, we would say that Portfolio A in Exhibit 7.15 *dominates* Portfolio

Exhibit 7.14 Numerous Portfolio Combinations of Available Assets

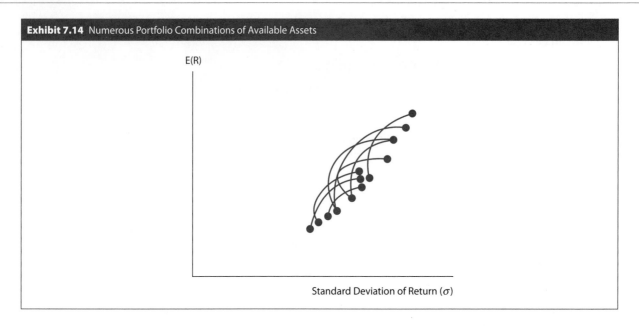

Exhibit 7.15 Efficient Frontier for Alternative Portfolios

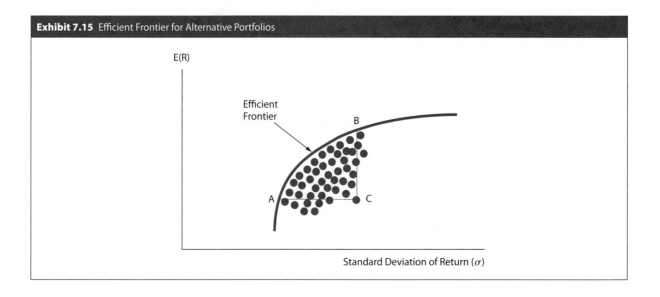

C because it has an equal rate of return but substantially less risk. Similarly, Portfolio B dominates Portfolio C because it has equal risk but a higher expected rate of return. Because of the benefits of diversification among imperfectly correlated assets, we would expect the efficient frontier to be made up of *portfolios* of investments rather than individual securities. Two possible exceptions arise at the end points, which represent the asset with the highest return and the asset with the lowest risk.

As an investor, you will target a point along the efficient frontier based on your *utility function,* which reflects your attitude toward risk. No portfolio on the efficient frontier can dominate any other portfolio on the efficient frontier. All of these portfolios have different return and risk measures, with expected rates of return that increase with higher risk.

Exhibit 7.16 Selecting an Optimal Risky Portfolio

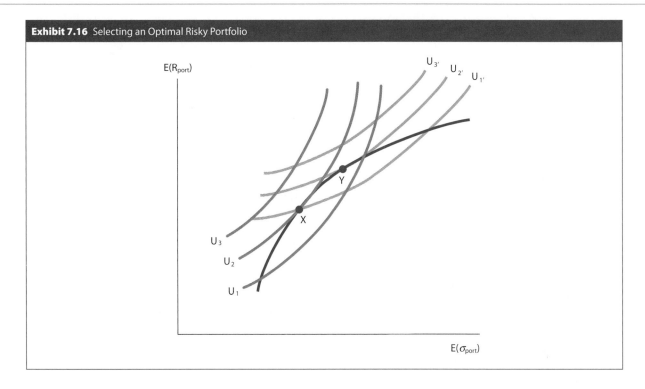

7.2.9 The Efficient Frontier and Investor Utility

The curve in Exhibit 7.15 shows that the slope of the efficient frontier curve decreases steadily as we move upward. This implies that adding equal increments of risk as we move up the efficient frontier gives diminishing increments of expected return. To evaluate this situation, we calculate the slope of the efficient frontier as follows:

7.11
$$\frac{\Delta E(R_{port})}{\Delta E(\sigma_{port})}$$

An individual investor's utility curves specify the trade-offs he or she is willing to make between expected return and risk. In conjunction with the efficient frontier, these utility curves determine which *particular* portfolio on the efficient frontier best suits an individual investor. Two investors will choose the same portfolio from the efficient set only if their utility curves are identical.

Exhibit 7.16 shows two sets of utility curves along with an efficient frontier of investments. The curves labeled U_1, U_2, and U_3 are for a strongly risk-averse investor. These utility curves are quite steep, indicating that the investor will not tolerate much additional risk to obtain additional returns. The investor is equally disposed toward any E(R), E(σ) combinations along the specific utility curve U_1.

The curves labeled ($U_{3'}$, $U_{2'}$, $U_{1'}$) characterize a less risk-averse investor. Such an investor is willing to tolerate a bit more risk to get a higher expected return.

The **optimal portfolio** is the efficient portfolio that has the highest utility for a given investor. It lies at the point of tangency between the efficient frontier and the U_1 curve with the highest possible utility. A conservative investor's highest utility is at Point X in Exhibit 7.16, where the U_2 curve just touches the efficient frontier. A less risk-averse investor's highest utility occurs at Point Y, which represents a portfolio on the efficient frontier with higher expected returns and higher risk than the portfolio at X.

• • • • SUMMARY • • • •

- The basic Markowitz portfolio model derives the expected rate of return for a portfolio of assets and a measure of expected risk, which is the standard deviation of expected rates of return. Markowitz showed that the expected rate of return of a portfolio is the weighted average of the expected return for the individual investments in the portfolio. The standard deviation of a portfolio is a function not only of the standard deviations for the individual investments but *also* of the covariance between the rates of return for all the pairs of assets in the portfolio. In a large portfolio, these covariances are the important factors.
- Different weights or amounts of a portfolio held in various assets yield a curve of potential combinations. Correlation coefficients among assets are the critical factor to consider when selecting investments. Investors can maintain their rate of return while reducing the risk level of their portfolio by combining assets or portfolios that have low-positive or negative correlation.
- Assuming numerous assets and a multitude of combination curves, the efficient frontier is the envelope curve that encompasses all of the best combinations. It defines the set of portfolios that has the highest expected return for each given level of risk or the minimum risk for each given level of return. From this set of dominant portfolios, investors select the one that lies at the point of tangency between the efficient frontier and their highest utility curve. Because risk–return utility functions differ, the point of tangency and, therefore, the portfolio choice will differ among investors.

At this point, you understand that an optimum portfolio is a combination of investments, each having desirable individual risk–return characteristics that also fit together based on their correlations. This deeper understanding of portfolio theory should lead you to reflect back on our earlier discussion of global investing. Because many foreign stock and bond investments provide superior rates of return compared with U.S. securities *and* have low correlations with portfolios of U.S. stocks and bonds (as shown in Chapter 3), including these foreign securities in your portfolio will help you to reduce the overall risk of your portfolio while possibly increasing your rate of return.

• • • • SUGGESTED READINGS • • • •

Elton, Edwin J., Martin J. Gruber, Stephen J. Brown, and William N. Goetzmann. *Modern Portfolio Theory and Investment Analysis*, 6th ed. New York: Wiley, 2003.

Farrell, James L., Jr. *Portfolio Management: Theory and Application*, 2nd ed. New York: McGraw-Hill, 1997.

John L. Masinn, Donald L. Tuttle, Jerold E. Pinto, and Dennis W. Mcleavy, *Managing Investment Portfolios: A Dynamic Process*, 3rd ed. Hoboken, NJ: John Wiley & Sons, 2007.

• • • • QUESTIONS • • • •

1. Why do most investors hold diversified portfolios?
2. What is covariance, and why is it important in portfolio theory?
3. Why do most assets of the same type show positive covariances of returns with each other? Would you expect positive covariances of returns between *different* types of assets such as returns on Treasury bills, General Electric common stock, and commercial real estate? Why or why not?
4. What is the relationship between covariance and the correlation coefficient?
5. Explain the shape of the efficient frontier.
6. Draw a properly labeled graph of the Markowitz efficient frontier. Describe the efficient frontier in exact terms. Discuss the concept of dominant portfolios, and show an example of one on your graph.
7. Assume you want to run a computer program to derive the efficient frontier for your feasible set of stocks. What information must you input to the program?
8. Why are investors' utility curves important in portfolio theory?
9. Explain how a given investor chooses an optimal portfolio. Will this choice always be a diversified portfolio, or could it be a single asset? Explain your answer.
10. Assume that you and a business associate develop an efficient frontier for a set of investments. Why might the two of you select different portfolios on the frontier?
11. Draw a hypothetical graph of an efficient frontier of U.S. common stocks. On the same graph, draw an efficient frontier assuming the inclusion of U.S. bonds as well. Finally, on the same graph, draw an

efficient frontier that includes U.S. common stocks, U.S. bonds, and stocks and bonds from around the world. Discuss the differences in these frontiers.

12. Stocks K, L, and M each have the same expected return and standard deviation. The correlation coefficients between each pair of these stocks are:

$$K \text{ and } L \text{ correlation coefficient} = +0.8$$
$$K \text{ and } M \text{ correlation coefficient} = +0.2$$
$$L \text{ and } M \text{ correlation coefficient} = -0.4$$

Given these correlations, a portfolio constructed of which pair of stocks will have the lowest standard deviation? Explain.

13. **CFA EXAMINATION LEVEL II** A three-asset portfolio has the following characteristics.

Asset	Expected Return	Expected Standard Deviation	Weight
X	0.15	0.22	0.50
Y	0.10	0.08	0.40
Z	0.06	0.03	0.10

The expected return on this three-asset portfolio is
   a. 10.3%
   b. 11.0%
   c. 12.1%
   d. 14.8% (2 minutes)

5. **CFA EXAMINATION LEVEL II** An investor is considering adding another investment to a portfolio. To achieve the maximum diversification benefits, the investor should add, if possible, an investment that has which of the following correlation coefficients with the other investments in the portfolio?
   a. −1.0
   b. −0.5
   c.   0.0
   d. +1.0 (1 minute)

• • • • PROBLEMS • • • •

1. The standard deviation of Shamrock Corp. stock is 19 percent. The standard deviation of Sophie Co. stock is 14 percent. The covariance between these two stocks is 100. What is the correlation between Shamrock and Sophie stock?

2. You are considering two assets with the following characteristics.

$$E(R_1) = 0.15 \quad E(\sigma_1) = 0.10 \quad w_1 = 0.5$$
$$E(R_2) = 0.20 \quad E(\sigma_2) = 0.20 \quad w_2 = 0.5$$

Compute the mean and standard deviation of two portfolios if $r_{1,2}$ = 0.40 and -0.60, respectively. Plot the two portfolios on a risk–return graph and briefly explain the results.

3. The following are monthly percentage price changes for four market indexes.

Month	DJIA	S&P 500	Russell 2000	Nikkei
1	0.03	0.02	0.04	0.04
2	0.07	0.06	0.10	−0.02
3	−0.02	−0.01	−0.04	0.07
4	0.01	0.03	0.03	0.02
5	0.05	0.04	0.11	0.02
6	−0.06	−0.04	−0.08	0.06

Compute the following.
   a. Average monthly rate of return for each index
   b. Standard deviation for each index

    c. Covariance between the rates of return for the following indexes:
       DJIA–S&P 500
       S&P 500–Russell 2000
       S&P 500–Nikkei
       Russell 2000–Nikkei
    d. The correlation coefficients for the same four combinations
    e. Using the answers from parts (a), (b), and (d), calculate the expected return and standard deviation of a portfolio consisting of equal parts of (1) the S&P and the Russell 2000 and (2) the S&P and the Nikkei. Discuss the two portfolios.

4. The following are the monthly rates of return for Madison Cookies and for Sophie Electric during a six-month period.

Month	Madison Cookies	Sophie Electric
1	−0.04	0.07
2	0.06	−0.02
3	−0.07	−0.10
4	0.12	0.15
5	−0.02	−0.06
6	0.05	0.02

    Compute the following.
    a. Average monthly rate of return $\overline{R}_i$ for each stock
    b. Standard deviation of returns for each stock
    c. Covariance between the rates of return
    d. The correlation coefficient between the rates of return

    What level of correlation did you expect? How did your expectations compare with the computed correlation? Would these two stocks offer a good chance for diversification? Why or why not?

5. Given: $E(R_1) = 0.12$
              $E(R_2) = 0.16$
              $E(\sigma_1) = 0.04$
              $E(\sigma_2) = 0.06$

    Calculate the expected returns and expected standard deviations of a two-stock portfolio having a correlation coefficient of 0.70 under the following conditions.
    a. $w_1 = 1.00$
    b. $w_1 = 0.75$
    c. $w_1 = 0.50$
    d. $w_1 = 0.25$
    e. $w_1 = 0.05$

    Plot the results on a return–risk graph. Without calculations, draw in what the curve would look like first if the correlation coefficient had been 0.00 and then if it had been −0.70.

6. Given the following market values of stocks in your portfolio and their expected rates of return, what is the expected rate of return for your common stock portfolio?

Stock	Market Value ($ Mil.)	$E(R_i)$
Disney	$15,000	0.14
Starbucks	17,000	−0.04
Harley Davidson	32,000	0.18
Intel	23,000	0.16
Walgreens	7,000	0.12

7. Given: $E(R_1) = 0.10$
              $E(R_2) = 0.15$
              $E(\sigma_1) = 0.03$
              $E(\sigma_2) = 0.05$

    Calculate the expected returns and expected standard deviations of a two-stock portfolio in which Stock 1 has a weight of 60 percent under the following conditions.
    a. $r_{1,2} = 1.00$
    b. $r_{1,2} = 0.75$
    c. $r_{1,2} = 0.25$
    d. $r_{1,2} = 0.00$

e. $r_{1,2} = -0.25$

f. $r_{1,2} = -0.75$

g. $r_{1,2} = -1.00$

8. Considering the world economic outlook for the coming year and estimates of sales and earning for the pharmaceutical industry, you expect the rate of return for Lauren Labs common stock to range between -20 percent and $+40$ percent with the following probabilities.

Probability	Possible Returns
0.10	−0.20
0.15	−0.05
0.20	0.10
0.25	0.15
0.20	0.20
0.10	0.40

Compute the expected rate of return $E(R_i)$ for Lauren Labs.

THOMSON ONE | Business School Edition

1. Collect daily price data for the past 30 trading days and compute the daily percentage price returns for each: Avon Products, Inc. (AVP), Best Buy Inc. (BBY), and Cisco Systems (CSCO).
2. Compute the mean daily return for each stock and the standard deviation of daily returns.
3. Compute the covariance and correlations between the three possible pairs.
4. Assuming equal weight between each pair of stocks, compute the mean daily return and the standard deviation of each of the three portfolios.
5. Create a risk–return scatterplot and enter the average daily return (vertical axis) and standard deviation (horizontal axis) for the three individual stocks and the three portfolios. Briefly discuss the results based on the material in this chapter.

· · · · • APPENDIX: CHAPTER 7 • · • · ·

APPENDIX ·

A. Proof That Minimum Portfolio Variance Occurs with Equal Weights When Securities Have Equal Variance

When $\sigma_1 = \sigma_2$, we have:

$$\sigma_{port}^2 = w_1^2(\sigma_1)^2 + (1 - w_1)^2(\sigma_1)^2 - 2w_1(1 - w_1)r_{1,2}(\sigma_1)^2$$

$$= (\sigma_1)^2[w_1^2 + 1 - 2w_1 + w_1^2 + 2w_1 r_{1,2} - 2w_1^2 r_{1,2}]$$

$$= (\sigma_1)^2[2w_1^2 + 1 - 2w_1 + 2w_1 r_{1,2} - 2w_1^2 r_{1,2}]$$

For this to be a minimum,

$$\frac{\partial(\sigma_{port}^2)}{\partial w_1} = 0 = (\sigma_1)^2[4w_1 \times 2 + 2r_{1,2} \times 4w_1 r_{1,2}]$$

Assuming $(\sigma_1)^2 > 0$,

$$4w_1 - 2 + 2r_{1,2} - 4w_1 r_{1,2} = 0$$

$$4w_1(1 - r_{1,2}) - 2(1 - r_{1,2}) = 0$$

from which

$$w_1 \frac{2(1 - r_{1,2})}{4(1 - r_{1,2})} = \frac{1}{2}$$

regardless of $r_{1,2}$. Thus, if $\sigma_1 = \sigma_2$, σ^2_{port} will *always* be minimized by choosing $w_1 = w_2 = 1/2$, regardless of the value of $r_{1,2}$, except when $r_{1,2} = +1$ (in which case $\sigma_{port} = \sigma_1 = \sigma_2$). This can be verified by checking the second-order condition

$$\frac{\partial(\sigma^2_{port})}{\partial w_1^2} > 0$$

Problem

1. The following information applies to Questions 1a and 1b. The general equation for the weight of the first security to achieve minimum variance (in a two-stock portfolio) is given by

$$w_1 = \frac{(\sigma_2)^2 - r_{1,2}(\sigma_1)(\sigma_2)}{(\sigma_1)^2 + (\sigma_2)^2 - 2r_{1,2}(\sigma_1)(\sigma_2)}$$

1a. Show that $w_1 = 0.5$ when $\sigma_1 = \sigma_2$.
1b. What is the weight of Security 1 that gives minimum portfolio variance when $r_{1,2} = 0.5$, $\sigma_1 = 0.04$, and $\sigma_2 = 0.06$?

B. Derivation of Weights That Will Give Zero Variance When Correlation Equals –1.00

$$\sigma^2_{port} = w_1^2(\sigma_1)^2 + (1 - w_1)^2(\sigma_2)^2 + 2w_1(1 - w_1)r_{1,2}(\sigma_1)(\sigma_2)$$

$$= w_1^2(\sigma_1)^2 + (\sigma_2)^2 - 2w_1(\sigma_2) - w_1^2(\sigma_2)^2 + 2w_1 r_{1,2}(\sigma_1)(\sigma_2) - 2w_1^2 r_{1,2}(\sigma_1)(\sigma_2)$$

If $r_{1,2} = 1$, this can be rearranged and expressed as

$$\sigma^2_{port} = w_1^2[(\sigma_1)^2 + 2(\sigma_1)(\sigma_2) + (\sigma_2)^2] - 2w[(\sigma_2)^2 + (\sigma_1)(\sigma_2)] + (\sigma_2)^2$$

$$= w_1^2[(\sigma_1) + (\sigma_2)]^2 - 2w_1(\sigma_2)[(\sigma_1) - (\sigma_2)] + (\sigma_2)^2$$

$$= \{w_1[(\sigma_1) + (\sigma_2)] - (\sigma_2)^2\}$$

We want to find the weight, w_1, which will reduce (σ^2_{port}) to *zero*; therefore,

$$w_1[(\sigma_1) + (\sigma_2)] - (\sigma_2) = 0$$

which yields

$$w_1 = \frac{(\sigma_2)}{(\sigma_1) + (\sigma_2)}, \text{ and } w_2 = 1 - w_1 = \frac{(\sigma_1)}{(\sigma_1) + (\sigma_2)}$$

Problem

1. Given two assets with the following characteristics:

$$E(R_1) = 0.12 \qquad \sigma_1 = 0.04$$
$$E(R_2) = 0.16 \qquad \sigma_2 = 0.06$$

Assume that $r_{1,2} = -1.00$. What is the weight that would yield a zero variance for the portfolio?

CHAPTER 8

An Introduction to Asset Pricing Models

After you read this chapter, you should be able to answer the following questions:

- How does capital market theory extend Markowitz portfolio theory with the addition of a risk-free asset?
- What are the other critical assumptions underlying captial market theory?
- What is the capital market line (CML), and how does it enhance our understanding of the relationship between risk and expected return?
- What is the market portfolio, and what role does it play in the investment process implied by the CML?
- Under what conditions does the CML recommend the use of leverage in forming an investor's preferred strategy?
- What is the difference between systematic and unsystematic risk, and how does that relate to the concept of diversification?
- How does the capital asset pricing model (CAPM) extend the results of captial market theory?
- What special role does beta play in the CAPM, and how do investors calculate a security's characteristic line in practice?
- What is the security market line (SML), and what are the similarities and differences between the SML and CML?
- How can the SML be used to evaluate whether securities are properly priced?
- What assumptions are necessary for the CAPM, and what impact does relaxing those assumptions have?
- What do the various empirical tests of the CAPM allow us to conclude?
- Does the selection of a proxy for the market portfolio matter?

Following the development of portfolio theory by Markowitz, two major theories have been derived for the valuation of risky assets. In this chapter, we introduce the first of these models—the capital asset pricing model (CAPM). The background on the CAPM is important at this point in the book because the risk measure it implies is a necessary input for much of our subsequent discussion. The presentation concerns capital market theory and the capital asset pricing model that was developed almost concurrently by three individuals. An alternative asset valuation model—the arbitrage pricing theory (APT)—has led to the development of numerous other multifactor models and is the subject of Chapter 9.

8.1 Capital Market Theory: An Overview

Because capital market theory builds directly on the portfolio theory we developed in Chapter 7, this chapter begins where our discussion of the Markowitz efficient frontier ended. In particular, capital market theory extends portfolio theory by developing a model for pricing all risky assets. The final product, the **capital asset pricing model (CAPM)**, will allow you to determine the required rate of return for any risky asset. As we will see, this development depends critically on the existence of a risk-free asset, which in turn will lead to the designation of the **market portfolio,** a collection of all of the risky assets in the marketplace that assumes a special role in asset pricing theory.

8.1.1 Background for Capital Market Theory

With any theory, it is necessary to articulate a set of assumptions that specify how the world is expected to act. This allows one to concentrate on developing an explanation for how market participants will respond to changes in the environment. In this section, we consider the main assumptions that underlie the development of capital market theory.

Assumptions of Capital Market Theory Because capital market theory builds on the Markowitz portfolio model, it requires the same assumptions, along with some additional ones:

1. All investors are Markowitz-efficient in that they seek to invest in tangent points on the efficient frontier. The exact location of this tangent point and, therefore, the specific portfolio selected will depend on the individual investor's risk–return utility function.
2. Investors can borrow or lend any amount of money at the risk-free rate of return (RFR). (Clearly, it is always possible to lend money at the nominal risk-free rate by buying risk-free securities such as government T-bills. It is not always possible to borrow at this risk-free rate, but we will see that assuming a higher borrowing rate does not change the general results.)
3. All investors have homogeneous expectations; that is, they estimate identical probability distributions for future rates of return. Again, this assumption can be relaxed with minimal effect.
4. All investors have the same one-period time horizon such as one month or one year. The model will be developed for a single hypothetical period, and its results could be affected by a different assumption, since it requires investors to derive risk measures and risk-free assets that are consistent with their investment horizons.
5. All investments are infinitely divisible, which means that it is possible to buy or sell fractional shares of any asset or portfolio. This assumption allows us to discuss investment alternatives as continuous curves. Changing it would have little impact on the theory.
6. There are no taxes or transaction costs involved in buying or selling assets. This is a reasonable assumption in many instances. Neither pension funds nor charitable foundations have to pay taxes, and the transaction costs for most financial institutions are less than 1 percent on most financial instruments. Again, relaxing this assumption does not change the basic result.
7. There is no inflation or any change in interest rates, or inflation is fully anticipated. This is a reasonable initial assumption, and it can be modified.
8. Capital markets are in equilibrium. This means that we begin with all investments properly priced in line with their risk levels.

Some of these assumptions may seem unrealistic, but keep in mind two things. First, as mentioned, relaxing them would have only a minor effect on the model and would not change its main implications or conclusions. Second, a theory should never be judged on the basis of its assumptions but rather on how well it explains and helps us predict behavior in the real world. If this theory and the model it implies help us explain the rates of return on a wide variety of risky assets, it is useful, even if some of its assumptions are unrealistic.

Development of Capital Market Theory The major factor that allowed portfolio theory to develop into capital market theory is the concept of a risk-free asset. Following the development of the Markowitz portfolio model, several authors considered the implications of assuming the existence of a **risk-free asset**, that is, an asset with *zero variance*. As we will show, such an asset would have zero correlation with all other risky assets and would provide the *risk-free rate of return (RFR)*.

This assumption of a risk-free asset allows us to derive a generalized theory of capital asset pricing under conditions of uncertainty from the Markowitz portfolio theory. This achievement is generally attributed to William Sharpe (1964), who received a Nobel Prize for it, but Lintner (1965) and Mossin (1966) derived similar theories independently. Consequently, you may see references to the Sharpe-Lintner-Mossin capital asset pricing model.

8.1.2 Developing the Capital Market Line

We have defined a **risky asset** as one from which future returns are uncertain, and we have measured this uncertainty by the variance, or standard deviation, of expected returns. Because the expected return on a risk-free asset is entirely certain, the standard deviation of its expected return is zero ($\sigma_{RF} = 0$). The rate of return earned on such an asset should be the risk-free rate of return (RFR), which, as we discussed in Chapter 1, should equal the expected long-run growth rate of the economy with an adjustment for short-run liquidity. We now show what happens when we introduce this risk-free asset into the risky world of the Markowitz portfolio model.

Covariance with a Risk-Free Asset   Recall that the covariance between two sets of returns is

$$\text{Cov}_{ij} = \sum_{i=1}^{n} [R_i - E(R_i)][R_j - E(R_j)]/n$$

Assume for the moment that Asset i in this formula is the risk-free asset. Because the returns for the risk-free asset are certain, ($\sigma_{RF} = 0$), $R_i = E(R_i)$ during all periods. Thus, $R_i - E(R_i)$ will equal zero, and the product of this expression with any other expression will equal zero. Consequently, the covariance of the risk-free asset with any risky asset or portfolio of assets will always equal zero. Similarly, the correlation between any risky asset i, and the risk-free asset, RF, would be zero because it is equal to

$$r_{RF,i} = \text{Cov}_{RF,i}/\sigma_{RF}\sigma_j$$

Combining a Risk-Free Asset with a Risky Portfolio   What happens to the expected rate of return and the standard deviation of returns when you combine a risk-free asset with a portfolio of risky assets such as those that exist on the Markowitz efficient frontier?

Expected Return   Like the expected return for a portfolio of two risky assets, the expected rate of return for a portfolio that includes a risk-free asset with a collection of risky assets (call it Portfolio M) is the weighted average of the two returns:

$$E(R_{port}) = w_{RF}(RFR) + (1 - w_{RF})E(R_M)$$

where:

w_{RF} = the proportion of the portfolio invested in the risk-free asset

$E(R_M)$ = the expected rate of return on risky Portfolio M

Standard Deviation   Recall from Chapter 7 that the expected variance for a two-asset portfolio is

$$\sigma_{port}^2 = w_1^2\sigma_1^2 + w_2^2\sigma_2^2 + 2w_1 w_2\, r_{1,2}\sigma_1\sigma_2$$

Substituting the risk-free asset for Security 1, and the risky asset portfolio for Security 2, this formula would become

$$\sigma_{port}^2 = w_{RF}^2\sigma_{RF}^2 + (1 - w_{RF})^2\sigma_M^2 + 2w_{RF}(1 - w_{RF})r_{RF,M}\,\sigma_{RF}\sigma_M$$

We know that the variance of the risk-free asset is zero, that is, $\sigma_{RF}^2 = 0$. Because the correlation between the risk-free asset and any risky asset, M, is also zero, the factor r_{RFM} in the preceding equation also equals zero. Therefore, any component of the variance formula that has either of these terms will equal zero. When you make these adjustments, the formula becomes

$$\sigma^2_{\text{port}} = (1 - w_{\text{RF}})^2 \sigma^2_{\text{M}}$$

The standard deviation is

$$\sigma_{\text{port}} = \sqrt{(1 - w_{\text{RF}})^2 \sigma^2_{\text{M}}}$$
$$= (1 - w_{\text{RF}})\sigma_{\text{M}}$$

Therefore, the standard deviation of a portfolio that combines the risk-free asset with risky assets is *the linear proportion of the standard deviation of the risky asset portfolio.*

The Risk–Return Combination With these results, we can develop the risk–return relationship between $E(R_{\text{port}})$ and σ_{port} by using a few algebraic manipulations

$$E(R_{\text{port}}) = (w_{\text{RF}})(RFR) + (1 - w_{\text{RF}})\,E(R_{\text{M}}) + \{RFR - RFR\}$$
$$= RFR - (1 - w_{\text{RF}})RFR + (1 - w_{\text{RF}})E(R_{\text{M}})$$
$$= RFR + (1 - w_{\text{RF}})[E(R_{\text{M}}) - RFR]$$
$$= RFR + (1 - w_{\text{RF}})\,\{\sigma_{\text{M}} / \sigma_{\text{M}}\}\,[E(R_{\text{M}}) - RFR]$$

so that

8.1
$$E(R_{\text{port}}) = RFR + \sigma_{\text{port}}\left[\frac{E(R_{\text{M}}) - RFR}{\sigma_{\text{M}}}\right]$$

Equation 8.1 is the primary result of capital market theory. It can be interpreted as follows: Investors who allocate their money between a riskless security and the risky Portfolio M can expect a return equal to the risk-free rate plus compensation for the number of risk units (σ_{port}) they accept.

This outcome is consistent with the concept underlying all of investment theory that investors perform two functions in the capital markets for which they can expect to be rewarded. First, they allow someone else to use their money, for which they receive the risk-free rate of interest. Second, they bear the risk that the returns they have been promised in exchange for their invested capital will not be repaid. The term, $[E(R_{\text{M}}) - RFR]/\sigma_{\text{M}}$, is the expected compensation per unit of risk taken, which is more commonly referred to as the investor's expected *risk premium* per unit of risk.

The Capital Market Line The risk–return relationship shown in Equation 8.1 holds for every combination of the risk-free asset with *any* collection of risky assets. However, investors would obviously like to maximize their expected compensation for bearing risk (i.e., they would like to maximize the risk premium they receive). Let us now assume that Portfolio M is the single collection of risky assets that happens to maximize this risk premium. With this assumption, Portfolio M is called the *market portfolio* and, by definition, it contains all risky assets held anywhere in the marketplace. It has the property of receiving the highest level of expected return (in excess of the risk-free rate) per unit of risk for any available portfolio of risky assets. Under these conditions, Equation 8.1 is called the **capital market line (CML)**

Exhibit 8.1 shows the various possibilities when a risk-free asset is combined with alternative risky combinations of assets along the Markowitz efficient frontier. Each of the straight lines depicted represents mixtures of a risky portfolio with the riskless asset. For instance, the risk-free asset could be combined in various weights with Portfolio A, as shown by the straight line *RFR* − A. Any combination on this line would dominate portfolio possibilities that fall below it because it would have a higher expected return for the same level of risk. Similarly, any combination of the risk-free asset and Portfolio A is dominated by some mixture of the risk-free asset and Portfolio B.

You can continue to draw lines from *RFR* to the efficient frontier with increasingly higher slopes until you reach the point of tangency at Portfolio M. The set of portfolio possibilities along Line *RFR*-M—which is the CML—dominates *all* other feasible combinations that investors could form. For example, Point C could be established by investing half of your assets in the riskless security (i.e., lending at *RFR*) and the other half in Portfolio M. Notice in Exhibit 8.1 that there is no way to invest your money and achieve a higher expected return for the same level of risk (σ_c). In this sense, *the CML represents a new efficient frontier* that results from combining the Markowitz efficient frontier of risky assets with the ability to invest in the risk-free security. Finally, the slope of the CML is $[E(R_M) - RFR]/\sigma_M$, which is the maximum risk premium compensation that investors can expect for each unit of risk they bear.

Risk–Return Possibilities with Leverage An investor may want to attain a higher expected return than is available at Point M in exchange for accepting higher risk. One alternative would be to invest in one of the risky asset portfolios on the efficient frontier beyond Point M such as the portfolio at Point D. A second alternative is to add *leverage* to the portfolio by *borrowing* money at the risk-free rate and investing the proceeds in the risky asset portfolio at Point M; this is depicted as Point E. What effect would this have on the return and risk for your portfolio?

If you borrow an amount equal to 50 percent of your original wealth at the risk-free rate, w_{RF} will not be a positive fraction but, rather, a negative 50 percent ($w_{RF} = -0.50$). The effect on the expected return for your portfolio is:

$$E(R_{port}) = w_{RF}(RFR) + (1 - w_{RF})E(R_M)$$
$$= -0.50(RFR) + [1 - (-0.50)]E(R_M)$$
$$= -0.50(RFR) + 1.50E(R_M)$$

Exhibit 8.1 Portfolio Possibilities Combining the Risk-Free Asset and Risky Portfolios on the Efficient Frontier

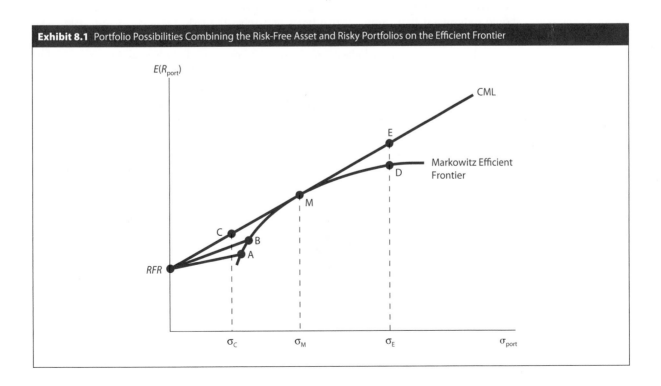

The return will increase in a *linear* fashion along the CML because the gross return increases by 50 percent, but you must pay interest at the *RFR* on the money borrowed. If $E(RFR) = 0.06$ and $E(R_M) = 0.12$, the return on your leveraged portfolio would be:

$$E(R_{port}) = -0.50(0.06) + 1.5(0.12)$$
$$= -0.03 + 0.18$$
$$= 0.15$$

The effect on the standard deviation of the leveraged portfolio is similar.

$$\sigma_{port} = (1 - w_{RF})\, \sigma_M$$
$$= [1 - (-0.50)]\, \sigma_M = 1.50\sigma_M$$

where:

σ_M = the standard deviation of Portfolio M

Therefore, *both return and risk increase in a linear fashion along the CML*. This is shown in Exhibit 8.2.

Our discussion of portfolio theory stated that, when two assets are perfectly correlated, the set of portfolio possibilities falls along a straight line. Therefore, because the CML is a straight line, it implies that all the portfolios on the CML are perfectly positively correlated. This positive correlation occurs because all portfolios on the CML combine the risky asset Portfolio M and the risk-free asset. You either invest part of your money in the risk-free asset (i.e., you *lend* at the *RFR*) and the rest in the risky asset Portfolio M, or you *borrow* at the risk-free rate and invest these funds in the risky asset portfolio. In either case, all the variability comes from the risky asset M portfolio. The only difference between the alternative portfolios on the CML is the magnitude of that variability, which is caused by the proportion of the risky asset portfolio held in the total portfolio.

8.1.3 Risk, Diversification, and the Market Portfolio

The investment prescription that emerges from capital market theory is clear-cut: Investors should only invest their funds in two types of assets—the risk-free security and risky asset Portfolio M—with the weights of these two holdings determined by the investors' tolerance for risk. Because of the special place that the market Portfolio M holds to all investors, it must contain *all risky assets* for which there is any value in the marketplace. This includes not just

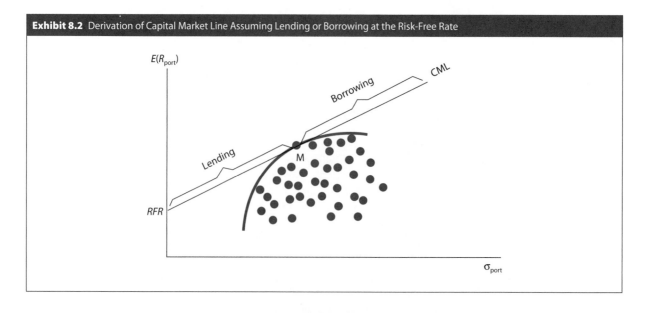

Exhibit 8.2 Derivation of Capital Market Line Assuming Lending or Borrowing at the Risk-Free Rate

U.S. common stocks, but also non-U.S. stocks, U.S. and non-U.S. bonds, real estate, private equity, options and futures contracts, art, antiques, and so on. Further, these assets should be represented in Portfolio M in proportion to their relative market values.

Since the market portfolio contains all risky assets, it is a **completely diversified portfolio,** which means that all risk unique to individual assets in the portfolio is diversified away. Specifically, the unique risk—which is often called **unsystematic risk**—of any single asset is offset by the unique variability of all of the other holdings in the portfolio. This implies that only **systematic risk**, defined as the variability in all risky assets caused by macroeconomic variables, remains in Portfolio M. Systematic risk can be measured by the standard deviation of returns to the market portfolio and it changes over time whenever there are changes in the underlying economic forces that affect the valuation of all risky assets.[1] Such economic forces would be variability of money supply growth, interest rate volatility, and variability in industrial production or corporate earnings.

How to Measure Diversification   As noted earlier, all portfolios on the CML are perfectly positively correlated, which means that all portfolios on the CML are perfectly correlated with the completely diversified market Portfolio M. Lorie (1975) suggests a measure of diversification. Specifically, a completely diversified portfolio would have a correlation with the market portfolio of +1.00. This is logical because complete diversification means the elimination of all the unsystematic or unique risk. Once you have eliminated all unsystematic risk, only systematic risk is left, which cannot be diversified away. Therefore, completely diversified portfolios would correlate perfectly with the market portfolio, which has only systematic risk.

Diversification and the Elimination of Unsystematic Risk   As discussed in Chapter 7, the purpose of diversification is to reduce the standard deviation of the total portfolio. This assumes imperfect correlations among securities. Ideally, as you add securities, the average covariance for the portfolio declines. How many securities must be included to arrive at a completely diversified portfolio? To discover the answer, you must observe what happens as you increase the sample size of the portfolio by adding securities that have some positive correlation. The typical correlation between U.S. securities ranges from 0.20 to 0.60.

One set of studies examined the average standard deviation for numerous portfolios of randomly selected stocks of different sample sizes. Evans and Archer (1968) and Tole (1982) computed the standard deviation for portfolios of increasing size up to 20 stocks. The results indicated that the major benefits of diversification were achieved rather quickly, with about 90 percent of the maximum benefit of diversification derived from portfolios of 12 to 18 stocks. Exhibit 8.3 shows a stylized depiction of this effect.

Two subsequent studies have modified this finding. Statman (1987) considered the trade-off between the diversification benefits and additional transaction costs involved with increasing the size of a portfolio. He concluded that a well-diversified portfolio must contain at least 30–40 stocks. Campbell, Lettau, Malkiel, and Xu (2001) demonstrated that because the idiosyncratic portion of an individual stock's total risk has been increasing in recent years, it now takes more stocks in a portfolio to achieve the same level of diversification. For instance, they showed that the level of diversification that was possible with only 20 stocks in the 1960s would require about 50 stocks by the late 1990s.

The important point to remember is that, by adding stocks to the portfolio that are not perfectly correlated with stocks in the portfolio, you can reduce the overall standard deviation of the portfolio, which will eventually reach the level of the market portfolio. At that point, you will have diversified away all unsystematic risk, but you still have market or systematic risk. You cannot eliminate the variability and uncertainty of macroeconomic factors that affect all risky assets. Further, you can attain a lower level of systematic risk by diversifying globally

---

[1] For analyses of changes in the standard deviation (volatility) of returns for stocks and bonds in the United States, see Schwert (1989), Ineichen (2000), Reilly, Wright, and Chan (2000), and Ang, Hodrick, Xing, and Zhang (2006).

Exhibit 8.3 Number of Stocks in a Portfolio and the Standard Deviation of Portfolio Return

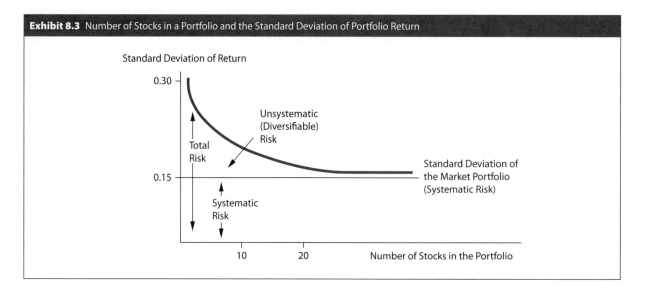

versus only diversifying within the United States because some of the systematic risk factors in the U.S. market (such as U.S. monetary policy) are not perfectly correlated with systematic risk variables in other countries such as Germany and Japan. As a result, if you diversify globally, you eventually get down to a world systematic risk level.

The CML and the Separation Theorem As we have seen, the CML leads all investors to invest in the same risky asset Portfolio M. Individual investors should only differ regarding their position on the CML, which depends on their risk preferences. In turn, how they get to a point on the CML is based on their *financing decisions*. If you are relatively risk averse, you will lend some part of your portfolio at the *RFR* by buying some risk-free securities and investing the remainder in the market portfolio of risky assets (e.g., Point C in Exhibit 8.1). In contrast, if you prefer more risk, you might borrow funds at the *RFR* and invest everything (all of your capital plus what you borrowed) in the market portfolio (Point E in Exhibit 8.1). This financing decision provides more risk but greater expected returns than the market portfolio. Because portfolios on the CML dominate other portfolio possibilities, the CML becomes the efficient frontier of portfolios, and investors decide where they want to be along this efficient frontier. Tobin (1958) called this division of the investment decision from the financing decision the **separation theorem**. Specifically, to be somewhere on the CML efficient frontier, you initially decide to invest in the market Portfolio M, which means that you will be on the CML. This is your *investment* decision. Subsequently, based on your risk preferences, you make a separate *financing* decision either to borrow or to lend to attain your preferred risk position on the CML.

A Risk Measure for the CML In discussing the Markowitz portfolio model, we noted that the relevant risk to consider when adding a security to a portfolio is *its average covariance with all other assets in the portfolio*. In this chapter, we have shown that *the only relevant portfolio is the market Portfolio M*. Together, this means that the only important consideration for any individual risky asset is its average covariance with all the risky assets in Portfolio M or *the asset's covariance with the market portfolio*. This covariance, then, is the relevant risk measure for an individual risky asset.

Because all individual risky assets are a part of the market portfolio, one can describe their rates of return in relation to the returns to Portfolio M using the following linear model:

8.2
$$R_{it} = a_i + b_i R_{Mt} + \varepsilon$$

where:

$R_{i,t}$ = return for asset i during period t
a_i = constant term for asset i
b_i = slope coefficient for asset i
R_{Mt} = return for Portfolio M during period t
ε = random error term

The variance of returns for a risky asset can similarly be described as

8.3
$$\begin{aligned} \text{Var}(R_{it}) &= \text{Var}(a_i + b_i R_{Mt} + \varepsilon) \\ &= \text{Var}(a_i) + \text{Var}(b_i R_{Mt}) + \text{Var}(\varepsilon) \\ &= 0 + \text{Var}(b_i R_{Mt}) + \text{Var}(\varepsilon) \end{aligned}$$

Note that $\text{Var}(b_i R_{Mt})$ is the variance of return for an asset related to the variance of the market return, or the asset's *systematic variance or risk*. Also, $\text{Var}(\varepsilon)$ is the residual variance of return for the individual asset that is not related to the market portfolio. This residual variance is the variability that we have referred to as the unsystematic or *unique risk* because it arises from the unique features of the asset. Therefore:

$$\text{Var}(R_{i,t}) = \text{Systematic Variance} + \text{Unsystematic Variance}$$

We know that a completely diversified portfolio has had all of its unsystematic variance eliminated. Therefore, the unsystematic variance of an asset is not relevant to investors, because they can eliminate it when holding an asset as part of a broad-based portfolio. As a consequence, investors should not expect to receive compensation for bearing this unsystematic risk. Only the systematic variance is relevant because it cannot be diversified away, because it is caused by economic forces that affect all risky assets.

8.1.4 Investing with the CML: An Example

After doing considerable research on current capital market conditions, you have estimated the investment characteristics for six different combinations of risky assets. Exhibit 8.4 lists your expected return and standard deviation forecasts for these portfolios. You have also established that each of these portfolios is completely diversified so that its volatility estimate represents systematic risk only. The risk-free rate at the time of your analysis is 4 percent.

Based on your forecasts for $E(R)$ and σ alone, none of these portfolios clearly dominates the others since higher levels of expected return always come at the cost of higher levels of risk. Which portfolio offers the best trade-off between risk and return? The last column in Exhibit 8.4 calculates the ratio of the expected risk premium $(E(R) - RFR)$ to volatility (σ) for each portfolio. As explained earlier, this ratio can be interpreted as the *amount of compensation that investors can expect for each unit of risk* they assume in a particular portfolio. For example, Portfolio 2 offers investors 0.429 ($= [7 - 4]/7$) units of compensation per unit of risk while the comparable ratio for Portfolio 6 is lower at 0.393 ($= [15 - 4]/28$) despite promising a much higher overall return.

By this measure, it is clear that Portfolio 3 offers investors the best combination of risk and return. No other feasible collection of risky assets in this comparison can match the 0.500 units of expected risk premium per unit of risk promised by Portfolio 3. Consequently, Portfolio 3 should be considered as the market portfolio. Capital market theory would recommend that you only consider two alternatives when investing your funds: (i) lending or borrowing in the riskless security at 4 percent and (ii) buying Portfolio 3.

Suppose now that given your risk tolerance you are willing to assume a standard deviation of 8.5 percent. How should you go about investing your money, according to the CML? First, using Equation 8.1, the return you can expect is:

$$4\% + (8.5\%)(0.500) = 8.25\%$$

Exhibit 8.4 Investment Characteristics for Portfolios of Risky Assets (RFR-5.4%)

Portfolio	Expected Return	Standard Deviation	$[E(R) - RFR]/\sigma$
1	5%	5%	0.200
2	7	7	0.429
3	9	10	0.500
4	11	15	0.467
5	13	21	0.429
6	15	28	0.393

As we have seen, there is no way for you to obtain a higher expected return under the current conditions without assuming more risk. Second, the investment strategy necessary to achieve this return can be found by solving:

$$8.25\% = w_{RF}(4\%) + (1 - w_{RF})(9\%)$$

or $w_{RF} = (9 - 8.25)/(9 - 4) = 0.15$. This means that you would need to invest 15 percent of your funds in the riskless asset and the remaining 85 percent in Portfolio 3. Finally, notice that the expected risk premium per unit of risk for this position is 0.500 ($=[8.25 - 4]/8.5$), the same as Portfolio 3. In fact, all points along the CML will have the same risk–return trade-off as the market portfolio since this ratio is the slope of the CML.

As a last extension, consider what would happen if you were willing to take on a risk level of $\sigma = 15$ percent. From Exhibit 8.4, you could realize an expected return of 11 percent if you placed 100 percent of funds in Portfolio 4. However, you can do better than this by following the investment prescription of the CML. Specifically, for a risk level of 15 percent, you can obtain an expected return of:

$$4\% + (15\%)(0.500) = 11.5\%.$$

This goal is greater than the expected return offered by a 100 percent investment in the market portfolio (i.e., 9 percent), so you will have to use leverage to achieve it. Specifically, solving for the investment weights along the CML leaves $w_{RF} = (9 - 11.5)/(9 - 4) = -0.50$ and $(1 - w_{RF}) = 1.50$. Thus, for each dollar you currently have to invest, you will need to borrow an additional 50 cents and place all of these funds in Portfolio 3.

· ·

8.2 The Capital Asset Pricing Model

Capital market theory represented a major step forward in how investors should think about the investment process. The formula for the CML (Equation 8.1) offers a precise way of calculating the return that investors can expect for (1) providing their financial capital (RFR), and (2) bearing σ_{port} units of risk ($[E(R_M) - RFR]/\sigma_M$). This last expression is especially significant because it offers a tangible measurement for the expected risk premium prevailing in the marketplace.

Unfortunately, capital market theory is an incomplete explanation for the relationship that exists between risk and return. To understand why, recall that the CML defined the risk an investor bears by the total volatility (σ) of the investment. However, since we have seen that investors cannot expect to be compensated for any portion of risk that they could have diversified away (i.e., unsystematic risk), the CML must be based on the assumption that investors only hold *fully diversified portfolios,* for which total risk and systematic risk are the same thing. The limitation is that the CML cannot provide an explanation for the risk–return trade-off for *individual* risky assets because the standard deviation measures for these securities will contain a substantial amount of unique risk.

The **capital asset pricing model (CAPM)** extends capital market theory in a way that allows investors to evaluate the risk–return trade-off for both diversified portfolios *and* individual securities. To do this, the CAPM redefines the relevant measure of risk from total volatility to just the nondiversifiable portion of that total volatility (i.e., systematic risk). This new risk measure is called the **beta** coefficient and it calculates the level of a security's systematic risk compared to that of the market portfolio. Using beta as the relevant measure of risk, the CAPM then redefines the expected risk premium per unit of risk in a commensurate fashion. This in turn leads once again to an expression of the expected return that can be decomposed into (1) the risk-free rate and (2) the expected risk premium.

8.2.1 A Conceptual Development of the CAPM

As noted earlier, Sharpe (1964), along with Lintner (1965) and Mossin (1966), developed the CAPM in a formal way. In addition to the assumptions listed before, the CAPM requires others, such as that asset returns come from a Normal probability distribution. Rather than repeat the mathematical derivation of the CAPM, we will present a conceptual development of the model that emphasizes its role in the natural progression that began with the Markowitz portfolio theory.

Recall that the CML expressed the risk–return trade-off for fully diversified portfolios as follows:

$$E(R_{port}) = RFR + \sigma_{port}\left[\frac{E(R_M) - RFR}{\sigma_M}\right]$$

When trying to extend this expression to allow for the evaluation of any individual risky asset i, the logical temptation is to simply replace the standard deviation of the portfolio (σ_{port}) with that of the single security (σ_i). However, as explained above, this would overstate the relevant level of risk in the i-th security because it does not take into account how much of that volatility the investor could diversify away by combining that asset with other holdings. One way to address this concern is to "shrink" the level of σ_i to include only the portion of risk in Security i that is systematically related to the risk in the market portfolio. This can be done by multiplying σ_i by the correlation coefficient between the returns to Security i and the market portfolio (r_{iM}). Inserting this product into the CML and adapting the notation for the i-th individual asset leaves:

$$E(R_i) = RFR + (\sigma_i r_{iM})\left[\frac{E(R_M) - RFR}{\sigma_M}\right]$$

This expression can be rearranged as:

$$E(R_i) = RFR + \left(\frac{\sigma_i r_{iM}}{\sigma_M}\right)[E(R_M) - RFR]$$

or:

8.4
$$E(R_i) = RFR + \beta_i[E(R_M) - RFR].$$

Equation 8.4 is the CAPM. Notice in particular that the CAPM redefines risk in terms of a security's beta (β_i), which captures the nondiversifiable portion ofthat stock's risk *relative to the market as a whole*. Because of this, beta can be thought of as *indexing* the asset's systematic risk to that of the market portfolio. This leads to a very convenient interpretation: A stock with a beta of 1.20 has a level of systematic risk that is 20% greater than the average for the entire market, while a stock with a beta of 0.70 is 30% less risky than the market. By definition, the market portfolio itself will always have a beta of 1.00.

Indexing the systematic risk of an individual security to the market has another nice feature as well. From Equation 8.4, it is clear that the CAPM once again expresses the expected return for an investment as the sum of the risk-free rate and the expected risk premium. However, rather than calculate a different risk premium for every separate security that exists, the CAPM states that only the overall **market risk premium** ($E(R_M) - RFR$) matters and that this quantity can then be adapted to any risky asset by scaling it up or down according to that asset's riskiness relative to the market (β_i). As we will see, this substantially reduces the number of calculations that investors must make when evaluating potential investments for their portfolios.

8.2.2 The Security Market Line

The CAPM can also be illustrated in graphical form as the **security market line** (SML). This is shown in Exhibit 8.5. Like the CML, the SML expresses the trade-off between risk and expected return as a straight line intersecting the vertical axis (i.e., zero-risk point) at the risk-free rate. However, there are two important differences between the CML and the SML. First, the CML measures risk by the standard deviation (i.e., total risk) of the investment while the SML explicitly considers only the systematic component of an investment's volatility. Second, as a consequence of the first point, the CML can only be applied to portfolio holdings that are already fully diversified, whereas the SML can be applied to any individual asset or collection of assets.

Determining the Expected Rate of Return for a Risky Asset   To demonstrate how you would compute expected or required rates of return, consider the following example stocks assuming you have already computed betas:

Stock	Beta
A	0.70
B	1.00
C	1.15
D	1.40
E	−0.30

Assume that we expect the economy's *RFR* to be 5 percent (0.05) and the expected return on the market portfolio ($E(R_M)$) to be 9 percent (0.09). This implies a market risk premium of 4 percent (0.04). With these inputs, the SML would yield the following required rates of return for these five stocks:

$$E(R_i) = RFR + \beta_i(E(R_M) - RFR)$$
$$E(R_A) = 0.05 + 0.70\,(0.09 - 0.05)$$
$$= 0.078 = 7.80\%$$
$$E(R_B) = 0.05 + 1.00\,(0.09 - 0.05)$$
$$= 0.09 = 9.00\%$$

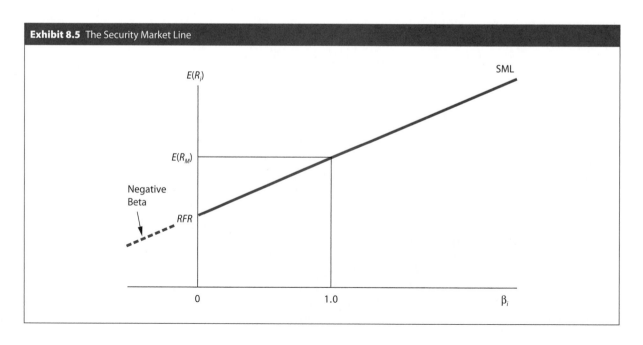

Exhibit 8.5 The Security Market Line

$$E(R_C) = 0.05 + 1.15 \,(0.09 - 0.05)$$
$$= 0.096 = 9.60\%$$
$$E(R_D) = 0.05 + 1.40 \,(0.09 - 0.05)$$
$$= 0.106 = 10.60\%$$
$$E(R_E) = 0.05 + (-0.30) \,(0.09 - 0.05)$$
$$= 0.05 - 0.012$$
$$= 0.038 = 3.8\%$$

Stock A has lower risk than the aggregate market, so you should not expect its return to be as high as the return on the market portfolio of risky assets. You should expect Stock A to return 7.80 percent. Stock B has systematic risk equal to the market's (beta = 1.00), so its required rate of return should likewise be equal to the expected market return (9 percent). Stocks C and D have systematic risk greater than the market's, so they should provide returns consistent with their risk. Finally, Stock E has a *negative* beta (which is quite rare in practice), so its required rate of return, if such a stock could be found, would be below the *RFR* of 5 percent.

In equilibrium, *all* assets and *all* portfolios of assets should plot on the SML. That is, all assets should be priced so that their **estimated rates of return**, which are the actual holding period rates of return that you anticipate, are consistent with their levels of systematic risk. Any security with an estimated rate of return that plots above the SML would be considered undervalued because it implies that you *estimated* you would receive a rate of return on the security that is above its *required* rate of return based on its systematic risk. In contrast, assets with estimated rates of return that plot below the SML would be considered overvalued. This position relative to the SML implies that your estimated rate of return is below what you should require based on the asset's systematic risk.

In a completely efficient market, you would not expect any assets to plot off the SML because, in equilibrium, all stocks should provide holding period returns that are equal to their required rates of return. Alternatively, a market that is fairly efficient but not completely efficient may misprice certain assets because not everyone will be aware of all the relevant information for an asset. As we discussed in Chapter 6, a superior investor has the ability to derive value estimates for assets that consistently outperform the consensus market evaluation. As a result, such an investor will earn better rates of return than the average investor on a risk-adjusted basis.

Identifying Undervalued and Overvalued Assets Now that we understand how to compute the rate of return one should expect or require for a specific risky asset using the SML, we can compare this *required* rate of return to the asset's *estimated* rate of return over a specific investment horizon to determine whether it would be an appropriate investment. To make this comparison, you need an independent estimate of the return outlook for the security based on either fundamental or technical analysis techniques, which will be discussed in subsequent chapters.

Assume that analysts at a major brokerage firm have been following the five stocks in the preceding example. Based on extensive fundamental analysis, they provide you with expected price and dividend information for the next year, as shown in Exhibit 8.6. Given these projections, you can compute an estimated rate of return for each stock by summing the expected capital gain ($[P_{t+1} - P_t]/P_t$) and the expected dividend yield (D_{t+1}/P_t). For example, the analysts' estimated future return for Stock A is 8.00 percent ($=[26 - 25]/25 + 1/25$).

Exhibit 8.7 summarizes the relationship between the required rate of return for each stock based on its systematic risk as computed earlier, and its estimated rate of return. This difference between estimated return and expected return is sometimes referred to as a stock's expected *alpha* or its excess return. This alpha can be positive (the stock is undervalued) or negative (the stock is overvalued). If the alpha is zero, the stock is on the SML and is properly valued in line with its systematic risk.

Exhibit 8.6 Price, Dividend, and Rate of Return Estimates

Stock	Current Price (P_t)	Expected Price (P_{t+1})	Expected Dividend (D_{t+1})	Estimated Future Rate of Return (Percent)
A	25	26	1.00	8.00%
B	40	42	0.50	6.20
C	33	37	1.00	15.15
D	64	66	1.10	5.16
E	50	53	—	6.00

Exhibit 8.7 Comparison of Required Rate of Return to Estimated Rate of Return (*RFR* = 5%)

Stock	Beta	Required Return $E(R_i)$	Estimated Return	Estimated Return Minus $E(R_i)$	Evaluation
A	0.70	7.80	8.00	0.20	Properly valued
B	1.00	9.00	6.20	−2.80	Overvalued
C	1.15	9.60	15.15	5.55	Undervalued
D	1.40	10.60	5.16	−5.44	Overvalued
E	−0.30	3.80	6.00	2.20	Undervalued

Plotting these estimated rates of return and stock betas on the SML gives Exhibit 8.8. Stock A is almost exactly on the line, so it is considered properly valued because its estimated rate of return is almost equal to its required rate of return. Stocks B and D are considered overvalued because their estimated rates of return during the coming period are substantially less than what an investor should expect for the risk involved. As a result, they plot below the SML. In contrast, Stocks C and E are expected to provide rates of return greater than we would require based on their systematic risk. Therefore, both stocks plot above the SML, indicating that they are undervalued.

Exhibit 8.8 Plot of Estimated Returns on SML Graph

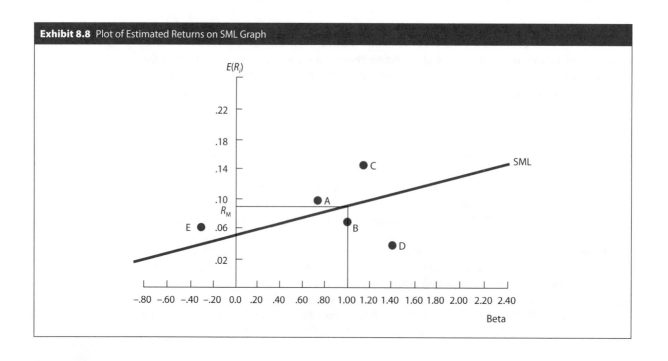

If you trusted these analysts to forecast estimated returns, you would take no action regarding Stock A, but you would buy Stocks C and E and sell Stocks B and D. You might even sell Stocks B and D short if you favored such aggressive tactics.

Calculating Systematic Risk There are two ways that a stock's beta can be calculated in practice. First, given our conceptual discussion of the CAPM, a beta coefficient for Security i can be calculated directly from the following formula:

8.5
$$\sigma_i = \left(\frac{\sigma_i}{\sigma_M}\right)(r_{iM}) = \frac{\text{Cov}(R_i, R_M)}{\sigma_M^2}$$

where, in addition to the terms defined earlier, σ_M^2 is the return variance for the market portfolio and $\text{Cov}(R_i, R_M)$ is the covariance between returns to the Security i and the market.

Alternatively, security betas can also be estimated as the slope coefficient in a regression equation between the returns to the security (R_{it}) over time and the returns (R_{Mt}) to the market portfolio:

8.6
$$R_{it} = a_i + \beta_i(R_{Mt}) + e_{it}$$

where a_i is the intercept of the regression and e_{it} is the random error term that accounts for the fact that not all of Security i's risk is systematically related to the market. Equation 8.6 is known as the security's **characteristic line** with the market portfolio.

Equations 8.5 and 8.6 will produce the same estimate of β_i for any given sample of security and market portfolio returns. However, the regression-based method in Equation 8.6 is often preferred because it is a formal estimation process, meaning that the statistical reliability of the estimate can be assessed (i.e., a t-statistic on the β_i estimate can be evaluated).

The Impact of the Time Interval In practice, the number of observations and the time interval used in the regression vary widely. For example, Morningstar derives characteristic lines for common stocks using monthly returns for the most recent five-year period (60 observations). Reuters Analytics calculates stock betas using daily returns over the prior two years (504 observations). Bloomberg uses two years of weekly returns (104 observations) in its basic calculations, although its system allows the user to select daily, weekly, monthly, quarterly, or annual returns over other time horizons. Because there is no theoretically correct time interval for this estimation, we must make a trade-off between enough observations to eliminate the impact of random rates of return and an excessive length of time, such as 15 or 20 years, over which the subject company may have changed dramatically. Remember that what you really want is the *expected* systematic risk for the potential investment. In this process, you are analyzing historical data to help you derive a reasonable estimate of the asset's future level of systematic risk.

Reilly and Wright (1988) analyzed the differential effects of return computation, market index, and the time interval and showed that the major cause of the differences in beta was the use of monthly versus weekly return intervals. Also, the interval effect depended on the sizes of the firms. The shorter weekly interval caused a larger beta for large firms and a smaller beta for small firms. Handa, Kothari, and Wasley (1989) concurred with this conclusion and showed that the reason was that an asset's covariance with the market and the market's return variance did not change proportionally with the return interval. They also confirmed that firm size influenced the effect.

The Effect of the Market Proxy Another significant decision when computing an asset's characteristic line is which indicator series to use as a proxy for the market portfolio of all risky assets. Most investigators use the Standard & Poor's 500 Composite Index as a proxy for the market portfolio, because the stocks in this index encompass a large proportion of the total market value of U.S. stocks and it is a value-weighted series, which is consistent with the theoretical market series. Still, this series is dominated by large-cap U.S. stocks, most of them listed on the NYSE. Previously, it was noted that the market portfolio of all risky assets should include U.S.

Exhibit 8.9 Computation of Beta for Procter & Gamble with Selected Indexes

Date	INDEX			RETURN			S&P 500 (SPX) $R_{SPX} -$ Avg. R_{SPX} (1)	MSCI World (MXWO) $R_{MXWO} -$ Avg. R_{MXWO} (2)	PG $R_{PG} -$ Avg. R_{PG} (3)	(4)[a]	(5)[b]
	SPX	MXWO	PG	SPX	MXWO	PG					
Jun-06	1270.20	1319.93	55.60	—	—	—					
Jul-06	1276.66	1327.23	56.20	0.51	0.55	1.08	-0.92	-1.09	0.22	-0.21	-0.24
Aug-06	1303.82	1358.87	61.90	2.13	2.38	10.14	0.70	0.74	9.29	6.47	6.91
Sep-06	1335.85	1373.37	61.98	2.46	1.07	0.13	1.03	-0.57	-0.73	-0.74	0.42
Oct-06	1377.94	1422.93	63.39	3.15	3.61	2.27	1.72	1.97	1.42	2.44	2.80
Nov-06	1400.63	1455.17	62.79	1.65	2.27	-0.95	0.22	0.63	-1.80	-0.39	-1.13
Dec-06	1418.30	1483.58	64.27	1.26	1.95	2.36	-0.17	0.31	1.50	-0.25	0.47
Jan-07	1438.24	1500.23	64.87	1.41	1.12	0.93	-0.03	-0.52	0.08	0.00	-0.04
Feb-07	1406.82	1490.44	63.49	-2.18	-0.65	-2.13	-3.62	-2.29	-2.98	10.78	6.83
Mar-07	1420.86	1514.18	63.16	1.00	1.59	-0.52	-0.43	-0.05	-1.37	0.60	0.06
Apr-07	1482.37	1577.86	64.40	4.33	4.21	1.96	2.90	2.57	1.11	3.21	2.85
May-07	1530.62	1616.87	63.55	3.25	2.47	-1.32	1.82	0.83	-2.17	-3.97	-1.81
Jun-07	1503.35	1602.36	61.19	-1.78	-0.90	-3.71	-3.21	-2.54	-4.57	14.68	11.59
										Total = 32.61	28.71
Average				1.43	1.64	0.85					
Standard Deviation				1.84	1.46	3.32					

$Cov_{(PG,SPX)} = 32.61/12 = 2.72$

$Cov_{(PG,MXWO)} = 28.71/12 = 2.39$

$Correlation\ Coeff._{(PG,SPX)} = 2.72/(1.84 \times 3.32) = 0.44$

$Var_{(SPX)} = StdDev^2_{(SPX)} = (1.84)^2 = 3.39$

$Var_{(MXWO)} = StdDev^2_{(MXWO)} = (1.46)^2 = 2.14$

$Beta_{(PG,SPX)} = 2.72/3.39 = 0.80$

$Beta_{(PG,MXWO)} = 2.39/2.14 = 1.12$

$Correlation\ Coeff._{(PG,MXWO)} = 2.39/(1.46 \times 3.32) = 0.49$

$Intercept_{(PG,SPX)} = 0.85 - (0.80 \times 1.43) = -0.29$

$Intercept_{(PG,MXWO)} = 0.85 - (1.12 \times 1.64) = -0.98$

[a] Column 4 is equal to Column 1 multiplied by Column 3.
[b] Column 5 is equal to Column 2 multiplied by Column 3.

Exhibit 8.10 Characteristic Line and Scatterplot of Procter & Gamble (PG) with the S&P 500 Index (SPX): July 2006–June 2007

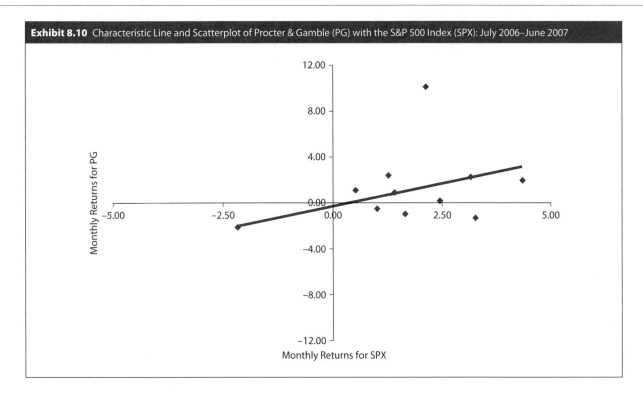

stocks and bonds, non-U.S. stocks and bonds, real estate, coins, stamps, art, antiques, and any other marketable risky asset from around the world.[2]

Computing a Characteristic Line: An Example The following example shows how you would estimate a characteristic line for Procter & Gamble (PG) using monthly return data from July 2006 to June 2007.[3] Twelve monthly rates are not typically considered sufficient for statistical purposes, but they are adequate for demonstration purposes. We calculate betas for PG using two different proxies for the market portfolio: (1) the S&P 500 (SPX), an index of stocks mostly domiciled in the United States, and (2) the MSCI World Equity (MXWO) index, which represents a global portfolio of stocks.

Exhibit 8.9 lists monthly price changes for PG, SPX, and MXWO, which are computed using month-end closing prices. Exhibit 8.10 shows a scatterplot of these return data for PG and SPX, while Exhibit 8.11 contains a similar display for PG and MXWO. During this 12-month period, there was only one month when the PG return diverged greatly from the S&P 500 index series. As a result, the calculation in Exhibit 8.9 shows that the covariance between PG and SPX was positive (2.72). The covariance divided by the variance of SPX (3.39) equals PG's beta compared to the S&P 500. For this period, the beta was 0.80, indicating that PG was less risky than the aggregate market. The intercept for this characteristic line is –0.29, calculated as the average monthly return for PG (0.85) less the product of the average monthly return for SPX (1.43) and the beta coefficient. The fact that most of the observations plotted in Exhibit 8.10 are reasonably close to the characteristic line is consistent with the correlation coefficient between PG and SPX of 0.44.

[2]Substantial discussion surrounds the market proxy used and its impact on the empirical results and usefulness of the CAPM. This concern is discussed further and demonstrated in the subsequent section on computing an asset's characteristic line. The effect of the market proxy is also considered when we discuss the arbitrage pricing theory (APT) in Chapter 9 and in Chapter 25 when we discuss the evaluation of portfolio performance.

[3]The returns used in this example are based solely on monthly price changes for PG and two indexes (S&P 500 and MSCI World Equity); they do not include dividends. This is done for simplicity but it is also based on Sharpe and Cooper's (1972a) finding that betas derived from returns with and without dividends have a correlation coefficient of 0.99.

Exhibit 8.11 Characteristic Line and Scatterplot of Procter & Gamble (PG) with the MSCI World Index (MXWO): July 2006–June 2007

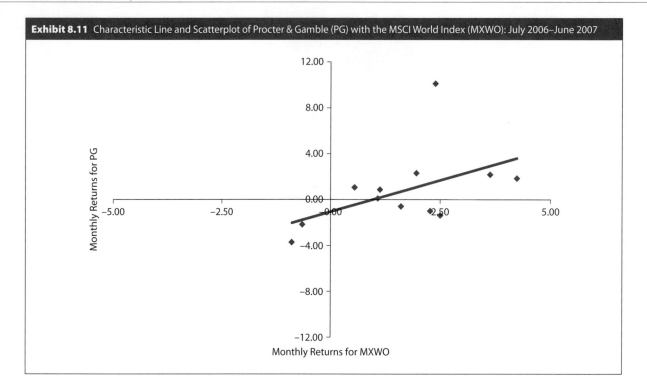

How does this analysis change if we use a different market proxy? Exhibit 8.9 also lists calculations for the PG beta using a global equity index as a market portfolio. Two things change when this substitution is made. First, notice that the volatility of the MSCI World index (2.14) was substantially lower than the S&P 500 over this period. Second, the covariance between PG and MXWO (2.39) is also lower, although the overall correlation coefficient between the two is higher (0.49) than between PG and SPX. Taken together, the lower volatility of the World index has a greater effect than the lower covariance statistic, so the beta coefficient between PG and MXWO is 1.12, substantially larger than when the S&P 500 was used as the market proxy. In fact, notice that the interpretation of the nature of PG's relative systematic risk changes dramatically with this new index. Rather than being 20 percent *less* risky than the domestic equity market, PG is now seen as being 12 percent *more* risky than the global index.

Beyond demonstrating the computations involved in the process, the important point illustrated in this example is that the proper selection of a proxy for the market portfolio is of vital importance when measuring risk. Reilly and Akhtar (1995) showed that beta differences of this magnitude are to be expected when comparing the stock of any company to both U.S. and World equity indexes. Further, even more extreme differences are possible when stock betas are calculated relative to market proxies that contain other asset classes, such as fixed-income securities or real estate.

8.3 Relaxing the Assumptions

Earlier in the chapter, several assumptions were set forth related to the CAPM. In this section, we discuss the impact on the capital market line (CML) and the security market line (SML) when we relax several of these assumptions.

8.3.1 Differential Borrowing and Lending Rates

One of the first assumptions of the CAPM was that investors could borrow and lend any amount of money at the risk-free rate. It is reasonable to assume that investors can *lend* unlimited

Exhibit 8.12 Investment Alternatives When the Cost of Borrowing Is Higher Than the Cost of Lending

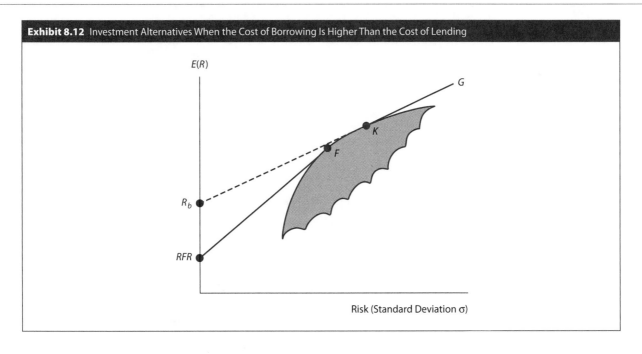

amounts at the risk-free rate by buying government securities (e.g., T-bills). In contrast, it is quite unlikely that investors can *borrow* unlimited amounts at the T-bill rate. For example, when T-bills are yielding 4 percent, most individuals would have to pay about 6 or 7 percent to borrow at a bank.

Because of this differential, there will be two different lines going to the Markowitz efficient frontier, as shown in Exhibit 8.12. The segment *RFR–F* indicates the investment opportunities available when an investor combines risk-free assets (i.e., lending at the *RFR*) and Portfolio F on the Markowitz efficient frontier. It is not possible to extend this line any farther if you cannot borrow at this risk-free rate to acquire further units of Portfolio F. If you can borrow at R_b, the point of tangency from this rate would be on the curve at Portfolio K. This indicates that you could borrow at R_b and use the proceeds to invest in Portfolio K to extend the CML along the line segment *K–G*. Therefore, the CML is made up of *RFR–F–K–G;* that is, a line segment (*RFR–F*), a curve segment (*F–K*), and another line segment (*K–G*). As noted by Brennan (1969), this implies that you can either lend or borrow, but the borrowing portfolios are not as profitable as when it was assumed that you could borrow at the *RFR*. In this instance, because you must pay a borrowing rate that is higher than the *RFR,* your net return is less—that is, the slope of the borrowing line (*K–G*) is below that for *RFR–F*.

8.3.2 Zero-Beta Model

If the market portfolio (M) is mean-variance efficient (i.e., it has the lowest risk for a given level of return among the attainable set of portfolios), an alternative model, derived by Black (1972), does not require a risk-free asset. Within the set of feasible alternative portfolios, several exist where the returns are completely uncorrelated with the market portfolio; the beta of these portfolios with the market portfolio is zero. Among the several zero-beta portfolios, you would select the one with minimum variance. Although this portfolio does not have any systematic risk, it does have some unsystematic risk. The availability of this zero-beta portfolio will not affect the CML, but it will allow construction of a linear SML, as shown in Exhibit 8.13. The combinations of this zero-beta portfolio and the market portfolio will be a linear relationship in return and risk because the covariance between the zero-beta portfolio (R_z) and the market portfolio is similar to what it was with the risk-free asset. Assuming the return for the zero-beta portfolio is greater than that for a risk-free asset, the slope of the line through the market

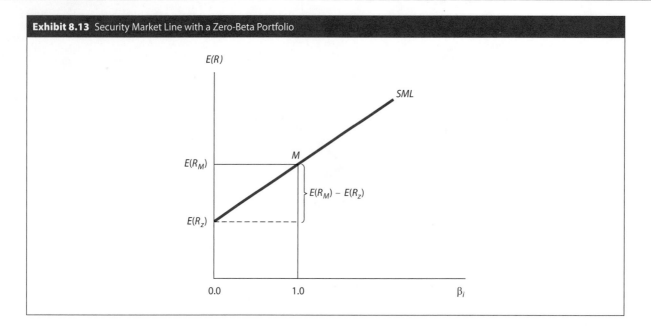

Exhibit 8.13 Security Market Line with a Zero-Beta Portfolio

portfolio would not be as steep; that is, the market risk premium would be smaller. The equation for this zero-beta CAPM line would be:

8.7
$$E(R_i) = E(R_z) + B_i[E(R_M) - E(R_z)]$$

Obviously, the risk premiums for individual assets would be a function of the beta for the individual security and the market risk premium:

$$[E(R_M) - E(R_z)]$$

Several studies have specifically tested this model with its higher intercept and flatter slope and had conflicting results. Specifically, studies by Gibbons (1982) and Shanken (1985b) rejected the model, while a study by Stambaugh (1982) supported the zero-beta CAPM.

8.3.3 Transaction Costs

The CAPM assumes that there are no transaction costs, so investors will buy or sell mispriced securities until they plot on the SML. If there are transaction costs, investors will not correct all mispricing because in some instances the cost of buying and selling the mispriced security will exceed any potential excess return. Therefore, securities will plot very close to the SML, but not exactly on it. Thus, the SML will be a band of securities, as shown in Exhibit 8.14, rather than a single line. Obviously, the width of the band is a function of the amount of the transaction costs. In a world with a large proportion of trading by institutions at pennies per share and with discount brokers available for individual investors, the band should be quite narrow.

Dimson (1979) considered how transaction costs affect the extent of diversification by investors. Earlier in the chapter, we discussed the relationship between the number of stocks in a portfolio and the variance of the portfolio. Initially, the variance declined rapidly, approaching about 90 percent of complete diversification with around 20 securities. An important question is, How many securities must be added to derive the last 10 percent? Because of transaction costs, Brennan and Subramanyam (1996) show that at some point the additional cost of diversification would exceed its benefit, especially when considering the costs of monitoring and analyzing the added securities. Degennaro and Robotti (2007) demonstrate that transaction costs can reduce the slope of the CML.

8.3.4 Heterogeneous Expectations and Planning Periods

If all investors had different expectations about risk and return, each would have a unique CML or SML, and the composite graph would be a set (band) of lines with a breadth determined by the divergence of expectations. If all investors had similar information and background, the band would be reasonably narrow.

The impact of *planning periods* is similar. Recall that the CAPM is a one-period model, corresponding to the planning period for the individual investor. Thus, if you are using a one-year planning period, your CML and SML could differ from someone with a one-month planning period.

8.3.5 Taxes

The expected returns in the CAPM are pretax returns. In fact, the actual returns for most investors are affected as follows:

8.8
$$E\left(R_i(AT)\right) = \frac{(P_e - P_b) \times (1 - T_{cg}) + (Div) \times (1 - T_i)}{P_b}$$

where:

$R_i(AT)$ = after-tax rate of return
P_e = ending price
P_b = beginning price
T_{cg} = tax on capital gain or loss
Div = dividend paid during period
T_i = tax on ordinary income

Clearly, tax rates differ between individuals and institutions. For institutions that do not pay taxes, the original pretax model is correctly specified—that is, T_{cg} and T_i take on values of zero. As noted by Black and Scholes (1979) and Litzenberger and Ramaswamy (1979), because investors have heavy tax burdens, this could cause major differences in the CML and SML

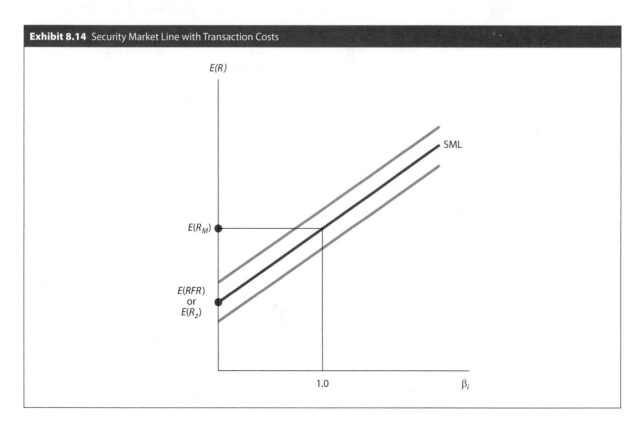

Exhibit 8.14 Security Market Line with Transaction Costs

among investors. Studies by Elton, Gruber, and Rentzler (1983); Miller and Scholes (1982); and Christie (1990) have examined the effect of the differential taxes on dividends versus capital gains but the evidence is inconclusive.

8.4 Additional Empirical Tests of the CAPM

When testing the CAPM, there are two major questions. First, *How stable is the measure of systematic risk (beta)?* Because beta is our principal risk measure, it is important to know whether past betas can be used as estimates of future betas. Second, *Is there a positive linear relationship as hypothesized between beta and the rate of return on risky assets?* More specifically, how well do returns conform to the SML in Equation 8.4

$$E(R_i) = RFR + \beta_i[E(R_M) - RFR]$$

Some specific questions might include:

- Does the intercept approximate the prevailing *RFR?*
- Was the slope of the line positive and was it consistent with the slope implied by the prevailing risk premium $(E(R_M) - RFR)?$

8.4.1 Stability of Beta

Numerous studies have examined the stability of beta and generally concluded that the risk measure was *not* stable for individual stocks, but the stability of the beta for *portfolios* of stocks increased dramatically. Further, the larger the portfolio (e.g., over 50 stocks) and the longer the period (over 26 weeks), the more stable the beta estimate. Also, the betas tended to regress toward the mean. Specifically, high-beta portfolios tended to decline over time toward unity (1.00), whereas low-beta portfolios tended to increase over time toward unity.

Carpenter and Upton (1981) considered the influence of the trading volume on beta stability and contended that predictions were slightly better using the volume-adjusted betas. A small-firm effect wherein the beta for low-volume securities was biased downward was documented by Ibbotson, Kaplan, and Peterson (1997).

8.4.2 Relationship between Systematic Risk and Return

The ultimate question regarding the CAPM is whether it is useful in explaining the return on risky assets. Specifically, is there a positive linear relationship between the systematic risk and the rates of return on these risky assets? Sharpe and Cooper (1972b) found a positive relationship between return and risk, although it was not completely linear.

Because of the statistical problems with individual stocks, Black, Jensen, and Scholes (1972) examined the risk and return for portfolios of stocks and found a positive linear relationship between monthly excess return and portfolio beta, although the intercept was higher than the zero value expected. Exhibit 8.15 contains charts from this study, which show that (1) most of the measured SMLs had a positive slope, (2) the slopes change between periods, (3) the intercepts are not zero, and (4) the intercepts change between periods.

Effect of Skewness on the Relationship   Beyond the analysis of return and beta, several authors also have considered the impact of skewness on expected returns. Skewness reflects the presence of too many large positive or negative observations in a distribution. A normal distribution is symmetric, which means that balance exists between positive and negative observations. In contrast, positive skewness indicates an abnormal number of large positive price changes.

Investigators contended that skewness helped explain the prior results wherein the model appeared to underprice low-beta stocks (so investors received returns above expectations) and overprice high-beta stocks (so investors received returns lower than expected). Some early results confirmed these expectations, but also found that high-beta stocks had high-positive skewness, which implied that investors prefer stocks with high-positive skewness that provide an opportunity for very large returns.

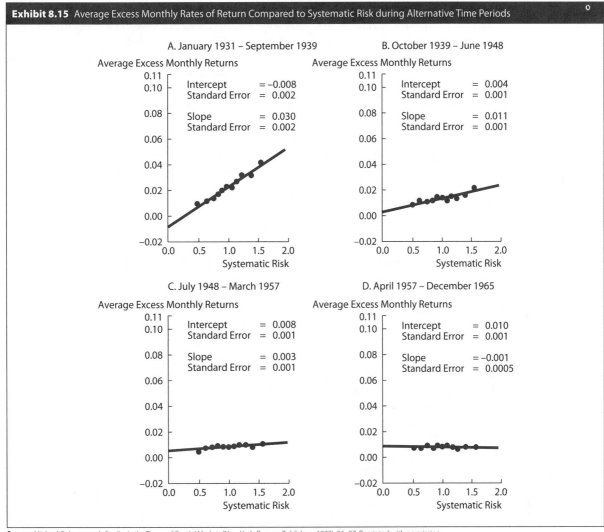

Exhibit 8.15 Average Excess Monthly Rates of Return Compared to Systematic Risk during Alternative Time Periods

Source: Michael C. Jenson, ed., *Studies in the Theory of Captial Markets* (New York: Praeger Publishers, 1972): 96–97. Reprinted with permission.

Kraus and Litzenberger (1976) tested a CAPM with a skewness term and confirmed that investors are willing to pay for positive skewness. The importance of skewness was supported in studies by Sears and Wei (1988) and subsequently by Lim (1989).

Effect of Size, P/E, and Leverage In the efficient markets hypothesis (EMH) chapter, we discussed the size effect (the small-firm anomaly) and the P/E effect and showed that these variables have an inverse impact on returns after considering the CAPM. These results imply that size and P/E are additional risk factors that need to be considered along with beta. Specifically, expected returns are a positive function of beta, but investors also require higher returns from relatively small firms and for stocks with relatively low P/E ratios.

Bhandari (1988) found that financial leverage also helps explain the cross section of average returns after both beta and size are considered. This implies a multivariate CAPM with three risk variables: beta, size, and financial leverage.

Effect of Book-to-Market Value Fama and French (1992) evaluated the joint roles of market beta, size, E/P, financial leverage, and the book-to-market equity ratio in the cross-section of average returns on the NYSE, AMEX, and NASDAQ stocks. While some earlier studies found a significant positive relationship between returns and beta, this study finds that the relationship between beta and the average rate of return disappears during the recent period

1963 to 1990, even when beta is used alone to explain average returns. In contrast, univariate tests between average returns and size, leverage, E/P, and book-to-market equity (BE/ME) indicate that all of these variables are significant and have the expected sign.

In the multivariate tests, the results showed that the negative relationship between size [In (ME)] and average returns is robust to the inclusion of other variables. Further, the positive relation between BE/ME and average returns also persists when the other variables are included. Interestingly, when both of these variables are included, the book-to-market value ratio (BE/ME) has the consistently stronger role in explaining average returns.

Fama and French concluded that size and book-to-market equity capture the cross-sectional variation in average stock returns associated with size, E/P, book-to-market equity, and leverage. Moreover, of the two variables, the book-to-market equity ratio appears to subsume E/P and leverage. Following these results, Fama and French (1993) suggested the use of a three-factor CAPM model. This model was used by Fama and French (1996) to explain a number of the anomalies from prior studies.[4]

8.4.3 Summary of CAPM Risk–Return Empirical Results

Most of the early evidence regarding the relationship between rates of return and systematic risk of portfolios supported the CAPM; there was evidence that the intercepts were generally higher than implied by the *RFR* that prevailed, which is either consistent with a zero-beta model or the existence of higher borrowing rates. To explain these unusual returns, additional variables were considered including the third moment of the distribution (skewness). The results indicated that positive skewness and high betas were correlated.

The literature provided extensive evidence that size, the P/E ratio, financial leverage, and the book-to-market value ratio have explanatory power regarding returns beyond beta. The Fama-French study concluded that the two dominant variables were size and the book-value to market-value ratio.

In contrast to Fama and French, who measure beta with monthly returns, Kothari, Shanken, and Sloan (1995) measured beta with annual returns to avoid trading problems and found substantial compensation for beta risk. They suggested that the results obtained by Fama and French may have been time period–specific and might not be significant over a longer period. Pettengill, Dundaram, and Matthur (1995) noted that empirical studies typically use realized returns to test the CAPM model when theory specifies expected returns. When they adjusted for negative market excess returns, they found a consistent and significant relationship between beta and rates of return. When Jagannathan and Wang (1996) employed a conditional CAPM that allows for changes in betas and in the market risk premium, this model performed well in explaining the cross section of returns. Grundy and Malkiel (1996) also contend that beta is a very useful measure of risk during declining markets, which is when it is most important. Finally, when Reilly and Wright (2004) examined the risk-adjusted performance for 31 different asset classes utilizing betas computed using a very broad proxy for the market portfolio, the risk–return relationship was significant and as expected in theory.

8.5 The Market Portfolio: Theory versus Practice

Throughout our presentation of the CAPM, we noted that the market portfolio included *all* the risky assets in the economy. Further, in equilibrium, the various assets would be included in the portfolio in proportion to their market value. Therefore, this market portfolio should contain not only U.S. stocks and bonds but also real estate, options, art, foreign stocks and bonds, and so on, with weights equal to their relative market value.

Although this concept of a market portfolio is reasonable in theory, it is difficult to implement when testing or using the CAPM. The easy part is getting an index series for U.S. and

---

[4]This three-factor model by Fama and French is discussed further and demonstrated in Chapter 9, which deals with multifactor models of risk and return.

foreign stocks and bonds. Because of the difficulty in deriving series that are available monthly in a timely fashion for numerous other assets, most studies have been limited to using a stock or bond series alone. In fact, the vast majority of studies have chosen an index limited to only U.S. stocks, which constitutes *less than 20 percent* of a truly global risky asset portfolio. At best, it is then assumed that the particular series used as a proxy for the market portfolio was highly correlated with the true market portfolio.

Most researchers recognize this potential problem but assume that the deficiency is not serious. Several articles by Roll (1977a, 1978, 1980, 1981), however, concluded that the use of these indexes as a proxy for the market portfolio had very serious implications for tests of the CAPM and especially for using the model when evaluating portfolio performance. Roll referred to this problem as a **benchmark error** because the practice is to compare the performance of a portfolio manager to the return of an unmanaged portfolio of equal risk—that is, the market portfolio adjusted for risk would be the benchmark. Roll's point is that, if the benchmark is incorrectly specified, you cannot measure the performance of a portfolio manager properly. A mistakenly specified market portfolio can have two effects. First, the beta computed for alternative portfolios would be wrong because the market portfolio used to compute the portfolio's systematic risk is inappropriate. Second, the SML derived would be wrong because it goes from the *RFR* through the improperly specified M portfolio. Exhibit 8.16 shows an example where the true portfolio risk (β_T) is underestimated (β_e), possibly because of the proxy market portfolio used in computing the estimated beta. As shown, the portfolio being evaluated may appear to be above the SML using β_e, which would imply superior management. If, in fact, the true risk (β_T) is greater, the portfolio being evaluated will shift to the right and be below the SML, which would indicate inferior performance.

Exhibit 8.17 indicates that the intercept and slope will differ if (1) there is an error in selecting a proper risk-free asset and (2) if the market portfolio selected is not the correct mean-variance efficient portfolio. Obviously, it is very possible that under these conditions, a portfolio judged to be superior relative to the first SML (i.e., the portfolio plotted above the measured SML) could be inferior relative to the true SML (i.e., the portfolio would plot below the true SML).

Roll contends that a test of the CAPM requires an analysis of whether the proxy used to represent the market portfolio is mean-variance efficient (on the Markowitz efficient frontier) and whether it is the true optimum market portfolio. Roll showed that if the proxy market

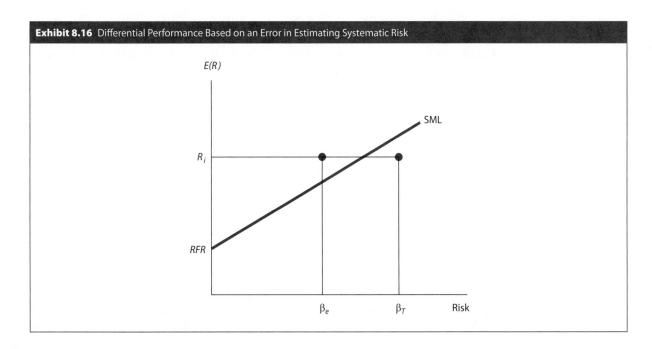

Exhibit 8.16 Differential Performance Based on an Error in Estimating Systematic Risk

Exhibit 8.17   Differential SML Based on Measured Risk-Free Asset and Proxy Market Portfolio

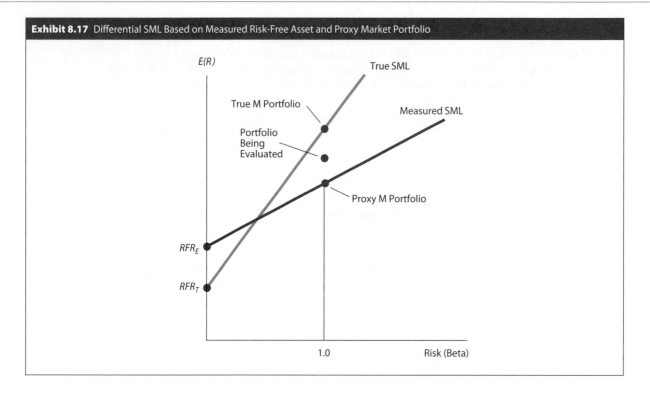

portfolio (e.g., the S&P 500 index) is mean-variance efficient, it is mathematically possible to show a linear relationship between returns and betas derived with this portfolio.

A demonstration of the impact of the benchmark problem is provided in a study by Reilly and Akhtar (1995). Exhibit 8.18 shows the substantial difference in average beta for the 30 stocks in the DJIA during three alternative periods using two different proxies for the market portfolio: (1) the S&P 500 Index, and (2) the Brinson Partners Global Security Market Index (GSMI). The GSMI includes not only U.S. and international stocks but also U.S. and international bonds. The results are as expected because, as we know from earlier discussions, beta for Security i is equal to:

$$\text{Beta}_i = \frac{\text{Cov}_{i,M}}{\sigma_M^2}$$

Consequently, as we change from an all–U.S. stock index to a world stock and bond index (GSMI), we would expect the covariance with U.S. stocks to decline. The other component of beta is the variance for the market portfolio. As shown in Exhibit 8.18, although the covariance between the U.S. stocks and the GSMI is lower, the variance of the GSMI market portfolio, which is highly diversified with stocks *and* bonds from around the world, is substantially lower (about 25 to 33 percent). As a result, the beta is substantially larger (about 27 to 48 percent larger) when the Brinson GSMI is used rather than the S&P 500 Index. Notably, the Brinson GSMI has a composition of assets that is substantially closer to the true M portfolio than the S&P 500 proxy that contains only U.S. stocks.

There also was a difference in the SMLs implied by each of the market proxies. Exhibit 8.19 contains the average *RFR*, the market returns, and the slope of the SML during three time periods for the two indexes. Clearly, the slopes differ dramatically among the alternative indexes and over time. Needless to say, the benchmark used does make a difference.

In summary, an incorrect market proxy will affect both the beta risk measures and the position and slope of the SML that is used to evaluate portfolio performance. In general, the errors will tend to overestimate the performance of portfolio managers because the proxy used for the market portfolio is probably not as efficient as the true market portfolio, so the slope of the SML will be underestimated. Also, the beta measure generally will be underestimated

Exhibit 8.18 The Average Beta for the 30 Stocks in the Dow Jones Industrial Average during Alternative Time Periods Using Different Proxies for the Market Portfolio

Time Period	ALTERNATIVE MARKET PROXIES	
	S&P 500	Brinson GSMI
2000–2004		
Average beta	0.961	1.305
Mean index return	–0.006	0.001
Standard deviation of index returns	0.048	0.031
1989–1994		
Average beta	0.991	1.264
Mean index return	0.010	0.008
Standard deviation of index returns	0.036	0.026
1983–1988		
Average beta	0.820	1.215
Mean index return	0.014	0.014
Standard deviation of index returns	0.049	0.031

Source: Adapted from Frank K. Reilly and Rashid A. Akhtar, "The Benchmark Error Problem with Global Capital Markets," *Journal of Portfolio Management* 22, no. 1 (Fall 1995): 33–52. The updated results were provided by Frank K. Reilly. This copyrighted material is reprinted with permission from *Journal of Portfolio Management,* a publication of Institutional Investor, Inc.

Exhibit 8.19 Components of Security Market Lines Using Alternative Market Proxies

	2000–2004			1989–1994			1983–1988		
	R_M	RFR	$(R_M - RFR)$	R_M	RFR	$(R_M - RFR)$	R_M	RFR	$(R_M - RFR)$
S&P 500	–2.01	3.05	–5.06	13.07	5.71	7.36	18.20	8.31	9.90
Brinson GSMI	3.02	3.05	–0.03	10.18	5.71	4.48	18.53	8.31	10.22

Source: Adapted from Frank K. Reilly and Rashid A. Akhtar, "The Benchmark Error Problem with Global Capital Markets," *Journal of Portfolio Management* 22, no. 1 (Fall 1995): 33–52. The updated results were provided by Frank K. Reilly. This copyrighted material is reprinted with permission from *Journal of Portfolio Management,* a publication of Institutional Investor, Inc.

because the true market portfolio will have a lower variance than the typical market proxy because the true market portfolio is more diversified. However, recognize that benchmark problems do not invalidate the CAPM as *a normative model of asset pricing*; they only indicate a problem in *measurement* when attempting to test the theory and when using this model for evaluating portfolio performance.

• • • • SUMMARY • • • •

- Capital market theory expanded the concepts introduced by Markowitz portfolio theory by introducing the notion that investors could borrow or lend at the risk-free rate in addition to forming efficient portfolios of risky assets. This insight led to the development of the *capital market line (CML)*, which can be viewed as a new efficient frontier that emanates from the risk-free rate and is tangent to the old Markowitz efficient frontier. The point of tangency is called the market portfolio.

- The CML's main contribution is the relationship it specifies between the risk and expected return of a well-diversified portfolio. The CML makes it clear that the market portfolio is the single collection of risky assets that maximizes the ratio of expected risk premium to portfolio volatility. The

investment prescription of the CML is that investors cannot do better, on average, than when they divide their investment funds between (1) the riskless asset and (2) the market portfolio.

- The CML is a model of the risk–return trade-off that only applies to portfolios that have diversified away all unsystematic risk. The *capital asset pricing model (CAPM)* generalizes this relationship to individual securities as well as entire portfolios. To make this extension, the CAPM redefines the relevant measure of risk as beta, which is the systematic component of a secutiry's volatility relative to that of the market portfolio. Like the CML, the *security market line (SML)* shows that the relationship between risk and expected return is a straight line with a positive slope.

The SML provides investors with a tool for judging whether securities are undervalued or overvalued given their level of systematic (beta) risk.
- The CAPM has been subjected to extensive empirical testing with mixed findings. Early tests substantiated the positive relationship between returns and measures of systematic

risk, although subsequent studies indicated that the single-beta model needed to be supplemented with additional dimensions of risk (e.g., skewness, firm size, P/E, book value/market value). Another challenge confronting the CAPM in practive is the benchmark error problem that results from improperly specifying a proxy for the market portfolio.

• • • • SUGGESTED READINGS • • • •

Black, Fischer. 1972. "Capital Market Equilibrium with Restricted Borrowing." *Journal of Business* 45, no. 3 (July): 444–455.

Campbell, John Y., and John Ammer. 1993. "What Moves the Stock and Bond Markets? A Variance Decomposition for Long-Term Asset Returns." *Journal of Finance* 48, no. 1 (March): 3–38.

Elton, Edwin J., Martin J. Gruber, Stephen J. Brown, and William N. Goetzmann. 2006. *Modern Portfolio Theory and Investment Analysis,* 7th ed. New York: Wiley.

Sharpe, William F. 2007. *Investors and Markets: Portfolio Choices, Asset Prices, and Investment Advice.* Princeton, NJ: Princeton University Press.

• • • • QUESTIONS • • • •

1. Draw a graph that shows what happens to the Markowitz efficient frontier when you combine a riskfree asset with alternative risky asset portfolios on the Markowitz efficient frontier. Explain why the line from the *RFR* that is tangent to the efficient frontier defines the dominant set of portfolio possibilities.

2. What changes would you expect in the standard deviation for a portfolio of between 4 and 10 stocks, between 10 and 20 stocks, and between 50 and 100 stocks?

3. The capital asset pricing model (CAPM) contends that there is systematic and unsystematic risk for an individual security. Which is the relevant risk variable and why is it relevant? Why is the other risk variable not relevant?

4. What are the similarities and differences between the CML and SML as models of the risk–return trade-off?

 5. **CFA EXAMINATION LEVEL I** Identify and briefly discuss *three* criticisms of beta as used in the capital asset pricing model (CAPM). [6 minutes]

 6. **CFA EXAMINATION LEVEL I** Briefly explain whether investors should expect a higher return from holding Portfolio A versus Portfolio B under capital asset pricing theory (CAPM). Assume that both portfolios are fully diversified. [6 minutes]

	Portfolio A	Portfolio B
Systematic risk (beta)	1.0	1.0
Specific risk for each individual security	High	Low

7. **CFA EXAMINATION LEVEL II** You have recently been appointed chief investment officer of a major charitable foundation. Its large endowment fund is currently invested in a broadly diversified portfolio of stocks (60 percent) and bonds (40 percent). The foundation's board of trustees is a group of prominent individuals whose knowledge of modern investment theory and practice is superficial. You decide a discussion of basic investment principles would be helpful.

   a. Explain the concepts of *specific risk, systematic risk, variance, covariance, standard deviation,* and *beta* as they relate to investment management. [12 minutes]

   You believe that the addition of other asset classes to the endowment portfolio would improve the portfolio by reducing risk and enhancing return. You are aware that depressed conditions in U.S. real estate markets are providing opportunities for property acquisition at levels of expected return that are unusually high by historical standards. You believe that an investment in U.S. real estate would be both appropriate and timely, and have decided to recommend a 20 percent position be established with funds taken equally from stocks and bonds.

Preliminary discussions revealed that several trustees believe real estate is too risky to include in the portfolio. The board chairman, however, has scheduled a special meeting for further discussion of the matter and has asked you to provide background information that will clarify the risk issue.

To assist you, the following expectational data have been developed:

Asset Class	Return	Standard Deviation	CORRELATION MATRIX			
			U.S. Stocks	U.S. Bonds	U.S. Real Estate	U.S. T-Bills
U.S. Stocks	12.0%	21.0%	1.00			
U.S. Bonds	8.0	10.5	0.14	1.00		
U.S. Real Estate	12.0	9.0	−0.04	−0.03	1.00	
U.S. Treasury Bills	4.0	0.0	−0.05	−0.03	0.25	1.00

b. Explain the effect on *both* portfolio risk *and* return that would result from the addition of U.S. real estate. Include in your answer *two* reasons for any change you expect in portfolio risk. (Note: It is *not* necessary to compute expected risk and return.) [8 minutes]

c. Your understanding of capital market theory causes you to doubt the validity of the expected return and risk for U.S. real estate. Justify your skepticism. [5 minutes]

8. Draw an ideal SML. Based on the early empirical results, what did the actual risk–return relationship look like relative to the ideal relationship implied by the CAPM?

9. According to the CAPM, what assets are included in the market portfolio, and what are the relative weightings? In empirical studies of the CAPM, what are the typical proxies used for the market portfolio? Assuming that the empirical proxy for the market portfolio is not a good proxy, what factors related to the CAPM will be affected?

10. Some studies related to the efficient market hypothesis generated results that implied additional factors beyond beta should be considered to estimate expected returns. What are these other variables and why should they be considered?

• • • PROBLEMS • • • •

1. Draw the security market line for each of the following conditions:
   a. (1) $RFR = 0.08$; $R_M(\text{proxy}) = 0.12$
      (2) $R_z = 0.06$; $R_M(\text{true}) = 0.15$
   b. Rader Tire has the following results for the last six periods. Calculate and compare the betas using each index.

Period	Rader Tire (%)	RATES OF RETURN Proxy Specific Index (%)	True General Index (%)
1	29	12	15
2	12	10	13
3	−12	−9	−8
4	17	14	18
5	20	25	28
6	−5	−10	0

   c. If the current period return for the market is 12 percent and for Rader Tire it is 11 percent, are superior results being obtained for either index beta?

2. You are an analyst for a large public pension fund and you have been assigned the task of evaluating two different external portfolio managers (Y and Z). You consider the following historical average return, standard deviation, and CAPM beta estimates for these two managers over the past five years:

Portfolio	Actual Ave. Return	Standard Deviation	Beta
Manager Y	10.20%	12.00%	1.20
Manager Z	8.80%	9.90%	0.80

Additionally, your estimate for the risk premium for the market portfolio is 5.00% and the risk-free rate is currently 4.50%.

a. For both Manager Y and Manager Z, calculate the expected return using the CAPM. Express your answers to the nearest basis point (i.e., xx.xx%).

b. Calculate each fund manaer's average "alpha" (i.e., actual return minus expected return) over the five-year holding period. Show graphically where these alpha statistics would plot on the security market line (SML).

c. Explain whether you can conclude from the information in Part b if: (i) either manager outperformed the other on a risk-adjusted basis, and (ii) either manager outperformed market expectations in general.

3. Given the following results, indicate what will happen to the beta for Sophie Fashion Co., relative to the market proxy, compared to the beta relative to the true market portfolio:

| | YEARLY RATES OF RETURN | | |
Year	Sophie Fashion (%)	Market Proxy (%)	True Market (%)
1	10	8	6
2	20	14	11
3	−14	−10	−7
4	−20	−18	−12
5	15	12	10

Discuss the reason for the differences in the measured betas for Sophie Fashion Co. Does the suggested relationship appear reasonable? Why or why not?

4. Based on five years of monthly data, you derive the following information for the companies listed:

Company	a_i (Intercept)	σ_i	r_{iM}
Intel	0.22	12.10%	0.72
Ford	0.10	14.60	0.33
Anheuser Busch	0.17	7.60	0.55
Merck	0.05	10.20	0.60
S&P 500	0.00	5.50	1.00

a. Compute the beta coefficient for each stock.

b. Assuming a risk-free rate of 8 percent and an expected return for the market portfolio of 15 percent, compute the expected (required) return for all the stocks and plot them on the SML.

c. Plot the following estimated returns for the next year on the SML and indicate which stocks are undervalued or overvalued.
  • Intel—20 percent
  • Ford—15 perent
  • Anheuser Busch—19 percent
  • Merck—10 percent

5. **CFA EXAMINATION LEVEL II** An analyst expects a risk-free return of 4.5 percent, a market return of 14.5 percent, and the returns for Stocks A and B that are shown in the following table.

| | STOCK INFORMATION | |
Stock	Beta	Analyst's Estimated Return
A	1.2	16%
B	0.8	14%

a. Show on the graph provided in the answer book:
  (1) Where Stocks A and B would plot on the security market line (SML) if they were fairly valued using the capital asset pricing model (CAPM)
  (2) Where Stocks A and B actually plot on the same graph according to the returns estimated by the analyst and shown in the table [6 minutes]

b. State whether Stocks A and B are undervalued or overvalued if the analyst uses the SML for strategic investment decisions. [4 minutes]

6. You are evaluating various investment opportunities currently available and you have calculated expected returns and standard deviations for five different well-diversified portfolios of risky assets:

Portfolio	Expected Return	Standard Deviation
Q	7.8%	10.5%
R	10.0	14.0
S	4.6	5.0
T	11.7	18.5
U	6.2	7.5

a. For each portolio, calculate the risk premium per unit of risk that you expect to receive ([E(R) – RFR]/σ). Assume that the risk-free rate is 3.0%.

b. Using your computations in Part a, explain which of these five portfolios is most likely to be the market portfolio. Use your calculations to draw the capital market line (CML).

c. If you are only willing to make an investment with σ = 7.0%, is it possible for you to earn a return of 7.0%?

d. What is the minimum level of risk that would be necessary for an investment to earn 7.0%? What is the composition of the portfolio along the CML that will generate that expected return?

e. Suppose you are now willing to make an investment with σ = 18.2%. What would be the investment proportions in the riskless asset and the market portfolio for this portfolio? What is the expected return for this portfolio?

7. **CFA EXAMINATION LEVEL II** The following information describes the expected return and risk relationship for the stocks of two of WAH's competitors.

	Expected Return	Standard Deviation	Beta
Stock X	12.0%	20%	1.3
Stock Y	9.0	15	0.7
Market Index	10.0	12	1.0
Risk-free rate	5.0		

Using only the data shown in the preceding table:

a. Draw and label a graph showing the security market line and position Stocks X and Y relative to it. [5 minutes]

b. Compute the alphas *both* for Stock X *and* for Stock Y. Show your work. [4 minutes]

c. Assume that the risk-free rate increases to 7 percent, with the other data in the preceding matrix remaining unchanged. Select the stock providing the higher expected risk-adjusted return and justify your selection. Show your calculations. [6 minutes]

8a. You expect an *RFR* of 10 percent and the market return (R_M) of 14 percent. Compute the expected return for the following stocks, and plot them on an SML graph.

Stock	Beta	$E(R_i)$
U	0.85	
N	1.25	
D	−0.20	

b. You ask a stockbroker what the firm's research department expects for these three stocks. The broker responds with the following information:

Stock	Current Price	Expected Price	Expected Dividend
U	22	24	0.75
N	48	51	2.00
D	37	40	1.25

Plot your estimated returns on the graph from Part a and indicate what actions you would take with regard to these stocks. Explain your decisions.

9. The following are the historic returns for the Chelle Computer Company:

Year	Chelle Computer	General Index
1	37	15
2	9	13
3	−11	14
4	8	−9
5	11	12
6	4	9

Based on this information, compute the following:

a. The correlation coefficient between Chelle Computer and the General Index.

b. The standard deviation for the company and the index.

c. The beta for the Chelle Computer Company.

10. Assume that you expect the economy's rate of inflation to be 3 percent, giving an *RFR* of 6 percent and a market return (R_M) of 12 percent.

a. Draw the SML under these assumptions.

b. Subsequently, you expect the rate of inflation to increase from 3 percent to 6 percent. What effect would this have on the *RFR* and the R_M? Draw another SML on the graph from Part a.

c. Draw an SML on the same graph to reflect an *RFR* of 9 percent and an R_M of 17 percent. How does this SML differ from that derived in Part b? Explain what has transpired.

THOMSON ONE | Business School Edition

1. You want to evaluate the recent investment performance for two stocks—Walgreen and Exxon Mobil—relative to the S&P 500 index.

a. Under the "Companies" tab, look up the ticker symbols for Walgreen and Exxon Mobil.

b. For each firm, as well as for the S&P 500 index, download *daily* price information for the past year using the menu options available under the "Prices" tab for each company.

c. For each firm, calculate the set of *daily* returns that correspond to these daily price series.

d. Using *daily* returns for the past year, calculate the beta coefficient for Walgreen and Exxon Mobil compared to the S&P 500 index. (Note: You can either build your own spreadsheet model to perform these calculations or use Excel's built-in functions for "Slope" or "Regression.")

e. Based on your results in Part d, which stock appears to be the riskiest?

2. To evaluate how sensitive beta estimates are to the period over which returns are measured, you now want to repeat the analysis in the last problem using *weekly* data over the past year.

a. For each firm, as well as for the S&P 500 index, download *weekly* price information for the past year using the menu options available in the Prices tab for each company.

b. For each firm, calculate the set of *weekly* returns that correspond to these daily price series.

c. Using *weekly* returns for the past year, calculate the beta for Walgreen and Exxon Mobil compared to the S&P 500 index.

d. How do your beta estimates for Walgreen and Exxon Mobil differ when using daily versus weekly data in the estimation process? Does your conclusion change about which stock is the riskiest?

3. You would now like to evaluate the impact that the choice of index used for the market portfolio proxy has on the beta estimation process.

a. Collect *monthly* price data for Walgreen and Exxon Mobil for the past *five years* and use this information to compute monthly returns over that period.

b. Collect montly price data for the S&P 500 index and MSCI World index (based in U.S. dollars) for the past five years and compute monthly returns for both series. (Note: You can access the information for a wide variety of different indexes under the main "Indices" tab.)

c. Calculate betas for both stocks compared to the S&P 500 index.

d. Calculate betas for both stocks compared to the MSCI World index.

e. Compare the two beta estimates for each stock and explain why they would differ from one another.

CHAPTER 9

Multifactor Models of Risk and Return

After you read this chapter, you should be able to answer the following questions:

- What are the deficiencies of the capital asset pricing model (CAPM) as an explanation of the relationship between risk and expected asset returns?
- What is the arbitrage pricing theory (APT) and how is it similar and different from the CAPM?
- What are the strengths and weaknesses of the APT as a theory of how risk and expected return are related?
- How can the APT be used in the security valuation process?
- How do you test the APT by examining anomalies found with the CAPM and why do some authors contend that the APT model is untestable?
- What are multifactor models and how are they related to the APT?
- What are the steps necessary in developing a usable multifactor model?
- What are the two primary approaches employed in defining common risk factors?
- What are the main macroeconomic variables used in practice as risk factors?
- What are the main security characteristic-oriented variables used in practice as risk factors?
- How can multifactor models be used to identify the investment "bets" that an active portfolio manager is making relative to a benchmark?
- How are multifactor models used to estimate the expected risk premium of a security or portfolio?

Chapter 7 and Chapter 8 introduced Markowitz portfolio theory and the capital asset pricing model (CAPM), which represent the foundation for understanding the connection between risk and expected return in financial markets. This chapter considers several extensions of this framework. Specifically, whereas the CAPM designated a single risk factor to account for the volatility inherent in an individual security or portfolio of securities, in this chapter we develop the intuition and application of *multifactor* explanations of risk and return. We begin with an explanation of the leading alternative to the CAPM—the arbitrage pricing theory (APT), which was developed by Stephen Ross. The chief difference between the CAPM and the APT is that the latter specifies several risk factors, thereby allowing for an expanded definition of systematic investment risk than that implied by the CAPM's single market portfolio.

After developing the conceptual basis for the APT in the next section and contrasting its major assumptions with those of the CAPM, we also examine the empirical evidence supporting the theory. One of the practical challenges that an investor faces when attempting to implement the APT is that the risk factors in the model are not defined in terms of their quantity (i.e., how many there are) or their identity (i.e., what they are). We conclude the chapter by discussing how investors use **multifactor models**, which can be viewed as attempts to convert the APT into a working tool for security analysis, thus turning theory into practice. A wide variety of factor models are currently in use. These models differ primarily in how they represent the risk factor and can be grouped broadly into those models that use *macroeconomic* factor definitions and those that specify *microeconomic* factors. Examples of the different approaches used in developing multifactor explanations of risk and return illustrate the myriad forms these models can assume.

9.1 Arbitrage Pricing Theory

The last chapter highlighted many of the ways in which the CAPM has contributed to the investment management field. In many respects, the CAPM has been one of the most useful—and frequently used—financial economic theories ever developed. However, many of the empirical studies cited point out some of the deficiencies in the model as an explanation of the link between risk and return. For example, tests of the CAPM indicated that the beta coefficients for individual securities were not stable but that portfolio betas generally were stable. There was mixed support for a positive linear relationship between rates of return and systematic risk for portfolios of stock, with some recent evidence indicating the need to consider additional risk variables or a need for different risk proxies. In addition, several papers criticized the tests of the model and the usefulness of the model in portfolio evaluation because of its dependence on a market portfolio of risky assets that is not currently available.

One major challenge to the CAPM was the set of results suggesting that it is possible to use knowledge of certain firm or security characteristics to develop profitable trading strategies, even after adjusting for investment risk as measured by beta. Banz (1981) showed that portfolios of stocks with low market capitalizations (i.e., "small" stocks) outperformed "large" stock portfolios on a risk-adjusted basis, and Basu (1977) documented that stocks with low price-earnings (P/E) ratios similarly outperformed high P/E stocks. More recent work by Fama and French (1992) also demonstrates that "value" stocks (i.e., those with high book value-to-market price ratios) tend to produce larger risk-adjusted returns than "growth" stocks (i.e., those with low book-to-market ratios). In an efficient market, these return differentials should not occur, meaning that either: (1) markets are not particularly efficient for extended periods of time (i.e., investors have been ignoring profitable investment opportunities for decades), or (2) market prices are efficient but there is something wrong with the way the single-factor models such as the CAPM measure risk.

Given the implausibility of the first possibility, in the early 1970s, financial economists began to consider the implications of the second. The academic community searched for an alternative asset pricing theory to the CAPM that was reasonably intuitive, required only limited assumptions, and allowed for multiple dimensions of investment risk. The result was the **arbitrage pricing theory (APT)**, which was developed by Ross (1976, 1977) in the mid-1970s and has three major assumptions:

1. Capital markets are perfectly competitive.
2. Investors always prefer more wealth to less wealth with certainty.
3. The stochastic process generating asset returns can be expressed as a linear function of a set of K risk factors (or indexes), and all unsystematic risk is diversified away.

Equally important, the following major assumptions—which were used in the development of the CAPM—are *not* required: (1) Investors possess quadratic utility functions, (2) normally distributed security returns, and (3) a market portfolio that contains all risky assets and is mean-variance efficient. Obviously, if such a model is simpler and can also explain differential security prices, it will be considered a superior theory to the CAPM.

Prior to discussing the empirical tests of the APT, we provide a brief review of the basics of the model. The theory assumes that the stochastic process generating asset returns can be represented as a K factor model of the form:

9.1
$$R_i = E(R_i) + b_{i1}\delta_1 + b_{i2}\delta_2 + \cdots + b_{ik}\delta_k + \varepsilon_i \text{ for } i = 1 \text{ to } n$$

where:

R_i = the actual return on asset i during a specified time period, $i = 1, 2, 3, \ldots n$

$E(R_i)$ = the expected return for asset i if all the risk factors have zero changes

b_{ij} = the reaction in asset i's returns to movements in a common risk factor j

δ_k = a set of common factors or indexes with a zero mean that influences the returns on all assets

ε_i = a unique effect on asset i's return (i.e., a random error term that, by assumption, is completely diversifiable in large portfolios and has a mean of zero)

n = number of assets

Two terms require elaboration: δ_j and b_{ij}. As indicated, δ terms are the multiple risk factors expected to have an impact on the returns to *all* assets. Examples of these factors might include inflation, growth in gross domestic product (GDP), major political upheavals, or changes in interest rates. The APT contends that there are many such factors that affect returns, in contrast to the CAPM, where the only relevant risk to measure is the covariance of the asset with the market portfolio (i.e., the asset's beta).

Given these common factors, the b_{ij} terms determine how each asset reacts to the jth particular common factor. Although all assets may be affected by growth in GDP, the impact (i.e., reaction) to a factor will differ. For example, stocks of cyclical firms will have larger b_{ij} terms for the "growth in GDP" factor than will noncyclical firms, such as grocery store chains. Likewise, all stocks are affected by changes in interest rates; however, some experience larger impacts. An interest-sensitive stock might have a b_j interest of 2.0 or more, whereas a stock that is relatively insensitive to interest rates have a b_j of 0.5. Other examples of common factors include changes in unemployment rates, exchange rates, and yield curve shifts. Note, however, that when we apply the theory, *the factors are not identified.* That is, when we discuss the empirical studies of the APT, the investigators will claim that they found three, four, or five factors that affect security returns, but *they will give no indication of what these factors represent.*

Similar to the CAPM model, the APT assumes that the unique effects (ε_i) are independent and will be diversified away in a large portfolio. The APT requires that in equilibrium the return on a zero-investment, zero-systematic-risk portfolio is zero when the unique effects are fully diversified. This assumption (and some theoretical manipulation using linear algebra) implies that the expected return on any asset i (i.e., $E(R_i)$), can be expressed as:

$$E(R_i) = \lambda_0 + \lambda_1 b_{i1} + \lambda_2 b_{i2} + \cdots + \lambda_k b_{ik} \quad \text{(APT)}$$

where:

λ_0 = the expected return on an asset with zero systematic risk

λ_j = the risk premium related to the jth common risk factor

b_{ij} = the pricing relationship between the risk premium and the asset; that is, how responsive asset i is to the jth common factor. (These are called factor betas or factor loadings.)

This equation represents the fundamental result of the APT. It is useful to compare the form of the APT's specification of the expected return-risk relationship with that of the CAPM from Chapter 8.

$$E(R_i) = RFR + \beta_i[E(R_M) - RFR] \quad \text{(CAPM)}$$

Exhibit 9.1 contrasts the relevant features of the two models. It should be clear that the ultimate difference between these two theories lies in the way systematic investment risk is defined: a single, market-wide risk factor for the CAPM versus a few (or several) factors in the APT that capture the salient nuances of that market-wide risk. However, both theories specify linear models based on the common belief that investors are compensated for performing two

Exhibit 9.1 Comparing the Capital Asset Pricing Model (CAPM) and the Arbitrage Pricing Theory (APT)

	CAPM	APT
Form of Equation	Linear	Linear
Number of Risk Factors	1	$K\ (\geq 1)$
Factor Risk Premium	$[E(R_M) - RFR]$	$\{\lambda_j\}$
Factor Risk Sensitivity	β_i	$\{b_{ij}\}$
"Zero-Beta" Return	RFR	λ_0

Exhibit 9.2 The Relationship between Expected Return and Two Common Risk Factors ($\lambda_0 = 4\%$, $\lambda_1 = 2\%$, $\lambda_2 = 3\%$)

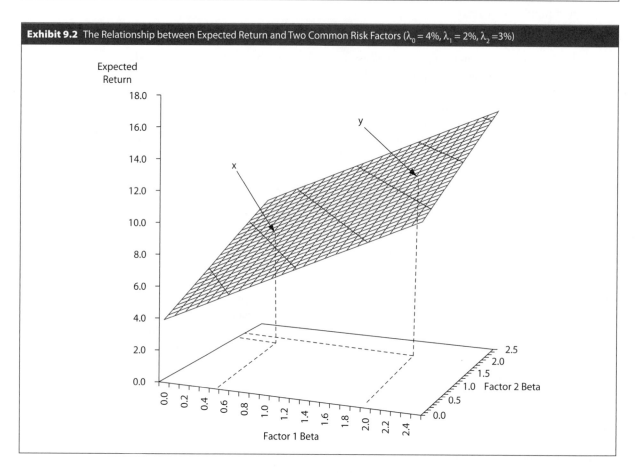

functions: committing capital and bearing risk. Finally, notice that the equation for the APT suggests a relationship that is analogous to the security market line associated with the CAPM. However, instead of a line connecting risk and expected return, the APT implies a *security market plane* with $(K + 1)$ dimensions—K risk factors and one additional dimension for the security's expected return. Exhibit 9.2 illustrates this relationship for two risk factors (i.e., $K = 2$).

9.1.1 Using the APT

As noted earlier, the primary challenge with using the APT in security valuation is identifying the risk factors. The complexities of this issue are addressed later, so to illustrate how the model works we will assume that there are two common factors: one related to unexpected changes in the level of inflation and another related to unanticipated changes in the real level of GDP. If the risk premium related to GDP sensitivity is 0.03 and a stock that is sensitive to GDP has a b_j (where j represents the GDP factor) of 1.5, this means that this factor would cause the stock's expected return to increase by 4.5 percent (= 1.5×0.03).

To develop this notion further, consider the following example of two stocks and a two-factor model. First, consider these risk factor definitions and sensitivities:

δ_1 = unanticipated changes in the rate of inflation. The risk premium related to this factor is 2 percent for every 1 percent change in the rate ($\lambda_1 = 0.02$)

δ_2 = unexpected changes in the growth rate of real GDP. The average risk premium related to this factor is 3 percent for every 1 percent change in the rate of growth ($\lambda_2 = 0.03$)

λ_0 = the rate of return on a zero-systematic risk asset (i.e., zero beta) is 4 percent ($\lambda_0 = 0.04$)

Assume also that there are two assets (x and y) that have the following sensitivities to these common risk factors:

b_{x1} = the response of asset x to changes in the inflation factor is 0.50 ($b_{x1} = 0.50$)
b_{x2} = the response of asset x to changes in the GDP factor is 1.50 ($b_{x2} = 1.50$)
b_{y1} = the response of asset y to changes in the inflation factor is 2.00 ($b_{y1} = 2.00$)
b_{y2} = the response of asset y to changes in the GDP factor is 1.75 ($b_{y2} = 1.75$)

These factor sensitivities can be interpreted in much the same way as beta in the CAPM; that is, the higher the level of b_{ij}, the greater the sensitivity of asset i to changes in the jth risk factor. Thus, the response coefficients listed indicate that asset y is a higher risk asset than asset x, and, therefore, its expected return should be greater. The overall expected return equation will be:

$$E(R_i) = \lambda_0 + \lambda_1 b_{i1} + \lambda_2 b_{i2}$$
$$= 0.04 + (0.02)b_{i1} + (0.03)b_{i2}$$

Therefore, for assets x and y:

$$E(R_x) = 0.04 + (0.02)(0.50) + (0.03)(1.50)$$
$$= 0.0950 = 9.50\%$$

and

$$E(R_y) = 0.04 + (0.02)(2.00) + (0.03)(1.75)$$
$$= 0.1325 = 13.25\%$$

The positions of the factor loadings and expected returns for these two assets are illustrated in Exhibit 9.2. If the prices of the two assets do not reflect these expected returns, we would expect investors to enter into arbitrage arrangements whereby they would sell overpriced assets short and use the proceeds to purchase the underpriced assets until the relevant prices were corrected. Given these linear relationships, it should be possible to find an asset or a combination of assets with equal risk to the mispriced asset, yet providing a higher expected return.

9.1.2 Security Valuation with the APT: An Example

Suppose that three stocks (A, B, and C) and two common systematic risk factors (1 and 2) have the following relationship (for simplicity, it is assumed that the zero-beta return (λ_0) equals zero):

$$E(R_A) = (0.80)\lambda_1 + (0.90)\lambda_2$$
$$E(R_B) = (-0.20)\lambda_1 + (1.30)\lambda_2$$
$$E(R_C) = (1.80)\lambda_1 + (0.50)\lambda_2$$

If $\lambda_1 = 4\%$ and $\lambda_2 = 5\%$, then the returns expected by the market over the next year can be expressed:

$$E(R_A) = (0.80)(4\%) + (0.90)(5\%) = 7.7\%$$
$$E(R_B) = (-0.20)(4\%) + (1.30)(5\%) = 5.7\%$$
$$E(R_C) = (1.80)(4\%) + (0.50)(5\%) = 9.7\%$$

which, assuming that all three stocks are currently priced at $35 and do not pay a dividend, implies the following expected prices a year from now:

$$E(P_A) = \$35(1.077) = \$37.70$$
$$E(P_B) = \$35(1.057) = \$37.00$$
$$E(P_C) = \$35(1.097) = \$38.40$$

Now, suppose you "know" that in one year the actual prices of stocks A, B, and C will be $37.20, $37.80, and $38.50. How can you take advantage of what you consider to be a market mispricing?

According to your forecasts of future prices, Stock A will not achieve a price level in one year consistent with investor return expectations. Accordingly, you conclude that at a current price of $35 a share, Stock A is *overvalued*. Similarly, Stock B is *undervalued* and Stock C is (slightly) *undervalued*. Consequently, any investment strategy designed to take advantage of these discrepancies will, at the very least, need to consider purchasing Stocks B and C while short selling Stock A.

The idea of *riskless arbitrage* is to assemble a portfolio that: (1) requires no net wealth invested initially and (2) will bear no systematic or unsystematic risk but (3) still earns a profit. Letting w_i represent the percentage investment in security i, the conditions that must be satisfied can be written formally as follows:

1. $\Sigma_i w_i = 0$ [i.e., no net wealth invested]
2. $\Sigma_i w_i b_{ij} = 0$ for all K factors [i.e., no systematic risk] and w_i is "small" for all i [i.e., unsystematic risk is fully diversified]
3. $\Sigma_i w_i R_i > 0$ [i.e., the actual portfolio return is positive]

In this example, since Stock A is the only one that is overvalued, assume that it is the only one that actually is short sold. The proceeds from the short sale of Stock A can then be used to purchase the two undervalued securities, Stocks B and C. To illustrate this process, consider the following investment proportions:

$$w_A = -1.0$$
$$w_B = +0.5$$
$$w_C = +0.5$$

These investment weights imply the creation of a portfolio that is *short two shares of Stock A for each one share of Stock B and one share of Stock C held long*. Notice that this portfolio meets the net investment and risk mandates of an arbitrage-based trade:

Net Initial Investment:	
Short 2 shares of A:	+70
Purchase 1 share of B:	−35
Purchase 1 share of C:	−35
Net investment:	0

Net Exposure to Risk Factors:

	Factor 1	Factor 2
Weighted exposure from Stock A:	$(-1.0)(0.8)$	$(-1.0)(0.9)$
Weighted exposure from Stock B:	$(0.5)(-0.2)$	$(0.5)(1.3)$
Weighted exposure from Stock C:	$(0.5)(1.8)$	$(0.5)(0.5)$
Net risk exposure:	0	0

Assuming prices in one year actually rise to the levels that you initially "knew" they would, your net profit from covering the short position and liquidating the two long holdings will be:
Net Profit:

$$[2(35) - 2(37.20)] + [37.80 - 35] + [38.50 - 35] = \$1.90$$

Thus, from a portfolio in which you invested no net wealth and assumed no net risk, you have realized a positive profit. This is the essence of arbitrage investing and is an example of the "long-short" trading strategies often employed by hedge funds.

Finally, if everyone else in the market today begins to believe the way you do about the future price levels of A, B, and C—but do not revise their forecasts about the expected factor returns or factor betas for the individual stocks—then the current prices for the three stocks will be adjusted by the resulting volume of arbitrage trading to:

$$P_A = (\$37.20) \div (1.077) = \$34.54$$
$$P_B = (\$37.80) \div (1.057) = \$35.76$$
$$P_C = (\$38.50) \div (1.097) = \$35.10$$

Thus, the price of Stock A will be bid down while the prices of Stocks B and C will be bid up until arbitrage trading in the current market is no longer profitable.

9.1.3 Empirical Tests of the APT

Although the APT is considerably newer than the CAPM, it has undergone numerous empirical studies. A brief overview of this literature is provided below. In discussing the empirical tests, remember the crucial earlier caveat that when applying the theory, we do not know what the factors generated by the formal model actually represent. This becomes a major point in some discussions of test results.

Roll and Ross Study   Roll and Ross (1980) produced one of the first large-scale empirical tests of the APT. Their methodology followed a two-step procedure:

1. Estimate expected returns and factor coefficients from time-series data on individual asset returns.
2. Use these estimates to test the basic cross-sectional pricing conclusion implied by the APT. Specifically, are the expected returns for these assets consistent with the common factors derived in Step 1?

The authors tested the following pricing relationship:

H_0: There exist nonzero constants $(\lambda_0, \lambda_i, \ldots \lambda_k)$ such that for any asset i:
$$[E(R_i) - \lambda_0] = \lambda_1 b_{i1} + \lambda_2 b_{i2} + \cdots + \lambda_k b_{ik}$$

The specific b_i coefficients were estimated using the statistical technique of *factor analysis*, which forms "portfolios" of the underlying assets (i.e., factors) based on the correlations in the underlying returns. Their database consisted of daily returns for the period from 1962 through 1972. Stocks were put into 42 portfolios of 30 stocks each (1,260 stocks) by alphabetical order.

The initial estimation of the factor model indicated that the maximum reasonable number of factors was five. The factors derived were applied to all 42 portfolios, with the understanding that the importance of the various factors might differ among portfolios (e.g., the first factor in Portfolio A might not be first in Portfolio B). Assuming a risk-free rate of 6 percent ($\lambda_0 = 0.06$), the subsequent analysis revealed the existence of at least three meaningful factors but probably not more than four. However, when they allowed the model to estimate the risk-free rate (λ_0), only two factors were consistently significant.

Roll and Ross also tested whether the three or four factors that affect Group A were the same as the factors that affect Group B. The analysis involved testing for cross-sectional consistency by examining whether the λ_0 terms for the 42 groups are similar. The results yielded no evidence that the intercept terms were different. The authors concluded that the evidence generally supported the APT but acknowledged that their tests were not conclusive.

Extensions of the Roll-Ross Tests Cho, Elton, and Gruber (1984) tested the APT by examining the number of factors in the return-generating process that were priced. They examined different sets of data to determine what happened to the number of factors priced in the model compared to prior studies that found between three and five significant factors. The authors concluded that even when returns were generated by a two-factor model, two or three factors are required to explain the returns. These results support the APT model because it allows for the consideration of these additional factors, which is not possible with the classical CAPM.

Dhrymes, Friend, and Gultekin (1984) reexamined the methodology used in prior studies and contended that these techniques have several major limitations. They found *no* relationship between the factor loadings for groups of 30 stocks and for a group of 240 stocks. Also, they could not identify the actual number of factors that characterize the return-generating process. When they applied the model to portfolios of different sizes, the number of factors changed. For example, for 15 securities, it is a two-factor model; for 30 securities, a three-factor model; for 45, a four-factor model; for 60, a six-factor model; and for 90, a nine-factor model.

Roll and Ross (1984) acknowledged that the number of risk factors differ with 30 stocks versus 240 but contended that the important consideration is whether the resulting estimates are *consistent* because it is not feasible to consider all of the stocks at once. When they tested for consistency, the APT was generally supported. They point out that the number of factors is a secondary issue compared to how well the model explains expected security returns compared to alternative models. The relevant question is: How many of these factors are significant in a diversified portfolio?

Dhrymes, Friend, Gultekin, and Gultekin (1985) repeated the prior tests for larger groups of securities. When they increased the number of securities in each group, both the number of factors that entered the model and the number of statistically significant (i.e., "priced") factors increased, although most factors are not priced. These results confirmed their earlier findings. In addition, they found that the unique or total standard deviation for a period was as good at predicting subsequent returns as the factor loadings. These results are not favorable to the empirical relevance of APT because they indicate extreme instability in the relationships and suggest that the risk-free rate implied by the model depends on group size and the number of observations.

Finally, Connor and Korajczyk (1993) argued that most tests for the number of priced risk factors are valid only for strict factor models in which diversifiable returns are uncorrelated across the set of stocks in the sample. They developed a test that identifies the number of factors in a model that does allow the unsystematic components of risk to be correlated across assets. Using this framework, they showed that between one and six priced factors exist for their sample of NYSE- and ASE-listed stocks.

The APT and Stock Market Anomalies An alternative set of tests of the APT considers how well the theory explains pricing anomalies that are not explained by a competing model (i.e., the CAPM). Two anomalies considered are the **small-firm effect** and the **January effect**.

APT Tests of the Small-Firm Effect Reinganum (1981) addressed the APT's ability to account for the differences in average returns between small firms and large firms. He contended that this anomaly, which could not be explained by the CAPM, should be explained by the APT if the latter was to be considered a superior theory. The critical element of Reinganum's test procedure involved sorting stocks into 10 separate portfolios based on market capitalization. According to the APT, these size-based portfolios should possess identical average excess returns.

The test results were clearly inconsistent with the APT. Specifically, the average excess returns of the 10 portfolios were not equal to zero for either a three-, four-, or five-factor model. The small-firm portfolio experienced a positive and statistically significant average excess return, whereas the large-firm portfolio had a statistically significant negative average excess return. The mean difference in excess returns between the small and large firms was about 25 percent a year. Also, the mean excess returns of smallest through largest portfolios were perfectly inversely ordered with firm size.

In contrast to Reinganum's work, Chen (1983) compared the APT model to the CAPM and provided contrary evidence related to the small-firm effect. The analysis employed 180 stocks and 5 factors. Chen's test of the two models for performance measurement was based on the contention that if the CAPM does not capture all the information related to returns, this remaining information will be in the residual series. In turn, if the APT can provide factors to explain these residual returns, it will be superior. He concluded that the CAPM was misspecified and that the missing price information was picked up by the APT.

APT Tests of the January Effect Given the so-called January effect, where returns in January are significantly larger than in any other month, Gultekin and Gultekin (1987) tested the ability of the APT model to adjust for this anomaly. The APT model was estimated separately for each month, and risk premia were *always* significant in January but rarely priced in other months. They concluded that the APT model can explain the risk–return relation only in January, meaning that the APT model does not explain this anomaly any better than the CAPM.

Burmeister and McElroy (1988) estimated a linear factor model, the APT, and the CAPM. They found a significant January effect that was not captured by any of the models. When they moved beyond the January effect, however, they rejected the CAPM in favor of the APT. Kramer (1994) shows that an empirical form of the APT accounts for the January seasonal effect in average stock returns while the CAPM cannot.

Is the APT Even Testable?
Similar to Roll's critique of the CAPM, Shanken (1982) challenged whether it is possible for the APT to be empirically verified at all. He questioned whether the APT is more susceptible to testing than the CAPM based on the usual empirical test that determines whether asset returns conform to a K factor model. One problem is that if stock returns are not explained by such a model, it is not considered a rejection of the model; however, if the factors do explain returns, it is considered support. Also, equivalent sets of securities may conform to different factor structures, meaning that the APT may yield different empirical implications regarding the expected returns for a given set of securities. Unfortunately, this implies that the theory cannot explain differential returns between securities because it cannot identify the relevant factor structure that explains the differential returns. This need to identify the relevant factor structure that affects asset returns is similar to the CAPM benchmark problem.

Dybvig and Ross (1985) replied by suggesting that the APT is testable as an equality rather than the "empirical APT" proposed by Shanken. Shanken (1985a) responded that what has emerged is a set of equilibrium APT pricing models that are testable but that arbitrage-based models are not testable as originally specified.

Alternative Techniques for Testing the APT
In addition to the test procedures just described, other researchers have proposed alternative statistical techniques for testing the APT

model. Jobson (1982) proposes that the APT be tested using a multivariate linear regression model. Brown and Weinstein (1983) propose an approach to estimating and testing asset pricing models using a bilinear paradigm. Geweke and Zhou (1996) produce an exact Bayesian framework for testing the APT and conclude that there is little reduction in pricing error from including additional factors beyond the first one. A number of subsequent papers have proposed new methodologies for testing the APT.[1]

9.2 Multifactor Models and Risk Estimation

When it comes to putting theory into practice, one advantage of the CAPM framework is that the identity of the single risk factor (i.e., the excess return to the market portfolio) is well specified. The empirical challenge in implementing the CAPM is to accurately estimate the market portfolio, a process that first requires identifying the relevant investment universe. As we saw in the last chapter, this is not a trivial problem as an improperly chosen proxy for the market portfolio (e.g., using the S&P 500 index to represent the market when evaluating a fixed-income portfolio) can lead to erroneous judgments. However, we also saw that once the returns to an acceptable surrogate for the market portfolio are identified (i.e., R_m), the process for estimating the parameters of the CAPM is straightforward and can be accomplished by either of the following regression equations:

1. A security or portfolio's *characteristic line* can be estimated via regression techniques using the *single-index market model*:

$$R_{it} = a_i + b_i R_{mt} + e_t$$

2. Alternatively, this equation can also be estimated in *excess return form* by netting the riskfree rate from the period t returns to security i and the market portfolio:

$$(R_{it} - RFR_t) = \alpha_i + b_i(R_{mt} - RFR_t) + e_{it}$$

In contrast to the CAPM, the primary practical problem associated with implementing the APT is that neither the identity nor the exact number of the underlying risk factors are developed by theory and therefore must be specified in an ad hoc manner. Said differently, before the APT can be used to value securities or measure investment performance, the investor must fill in a considerable amount of missing information about the fundamental relationship between risk and expected return.

As discussed earlier, the first attempts to implement a usable form of the APT relied on multivariate statistical techniques, such as principal components analysis and factor analysis, wherein many periods of realized returns for large number of securities are analyzed simultaneously in order to detect recognizable patterns of behavior. A consistent finding of these studies is that there appear to be as many as three or four "priced" (i.e., statistically significant) factors, although researchers were not able to establish that the same set of factors was generated by different subsets of their sample. Indeed, we also saw that the inability to identify the risk factors is a major limitation to the usefulness of the APT. Jones (2001) and Ludvigson and Ng (2007) provide some recent extensions along these lines.

A different approach to developing an empirical model that captures the essence of the APT relies on the direct specification of the form of the relationship to be estimated. That is, in a *multifactor model*, the investor chooses the exact number and identity of risk factors in the following equation:

9.2
$$R_{it} = a_i + [b_{i1}F_{1t} + b_{i2}F_{2t} + \cdots + b_{iK}F_{Kt}] + e_{it}$$

---

[1]Among these papers are works by Cho (1984), McCulloch and Rossi (1990), and Shakla and Trzcinka (1990).

where F_{jt} is the period t return to the jth designated risk factor and R_{it} can be measured as either a nominal or excess return to security i. The advantage of this approach is that the investor knows precisely how many and what things need to be estimated to fit the regression equation. The major disadvantage of a multifactor model is that it is developed with little theoretical guidance as to the true nature of the risk–return relationship. In this sense, developing a useful factor model is as much an art form as it is a theoretical exercise.

9.2.1 Multifactor Models in Practice

A wide variety of empirical factor specifications have been employed in practice. A hallmark of each alternative model that has been developed is that it attempts to identify a set of economic influences that is simultaneously broad enough to capture the major nuances of investment risk but small enough to provide a workable solution to the analyst or investor. Two general approaches have been employed in this factor identification process. First, risk factors can be viewed as *macroeconomic* in nature; that is, they attempt to capture variations in the underlying reasons an asset's cash flows and investment returns might change over time (e.g., changes in inflation or real GDP growth in the example discussed earlier). On the other hand, risk factors can also be viewed at a *microeconomic* level by focusing on relevant characteristics of the securities themselves, such as the size of the firm in question or some of its financial ratios. A few examples representative of both of these approaches are discussed in the following sections.

Macroeconomic-Based Risk Factor Models One particularly influential model was developed by Chen, Roll, and Ross (1986), who hypothesized that security returns are governed by a set of broad economic influences in the following fashion:

9.3 $$R_{it} = a_i + [b_{i1}R_{mt} + b_{i2}\,MP_t + b_{i3}\,DEI_t + b_{i4}\,UI_t + b_{i5}\,UPR_t + b_{i6}UTS_t] + e_{it}$$

where:

R_m = the return on a value-weighted index of NYSE-listed stocks
MP = the monthly growth rate in U.S. industrial production
DEI = the change in inflation, measured by the U.S. consumer price index
UI = the difference between actual and expected levels of inflation
UPR = the unanticipated change in the bond credit spread (Baa yield - RFR)
UTS = the unanticipated term structure shift (long-term less short-term RFR)

In estimating this model, the authors used a series of monthly returns for a large collection of securities from the Center for Research in Security Prices (CRSP) database over the period 1958–1984. Exhibit 9.3 shows the factor sensitivities (along with the associated t-statistics in parentheses) that they established. Notice two things about these findings. First, the economic significance of the designated risk factors changed dramatically over time. For instance, the inflation factors (*DEI* and *UI*) appear to only be relevant during the 1968–1977 period. Second,

Exhibit 9.3 Estimating a Multifactor Model with Macroeconomic Risk Factors

Period	Constant	R_M	MP	DEI	UI	UPR	UTS
1958–1984	10.71	−2.40	11.76	−0.12	−0.80	8.27	−5.91
	(2.76)	(−0.63)	(3.05)	(−1.60)	(−2.38)	(2.97)	(−1.88)
1958–1967	9.53	1.36	12.39	0.01	−0.21	5.20	−0.09
	(1.98)	(0.28)	(1.79)	(0.06)	(−0.42)	(1.82)	(−0.04)
1968–1977	8.58	−5.27	13.47	−0.26	−1.42	12.90	−11.71
	(1.17)	(−0.72)	(2.04)	(−3.24)	(−3.11)	(2.96)	(−2.30)
1978–1984	15.45	−3.68	8.40	−0.12	−0.74	6.06	−5.93
	(1.87)	(−0.49)	(1.43)	(−0.46)	(−0.87)	(0.78)	(−0.64)

Source: Nai-fu Chen, Richard Roll, and Stephen A. Ross, "Economic Forces and the Stock Market," *Journal of Business* 59, no. 3 (April 1986).

the parameter on the stock market proxy is never significant, suggesting that it contributes little to the explanation beyond the information contained in the other macroeconomic risk factors.

Burmeister, Roll, and Ross (1994) analyzed the predictive ability of a model based on a different set of macroeconomic factors. Specifically, they define the following five risk exposures: (1) *confidence risk,* based on unanticipated changes in the willingness of investors to take on investment risk; (2) *time horizon risk,* which is the unanticipated changes in investors' desired time to receive payouts; (3) *inflation risk,* based on a combination of the unexpected components of short-term and long-term inflation rates; (4) *business cycle risk,* which represents unanticipated changes in the level of overall business activity; and (5) *market-timing risk,* defined as the part of the Standard & Poor's 500 total return that is not explained by the other four macroeconomic factors. Using monthly data through the first quarter of 1992, the authors estimated risk premia (i.e., the market "price" of risk) for these factors:

Risk Factor	Risk Premium
Confidence	2.59%
Time horizon	−0.66
Inflation	−4.32
Business cycle	1.49
Market timing	3.61

They also compared the factor sensitivities for several different individual stocks and stock portfolios. Panel A and Panel B of Exhibit 9.4 show these factor beta estimates for a particular stock (Reebok International Ltd.) versus the S&P 500 index and for a portfolio of small-cap firms versus a portfolio of large-cap firms. Also included in these graphs is the security's or portfolio's exposure to the BIRR composite risk index, which is designed to indicate which position has the most overall systematic risk. These comparisons highlight how a multifactor model can help investors distinguish the nature of the risk they are assuming when they hold with a particular position. For instance, notice that Reebok has greater exposures to all sources of risk than the S&P 500, with the incremental difference in the business cycle exposure being particularly dramatic. Additionally, smaller firms are more exposed to business cycle and confidence risk than larger firms but less exposed to horizon risk.

Microeconomic-Based Risk Factor Models In contrast to macroeconomic-based explanations of the connection between risk and expected return, it is also possible to specify risk in microeconomic terms using proxy variables that concentrate on certain characteristics of the underlying sample of securities. Typical of this *characteristic-based approach* to forming a multifactor model is the work of Fama and French (1993), who use the following functional form:

9.4 $$(R_{it} - RFR_t) = \alpha_i + b_{i1}(R_{mt} - RFR_t) + b_{i2}SMB_t + b_{i3}HML_t + e_{it}$$

where, in addition to the excess return on a stock market portfolio, two other risk factor proxies are defined:

SMB (i.e., small minus big) is the return to a portfolio of small capitalization stocks less the return to a portfolio of large capitalization stocks

HML (i.e., high minus low) is the return to a portfolio of stocks with high ratios of book-to-market values less the return to a portfolio of low book-to-market value stocks

In this specification, *SMB* is designed to capture elements of risk associated with firm size while *HML* is intended to distinguish risk differentials associated with "growth" (i.e., low book-to-market ratio) and "value" (i.e., high book-to-market) firms. As we saw earlier, these are two dimensions of a security—or portfolio of securities—that have consistently been shown to matter when evaluating investment performance. Also, notice that without *SMB* and *HML* this model reduces to the excess returns form of the single-index market model.

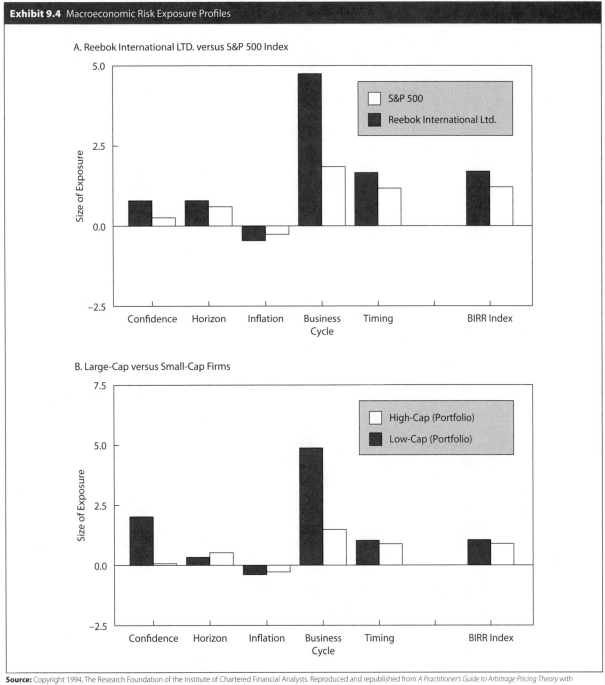

Exhibit 9.4 Macroeconomic Risk Exposure Profiles

A. Reebok International LTD. versus S&P 500 Index

B. Large-Cap versus Small-Cap Firms

Fama and French examined the behavior of a broad sample of stocks grouped into quintile portfolios by their price to earnings (P/E) ratios on a yearly basis over the period from July 1963 to December 1991. The results for both the single-index and multifactor versions of the model for the two extreme quintiles are shown in Exhibit 9.5 (*t*-statistics for the estimated coefficients are listed parenthetically). Notice that while the estimated beta from the single-factor model indicates that there are substantial differences between low and high P/E stocks (i.e., 0.94 vs. 1.10), this gap is dramatically reduced in the multifactor specification (i.e., 1.03 vs. 0.99). This

Exhibit 9.5 Estimating a Multifactor Model with Characteristic-Based Risk Factors

Portfolio	Constant	Market (1) Single-Index Model	SMB	HML	R²
Lowest P/E	0.46	0.94	—	—	0.78
	(3.69)	(34.73)			
Highest P/E	−0.20	1.10	—	—	0.91
	(−2.35)	(57.42)			
(2) Multifactor Model					
Lowest P/E	0.08	1.03	0.24	0.67	0.91
	(1.01)	(51.56)	(8.34)	(19.62)	
Highest P/E	0.04	0.99	−0.01	−0.50	0.96
	(0.70)	(66.78)	(−0.55)	(−19.73)	

Source: Reprinted from Eugene F. Fama and Kenneth R. French, "Common Risk Factors in the Returns on Stocks and Bonds," *Journal of Financial Economics* 33, no. 1 (January 1993), with permission from Elsevier Science.

suggests that the market portfolio in a one-factor model serves as a proxy for some, but not all, of the additional risk dimensions provided by *SMB* and *HML*. Further, low P/E stocks tend to be positively correlated with the small-firm premium, but the reverse is not reliably true for high P/E stocks. Finally, low P/E stocks also tend to have high book-to-market ratios while high P/E stocks tend to have low book-to-market ratios (i.e., estimated *HML* parameters of 0.67 and −0.50, respectively). Not surprisingly, relative levels of P-E and book-to-market ratios are both commonly employed in practice to classify growth and value stocks.

Carhart (1997) directly extends the Fama-French three-factor model by including a fourth common risk factor that accounts fot the tendency for firms with positive (negative) past returns to produce positive (negative) future returns. He calls this additional risk dimension a *price momentum factor* and estimates it by taking the average return to a set of stocks with the best performance over the prior year minus the average return to stocks with the worst returns. In this fashion, Carhart defines the momentum factor—labeled here as *MOM*—in a fashion similar to *SMB* and *HML*. Formally, the model he proposes is :

9.5 $(R_{it} - RFR_t) = \alpha_i + b_{i1}(R_{mt} - RFR_t) + b_{i2}SMB_t + b_{i3}HML_t + b_{i4}MOM_t + e_{it}$

He demonstrates that the typical factor sensitivity (i.e., factor beta) for the momentum variable is positive and its inclusion into the Fama-French model increases explanatory power by as much as 15 percent. Equation 9.5 is often referred to as the four-factor Fama-French model.

Extensions of Characteristic-Based Risk Factor Models Another type of security characteristic-based method for defining systematic risk exposures involves the use of index portfolios (e.g., S&P 500, Wilshire 5000) as common factors. Intuitively, if the indexes themselves are designed to emphasize certain investment characteristics, they can act as proxies for the underlying exposure that determines returns to that characteristic. Examples of this include the Russell 1000 Growth index, which emphasizes large-cap stocks with low book-to-market ratios, or the EAFE (Europe, Australia, and the Far East) index that selects a variety of companies that are domiciled outside the United States. Typical of these index-based factor models is the work of Elton, Gruber, and Blake (1996), who rely on four indexes: the S&P 500, the Lehman Brothers aggregate bond index, the Prudential Bache index of the difference between large- and small-cap stocks, and the Prudential Bache index of the difference between value and growth stocks. Ferson and Schadt (1996) have developed an interesting variation on this approach, which, in addition to using stock and bond indexes as risk factors, also includes other "public information" variables, such as the shape of the yield curve and dividend payouts.

BARRA, a leading risk forecasting and investment consulting firm, provides a final example of the microeconomic approach to building a multifactor model. The model they employ for

> **Exhibit 9.6** Description of BARRA Characteristic-Based Risk Factors
>
> - **Volatility (VOL)** Captures both long-term and short-term dimensions of relative return variability
> - **Momentum (MOM)** Differentiates between stocks with positive and negative excess returns in the recent past
> - **Size (SIZ)** Based on a firm's relative market capitalization
> - **Size Nonlinearity (SNL)** Captures deviations from linearity in the relationship between returns and firm size
> - **Trading Activity (TRA)** Measures the relative trading in a stock, based on the premise that more actively traded stocks are more likely to be those with greater interest from institutional investors
> - **Growth (GRO)** Uses historical growth and profitability measures to predict future earnings growth
> - **Earnings Yield (EYL)** Combines current and historical earnings-to-price ratios with analyst forecasts under the assumption that stocks with similar earnings yields produce similar returns
> - **Value (VAL)** Based on relative book-to-market ratios
> - **Earnings Variability (EVR)** Measures the variability in earnings and cash flows using both historical values and analyst forecasts
> - **Leverage (LEV)** Measures the relative financial leverage of a company
> - **Currency Sensitivity (CUR)** Based on the relative sensitivity of a company's stock return to movements in a basket of foreign currencies
> - **Dividend Yield (YLD)** Computes a measure of the predicted dividend yield using a firm's past dividend and stock price history
> - **Nonestimation Indicator (NEU)** Uses returns to firms outside the equity universe to account for risk dimensions not captured by the other risk factors

Source: Adapted from BARRA U.S Equity Model Version 3 (E3) Handbook.

analyzing U.S. equities includes as risk factors several characteristic-based variables and more than 50 industry indexes.[2] Exhibit 9.6 provides a brief description of the characteristic-based factors representative of the BARRA approach to decomposing investment risk. One useful application for this model is to understand where the investment "bets" in an actively managed portfolio are being placed relative to a performance benchmark. Exhibit 9.7 illustrates this for a small-cap-oriented mutual fund (POOL2) versus the S&P 500 index (SAP500). As you would expect, there are dramatic differences between the fund and the benchmark in terms of the firm-size risk factors (i.e., size, SIZ, and size nonlinearity, SNL). However, it also appears that POOL2 holds companies with substantially different leverage (LEV) and momentum (MOM) exposures from the index.

Connor (1995) has analyzed the ability of the BARRA model to explain the returns generated by a sample of U.S. stocks over the period from 1985 to 1993. He found that the industry indexes, taken collectively, provided about four times the explanatory power as any single characteristic-based factor, followed in importance by volatility, growth, dividend yield, and momentum. Overall, the BARRA model was able to explain slightly more return variability than the other models to which it was compared, in part because of the large number of factors it employs.

9.2.2 Estimating Risk in a Multifactor Setting: Examples

Estimating Expected Returns for Individual Stocks One direct way to employ a multifactor risk model is to use it to estimate the expected return for an individual stock position. In order to do this, the following steps must be taken: (1) a specific set of K common risk factors (or their proxies) must be identified, (2) the risk premia (F_j) for the factors must be estimated, (3) the sensitivities (b_{ij}) of the ith stock to each of those K factors must be estimated, and (4) the expected returns can be calculated by combining the results of the previous steps in the appropriate way.

[2]A more complete description of the BARRA approach to analyzing investment risk can be found in Richard Grinold and Ronald N. Kahn (1994).

Exhibit 9.7 BARRA Risk Decomposition for a Small-Cap Fund versus S&P 500

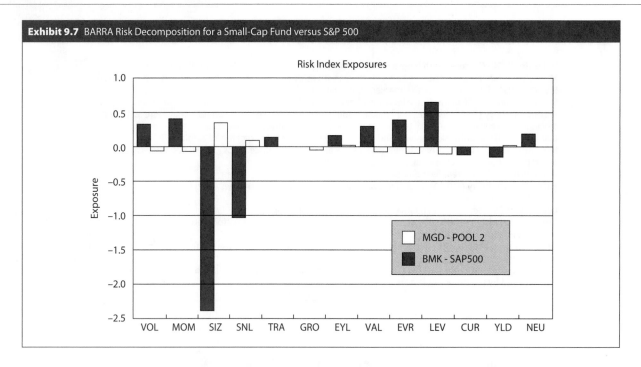

As an example of this process, we will use both the three-factor and four-factor versions of the Fama-French model discussed earlier. This immediately solves the first step by designating proxies for the four common risk factors: the excess return on the market portfolio (R_m), the return differential between small and large capitalization stocks (*SMB*), the return differential between high and low book-to-market stocks (*HML*), and the return differential between stocks with the highest and lowest past returns (*MOM*). The second step is often addressed in practice by using historical return data to calculate the average values for each of the risk factors. However, it is important to recognize that these averages can vary tremendously depending on the time period the investor selects. For the four factors just described, the first panel of Exhibit 9.8 lists the average annual factor risk premia over three different time frames: a 10-year period ending in December 2006, a 20-year period ending in December 2006, and a 80-year period ending in December 2006.[3] Notice that these data confirm that small stocks earned higher returns than large stocks, on average, and value stocks outperformed growth stocks (i.e., positive risk premia for the *SMB* and *HML* factors).

To illustrate the final steps involved in estimating expected stock returns, risk factor sensitivities were estimated by regression analysis for three different stocks using monthly return data over the period January 2001 to December 2006. The three stocks were General Electric (GE), a multinational conglomerate, ConAgra Foods (CAG), a packaged foods company, and CSX Corporation (CSX), a railroad firm. The estimated factor betas are listed in Panel B of Exhibit 9.8 for the three-factor model and in Panel C for the four-factor version of the equation.

These factor betas provide some interesting comparisons between the three stocks. First, the positive coefficients on the market factor indicate that all of these companies are positively correlated with general movements in the stock market. The coefficients on the *SMB* factor confirm that GE and CAG produce returns consistent with large-cap stocks (i.e., negative *SMB* exposures), while CSX acts like a small-cap or mid-cap stock. Further, CAG and CSX are more

[3] The data in these calculations are available from Professor Kenneth French's Web site at http://mba.tuck.dartmouth.edu/pages/faculty/ken.french.

Exhibit 9.8 Estimates for Risk Factor Premia, Factor Sensitivities and Expected Returns

A. Risk Factor Premium Estimates Using Historical and Hypothetical Data

Risk Factor	Historical: 1997–2006	Historical: 1987–2006	Historical: 1927–2006	Hypothetical Forecast
Market	6.83%	8.28%	8.30%	7.00%
SMB	3.49	1.09	3.70	2.00
HML	7.53	5.36	5.25	3.00
MOM	9.74	10.11	10.73	4.00

B. Estimates of Factor Sensitivities and Expected Risk Premia: Three-Factor Model

	GE	CAG	CSX
Factor:			
Market	0.826	0.565	0.906
SMB	−0.660	−0.120	0.089
HML	−0.245	0.117	0.370
E(Risk Prem):			
87–06	4.80%	5.18%	9.59%
Hypothetical	3.72	4.07	7.64

C. Estimates of Factor Sensitivities and Expected Risk Premia: Four-Factor Model

	GE	CAG	CSX
Factor:			
Market	0.777	0.593	0.804
SMB	−0.655	−0.123	0.100
HML	−0.186	0.084	0.496
MOM	−0.074	0.042	−0.158
E(Risk Prem):			
87–06	3.97%	5.65%	7.83%
Hypothetical	3.27	4.32	6.68

likely to be considered value stocks (i.e., positive HML exposures) while GE can be considered a growth-oriented stock. Finally, only CAG exhibited positive price momentum—albeit slight—during this time period (i.e., positive MOM exposure in Panel C).

Whichever specific factor risk estimates are used, the expected return for any stock in excess of the risk-free rate (i.e., the stock's expected risk premium) can be calculated with either the three-factor or four-factor version of the formula:

9.6 $$[E(R_i) - RFR] = b_{im}\lambda_m + b_{iSMB}\lambda_{SMB} + b_{iHML}\lambda_{HML} + b_{iMOM}\lambda_{MOM}$$

In Panels B and C of Exhibit 9.8, these expected excess return calculations are summarized for all three stocks using two different factor risk premia estimates: (1) historical data from the 1987–2006 period, and (2) a set of hypothetical forecasts. For example, the expected risk premium estimates for CAG using the historical risk factor data are:

Three-Factor: $[E(R) - RFR] = (0.565)(8.28) + (-0.120)(1.09) + (0.117)(5.36)$
$$= 5.18\%$$
Four-Factor: $[E(R) - RFR] = (0.593)(8.28) + (-0.123)(1.09) + (0.084)(5.36) + (0.042)(10.11)$
$$= 5.65\%$$

Notice three things about the forecasts in Exhibit 9.8. First, for any factor model and set of risk factor forecasts, the comparative excess return estimates across the stocks appear to be reasonable. Second, the forecasted expected stock returns generated by the hypothetical factor estimates are uniformly lower than those produced by using historical data. Finally, the three-factor and four-factor models produce fairly comparable forecasts for GE and CAG, but not for CSX where ignoring the larger MOM exposure matters more.

Comparing Mutual Fund Risk Exposures To get a better sense of how risk factor sensitivity is estimated at the portfolio level, consider the returns produced by two popular mutual funds: Fidelity's Magellan Fund (FMAGX) and T. Rowe Price's Mid-Cap Value Fund (TRMCX). Morningstar Inc., an independent stock and mutual fund advisory service, classifies FMAGX's investment style into the "large-cap growth" category. This means that the typical equity holding of FMAGX is characterized as a large market capitalization firm whose P/E and book-to-market ratios exceed those of the average firm in the market. Exhibit 9.9 shows a sample page for FMAGX from Morningstar's public-access Web site and shows graphically where the fund fits into the investment "style box" as of the reporting date in 2007. Conversely, as shown in Exhibit 9.10, Morningstar plots TRMCX into the "mid-cap blend" category—despite the fund's name—meaning that the portfolio generally emphasizes smaller companies than does FMAGX as well as those that fall somewhere in the middle of the value-growth spectrum. Thus, assuming that Morningstar's classification system is meaningful, the two funds should differ in the relative sensitivities to both the SMB and HML factors.

Using monthly returns from January 2003 to December 2006, the risk parameters for both funds were estimated relative to three different specifications: (1) a single-factor model using the Standard & Poor's 500 index as proxy for the market portfolio, (2) a single-factor model using a broader composite index of the U.S. stock market as a market proxy, and (3) the Fama-French three-factor model using the U.S. market composite. The results of these estimations are summarized in Exhibit 9.11, with t-statistics shown in parentheses.

From both versions of the one-factor market model, it is apparent that FMAGX and TRMCX differ substantially in their systematic risk. In particular, the beta coefficients for TRMCX indicate higher than average market risk (i.e., substantially greater than 1.00), regardless of how the market portfolio is proxied. Additionally, notice that during January 2003–December 2006, the beta estimates for the two funds are higher when the market portfolio is defined by the S&P 500 rather than the U.S. Composite index (e.g., 1.02 versus 0.94 for FMAGX). This suggests that S&P 500 was the less volatile of the two market indicators over this time period.

The multifactor model gives a much better sense of how FMAGX's and TRMCX's risk exposures actually differ from one another. First, notice that including the *SMB* and *HML* factors does not greatly affect the systematic market exposures of the two funds. For instance, the beta relative to the U.S. Composite index for TRMCX is 1.12 in the single-index model, but changes only slightly to 1.11 when estimated as part of the broader three-factor model.

A second implication of the multifactor equation is how the funds should react to the *HML* variable. Consistent with its Morningstar style category, FMAGX is tilted toward holding growth-oriented stocks. The fund's *HML* sensitivity of −0.18 is statistically significant, which shows that FMAGX's returns move inversely to a risk factor that, by its construction, is implicitly long in value stocks and short in growth stocks. (Recall that a low book-to-market ratio, like a high P/E ratio, is characteristic of a growth-oriented stock.) On the other hand, the *HML* coefficient for TRMCX is positive (i.e., 0.16) but of lesser statistical reliability, which is as expected for a fund that tends to hold both growth and value stocks but with a slight bias toward the latter. Notice in Exhibit 9.10 that Morningstar places its "fund centroid" at the extreme left edge of the mid-cap blend cell in the style box.

Finally, the Morningstar classification system also implies that FMAGX and TRMCX should differ in their sensitivity to the SMB risk factor. At first glance, this also is the case: FMAGX has a *SMB* sensitivity of −0.06, suggesting a slight tilt toward stocks that have larger market capitalizations, while TRMCX, with a *SMB* sensitivity of 0.04, indicates a tendency toward holding smaller stocks. However, neither of these factor sensitivity estimates is statistically significant, meaning that the returns to each portfolio act more like those of a mid-cap fund. Of course, given their respective style box placements, this outcome is more expected from TRMCX than FMAGX.

Exhibit 9.9 Morningstar Snapshot Report for Fidelity Magellan (FMAGX) Fund

Performance
Growth of $10,000   07-31-07

	2003	2004	2005	2006	2007
● Fund	24.8	7.5	6.4	7.2	8.8
● +/− Cat	-4.5	-0.9	-0.6	0.0	2.4
● +/− S&P 500 TR	-3.9	-3.4	1.5	-8.6	5.1

Trailing Returns %   08-29-07

	YTD	3 year	5 year
Fund	8.85	10.48	9.83
+/− S&P 500 TR	4.39	-1.30	-1.97

Key Stats

Morningstar Category	**Morningstar Rating**
Large Growth	★★★
Nav (08-29-07)	**Day Change**
$92.16	$2.50
Total Assets($mil)	**Expense Ratio %** ▶▶
42,836	$2.50
Front Load %	**Deferred Load %**
None *	None *
Yield % (TTM)	**Min Investment**
0.35	closed
Manager	**Start Date**
Harry Lange	10-31-05

* Closed to new investors

Portfolio Analysis   03-31-07

Morningstat Style Box ⍰

Value Blend Growth

Average Mkt Cap $Mil

24,194

Price/Prospective
Earnings

18.4

Ownership Zone ⍰

Value Blend Growth

● Fund centroid
represents weighted
average of domestic
stock holdings

● Zone represents 75%
of fund's domestic
stock holdings

Sector Breakdown (% of stocks) ⍰

⚙	**Information**	31.08
	Software	3.93
	Hardware	22.14
	Media	1.36
	Telecommunications	3.65
⛃	**Service**	47.03
	Healthcare	11.84
	Consumer Services	9.14
	Business Services	10.60
	Financial Services	15.46
🏭	**Manufacturing**	21.89
	Consumer Goods	3.94
	Industrial Materials	10.01
	Energy	7.65
	Utilities	0.30

Asset Allocation %

Cash	1.1
Stocks	98.9
Bonds	0.0
Other	0.0

Annual Turnover %	41
% Assets in Top 10	25.46

Top 5 Holdings Get Price Quotes

	Sector	YTD Return %	% Net Assets
Nokia Corporation ADR*	Hardware	61.89	4.92 %
Corning Inc.*	Hardware	26.89	3.97 %
Google, Inc.*	Business Services	11.38	2.88 %
⊕ Seagate Technology*	Hardware	-2.98	2.57 %
⊖ American International Group*	Financial Services	-7.28	2.54 %

Exhibit 9.10 Morningstar Snapshot Report for T. Rowe Price Mid-Cap Value (TRMCX) Fund

Performance
Growth of $10,000   07-31-07

	2003	2004	2005	2006	2007
● Fund	39.0	20.6	7.7	20.2	3.3
◔ +/– Cat	3.5	1.6	–0.9	4.4	–0.8
● +/– S&P 500 TR	10.3	9.7	2.8	4.5	–0.3

Trailing Returns %   08-29-07

	YTD	3 year	5 year
Fund	2.60	15.16	17.11
+/– S&P 500 TR	–1.86	3.38	5.31

Key Stats

Morningstar Category	**Morningstar Rating**
Mid-Cap Value	★★★★

Nav (08-29-07)   **Day Change**
$26.08 $0.53

Total Assets($mil)   **Expense Ratio %** ▶▶
8,111   0.80

Front Load %   **Deferred Load %**
None *   None *

Yield % (TTM)   **Min Investment**
0.87   closed

Manager   **Start Date**
David J. Wallack   12-31-00

* Closed to new investors

Portfolio Analysis   06-30-07

Morningstat Style Box ?

Average Mkt Cap $Mil

5,915

Price/Prospective Earnings

17.9

Ownership Zone ?

● Fund centroid represents weighted average of domestic stock holdings

◔ Zone represents 75% of fund's domestic stock holdings

Sector Breakdown (% of stocks) ?

Information	18.87
Software	0.62
Hardware	9.56
Media	8.69
Telecommunications	0.00
Service	43.96
Healthcare	9.96
Consumer Services	7.95
Business Services	6.45
Financial Services	19.60
Manufacturing	37.17
Consumer Goods	10.79
Industrial Materials	14.38
Energy	6.13
Utilities	5.87

Asset Allocation %

Cash	5.8
Stocks	92.8
Bonds	0.0
Other	1.5

Annual Turnover %   62

% Assets in Top 10   17.69

Top 5 Holdings   Get Price Quotes

	Sector	YTD Return %	% Net Assets
⊖ Marsh & McLennan Companies*	Financial Services	–12.50	2.23 %
International Paper Co.*	Industrial Materials	2.98	2.03 %
⊕ Nalco Holding Company*	Industrial Materials	32.67	1.91 %
⊕ Southwest Airlines, Co.*	Business Servicestt	–0.10	1.90 %
Murphy Oil Corporation*	Energy	19.66	1.75 %

Exhibit 9.11 Risk Factor Estimates for FMAGX and TRMCX

Mutual Fund	Constant	Market	SMB	HML	R^2
(1) Single-Index Market Model (Market = S&P 500)					
FMAGX	−0.12	1.02	—	—	0.87
	(−0.79)	(17.62)			
TRMCX	0.49	1.20	—	—	0.87
	(2.79)	(17.37)			
(2) Single-Index Market Model (Market = U.S. Composite)					
FMAGX	−0.37	0.94	—	—	0.90
	(−2.71)	(19.93)			
TRMCX	0.18	1.12	—	—	0.91
	(1.19)	(21.06)			
(3) Multifactor Model (Market = U.S. Composite)					
FMAGX	−0.24	0.97	−0.06	−0.18	0.91
	(−1.68)	(16.56)	(−0.92)	(−2.27)	
TRMCX	0.07	1.11	0.04	0.16	0.91
	(0.43)	(16.51)	(0.52)	(1.71)	

• • • • SUMMARY • • • •

- Although the CAPM is an elegant and appealing explanation for the way in which investment risk and expected return are related, a number of empirical anomalies—such as the small-firm effect—have caused financial economists to seek other answers. Ross subsequently devised an alternative asset pricing model—the APT—that makes fewer assumptions than the CAPM and does not specifically require the designation of a market portfolio. Instead, the APT posits that expected security returns are related in a linear fashion to multiple common risk factors. Unfortunately, the theory does not offer guidance as to how many factors exist or what their identities might be. The results from the empirical tests of the APT have thus far been mixed.

- Given that the common risk factors are not identified, the APT is difficult to put into practice in a theoretically rigorous fashion. Multifactor models of risk and return attempt to bridge this gap by specifying a set of variables that are thought to capture the essence of the systematic risk exposures that exist in the capital market. There have been a number of alternative risk factors suggested and tested by financial researchers. One general approach has been to use macroeconomic variables—such as unexpected inflation, changes in consumer confidence, unanticipated shifts in the yield curve, or unexpected changes in real GDP—as surrogates for the types of exposures that will have an impact on all securities. Once selected, historical data are often employed to determine the risk premium (i.e., market "price") for each common factor.

- A second approach to proxying for the risk exposures in a multifactor model has focused on the characteristics of the securities themselves. Typical of this sort of microeconomic approach is the work of Fama and French, who posit that three risk factors should be employed: the excess returns to a broad market index, the return difference between portfolios of small- and large-cap stocks, and the return difference between portfolios of value- and growth-oriented stocks. One immediate advantage of this specification is that it accounts directly for some of the anomalies that plagued the CAPM (i.e., the small-firm effect). Another advantage of the characteristic-based approach to forming factor models is the flexibility to modify the equation to changing market conditions. For instance, the Fama-French model has been expanded to include a factor accounting for stock return momentum.

- It is probably safe to assume that both the CAPM and APT will continue to be used to value capital assets. Coincident with their use will be further empirical tests of both theories, the ultimate goal being to determine which theory does the best job of explaining current returns and predicting future ones. Notably, although the APT model requires fewer assumptions and considers multiple factors to explain the risk of an asset, the CAPM has an advantage in that its single risk factor is well defined. Future work in this area will continue to seek to identify the set of factors that best captures the relevant dimension of investment risk as well as explore the intertemporal dynamics of the models (e.g., factor betas and risk premia that change over time).

• • • • SUGGESTED READINGS • • • •

Elton, Edwin J., Martin J. Gruber, Stephen J. Brown, and William N. Goetzmann. *Modern Portfolio Theory and Investment Analysis,* 6th ed. New York: John Wiley & Sons, 2003.

Grinold, Richard C., and Ronald N. Kahn. *Active Portfolio Management,* 2nd ed. New York: McGraw-Hill, 2000.

Lehmann, B. N., and D. M. Modest. "The Empirical Foundations of the Arbitrage Pricing Theory." *Journal of Financial Economics* 21, no. 3 (September 1988).

Peavy, John, ed. *A Practitioner's Guide to Factor Models.* Charlottesville, VA: Research Foundation of the CFA Institute, 1994.

Sharpe, William F. "Factor Models, CAPMs, and the APT." *Journal of Portfolio Management* 11, no. 1 (Fall 1984).

• • • • QUESTIONS • • • •

1. Both the capital asset pricing model and the arbitrage pricing theory rely on the proposition that a no-risk, no-wealth investment should earn, on average, no return. Explain why this should be the case, being sure to describe briefly the similarities and differences between the CAPM and the APT. Also, using either of these theories, explain how superior investment performance can be established.

2. **CFA EXAMINATION LEVEL III** You are an investment officer at Pegasus Securities and are preparing for the next meeting of the investment committee. Several committee members are interested in reviewing two asset pricing models—the capital asset pricing model (CAPM) and the arbitrage pricing theory (APT)—and their use in portfolio management and stock selection.
   a. Describe both the CAPM and the APT, and identify the factor(s) that determines returns in each.
   b. "The APT model is more general than the CAPM." Explain how this observation has meaning in the stock selection process.

3. The *small-firm effect* refers to the observed tendency for stock prices to behave in a manner that is contrary to normal expectations. Describe this effect and discuss whether it represents sufficient information to conclude that the stock market does not operate efficiently. In formulating your response, consider: (a) what it means for the stock market to be inefficient, and (b) what role the measurement of risk plays in your conclusions about each effect.

4. Some studies related to the efficient market hypothesis generated results that implied additional factors beyond beta should be considered to estimate expected returns. What are these other variables and why should they be considered?

5. Suppose you are considering the purchase of shares in the XYZ mutual fund. As part of your investment analysis, you regress XYZ's monthly returns for the past five years against the three factors specified in the Fama and French models. This procedure generates the following coefficient estimates: market factor = 1.2, *SMB* factor = –0.3, *HML* factor = 1.4. Explain what each of these coefficient values means. What types of stocks is XYZ likely to be holding?

6. **CFA EXAMINATION LEVEL III** As the manager of a large, broadly diversified portfolio of stocks and bonds, you realize that changes in certain macroeconomic variables may directly affect the performance of your portfolio. You are considering using an arbitrage pricing theory (APT) approach to strategic portfolio planning and want to analyze the possible impacts of the following four factors:
   • Industrial production
   • Inflation
   • Risk premia or quality spreads
   • Yield curve shifts
   Indicate how each of these four factors influences the cash flows and/or the discount rates in the traditional discounted cash flow model. Explain how unanticipated changes in each of these four factors could affect portfolio returns.

7. Describe the intuition underlying: (a) the macroeconomic approach to identifying risk factors, and (b) the microeconomic (i.e., characteristic-based) approach to identifying risk factors. Is it conceptually and practically possible for these two approaches to lead to the same estimate of expected return for any given security?

8. How can multifactor models be used to help investors understand the relative risk exposures in their portfolios relative to a benchmark portfolio? Support your answer with examples using both macro-economic and microeconomic approaches to factor identification.

9. Consider the following questions related to empirical tests of the APT:
   a. Briefly discuss one study that does not support the APT. Briefly discuss a study that does support the APT. Which position seems more plausible?
   b. Briefly discuss why Shanken contends that the APT is not testable. What is the contrary view to Shanken's position?

 10. **CFA EXAMINATION LEVEL II** Jeffrey Bruner, CFA, uses the capital asset pricing model (CAPM) to help identify mispriced securities. A consultant suggests Bruner use the arbitrage pricing theory (APT) instead. In comparing the CAPM and the APT, the consultant made the following arguments:
   a. Both the CAPM and the APT require a mean-variance efficient market portfolio.
   b. Neither the CAPM nor the APT assumes normally distributed security returns.
   c. The CAPM assumes that one specific factor explains security returns, but the APT does not.
   State whether *each* of the consultant's arguments is correct or incorrect. Indicate, for each incorrect argument, why the argument is incorrect.

• • • • PROBLEMS • • • •

1. Consider the following data for two risk factors (1 and 2) and two securities (J and L):

$$\lambda_0 = 0.05 \qquad b_{J1} = 0.80$$
$$\lambda_1 = 0.02 \qquad b_{J2} = 1.40$$
$$\lambda_2 = 0.04 \qquad b_{L1} = 1.60$$
$$\qquad\qquad\qquad b_{L2} = 2.25$$

   a. Compute the expected returns for both securities.
   b. Suppose that Security J is currently priced at $22.50 while the price of Security L is $15.00. Further, it is expected that both securities will pay a dividend of $0.75 during the coming year. What is the expected price of each security one year from now?

2. Exhibit 9.8 demonstrated how the Fama-French three-factor and four-factor models could be used to estimate the expected excess returns for three stocks (GE, CAG and CSX). Specifically, using return data from 2001 to 2006, the following equations were estimated:

Three-Factor Model:

$$\text{GE:} \quad [E(R) - RFR] = (0.826)(\lambda_m) + (-0.660)(\lambda_{SMB}) + (-0.245)(\lambda_{HML})$$
$$\text{CAG:} [E(R) - RFR] = (0.565)(\lambda_m) + (-0.120)(\lambda_{SMB}) + (0.117)(\lambda_{HML})$$
$$\text{CSX:} [E(R) - RFR] = (0.906)(\lambda_m) + (0.089)(\lambda_{SMB}) + (0.370)(\lambda_{HML})$$

Four-Factor Model:

$$\text{GE:} \quad [E(R) - RFR] = (0.777)(\lambda_m) + (-0.655)(\lambda_{SMB}) + (-0.186)(\lambda_{HML}) + (-0.074)(\lambda_{MOM})$$
$$\text{CAG:} [E(R) - RFR] = (0.593)(\lambda_m) + (-0.123)(\lambda_{SMB}) + (0.084)(\lambda_{HML}) + (0.042)(\lambda_{MOM})$$
$$\text{CSX:} [E(R) - RFR] = (0.804)(\lambda_m) + (0.100)(\lambda_{SMB}) + (0.496)(\lambda_{HML}) + (-0.158)(\lambda_{MOM})$$

Using the estimated factor risk premia of $\lambda_m = 8.28\%$, $\lambda_{SMB} = 1.09\%$, $\lambda_{HML} = 5.36\%$ and $\lambda_{MOM} = 10.11\%$, it was then shown that the expected excess returns for the three stocks were 4.80%, 5.18%, and 9.59% (three-factor model) or 3.97%, 5.65%, and 7.83% (four-factor model), respectively.

   a. Exhibit 9.8 also lists historical factor risk prices from two different time frames: (1) 1997–2006 ($\lambda_m = 6.83\%$, $\lambda_{SMB} = 3.49\%$, and $\lambda_{HML} = 7.53\%$), and (2) 1927–2006 ($\lambda_m = 8.30\%$, $\lambda_{SMB} = 3.70\%$, and $\lambda_{HML} = 5.25\%$). Calculate the expected excess returns for GE, CAG, and CSX using both of these alternative sets of factor risk premia *in conjunction with the three-factor risk model.*
   b. Exhibit 9.8 also lists historical estimates for the MOM risk factor: (i) $\lambda_{MOM} = 9.74\%$ (1997–2006), and (2) $\lambda_{MOM} = 10.73\%$ (1927–2006). Using this additional information, calculate the expected excess returns for GE, CAG, and CSX *in conjunction with the four-factor risk model.*

c. Do all of the expected excess returns you calculated in Part a and Part b make sense? If not, identify which ones seem inconsistent with asset pricing theory and discuss why.

d. Would you expect the factor betas to remain constant over time? Discuss how and why these coefficients might change in response to changing market conditions.

3. You have been assigned the task of estimating the expected returns for three different stocks: QRS, TUV, and WXY. Your preliminary analysis has established the historical risk premiums associated with three risk factors that could potentially be included in your calculations: the excess return on a proxy for the market portfolio (MKT), and two variables capturing general macroeconomic exposures (MACRO1 and MACRO2). These values are: $\lambda_{MKT} = 7.5\%$, $\lambda_{MACRO1} = -0.3\%$, and $\lambda_{MACRO2} = 0.6\%$. You have also estimated the following factor betas (i.e., loadings) for all three stocks with respect to each of these potential risk factors:

FACTOR LOADING

Stock	MKT	MACRO1	MACRO2
QRS	1.24	−0.42	0.00
TUV	0.91	0.54	0.23
WXY	1.03	−0.09	0.00

a. Calculate expected returns for the three stocks using just the MKT risk factor. Assume a risk-free rate of 4.5%.

b. Calculate the expected returns for the three stocks using all three risk factors and the same 4.5% risk-free rate.

c. Discuss the differences between the expected return estimates from the single-factor model and those from the multifactor model. Which estimates are most likely to be more useful in practice?

d. What sort of exposure might MACRO2 represent? Given the estimated factor betas, is it really reasonable to consider it a common (i.e., systematic) risk factor?

4. Consider the following information about two stocks (D and E) and two common risk factors (1 and 2):

Stock	b_{i1}	b_{i2}	$E(R_i)$
D	1.2	3.4	13.1%
E	2.6	2.6	15.4%

a. Assuming that the risk-free rate is 5.0%, calculate the levels of the factor risk premia that are consistent with the reported values for the factor betas and the expected returns for the two stocks.

b. You expect that in one year the prices for Stocks D and E will be $55 and $36, respectively. Also, neither stock is expected to pay a dividend over the next year. What should the price of each stock be today to be consistent with the expected return levels listed at the beginning of the problem?

c. Suppose now that the risk premium for Factor 1 that you calculated in Part a suddenly increases by 0.25% (i.e., from $x\%$ to $(x +0.25)\%$, where x is the value established in Part a). What are the new expected returns for Stocks D and E?

d. If the increase in the Factor 1 risk premium in Part c does not cause you to change your opinion about what the stock prices will be in one year, what adjustment will be necessary in the current (i.e., today's) prices?

5. Suppose that three stocks (A, B, and C) and two common risk factors (1 and 2) have the following relationship:

$$E(R_A) = (1.1)\,\lambda_1 + (0.8)\,\lambda_2$$
$$E(R_B) = (0.7)\,\lambda_1 + (0.6)\,\lambda_2$$
$$E(R_C) = (0.3)\,\lambda_1 + (0.4)\,\lambda_2$$

a. If $\lambda_1 = 4\%$ and $\lambda_2 = 2\%$, what are the prices expected next year for each of the stocks? Assume that all three stocks currently sell for $30 and will not pay a dividend in the next year.

b. Suppose that you know that next year the prices for Stocks A, B, and C will actually be $31.50, $35.00, and $30.50. Create and demonstrate a riskless, arbitrage investment to take advantage of these mispriced securities. What is the profit from your investment? You may assume that you can use the proceeds from any necessary short sale.

Problems 6 and 7 refer to the data contained in Exhibit 9.12, which lists 30 monthly excess returns to two different actively managed stock portfolios (A and B) and three different common risk factors (1, 2, and 3). (Note: You may find it useful to use a computer spreadsheet program such as Microsoft Excel to calculate your answers.)

6. a. Compute the average monthly return and monthly standard return deviation for each portfolio and all three risk factors. Also state these values on an annualized basis. (Hint: Monthly returns can be annualized by multiplying them by 12, while monthly standard deviations can be annualized by multiplying them by the square root of 12.)

b. Based on the return and standard deviation calculations for the two portfolios from Part a, is it clear whether one portfolio outperformed the other over this time period?

c. Calculate the correlation coefficients between each pair of the common risk factors (i.e., 1 & 2, 1 & 3, and 2 & 3).

d. In theory, what should be the value of the correlation coefficient between the common risk factors? Explain why.

e. How close do the estimates from Part b come to satisfying this theoretical condition? What conceptual problem(s) is created by a deviation of the estimated factor correlation coefficients from their theoretical levels?

7. a. Using regression analysis, calculate the factor betas of each stock associated with each of the common risk factors. Which of these coefficients are statistically significant?

b. How well does the factor model explain the variation in portfolio returns? On what basis can you make an evaluation of this nature?

c. Suppose you are now told that the three factors in Exhibit 9.12 represent the risk exposures in the Fama-French characteristic-based model (i.e., excess market, *SMB,* and *HML*). Based on your regression results, which one of these factors is the most likely to be the market factor? Explain why.

d. Suppose it is further revealed that Factor 3 is the *HML* factor. Which of the two portfolios is most likely to be a growth-oriented fund and which is a value-oriented fund? Explain why.

Exhibit 9.12 Monthly Excess Return Data for Two Portfolios and Three Risk Factors

Period	Portfolio A	Portfolio B	Factor 1	Factor 2	Factor 3
1	1.08%	0.00%	0.01%	−1.01%	−1.67%
2	7.58	6.62	6.89	0.29	−1.23
3	5.03	6.01	4.75	−1.45	1.92
4	1.16	0.36	0.66	0.41	0.22
5	−1.98	−1.58	−2.95	−3.62	4.29
6	4.26	2.39	2.86	−3.40	−1.54
7	−0.75	−2.47	−2.72	−4.51	−1.79
8	−15.49	−15.46	−16.11	−5.92	5.69
9	6.05	4.06	5.95	0.02	−3.76
10	7.70	6.75	7.11	−3.36	−2.85
11	7.76	5.52	5.86	1.36	−3.68
12	9.62	4.89	5.94	−0.31	−4.95
13	5.25	2.73	3.47	1.15	−6.16
14	−3.19	−0.55	−4.15	−5.59	1.66
15	5.40	2.59	3.32	−3.82	−3.04
16	2.39	7.26	4.47	2.89	2.80
17	−2.87	0.10	−2.39	3.46	3.08
18	6.52	3.66	4.72	3.42	−4.33
19	−3.37	−0.60	−3.45	2.01	0.70
20	−1.24	−4.06	−1.35	−1.16	−1.26
21	−1.48	0.15	−2.68	3.23	−3.18
22	6.01	5.29	5.80	−6.53	−3.19
23	2.05	2.28	3.20	7.71	−8.09
24	7.20	7.09	7.83	6.98	−9.05
25	−4.81	−2.79	−4.43	4.08	−0.16
26	1.00	−2.04	2.55	21.49	−12.03
27	9.05	5.25	5.13	−16.69	7.81
28	−4.31	−2.96	−6.24	−7.53	8.59
29	−3.36	−0.63	−4.27	−5.86	5.38
30	3.86	1.80	4.67	13.31	−8.78

THOMSON ONE | Business School Edition

1. You would like to evaluate the historical relationship between value-oriented and growth-oriented stocks that form the basis for the HML risk factor in the Fama-French multi-factor model. The proxies you choose are the S&P 500/Barra Value index and the S&P 500/Barra Growth index, respectively.
   a. Under the "Indices" tab, download *weekly* price information for the five-year period from July 2, 2001 to June 30, 2006 for each index.
   b. For each index, calculate the set of *weekly* returns that correspond to these weekly price series.
   c. Calculate the average weekly return and the return standard deviation for each index series. Which equity investment style (i.e., value versus growth) appears to have been the most successful over this sample period?
   d. Suppose that you are considering forming a hedge fund employing a strategy of always being long in value stocks and short in growth stocks. Evaluate the potential success of this strategy by taking the weekly difference in returns between the value and growth indexes you analyzed above. What is the average return and return standard deviation for the return differential series?
   e. Plot the return differential series you calculated in Part e, using the return differential on the vertical axis and time on the horizontal axis. What do you conclude about the viability of the "long value, short growth" investment strategy?

2. You would also like to evaluate the historical relationship between small cap-oriented and large cap-oriented stocks that form the basis for the SMB risk factor in the Fama-French multifactor model. The proxies you choose are the S&P 600 Small Cap index and the S&P 500 index, respectively.
   a. Under the "Indices" tab, download *weekly* price information for the most recent five-year period available for each index.
   b. For each index, calculate the set of *weekly* returns that correspond to these weekly price series.
   c. Calculate the average weekly return and the return standard deviation for each index series. Which equity investment style (i.e., small cap versus large cap) appears to have been the most successful over this sample period?
   d. Suppose that you are considering forming a hedge fund employing a strategy of always being long in small cap stocks and short in large cap stocks. Evaluate the potential success of this strategy by taking the weekly difference in returns between the small cap and large cap indexes you analyzed above. What is the average return and return standard deviation for the return differential series?
   e. Plot the return differential series you calculated in Part e, using the return differential on the vertical axis and time on the horizontal axis. What do you conclude about the viability of the "long small cap, short large cap" investment strategy?

PART 3
Valuation Principles and Practices

CHAPTER 10
Analysis of Financial Statements

CHAPTER 11
An Introduction to Security Valuation

In Parts 1 and 2 you learned the purpose of investing and the importance of an appropriate asset allocation decision. You also learned about the numerous investment instruments available on a global basis and the background regarding the institutional characteristics of the capital markets. In addition, you are now aware of the major developments in investment theory as they relate to efficient capital markets, portfolio theory, capital asset pricing, and multifactor valuation models. Therefore, at this point you are in a position to consider the theory and practice of estimating the value of various securities, which is the heart of investing and leads to the construction of a portfolio that is consistent with your risk–return objectives. You will recall that the investment decision is based on a comparison of an asset's intrinsic value and its market price.

The major source of information regarding a stock or bond is the corporation's financial statements. Chapter 10 considers what financial statements are available and what information they provide, followed by a discussion of the financial ratios used to answer several important questions about a firm's liquidity, its operating performance, its risk profile, and its growth potential.

Chapter 11 considers the basic principles of valuation and applies those principles to the valuation of bonds, preferred stock, and common stock. Because it is recognized that the valuation of common stock is the most challenging task, we present two general approaches to equity valuation (discounted cash flow models and relative valuation ratios) and several techniques for each of these approaches. We conclude this chapter by reviewing the basic factors that influence the two critical variables that determine the intrinsic value of an asset irrespective of the valuation model: (1) the required rate of return for an investment, and (2) the estimated growth rate of earnings, dividends, and cash flows for the investment.

When you master these two chapters, you will have the tools and the theoretical understanding to apply the valuation models to the range of entities included in the top-down approach—the aggregate market, alternative industries, and individual companies and stocks. These specific valuations are the topics considered in Part 4.

CHAPTER 10

Analysis of Financial Statements

After you read this chapter, you should be able to answer the following questions:

- What are the major financial statements provided by firms and what specific information does each of them contain?
- Why do we use financial ratios to examine the performance of a firm, and why is it important to examine performance relative to the economy and to a firm's industry?
- What are the major categories for financial ratios and what questions are answered by the ratios in these categories?
- What specific ratios help determine a firm's internal liquidity, operating performance, risk profile, and growth potential?
- How can DuPont analysis help evaluate a firm's past and future return on equity?
- What is a quality balance sheet or income statement?
- Why should you engage in financial statement analysis if markets are efficient and forward-looking?
- What major financial ratios are used by analysts in the following areas: stock valuation, estimating and evaluating systematic risk, predicting the credit ratings on bonds, and the probability of bankruptcy?

You have probably already noted that this is a fairly long chapter with several financial statements and numerous financial ratios. The reason for this extensive discussion of how to analyze financial statements is that our ultimate goal (as noted earlier) is to construct a portfolio of investments that will provide rates of return that are consistent with the risk of the portfolio. In turn, to determine the expected rates of return on different assets we must *estimate the future value* of each asset since a major component of the rate of return is the change in value for the asset over time. Therefore, the crux of investments is *valuation.* Although we consider various valuation models for common stocks in the next chapter, you are already aware that the value of any earning asset is the present value of the expected cash flows generated by the asset. Therefore, as noted in previous chapters, to estimate the value of an asset we must derive an estimate of the discount rate for the asset (the required rate of return) and its expected cash flows. The main source of the information needed to make these two estimates is the financial statements. To derive an estimate of the required rate of return, we need to understand the business and financial risk of the firm. To estimate future cash flows, we must understand the composition of cash flows and what will contribute to the short-run and long-run growth of these cash flows. Financial statements, business and financial risk, and analysis of the composition and growth of cash flow are all topics of this chapter. In other words, a primary purpose of this chapter is to help you understand how to estimate the variables in alternative valuation models.

Financial statements are also the main source of information when deciding whether to lend money to a firm (invest in its bonds) or to buy warrants or options on a firm's stock. In this chapter, we first introduce a corporation's major financial statements and discuss why and how financial ratios are useful. We also provide example computations of ratios that reflect internal liquidity, operating performance, risk analysis, and growth analysis. In addition, we address four major areas in investments where financial ratios have been effectively employed.

Our example in this chapter is Walgreens Co., the largest retail drugstore chain in the United States. It operates in 48 states and Puerto Rico. Pharmacy prescription sales generate over 65 percent of total sales. The firm leads its industry (retail drugstores) in sales, profit, and store growth. The firm's goal is to be America's most convenient and technologically advanced health-care retailer. It takes great pride in its steady sales and earnings growth that have been reflected in outstanding stock performance—e.g., dividends have increased in each of the past 32 years and, since 1980, the stock has been split two-for-one seven times.

10.1 Major Financial Statements

Financial statements are intended to provide information on the resources available to management, how these resources were financed, and what the firm accomplished with them. Corporate shareholder annual and quarterly reports include three required financial statements: the balance sheet, the income statement, and the statement of cash flows. In addition, reports that must be filed with the Securities and Exchange Commission (SEC) (for example, the 10-K and 10-Q reports) carry detailed information about the firm, such as information on loan agreements and data on product line and subsidiary performance. Information from the basic financial statements can be used to calculate financial ratios and to analyze the operations of the firm to determine what factors influence a firm's earnings, cash flows, and risk characteristics.

10.1.1 Generally Accepted Accounting Principles

Among the input used to construct the financial statements are **generally accepted accounting principles (GAAP)**, which are formulated by the Financial Accounting Standards Board (FASB). The FASB recognizes that it would be improper for all companies to use identical and restrictive accounting principles. Some flexibility and choice are needed because industries and firms within industries differ in their operating environments. Therefore, the FASB allows companies some flexibility to choose among appropriate GAAP. This flexibility allows the firm's managers to choose accounting standards that best reflect company practice. On the negative side, this flexibility can allow firms to appear healthier than they really are.[1] Given this possibility, the financial analyst must rigorously analyze the available financial information to separate those firms that *appear* attractive from those that actually are in good financial shape.

Fortunately, the FASB requires that financial statements include footnotes that indicate which accounting principles were used by the firm. Because accounting principles frequently differ among firms, the footnote information assists the financial analyst in adjusting the financial statements of companies so the analyst can better compare "apples with apples."

10.1.2 Balance Sheet

The **balance sheet** shows what resources (assets) the firm controls and how it has financed these assets. Specifically, it indicates the current and fixed assets available to the firm *at a point in time* (the end of the fiscal year or the end of a quarter). In most cases, the firm owns these assets, but some firms lease assets on a long-term basis. How the firm has financed the acquisition of these assets is indicated by its mixture of current liabilities (accounts payable or short-term borrowing), long-term liabilities (fixed debt and leases), and owners' equity (preferred stock, common stock, and retained earnings).

The balance sheet for Walgreens in Exhibit 10.1 represents the *stock* of assets and its financing mix as of the end of Walgreen Co.'s fiscal year, August 31, 2005, 2006, and 2007.

---

[1] The Enron fiasco clearly makes this point. For a general discussion on this topic, see Byrnes and Henry (2001), Henry (2001), and McNamee (2002).

Exhibit 10.1 Walgreen Co. and Subsidiaries Consolidated Balance Sheet ($ Millions), Years Ended August 31, 2007, 2006, and 2005

	2007	2006	2005
Cash, and cash equivalents	254.8	919.9	576.8
Short-term investments – available for sale	-	415.1	494.8
Accounts receivable, net	2,236.5	2,062.7	1,396.3
Inventories	6,790.5	6,050.4	5,592.7
Other current assets	228.7	257.3	255.9
Total current assets	9,510.5	9,705.4	8,316.5
Property, plant, and equipment, gross	10,976.5	9,287.0	8,150.2
Less accumulated depreciation and amortization	(2,776.6)	(2,338.1)	(1,985.2)
Property, plant, and equipment, net	8,199.9	6,948.9	6,165.0
Goodwill	1,060.2	168.4	10.3
Other noncurrent assets	543.0	308.4	117.0
Total assets	19,313.6	17,131.1	14,608.8
Short-term borrowings	878.5	-	-
Trade accounts payable	3,733.3	4,039.2	2,918.2
Accrued expenses and other liabilities	2,104.4	1,713.3	1,491.9
Income taxes	28.1	2.8	70.9
Total current liabilities	6,744.3	5,755.3	4,481.0
Deferred income taxes	158.2	141.1	240.4
Other non-current liabilities	1,306.8	1,118.9	997.7
Total Non-current Liabilities	1,465.0	1,260.0	1,238.1
Preferred stock, $.0625 par value; authorized 32 million shares; non outstanding	-	-	-
Common stock, $.078125 par value; authorized 3.2 billion shares; issued 1,205,400,000 in 2007, 2006, 2005.	80.1	80.1	80.1
Paid-in capital	558.8	558.5	565.0
Employee stock loan receivable	(51.6)	(70.3)	(76.8)
Retained earnings	12,026.8	10,311.7	8,836.3
Accumulated other comprehensive loss	(3.9)	-	-
Treasury stock at cost, 34,258,643 shares in 2007 17,537,881 shares in 2006, and 11,887,953 shares in 2005.	(1,505.9)	(764.2)	(514.9)
Total Shareholders' Equity	11,104.3	10,115.8	8,889.7
Total Liabilities and Shareholders' Equity	19,313.6	17,131.1	14,608.8

Source: Reprinted with permission from Walgreen Co., Deerfield, IL.

10.1.3 Income Statement

The **income statement** contains information on the operating performance of the firm during some *period of time* (a quarter or a year). In contrast to the balance sheet, which is at a fixed point in time, the income statement indicates the *flow* of sales, expenses, and earnings during a period of time. The income statement for Walgreens for the years 2005, 2006, and 2007 appears in Exhibit 10.2. We concentrate on earnings from operations after tax as the relevant net earnings figure. For Walgreens, this is typically the same as net income because the firm generally has no nonrecurring or unusual income or expense items.

10.1.4 Statement of Cash Flows

Our earlier discussion on valuation indicates that cash flows are a critical input that firms are required to provide. The statement of cash flows integrates the effects on the firm's cash flow of income flows (based on the most recent year's income statement) and changes on the balance sheet (based on the two most recent annual balance sheets). Analysts use these cash flow values to estimate the value of a firm and to evaluate the risk and return of the firm's bonds and stock.

Exhibit 10.2   Walgreen Co. and Subsidiaries Consolidated Statement of Earnings and Shareholders' Equity ($ Millions, Except per Share Data), Years Ended August 31, 2007, 2006, and 2005

	2007	2006	2005
Net sales	53,762.0	47,409.0	42,201.6
Cost of sales	38,518.1	34,240.4	30,413.8
Gross profit	15,243.9	13,168.6	11,787.8
Selling, occupancy, and administrative expense	12,093.2	10,467.1	9,363.8
Operating profit (EBIT)	3,150.7	2,701.5	2,424.0
Interest income, net	38.4	52.6	31.6
Operating income before income taxes	3,189.1	2,754.1	2,455.6
Provision for income taxes	1,147.8	1,003.5	896.1
Reported net income	2,041.3	1,750.6	1,559.5
Reported net income available for common	2,041.3	1,750.6	1,559.5
Net earnings (loss) per share-Basic	2.04	1.73	1.53
Net earnings (loss) per share-Diluted	2.03	1.72	1.52
Average number of common shares outstanding (millions)	998.6	1,010.3	1,019.7
Dilutive effect of stock options (millions)	7.7	9.1	8.7
Average shares outstanding assuming dilution (millions)	1,006.3	1,019.4	1,028.3

Source: Reprinted with permission from Walgreen Co., Deerfield, IL.

The statement of cash flows has three sections: cash flows from operating activities, cash flows from investing activities, and cash flows from financing activities. The total cash flows from the three sections is the net change in the cash position of the firm that should equal the difference in the cash balance between the ending and beginning balance sheets. The statements of cash flow for Walgreens for 2005, 2006, and 2007 appear in Exhibit 10.3.

Cash Flows from Operating Activities   This section of the statement lists the sources and uses of cash that arise from the normal operations of a firm. The net cash flow from operations is computed as the net income reported on the income statement including changes in net working capital items (i.e., receivables, inventories, and so on) plus adjustments for noncash revenues and expenses (such as depreciation), or:

10.1   Cash Flow from Operating Activities=Net Income + Noncash Revenue and Expenses
+ Changes in Net Working Capital Items

Consistent with our previous discussion, the cash account is not included in the calculations of cash flow from operations. Notably, Walgreens has been able to generate consistently large and growing cash flows from operations even after accounting for consistent substantial increases in accounts receivable and inventory required by the firm's growth.

Cash Flows from Investing Activities   A firm makes investments in both its own noncurrent and fixed assets and the equity of other firms (which may be subsidiaries or joint ventures of the parent firm. They are listed in the "investment" account of the balance sheet). Increases and decreases in these noncurrent accounts are considered investment activities. The cash flow from investing activities is the change in gross plant and equipment plus the change in the investment account. The changes are positive if they represent a source of funds (e.g., sale of some plant and/or equipment); otherwise they are negative. The dollar changes in these accounts are computed using the firm's two most recent balance sheets. Most firms (including Walgreens) experience negative cash flows from investments due to significant capital expenditures.

Cash Flows from Financing Activities   Cash inflows are created by increasing notes payable and long-term liability and equity accounts, such as bond and stock issues. Financing uses (outflows) include decreases in such accounts (that is, paying down liability accounts or the

Exhibit 10.3 Walgreen Company and Subsidiaries Consolidated Statements of Cash Flows for the Years Ended August 31, 2007, 2006, and 2005 *(In Millions)*

		2007	2006	2005
Cash Flows from Operating Activities	Net earnings	$ 2,041.3	$ 1,750.6	$ 1,559.5
	Adjustments to reconcile net income to net cash provided by operating activities –			
	Depreciation and amortization	675.9	572.2	482.1
	Deferred income taxes	23.2	(104.0)	(70.8)
	Stock compensation expense	74.2	102.5	—
	Income tax savings from employee stock plans	6.1	8.1	33.9
	Other	3.3	(19.3)	(6.7)
	Changes in operating assets and liabilities –			
	Inventories	(676.2)	(375.7)	(854.0)
	Trade accounts payable	(128.3)	875.6	276.7
	Accounts receivable, net	(40.4)	(618.5)	(224.9)
	Accrued expenses and other liabilities	276.9	204.5	105.3
	Other assets	(28.9)	(8.5)	(78.1)
	Other non-current liabilities	104.3	120.5	143.2
	Income taxes	25.3	(68.4)	5.0
	Net cash provided by operating activities	2,356.7	2,439.6	1,371.2
Cash Flows from Investing Activities	Purchases of short-term investments – available for sale	(6,396.9)	(12.282.4)	(10,742.0)
	Proceeds from sales of short-term investments – available for sale	6,826.0	12,338.4	11,519.9
	Additions to property and equipment	(1,785.3)	(1,337.8)	(1,237.5)
	Proceeds from sale of assets	40.8	23.0	15.5
	Business and intangible asset acquisitions, net of cash received	(1,085.8)	(485.4)	—
	Net proceeds from corporate-owned life insurance policies	5.5	10.7	10.1
	Net cash used for investing activities	(2,395.7)	(1,683.5)	(434.0)
Cash Flows from Financing Activities	Net proceeds from short-term borrowings	850.0	—	—
	Payments of debt	(141.2)	—	—
	Stock purchases	(1,063.5)	(668.8)	(781.8)
	Proceeds related to employee stock plans	266.1	319.1	177.5
	Cash dividends paid	(310.2)	(262.9)	(214.5)
	Bank overdrafts	(213.9)	213.9	—
	Other	(13.4)	(14.3)	14.4
	Net cash used for financing activities	(626.1)	(413.0)	(804.4)
Changes in Cash and Cash Equivalents	Net increase (decrease) in cash and cash equivalents	(665.1)	343.1	132.8
	Cash and cash equivalents at beginning of year	919.9	576.8	444.0
	Cash and cash equivalents at end of year	$ 254.8	$ 919.9	$ 576.8

Source: Reprinted with permission from Walgreen Co., Deerfield, IL.

repurchase of common shares). Dividend payments are a significant financing cash outflow. For Walgreens and for many firms, the repurchase of shares has also been a major financing outflow in recent years.

The total cash flows from operating, investing, and financing activities are the net increase or decrease in the firm's cash. In the case of Walgreens during 2007, it is shown that although the firm had strong cash flow from operations, it experienced an increase in a cash outflow for investments due to asset acquisitions and an outflow from financing caused by heavy share repurchases partially offset by short-term borrowing. The overall effect was a decline in the firm's cash balance. The statement of cash flows provides cash flow detail that is lacking in the balance sheet and income statement.

10.1.5 Measures of Cash Flow

There are several cash flow measures an analyst can use to determine the underlying health of the corporation. You should become familiar with these alternative measures.

Traditional Cash Flow The traditional measure of cash flow equals net income plus depreciation expense and deferred taxes. But as we have just seen, it is also necessary to adjust for changes in operating (current) assets and liabilities that either use or provide cash. These changes can add to or subtract from the cash flow estimated from the traditional measure of cash flow: net income plus noncash expenses.

The table below compares the cash flow from operations figures (Exhibit 10.3) to the traditional cash flow figures for Walgreens from 2005 to 2007.

	Traditional Cash Flow Equals Net Income + Depreciation + Change in Deferred Taxes	Cash Flow from Operations from Statement of Cash Flows
2007	2,734.3	2,356.7
2006	2,223.5	2,439.6
2005	2,007.9	1,371.2

In two of the three years the cash flow from operations was less than the traditional cash flow estimate because of the several adjustments needed to arrive at cash flow from operations. Therefore, using this more exact measure of cash flow for these two years, the Walgreens ratios would not have been as strong. For many firms, this is fairly typical because the effect of working capital changes is often a large negative cash flow due to necessary increases in receivables or inventory to support sales growth (especially for high-growth companies).

Free Cash Flow **Free cash flow** modifies cash flow from operations to recognize that some investing and financing activities are critical to the firm. It is assumed that these expenditures must be made before a firm can use its cash flow for other purposes such as reducing debt outstanding or repurchasing common stock. Two additional items are considered: (1) capital expenditures (an investing expenditure) and (2) the disposition of property and equipment (a divestment source of cash). These two items are used to modify Walgreen Co.'s cash flow from operations as follows (most analysts only subtract net capital expenditures, but conservative analysts also subtract dividends).

	Cash Flow from Operations	−	Capital Expenditures	+	Disposition of Property and Equipment	=	Free Cash Flow
2007	2,356.7	−	1,785.3	+	40.8	=	612.2
2006	2,439.6	−	1,337.8	+	23.0	=	1,124.8
2005	1,371.2	−	1,237.5	+	15.5	=	149.2

For firms involved in leveraged buyouts, this free cash flow number is critical because the new owners typically want to use the firm's free cash flow as funds available for retiring outstanding debt. It is not unusual for a firm's free cash flow to be a negative value. For Walgreens, the free cash flow value has been positive but not large because of significant capital expenditures related to store growth. Notably, this free cash flow value or a variation of it will be used in the subsequent cash flow valuation models.[2]

EBITDA The widely-used EBITDA (earnings before interest, taxes, depreciation, and amortization) measure of cash flow is extremely liberal. This very generous measure of operating earnings does not consider any of the adjustments noted previously. Specifically, it adds back depreciation and amortization (as in the traditional measure) along with both interest expense and taxes, but does not consider the effect of changes in working capital items (such as additions to receivables

[2] As we will show in the next chapter, small modifications of this free cash flow—called free cash flow to equity (FCFE), free cash flow to the firm (FCFF), and net operating profits less applicable taxes (NOPLAT)—are used in valuation models and also the economic value added (EVA) model.

and inventory) or the significant impact of capital expenditures. The following table, which compares this measure to the other three measures of cash flow for Walgreens, demonstrates the large differences among these measures. Notably, because EBITDA does not consider several of these necessary expenditures, it consistently has the highest value among cash flow measures.

Year	EBITDA	Traditional Cash Flow	Cash Flow from Operations	Free Cash Flow
2007	3,826.6	2,734.3	2,356.7	612.2
2006	3,273.7	2,223.5	2,434.6	1,124.8
2005	2,906.1	2,007.9	1,371.2	149.2

Some analysts have used EBITDA as a proxy for cash flow and a metric for valuation similar to earnings—that is, they refer to EBITDA multiples as other analysts would refer to price-earnings (P/E) multiples. Yet given what this measure does not consider, this is a very questionable practice and the authors do *not* recommend using EBITDA.[3]

10.1.6 Purpose of Financial Statement Analysis

Financial statement analysis seeks to evaluate management performance in several important areas, including profitability, efficiency, and risk. Although we will necessarily analyze historical data, the ultimate goal of this analysis is to provide insights that will help us to project *future* management performance, including pro forma balance sheets, income statements, cash flows, and risk. It is the firm's *expected future* performance that determines whether we should lend money to a firm or invest in it.

10.2 Analysis of Financial Ratios

Analysts use financial ratios because numbers in isolation typically convey little meaning. For example, knowing that a firm earned a net income of $100,000 is not very informative unless we also know the sales figure that generated this income ($1 million or $10 million) and the assets or capital committed to the enterprise. Thus, ratios are intended to provide meaningful *relationships* between individual values in the financial statements.

Because the major financial statements report numerous individual items, it is possible to produce a vast number of potential ratios, many of which will have little value. Therefore, we limit our examination to the most relevant ratios and group them into categories that will provide information on important economic characteristics of the firm.

10.2.1 Importance of Relative Financial Ratios

Just as a single number from a financial statement is of little use, an individual financial ratio has little value except in relation to comparable ratios for other entities. That is, *only relative financial ratios are relevant.* Therefore, it is important to compare a firm's performance relative to

- The aggregate economy
- Its industry or industries
- Its major competitors within the industry
- Its past performance (time-series analysis)

The comparison to the aggregate economy is important because almost all firms are influenced by economic fluctuations. For example, it is unreasonable to expect an increase in the profit margin for a firm during a recession; a stable margin might be encouraging under such conditions. In contrast, a small increase in a firm's profit margin during a major business expansion may be a sign of weakness. Thus, this analysis that considers the economic environment helps

---

[3] For a detailed discussion of the problems with using EBITDA, see Greenberg (2000).

investors understand how a firm reacts to the business cycle and should improve an *estimate* of the future performance of the firm during subsequent business cycles.

Probably the most significant comparison relates a firm's performance to that of its industry. Different industries affect the firms within them differently, but this relationship is always significant. The industry effect is strongest for industries with homogeneous products such as steel, rubber, glass, and wood products, because all firms within these industries experience coincidental shifts in demand. In addition, these firms employ fairly similar technology and production processes. As a result, even the best-managed steel firm experiences a decline in sales and profit margins during a recession. In such a case, the relevant question is not whether sales and margins declined, but how bad was the decline relative to other steel firms? In addition, investors should examine an industry's performance relative to the economy to understand how the industry responds to the business cycle, as discussed in Chapter 13.

When comparing a firm's financial ratios to industry ratios, investors may not want to use the average (mean) industry value when there is wide variation among firms in the industry. Alternatively, if we believe that a firm has a unique component, a **cross-sectional analysis** in which we compare the firm to a subset of industry firms comparable in size or characteristics, may be appropriate. As an example, we would compare the performance of Kroger to that of other national food chains rather than regional food chains or specialty food chains.

Another practical problem with comparing a firm to its industry is that many large firms are multi-industry. Inappropriate comparisons can arise when a multi-industry firm is evaluated against the ratios from a single industry. To mitigate this problem, we can use a cross-sectional analysis that compares the firm against a rival that operates in many of the same industries. Alternatively, we can construct composite industry average ratios for the firm. To do this, we use the firm's annual report or 10-K filing to identify each industry in which the firm operates and the proportion of total firm sales and operating earnings derived from each industry. The composite industry ratios would be the weighted-average ratios based on the proportion of firm sales and operating earnings derived from each industry.

Finally, **time-series analysis,** in which we examine a firm's relative performance over time to determine whether it is progressing or declining, is helpful when estimating future performance. Calculating the five or 10 year average of a ratio without considering the time-series trend can result in misleading conclusions. For example, an average rate of return of 10 percent can be the result of rates of return that have increased from 5 percent to 15 percent over time or the result of a series that declined from 15 percent to 5 percent. Obviously, the difference in the trend for these series would have a major impact on our estimate for the future. Ideally, an analyst should examine a firm's time series of *relative* financial ratios compared to its industry and the economy.

10.3 Computation of Financial Ratios

In the following discussion, we divide the financial ratios into five major categories that underscore the important economic characteristics of a firm. The five categories are

1.   Common size statements
2.   Internal liquidity (solvency)
3.   Operating performance
     a.   Operating efficiency
     b.   Operating profitability
4.   Risk analysis
     a.   Business risk
     b.   Financial risk
     c.   External liquidity risk
5.   Growth analysis

10.3.1 Common Size Statements

Common size statements normalize balance sheet and income statement items to allow easier comparison of different sized firms. A common size *balance sheet* expresses all balance sheet accounts as a *percentage of total assets.* A common size *income statement* expresses all income statement items as a *percentage of sales.* Exhibit 10.4 is the common size balance sheet for Walgreens, and Exhibit 10.5 contains the common size income statement. Common size ratios are useful to quickly compare two different sized firms and to examine trends over time within a single firm. Common size statements also give insight into a firm's financial condition, for example, the proportion of liquid assets or the proportion of short-term liabilities, and the percentage of sales consumed by production costs or interest expense. In the case of Walgreens, the common size balance sheet shows a decline in the percent of current assets (due to a significant decline in the cash balance partially offset by an increase in receivables). Alternatively, the common size income statement shows that Walgreen Co.'s cost of goods sold and its selling and administrative expenses were quite stable from 2003 to 2007 in proportion to sales. As a result of this stability, the firm has experienced virtually a constant operating profit margin before and after taxes. The stability of Walgreens wherein it experienced strong growth in sales (over 14 percent a year) *and* a constant profit margin is very impressive.

Exhibit 10.4 Walgreen Co. and Subsidiaries Common Size Balance Sheet ($ Millions), Years Ended August 31, 2003–2007

	2007	2006	2005	2004	2003
Cash, and cash equivalents	1.32%	5.37%	3.95%	3.33%	10.88%
Short-term investments – available for sale	0.00%	2.42%	3.39%	9.38%	0.00%
Accounts receivable, net	11.58%	12.04%	9.56%	8.76%	8.73%
Inventories	35.16%	35.32%	38.28%	35.52%	36.05%
Other current assets	1.18%	1.50%	1.75%	1.21%	1.03%
Total current assets	49.24%	56.65%	56.93%	58.19%	56.70%
Property, plant, and equipment, gross	56.83%	54.21%	55.79%	58.17%	54.58%
Less accumulated depreciation and amortization	−14.38%	−13.65%	−13.59%	−12.35%	−12.20%
Property, plant, and equipment, net	42.46%	40.56%	42.20%	40.82%	42.38%
Goodwill	5.49%	0.98%	0.07%	0.08%	0.09%
Other noncurrent assets	2.81%	1.80%	0.80%	0.91%	0.84%
Total assets	100.00%	100.00%	100.00%	100.00%	100.00%
Short-term borrowings	4.55%	0.00%	0.00%	0.00%	0.00%
Trade accounts payable	19.33%	23.58%	19.98%	19.80%	20.66%
Accrued expenses and other liabilities	10.90%	10.00%	10.21%	10.27%	9.93%
Income taxes	0.15%	0.02%	0.49%	0.49%	0.91%
Total current liabilities	34.92%	33.60%	30.67%	30.56%	31.50%
Deferred income taxes	0.82%	0.82%	1.65%	2.05%	1.55%
Other non-current liabilities	6.77%	6.53%	6.83%	6.37%	5.89%
Total Non-current Liabilities	7.59%	7.36%	8.48%	8.43%	7.44%
Preferred stock, $.0625 par value; authorized 32 million shares; non outstanding	0.00%	0.00%	0.00%	0.00%	0.00%
Common stock, $.078125 par value; authorized 3.2 billion shares; issued 1,205,400,000 in 2007-2005 and 1,024,908,276 in 2004-2003	0.41%	0.47%	0.55%	0.60%	0.69%
Paid-in capital	2.89%	3.26%	3.87%	4.74%	5.99%
Employee stock loan receivable	−0.27%	−0.41%	−0.53%	0.00%	0.00%
Retained earnings	62.27%	60.19%	60.49%	56.24%	54.39%
Accumulated other comprehensive loss	−0.02%	0.00%	0.00%	0.00%	0.00%
Treasury stock at cost, 34,258,643 shares in 2007 17,537,881 shares in 2006, 11,887,953 shares in 2005, and 2,107,263 shares in 2004.	−7.80%	−4.46%	−3.52%	−0.57%	0.00%
Total Shareholders' Equity	57.49%	59.05%	60.85%	61.01%	61.06%
Total Liabilities and Shareholders' Equity	100.00%	100.00%	100.00%	100.00%	100.00%

Source: Information calculated using publicly available data of Walgreen Co. Reprinted with the permission of Walgreen Co.

Exhibit 10.5 Walgreen Co. and Subsidiaries Common Size Statement of Income ($ Millions, Except per Share Data), Years Ended August 31, 2003–2007

	2007	%	2006	%	2005	%	2004	%	2003	%
Net sales	53,762.0	100.00	47,409.0	100.00	42,201.6	100.00	37,508.2	100.00	32,505.4	100.00
Cost of sales	38,518.1	71.65	34,240.4	72.22	30,413.8	72.07	27,310.4	72.81	23,706.2	72.93
Gross profit	15,243.9	28.35	13,168.6	27.78	11,787.8	27.78	10,197.8	27.19	8,799.2	27.07
Selling, occupancy, and administrative expense	12,093.2	22.49	10,467.1	22.08	9,363.8	22.19	8,055.4	21.48	6,938.3	21.35
Operating profit (EBIT)	3,150.7	5.86	2,701.5	5.70	2,424.0	5.74	2,142.4	5.71	1,860.9	5.72
Interest income, Net	38.4	0.07	52.6	0.11	31.6	0.07	17.3	0.05	10.8	0.03
Earning before income tax provision	3,189.1	5.93	2,754.1	5.81	2,455.6	5.82	2,159.7	5.76	1,871.7	5.76
Provision for income taxes	1,147.8	2.13	1,003.5	2.12	896.1	2.12	809.9	2.16	706.6	2.17
Reported net income	2,041.3	3.80	1,750.6	3.69	1,559.5	3.70	1,349.8	3.60	1,165.1	3.58

Source: Information calculated using publicly available data of Walgreen Co. Reprinted with the permission of Walgreen Co.

· ·
10.4 Evaluating Internal Liquidity

Internal liquidity (solvency) ratios are intended to indicate the ability of the firm to meet future short-term financial obligations. They compare near-term financial obligations, such as accounts payable or notes payable, to current assets or cash flows that will be available to meet these obligations.

10.4.1 Internal Liquidity Ratios

Current Ratio Clearly the best-known liquidity measure is the current ratio, which examines the relationship between current assets and current liabilities as follows:

10.2
$$\text{Current Ratio} = \frac{\text{Current Assets}}{\text{Current Liabilities}}$$

For Walgreens, the current ratios (in thousands of dollars) were:

$$2007: \frac{9,510}{6,744} = 1.41$$

$$2006: \frac{9,705}{5,755} = 1.69$$

$$2005: \frac{8,316}{4,481} = 1.86$$

These current ratios experienced a consistent decline during the three years but still are consistent with the typical current ratio. As always, it is important to compare these values with similar figures for the firm's industry and the aggregate market. If the ratios differ from the industry results, we need to determine what might explain it in terms of specific current assets and liabilities. (We will discuss comparative analysis in a later section.)

Quick Ratio Some observers question using total current assets to gauge the ability of a firm to meet its current obligations because inventories and some other current assets might not be very liquid. They prefer the quick ratio, which relates current liabilities to only relatively liquid current assets (cash items and accounts receivable) as follows:

10.3
$$\text{Quick Ratio} = \frac{\text{Cash} + \text{Marketable Securities} + \text{Receivables}}{\text{Current Liabilities}}$$

Walgreen Co.'s quick ratios were

$$2007: \frac{2,491}{6,744} = 0.37$$

$$2006: \frac{3,398}{5,755} = 0.59$$

$$2005: \frac{2,468}{4,481} = 0.55$$

These quick ratios were respectable and declined over the three years mainly due to the lower cash balances discussed earlier. As before, we should compare these values to other firms in the industry and to the aggregate economy.

Cash Ratio The most conservative liquidity ratio is the cash ratio, which relates the firm's cash and short-term marketable securities to its current liabilities as follows:

10.4
$$\text{Cash Ratio} = \frac{\text{Cash and Marketable Securities}}{\text{Current Liabilities}}$$

Walgreens Co.'s cash ratios were

$$2007: \frac{254.8}{6,744.3} = 0.04$$

$$2006: \frac{1,335.0}{5,755.3} = 0.23$$

$$2005: \frac{1,071.6}{4,481.0} = 0.24$$

The cash ratios declined substantially from 2005 to 2007, to where they might be of concern except for the firm's very stable growth of sales and earnings, with significant operating cash flows. In addition, the firm has strong bank lines of credit.

Receivables Turnover In addition to examining total liquid assets, it is useful to analyze the quality (liquidity) of the accounts receivable by calculating how often the firm's receivables turn over, which implies an average collection period. The faster these accounts are paid, the sooner the firm gets the funds to pay off its own current liabilities. Receivables turnover is computed as

10.5 $$\text{Receivable Turnover} = \frac{\text{Net Annual Sales}}{\text{Average Receivables}}$$

The average receivables figure is typically equal to the beginning receivables figure plus the ending value divided by two. Receivables turnover ratios for Walgreens were

$$2007: \frac{53,762}{(2,237 + 2,063)/2} = 25.01 \text{ times}$$

$$2006: \frac{47,409}{(2,063 + 1,396)/2} = 27.41 \text{ times}$$

We cannot compute a turnover value for 2005 because the tables used do not include a beginning receivables figure for 2005 (that is, we lack the ending receivables figure for 2004).

Given these annual receivables turnover figures, the average collection period is

10.6 $$\text{Average Receivable Collection Period} = \frac{365 \text{ Days}}{\text{Annual Receivables Turnover}}$$

For Walgreens,

$$2007: \frac{365}{25.01} = 14.59 \text{ days}$$

$$2006: \frac{365}{27.41} = 13.32 \text{ days}$$

These results indicate that Walgreens currently collects its accounts receivable in about 14 days, on average. To determine whether these account collection numbers are good or bad, it is essential that they be related to the firm's credit policy and to comparable numbers for other firms in the industry. The point is, the receivables collection period value varies dramatically for different firms (e.g., from 10 to over 60), and it is mainly due to the product and the industry. An industry comparison would indicate similar rapid collection periods for other drugstore chains, since most sales are for cash. The reason for a gradual increase in the collection period over several years (since 2000) is that a significant change has occurred in pharmacy sales. Specifically, a growing proportion of pharmacy sales (currently about 92 percent) are now to a third party so they are reimbursed with a lag by a managed-care or insurance company, which has caused the increase in receivables and the collection period.

The receivables turnover is one of the ratios in which a firm *does not want to deviate too much from the norm*. In an industry where the norm is 40 days, a collection period of 80 days would indicate slow-paying customers, which increases the capital tied up in receivables and the possibility of bad debts. Therefore, the firm wants to be somewhat below the norm (for example, 35 days vs. 40 days). At the same time, a figure *substantially below* the norm (e.g., 20 days) might indicate overly stringent credit terms relative to the competition, which could be detrimental to sales in the long-run.

10.4.2 Inventory Turnover

We should also examine the liquidity of inventory based on the firm's inventory turnover (i.e., how many times it is sold during a year) and the implied processing time. Inventory turnover can be calculated relative to sales or cost of goods sold. The preferred turnover ratio is relative to cost of goods sold (CGS), which does not include the profit implied in sales.

10.7
$$\text{Inventory Turnover} = \frac{\text{CGS}}{\text{Average Inventory}}$$

For Walgreens, the inventory turnover ratios were

$$2007: \frac{38,518}{(6,790 + 6,050)/2} = 6.00 \text{ times}$$

$$2006: \frac{34,740}{(6,050 + 5,543)/2} = 5.88 \text{ times}$$

Given these turnover values, we can compute the average inventory processing time as follows:

10.8
$$\text{Average Inventory Processing Period} = \frac{365}{\text{Annual Inventory Turnover}}$$

For Walgreens,

$$2007: \frac{365}{6.00} = 60.8 \text{ days}$$

$$2006: \frac{365}{5.88} = 62.1 \text{ days}$$

Although this seems like a low turnover figure, it is encouraging that the inventory processing period has been very stable. Still, it is essential to examine this turnover ratio relative to an industry norm and/or the firm's prime competition. Notably, this ratio will also be affected by the products carried by the chain—for instance, if a drugstore chain adds high-profit margin items, such as cosmetics and liquor, these products may have a lower turnover.

As with receivables, a firm does not want an extremely low inventory turnover value and long processing time, because this implies that capital is being tied up in inventory and could signal obsolete inventory (especially for firms in the technology sector). Alternatively, an abnormally high inventory turnover and a short processing time could mean inadequate inventory that could lead to outages, backorders, and slow delivery to customers, which would eventually have an adverse effect on sales.

Cash Conversion Cycle A very useful measure of overall internal liquidity is the cash conversion cycle, which combines information from the receivables turnover, the inventory turnover, and the accounts payable turnover. Cash is tied up in assets for a certain number of days. Specifically, cash is committed to receivables for the collection period and in inventory for a number of days—the inventory processing period. At the same time, the firm receives an offset to this capital commitment from its own suppliers who provide interest-free loans to the firm by carrying the firm's payables. Specifically, the payables' payment period is equal to 365 divided by the payables' turnover ratio. In turn, the payables turnover ratio is

10.9 $$\text{Payables Turnover Ratio} = \frac{\text{Cost of Goods Sold}}{\text{Average Trade Payables}}$$

For Walgreens, the payables turnover ratios were

$$2007: \frac{38,518}{(3,733 + 4,039)/2} = 9.91 \text{ times}$$

$$2006: \frac{34,240}{(4,039 + 2,918)/2} = 9.84 \text{ times}$$

10.10 $$\text{Payables Payment Period} = \frac{365 \text{ days}}{\text{Payable Turnover}}$$

$$2007: \frac{365}{9.91} = 36.8 \text{ days}$$

$$2006: \frac{365}{9.84} = 37.1 \text{ days}$$

Therefore, the cash conversion cycle for Walgreens (with components rounded) equals:

Year	Receivables Collection Days	+	Inventory Processing Days	−	Payables Payment Period	=	Cash Conversion Cycle
2007	15	+	61	−	37	=	39 days
2006	13	+	62	−	37	=	38 days

Walgreens has experienced stability in its receivables days and in its inventory processing days and is also consistent in paying its bills. The overall result is stability in its cash conversion cycle. Although the overall cash conversion cycle appears to be quite good (about 38 days), as always we should examine the firm's long-term trend and compare it to other drugstore chains.

10.5 Evaluating Operating Performance

The operating performance ratios can be divided into two subcategories: (1) **operating efficiency ratios** and (2) **operating profitability ratios**. Efficiency ratios examine how the management uses its assets and capital, measured by dollars of sales generated by various asset or capital categories. Profitability ratios analyze the profits as a percentage of sales and as a percentage of the assets and capital employed.

10.5.1 Operating Efficiency Ratios

Total Asset Turnover The total asset turnover ratio indicates the effectiveness of the firm's use of its total asset base (net assets equals gross assets minus depreciation on fixed assets). It is computed as

10.11 $$\text{Total Asset Turnover} = \frac{\text{Net Sales}}{\text{Average Total Net Assets}}$$

Walgreen Co.'s total asset turnover values were

$$2007: \frac{53,762}{(19,314 + 17,131)/2} = 2.95 \text{ times}$$

$$2006: \frac{47,409}{(17,131 + 14,609)/2} = 2.99 \text{ times}$$

This ratio must be compared to that of other firms *within* an industry because it varies substantially between industries. For example, total asset turnover ratios range from less than 1 for large, capital-intensive industries (steel, autos, and heavy manufacturing companies) to over 10 for some retailing or service operations. It also can be affected by the use of leased facilities.

Again, we must consider a *range* of turnover values consistent with the industry. It is poor management to have an exceedingly high asset turnover relative to the industry because this might imply too few assets for the potential business (sales), or it could be due to the use of outdated, fully depreciated assets. It is equally poor management to have an extremely low asset turnover because this implies that the firm is tying up capital in excess assets relative to the needs of the firm and compared with its competitors.

Beyond the analysis of the firm's total asset base, it is insightful to examine the utilization of some specific assets, such as receivables, inventories, and fixed assets. This detailed analysis is especially important if the firm has experienced a major decline in its total asset turnover because we want to know the cause of the decline, that is, which of the component turnovers (receivables, inventory, fixed assets) contributed to the decline. We have already examined the very stable receivables and inventory turnover as part of our liquidity analysis; we now examine the fixed asset turnover ratio.

Net Fixed Asset Turnover   The net fixed asset turnover ratio reflects the firm's utilization of fixed assets.[4] It is computed as

10.12 $$\text{Fixed Asset Turnover} = \frac{\text{Net Sales}}{\text{Average Net Fixed Assets}}$$

Walgreen Co.'s fixed asset turnover ratios were

$$2007: \frac{53,762}{(9,803 + 7,426)/2} = 6.24 \text{ times}$$

$$2006: \frac{47,409}{(7,426 + 6,292)/2} = 6.91 \text{ times}$$

These turnover ratios, which indicate a small decrease for Walgreens during the last few years, must be compared with industry competitors and should consider the impact of leased assets (this is especially significant for retail firms and will be discussed subsequently). Again, an abnormally low turnover implies capital tied up in excessive fixed assets. An abnormally high asset turnover ratio can indicate a lack of productive capacity to meet sales demand, or it might imply the use of an old, fully depreciated plant or equipment that may be obsolete.[5]

Equity Turnover   In addition to specific asset turnover ratios, it is useful to examine the turnover for capital components. An important one, equity turnover, is computed as

10.13 $$\text{Equity Turnover} = \frac{\text{Net Sales}}{\text{Average Equity}}$$

---

[4] When analyzing asset turnover it is important to be aware of intangible assets such as goodwill or patents that can be substantial items. In such cases, analysts will often consider only "tangible" assets or "operating" assets. In the case of Walgreens this is not a problem.

[5] The "DuPont System" section of this chapter contains an analysis of this total asset turnover ratio over a longer term.

Equity includes preferred and common stock, paid-in capital, and total retained earnings.[6] This ratio differs from total asset turnover in that it excludes current liabilities and long-term debt. Therefore, when examining this series, it is very important to consider the firm's capital structure ratios, because the firm can increase (or decrease) its equity turnover ratio by increasing (or decreasing) its proportion of debt capital.

Walgreen Co.'s equity turnover ratios were

$$2007: \frac{53,762}{(11,104 + 10,116)/2} = 5.07 \text{ times}$$

$$2006: \frac{47,409}{(10,116 + 8,890)/2} = 4.99 \text{ times}$$

This ratio has increased slightly during the past several years. In our later analysis of sustainable growth, we examine the variables that affect the equity turnover ratio to understand what variables might cause changes.

Following an analysis of the firm's operating efficiency, the next step is to examine its profitability in relation to its sales and capital.

10.5.2 Operating Profitability Ratios

There are two facets of profitability: (1) the rate of profit on sales (profit margin) and (2) the percentage return on capital employed. The analysis of profitability of sales actually entails several component profit margins that consider various expense categories. These component margins provide important information relative to the final net profit margin. Thus, if we determine that a firm has experienced a significant increase or decrease in its net profit margin, the analysis of the component profit margins will help us to determine the specific causes of the change. Therefore, we will briefly discuss each of the margins but will defer calculations and comments on the trends until we discuss the common size income statement.

Gross Profit Margin Gross profit equals net sales minus the cost of goods sold. The gross profit margin is computed as

10.14
$$\text{Gross Profit Margin} = \frac{\text{Gross Profit}}{\text{Net Sales}}$$

This ratio indicates the basic cost structure of the firm. An analysis of this ratio over time shows the firm's relative cost–price position. As always, we must compare these margins to comparable industry results and to major competitors. Notably, this margin can also be impacted by a change in the firm's product mix toward higher or lower profit margin items.

Operating Profit Margin Operating profit is gross profit minus sales, general, and administrative (SG&A) expenses. It is also referred to as EBIT—earnings before interest and taxes.

10.15
$$\text{Operating Profit Margin} = \frac{\text{Operating Profit}}{\text{Net Sales}}$$

The variability of the operating profit margin over time is a prime indicator of the business risk for a firm. Again, this volatility should be compared to similar ratios for competitors and the industry.

There are two additional deductions from operating profit—interest expense and net foreign exchange loss. After these deductions, we have income before income taxes.

---

[6] Some investors prefer to consider only *owner's* equity, which would not include preferred stock.

Some investors add back to the operating income value (EBIT) the firm's depreciation expense and compute a profit margin that consists of earnings before interest, taxes, depreciation, and amortization (EBITDA). This alternative operating profit margin has been used by some analysts as a proxy for pretax cash flow. As noted earlier, we do *not* recommend the use of this series because it is a biased cash flow estimate.

Net Profit Margin This margin relates after-tax net income to sales. In the case of Walgreens, this is the same as operating income after taxes, because the firm does *not* have any significant nonoperating adjustments. This margin is equal to

10.16
$$\text{Net Profit Margin} = \frac{\text{Net Income}}{\text{Net Sales}}$$

This ratio should be computed using sales and earnings from *continuing* operations, because our analysis seeks to derive insights about *future* expectations. Therefore, we do not consider earnings from discontinued operations, or the gain or loss from the sale of these operations. Likewise, you do not want to include any nonrecurring income or expenses.

Common Size Income Statement As noted earlier, these profit margin ratios are basically included in a common size income statement, which lists all expense and income items as a percentage of sales. This statement provides useful insights regarding the trends in cost figures and profit margins.

Exhibit 10.5 shows a common size statement for Walgreens for 2003–2007. As noted earlier in the chapter when Exhibit 10.5 was presented, the most striking characteristic of the various profit margins for Walgreens (gross, operating, and net) is the *significant stability* in those margins over time. This stability is notable because the firm has experienced a significant growth rate of sales during this period (about 14 percent a year), and it is generally a challenge to control costs when growing rapidly.

Beyond the analysis of earnings on sales, the ultimate measure of management performance is the profits earned on the assets or the capital committed to the enterprise. Several ratios help us evaluate this important relationship.

Return on Total Invested Capital The return on total invested capital ratio (referred to as ROIC) relates the firm's earnings to all the invested capital involved in the enterprise (debt, preferred stock, and common stock). Therefore, the earnings figure used is the net income from continuing operations (before any dividends) *plus* the interest paid on debt. While there might be a tendency to equate total capital with total assets, most analysts differentiate due to the term *invested capital*, which does *not* include non-interest-bearing liabilities such as trade accounts payable, accrued expenses, income taxes payable, and deferred income taxes. In contrast, short-term debt such as bank borrowings and principal payments due on long-term debt are interest bearing and would be included as invested capital. Therefore, the ratio would be:

10.17
$$\text{Return on Total Invested Capital} = \frac{\text{Net Income} + \text{Interest Expense}}{\text{Average Total Invested Capital*}}$$

*Interest bearing debt plus shareholders' equity

Walgreens incurred interest expense for long- and short-term debt. The gross interest expense value used in this ratio differs from the net interest expense item in the income statement, which is measured as gross interest expense minus interest income.[7]

---

[7] Subsequently, in connection with the analysis of financial risk, we discuss why and how to capitalize the operating lease payments that are reported in footnotes. When we do this, we will add this capitalized value to the balance sheet in terms of additional leased assets and also lease obligations along with the implied interest on the leases. At that point, we demonstrate the affect of this on the firm's ROIC and several other financial ratios—mainly financial risk ratios.

Walgreen Co.'s rates of return on total invested capital (ROIC) were

$$2007: \frac{2{,}041 + 0.7}{(13{,}448 + 11{,}235)/2} = 16.55\%$$

$$2006: \frac{1{,}751 + 0.0}{(11{,}235 + 9{,}887)/2} = 16.58\%$$

This ratio indicates the firm's return on all its invested capital. It should be compared with the ratio for other firms in the industry and the economy. For Walgreens, the results are stable, with a small increase during the last several years.

Return on Owner's Equity   The return on owner's equity (ROE) ratio is extremely important to the owner of the enterprise (the common stockholder) because it indicates the rate of return that management has earned on the capital provided by stockholders after accounting for payments to all other capital suppliers. If we consider all equity (including preferred stock), this return would equal

10.18 $$\text{Return on Total Equity} = \frac{\text{Net Income}}{\text{Average Total Equity}}$$

If we are concerned only with owner's equity (the common stockholder's equity), the ratio would be[8]

10.19 $$\text{Return on Owner's Equity} = \frac{\text{Net Income} - \text{Preferred Dividend}}{\text{Average Common Equity}}$$

Walgreens generated return on owner's equity of

$$2007: \frac{2{,}041 - 0}{(11{,}104 + 10{,}116)/2} = 19.24\%$$

$$2006: \frac{1{,}751 - 0}{(10{,}116 + 8{,}860)/2} = 18.42\%$$

This ratio reflects the rate of return on the stockholder's capital. It should be consistent with the firm's overall business risk, but it also should reflect the financial risk assumed by the common stockholder because of the prior claims of the firm's bondholders.

The DuPont System   The importance of ROE as an indicator of performance makes it desirable to divide the ratio into several component ratios that provide insights into the causes of a firm's ROE or any changes in it. This breakdown is generally referred to as the **DuPont System**. First, the return on equity (ROE) ratio can be broken down into two ratios that we have discussed—net profit margin and equity turnover.

10.20 $$\text{ROE} = \frac{\text{Net Income}}{\text{Common Equity}} = \frac{\text{Net Income}}{\text{Net Sales}} \times \frac{\text{Net Sales}}{\text{Common Equity}}$$

This breakdown is an identity because we have both multiplied and divided by net sales. To maintain the identity, the common equity value used is the year-end figure rather than the average of the beginning and ending value.[9] This identity reveals that ROE equals the net profit

---

[8] In the case of Walgreens, return on total equity and return on owner's equity is the same, since there is no preferred stock outstanding (it is authorized but not issued).

[9] The effect of using the year-end equity rather than the average for the year will cause a lower ROE since the equity is generally increasing over time. Two points regarding this difference: First, the conservative bias is generally small—for Walgreens (which is growing fast), the average equity result above for 2007 was 19.24% versus 18.38% using the year-end equity. Second, the important trend results will be evident, along with the component trends that are very important.

margin times the equity turnover, which implies that a firm can improve its return on equity by *either* using its equity more efficiently (increasing its equity turnover) *or* by becoming more profitable (increasing its net profit margin).

As noted previously, a firm's equity turnover is affected by its capital structure. Specifically, a firm can increase its equity turnover by employing a higher proportion of debt capital. We can see this effect by considering the following relationship:

10.21
$$\frac{\text{Net Sales}}{\text{Common Equity}} = \frac{\text{Net Sales}}{\text{Total Assets}} \times \frac{\text{Total Assets}}{\text{Common Equity}}$$

Similar to the prior breakdown, this is an identity because we have both multiplied and divided the equity turnover ratio by total assets. This equation indicates that the equity turnover ratio equals the firm's *total asset turnover* (a measure of efficiency) times the ratio of *total assets to equity* (a measure of financial leverage). Specifically, this financial leverage ratio indicates the proportion of total assets financed with debt. *All assets have to be financed by either equity or some form of debt* (either current liabilities or long-term debt). Therefore, the higher the ratio of assets to equity, the higher the proportion of debt to equity. A total asset–equity ratio of 2, for example, indicates that for every two dollars of assets there is a dollar of equity, which means the firm financed one-half of its assets with equity and the other half with debt. Likewise, a total asset–equity ratio of 3 indicates that only one-third of total assets was financed with equity and two-thirds must have been financed with debt. Thus a firm can increase its equity turnover either by increasing its total asset turnover (becoming more efficient) or by increasing its financial leverage ratio (financing assets with a higher proportion of debt capital). This financial leverage ratio is also referred to as the financial leverage multiplier, because the first two ratios (profit margin times total asset turnover) equal return on total assets (ROTA), and ROTA times the financial leverage multiplier equals ROE.

Combining these two breakdowns, we see that a firm's ROE is composed of three ratios, as follows:

10.22
$$\frac{\text{Net Income}}{\text{Common Equity}} = \frac{\text{Net Income}}{\text{Net Sales}} \times \frac{\text{Net Sales}}{\text{Total Assets}} \times \frac{\text{Total Assets}}{\text{Common Equity}}$$

$$= \frac{\text{Profit}}{\text{Margin}} \times \frac{\text{Total Asset}}{\text{Turnover}} \times \frac{\text{Financial}}{\text{Leverage}}$$

As an example of this important set of relationships, the data in Exhibit 10.6 indicate what has happened to the ROE for Walgreens and the components of its ROE during the 26-year period from 1982 to 2007. As noted, these ratio values employ year-end balance sheet figures (assets and equity) rather than the average of beginning and ending data, so they will differ from our individual ratio computations.

The DuPont results in Exhibit 10.6 indicate several significant trends:

1. The total asset turnover ratio was relatively stable: a total range of 2.77 to 3.31, with a small decline in the ratio to its level in 2007 of 2.78.
2. The profit margin series experienced a consistent increase from 2.75 to its peak value of 3.80 in 2007.
3. The product of the total asset turnover and the net profit margin is equal to return on total assets (ROTA), which experienced an overall increase from 9.09 percent to a peak of 10.94 percent in 2000, followed by a small decline to 10.57 percent in 2007.
4. The financial leverage multiplier (total assets/equity) experienced an overall decline from 2.06 to 1.74. Notably, most of this debt is trade credit, which is non-interest-bearing. The fact is, the firm has almost no interest-bearing debt, except for the long-term leases on drugstores that are not on the formal balance sheet but are discussed and analyzed in the subsequent financial risk section.

Exhibit 10.6 Components of Return on Total Equity for Walgreen Co.[a]

Year	(1) Sales/Total Assets (Times)	(2) Net Profit Margin (Percent)	(3)[b] Return On Total Assets (Percent)	(4) Total Assets/Equity (Times)	(5)[c] Return On Equity (Percent)
1982	3.31	2.75	9.09	2.06	18.73
1983	3.29	2.96	9.72	2.04	19.84
1984	3.26	3.11	10.16	2.03	20.60
1985	3.29	2.98	9.79	2.00	19.58
1986	3.06	2.82	8.62	2.16	18.64
1987	3.14	2.42	7.60	2.19	16.63
1988	3.23	2.64	8.54	2.12	18.12
1989	3.20	2.87	9.18	2.04	18.74
1990	3.16	2.89	9.12	2.02	18.42
1991	3.21	2.90	9.31	1.94	18.04
1992	3.15	2.95	9.30	1.92	17.90
1993	3.27	2.67	8.74	1.84	16.07
1994	3.17	3.05	9.69	1.85	17.91
1995	3.20	3.09	9.86	1.81	17.85
1996	3.24	3.16	10.23	1.78	18.19
1997	3.18	3.26	10.37	1.77	18.35
1998	3.12	3.34	10.42	1.72	17.93
1999	3.02	3.50	10.57	1.70	17.91
2000	2.99	3.66	10.94	1.68	18.35
2001	2.79	3.60	10.03	1.70	17.01
2002	2.90	3.55	10.32	1.59	16.36
2003	2.79	3.58	10.00	1.64	16.37
2004	2.81	3.60	10.11	1.64	16.58
2005	2.89	3.70	10.68	1.64	17.54
2006	2.77	3.69	10.22	1.69	17.31
2007	2.78	3.80	10.57	1.74	18.38

[a]Ratios use year-end data for total assets and common equity rather than averages of the year.
[b]Column (3) is equal to column (1) times column (2).
[c]Column (5) is equal to column (3) times column (4).

Note: When you multiply the three component ratios, this product may not be equal to the ROE based on year-end statements due to the rounding of the three ratios.

5. Finally, as a result of the overall increase in ROTA and a clear decline in financial leverage, the firm's ROE has experienced a very small decline overall, beginning at 18.73 and ending at 18.38.

An Extended Dupont System Beyond the original DuPont system, some analysts have suggested using an extended DuPont system,[10] which provides additional insights into the effect of financial leverage on the firm and also pinpoints the effect of income taxes on the firm's ROE. Because both financial leverage and tax rates have changed dramatically over the past decade, these additional insights are important. The concept and use of the model is the same as the basic DuPont system except for a further breakdown of components.

In the prior presentation, we started with the ROE and divided it into components. In contrast, we now begin with the operating profit margin (EBIT divided by sales) and introduce additional ratios to derive an ROE value. Combining the operating profit margin and the total asset turnover ratio yields the following:

$$\frac{EBIT}{Net\ Sales} \times \frac{Net\ Sales}{Total\ Assets} = \frac{EBIT}{Total\ Assets}$$

[10] The original DuPont system was the three-component breakdown discussed in the prior section. Because this extended analysis also involves the components of ROE, some still refer to it as the DuPont system. In our presentation, we refer to it as the extended DuPont system to differentiate it from the original three-component analysis.

This ratio is the operating profit return on total assets. To consider the negative effects of financial leverage, we examine the effect of interest expense as a percentage of total assets:

$$\frac{\text{EBIT}}{\text{Total Assets}} - \frac{\text{Interest Expense}}{\text{Total Assets}} = \frac{\text{Net Before Tax (NBT)}}{\text{Total Assets}}$$

We consider the positive effect of financial leverage with the financial leverage multiplier as follows:

$$\frac{\text{Net Before Tax (NBT)}}{\text{Total Assets}} \times \frac{\text{Total Assets}}{\text{Common Equity}} = \frac{\text{Net Before Tax (NBT)}}{\text{Common Equity}}$$

This indicates the pretax return on equity. Finally, to arrive at ROE, we must consider the tax-rate effect. We do this by multiplying the pre-tax ROE by a tax-retention rate as follows:

$$\frac{\text{Net Before Tax}}{\text{Common Equity}} \times \left(100\% - \frac{\text{Income Taxes}}{\text{Net Before Tax}}\right) = \frac{\text{Net Income}}{\text{Common Equity}}$$

In summary, we have the following five components:

1. $\dfrac{\text{EBIT}}{\text{Sales}}$ = Operating Profit Margin

2. $\dfrac{\text{Sales}}{\text{Total Assets}}$ = Total Asset Turnover

3. $\dfrac{\text{Interest Expense}}{\text{Total Assets}}$ = Interest Expense Rate

4. $\dfrac{\text{Total Assets}}{\text{Common Equity}}$ = Financial Leverage Multiplier

5. $\left(100\% - \dfrac{\text{Income Taxes}}{\text{Net Before Tax}}\right)$ = Tax Retention Rate

To demonstrate the use of this extended DuPont system, Exhibit 10.7 contains the calculations, using the five components for the years 1982 through 2007. The first column indicates that the firm's operating profit margin peaked in 1985, subsequently declined to a low point in 1990, followed by an increase to a new peak of 5.86 percent in 2007. We know from the prior discussion that the firm's total asset turnover (Column 2) experienced an overall decline to 2.77–2.78 in 2006–2007. The resulting operating profit return on assets declined to a low point in 2001 followed by a partial recovery through 2007. As discussed, because of virtually no interest-bearing debt (except off-balance-sheet leases), Column 4 shows zero negative impact on leverage.

Column 5 reflects the firm's operating performance before the positive impact of financing (the leverage multiplier) and the impact of taxes. These results are often identical to Column 3 due to no debt but can differ due to interest income. Column 6 reflects the steady decline in non-lease financial leverage. As a result of the reduced leverage multiplier, the before-tax ROE in Column 7 has declined since 1984. Column 8 shows the strong positive effect of lower tax rates, which caused a higher tax-retention rate that increased from the mid-50 percent range to the recent 64 percent rate.

In summary, this breakdown helps you to understand *what* happened to a firm's ROE and *why* it happened. The intent is to determine what happened to the firm's internal operating results, what has been the negative and positive effect of its financial leverage policy, and what was the effect of external government tax policy. Although the two breakdowns should provide the same ending value, they typically differ by small amounts because of the rounding of components.

Exhibit 10.7   Extended DuPont System Analysis for Walgreens: 1982–2007[a]

	1	2	3	4	5	6	7	8	9
Year	EBIT/ Sales (Percent)	Sales/ Total Assets (Times)	EBIT/ Total Assets (Percent)[b]	Interest Expense/ Total Assets (Percent)	Net before Tax/ Total Assets (Percent)[c]	Total Assets/ Common Equity (Times)	Net before Tax/ Common Equity (Percent)[d]	Tax Retention Rate	Return on Equity (Percent)[e]
1982	4.32	3.31	14.30	(0.85)	15.15	2.06	31.20	0.60	18.75
1983	5.16	3.29	17.00	0.25	16.75	2.04	34.20	0.56	19.30
1984	5.57	3.26	18.20	(0.24)	18.44	2.03	37.40	0.55	20.65
1985	5.63	3.29	18.50	0.43	18.07	2.00	36.10	0.54	19.57
1986	5.37	3.06	16.40	0.74	15.66	2.16	33.90	0.55	18.63
1987	4.92	3.14	15.50	1.22	14.28	2.19	31.30	0.53	16.69
1988	4.59	3.23	14.80	1.01	13.79	2.12	29.30	0.62	18.10
1989	4.71	3.20	15.10	0.57	14.53	2.04	29.70	0.63	18.79
1990	4.70	3.16	14.90	0.17	14.73	2.02	29.80	0.62	18.52
1991	4.77	3.21	15.30	0.44	14.86	1.94	28.80	0.63	18.00
1992	4.80	3.15	15.10	0.23	14.87	1.92	28.60	0.62	17.87
1993	4.90	3.31	16.20	0.26	15.94	1.82	29.00	0.61	17.80
1994	4.93	3.21	15.90	(0.10)	16.00	1.83	29.20	0.62	17.96
1995	5.00	3.20	15.99	0.04	15.95	1.81	28.90	0.61	17.70
1996	5.13	3.24	16.62	0.06	16.56	1.78	29.50	0.61	18.07
1997	5.30	3.18	16.85	0.05	16.80	1.77	29.74	0.61	18.14
1998	5.46	3.12	17.04	0.02	17.02	1.72	29.28	0.61	17.93
1999	5.69	3.02	17.19	0.00	17.19	1.70	29.22	0.61	17.83
2000	5.77	2.99	17.25	0.00	17.25	1.68	28.98	0.61	17.78
2001	5.68	2.79	15.84	0.00	16.11	1.70	27.33	0.62	17.07
2002	5.66	2.90	16.57	0.00	16.57	1.62	26.28	0.62	16.36
2003	5.69	2.79	15.71	0.00	16.20	1.62	26.25	0.62	16.34
2004	5.67	2.81	15.94	0.00	16.31	1.62	26.45	0.62	16.53
2005	5.74	2.89	16.59	0.00	16.81	1.64	27.67	0.64	17.54
2006	5.70	2.77	15.77	0.00	16.08	1.69	27.23	0.64	17.31
2007	5.86	2.78	16.31	0.00	16.51	1.74	28.72	0.64	18.38

[a]The percents in this table may not be the same as in Exhibit 10.6 due to rounding.
[b]Column 3 is equal to Column 1 times Column 2.
[c]Column 5 is equal to Column 3 minus Column 4.
[d]Column 7 is equal to Column 5 times Column 6.
[e]Column 9 is equal to Column 7 times Column 8.

10.6 Risk Analysis

Risk analysis examines the uncertainty of income flows for the total firm and for the individual sources of capital (that is, debt, preferred stock, and common stock). The typical approach examines the major factors that cause a firm's income flows to vary. More volatile income flows mean greater risk (uncertainty) facing the investor.

The total risk of the firm has two internal components: business risk and financial risk. We first discuss the concept of business risk: how to measure it, what causes it, and how to measure its individual causes. Then we consider financial risk and the several ratios by which we measure it. Following this analysis of a firm's internal risk factors, we discuss an important external risk factor, external liquidity risk—that is, the ability to buy or sell the firm's stock in the secondary equity market.

10.6.1 Business Risk

Recall that **business risk**[11] is the uncertainty of operating income caused by the firm's industry. In turn, this uncertainty is due to the firm's variability of operating earnings caused by

[11] For further discussion of this topic, see Brigham and Gapenski (2006), Chapters 6 and 10.

its products, customers, and the way it produces its products. Specifically, a firm's operating earnings vary over time and its business risk is measured by the volatility of the firm's operating income over time, which is due to two factors: (1) the volatility of the firm's sales over time, and (2) how the firm produces its products in terms of its mix of fixed and variable costs—that is, its operating leverage. Specifically, a firm's operating earnings vary over time because its sales and production costs vary. As an example, the earnings for a steel firm will probably vary more than those of a grocery chain because (1) over the business cycle, steel sales are more volatile than grocery sales; and (2) the steel firm's large fixed production costs (high operating leverage) make its earnings vary more than its sales.

Business risk is generally measured by the variability of the firm's operating income over time determined by the standard deviation of the historical operating earnings series. You will recall from Chapter 1 that the standard deviation is influenced by the size of the numbers, so investors standardize this measure of volatility by dividing it by the mean value for the series (i.e., the average operating earnings). The resulting ratio of the standard deviation of operating earnings divided by the average operating earnings is the coefficient of variation (CV) of operating earnings:

$$\text{Business Risk} = f(\text{Coefficient of Variation of Operating Earnings})$$

$$= \frac{\text{Standard Deviation of Operating Earnings (OE)}}{\text{Mean Operating Earnings}}$$

$$= \frac{\sqrt{\sum_{i=1}^{n}(OE_i - \overline{OE})^2/n}}{\sum_{i=1}^{n}OE_i/n}$$

The CV of operating earnings allows comparisons between standardized measures of business risk for firms of different sizes. To compute the CV of operating earnings, you need a minimum of 5 years up to about 10 years. Less than 5 years is not very meaningful, and data more than 10 years old are typically out of date. Besides measuring overall business risk, it is very insightful to examine the two factors that contribute to the variability of operating earnings: sales variability and operating leverage.

Sales Variability Sales variability is the prime determinant of operating earnings variability. In turn, the variability of sales is mainly caused by a firm's industry and is largely outside the control of management. For example, sales for a firm in a cyclical industry, such as automobiles or steel, will be quite volatile over the business cycle compared to sales of a firm in a noncyclical industry, such as retail food or hospital supplies. Like operating earnings, the variability of a firm's sales is typically measured by the CV of sales during the most recent 5 to 10 years. The CV of sales equals the standard deviation of sales divided by the mean sales for the period.

$$\text{Sales Volatility} = f(\text{Coefficient of Variation of Sales})$$

$$= \frac{\sqrt{\sum_{i=1}^{n}(S_i - \overline{S})^2/n}}{\sum_{i=1}^{n}S_i/n}$$

Adjusting Volatility Measures for Growth Besides normalizing the standard deviation of EBIT and sales for size by computing the CV, it is also important to recognize that the standard deviation is measured relative to the mean value for the series—that is, it computes deviations from "expected value." The problem arises for firms that experience significant growth that will create very large deviations from the mean for the series even if it is *constant* growth. The way to avoid this bias due to growth is to measure deviations from the growth path of the series. For details, see Appendix C of this chapter, which demonstrates this adjustment using 10 years of data for Walgreens.

Operating Leverage The variability of a firm's operating earnings also depends on its mixture of production costs. Total production costs of a firm with no *fixed* production costs would vary directly with sales, and operating profits would be a constant proportion of sales. In such an example, the firm's operating profit margin would be constant and its operating profits would have the same relative volatility as its sales. Realistically, firms always have some fixed production costs such as buildings, machinery, or relatively permanent personnel. Fixed production costs cause operating profits to vary more than sales over the business cycle. Specifically, during slow periods, operating profits will decline by a larger percentage than sales, while during an economic expansion, operating profits will increase by a larger percentage than sales.

The employment of fixed production costs is referred to as **operating leverage**. Clearly, greater operating leverage (caused by a higher proportion of fixed production costs) makes the operating earnings series more volatile relative to the sales series (see Lee, Finnerty, and Norton, 2006). This basic relationship between operating profit and sales leads us to measure operating leverage as the average of the annual percentage change in operating earnings relative to the percentage change in sales during a specified period as follows:

$$\text{Operating Leverage} = \frac{\sum_{i=1}^{n} \left| \frac{\%\Delta OE}{\%\Delta S} \right|}{n}$$

We take the absolute value of the percentage changes because the two series can move in opposite directions. The direction of the change is not important, but the relative size of the change is relevant. By implication, the more volatile the operating earnings as compared to the volatility of sales, the greater the firm's operating leverage. Again, Appendix C to this chapter contains an example of this computation for Walgreens.

10.6.2 Financial Risk

Financial risk you will recall, is the additional uncertainty of returns to equity holders due to a firm's use of fixed financial obligation securities. This financial uncertainty is in addition to the firm's business risk. When a firm sells bonds to raise capital, the interest payments on this capital precede the computation of common stock earnings, and these interest payments are fixed contractual obligations. As with operating leverage, during an economic expansion, the net earnings available for common stock after the fixed interest payments will experience a larger percentage increase than operating earnings. In contrast, during a business decline, the earnings available to stockholders will decline by a larger percentage than operating earnings because of these fixed financial costs (i.e., interest payments). Notably, as a firm increases its relative debt financing with fixed contractual obligations, it increases its financial risk and the possibility of default and bankruptcy.

Relationship between Business Risk and Financial Risk A very important point to remember is that *the acceptable level of financial risk for a firm depends on its business risk.* If the firm has low business risk (i.e., stable operating earnings), investors are willing to accept higher financial risk. For example, retail food companies typically have stable operating earnings over time, which implies *low* business risk, and means that investors and bond-rating firms will allow the firms to have *higher* financial risk. In contrast, if a firm is in an industry that is subject to high business risk (i.e., it experiences high sales volatility and it has high operating leverage), such as steel, auto, and airline companies, an investor would *not* want these firms to also have high financial risk. The two risks would compound and the probability of bankruptcy would be substantial.[12]

In our analysis, we employ three sets of financial ratios to measure financial risk, and *all three* sets should be considered. First, there are balance sheet ratios that indicate compared the proportion of capital derived from debt securities to equity capital. Second are ratios that compare the earnings or cash flows available to the required fixed financial charges. Third are ratios that consider the cash flows available and relate these cash flows to the book value of the outstanding debt. Before we discuss and demonstrate these financial risk ratios, it is necessary to consider the topic of operating lease obligations.

Consideration of Lease Obligations   Many firms lease facilities (buildings) and equipment rather than borrow the funds and purchase the assets—it is basically a lease or borrow decision since the lease contract is like a bond obligation. The accounting for the lease obligation depends on the type of lease. If it is a *capital* lease, the value of the asset and the lease obligation is included on the balance sheet as an asset and liability. If it is an *operating* lease, it is noted in the footnotes but is not specifically included on the balance sheet.[13] Because operating leases are a form of financing used extensively by retailers (such as Walgreens, Sears, and McDonald's) and airlines, it is necessary to recognize this obligation, capitalize estimated future lease payments, and include this capitalized lease value on the balance sheet as both an asset and a long-term liability. In the following subsection, we discuss how to do this, and demonstrate the significant impact this adjustment can have on several financial risk ratios.

Capitalizing Operating Leases   Capitalizing leases basically involves an estimate of the present value of a firm's future required lease payments. Therefore, an analyst must estimate: (1) an appropriate discount rate (typically the firm's long-term debt rate) and (2) the firm's future lease payment obligations as specified in a footnote.

An estimate of the discounted value of the future lease payments can be done one of two ways: (1) a multiple of the forthcoming minimum lease payments or (2) the discounted value of the future lease payments provided in the annual report at the firm's cost of long-term debt. The traditional multiple technique multiplies the minimum lease payment in year $t + 1$ by 8. In the case of Walgreens, the future minimum lease payments in the annual report for the year 2007 are as follows:

Years Relating to Year-End	1	2	3	4	5	Later
Minimum Payments ($ millions)	1,647.3	1,723.5	1,711.3	1,687.7	1,661.7	20,704.4

Given these data, the estimate using the multiple technique would produce an estimate of $8 \times \$1,647.3$ million $= \$13.18$ billion. To *derive* an estimate using the discounted value technique, we need to estimate the firm's cost of long-term debt and consider how to handle the lump-sum later payments. Our debt rate estimate is 7.00 percent, which is consistent with the prevailing interest rate on 20-year, A-rated corporate bonds, which is conservative for Walgreens (as of August 31, 2007, the long-term debt rating was Aa3 by Moody's and A+ by Standard & Poor's). For the later lump-sum payment, we need to derive a reasonable estimate regarding how many years to assume for this payout. A liberal assumption is that the lump-sum payment is spread evenly over 15 years, based on the standard building lease for Walgreens of 20 years ($20,704.4/15 = 1,380$ million per year). An alternative estimate of the spread period is derived

[12] Support for this specific relationship is found in a set of tables (see Standard & Poor, 2002, p. 57) that suggest specific required financial risk ratios necessary for a firm to be considered for a specific bond rating. The required ratios differ on the basis of the perceived business risk of the firm.
[13] A discussion of the technical factors that will cause a lease to be capital versus operating is beyond the scope of this book, but it is covered in most intermediate accounting texts.

by dividing the lump-sum payment in the "later" period by the $t + 5$ payment, which implies a time estimate ($20,704.4/1,661.7 = 12.46$). If we round this down to 12 years, we have an annual payment of $20,704.4/12 = 1,725$ million per year for 12 years.

If we discount at 7.00 percent all the annual flows and the "later" flows over 15 years, we derive an estimate of the lease debt of $15.88 *billion*. A similar computation using the 12-year spread indicates an estimate of lease debt of $16.68 *billion*. Therefore, we have the following three estimates:[14]

8 times the $t + 1$ lease payment	$13.18 billion
Discounting the lease payments assuming a 15-year spread	$15.88 billion
Discounting the lease payments assuming a 12-year spread	$16.68 billion

We will use the $15.88 billion discounted lease payment estimate since this estimate is midway between the liberal multiple method and the conservative discounting method that assumes a 12-year spread. If we add this amount (or that estimated by the other methods) to both fixed assets and long-term debt we will have a better measure of the assets utilized by the firm and the complete funding of the assets (recognition of substantially more debt).

Implied Interest for Leased Assets When computing the return on total capital (ROTC) that considers these leased assets, we must also add the implied interest expense for the leases. The interest expense component of a lease is typically estimated by bond-rating agencies and many other analysts as equal to one-third of the lease payment in year $t + 1$ (in our example, $1,647 million/3 = \$549$ million).

An alternative to this rule of thumb would be to derive a specific estimate based on an estimate of the firm's cost of debt capital (7.00 percent) and the estimate of the present value (PV) of the lease obligation, as follows:

Estimating Technique	PV of Lease Obligation ($ Billion)	Interest Expense at 7.00 Percent ($ Million)
8 times estimate of $t+1$ payment	13.18	923
PV with 15-year spread	15.88	1,112
PV with 12-year spread	16.68	1,168

Notably, all of these estimates of the implied interest expense are substantially higher than the one-third rule-of-thumb estimate of $549 million. Again, the rule of thumb underestimates the financial leverage related to these lease obligations.

To calculate the ROTC for 2006 and 2007, we need to compute the value of the lease obligations and the implied interest expense for the three years (2005, 2006, and 2007) as follows:

Year	Estimate of PV of Lease Obligation[a] ($ Billion)	Estimate of Interest Component of Lease[b] ($ Million)
2007	15.88	1,112
2006	14.40	1,008
2005	13.13	919

[a]See calculations in Appendix B.
[b]Equal to 0.07 of the PV of lease obligation.

Adding these values to the prior ratios results in the following lease-adjusted return on total invested capital (ROIC) values:

$$2007: \frac{2,041 + 0.7 + 1,112}{(32,775 + 25,635)/2} = 10.80\%$$

[14] Notably, the "8 times" estimate almost always provides the lowest estimate of debt value, which means that this rule of thumb will tend to underestimate the financial leverage for these firms and the resulting implied interest expense. As noted, we have opted to use the discounted value of future lease payments, assuming a 15-year spread of the later payments. The computations are demonstrated in Appendix A.

$$2006: \frac{1,751 + 0.0 + 1,008}{(25,635 + 23,021)/2} = 11.34\%$$

As shown, the ROICs that include the leased assets and lease debt are lower (about 11 percent versus over 16 percent), but they are still quite reasonable.

Implied Depreciation on Leased Assets Another factor is the implied depreciation expense that would be taken if these were not leased assets. One way to calculate this value is to simply use the typical term of the lease or weighted-average term. In the case of Walgreens, this is reasonably clear since almost all leases are 20-year leases on buildings. However, if the value were not clear, a second alternative would be the average percent of depreciation as a percent of beginning-of-year net fixed assets. In the case of Walgreens, for 2007 this would be

Depreciation (2007) $676 million; Net Fixed Assets at End of 2006: $6,949

This implies a percent of 0.0973 (676/6,949), which is clearly higher than the 5 percent on buildings. Obviously, Walgreens has many assets being depreciated over shorter lives. For these calculations related to leases on buildings, we assume the 20-year life as follows:

Year	Estimate of PV of Lease Obligation ($ Billion)	Estimate of Implied Depreciation Expense of Lease* ($ Million)
2007	15.88	794
2006	14.40	720
2005	13.13	657

*Assumes straight-line depreciation over a 20-year life.

These implied depreciation charges should be included in ratios that include depreciation expenses.

10.6.3 Proportion of Debt (Balance Sheet) Ratios

The proportion of debt ratios indicate what proportion of the firm's capital is derived from debt compared to other sources of capital, such as preferred stock, common stock, and retained earnings. A higher proportion of debt capital compared to equity capital makes earnings more volatile (i.e., more financial leverage) and increases the probability that a firm could default on the debt. Therefore, higher proportion of debt ratios indicate greater financial risk. The following are the major proportion of debt ratios used to measure financial risk.

Debt–Equity Ratio   The debt–equity ratio is

10.23
$$\text{Debt–Equity Ratio} = \frac{\text{Total Long–Term Debt}}{\text{Total Equity}}$$

The debt figure includes all long-term fixed obligations, including subordinated convertible bonds. The equity typically is the book value of equity and includes preferred stock, common stock, and retained earnings. Some analysts prefer to exclude preferred stock and consider only common equity. Total equity is preferable if some of the firms being analyzed have preferred stock.

Notably, debt ratios can be computed *with and without deferred taxes.* Most balance sheets include an accumulated deferred tax figure. There is some controversy regarding whether these deferred taxes should be treated as a liability or as part of permanent capital. Some argue that if the deferred tax has accumulated because of the difference in accelerated and straight-line depreciation, this liability may never be paid. That is, as long as the firm continues to grow and add new assets, this total deferred tax account continues to grow. Alternatively, if the deferred tax account is caused by differences in the recognition of income on long-term contracts, there will be a reversal and this liability must eventually be paid. As suggested by White, Sondhi, and Fried (2003), to resolve this question, the analyst must determine the reason for the deferred tax account and examine its long-term trend. Walgreen Co.'s deferred tax account is because of a depreciation difference and it has typically grown over time.

A second consideration when computing debt ratios is the existence of operating leases. As noted, given a firm like Walgreens with extensive leased facilities, it is necessary to include an estimate of the present value of the lease payments as long-term debt.

To show the effect of these two significant items on the financial risk of Walgreens, we define the ratios to include both of these factors, but they will be broken out to identify the effect of each of the components of total debt. Thus, the debt–equity ratio is

10.24
$$\text{Debt–Equity Ratio} = \frac{\text{Total Long-Term Debt}}{\text{Total Equity}}$$

$$= \frac{\text{Noncurrent Liabilities} + \text{Deferred Taxes} + \text{PV of Lease Obligations}}{\text{Total Equity}}$$

For Walgreens, the debt–equity ratios were

$$2007: \frac{1{,}307 + 158 + 15{,}878}{11{,}104} = \frac{17{,}343}{11{,}104} = 156.2\%$$

$$2006: \frac{1{,}119 + 141 + 14{,}400}{10{,}116} = \frac{15{,}660}{10{,}116} = 154.8\%$$

$$2005: \frac{998 + 240 + 13{,}133}{8{,}890} = \frac{14{,}371}{8{,}890} = 161.7\%$$

These ratios demonstrate the significant impact of including the present value of the lease payments as part of long-term debt—for example, the debt–equity percent for 2007 went from about 13 percent without lease obligations to over 156 percent when capitalized leases are included.

Long-Term Debt–Total Capital Ratio The long-term debt–total capital ratio indicates the proportion of long-term capital derived from long-term debt capital. It is computed as

10.25
$$\text{Long-Term Debt} - \text{Total Capital Ratio} = \frac{\text{Total Long-Term Debt}}{\text{Total Long-Term Capital}}$$

The total long-term debt values are the same as above. The total long-term capital would include all long-term debt, any preferred stock, and total equity. The long-term debt–total capital ratios for Walgreens were

Including Deferred Taxes and Lease Obligations as Long-Term Debt

$$2007: \frac{17{,}343}{17{,}343 + 11{,}104} = 61.0\%$$

$$2006: \frac{15{,}660}{15{,}660 + 10{,}116} = 60.8\%$$

$$2005: \frac{14{,}372}{14{,}372 + 8{,}890} = 61.8\%$$

Again, this ratio, which includes the present value of lease obligations, shows that a significant percent of long-term capital is debt obligations (about 61 percent). This differs substantially from a ratio without the lease obligations.

Total Debt–Total Capital Ratios In many cases, it is useful to compare *total* debt to *total* invested capital. Earlier when we computed return on invested capital, we did not consider non-interest-bearing capital such as accounts payable, accrued expenses, income taxes payable, or deferred taxes (caused by depreciation). In such a case, total debt would be long-term debt (without deferred taxes), which would be other noncurrent liabilities plus capitalized leases. Total capital would be this interest-bearing debt plus shareholders' equity, as follows:

$$\text{Total Debt-Total Capital Ratio} = \frac{\text{Total Interest-Bearing Debt}}{\text{Total Invested Capital}}$$

$$= \frac{\text{Capitalized Leases} + \text{Noncurrent Liabilities}}{\text{Total Interest-Bearing Debt} + \text{Shareholders' Equity}}$$

$$2007: \frac{15,878 + 1,307}{15,878 + 1,307 + 11,104} = \frac{17,185}{28,289} = 60.7\%$$

$$2006: \frac{14,400 + 1,119}{14,400 + 1,119 + 10,116} = \frac{15,519}{25,635} = 60.5\%$$

$$2005: \frac{13,133 + 998}{13,133 + 998 + 8,890} = \frac{14,131}{23,021} = 61.4\%$$

While these adjustments cause the debt percents to be slightly lower, they are still quite high. These ratios confirm the importance of considering the impact of lease obligations on the financial risk of firms like Walgreens that employ lease financing.

10.6.4 Earnings and Cash Flow Coverage Ratios

In addition to ratios that indicate the proportion of debt on the balance sheet, investors are very conscious of ratios that relate the *flow* of earnings or cash flows available to meet the required interest and lease payments. A higher ratio of available earnings or cash flow relative to fixed financial charges indicates lower financial risk.

Interest Coverage Ratio The standard interest coverage ratio is computed as

10.26 $$\text{Interest Coverage} = \frac{\text{Income before Interest and Taxes (EBIT)}}{\text{Debt Interest Charges}}$$

$$= \frac{\text{Net Income} + \text{Income Taxes} + \text{Gross Interest Expense}}{\text{Gross Interest Expense}}$$

This ratio indicates how many times the fixed interest charges are earned, based on the earnings available to pay these expenses.[15] Alternatively, one minus the reciprocal of the interest coverage ratio indicates how far earnings could decline before it would be impossible to pay the interest charges from current earnings. For example, a coverage ratio of 5 means that earnings could decline by 80 percent (1 minus ⅕), and the firm could still pay its fixed financial charges. Again, for firms like Walgreens that have heavy lease obligations, it is necessary to consider the impact of the lease obligations on this ratio because if we only consider Walgreen Co.'s public interest-bearing debt, the interest cost is less than a half-million dollars and the coverage ratio exceeds 3,000 times. In contrast, if we recognize the lease obligations as debt and include the

---

[15] The interest expense for Walgreens other than for leased assets is clearly insignificant (about $200,000), so it is not included in the computations although it is in the formulas to be considered for other firms. It is important to use "gross" interest expense rather than "net" interest expense that equals gross interest expense minus interest income, which is often reported in income statements. The interest income is a component of other income and is included in the net income value.

implied interest on the capitalized leases as computed earlier, the coverage ratio would be restated as follows:

10.27

$$\frac{\text{Fixed Financial}}{\text{Cost Coverage}} = \frac{\text{Net Income} + \text{Income Taxes} + \text{Interest Expense} + \text{Implied Lease Interest}}{\text{Gross Interest Expense} + \text{Implied Lease Interest}}$$

Hence, the fixed financial cost coverage ratios for Walgreens were

$$2007: \frac{2{,}041 + 1{,}148 + 1{,}112}{1{,}112} = \frac{4{,}301}{1{,}112} = 3.87 \text{ times}$$

$$2006: \frac{1{,}751 + 1{,}004 + 1{,}008}{1{,}008} = \frac{3{,}763}{1{,}008} = 3.73 \text{ times}$$

$$2005: \frac{1{,}560 + 896 + 919}{919} = \frac{3{,}375}{919} = 3.67 \text{ times}$$

These fixed financial cost coverage ratios show a substantially different picture than the coverage ratios that do not consider the impact of the lease obligations. Even so, these coverage ratios are not unreasonable for a firm with very low business risk.

The trend of Walgreen Co.'s coverage ratios has been consistent with the overall trend in the proportion of debt ratios. The point is, the proportion of debt ratios and the earnings flow ratios do not always give consistent results because the proportion of debt ratios are not sensitive to changes in earnings or to changes in the interest rates on the debt. For example, if interest rates increase or if the firm replaces old debt with new debt that has a higher interest rate, no change would occur in the proportion of debt ratios, but the interest coverage ratio would decline. Also, the interest coverage ratio is sensitive to an increase or decrease in earnings. Therefore, the results using balance sheet ratios and coverage ratios can differ. Given a difference between the two sets of ratios, we have a strong preference for the earning or cash flow coverage ratios that reflect the ability of the firm to meet its financial obligations.

Alternatives to these earnings coverage ratios are several ratios that relate the cash flow available from operations to either interest expense or total fixed charges.

Cash Flow Coverage Ratio The motivation for this ratio is that a firm's earnings and cash flow typically will differ substantially (these differences have been noted and will be considered in a subsequent section). The cash flow value used is the cash flow from operating activities figure contained in the cash flow statement. As such, it includes depreciation expense, deferred taxes, and the impact of all working capital changes. Again, it is appropriate to specify the ratio in terms of total fixed financial costs including leases, as follows:

10.28   Cash Flow Coverage of Fixed Financial Cost

$$= \frac{\text{Net Cash Flow from Operating Activities} + \text{Interest Expense} + \text{Implied Lease Interest}}{\text{Interest Expense} + \text{Implied Lease Interest}}$$

We use the values given in the cash flow statement, since we are specifically interested in the cash flow effect and again do not include the insignificant interest expense.

The cash flow coverage ratios for Walgreens were:

$$2007: \frac{2{,}357 + 1{,}112}{1{,}112} = 3.12 \text{ times}$$

$$2006: \frac{2{,}440 + 1{,}008}{1{,}008} = 3.42 \text{ times}$$

$$2005: \frac{1{,}371 + 919}{919} = 2.49 \text{ times}$$

While these coverage ratios are not alarming for a firm with very low business risk, it is note-worthy that they were up and down over the past three years.

10.6.5 Cash Flow–Outstanding Debt Ratios

Cash Flow–Long-Term Debt Ratio Several studies have used a ratio that relates cash flow to a firm's outstanding debt. The cash flow–outstanding debt ratios are unique because they relate the *flow* of earnings plus noncash expenses to the *stock* of outstanding debt. These ratios have been significant variables in numerous studies concerned with predicting bankrupt-cies and bond ratings. (These studies are listed in the reference section.) Again, the cash flow figure we use is the cash flow from operating activities. Obviously, the higher the percent of cash flow to long-term debt, the stronger the company—i.e., the lower its financial risk. This ratio would be computed as

$$\frac{\text{Cash Flow}}{\text{Long-Term Debt}} = \frac{\text{Cash Flow from Operating Activities}}{\text{Book Value of Long-Term Debt} + \text{Present Value of Lease Obligations}}$$

10.29

For Walgreens, the ratios were as follows, assuming that deferred taxes are not included, since they are not interest-bearing. Thus, the long-term debt is noncurrent liabilities and the lease obligations:

$$2007: \frac{2,357}{1,307 + 15,878} = 13.7\%$$

$$2006: \frac{2,440}{1,119 + 14,400} = 16.8\%$$

$$2005: \frac{1,371}{998 + 13,133} = 9.7\%$$

Cash Flow–Total Debt Ratio Investors also should consider the relationship of cash flow to *total* debt to check that a firm has not had a significant increase in its short-term borrowing.

10.30 $$\frac{\text{Cash Flow}}{\text{Total Debt}} = \frac{\text{Cash Flow from Operating Activities}}{\text{Total Long-Term Debt} + \text{Interest-Bearing Current Liabilities}}$$

For Walgreens, these ratios are the same as with long-term debt because the firm does not have any interest-bearing short-term debt. When firms do have short-term debt, the percents for this ratio will be lower; how much lower will indicate the amount of short-term borrowing by the firm. As before, it is important to compare these flow ratios with similar ratios for other companies in the industry and with the overall economy to gauge the firm's relative perfor-mance over a period of 5 to 10 years.

Alternative Measures of Cash Flow[16] As noted, many past studies that included a cash flow variable used the traditional measure of cash flow. The requirement that companies must prepare and report the statement of cash flows to stockholders has raised interest in other exact measures of cash flow. The first alternative measure is the *cash flow from operations,* which is taken directly from the statement of cash flows and is the one we have used. A second alternative measure is *free cash flow,* which is a modification of the cash flow from operations—that is, capital expenditures (minus the cash flow from the sale of assets) are also deducted. Finally, some analysts also subtract dividends. The following table summarizes the values for Walgreens derived earlier in the section entitled "Measures of Cash Flow."

---

[16] A list of studies in which financial ratios or cash flow variables are used to predict bankruptcies or bond ratings is included in the reference section.

Year	Traditional Cash Flow	Cash Flow from Operations	Net Cap Exp	FREE CASH FLOW		
				Before Div.	Div.	After Div.
2007	2,734	2,357	1,785	612	310	302
2006	2,224	2,440	1,315	1,125	263	862
2005	2,008	1,371	1,222	149	215	(65)

As shown, Walgreens has strong cash flow from operations even after considering significant working capital requirements. In addition, the firm experiences positive free cash flow before dividends after substantial net capital expenditures necessitated by the firm's growth. Finally, the firm generally has positive free cash flows even after considering a growing dividend payout.

10.6.6 External Market Liquidity Risk

External Market Liquidity Defined In Chapter 1 we discussed external market liquidity as the ability to buy or sell an asset quickly with little price change from a prior transaction assuming no new information. GE and Pfizer are examples of liquid common stocks because investors can sell them quickly with little price change from the prior trade. Investors might be able to sell an illiquid stock quickly, but the price would be significantly different from the prior price. Alternatively, the broker might be able to get a specified price, but it could take several days to do it.

Determinants of External Market Liquidity Investors should know the liquidity characteristics of the securities they currently own or may buy because liquidity can be important if they want to change the composition of their portfolios. Although the major determinants of market liquidity are reflected in market trading data, several internal corporate variables are good proxies for these market variables. The most important determinant of external market liquidity is the number of shares or the dollar value of shares traded (the dollar value adjusts for different price levels). More trading activity indicates a greater probability that one can find someone to take the other side of a desired transaction. A very good measure that is usually available is **trading turnover** (the percentage of outstanding shares traded during a period of time), which indicates relative trading activity. The specific measure of trading turnover is

$$\text{Trading Turnover} = \frac{\text{Number of Shares Traded during the Year}}{\text{Average Number of Shares Outstanding during the Year}}$$

The average shares outstanding is typically estimated as the mean of the shares outstanding (in thousands) at the beginning and end of the fiscal year. For Walgreens, the trading turnover values were:

$$2007: \frac{887,296}{(991.141 + 1,007,862)/2} = \frac{887,296}{999.502} = 89\%$$

$$2006: \frac{812,365}{(1,007,862 + 1,013,512)/2} = \frac{812,365}{1,010,687} = 80\%$$

$$2006: \frac{784,693}{(1,013,512 + 1,023,293)/2} = \frac{784,693}{1,018,403} = 77\%$$

This compares with the average turnover for the NYSE of about 90 percent. Another measure of market liquidity is the bid–ask spread, where a smaller spread indicates greater liquidity. In addition, certain corporate variables are correlated with these trading variables:

1. Total market value of common shares outstanding.
2. Number of security owners.

Numerous studies have shown that the main determinant of the bid–ask spread (besides price) is the dollar value of trading, which is highly correlated with the market value of the outstanding securities.[17]

[17] Studies on this topic were discussed in Chapter 4.

We can estimate the market value of Walgreen Co.'s outstanding stock as the average number of shares outstanding during the year (as computed above) times the average market price for the year (equal to the high price plus the low price divided by 2) as follows:[18]

$$2007: \ 999{,}502 \times \frac{51 + 37}{2} = \$43.98 \text{ billion}$$

$$2006: \ 1{,}010{,}687 \times \frac{49 + 40}{2} = \$44.98 \text{ billion}$$

$$2005: \ 1{,}018{,}403 \times \frac{48 + 36}{2} = \$42.77 \text{ billion}$$

These market values clearly would place Walgreens in the large-cap category, which usually begins at about $5 billion. Walgreens stockholders number 101,000, including more than 650 institutions that own approximately 56 percent of the outstanding stock. These large values for total market value, the number of stockholders, institutional holders, and strong trading turnover indicate a highly liquid market in Walgreens stock, which implies low external liquidity risk.

10.7 Analysis of Growth Potential

10.7.1 Importance of Growth Analysis

The analysis of **sustainable growth potential** examines ratios that indicate how fast a firm should grow. Analysis of a firm's growth potential is important for both lenders and owners. Owners know that the value of the firm depends on its future growth in earnings, cash flow, and dividends. In the following chapter, we discuss various valuation models that are based on alternative cash flows, the investor's required rate of return for the stock, and the firm's expected growth rate of earnings and cash flows.

Creditors also are interested in a firm's growth potential because the firm's future success is the major determinant of its ability to pay obligations, and the firm's future success is influenced by its growth. Some credit analysis ratios measure the book value of a firm's assets relative to its financial obligations, assuming that the firm can sell these assets to pay off the loan in case of default. Selling assets in a forced liquidation will typically yield only about 10 to 15 cents on the dollar. Currently, it is widely recognized that the more relevant analysis is the ability of the firm to pay off its obligations as an ongoing enterprise, which is impacted by its growth potential. This analysis of growth is also relevant to changes of bond ratings.

10.7.2 Determinants of Growth

The growth of business, like the growth on any economic entity, including the aggregate economy, depends on

1. The amount of resources retained and reinvested in the entity
2. The rate of return earned on the reinvested funds

The more a firm reinvests, the greater its potential for growth. Alternatively, for a given level of reinvestment, a firm will grow faster if it earns a higher rate of return on the funds reinvested. Therefore, the growth rate of equity earnings and cash flows is a function of two variables: (1) the percentage of net earnings retained (the firm's retention rate) and (2) the rate of return earned on the firm's equity capital (the firm's ROE), because when earnings are retained they become part of the firm's equity.

[18] These stock prices (which are for the calendar year) are rounded to the nearest whole dollar.

10.31 $g = \text{Percentage of Earnings Retained} \times \text{Return on Equity} = RR \times ROE$

where:

g = potential (i.e., sustainable) growth rate
RR = the retention rate of earnings
ROE = the firm's return on equity

The retention rate is a decision by the board of directors based on the investment opportunities available to the firm. Theory suggests that the firm should retain earnings and reinvest them as long as the expected rate of return on the investment exceeds the firm's cost of capital.

As discussed earlier regarding the DuPont System, a firm's ROE is a function of three components:

- Net profit margin
- Total asset turnover
- Financial leverage (total assets/equity)

Therefore, a firm can increase its ROE by increasing its profit margin, by becoming more efficient (increasing its total asset turnover), or by increasing its financial leverage (and its financial risk). As discussed, investors should examine and estimate each of the components when estimating the ROE for a firm.

The sustainable growth potential analysis for Walgreens begins with the retention rate (RR):

10.32 $\text{Retention Rate} = 1 - \dfrac{\text{Dividends Declared}}{\text{Net Earnings}}$

Walgreens RR figures were

$$2007: \quad 1 - \frac{326.2}{2,041.3} = 0.84$$

$$2006: \quad 1 - \frac{275.2}{1,750.6} = 0.84$$

$$2005: \quad 1 - \frac{226.5}{1,559.5} = 0.85$$

The historical results in Exhibit 10.8 indicate that the retention rate for Walgreens has been relatively stable during the 26-year period. Specifically, it has almost always been in excess of 70 percent, prior to its recent increases to about 84 percent.

Exhibit 10.6 contains the three components of ROE for the period 1982–2007. Exhibit 10.8 contains the two factors that determine a firm's growth potential and the implied growth rate during the past 26 years. Overall, Walgreens experienced a slight decline in its growth potential during the early 1990s, but since 1999 the firm has experienced a potential growth rate of almost 14 percent or above which is very consistent with its actual performance.

Exhibit 10.8 reinforces our understanding of the importance of the firm's ROE. Walgreen Co.'s retention rate was quite stable throughout the period with an increase during the last eight years. Even with this, it has been the firm's ROE that has mainly determined its sustainable growth rate. This analysis indicates that the important consideration is *the long-run outlook for the components of return on equity.* Investors need to *project* changes in each of the components of ROE and employ these projections to estimate an ROE to use in the growth model along with an estimate of the firm's long-run retention rate. We will come back to these concepts on numerous occasions when discussing stock valuation. This detailed analysis of ROE is extremely important for growth companies where the ROEs are notably above average for the economy and, therefore, vulnerable to competition.

Exhibit 10.8 Walgreen Co. Components of Growth and the Implied Sustainable Growth Rate

Year	(1) Retention Rate	(2) Return on Equity[a]	(3)[b] Sustainable Growth Rate
1982	0.72	18.73	13.49
1983	0.74	19.84	14.68
1984	0.74	20.60	15.24
1985	0.71	19.58	13.90
1986	0.70	18.64	13.05
1987	0.68	16.63	11.31
1988	0.71	18.12	12.87
1989	0.73	18.74	13.68
1990	0.72	18.42	13.26
1991	0.71	18.04	12.81
1992	0.71	17.90	12.71
1993	0.67	16.07	10.77
1994	0.70	17.91	12.54
1995	0.69	17.85	12.32
1996	0.71	18.19	12.91
1997	0.73	18.35	13.40
1998	0.75	17.93	13.44
1999	0.79	17.91	14.15
2000	0.82	18.35	15.05
2001	0.84	17.01	14.29
2002	0.85	16.36	13.91
2003	0.86	16.37	14.08
2004	0.86	16.58	14.26
2005	0.85	17.51	15.09
2006	0.84	17.31	14.71
2007	0.84	18.38	15.62

[a]From Exhibit 10.6.
[b]Column (3) is equal to column (1) times column (2).

10.8 Comparative Analysis of Ratios

We have discussed the importance of comparative analysis, but so far we have concentrated on the selection and computation of specific ratios. Exhibit 10.9 contains most of the ratios discussed for Walgreens, the retail drugstore industry (as derived from the *S&P Analysts Handbook*), and the S&P Industrials Index. The three-year comparison should provide some insights, although we typically would want to examine data for a 5- to 10-year period. It was necessary to do the comparison for the period 2004–2006 because industry and market data from Standard and Poor's were not available for 2007 at the time of this writing.

10.8.1 Internal Liquidity

The three basic ratios (current ratio, quick ratio, and cash ratio) provided mixed results regarding liquidity for Walgreens relative to the industry and market. The current ratio is generally above both the industry and the market. The firm's receivables collection period is substantially faster than the S&P Industrials and below the retail drugstore industry. Because the collection period has been fairly steady, the difference is due to the firm's basic credit policy related to third-party payers of prescriptions as noted previously.

Overall, the comparisons indicate reasonably strong internal liquidity. An additional positive liquidity factor is the firm's ability to sell high-grade commercial paper and several major bank credit lines.

10.8.2 Operating Performance

This segment of the analysis considers efficiency ratios (turnovers) and profitability ratios. The major comparison is relative to the industry. Walgreen Co.'s turnover ratios were consistently above those of the retail drugstore industry.

Exhibit 10.9 Summary of Financial Ratios for Walgreens, S&P Retail Drugstores, and the S&P Industrials Index: 2004–2006

	2006			2005			2004		
	Walgreens	Drugstores	S&P Industrials	Walgreens	Drugstores	S&P Industrials	Walgreens	Drugstores	S&P Industrials
Internal Liquidity									
Current Ratio	1.69	1.52	1.48	1.86	1.77	1.32	1.90	1.71	1.20
Quick Ratio	0.64	0.44	1.20	0.61	0.48	1.07	0.74	0.50	1.00
Cash Ratio	0.16	0.10	0.14	0.13	0.15	0.13	0.42	0.18	0.15
Receivables turnover	7.84	19.84	1.80	7.55	24.16	1.99	7.92	22.49	1.85
Average collection period	46.58	18.40	202.35	48.37	15.11	183.88	46.11	16.23	197.02
Working Capital—Sales	0.08	0.08	0.25	0.09	0.09	0.17	0.10	0.10	0.13
Operating Performance									
Total asset turnover	2.77	2.68	0.62	2.89	2.69	0.58	2.81	2.69	0.55
Inventory turnover (sales)	7.84	7.13	10.31	7.55	6.95	11.11	7.92	6.95	11.44
Working capital turnover	12.00	13.09	4.04	11.00	10.62	5.78	10.17	10.19	7.66
Net fixed asset turnover	6.38	5.19	1.12	6.71	5.94	0.99	6.72	5.59	0.88
Equity turnover	4.99	5.58	2.16	4.93	6.03	2.11	4.86	6.15	2.16
Profitability									
Gross profit margin	27.78%	NA	NA	27.93%	NA	NA	27.19%	NA	NA
Operating profit margin	5.70%	8.48%	18.91%	5.74%	9.87%	18.07%	5.71%	9.08%	16.95%
Net profit margin	3.69%	3.45%	8.48%	3.70%	3.49%	7.66%	3.63%	3.40%	6.50%
Return on total capital	14.53%	15.79%	7.64%	14.58%	17.71%	6.79%	13.94%	17.81%	5.67%
Return on owners' equity	17.31%	19.22%	18.36%	17.54%	21.06%	16.17%	16.53%	20.90%	14.03%
Financial risk									
Debt–equity ratio	154.80%	14.39%	98.94%	161.70%	9.19%	90.30%	165.00%	12.57%	100.16%
Long-term debt–long-term capital	60.80%	15.20%	50.61%	61.80%	10.61%	46.86%	62.00%	15.27%	51.82%
Total debt—total capital	60.50%	12.51%	49.71%	61.90%	8.37%	47.41%	61.10%	11.11%	50.00%
Interest coverage	3.73	34.28	5.83	3.67	68.38	6.13	3.50	99.68	6.13
Cash flow—long-term debt	0.17	1.83	0.35	0.10	2.94	0.35	0.11	2.09	0.28
Cash flow—total debt	0.17	1.04	0.23	0.10	2.14	0.23	0.11	1.41	0.19
Growth Analysis									
Retention rate	84.28%	88.63%	39.83%	79.81%	79.76%	59.94%	86.30%	85.04%	78.01%
Return on equity	17.31%	19.22%	18.36%	17.54%	21.06%	16.17%	16.53%	20.90%	14.03%
Total asset turnover	2.77	2.68	0.62	2.89	2.69	0.58	2.81	2.69	0.55
Total asset—equity	1.69	1.92	3.50	1.64	2.32	3.54	1.62	2.16	3.73
Net profit margin	3.69%	3.45%	8.48%	3.70%	3.49%	7.66%	3.63%	3.40%	6.50%
Sustainable growth rate	14.59%	17.03%	7.31%	14.00%	16.80%	9.69%	14.27%	17.78%	10.94%

The comparison of profitability from sales was mixed. Operating profit margins were consistently lower than the industry, but net margins beat the industry performance. The strong profit margin was in spite of the higher growth rate of new stores relative to the competition, and the fact that new stores require 18 to 24 months to reach the firm's "normal" profit rate.

The profit performance related to invested capital was historically strong. The return on total capital (including capitalized leases) for Walgreens was consistently above both the S&P Industrials and the retail drugstore industry. Walgreens likewise always attained higher ROEs than the market but not its industry.

10.8.3 Risk Analysis

Walgreen Co.'s financial risk ratios, measured in terms of proportion of debt, were consistently inferior to those of the industry and the market when both deferred taxes and capitalized leases were included as long-term debt for Walgreens, but it was not possible to do a comparable adjustment of lease obligations for the S&P Industrials or the industry. Such an adjustment would have a significant impact on the industry results. Similarly, the financial risk ratios that use cash flow for Walgreens were below the market and its industry. These comparisons indicate that Walgreens has a fair amount of financial risk, but it is not of major concern because the firm has very low business risk. Notably, there are no specific comparative ratios available for both business and external liquidity risk. (Specifically, the analysis of relative sales and EBIT volatility adjusted for growth as demonstrated in the appendix indicated that the adjusted volatility for Walgreens was very low, indicating low business risk.) Also, the Walgreen stock trading turnover and market value data indicated low external liquidity risk.

10.8.4 Growth Analysis

Walgreens had recently experienced a sustainable growth rate below its industry because of a lower ROE, but substantially above the aggregate market, based on both a higher ROE and a consistently higher retention rate. In sum, Walgreens has adequate liquidity; a good operating record, including a very consistent growth record that implies low business risk; above-average financial risk when we consider the leases on stores; and above-average growth performance relative to the aggregate market. Your success as an investor depends on how well you use these historical numbers to derive meaningful *estimates* of *future* performance for use in a valuation model. As noted previously, everybody is generally aware of the valuation models, so it is the individual who can provide the best *estimates* of relevant valuation variables (including the *rate* of growth and the *duration* of growth) who will experience superior risk-adjusted performance.

10.9 Analysis of Non-U.S. Financial Statements

As we have stressed several times, your portfolio should encompass other economies and markets, numerous global industries, and many foreign firms in these global industries. However, because accounting conventions differ among countries, non-U.S. financial statements will differ from those in this chapter and from what you will see in a typical accounting course. While it is beyond the scope of this text to discuss these alternative accounting conventions in detail, we encourage you to examine the sources in the "Suggested Readings" section entitled *Analysis of International Financial Statements.*

10.10 The Quality of Financial Statements

Analysts sometimes speak of the quality of a firm's earnings or the quality of a firm's balance sheet. In general, **quality financial statements** are a good reflection of reality; accounting tricks and one-time changes are not used to make the firm appear stronger than it really is. Some factors that lead to lower-quality financial statements were mentioned previously when we discussed ratio analysis. Other quality influences are discussed here and in Palepu, Healy, and Bernard (2007, Chapter 3).

10.10.1 Balance Sheet

A high-quality balance sheet typically has limited use of debt or leverage. Therefore, the potential of financial distress resulting from excessive debt is quite low. Little use of debt also implies the firm has unused borrowing capacity, which implies that the firm can draw on that unused capacity to make profitable investments.

A quality balance sheet contains assets with market values greater than their book value. The capability of management and the existence of intangible assets—such as goodwill, trademarks, or patents—will make the market value of the firm's assets exceed their book values. In general, as a result of inflation and historical cost accounting, we might expect the market value of assets to exceed their book values. Overpriced assets on the books occur when a firm has outdated, technologically inferior assets; obsolete inventory; and nonperforming assets such as a bank that has not written off nonperforming loans.

The presence of off-balance-sheet liabilities also harms the quality of a balance sheet. Such liabilities may include joint ventures and loan commitments or guarantees to subsidiaries, which are discussed in Stickney, Brown, and Wahlen (2007, Chapter 6).

10.10.2 Income Statement

High-quality earnings are *repeatable* earnings. For example, they arise from sales to customers who are expected to do repeat business with the firm and from costs that are not artificially low as a result of unusual and short-lived input price reductions. One-time and nonrecurring items—such as accounting changes, mergers, and asset sales—should be ignored when examining earnings. Unexpected exchange rate fluctuations that work in the firm's favor to raise revenues or reduce costs should also be viewed as nonrecurring.

High-quality earnings result from the use of conservative accounting principles that do not result in overstated revenues and understated costs. The closer the earnings are to cash, the higher the quality of the income statement. Suppose a firm sells furniture on credit by allowing customers to make monthly payments. A higher-quality income statement will recognize revenue using the "installment" principle; that is, as the cash is collected each month, in turn, annual sales will reflect only the cash collected from sales during the year. A lower-quality income statement will recognize 100 percent of the revenue at the time of sale, even though payments may stretch well into next year. A detailed discussion of income items is in Stickney, Brown, and Wahlen (2007, Chapter 5).

10.10.3 Footnotes

A word to the wise: **read the footnotes!** The purpose of the footnotes (that have come to include three or more pages in most annual reports) is to provide information on how the firm handles balance sheet and income items. While the footnotes may not reveal everything you should know (e.g., Enron), if you do not read them you cannot hope to be informed. The fact is, many analysts recommend that you should read an annual report *backward,* so that you read the footnotes first!

· ·

10.11 The Value of Financial Statement Analysis

Financial statements, by their nature, are backward-looking. They report the firm's assets, liabilities, and equity as of a certain (past) date; they report a firm's revenues, expenses, or cash flows over some (past) time period. An efficient capital market will have already incorporated this past information into security prices; so it may seem, at first glance, that analysis of a firm's financial statements and ratios is a waste of the analyst's time.

The fact is, the opposite is true. Analysis of financial statements allows the analyst to gain knowledge of a firm's operating and financial strategy and structure. This, in turn, assists the analyst in determining the effects of *future* events on the firm's cash flows. Combining knowledge of the firm's operating and financial leverage, its strategy, and possible macro- and microeconomic scenarios is necessary to determine an appropriate market value for the firm's stock. Combining the analysis of historical data with potential future scenarios allows analysts to evaluate the risks facing the firm and then to develop an expected return and cash flow forecast based on these risks. The final outcome of the process, as future chapters will detail, is the determination of the firm's current intrinsic value based on expected cash flows, which is compared to the stock's current market price to determine your investment decision. The point is, the detailed analysis of the historical results ensures a better estimation of the expected cash flows and an appropriate discount rate which in turn leads to a superior estimate of the intrinsic value of the firm.

10.12 Specific Uses of Financial Ratios

In addition to measuring firm performance and risk, financial ratios have been used in three major areas in investments: (1) stock valuation, (2) assigning credit quality ratings on bonds, and (3) predicting insolvency (bankruptcy) of firms.

10.12.1 Stock Valuation Models

As we will discuss in the following chapter, most valuation models attempt to derive a value based on one of several present value of cash flow models or appropriate relative valuation ratios for a stock. As will be noted, all the valuation models require an estimate of the expected growth rate of earnings, cash flows, or dividends and the required rate of return on the stock. Clearly, financial ratios can help in estimating these critical inputs. The growth rate estimate for earnings, cash flow, or dividends employs the ratios discussed in the potential growth rate section.

When estimating the required rate of return on an investment (i.e., either the cost of equity, *k*, or the weighted average cost of capital, WACC), recall that these estimates depend on the risk premium for the security, which is a function of business risk, financial risk, and liquidity risk. Business risk typically is measured in terms of earnings variability; financial risk is identified by either the debt proportion ratios or the earnings or cash flow ratios. Insights regarding a stock's liquidity risk can be obtained from the external liquidity measures we discussed.

The typical empirical valuation model has examined a cross section of companies and used a multiple regression model that relates one of the relative valuations ratios for the sample firms to some of the following corporate variables (the averages generally consider the past 5 or 10 years).[19]

Financial Ratios

1. Average debt–equity
2. Average interest coverage
3. Average dividend payout
4. Average return on equity
5. Average retention rate
6. Average market price to book value

---

[19] A list of studies in this area appears in the "Suggested Readings" section at the end of the chapter.

7. Average market price to cash flow
8. Average market price to sales

Variability Measures

1. Coefficient of variation of operating earnings
2. Coefficient of variation of sales
3. Coefficient of variation of net income
4. Systematic risk (beta)

Nonratio Variable

1. Average growth rate of earnings and cash flows

An alternative use of these ratios is to act as a filter to derive a subset of stocks to analyze from some total universe of stocks. For example, starting with a universe of 5,000 stocks, you would screen on the basis of consistent growth rates, profitability, and stability to generate a subset of 250 stocks that you would analyze in depth.

10.12.2 Estimating the Ratings on Bonds

As discussed in Chapter 3, three financial services assign credit ratings to bonds on the basis of the issuing company's ability to meet all its obligations related to the bond. An AAA or Aaa rating indicates high quality and almost no chance of default, whereas a C rating indicates the bond is already in default. Numerous studies have used financial ratios to predict the rating to be assigned to a bond.[20] The major financial variables considered in these studies were as follows:

Financial Ratios

1. Long-term debt–total assets
2. Total debt–total capital
3. Net income plus depreciation (cash flow)–long-term senior debt
4. Cash flow–total debt
5. Earnings before interest and taxes (EBIT)–interest expense (fixed charge coverage)
6. Cash flow from operations plus interest–interest expense
7. Market value of stock–par value of bonds
8. Net operating profit–sales
9. Net income–owners' equity (ROE)
10. Net income–total assets (ROA)
11. Working capital–sales
12. Sales–net worth (equity turnover)

Variability Measures

1. Coefficient of variation of sales
2. Coefficient of variation of operating earnings
3. Coefficient of variation of net earnings
4. Coefficient of variation of return on assets

Nonratio Variables

1. Subordination of the issue
2. Size of the firm (total assets)
3. Issue size for alternative bond issues
4. Par value of all publicly traded bonds of the firm

---

[20] A list of studies in this area appears in the "Suggested Readings" section at the end of the chapter.

10.12.3 Predicting Insolvency (Bankruptcy)

Analysts have always been interested in using financial ratios to identify firms that might default on a loan or declare bankruptcy.[21] The typical study examines a sample of firms that have declared bankruptcy against a matched sample of firms in the same industry and of comparable size that have not failed. The analysis involves examining a number of financial ratios expected to reflect declining liquidity for several years prior to the declaration of bankruptcy. The goal is to determine which set of ratios correctly predict that a firm will be in the bankrupt or nonbankrupt group. The better models have typically correctly classified more than 80 percent of the firms one year prior to failure. Some of the financial ratios included in successful models were as follows:

Financial Ratios

1. Cash flow–total debt
2. Cash flow–long-term debt
3. Sales–total assets*
4. Net income–total assets
5. EBIT/total assets*
6. Total debt/total assets
7. Market value of stock–book value of debt*
8. Working capital–total assets*
9. Retained earnings–total assets*
10. Current ratio
11. Working capital–sales

In addition to the several studies that have used financial ratios to predict bond ratings and failures, other studies have also used cash flow variables or a combination of financial ratios and cash flow variables for these predictions, and the results have been quite successful. These studies are listed in the "Suggested Readings" section at the end of the chapter. The five ratios designated by an asterisk (*) are the ratios used in the well-known Altman Z-score model (Altman, 1968).

10.12.4 Limitations of Financial Ratios

We must reinforce an earlier point: you should always consider *relative* financial ratios. In addition, you should be aware of other questions and limitations of financial ratios:

1. Are alternative firms' accounting treatments comparable? As you know from prior accounting courses, there are several generally accepted methods for treating various accounting items, and the alternatives can cause a difference in results for the same event. Therefore, you should check on the accounting treatment of significant items and adjust the values for major differences. Comparability becomes a critical consideration when dealing with non-U.S. firms.
2. How homogeneous is the firm? Many companies have divisions that operate in different industries, which can make it difficult to derive comparable industry ratios.
3. Are the implied results consistent? It is important to develop a total profile of the firm and not depend on only one set of ratios (for example, internal liquidity ratios). As an example, a firm may be having short-term liquidity problems but be very profitable—the profitability will eventually alleviate the short-run liquidity problems.
4. Is the ratio within a reasonable range for the industry? As noted on several occasions, you typically want to consider a *range* of appropriate values for the ratio because a value that is either too high or too low for the industry can be a problem.

---

[21] A list of studies on this topic appears in the "Suggested Readings" section at the end of the chapter.

• • • • SUMMARY • • • •

- The overall purpose of financial statement analysis is to help investors make decisions on investing in a firm's bonds or stock. Financial ratios should be examined relative to the economy, the firm's industry, the firm's main competitors, and the firm's past relative ratios.
- The specific ratios can be divided into four categories, depending on the purpose of the analysis: internal liquidity, operating performance, risk analysis, and growth analysis.
- When analyzing the financial statements for non-U.S. firms, analysts must consider differences in format and in accounting principles that cause different values for specific ratios.

- Three major uses of financial ratios are (1) stock valuation, (2) assigning credit ratings on bonds, and (3) predicting insolvency (bankruptcy).
- A final caveat: you can envision numerous financial ratios to examine almost every possible relationship. The goal is not more ratios, but to limit and group the ratios so you can examine them in a meaningful way. This entails analyzing the ratios over time relative to the economy, the industry, or the past. You should concentrate on deriving better comparisons for a limited number of ratios that provide insights into the questions of interest to you.

• • • • SUGGESTED READINGS • • • •

General

Beaver, William H. *Financial Reporting: An Accounting Revolution.* Englewood Cliffs, NJ: Prentice Hall, 1989.

Bernstein, Leopold A., and John J. Wild. *Financial Statement Analysis: Theory, Application, and Interpretation*, 6th ed. Homewood, IL: Irwin/McGraw-Hill, 1997.

Fridson, Martin, and Fernando Alvarez. *Financial Statement Analysis*, 3rd ed. New York: Wiley, 2002.

Heckel, Kenneth S., and Joshua Livnat. *Cash Flow and Security Analysis*, 2nd ed. Burr Ridge, IL: Business One Irwin, 1996.

Helfert, Erich A. *Techniques of Financial Analysis*, 11th ed. New York: McGraw-Hill, 2002.

Higgins, Robert C. *Analysis of Financial Management*, 5th ed. Chicago: Irwin, 1998.

Peterson, Pamela P., and Frank J. Fabozzi. *Analysis of Financial Statements*. New Hope, PA: Frank J. Fabozzi Associates, 1999.

Analysis of International Financial Statements

Choi, Frederick D. S., Carol Ann Frost, and Gary Meek. *International Accounting*. Englewood Cliffs, NJ: Prentice Hall, 2000.

Iqbal, M. Zafar. *International Accounting: A Global Approach*. Cincinnati: South-Western, 2002.

Rueschhoff, Norlin, and David Strupeck. "Equity Returns: Local GAAP versus US GAAP for Foreign Issuers from Developing Countries," *Journal of International Accounting* 33, no. 3 (Spring 2000).

Saudagaran, Shakrokh. *International Accounting: A User Perspective*. Cincinnati: South-Western, 2001.

Financial Ratios and Stock Valuation Models

Copeland, Tom, Tim Koller, Marc Goedhart, and David Wessels. *Valuation: Measuring and Managing the Value of Companies*, 4th ed. New York: Wiley, 2005.

Damodaran, Aswath. *Damodaran on Valuation*, 2nd ed. New York: Wiley, 2006.

Danielson, M. G. "A Simple Valuation Model and Growth Expectations." *Financial Analysts Journal* 54, no. 3 (May–June 1998).

Farrell, James L. "The Dividend Discount Model: A Primer." *Financial Analysts Journal* 41, no. 6 (November–December 1985).

Kaplan, S. N., and R. S. Ruback. "The Valuation of Cash Flow Forecasts: An Empirical Analysis." *Journal of Finance* 50, no. 4 (September 1995).

Penman, S. H. "The Articulation of Price–Earnings Ratios and Market-to-Book Ratios and the Evaluation of Growth." *Journal of Accounting Research* 34, no. 2 (Spring 1996).

Financial Ratios and Bond Ratings

Cantor, R., and F. Packer. "The Credit Rating Industry." *Journal of Fixed Income* 5, no. 3 (December 1995).

Fisher, Lawrence. "Determinants of Risk Premiums on Corporate Bonds." *Journal of Political Economy* 67, no. 3 (June 1959).

Gentry, James A., David T. Whitford, and Paul Newbold. "Predicting Industrial Bond Ratings with a Probit Model and Funds Flow Components." *Financial Review* 23, no. 3 (August 1988).

Standard and Poor's Corporation. "Corporate Ratings Criteria," 2007.

Zhou, Chunsheng. "Credit Rating and Corporate Defaults." *Journal of Fixed Income* 11, no. 3 (December 2001).

Financial Ratios and Corporate Bankruptcy

Altman, Edward I. "Financial Ratios, Discriminant Analysis, and the Prediction of Corporate Bankruptcy." *Journal of Finance* 23, no. 4 (September 1968).

Altman, Edward I., and Edith Hotchkiss. *Corporate Financial Distress and Bankruptcy*, 3rd ed. New York: Wiley, 2006.

Aziz, A., and G. H. Lawson. "Cash Flow Reporting and Financial Distress Models: Testing of Hypothesis." *Financial Management* 18, no. 1 (Spring 1989).

Beaver, William H. "Financial Ratios as Predictors of Failure." *Empirical Research in Accounting: Selected Studies,* 1966, supplement to vol. 4, *Journal of Accounting Research.*

Beaver, William H. "Market Prices, Financial Ratios, and the Prediction of Failure," *Journal of Accounting Research* 6, no. 2 (Autumn 1968).

Caouette, J. B., E. I. Altman, and P. Narayanan. *Managing Credit Risk.* New York: Wiley, 1998.

De Servigney, Arnaud, and Olivier Renault. *Measuring and Managing Credit Risk.* New York: McGraw-Hill, 2004.

Dumbolena, I. G., and J. M. Shulman. "A Primary Rule of Detecting Bankruptcy: Watch the Cash." *Financial Analysts Journal* 44, no. 5 (September–October 1988).

Gentry, James A., Paul Newbold, and David T. Whitford. "Classifying Bankrupt Firms with Funds Flow Components." *Journal of Accounting Research* 23, no. 1 (Spring 1985).

Gentry, James A., Paul Newbold, and David T. Whitford. "Predicting Bankruptcy: If Cash Flow's Not the Bottom Line, What Is?" *Financial Analysts Journal* 41, no. 5 (September–October 1985).

Gombola, M. F., M. E. Haskins, J. E. Katz, and D. D. Williams. "Cash Flow in Bankruptcy Prediction." *Financial Management* 16, no. 4 (Winter 1987).

Helwege, J., and P. Kleiman. "Understanding High Yield Bond Default Rates." *Journal of Fixed Income* 7, no. 1 (June 1997).

Jonsson, J. G., and M. S. Fridson. "Forecasting Default Rates on High Yield Bonds." *Journal of Fixed Income* 6, no. 1 (June 1996).

Reilly, Frank K. "Using Cash Flows and Financial Ratios to Predict Bankruptcies." In *Analyzing Investment Opportunities in Distressed and Bankrupt Companies.* ed. Thomas A. Bowman. Charlottesville, VA: Institute of Chartered Financial Analysts, 1991.

• • • • QUESTIONS • • • •

1. Discuss briefly two decisions that require the analysis of financial statements.
2. Why do analysts use financial ratios rather than the absolute numbers? Give an example.
3. Besides comparing a company's performance to its total industry, discuss what other comparisons should be considered *within* the industry.
4. How might a jewelry store and a grocery store differ in terms of asset turnover and profit margin? Would you expect their return on total assets to differ assuming equal business risk? Discuss.
5. Describe the components of business risk, and discuss how the components affect the variability of operating earnings (EBIT).
6. Would you expect a steel company or a retail food chain to have greater business risk? Discuss this expectation in terms of the components of business risk.
7. When examining a firm's financial structure, would you be concerned with the firm's business risk? Why or why not?
8. Give an example of how a cash flow ratio might differ from a proportion of debt ratio. Assuming these ratios differ for a firm (for example, the cash flow ratios indicate high financial risk, while the proportion of debt ratio indicates low risk), which ratios would you follow? Justify your choice.
9. Why is the analysis of growth potential important to the common stockholder? Why is it important to the debt investor?
10. Discuss the general factors that determine the rate of growth of *any* economic unit.
11. A firm is earning 24 percent on equity and has low business and financial risk. Discuss why you would expect it to have a high or low retention rate.
12. The Gold Company earned 18 percent on equity, whereas the Blue Company earned only 14 percent on equity. Does this mean that Gold will grow faster than Blue? Explain.
13. In terms of the factors that determine market liquidity, why do investors consider real estate to be a relatively illiquid asset?
14. Discuss some internal company factors that would indicate a firm's market liquidity.
15. Select one of the limitations of ratio analysis and indicate why you believe it is a major concern.

• • • • PROBLEMS • • • •

1. The Shamrock Vegetable Company has the following results.

Net sales	$6,000,000
Net total assets	4,000,000
Depreciation	160,000
Net income	400,000
Long-term debt	2,000,000
Equity	1,160,000
Dividends	160,000

   a. Compute Shamrock's ROE directly. Confirm this using the three components.
   b. Using the ROE computed in part (a), what is the expected sustainable growth rate for Shamrock?
   c. Assuming the firm's net profit margin went to 0.04, what would happen to Shamrock's ROE?
   d. Using the ROE in part (c), what is the expected sustainable growth rate? What if dividends were only $40,000?

2. Three companies have the following results during the recent period.

	K	L	M
Net profit margin	0.04	0.06	0.10
Total assets turnover	2.20	2.00	1.40
Total assets/equity	2.40	2.20	1.50

   a. Derive for each its return on equity based on the three DuPont components.
   b. Given the following earnings and dividends, compute the estimated sustainable growth rate for each firm.

	K	L	M
Earnings/share	2.75	3.00	4.50
Dividends/share	1.25	1.00	1.00

3. Given the following balance sheet, fill in the ratio values for 2010 and discuss how these results compare with both the industry average and prior average performance of Sophie Enterprises.

**SOPHIE ENTERPRISES CONSOLIDATED BALANCE SHEET, YEARS
ENDED DECEMBER 31, 2009 AND 2010**

ASSETS ($ THOUSANDS)	2010	2009
Cash	$ 100	$ 90
Receivables	220	170
Inventories	330	230
Total current assets	650	490
Property, plant, and equipment	1,850	1,650
Depreciation	330	225
Net properties	1,500	1,425
Intangibles	150	150
Total assets	2,300	2,065

LIABILITIES AND SHAREHOLDERS' EQUITY

	2010	2009
Accounts payable	$ 85	$ 105
Short-term bank notes	125	110
Current portion of long-term debt	75	—
Accruals	65	85
Total current liabilities	350	300
Long-term debt	625	540
Deferred taxes	100	80
Preferred stock (10%, $100 par)	150	150
Common stock ($2 par, 100,000 issued)	200	200
Additional paid-in capital	325	325
Retained earnings	550	470
Common shareholders' equity	10,75	995
Total liabilities and shareholders' equity	2,300	2,065

SOPHIE ENTERPRISES CONSOLIDATED STATEMENT OF INCOME, YEARS ENDED DECEMBER 31, 2009 AND 2010 ($ THOUSANDS)

	2010	2009
Net sales	$3,500	$2,990
Cost of goods sold	2,135	1,823
Selling, general, and administrative expenses	1,107	974
Operating profit	258	193
Net interest expense	62	54
Income from operations	195	139
Income taxes	66	47
Net income	129	91
Preferred dividends	15	15
Net income available for common shares	114	76
Dividends declared	40	30

	Sophie (2010)	Sophie's Average	Industry Average
Current ratio	——	2.000	2.200
Quick ratio	——	1.000	1.100
Receivables turnover	——	18.000	18.000
Average collection period	——	20.000	20.000
Total asset turnover	——	1.500	1.400
Inventory turnover	——	11.000	12.500
Fixed-asset turnover	——	2.500	2.400
Equity turnover	——	3.200	3.000
Gross profit margin	——	0.400	0.350
Operating profit margin	——	8.000	7.500
Return on capital	——	0.107	0.120
Return on equity	——	0.118	0.126
Return on common equity	——	0.128	0.135
Debt–equity ratio	——	0.600	0.500
Debt–total capital ratio	——	0.400	0.370
Interest coverage	——	4.000	4.500
Fixed charge coverage	——	3.000	4.000
Cash flow–long-term debt	——	0.400	0.450
Cash flow–total debt	——	0.250	0.300
Retention rate	——	0.350	0.400

4. **CFA EXAMINATION LEVEL I (ADAPTED)** (Question 4 is composed of two parts, for a total of 20 minutes.) The DuPont formula defines the net return on shareholders' equity as a function of the following components:
   - Operating margin
   - Asset turnover
   - Interest burden
   - Financial leverage
   - Income tax rate

   Using *only* the data in the table shown below:
   a. Calculate *each* of the *five* components listed above for 2005 and 2009, and calculate the return on equity (ROE) for 2005 *and* 2009, using all of the *five* components. Show calculations. (15 minutes)
   a. Briefly discuss the impact of the changes in asset turnover *and* financial leverage on the change in ROE from 2005 to 2009. (5 minutes)

	2005	2009
INCOME STATEMENT DATA		
Revenues	$542	$979
Operating income	38	76
Depreciation and amortization	3	9
Interest expense	3	0
Pretax income	32	67
Income taxes	13	37
Net income after tax	19	30

	2005	2009
BALANCE SHEET DATA		
Fixed assets	$ 41	$ 70
Total assets	245	291
Working capital	123	157
Total debt	16	0
Total shareholders' equity	159	220

5. **CFA EXAMINATION LEVEL II** Mike Smith, CFA, an analyst with Blue River Investments, is considering buying a Montrose Cable Company corporate bond. He has collected the following balance sheet and income statement information for Montrose as shown in Exhibit 10.10. He has also calculated the three ratios shown in Exhibit 10.11, which indicate that the bond is currently rated "A" according to the firm's internal bond-rating criteria shown in Exhibit 10.13.

  Smith has decided to consider some off-balance-sheet items in his credit analysis, as shown in Exhibit 10.12. Specifically, Smith wishes to evaluate the impact of each of the off-balance-sheet items on each of the ratios found in Exhibit 10.11.

  a. Calculate the combined effect of the *three* off-balance-sheet items in Exhibit 10.12 on *each* of the following *three* financial ratios shown in Exhibit 10.11.
    i.   EBITDA/interest expense
    ii. Long-term debt/equity
    iii. Current assets/current liabilities (9 minutes)

  The bond is currently trading at a credit premium of 55 basis points. Using the internal bond-rating criteria in Exhibit 10.13, Smith wants to evaluate whether or not the credit yield premium incorporates the effect of the off-balance-sheet items.

  b. State and justify whether or not the current credit yield premium compensates Smith for the credit risk of the bond based on the internal bond-rating criteria found in Exhibit 10.13. (6 minutes)

Exhibit 10.10 Montrose Cable Company Year Ended March 31, 1999 (US$ Thousands)

Balance Sheet

Current assets	$ 4,735
Fixed assets	43,225
Total assets	$47,960
Current liabilities	$ 4,500
Long-term debt	10,000
Total liabilities	$14,500
Shareholders' equity	33,460
Total liabilities and shareholder's equity	$47,960

Income Statement

Revenue	$18,500
Operating and administrative expenses	14,050
Operating income	$ 4,450
Depreciation and amortization	1,675
Interest expense	942
Income before income taxes	$ 1,833
Taxes	641
Net income	$ 1,192

Exhibit 10.11 Selected Ratios and Credit Yield Premium Data for Montrose

EBITDA/interest expense	4.72
Long-term debt/equity	0.30
Current assets/current liabilities	1.05
Credit yield premium over U.S. Treasuries	55 basis points

Exhibit 10.12 Montrose Off-Balance-Sheet Items

- Montrose has guaranteed the long-term debt (principal only) of an unconsolidated affiliate. This obligation has a present value of $995,000.
- Montrose has sold $500,000 of accounts receivable with recourse at a yield of 8 percent.
- Montrose is a lessee in a new noncancelable operating leasing agreement to finance transmission equipment. The discounted present value of the lease payments is $6,144,000 using an interest rate of 10 percent. The annual payment will be $1,000,000.

Exhibit 10.13 Blue River Investments: Internal Bond-Rating Criteria and Credit Yield Premium Data

Bond Rating	Interest Coverage (EBITDA/ interest expense)	Leverage (Long-term debt/equity)	Current Ratio (Current assets/ current liabilities)	Credit Yield Premium over U.S. Treasuries (in basis points)
AA	5.00 to 6.00	0.25 to 0.30	1.15 to 1.25	30 bps
A	4.00 to 5.00	0.30 to 0.40	1.00 to 1.15	50 bps
BBB	3.00 to 4.00	0.40 to 0.50	0.90 to 1.00	100 bps
BB	2.00 to 3.00	0.50 to 0.60	0.75 to 0.90	125 bps

THOMSON ONE | Business School Edition

1. Update the ratio analysis for Walgreens presented in this chapter.
2. In Chapter 7 you made a retail sales stock index using price and share data from Amazon (AMZN), Family Dollar (FDO), J.C. Penney (JCP), Target (TGT), and Wal-Mart (WMT). Now download balance sheet and income statement data into a spreadsheet and sum similar accounting categories to create an industry balance sheet and an industry income statement. Compute the following ratios and compare the performance of Wal-Mart's ratios against the industry ratios:
   a. Current ratio
   b. Inventory turnover
   c. Total asset turnover
   d. Net profit margin
   e. Debt-equity
3. Using common-size financial statements, compare the operating characteristics of a retail firm (Walgreens), a technology firm (Microsoft), and one involved in oil production and distribution (ExxonMobil).
4. Using the firms in Problem 3, compare their returns on equity using DuPont analysis.
5. Find Walgreen Co.'s peers using Thomson One: Business School Edition. Click on "financials" and review the financial ratios of Walgreens and its peers. Comment on the strengths and weaknesses of Walgreens compared to these firms.

APPENDIX: CHAPTER 10

Exhibit 10 A. Computation of Present Value of Lease Payments for Walgreens as of September 1, 2007 (Discount Rate of 7%)

	PRESENT VALUE ASSUMING 15-YEAR SPREAD OF LUMP SUM		PRESENT VALUE ASSUMING 12-YEAR SPREAD OF LUMP SUM	
Year	**Payment $ Mil.**	**Present Value of Payment $ Mil.**	**Payment $ Mil.**	**Present Value of Payment $ Mil.**
2008	1647	1540	1647	1540
2009	1724	1505	1724	1505
2010	1711	1397	1711	1397
2011	1688	1288	1688	1288
2012	1662	1185	1662	1185
2013	1380	920	1725	1150
2014	1380	860	1725	1074
2015	1380	803	1725	1004
2016	1380	751	1725	938
2017	1380	702	1725	877
2018	1380	656	1725	820
2019	1380	613	1725	766
2020	1380	573	1725	716
2021	1380	535	1725	669
2022	1380	500	1725	625
2023	1380	468	1725	584
2024	1380	437	1725	546
2025	1380	408		
2026	1380	382		
2027	1380	357		
Total		$15,878		$16,685

B. Computation of Operating Lease Obligations for Walgreens for 2007, 2006, 2005 (7% Debt Rate, 15-Year Amortization Period)

2007			2006			2005		
Year	**Payment $ Mil.**	**PV of Pmt. $ Mil.**		**Payment $ Mil.**	**PV of Pmt. $ Mil.**		**Payment $ Mil.**	**PV of Pmt. $ Mil.**
2008	1647	1540	2007	1496	1398	2006	1390	1299
2009	1724	1535	2008	1550	1353	2007	1436	1294
2010	1711	1597	2009	1538	1255	2008	1396	1140
2011	1688	1288	2010	1515	1156	2009	1370	1045
2012	1662	1185	2011	1492	1064	2010	1347	960
2013	1380	920	2012	1259	839	2011	1145	763
2014	1380	860	2013	1259	784	2012	1145	713
2015	1380	803	2014	1259	733	2013	1145	666
2016	1380	751	2015	1259	685	2014	1145	623
2017	1380	702	2016	1259	640	2015	1145	582
2018	1380	656	2017	1259	598	2016	1145	544
2019	1380	613	2018	1259	559	2017	1145	508
2020	1380	573	2019	1259	522	2018	1145	475
2021	1380	535	2020	1259	488	2019	1145	444
2022	1380	500	2021	1259	456	2020	1145	415
2023	1380	468	2022	1259	426	2021	1145	388
2024	1380	437	2023	1259	398	2022	1145	362
2025	1380	408	2024	1259	372	2023	1145	339
2026	1380	382	2025	1259	348	2024	1145	317
2027	1380	357	2026	1259	325	2025	1145	296
Totals		$15,878			$14,400			$13,133

Appendix 10C Adjusting Volatility Measure for Growth

C. As indicated in footnote 11, when computing the volatility of sales and/or operating earnings it is important to consider the effect of growth on the volatility of a series. For example, if you are analyzing the sales data for a company that is growing at a constant 15 percent a year and you compute the standard deviation of the series, you will derive a large measure of volatility because the deviations are being measured from the overall mean of the series. Therefore, the firm's sales during the initial years will be substantially below the mean and the firm's sales in the latter years will be substantially above the mean. The way to avoid this problem is to examine the deviations from a growth series that takes account of either linear growth or compound growth, as shown in Exhibit 10C.1. Notably, in all three calculations the variability measures are compared to the mean value for the series to derive a relative measure of volatility. As shown with the Walgreen example for sales in Exhibit 10C.1, the coefficient of variation based on the standard deviation from the mean with no adjustment for growth indicates a significant level of sales volatility (46%), in contrast to the volatility assuming linear growth, where the relative measure of volatility declines to 14 percent. Finally, when you compute the firm's sales deviation from a compound growth curve of 15 percent, the relative volatility is only 4 percent, which indicates fairly low sales volatility when the measurement considers constant compound growth.

The results then we measure the volatility of operating earnings (EBIT) are similar. Specifically, the relative volatility is 50 percent when compared to the overall mean, 14 percent when examined relative to the linear growth curve, and only 6 percent when computed relative to the compound growth curve of almost 20 percent a year. This implies what can be seen in the graphs—the growth rates for sales and operating earnings are fairly high, but they are also quite constant, which means that there is not the uncertainty (risk) implied if the volatility is measured relative to the overall mean.

Measuring Operating Leverage. In addition to examining sales and operating income (EBIT) realtive to its growth curve, we also discussed a specific measure of operating leverage that computes the average of the annual ratios of percent change in EBIT relative to the percent change in sales with the understanding that the higher this average ratio (i.e., the more volatile EBIT is relative to the volatility of sales), the greater the operating leverage caused by fixed operating expenses. Consider that if a firm has only variable operating expense, this ratio should be theoretically equal to unity (1.00). In the case of Walgreens, it is shown in Exhibit 10C.2 that the annual ratio varied from 0.88 to 1.31, 7 of 10 years the ratio exceeded 1.00, and the overall mean of the annual ratios was 1.073, which would be considered a fairly low operating leverage value consistent with Walgreen's overall low business risk as indicated by the low relative volatility of operating earnings.

Exhibit 10C.1 Calculation of Sales and Operating Earnings Volatility for Walgreens from Arithmetic Mean, from Linear Growth Curve, and from a Compound Growth Curve

Walgreens

	1996	1997	1998	1999	2000	2001	2002	2003	2004	2005	2006	2007
Sales	11,778	13,363	15,307	17,839	21,207	24,623	28,681	32,505	37,508	42,202	47,409	53,762
EBIT	604.0	706	835	1,015	1,224	1,398	1,624	1,848	2,143	2,424	2,702	3,151

	1996	1997	1998	1999	2000	2001	2002	2003	2004	2005	2006	2007	
Sales	11,778.0	13,363.0	15,307.0	17,839.0	21,207.0	24,623.0	29,681.0	32,505.0	37,508.0	42,202.0	47,409.0	53,762.0	
Linear	11,778.0	15,594.7	19,411.5	23,228.2	27,044.9	30,861.6	34,678.4	38,495.1	42,311.8	46,128.5	49,945.3	53,762.0	
Constant Growth	11,778.0	13,521.3	15,522.6	17,820.1	20,457.6	23,485.5	26,961.6	30,852.2	35,533.5	40,792.8	46,830.6	53,762.0	1.15
vs. Mean	48%												
	0	4980607	16846547	29043281	34081183	38920584	35968371	35881189	23076669	15417759	6432790	0	
vs. Linear	14%												
	0	25048	46463	359	561594	1203812	2956182	2411040	3898647	1985768	334560	0	
vs. C.G.	4%												

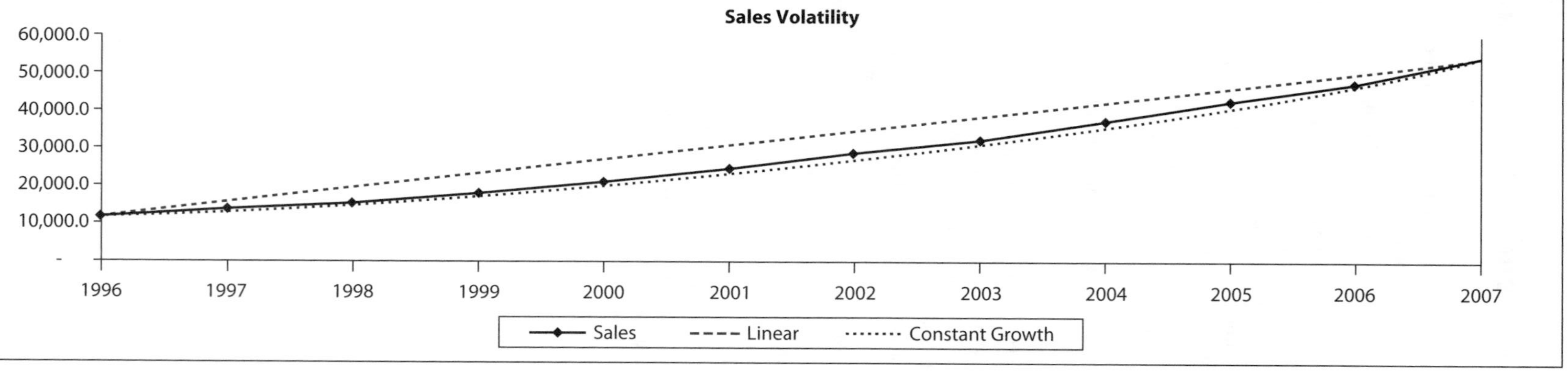

(*Continued*)

Exhibit 10C.1 (continued)

Walgreens

	1996	1997	1998	1999	2000	2001	2002	2003	2004	2005	2006	2007	1.20
EBIT	604.0	708.0	835.0	1,015.0	1,224.0	1,396.0	1,624.0	1,848.0	2,143.0	2,424.0	2,702.0	3,151.0	
Linear	604.0	835.5	1,067.1	1,298.6	1,530.2	1,761.7	1,993.3	2,224.8	2,456.4	2,687.9	2,919.5	3,151.0	
Constant Growth	604.0	701.9	815.6	947.6	1,101.3	1,279.6	1,487.1	1,728.1	2,008.1	2,333.5	2,711.6	3,151.0	
vs. Mean	50%	0	16266	53866	80450	93747	132298	136362	141992	98197	69648	47286	0
vs. Linear	14%	0	38	376	4522	15050	13976	18730	14373	18191	8188	93	0
vs. C.G.	6%												

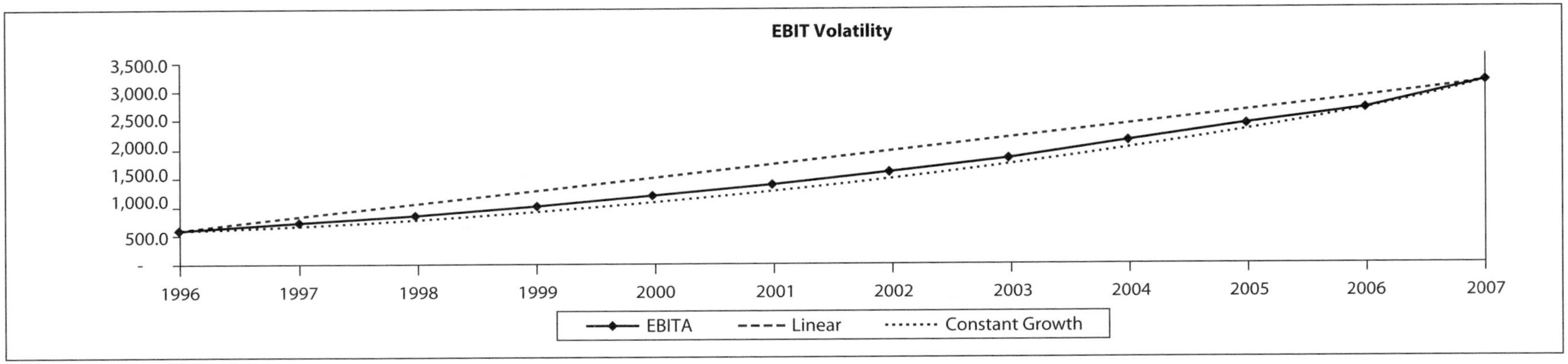

EBIT Volatility

— EBITA   ---- Linear   ⋯⋯ Constant Growth

Exhibit 10 C.2 Calculation of Operating Leverage for Walgreens

	1998	1999	2000	2001	2002	2003	2004	2005	2006	2007
EBIT	835,000	1,015,400	1,224,100	1,398,300	1,624,200	1,848,300	2,142,700	2,424,000	2,701,500	3,150,700
Net sales	15,307,000	17,838,800	21,206,900	24,623,000	28,681,100	32,505,400	37,508,200	42,201,600	47,409,000	53,762,000
	1998	1999	2000	2001	2002	2003	2004	2005	2006	2007
% Change EBIT	17.28%	21.60%	20.55%	14.23%	16.16%	13.80%	15.93%	13.13%	11.45%	16.63%
% change Sales	14.55%	16.54%	18.88%	16.11%	16.48%	13.33%	15.39%	12.51%	12.34%	13.40%
Ratio:										
% change EBIT/ % Change Sales	1.19	1.31	1.09	0.88	0.98	1.03	1.03	1.05	0.93	1.24

Legend:
— % Change EBIT
— % Change Sales

Mean of Annual Operating Leverage Ratios $= \sum\limits_{i-} \dfrac{\% \Delta \text{EBIT}}{\% \Delta \text{Sales}} \Big/ N = \dfrac{10.73}{10} = 1.073$

CHAPTER 11

An Introduction to Security Valuation

After you read this chapter, you should be able to answer the following questions:

- What are the two major approaches to the investment process?
- What are the specifics and logic of the top-down (three-step) approach?
- What empirical evidence supports the usefulness of the top-down approach?
- When valuing an asset, what are the required inputs?
- After you have valued an asset, what is the investment decision process?
- How do you determine the value of bonds?
- How do you determine the value of preferred stock?
- What are the two primary approaches to the valuation of common stock?
- Under what conditions is it best to use the present value of cash flow approach for valuing a company's equity?
- Under what conditions is it best to use the relative valuation techniques for valuing a company's equity?
- How do you apply the discounted cash flow valuation approach, and what are the major discounted cash flow valuation techniques?
- What is the dividend discount model (DDM), and what is its logic?
- What is the effect of the assumptions of the DDM when valuing a growth company?
- How do you apply the DDM to the valuation of a firm that is expected to experience temporary supernormal growth?
- How do you apply the present value of operating cash flow technique?
- How do you apply the present value of free cash flow to equity technique?
- How do you apply the relative valuation approach?
- What are the major relative valuation ratios?
- How can you use the DDM to develop an earnings multiplier model?
- What does the DDM model imply are the factors that determine a stock's *P/E* ratio?
- What two general variables need to be estimated in any valuation approach?
- How do you estimate the major inputs to the stock valuation models: (1) the required rate of return and (2) the expected growth rate of earnings, cash flows, or dividends?
- What additional factors must be considered when estimating the required rate of return and growth rate for a foreign security?

At the start of this book, we defined an investment as a commitment of funds for a period of time to derive a rate of return that would compensate the investor for the time during which the funds are invested, for the expected rate of inflation during the investment horizon, and for the uncertainty involved. From this definition, we know that the first step in making an investment is determining your required rate of return.

Once you have determined this rate, some investment alternatives, such as savings accounts and T-bills, are fairly easy to evaluate because they provide stated cash flows. Most investments have expected cash flows and a stated market price (for example, common stock), and you must estimate a value for the investment to determine if its current market price is consistent with your estimated intrinsic value. You must estimate the intrinsic value of the security based on its expected cash flows and your required rate of return. After you have completed estimating a security's intrinsic value, you compare this estimated intrinsic value to the prevailing market price to decide whether you want to buy the security or not.

This **investment decision process** is similar to the process you follow when deciding on a corporate investment or when shopping for clothes, a stereo, or a car. In each case, you examine the item and decide how much it is worth to you (its value). If the price equals its estimated value or is less, you would buy it. The same technique applies to securities except that the determination of a security's value is more formal.

We start our investigation of security valuation by discussing the **valuation process**. There are two general approaches to the valuation process: (1) the top-down, three-step approach; or (2) the bottom-up, stock valuation, stockpicking approach. Both of these approaches can be implemented by either fundamentalists or technicians. The difference between the two approaches is the perceived importance of the economy and a firm's industry on the valuation of a firm and its stock.

Advocates of the top-down, three-step approach believe that both the economy/market and the industry effect have a significant impact on the total returns for individual stocks. In contrast, those who employ the bottom-up, stockpicking approach contend that it is possible to find stocks that are undervalued relative to their market price, and these stocks will provide superior returns *regardless* of the market and industry outlook.

Both of these approaches have numerous supporters, and advocates of both approaches have been quite successful.[1] In this book, we advocate and present the top-down, three-step approach because of its logic and empirical support. Although we believe that a portfolio manager or an investor can be successful using the bottom-up approach, we believe that it is more difficult to be successful because these stockpickers are ignoring substantial information from an analysis of the outlook for the market and the firm's industry.

Although we know that the value of a security is determined by its quality and profit potential, we also believe that the economic environment and the performance of a firm's industry influence the value of a security and its rate of return. Because of the importance of these economic and industry factors, we present an overview of the valuation process that describes these influences and explains how they can be incorporated into the analysis of a security's value. Subsequently, we describe the theory of value and emphasize the factors that affect the value of individual securities.

Next, we apply these valuation concepts to the valuation of different assets—bonds, preferred stock, and common stock. In this section, we show how the valuation models help investors calculate how much they should pay for these assets. In the final section, we emphasize the estimation of the variables that affect value (the required rate of return and the expected growth rate of cash flows). We conclude with a discussion of additional factors that must be considered when evaluating international securities.

11.1 An Overview of the Valuation Process

Psychologists suggest that the success or failure of an individual can be caused as much by his or her social, economic, and family environment as by genetic gifts. Extending this idea to the valuation of securities means we should consider a firm's economic and industry environment during the valuation process. Regardless of the qualities or capabilities of a firm and its management, the economic and industry environment will have a major influence on the success of a firm and the realized rate of return on its stock.

As an example, assume you own shares of the strongest and most successful firm producing home furnishings. If you own the shares during a strong economic expansion, the sales and earnings of the firm will increase and your rate of return on the stock should be quite high. In

---

[1] For the history and selection process of a legendary stockpicker, see Hagstrom (2001) or Lowenstein (1995).

contrast, if you own the same stock during a major economic recession, the sales, earnings and cash flows of this firm (and probably most or all of the firms in the industry) would likely experience a decline and the price of its stock would be stable or decline. Therefore, when assessing the future value of a security, it is necessary to analyze the outlook for the aggregate economy and the firm's specific industry.

The valuation process is like the chicken-and-egg dilemma. Do you start by analyzing the macroeconomy and various industries before individual stocks, or do you begin with individual securities and gradually combine these firms into industries and the industries into the entire economy? For reasons discussed in the next section, we contend that the discussion should begin with an analysis of aggregate economies and overall securities markets and progress to different industries with a global perspective. Only after a thorough analysis of a global industry are you in a position to properly evaluate the securities issued by individual firms within the better industries. Thus, we recommend a three-step, top-down valuation process in which you first examine the influence of the general economy on all firms and the security markets, then analyze the prospects for alternative global industries in this economic environment, and finally turn to the analysis of individual firms in the alternative industries and to the common stock of these firms. Exhibit 11.1 indicates the procedure recommended.

11.2 Why a Three-Step Valuation Process?

11.2.1 General Economic Influences

Monetary and fiscal policy measures enacted by various agencies of national governments influence the aggregate economies of those countries. The resulting economic conditions influence all industries and companies within the economies.

Exhibit 11.1 Overview of the Investment Process

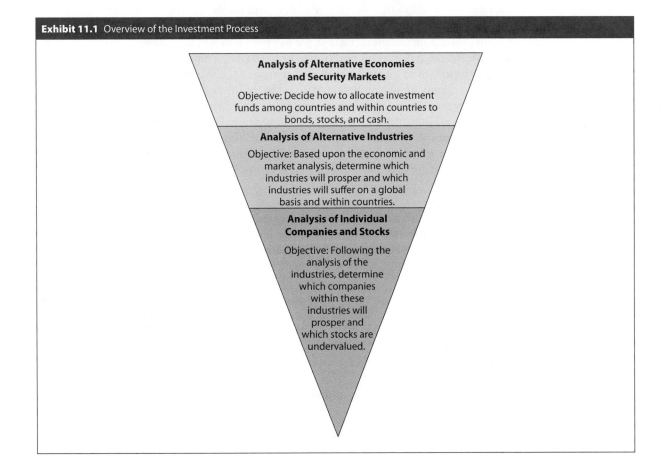

Analysis of Alternative Economies and Security Markets

Objective: Decide how to allocate investment funds among countries and within countries to bonds, stocks, and cash.

Analysis of Alternative Industries

Objective: Based upon the economic and market analysis, determine which industries will prosper and which industries will suffer on a global basis and within countries.

Analysis of Individual Companies and Stocks

Objective: Following the analysis of the industries, determine which companies within these industries will prosper and which stocks are undervalued.

Fiscal policy initiatives, such as tax credits or tax cuts, can encourage spending, whereas additional taxes on income, gasoline, cigarettes, and liquor can discourage spending. Increases or decreases in government spending on defense, on unemployment insurance, retraining programs, or on highways also influence the general economy. These fiscal policies influence the business environment for firms that rely directly on such government expenditures. In addition, we know that government spending has a strong *multiplier effect*. For example, increases in road building increase the demand for earthmoving equipment and concrete materials. As a result, in addition to construction workers, the employees of industries that supply the equipment and materials have more to spend on consumer goods, which raises the demand for consumer goods, which, in turn, affects another set of suppliers.

Monetary policy produces similar economic changes. A restrictive monetary policy that reduces the growth rate of the money supply reduces the supply of funds for working capital and expansion for all businesses. Alternatively, a restrictive monetary policy that targets interest rates would raise market interest rates and therefore firms' costs and make it more expensive for individuals to finance home mortgages and to purchase other durable goods, such as autos and appliances. Monetary policy therefore affects all segments of an economy and that economy's relationship with other economies.

Any economic analysis requires the consideration of inflation. As discussed, inflation causes differences between real and nominal interest rates and changes the spending and savings behavior of consumers and corporations. In addition, unexpected changes in the rate of inflation make it difficult for firms to plan, which inhibits growth and innovation. Beyond the impact on the domestic economy, differential inflation and interest rates also influence the trade balance between countries and the exchange rate for currencies.

In addition to monetary and fiscal policy actions, such events as war, political upheavals in foreign countries, or international monetary devaluations produce changes in the business environment that add to the uncertainty of sales and earnings expectations and therefore the risk premium required by investors. For example, the political uncertainty in Russia during the late 1990s caused a significant increase in the risk premium for investors in Russia and a reduction in investment and spending in Russia. In contrast, the end of apartheid in South Africa and its open election in the mid-1990s were viewed as positive events and led to a significant increase in economic activity in the country. Similarly, the peace accord in Northern Ireland in the late 1990s caused a major influx of investment and tourist dollars.

In short, it is difficult to conceive of any industry or company that can avoid the impact of macroeconomic developments that affect the total economy. Because aggregate economic events have a profound effect on all industries and companies within these industries, these macroeconomic factors should be considered before industries are analyzed.

Taking a global portfolio perspective, the asset allocation for a country within a global portfolio will be affected by its economic outlook. If a recession is imminent in a country, you would expect a negative impact on its security prices. Because of these economic expectations, investors would be apprehensive about investing in most industries in the country. Given these expectations, the country will be **underweighted** in portfolios relative to its weight based on its market value. Further, given these pessimistic expectations, any funds invested in the country would be directed to low-risk sectors (industries) of the economy.

In contrast, optimistic economic and stock market outlooks for a given country should lead an investor to increase the overall allocation to this country (**overweight** the country compared to its weights determined by its relative market value).[2] After allocating funds among countries, the investor looks for outstanding industries in each country. This search for the best industries is enhanced by the economic analysis because the future performance of most industries depends on the country's economic outlook *and* the industry's expected relationship to the economy during the particular phase of the business cycle.

---

[2] We will show an example of a global asset allocation in Chapter 12.

11.2.2 Industry Influences

The second step in the valuation process is to identify global industries that will prosper or suffer in the long run or during the expected near-term economic environment. Examples of conditions that affect specific industries are strikes within a major producing country, import or export quotas or taxes, a worldwide shortage or an excess supply of a resource or product, or government-imposed regulations on an industry.

You should remember that alternative industries react to economic changes at different points in the business cycle. For example, firms typically increase capital expenditures when they are operating at full capacity at the peak of the economic cycle. Therefore, industries that provide plant and equipment will typically be affected toward the end of a cycle. In addition, alternative industries have different responses to the business cycle. As an example, cyclical industries, such as steel or autos, typically do much better than the aggregate economy during expansions, but they suffer more during contractions. In contrast, noncyclical industries, such as retail food and household products, would not experience a significant decline during a recession but also would not experience a strong increase during an economic expansion.

Another factor that will have a differential effect on industries is demographics. For example, it is widely recognized that the U.S. population is weighted toward baby boomers in their late 50s and that there has been a large surge in the number of citizens over age 65. These two groups have heavy demand for second homes and medical care and the industries related to these segments (e.g., home furnishings and pharmaceuticals).

Firms that sell in international markets can benefit or suffer as foreign economies shift. An industry with a substantial worldwide market might experience low demand in its domestic market but benefit from growing demand in its international market. As an example, much of the growth for Coca-Cola and Pepsi and the fast-food chains, such as McDonald's and Burger King, has come from international expansion in Europe and the Far East.

In general, an industry's prospects within the global business environment will determine how well or poorly an individual firm will fare, so industry analysis should precede company analysis. Few companies perform well in a poor industry, so even the best company in an industry with a negative outlook is a bad prospect for investment. For example, a poor sales and earnings outlook in the farm equipment industry would have a negative impact on Deere and Co., a well-managed firm and probably the best firm in its industry. Though Deere would likely perform better than other firms in the industry (some might go bankrupt), its earnings and stock performance would still fall far short of its past performance, and the company would probably do poorly compared to firms in most other industries.

Notably, even money managers who are essentially "stockpickers" consider industry analysis important because it determines a firm's business risk due to sales volatility and operating leverage, and its profitability is impacted by the competitive environment in the industry.

11.2.3 Company Analysis

After determining an industry's outlook, an investor can analyze and compare an individual firms' performance relative to the entire industry using financial ratios and cash flow values. As we discussed in Chapter 10, many financial ratios for firms are valid only when they are compared to the performance of their industries.

You undertake company analysis to identify the best company in a promising industry. This involves examining a firm's past performance, but more important, its future prospects. After you understand the firm and its outlook, you can estimate its value using one of several valuation models. An important point that will be emphasized is that it is your estimated inputs to the valuation models that are critical, and the quality of these inputs depends on your prior market–industry–company analysis. In the final step, you compare your estimated intrinsic value to the prevailing market price of the firm's stock and decide whether its stock is a good investment.

Your final goal is to select the best stock within a desirable industry and include it in your portfolio based on its relationship (correlation) with all other assets in your portfolio. As we discuss in more detail in Chapter 14, the best stock for investment purposes may not necessarily be issued by the best company because the stock of the finest company in an industry may be overpriced, which would cause it to be a poor investment. You cannot know whether a security is undervalued or overvalued until you have thoroughly analyzed the company, estimated its intrinsic value, and compared your estimated intrinsic value to the market price of the firm's stock.

11.2.4 Does the Three-Step Process Work?

Although you might agree with the logic of the three-step investment process, you might wonder how well this process works in selecting investments. The results of several academic studies have supported this technique. First, studies indicated that most changes in an individual firm's *earnings* could be attributed to changes in aggregate corporate earnings and changes in the firm's industry, with the aggregate earnings changes being more important. Although the relative influence of the general economy and the industry on a firm's earnings varied among individual firms, the results consistently demonstrated that the economic environment had a significant effect on firm earnings.

Second, studies by Moore and Cullity (1988) and Siegel (1991) found a relationship between aggregate stock prices and various economic series, such as employment, income, or production. These results supported the view that a relationship exists between stock prices and economic expansions and contractions.

Third, an analysis of the relationship between *rates of return* for the aggregate stock market, alternative industries, and individual stocks showed that most of the changes in rates of return for individual stocks could be explained by changes in the rates of return for the aggregate stock market and the stock's industry. As shown by Meyers (1973), although the importance of the market effect tended to decline over time and the significance of the industry effect varied among industries, the combined market-industry effect on an individual stock's rate of return was still important.

These results from academic studies support the use of the three-step investment process. This investment decision approach is consistent with the discussion in Chapter 2, which contended that the most important decision is the asset allocation decision.[3] The asset allocation specifies: (1) what proportion of your portfolio will be invested in various nations' economies; (2) within each country, how you will divide your assets among stocks, bonds, or other assets; and (3) your industry selections, based on which industries are expected to prosper in the projected economic environment. We provide an example of global asset allocation in Chapter 12.

Now that we have described and justified the three-step process, we need to consider the theory of valuation. The application of this theory allows us to compute estimated intrinsic values for the market, for alternative industries, and for the stocks of individual firms. Finally, we compare these estimated intrinsic values to current market prices and determine appropriate investment decisions.

· ·

11.3 Theory of Valuation

You may recall from your studies in accounting, economics, or corporate finance that the value of an asset is the present value of its expected returns. Specifically, you expect an asset to provide a stream of returns during the period of time you own it. To convert this estimated stream

---

[3] The classic studies that established the importance of asset allocation are Brinson, Hood, and Beebower (1986), followed by Brinson, Singer, and Beebower (1991). A subsequent well-regarded application of these concepts is contained in Cohen (1996).

of returns to a value for the security, you must discount this stream at your required rate of return. This process of valuation requires estimates of (1) the stream of expected returns and (2) the required rate of return on the investment (its discount rate).

11.3.1 Stream of Expected Returns (Cash Flows)

An estimate of the expected returns from an investment encompasses not only the size but also the form, time pattern, and the uncertainty of returns, which affect the required rate of return.

Form of Returns The returns from an investment can take many forms, including earnings, cash flows, dividends, interest payments, or capital gains (increases in value) during a period. We will consider several alternative valuation techniques that use different forms of returns. As an example, one common stock valuation model applies a multiplier to a firm's earnings, whereas another valuation model computes the present value of a firm's operating cash flows, and a third model estimates the present value of dividend payments. Returns or cash flows can come in many forms, and you must consider all of them to evaluate an investment accurately.

Time Pattern and Growth Rate of Returns You cannot calculate an accurate value for a security unless you can estimate when you will receive the returns or cash flows. Because money has a time value, you must estimate the time pattern and growth rate of returns (cash flows) from an investment. This knowledge will make it possible to properly value the stream of returns relative to alternative investments with a different time pattern and growth rate of returns or cash flows.

11.3.2 Required Rate of Return

Uncertainty of Returns (Cash Flows) You will recall from Chapter 1 that the required rate of return on an investment is determined by (1) the economy's real risk-free rate of return, plus (2) the expected rate of inflation during the holding period, plus (3) a risk premium that is determined by the uncertainty of returns. All investments are affected by the risk-free rate and the expected rate of inflation because these two variables determine the nominal risk-free rate. Therefore, the factor that causes a difference in required rates of return is the risk premium for alternative investments. In turn, this risk premium depends on the uncertainty of returns or cash flows from an investment.

We can identify the sources of the uncertainty of returns by the internal characteristics of assets or by market-determined factors. Earlier, we subdivided the internal characteristics for a firm into business risk (BR), financial risk (FR), liquidity risk (LR), exchange rate risk (ERR), and country risk (CR). The market-determined risk measures are the systematic risk of the asset (its beta), or a set of multiple risk factors that were discussed in Chapter 9.

11.3.3 Investment Decision Process: A Comparison of Estimated Values and Market Prices

To ensure that you receive your required return on an investment, you must estimate the intrinsic value of the investment at your required rate of return and then compare this estimated intrinsic value to the prevailing market price. You should not buy an investment if its market price exceeds your estimated value because the difference will prevent you from receiving your required rate of return on the investment. In contrast, if the estimated intrinsic value of the investment exceeds the market price, you should buy the investment. In summary:

> If Estimated Intrinsic Value > Market Price, Buy
> If Estimated Intrinsic Value < Market Price, Don't Buy or Sell If You Own It.

For example, assume you read about a firm that produces athletic shoes and its stock is listed on the NYSE. Using one of the valuation models we will discuss and making estimates of the earnings, or cash flows, and the growth of these variables based on the company's annual report and other information, you estimate the company's intrinsic stock value using your required rate of return as $20 a share. After estimating this value, you look in the paper and see that the stock is currently being traded at $15 a share. You would want to buy this stock because you think it is worth $20 a share and you can buy it for $15 a share. In contrast, if the current market price were $25 a share, you would not want to buy the stock because, based upon your valuation, it is overvalued.

The theory of value provides a common framework for the valuation of all investments. Different applications of this theory generate different estimated values for alternative investments because of the different payment streams and characteristics of the securities. The interest and principal payments on a bond differ substantially from the expected dividends and future selling price for a common stock. The initial discussion that follows applies the discounted cash flow method to bonds, preferred stock, and common stock. This presentation demonstrates that the same basic model is useful across a range of investments. Subsequently, because of the difficulty in estimating the value of common stock, we consider two general approaches and numerous techniques for the valuation of stock.

. . . .

11.4 Valuation of Alternative Investments

11.4.1 Valuation of Bonds

Calculating the value of bonds is relatively easy because the size and time pattern of cash flows from the bond over its life are known. A bond typically promises

1. Interest payments every six months equal to one-half the coupon rate times the face value of the bond
2. The payment of the principal on the bond's maturity date

As an example, in 2009, a $10,000 bond due in 2024 with a 10 percent coupon will pay $500 every six months for its 15-year life. In addition, the bond issuer promises to pay the $10,000 principal at maturity in 2024. Therefore, assuming the bond issuer does not default, the investor knows what payments (cash flows) will be made and when they will be made.

Applying the valuation theory—which states that the value of any asset is the present value of its cash flows—the value of the bond is the present value of the interest payments, which we can think of as an annuity of $500 every six months for 15 years, and the present value of the principal payment, which in this case is the present value of $10,000 to be paid at the end of 15 years. The only unknown for this asset (assuming the borrower does not default) is the required rate of return that should be used to discount the expected stream of returns (cash flows). If the prevailing nominal risk-free rate is 7 percent and the investor requires a 3 percent risk premium on this bond because there is some probability of default, the required rate of return would be 10 percent.

The present value of the semiannual interest payments is an annuity for 30 periods (15 years every six months) at one-half the required return (5 percent)[4]:

$$\$500 \times 15.3725 = \$7,686$$
(Present Value of Interest Payments at 10 Percent)

The present value of the principal is likewise discounted at 5 percent for 30 periods[5]:

$$\$10,000 \times 0.2314 = \$2,314$$
(Present Value of the Principal Payment at 10 Percent)

---

[4] The annuity factors and present value factors are contained in Appendix C at the end of the book.
[5] If we used annual compounding, this would be 0.239 rather than 0.2314. We use semiannual compounding because it is consistent with the interest payments and is used in practice.

This can be summarized as follows:

Present Value of Interest Payments $500 × 15.3725   = $ 7,686
Present Value of Principal Payment $10,000 × 0.2314 =   2,314
Total Present Value of Bond at 10 Percent   = $10,000

This is the amount that an investor should be willing to pay for this bond, assuming that the required rate of return on a bond of this risk class is 10 percent. If the market price of the bond is above this value, the investor should not buy it because the promised yield to maturity at this higher price will be less than the investor's required rate of return.

Alternatively, assuming an investor requires a 12 percent return on this bond, its value would be:

$500 × 13.7648 = $6,882
$10,000 × 0.1741 =   1,741
Total Present Value of Bond at 12 Percent = $8,623

This example shows that if you want a higher rate of return, you will not pay as much for an asset; that is, a given stream of cash flows has a lower value to you. It is this characteristic that leads to the often-used phrase that the prices of bonds move in an opposite direction of yields. As before, you would compare this computed present value to the market price of the bond to determine whether you should invest in it.[6]

11.4.2 Valuation of Preferred Stock

The owner of a preferred stock receives a promise to pay a stated dividend, usually each quarter, for an infinite period. Preferred stock is a **perpetuity** because it has no maturity. As was true with a bond, stated payments are made on specified dates although the issuer of this stock does not have the same legal obligation to pay investors as do issuers of bonds. Payments are made only after the firm meets its bond interest payments. Because this reduced legal obligation increases the uncertainty of returns, investors should require a higher rate of return on a firm's preferred stock than on its bonds. Although this differential in required return should exist in theory, it generally does not exist in practice because of the tax treatment accorded dividends paid to corporations. As described in Chapter 3, 80 percent of intercompany preferred dividends are tax-exempt, making the effective tax rate on preferred dividends about 6.8 percent, assuming a corporate tax rate of 34 percent. This tax advantage stimulates the demand for preferred stocks by corporations; and, because of this demand, the yield on preferred stocks has generally been below that on the highest-grade corporate bonds.

Because preferred stock is a perpetuity, its value is simply the stated annual dividend divided by the required rate of return on preferred stock (k_p) as follows:

$$V = \frac{\text{Dividend}}{k_p}$$

Consider a preferred stock has a $100 par value and a dividend of $8 a year. Because of the expected rate of inflation, the uncertainty of the dividend payment, and the tax advantage to you as a corporate investor, assume that your required rate of return on this stock is 9 percent. Therefore, the value of this preferred stock to you is

$$V = \frac{\$8}{0.09}$$
$$= \$88.89$$

---

[6] To test your mastery of bond valuation, check that if the required rate of return were 8 percent, the value of this bond would be $11,729.

Given this estimated value, you would inquire about the current market price to decide whether you would want to buy this preferred stock. If the current market price is $95, you would decide against a purchase, whereas if it is $80, you would buy the stock. Also, given the market price of preferred stock, you can derive its promised yield. Assuming a current market price of $85, the promised yield would be

$$k_p = \frac{\text{Dividend}}{\text{Price}} = \frac{\$8}{\$85.00} = 0.0941$$

11.4.3 Approaches to the Valuation of Common Stock

Because of the complexity and importance of valuing common stock, various valuation techniques have been devised over time. These techniques fall into one of two general approaches: (1) the discounted cash flow valuation techniques, where the value of the stock is estimated based upon the present value of some measure of cash flow, including dividends, operating cash flow, and free cash flow; and (2) the relative valuation techniques, where the value of a stock is estimated based upon its current price relative to variables considered to be significant to valuation, such as earnings, cash flow, book value, or sales. Exhibit 11.2 provides a visual presentation of the alternative approaches and specific techniques.

An important point is that *both of these approaches and all of these valuation techniques have several common factors.* First, all of them are significantly affected by the investor's *required rate of return* on the stock because this rate becomes the discount rate or is a major component of the discount rate. Second, all valuation approaches are affected by *the estimated growth rate of the variable* used in the valuation technique—for example, dividends, earnings, cash flow, or sales. As noted in the efficient market discussion, both of these critical variables must be *estimated.* As a result, different analysts using the same valuation techniques will derive different estimates of value for a stock because they have different estimates for these critical variable inputs. Put another way, you should assume that most investors are aware of the valuation models and it is the *inputs* to the models that make a difference—that is, your estimates of the discount rate and the growth rate of earnings and cash flows. If you are better at estimating these inputs, you will be a superior analyst.

The following discussion of equity valuation techniques considers the specific models and the theoretical and practical strengths and weaknesses of each of them. Notably, the authors'

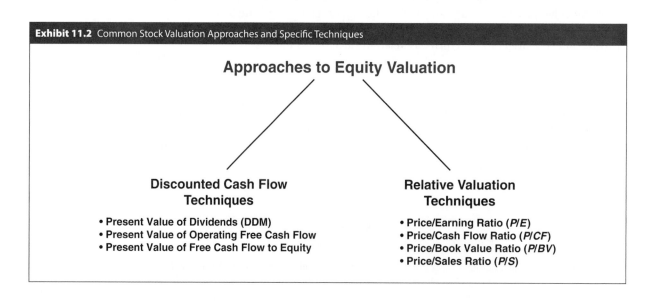

Exhibit 11.2 Common Stock Valuation Approaches and Specific Techniques

Approaches to Equity Valuation

Discounted Cash Flow Techniques

• Present Value of Dividends (DDM)
• Present Value of Operating Free Cash Flow
• Present Value of Free Cash Flow to Equity

Relative Valuation Techniques

• Price/Earning Ratio (*P/E*)
• Price/Cash Flow Ratio (*P/CF*)
• Price/Book Value Ratio (*P/BV*)
• Price/Sales Ratio (*P/S*)

intent is to present these two approaches as complementary, *not* competitive, approaches—that is, you should learn and use both of them.

11.4.4 Why and When to Use the Discounted Cash Flow Valuation Approach

These discounted cash flow valuation techniques are obvious choices for valuation because they are the epitome of how we describe value—that is, the present value of expected cash flows. The major difference between the alternative techniques is how one specifies cash flow—that is, the measure of cash flow used.

The cleanest and most straightforward measure of cash flow is *dividends* because these are clearly cash flows that go directly to the investor, which implies that you should use *the cost of equity* as the discount rate. However, this dividend technique is difficult to apply to firms that do not pay dividends during periods of high growth, or that currently pay very limited dividends because they have high rate of return investment alternatives available. On the other hand, an advantage is that the reduced form of the dividend discount model (DDM) is very useful when discussing valuation for a stable, mature entity where the assumption of relatively constant growth for the long term is appropriate (a good example is the aggregate stock market).

The second specification of cash flow is the *operating free cash flow,* which is generally described as cash flows after direct costs (cost of goods and S, G & A expenses) and after allowing for cash flows to support working capital outlays and capital expenditures required for future growth, but before any payments to capital suppliers. Because we are dealing with the cash flows available for all capital suppliers, the discount rate employed is the firm's *weighted average cost of capital* (WACC). This is a very useful model when comparing firms with diverse capital structures because you determine the value of the total firm (the entity value) and then subtract the value of the firm's debt obligations to arrive at a value for the firm's equity.

The third cash flow measure is *free cash flow to equity,* which is a measure of cash flows similar to the operating free cash flow described above, but after payments to debt holders, which means that these are cash flows available to equity owners. Therefore, the appropriate discount rate is the firm's *cost of equity.*

Beyond being theoretically correct, these models allow a substantial amount of flexibility in terms of changes in sales and expenses that implies changing growth rates over time. Once you understand how to compute each measure of cash flow, you can estimate cash flow for each year by constructing a pro forma statement for each year or you can estimate overall growth rates for the alternative cash flow values as we will demonstrate with the DDM.

A potential difficulty with these cash flow techniques is that they are very dependent on the two significant inputs—(1) the growth rates of cash flows (both the *rate* of growth and the *duration* of growth) and (2) the estimate of the discount rate. As we will show in several instances, a small change in either of these values can have a significant impact on the estimated value. As noted earlier, everyone knows and uses similar valuation models, but it is the *inputs* that are critical—GIGO: garbage in, garbage out! This is similar to the discussion in Chapter 6 regarding being a superior analyst in a world with an efficient market.

11.4.5 Why and When to Use the Relative Valuation Techniques

As noted, a benefit but also a potential problem with the discounted cash flow valuation models is that it is possible to derive intrinsic values that are substantially above or below prevailing prices depending on how you adjust your estimated inputs to the prevailing environment. An advantage of the relative valuation techniques is that they provide information about how the market is *currently* valuing stock at several levels—that is, the aggregate market, alternative industries, and individual stocks within industries. Following this chapter, which provides the background for these two approaches, we will demonstrate the alternative relative valuation ratios for the aggregate market, for an industry relative to the market, and for an individual company relative to the aggregate market, to its industry, and to other stocks in its industry.

The good news is that this relative valuation approach provides information on how the market is currently valuing securities. The bad news is that it is providing information on current valuation. The point is, the relative valuation approach provides this information on current valuation, but it does not provide guidance on whether these current valuations are appropriate—that is, *all* valuations at a point in time could be too high or too low. For example, assume that the market becomes significantly overvalued. If you were to compare the value for an industry to the very overvalued market, you might contend based on such a comparison that an industry is undervalued relative to the market. Unfortunately, your judgment may be wrong because of the benchmark you are using—that is, you might be comparing a fully valued industry to a *very* overvalued market. Alternatively, if you compare an undervalued industry to an aggregate market that is *grossly* undervalued, the industry will appear overvalued by comparison.

Put another way, the relative valuation techniques are appropriate to consider under two conditions:

1. You have a good set of comparable entities—that is, comparable companies that are similar in terms of industry, size, and, it is hoped, risk.
2. The aggregate market and the company's industry are not at a valuation extreme—that is, they are not either seriously undervalued or overvalued.

11.4.6 Discounted Cash Flow Valuation Techniques

All of these valuation techniques are based on the basic valuation model, which asserts that the value of an asset is the present value of its expected future cash flows as follows:

$$V_j = \sum_{t=1}^{n} \frac{CF_t}{(1 + k)^t}$$

where:

V_j = value of Stock j
n = life of the asset
CF_t = cash flow in Period t
k = the discount rate that is equal to the investors' required rate of return for Asset j, which is determined by the uncertainty (risk) of the asset's cash flows

As noted, the specific cash flows used will differ between techniques. They range from dividends (the best-known model) to operating free cash flow and free cash flow to equity. We begin with a fairly detailed presentation of the present-value-of-dividend model, referred to as the dividend discount model (DDM), because it is intuitively appealing and is the best-known model. Also, its general approach is similar to the other discounted cash flow models.

The Dividend Discount Model (DDM) The dividend discount model assumes that the value of a share of common stock is the present value of all future dividends as follows:[7]

$$V_j = \frac{D_1}{(1 + k)} + \frac{D_2}{(1 + k)^2} + \frac{D_3}{(1 + k)^3} + \cdots + \frac{D_\infty}{(1 + k)^\infty}$$

$$= \sum_{t=1}^{n} \frac{D_t}{(1 + k)^t}$$

where:

V_j = value of common Stock j
D_t = dividend during Period t
k = required rate of return on Stock j

[7] This model was initially set forth in Williams (1938) and subsequently reintroduced and expanded by Gordon (1962).

An obvious question is: What happens when the stock is not held for an infinite period? A sale of the stock at the end of Year 2 would imply the following formula:

$$V_j = \frac{D_1}{(1+k)} + \frac{D_2}{(1+k)^2} + \frac{SP_{j2}}{(1+k)^2}$$

The value is equal to the two dividend payments during Years 1 and 2 plus the sale price (SP) for stock j at the end of Year 2. The expected selling price of stock j at the end of Year 2 (SP_{j2}) is simply the value of all remaining dividend payments.

$$SP_{j2} = \frac{D_3}{(1+k)} + \frac{D_2}{(1+k)^2} + \cdots + \frac{D_\infty}{(1+k)^\infty}$$

If SP_{j2} is discounted back to the present by $1/(1+k)^2$, this equation becomes

$$PV(SP_{j2}) = \frac{\dfrac{D_3}{(1+k)} + \dfrac{D_4}{(1+k)^2} + \cdots + \dfrac{D_\infty}{(1+k)^\infty}}{(1+k)^2}$$

$$= \frac{D_3}{(1+k)^3} + \frac{D_4}{(1+k)^4} + \cdots + \frac{D_\infty}{(1+k)^\infty}$$

which is simply an extension of the original equation. Whenever the stock is sold, its value (that is, the sale price at that time) will be the present value of all future dividends. When this ending value is discounted back to the present, you are back to the original dividend discount model.

What about stocks that pay no dividends? Again, the concept is the same, except that some of the early dividend payments are zero. Notably, there are expectations that *at some point* the firm will start paying dividends. If investors lacked such an expectation, nobody would be willing to buy the security. It would have zero value. A firm with a non-dividend-paying stock is reinvesting its capital in very profitable projects rather than paying current dividends so that its earnings and dividend stream will be larger and grow faster in the future. In this case, we would apply the DDM as:

$$V_j = \frac{D_1}{(1+k)} + \frac{D_2}{(1+k)^2} + \frac{D_3}{(1+k)^3} + \cdots + \frac{D_\infty}{(1+k)^\infty}$$

where:

$$D_1 = 0;\ D_2 = 0$$

The investor expects that when the firm starts paying dividends in Period 3, it will be a large initial amount and dividends will grow faster than those of a comparable stock that had paid out dividends. The stock has value because of these *future* dividends. We will apply this model to several cases having different holding periods that will show you how it works.

One-Year Holding Period   Assume an investor wants to buy the stock, hold it for one year, and then sell it. To determine the value of the stock—that is, how much the investor should be willing to pay for it—using the DDM, we must estimate the dividend to be received during the period, the expected sale price at the end of the holding period, and the investor's required rate of return.

To estimate the dividend for the coming year, adjust the current dividend for expectations regarding the change in the dividend during the year. Assume the company we are analyzing earned $2.50 a share last year and paid a dividend of $1 a share. Assume further that the firm has been fairly consistent in maintaining this 40 percent payout over time. The consensus of financial analysts is that the firm will earn about $2.75 during the coming year and will raise its dividend to $1.10 per share.

A crucial estimate is the expected selling price for the stock a year from now. You can estimate this expected selling price by one or more of three alternative procedures. In the first, you can apply the dividend discount model where you estimate the specific dividend payments for a number of years into the future and calculate the value of the stock from these estimates. In the second procedure, the earnings multiplier model, you multiply the future expected earnings for the stock by an earnings multiple, which you likewise estimate, to find an expected sale price. We will discuss the earnings multiple model in a later section of the chapter.

In the third method you estimate the firm's future earnings and its dividend payout ratio to arrive at an estimate of its expected dividend at your sale date. Given this dividend and an estimate of the dividend yield on stocks, you can derive a price estimate.

Given the estimated earnings and dividend above (earnings of $2.75, and dividend of $1.10), we can use the earnings multiplier and the dividend yield procedures as follows:

The long-run forward P/E of stocks is between 12 and 16. Using the midpoint of 14, we get an estimated price of:

$$14 \times \$2.75 = \$35.50$$

The long-run dividend yield on stocks has been between 1.50 percent and 5.00 percent, but in recent years (since 1980) it has been 1.50 to 4.00 percent, which implies a midpoint of 2.75 percent. Using this estimate with the $1.10 dividend gives an estimated price of:

$$\frac{\$1.10}{0.0275} = \$40.00$$

The average of these two estimates is $37.75, which is rounded to $38.

Finally, you must determine the required rate of return. As discussed before, the nominal risk-free rate is determined by the real risk-free rate and the expected rate of inflation. A widely used proxy for this rate is the promised yield on 10-year government bonds because the typical investment horizon (expected holding period) is 5 to 10 years. You estimate the stock's risk premium by comparing its risk level to the risk of other potential investments. In later chapters, we discuss how you can estimate this risk. For the moment, assume that 10-year government bonds are yielding 6 percent, and you believe that a 4 percent risk premium over the yield of these bonds is appropriate for this stock. Thus, you specify a required rate of return of 10 percent.

In summary, you have estimated the dividend at $1.10 (payable at year end), an ending sale price of $38, and a required rate of return of 10 percent. Given these inputs, you would estimate the value of this stock as follows:

$$V_1 = \frac{\$1.10}{(1 + 0.10)} + \frac{\$38.00}{(1 + 0.10)}$$

$$= \frac{\$1.10}{1.10} + \frac{\$38.00}{1.10}$$

$$= \$1.00 + 34.55$$

$$= \$35.55$$

Note that we have not mentioned the current market price of the stock. This is because the market price is not relevant to you as an investor except as a comparison to the independently derived intrinsic value based on your estimates of the relevant variables. Once we have calculated the stock's intrinsic value as $35.55 we can compare it to the market price and apply the investment decision rule: If the stock's market price is more than $35.55, do not buy; if it is equal to or less than $35.55, buy.

Multiple-Year Holding Period If you anticipate holding the stock for several years and then selling it, the valuation estimate is harder. You must forecast several future dividend payments and estimate the sale price of the stock several years in the future.

The difficulty with estimating future dividend payments is that the future stream can have numerous forms. The exact estimate of the future dividends depends on two projections. The first is your outlook for earnings growth because earnings are the source of dividends. The second projection is the firm's dividend policy, which can take several forms. A firm can have a constant percent payout of earnings each year, which implies a change in dividend each year, or the firm could follow a step pattern in which it increases the dividend rate by a constant dollar amount each year or every two or three years. The easiest dividend policy is to assume that the firm enjoys a constant growth rate in earnings and maintains a constant dividend payout. This set of assumptions implies that the dividend stream will experience a constant growth rate that is equal to the earnings growth rate. Clearly, the important estimate by the analyst is the growth rate of earnings, which will provide the dividend estimates and ending estimates for earnings and the dividends that are used to derive the ending price estimate as above. As before, the estimated intrinsic value is simply the discounted value of these cash flows at your required cost of equity. Finally, compare this estimated intrinsic value for the stock to its current market price to determine whether you should buy it.

At this point, you should recognize that the valuation procedure discussed here is similar to that used in corporate finance when making investment decisions, except that the cash flows are from dividends instead of returns to an investment project. Also, rather than estimating the scrap value or salvage value of a corporate asset, we are estimating the ending sale price for the stock. Finally, rather than discounting cash flows using the firm's cost of capital, we use the individual's required rate of return on the company's equity. In both cases, we are looking for excess present value, which means that the present value of expected cash inflows—that is, the estimated intrinsic value of the asset—exceeds the present value of cash outflows, which is the market price of the asset.

Infinite Period Model We can extend the multiperiod model by extending our estimates of dividends but the benefits derived from these extensions would be minimal. Instead, we will move to the infinite period dividend discount model, which assumes that investors estimate future dividend payments for an infinite number of periods.

Needless to say, this is a formidable task. We must make some simplifying assumptions about this future stream of dividends to make the task viable. The easiest assumption is that *the future dividend stream will grow at a constant rate for an infinite period*. This is a rather heroic assumption in many instances, but where it does hold, we can use the model to value individual stocks as well as the aggregate market and alternative industries. This model is generalized as follows:

$$V_j = \frac{D_0(1 + g)}{(1 + k)} + \frac{D_0(1 + g)^2}{(1 + k)^2} + \cdots + \frac{D_0(1 + g)^n}{(1 + k)^n}$$

where:

V_j = the value of Stock j
D_0 = the dividend payment in the current period
g = the constant growth rate of dividends
k = the required rate of return on Stock j
n = the number of periods, which we assume to be infinite

In the appendix to this chapter, we show that with certain assumptions, this infinite period constant growth rate model can be simplified to the following expression (referred to as the reduced form DDM):

$$V_j = \frac{D_1}{k - g}$$

You will probably recognize this formula as one that is widely used in corporate finance to estimate the cost of equity capital for the firm—that is, $k = D/V + g$.

To use this model for valuation, you must estimate (1) the required rate of return (k) and (2) the expected constant growth rate of dividends (g). After estimating g, it is a simple matter to estimate D_1, because it is the current dividend (D_0) times ($1 + g$).

Consider the example of a stock with a current dividend of $1 a share. You believe that, over the long run, this company's earnings and dividends will grow at 7 percent; your estimate of g is 0.07, which implies that you expect the dividend next year (D_1) to be $1.07. For the long run, you expect a nominal risk-free rate of about 6 percent and a risk premium for this stock of 5 percent. Therefore, you set your long-run required rate of return on this stock at 11 percent; your estimate of k is 0.11. To summarize the relevant estimates:

$$g = 0.07$$
$$k = 0.11$$
$$D_1 = \$1.07 (\$1.00 \times 1.07)$$
$$V = \frac{\$1.07}{0.11 - 0.07}$$
$$= \frac{\$1.07}{0.04}$$
$$= \$26.75$$

A small change in any of the original estimates will have a large impact on V, as shown by the following examples:

1. $g = 0.07; k = 0.12; D_1 = \$1.07$. (We assume an increase in k.)
$$V = \frac{\$1.07}{0.12 - 0.07}$$
$$= \frac{\$1.07}{0.05}$$
$$= \$21.40$$

2. $g = 0.08; k = 0.11; D_1 = \$1.08$ (We assume an increase in g.)
$$V = \frac{\$1.08}{0.11 - 0.08}$$
$$= \frac{\$1.08}{0.03}$$
$$= \$36.00$$

These examples show that as small a change as 1 percent in either g or k produces a large difference in the estimated value of the stock. The crucial relationship that determines the value of the stock is the *spread between the required rate of return* (k) *and the expected growth rate of dividends* (g). Anything that causes a decline in the spread will cause an increase in the computed value, whereas any increase in the spread will decrease the computed value of the stock.

11.4.7 Infinite Period DDM and Growth Companies

As noted in the Appendix, the infinite period DDM has the following assumptions:

1. Dividends grow at a constant rate.
2. The constant growth rate will continue for an infinite period.
3. The required rate of return (k) *is greater than the infinite growth rate* (g). If it is not, the model gives meaningless results because the denominator becomes negative.

What is the effect of these assumptions if you want to use this model to value the stock of growth companies, such as Intel, Pfizer, Microsoft, Apple, and Google? **Growth companies** are firms that have the opportunities and abilities to earn rates of return on investments that are consistently above their required rates of return.[8] You will recall from corporate finance that the required rate of return for a corporation is its weighted average cost of capital (WACC). An example might be Intel, which has a WACC of about 12 percent, but is currently earning about 20 percent on its invested capital. Therefore, we would consider Intel a growth company. To exploit these outstanding investment opportunities, these growth firms generally retain a high percentage of earnings for reinvestment, and their earnings will grow faster than those of the typical firm. You will recall from the discussion in Chapter 10 that a firm's sustainable growth is a function of its retention rate and its return on equity (ROE). Notably, as discussed subsequently, the earnings growth pattern for these growth companies is inconsistent with the assumptions of the infinite period DDM.

First, the infinite period DDM assumes dividends will grow at a constant rate for an infinite period. This assumption seldom holds for companies currently growing at above-average rates. As an example, both Apple and Google have grown at rates in excess of 20 percent a year for several years. It is unlikely that they can maintain such extreme rates of growth because of the inability to continue earning the ROEs implied by this growth for an infinite period in an economy where other firms will compete with them for these high rates of return.

Second, during the periods when these firms experience abnormally high rates of growth, their rates of growth probably exceed their required rates of return. There is *no* automatic relationship between growth and risk; a high-growth company is not necessarily a high-risk company. In fact, a firm growing at a high *constant rate* would have lower risk (less uncertainty) than a low-growth firm with an unstable earnings pattern.

In summary, some firms experience periods of abnormally high rates of growth for some finite periods of time. The infinite period DDM cannot be used to value these true growth firms because these high-growth conditions are temporary and therefore inconsistent with the assumptions of the DDM. In the following section, we discuss how to adjust the DDM to value a firm with temporary supernormal growth. In Chapter 14 we will discuss additional models used for estimating the stock value of growth companies.

11.4.8 Valuation with Temporary Supernormal Growth

Thus far, we have considered how to value a firm with different growth rates for short periods of time (one to three years) and how to value a stock using a model that assumes a constant growth rate for an infinite period. As noted, the assumptions of the model make it impossible to use the infinite period constant growth model to value true growth companies. The point is, in a competitive free enterprise economy, it is not reasonable to expect a company to permanently maintain a growth rate higher than its required rate of return because competition will eventually enter this apparently lucrative business, which will reduce the firm's profit margins and therefore its ROE and growth rate. Therefore, after a few years of exceptional growth—that is, a period of temporary supernormal growth—a firm's growth rate is expected to decline. Eventually its growth rate is expected to stabilize at a constant level consistent with the assumptions of the infinite period DDM.

To determine the value of a temporary supernormal growth company, you must combine the previous models. In analyzing the initial years of exceptional growth, you examine each year individually. If the company is expected to have two or three stages of supernormal growth, you must examine each year during these stages of growth. When the firm's growth rate stabilizes at a rate below the required rate of return, you can compute the remaining value of the firm assuming constant growth using the DDM and discount this lump-sum constant growth value back to the present. The technique should become clear as you work through the following example.

---

[8] Growth companies are discussed in Salomon (1963) and Miller and Modigliani (1961). Models to value growth companies are discussed in Chapter 14.

The Bourke Company has a current dividend (D_0) of $2 a share. The following are the expected annual growth rates for dividends.

Year	Dividend Growth Rate
1–3	25%
4–6	20
7–9	15
10 on	9

The required rate of return for the stock (the company's cost of equity) is 14 percent. Therefore, the value equation becomes (Exhibit 11.3 presents it in a table):

$$V_j = \frac{2.00(1.25)}{1.14} + \frac{2.00(1.25)^2}{(1.14)^2} + \frac{2.00(1.25)^3}{(1.14)^3}$$

$$+ \frac{2.00(1.25)^3(1.20)}{(1.14)^4} + \frac{2.00(1.25)^3(1.20)^2}{(1.14)^5}$$

$$+ \frac{2.00(1.25)^3(1.20)^3}{(1.14)^6} + \frac{2.00(1.25)^3(1.20)^3(1.15)}{(1.14)^7}$$

$$+ \frac{2.00(1.25)^3(1.20)^3(1.15)^2}{(1.14)^8} + \frac{2.00(1.25)^3(1.20)^3(1.15)^3}{(1.14)^9}$$

$$+ \frac{\dfrac{2.00(1.25)^3(1.20)^3(1.15)^3(1.09)}{(0.14 - 0.09)}}{(1.14)^9}$$

The computations in Exhibit 11.3 indicate that the total value of the stock is $94.36. As before, you would compare this estimate of intrinsic value to the market price of the stock when deciding whether to purchase the stock. The difficult part of the valuation is estimating both the supernormal *growth rates* and determining *how long* each of the growth rates will last.

To summarize this section, the initial present value of cash flow stock valuation model considered was the dividend discount model (DDM). After explaining the basic model and the derivation of its reduced form, we noted that the infinite period DDM cannot be applied to the valuation of stock for growth companies because the abnormally high growth rate of earnings

Exhibit 11.3 Computation of Value for the Stock of a Company with Temporary Supernormal Growth

Year	Dividend	Discount Factor (14 percent)	Present Value
1	$ 2.50	0.8772	$ 2.193
2	3.12	0.7695	2.401
3	3.91	0.6750	2.639
4	4.69	0.5921	2.777
5	5.63	0.5194	2.924
6	6.76	0.4556	3.080
7	7.77	0.3996	3.105
8	8.94	0.3506	3.134
9	10.28	0.3075[b]	3.161
10	11.21		
	$224.20[a]	0.3075[b]	68.941
		Total value =	$94.355

[a] Value of dividend stream for Year 10 and all future dividends (that is, $11.21/(0.14 − 0.09) = $224.20).

[b] The discount factor is the ninth-year factor because the valuation of the remaining stream is made at the end of Year 9 to reflect the dividend in Year 10 and all future dividends.

for the growth company is inconsistent with the assumptions of the infinite period constant growth DDM model. Subsequently we modified the DDM model to evaluate companies with temporary supernormal growth. In the following sections, we discuss the other present value of cash flow techniques assuming a similar set of scenarios.

11.4.9 Present Value of Operating Free Cash Flows

In this model, you are deriving the value of the total firm because you are discounting the operating free cash flows prior to the payment of interest to the debt holders but after deducting funds needed to maintain the firm's asset base (capital expenditures). Also, because you are discounting the total firm's operating free cash flow, you would use the firm's weighted average cost of capital (*WACC*) as your discount rate. Therefore, once you estimate the value of the total firm, you subtract the value of debt, assuming your goal is to estimate the value of the firm's equity. The total value of the firm is equal to:

$$V_j = \sum_{t=1}^{n} \frac{OFCF_t}{(1 + WACC_j)^t}$$

where:

V_j = value of Firm j
n = number of periods assumed to be infinite
$OFCF_t$ = the firm's operating free cash flow in Period t. The detailed specification of operating free cash flow will be discussed in Chapter 14.
$WACC_j$ = Firm j's weighted average cost of capital. The computation of the firm's *WACC* will be discussed in Chapter 14.

Similar to the process with the DDM, it is possible to envision this as a model that requires estimates for an infinite period. Alternatively, if you are dealing with a mature firm whereby its operating cash flows have reached a stage of stable growth, you can adapt the infinite period constant growth DDM model as follows:

$$V_j = \frac{OFCF_1}{WACC_j - g_{OFCF}}$$

where:

$OFCF_1$ = operating free cash flow in Period 1 equal to $OFCF_0(1 + g_{OFCF})$
g_{OFCF} = long-term constant growth rate of operating free cash flow

Alternatively, assuming that the firm is expected to experience several different rates of growth for *OFCF*, these estimates can be divided into three or four stages, as demonstrated with the temporary supernormal dividend growth model. Similar to the dividend model, the analyst must estimate the *rate* of growth and the *duration* of growth for each of these periods of supernormal growth as follows:

Year	*OFCF* Growth Rate
1–4	20%
5–7	15
8–10	10
11 on	6

Therefore, the calculations would estimate the specific *OFCF*s for each year through Year 10 based on the expected growth rates, but you would use the infinite growth model estimate when the growth rate reached stability after Year 10. As noted, after determining the value of the total firm V_j, you must subtract the value of all nonequity items, including accounts payable, total interest-bearing debt, deferred taxes, and preferred stock, to arrive at the estimated value of the firm's equity. This calculation is demonstrated in Chapter 14.

11.4.10 Present Value of Free Cash Flows to Equity

The third discounted cash flow technique deals with "free" cash flows to equity, which would be derived *after* operating free cash flows have been adjusted for debt payments (interest and principal). Also, these cash flows precede dividend payments to the common stockholder. Such cash flows are referred to as free because they are what is left after providing the funds needed to maintain the firm's asset base (similar to operating free cash flow). They are specified as free cash flows to equity because they also adjust for payments to debt holders and to preferred stockholders.

Notably, because these are cash flows available to equity owners, the discount rate used is the firm's cost of equity (*k*) rather than the firm's *WACC*.

$$V_j = \sum_{t=1}^{n} \frac{FCFE_t}{(1 + k_j)^t}$$

where:

V_j = value of the stock of Firm *j*
n = number of periods assumed to be infinite
$FCFE_t$ = the firm's free cash flow to equity in Period *t*. The detailed specification of free cash flow to equity is discussed in Chapter 14.

Again, how an analyst would implement this general model depends upon the firm's position in its life cycle. That is, if the firm is expected to experience stable growth, analysts can use the infinite growth model. In contrast, if the firm is expected to experience a period of temporary supernormal growth, analysts should use the multistage growth model similar to the process used with dividends and for operating free cash flow.

. . . .

11.5 Relative Valuation Techniques

In contrast to the various discounted cash flow techniques that attempt to estimate a specific value for a stock based on its estimated growth rates and its discount rate, the relative valuation techniques implicitly contend that it is possible to determine the value of an economic entity (i.e., the market, an industry, or a company) by comparing it to similar entities on the basis of several relative ratios that compare its stock price to relevant variables that affect a stock's value, such as earnings, cash flow, book value, and sales. Therefore, in this section, we discuss the following relative valuation ratios: (1) price/earnings (*P/E*), (2) price/cash flow (*P/CF*), (3) price/book value (*P/BV*), and price/sales (*P/S*). We begin with the *P/E* ratio, also referred to as the earnings multiplier model, because it is the most popular relative valuation ratio. In addition, we will show that the *P/E* ratio can be directly related to the DDM in a manner that indicates the variables that affect the *P/E* ratio.

11.5.1 Earnings Multiplier Model

As noted, many investors prefer to estimate the value of common stock using an **earnings multiplier model**. The reasoning for this approach recalls the basic concept that the value of any investment is the present value of future returns. In the case of common stocks, the returns that investors are entitled to receive are the net earnings of the firm. Therefore, one way investors can estimate value is by determining how many dollars they are willing to pay for a dollar of expected earnings (typically represented by the estimated earnings during the following 12-month period or an estimate of "normalized earnings"). For example, if investors are willing to pay 10 times expected or "normal" earnings, they would value a stock they expect to earn $2 a share during the following year at $20. You can compute the prevailing earnings multiplier, also referred to as the **price/earnings (P/E) ratio**, as follows:

$$\text{Earnings Multiplier} = \text{Price/Earnings Ratio}$$
$$= \frac{\text{Current Market Price}}{\text{Expected 12-Month Earnings}}$$

This computation of the current earnings multiplier (P/E ratio) indicates the prevailing attitude of investors toward a stock's value. Investors must decide if they agree with the prevailing P/E ratio (that is, is the earnings multiplier too high or too low?) based upon how it compares to the P/E ratio for the aggregate market, for the firm's industry, and for similar firms and stocks.

To answer this question in a defensible manner, we must consider what influences the earnings multiplier (P/E ratio) over time. For example, over time the aggregate stock market P/E ratio, as represented by the S&P Industrials Index, has varied from about 6 times earnings to about 30 times earnings.[9] The infinite period dividend discount model can be used to indicate the variables that should determine the value of the P/E ratio as follows:[10]

$$P_i = \frac{D_1}{k - g}$$

If we divide both sides of the equation by E_1 (expected earnings during the next 12 months), the result is

$$\frac{P_i}{E_1} = \frac{D_1/E_1}{k - g}$$

Thus, this model implies that the P/E ratio is determined by

1. The *expected* dividend payout ratio (dividends divided by earnings)
2. The *estimated* required rate of return on the stock (k)
3. The *expected* growth rate of dividends for the stock (g)

As an example, if we assume a stock has an expected dividend payout of 50 percent, a required rate of return of 12 percent, and an expected growth rate for dividends of 8 percent, this would imply that the stock's P/E ratio should be:

$$D/E = 0.50; k = 0.12; g = 0.08$$
$$P/E = \frac{0.50}{0.12 - 0.08}$$
$$= 0.50/0.04$$
$$= 12.5$$

---

[9] When computing historical P/E ratios, the practice is to use earnings for the past 12 months rather than expected earnings. Although this practice of using historical earnings will influence the level, it demonstrates the changes in the P/E ratio over time. Although it may be appropriate to use historical P/E ratios for past comparison, we strongly believe that investment decisions should emphasize future or forward P/E ratios that use *expected* earnings.

[10] In this formulation of the model we use P rather than V (that is, the value is stated as the estimated price of the stock). Although the factors that determine the P/E are the same for growth companies, this formula cannot be used to estimate a specific value because these firms often do not have dividends, the infinite growth rate assumption is not valid, and the ($k - g$) assumptions don't apply.

Again, a small difference in either k or g or both will have a large impact on the earnings multiplier, as shown in the following three examples.

1. $D/E = 0.50$; $k = 0.13$; $g = 0.08$. (In this example, we assume a higher k for the stock.)

$$P/E = \frac{0.50}{0.13 - 0.08}$$
$$= \frac{0.50}{0.05}$$
$$= 10$$

2. $D/E = 0.50$; $k = 0.12$; $g = 0.09$. (In this example, we assume a higher g for the stock and the original k.)

$$P/E = \frac{0.50}{0.12 - 0.09}$$
$$= \frac{0.50}{0.03}$$
$$= 16.7$$

3. $D/E = 0.50$; $k = 0.11$; $g = 0.09$. (In this example, we assume a fairly optimistic scenario where the k for the stock is only 11 percent and there is a higher expected growth rate of dividends of 9 percent.)

$$P/E = \frac{0.50}{0.11 - 0.09}$$
$$= \frac{0.50}{0.02}$$
$$= 25$$

As before, *the spread between k and g is the main determinant of the size of the P/E ratio.* Although the dividend payout ratio has an impact, we are generally referring to a firm's long-run target payout, which is typically rather stable with little effect on year-to-year changes in the *P/E* ratio (earnings multiplier).

After estimating the earnings multiple, you would apply it to your estimate of earnings for the next year (E_1) to arrive at an estimated value. In turn, E_1 is based on the earnings for the current year (E_0) and your expected growth rate of earnings. Using these two estimates, you would compute an estimated value of the stock and compare this estimated value to its market price.

Consider the following estimates for an example firm:

$$D/E = 0.50$$
$$k = 0.12$$
$$g = 0.09$$
$$E_0 = \$2.00$$

Using these estimates, you would compute an earnings multiple of:

$$P/E = \frac{0.50}{0.12 - 0.09} = \frac{0.50}{0.03} = 16.7$$

Given current earnings (E_0) of \$2.00 and a g of 9 percent, you would expect E_1 to be \$2.18. Therefore, you would estimate the value (price) of the stock as

$$V = 16.7 \times \$2.18$$
$$= \$36.41$$

As before, you would compare this estimated value of the stock to its current market price to decide whether you should invest in it. This estimate of value is referred to as a two-step process because it requires you to estimate future earnings (E_1) and a P/E ratio based on expectations of k and g. These two estimates are discussed in Chapter 14.

11.5.2 The Price/Cash Flow Ratio

The growth in popularity of the relative price/cash flow valuation ratio can be traced to concern over the propensity of some firms to manipulate earnings per share, whereas cash flow values are generally less prone to manipulation. Also, as noted, cash flow values are important in fundamental valuation (when computing the present value of cash flow), and they are critical when doing credit analysis where "cash is king." The price to cash flow ratio is computed as follows:

$$P/CF_j = \frac{P_t}{CF_{t+1}}$$

where:

> P/CF_j = the price/cash flow ratio for Firm j
> P_t = the price of the stock in Period t
> CF_{t+1} = the expected cash flow per share for Firm j

Regarding what variables affect this valuation ratio, the factors are similar to the P/E ratio. Specifically, the main variables should be: (1) the expected growth rate of the cash flow variable used, and (2) the risk of the stock as indicated by the uncertainty or variability of the cash flow series over time. The specific cash flow measure used will vary depending upon the nature of the company and industry and which cash flow specification (for example, operating cash flow or free cash flow) is the best measure of performance for this industry.[11] An appropriate ratio can also be affected by the firm's capital structure.

11.5.3 The Price/Book Value Ratio

The price/book value (P/BV) ratio has been widely used for many years by analysts in the banking industry as a measure of relative value. The book value of a bank is typically considered a good indicator of intrinsic value because most bank assets, such as bonds and commercial loans, have a value equal to book value. This ratio gained in popularity and credibility as a relative valuation technique for all types of firms based upon a study by Fama and French (1992) that indicated a significant inverse relationship between P/BV ratios and excess rates of return for a cross section of stocks. The P/BV ratio is specified as follows:

$$P/BV_j = \frac{P_t}{BV_{t+1}}$$

where:

> P/BV_j = the price/book value ratio for Firm j
> P_t = the price of the stock in Period t
> BV_{t+1} = the estimated end-of-year book value per share for Firm j

As with other relative valuation ratios, it is important to match the current price with the future book value that is expected to prevail at the end of the year. The difficulty is that this future book value is not generally available. One can derive an estimate of the end-of-year book value based upon an estimate of net earnings minus the expected dividends (which is added to retained earnings). The growth rate for the series can be estimated using the growth rate implied by the sustainable growth formula: g = (ROE) (Retention Rate).

---

[11] While there has been a tendency to employ EBITDA as the proxy for cash flow, we do not recommend or encourage this because of the strong upward bias of this series compared to other cash flow measures, as noted in Chapter 10.

Regarding what factors determine the size of the *P/BV* ratio, it is a function of the firm's ROE relative to its cost of equity since the ratio would be one if they were equal—that is, if the firm earned its required return on equity. In contrast, if the firm's ROE is much larger than its cost of equity, it is a growth company and investors should be willing to pay a premium price over its book value for the stock.

11.5.4 The Price/Sales Ratio

The price/sales (*P/S*) ratio has a volatile history. It was a favorite of Phillip Fisher (1984), a well-known money manager in the late 1950s, as well as his son Kenneth Fisher (1984) and Sanchek and Martin (1987). Recently, the *P/S* ratio has been suggested as useful by Martin Leibowitz (1997), a widely admired stock and bond portfolio manager. These advocates consider this ratio meaningful and useful for two reasons. First, they believe that strong and consistent sales growth is a requirement for a growth company. Although they note the importance of an above-average profit margin, they contend that *the growth process must begin with sales.* Second, given all the data in the balance sheet and income statement, sales information is subject to less manipulation than any other data item. The specific *P/S* ratio is:

$$P/S_j = \frac{P_t}{S_{t+1}}$$

where:

P/S_j = the price to sales ratio for Firm j
P_t = the price of the stock in Period t
S_{t+1} = the expected sales per share for Firm j

Again, it is important to match the current stock price with the firm's *expected* sales per share, which may be difficult to derive for a large cross section of stocks. Two caveats are relevant to the price to sales ratio. First, this particular relative valuation ratio varies dramatically by industry. For example, the sales per share for retail firms, such as Kroger or Wal-Mart, are typically much higher than sales per share for computer or microchip firms. The second consideration is the profit margin on sales. The point is, retail food stores have high sales per share, which will cause a low *P/S* ratio, which is considered good until one realizes that these firms have low net profit margins. Therefore, your relative valuation analysis using the *P/S* ratio should be between firms in the same or similar industries.

11.5.5 Implementing the Relative Valuation Technique

To properly implement the relative valuation technique, it is essential not only to compare the various ratios but also to understand what factors affect each of the valuation ratios and, therefore, know why they should differ. The first step is to compare the valuation ratio over time (e.g., the *P/E* ratio) for a company to the comparable ratio for the market, for the stock's industry, and to other stocks in the industry to determine how it compares—that is, is it similar to these other *P/Es*, or is it consistently at a premium or discount? Beyond knowing the overall relationship to the market, industry, and competitors, the real analysis is involved in understanding *why* the ratio has this relationship or why it should *not* have this relationship and the implications of this mismatch. Specifically, the second step is to explain the relationship. To do this, you need to understand what factors determine the specific valuation ratio and then compare these factors for the stock being valued versus the same factors for the market, industry, and other stocks.

To illustrate this process, consider the following example wherein you want to value the stock of a pharmaceutical company and, you decide to employ the *P/E* relative valuation technique. As part of this analysis, you compare the *P/E* ratios for this firm over time (e.g., the last 15 years) to similar ratios for the S&P Industrials, the pharmaceutical industry, and specific competitors. This comparison indicates that the company *P/E* ratios are consistently above all the other sets. Following this initial observation, the second part of the analysis considers whether the fundamental factors that affect the *P/E* ratio (i.e., the firm's growth rate and its required rate of return) justify the higher *P/E*. A positive scenario would be that the firm had a historical and expected growth rate that was substantially above all the comparables and your risk analysis indicates it should have a lower required rate of return. This would indicate that the higher *P/E* ratio is justified; the subsequent question that needs to be considered is, how much higher should the *P/E* ratio be? Alternatively, the negative scenario for this stock with a *P/E* ratio above most comparables would be if the company's expected growth rate was equal to or lower than the industry and competitors' while its required *k* was higher than for the industry and competitors. This set of conditions would signal a stock that is apparently overpriced based on the fundamental factors that determine a stock's *P/E* ratio.

In subsequent sections, we discuss how an analyst arrives at estimates for *g* and *k,* and we demonstrate the process in subsequent chapters. At this point, the reader should understand the overall process required by the relative valuation technique.

11.6 Estimating the Inputs: The Required Rate of Return and the Expected Growth Rate of Valuation Variables

This section deals with estimating two inputs that are critical to the valuation process irrespective of which approach or technique is being used: the required rate of return (*k*) and the expected growth rate of earnings and other valuation variables—that is, book value, cash flow, sales, and dividends.

We will review these factors and discuss how the estimation of these variables differs for domestic versus foreign securities. Although the valuation procedure is the same for securities around the world, *k* and *g* differ among countries. Therefore, we will review the components of the required rate of return for U.S. securities and then consider the components for foreign securities. Subsequently, we consider the estimation of the growth rate of earnings, cash flow, and dividends for domestic stocks and then for foreign stocks.

11.6.1 Required Rate of Return (*k*)

This discussion reviews the determinants of the nominal required rate of return on an investment, including a consideration of factors for non-U.S. markets. This required rate of return will be the discount rate for most cash flow models and affects all the relative valuation techniques. There is a difference in the discount rate when you are employing the present value of operating free cash flow technique because as noted, it uses the weighted average cost of capital (*WACC*). Notably, the cost of equity is a critical input to estimating the firm's *WACC*.

Recall that three factors influence an equity investor's required rate of return (*k*):

1. The economy's real risk-free rate (*RRFR*)
2. The expected rate of inflation (*I*)
3. A risk premium (*RP*)

The Economy's Real Risk-Free Rate This is the absolute minimum rate that an investor should require. It depends on the real growth rate of the investor's home economy because capital invested should grow at least as fast as the economy. As noted previously, this rate can be affected for short periods of time by temporary tightness or ease in the capital markets.

The Expected Rate of Inflation Investors are interested in real rates of return that will allow them to increase their rate of consumption. Therefore, if investors expect a given rate of inflation, they should increase their required *nominal* risk-free rate of return (*NRFR*) to reflect any expected inflation as follows:

$$NRFR = \left[[1 + RRFR]\,[1 + E(I)]\right] - 1$$

where:

$E(I)$ = expected rate of inflation

The two factors that determine the *NRFR* affect all investments, from U.S. government securities to highly speculative land deals. Investors who hope to calculate security values accurately must carefully estimate the expected rate of inflation. Not only does the *NRFR* affect all investments, but, as shown in Chapter 1, its extreme volatility makes its estimation difficult.

The Risk Premium   The risk premium (*RP*) causes differences in the required rates of return among alternative investments that range from government bonds to corporate bonds to common stocks. The *RP* also explains the difference in the expected return among securities of the same type. For example, this is the reason corporate bonds with different ratings of Aaa, Aa, or A have different yields, and why different common stocks have widely varying *P/E* ratios despite similar growth expectations.

In Chapter 1, we noted that investors demand a risk premium because of the uncertainty of returns expected from an investment. A measure of this uncertainty of returns was the dispersion of expected returns. We suggested several internal factors that influence a firm's variability of returns, such as its business risk, financial risk, and liquidity risk. We noted that securities of foreign firms or of domestic companies with significant foreign sales and earnings (e.g., Coca-Cola and McDonald's) have additional risk factors, including exchange rate risk and country (political) risk.

Changes in the Risk Premium   Because different securities (e.g., government bonds and common stocks) have different patterns of returns and different guarantees to investors, we expect their risk premiums to differ. In addition, a fact that is less recognized is that the risk premiums for the same securities can *change over time*. For example, Exhibit 11.4 shows the spread between the yields to maturity for Aaa-rated corporate bonds and Baa-rated corporate bonds from 1974 through 2007. This yield spread, or difference in yield, is a measure of the risk premium for investing in higher-risk bonds (Baa) compared to low-risk bonds (Aaa). As shown, the yield spread varied from about 0.40 percent to 2.69 percent (from less than one-half of 1 percent to almost 3 percent).

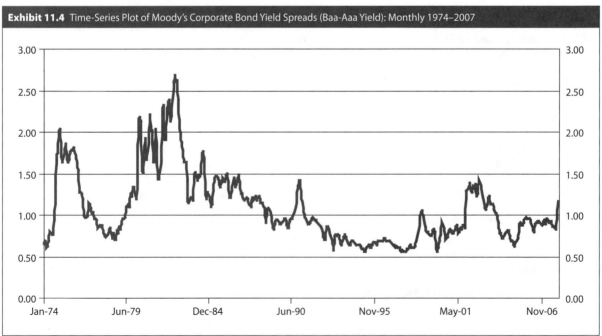

Exhibit 11.4   Time-Series Plot of Moody's Corporate Bond Yield Spreads (Baa-Aaa Yield): Monthly 1974–2007

Source: Prepared by authors using data from Lehman Brothers.

Exhibit 11.5 contains a plot of the *ratio* of the yields for the same period, which indicates the percentage risk premium of Baa bonds compared to Aaa bonds. We consider this because you might expect a larger difference in yield between Baa and Aaa bonds if Aaa bonds are yielding 12 percent rather than 6 percent. The yield ratio in Exhibit 11.5 adjusts for this size difference. This shows that even adjusting for the yield level difference, the risk premium ratio varies from about 1.06 to 1.56— a 6 percent premium to a 56 percent premium over the base yield on Aaa bonds. This significant change in the credit risk premium over time occurs because either investors perceive a change in the level of risk of Baa bonds compared to Aaa bonds or there is a change in the amount of return that investors require to accept the same risk differential. In either case, this change in the risk premium for a set of assets implies a change in the slope of the security market line (SML) as demonstrated in Chapter 1.

In Chapter 12, we will discuss the controversy regarding estimates of the equity market risk premium and the question of possible changes in the long-run equity risk premium.

11.6.2 Estimating the Required Return for Foreign Securities

Our discussion of the required rate of return for investments has been limited to the domestic market. Although the basic valuation model and its variables are the same around the world, there are significant differences in the values for specific variables. This section points out where these differences occur.

Foreign Real RFR   Because the *RRFR* in other countries should be determined by the real growth rate within the particular economy, the estimated rate can vary substantially among countries due to differences in an economy's real growth rate. An example of differences in the real growth rate of gross domestic product (GDP) can be seen from growth expectations for 2008 real GDP contained in the *IMF World Economic Outlook* as shown in Exhibit 11.6. There is a range of estimates for 2008 of about 1.7 percent (that is, 1.9 percent for Germany and Japan compared to 3.6 percent for the United States with the Euro Zone estimated at about 2.3 percent). This difference in the expected growth rates of real GDP implies a substantial difference in the RRFR for these countries.[12]

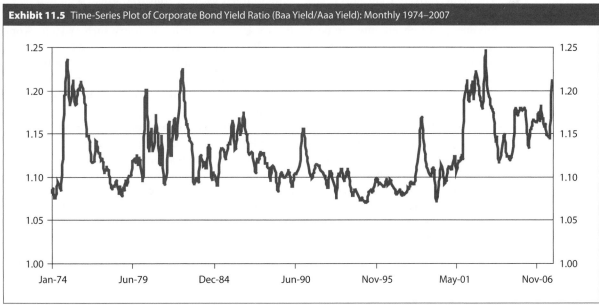

Exhibit 11.5   Time-Series Plot of Corporate Bond Yield Ratio (Baa Yield/Aaa Yield): Monthly 1974–2007

Source: Prepared by authors using data from Lehman Brothers.

[12] All the estimates of real growth and inflation are from the *IMF World Economic Outlook* (April, 2007).

Inflation Rate   To estimate the *NRFR* for a country, you must also estimate its expected rate of inflation and adjust the *NRFR* for this expectation. Again, this rate of inflation typically varies substantially among countries. The price change data show that the expected rate of inflation during 2008 varied from zero percent in Japan to 2.4 percent in the United States. Assuming equal real growth, this inflation estimate implies a difference in the nominal required rate of return between Japan and the United States of 2.4 percent. Such a difference in *k* can have a substantial impact on estimated values, as demonstrated earlier. Again, you must make a separate estimate for each individual country in which you are evaluating securities.

To demonstrate the combined impact of differences in real growth and expected inflation, Exhibit 11.6 shows the results of the following computation for four countries and the Euro Area based on the year 2008 estimates:

$$NRFR = [(1 + \text{Real Growth}) \times (1 + \text{Expected Inflation})] - 1$$

Given the differences between countries in the two components, the range in the *NRFR* of 4.2 percent is not surprising (6.1 percent for the United States versus 1.9 percent for Japan). As demonstrated earlier, such a difference in *k* for an investment will have a significant impact on its value.

Risk Premium   You must also derive an equity risk premium for the investments in each country. Again, the five risk components differ substantially between countries: business risk, financial risk, liquidity risk, exchange rate risk, and country risk. *Business risk* can vary because it is a function of the variability of economic activity within a country and of the operating leverage used by firms within the country. Firms in different countries assume significantly different *financial risk* as well. For example, Japanese firms use substantially more financial leverage than U.S. or U.K. firms. Regarding *liquidity risk,* the U.S. capital markets are acknowledged to be the most liquid in the world, with Japan and the United Kingdom being close behind. In contrast, some emerging markets are quite illiquid and in such cases investors need to add a significant liquidity risk premium.

When investing globally, you also must estimate *exchange rate risk,* which is the additional uncertainty of returns caused by changes in the exchange rates for the currency of another country. This uncertainty can be small for a U.S. investor in a country such as Hong Kong because the currency is pegged to the U.S. dollar. In contrast, in some countries, substantial volatility in the exchange rate over time can mean significant differences in the domestic return for the country and return in U.S. dollars.[13] The level of volatility for the exchange rate differs between countries. The greater the uncertainty regarding future changes in the exchange rate, the larger the exchange rate risk for the country.[14]

Recall that *country risk* arises from unexpected events in a country, such as upheavals in its political or economic environment. Examples of political disruptions occurred in Zimbabwe during 2008 when there was substantial turmoil about the presidential election when the opposition candidate withdrew. Similarly, there was significant political unrest in Thailand during 2008 that led to riots. Such political unrest or a change in the economic environment creates uncertainties that increase the risk of investments in these countries. Before investing in such countries, investors must evaluate the additional returns they should require to accept this increased uncertainty.

---

[13] Although we generally refer to these as domestic and U.S. dollar returns, you will also see references to *hedged* returns (for example, domestic) and *unhedged* returns (returns in U.S. dollars). In some cases, the hedged returns will adjust for the cost of hedging.

[14] For a thorough analysis of exchange rate determination and forecasting models, see Rosenberg (1996).

Exhibit 11.6 Estimates of Year 2008 Nominal RFR for Major Countries

Country	Real Growth in GDP	Expected Inflation	Nominal RFR
United States	1.9	2.3	4.2
Japan	1.7	0.5	2.2
Germany	2.0	2.0	4.0
United Kingdom	2.3	2.0	4.3
Euro Area	2.1	2.0	4.1

Source: Prepared by authors using data from *IMF World Economic Outlook* (October, 2007).

Thus, when estimating required rates of return on foreign investments, you must assign a unique risk premium for each country.

11.6.3 Expected Growth Rates

After arriving at a required rate of return, the investor must estimate the growth rate of sales, cash flows, earnings, and dividends because the alternative valuation models for common stock depend heavily on good estimates of growth (g) for these variables. The initial procedure we describe here is a brief summary of the presentation in Chapter 10, where we used financial ratios to measure a firm's growth potential. Subsequently, we discuss the use of historical growth rates as an input to the estimate.

Estimating Growth from Fundamentals The growth rate of dividends is determined by the growth rate of earnings and the proportion of earnings paid out in dividends (the payout ratio). Over the short run, dividends can grow faster or slower than earnings if the firm changes its payout ratio. Specifically, if a firm's earnings grow at 6 percent a year and it pays out exactly 50 percent of earnings in dividends, then the firm's dividends will likewise grow at 6 percent a year. Alternatively, if a firm's earnings grow at 6 percent a year and the firm increases its payout, then during the period when the payout ratio increases, dividends will grow faster than earnings. In contrast, if the firm reduces its payout ratio, dividends will grow slower than earnings for a period of time. Because there is a limit to how long this difference in growth rates can continue, most investors assume that the long-run dividend payout ratio is fairly stable. Therefore, our analysis of the growth rate of dividends concentrates on an analysis of the growth rate of equity earnings. Also, as will be shown in Chapter 14, equity earnings are the major factor driving the operating cash flows or the free cash flows for the firm.

When a firm retains earnings and acquires additional assets, if it earns some positive rate of return on these additional assets, the total earnings of the firm will increase because its asset base is larger. How rapidly a firm's earnings increase depends on (1) the proportion of earnings it retains and reinvests in new assets and (2) the rate of return it earns on these new assets. Specifically, the growth rate (g) of equity earnings (that is, earnings per share) without any external financing is equal to the percentage of net earnings retained (the retention rate, which equals 1 – the payout ratio) times the rate of return on equity capital.

$$g = (\text{Retention Rate}) \times (\text{Return on Equity})$$
$$= RR \times ROE$$

Therefore, a firm can increase its growth rate by increasing its retention rate (reducing its payout ratio) and investing these added funds at its historic *ROE*. Alternatively, the firm can maintain its retention rate but increase its *ROE*. For example, if a firm retains 50 percent of net earnings and consistently has an *ROE* of 10 percent, its net earnings will grow at the rate of 5 percent a year, as follows:

$$g = RR \times ROE$$
$$= 0.50 \times 0.10$$
$$= 0.05$$

If, however, the firm increases its retention rate to 75 percent and is able to invest these additional funds in projects that likewise earn 10 percent, its growth rate will increase to 7.5 percent, as follows:

$$g = 0.75 \times 0.10$$
$$= 0.075$$

If, instead, the firm continues to reinvest 50 percent of its earnings but is able to earn a higher rate of return on these investments, say 15 percent, it can likewise increase its growth rate, as follows:

$$g = 0.50 \times 0.15$$
$$= 0.075$$

Breakdown of *ROE* Although the retention rate is a management decision, changes in the firm's *ROE* result from changes in its operating performance or its financial leverage. As discussed in Chapter 10, we can divide the *ROE* ratio into three components:

$$ROE = \frac{\text{Net Income}}{\text{Sales}} \times \frac{\text{Sales}}{\text{Total Assets}} \times \frac{\text{Total Assets}}{\text{Equity}}$$

$$= \frac{\text{Profit}}{\text{Margin}} \times \frac{\text{Total Asset}}{\text{Turnover}} \times \frac{\text{Financial}}{\text{Leverage}}$$

This breakdown allows us to consider the three factors that determine a firm's *ROE*.[15] Because it is a multiplicative relationship, an increase in any of the three ratios will cause an increase in *ROE*. The first two of the three ratios reflect operating performance, and the third one indicates a firm's financing decision.

The first operating ratio, net profit margin, indicates the firm's profitability on sales. This ratio changes over time for some companies and is highly sensitive to the business cycle. For growth companies, this is one of the first ratios to decline because the increased competition increases the supply of the goods or services and forces price cutting, which leads to lower profit margins. Also, during recessions, profit margins decline because of price cutting or because of higher percentages of fixed costs due to lower sales.

The second component, total asset turnover, is the ultimate indicator of operating efficiency and reflects the asset and capital requirements of the business. Although this ratio varies dramatically by industry, within an industry it is an excellent indicator of management's operating efficiency.

The product of these first two components (profit margin and total asset turnover) equals the firm's return on assets (*ROA*), which reflects the firm's operating performance before the financing impact.[16]

[15] You will recall from Chapter 10 (Exhibit 10.7) that it is possible to employ an extended DuPont system that involves eight ratios. For purposes of this discussion, the three ratios indicate the significant factors and differences among countries.
[16] In Chapter 13, we discuss a study that analyzes why and how alternative industries differ regarding the return on assets and the two components of ROA.

The final component, total assets/equity, does not measure operating performance but, rather, financial leverage. Specifically, it indicates how management has decided to finance the firm. In turn, this management decision regarding the financing of assets can contribute to a higher *ROE*, but it also has financial risk implications for the stockholder.

Knowing this breakdown of *ROE*, you must examine past results and expectations for a firm and develop *estimates* of the three components and therefore an estimate of a firm's *ROE*. This estimate of *ROE* combined with the firm's expected retention rate will indicate its future growth potential. Finally, it is important to note that when estimating growth, it is necessary to estimate, not only the *rate* of growth, but also the *duration* of growth (how long can the firm sustain this rate of growth?). Clearly, the higher the rate of growth the more significant the estimate of the duration of growth to the ultimate value of the stock. Also, a high rate of growth generally requires a high ROE, which is difficult to sustain because numerous competitors want to experience these high rates of return.

Estimating Growth Based on History Although the authors have a strong bias in favor of using the fundamentals to estimate future growth, which involves estimating the components of *ROE*, we also believe in using all the information available to make this critical estimate. Therefore, we suggest that analysts also consider the historical growth rate of sales, earnings, cash flow, and dividends and consider not only the different rates of growth, but also the variability in the growth pattern over time for these series.

Although we demonstrate these computations for the market, for an industry, and for a company in subsequent chapters, the following discussion considers some suggestions on alternative calculations. In terms of the relevant period to consider, one is struck by the cliché "more is better" as long as you recognize that "recent is relevant." Specifically, about 20 years of annual observations would be ideal, but it is important to consider subperiods as well as the total period—that is, 20 years, two 10-year periods, and four 5-year periods would indicate the overall growth rate but also would indicate if there were any *changes* in the growth rate during the critical recent periods.

The specific measurement can be done using one or more of three techniques: (1) arithmetic or geometric average of annual percentage changes, (2) linear regression models, and (3) log-linear regression models. Irrespective of the measurement techniques used, we strongly encourage a time-series plot of the annual percentage changes.

The arithmetic or geometric average technique involves computing the annual percentage change and then computing either the simple arithmetic average or the geometric average of these values for the alternative periods. As you will recall from the discussion in Chapter 3, the arithmetic average will always be a higher value than the geometric average (except when the annual values are constant) and the difference between the arithmetic and geometric average values will increase with volatility. As noted previously, we generally prefer the geometric mean because it provides the average annual compound growth rate.

The linear regression model goes well with the suggested time-series plot and is as follows:

$$EPS_t = a + bt$$

where:

EPS_t = earnings per period in Period t
  t = year t where t goes from 1 to n
  b = the coefficient that indicates the average absolute change in the series during the period

It would be very informative to superimpose this regression line on the time-series plot because it would provide insights on changes in absolute growth.

The log-linear model considers that the series might be better described in terms of a constant *growth rate*. This model is as follows:

$$ln(EPS_t) = a + bt$$

where:

$ln(EPS_t)$ = the natural logarithm of earnings per share in Period t
b = the coefficient that indicates *the average percentage change* in the series during the period

The analysis of these historical growth rates both visually with the time-series graph and the alternative calculations should provide you with significant insights into the trend of the growth rates as well as the *variability* of the growth rates over time. As discussed in Chapter 10 and demonstrated in Appendix 10C, this could provide information on the unit's business risk with the analysis of sales and EBIT growth.

11.6.4 Estimating Dividend Growth for Foreign Stocks

The underlying factors that determine the growth rates for foreign stocks are similar to those for U.S. stocks, but the value of the equation's components may differ substantially from what is common in the United States. The differences in the retention rate or the components of *ROE* result from differences in accounting practices as well as alternative management performance or philosophy. Therefore, it is important to determine the different values for the ratios and the reasons for the differences.

Retention Rates The retention rates for foreign corporations differ within countries, but differences also exist among countries due to differences in the countries' investment opportunities. As an example, firms in Japan have a higher retention rate than firms in the United States, whereas the rate of retention in France is much lower. Therefore, you need to examine the retention rates for a number of firms in a country as a background for estimating the standard rate within a country.

Net Profit Margin The net profit margin of foreign firms can differ because of different accounting conventions between countries. As noted in Chapter 10, foreign accounting rules allow firms to recognize revenue and allocate expenses differently from U.S. firms. For example, German firms are allowed to build up large reserves for various reasons. As a result, they report low earnings for tax purposes. Also, different foreign depreciation practices require adjustment of earnings and cash flows.

Total Asset Turnover Total asset turnover can likewise differ among countries because of different accounting conventions on the reporting of asset values at cost or market values. For example, in Japan, a large part of the market values for some firms comes from their real estate holdings and their common stock investments in other firms. These assets are reported at cost, which typically substantially understates their true value. This also means that the total asset turnover ratio for these firms is substantially overstated.

This ratio will also be impacted by leases that are not capitalized on the balance sheet—that is, if leases are not capitalized, both assets and liabilities are understated.

Total Asset/Equity Ratio This ratio, a measure of financial leverage, differs among countries because of differences in economic environments, tax laws, management philosophies regarding corporate debt, and accounting conventions. In several countries, the attitude toward debt is much more liberal than in the United States. A prime example is Japan, where debt as a percentage of total assets is almost 50 percent higher than this ratio in the United States. Notably, most corporate debt in Japan entails borrowing from banks at fairly low rates of interest. Balance sheet debt ratios may be higher in Japan than in the United States or other countries; but, because of the lower interest rates in Japan, the fixed-charge coverage ratios, such as the times interest earned ratio, might be similar to those in other countries. The point is, it is important to consider the several cash flow financial risk ratios along with the balance sheet debt ratios.

Consequently, when analyzing a foreign stock market or an individual foreign stock that involves estimating the growth rate for earnings and dividends, you must consider the three components of the *ROE* just as you would for a U.S. stock but recognize that the financial ratios for foreign firms can differ from those of U.S. firms, as discussed in Chapter 10 references. Subsequent chapters on valuation applied to the aggregate market, to various industries, and to companies contain examples of these differences.

• • • • SUMMARY • • • •

- As an investor, you want to select investments that will provide a rate of return that compensates you for your time, the expected rate of inflation, and the risk involved. To help you find these investments, this chapter considers the theory of valuation by which you derive the value of an investment using your required rate of return. We consider the two investment decision processes, which are the top-down, three-step approach and the bottom-up, stockpicking approach. Although it is recognized that either process can provide abnormal positive returns if the analyst is superior, we feel that a preferable approach is the top-down approach in which you initially consider the aggregate economy and market, then examine alternative global industries, and finally analyze individual firms and their stocks.
- We apply the valuation theory to a range of investments, including bonds, preferred stock, and common stock. Because the valuation of common stock is more complex and

difficult, we suggest two alternative approaches (the present value of cash flows and the relative valuation approach) and several techniques for each of these approaches. Notably, these are *not* competitive approaches and we suggest that both approaches be used. Although we suggest using several different valuation models, the investment decision rule is always the same: If the estimated intrinsic value of the investment is greater than the market price, you should buy the investment; if the estimated intrinsic value of an investment is less than its market price, you should not invest in it and if you own it, you should sell it.
- We conclude with a review of factors that you need to consider when estimating the value of stock with either approach—your required rate of return on an investment and the growth rate of earnings, cash flow, and dividends. Finally, we consider some unique factors that affect the application of these valuation models to foreign stocks.

• • • • SUGGESTED READINGS • • • •

Arzac, Enrique. *Valuations for Mergers, Buyouts, and Restructuring.* New York: Wiley, 2005.

Billingsley, Randall, ed. *Corporate Financial Decision Making and Equity Analysis.* Proceedings of a seminar by the Association of Investment Management and Research. Charlottesville, VA: AIMR, 1995.

Damodaran, Aswath. *Damodaran on Valuation,* 2nd ed. New York: Wiley, 2006.

Damodaran, Aswath. *Investment Valuation,* 2nd ed. New York: Wiley, 2002.

Fogler, H. Russell, ed. *Blending Quantitative and Traditional Equity Analysis.* Proceedings of a seminar by the Association of Investment Management and Research. Charlottesville, VA: AIMR, 1994.

Helfert, Erich A. *Techniques of Financial Analysis,* 11th ed. New York: McGraw-Hill Irwin, 2002.

Higgins, Robert C. *Analysis for Financial Management,* 8th ed. New York: McGraw-Hill Irwin, 2005.

Koller, Tim, Marc Goedhart, and David Wessels. *Valuation: Measuring and Managing the Value of Companies,* 4th ed. New York: Wiley, 2005.

Palepu, Krishna, and Paul Healy. *Business Analysis and Valuation,* 4th ed. Cincinnati, OH: South-Western, 2007.

Squires, Jan, ed. *Equity Research and Valuation Techniques.* Proceedings of a seminar by the Association of Investment Management and Research. Charlottesville, VA: AIMR, 1997.

Squires, Jan, ed. *Practical Issues in Equity Analysis.* Conference proceedings by the Association of Investment Management and Research. Charlottesville, VA: AIMR, 2000.

Stowe, J. D., T. R. Robinson, J. E. Pinto, and D. W. McLeavey. *Analysis of Equity Investments: Valuation.* Charlottesville, VA: Association of Investment Management and Research; 2002.

Sullivan, Rodney N., ed. *Equity Analysis Issues, Lessons, and Techniques.* Proceedings of a seminar by AIMR, Charlottesville, VA: AIMR, 2003.

• • • • QUESTIONS • • • •

1. Discuss the difference between the top-down and bottom-up approaches. What is the major assumption that causes the difference in these two approaches?
2. What is the benefit of analyzing the market and alternative industries before individual securities?
3. Discuss why you would not expect all industries to have a similar relationship to the economy. Give an example of two industries that have different relationships to the economy.
4. Discuss why estimating the value for a bond is easier than estimating the value for common stock.
5. Would you expect the required rate of return for a U.S. investor in U.S. common stocks to be the same as the required rate of return on Japanese common stocks? What factors would determine the required rate of return for stocks in the United States versus Japan?
6. Would you expect the nominal *RFR* in the United States to be the same as in Germany? Discuss your reasoning in detail.
7. Would you expect the risk premium for an investment in an Indonesian stock to be the same as that for a stock from the United Kingdom? Discuss your specific reasoning.
8. Would you expect the risk premium for an investment in a stock from Singapore to be the same as that for a stock from the United States? Discuss your specific reasoning.
9. Give an example of a stock where it would be appropriate to use the reduced form DDM for valuation and discuss why you feel that it is appropriate. Similarly, give an example and discuss a stock where it would not be appropriate to use the reduced form DDM.
10. Give an example of and discuss a stock that has temporary, supernormal growth where it would be appropriate (necessary) to use the modified DDM.
11. Under what conditions will it be ideal to use one or several of the relative valuation ratios to evaluate a stock?
12. Discuss a scenario where it would be appropriate to use one of the present value of cash flow techniques for the valuation.
13. Discuss why the two valuation approaches (present value of cash flows and the relative valuation ratios) are competitive or complementary.

• • • • PROBLEMS • • • •

1. What is the value to you of a 9 percent coupon bond with a par value of $10,000 that matures in 10 years if you require a 7 percent return? Use semiannual compounding.
2. What would be the value of the bond in Problem 1 if you required an 11 percent rate of return?
3. The preferred stock of the Clarence Radiology Company has a par value of $100 and a $9 dividend rate. You require an 11 percent rate of return on this stock. What is the maximum price you would pay for it? Would you buy it at a market price of $96?
4. The Baron Basketball Company (BBC) earned $10 a share last year and paid a dividend of $6 a share. Next year, you expect BBC to earn $11 and continue its payout ratio. Assume that you expect to sell the stock for $132 a year from now. If you require 12 percent on this stock, how much would you be willing to pay for it?
5. Given the expected earnings and dividend payments in Problem 4, if you expected a selling price of $110 and required an 8 percent return on this investment, how much would you pay for the BBC stock?
6. Over the long run, you expect dividends for BBC in Problem 4 to grow at 8 percent and you require 11 percent on the stock. Using the infinite period DDM, how much would you pay for this stock?
7. Based on new information regarding the popularity of basketball, you revise your growth estimate for BBC to 9 percent. What is the maximum *P/E* ratio you will apply to BBC, and what is the maximum price you will pay for the stock?
8. The Shamrock Dogfood Company (SDC) has consistently paid out 40 percent of its earnings in dividends. The company's return on equity is 16 percent. What would you estimate as its dividend growth rate?
9. Given the low risk in dog food, your required rate of return on SDC is 13 percent. What *P/E* ratio would you apply to the firm's earnings?

10. What *P/E* ratio would you apply if you learned that SDC had decided to increase its payout to 50 percent? (Hint: This change in payout has multiple effects.)

11. Discuss three ways a firm can increase its *ROE*. Make up an example to illustrate your discussion.

12. It is widely known that grocery chains have low profit margins—on average they earn about 1 percent on sales. How would you explain the fact that their *ROE* is about 12 percent? Does this seem logical?

13. Compute a recent five-year average of the following ratios for three companies of your choice (attempt to select diverse firms):
    a. Retention rate
    b. Net profit margin
    c. Equity turnover
    d. Total asset turnover
    e. Total assets/equity
    Based on these ratios, explain which firm should have the highest growth rate of earnings.

14. You have been reading about the Madison Computer Company (MCC), which currently retains 90 percent of its earnings ($5 a share this year). It earns an *ROE* of almost 30 percent. Assuming a required rate of return of 14 percent, how much would you pay for MCC on the basis of the earnings multiplier model? Discuss your answer. What would you pay for Madison Computer if its retention rate was 60 percent and its *ROE* was 19 percent? Show your work.

15. Gentry Can Company's (GCC) latest annual dividend of $1.25 a share was paid yesterday and maintained its historic 7 percent annual rate of growth. You plan to purchase the stock today because you believe that the dividend growth rate will increase to 8 percent for the next three years and the selling price of the stock will be $40 per share at the end of that time.
    a. How much should you be willing to pay for the GCC stock if you require a 12 percent return?
    b. What is the maximum price you should be willing to pay for the GCC stock if you believe that the 8 percent growth rate can be maintained indefinitely and you require a 12 percent return?
    c. If the 8 percent rate of growth is achieved, what will the price be at the end of Year 3, assuming the conditions in Part b?

16. In the *Federal Reserve Bulletin,* find the average yield of AAA and BBB bonds for a recent month. Compute the risk premium (in basis points) and the percentage risk premium on BBB bonds relative to AAA bonds. Discuss how these values compare to those shown in Exhibits 11.4 and 11.5.

THOMSON ONE | Business School Edition

1. Using Ford (F), General Electric (GE), McDonald's (MCD), Nike (NKE), and Walgreens (WAG), find the five-year estimate for net income growth (LTG) dividend yield, *P/E*, Price/Cash Flow, and Price/Book Value ratios. Do a spreadsheet listing each of these values for each company and briefly comment on the differences between each item.

2. Assume that the five-year estimates for net income growth for General Electric, McDonald's, and Walgreens are the same as their dividend growth rates—that is, earnings and dividends grow at the same rate.
    a. For each of these three firms, estimate the dollar amount of dividends per share over each of the next five years.
    b. Find the present value of each dividend stream from part a. Use a discount rate of 10 percent for each firm. (This is a simplification; in reality we would need to estimate the required rate of return for each firm.)
    c. For each firm, compare its current stock price with the estimated present value of its dividends over the next five years. Given our assumptions, what proportion of the stock price arises from cash flows *beyond* the next five years?

3. For each of the five firms, using the beta provided in the database, compute the stock's required return on equity (*K*) using the following *SML* equation.

$$E(R) = RFR + \beta_i (R_m - RFR)$$
$$= 0.05 + \beta_i (0.09 - 0.05)$$

4. Knowing that a stock's *P/E* ratio is mainly determined by *K* and *g*, show in a table the following for each of the five stocks:

Stock	*Current Forward P/E	LTG	K

$$^*\text{Forward } P/E = \frac{\text{Current } P}{EPS_{t+1}}$$

Comment on the stocks that appear to be relatively high priced or low priced and why you label them as such.

• • • • • APPENDIX: CHAPTER 11 • • • • •

Derivation of Constant Growth Dividend Discount Model (DDM)

The basic model is

$$P_0 = \frac{D_1}{(1+k)^1} + \frac{D_2}{(1+k)^2} + \frac{D_3}{(1+k)^3} + \cdots + \frac{D_n}{(1+k)^n}$$

where:

P_0 = current price
D_i = expected dividend in Period i
k = required rate of return on Asset j

If growth rate (g) is constant,

$$P_0 = \frac{D_0(1+g)^1}{(1+k)^1} + \frac{D_0(1+g)^2}{(1+k)^2} + \cdots + \frac{D_0(1+g)^n}{(1+k)^n}$$

This can be written

$$P_0 = D_0\left[\frac{(1+g)}{(1+k)} + \frac{(1+g)^2}{(1+k)^2} + \frac{(1+g)^3}{(1+k)^3} + \cdots + \frac{(1+g)^n}{(1+k)^n}\right]$$

Multiply both sides of the equation by $\frac{1+k}{1+g}$.

$$\left[\frac{(1+k)}{(1+g)}\right]P_0 = D_0\left[1 + \frac{(1+g)}{(1+k)} + \frac{(1+g)^2}{(1+k)^2} + \cdots + \frac{(1+g)^{n-1}}{(1+k)^{n-1}}\right]$$

Subtract the previous equation from this equation:

$$\left[\frac{(1+k)}{(1+g)} - 1\right]P_0 = D_0\left[1 - \frac{(1+g)^n}{(1+k)^n}\right]$$

$$\left[\frac{(1+k) - (1+g)}{(1+g)}\right]P_0 = D_0\left[1 - \frac{(1+g)^n}{(1+k)^n}\right]$$

Assuming $k > g$, as $n \rightarrow \infty$, the term in brackets on the right side of the equation goes to 1, leaving:

$$\left[\frac{(1 + k) - (1 + g)}{(1 + g)}\right] P_0 = D_0$$

This simplifies to

$$\left[\frac{(1 + k - 1 - g)}{(1 + g)}\right] P_0 = D_0$$

which equals

$$\left[\frac{k - g}{(1 + g)}\right] P_0 = D_0$$

This equals

$$(k - g)P_0 = D_0(1 + g)$$
$$D_0(1 + g) = D_1$$

so:

$$(k - g)P_0 = D_1$$
$$P_0 = \frac{D_1}{k - g}$$

Remember, this model assumes

- A constant growth rate
- An infinite time period
- The required return on the investment (k) is greater than the expected growth rate (g)

PART 4
Analysis and Management of Common Stocks

CHAPTER 12
Macroanalysis and Microvaluation of the Stock Market

CHAPTER 13
Industry Analysis

CHAPTER 14
Company Analysis and Stock Valuation

CHAPTER 15
Technical Analysis

CHAPTER 16
Equity Portfolio Management Strategies

In Part 3 we considered the basic valuation principles and practices applied to all securities and how this was applied to the global asset allocation decision. In Part 4, we apply these same valuation principles and practices to the analysis and management of common stocks. The objective is to be in position to make the critical risk–return decision at the market-industry-company stock level.

You will recall from Chapter 11 that successful investment requires several steps, beginning with a valuation of the aggregate economy and market and the examination of various industries and concluding with the analysis of individual companies and their securities. Globalization of the capital markets has definitely complicated this process wherein it is now necessary to consider markets on a worldwide basis followed by the analysis of *world* industries that involve numerous, complex foreign companies.

In Chapter 12, we begin the three-step, top-down approach and discuss how to analyze the aggregate stock market using the two general valuation approaches introduced in Chapter 11— the present value of cash flow models and the relative valuation ratios. In Chapter 13, we again demonstrate these two approaches to the valuation of an industry.

Chapter 14 on company analysis begins with a discussion of the difference between a company and its stock. In many instances, the common stock of a very fine company (possibly a true growth company) may not be a good investment, which is why we emphasize that company analysis and stock selection are two separate but dependent activities. Once again, the analysis procedure is built on the two valuation approaches employed for the market and alternative industries. We also consider other techniques, such as economic value added (EVA), that provide insights regarding the economic success of a firm and its management. The overall goal of this procedure is to select one of the best companies in a superior industry during a favorable market environment.

It was noted in Chapter 11 that it is not feasible to use the standard dividend discount model to value the stock of true growth companies. Therefore, in Chapter 14 we discuss several valuation models that have been specifically developed for the analysis and valuation of growth companies.

Throughout this section, we refer back to the semi-strong efficient market hypothesis. Recall that, although many studies support this hypothesis, there is a growing literature dealing with anomalies related to this hypothesis. Therefore, in this section we provide a consistent and justifiable valuation process that can be used to find undervalued securities. You should never forget that the output of alternative valuation models is only as good as the estimated inputs and *the superior analyst is the one who provides (1) the best estimates of the required rate of return on a security based upon its risks and (2) the expected growth rate of future cash flows.*

Chapter 15 deals with technical analysis, an alternative or supplement to the fundamental approach discussed in the prior chapters. Rather than estimating value based on fundamental variables, the technical analyst believes that it is possible to project future stock price movements based on past stock price changes or other stock market data. Various techniques used by technical analysts for U.S. and world markets are discussed and demonstrated.

Chapter 16 deals with equity portfolio management strategies. We begin with a general discussion of passive versus active management styles. This is followed by a specific discussion of indexing, including the selection of an appropriate benchmark index, and the various methods of index portfolio investing used in practice. The concept of *tracking error* is introduced as a means of assessing how well an investor has replicated the benchmark portfolio.

The overview of active equity portfolio management strategies includes a discussion of how one constructs a portfolio that reflects the client's risk–return objectives and constraints from three different perspectives: fundamental analysis (e.g., asset class and sector rotation, stock under- and overvaluation), technical analysis (e.g., overreaction, price momentum), and anomaly and attribute analysis (e.g., earnings momentum, firm size). In this discussion, we pay special attention to the conceptual and practical differences between forming portfolios based on both value-oriented and growth-oriented investment styles. Notably, all of these approaches should consider global opportunities.

We conclude Chapter 16 with a discussion of how the equity portfolio management decision fits into the investor's overall asset allocation strategy. After discussing the integrated approach to asset allocation, we examine strategic, tactical, and insured allocation strategies. Finally, we present the basic intuition for how investors can use *derivative instruments* (such as futures and option contracts) to alter the risk and return characteristics of their equity portfolios.

CHAPTER 12

Macroanalysis and Microvaluation of the Stock Market

After you read this chapter, you should be able to answer the following questions:

- What are the expected and the empirical relationships between economic activity and security markets?
- What is the macroeconomic approach to estimating future market returns?
- What are the major macroeconomic techniques used to project the securities market?
- What is the leading economic indicator approach? What are its uses and shortcomings?
- What are the expected and the empirical relationships between the growth of the money supply and stock prices?
- by excess liquidity, and how is it measured?
- t of monetary policy on stock prices in the United States and around the world?
- xpected and the empirical relationships between inflation, interest rates, and
- xpected and the empirical relationships between inflation and stock prices?
- sic valuation variables differ among countries?
- hould be considered when analyzing the outlook for a foreign economy and ond market?
- set allocation procedure for a global portfolio?
- sset allocation, what is meant by normal weighting, underweighting, and
- ply the dividend discount model (DDM) to the valuation of the aggregate stock
- e the prevailing value of the market as represented by the S&P Industrials Index he reduced form DDM?
- e the prevailing value of the aggregate stock market based upon the present cash flow to equity (FCFE) model?
- mponents are involved in the two-part valuation procedure?
- components in the valuation procedure, which is more volatile?
- re involved in estimating the earnings per share for an aggregate market series?
- es affect the aggregate operating profit margin and how do they affect it?
- es determine the level and changes in the market earnings multiplier?
- appened to the values for the other relative valuation ratios—that is, the *P/BV*, S ratios?
- onal factors must be considered when you apply this microanalysis approach to n of stock markets around the world?

12.1 The Components of Market Analysis

In Chapter 11 we introduced the top-down, three-step market-industry-company investment process. This chapter is concerned with the market analysis portion of this process. In turn, this market analysis has two components: (1) the macroanalysis of the relationship between the aggregate securities markets and the aggregate economy, and (2) the specific microvaluation of the stock market employing the valuation approaches introduced in Chapter 11.

The macroanalysis is in response to the belief that *security markets reflect what is expected to go on in the economy,* because the value of an investment is determined by its expected cash flows and its expected required rate of return (i.e., its discount rate). Clearly, both of these valuation factors are influenced by the aggregate economic environment. The objective is to consider what specific variables and economic series should be considered when attempting to project future market movements. This macroeconomy and market analysis provides important insights for our subsequent industry and company analysis.

The microanalysis builds on these macroinsights by deriving a specific valuation for the market using the approaches discussed. The result is an estimated intrinsic value for a market indicator series, leading to the decision rule wherein this intrinsic value is compared to the current market value and an appropriate decision regarding the aggregate U.S. stock market. Specifically, the decision is how to weight the U.S. stock market in a global asset portfolio—that is, underweight, market weight, or overweight the U.S. stock market depending on whether it is currently overvalued, properly valued, or undervalued.

12.2 Macromarket Analysis

Fluctuations in security markets are related to changes in expectations for the aggregate economy. The prices of government and investment-grade corporate bonds are determined by the level of interest rates, which is influenced by overall economic activity and Federal Reserve policy. Aggregate stock prices reflect investor expectations about corporate performance in terms of earnings, cash flows, and the required rate of return by investors. All of these expectations are heavily impacted by the economic outlook.

Given the expected relationship between security markets and the economy, this section has four subsections: (1) documentation of the relationship between the economy and stock prices, (2) presentation of several economic series that provide specific insights related to the stock market; (3) specific discussion of the macroeconomic impact of inflation and interest rates on security prices, and (4) brief consideration of what additional factors should be analyzed when dealing with world security markets.

12.2.1 Economic Activity and Security Markets

In its monitoring of business cycles, the National Bureau of Economic Research (NBER) has examined the relationship of alternative economic series to the behavior of the entire economy and has classified numerous economic series into three groups: leading, coincident, and lagging indicator series. Further, extensive analysis of the relationship between the economy and the stock market has shown that stock prices are one of the better leading indicator series.

The evidence by Moore and Cullity (1988) and Siegel (1991) not only has indicated a strong relationship between stock prices and the economy but also has shown that stock prices consistently turn *before* the economy does. The data in Exhibit 12.1 document this relationship, beginning in the 1950s.

There are two possible reasons why stock prices lead the economy. One is that stock prices reflect *expectations* of earnings, dividends, and interest rates. As investors attempt to estimate these future variables, their stock price decisions reflect expectations for *future* economic activity, not past or current activity. A second possible reason is that the stock market reacts to various leading indicator series, the most important being corporate earnings, corporate profit margins, interest rates, and changes in the growth rate of the money supply. Because these series tend to lead the economy, when investors adjust stock prices to reflect these leading economic series, *expectations* for stock prices become a leading series as well.

Exhibit 12.2 Economic Series Included in the Conference Board Indicators

Leading Index

1. Average weekly hours of manufacturing workers
2. Average weekly initial claims for unemployment insurance
3. Real value of manufacturers' new orders for consumer goods and materials
4. Index of consumer expectations
5. Index of 500 common stock prices
6. Manufacturers' new orders, nondefense capital goods in 1992 dollars
7. Index of new private housing starts authorized by local building permits
8. Vendor performance (the percentage of companies receiving delivery later than the industry average)
9. Real money supply, M2
10. Interest rate spread, 10-year Treasury bonds less federal funds rate

Coincident Index

1. Number of employees on nonagricultural payrolls
2. Personal income less transfer payments, expressed in 1992 dollars
3. Index of industrial production
4. Manufacturing and trade sales, expressed in 1992 dollars

Lagging Index

1. Average duration of unemployment
2. Ratio of manufacturing and trade inventories to sales
3. Percentage change in the labor cost per unit of output in manufacturing
4. Average prime rate charged by banks
5. Commercial and industrial loans outstanding
6. Ratio of consumer installment credit outstanding to personal income
7. Change in the consumer price index (inflation rate) for services

A final category, *selected series,* includes economic series that are expected to influence aggregate economic activity but do not fall neatly into one of the three main groups. This includes such series as U.S. balance of payments and federal surplus or deficit.[1]

Composite Series and Ratio of Series In addition to the individual economic series in each category, a composite time series combines these economic series—for example, the ***composite leading indicator index.*** This composite leading indicator series is widely reported in the press each month as an indicator of the current and future state of the economy. There also are composite coincident and lagging indicator series.

Some analysts have used a *ratio* of these composite series, contending that the ratio of the composite coincident series divided by the composite lagging series acts like a leading series, in some instances even leading the composite leading series. The rationale for expecting this leading relationship for the ratio is that the coincident series should turn before the lagging series, and the ratio of the two series will be quite sensitive to such changes. As a result, this ratio series is expected to lead both of the individual composite series, especially at turning points.

Although movements for this ratio series are generally parallel to those of the leading series, its real value comes when it diverges from the composite leading indicator series because this divergence signals a change in the normal relationship between the indicator series. For example, if the leading indicator series has been rising for a period of time, you

[1]While the cyclial indicator approach and the placement of economic series into the three categories was done by the NBER beginning in the 1930s, the publication and maintenance of the database was transferred to the Conference Board in the late 1990s, so current references willl be to the Conference Board.

Exhibit 12.1 Timing Relationships between Stock Market and Business Cycle Peaks and Troughs

Peak	Trough
Nov-83	Jun-84
Aug-87	Oct-87
Jul-90	Oct-90
Jul-98	Aug-98
Jan-00	Mar-00
Sep-00	Mar-01
May-01	Oct-02
Nov-02	Mar-03
Oct-07	Jan-08

Because stock prices lead the aggregate economy, our macroeconomic approach to market analysis concentrates on economic series that lead the economy by more than stock prices do. First, we discuss cyclical indicator approaches developed by various research groups. Next, we consider the money supply, as well as other measures of monetary liquidity and policy. Finally, we discuss the research related to a number of economic series expected to affect security returns (e.g., production, inflation, and risk premiums).

12.2.2 Economic Series and Stock Prices

As noted, because research has documented that peaks and troughs in stock prices tend to occur prior to peaks and troughs in the economy, our consideration of relevant economic series concentrates on two broad categories of economic series that likewise lead the economy and should provide some insights regarding the future trend of stocks. The first are sets of economic series suggested by the National Bureau of Economic Research. The second are alternative monetary series influenced by the Federal Reserve.

12.2.3 The Cyclical Indicator Approach

The cyclical indicator approach to monitoring and forecasting the economy is built on the belief that the aggregate economy experiences periods of expansion and contraction that can be identified by the movements in specific economic series.

Cyclical Indicator Categories The NBER examined the behavior of hundreds of economic time series in relation to past business cycles and grouped various economic series into three major categories based on their relationship to the business cycle.

The first category, **leading indicators**, includes economic series that usually reach peaks or troughs before corresponding peaks or troughs in aggregate economic activity. The group currently includes the 10 series shown in Exhibit 12.2. Included are common stock prices, which have a median lead of four months at peaks and troughs and the money supply in constant (1992) dollars, which has a median lead of five months at peaks and four months at troughs.

The second category, **coincident indicators**, includes four economic time series that have peaks and troughs that roughly coincide with the peaks and troughs in the business cycle. As one might expect, many of these economic time series are used to define the business cycle.

The third category, **lagging indicators**, includes seven series that experience their peaks and troughs after those of the aggregate economy. A listing of the coincident and lagging series also appears in Exhibit 12.2.

Exhibit 12.3 Indicator Series Performance

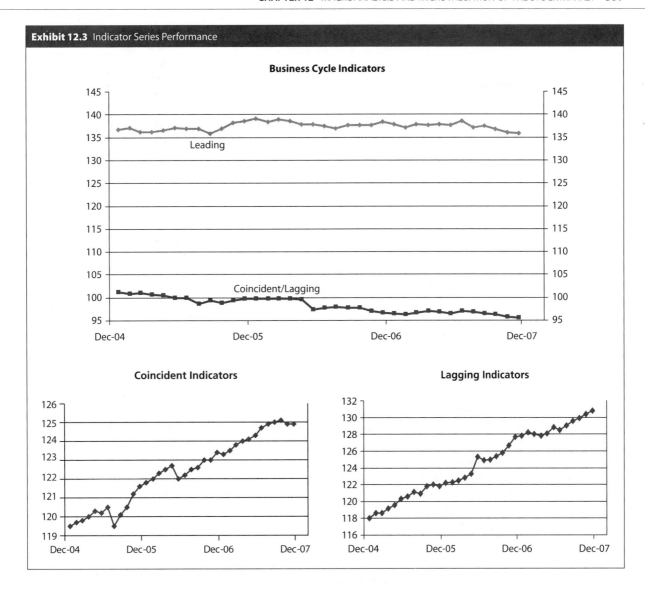

would expect both the coincident and lagging series also to be rising, but the coincident series should be rising faster than the lagging series, so the ratio of the coincident to the lagging series should likewise be rising. In contrast, assume the composite leading indicator series is rising but the ratio of coincident to lagging series is flattening out or declining. This change in trend in the ratio series could occur because the coincident series is not rising as fast as the lagging indicator series or because the coincident series has turned down. Either scenario would indicate a possible end to an economic expansion or at least a less-robust expansion.

An example of such a divergence shows up in Exhibit 12.3. During the last several months of 2007 the coincident/lagging series index declined before the leading series index based on a coincident series index that declined slightly for several months and a lagging index that continued to rise. It appears that this most recent divergence was a precursor to the slowdown/recession subsequently experienced by the U.S. economy during 2008.

Analytical Measures of Performance   Certain analytical measures have been suggested for examining behavior within an economic series.

Diffusion Indexes   As the name implies, ***diffusion indexes*** indicate how pervasive a given movement is in a series. Diffusion index values are measured by computing the percentage of reporting units in a series that indicate a given result. For example, if 100 companies constitute the sample reporting new orders for equipment, the diffusion index for this series would indicate what proportion of the 100 companies was reporting higher orders during an expansion. In addition to knowing that aggregate new orders are increasing, it is helpful to know whether 55 percent or 95 percent of the companies in the sample are reporting higher orders. This information on the pervasiveness of the increase in new orders would help you project the future length and strength of the increase and the impact on the expansion.

You also would want to know the prevailing *trend* for a diffusion index. The diffusion index for a series almost always reaches its peak or trough before the peak or trough in the corresponding aggregate series. Therefore, the trend of the diffusion index for a series helps predict the behavior of the series itself.

Besides diffusion indexes for individual series, a diffusion index that shows the percentage of the 10 leading indicators rising or falling is used as an indicator of the future state of the economy.

Rates of Change   Knowing whether a series is increasing is useful, but knowing that a 7 percent increase one month followed a 10 percent increase the previous month indicates the series is growing but at a declining rate. Similar to the diffusion index, the rate of change values for a series reaches peaks or troughs prior to the peak or trough in the aggregate series.

Comparison with Previous Cycles   A set of tables and charts shows the movements of individual series during the current business cycle and compares these movements to previous cycles for the same economic series. This comparison reveals whether a given series is moving slower or faster than during prior cycles. This information can be useful because, typically, movements in the initial months of an expansion or contraction indicate their ultimate length and strength.

Limitations of the Cyclical Indicator Approach   The Conference Board acknowledges the following limitations that are also discussed in Koenis and Emery (1991):

False Signals   This is when a series that is moving in one direction suddenly reverses and nullifies a prior signal or hesitates, which is difficult to interpret. High variability in a series causes this problem.

Currency of the Data and Revisions   Some data series take time to be reported, but a bigger problem are revisions in data especially if the revision changes the direction implied by the original data.

Economic Sectors Not Represented   Examples include the service sector, import-exports, data, and many international series.

Other Leading Indicator Series   The Center for International Business Conditions Research (CIBCR) at the Columbia Graduate School of Business has developed the following additional leading indicator series.

Long-Leading Index It is intended to provide earlier signals of major turning points in the economy.

Leading Employment Index It is meant to forecast changes in U.S. employment.

Leading Inflation Index It is intended to forecast U.S. inflation.

International Leading Indicator Series This is a set of composite leading indicators for eight other major industrial countries: Canada, Germany, France, the United Kingdom, Italy, Japan, Australia, and Taiwan (Republic of China). The series are comparable in data and analysis to the leading series for the United States.

Surveys of Sentiment and Expectations Consumer expectations are considered relevant as the economy approaches cyclical turning points. Two surveys of consumer expectations are reported monthly. The University of Michigan Consumer Sentiment Index and the Conference Board Consumer Confidence Index both query a sample of households on their expectations. Although the two indexes deviate from month to month, over longer time periods they track each other fairly closely. Both indexes are meant to be leading indicators of the economy.

Other surveys of business expectations focus on firms' capital spending or inventory investment plans. The problem with survey data is that individuals' and firms' reported plans may not come to fruition.

Economic statistics released by the government are another source of helpful information about current economic trends. Every Monday, The *Wall Street Journal* publishes a short commentary, "Tracking the Economy." The feature reports statistics that will be released during the coming weeks, their previous values, and their consensus forecasts. As implied by our discussion of efficient markets, investors react to economic surprises wherein the actual results deviate from the consensus forecasts (expectations).

12.2.4 Monetary Variables, the Economy, and Stock Prices

Many academic and professional observers hypothesize a close relationship between stock prices and various monetary variables that are influenced by monetary policy. The best-known monetary variable is the *money supply*. You will recall from your economics course that there are numerous measures of the money supply and the Federal Reserve controls the money supply through various tools, the most useful of which is open market operations.

12.2.5 Money Supply and the Economy

In their classic work on the monetary history of the United States, Friedman and Schwartz (1963) thoroughly documented that declines in the rate of growth of the money supply have preceded business contractions, while increases in the growth rate of the money supply have consistently preceded economic expansions.

Friedman (1969) suggests a transmission mechanism through which changes in the growth rate of the money supply affect the aggregate economy. He hypothesizes that, to implement planned changes in monetary policy, the Federal Reserve engages in open market operations, buying or selling Treasury bonds to adjust bank reserves and, eventually, the money supply. Because the Fed deals in government bonds, the initial liquidity impact when the Fed buys bonds affects the government bond market, creating excess liquidity for those who sold bonds to the Fed. The result of the bond purchases is an increase in bond prices and lower interest rates. Rising government bond prices subsequently filter down to corporate bonds, and this change in liquidity eventually affects common stocks and then the real goods market. There is the opposite effect if the Fed sells bonds to reduce bank reserves and the money supply. The impact of changes in money supply growth on stock prices is really part of the transmission process whereby money supply affects the aggregate economy. This liquidity transmission scenario implies that the effect of a change in monetary policy initially appears in financial markets (bonds and stocks) and only later in the aggregate economy.

12.2.6 Money Supply and Stock Prices

Numerous studies have tested the relationship suggested by this transmission mechanism. Specifically, do changes in the growth rate of the money supply precede changes in stock prices? The results of these studies have tended to change over time. The initial studies by Sprinkel (1971), Keran (1971), and Homa and Jaffe (1971) generally indicated a strong *leading* relationship between money supply changes and stock prices.

Subsequent studies by Cooper (1974) and Rozeff (1974) questioned these findings because they found a relationship between the money supply and stock prices, but they found that changes in the growth rate of the money supply consistently *lagged* stock returns by about one to three months.

Davidson and Froyer (1982) and Hafer (1985) examined the relationship of stock returns to anticipated and unanticipated money supply growth and found that stock prices adjust very quickly to unexpected changes in money supply growth. This implies that to take advantage of this relationship it is necessary to *forecast unanticipated changes* in money supply growth.

12.2.7 Monetary Policy and Stock Returns

Following more than a decade of limited research on this topic, the recent focus had been on monetary policy rather that only money supply. Several studies by Jensen, Johnson, and Mercer (JJM) (1996, 1997, 1998, 2000) showed that the results of several earlier studies that examined the relationship between some economic or company variables and stock returns can be significantly affected by the prevailing monetary environment. Specifically, JJM showed that the business conditions proxies suggested by Fama and French (1989) (i.e., the term spread, dividend yield, and the default spread) have a different effect on stock returns depending on the prevailing monetary policy. Notably JJM contend that monetary policy is best indicated by discount rate changes (i.e., declining discount rates imply an easy monetary policy, while rising discount rates imply a restrictive policy). The JJM studies also show that the relationship between stock price returns and both size and the price-to-book value ratio that was found in studies by Fama and French (1995), and Fairfield (1994) only holds during periods of easy monetary policy. A subsequent study by Thorbecke (1997) that examined how stock returns respond to monetary policy shocks indicated that expansionary monetary policy increases ex-post stock returns. Patelis (1997) examined whether shifts in monetary policy affect the predictability of excess stock returns and found that monetary policy variables were significant predictors of future stock returns along with dividend yield.

12.2.8 Inflation, Interest Rates, and Security Prices

Because this chapter is concerned with the macroeconomic analysis of security markets, we should examine the macroeconomic impact of inflation and interest rates. We have noted throughout the book the critical role of expected inflation and nominal interest rates in determining the required rate of return used to derive the value of all investments. We would expect these variables that are very important in microeconomic valuation to also affect changes in the aggregate markets.

Inflation and Interest Rates Exhibit 12.4 contains a plot of long-term interest rates (the 10-year Treasury note) and the year-to-year percentage change in the consumer price index (CPI, a measure of inflation). This graph demonstrates the relationship between inflation and interest rates. We contended in our earlier discussion that when investors anticipated an increase in the rate of inflation, we would expect them to increase their required rates of return by a similar amount to derive constant real rates of return. The time-series graph of the promised yield of Treasury bonds and the annual rate of inflation in Exhibit 12.4 confirms the expected relationship overall. If the relationship was perfect and investors were accurate in their *predictions* of future inflation, the difference between the interest rate and the inflation rate (the

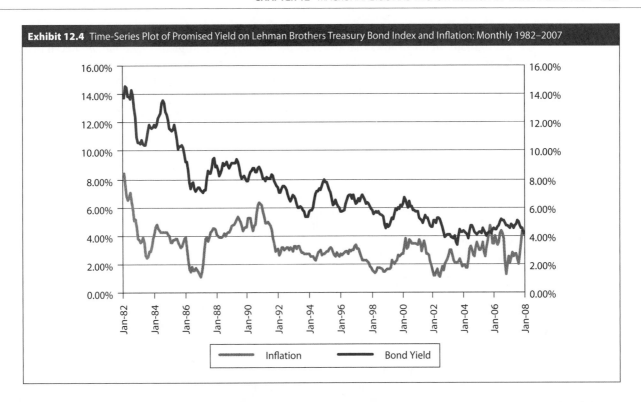

Exhibit 12.4 Time-Series Plot of Promised Yield on Lehman Brothers Treasury Bond Index and Inflation: Monthly 1982–2007

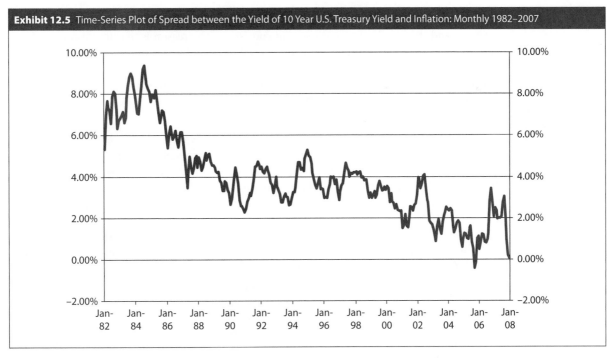

Exhibit 12.5 Time-Series Plot of Spread between the Yield of 10 Year U.S. Treasury Yield and Inflation: Monthly 1982–2007

spread between them) would be fairly constant, reflecting the real return on Treasury bonds. Notably, the spread between these two curves changes over time as shown in Exhibit 12.5. Although the two curves generally move together, during 1983–1985, the real rates of return on these Treasury bonds were in the 8 to 9 precent range, which clearly exceeds what most investors would expect on zero credit risk bonds. In sharp contrast, during 2006–2007, the real rate declines to zero, which is likewise not reasonable.

This change in spread does not mean that there is not a relationship between inflation and interest rates; it only shows that *investors are not very good at predicting inflation.* Recall that the theoretical relationship is between *expected* inflation and interest rates, which is in contrast to these data that reflect actual inflation. Apparently, investors overestimated the rate of inflation during 1980–1983 when inflation declined rapidly, so they underpaid for bonds and experienced abnormally high real rates of return and underestimated inflation during 2001–2007 so they overpaid for Treasury bonds and received low real rates of return.

Interest Rates and Bond Prices The relationship between interest rates and bond prices is clearly negative because the only variable that changes in the valuation model is the discount factor. Specifically, the expected cash flows from a straight noncallable bond would not change, so an increase in interest rates will cause a decline in bond prices and a decline in interest rates will boost bond prices. For example, if you own a 10-year bond with a coupon of 10 percent, when interest rates increase from 10 percent to 12 percent, the price of this bond will decline from $1,000 (par) to $885. In contrast, if rates decline from 10 percent to 8 percent, the price of the bond will increase from $1,000 to $1,136.

The size of the price change will depend on the characteristics of the bond. As will be discussed in Chapter 19, a longer-term bond will experience a larger price change for a change in interest rates. Therefore, we can anticipate a negative relationship between inflation and the rates of return on bonds because inflation generally has a direct effect on interest rates; and, in turn, interest rates have an inverse effect on bond prices and rates of return. One example of empirical verification for this negative relationship is provided in Exhibit 3.10, which shows a correlation of -0.11 between inflation and rates of return on long-term investment-grade bonds.

Inflation, Interest Rates, and Stock Prices The relationship between inflation, interest rates, and stock prices is not direct and consistent. The reason is that the cash flows from stocks can change along with inflation and interest rates, and we cannot be certain whether this change in cash flows will augment or offset the change in interest rates. To demonstrate this, consider the following potential scenarios following an increase in the rate of inflation and the effect of this on stock prices based on the DDM.

1. *The positive scenario.* Interest rates rise due to an increase in the rate of inflation, and corporate earnings likewise experience an increase in growth because firms are able to increase prices in line with cost increases. In this case, stock prices might be fairly stable because the negative effect of an increase in the required rate of return (k) is partially or wholly offset by the increase in the growth rate of earnings and dividends (g), which causes an increase in the value of stocks. As a result, the returns on stock increase in line with the rate of inflation.

2. *Mild negative scenario.* Interest rates and the required return k increase due to inflation, but expected cash flows continue to grow at the prior rate assuming small increases in prices at rates below the increase in the inflation rate and cost increases. This would cause a decline in stock prices similar to what happens with a bond. The required rate of return (k) would increase, but the growth rate of dividends (g) would be constant. As a result, the $k–g$ spread discussed in Chapter 11 would widen and stock prices would decline.

3. *Very negative scenario.* Interest rates and the required return k increase due to inflation, while the growth rate of cash flows decline because during the period of inflation the costs of production increase, but many firms are not able to increase prices at all, which causes a major decline in profit margins. Given this scenario, stock prices will experience a significant decline because k will increase and g will decline, causing a large increase in the $k–g$ spread.

In contrast to these scenarios, you can envision a comparable set of scenarios when inflation and interest rates decline. The relationship between inflation, interest rates, and stock prices is not as direct or consistent as the relationship between interest rates and bond prices. The point is, the effect of interest rate changes on stock prices will depend on what caused the change in interest rates and the effect of this event on the expected cash flows on common stock.

Notably, the actual relationship between inflation, interest rates, and stock prices is an empirical question and *the effect varies over time.* Therefore, although there has generally been a significant *negative* relationship between inflation, interest rates, and the returns on stock, as shown in Chapter 3 (Exhibit 3.10), this is not always true as shown by Reilly (1975), Jaffee and Mandelker (1976), and Fama (1981). In addition, even when the negative relationship is true for the overall market, certain industries may have earnings, cash flows, and dividends that react positively to inflation and interest rate changes. In such an instance, their stock prices would be positively correlated with inflation and interest rates as demonstrated by Reilly, Wright, and Johnson (2005).

12.2.9 Analysis of World Security Markets

Although we have focused on the U.S. market to demonstrate the macroeconomic approach to forecasting movements in the securities markets, you must also consider a similar analysis for numerous foreign markets, including those in Japan, Canada, the United Kingdom, and Germany. While it is not feasible to consider the full macroanalysis, the following discussion considers some of the variables and economic series and some differences that will cause the macromarket analysis to imply a different outlook for alternative countries compared to the United States.

Leading economic series are available for virtually all the developed countries, and the empirical relationships to the economy are quite similar to those of the United States.

Real GDP growth is typically consistent with what is implied by the leading series. Notably, the growth rate outlook will vary between countries by at least 4 percent ranging from about 1 percent to over 5 percent (e.g., China). Recall that these estimates of real GDP growth will impact both the country's real rate of interest and the growth of its sales and earning cash flows.

The monetary environment of a country will clearly differ from the United States because the monetary authority in each country will be responsive to the economic outlook for *its* country, which is typically different from that of the United States.

The inflation outlook will depend on the monetary environment—that is, the ease or tightness of monetary policy. It also will be impacted by the economic environment and the point on the business cycle (recession or expansion). Again, there will be a wide range for the expected rate of inflation among countries, and the impact of these different inflation rates on security values will be as described earlier for the United States.

Similar to the United States, if you have a good understanding of the outlook for each of these critical macroeconomic variables, you will also have a view on the outlook for the bond and stock market for the country and be in a better position to derive a microestimate of the future value for the country's financial markets.

- -

12.3 Microvaluation Analysis

In this section, building on the macroanalysis of the economy and the implications of this for the stock market, we estimate specific values for an aggregate stock market series using the various valuation models presented in Chapter 11. Therefore, this section has four subsections in which the four sets of valuation techniques are employed: (1) the dividend discount model (DDM), (2) the free cash flow to equity model, (3) the earnings multiplier technique, and (4) the other relative valuation ratios. Note that the first two subsections consider two of the present value of cash flow approaches presented in Chapter 11, while the last two subsections employ the four relative valuation ratios from Chapter 11. Notably, we do not demonstrate the operating free cash flow model because of space constraints and the difficulty of estimating debt for the S&P industrials. Also, we do not use the other relative valuation ratios to derive a specific value of the market; rather, we discuss the trends for these ratios during the past 12 years to help you become familiar with them so that you can use these relative valuation ratios in subsequent industry and company stock analysis. Specifically, you will want to compare the relative valuation ratios for an industry or company to the relative valuation ratios for the market. We finish the chapter with a discussion of unique factors that should be considered when applying these valuation techniques to foreign markets.

12.3.1 Applying the DDM Valuation Model to the Market

In Chapter 11, we employed the dividend discount model (DDM), which estimated the value of the stock (V_j) assuming a constant growth rate of dividends for an infinite period.

12.1
$$V_j = \frac{D_0(1+g)}{(1+k)} + \frac{D_0(1+g)^2}{(1+k)^2} + \cdots + \frac{D_0(1+g)^n}{(1+k)^n}$$

where:

V_j = the value of stock j
D_0 = the dividend payment in the current period
g = the constant growth rate of dividends
k = the required rate of return on stock j
n = the number of periods, which is assumed to be infinite

This model, which has been used extensively for the fundamental analysis of common stock, can also be used to value a stock market series. In the appendix to Chapter 11, it was shown that this model can be simplified to the following reduced form expression:

12.2
$$V_j = P_j = \frac{D_1}{k - g}$$

where:

P_j = the price of stock j
D_1 = dividend in Period 1, which is equal to: $D_0(1 + g)$
k = the required rate of return for stock j
g = the constant growth rate of dividends

This model suggests that the parameters to be estimated are (1) the required rate of return *(k)* and (2) the expected growth rate of dividends *(g)*. After estimating g, it is simple to estimate D_1 because it is equal to the current dividend (D_0) times $(1 + g)$.

Market Valuation Using the Reduced Form DDM In this section we will apply the model to the valuation of the S&P Industrials Index as of mid-2008. As noted, the critical estimates are the prevailing k and g for the U.S. equity market. The estimate of D_1 is the current D_0 for the latest 52-week period times $(1 + g)$. As of mid-2008, the recent trailing 52-week dividend estimate in *Barron's* was $28.50.

As discussed previously, the estimate of k is a function of the nominal risk-free rate *(NRFR)* plus a market risk premium. Because both of these components are subject to interpretation, we will consider a range of values.

The Nominal Risk-Free Rate The alternatives for the *NRFR* are based upon the theoretical specifications that it should be a zero-coupon, default-free asset with a time to maturity that approximates the investor's holding period. The point is, such an asset would provide the asset's promised return (i.e., its yield to maturity) because there is no default risk, no reinvestment risk because it is a zero-coupon security, and no price risk because the asset matures at the end of the holding period. The range of suggested maturities goes from a three-month T-bill to an intermediate government bond (e.g., a 10-year Treasury bill), to the long-term government bond (e.g., a 30-year Treasury bond). As of mid-2008, these yields were:

3-month Treasury bill:	2.60%
10-year Treasury note:	3.80%
30-year Treasury bond:	4.60%

The Equity Risk Premium   The attitude toward the estimation of the equity risk premium has undergone significant changes during the 1990s. The initial empirical estimate of an equity risk premium was provided by the pioneering work of Ibbotson and Sinquefield (1982) in their monograph for the Financial Analysts Research Foundation. They estimated the risk premium on common stock as the arithmetic mean of the difference in the annual rate of return from stocks minus the return on Treasury bills. Although the original estimate was for 1926–1981, this estimated risk premium has been updated annually in a yearbook provided by Ibbotson Associates (annual). For example, the equity risk premium as of 2008 for 1926–2007 was 8.5 percent using the arithmetic mean of the annual values and 6.7 percent using the geometric mean of the annual values. The geometric mean is appropriate for long-run asset class comparisons, whereas the arithmetic mean is what you would use to estimate the premium for a given year (e.g., the *expected* performance next year). Because our application is to the long-term DDM model, the geometric mean value would probably be more appropriate, which implies using the 6.7 percent risk premium value.

An additional adjustment is suggested to reflect the belief that the typical investment horizon is longer than that implied by the T-bill rate. Assuming that most investors consider the intermediate time frame (5–10 years) a more appropriate investment horizon, the risk premium should be computed as the stock return less the return on intermediate government bonds. Given the typical upward-sloping yield curve, it is not surprising that this measure of the risk premium is about 1.5 percent less than the T-bill premium—that is, the arithmetic mean of the annual risk premiums relative to intermediate government bonds was 6.8 percent from 1926–2007 and the geometric mean of the annual risk premiums was 5.1 percent. In recent years, Ibbotson Associates has also provided a long-horizon risk premium estimate that employs the long-term government bond return. The arithmetic average for this series was 5.8 percent, and the geometric average was 4.7 percent. Therefore, the long-term historical risk premium to use should be about *4.9 percent.*

Several authors have contended that there are problems with this estimate in a dynamic real-world environment. The major criticism articulated by Rozeff (1984) is that the time period is *too long* and causes the *market risk premium to be almost a constant value.* Given that we are dealing with an average value that encompasses almost 82 years, this technique will not reflect any changes over time. There are ways to adjust for this constant value problem, and there are other estimation approaches that have been suggested.

The first suggestion to adjust for the constant value is to use a constant period moving average for the Ibbotson-Sinquefield technique—for example, instead of using a single mean value for the total period since 1926, employ a 20-year moving average of the series. This would reflect any trends in the series over time. The authors computed such a series employing a moving average and using the intermediate bond return as the risk-free asset. The time-series plots clearly demonstrated that the risk premium series was not stable since the 20-year moving average values varied from about 1 percent to 16 percent. Notably, given how the risk premium is computed, it increases during years when the market does well and declines during poor performing periods. This is clearly counterintuitive to expectations.

The paper by Rozeff (1984) discusses the equity risk premium concept similar to the presentation in this book. This is followed by a review of alternative measures of the risk premium, including the Ibbotson-Sinquefield series, an estimate using the CAPM, and a brief consideration of the default risk premium (referred to as the credit risk series).

The credit risk premium concept has been referred to on several occasions in this book when discussing changes in the capital market risk premium. The notion is that changes in the absolute or percentage spread between the yield on BBB and AAA bonds indicate a change in the required rate of return by investors for accepting credit risk. Further, this change in the credit risk premium implies a change in the slope of the security market line (SML). The percent yield spread is considered a preferable measure because it adjusts for the level of yields. An advantage of the credit risk measure is that it is based on current market results and reflects prevailing investor attitudes. For a recent plot of this credit yield spread, see Exhibit 1.9, which indicates a very volatile series with peaks in 1976 and 2003.

An alternative estimate of the equity risk premium is suggested by Reichenstein and Rich (1993). They employ the Value Line forecast of dividends and capital gains. This estimated total market return less the short-term government bond yield is shown to provide better and more consistent results than an earnings price value or dividend yield, although it provides consistently biased results that can be adjusted.

A comparison used by Woolridge (1995) to justify a change in the equity risk premium is the relative volatility of stocks versus bonds. Woolridge argues that the risk premium for equity has declined from the 6 percent estimate based on the Ibbotson-Sinquefield data to about 2.5 percent because of the *increase* in bond market volatility relative to stock volatility.[2] Specifically, the equity risk premium spread has declined, not because stocks have become less volatile but because bonds have become more volatile. Thus, the difference in risk between the two asset classes is less than before, so the risk premium spread has declined. A study by Claus and Thomas (2001) derives an estimate of the equity risk premium from the discount rate that equates market valuations with prevailing expectations of future flows. Their results indicate a risk premium between 1985 and 1998 of 3 percent or less.

In summary, if you use the current intermediate government bond rate as your estimate of the minimal *NRFR*, these studies indicate that the equity risk premium should be somewhere between 2.5 percent and 6.0 percent, depending on the current environment. In turn, you can derive an indicator of the current environment by examining the prevailing credit risk spread, or the relative volatility of bonds versus stocks.

Once you have estimated the required rate of return for the current period, you must determine whether the expected rate of inflation or the risk premium on common stock will change during your investment horizon.

The Current Estimate of Risk Premium and k The prior discussion indicated that the total range for the equity risk premium is from about 2.5 precent to about 6.0 percent. To apply these results, we employ three alternative risk premiums of 2, 4, and 6 percent. If we combine these risk premiums with the prior nominal risk-free rates for government bonds, we derive the following matrix of required rates of return *(k)* for the S&P Industrials Index:

	RISK PREMIUMS		
Nominal *RFR*	**0.02**	**0.04**	**0.06**
0.026	0.046	0.066	0.086
0.038	0.058	0.078	0.098
0.046	0.066	0.086	0.106

The matrix indicates a range of *k* from 0.046 (4.6 percent) to 0.016 (10.6 percent). The low required rate of return assumes investors have a very short-run horizon and a very small risk premium, while the high required return implies a long-run horizon and the very large long-run historical risk premium of Ibbotson-Sinquefield.

---

[2] For an analysis of relative volatility of bonds versus stocks that is consistent with the Woolridge contention, see Reilly, Wright, and Chan (2000).

For purposes of our subsequent estimate, we will use the diagonal values from this matrix: 0.046, 0.078, 0.106, which are equal to: 4.6, 7.8, and 10.6 percemt.

The Dividend Growth Rate   The earnings multiple that is applied to next year's earnings must take into account the expected growth rate (g) for common dividends.[3] There is a positive relationship between the earnings multiplier and the growth rate of earnings and dividends— the higher the expected growth rate, the higher the multiple.[4] When estimating g, you should consider the current expected rate of growth and estimate any *changes* in the growth rate. Such changes in expectations indicate a change in the relationship between k and g and will have a profound effect on the earnings multiplier.

As discussed in Chapters 10 and 11, a firm's growth rate is equal to (1) the proportion of earnings retained and reinvested by the firm—that is, its retention rate *(b)*—times (2) the rate of return earned on investments *(ROE)*. An increase in either or both of these variables causes an increase in the expected growth rate (g) and an increase in the earnings multiplier. Therefore, the expected growth rate can be stated as:

12.3
$$g = f(b, ROE)$$

where:

g = expected growth rate
b = the expected retention rate equal to 1 − D/E
ROE = the expected return on equity investments

Therefore, to estimate the expected growth rate, you need to estimate changes in the retention rate *(b)* and the return on equity *(ROE)*. The plot in Exhibit 12.6 shows that the retention rate has become relatively high. Because the valuation model is a long-run model, you should estimate only relatively permanent changes, although short-run changes can affect expectations.

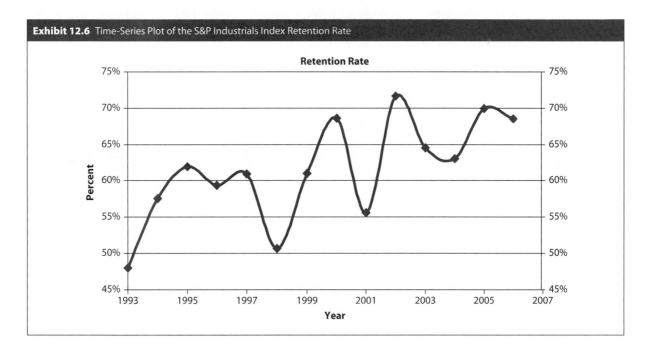

Exhibit 12.6   Time-Series Plot of the S&P Industrials Index Retention Rate

---

[3] You know that the g in the valuation model is the expected growth rate for dividends. In our discussion, we assume a relatively constant dividend-payout ratio (dividend/earnings), so the growth of dividends is dependent on the growth in earnings.

[4] A paper that specifically examines this relationship is Fairfield (1994).

Specifically, you should recognize that the annual retention rate, which has been volatile and generally increases (between 48 and 70 percent), is heavily impacted by annual earnings changes (as will be discussed in the dividend payout section).

The second variable that affects *g* is changes in the return on equity *(ROE)*.

As discussed in Chapter 10, the *ROE* can be broken down using the three-component DuPont analysis as follows:

$$12.4 \qquad ROE = \frac{\text{Net Income}}{\text{Equity}} = \frac{\text{Net Income}}{\text{Sales}} \times \frac{\text{Sales}}{\text{Total Assets}} \times \frac{\text{Total Assets}}{\text{Equity}}$$

$$= \frac{\text{Net Profit}}{\text{Margin}} \times \frac{\text{Total Asset}}{\text{Turnover}} \times \frac{\text{Financial}}{\text{Leverage}}$$

This equation shows that the *ROE* increases if either the total asset turnover or the profit margin increases. In addition, you can increase *ROE* by increasing financial leverage. Because the S&P Industrials series includes the required historical information only since 1993, we examine this three-component breakdown of *ROE* for this 14-year period 1993–2006 (2007 date are not available until late in 2008).

As shown in Exhibit 12.7, the *ROE* for the S&P Industrials series during the period 1993–2006 experienced its lowest value during the recession in 2001 and its peak in 1995. An analysis of the three components of *ROE* indicates what contributed to the changes over time. First, an analysis of Exhibits 12.7 and 12.8 shows that the profit margin over time was a major factor explaining the overall pattern of *ROE* since 1993. The second component, total asset turnover, (Exhibit 12.9) experienced a peak of about 95 percent in 1996, a declined to a trough in 2002, and then an increase to finish at 85 percent in 2006. Combining these two variables (*PM* and *TATO*) equals return on total assets (*ROTA*) (Exhibit 12.7) that experienced an overall increase from about 4 percent in 1993 to 6 percent in 2006. Finally, the total assets/equity ratio (in Exhibit 12.10) that reflects financial leverage experienced an almost constant decline over this period from about 3.6 times to 2.6 times. Therefore, the *ROE* both started and ended at about 16 percent based upon an overall increase in the profit margin offset by declines in both total asset turnover and financial leverage.

The point is, an investor needs to estimate the long-term outlook for *ROE*, which in turn requires a long-term estimate for each of the three component ratios. Once that is established, multiply this long-term estimate of *ROE* by your estimate of *b*, the retention rate, to calculate an estimate of the long-term growth rate *(g)* of U.S. Industrial firms. For example, if you estimate

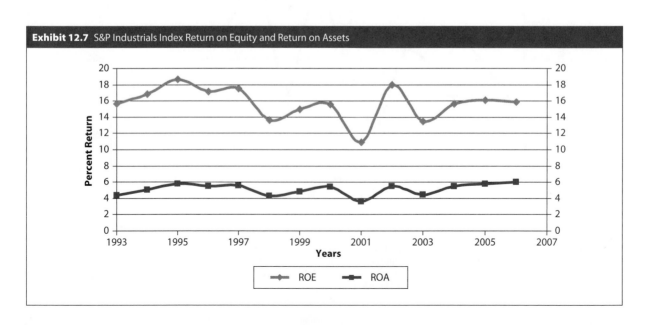

Exhibit 12.7 S&P Industrials Index Return on Equity and Return on Assets

Exhibit 12.8 S&P Industrials Index Net Profit Margin (NPM)

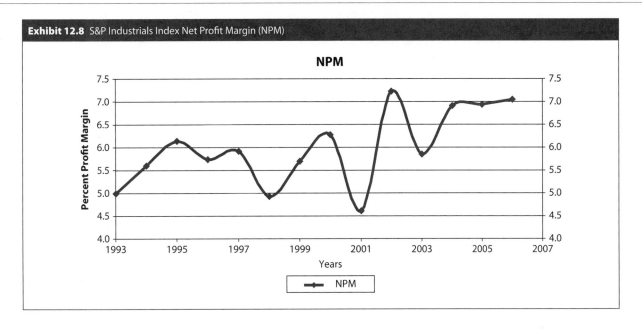

Exhibit 12.9 S&P Industrials Index Total Asset Turnover (TATO)

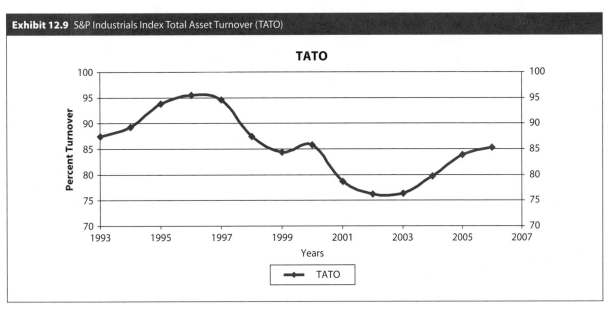

that the *long-run* retention rate of firms will be 55 percent and their *ROE* will be about 13 percent, this means you would expect the long-run growth rate to be about 7.1 percent, as follows:

$$g = b \times ROE$$
$$= 0.55 \times 0.13$$
$$= 0.071 = 7.1\%$$

Combining the Estimates If we combine the several estimates, they are as follows:

$$D_0 = \$28.50$$
$$k = 0.046 \text{ or } 0.078 \text{ or } 0.106$$
$$g = 0.071$$
$$D_1 = 28.50 \,(1 + g) = 28.50 \,(1.071) = 30.52$$

Exhibit 12.10 S&P Industrials Index Total Assets/Equity Ratio

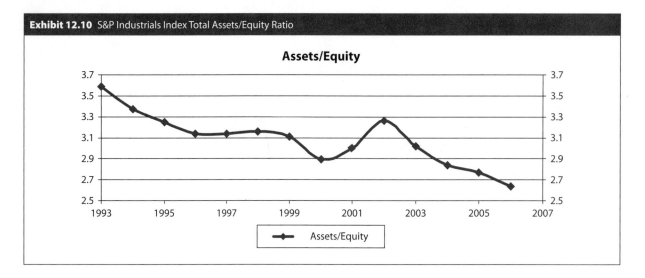

Using these inputs for the reduced form DDM indicates the following three estimates of market value:

$$1. \quad \frac{30.52}{0.046 - 0.071} = \frac{30.52}{-0.025} = Meaningless \ (g > k)$$

$$2. \quad \frac{30.52}{0.078 - 0.071} = \frac{30.52}{0.007} = 4,360$$

$$3. \quad \frac{30.52}{0.106 - 0.071} = \frac{30.52}{0.035} = 872$$

As noted, the first estimate is meaningless since the growth rate exceeds the required return k. The second estimate that has a $(k–g)$ spread of only 0.007 indicates a valuation of 4,360, which exceeds the market price of February 2008 (assumed to be the current market price) of 1,650. Finally, the third estimated that has a $(k–g)$ spread of 0.035 indicates a value of 872, which is substantially below the market price of 1,650. Assuming the dividend value of $30.52 is reasonable, one needs to consider what $k–g$ spread is necessary to justify the prevailing market value. Consider the following values:

$$\frac{30.52}{0.017} = 1,795$$

$$\frac{30.52}{0.018} = 1,696$$

$$\frac{30.52}{0.019} = 1,606$$

It appears that the current market value implies (requires) a $k–g$ spread very close to 1.8 percent, which means either a k below 0.095 or an expected growth rate above 0.071. Since the 7.1 percent long-run growth rate appears fairly aggressive (optimistic), the most likely adjustment would be a k approaching 0.089. A more conservative growth estimate would mean a lower required k.

12.3.2 Market Valuation Using the Free Cash Flow to Equity (FCFE) Model

As indicated earlier, we will derive an estimate using this FCFE model under two scenarios: (1) a constant growth rate from the present and then (2) a two-stage growth rate assumption.

Exhibit 12.11 Components of Free Cash Flow to Equity for the S&P Industrials Index: 1993–2006

Year	Net Income	Depreciation Expense	Capital Expenditures	Working Capital	Changes in Working Capital	Principal Repayment	New Debt Issued	Total FCFE
1993	31.02	34.10	42.85	64.43	N/A	6.99		N/A
1994	36.64	35.79	45.83	86.37	21.94		13.46	18.12
1995	43.36	39.54	51.85	92.70	6.33		20.91	45.63
1996	41.69	39.55	56.75	89.60	−3.10	2.61		24.98
1997	44.43	40.62	60.37	78.63	−10.97		15.33	50.98
1998	36.96	44.83	61.34	71.71	−6.92		20.18	47.55
1999	46.28	47.54	61.45	76.87	5.16		37.41	64.62
2000	53.56	50.13	62.19	59.91	−16.96		1.19	59.65
2001	37.41	50.24	62.19	83.28	23.37		27.91	30.00
2002	56.51	41.68	48.23	104.39	21.11		4.26	33.11
2003	49.52	42.98	44.82	124.45	20.06		11.78	39.40
2004	65.22	44.35	49.01	140.29	15.84		14.30	59.02
2005	72.41	45.83	55.30	151.89	11.60		9.69	61.03
2006	79.11	48.89	66.20	145.16	−6.73	8.41		60.12

Source: Adapted from *S & P Analysts Handbook.*

The Constant Growth FCFE Model To begin, the FCFE is defined (measured) as follows:[5]

Net Income
  + Depreciation expense
  − Capital expenditures
  − Δ in working capital
  − Principal debt repayments
  + New debt issues

This technique attempts to determine the free cash flow that is available to the stockholders after payments to all other capital suppliers and after providing for the continued growth of the firm. The FCFE data for the S&P Industrials Index for the period 1994–2006 are contained in Exhibit 12.11.

Although there was overall growth in the FCFE series for the period 1994–2006 of about 7 percent, there was also substantial variation from a low point in 1994 to a peak of 64.62 in 1999, followed by three much lower values in 2001–2003. A major cause of the poor results were the large working capital additions. Preliminary indications for 2007 point toward strong earnings, reasonable capital expenditures and working capital increases, and a "best" estimate for FCFE of about 65.00. Therefore, for the constant growth version of the model, we will use the growth estimate used in the DDM as follows:

$$g = 0.077$$
$$k = 0.078; 0.106$$
$$FCFE_0 = \$65.00 \text{ (estimate for 2007)}$$
$$FCFE_1 = (\$65.00)(1.07) = \$69.55 \text{ (estimate for 2008)}$$

Equity Values:

$$\frac{69.55}{0.078 - 0.070} = \frac{69.55}{0.008} = 8,694$$

$$\frac{69.55}{0.106 - 0.070} = \frac{69.55}{0.036} = 1,987$$

[5] For further discussion and detail, see Damodaran (1994).

In contrast to the DDM results, this model indicates that the market at its current price of about 1,650 is undervalued even if one assumes a cost of equity of 10.6 percent. Recall that this 10.6 percent k is based on a long-term bond rate of 4.60 percent and an equity risk premium of 6.00 percent.

Alternatively, if we assume that FCFE does not grow by 7 percent in 2008, but only by 4 percent because of the slowdown/recession, and a lower perpetual growth rate of 6.5 percent, the values decline as follows:

$$\frac{67.60}{0.078 - 0.065} = \frac{67.60}{0.013} = 5,200$$

$$\frac{67.60}{0.106 - 0.065} = \frac{67.60}{0.041} = 1,649$$

Finally, if we assume the lower estimate of FCFE (67.60) and 6.0 percent perpetual growth, the values are:

$$\frac{67.60}{0.078 - 0.060} = \frac{67.60}{0.018} = 3,756$$

$$\frac{67.60}{0.106 - 0.060} = \frac{67.60}{0.046} = 1,470$$

Needless to say, the valuations and the investment decisions given the current market value of 1,650 are very sensitive to the estimate of k and g and the resulting spread.

The Two-Stage Growth FCFE Model As noted above, if one considers the total period 1994–2006, the average annual percentage growth is about 8 percent. To demonstrate this two-stage model, we assume the following above-average growth rates during the next five years (the first stage) followed by a second stage of constant growth at 6 percent.

2008—8.5%

2009—8%

2010—7.5%

2011—7.0%

2012—6.5%

2013 onward—6.0%

Assuming a k of 9.0 percent and a FCFE of $65.00 in 2007, the computations are as follows:

		Two-Stage Valuation	
Year	**FCFE**	**Discount Factors at 0.090**	**Present Value**
2008	70.52	0.9174	64.70
2009	76.16	0.8417	64.10
2010	81.87	0.7722	63.22
2011	87.60	0.7084	62.06
2012	93.30	0.6499	60.64
Continuing Value[a]	3,297	0.6499	2,143.00
		Total *PV*	2,458

$$\frac{^{a}93.30\,(1.06)}{0.09 - 0.06} = \frac{98.90}{0.03} = 3,297$$

As can be seen, this set of assumptions indicates an intrinsic value of 2,458 which exceeds the current market price of the market (1,650), which implies the following: (1) the market is undervalued at this time, and (2) investors who acquire a diversified portfolio of U.S. stocks at these prices should derive a long-run annual rate of return in excess of 9.0 percent. It is also possible to approximate this market return using the k estimate from the DDM as follows:

12.5
$$k = \frac{D}{p} + g$$

Combining the current dividend yield of about 1.8 percent and the expected long-run g of 7.0 percent implies a return of 8.8 percent. Notably, this estimated return is higher than what is expected by Emmons (1999) who derives expected earnings growth based on the growth of nominal GDP of about 6 percent plus a dividend yield of 1.3 percent to arrive at a return estimate of about 7 percent (he stipulates a range of 5 to 7 percent).

The next section will discuss and demonstrate the four alternative relative valuation ratios as follows: (1) the price/earnings ratio (*P/E*), (2) the price/book value ratio (*P/BV*), (3) the price/cash flow ratio (*P/CF*), and (4) the price/sales ratio (*P/S*). We begin with the *P/E* ratio because it is the most well known and because it can be derived from the DDM. Also this model can be used to derive a specific market value.

12.4 Valuation Using the Earnings Multiplier Approach

12.4.1 Two-Part Valuation Procedure

We use the earnings multiplier version of the dividend discount model to value the stock market because it is a theoretically correct model of value assuming a constant growth rate of dividends for an infinite time period. The point is, these are reasonable assumptions for the aggregate stock market.[6] Also, this valuation technique is consistently used in practice.

Recall that k and g are independent variables because k depends heavily on risk, whereas g is a function of the retention rate and the *ROE*. Therefore, this spread between k and g can and does change over time. The following equations imply an estimate of this spread at a point in time equal to the prevailing dividend yield:

$$P_j = \frac{D_1}{k - g}$$
$$P_j/D_1 = 1/k - g$$
$$D_1/P_j = k - g$$

Although the dividend yield gives an estimate of the size of the prevailing spread, it does not indicate the values for the two individual components (k and g) or what caused the *change* in the spread. More important, it says nothing about what the spread *should* be, which is the critical value that must be determined based upon estimating values for k and g.

12.4.2 Importance of Both Components of Value

The ultimate objective of this microanalysis is to estimate the intrinsic market value for a major stock market series, such as the S&P Industrials Index. This estimation process has two equally important steps:

1. Estimating the future earnings per share for the stock market series
2. Estimating the appropriate earnings multiplier for the stock market series based on long-run estimates of k and g.[7]

[6] Recall that these assumptions may be unrealistic for many stocks, especially for stocks of growth companies. We consider these problems for growth companies and discuss alternative growth company valuation models that consider such conditions in Chapter 14.
[7] Our emphasis will be on *estimating future values* for EPS, as well as estimating a *forward* earnings multiple using estimates of k and g. We will show the relevant variables and provide a procedural framework, but the final estimate depends on the ability of the analyst.

Some analysts have concentrated on estimating the earnings for a market series with little consideration of changes in the earnings multiplier for the series. An investor who considers only the earnings for the series and ignores the earnings multiplier (i.e., the *P/E* ratio), assumes that the earnings multiplier will be relatively constant over time. If this were correct, stock prices would generally move in line with earnings. The fallacy of this assumption is obvious when one examines data for the two components during the period from 1993–2006, as shown in Exhibit 12.12.

The year-end stock price is the closing value for the S&P Industrials Index on the last trading day of the year. The next column is the percentage change in price for the year. The earnings figure is the earnings per share during the year for the S&P Industrials Index, and the next column shows the percentage change from the prior year. The fifth column is the historical earnings multiplier at the end of the year, which is equal to the year-end value for the S&P Industrials Index divided by the *historical* earnings for that year. As an example, at the end of 1993, the S&P Industrials Index was equal to 540.19 and the earnings per share for the firms that made up the series were 31.02 for the 12 months ending 12/31/93. This implies an earnings multiplier of 17.42 (540.19/31.02). Although this may not be the ideal measure of the multiplier, it is consistent in its measurement and shows the changes in the relationship between stock prices and earnings over time. An alternative measure is the *forward* multiplier using *next* year's earnings (i.e., stock price as of 12/31/93 versus earnings for the 12 months ending 12/31/94). This forward *P/E* series likewise experiences substantial annual changes and is the multiple we will be estimating. Typically, it is a smaller value and less volatile than the historical multiple because it considers future earnings that are generally higher.

There have been numerous striking examples where annual stock price movements for the S&P Industrials Index were opposite to earnings changes during the same year as follows:

- 1998 profits *decreased* by almost 17 percent; stock prices *increased* almost 32 percent.
- 2000 profits *increased* almost 16 percent; stock prices *declined* over 17 percent.
- 2002 profits *increased* over 51 percent; stock prices *declined* over 24 percent.
- 2003 profits *decreased* over 12 percent; stock prices *increased* over 26 percent.

During each of these years, the major influences on stock price movements came from changes in the forward earnings multiplier. The greater volatility of the multiplier series compared to the earnings per share series can be seen from the summary figures at the bottom of Exhibit 12.12 and from the graph of the forward earnings multiplier in Exhibit 12.13. The standard deviation of annual changes for the forward earnings multiplier series is much larger than the standard deviation of EPS changes (25.22 vs. 21.59). The same is true for the relative volatility measures of the coefficient of variability. Also, the standard deviation of the forward multiplier series without signs is larger than for the EPS series (35.56 vs. 28.89). Therefore, these figures show that, of the two estimates required for market valuation, *the forward earnings multiplier is the more volatile component.*

The point of this discussion is not to reduce the importance of the earnings estimate but to note that the estimation of the intrinsic market value requires two separate estimates and *both* are important and necessary. Therefore, we initially consider a procedure for estimating aggregate earnings followed by the procedure for estimating the forward market earnings multiplier.

12.5 Estimating Expected Earnings per Share

The estimate of expected earnings per share for the market series will consider the outlook for the aggregate economy and for the corporate sector. This requires the following steps:

1. Estimate sales per share for a stock market series, such as the S&P Industrials Index. This estimate of sales involves estimating gross domestic product (GDP) because of the relationship between industrial firm sales and aggregate economic activity. Therefore, we will initially consider sources for an estimate of GDP.

Exhibit 12.12 Annual Changes in Stock Prices, Corporate Earnings, and the Earnings Multiplier for S&P Industrials Index: 1993–2006

Year	Year-End Stock Price	% Change	Earnings Per Share	% Change	Year-End Earnings Multiple	% Change	Earnings Multiple (*t*+1)	% Change
1993	540.19		31.02		17.42		14.74	
1994	547.51	1.36%	36.64	18.13%	14.94	−14.20%	12.63	−14.35%
1995	721.19	31.72%	43.36	18.34%	16.63	−11.31%	17.30	36.99%
1996	869.97	20.63%	41.69	−3.84%	20.87	25.45%	19.58	13.21%
1997	1,121.38	28.90%	44.43	6.56%	25.24	20.97%	30.34	54.93%
1998	1,479.16	31.91%	36.96	−16.80%	40.02	58.54%	31.96	5.35%
1999	1,841.92	24.52%	46.28	−25.21%	39.80	−0.55%	34.39	7.60%
2000	1,527.86	−17.05%	53.56	15.73%	28.53	−28.32%	40.84	18.76%
2001	1,333.94	−12.69%	37.41	−30.15%	35.66	25.00%	23.60	−42.21%
2002	1,005.99	−24.59%	56.51	51.07%	17.80	−50.08%	20.31	−13.94%
2003	1,271.07	26.35%	49.52	−12.37%	25.67	44.19%	19.49	−4.07%
2004	1,380.33	8.60%	65.22	31.71%	21.16	−17.55%	19.06	−2.17%
2005	1,413.00	2.37%	72.41	11.01%	19.52	−7.79%	17.86	−6.31%
2006	1,595.62	12.92%	79.11	9.26%	20.17	3.36%	N/A	N/A
With Signs								
Mean		10.38%		9.53%		5.41%		4.48%
Std. Deviation		19.33%		21.59%		29.91%		25.22%
Coefficient of Var.		3.74%		4.66%		8.94%		6.36%
Without Signs								
Mean		18.74%		28.71%		30.81%		27.80%
Std. Deviation		10.49%		28.89%		34.71%		35.56%
Coefficient of Var.		1.10%		8.93%		12.05%		12.64%

Exhibit 12.13 Year-End Earnings Multiple for the S&P Industrials Index Based on Forward Earnings: 1993–2005

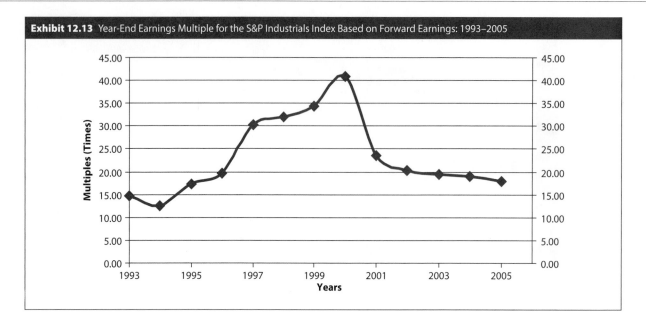

2. Estimate the operating profit margin for the series, which equals operating profit divided by sales. Given the data available from Standard and Poor's, we will define operating profit as earnings before interest, taxes, and depreciation (EBITDA).
3. Estimate depreciation per share for the next year.
4. Estimate interest expense per share for the next year.
5. Estimate the corporate tax rate for the next year.

These steps will lead to an estimate of net earnings per share that will be combined with an estimate of the forward earnings multiplier to arrive at an estimate of the current intrinsic value for the stock market series.

12.5.1 Estimating Gross Domestic Product

GDP is a measure of aggregate economic output or activity. Therefore, one would expect aggregate corporate sales to be related to GDP. We begin our estimate of sales with a prediction of nominal GDP from one of several banks or financial service firms that regularly publish such estimates. We use this nominal GDP projection, to estimate corporate sales based on the historical relationship between S&P Industrials Index sales per share and aggregate economic activity (GDP).[8]

12.5.2 Estimating Sales per Share for a Market Series

As noted, we will use a sales figure for an existing stock market series—the S&P Industrials Index.[9] Exhibit 12.14 contains the annual nominal GDP and sales per share for the S&P Industrials Index and yearly percent changes in the two series. Generally, a large proportion of the percentage changes in Industrial sales per share can be explained by percentage changes

[8] This would include projections by Standard & Poor's appearing late in the year in the *Outlook;* and projections by several of the large investment firms, such as Goldman, Sachs, & Company ("The Pocket Chartroom") or Merrill Lynch, as well as by banks. The *Wall Street Journal* publishes a survey of over 50 economists every 6 months that includes estimates of various interest rates, GDP and inflation.

[9] Sales per share figures are available from 1993 in Standard & Poor's *Analyst's Handbook* (New York: Standard & Poor's Corporation). Because the composite series include numerous companies of different sizes, all data are on a per-share basis. The book is updated annually.

Exhibit 12.14 Norminal GDP and S&P Industrial Index Sales per Share: 1993–2006

Year	S&P Net Sales $	S&P Net Sales %Δ	GDP $	GDP %Δ
1993	622.12	3.60%	6657.40	5.10%
1994	653.75	5.08%	7072.20	6.23%
1995	706.13	8.01%	7397.70	4.60%
1996	727.40	3.01%	7816.90	5.67%
1997	750.71	3.20%	8304.30	6.24%
1998	750.48	−0.03%	8747.00	5.33%
1999	812.00	8.20%	9268.40	5.96%
2000	853.86	5.16%	9817.00	5.92%
2001	811.04	−5.01%	10128.00	3.17%
2002	781.65	−3.62%	10496.60	3.64%
2003	847.38	8.41%	10960.80	4.42%
2004	944.36	11.44%	11685.90	6.62%
2005	1043.61	10.51%	12433.90	6.40%
2006	1123.34	7.64%	13194.70	6.12%

in nominal GDP. The relationship is not stronger because (1) the S&P Industrials Index sales series is more volatile than the GDP series and (2) the nominal GDP series never experienced a decline. The equation for the least-squares regression line relating annual percentage changes (% Δ) in the two series for the period 1993–2006 is

$$\% \Delta \text{ S\&P Industrials Index Sales}_t = -0.126 + 3.22 \,(\% \Delta \text{ in Nominal GDP}_t)$$

$$\text{Adj. } R^2 = 0.48$$

These results indicate that about 48 percent of the variance in percentage changes in S&P Industrial sales can be explained by percentage changes in nominal GDP. Thus, given an estimate of the percentage change in nominal GDP for next year, we can estimate the percentage

Exhibit 12.15 Scatterplot of Annual Percentage Changes in S&P Industrials Index Sales and in Nominal GDP

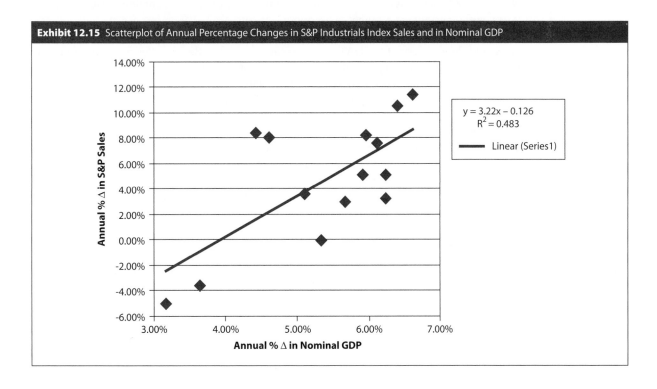

$y = 3.22x - 0.126$
$R^2 = 0.483$
—— Linear (Series1)

change in sales for the S&P Industrials Index series and therefore the sales per share. For example, the consensus estimate for economists is that during 2007 nominal GDP increased by approximately 5.8 percent (a 3.0 percent increase in real GDP plus 2.8 percent inflation). This estimate, combined with the regression, implies the following increase in S&P Industrial sales for 2007:

$$\% \Delta \text{ S\&P Industrials Index Sales} = -0.126 + 3.22 \,(0.058)$$

$$= 0.0608$$

$$= 6.08\%$$

Because of the dramatic slowdown in the fourth quarter, we use an estimate of 6 percent.

Given the significant uncertainty in the economy during early 2008, we estimate that nominal GDP in 2008 will only increase by 4.0 percent which implies an S&P sales growth of about 4.0 percent. Notably, this is referred to as a *point estimate of sales* because it is based on a point estimate of GDP. Although we know there is actually a *distribution* of estimates for GDP, we have used the mean value, or expected value, as our point estimate. In actual practice, you would probably consider several estimates and assign probabilities to each of them.

12.5.3 Alternative Estimates of Corporate Net Profits

Once sales per share for the market series have been estimated, the difficult estimate is the profit margin. Exhibit 12.16 contains the data on the operating earnings components. Three alternative procedures are possible depending on the desired level of aggregation.

The first is a direct estimate of the *net* profit margin based on recent trends. As shown in Exhibit 12.16, the net profit margin series is quite volatile because of changes in depreciation, interest, and the tax rate over time. As such, it is the most difficult series to estimate.

The second procedure would attempt to estimate the *net before tax* (NBT) profit margin. Once the NBT margin is derived, a separate estimate of the tax rate is obtained based on recent tax rates and current government tax pronouncements.

The third method estimates an *operating* profit margin, defined as earnings before interest, taxes, and depreciation (EBITDA), as a percentage of sales. Because this measure of operating earnings as a percentage of sales is not influenced by changes in depreciation allowances, interest expense, or tax rates, it should be a more stable series compared to either the net profit margin or net before tax margin series. We begin our analysis by estimating this operating profit margin series.

After estimating this operating profit margin, we multiply it by the sales estimate to derive a dollar estimate of operating earnings (EBITDA). Subsequently, we will derive separate estimates of depreciation and interest expenses, which are subtracted from the EBITDA to arrive at earnings before taxes *(EBT)*. Finally, we estimate the expected tax rate *(T)* and multiply *EBT* times $(1 - T)$ to get our estimate of net income. The following sections discuss the details of estimating earnings per share beginning with the operating profit margin.

12.5.4 Estimating Aggregate Operating Profit Margin

Finkel and Tuttle (1971) hypothesized that the following four variables affected the aggregate profit margin:

1. Capacity utilization rate
2. Unit labor costs
3. Rate of inflation
4. Foreign competition

Exhibit 12.16 Industrials Index Sales per Share and Components of Operating Profit Margin: 1993–2006

Year	Net Sales	EBITDA[a]		Depreciation		Interest		Income Tax		Net Income[b]	
		P/S	% of Sales	P/S	% of Sales	P/S	% of Sales	P/S	Tax Rate	P/S	% of Sales
1993	622.12	87.85	14.12%	34.10	5.48%	13.41	2.16%	14.16	36.79%	31.02	4.99%
1994	653.75	104.28	15.95%	35.79	5.47%	14.82	2.27%	20.57	35.76%	36.64	5.60%
1995	706.13	115.65	16.38%	39.54	5.60%	15.78	2.23%	22.78	35.85%	43.36	6.14%
1996	727.40	118.46	16.29%	39.55	5.44%	14.61	2.01%	24.97	35.90%	41.69	5.73%
1997	750.71	123.31	16.43%	40.62	5.41%	13.89	1.85%	24.50	36.26%	44.43	5.92%
1998	750.48	123.74	16.49%	44.83	5.97%	14.85	1.98%	22.98	34.69%	36.96	4.93%
1999	812.00	139.16	17.14%	47.54	5.85%	15.71	1.93%	28.95	36.12%	46.28	5.70%
2000	853.86	150.40	17.61%	50.13	5.87%	17.65	2.07%	32.98	37.00%	53.56	6.27%
2001	811.04	125.46	15.47%	50.24	6.19%	16.51	2.04%	17.80	35.65%	37.41	4.61%
2002	781.65	122.59	15.68%	41.68	5.33%	15.26	1.95%	20.13	34.30%	56.51	7.23%
2003	847.38	135.30	15.97%	42.98	5.07%	16.48	1.94%	24.07	32.97%	49.52	5.84%
2004	944.36	155.57	16.47%	44.35	4.70%	16.95	1.79%	28.73	31.68%	65.22	6.91%
2005	1043.61	172.26	16.51%	45.83	4.39%	19.48	1.87%	36.84	32.24%	72.41	6.94%
2006	1123.34	190.28	16.94%	48.89	4.35%	22.10	1.97%	40.66	31.74%	79.11	7.04%

[a] This is used as an estimate of operating earnings.
[b] This net income is adjusted for "special items" and minority interest and is used in subsequent exhibits.

Exhibit 12.17 Variables That Affect the Aggregate Profit Margin: Capacity Utilization Rate, Percentage Change in Compensation, Productivity, Unit Labor Cost, and Consumer Price Index: 1993–2006

Year	Utilization Rate (MFG.) Percent	Compensation/ Work Hours % Change	Output/ Work Hours % Change	Unit Labor Costs % Change	Rate of Inflation Percent
1993	81.4	2.0	0.4	1.6	2.7
1994	83.6	1.7	1.1	0.5	2.7
1995	84.0	2.1	0.5	1.6	2.5
1996	83.1	3.4	2.7	0.7	3.3
1997	83.9	3.1	1.6	1.4	1.7
1998	82.8	6.0	2.8	3.1	1.6
1999	81.9	4.7	2.9	1.8	2.7
2000	81.7	7.2	2.8	4.2	3.4
2001	76.1	4.0	2.5	1.5	1.6
2002	74.8	3.6	4.1	−0.5	2.4
2003	76.1	4.0	3.7	0.3	1.9
2004	78.1	3.6	2.7	0.9	3.3
2005	80.2	4.0	1.9	2.0	3.4
2006	81.7	3.9	1.0	2.9	2.5

Capacity Utilization Rate One would expect a positive relationship between the capacity utilization rate and the profit margin because if production increases as a proportion of total capacity, there is a decrease in per-unit fixed production costs and fixed financial costs. The relationship may not be completely linear at very high rates of capacity utilization because operating diseconomies are introduced as firms are forced to use marginal labor and/or older plant and equipment to reach the higher capacity. The figures in Exhibit 12.17 indicate that capacity utilization ranged from a peak of 84.0 percent in 1995 to a trough of 74.8 percent in 2002 following the 2001 recession.

Unit Labor Cost The change in unit labor cost is a compound effect of two individual factors: (1) changes in wages per hour and (2) changes in worker productivity. Wage costs per hour typically increase every year by varying amounts depending on the economic environment. As shown in Exhibit 12.17, the annual percentage increase in compensation per hour varied from 1.7 percent in 1994 to 7.2 percent in 2000. If workers did not become more productive, this increase in per-hour wage costs would be the increase in per-unit labor cost. Fortunately, because of advances in technology and greater mechanization, the output per hour (the measure of labor productivity) has increased over time—our labor force has become *more productive.* If wages per hour increase by 5 percent and labor productivity increases by 5 percent, there would be no increase in unit labor costs because the workers would offset wage increases by producing more. Therefore, the increase in *per-unit labor cost* is a function of the percentage change in hourly wages minus the increase in productivity during the period. The actual relationship is not this exact due to measurement problems, but it is close as indicated by the data in Exhibit 12.17. For example, during 2001, wage rates increased by 4.0 percent, productivity increased by only 2.5 percent because of the recession, and therefore, unit labor costs increased by 1.5 percent. In contrast, during 2002 compensation increased by 3.6 percent but productivity rose at a 4.1 percent rate so that unit labor costs actually declined by 0.5 percent. Because unit labor is the major variable cost of a firm, one would expect a *negative* relationship between the operating profit margin and percentage changes in unit labor cost—that is, during years with small (below-average) changes in unit labor cost, (e.g., 1994, 1996, 2002 and 2003), we should observe above-average operating profit margins.

Rate of Inflation The precise effect of inflation on the aggregate profit margin is unresolved. Finkel and Tuttle hypothesized a positive relationship between inflation and the profit margin. They contended that a higher level of inflation increases the ability of firms to pass higher costs on to the consumer and thereby raise their profit margin. Second, assuming the classic demand-pull inflation, the increase in prices would indicate an increase in general economic activity, which typically is accompanied by higher margins.

In contrast, many observers doubt that most businesses can consistently increase prices in line with rising costs. Assuming a 5 percent rate of inflation that impacts costs, the question is whether all firms can *completely* pass these cost increases along to their customers. If a firm increases prices at the same rate as cost increases, there will be a *constant* profit margin, *not* an increase. Only if a firm can raise prices by *more than* cost increases can it increase its margin. Many firms are not able to raise prices in line with increased costs because of the elasticity of demand for their products[10] which will cause the profit margin to decline. Given the alternative scenarios, it is contended that very few firms will be able to increase their profit margins and not that many will hold them constant. Assuming this scenario, one would expect the aggregate profit margin to decline when there is an increase in the rate of inflation.

Given the contrasting expectations, one needs to consider the empirical evidence to determine the relationship between inflation and the operating profit margin.

Foreign Competition   Finkel and Tuttle (1971) contend that export markets are more competitive than domestic markets, so export sales are made at a lower margin. This implies that lower exports by U.S. firms would increase profit margins. In contrast, Gray (1976) believed that only exports between independent firms should be considered and they should be examined relative to total output exported. Further, he felt that imports could have an important negative impact on the operating profit margin because they influence the selling price of all competing domestic products. Given these divergent expectations regarding the ultimate effect of foreign trade on the operating profit margin, this is likewise an empirical question.

Our analysis of the annual data for the period 1977 to 2006 confirmed that the relationship between the operating profit margin and the capacity utilization rate was always significant and positive. In addition, the relationship between the unit labor cost and the operating profit margin was always negative and significant. Alternatively, the rate of inflation and foreign trade variables were never significant in the multiple regression. Finally, the univariate correlation between the profit margin and inflation was consistently *negative*.

Therefore, given these empirical results, when estimating the operating profit margin, you should concentrate on the capacity utilization rate for the economy and the rate of change in unit labor cost. As an example, consider what will happen at two extremes of the business cycle. Coming out of a recession, capacity utilization will be increasing while unit labor costs will rise very slowly due to increased labor productivity. Given this scenario, you should expect an increase in the operating profit margin.

In contrast, at the peak of the business cycle, firms will be operating at full capacity, so there will be declines in capacity utilization. Also due to inflation, there will be large wage increases and small increases in labor productivity which will result in large increases in unit labor cost. Overall, you should expect a major decline in the operating profit margin at the peak of a business cycle.

How do you use this information to estimate an operating profit margin? The most important estimate is *the direction of the change from current levels.* The size of the estimated change will depend on where the economy is in the business cycle and the direction and size of the expected changes in capacity utilization and unit labor cost.

After estimating the operating profit margin, you can calculate the dollar value of EBITDA by applying this operating profit margin estimate to the estimated sales-per-share figure. The next step is to estimate depreciation per share.

---

[10] An extreme example of this inability is regulated industries that may not be able to raise prices at all until after lengthy hearings before regulatory agencies. Even then, the increase in rates may not match the cost increase.

12.5.5 Estimating Depreciation Expense

As shown in Exhibit 12.18, the depreciation expense per share series has declined only once since 1992 (in 2002) for noneconomic reasons. This is not surprising, because depreciation expense is an estimate of the fixed-cost expense related to corporate total fixed assets that naturally increases over time. Therefore, the relevant question is *not* whether depreciation expense will increase or decrease but by *how much will it increase?*

There are two suggestions for estimating depreciation expense. First, you can use time-series analysis, which involves using the recent trend as a guide to the future increase. Because a column in Exhibit 12.16 shows depreciation as a percent of sales, you might consider this an estimating approach—this would be a *mistake.* Depreciation is clearly a *fixed* expense, which means that it should not vary with sales. As shown in Exhibit 12.16, depreciation as a percentage of sales has varied from 4.65 percent to 5.84 percent, which is consistent with its fixed nature.

A second alternative that is preferable is to estimate depreciation expense by estimating property, plant, and equipment *(PPE)* and then apply an historical depreciation rate to the *PPE* account. This technique requires two steps. First, estimate the *PPE* account based on the relationship between sales and *PPE*—that is, the expected *PPE* turnover. The historical *PPE* turnover series in Exhibit 12.19 has experienced an overall increase from about 2.40 to over 3.20 in 2006 (see Exhibit 12.20). Therefore, given your estimate for sales you can derive an estimate of *PPE.* The second estimate is the ratio of depreciation to net *PPE,* which is in Exhibit 12.19 and plotted in Exhibit 12.21. As shown, this ratio increased from about 13.5 percent to almost 18 percent in 2000, followed by a decline to almost 14 percent in 2006. Therefore, you can estimate depreciation expense based on estimates of net *PPE* and the ratio of depreciation to net *PPE.*

After you have estimated the depreciation expense, you subtract it from the operating profit estimate to get an estimate of EBIT.

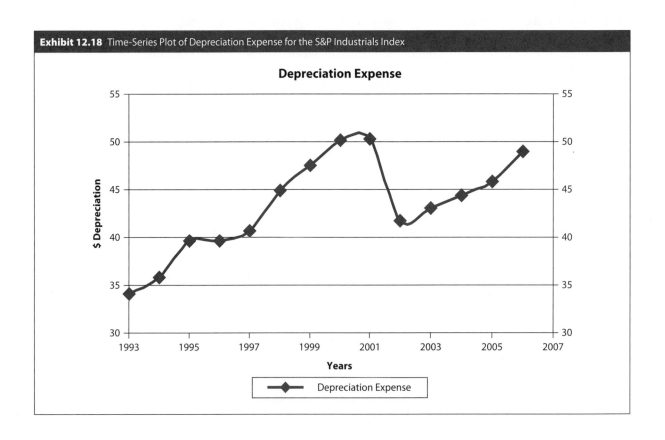

Exhibit 12.18 Time-Series Plot of Depreciation Expense for the S&P Industrials Index

Exhibit 12.19 Inputs Required to Estimate Depreciation Expense and Interest Expense for the S&P Industrials Index

Year	Deprec. Expense	Net PPE	Sales/ Net PPE	Deprec. Exp./ Net PPE	Interest Expense	Total Asset Turnover	L-T Debt	L-T Debt/ Assets	Int Exp./ L-T Debt	L-T Govt. Bond Yield
1993	34.10	254.15	2.45	0.13	13.41	0.87	139.70	0.20	0.10	5.87
1994	35.79	258.97	2.52	0.14	14.82	0.89	143.34	0.20	0.10	7.09
1995	39.54	268.66	2.63	0.15	15.78	0.94	156.44	0.21	0.10	6.57
1996	39.55	266.78	2.73	0.15	14.61	0.95	153.59	0.20	0.10	6.44
1997	40.62	271.97	2.76	0.15	13.89	0.95	160.42	0.20	0.09	6.35
1998	44.83	275.22	2.73	0.16	14.85	0.88	174.56	0.20	0.09	5.26
1999	47.54	286.26	2.84	0.17	15.71	0.84	193.83	0.20	0.08	5.65
2000	50.13	282.90	3.02	0.18	17.65	0.86	195.21	0.20	0.09	6.03
2001	50.24	287.36	2.82	0.17	16.51	0.79	229.45	0.22	0.07	5.02
2002	41.68	279.62	2.80	0.15	15.26	0.76	246.99	0.24	0.06	4.61
2003	42.98	292.06	2.90	0.15	16.48	0.76	251.34	0.23	0.07	4.01
2004	44.35	299.51	3.15	0.15	16.95	0.80	253.33	0.21	0.07	4.27
2005	45.83	311.32	3.35	0.15	19.48	0.84	253.39	0.20	0.08	4.29
2006	48.89	347.36	3.23	0.14	22.10	0.85	254.25	0.19	0.09	4.80

Source: Adapted by authors from *S&P Analysts Handbook* (New York: Standard Poor's, 2007).

Exhibit 12.20 Time-Series Plot of the Ratio of Sales to *PPE* (*PPE* Turnover) for the S&P Industrials Index

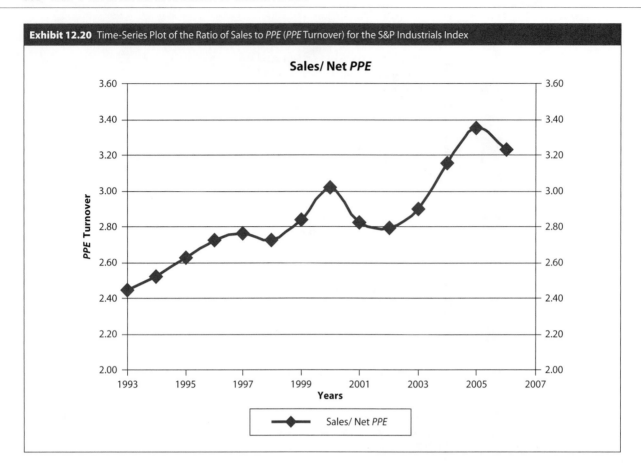

12.5.6 Estimating Interest Expense

The estimate of interest expense should be based on an estimate of debt outstanding (will it grow and by how much?) and the level of interest rates (do you expect interest rates to increase or decline in the future?).

The point is, to estimate interest expense you need to estimate both of these components (the amount of debt outstanding and the average interest rate on this debt) and determine the joint effect. The basic data is listed in Exhibit 12.19. The time-series plot of debt outstanding (Exhibit 12.22) shows an overall increase, but also a flattening during the recent period 2003–2006. Finally, a time-series plot of the average interest rate on debt in Exhibit 12.23 indicates an overall decline to a trough in 2002 followed by a steady increase to almost 9 percent in 2006.

An estimate of debt outstanding requires two estimates: (1) the value of total assets for the firm based upon the firm's expected total asset turnover and (2) the expected capital structure based upon the average total debt to total asset ratio. Both of these ratios are included in Exhibit 12.19.

Similar to depreciation, interest expense is a fixed expense that is impacted by corporate financing decisions and the cost of debt (i.e., interest rates). Therefore, interest expense as a percent of sales should *not* be used when estimating interest expense.

After you have estimated the interest expense figure (time-series plot in Exhibit 12.24) this value is subtracted from the EBIT per share value to arrive at an estimate of EBT.

Exhibit 12.21 Time-Series Plot of the Ratio of Depreciation Expenses to *PPE* Account for the S&P Industrials Index

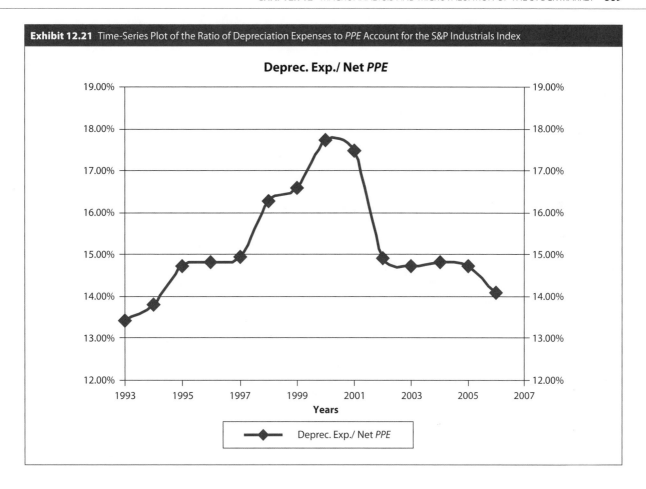

12.5.7 Estimating the Tax Rate

This is the final step in estimating the earnings per share for the S&P Industrials Index series. As shown in Exhibit 12.16, the average tax rate during the 14-year period was about 33 percent, which is also consistent with the tendency to move between 31 and 35 percent.

Estimating the future tax rate is difficult because it depends on political action. You must evaluate the current tax rate and recent tax legislation that affects business firms (e.g., tax credits). Once you have estimated the tax rate *(T)*, you multiply one minus this tax rate $(1 - T)$ times the EBT per share figure to derive an estimate of the net income per share for the S&P Industrials Index series.

In the next section, we demonstrate this procedure by estimating S&P Industrial earnings per share for 2008.

12.5.8 Calculating Earnings per Share: An Example

The following demonstration emphasizes the procedure rather than the actual numbers. A practicing analyst would provide a long, detailed analysis. In this example, we estimate earnings per share for the S&P Industrials Index during 2008 using 2007 data (most of which is estimated).

Exhibit 12.22 Time-Series Plot of Debt Outstanding for the S&P Industrials Index

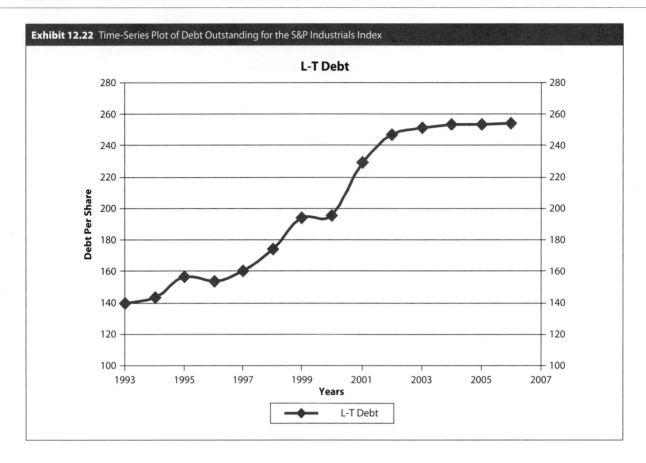

Step 1 Nominal GDP for 2008 is based on an estimate of 5.8 percent growth for 2007, which implies GDP of approximately $13.980 billion. In 2007, the economy was in the sixth year of an expansion following the recession in 2001. The current question is, how strong will 2008 be given the expected slowdown/recession? Recent date have indicated that overall growth in 2008 will definitely not be as strong as 2007— expectations are for real GDP to increase by 1.3 percent in 2008 and for inflation to be 2.7 percent, resulting in an estimated nominal increase of 4.0 percent to $14,540 billion.

Step 2 Corporate sales have had a strong relationship with nominal GDP as shown in Exhibit 12.14. During 2007, when nominal GDP increased by about 5.8 percent, the regression model indicated that S&P sales should increase by about 6 percent to an estimated $1,190 per share. In 2008 with GDP rising about 4.0 percent, the Sales-GDP model generates an expection that S&P sales should only increase by about 1 percent to $1,202 per share.

Step 3 We estimate a small increase in the operating margin during 2007 to about 17 percent. In 2008, we expect a decline in capacity utilization from the recent high point of 82.5 percent at the end of 2007. As noted, this will have a negative impact on the operating margin. Unit labor cost is expected to experience an increase of about 2.0 percent in 2007, followed by a larger increase in 2008 because of slightly lower wage increase but much lower productivity gains during the slowdown/recession. This will also have a clear negative effect on the margin. These two negative factors should cause a decrease in the operating profit margin for 2008 to about 16.00 percent, which implies operating profit of $192(0.16 $\times$ $1,202).

Exhibit 12.23 Time-Series Plot of Interest Rate on Debt Outstanding for the S&P Industrials Index

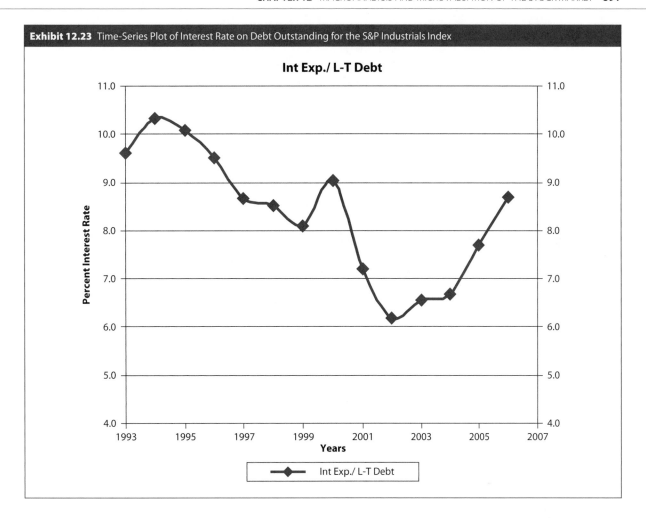

Step 4 The depreciation expense during 2007 was approximately $51 per share. As noted, we estimate sales in 2008 at $1,202 and the *PPE* turnover has been increasing steadily to almost 3.30 times. We expect a further increase in the *PPE* turnover to 3.40, which implies *PPE* of $354 (1202 ÷ 3.40). The depreciation/*PPE* ratio (percent) has been steady at about 15 percent and we assume this will continue in 2008. This implies depreciation expense for 2008 of $53 (0.15 × $354). Thus, the estimated EBIT is $139 ($192 − $53).

Step 5 Interest expense has experienced relatively small increases the last several years because increases in debt outstanding were partially offset by lower interest rates. In 2008 the sales estimate of $1202 and a total asset turnover of 0.86 indicates total assets of $1,398. The percent of long-term debt financing of assets has declined to 19 percent and we expect a further decline to 18.5 percent which implies long-term debt of $259 (0.185 × $1,398). During recent years the rate of interest on debt has increased steadily to over 9 percent and we expect continued increases to 9.5 percent, which implies that interest expense in 2008 will be almost $25 (0.095 × $259). Therefore, EBT is estimated to be $114 ($139 − $25).

Step 6 The tax rate suggested by our earlier analysis was 32.0 percent. Using this rate for 2008 we get net income for 2008 of $77.52 ($114 × 0.68). For simplicity, we will round this to an EPS estimate of $78.

Exhibit 12.24   Time-Series Plot of Interest Expense for the S&P Industrials Index

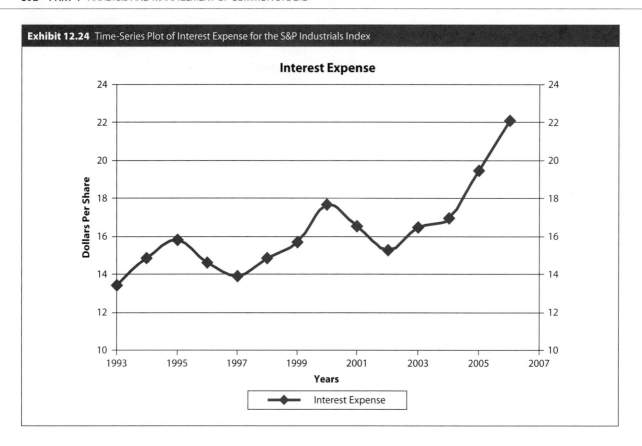

These estimates can be summarized as follows:

Sales	$1202
EBITDA	192
Depreciation Expense	53
EBIT	139
Interest Expense	25
EBT	114
Taxes	36.50
Net Income (EPS)	77.50
Final EPS estimate	$78

12.6 Estimating the Stock Market Earnings Multiplier

Given our estimate of earnings per share, the next step is to estimate an earnings multiplier. A combination of the earnings per share estimate times the estimated forward earnings multiplier provides an estimate of the intrinsic value for the stock market series. Similar to the investment decision rule with the cash flow valuations, if the intrinsic value based on the forward P/E ratio and estimated EPS is greater than the current market price, we should overweight U.S. common stocks; if the value is below the market price we should underweight U.S. common stocks.

Our prior discussion of Exhibit 12.12 indicated that the earnings multiplier (i.e., P/E ratio) over time has been more volatile than the earnings per share series because the multiplier is very sensitive to changes in the spread between k and g. We will examine each of the variables in the P/E ratio equation to determine why they change and demonstrate how an investor would estimate a value for the earnings multiplier.

12.6.1 Determinants of the Earnings Multiplier

Recall the variables that influence the earnings multiplier or the *P/E* ratio based on the dividend discount model:

12.6
$$P/E = \frac{D_1/E_1}{k - g}$$

where:

D_1 = dividends expected in Period 1, which is equal to $D_0 (1 + g)$
E_1 = earnings expected in Period 1
D_1/E_1 = the dividend-payout ratio expected in Period 1
k = the required rate of return on the stock
g = the expected growth rate of dividends for the stock

Therefore, the major variables that affect the aggregate stock market earnings multiplier in a country are

- The composite dividend-payout ratio for common stocks in a country
- The required rate of return on common stock in the country being analyzed
- The expected growth rate of dividends for the stocks in the country being analyzed

Because this equation is derived from the dividend discount model, it assumes constant growth for an infinite period. Also, the required rate of return is the long-term estimate. Therefore, the *k* and *g* projections are *long-term estimates*. Thus, although these variables can be impacted by near-term events, they should not experience major changes on a year-to-year basis.

It is easier to discuss the dividend-payout ratio after we have considered both *k* and *g*. There, we consider *k* and *g* before D_1/E_1.

12.6.2 Estimating the Required Rate of Return (*k*)

The multiplier equation indicates that the earnings multiplier is inversely related to the required rate of return.

Earlier in the chapter, we discussed what determines *k* and we derived a range of estimates of *k* as follows:

NRFR	Risk Premium	Estimated k	Description
0.026	0.02	0.046	Short-term *RFR* and small risk premium
0.038	0.04	0.078	Intermediate *RFR* and midrange risk premium
0.046	0.06	0.106	Long-term *RFR* and historical risk premium

12.6.3 Estimating the Growth Rate of Dividends (*g*)

Earlier we discussed the estimated growth rate of earnings and dividends using Equation 12.4 as follows:

$$g = b \times \text{ROE}$$

After discussing dividend payouts over the business cycle, we suggested using a long-run retention rate (*b*) of 55 percent.

We estimated a long-run *ROE* based upon an analysis of the three components of the DuPont analysis of 13 percent. The combined result was

$$g = 0.55 \times 0.13$$
$$= 0.071 = 7.1\%$$

Given these estimates of *k, g,* and dividend payout (1 minus the retention rate of 0.55), the following section discusses the estimation of the earnings multiples.

12.6.4 Estimating the Dividend-Payout Ratio (D_1/E_1)

Based on the *P/E* equation, there is a positive relationship between the dividend-payout ratio and the *P/E* ratio. Therefore, if the $k - g$ spread is constant and this dividend-payout ratio increases, there will be an increase in the earnings multiplier. Recall that the dividend-payout ratio is equal to one minus the earnings retention rate *(b)*. Therefore, if the dividend-payout *increases,* there will be a *decline* in the earnings retention rate *(b)*, which will cause a *decline* in the growth rate *(g)*. Thus, there is a partial offset between changes in the dividend-payout rate and the expected growth rate *(g)*.

In the discussion of the growth rate, we indicated that the retention rate was high in the 1970s, declined in the early 1980s, and has increased again since 1993. This increase in the retention rate implies that the payout ratio has declined recently.

Dividend Payout Rate—Active or Residual Decision? When estimating the dividend payout for the aggregate market or an individual firm, you must consider whether the dividend payout rate is (1) an *active* decision of management (and the board of directors) or (2) a *residual* outcome because the active decision is the dividend payment. Obviously, if the dividend payout rate is the active decision, the dividend payment would vary over time in line with earnings. In contrast, if the dividend payment is the active decision, the dividend payout rate is a residual outcome. In this latter case, the dividend payments would be reasonably stable and show fairly steady increases while the dividend-payout ratio would be very volatile because it would be dictated by the earnings. That is, the dividend payout rate would increase dramatically during periods of low earnings and decline significantly during periods high earnings growth.

The time-series plots in Exhibits 12.25 and 12.26 support the residual payout theory because they show fairly constant changes in dividend payments (Exhibit 12.25) but high volatility for

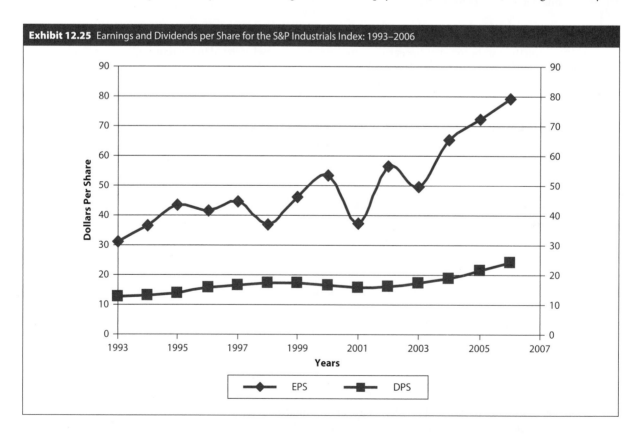

Exhibit 12.25 Earnings and Dividends per Share for the S&P Industrials Index: 1993–2006

Exhibit 12.26 Time-Series Plot for the S&P Industrial Index Dividend Payout Ratio: 1993–2006

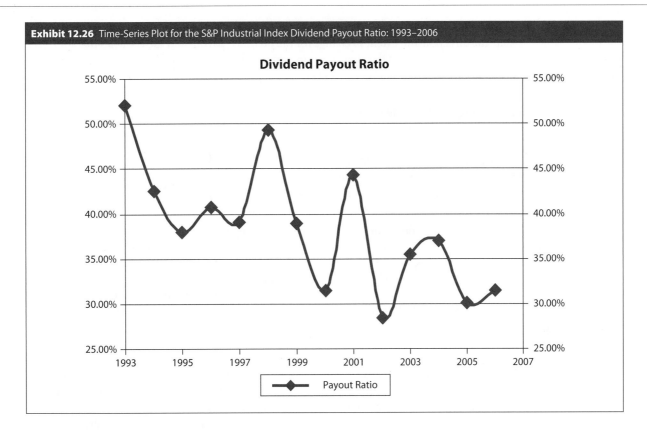

the dividend-payout ratio in Exhibit 12.26. Specifically, the dividend payout declined during the economic expansion of 1993–2000, increased during the 2001 recession, and declined during the economic recovery in 2002–2006. This implies that the annual dividend payout is inversely related to earnings changes. Therefore, when estimating the dividend-payout ratio, you should estimate the dividend payment using time-series analysis and relate this estimated divided to the earnings estimate. It is important *not* to emphasize the volatile annual dividend payout changes but use a *long-run perspective* regarding the dividend–payout ratio over the business cycle.

Further, you should consider the *secular* trend in the payout ratio, which appears to be declining because corporations are increasing the retention rate for the following reasons. First, given the strong *ROE* over the past decade, one could argue that corporations have more profitable investment opportunities, which justifies lower dividend payouts. Second, corporations are repurchasing stock, which is a more tax-efficient way to reward the stockholder. The result of repurchases is fewer shares, higher earnings per share, and higher valuation, which is not taxed like dividends to the shareholder.

12.6.5 Estimating an Earnings Multiplier: An Example

There are two ways to estimate the earnings multiplier. The first approach begins with the current earnings multiplier and estimates the direction and amount of change based on expected changes in the three major components.

The second approach estimates a specific value for the earnings multiplier based on specific estimates for the three components in the *P/E* ratio equation. This approach typically involves deriving several estimates based on optimistic or pessimistic scenarios.

The Direction of Change Approach Begin with the current earnings multiplier and estimate the direction and extent of change for the dividend payout and the variables that influence k and g. The direction of the change is more important than its size.

The variables that must be estimated are

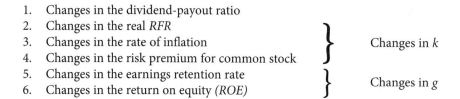

1. Changes in the dividend-payout ratio
2. Changes in the real *RFR*
3. Changes in the rate of inflation
4. Changes in the risk premium for common stock   } Changes in k
5. Changes in the earnings retention rate
6. Changes in the return on equity *(ROE)*   } Changes in g

The changes envisioned for 2008 will be heavily impacted by a slowdown/recession widely projected for 2008. The dividend-payout ratio has been declining for several years because of the strong earnings growth. In contrast, the earnings growth in 2008 in expected to be below the long-term average, so the payout ratio should increase.

Given the three variables that affect the required rate of return on common stocks (k), we expect a small decline in the real *RFR* in 2008 consistent with a small decline in the real growth rate. The rate of inflation during 2007 was 2.6 percent and is expected to increase in 2008. Finally, the equity risk premium is expected to increase in 2008 after a significant decrease during early 2007 followed by increases due to the "credit crises" in the fourth quarter. Therefore, overall we expect an increase in k during 2008.

The last two factors in the earnings multiplier estimate relate to the growth rate. As discussed, we expect a higher payout rate, which implies a lower retention rate. The outlook is for a decline in the aggregate *ROE* during 2008. Specifically, both the profit margin and the total asset turnover are expected to decline given the expected slowdown/recession in 2008. Finally, we envision a small decline in the financial leverage ratio as firms work to reduce their financial risk given the negative economic environment. The overall result should be a definite decrease in the *ROE* during 2008. Therefore, with a decrease in both the retention rate and in *ROE,* we envision a significant decline in the expected growth rate. In summary, we expect

*   An increase in the payout ratio
*   An increase in the required rate of return
*   A clear decline in the expected growth rate

Overall, this would imply a definite decline in the earnings multiplier. The forward earnings multiplier early in 2008 is about 18 times. This discussion would indicate that the multiplier would be about 15 to 16 times by the end of 2008.

Specific Estimate Approach This approach derives specific estimates for the earnings multiplier based on a range of estimates for: dividend payout (D/E), required rate of return (k), and expected growth (g). Although the payout ratio has fluctuated between 35 and 55 percent during the past 10 years, we expect it to be at the upper end of the range (55 percent) due to the earnings decline envisioned for 2008.

As discussed, the required rate (k) can be estimated using the interest rate on government bonds plus a risk premium for common stocks between 2 and 6 percent. As noted earlier, in early 2008, the rate on T-bills was about 2.60 percent, the rate on 10-year government bonds was about 3.80 percent, and the rate on long-term bonds was 4.60 percent. Notably, these interest rates are at the low end of the range for the past 20 years, and most observers expect a small increase during the year. Assuming an adjustment to reflect this, you could conceive of the following possibilities:

		Expected at Year End 2008
A. 10-year government bonds		4.0%
High-risk premium		6.0
	Estimated k	10.0%
B. 10-year government bonds		4.0%
Low-risk premium		2.0
	Estimated k	6.0%
C. 10-year government bonds		4.0%
Medium-risk premium		4.0
	Estimated k	8.0%

Therefore, the required return (k) could be in the range of 6 to 10 percent.

The estimate of growth should be based on the current and expected return on equity *(ROE)* and the rate of retention. The graph in Exhibit 12.27 shows that the *ROE* for the S&P Industrials Index was in the 14 to 20 percent range during the period 1992–2006, but it has been trading down since 1997 and ended at the low point. Assuming that 2008 is between an economic slowdown and recession, a range of 12 to 15 percent for the *ROE* seems appropriate. As indicated earlier, the retention rate has been between 50 and 70 percent. Therefore, a conservative estimate of the growth rate would combine the 50 percent retention rate and an *ROE* of 12 percent: $0.50 \times 0.12 = 0.06$. An optimistic growth rate estimate would combine the 70 percent retention rate and a 15 percent *ROE*: $0.70 \times 0.15 = 0.105$. To summarize,

Dividend/earnings	0.50–0.70
Government securities	0.026–0.046
Equity risk premium	0.020–0.060
Required return (k)	0.06–0.10
ROE	0.12–0.15
Sustainable growth	0.06–0.105

By combining the more optimistic figures (with a positive $k - g$ spread), we can derive a reasonably generous estimate. Using the pessimistic estimates, we can derive a fairly conservative estimate. The dividend-payout (D/E) figure should be consistent with the retention rate.

The fact is, it is not feasible to combine the maximum components because it would generate a negative k–g spread, which is undefined. The most reasonable spread is 2 percent, which provides the following result.

$$\text{High Estimate: } D/E = 0.50$$
$$k = 0.09$$
$$g = 0.07 \ (0.50 \times 0.14)$$

$$P/E = \frac{0.50}{0.090 - 0.07} = \frac{0.50}{0.02} = 25 \text{ times}$$

Obviously, if we assume a spread of only 1 percent, the estimated P/E would be 50 times, which is unrealistic for the aggregate stock market.

$$\text{Low Estimate: } D/E = 0.60$$
$$k = 0.10$$
$$g = 0.06$$

$$P/E = \frac{0.60}{0.10 - 0.06} = \frac{0.60}{0.04} = 15 \text{ times}$$

Therefore, these data imply a range of earnings multiplier from about 15 times to about 25 times with a midrange of about 20 times. The low estimate is consistent with the expectation of a *P/E* ratio range of 15–16 derived from the direction of change approach.

Exhibit 12.27 Relative Valuation Ratios for the S&P Industrials Index: 1993–2006

	Price/ Book Value		Price/Cash Flow (EBITDA)		Price/Sales		Price/Earnings	
	t	*t* + 1	*t*	*t* + 1	*t*	*t* + 1	*t*	*t* + 1
1993	2.81	2.56	6.15	5.18	0.87	0.83	17.42	14.74
1994	2.59	2.41	5.25	4.73	0.84	0.78	14.94	12.63
1995	3.17	3.02	6.24	6.09	1.02	0.99	16.63	17.30
1996	3.64	3.51	7.34	7.06	1.20	1.16	20.87	19.58
1997	4.52	4.24	9.09	9.06	1.49	1.49	25.24	30.34
1998	5.58	4.90	11.95	10.63	1.97	1.82	40.02	31.96
1999	6.09	5.46	13.24	12.25	2.27	2.16	39.80	34.39
2000	4.52	4.39	10.16	12.18	1.79	1.88	28.53	40.84
2001	3.82	4.29	10.63	10.88	1.64	1.71	35.66	23.60
2002	3.23	2.77	8.21	7.44	1.29	1.19	17.80	20.31
2003	3.49	3.13	9.39	8.17	1.50	1.35	25.67	19.49
2004	3.40	3.08	8.87	8.01	1.46	1.32	21.16	19.06
2005	3.14	2.87	8.20	7.43	1.35	1.26	19.52	17.86
2006	3.24	NA	8.39	NA	1.42	NA	20.17	NA

NA—not available.

12.6.6 Calculating an Estimate of the Value for the Market Series

Previously, we estimated the earnings per share for Standard and Poor's Industrials Index of $58. Clearly, it would have been possible to derive additional earnings estimates.

In our work with the *P/E*, we developed several estimates for the price/earnings multiplier that varied from about 15 to 25. At this point, we can combine these estimates of an earnings per share of $78 and the several earnings multipliers and calculate the following estimates of intrinsic value for Standard & Poor's Industrials Index series:

$$15.0 \times \$78 = 1{,}170$$
$$17.5 \times \$78 = 1{,}365$$
$$20.0 \times \$78 = 1{,}560$$
$$22.5 \times \$78 = 1{,}755$$
$$25.0 \times \$78 = 1{,}950$$

You would compare these several intrinsic value estimates to the current price of the market, which is about 1,650—that is, two of the valuations indicate a buy and one is fairly close. Alternatively, the current market is selling for a *P/E* of 21.2 (1,650/78), which is close to the midrange *P/E* estimate.

This example is intended to help you understand the estimation procedure. The estimation of values for *D/E, k,* and *g* was not as extensive as the process used by professional analysts. In addition, we used a point estimate for earnings per share rather than a range of estimates (pessimistic, optimistic, most likely), which would have been preferable. Our discussion has provided the skeleton of the process that includes the theoretical background that forms the foundation for the fundamental analysis of stocks. It is important to understand *the relevant variables and how they relate to the critical estimates of earnings per share and the earnings multiplier.* Notably, the two critical estimates that are necessary for both the present value of cash flow models and the earnings multiplier approach are *k* and *g*—that is, the required rate of return discount rate and the expected growth rate of earnings, cash flow, and dividends.

12.6.7 Using Other Relative Valuation Ratios

In addition to the *P/E* ratio, several other ratios are used by investors as indicators of relative value. Specifically, when doing an industry and company stock analysis, analysts compare these valuation ratios to similar ratios for the aggregate market, other industries, and other stocks in an industry. Therefore, it is important to become familiar with the computation and historical movements for these ratios. The other relative valuation ratios considered are

- Price-to-book-value ratio (*P/BV*)
- Price-to-cash-flow ratio (*P/CF*)
- Price-to-sales ratio (*P/S*)

Calculation of Relative Valuation Ratios The calculation of each of these ratios is generally straightforward with some differences in the measurement of the valuation variable (i.e., *BV, CF,* or *S*). Again, it is necessary to decide whether one uses historical data or forward values—that is, do you compare current price to the *historical* valuation variable (e.g., cash flow for the prior year) or the *future expected* variable (e.g., the expected cash flow for the industry or company). As before, the authors prefer forward valuation ratios.

When computing the *price-to-book-value (P/BV) ratio* for current valuation purposes, it is equal to the current stock price divided by the equity book value per share of the entity. In the current case, because we are computing the relative valuation ratios for historical exposition purposes, we use the *average price*, which is equal to the average of the high and low prices for the year. Again, you must determine whether you want to use historical book value (i.e., compare the average stock price for Year *t* to the book value at the end of Year *t*) or use future book value (i.e., average stock price for Year *t* to *estimated* book value for Year *t* + 1). Similar to the *P/E* ratio, when you compute a future ratio, the ratio will generally be lower and less volatile. Both sets of *P/BV* ratios are contained in Exhibit 12.27 and plotted in Exhibit 12.28. The future ratios are computed using *actual* values for Period *t* + 1 except for the last year (2006) that would have required 2007 values that were not available.

The *price-to-cash-flow (P/CF) ratio* is equal to the average stock price for Year *t* divided by either the historical or the estimated cash flow per share. Similar to most analysts, we use

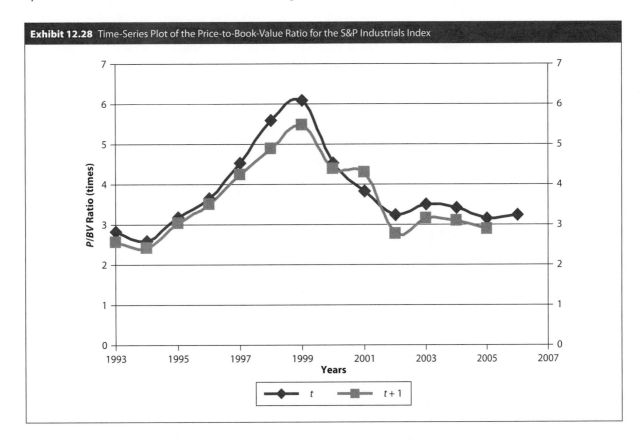

Exhibit 12.28 Time-Series Plot of the Price-to-Book-Value Ratio for the S&P Industrials Index

Exhibit 12.29 Time-Series Plot of the Price-to-Cash-Flow Ratio for the S&P Industrials Index

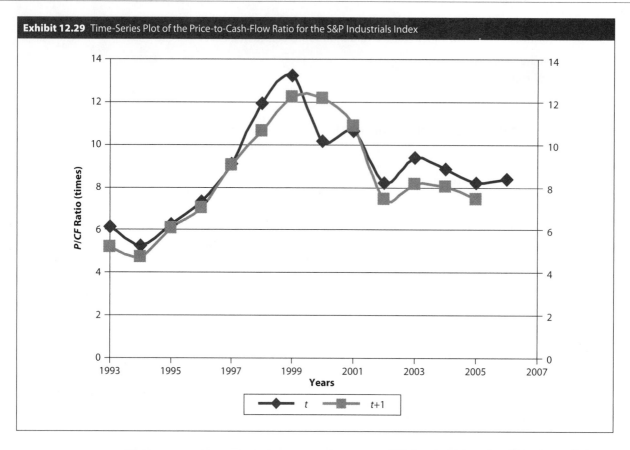

EBITDA for demonstration purposes, even though it is a very imperfect measure of cash flow. Again, we use actual EBITDA in Period $t + 1$ for the future ratio except for the final year. The data are in Exhibit 12.27 and plotted in Exhibit 12.29.

The *price-to-sales* (*P/S*) *ratio* is equal to the average stock price for Year t divided by net sales per share during Year t or an estimate of sales per share for Year $t + 1$. Again, for the future *P/S* ratio, we use sales per share during Period $t + 1$ except for the final year. The results are in Exhibit 12.27 and plotted in Exhibit 12.30.

As shown, all the future ratios experienced significant increases through 1999 followed by declines to levels above beginning values.

Relative Valuation Ratio	Approximate Beginning Value (1993)	Approximate Ending Value (2005)
Price/Earnings	14.74	17.86
Price/Book Value	2.56	2.87
Price/Cash Flow	5.18	7.43
Price/Sales	0.83	1.26

To understand these higher valuation ratios, it is necessary to consider what factors drive the particular valuation ratio and whether these factors have changed over time. In the case of the *P/E* ratio, we know from DDM that the relevant variables are k and g for the economic unit. Therefore, when attempting to explain why the market *P/E* ratio has gone from about 15 times to 18 times, you would consider what has happened to these two variables. Without going into detail, we know that k has declined over time due to lower inflation and some evidence that the market risk premium has declined. In addition, the aggregate *ROE* has been fairly stable so the expected growth rate has been constant. In summary, the k–g spread has declined so a higher *P/E* is justified. How much higher it should be is subject to estimation and debate. Subsequently, we will discuss the relevant factors for the other ratios.

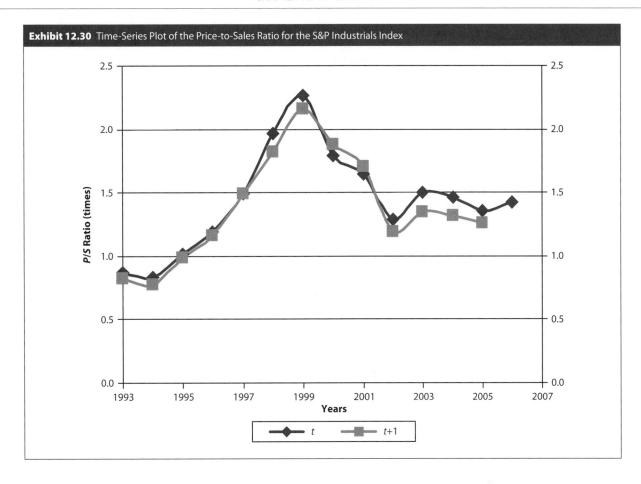

Exhibit 12.30 Time-Series Plot of the Price-to-Sales Ratio for the S&P Industrials Index

The plots also show considerable consistency between the time series using historical and future expected data. Again, the authors have a definite perference for using the *future* valuation variables because when investors buy a stock, they are buying future earnings, cash flows, book values, or sales. Although it is not easy to obtain estimates for these alternative valuation variables, you need to think in these terms when using these ratios for valuation. Similar to valuations using the *P/E* ratio, you must estimate the valuation variable (i.e., *BV, CF,* or Sales per share) and then apply an appropriate *future* multiple to the valuation variable to derive an estimate of intrinsic value.

12.7 Microvaluation of World Markets

Similar to our discussion at the end of the macroeconomic analysis of the market, we need to briefly consider some of the unique factors when deriving a microvaluation for markets outside the United States.

It is crucial to keep three important factors in mind. First, the basic valuation model and concepts apply globally. Specifically, value is still based on the discounted value of future cash flows whether you are in New York, London, Moscow, or Beijing. Also, the ultimate decision is still based on the relationship between estimated intrinsic value and the market price.

Second, while the models and concepts are the same, the input values can and will vary dramatically across countries, which means that values will differ and opportunities will differ—for example, when stocks appear overpriced in the United States they may be undervalued in Japan or Australia.

Third, the valuation of nondomestic markets will almost certainly be more onerous because of several additional variables or constraints that must be considered. The most obvious is that you must estimate a value in the local currency but also estimate potential changes in the value of the foreign currency relative to the U.S. dollar. The difficulty of estimating these changes or attempting to hedge this currency risk (if it is possible) becomes an added risk factor discussed in Chapter 1—exchange rate risk.

It is also necessary to consider country or political risk, which can be very significant in many countries. This risk generally *cannot* be hedged away.

Notably, investors in U.S. stocks generally do not think about this risk even during elections. The only change has been terrorist risk since the 9/11 event, a risk which is present around the world. The point is, country risk must be evaluated and estimated when investing outside the United States.

As a result of the two added risk factors (exchange rate risk and country risk), the required rate of return on foreign securities will generally be higher than for domestic stock. Notably, these added risks can be offset by higher growth expectations, such as in China and India. As always, it is the individual who does the best estimates of these critical valuation variables (k and g) who will be the superior analyst.

Another added burden relates to different accounting conventions in alternative countries. Therefore, you must understand how firms in a country account for various items and how this impacts cash flows, etc. The good news is the constant movement toward international accounting standards should substantially reduce this problem—when the international standards become resolved and are widely adopted.

In summary, as money management becomes more global and industry analysis requires global constituents, you will need to evaluate stock markets around the globe and keep these added factors in mind.

• • • • SUMMARY • • • •

In earlier chapters, we emphasized the importance of analyzing the aggregate markets before any industry or company analysis. You must assess the economic and security market outlooks and their implications regarding the bond, stock, and cash components of your portfolio. Then you proceed to consider the best industry or company.

- Two techniques are used to make the market decision: (1) the macroeconomic technique, which is based on the relationship between the aggregate economy and the stock market; (2) the microeconomic technique, which determines future market values by applying the two valuation approaches discussed in Chapter 11 to the aggregate stock market.
- The economy and the stock market have a strong, consistent relationship, but the stock market generally turns before the economy does. Therefore, the best macroeconomic projection techniques use economic series that likewise lead the economy, and possibly the stock market. The Conference Board leading indicator series (which includes stock prices) is one possibility.
- The money supply has been suggested as a predictor of aggregate market behavior based on its relationship to the economy. Some early studies indicated a strong relationship and suggested that money supply changes turned before stock prices. Subsequent studies confirmed the link between money supply and stock prices, but indicated that stock prices turn with or before money supply changes.

Recent results show that the monetary policy environment has an important impact on security market returns and also affects how stocks relate to other variables.

- Our microanalysis of the U.S. equity market considered both approaches to equity analysis—the present value of cash flow techniques and the relative valuation ratio techniques. The cash flow techniques provided a range of estimates, most of which indicated that the market was fully valued, which implies that the rates of return on common stock in the near term will be lower than the long-run historical returns.
- We considered four relative valuation ratios, including the earnings multiple (*P/E*) approach where we discussed a two-step approach (that included estimating EPS and the *P/E* ratio) and generated a specific intrinsic market value. The other three ratios (*P/BV*; *P/CF*; and *P/S*) were defined and explained in anticipation of using them during industry and company analysis where the relative valuation technique compares an industry to the market and relates a company to both its industry and the aggregate market. The goal is to evaluate the relative value position of an industry or a stock. This initial analysis of the valuation ratios was intended to demonstrate the computations involved. Subsequent analysis will consider what variables drive these relative valuation ratios and evaluate whether these variables have changed in a way that justifies current values.

- Finally, because we know it is necessary to do a similar analysis for non-U.S. markets, we discussed some of the additional factors involved in non-U.S. market analysis.

Following this aggregate market analysis, the next step is industry analysis, which is considered in the following chapter.

• • • • SUGGESTED READINGS • • • •

Diermeier, Jeffrey J. "Capital Market Expectations: The Macro Factors." In *Managing Investment Portfolios: A Dynamic Process,* 2nd ed., eds. John L. Maginn and Donald L. Tuttle. Boston: Warren Gorham and Lamont, 1990.

Fama, Eugene F., and Kenneth French. "Business Conditions and Expected Returns on Stocks and Bonds." *Journal of Financial Economics* 25, no. 1 (November 1989).

Finnerty, John D., and Dean Leistikow. "The Behavior of Equity and Debt Risk Premiums." *Journal of Portfolio Management* 19, no. 4 (Summer 1993).

Shackalford, Aaron L., ed. *Economic Analysis for Investment Professionals.* Charlottesville, VA: AIMR, 1997.

Solnik, Bruno. *Predictable Time-Varying Components of International Asset Returns.* Charlottesville, VA: AIMR, 1993.

• • • • QUESTIONS • • • •

1. Why would you expect a relationship between economic activity and stock price movements?

2. At a lunch with some business associates, you discuss the reason for the relationship between the economy and the stock market. One of your associates contends that she has heard that stock prices typically turn before the economy does. How would you explain this phenomenon?

3. Explain the following statements: (a) There is a strong, consistent relationship between money supply changes and stock prices. (b) Money supply changes cannot be used to predict stock price movements.

4. You are informed of the following estimates: nominal money supply is expected to grow at a rate of 7 percent, and GDP is estimated to grow at 4 percent. Explain what you think will happen to stock prices during this period and the reason for your expectation.

5. The current rate of inflation is 3 percent, and long-term Treasury bonds are yielding 7 percent. You estimate that the rate of inflation will increase to 6 percent. What do you expect to happen to long-term bond yields? Compute the effect of this change in inflation on the price of a 15-year, 10 percent coupon bond with a current yield to maturity of 8 percent.

6. Some observers contend that it is harder to estimate the effect of a change in interest rates on common stocks than on bonds. Discuss this contention.

7. An investor is convinced that the stock market will experience a substantial increase next year because corporate earnings are expected to rise by at least 12 percent. Do you agree or disagree? Why or why not?

8. Find at least three sources of historical information on nominal and real GDP. Find two sources of an annual estimate of nominal GDP.

9. To arrive at an estimate of the *net profit margin*, why would you spend time estimating the operating profit margin and work down?

10. You are convinced that capacity utilization next year will decline from 82 percent to about 79 percent. Explain what effect this change will have on the operating profit margin.

11. You see an estimate that hourly wage rates will increase by 6 percent next year. How does this affect your estimate of the operating profit margin? What other information do you need to determine the effect of this wage rate increase and why do you need it?

12. It is estimated that, next year, hourly wage rates will increase by 7 percent and productivity will increase by 5 percent. What would you expect to happen to unit labor cost? Discuss how this unit labor cost estimate would influence your estimate of the operating profit margin.

13. Assume that each of the following changes is independent (i.e., except for this change, all other factors remain unchanged). In each case, indicate what will happen to the earnings multiplier and explain why.
    a. The return on equity increases
    b. The aggregate debt–equity ratio declines
    c. Overall productivity of capital increases
    d. The dividend-payout ratio declines

• • • • PROBLEMS • • • •

1. Prepare a table showing the percentage change for each of the last 10 years in (a) the Consumer Price Index (all items), (b) nominal GDP, (c) real GDP (in constant dollars), and (d) the GDP deflator. Discuss how much of nominal growth was due to *real* growth and how much was due to inflation.

2. **CFA EXAMINATION LEVEL I** There has been considerable growth in recent years in the use of economic analysis in investment management. Further significant expansion may lie ahead as financial analysts develop greater skills in economic analysis and these analyses are integrated more into the investment decision-making process. The following questions address the use of economic analysis in the investment decision-making process:

   a. (1) Differentiate among leading, lagging, and coincident indicators of economic activity, and give an example of each.

      (2) Indicate whether the leading indicators are one of the best tools for achieving above-average investment results. Briefly justify your conclusion.

   b. Interest rate projections are used in investment management for a variety of purposes. Identify three significant reasons why interest rate forecasts may be important in reaching investment conclusions.

   c. Assume you are a fundamental research analyst following the automobile industry for a large brokerage firm. Identify and briefly explain the relevance of three major economic time series, economic indicators, or economic data items that would be significant to automotive industry and company research.

4. **CFA EXAMINATION LEVEL III** A U.S. pension plan hired two offshore firms to manage the non-U.S. equity portion of its total portfolio. Each firm was free to own stocks in any country market included in Capital International's Europe, Australia, and Far East Index (EAFE) and free to use any form of dollar and/or nondollar cash or bonds as an equity substitute or reserve. After three years had elapsed, the records of the managers and the EAFE Index were as shown:

SUMMARY: CONTRIBUTIONS TO RETURN

	Currency	Country Selection	Stock Selection	Cash/Bond Allocation	Total Return Recorded
Manager A	(9.0%)	19.7%	3.1%	0.6%	14.4%
Manager B	(7.4)	14.2	6.0	2.8	15.6
Composite of A&B	(8.2)	16.9	4.5	1.7	15.0
EAFE Index	(12.9)	19.9	–	–	7.0

You are a member of the plan sponsor's pension committee, which will soon meet with the plan's consultant to review manager performance. In preparation for this meeting, you go through the following analysis:

   a. Briefly describe the strengths and weaknesses of each manager, relative to the EAFE Index data.

   b. Briefly explain the meaning of the data in the Currency column.

4. You are told that nominal GDP will increase by about 10 percent next year. Using Exhibit 12.14 and the regression equation, what increase would you expect in corporate sales? How would this estimate change if you gave more weight to the recent observations?

5. Currently, the dividend-payout ratio (*D/E*) for the aggregate market is 60 percent, the required return (*k*) is 11 percent, and the expected growth rate for dividends (*g*) is 5 percent.

   a. Compute the current earnings multiplier.

   b. You expect the *D/E* ratio to decline to 50 percent, but you assume there will be no other changes. What will be the *P/E*?

   c. Starting with the initial conditions, you expect the dividend-payout ratio to be constant, the rate of inflation to increase by 3 percent, and the growth rate to increase by 2 percent. Compute the expected *P/E*.

   d. Starting with the initial conditions, you expect the dividend-payout ratio to be constant, the rate of inflation to decline by 3 percent, and the growth rate to decline by 1 percent. Compute the expected *P/E*.

6. As an analyst for Charlotte, Chelle, and Denise, you are forecasting the market *P/E* ratio using the dividend discount model. Because the economy has been expanding for 9 years, you expect the

dividend-payout ratio will be at its low of 40 percent and that long-term government bond rates will rise to 7 percent. Because investors are becoming less risk averse, the equity risk premium will decline to 3 percent. As a result, investors will require a 10 percent return, and the return on equity will be 12 percent.

a. What is the expected growth rate?

b. What is your expectation of the market *P/E* ratio?

c. What will be the value for the market index if the expectation is for earnings per share of $80?

7. You are given the following estimated per share data related to the S&P Industrials Index for the year 2010:

Sales	$1,320.00
Depreciation	58.00
Interest expense	28.00

You are also informed that the estimated operating profit margin is 0.16 and the tax rate is 32 percent.

a. Compute the estimated EPS for 2010.

b. Assume that a member of the research committee for your firm feels that it is important to consider a range of operating profit margin (OPM) estimates. Therefore, you are asked to derive both optimistic and pessimistic EPS estimates using 0.15 and 0.17 for the OPM and holding everything else constant.

8. Given the three EPS estimates in Problem 7, you are also given the following estimates related to the market earnings multiple:

	Pessimistic	**Consensus**	**Optimistic**
D/E	0.65	0.55	0.45
Nominal *RFR*	0.10	0.09	0.08
Risk premium	0.05	0.04	0.03
ROE	0.11	0.13	0.15

a. Based on the three EPS and *P/E* estimates, compute the high, low, and consensus intrinsic market value for the S&P Industrials Index in 2010.

b. Assuming that the S&P Industrials Index at the beginning of the year was priced at 1,950, compute your estimated rate of return under the three scenarios from Part a. Assuming your required rate of return is equal to the consensus, how would you weight the S&P Industrials Index in your global portfolio?

9. You are analyzing the U.S. equity market based upon the S&P Industrials Index and using the present value of free cash flow to equity technique. Your inputs are as follows:

Beginning FCFE: $80
k = 0.09

Growth Rate:	
Year 1–3:	9%
4–6:	8%
7 and beyond	7%

a. Assuming that the current value for the S&P Industrials Index is 1,950, would you underweight, overweight, or market weight the U.S. equity market?

b. Assume that there is a 1 percent increase in the rate of inflation—what would be the market's value and how would you weight the U.S. market? State your assumptions.

CHAPTER 13

Industry Analysis*

After you read this chapter, you should be able to answer the following questions:

- Is there a difference between the returns for alternative industries during specific time periods? What is the implication of these results for industry analysis?
- Is there consistency in the returns for individual industries over time? What do these results imply regarding industry analysis?
- Is the performance for firms within an industry consistent? What is the implication of these results for industry and company analysis?
- Is there a difference in risk among industries? What are the implications of these results for industry analysis?
- What happens to risk for individual industries over time? What does this imply for industry analysis?
- What are the stages in the industrial life cycle and how does the stage in an industry's life cycle affect the sales estimate for an industry?
- What are the five basic competitive forces that determine the intensity of competition in an industry and, thus, its rate of return on capital?
- How does an analyst determine the value of an industry using the DDM assuming constant growth or two-stage growth?
- How does an analyst determine the value of an industry using the free cash flow to equity (FCFE) model assuming constant growth or two-stage growth?
- What are the steps involved in estimating earnings per share for an industry?
- How does the procedure for estimating the operating profit margin differ for the aggregate market versus an industry?
- What is involved in a macroanalysis of the industry earnings multiplier?
- What are the steps in the microanalysis of an industry earnings multiplier?
- How do you determine if an industry's estimated multiplier is relatively high or low?
- How do analysts compare relative valuation ratios such as *P/BV, P/CF,* and *P/S* to comparable market ratios?
- How do industries differ in terms of what dictates their return on assets?
- What are some of the unique factors that must be considered in global industry analysis?

When asked about his or her job, a securities analyst typically will reply that he or she is an oil analyst, a retail analyst, or a computer analyst. A widely read trade publication, *The Institutional Investor*, selects an All-American analyst team each year based on industry groups. Investment managers talk about being in or out of the metals, the autos, or the utilities. This constant reference to industry groups is because most professional investors are extremely conscious of differences among alternative industries and organize their analyses and portfolio decisions according to industry groups.

* The authors acknowledge input to the discussions on "The Business Cycle and Industry Sectors" and "Structural Economic Changes" provided by Professor Edgar Norton of Illinois State University.

We acknowledge the importance of industry analysis as a component of the three-step fundamental analysis procedure initiated in Chapter 11. Industry analysis is the second step as we progress toward selecting specific firms and stocks for our investment portfolio. In Chapter 12, we did a macroanalysis and valuation of the stock market to decide whether the expected rate of return from investing in common stocks was equal to or greater than our required rate of return—that is, should we overweight, market weight, or underweight stocks? In this chapter, we analyze different industries to determine if the intrinsic value of an industry is equal to or greater than its market price. Based on this relationship, we decide how to weight the industry in our stock portfolio. In Chapter 14, we analyze the individual companies and stocks within alternative industries.

In the first section, we discuss the results of several studies that identify the benefits and uses of industry analysis. Similar to the market analysis that considered both macroeconomic factors and microvaluation, we consider several industry macroanalysis topics such as the differential impact of the business cycle on alternative industries, how various structural economic changes affect different industries, understanding an industry's life cycle, and evaluating the competitive environment in an industry. This macroanalysis is crucial to an overall understanding of what factors determine risk and return in an industry.

Following this, the bulk of the chapter considers the microvaluation of the retail industry including a demonstration of both the cash flow models and the relative valuation ratios introduced earlier in Chapter 11. We conclude the chapter with a discussion of global industry analysis, because many industries transcend U.S. borders and compete on a worldwide basis.

. . . .

13.1 Why Do Industry Analysis?

Investment practitioners perform industry analysis because they believe it helps them isolate investment opportunities that have favorable return–risk characteristics. We likewise have recommended it as part of our three-step, top-down investment analysis approach. What exactly do we learn from an industry analysis? Can we spot trends in industries that make them good investments? Are there unique patterns in the rates of return and risk measures over time in different industries? In this section, we survey the results of studies that addressed the following set of questions designed to pinpoint the benefits and limitations of industry analysis:

- Is there a difference between the returns for alternative industries during specific time periods?
- Will an industry that performs well in one period continue to perform well in the future? That is, can we use past relationships between the market and an individual industry to predict future trends for the industry?
- Is the performance of firms within an industry consistent over time?

Several studies also considered questions related to risk:

- Is there a difference in the risk for alternative industries?
- Does the risk for individual industries vary, or does it remain relatively constant over time?

Based on the results of these studies, we come to some general conclusions about the value of industry analysis. In addition, this assessment helps us interpret the results of our subsequent industry valuation.

13.1.1 Cross-Sectional Industry Performance

To find out if the rates of return among different industries varied during a given period (e.g., during the year 2009), researchers compared the performance of alternative industries during a specific time period. Similar performance during specific time periods for different industries would indicate that industry analysis is not necessary. For example, assume that during 2009, the aggregate stock market experienced a rate of return of 10 percent and the returns for *all* industries were bunched between 9 percent and 11 percent. If this similarity in performance persisted over time, you might question whether it was worthwhile to do industry analysis to find an industry that would return 11 percent when random selection would provide a return of about 10 percent (the average return).

Studies of the annual performance by numerous industries found that different industries have consistently shown *wide dispersion in their rates of return*. A specific example is the year 2007. As shown in Exhibit 13.1, although the aggregate stock market experienced a percent price change of about 3.5 (the S&P 500) the industry performance ranged from 83.05 percent (heavy construction) to −55.86 percent (home construction). The consistency of these results is confirmed in Exhibit 13.2 for the recent eight years—the average high industry change is 81 percent and the average low change is −43 percent. These results imply that industry analysis is important and necessary to uncover these substantial performance differences—that is, it helps identify both unprofitable and profitable opportunities.

13.1.2 Industry Performance over Time

Another set of studies questioned whether industries that perform well in one time period would perform well in subsequent time periods, or outperform the aggregate market in the later time period. Investigators found *almost no association* in industry performance year to year or over sequential rising or falling markets.

These time-series studies imply that past performance alone does *not* project future industry performance. The results do *not*, however, negate the usefulness of industry analysis. They simply confirm that variables that affect industry performance change over time and each year you must estimate the current intrinsic value for each industry based on future estimates of relevant variables and compare this to the market price.

13.1.3 Performance of the Companies within an Industry

Other studies examined whether there is consistency in the performance of companies within an industry. If all the firms within an industry performed consistently during a specified time

---

Exhibit 13.1 How the Dow Jones U.S. Industry Groups Fared during 2007

Top Ten Performers % change 12/31/06 to 12/31/07		Bottom Ten Performers % change 12/31/06 to 12/31/07	
Heavy Construction	83.05	Home Construction	−55.86
General Mining	67.05	Mortgage Finance	−50.36
Coal	62.24	Specialty Finance	−40.05
Specialty Chemicals	43.55	Airlines	−36.92
Nonferrous Metals	42.36	Home Improvement Retailers	−31.14
Oil Equipment & Services	41.82	Real Estate Hldng & Dev	−28.64
Exploration & Production	39.14	Banks	−28.08
Commercial Vehicles & Trucks	38.88	Consumer Finance	−26.58
Steel	37.68	Bus. Trning & Employ Agncys	−24.50
Computer Hardware	32.42	Clothing & Accessories	−24.03

Exhibit 13.2 Annual Range of Industry Performance[1] Relative to the Aggregate Market (S&P 500) 2000–2007

Year	S&P 500	High Industry		Low Industry		Total Range
2000	−10.14	Tobacco	85.92	Consumer Services	−65.52	151.44%
2001	−13.04	Consumer Services	57.12	Gas Utilities	−71.60	128.72%
2002	−23.37	Precious Metals	40.48	Pipelines	−66.04	106.52%
2003	26.38	Mining	156.68	Fixed Line Communication	−3.78	160.46%
2004	8.99	General Mining	97.15	Semiconductors	−21.65	118.80%
2005	3.00	Oil & Gas Exploration	64.22	Automobiles	−38.97	103.19%
2006	13.63	Steel	61.66	Home Construction	−20.69	82.35%
2007	3.53	Heavy Construction	83.05	Home Construction	−55.86	138.91%
	Average =		80.79		−43.01	123.80%

[1]Performance is measured by the percent change in the industry index value during the year. Therefore, they are only price changes, not total return that would include dividend.

period, you would not need to do company analysis. Specifically, industry analysis alone would be enough because given a profitable industry you would know that all the stocks in that industry would do well.

These studies typically have found *wide dispersion* in the performance among companies in most industries. Studies by Meyers (1973) and Livingston (1977) provided evidence of an industry effect in specific industries, such as oil or autos, but also showed that the industry effect has been declining over time.

Implication of Dispersion within Industries Some observers have contended that industry analysis is useless because all firms in an industry do not move together. Obviously, consistent firm performance in an industry would be ideal, as noted, because you would not need to do company analysis. For industries that have a strong, consistent industry influence, such as oil, gold, steel, autos, and railroads, company analysis is less critical than industry analysis.

Because there is not a strong industry influence across firms means that a thorough *company* analysis is still necessary. Still, industry analysis is valuable because it is much easier to select a superior company from a good industry than to find a good company in a poor industry. By selecting the best stocks within a strong industry, you avoid the risk that your analysis and selection of a good company will be offset by poor industry performance.

13.1.4 Differences in Industry Risk

Although numerous studies have examined industry returns, few studies have examined industry risk measures. The studies on industry risk investigated two questions: (1) Does risk differ among industries during a given time period? (2) Are industry risk measures stable over time? The studies of risk dispersion found a wide range of risk among different industries and the differences in industry risk typically widened during rising and falling markets. The results on risk stability were positive—the risk measures for individual industries over time were *reasonably stable.*

Therefore, although risk measures for different industries showed substantial dispersion during a period of time, individual industries' risk measures are stable over time. Hence, the analysis of industry risk is necessary, but this analysis of risk is useful when estimating the future risk for an industry.

13.1.5 Summary of Research on Industry Analysis

The conclusions of the studies dealing with industry analysis are:

- During any time period, the returns for different industries vary within a wide range, which means that industry analysis is an important part of the investment process.
- The rates of return for individual industries vary over time, so we cannot simply extrapolate past industry performance into the future.
- The rates of return of firms within industries also vary, so analysis of individual companies in an industry is a necessary follow-up to industry analysis.
- During any time period, different industries' risk levels vary within wide ranges, so we must examine and estimate the risk factors for alternative industries.
- Risk measures for different industries remain fairly constant over time, so the historical risk analysis is useful when estimating future risk.

13.1.6 Industry Analysis Process

An important question is, How should you structure your industry analysis? In our previous analysis of the economy and the aggregate equity market, we contended that it is necessary to examine the macroeconomy for two related reasons. First, although the security markets tend to move ahead of the aggregate economy, we know that security markets reflect the strength or weakness of the economy. Second, most of the variables that determine value for the security markets are macrovariables such as interest rates, GDP, and corporate earnings. Therefore, our analysis of the aggregate equity market contained two components—one dealing with macrovariables such as leading indicators and monetary policy and a second facet being micro-analysis of specific variables that affect valuation.

The point is, the industry analysis process is similar—first is a *macroanalysis* of the industry to determine how this industry relates to the business cycle and what economic variables drive this industry. This macroanalysis will make the microvaluation component easier wherein we use the several valuation techniques introduced earlier. As noted, macroanalysis of the industry will make the estimation of the valuation inputs of a discount rate and expected growth for earnings and cash flows easier and more accurate.

The specific macroanalysis topics are:

1. The business cycle and industry sectors
2. Structural economic changes and alternative industries
3. Evaluating an industry's life cycle
4. Analysis of the competitive environment in an industry

13.2 The Business Cycle and Industry Sectors

Economic trends can and do affect industry performance. Our objective is to monitor the economy and gauge the implications of new information on our economic outlook and industry analysis. Recall that in order to beat the market on a risk-adjusted basis, our forecasts must differ from the market consensus *and* we must be correct more often than not.

Economic trends can take two basic forms: **cyclical changes** that arise from the ups and downs of the business cycle, and **structural changes** when the economy is undergoing a major change in how it functions. For example, excess labor or capital may exist in some sectors whereas shortages of labor and capital exist elsewhere. The "downsizing" of corporate America during the 1990s, transitions from socialist to market economies in Eastern Europe, and the transition in the United States from a manufacturing to a service economy are all examples of structural change.[1] Industry analysts must examine structural economic changes for the implications they have for an industry under review.

While industry performance is related to the stage of the business cycle, the real challenge is that every business cycle is different and those who look only at history miss the evolving trends that will determine future market and industry performance.

Switching industry groups over the course of a business cycle is known as a *rotation strategy*. When trying to determine which industry groups will benefit from the next stage of the business cycle, investors need to monitor economic trends and changes in industry characteristics.

Exhibit 13.3 presents a stylized graphic of which industry groups typically perform well in the different stages of the business cycle. For example, toward the end of a recession, financial stocks rise in value because investors anticipate that banks' earnings will rise as both the economy and loan demand recover. Brokerage houses become attractive investments because their sales and earnings are expected to rise as investors trade securities, businesses sell debt and equity, and there are more mergers during the economic recovery. These industry expectations assume that when the recession ends there will be an increase in loan demand, housing construction, and security offerings.

Once the economy begins its recovery, consumer durable firms that produce items such as cars, personal computers, refrigerators, lawn tractors, and snow blowers, become attractive investments because a reviving economy will increase consumer confidence and disposable income. Once businesses recognize the economic recovery, they think about modernizing, renovating, or purchasing new equipment to satisfy rising demand and reduce costs. Thus, capital goods industries such as heavy equipment manufacturers, machine tool makers, and airplane manufacturers become attractive.

---

[1] An excellent discussion of structural changes in the U.S. economy and the implications of these changes for the business cycle, the stock market, and some specific industries is contained in Dudley and McKelvey (1997).

Exhibit 13.3 The Stock Market and the Business Cycle

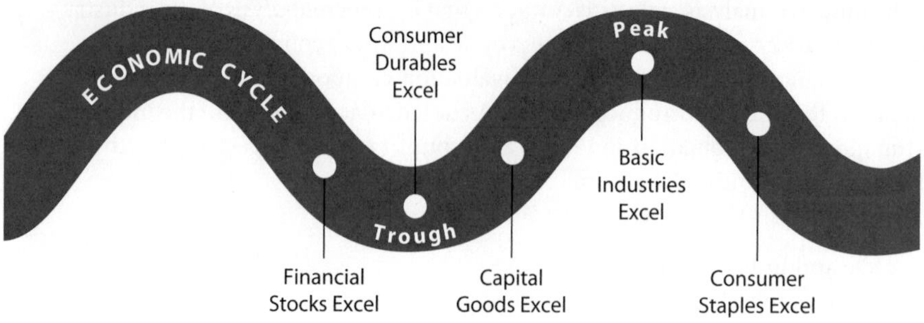

Source: Susan E. Kuhn, "Stocks Are Still Your Best Buy," *Fortune*, 21 March 1994, 140.

Cyclical industries whose sales rise and fall along with general economic activity are attractive investments during the early stages of an economic recovery because of their high degree of operating leverage, which means that they benefit greatly from the sales increases during an economic expansion.[2] Industries with high financial leverage likewise benefit from rising sales volume.[3]

Traditionally, toward the business cycle peak, inflation increases as demand starts to outstrip supply. Basic materials industries such as oil, metals, and timber, which transform raw materials into finished products, become investor favorites. Because inflation has little influence on the cost of extracting these products and they can increase prices, these industries experience higher profit margins.

During a recession, some industries do better than others. Consumer staples, such as pharmaceuticals, food, and beverages, outperform other sectors during a recession because, although overall spending may decline, people still spend money on necessities so these "defensive" industries generally maintain their values. Similarly, if a weak domestic economy causes a weak currency, industries that export to growing economies benefit because their goods become more cost competitive.

We have identified certain industries that are typically attractive investments over the business cycle. Remember, you should not invest based upon the current economic environment because the efficient market has already incorporated current economic news into security prices. Rather, you must *forecast* important economic variables and invest accordingly. The following subsections consider how changes in several important economic variables may affect different industries.

13.2.1 Inflation

As noted in several chapters, higher inflation is generally negative for stocks, because it causes higher market interest rates, more uncertainty about future prices and costs, and harms firms that cannot pass through cost increases. Although these adverse effects are true for most industries, there are some industries that benefit from inflation. Natural resource industries benefit *if* their production costs do not rise with inflation, because their output will likely sell at higher prices. Industries with high operating leverage benefit because many of their costs are fixed in nominal (current dollar) terms whereas revenues increase with inflation. Industries with high financial leverage may also gain, because their debts are repaid in cheaper dollars.

[2] As discussed in Chapter 1, operating leverage arises from the existence of fixed costs in a firm's operating structure. Industries with large fixed expenses will have high degrees of operating leverage. This means a small percentage change in sales can result in a large percentage change in operating income.

[3] As noted in Chapter 10, financial leverage arises from fixed financial costs (that is, interest expense) in a firm's capital structure. Industries that have extensive debt financing (such as banks or utilities) will have net income that is sensitive to small changes in operating income.

13.2.2 Interest Rates

Financial institutions, including banks, are typically adversely impacted by higher rates because they find it difficult to pass on these higher rates to customers (i.e., lagged adjustment). High interest rates clearly harm the housing and the construction industry, but they might benefit industries that supply the do-it-yourselfer. High interest rates also benefit retirees whose income is dependent on interest income. A study by Reilly, Wright, and Johnson (2007) examines the interest rate sensitivity of a large cross-section of industries and types of stocks.

13.2.3 International Economics

Both domestic and international events affect the value of the U.S. dollar. A weaker U.S. dollar helps U.S. industries because their exports become comparatively cheaper in overseas markets while the goods of foreign competitors become more expensive in the United States. A stronger dollar has an opposite effect. Economic growth in world regions or specific countries benefits industries that have a large presence in those areas. The creation of free trade zones, such as the European Community and the North American Free Trade Zone, assist industries that produce goods and services that previously faced quotas or tariffs in partner countries.

13.2.4 Consumer Sentiment

Because it comprises about two-thirds of GDP, consumption spending has a large impact on the economy. Optimistic consumers are more willing to spend and borrow money for expensive goods, such as houses, cars, new clothes, and furniture. Therefore, the performance of consumer cyclical industries will be affected by changes in consumer sentiment and by consumers' willingness and ability to borrow and spend money.

· ·
13.3 Structural Economic Changes and Alternative Industries

Influences other than the economy are part of the business environment. Demographics, changes in technology, and political and regulatory environments also can have a significant effect on the cash flow and risk prospects of different industries.

13.3.1 Demographics

In the past 50 years, the United States has had a baby boom and a baby bust and is now enjoying a baby boomlet as members of the baby-boom generation (those born between the end of World War II and the early 1960s) have children. The influx of the baby boom and the "graying of the baby boom" have had a large impact on U.S. consumption, from advertising strategies to house construction to concerns over social security and health care. The study of demographics includes much more than population growth and age distributions. Demographics also includes the geographical distribution of people, the changing ethnic mix in a society, and changes in income distribution. Therefore, industry analysts need to carefully study demographic trends and project their effect on different industries.

During the period from 1990 to 2008, the fastest-growing age groups in the United States were those in their 40s and 50s, teens, and those over 70; among the declining groups were those between ages 18 and 24. As of the early 2000s, more than one in eight Americans are 65 years of age or older. The changing age profile of Americans has implications for resource availability, namely, a possible shortage of entry-level workers leading to an increase in labor costs and difficulty in finding qualified persons to replace the retiring baby boomers. The aging U.S. population also affects U.S. savings patterns, because people in the 40 to 60 age bracket usually save more than younger people. This is good for the financial services industry, which offers assistance to those who want to invest their savings. Alternatively, fewer younger workers and more "saving seniors" may have a negative impact on some industries, such as the retailing industry.

13.3.2 Lifestyles

Lifestyles deal with how people live, work, form households, consume, enjoy leisure, and educate themselves. Consumer behavior is affected by trends and fads. The rise and fall of designer jeans, chinos, and other styles in clothes illustrate the sensitivity of some markets to changes in consumer tastes. The increase in divorce rates, dual-career families, population shifts away from cities, and computer-based education and entertainment have influenced numerous industries, including housing, restaurants, automobiles, catalog shopping, services, and home entertainment. From an international perspective, some U.S.-brand goods—from blue jeans to movies—have a high demand overseas. They are perceived to be more in style and perhaps higher quality than items produced domestically. Several industries have benefited from this positive brand reputation.

13.3.3 Technology

Technology can affect numerous industry factors including the product or service and how it is produced and delivered. There are numerous examples of changes due to technological innovations. For example, demand has fallen for carburetors on cars because of electronic fuel-injection technology. The engineering process has changed because of the advent of computer-aided design and manufacturing. Perpetual improvement of designs in the semiconductor and microprocessor industry has made that industry a difficult one to evaluate. Innovations in process technology allowed steel minimills to grow at the expense of large steel producers. Advances in technology allow some plant sites and buildings to generate their own electricity, bypassing their need for power from the local electric utility. Trucks have reduced railroads' market share in the long-distance carrier industry. The information superhighway is becoming a reality and encouraging linkages between telecommunications and cable television systems. Changes in technology have spurred capital spending in technological equipment as a way for firms to gain competitive advantages. The future effect of the Internet is astronomical.

The retailing industry is a wonderful example of how an industry can use new technology. Some forecasters envision relationship merchandising, in which customer databases will allow closer links between retail stores and customer needs. Rather than market research on aggregate consumer trends, specialized retailers offer products that consumers desire in preferred locations. Technology allows retailers to become more organizationally decentralized and geographically diversified. Major retailers use barcode scanning, which speeds the checkout process and allows the firm to track inventory and customer preferences. Credit cards allow firms to track customer purchases and send customized sales announcements. Electronic data interchange (EDI) allows the retailer to electronically communicate with suppliers to order new inventory and pay accounts payable. Electronic funds transfer allows retailers to move funds quickly and easily between local banks and headquarters.

It is essential for an analyst to become aware of how technology can be a benefit or threat to an industry.

13.3.4 Politics and Regulations

Because political change reflects social values, today's social trend may be tomorrow's law, regulation, or tax. The industry analyst needs to project and assess political changes relevant to the industry under study.

Some regulations and laws are based on economic reasoning. Due to utilities' positions as natural monopolies, their rates must be reviewed and approved by a regulatory body.[4] Some regulation involves social ends. For example, the Food and Drug Administration protects consumers by reviewing new drugs. Public and worker safety concerns spurred creation of the Consumer Product Safety Commission, the Environmental Protection Agency, and OSHA. Notably, heavy regulation of an industry can increase a firm's costs but also can restrict entry into the industry.

Regulatory changes have affected numerous industries. An example is the numerous regulations and inspections following the September 11, 2001, attacks. Changing regulations and

---

[4] Technology can change natural monopolies. We mentioned earlier how some firms are generating their own electrical power. Another example is that, currently, numerous states are allowing electric utilities to compete for customers.

technology are bringing participants in the financial services industry—banking, insurance, investment banking, and investment services—together.

Regulations and laws affect international commerce. International tax laws, tariffs, quotas, embargoes, and other trade barriers have a significant effect on some industries and global commerce.

Again, an interesting example is how the retail industry is affected by numerous regulatory factors. First, the minimum-wage law impacts many retail employees. A second factor is employer-paid health insurance, which dramatically impacts the labor costs of service industries, such as retailing. Third, because goods must first be delivered to the stores, regulations that affect the cost of shipping by airplane, ship, or truck will affect retailers' costs. Finally, lower tariffs and quotas will allow retailers to offer imported goods at lower prices (e.g., Wal-Mart), which will expand their international production (outsourcing).

13.4 Evaluating the Industry Life Cycle

An insightful analysis when predicting industry sales and trends in profitability is to view the industry over time and divide its development into stages similar to those that humans progress through: birth, adolescence, adulthood, middle age, old age. The number of stages in this **industry life cycle analysis** can vary based on how much detail you want. A five-stage model would include

1. Pioneering development
2. Rapid accelerating growth
3. Mature growth
4. Stabilization and market maturity
5. Deceleration of growth and decline

Exhibit 13.4 shows the growth path of sales during each stage. The vertical scale in logs reflects *rates* of growth, whereas the arithmetic horizontal scale has different widths representing

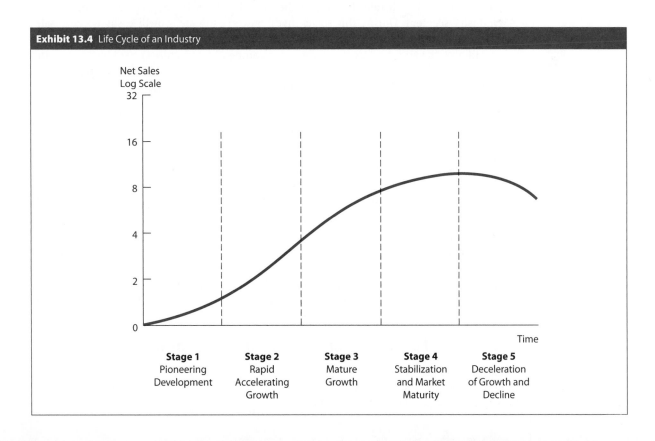

Exhibit 13.4 Life Cycle of an Industry

different, unequal time periods. To estimate industry sales, you must predict the length of time for each stage. This requires answers to such questions as: How long will an industry grow at an accelerating rate (Stage 2)? How long will it be in a mature growth phase (Stage 3) before its sales growth stabilizes (Stage 4) and then declines (Stage 5)?

Besides being useful when estimating sales, this industry life cycle analysis also provides insights into profit margins and earnings growth, although these profit measures may not parallel the sales growth. The profit margin series typically peaks very early in the total cycle and then levels off and declines as competition is attracted by the early success of the industry.

The following is a brief description of how these stages affect sales growth and profits:

1. *Pioneering development.* During this start-up stage, the industry experiences modest sales growth and very small or negative profits. The market for the industry's product or service during this stage is small, and the firms incur major development costs.

2. *Rapid accelerating growth.* During this rapid growth stage, a market develops for the product or service and demand becomes substantial. The limited number of firms in the industry face little competition, and firms can experience substantial backlogs and very high profit margins. The industry builds its productive capacity as sales grow at an increasing rate as the industry attempts to meet excess demand. High sales growth and high profit margins that increase as firms become more efficient cause industry and firm profits to explode (i.e., profits can grow at over 100 percent a year because of the low earnings base and the rapid growth of sales and margins).

3. *Mature growth.* The success in Stage 2 has satisfied most of the demand for the industry goods or service. Thus, future sales growth may be above normal but it no longer accelerates. For example, if the overall economy is growing at 8 percent, sales for this industry might grow at an above normal rate of 15 percent to 20 percent a year. Also, the rapid growth of sales and the high profit margins attract competitors to the industry, which causes an increase in supply and lower prices, which means that the profit margins begin to decline to normal levels.

4. *Stabilization and market maturity.* During this stage, which is probably the longest phase, the industry growth rate declines to the growth rate of the aggregate economy or its industry segment. During this stage, investors can estimate growth easily because sales correlate highly with an economic series. Although sales grow in line with the economy, profit growth varies by industry because the competitive structure varies by industry, and by individual firms within the industry because the ability to control costs differs among companies. Competition produces tight profit margins, and the rates of return on capital (e.g., return on assets, return on equity) eventually become equal to or slightly below the competitive level.

5. *Deceleration of growth and decline.* At this stage of maturity, the industry's sales growth declines because of shifts in demand or growth of substitutes. Profit margins continue to be squeezed, and some firms experience low profits or even losses. Firms that remain profitable may show very low rates of return on capital. Finally, investors begin thinking about alternative uses for the capital tied up in this industry.

Although these are general descriptions of the alternative life cycle stages, they should help you identify the stage your industry is in, which in turn should help you estimate its potential sales growth and profit margin. Obviously, everyone is looking for an industry in the early phases of Stage 2 and hopes to avoid industries in Stage 4 or Stage 5. Comparing the sales and earnings growth of an industry to similar growth in the economy should help you identify the industry's stage within the industrial life cycle.

13.5 Analysis of Industry Competition

Similar to the sales forecast that can be enhanced by the analysis of the industrial life cycle, an industry earnings forecast should be preceded by the analyses of the competitive structure for the industry. Specifically, a critical factor affecting the profit potential of an industry is the intensity of competition in the industry, as Porter (1980a, b, 1985) has discussed.

13.5.1 Competition and Expected Industry Returns

Porter's concept of **competitive strategy** is described as the search by a firm for a favorable competitive position in an industry. To create a profitable competitive strategy, a firm must first examine the basic competitive structure of its industry because the potential profitability of a firm is heavily influenced by the profitability of its industry. After determining the competitive structure of the industry, you examine the factors that determine the relative competitive position of a firm within its industry. In this section, we consider the competitive forces that determine the competitive structure of the industry. In the next chapter, our discussion of company analysis considers the factors that determine the relative competitive position of a firm within its industry.

Basic Competitive Forces   Porter believes that the **competitive environment** of an industry (the intensity of competition among the firms in that industry) determines the ability of the firms to sustain above-average rates of return on invested capital. As shown in Exhibit 13.5, he suggests that five competitive forces determine the intensity of competition and that the relative effect of each of these five factors can vary dramatically among industries.

1. *Rivalry among the existing competitors.* For each industry analyzed, you must judge if the rivalry among firms is currently intense and growing, or polite and stable. Rivalry increases when many firms of relatively equal size compete in an industry. When estimating the number and size of firms, be sure to include foreign competitors. Further, *slow growth* causes competitors to fight for market share and increases competition. *High fixed costs* stimulate the desire to sell at the full capacity, which can lead to price cutting and greater competition. Finally, look for *exit barriers,* such as specialized facilities or labor agreements. These can keep firms in the industry despite *below-average* or negative rates of return.

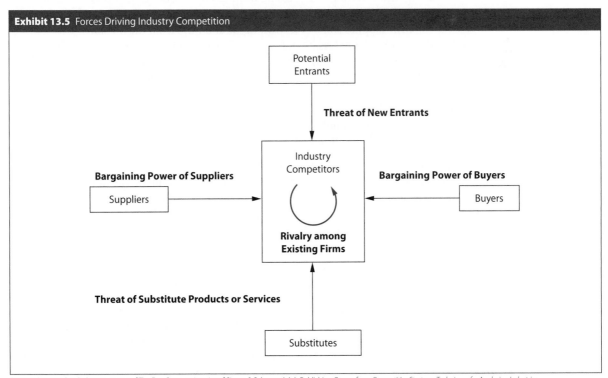

Exhibit 13.5 Forces Driving Industry Competition

Source: Reprinted with the permission of The Free Press, an imprint of Simon & Schuster Adult Publishing Group, from *Competitive Strategy: Techniques for Analyzing Industries and Competitors* by Michael E. Porter. Copyright © 1980, 1998 by The Free Press.

2. *Threat of new entrants.* Although an industry may have few competitors, you must determine the likelihood of firms entering the industry and increasing competition. *High barriers to entry,* such as low current prices relative to costs, keep the threat of new entrants low. Other barriers to entry include the need to invest large financial resources to compete and the availability of capital. Also, substantial economies of scale give a current industry member an advantage over a new firm. Further, entrants might be discouraged if success in the industry requires extensive distribution channels that are hard to build because of exclusive distribution contracts. Similarly, high costs of switching products or brands, such as those required to change a computer or telephone system, keep competition low. Finally, government policy can restrict entry by imposing licensing requirements or limiting access to materials (lumber, coal). Without some of these barriers, it might be very easy for competitors to enter an industry, increasing the competition and driving down potential rates of return.

3. *Threat of substitute products.* Substitute products limit the profit potential of an industry because they limit the prices firms in an industry can charge. Although almost everything has a substitute, you must determine how close the substitute is in price and function to the product in your industry. As an example, the threat of substitute glass containers hurts the metal container industry. Glass containers kept declining in price, forcing metal container prices and profits down. In the food industry, consumers constantly substitute between beef, pork, chicken, and fish. The more commoditylike the product, the greater the competition and the lower the profit margins.

4. *Bargaining power of buyers.* Buyers can influence the profitability of an industry because they can bid down prices or demand higher quality or more services by bargaining among competitors. Buyers become powerful when they purchase a large volume relative to the sales of a supplier (e.g., Wal-Mart, Home Depot). The most vulnerable firm is a one-customer firm that supplies a single large manufacturer, as is common for auto parts manufacturers or software developers. Buyers will be more conscious of the costs of items that represent a significant percentage of the firm's total costs. This consciousness increases if the buying firm is feeling cost pressure from its customers. Also, buyers who know a lot about the costs of supplying an industry will bargain more intensely—for example, when the buying firm supplies some of its own needs and buys from the outside.

5. *Bargaining power of suppliers.* Suppliers can alter future industry returns if they increase prices or reduce the quality of the product or the services they provide. The suppliers are more powerful if they are few and if they are more concentrated than the industry to which they sell and if they supply critical inputs to several industries for which few, if any, substitutes exist. In this instance, the suppliers are free to change prices and services they supply to the firms in an industry. When analyzing supplier bargaining power, be sure to consider labor's power within each industry.

An investor needs to analyze these competitive forces to determine the intensity of the competition in an industry and assess the effect of this competition on the industry's long-run profit potential. You should examine each of these factors and develop a relative competitive profile for each industry. You need to update this analysis of an industry's competitive environment over time, because an industry's competitive structure can and will change over time.

13.6 Estimating Industry Rates of Return

At this point, we have determined that industry analysis helps an investor select profitable investment opportunities and we have completed a thorough macroanalysis of the industry. Our next question is, How do we go about valuing an industry? Again, we consider the two equity valuation approaches introduced in Chapter 11—the present value of cash flows and the relative valuation ratios.

Although our investment decision is always the same, the form of the comparison depends on which valuation approach is being used. In the case of the present value of cash flow techniques, we compare the present value of the specified cash flow versus the prevailing value of the index and determine if we should underweight, equal weight, or overweight this global industry in our portfolio.

When we value the industry using the alternative valuation ratios, the only addition to the analysis is that we also compare our industry ratios to the market ratios presented in Chapter 12.

To demonstrate industry analysis, we use Standard and Poor's retailing index to represent industrywide data. This retailing index (hereinafter referred to as the RET industry) contains about 30 individual companies from several retailing sectors including two drug stores. Therefore, it should be reasonably familiar to most observers, and it is consistent with the subsequent company analysis of Walgreens.

13.6.1 Valuation Using the Reduced Form DDM

Recall that the reduced form DDM is

13.1
$$P_i = \frac{D_1}{k - g}$$

where:

P_i = the price of Industry i at Time t
D_1 = expected dividend for Industry i in Period 1 equal to $D_0 (1 + g)$
k = the required rate of return on the equity for Industry i
g = the expected long-run growth rate of earnings and dividend for Industry i

As always, *the two major estimates for any valuation model are k and g*. We will discuss each of these at this point and also use these estimates subsequently when applying the two-step, price/earnings ratio technique for valuation.

Estimating the Required Rate of Return *(k)* Because the required rate of return *(k)* on all investments is influenced by the risk-free rate and the expected inflation rate, the differentiating factor in this case is the risk premium for the retailing industry versus the market. In turn, we discussed the risk premium in terms of fundamental factors, including business risk *(BR)*, financial risk *(FR)*, liquidity risk *(LR)*, exchange rate risk *(ERR)*, and country (political) risk *(CR)*. Alternatively, you can estimate the risk premium based on the CAPM, which implies that the risk premium is a function of the systematic risk (beta) of the asset. Therefore, to derive an estimate of the industry's risk premium, you should examine the *BR, FR, LR, ERR*, and *CR* for the industry and compare these industry risk factors to those of the aggregate market. Alternatively, you can compute the systematic risk (beta) for the industry and compare this to the market beta of 1.0. Prior to calculating an industry beta, we briefly discuss the industry's fundamental risk factors.

Business risk is a function of relative sales volatility and operating leverage. As we will see when we examine the sales and earnings for the industry, the annual percentage changes in retailing sales were less volatile than aggregate sales as represented by PCE. Also, the OPM (operating profit margin) for retail stores was less volatile than for the S&P Industrials Index. Therefore, because both sales and the OPM for the retailing industry have been less volatile than the market, operating profits are substantially less volatile. This implies that the business risk for the retailing industry is *below average*.

The *financial risk* for this industry is difficult to judge because of widespread use of building leases in the industry that are not included on the balance sheet. As a result, the reported data on debt to total capital or interest coverage ratios indicate that the *FR* for this industry is substantially below the market. Assuming substantial use of long-term lease contracts, when these are capitalized, the retailing industry probably has financial risk *about equal* to the market. While the data is not available to capitalize leases for the industry, we showed how to do this in Chapter 10, and will demonstrate it for a company in Chapter 14.

To evaluate an industry's market *liquidity risk* you must estimate the liquidity risk for all the firms in the industry and derive a composite view. The fact is, there is substantial variation in market liquidity among the firms in this industry ranging from Walgreens and Wal-Mart that are fairly liquid compared to small specialty retail chains that are relatively illiquid. A conservative view is that the industry has *above-average* liquidity risk.

Exchange rate risk (ERR) is the uncertainty of earnings due to changes in exchange rates faced by firms in this industry that sell outside the United States. The amount of *ERR* is determined by what proportion of sales is non-U.S., how these sales are distributed among countries, and the exchange rate volatility for these countries. This risk could range from an industry with very limited international sales (e.g., a service industry that is not involved overseas) to a global industry (e.g., the chemical or pharmaceutical industry). For a truly global industry, you need to examine the distribution of sales among specific countries because the exchange rate risk varies among countries based on the volatility of exchange rates with the U.S. dollar. The *ERR* for the retailing industry would be relatively *low* because sales and earnings for retailing firms are mainly attributable to activity within the United States.

The existence of *country risk (CR)* is likewise a function of the proportion of foreign sales, the specific foreign countries involved, and the stability of the political/economic system in these countries. As noted, there is very little *CR* in the United Kingdom and Japan, but there can be substantial *CR* in China, Russia, or South Africa. Again, for the retailing industry, country risk would be relatively low because of limited foreign sales.

In summary, for the retailing industry, business risk is definitely below average, financial risk is at best equal to the market, liquidity risk is above average, and exchange rate risk and country risk are fairly low. The consensus is that the overall fundamental risk for the RET industry should be lower than for the aggregate market.

The *systematic risk* for the retailing (RET) industry is computed using the market model as follows:

13.2
$$\% \, \Delta \, \text{RET}_t = \alpha_i + \beta_i \, (\% \, \Delta \, \text{S\&P 500}_t)$$

where:

$\% \, \Delta \, \text{RET}_t$ = the percentage price change in the retailing (RET) index during month t
α_i = the regression intercept for the RET industry
β_i = the systematic risk measure for the RET industry equal to $\text{Cov}_{i,m}/\sigma_m^2$

To derive an estimate for the RET industry, the model specified was run with monthly data for the five-year period of 2003 to 2007. The results for this regression are as follows:

$\alpha_t = 0.003$	$R^2 = 0.71$
$\beta_t = 0.95$	$DW = 1.80$
t-value = 6.50	$F = 71.37$

The systematic risk ($\beta = 0.95$) for the RET industry is below unity, indicating a low-risk industry (i.e., risk less than the market). These results are consistent with the prior analysis of fundamental risk factors *(BR, FR, LR, ERR, CR)*.

Translating this systematic risk into a required rate of return estimate *(k)* calls for using the security market line model as follows:

13.3
$$k_i = \text{RFR} + \beta_i \, (R_m - \text{RFR})$$

Recall that in Chapter 12 we derived three estimates for the required market rate of return (based on alternative risk premiums) (0.048 −0.085−0.108). For our purposes here, it seems like the midpoint is reasonable—that is, a nominal *RFR* of 0.038 and an R_m of 0.078. This, combined with a beta for the industry at 0.95, indicates the following:

$$k = 0.038 + 0.95(0.04)$$
$$= 0.038 + 0.038$$
$$= 0.0760 = 7.60\%$$

For ease of computation, we will use a k of 8.0%. Both the fundamental risk analysis and the CAPM estimate implies below average risk and an industry earnings multiple *above* the market multiple, all other factors being equal.

Estimating the Expected Growth Rate (g)   Recall that earnings and dividend growth are determined by the retention rate and the return on equity.

$$g = f \text{ (Retention Rate and Return on Equity)}$$

Again, we employ the three components of ROE:

$$\frac{\text{Net Profit}}{\text{Equity}} = \frac{\text{Net Income}}{\text{Sales}} \times \frac{\text{Sales}}{\text{Total Assets}} \times \frac{\text{Total Assets}}{\text{Equity}}$$

$$= \frac{\text{Profit}}{\text{Margin}} \times \frac{\text{Total Asset}}{\text{Turnover}} \times \frac{\text{Financial}}{\text{Leverage}}$$

we examine each of these variables in Exhibit 13.5 to determine if they imply a different expected growth rate for RET versus the aggregate market (S&P Industrials Index).

Earnings Retention Rate   The data in Exhibit 13.5 indicate that the RET industry has a higher retention rate (79 percent versus 67 percent) which implies a potentially *higher* growth rate, all else being the same (i.e., equal *ROE*).

Return on Equity   Because the return on equity is a function of the net profit margin, total asset turnover, and financial leverage, these three variables are examined individually.

Historically, the data in Exhibit 13.5 show that the net profit margin for the S&P Industrials Index series has been consistently higher than the margin for the RET industry. This is not surprising because retail firms typically have lower profit margins but higher turnover.

As expected, the total asset turnover *(TAT)* for the RET industry was higher than the average industrial company. In Exhibit 13.6, the average *TAT* for the S&P Industrials Index was 0.86 versus 1.77 for the RET industry. Beyond the overall difference, as shown in Exhibit 13.6 the spread between the two series increased over the period because the industrials *TAT* experienced a small overall decline while the *TAT* for the RET industry experienced an overall increase, as shown in Exhibits 13.6 and 13.7. Multiplying the PM by the *TAT* indicates the industry's return on total assets *(ROTA).*[5]

$$\frac{\text{Net Income}}{\text{Sales}} \times \frac{\text{Sales}}{\text{Total Assets}} = \frac{\text{Net Income}}{\text{Total Assets}}$$

The results in Exhibit 13.6 indicate that the return on total assets *(ROTA)* for the S&P Industrials Index series went from 3.27 percent in 1993 to 6.47 percent in 2006 and averaged 4.68 percent, whereas the *ROTA* for the RET industry went from 4.07 percent to 8.15 percent and averaged 6.10 percent. Clearly, the industry *ROTA* results were superior on average.

The final component is the financial leverage multiplier (total assets/equity). As shown in Exhibits 13.6 and 13.8 both leverage multipliers experienced declines over the 14-year period—the industrials by 26 percent and the RET industry by 38 percent. Although the higher financial leverage multiplier implies greater financial risk for the S&P Industrials Index series, recall that the RET industry financial leverage is understated because the widely-used leases are not capitalized.

---

[5] The reader is encouraged to read Appendix 13B to this chapter, which contains a discussion of an article by Selling and Stickney (1989), wherein they analyze the components of *ROA* and relate this to an industry's economics and its strategy.

Exhibit 13.6 Earnings Multiplier for the S&P Industrials Index and the Retail Industry, and Influential Variables: 1993–2006

Year	Earnings Multiplier (t + 1)		Retention Rate		Net Profit Margin		Total Asset Turnover		Return on Total Assets		Total Assets / Equity		Return on Equity	
	S&P Ind	Retail	S&P Ind	Retail	S&P Ind	Retail	S&P Ind	Retail	S&P Ind	Retail	S&P Ind	Retail	S&P Ind	Retail
1993	14.74	18.4	47.96	71.74	4.99	3.13	0.87	1.32	3.27	4.07	3.59	3.35	15.65	13.86
1994	12.63	19.76	57.51	71.13	5.60	3.14	0.89	1.44	4.91	4.35	3.37	3.34	16.88	14.70
1995	17.30	16.04	61.95	67.91	6.14	2.43	0.94	1.58	5.19	4.08	3.25	2.76	18.68	11.43
1996	19.58	16.35	59.30	77.48	5.73	2.86	0.95	1.83	5.62	5.02	3.14	2.77	17.17	14.04
1997	30.34	18.70	60.88	78.20	5.92	3.01	0.95	1.85	5.33	5.38	3.14	2.70	17.55	14.60
1998	31.96	26.27	50.63	83.24	4.93	3.45	0.88	1.96	4.90	6.66	3.16	2.66	13.61	17.86
1999	34.39	41.65	60.98	83.70	5.70	3.61	0.84	2.02	5.22	6.91	3.11	2.60	14.96	18.07
2000	40.84	33.27	68.54	82.43	6.27	2.86	0.86	2.02	5.45	5.60	2.89	2.57	15.57	14.46
2001	23.60	26.54	55.60	82.68	4.61	2.57	0.79	2.00	1.79	4.92	3.00	2.61	10.90	12.86
2002	20.31	13.86	71.60	86.15	7.23	3.71	0.76	1.88	1.92	6.81	3.26	2.46	17.98	16.83
2003	19.49	18.47	64.52	85.12	5.84	5.02	0.76	1.67	4.29	7.27	3.02	2.23	13.46	16.22
2004	19.06	18.72	63.01	85.65	6.91	4.63	0.80	1.66	5.09	7.61	2.84	1.99	15.64	15.17
2005	17.86	16.24	69.95	83.66	6.94	5.18	0.84	1.70	6.06	8.53	2.77	2.15	16.12	18.34
2006	N/A	N/A	68.52	83.42	7.04	4.85	0.85	1.83	6.47	8.15	2.64	2.09	15.84	17.06
mean	23.24	21.87	61.50	80.18	5.99	3.60	0.86	1.77	4.68	6.10	3.08	2.59	15.71	15.39

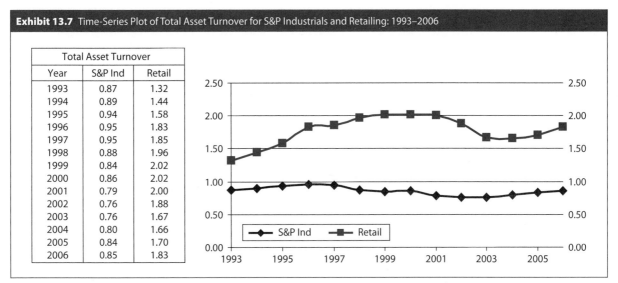

Exhibit 13.7 Time-Series Plot of Total Asset Turnover for S&P Industrials and Retailing: 1993–2006

Total Asset Turnover		
Year	S&P Ind	Retail
1993	0.87	1.32
1994	0.89	1.44
1995	0.94	1.58
1996	0.95	1.83
1997	0.95	1.85
1998	0.88	1.96
1999	0.84	2.02
2000	0.86	2.02
2001	0.79	2.00
2002	0.76	1.88
2003	0.76	1.67
2004	0.80	1.66
2005	0.84	1.70
2006	0.85	1.83

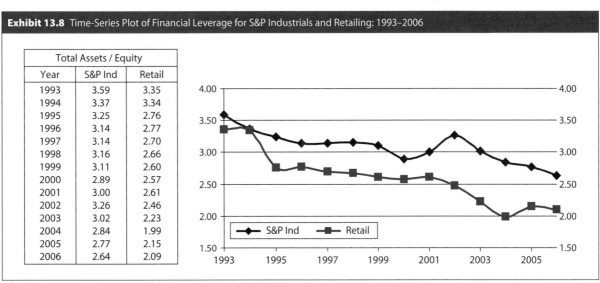

Exhibit 13.8 Time-Series Plot of Financial Leverage for S&P Industrials and Retailing: 1993–2006

Total Assets / Equity		
Year	S&P Ind	Retail
1993	3.59	3.35
1994	3.37	3.34
1995	3.25	2.76
1996	3.14	2.77
1997	3.14	2.70
1998	3.16	2.66
1999	3.11	2.60
2000	2.89	2.57
2001	3.00	2.61
2002	3.26	2.46
2003	3.02	2.23
2004	2.84	1.99
2005	2.77	2.15
2006	2.64	2.09

This final value of *ROE* in Exhibits 13.6 and 13.9 indicate that the best annual *ROE* varied by year until the last two years when the RET industry was higher. The average annual *ROE*s were quite close—15.71 percent for the industrials, 15.39 percent for the RET industry. These average percentages are quite consistent with what would be derived from multiplying the averages of the components from Exhibit 13.6 as follows:

ROE ESTIMATE BASED ON TOTAL PERIOD AVERAGES (1993–2006)

	Profit Margin		Total Asset Turnover		Total Assets/ Equity		ROE
S&P Industrials Index	5.99	×	0.86	×	3.08	=	15.87
RET Industry	3.60	×	1.77	×	2.59	=	16.50

Although examining the historical trends and the averages for each of the components is important, you should not forget that expectations of *future* performance will determine the *ROE* value for the industry. In the current case, this analysis of expectations is very important

Exhibit 13.9 Time-Series Plot of Return on Equity for the S&P Industrials Index and the Retail Industry: 1993–2006

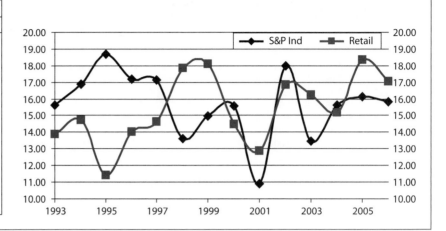

Return On Equity		
Year	S&P Ind	Retail
1993	15.65	13.86
1994	16.88	14.70
1995	18.68	11.43
1996	17.17	14.04
1997	17.55	14.60
1998	13.61	17.86
1999	14.96	18.07
2000	15.57	14.46
2001	10.90	12.86
2002	17.98	16.83
2003	13.46	16.22
2004	15.64	15.17
2005	16.12	18.34
2006	15.84	17.06

because of the positive change in relative *ROE* during the last two years (2005, 2006). As an analyst, it is necessary to determine whether this recent change is a permanent change in the relative performance of this industry versus the market. In this case, you should be encouraged because of the strong performance of the RET industry during 2005–2006. Specifically, if you use the results for the recent five-year period (2002–2006), the *ROE* results are:

ROE ESTIMATE BASED ON RECENT FIVE-YEAR AVERAGES (2002–2006)

	Profit Margin		Total Asset Turnover		Total Assets/ Equity		ROE
S&P Industrials Index	6.79	×	0.80	×	2.90	=	15.75
RET Industry	4.68	×	1.75	×	2.18	=	17.85

Notably, using the recent results, the *ROE* results for the RET industry are clearly superior to the industrials. Combining these recent *ROE* results with alternative retention rates provides interesting growth estimates:

GROWTH ESTIMATES BASED ON RECENT *ROE* WITH HISTORICAL AND RECENT RETENTION RATES

	Recent* ROE	Historical** RR	Estimated g	Recent* ROE	Recent* RR	Estimated g
S&P Industrials Index	15.75	0.62	9.77	15.75	0.68	10.71
RET Industry	17.85	0.80	14.28	17.85	0.85	15.17

*Recent five-year average.
**Total period average.

The point is, using full-period retention results indicates a higher *g* for the RET industry. Further, using the retention rates and *ROE* for the recent five-year period indicates a substantially higher *g* for the industry. Given the increase in *g* for the industry when we consider the recent results, it is probably appropriate to use a growth estimate for the RET industry that is above the long-run historical estimate—that is, we will assume a near-term growth rate of 13 percent, which is relatively conservative. Obviously, the best estimate of *g* would be based on an *estimate* of the three components of *ROE* for the *future* five years.

Exhibit 13.10 Dividend Discount Calculations

Year	Estimated Dividend	Discount Factor @ 8.0%	Present Value of Dividend
2008	5.85	—	—
2009	6.61	.9259	6.12
2010	7.47	.8573	6.40
2011	8.29	.7938	6.58
2012	9.20	.7350	6.76
2013	10.21	.6806	6.95
2014	11.13	.6302	7.01
2015	12.13	.5835	7.08
2016	13.22	.5402	7.14
Continuing Value[a]	1,415	.5402	764.38
			Total Value $818.42

[a]Constant Growth Rate = 7%

Continuing Value: $\dfrac{D_1}{k-g} = \dfrac{13.22\,(1.07)}{0.08-0.07} = \dfrac{14.15}{0.01} = 1{,}415$

Combining the Estimates At this point, we have the following estimates:

$$k = 0.080$$
$$g = 0.130$$
$$D_0 = \$5.18 \text{ (Estimated 2007 Dividends)}$$
$$D_1 = \$5.18 \times 1.13 = \$5.85 \text{ (Estimated Dividend for 2008)}$$

Because of the inequality between k and g (this g is above k and above the long-run market norm of about 7 percent and probably cannot be sustained), we need to evaluate this industry using the temporary growth company model discussed in Chapter 12. We will assume the following growth pattern:

2008–2010	0.130
2011–2013	0.110
2014–2016	0.090
2017–onward	0.070

Using these estimates of k and this growth pattern, the computation of value for the industry using the DDM is contained in Exhibit 13.10.

These computations imply a value of $818.42 compared to the stock price for the industry index of about $410 in early 2008. Therefore, according to this valuation model and these k and g estimates, this industry is currently almost 50 percent undervalued. As will be shown, a fairly small change in the $k - g$ spread can have a large effect on the estimated value.

If we assumed a constant growth rate of 7 percent from the beginning and a D_1 of $5.85, the value would be as follows:

$$P = \frac{5.85}{(0.080 - 0.070)} = \frac{5.85}{0.010} = 585.00$$

Notably this valuation likewise implies the industry is undervalued, even though it is a low estimate of value since it assumes the base growth rate of 7 percent from the beginning. The point is, the industry is undervalued assuming either strong growth in the next few years, or only market growth. Clearly, both valuations are dependent on the growth estimate—assuming 6 percent long-term growth would have a large impact on value.

13.6.2 Industry Valuation Using the Free Cash Flow to Equity (FCFE) Model

We initially define the FCFE series and present the series for the recent 14-year period, along with an estimate for 2007 in Exhibit 13.11. Given these data, we consider the historical growth rates for the components and for the final FCFE series as inputs to estimating future growth for the valuation models. You will recall that FCFE is defined (measured) as follows:

Net Income
  + Depreciation expense
  − Capital expenditures
  − Δ in working capital
  − Principal debt repayments
  + New debt issues

As noted, the FCFE data inputs and final annual value of FCFE for the RET industry for the period 1993–2007 is contained in Exhibit 13.11 along with 5-year and 10-year growth rates of the components. Using this data, we derive an estimate using the FCFE model under two scenarios: (1) a constant growth rate from the present, and (2) a two-stage growth rate assumption.

The Constant Growth Rate FCFE Model We know that the constant growth rate model requires that the growth rate (g) be lower than the required rate of return (k), which we have specified as 8.00 percent. In the current case, this is difficult because the 10-year growth rate exceeds this. Still, in order to use the model, we assume a 10 percent growth in 2008 and 6 percent long-run growth in subsequent years. The result is as follows:

$$g = 0.06 \text{ (Long-Run Growth Beginning in 2009)}$$

$$k = 0.080$$

$$\text{FCFE (2007)} = \$16.00$$

$$\text{FCFE (2008)} = \$16.00 \,(1.10) = \$17.60 = \text{FCFE}_0$$

$$V = \frac{\text{FCFE}_1}{k - g}$$

$$= \frac{17.60 \,(1.06)}{0.080 - 0.060} = \frac{18.66}{0.02}$$

$$= \$933$$

This $933 value exceeds the industry stock price of $410 that prevailed in early 2008. This implies that the industry is undervalued and should be overweighted in the portfolio. Notably, even if we assumed the long-run growth rate was only 5 percent, the estimated value would be $622, which would still imply that the industry is undervalued.

The Two-Stage Growth FCFE Model As before, we assume a period of above-average growth for several years followed by a second period of constant growth at 6 percent. The period of above-average growth will be as follows based on an estimated initial 9 percent growth rate of FCFE, which is lower than what was used for dividends because the FCFE series has been fairly erratic over the past 14 years including several years when the FCFE was negative.

2008	9%
2009	9%
2010	8%
2011	8%
2012	7%
2013	7%
2014–onward	6%

Exhibit 13.11 Components of Free Cash Flow to Equity for the Retail Industry

Year	Net Income	Depreciation Expense	Capital Expenditures	Working Capital	Change in Working Captial	Principal Repayment	New Debt Issues	Total FCFE
1993	5.45	2.76	7.37	23.18	1.93			−1.09
1994	6.20	3.05	8.51	25.52	2.34		2.11	0.51
1995	5.06	3.77	8.93	30.50	4.98		7.41	2.33
1996	6.67	4.27	8.28	29.54	−0.96		0.36	3.98
1997	7.56	4.80	9.06	29.99	0.45		1.17	4.02
1998	9.52	5.24	10.51	28.02	−1.97	1.64		4.58
1999	10.92	6.01	12.93	24.67	−3.35		3.26	10.61
2000	9.44	6.52	15.60	23.24	−1.43		2.73	4.52
2001	9.04	7.25	15.76	33.66	10.42		4.09	−5.80
2002	13.21	7.00	14.23	33.21	−0.45		3.53	9.96
2003	19.29	9.11	15.70	51.11	17.90		3.57	−1.63
2004	20.58	10.57	17.98	56.02	4.91	10.05		−1.79
2005	24.68	11.38	19.44	45.27	−10.75		2.21	29.58
2006	28.15	13.05	23.83	48.27	3.00		16.29	30.66
2007(e)	30.00	14.00	25.00	51.27	3.00			16.00
5-Year Growth Rate	25.51%	12.47%	8.62%	NM	NM	NM	NM	NM
10-Year Growth Rate	15.49%	11.82%	11.15%	NM	NM	NM	NM	NM

NM = Not Meaningful
(e) = estimate

Source: By the authors from data in *S&P Analysts Handbook*, 2007.

Exhibit 13.12 Computation of RET Industry Value Using the FCFE Model and Two–Stage Growth

Year	FCFE	Discount Factor @ 0.080	Present Value
2009	19.18	0.9259	17.76
2010	20.71	0.8573	17.75
2011	22.37	0.7938	17.76
2012	23.94	0.7350	17.60
2013	25.62	0.6806	17.44
Continuing Value[a]	1,358	0.6806	924.25
		Total Present Value	$1,012.56

[a] $\dfrac{25.62\,(1.06)}{0.08 - 0.06} = \dfrac{27.16}{0.02} = 1{,}358$

Assuming a k of 8.0 percent and an FCFE of $16.00 in 2007, $17.60 in 2008, and $19.18 in 2009, the value for the industry is as shown in Exhibit 13.12. These results are very encouraging for the industry because the computed value of $1,013 is substantially above the recent market price of about $410. This apparent undervaluation would indicate that the industry should be overweighted in the portfolio.

Notably, the alternative present value of cash flow models have generated the following intrinsic values:

Model	Computed Value
Constant growth DDM	$585
Two-stage growth DDM	$818
Constant growth FCFE	$933
Two-stage growth FCFE	$1,013

Notably, while there is a wide range of computed intrinsic values, all of them indicated that this industry is undervalued given its recent market price of $410.

· ·
13.7 Industry Analysis Using the Relative Valuation Approach

This section contains a discussion and demonstration of the relative valuation ratio techniques: (1) price/earnings ratios (*P/E*), (2) the price to book value ratios (*P/BV*), (3) price to cash flow ratios (*P/CF*), and (4) price to sales ratios (*P/S*). Again, we will begin with the detailed demonstration of the *P/E* ratio approach, which provides a specific intrinsic value that equals an estimate of future earnings per share and an industry multiple.

The analysis of the other relative valuation ratios is also more meaningful because we can compare the industry valuation ratios to the market valuation ratios while considering what factors affect the specific valuation ratios.

13.7.1 The Earnings Multiple Technique

Again, the earnings multiple technique involves (1) a detailed estimation of future earnings per share, and (2) an estimate of an appropriate earnings multiplier (*P/E* ratio) based on a consideration of *P/E* determinants derived from the DDM.

Estimating Earnings per Share   To estimate earnings per share, you must start by estimating sales per share. We initially describe three techniques that provide help and insights for the sales estimate. Next, we derive an estimate of earnings per share, which implies a net profit margin for the industry. As in Chapter 12, we begin the EPS estimate by estimating the operating profit margin and operating profits. Then we subtract estimates of depreciation expense and interest expense and finally apply a tax rate to arrive at an estimate of earnings per share.

Forecasting Sales per Share   Following the macroanalysis of the industry that included considering (1) how the industry is impacted by the business cycle, (2) what structural changes have occurred within the industry, and (3) where the industry is in its life cycle, the analyst would have a strong start regarding an industry sales estimate. The following discussion considers two general estimation techniques (time series and input-output analysis) and a primary technique that should be used for almost all industries (i.e., a specific analysis of the industry-economy relationship).

Time-Series Analysis   A simple time-series plot of the sales for an industry can be very informative regarding the pattern and the rate of growth for industry sales. Analyzing this series with an overlay of business cycle periods (expansions and recessions) and notations regarding major events will provide further insights. Finally, for many industries, you can extrapolate the time series to derive an estimate of sales. For industries that have experienced consistent growth, this can be an important estimate, especially if it is a new industry that has not developed a history with the economy. If the sales growth has been at a constant rate, you should use a semi-log scale where the constant growth shows as a straight line.

Input-Output Analysis   Input-output analysis provides useful insights regarding the outlook for an industry by identifying an industry's suppliers and customers. This will indicate (1) the future demand from customers and (2) the ability of suppliers to provide the goods and services required by the industry. The goal is to determine the long-run sales outlook for the industry's suppliers and its major customers. In the case of global industries, you must include worldwide suppliers and customers.

Industry-Economy Relationships   The most rigorous and useful analysis involves comparing sales for an industry with one or several economic series that are related to the goods and services produced by the industry. The specific question is, What economic variables influence the demand for this industry? You should think about numerous factors that impact industry sales,

Exhibit 13.13 S&P Retail Sales and Various Economic Series: 1993–2006

| Year | Retail Sales ($/Share) | Personal Consumption Expenditures ($ Billions) | PCE Food, Clothes, and Shoes ($ Billions) | Per Capita | | Food, Clothing, and Shoes as a Percentage of PCE |
				Personal Consumption Expenditures (Dollars)	PCE Food, Clothes, and Shoes (Dollars)	
1993	173.89	4,477.90	921.80	17,204.00	3,541.54	20.59
1994	197.21	4,743.30	958.70	18,004.00	3,638.91	20.21
1995	208.15	4,975.80	982.60	18,665.00	3,685.89	19.75
1996	232.82	5,256.80	1,018.90	19,490.00	3,777.65	19.38
1997	251.33	5,547.40	1,054.30	20,323.00	3,862.45	19.01
1998	276.12	5,879.50	1,100.70	21,291.00	3,985.88	18.72
1999	302.62	6,282.50	1,159.40	22,491.00	4,150.59	18.45
2000	329.76	6,739.40	1,222.90	23,860.00	4,329.52	18.15
2001	352.27	7,055.00	1,265.60	24,712.00	4,433.10	17.94
2002	355.62	7,350.70	1,305.40	25,483.00	4,525.49	17.76
2003	383.89	7,703.60	1,356.90	26,445.00	4,657.98	17.61
2004	444.61	8,195.90	1,438.10	27,868.00	4,889.88	17.55
2005	476.54	8,707.80	1,525.50	29,322.00	5,136.86	17.52
2006	580.68	9,224.50	1,616.50	30,765.00	5,391.25	17.52
Compound Annual Growth Rate	9.72%	5.72%	4.42%	4.57%	3.29%	−1.23%

how these economic variables will impact demand, and how they might interact. The following example demonstrates this industry-economy technique for the retailing industry (RET).

Demonstrating a Sales Forecast The RET industry includes retailers of basic necessities, including pharmaceuticals and medical supplies and nonmedical products, such as food, and clothing. Therefore, we want a series that (1) reflects broad consumption expenditures and (2) gives weight to food and clothing. The economic series we consider are personal consumption expenditures (PCE) and PCE food, clothing, and shoes. Exhibit 13.13 contains the aggregate and per-capita values for these two series.

These time-series data indicate that personal consumption expenditures (PCE) have experienced reasonably steady growth of about 5.7 percent a year during this period, while PCE food and clothes has grown at a slower rate of about 4.4 percent. As a result, food and clothes as a percentage of all PCE has declined from 20.6 percent in 1993 to only 17.5 percent in 2006. Obviously, as an analyst, you would be pleased because even though sales of food and clothing have grown slower than overall PCE, retail sales have grown faster than both of them at about 9.7 percent.

The scatterplot in Exhibit 13.14 indicates a strong linear relationship between retail sales per share and sales of food, clothing, and shoes. Although not shown, there also is a good relationship with PCE. Therefore, if you can accurately estimate changes in these economic series, you should be able to estimate sales for RET.

As the industry being analyzed becomes more specialized, you need a more unique economic series that reflects the demand for the industry's unique product. The selection of several appropriate economic series demonstrates an analyst's knowledge and innovation. Also, industry sales are often dependent on several components of the economy, so you should consider a multivariate model that would include two or more economic series. For example, if you are analyzing the tire industry, you would need to consider new-car production, new-truck production, and a series that would reflect the replacement tire demand for both cars and trucks.

You also should consider *per-capita* personal consumption expenditures. Although aggregate PCE increases each year, there also is an increase in the aggregate population, so the

Exhibit 13.14   Scatterplot of Retail Sales per Share and PCE—Food, Clothing, and Shoes: 1993–2006

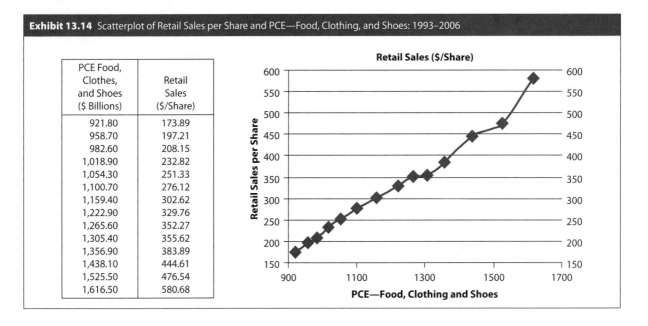

PCE Food, Clothes, and Shoes ($ Billions)	Retail Sales ($/Share)
921.80	173.89
958.70	197.21
982.60	208.15
1,018.90	232.82
1,054.30	251.33
1,100.70	276.12
1,159.40	302.62
1,222.90	329.76
1,265.60	352.27
1,305.40	355.62
1,356.90	383.89
1,438.10	444.61
1,525.50	476.54
1,616.50	580.68

increase in PCE per capita (the average PCE for each adult and child) will be less than for the aggregate series. For example, during 2006, aggregate PCE increased about 5.9 percent, but per-capita PCE increased only 4.9 percent. Finally, an analysis of the relationship between percent change in an economic variable and percent changes in industry sales will indicate how the two series move together and would be sensitive to any changes in the relationship. Using annual percentage changes provides the following regression model:

13.4 $\% \, \Delta \text{ Industry Sales} = \alpha_i + \beta_i \, (\% \, \Delta \text{ in Economic Series})$

The size of the β_i coefficient should indicate how closely the two series move together. Assuming the intercept (α_i) is close to zero, a slope (β_i) value of 1.00 would indicate relatively equal percent changes (e.g., a 10 percent increase in PCE typically is associated with a 10 percent increase in industry sales). A β_i larger than unity would imply that industry sales are more volatile than the economy is. This analysis and the levels relationship reflected in Exhibit 13.14 would help you find an economic series that closely reflects the demand for the industry's products; it also would indicate the form of the relationship.

As indicated, there was a good relationship between retail sales and PCE—Food, Clothing, and Shoes. The specific regression relationship was:

13.5 $\% \Delta \text{ Retail Sales} = -0.05 + 2.49 \, (\% \, \Delta \text{PCE—Food, Clothing, and Shoes})$
          $r^2 = 0.37$

Given the regression results, the specific sales forecast begins with an estimate of aggregate PCE growth for the years in question (i.e., 2007 and 2008). Because of the importance of PCE as a component of the economy, several estimates are available. The next step is to estimate the proportion of PCE spent on food, clothing, and shoes which has declined from 20.6 percent to 17.5 percent. You apply an estimate of this proportion to the PCE estimate and derive an estimate of the percent change in PCE—Food, Clothing, and Shoes that is used in the retail store sales regression model.

To demonstrate this process, we examined several economic sources which indicated that nominal PCE increased by 5.4 percent in 2007 (to $9,725 billion) and the projection was for an increase in 2008 of 4.5 percent to $10,163 billion. Regarding the percent of

Exhibit 13.15 Profit Margins and Component Expenses for the S&P Industrials Index and the Retail Industry

Year	EBITDA ($)		EBITDA Margin (%)		Depreciation Expense ($)		Interest Expense ($)		Tax Rate (%)		Net Profit Margin (%)	
	S&P Industrials	Retail	S&P Industrials	Retail	S&P Industrials	Retail	S&P Industrials	Retail	S&P Industrials	Retail	S&P Industrials	Retail
1993	87.85	10.87	14.12	6.25	34.10	2.76	13.41	2.43	36.79	33.29	4.99	3.13
1994	104.28	13.11	15.95	6.64	35.79	3.05	14.82	1.90	35.76	35.62	5.60	3.14
1995	115.65	14.12	16.38	6.78	39.54	3.77	15.78	2.81	35.85	39.26	6.14	2.43
1996	118.46	16.86	16.29	7.24	39.55	4.27	14.61	3.01	35.90	37.84	5.73	2.86
1997	123.31	18.65	16.43	7.42	40.62	4.80	13.89	2.60	36.26	38.18	5.92	3.00
1998	123.74	21.56	16.49	7.80	44.83	5.24	14.85	2.99	34.69	36.36	4.93	3.44
1999	139.16	25.46	17.14	8.41	47.54	6.01	15.71	2.76	36.12	38.27	5.70	3.60
2000	150.40	25.47	17.61	7.72	50.13	6.52	17.65	3.09	37.00	39.45	6.27	2.86
2001	125.46	26.77	15.47	7.60	50.24	7.25	16.51	3.18	35.65	40.88	4.61	2.56
2002	122.59	29.53	15.68	8.30	41.68	7.00	15.26	2.72	34.30	36.91	7.23	3.71
2003	135.30	40.08	15.97	10.43	42.98	9.11	16.48	3.33	32.97	36.82	5.84	5.02
2004	155.57	44.94	16.47	10.10	44.35	10.57	16.95	2.72	31.68	36.25	6.91	4.63
2005	172.26	51.91	16.51	10.89	45.83	11.38	19.48	2.66	32.24	35.51	6.94	5.18
2006	190.28	61.30	16.94	10.56	48.89	13.05	22.10	3.26	31.74	36.98	7.04	4.85

PCE spent on food, clothing, and shoes, we expect this proportion to continue to decline to 17.45 percent in 2007 and 17.40 in 2008. This implies values for PCE—Food, Clothing, and Shoes of $1,697 billion in 2007 and $1,768 billion in 2008, which implies growth of 4.9 percent in 2007 and 4.2 percent in 2008. Using these percentages in the Equation 13.5 regression provides retail stores sales growth estimates of 7.0 percent for 2007 ($620) and 5.0 percent for 2008 ($650). These sales growth rates are somewhat conservative relative to the long-run results in this industry, but reflect the economic slowdown/recession in 2008.

Forecasting Earnings per Share After the sales forecast, it is necessary to estimate the industry's profitability based on an analysis of the industry income statement. An analyst should also benefit from the prior macroanalysis that considered where the industry is in its life cycle, which impacts its profitability. How does this industry relate to the business cycle and what does this imply regarding profit margins at this point in the cycle? Most important, what did you conclude regarding the competitive environment in the industry and what does this mean for the profitability of sales?

Industry Profit Margin Forecast Similar to the aggregate market, the net profit margin is the most volatile and the hardest margin to estimate directly. Alternatively, it is suggested that you begin with the operating profit margin (EBITDA/Sales) and then estimate depreciation expense, interest expense, and the tax rate.

The Industry's Operating Profit Margin Recall that in the market analysis, we analyzed the factors that should influence the economy's operating profit margin, including capacity utilization, unit labor cost, inflation, and net exports. The most important variables were capacity utilization and unit labor cost. We cannot do such an analysis for most industries because the relevant variables typically are not available for individual industries. As an alternative, we can assume that movements in these industry profit margin variables are related to movements in similar economic variables. For example, assuming an increase in capacity utilization for the aggregate economies there is probably a comparable increase in utilization for the auto industry or the chemical industry. The same could be true for unit labor cost. If there is a stable relationship between these variables for the industry and the economy, you would expect a relationship to exist between the profit margins for the industry and the economy. Although it is not necessary that the relationship be completely linear, it is important for the relationship (whatever it is) to be generally stable.

The operating profit margin (*OPM*) for the S&P Industrials Index and the retail (RET) index is presented in Exhibit 13.15. The time-series plot in Exhibit 13.16 indicates that the S&P Industrials Index OPM experienced a steady increase from 1993 through 2000, followed by a strong decline during the recession year 2001. The margins have slowly recovered from 2002 through 2006. The *RET OPM* likewise experienced a fairly steady increase that peaked in 1999, followed by small declines in 2000 and 2001, a small recovery in 2002, a strong move in 2003 to over 10 percent that has persisted through 2006. The analysis of the relationship between the *OPM* for the market and industry using regression analysis was not useful, so it is not discussed. Apparently, the best estimate for the RET industry is the *OPM* time-series plot using what we know about the changing competitive environment and profit trends in the retail business. The point is, any quantitative analysis should be a supplement to the macroanalysis of the competitive environment for the industry.

Either regression analysis or time-series techniques can be useful tools, but *neither technique should be applied mechanically.* You should be aware of any unique factors affecting the industry, such as price wars, contract negotiations, building plans, or foreign competition. An analysis of these unique events is critical when estimating the gross profit margin or a range of industry profit margins (optimistic, pessimistic, most likely).

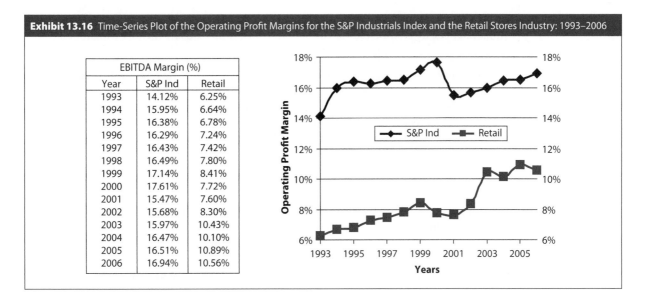

Exhibit 13.16 Time-Series Plot of the Operating Profit Margins for the S&P Industrials Index and the Retail Stores Industry: 1993–2006

EBITDA Margin (%)		
Year	S&P Ind	Retail
1993	14.12%	6.25%
1994	15.95%	6.64%
1995	16.38%	6.78%
1996	16.29%	7.24%
1997	16.43%	7.42%
1998	16.49%	7.80%
1999	17.14%	8.41%
2000	17.61%	7.72%
2001	15.47%	7.60%
2002	15.68%	8.30%
2003	15.97%	10.43%
2004	16.47%	10.10%
2005	16.51%	10.89%
2006	16.94%	10.56%

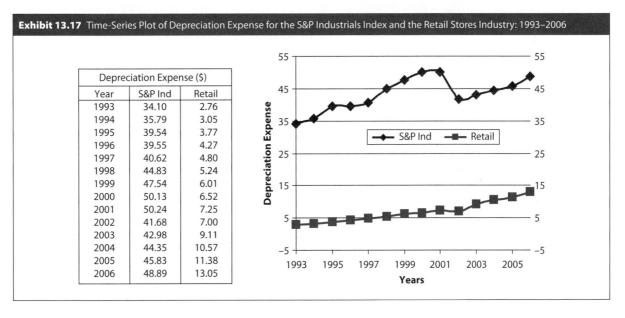

Exhibit 13.17 Time-Series Plot of Depreciation Expense for the S&P Industrials Index and the Retail Stores Industry: 1993–2006

Depreciation Expense ($)		
Year	S&P Ind	Retail
1993	34.10	2.76
1994	35.79	3.05
1995	39.54	3.77
1996	39.55	4.27
1997	40.62	4.80
1998	44.83	5.24
1999	47.54	6.01
2000	50.13	6.52
2001	50.24	7.25
2002	41.68	7.00
2003	42.98	9.11
2004	44.35	10.57
2005	45.83	11.38
2006	48.89	13.05

Beyond this estimation of the near-term *OPM,* it is important to consider the long-term profitability of the industry based on its competitive structure as discussed previously.

Industry Depreciation Estimating industry depreciation is easier because the series generally is increasing; so the only question is by how much. As shown in Exhibit 13.15, the depreciation series for RET increased every year but one since 1993. The time-series plots in Exhibit 13.17 relate depreciation for the S&P Industrials Index and the RET industry. To estimate depreciation expense, one can consider the two techniques used in the market analysis chapter (i.e., the time-series analysis and the specific estimate technique using the depreciation expense/*PPE* ratio) or an industry-market relationship.

An analysis of the graph, as well as regression analysis of levels and annual percentage changes, indicates that the relationship between this industry and the market is not good enough to use for an estimate. Although the market depreciation expense series increased at a fairly steady rate before 2002, the erratic change in 2002 calls into question the use of time-series estimates.

Exhibit 13.18 contains the components needed to derive a specific depreciation expense estimate similar to what we did for the S&P Industrials Index using the following four steps:

1. Calculate the annual *PPE* turnover for the RET industry.
2. Based upon your sales estimate and your expected *PPE* turnover ratio, estimate the expected *PPE* for next year.
3. Estimate the annual depreciation expense as a percent of *PPE* for the RET industry.
4. Estimate depreciation expense as follows:

$$(\text{Estimated } PPE) \times \text{Estimated} \left(\frac{\text{Depreciation Expense}}{PPE} \right) \text{Ratio}$$

For example, the *PPE* turnover has stabilized the last three years at about 4.20, which is what we will use. This turnover value combined with a per share sales estimate for 2008 of $650 implies a *PPE* estimate of $155. In turn, the depreciation expense/*PPE* ratio has been in the 9–10 percent range with the recent five-year average equal to 9.41. Therefore, we will use 9.4 percent. Applying this estimated percent to the *PPE* estimate of $155 implies a depreciation expense estimate of $14.50 ($155 × 0.094).

Subtracting an estimate of depreciation expense from the operating profit figure indicates the industry's net income before interest and taxes (EBIT).

Industry Interest Expense   An industry's interest expense will be a function of its financial leverage and interest rates. As shown in Exhibit 13.19, interest expense for the RET industry has always been relatively low and stable when compared to the S&P Industrials Index. Therefore, there is not a relationship between the two interest expense series. Therefore, you should derive your estimate based on two separate estimates: (1) changes in the amount of debt outstanding for this industry and (2) an estimate of interest rates (will they increase or decline?).

Estimating Interest Expense   The historical data needed to estimate interest expense are in Exhibit 13.19 and we can use the following steps:

1. Derive an estimate of the annual total asset turnover (*TAT*) for the RET industry.
2. Use your 2008 sales and *TAT* forecasts to estimate total assets.
3. Estimate the long-term (interest-bearing) debt as a percentage of total assets for the RET industry.
4. Use your estimate of total assets and the percent of long-term debt to total assets to estimate the dollar value of long-term debt.
5. Analyze and estimate the annual interest cost as a percentage of long-term debt based upon your prior estimate of market yields.
6. Estimate interest expense based on the following:

$$(\text{Estimated Interest Cost of Debt }) \times (\text{Estimated Long-Term Debt})$$

For example, our sales estimate of $650 and a *TAT* that has averaged about 1.70 over the recent years imply total assets of $382.00 next year. Long-term, interest-bearing debt has averaged about 21 percent of total assets for the RET industry but has declined to about 16 recently so we will use 18 percent for 2008, which implies debt of $69 (0.18 × $382). In turn, interest expense as a percentage of long-term debt during the recent period has been between 6 and 7 percent for the industry. Based on the expectation of a small decline in market interest rates during 2008, we would estimate a rate of 6.40 percent. This interest rate estimate combined with our long-term debt estimate of $69 implies interest expense of $4.40 (0.064 × $69).

Industry Tax Rate   As you might expect, tax rates differ between industries. An extreme example would be the oil industry, in which heavy depletion allowances cause lower taxes. Generally, you

Exhibit 13.18 Components for Deriving Specific Estimates for Depreciation Expense and Interest Expense for the Retail Industry

Year	Net Sales	Net PPE	PPE Turnover	Depreciation Expense	Depr. Exp./PPE	Total Assets	Total Asset Turnover	L.T. Debt	L.T. Debt / Total Assets	Interest Expense	Interest Exp./ L.T. Debt
1993	173.89	34.34	5.06	2.76	8.04	131.72	1.32	23.59	17.91	2.43	10.30
1994	197.21	38.40	5.14	3.05	7.94	140.71	1.40	25.01	17.77	1.90	7.60
1995	208.15	46.40	4.49	3.77	8.13	122.07	1.71	32.63	26.73	2.81	8.61
1996	232.82	50.66	4.60	4.27	8.43	131.46	1.77	32.62	24.81	3.01	9.23
1997	251.33	54.83	4.58	4.80	8.75	139.75	1.80	34.54	24.72	2.60	7.53
1998	276.12	57.03	4.84	5.24	9.19	141.99	1.94	34.65	24.40	2.99	8.63
1999	302.62	65.12	4.65	6.01	9.23	157.36	1.92	36.15	22.97	2.76	7.63
2000	329.76	72.87	4.53	6.52	8.95	168.00	1.96	36.99	22.02	3.09	8.35
2001	352.27	79.78	4.42	7.25	9.09	183.22	1.92	43.54	23.76	3.18	7.30
2002	355.62	80.82	4.40	7.00	8.66	193.45	1.84	44.96	23.24	2.72	6.05
2003	383.89	101.39	3.79	9.11	8.99	264.83	1.45	47.76	18.03	3.33	6.97
2004	444.61	105.21	4.23	10.57	10.05	270.00	1.65	41.13	15.23	2.72	6.61
2005	476.54	114.07	4.18	11.38	9.98	288.98	1.65	44.08	15.25	2.66	6.03
2006	580.68	139.11	4.17	13.05	9.38	345.38	1.68	59.17	17.13	3.26	5.51
Means	NM	NM	4.50	NM	8.91	NM	1.72	NM	21.00	NM	7.60

Exhibit 13.19 Time-Series Plot of Interest Expense for the S&P Industrials Index and the Retail Stores Industry: 1993–2006

Year	Retail	S&P Ind
1993	2.43	13.41
1994	1.90	14.82
1995	2.81	15.78
1996	3.01	14.61
1997	2.60	13.89
1998	2.99	14.85
1999	2.76	15.71
2000	3.09	17.65
2001	3.18	16.51
2002	2.72	15.26
2003	3.33	16.48
2004	2.72	16.95
2005	2.66	19.48
2006	3.26	22.10

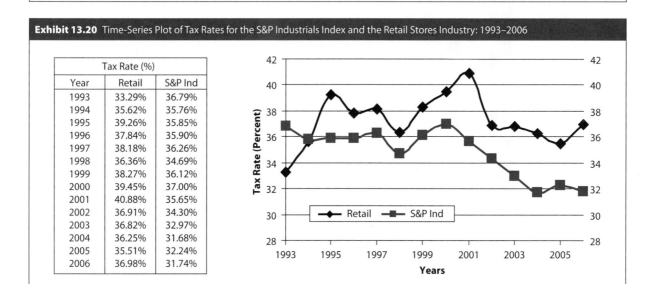

Exhibit 13.20 Time-Series Plot of Tax Rates for the S&P Industrials Index and the Retail Stores Industry: 1993–2006

	Tax Rate (%)	
Year	Retail	S&P Ind
1993	33.29%	36.79%
1994	35.62%	35.76%
1995	39.26%	35.85%
1996	37.84%	35.90%
1997	38.18%	36.26%
1998	36.36%	34.69%
1999	38.27%	36.12%
2000	39.45%	37.00%
2001	40.88%	35.65%
2002	36.91%	34.30%
2003	36.82%	32.97%
2004	36.25%	31.68%
2005	35.51%	32.24%
2006	36.98%	31.74%

can assume that tax law changes are consistent across industries. To see if this is valid, you need to examine the relationship of tax rates over time for your industry and the aggregate market to determine if you can use regression analysis in your estimation process. Alternatively, a time-series plot could provide a useful estimate.

Exhibit 13.20 indicates that the RET tax rate has been between 36 and 40 percent and has averaged 37 percent in recent years. Therefore, we would use 37 percent although you still need to consider pending national legislation and unique industry tax factors. Using this estimated tax rate, you multiply the *EBT* per share value by $(1 - 0.37)$ to get your estimate of earnings per share (*EPS*).

In addition to estimating *EPS*, you also should examine the industry's net profit margin as a check on your *EPS* estimate. A time-series plot of the net profit margin series for the industry and the S&P Industrials Index is contained in Exhibit 13.21. Notably, both series experienced an overall increase of about 2 percent, but the RET industry has been less volatile.

An Industry Earnings Estimate Example To help you understand the procedure, the following is an estimate of earnings per share for the RET industry. A practicing analyst would use this

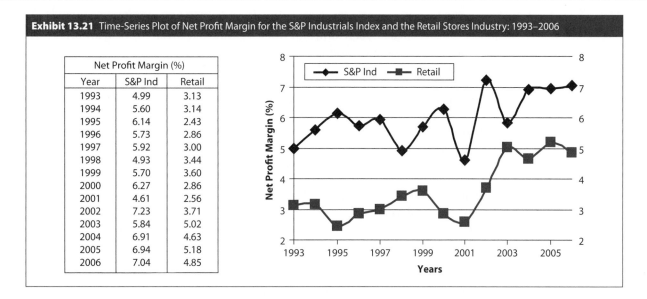

Exhibit 13.21 Time-Series Plot of Net Profit Margin for the S&P Industrials Index and the Retail Stores Industry: 1993–2006

Net Profit Margin (%)		
Year	S&P Ind	Retail
1993	4.99	3.13
1994	5.60	3.14
1995	6.14	2.43
1996	5.73	2.86
1997	5.92	3.00
1998	4.93	3.44
1999	5.70	3.60
2000	6.27	2.86
2001	4.61	2.56
2002	7.23	3.71
2003	5.84	5.02
2004	6.91	4.63
2005	6.94	5.18
2006	7.04	4.85

example as an *initial* estimate that would be modified based on his or her industry knowledge, current events, and expectations of unique factors.

Given that the best relationship was between RET sales and PCE—Food, Clothing, and Shoes, we demonstrated that with estimates of PCE and PCE—Food, Clothing, and Shoes as a percent of PCE we could derive an RET sales estimate of $650 per share.

As noted earlier, the OPM for the RET industry recovered from the recession in 2002 and then experienced strong performance in 2003 to over 10 percent and has been able to maintain this level through 2006. We estimate that this margin increased in 2007 to 10.70 percent, but will suffer a decline during the 2008 economic slowdown to 9 percent, which implies operating profits of $58.50 (0.09 × $650).

Earlier we derived a specific estimate for industry depreciation expense of $14.50 for 2008. Therefore, earnings before interest and taxes would be $44.00 ($58.50 − $14.50).

Given the declining yields during 2006 and the rates envisioned during 2008, our prior specific estimate of interest expense was $4.40 in 2008. Thus, *EBT* would be $39.60 ($44.00 − $4.40).

As noted earlier, the tax rate for the RET industry has been consistently about 37 percent during recent years and this seems appropriate for 2008. This implies net income of $24.95 ($39.60 × 0.63). This indicates a net profit margin for the RET industry of 3.84 percent ($24.95/$650.00), which is above the margin during the recession of 2001, but about equal to the 2002 margin.

Given an estimate of the industry's net income per share (for simplicity, we will round off the *EPS* estimate to $25 per share), your next step is to estimate the earnings multiplier for this industry.

Estimating an Industry Earnings Multiplier
This section discusses how to estimate an industry earnings multiplier using two alternative techniques: macroanalysis and microanalysis. In macroanalysis, you examine the relationship between the multiplier for the industry and the market. In microanalysis, you estimate the multiplier by examining the specific variables that influence it: (1) the dividend-payout ratio, (2) the required rate of return for the industry (k), and (3) the expected growth rate of earnings and dividends for the industry (g).

Macroanalysis of an Industry Multiplier: Why a Relationship? This subsection considers the relationship between the earnings multiplier (*P/E* ratio) for an industry to the *P/E* for the aggregate market. We *expect* a relationship based on the variables that influence the multiplier—the required rate of return, the expected growth rate of earnings and dividends, and the dividend-payout ratio. Specifically, as discussed, the required rate of return (k) is a function of the nominal risk-free rate plus a risk premium, and we know that the nominal risk-free rate is the same for all investment assets and is the major reason for changes in k. Also, while the risk premium, may differ between the market and an industry, any *changes* in the risk premium for the market and the industry are probably related.

Although the rate of growth (g) for an industry may differ from that of the market, and is a major reason for the difference in the level of the *P/E* ratio, *changes* in the growth expectations for many industries are related to changes in g for the market and other industries because they are driven by macroeconomic growth factors that affect the overall market and most industries. Therefore, changes in the *P/E* ratio for the aggregate market and alternative industries are caused by changes in the $k - g$ spread. In turn, these two variables have several components that move together, so we expect an overall (macro) relationship between changes in an industry's *P/E* and the market *P/E* ratio.

An examination of the relationship between the *P/E* ratios for 71 S&P industries and the S&P Industrials Index by Reilly and Zeller (1974) indicated a significant positive relationship between percentage changes in *P/E* ratios for most industries examined. Notably, because the significance of the relationship differed between alternative industries and the market, it is necessary to evaluate the quality of the relationship between the *P/E* ratios for a specific industry and the market before using this technique.

The results in Exhibits 13.6 and 13.22 for the RET industry indicate a relatively close relationship between the *P/E*s for the market and the RET industry, and the *P/E* ratios have been very similar during the final three years. Still, a crucial question that an analyst must consider is, Why has the RET multiplier been consistently smaller and should this differential continue? The following microanalysis should help us answer this question.

Microanalysis of an Industry Multiplier In Chapter 12, we estimated a future market earnings multiplier by estimating a range of values for the three variables (i.e., dividend payout, k, and g) that determine the multiplier and derived a range of *P/E* ratio estimates. In turn, these multipliers were used with our EPS estimate to compute a range of intrinsic values for the market index.

Exhibit 13.22 Time-Series Plot of Annual Average Future Earnings Multipliers for the S&P Industrials Index and the Retail Stores Industry: 1993–2005

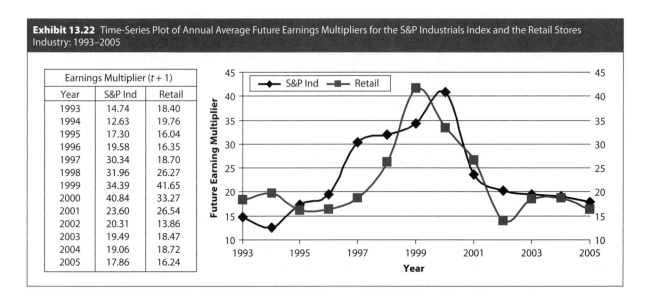

Earnings Multiplier ($t + 1$)		
Year	S&P Ind	Retail
1993	14.74	18.40
1994	12.63	19.76
1995	17.30	16.04
1996	19.58	16.35
1997	30.34	18.70
1998	31.96	26.27
1999	34.39	41.65
2000	40.84	33.27
2001	23.60	26.54
2002	20.31	13.86
2003	19.49	18.47
2004	19.06	18.72
2005	17.86	16.24

For the industry multiplier we could use the same approach, but it would not take advantage of the prior work on the stock market multiplier. Because the variables that affect the stock market and the industry multiplier are the same we can compare these variables.

Therefore, in our microanalysis, we estimage and compare the three variables that determine the industry earnings multiplier to the comparable values for the market *P/E*. This allows us to determine whether the industry earnings multiplier *should* be above, below, or equal to the market multiplier. Given this relationship, it is easier to estimate a specific industry *P/E* ratio. First we need to recall the recent historical relationship between the industry and market *P/E* ratios.

Industry Multiplier versus the Market Multiplier Recall from Exhibit 13.22 that the *P/E* ratios for the RET industry and the market generally moved together but during the recent three years the market *P/E* has consistently been slightly larger than the RET industry *P/E*. A comparative analysis of the factors that determine this earnings multiplier should help us determine if this is an appropriate relationship.

Comparing Dividend-Payout Ratios The data in Exhibit 13.6 indicates that the retention rate for retail stores has consistently been higher than for the market (80 percent versus 62 percent). This indicates a higher dividend payout for the S&P Industrials Index, which alone implies a higher multiplier for the S&P Industrials Index.

Comparing the Required Rates of Return Earlier we estimated the industry's required rate of return (k) assuming a beta of 0.95 for the RET industry, which was generally consistent with the fundamental risk characteristics of the industry. In turn, this beta in the prevailing SML implied a k of less than 8.00 percent, but we rounded it to 8.00 percent, which compares to the stock market k derived in Chapter 12 of 8.00 percent. This implies that all else being the same, the industry and market *P/E* should be the same.

Comparing the Expected Growth Rate (g) Previously, we likewise estimated an industry growth rate in connection with the present value of cash flow models. Using the relationship

$$g = \text{Retention Rate } (b) \times \text{Return on Equity } (ROE)$$
$$= (b) \times (ROE)$$

we estimated a g of over 12 percent based on long-run historical results, and a g of about 13 percent using the results for the recent five-year period of 1999–2003.

This 13 percent growth rate estimate compares to the growth rates for the S&P Industrials Index of between 10 and 11 percent (using the long-run retention rate or the recent five-year retention rate). Notably, the growth rates implied for both the industry (13 percent) and the market (10–11 percent) appear too high for any long-term period—that is, we typically use continuing growth rates of 5 to 6 percent. Therefore, while we would not use the higher growth rates for long-run estimates, the comparison appears valid for our purposes here. Specifically, the industry has a higher g than the market, which implies that based on growth the industry multiple would be higher than the market multiple.

In summary, a comparison of the dividend-payout ratios indicates that the market *P/E* ratio should be higher. The required returns are approximately equal. In contrast, the growth rate comparison clearly favors the industry multiple. Because of the significant difference in growth and the mathematical power of this variable, the consensus favors a higher industry multiple, which is not consistent with the recent relationship. Earlier it was discussed that the forward market multiple is currently about 16 times, which implies an industry multiplier in the 18 to 22 range.

Industry Estimates Value and Rate of Return At this point, we have an earlier estimate of industry earnings per share ($25.00) and an estimate for an industry earnings multiple in the

18 to 22 range. Because the multiple estimate is necessarily not specific, it seems appropriate to consider a range of intrinsic values as follows:

Optimistic Multiple:	22 × 25.00 = $550
Expected Multiple:	20 × 25.00 = $500
Pessimistic Multiple:	18 × 25.00 = $450

Given a current market price for the industry index of about $410, these results indicate that the industry is underpriced for all the scenarios. Put another way, while we envisioned *P/Es* of between 18 and 22, it is currently priced at 16.4 times, which is only slightly above the market *P/E* ratio.

13.8 Other Relative Valuation Ratios

Similar to the market analysis, we need to consider the other three relative valuation ratios (*P/BV; P/CF;* and *P/S*) and compare their performance over time relative to similar ratios for the aggregate stock market (the S&P Industrials Index).

Again, the calculations will employ the average annual price and *future* book value, cash flow, and sales. The input data derived for the industry and the S&P Industrials Index (from Chapter 12) with 10-year growth rates for each of these variables are contained in Exhibit 13.23. Notably, the subsequent comparison indicates that the compound growth rate for every RET industry variable is higher than the growth rate for the same market variable.

Exhibit 13.24 contains the four relative valuation ratios for the RET industry and for the S&P Industrials Index along with the ratio of the annual industry valuation ratio divided by the market valuation ratio. For each valuation ratio, you should examine the long-run industry-market relationship, including any changes in this relationship. Subsequently, the goal is to explain the overall relationship and consider any changes that have occurred and whether these changes can be explained based upon the factors that should determine the relative valuation ratio. The comparative *P/E* ratios will not be discussed again.

13.8.1 The Price/Book Value Ratio

Exhibit 13.25 shows the overall increase in the price/book value ratio experienced by both the market and the industry to a peak of about five times in 1999 followed by declines to a trough in 2003 after which they are virtually equal. Notably, the relationship between the industry and the market has almost always shown the market *P/BV* ratio larger than or equal to the RET industry ratio.

This relationship is difficult to explain because the *P/BV* ratio should reflect the ability of the market or an industry, to earn a ROE that exceeds its cost of equity. In fact we know that during the last five years the *ROE* for the industry has been larger than for the market while the cost of equity for the industry is lower (*B* = 0.95). This implies a larger return spread for the industry that should lead to a higher *P/BV* ratio for the industry relative to the market.

13.8.2 The Price/Cash Flow Ratio

As shown in Exhibit 13.24 and Exhibit 13.26, the *P/CF* ratio increased then declined to about 11 times for both series. The *P/CF* ratio is akin to the *P/E* ratio wherein it is driven by the growth rate and stability of the cash flow series. As shown in Exhibit 13.23, the growth rate of the industry *CF* has consistently been much higher than the market *CF* (i.e., 14 percent versus about 5 percent). The growth of the industry *CF* series was also more consistent. While the *P/CF* ratio relationship is in the right direction, the question is, does the substantial difference in consistent growth of *CF* for the industry justify a larger difference in the *P/CF* ratios?

Exhibit 13.23 Inputs for Relative Valuation Ratios: The Retail Stores Industry and the S&P Industrials Index: 1993–2006

Yr	Retail Stores Industry						S&P Industrials Index					
	Mean Price	EPS	Cash Flow P/S	Book Value P/S	Net Sales P/S	Dividend P/S	Mean Price	EPS	Cash Flow P/S	Book Value P/S	Net Sales P/S	Dividend P/S
1993	115.94	5.45	8.21	37.18	173.89	1.57	520.21	31.02	58.00	198.18	622.12	12.51
1994	109.67	6.20	9.26	40.53	197.21	1.71	536.52	36.64	72.39	217.11	653.75	13.01
1995	108.85	5.06	8.84	43.25	208.15	1.69	638.97	43.36	79.27	232.08	706.13	13.96
1996	117.46	6.67	10.94	46.75	232.82	1.45	795.01	41.69	82.89	242.82	727.40	15.58
1997	152.50	7.56	12.36	51.66	251.33	1.59	1006.12	44.43	83.73	253.14	750.71	16.72
1998	230.78	9.52	14.76	53.34	276.12	1.62	1285.73	36.96	87.38	271.52	750.48	17.28
1999	335.22	10.92	16.93	60.72	302.62	1.74	1651.82	53.56	97.73	309.45	812.00	17.40
2000	320.07	9.44	15.97	65.48	329.76	1.67	1692.85	46.28	105.09	343.95	853.86	16.59
2001	301.48	9.04	16.29	70.54	352.27	1.70	1363.30	37.41	68.58	343.27	811.04	15.85
2002	309.90	13.21	20.21	77.76	355.62	1.83	1133.05	56.51	61.59	314.38	781.65	16.18
2003	317.61	19.29	28.40	116.53	383.89	2.85	1097.27	49.52	90.88	367.97	847.38	17.23
2004	413.38	20.58	31.16	124.72	444.61	2.94	1294.47	65.22	104.76	417.05	944.36	18.75
2005	443.58	24.68	36.07	139.37	476.54	3.28	1375.37	72.41	121.36	449.30	1043.61	21.58
2006	464.24	28.15	41.21	159.16	580.68	4.63	1492.05	79.11	134.17	499.46	1123.34	24.28
10 yr G	14.73%	15.49%	14.18%	13.03%	9.57%	12.31%	6.50%	6.61%	4.93%	7.48%	4.44%	4.54%

Exhibit 13.24 Relative Valuation Ratios for the Retail Industry versus S&P Industrials: 1993–2005

Year	Price Earnings (t + 1)			Price Book Value (t + 1)			Price Cash Flow (t + 1)			Price Sales (t + 1)		
	Retail	S&P Ind	Ratio Ind/Mkt	Retail	S&P Ind	Ratio Ind/Mkt	Retail	S&P Ind	Ratio Ind/Mkt	Retail	S&P Ind	Ratio Ind/Mkt
1993	18.70	14.20	1.32	2.86	2.40	1.19	12.52	7.19	1.74	0.59	0.80	0.74
1994	21.67	12.37	1.75	2.54	2.31	1.10	12.41	6.77	1.83	0.53	0.76	0.69
1995	16.32	15.33	1.06	2.33	2.63	0.88	9.95	7.71	1.29	0.47	0.88	0.53
1996	15.54	17.89	0.87	2.27	3.14	0.72	9.50	9.49	1.00	0.47	1.06	0.44
1997	16.02	27.22	0.59	2.86	3.71	0.77	10.33	11.51	0.90	0.55	1.34	0.41
1998	21.13	27.78	0.76	3.80	4.15	0.91	13.63	13.16	1.04	0.76	1.58	0.48
1999	35.51	30.84	1.15	5.12	4.80	1.07	20.99	15.72	1.34	1.02	1.93	0.53
2000	35.41	45.25	0.78	4.54	4.93	0.92	19.65	24.68	0.80	0.91	2.09	0.44
2001	22.82	24.12	0.95	3.88	4.34	0.89	14.92	22.14	0.67	0.85	1.74	0.49
2002	16.07	22.88	0.70	2.66	3.08	0.86	10.91	12.47	0.88	0.81	1.34	0.60
2003	15.43	16.82	0.92	2.55	2.63	0.97	10.19	10.47	0.97	0.71	1.16	0.61
2004	16.75	17.88	0.94	2.97	2.88	1.03	11.46	10.67	1.07	0.87	1.24	0.70
2005	15.76	17.39	0.91	2.79	2.75	1.01	10.76	10.25	1.05	0.76	1.22	0.62

Exhibit 13.25 Time-Series Plot of Price/Book Value Ratios for the S&P Industrials Index and the Retail Stores Industry: 1993–2005

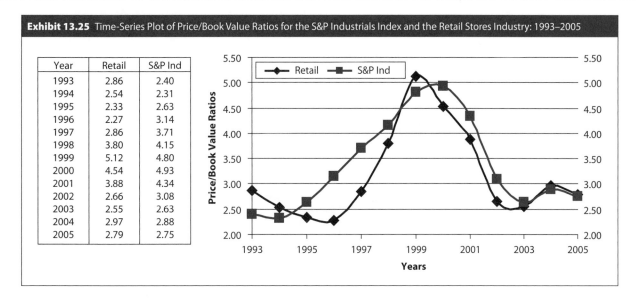

Year	Retail	S&P Ind
1993	2.86	2.40
1994	2.54	2.31
1995	2.33	2.63
1996	2.27	3.14
1997	2.86	3.71
1998	3.80	4.15
1999	5.12	4.80
2000	4.54	4.93
2001	3.88	4.34
2002	2.66	3.08
2003	2.55	2.63
2004	2.97	2.88
2005	2.79	2.75

Exhibit 13.26 Time-Series Plot of Price/Cash Flow Ratios for the S&P Industrials Index and the Retail Stores Industry: 1993–2005

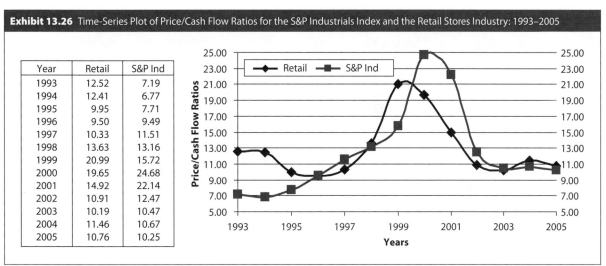

Year	Retail	S&P Ind
1993	12.52	7.19
1994	12.41	6.77
1995	9.95	7.71
1996	9.50	9.49
1997	10.33	11.51
1998	13.63	13.16
1999	20.99	15.72
2000	19.65	24.68
2001	14.92	22.14
2002	10.91	12.47
2003	10.19	10.47
2004	11.46	10.67
2005	10.76	10.25

13.8.3 The Price/Sales Ratio

As shown in Exhibits 13.24 and 13.27, the market *P/S* ratio has always been substantially higher (1.2 versus 0.8 at the end of the period). The *P/S* ratio should be impacted by three factors: (1) sales growth rate, (2) the uncertainty (risk) of sales growth, and (3) the profitability of sales (i.e., the net profit margin). Because the industry experienced a *higher* rate of growth for sales during the 10-year period, it is not the rate of growth. Both have experienced relatively low volatility in sales growth. In contrast, the profit margin (*PM*) has always been higher for the market, but the difference in profit margins has declined in recent years. Thus, the difference in the *P/S* ratio is questionable—i.e., should the market sales multiplier be 50 percent larger?

13.8.4 Summary of Industry/Market Ratios

Exhibit 13.28 contains the four industry-market ratios for each of the valuation ratios. These results indicate that investors' assessment of this industry relative to the market has declined over time because all the industry-market relative ratios declined. Only the price/*CF* ratio for the industry is above the market. Given that the industry has higher growth rates for these variables and lower risk characteristics, this indicates that possibly the industry is undervalued.

Exhibit 13.27 Time-Series Plot of Price/Sales Ratios for the S&P Industrials Index and the Retail Stores Industry: 1993–2005

Year	Retail	S&P Ind
1993	0.59	0.80
1994	0.53	0.76
1995	0.47	0.88
1996	0.47	1.06
1997	0.55	1.34
1998	0.76	1.58
1999	1.02	1.93
2000	0.91	2.09
2001	0.85	1.74
2002	0.81	1.34
2003	0.71	1.16
2004	0.87	1.24
2005	0.76	1.22

Exhibit 13.28 Time-Series Plot of the Industry-Market Relative Ratios of Valuation Ratios for the S&P Industrials Index and the Retail Stores Industry: 1993–2005

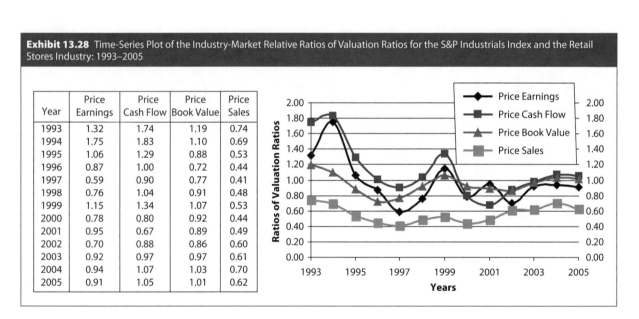

Year	Price Earnings	Price Cash Flow	Price Book Value	Price Sales
1993	1.32	1.74	1.19	0.74
1994	1.75	1.83	1.10	0.69
1995	1.06	1.29	0.88	0.53
1996	0.87	1.00	0.72	0.44
1997	0.59	0.90	0.77	0.41
1998	0.76	1.04	0.91	0.48
1999	1.15	1.34	1.07	0.53
2000	0.78	0.80	0.92	0.44
2001	0.95	0.67	0.89	0.49
2002	0.70	0.88	0.86	0.60
2003	0.92	0.97	0.97	0.61
2004	0.94	1.07	1.03	0.70
2005	0.91	1.05	1.01	0.62

13.9 Global Industry Analysis

Because so many firms are active in foreign markets and because the proportion of foreign sales is growing for many firms, it is necessary to consider the effects of foreign firms on industry returns. To see why this is so, consider the auto industry. Besides Ford and General Motors, the auto industry for a global investor includes numerous firms from Japan, Germany, Italy, and Korea, among others. Thus, we must extend our analysis to include global factors.

While space does not permit an example, the following major factors need to be analyzed in this context:

- The macroenvironment in the major producing and consuming countries for an industry. This will impact demand from these countries.

- An overall analysis of the significant global companies in the industry, the products they produce, and how successful they are in terms of the DuPont three-component analysis.
- Regarding company analysis, what are the accounting differences by country and how do these differences impact the relative valuation ratios? Because of accounting differences, it is typically not possible to directly compare many ratios across countries but only examine them over time within a country. This problem should be reduced as the use of international accounting standards grows.
- What is the effect of currency exchange rate trends for the major countries? Significant currency changes can affect the demand for U.S. products from specific countries and also impact costs assuming U.S. firms receive inputs from foreign firms.

Global industry analysis is growing in importance as documented by Cavaglia, Brightman, and Aked (2000). Specifically, prior research showed that country factors dominated industry factors in terms of explaining equity returns but the Cavaglia et al. (2000) study presented evidence that industry factors have been growing in importance and currently dominate country factors. In summary, it is important to carry out industry analysis on a global scale.

• • • • SUMMARY • • • •

- Several studies have examined industry performance and risk. They have found wide dispersion in the performance of alternative industries during specified time periods, implying that industry analysis can help identify superior investments. They also showed inconsistent industry performance over time, implying that looking at only past performance of an industry has little value in projecting future performance. Also, the performance by firms within industries typically is not very consistent, so you must analyze individual companies in an industry following the industry analysis.
- The analysis of industry risk indicated wide dispersion in the measures of risk for different industries but strong consistency in the risk measure over time for individual industries. These results imply that risk analysis and measurement are useful and necessary. The good news is that past risk measures are useful when estimating future risk.
- We discussed and demonstrated both approaches to the valuation of the RET industry. The present value of cash flow models indicated a fairly wide range of values.
- The four relative valuation ratio techniques also provided a range of results, including the two-step earnings multiple technique where the multiple results surrounded the current market price. All of the relative valuation ratios declined over time relative to the market.
- Industry analysis needs to be carried out on a global scale and must evaluate the effects of world supply, demand, and cost components for an industry but also different valuation levels due to accounting conventions. Finally, you must consider the impact of exchange rates on the total industry and the firms within it.

• • • • SUGGESTED READINGS • • • •

Goodman, D. A., and John W. Peavy, III. "Industry Relative Price-Earnings Ratios as Indicators of Investment Returns," *Financial Analysts Journal* 39, no. 2 (March–April 1983): 60–66.

Porter, Michael E. "How to Conduct an Industry Analysis." In *The Financial Analysts Handbook,* 2d ed., ed. Sumner N. Levine. Homewood, IL: Dow Jones–Irwin, 1988.

The following are proceedings from industry analysis seminars sponsored by the Association for Investment Management and Research (AIMR):

Balog, James (ed.). *The Health Care Industry.* Charlottesville, VA: AIMR, 1993.

Bhatia, Sanjiv, ed. *The Consumer Staples Industry.* Charlottesville, VA: AIMR, 1995.

Bhatia, Sanjiv, ed. *The Media Industry.* Charlottesville, VA: AIMR, 1996.

Petrie, Thomas, A. ed. *The Oil and Gas Industries.* Charlottesville, VA: AIMR, 1993.

Shasta, Theodore, ed. *The Automotive Industry.* Charlottesville, VA: AIMR, 1994.

• • • • QUESTIONS • • • •

1. Briefly describe the results of studies that examined the performance of alternative industries during specific time periods and discuss their implications for industry analysis.

2. Briefly describe the results of the studies that examined industry performance over time. Do these results complicate or simplify industry analysis?

3. Assume all the firms in a particular industry have consistently experienced similar rates of return. Discuss what this implies regarding the importance of industry and company analysis for this industry.

4. Discuss the contention that differences in the performance of various firms within an industry limit the usefulness of industry analysis.

5. Several studies have examined the difference in risk for alternative industries during a specified time period. Describe the results of these studies and discuss their implications for industry analysis.

6. What were the results when industry risk was examined during successive time periods? Discuss the implication of these results for industry analysis.

7. Assume the industry you are analyzing is in the fourth stage of the industrial life cycle. How would you react if your industry-economic analysis predicted that sales per share for this industry would increase by 20 percent? Discuss your reasoning.

8. Discuss at what stage in the industrial life cycle you would like to discover an industry. Justify your decision.

9. Give an example of an industry in Stage 2 of the industrial life cycle. Discuss your reasoning for putting the industry in Stage 2 and any evidence that caused you to select this stage for the industry.

10. Discuss an example of input-output analysis to predict the sales for the auto industry. Discuss how you would use input-output analysis to predict the costs of production for the auto industry.

11. Discuss the impact of substitute products on the steel industry's profitability.

12. Discuss the two variables that must be considered whether you are using the present value of cash flow approach or the relative valuation ratio approach to valuation. Why are these variables relevant for either valuation approach?

13. List the three variables that are relevant when attempting to determine whether the earnings multiple (*P/E* ratio) for an industry should be higher, equal to, or lower than the market multiple.

14. Discuss when you would use the two-stage growth FCFE model rather than the constant growth model.

15. You are examining the *P/CF* ratio for an industry compared to the market and find that the industry ratio has always been at a discount to the market—for example, the industry-market ratio of ratios is about 0.80. Discuss the variable(s) you would examine to explain this difference or to justify an increase in the industry-market ratio.

16. **CFA EXAMINATION LEVEL II** Elizabeth Coronado, CFA, is analyzing Nelson Motors, Inc., one of the largest and most profitable automobile manufacturers in North America. Since the mid-1990s, the fastest growing and most profitable product segment for Nelson has been its sport utility vehicles (SUV) line shown in the following exhibit.

    Coronado believes that applying the product life cycle model to Nelson's SUV product line will yield additional analytical insights into the company's recent rapid earnings growth.

    a. Identify the current product life cycle stage for the Raven, Hawk, and Eagle. Justify your choice of product life cycle stage by citing evidence from the following exhibit. [6 minutes]

    Because of the high expectations associated with the Eagle, Nelson Motors' current *P/E* is above its five-year historic range and above the auto industry *P/E*. An auto analyst states that "Nelson Motors has the best of both worlds:

    - increasing SUV profitability and
    - declining expected future earnings volatility."

NELSON MOTORS ANNUAL SUV PRODUCTION AND FINANCIAL DATA

	1990	1991	1992	1993	1994	1995	1996	1997	1998	1999E	2000E
SUV Units Sold in Thousands											
Raven	5	10	35	70	90	100	110	112	110	105	90
Hawk	—	—	—	—	3	10	20	45	63	68	69
Eagle	—	—	—	—	—	—	—	5	32	70	110
Profit per Vehicle in $ Thousands											
Raven	9	10	9	8	8	7	7	6	5	4	3
Hawk	—	—	—	—	6	7	8	7	7	8	7
Eagle	—	—	—	—	—	—	—	10	10	11	12
Profit per SUV Model in $ Millions											
Raven	45	100	315	560	720	700	770	672	550	420	270
Hawk	—	—	—	—	18	70	160	315	441	544	483
Eagle	—	—	—	—	—	—	—	50	320	770	1,320
Total SUV Division profit in $ millions	45	100	315	560	738	770	930	1,037	1,311	1,734	2,073
Total Nelson Motors profit in $ millions	1,125	1,250	1,575	1,600	1,994	1,974	2,214	2,357	2,960	3,470	3,989
SUV Division profit % of Nelson Motors profit	4%	8%	20%	35%	37%	39%	42%	44%	44%	50%	52%
Year over year % change in total SUV profit	—	122%	215%	78%	32%	4%	21%	12%	26%	32%	20%
Model percent of SUV Division Profit											
Raven	100%	100%	100%	100%	98%	91%	83%	65%	42%	24%	13%
Hawk	—	—	—	—	2%	9%	17%	30%	34%	31%	23%
Eagle	—	—	—	—	—	—	—	5%	24%	44%	64%

b. Evaluate *each* statement, using the data presented in the exhibit (6 minutes).

• • • • PROBLEMS • • • •

1. Select three industries from the S&P *Analysts Handbook* with different demand factors. For each industry, indicate what economic series you would use to predict the growth for the industry. Discuss why the economic series selected is relevant for this industry.

2. Prepare a scatterplot for one of the industries in Problem 1 of industry sales per share and observations from the economic series you suggested for this industry. Do this for the most recent 10 years using information available in the *Analysts Handbook*. Based on the results of the scatterplot, discuss whether the economic series was closely related to this industry's sales.

3. Based on an analysis of the results in Problem 2, discuss the stage of your industry in its life cycle.

4. Evaluate your industry in terms of the five factors that determine an industry's intensity of competition. Based on this analysis, what are your expectations about the industry's profitability in the short run (1 or 2 years) and the long run (5–10 years)?

5. Using the S&P *Analysts Handbook,* plot the latest 10-year history of the operating profit margin for the S&P Industrials Index versus the S&P industry of your choice. Is there a positive, negative, or zero correlation?

6. Using the S&P *Analysts Handbook,* calculate the means for the following variables of the S&P Industrials Index and the industry of your choice during the last 10 years:
   a. Price/earnings multiplier
   b. Retention rate
   c. Return on equity
   d. Equity turnover
   e. Net profit margin
   Briefly comment on how your industry and the S&P Industrials Index differ for each of the variables.

7. Prepare a table listing the variables that influence the earnings multiplier for your chosen industry and the S&P Industrials Index series for the most recent 10 years.
   a. Do the average dividend-payout ratios for your industry and the S&P Industrials Index differ? How should the dividend payout influence the difference between the multipliers?
   b. Based on the fundamental factors, would you expect the risk for this industry to differ from that for the market? In what direction, and why? Calculate the industry beta using monthly data for five years. Based on the fundamental factors and the computed systematic risk, how does this industry's risk compare to the market? What effect will this difference in risk have on the industry multiplier relative to the market multiplier?
   c. Analyze and discuss the different components of growth (retention rate, total asset turnover, total assets/equity, and profit margin) for your chosen industry and the S&P Industrials Index during the most recent 10 years. Based on this analysis, how would you expect the growth rate for your industry to compare with the growth rate for the S&P Industrials Index? How would this difference in expected growth affect the multiplier?

8. **CFA EXAMINATION LEVEL II** As a securities analyst, you have been asked to review a valuation of a closely held business—Wigwam Autoparts Heaven, Inc. (WAH), prepared by the Red Rocks Group (RRG). You are to give an opinion on the valuation and to support your opinion by analyzing each part of the valuation. WAH's sole business is automotive parts retailing.

   The RRG valuation includes a section called "Analysis of the Retail Autoparts Industry," based completely on the data in Table 1 and the following additional information.
   • WAH and its principal competitors each operated over 150 stores at year end 1994.
   • The average number of stores operated per company engaged in the retail autoparts industry is 5.3.
   • The major customer base for autoparts sold in retail stores consists of young owners of old vehicles. These owners do their own automotive maintenance out of economic necessity.
   a. One of RRG's conclusions is that the retail autoparts industry as a whole is in the stabilization stage of the industry life cycle. Discuss *three* relevant items of data from Table 1 that support this conclusion. [9 minutes]
   b. Another RRG conclusion is that WAH and its principal competitors are in the growth stage of their life cycle.

      Cite *three* relevant items of data from Table 13.1 that support this conclusion.

      Explain how WAH and its principal competitors can be in a growth stage while their industry as a whole is in the stabilization stage. [11 minutes]

9. You know the following about your industry (I) and the market (M):

ROE_i:	12%	ROE_M:	16%
RR_i:	0.60	RR_M:	0.55
$Beta_i$:	1.05	$Beta_M$:	1.00

   Discuss what difference you would expect in the *P/Es,* and explain why you expect this difference.

Table 13.1 Selected Retail Autoparts Industry Data

	1994	1993	1992	1991	1990	1989	1988	1987	1986	1985
Population 18–29 years old (percentage change)	−1.8%	−2.0%	−2.1%	−1.4%	−0.8%	−0.9%	−1.1%	−0.9%	−0.7%	−0.3%
Number of households with income more than $35,000 (percentage change)	6.0%	4.0%	8.0%	4.5%	2.7%	3.1%	1.6%	3.6%	4.2%	2.2%
Number of households with income less than $35,000 (percentage change)	3.0%	−1.0%	4.9%	2.3%	−1.4%	2.5%	1.4%	−1.3%	0.6%	0.1%
Number of cars 5–15 years old (percentage change)	0.9%	−1.3%	−6.0%	1.9%	3.3%	2.4%	−2.3%	−2.2%	−8.0%	1.6%
Automotive aftermarket industry retail sales (percentage change)	5.7%	1.9%	3.1%	3.7%	4.3%	2.6%	1.3%	0.2%	3.7%	2.4%
Consumer expenditures on automotive parts and accessories (percentage change)	2.4%	1.8%	2.1%	6.5%	3.6%	9.2%	1.3%	6.2%	6.7%	6.5%
Sales growth of retail auto parts companies with 100 or more stores	17.0%	16.0%	16.5%	14.0%	15.5%	16.8%	12.0%	15.7%	19.0%	16.0%
Market share of retail auto parts companies with 100 or more stores	19.0%	18.5%	18.3%	18.1%	17.0%	17.2%	17.0%	16.9%	15.0%	14.0%
Average operating margin of retail auto parts companies with 100 or more stores	12.0%	11.8%	11.2%	11.5%	10.6%	10.6%	10.0%	10.4%	9.8%	9.0%
Average operating margin of all retail auto parts companies	5.5%	5.7%	5.6%	5.8%	6.0%	6.5%	7.0%	7.2%	7.1%	7.2%

· · · · · APPENDIX: CHAPTER 13 · · · ·

A. Preparing an Industry Analysis: What Is an Industry?[6]

Identifying a company's industry can be difficult in today's business world. Although airlines, railroads, and utilities may be easy to categorize, what about manufacturing companies with three different divisions, none of which is dominant? Perhaps the best way to test whether a company fits into an industry grouping is to compare the operating results for the company and an industry. For our purposes, an industry is a group of companies with similar demand, supply, and operating characteristics.

The following is a set of guidelines for preparing an industry appraisal, including the topics to consider and some specific items to include.

Characteristics to Study

1. Price history reveals valuable long-term relationships.
   a. Price/earnings ratios
   b. Common stock yields
   c. Price/book value ratios
   d. Price/cash flow ratios
   e. Price/sales ratios
2. Operating data show comparisons of
   a. Return on total investment (*ROI*)
   b. Return on equity (*ROE*)
   c. Sales growth
   d. Trends in operating profit margin
   e. Evaluation of stage in industrial life cycle
   f. Book value per-share growth
   g. Earnings-per-share growth
   h. Profit margin trends (gross, operating, and net)
   i. Evaluation of exchange rate risk from foreign sales
3. Comparative results of alternative industries show
   a. Effects of business cycles on each industry group
   b. Secular trends affecting results
   c. Industry growth compared to other industries
   d. Regulatory changes
   e. Importance of overseas operations

Factors in Industry Analysis

Markets for Products
1. Trends in the markets for the industry's major products: historical and projected
2. Industry growth relative to GDP or other relevant economic series; possible changes from past trends
3. Shares of market for major products among domestic and global producers; changes in market shares in recent years; outlook for market share
4. Effect of imports on industry markets; share of market taken by imports; price and margin changes caused by imports; outlook for imports
5. Effect of exports on their markets; trends in export prices and units exported; outlook for exports
6. Expectations for the exchange rates in major non-U.S. countries; historical volatility of exchange rates; outlook for the level and volatility of exchange rates

Financial Performance
1. Capitalization ratios; ability to raise new capital; earnings retention rate; financial leverage
2. Ratio of fixed assets to capital invested; depreciation policies; capital turnover
3. Return on total capital; return on equity capital; components of ROE
4. Return on foreign investments; need for foreign capital

[6] Reprinted and adapted with permission of Stanley D. Ryals, CFA; Investment Council, Inc: La Crescenta, CA 91214.

Operations

1. Degrees of integration; cost advantages of integration; major supply contracts
2. Operating rates as a percentage of capacity; backlogs; new-order trends
3. Trends of industry consolidation
4. Trends in industry competition
5. New-product development; research and development expenditures in dollars and as a percentage of sales
6. Diversification; comparability of product lines

Management

1. Management depth and ability to develop from within; organizational structure
2. Board of directors: internal versus external members; compensation package
3. Flexibility to deal with product demand changes; ability to identify and eliminate losing operations
4. Record and outlook regarding labor relations
5. Dividend policy and historical progression

Sources of Industry Information

1. Independent industry journals
2. Industry and trade associations
3. Government reports and statistics
4. Independent research organizations
5. Brokerage house research
6. Financial publishers (S&P; Moody's; Value Line)

B. Insights on Analyzing Industry *ROAs*

Insights on Industry ROAs

Beyond the normal analysis of *ROA* as a component of *ROE* (*ROA* times Total Assets/Equity equals *ROE*), an article by Selling and Stickney provides some interesting insights for industry analysis based upon an analysis of the two components of the *ROA* ratio (profit margin and total asset turnover) and what these two components signal regarding the industry strategy.[7] Given the two components of the *ROA,* it is possible to graph each of these values as shown in Exhibit 13A.1 and determine what each component contributed to the *ROA* at the point of intersection. As shown, it is possible to draw a constant *ROA* curve, which demonstrates that it is possible to achieve an 8 percent (or 4 percent) *ROA* with numerous combinations of profit margin and asset turnover. The particular combination of profit margin and asset turnover is generally dictated by the nature of the industry and the strategy employed by management. For example, many industries necessarily require large capital inputs for equipment (e.g., steel, auto, heavy machinery manufacturers). Therefore, the asset turnover is necessarily low, which means the profit margin must be higher. The firms in such an industry are typically in the upper left segment of the graph (Segment *a*), and improvements of *ROA* in these industries are derived by increasing profit margins because it is difficult to increase asset turnover. In contrast, industries that have commodity-type products (e.g., retail food, paper, industrial chemicals) generally have low profit margins and succeed based upon high asset turnover. These industries are generally in the lower right segment of the graph (Segment *c*) and they attempt to improve their *ROA* by increasing their asset turnover rather than the profit margin (i.e., they are constrained by price competition). Industries in the middle segment *(b)* are in a more balanced position and can attempt to improve the *ROA* by increasing *either* the profit margin or the asset turnover.

It is very important for an analyst to understand the nature of the industry and what contributes to the industry's *ROA* as well as what this implies about the constraints and opportunities facing the firms in the industry.

---

[7] Thomas Selling and Cycle P. Stickney. "The Effects of Business Environment and Strategy on a Firm's Rate of Return on Assets," *Financial Analysts Journal* 45, no. 1 (January–February 1989): 43–52.

Exhibit 13A.1 *ROA*—The Trade-Off of Profit Margin and Asset Turnover

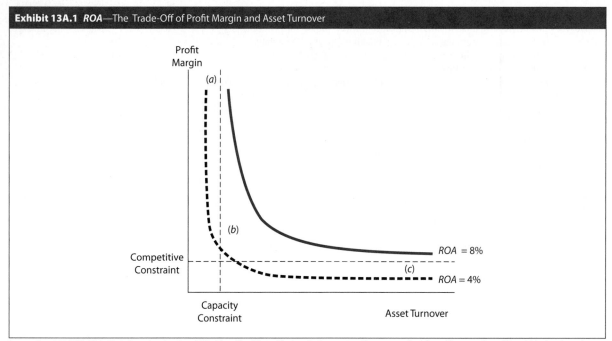

CHAPTER 14

Company Analysis and Stock Valuation*

After you read this chapter, you should be able to answer the following questions:

- Why is it important to differentiate between company analysis and stock valuation?
- What is the difference between a true growth company and a growth stock?
- How do we apply the two valuation approaches and the several valuation techniques to Walgreens?
- What techniques are useful when estimating the inputs to alternative valuation models?
- What techniques are useful when estimating company sales?
- How do we estimate the profit margins and earnings per share for a company?
- What factors are considered when estimating the earnings multiplier for a firm?
- What two specific competitive strategies can a firm use to cope with the competitive environment in its industry?
- In addition to the earnings multiplier, what are some other relative valuation ratios?
- How do we apply the several present value of cash flow models to the valuation of a company?
- What value-added measures are available to evaluate the performance of a firm?
- How do we compute economic value added (EVA), market value added (MVA), and the franchise value for a firm?
- What is the relationship between these value-added measures and changes in the market value of firms?
- What is the relationship between positive EVA and a growth company?
- Why is it inappropriate to use the standard dividend discount model (DDM) to value a true growth company?
- What is the difference between no growth, simple growth, and dynamic growth?
- What is the growth duration model and what information does it provide?
- How can we use the growth duration model to estimate the *P/E* for a growth company?
- How can you use site visits and interviews to gain unique insights not generally available?
- What are some factors that should lead you to sell a stock?
- What additional factors should be considered when analyzing a company on a global basis?

At this point, you have made two decisions about your investment in equity markets. First, after analyzing the economy and stock markets for several countries, you have decided what percent of your portfolio should be invested in common stocks. Second, after analyzing various industries, you have identified those that appear to offer above-average risk-adjusted performance over your investment horizon. The final questions in the fundamental analysis procedure are (1) which are the best companies within these desirable industries? and (2) are their stocks underpriced? Specifically, is the intrinsic value of the stock above its market value, or is the expected rate of return on the stock equal to or greater than its required rate of return?

* The authors acknowledge comments and suggestions on this chapter by Professor Edgar Norton of Illinois State University.

We begin with a discussion of the difference between company analysis and stock valuation. Company analysis should occur in the context of the prevailing economic and industry conditions. We discuss some competitive strategies that can help firms maximize returns in an industry's competitive environment. Most of the chapter involves a demonstrate of cash flow models and relative valuation ratios used to determine a stock's intrinsic value and determine whether it is an undervalued or overvalued stock. This is followed by a review of factors that will help you determine when to sell a stock that you own and discuss the pressures and influences that affect professional stock analysts. We conclude with a discussion of important factors to consider when analyzing foreign stocks.

· ·

14.1 Company Analysis versus Stock Valuation

This chapter is titled "Company Analysis and Stock Valuation" to convey the idea that the common stocks of good companies are not necessarily good investments. The point is, after analyzing a company and deriving an understanding of its strengths and risks, you need to compute the intrinsic value of the firm's stock and compare this to its market value to determine if the company's stock should be purchased. The stock of a wonderful firm with superior management and strong performance measured by sales and earnings growth can be priced so high that the intrinsic value of the stock is below its current market price and should not be acquired. In contrast, the stock of a company with less sales and earnings growth may have a market price that is below its intrinsic value. In this case, although the company is not as good, its stock could be the better investment.

The classic confusion concerns growth companies versus growth stocks. The stock of a growth company is not necessarily a growth stock. Recognition of this difference is absolutely essential for successful investing.

14.1.1 Growth Companies and Growth Stocks

Observers have historically defined growth companies as those that consistently experience above-average increases in sales and earnings. This definition has some limitations because many firms could qualify due to certain accounting procedures, mergers, or other external events.

In contrast, financial theorists such as Salomon (1963) and Miller and Modigliani (1961) define a **growth company** as a firm with the management ability and the opportunities to make investments that yield rates of return greater than the firm's required rate of return. This required rate of return is the firm's weighted average cost of capital (WACC). As an example, a growth company might be able to acquire capital at an average cost of 10 percent and yet have the management ability and the opportunity to invest those funds at rates of return of 15 to 20 percent. As a result of these superior investment opportunities, the firm's sales and earnings grow faster than those of similar risk firms and the overall economy. In addition, a growth company that has above-average investment opportunities should, and typically does, retain a large portion of its earnings to fund these superior investment projects (i.e., they have low dividend-payout ratios).

Growth stocks are *not* necessarily shares in growth companies. A **growth stock** is a stock with a higher expected rate of return than other stocks in the market with similar risk characteristics. The stock achieves this expected superior risk-adjusted rate of return because the market has undervalued it compared to other stocks. Although the stock market adjusts stock prices relatively quickly and accurately to reflect new information, available information is not always perfect or complete. Therefore, imperfect or incomplete information may cause a given stock to be undervalued or overvalued at a point in time.[1]

---

[1] An analyst is more likely to find such stocks outside the top tier of companies that are scrutinized by numerous analysts; in other words, look for neglected stocks.

If the stock is undervalued, its price should eventually increase to reflect its true fundamental value when the correct information becomes available. During this period of price adjustment, the stock's realized return will exceed the required return for a stock with its risk, and, during this period of adjustment, it will be a growth stock. Growth stocks are not necessarily limited to growth companies. A future growth stock can be the stock of any type of company; the stock need only be undervalued by the market.

The fact is, if investors recognize a growth company and discount its future earnings stream properly, the current market price of the growth company's stock will reflect its future earnings stream. Those who acquire the stock of a growth company at this correct market price will receive a rate of return consistent with the risk of the stock, even when the superior earnings growth is attained. In many instances, overeager investors tend to overestimate the expected growth rate of earnings and cash flows for the growth company and, therefore, inflate the price of a growth company's stock. Investors who pay the inflated stock price will earn a rate of return below the risk-adjusted required rate of return, despite the fact that the growth company experiences above-average growth of sales and earnings. Studies by Solt and Statman (1989), Shefrin and Statman (1995), and Clayman (1987) have examined the stock price performance for samples of growth companies and found that their stocks performed poorly—that is, the stocks of growth companies have generally *not* been growth stocks.

14.1.2 Defensive Companies and Stocks

Defensive companies are those whose future earnings are likely to withstand an economic downturn. One would expect them to have relatively low business risk and not excessive financial risk. Typical examples are public utilities or grocery chains—firms that supply basic consumer necessities.

There are two closely related concepts of a **defensive stock**. First, a defensive stock's rate of return is not expected to decline during an overall market decline, or decline less than the overall market. Second, our CAPM discussion indicated that an asset's relevant risk is its covariance with the market portfolio of risky assets—that is, an asset's systematic risk. A stock with low or negative systematic risk (a small positive or negative beta) may be considered a defensive stock according to this theory because its returns are unlikely to be harmed significantly in a bear market.

14.1.3 Cyclical Companies and Stocks

A **cyclical company's** sales and earnings will be heavily influenced by aggregate business activity. Examples would be firms in the steel, auto, or heavy machinery industries. Such companies will do well during economic expansions and poorly during economic contractions. This volatile earnings pattern is typically a function of the firm's business risk (both sales volatility and operating leverage) and can be compounded by financial risk.

A **cyclical stock** will experience changes in its rates of return greater than changes in overall market rates of return. In terms of the CAPM, these would be stocks that have high betas. The stock of a cyclical company, however, is not necessarily cyclical. A cyclical stock is the stock of any company that has returns that are more volatile than the overall market—that is, high-beta stocks that have high correlation with the aggregate market and greater volatility.

14.1.4 Speculative Companies and Stocks

A **speculative company** is one whose assets involve great risk but that also has a possibility of great gain. A good example of a speculative firm is one involved in oil exploration.

A **speculative stock** possesses a high probability of low or negative rates of return and a low probability of normal or high rates of return. Specifically, a speculative stock is one that is overpriced, leading to a high probability that during the future period when the market adjusts the stock price to its true value, it will experience either low or possibly negative rates of return. Such an expectation might be the case for an excellent growth company whose stock is selling at an extremely high price/earnings ratio—that is, it is substantially overvalued.

14.1.5 Value versus Growth Investing

Some analysts also divide stocks into growth stocks and value stocks. As we have discussed, growth stocks are companies that will experience above-average risk-adjusted rates of return because the stocks are undervalued. If the analyst does a good job in identifying such companies, investors in these stocks will reap the benefits of seeing their stock prices rise after other investors identify their earnings growth potential. **Value stocks** are those that appear to be undervalued for reasons other than earnings growth potential. Value stocks are usually identified by analysts as having low price-earning or price-book value ratios. Notably, in these comparisons between growth and value stocks, the specification of a growth stock is *not* consistent with our preceding discussion. In these discussions, a growth stock is generally specified as a stock of a company that is experiencing rapid growth of sales and earnings (e.g., Intel and Microsoft). As a result of this company performance, the stock typically has a high *P/E* and price-book-value ratio. Unfortunately, the specification does not consider the critical comparison we advocate between intrinsic value and market price. Therefore, these specifications will not be used in subsequent discussions of valuation.

The major point of this section is that you must initially examine a company in detail to determine its fundamantal characteristics and use this information to derive an estimate of the intrinsic value of its stock. When you compare this intrinsic value of the stock to its current market price you decide whether you should acquire it—that is, will it be a growth stock that provides a rate of return greater than what is consistent with its risk?

· ·

14.2 Economic, Industry, and Structural Links to Company Analysis

The analysis of companies and their stocks is the final step in the top-down approach to investing. Rather than selecting stocks only on the basis of company-specific factors (as with bottom-up analysis), top-down analysts review the current status and future outlook for domestic and international sectors of the economy. Based on this macroeconomic analysis, they identify industries that offer attractive returns in the expected future environment. Following this macroanalysis, we value the firms in the selected industries. Our analysis concentrates on the two significant determinants of a stock's intrinsic value: (1) growth of the firm's expected earnings and cash flows and (2) its risk and the appropriate discount rate.

14.2.1 Economic and Industry Influences

If economic trends are favorable for an industry, the company analysis should focus on firms in that industry that will benefit from these economic trends. Research analysts should become familiar with the cash flow and risk attributes of the firms they are studying. Given a period of economic-industry growth the most attractive firms in the industry will typically have high levels of operating and financial leverage wherein a modest percentage increase in revenue results in a must larger percentage rise in earnings and cash flow. The point is, firms in an industry will have varying sensitivities to economic variables, such as economic growth, interest rates, input costs, and exchange rates. Because each firm is different, an investor must determine the best candidates for purchase under expected economic conditions.

14.2.2 Structural Influences

In addition to economic variables, other factors, such as social trends, technology, and political and regulatory influences, can have a major effect on some firms in an industry. Some firms in the industry are able to take advantage of demographic changes or shifts in consumer tastes and lifestyles, or they can invest in technology to lower costs and better serve their customers. Such firms grow and succeed despite unfavorable industry or economic conditions. For example, Wal-Mart became the nation's leading retailer because of several smart management decisions.

The geographic location of many of its stores allowed it to benefit from regional population growth and lower labor costs. Its competitive strategy, which emphasized everyday low prices, was appealing to consumers concerned about the price and value of purchases. Finally, its technologically advanced inventory and ordering systems and its outstanding distribution system gave Wal-Mart a clear competitive (cost) advantage.

During the initial stage of an industry's life cycle, the original firms in the industry can refine their technologies and move down the learning curve. Subsequent followers may benefit from these initial actions and can learn from the leaders' mistakes and take the market lead away from them. Investors need to be aware of such leadership changes so they can evaluate companies and their stocks accordingly.

Political and regulatory events can create opportunities in an industry even during weak economic periods. Deregulation in trucking, airlines, and the financial services industries in the 1980s led to the creation of new companies with innovative strategies. As a result, sharp price declines following bad industry news may be a good buying opportunity for astute investors. Some stocks in an industry may deserve lower prices following some political or regulatory events; but, if the market also punishes the stock prices of good companies with smaller exposures to the bad news, then an alert analyst will identify buying opportunities of underpriced stocks within an industry.

The bottom line is that, although the economy plays a major role in determining overall market trends and industry groups display sensitivity to economic variables, other structural changes may counterbalance the economic effects, or company management may be able to minimize the impact of economic or industry events on a company. Analysts who are familiar with industry trends and company strategies can issue well-reasoned buy-and-sell recommendations irrespective of the economic forecast.

· ·

14.3 Company Analysis

This section groups various analysis components for discussion. The first subsection continues the Porter discussion of an industry's competitive environment. The basic SWOT analysis is intended to articulate a firm's strengths, weaknesses, opportunities, and threats. These two analyses should provide an understanding of a firm's overall *strategic* approach. Given this background, we demonstrate the two valuation approaches: (1) the present value of cash flows, and (2) relative valuation ratio techniques. The next section discusses the unique features of true growth companies and demonstrates several models that can be used to value growth companies. Following this, we discuss site visits to companies, how to prepare for a management interview, and suggestions on when to sell an asset. We conclude with a discussion of the evaluation of international companies and their stocks.

14.3.1 Firm Competitive Strategies

In describing competition within industries, we discussed the five competitive forces that could affect the competitive structure and profit potential of an industry. After you have determined the competitive structure of an industry, you should attempt to identify the specific competitive strategy employed by each firm in the industry.

A company's competitive strategy can either be *defensive* or *offensive*. A **defensive competitive strategy** involves positioning the firm to deflect the effect of the competitive forces in the industry. Examples may include investing in fixed assets and technology to lower production costs or creating a strong brand image with increased advertising expenditures.

An **offensive competitive strategy** is one in which the firm attempts to use its strengths to affect the competitive forces in the industry. For example, Wal-Mart used its buying power to obtain price concessions from its suppliers. This cost advantage, coupled with a superior delivery system to its stores, allowed Wal-Mart to grow against larger competitors and eventually become the leading U.S. retailer.

As an investor, you must understand the alternative competitive strategies available, determine each firm's strategy, judge whether the firm's strategy is reasonable for its industry, and, finally, evaluate how successful the firm is in implementing its strategy.

In the following sections, we discuss analyzing a firm's competitive position and strategy. The analyst must decide whether the firm's management is correctly positioning the firm to take advantage of industry and economic conditions. The analyst's opinion about management's decisions should ultimately be reflected in the analyst's estimates of the firm's growth of cash flow and earnings.

Porter (1980a, 1985) suggests two major competitive strategies: low-cost leadership and differentiation. These two competitive strategies dictate how a firm has decided to cope with the five competitive conditions that define an industry's environment. The strategies available and the ways of implementing them differ within each industry.

Low-Cost Strategy The firm that pursues the low-cost strategy is determined to become *the* low-cost producer and, hence, the cost leader in its industry. Cost advantages vary by industry and might include economies of scale, proprietary technology, or preferential access to raw materials. In order to benefit from cost leadership, the firm must command prices near the industry average, which means that it must differentiate itself about as well as other firms. If the firm discounts price too much, it could erode the superior rates of return available because of its low cost. During the past decade, Wal-Mart was considered a low-cost source. The firm achieved this by volume purchasing of merchandise and lower-cost operations. As a result, the firm charged less but still enjoyed higher profit margins and returns on capital than many of its competitors.

Differentiation Strategy With the differentiation strategy, a firm seeks to identify itself as unique in its industry in an area that is important to buyers. Again, the possibilities for differentiation vary widely by industry. A company can attempt to differentiate itself based on its distribution system (selling in stores, by mail order, or door-to-door) or some unique marketing approach. A firm employing the differentiation strategy will enjoy above-average rates of return only if the price premium attributable to its differentiation exceeds the extra cost of being unique. Therefore, when you analyze a firm using this strategy, you must determine whether the differentiating factor is truly unique, whether it is sustainable, what is its cost, and if the price premium derived from the uniqueness is greater than its cost (is the firm experiencing above-average rates of return?).

14.3.2 Focusing a Strategy

Whichever strategy it selects, a firm must determine where it will focus this strategy. Specifically, a firm must select segments in the industry and tailor its strategy to serve these specific groups. For example, a low-cost strategy would typically exploit cost advantages for certain segments of the industry, such as being the low-cost producer for the expensive segment of the market. Similarly, a differentiation focus would target the special needs of buyers in specific segments. For example, in the athletic shoe market, companies have attempted to develop shoes for unique sport segments, such as tennis, basketball, aerobics, or walkers and hikers, rather than offering only shoes for runners. Athletic shoe firms thought that participants in these alternative activities needed shoes with characteristics different from those desired by joggers. Equally important, they believed that these athletes would be willing to pay a premium for these special shoes. Again, you must ascertain if special possibilities exist, if they are being served by another firm, and if they can be priced to generate abnormal returns to the firm. Exhibit 14.1 details some of Porter's ideas for the skills, resources, and company organizational requirements needed to successfully develop a cost leadership or a differentiation strategy.

Next, you must determine which strategy the firm is pursuing and its success. Also, can the strategy be sustained? Further, you should evaluate a firm's competitive strategy over time,

Exhibit 14.1 Skills, Resources, and Organizational Requirements Needed to Successfully Apply Cost Leadership and Differentiation Strategies

Generic Strategy	Commonly Required Skills and Resources	Common Organizational Requirements
Overall cost leadership	Sustained capital investment and access to capital Process engineering skills Intense supervision of labor Products designed for ease in manufacture Low-cost distribution system	Tight cost control Frequent, detailed control reports Structured organization and responsibilities Incentives based on meeting strict quantitative targets
Differentiation	Strong marketing abilities Product engineering Creative flair Strong capability in basic research Corporate reputation for quality or technological leadership Long tradition in the industry or unique combination of skills drawn from other businesses Strong cooperation from channels	Strong coordination among functions in R&D, product development, and marketing Subjective measurement and incentives instead of quantitative measures Amenities to attract highly skilled labor, scientists, or creative people

Source: Adapted from *Competitive Strategy: Techniques for Analyzing Industries and Competitors* by Michael E. Porter.

because strategies need to change as an industry evolves; different strategies work during different phases of an industry's life cycle. For example, differentiation strategies may work for firms in an industry during the early growth stages. Subsequently, when the industry is in the mature stage, firms may try to lower their costs.

Through the analysis process, the analyst identifies what the company does well, what it doesn't do well, and where the firm is vulnerable to the five competitive forces. Some call this process developing a company's "story." This evaluation enables the analyst to determine the outlook and risks facing the firm. In summary, understanding the industry's competitive forces and the firm's strategy for dealing with them is the key to understanding how a company makes money and deriving an accurate and unique estimate of the firm's long-run cash flows and its risks.

Another framework for examining and understanding a firm's competitive position and its strategy is a company SWOT analysis.

14.3.3 SWOT Analysis

As before, **SWOT analysis** involves an examination of a firm's *s*trengths, *w*eaknesses, *o*pportunities, and *t*hreats. It should help you evaluate a firm's strategies to exploit its competitive advantages or defend against its weaknesses. Strengths and weaknesses involve identifying the firm's *internal* abilities or lack thereof. Opportunities and threats include *external* situations, such as competitive forces, discovery and development of new technologies, government regulations, and domestic and international economic trends.

The *strengths* of a company give the firm a comparative advantage in the marketplace. Perceived strengths can include good customer service, high-quality products, strong brand image, customer loyalty, innovative R&D, market leadership, or strong financial resources. To remain strengths, they must continue to be developed, maintained, and defended through prudent capital investment policies.

Weaknesses result when competitors have potentially exploitable advantages over the firm. Once weaknesses are identified, the firm can select strategies to mitigate or correct the weaknesses. For example, a firm that is only a domestic producer in a global market can make investments that will allow it to export or produce its product overseas. Another example would be a firm with poor financial resources that would form joint ventures with financially stronger firms.

Opportunities, or environmental factors that favor the firm, can include a growing market for the firm's products (domestic and international), shrinking competition, favorable exchange rate shifts, or identification of a new market or product segment.

Threats are environmental factors that can hinder the firm in achieving its goals. Examples would include a slowing domestic economy (or sluggish overseas economies for exporters), additional government regulation, an increase in industry competition, threats of entry, buyers or suppliers seeking to increase their bargaining power, or new technology that can obsolete the industry's product. By recognizing and understanding opportunities and threats, an investor can make informed decisions about how the firm can exploit opportunities and mitigate threats.

14.3.4 Some Lessons from Lynch

Peter Lynch (1989, 1993), the former portfolio manager of Fidelity Investments' highly successful Magellan Fund, looks for the following attributes when he analyzes firms.

Favorable Attributes of Firms The following attributes of firms may result in favorable stock market performance:

1. The firm's product is not faddish; it is one that consumers will continue to purchase over time.
2. The company has a sustainable comparative competitive advantage over its rivals.
3. The firm's industry or product has market stability. Therefore, it has little need to innovate or create product improvements or fear that it may lose a technological advantage. Market stability means less potential for entry.
4. The firm can benefit from cost reductions (for example, a computer manufacturer that uses technology provided by suppliers to deliver a faster and less-expensive product).
5. The firm buys back its shares or management purchases shares which indicates that its insiders are putting their money into the firm.

14.3.5 Tenets of Warren Buffett

The following tenets are from Robert Hagstrom (2001). The parenthetical comments are based on discussions in the book and Berkshire Hathaway annual report letters.

Business Tenets
*   Is the business simple and understandable?
    (This makes it easier to estimate future cash flows with a high degree of confidence.)
*   Does the business have a consistent operating history?
    (Again, cash flow estimates can be made with more confidence.)
*   Does the business have favorable long-term prospects?
    (Does the business have a franchise product or service that is needed or desired, has no close substitute, and is not regulated? This implies that the firm has pricing flexibility.)

Management Tenets
*   Is management rational?
    (Is the allocation of capital to projects that provide returns above the cost of capital? If not, does management pay capital to stockholders through dividends or the repurchase of stock?)
*   Is management candid with its shareholders?
    (Does management tell owners everything you would want to know?)
*   Does management resist the institutional imperative?
    (Does management not attempt to imitate the behavior of other managers?)

Financial Tenets
*   Focus on return on equity, not earnings per share.
    (Look for strong *ROE* with little or no debt.)

- Calculate owner earnings.
  (Owner earnings are basically equal to free cash flow after capital expenditures.)
- Look for a company with relatively high sustainable profit margins for its industry.
- Make sure the company has created at least one dollar of market value for every dollar retained.

Market Tenets
- What is the intrinsic value of the business?
  (Value is equal to future free cash flows discounted at a government bond rate. Using this low discount rate is considered appropriate because Warren Buffett is very confident of his cash flow estimates due to extensive analysis, and this confidence implies low risk.)
- Can the business be purchased at a significant discount to its fundamental intrinsic value?

The point is to make use of research on the competitive forces in an industry, a firm's responses to those forces, SWOT analysis, Lynch's suggestions, and Buffett's tenets.

14.4 Estimating Intrinsic Value

Now that the analysis of the economy, structural forces, the industry, the company, and its competitors is completed, it is time to estimate the intrinsic value of the firm's common stock. If the intrinsic value estimate exceeds the stock's current market price, the stock should be purchased. In contrast, if the current market price exceeds our intrinsic value estimate, we should avoid the stock or sell it if we own it.

As in Chapter 11, we will consider two general approaches to valuation and the following techniques.

Present Value of Cash Flows (PVCF)
1. Present value of dividends (DDM)
2. Present value of free cash flow to equity (FCFE)
3. Present value of free operating cash flow to the firm (FCFF)

Relative Valuation Techniques
1. Price/earnings ratio (*P/E*)
2. Price/cash flow ratio (*P/CF*)
3. Price/book value ratio (*P/BV*)
4. Price/sales ratio (*P/S*)

This section contains a brief presentation for each of these techniques as applied to Walgreens, the largest retail drugstore (RDS) chain in the United States. It operates 5,997 drugstores in 48 states and Puerto Rico. Its pharmacy operation generates over 64 percent of sales.

Although we limit our demonstration to Walgreens (whose ticker symbol is WAG), a complete company analysis would cover all the firms in the RDS industry to determine which stocks should perform the best. The objective is to estimate the expected return and risk for all the individual firms in the industry over your investment horizon. Initially we consider the present value of cash flow (PVCF) models. Exhibit 14.2 contains historical data for Walgreens required for the PVCF models.

14.4.1 Present Value of Dividends

As noted in Chapter 11 because determining the present value of all future dividends is difficult, analysts typically apply simplifying assumptions when employing the dividend discount models (DDMs). The typical assumption is that the stock's dividends will grow at a constant rate over time. Although unrealistic for fast-growing or cyclical firms, this assumption may be appropriate for many mature firms. More complex DDMs exist for more complicated growth forecasts including two-stage growth models (a period of fast growth followed by a period of

Exhibit 14.2 Walgreen Co.'s Input Data for Alternative Present Value of Cash Flow Models (Dollars in Millions, except per Share Data) 1983–2007

Year	Dividend Per Share	Net Income	Depreciation Expense	Capital Spending	Change in Working Capital	Principal Repayment	New Debt Issued	FCFE	EBIT	Tax Rate	FCFF	100% – Tax Rate	Time
1983	0.02	70	25	-71	-15	-3	0	6	147	45	20	55	1
1984	0.03	85	29	-68	-56	-3	0	-13	181	45	5	55	2
1985	0.03	94	34	-97	-61	-3	20	-13	209	46	-11	54	3
1986	0.03	103	44	-156	-72	-5	92	6	229	45	-58	55	4
1987	0.04	104	54	-122	-118	-4	5	-81	243	46	-55	54	5
1988	0.04	129	59	-114	49	-4	31	150	263	38	157	62	6
1989	0.05	154	64	-121	-97	-4	0	-4	301	37	36	63	7
1990	0.05	175	70	-192	-69	-4	0	-20	344	38	22	62	8
1991	0.06	195	84	-202	-129	-24	0	-76	381	38	-11	62	9
1992	0.07	221	92	-145	-32	-6	0	130	429	37	185	63	10
1993	0.08	245	105	-185	-28	-112	0	25	483	39	187	61	11
1994	0.09	282	118	-290	-58	-6	0	46	550	38	111	62	12
1995	0.10	321	132	-310	-104	-7	0	32	629	39	102	61	13
1996	0.11	372	147	-364	-116	0	2	41	725	39	109	61	14
1997	0.12	436	164	-485	34	-1	0	148	842	39	227	61	15
1998	0.13	511	189	-641	-143	0	0	-84	878	39	-59	61	16
1999	0.13	624	210	-696	-206	0	0	-68	1028	39	-65	61	17
2000	0.14	777	230	-1119	-140	0	0	-252	1264	39	-258	61	18
2001	0.14	886	269	-1237	-569	0	0	-651	1426	38	-653	62	19
2002	0.15	1019	307	-934	-830	0	0	-438	1637	38	-442	62	20
2003	0.16	1176	346	-795	-726	0	0	1	1889	38	-4	62	21
2004	0.18	1360	403	-940	-748	0	0	75	2176	38	64	62	22
2005	0.22	1560	482	-1238	-149	0	0	655	2456	36	667	64	23
2006	0.27	1751	572	-1338	-115	0	0	870	2754	36	882	64	24
2007	0.33	2041	676	-1785	1184	0	879	2995	3189	36	2116	64	25
10 yr Growth Rate	10.65%	16.69%	15.22%	13.92%					14.24%		25.03%		

constant growth) and three-stage growth models (a period of fast growth followed by a period of diminishing growth rates followed by a period of constant growth).[2]

Recall that the constant growth DDM implies that when dividends grow at a constant rate, a stock's price should equal next year's dividend, D_1, divided by investors' required rate of return on the stock (k) minus the dividend growth rate (g):

14.1   Intrinsic Value $= D_1 / (k - g)$

Assuming constant dividend growth, next year's dividend (D_1) should equal the current dividend, D_0, increased by the constant dividend growth rate: $D_1 = D_0 (1 + g)$. Because the current dividend is known, to estimate intrinsic value we need only estimate the dividend growth rate and investors' required rate of return.

Growth Rate Estimates If the stock has had fairly constant dividend growth over the past 5 to 10 years, one estimate of the constant growth rate is to use the actual growth of dividends over this period. The average compound rate of growth is found by computing

14.2   Average Dividend Growth Rate $= \sqrt[n]{\dfrac{D_n}{D_0}} - 1$

In the case of Walgreens, the 1983 dividend (D_0) was \$0.02 a share and the 2007 dividend (D_{24}) was \$0.33 a share. The average dividend growth rate was

$$\sqrt[24]{\dfrac{\$0.33}{0.02}} - 1 = \sqrt[24]{16.50} - 1 = 0.1233$$

$$= 12.33\%$$

or 12.33 percent. Clearly, blindly plugging historical growth rates into our formulas ignores our analysis of economic, structural, industry, and company influences. Our analysis may have indicated that growth is expected to increase or decrease due to such factors as changes in government programs, demographic shifts, or changes in product mix. The historical growth rate may need to be raised or lowered to incorporate our findings.

In Chapter 10, we learned other ways to estimate future growth. The sustainable growth rate

14.3 $g = RR \times ROE$

assumes the firm will maintain a constant debt-equity ratio as it finances asset growth. ROE is the product of the net profit margin, total asset turnover, and the financial leverage multiplier. Thus, a firm's future growth rate and its components of ROE can be compared to those of its competitors, its industry, and the market. For Walgreens, the sustainable growth rate calculation using the average data for the recent three years: 2005–2007.[3]

$$g = RR \times ROE = 0.84 \times .177$$

$$= 0.1487 = 14.87\%$$

The dividend growth rate will be influenced by the age of the industry life cycle, structural changes, industry competition and economic trends. Economic-industry-firm analysis provides valuable information regarding future trends in dividend growth. Information derived about management's plans to expand the firm, diversify into new areas, or change dividend policy can provide useful information about the firm's dividend policy. Averaging the historical growth rate of dividends (12.33 percent) and the implied sustainable growth estimate of 14.87

---

[2] These were discussed in Chapter 11.

[3] This sustainable growth rate value differs from the one in Chapter 10 because this calculation uses year-end values for *ROE*, whereas in Chapter 10, the equity value is an average of the beginning and ending values.

percent indicates a value of 13.60 percent. Although we feel that a firm's *ROE* is the critical growth factor and give this estimate more weight, we will use a conservative 13 percent for Walgreen Co.'s estimated *g*.

Required Rate of Return Estimate We know an investor's required rate of return has two basic components: the nominal risk-free interest rate and a risk premium. If the market is efficient, over time the return earned by investors should compensate them for the risk of the investment.

Notably, we must estimate *future* risk premiums to determine the stock's current intrinsic value. Estimates of the nominal risk-free interest rate are available from the initial analysis of the economy during the top-down approach. The risk premium of the firm must rely on other information including evaluation of the financial statements and capital market relationships.

In Chapter 10, we examined ratios that measure business risk, financial risk, liquidity risk, exchange rate risk, and country risk. These measures can be compared against the firm's major competitors, its industry, and the overall market. This fundamental comparison should indicate if the firm deserves a higher or lower risk premium than the overall market, other firms in the industry, or the firm's historical risk premium. Accounting-based risk measures use historical data, whereas investment analysis requires an estimate of the future, including any information uncovered during the top-down process that would lead to higher or lower risk estimates.

For a market-based risk estimate, the firm's characteristic line is estimated by regressing market returns on the stock's returns. The slope of this regression line is the stock's measure of systematic risk. Estimates of the economy's risk-free rate, the future long-run market return, and an estimate of the stock's beta help estimate next year's required rate of return:

14.4
$$E(R_{stock}) = E(RFR) + \beta_{stock}[E(R_{market}) - E(RFR)]$$

We begin with an estimate of beta using historical market information. Because beta is affected by changes in a firm's business and financial risks, as well as other influences, an investor should increase or lower the historical beta estimate based on his or her analysis of the firm's *future* risk characteristics.

To demonstrate the estimate of the required rate of return equation for Walgreens, we make several assumptions regarding components of the security market line (SML). First, the prevailing nominal risk-free rate *(RFR)* is estimated at about 3.8 percent—the current yield to maturity for the intermediate-term (10 year) government bond. The expected equity market rate of return (R_M) depends on the expected market risk premium on stocks. As noted earlier, this is a very controversial topic wherein the estimates range from a high of about 8 percent to a low of about 3 percent. The authors reject both of these extreme values and will use a 4.0 percent mid-range risk premium (0.040) as discussed in Chapter 12. The final estimate is the firm's systematic risk value (beta), based upon the following regression model (the characteristic line):

14.5
$$R_{WAG} = \alpha + \beta_{WAG} R_M$$

where:

R_{WAG} = monthly rate of return for Walgreens
α = constant term
β_{WAG} = beta coefficient for Walgreens
equal to $\dfrac{Cov_{W,M}}{\sigma_M^2}$
R_M = monthly rates of return for a market proxy—typically the S&P 500 Index

When this regression was run using monthly rates of return during the five-year period 2003–2007 (60 observations), the beta coefficient was estimated at 0.90.

Reflecting the discussion in Chapter 12, we put together the *RFR* of 0.038 and the market risk premium of 0.040, which implies an expected market return (R_M) of 0.078. This, combined with the Walgreen Co.'s beta of 0.90, indicates the following expected rate of return for Walgreens:

$$E(R) = RFR + \beta_i(R_M - RFR)$$
$$= 0.038 + 0.90\,(0.04)$$
$$= 0.038 + 0.036$$
$$= 0.081 = 8.1\%$$
$$= 0.074 = 7.4\%$$

Given that the 10-year Treasury yield is currently at an abnormally low value and we assumed a market risk premium at the low end of the historical range, we will round this to 8 percent for our intrinsic valuations.

14.4.2 Present Value of Dividends Model (DDM)

At this point, the analyst would face a problem: The intent was to use the basic DDM, which assumed a constant growth rate for an infinite period. You will recall that the model also required that $k > g$ (the required rate of return is larger than the expected growth rate), which is not true in this case because $k = 8$ percent and $g = 13$ percent (as computed earlier). Therefore, the analyst must employ a two- or three-stage growth model. Because of the fairly large difference between the current growth rate of 13 percent and the long-run constant growth rate of 7 percent, it seems reasonable to use a three-stage growth model, which includes a gradual transition period. We assume that the growth periods are as follows:

g_1 = 5 years (growing at 13 percent a year)
g_2 = 6 years (during this period it is assumed that the growth rate declines 1 percent per year for 6 years)
g_3 = constant perpetual growth of 7 percent

Therefore, beginning with 2008 when dividends were expected to be $0.37(0.33 × 1.13), the future dividend payments will be as follows (the growth rates are in parentheses):

	HIGH-GROWTH PERIOD					DECLINING-GROWTH PERIOD			
Year	Gr. Rate	Div.	8% PV Factor	PV	Year	Gr. Rate	Div.	8% PV Factor	PV
2009	(13%)	0.42	0.855	0.36	2014	(12%)	0.76	.585	0.44
2010	(13%)	0.47	0.794	0.37	2015	(11%)	0.85	.541	0.46
2011	(13%)	0.53	0.735	0.39	2016	(10%)	0.93	.500	0.47
2012	(13%)	0.60	0.680	0.41	2017	(9%)	1.01	.463	0.47
2013	(13%)	0.68	0.629	0.43	2018	(8%)	1.09	.429	0.47
					2019	(7%)	1.17	.397	0.46
			Sum	1.96				Sum	2.77

Constant Growth Period:

$$P_{2020} = \frac{1.17(1.07)}{0.08 - 0.07} = \frac{1.25}{0.01} = \$125.00 \times 0.397 = 49.62$$

The total value of the stock is the sum of the three present-value streams discounted at 8 percent:

1. Present value of high-growth period dividends $1.96
2. Present value of declining-growth period dividends   2.77
3. Present value of constant-growth period dividends   49.62

   Total present value of dividends $54.35

The estimated value based on the DDM ($54.35) is substantially above the market price in mid-2008 of about $37.00. This estimated value also implies a *P/E* ratio based on expected earnings in 2008 of about $2.20 per share (that is, about 24.7 times earnings) compared to the prevailing market *P/E* of about 18 times 2008 earnings. In a subsequent section on relative valuation techniques, we compare Walgreen Co.'s *P/E* ratio to that of its industry and the market.

14.4.3 Present Value of Free Cash Flow to Equity

As noted in Chapter 11, this technique resembles a present value of earnings concept except that it considers the capital expenditures required to maintain and grow the firm and the change in working capital required for a growing firm (that is, an increase in accounts receivable and inventory). The specific definition of free cash flow to equity (FCFE) is:

$$\text{Net Income} + \text{Depreciation Expense} - \text{Capital Expenditures}$$
$$- \Delta \text{ in Working Capital} - \text{Principal Debt Repayments}$$
$$+ \text{New Debt Issues}$$

This technique attempts to determine the free cash flow that is available to the stockholders after payments to all other capital suppliers and after providing for the continued growth of the firm. As noted in Chapter 11, given the current FCFE values, the alternative forms of the model are similar to those available for the DDM, which in turn depends on the firm's growth prospects. Specifically, if the firm is in its mature, constant-growth phase, it is possible to use a model similar to the reduced form DDM:

14.6
$$\text{Value} = \frac{\text{FCFE}_1}{k - g_{\text{FCFE}}}$$

where:

$$\text{FCFE} = \text{the expected free cash flow to equity in Period 1}$$
$$k = \text{the required rate of return on equity for the firm}$$
$$g_{\text{FCFE}} = \text{the expected constant growth rate of free cash flow to equity for the firm}$$

We already know from the prior dividend model that the firm's net income has grown at a rate (about 13 percent) that exceeds the required rate of return. In the case of FCFE, it is necessary to consider the effect of capital expenditures relative to depreciation and changes in working capital as well as debt repayments and new debt issues. The historical data in Exhibit 14.2 shows a growth rate that exceeded 20 percent during some periods since 1983, in contrast to the negative values in 1998–2002. The reason for the dramatic change is the very heavy capital expenditures and the significant working capital requirements during these years. The firm subsequently reduced the growth rate of stores due to the prevailing shortage of pharmacists. While Walgreens continued adding stores, the slower rate of growth and a reduction in the growth of inventory allowed the firm to increase its positive cash flows. Notably, 2007 was unusual because of an inflow from working capital and a new bond issue. Without these items it would have been about $812 million. Thus, it is estimated that in 2008 the FCFE will be about $780 million. Such volatility makes it appropriate to use the conservative 13 percent growth rate going forward after 2008. The following example again uses a three-stage growth model with characteristics similar to the dividend growth model except that constant growth will only be 6 percent.

$g_1 = 13$ percent for the five years after 2008
$g_2 = $ a constantly declining growth rate to 6 percent over seven years
$k = 8$ percent cost of equity

The specific estimates of annual FCFE, beginning with the estimated value of $780 million in 2008 are as follows:

	HIGH-GROWTH PERIOD					DECLINING-GROWTH PERIOD			
Year	**Growth Rate**	**$ Million**	**8% PV Factor**	**PV @ 8%**	**Year**	**Growht Rate**	**$ Million**	**8% PV Factor**	**PV@ 8%**
2009	(13%)	881	0.855	753	2014	(12%)	1,609	0.585	941
2010	(13%)	996	0.794	791	2015	(11%)	1,786	0.541	966
2011	(13%)	1,125	0.735	827	2016	(10%)	1,965	0.500	982
2012	(13%)	1,271	0.680	864	2017	(9%)	2,142	0.463	992
2013	(13%)	1,437	0.629	904	2018	(8%)	2,313	0.429	992
					2019	(7%)	2,475	0.397	983
					2020	(6%)	2,624	0.368	966
			Total	$4,139				Total	$6,822

$$\text{Constant Growth Period Value} = \frac{2{,}624(1.06)}{0.08 - 0.06} = \frac{2{,}781}{0.02} = 139{,}050$$

$$\text{PV@8\%} = \$139{,}050 \times 0.368 = \$51{,}170$$

The total value of the stock is the sum of the three present-value streams discounted at 8 percent:

	$Million
1. Present value of high-growth FCFEs	4,139
2. Present value of declining-growth FCFEs	6,822
3. Present value of constant-growth FCFEs	51,170
Total present value of FCFE	62,131

The outstanding shares in 2007 were approximately 1,006 million. Therefore, the per share value, based on the present value of FCFE is $61.76 (62,131/1,006). Again, the estimated value is above the prevailing market price of about $37.00. This estimated value implies a *P/E* ratio of about 28 times estimated 2008 earnings of $2.20 per share.

14.4.4 Present Value of Operating Free Cash Flow

This is also referred to as *free cash flow to the firm* (FCFF) by Damodaran (1994) and *the entity DCF model* by Copeland et al. (2005). The object is to determine a value for the total firm and subtract the value of the firm's debt obligations to arrive at a value for the firm's equity. Notably, in this valuation technique, we discount the firm's operating free cash flow to the firm (FCFF) at the firm's weighted average cost of capital (WACC) rather than its cost of equity.

Operating free cash flow or free cash flow to the firm is equal to

EBIT $(1 - \text{Tax Rate})$ + Depreciation Expense
$- $ Capital Expenditures $- \Delta$ in Working Capital
$- \Delta$ in other assets

This is the cash flow generated by a company's operations and available to all who have provided capital to the firm—both equity and debt. As noted, because it is the cash flow available to *all capital suppliers,* it is discounted at the firm's WACC.

Again, the alternative specifications of this operating FCF model are similar to the DDM—that is, the specification depends upon the firm's growth prospects. Assuming an expectation of constant growth, you can use the reduced form model:

14.7
$$\text{Firm Value} = \frac{\text{FCFF}_1}{\text{WACC} - g_{\text{FCFF}}} \quad \text{or} \quad \frac{\text{OFCF}_1}{\text{WACC} - g_{\text{OFCF}}}$$

where:

FCFF_1 = the free cash flow for the firm in Period 1
OFCF_1 = the firm's operating free cash flow in Period 1
WACC = the firm's weighted average cost of capital
g_{FCFF} = the constant infinite growth rate of free cash flow for the firm
g_{OFCF} = the constant infinite growth rate of operating free cash flow

As noted in Exhibit 14.2, the compound annual growth rate for operating free cash flow (free cash flow to the firm) during the 24-year period was not meaningful because it was negative between 1998 and 2003 and the became very large in 2007 due to a large decline in working capital. Under more normal conditions, it is estimated it will be $700 million during the recession/slowdown in 2008. An alternative measure of long-run growth is the growth implied by the equation:

14.8
$$g = (RR)(ROIC)$$

where:

RR = the average retention rate
$ROIC$ = EBIT (1 − Tax Rate)/Total Capital

For Walgreens, the recent retention rate is about 84 percent and

$$ROIC = \frac{\text{EBIT}(1 - \text{Tax Rate})}{\text{Total Capital}} = \frac{3{,}189 \times (0.64)}{(11{,}376 + 12{,}569)/2} = \frac{2{,}041}{11{,}972} = 0.1705$$

$$= 17.05\%$$

Therefore,

$$g = (0.84)(0.1705)$$
$$= 0.1432 = 14.32\%$$

Given the expensive initiatives planned by Walgreens and the intensive competition from CVS, we will round this down to a beginning growth estimate for OFCF/FCFF of 13 percent.

Calculation of WACC   We calculate the discount rate (i.e., the firm's WACC) using the following formula:

14.9
$$\text{WACC} = W_E k + W_D i$$

where:

W_E = the proportion of equity in total capital
k = the after-tax cost of equity (from the SML)
W_D = the proportion of debt in total capital[4]
i = the after-tax cost of debt[5]

Recall from corporate finance courses that there are differences of opinion regarding how one should estimate the debt and equity weights—that is, using proportions based upon relative book values or based on relative market value weights. Without getting into the reasons for each choice, it is important to recognize that the use of market value weights will almost always

---

[4] The proportions of debt and equity capital used in the WACC estimate will be computed using both book value weights that consider the value of capitalized lease payments as debt, and market value weights.
[5] For this estimate, we use the prevailing interest rate on corporate A-rated bonds (7 percent), and Walgreen Co.'s (ticker symbol WAG) recent tax rate of 36 percent.

result in a higher WACC because it will imply more equity financing since most firms have a *P/BV* ratio greater than one (for Walgreens the *P/BV* ratio is currently in excess of 4.0). To demonstrate this, we compute a WACC using both weightings. The cost of debt and cost of equity will be the same for both sets.

WACC Using Book Value Weights

k_e = 0.080 (from prior SML calculation)

k_d = 0.042 (current interest rate of 7% and recent tax rate of 36% for WAG)
$$0.07 \times (1 - 0.36) = 0.045$$

W_d = 0.30 (including leases)

W_e = 0.70

$$WACC = (W_d \times k_d) + (W_e \times k_e)$$
$$= (0.30 \times 0.045) + (0.70 \times 0.080)$$
$$= 0.013 + 0.056 = 0.069 = 6.90\%$$

WACC Using Market Value Weights

k_e = 0.080 W_e = 0.90

k_d = 0.043 W_d = 0.10

$$WACC = (W_d \times k_d) + (W_e \times k_e)$$
$$= (0.10 \times 0.045) + (0.90 \times 0.080)$$
$$= 0.0045 + 0.072 = 0.0765 = 7.65\%$$

Therefore, we have a range of 6.90 percent to 7.5 percent and an average of 7.28 percent. We will use a WACC of 7.5 percent in the demonstration.

Again, because the expected growth rate of operating free cash flow (13 percent) is greater than the firm's WACC, we cannot use the reduced form model that assumes constant growth at this relatively high rate for an infinite period. Therefore, the following demonstration will employ the three-stage growth model with the following growth duration assumptions.

Given the firm's WACC, we will use the following growth estimates for a three-stage growth model:

g_1 = 13 percent for four years

g_2 = a constantly declining rate to 6 percent over seven years.[6]

The specific estimates for future OFCF (or FCFF) are as follows, beginning from the 2008 value of $700 million.

	HIGH-GROWTH PERIOD					DECLINING-GROWTH PERIOD			
Year	Growth Rate	FCFF	PV Factor @ 7.5%	PV @ 7.5%	Year	Growth Rate	FCFF	PV Factor @ 7.5%	PV @ 7.5%
2008	—	700	—	—	2013	(12%)	1278	0.697	891
2009	(13%)	791	0.930	736	2014	(11%)	1419	0.648	920
2010	(13%)	894	0.865	773	2015	(10%)	1560	0.603	935
2011	(13%)	1010	0.805	813	2016	(9%)	1701	0.561	954
2012	(13%)	1141	0.749	855	2017	(8%)	1837	0.522	959
					2018	(7%)	1966	0.486	955
					2019	(6%)	2083	0.452	942
			Total	3,177				Total	6,556

$$\text{Constant Growth Period Value} = \frac{2,083(1.06)}{0.075 - 0.060} = \frac{2,208}{0.015} = 147,200$$

$$\text{PV @ 7.5\%} = \$147,200 \times 0.452 = 66,534$$

---

[6] This growth rate assumption implies that we do not believe that FCFF can grow as long at 13 percent as FCFE. Given a beginning growth rate of 13 percent for only four years and a long-run rate of 6 percent means that the growth rate will decline by 0.01 per year as shown in the following example.

Thus, the total value of the firm is:

	$ Million
1. Present value of high-growth cash flows	3,177
2. Present value of declining-growth cash flows	6,556
3. Present value of constant-growth cash flows	66,534
Total present value of operating FCF (FCFF)	$76,267

Recall that the value of equity is the total value of the firm (PV of OFCF) minus the current market value of debt, which is the present value of debt payments at the firm's cost of debt (0.07). The values are as follows:

Total present value of operating FCF	$ 76,267
Minus: Value of debt[7]	20,793
Value of equity	$ 55,474
Number of common shares	1,006 million
Value of equity per share	$ 55.14

Again, this estimated value compares to the recent market value of about $37.00. The $55.14 value implies a *P/E* of about 25 times estimated 2008 earnings of $2.20 per share.

To summarize, the valuations derived from the present value of cash flow techniques are as follows:

Present value of dividends	$54.35
Present value of FCFE	$61.76
Present value of OFCF (or the PV of FCFF)	$55.14

All of these prices must be compared to the prevailing market price of $37.00 to determine the investment decision.

14.4.5 Relative Valuation Ratio Techniques

In this section, we present the data required to compute the several relative valuation ratios and demonstrate the use of these relative valuation ratio techniques for Walgreens compared to the Retail Stores (RS) industry and the S&P Industrials Index.

Exhibit 14.3 contains the basic data required to compute the relative valuation ratios, and Exhibit 14.4 contains the four sets of relative valuation ratios for Walgreens, its industry, and the aggregate market. This exhibit also contains a comparison of the company ratios to similar ratios for the company's industry and the market. This comparison indicates the changes in the relative valuation ratios over time and helps determine if the current valuation ratio for the company (Walgreens) is reasonable based on the financial characteristics of the firm versus its industry and the market. To aid in the analysis, four graphs contain the time series of the relative valuation ratios for the company, its industry, and the market. Four additional graphs show the relationship between the relative valuation ratios: for the company compared to its industry and for the company compared to the stock market. We begin with the *P/E* ratio approach where we derive an intrinsic value for the stock based upon an estimate of future EPS and an earnings multiple (*P/E*) for the stock that reflects future expectations for WAG compared to its industry and the market.

14.5 Estimating Company Earnings per Share

An estimate of the earnings per share for the company is a function of the sales forecast and the estimated profit margin. The sales forecast includes an analysis of the relationship of company sales to various relevant economic series and to the RS industry series. These comparisons indicate how the company is performing relative to the economy and its competition.

[7] This long-term debt value from Chapter 10 includes the present value of minimum lease payments discounted at the firm's cost of debt (7 percent).

Exhibit 14.3 Inputs for Relative Valuation Technique: Walgreens, Retail Stores Industry and the S&P Industrials Index: 1993–2006

Year	Walgreens					Retail Stores Industry					S&P Industrials Index				
	Mean Price	EPS	Cash Flow P/S	Book Value P/S	Net Sales P/S	Mean Price	EPS	Cash Flow P/S	Book Value P/S	Net Sales P/S	Mean Price	EPS	Cash Flow P/S	Book Value P/S	Net Sales P/S
1993	4.41	0.22	0.31	1.39	8.38	115.94	5.45	8.21	37.18	173.89	520.21	31.02	58.00	198.18	622.12
1994	4.48	0.29	0.36	1.59	9.34	109.67	6.20	9.26	40.53	197.21	536.52	36.64	72.39	217.11	653.75
1995	5.85	0.33	0.35	1.81	10.50	108.85	5.06	8.84	43.25	208.15	638.97	43.36	79.27	232.08	706.13
1996	8.09	0.38	0.41	2.06	11.85	117.46	6.67	10.94	46.75	232.82	795.01	41.69	82.89	242.82	727.40
1997	12.02	0.44	0.65	2.38	13.41	152.50	7.56	12.36	51.66	251.33	1006.12	44.43	83.73	253.14	750.71
1998	19.94	0.52	0.58	2.87	15.43	230.78	9.52	14.76	53.34	276.12	1285.73	36.96	87.38	271.52	750.48
1999	26.13	0.62	0.62	3.48	17.83	335.22	10.92	16.93	60.72	302.62	1651.82	46.28	97.73	309.45	812.00
2000	31.37	0.77	0.96	4.20	21.05	320.07	9.44	15.97	65.48	329.76	1692.85	53.56	105.09	343.95	853.86
2001	35.94	0.87	0.71	5.12	24.23	301.48	9.04	16.29	70.54	352.27	1363.30	37.41	68.58	343.27	811.04
2002	34.25	1.00	1.44	6.09	28.05	309.90	13.21	20.21	77.76	355.62	1133.05	56.51	61.59	314.38	781.65
2003	30.87	1.15	1.46	7.02	31.72	317.61	19.29	28.40	116.53	383.89	1097.27	49.52	90.88	367.97	847.38
2004	34.92	1.33	1.61	8.03	36.61	413.38	20.58	31.16	124.72	444.61	1294.47	65.22	104.76	417.05	944.36
2005	44.05	1.53	1.34	8.72	41.39	443.58	24.68	36.07	139.37	476.54	1375.37	72.41	121.36	449.30	1043.61
2006	43.84	1.73	2.41	10.01	46.93	464.24	28.15	41.21	159.16	580.68	1492.05	79.11	134.17	499.46	1123.34
10 yr Growth Rate	18.40%	16.52%	19.29%	17.15%	14.75%	14.73%	15.49%	14.18%	13.03%	9.57%	6.50%	6.61%	4.93%	7.48%	4.44%

Exhibit 14.4 Relative Valuation Variables: Walgreens, Retail Store Industry, and S&P Industrials Index: 1993–2006

Price/Earnings Ratio

Year	Walgreens	Retail Store	Ratio Co/Ind.	S&P Ind.	Ratio Co/Mkt
1993	19.70	21.27	0.93	16.77	1.17
1994	15.71	17.69	0.89	14.64	1.07
1995	18.00	21.51	0.84	14.74	1.22
1996	21.59	17.61	1.23	19.07	1.13
1997	27.32	20.17	1.35	22.65	1.21
1998	38.71	24.24	1.60	34.78	1.11
1999	42.15	30.70	1.37	35.69	1.18
2000	40.74	33.91	1.20	31.61	1.29
2001	41.31	33.35	1.24	36.44	1.13
2002	34.25	23.46	1.46	20.05	1.71
2003	26.85	16.47	1.63	22.16	1.21
2004	26.25	20.09	1.31	19.85	1.32
2005	28.79	17.97	1.60	19.00	1.52
2006	25.34	16.49	1.54	18.86	1.34
Mean	29.05	22.49	1.30	23.31	1.26

Price/Cash Flow Ratio

Year	Walgreens	Retail Store	Ratio Co/Ind.	S&P Ind.	Ratio Co/Mkt
1993	14.24	14.12	1.01	8.97	1.59
1994	12.46	11.84	1.05	7.41	1.68
1995	16.79	12.31	1.36	8.06	2.08
1996	19.56	10.74	1.82	9.59	2.04
1997	18.43	12.34	1.49	12.02	1.53
1998	34.64	15.64	2.22	14.71	2.35
1999	41.81	19.80	2.11	16.90	2.47
2000	32.52	20.04	1.62	16.11	2.02
2001	50.79	18.51	2.74	19.88	2.55
2002	23.77	15.33	1.55	18.40	1.29
2003	21.22	11.18	1.90	12.07	1.76
2004	21.64	13.27	1.63	12.36	1.75
2005	32.76	12.30	2.66	11.33	2.89
2006	18.16	11.27	1.61	11.12	1.63
Mean	25.63	14.19	1.77	12.78	1.98

Price/Book Value Ratio

Year	Walgreens	Retail Store	Ratio Co/Ind.	S&P Ind.	Ratio Co/Mkt
1993	3.17	3.12	1.02	2.62	1.21
1994	2.81	2.71	1.04	2.47	1.14
1995	3.23	2.52	1.28	2.75	1.17
1996	3.94	2.51	1.57	3.27	1.20
1997	5.05	2.95	1.71	3.97	1.27
1998	6.94	4.33	1.60	4.74	1.47
1999	7.50	5.52	1.36	5.34	1.41
2000	7.46	4.89	1.53	4.92	1.52
2001	7.01	4.27	1.64	3.97	1.77
2002	5.62	3.99	1.41	3.60	1.56
2003	4.40	2.73	1.61	2.98	1.47
2004	4.35	3.31	1.31	3.10	1.40
2005	5.05	3.18	1.59	3.06	1.65
2006	4.38	2.92	1.50	2.99	1.47
Mean	5.07	3.50	1.44	3.56	1.41

Price/Sales Ratio

Year	Walgreens	Retail Store	Ratio Co/Ind.	S&P Ind.	Ratio Co/Mkt
1993	0.53	0.67	0.79	0.84	0.63
1994	0.48	0.56	0.86	0.82	0.58
1995	0.56	0.52	1.07	0.90	0.62
1996	0.68	0.50	1.35	1.09	0.62
1997	0.90	0.61	1.48	1.34	0.67
1998	1.29	0.84	1.55	1.71	0.75
1999	1.47	1.11	1.32	2.03	0.72
2000	1.49	0.97	1.54	1.98	0.75
2001	1.48	0.86	1.73	1.68	0.88
2002	1.22	0.87	1.40	1.45	0.84
2003	0.97	0.83	1.18	1.29	0.75
2004	0.95	0.93	1.03	1.37	0.70
2005	1.06	0.93	1.14	1.32	0.81
2006	0.93	0.80	1.17	1.33	0.70
Mean	1.00	0.78	1.26	1.37	0.72

14.5.1 Company Sales Forecast

Besides providing background on the company, these relationships can help us develop specific sales forecasts for Walgreens.

Exhibit 14.5 contains data on sales for Walgreens from its annual report, sales per share for the RS industry, and several personal consumption expenditure (PCE) series for the period 1993 to 2006.

To examine the relationship of Walgreen Co.'s sales to the economy, we considered several alternative series. The series that had the strongest relationship was personal consumption expenditure for medicine (PCE medical care).[8] The scatterplot of Walgreen Co.'s sales and the PCE medical care expenditures contained in Exhibit 14.6 indicates a strong linear relationship, including the fact that Walgreen Co.'s sales grew faster than PCE medical care (i.e., 14.94 percent versus 6.66 percent). As a result, Walgreen Co.'s sales have gone from about 1.2 percent of PCE medical care to 3.0 percent.

We also compared Walgreen Co.'s sales and sales per share for the RS industry. Unfortunately, it did not reflect as strong a relationship and is not used subsequently.

The figures in the last column of Exhibit 14.5 indicate that during this period, the proportion of PCE allocated to medical care went from almost 16 percent in 1993 to 17.2 percent in 2006. The increasing proportion of PCE spent on medical care is a function of the growing proportion of the population over 65 and the rising cost of medical care. Because Walgreen Co.'s sales are growing faster than medical expenditures, these increases should continue to be beneficial for Walgreens because about 65 percent of its sales are prescriptions. Notably, these increases in medical care expenditures continued during the economic recession in 2001–2002.

As shown in Exhibit 14.7, the internal sales growth for Walgreens going back to 1977, resulted from an increase in the number of stores (from 626 in 1977 to 5,997 in 2007) and an annual increase in the sales per store of 5 percent because of the upgrading of stores. The net increase in stores each year includes numerous new, large stores and the closing of many smaller stores. As a result, the average size of stores has increased. More important, the firm has continued to increase its sales per thousand square feet at over 4 percent a year. This is a

Exhibit 14.5 Walgreens, S&P Retail Drugstore Sales, and Various Economic Series: 1993–2006

Year	Sales Walgreens ($ millions)	Retail Sales ($/Share)	Personal Consumption Expenditures ($ Billions)	PCE Medical Care ($ Billions)	Medical Care as a Percentage of PCE
1993	8,295	173.89	4,477.90	715.1	15.97%
1994	9,235	197.21	4,743.30	752.9	15.87%
1995	10,395	208.15	4,975.80	797.9	16.04%
1996	11,778	232.82	5,256.80	833.5	15.86%
1997	13,363	251.33	5,547.40	873.0	15.74%
1998	15,307	276.12	5,879.50	921.4	15.67%
1999	17,839	302.62	6,282.50	961.1	15.30%
2000	21,207	329.76	6,739.40	1,026.8	15.24%
2001	24,623	352.27	7,055.00	1,113.8	15.79%
2002	28,681	355.62	7,350.70	1,206.2	16.41%
2003	32,505	383.89	7,703.60	1,300.5	16.88%
2004	37,508	444.61	8,195.90	1,395.5	17.03%
2005	42,202	476.54	8,707.80	1,492.6	17.14%
2006	47,409	580.68	9,224.50	1,587.7	17.21%
10 yr Growth Rate	14.94%	9.57%	5.78%	6.66%	0.82%

[8] The relationship between Walgreen Co.'s sales and total PCE or per capital PCE was significant but not as strong as PCE medical care.

Exhibit 14.6 Scatter Plot of Walgreen Co.'s Sales and PCE Medical Care: 1993–2006

PCE Medical Care ($ Billions)	Sales Walgreens ($ millions)
715.1	8,295
752.9	9,235
797.9	10,395
833.5	11,778
873.0	13,363
921.4	15,307
961.1	17,839
1,026.8	21,207
1,113.8	24,623
1,206.2	28,681
1,300.5	32,505
1,395.5	37,508
1,492.6	42,202
1,587.7	47,409

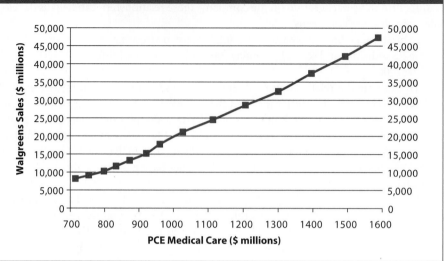

Exhibit 14.7 Sales, Number of Stores, and Sales Area for Walgreens: 1997–2007

Year	Sales Walgreens ($ millions)	Number of Stores	Annual Sales per Store ($ Millions)	Total Store Area (000 Sq. Ft.)	Area per Store (000 Sq. Ft.)	Avg. Sales per Thousand Sq. Ft.
1977	1,223.2	626	1.95	5,188	8.29	235.77
1978	1,192.9	641	1.86	5,390	8.41	221.32
1979	1,334.5	688	1.94	5,851	8.50	228.08
1980	1,530.7	739	2.07	6,305	8.53	242.78
1981	1,743.5	821	2.12	7,209	8.78	241.85
1982	2,039.5	883	2.31	7,815	8.85	260.97
1983	2,360.6	941	2.51	8,402	8.93	280.96
1984	2,744.6	1,002	2.74	9,002	8.98	304.89
1985	3,161.9	1,095	2.89	10,010	9.14	315.87
1986	3,660.6	1,273	2.88	11,895	9.34	307.74
1987	4,281.6	1,356	3.16	12,844	9.47	333.35
1988	4,883.5	1,416	3.45	13,549	9.57	360.43
1989	5,380.1	1,484	3.63	14,272	9.62	376.97
1990	6,047.5	1,564	3.87	15,105	9.66	400.36
1991	6,733.0	1,646	4.09	15,877	9.65	424.07
1992	7,475.0	1,736	4.31	16,811	9.68	444.65
1993	8,294.8	1,836	4.52	17,950	9.78	462.11
1994	9,235.0	1,968	4.69	19,342	9.83	477.46
1995	10,395.1	2,085	4.99	20,731	9.94	501.43
1996	11,778.4	2,193	5.37	22,124	10.09	532.38
1997	13,363.0	2,358	5.67	23,935	10.15	558.30
1998	15,307.0	2,549	6.01	26,024	10.21	588.19
1999	17,838.8	2,821	6.32	29,230	10.36	610.29
2000	21,206.9	3,165	6.70	33,684	10.64	629.58
2001	24,623.0	3,520	7.00	38,226	10.86	644.14
2002	28,681.1	3,883	7.39	42,672	10.99	672.13
2003	32,505.4	4,252	7.64	46,733	10.99	695.56
2004	37,508.2	4,613	8.13	50,926	11.04	736.52
2005	42,201.6	4,985	8.47	55,385	11.11	761.97
2006	47,409.0	5,461	8.68	60,795	11.13	779.82
2007	53,762.0	5,997	8.96	66,386	11.07	809.84
Average Annual rate of growth (%)	12.98%	7.56%	5.04%	8.57%	0.94%	4.06%

critical statistic in the retailing industry. The fact that Walgreens has been able to experience consistent growth in this metric is significant evidence of strong management.

Sample Estimate of Walgreen Co.'s Sales   The foregoing analysis indicates that you should use the Walgreens–PCE medical care graph. To estimate PCE medical care, you need to initially project total PCE and then estimate how much would be included in the medical care component. As noted in Chapter 13 (industry analysis), for 2008 economists were forecasting an increase in PCE of only 4.5 percent to $10,163 billion due to the recession. In addition, we estimated that the percentage of PCE spent on medical care at about 17.4 percent. This implies an estimate for PCE medical care of $1,768 billion, a 5.0 percent increase from 2007. In turn, Exhibit 14.6, which shows the historical relationship between PCE medical care and Walgreen Co.'s sales, implies an 11 percent increase in Walgreens sales to about $59.68 billion (53.76 × 1.11).

Because Walgreens provides data on square footage and the number of stores, it allows us to use the data in Exhibit 14.7 to compute alternative sales estimates to support the prior estimate. If we assume an increase in store area during 2008 of about 5 million square feet (which is less than in recent years), the firm's total sales area would be about 71.4 million square feet. As noted, sales per square foot have likewise increased. Assuming a conservative increase to $830 of sales per thousand square feet implies a sales forecast of $59.26 billion for 2008, an 11 percent increase over 2007 sales of $53.76 billion.

Another internal estimate employs the number of stores and sales per store. Walgreens is expected to open 560 stores during 2008 and close 75 stores, which implies a net addition of 485 stores, resulting in 6,482 stores at the end of 2008. Assuming sales per store likewise continue to increase from $8.96 million to $9.10 million indicates an estimate of $59.0 billion (6,482 × $9.10), an increase of 11 percent over 2007.

Therefore, the three estimates were:

PCE Medical Care	$59.68 billion
Sales per Square Foot	$59.26 billion
Sales per Store	$59.00 billion

Given the three estimates, the preference is for the low estimate of $59 billion. We use the conservative estimate because of the growing consensus that the U.S. economy will experience a recession in 2008.

14.5.2 Estimating the Company Profit Margin

The next step in projecting earnings per share is to estimate the firm's net profit margin, which should include three considerations: (1) identification and evaluation of the firm's specific competitive strategy—that is, either low-cost or differentiation; (2) the firm's internal performance, including general company trends and consideration of any problems that might affect its future performance; and (3) the firm's relationship with its industry, which should indicate whether the company's past performance is attributable to its industry or if it is unique to the firm. These examinations should help us understand the firm's past performance but should also provide the background to make a meaningful estimate for the future. In this analysis, we only consider the company-economy relationship briefly because the significant economywide profit factors are reflected in the industry results.

14.6 Walgreen Co.'s Competitive Strategies

Over the years, has Walgreens pursued a low-cost strategy or has the firm attempted to differentiate itself from its competitors in some unique way? Based on its annual reports, Walgreens has pursued both strategies with different segments of its business. The firm's size and buying power allow it to be a cost leader for some of its nonprescription products, such as liquor, ice cream, candy, and soft drinks. These items are advertised heavily to attract customer traffic and to build consumer loyalty. At the same time, Walgreens has attempted to build a very strong franchise in the medical prescription business based on differentiation in service. Computer technology in the prescription area makes it possible for the firm to distinguish itself by providing outstanding service to its prescription customers. Specifically, the firm refers to itself as the nation's prescription druggist based on the number of prescriptions it fills and a nationwide computer system that allows customers to have their prescriptions filled at any of the 5,997 Walgreen Co.'s drugstores in the country. This service leadership in the growing medical field is a major goal.

14.6.1 The Internal Performance

Profit margin figures for Walgreens and the RS industry are in Exhibit 14.8. The net profit margins for Walgreens increased from 2.67 percent to 3.69 percent. The margins for the RS industry likewise experienced an overall increase. To predict future values, you need to determine the reasons for the increase in the industry profit margin and, more important, what factors have contributed to Walgreen Co.'s strong positive performance.

Industry Factors Industry profit margins were relatively flat in the late 1990s due to price discounting by aggressive regional drug chains.[9] The discussion in Chapter 13 suggested this as one of the competitive structure conditions that affect long-run profitability. On a positive note, industry analysts have observed that price cutting has subsided, and they foresee relative price stability following a period of consolidation in which CVS has acquired several of the smaller, less profitable chains. In addition, drugstores have tended toward a more profitable product mix featuring high-profit-margin items, such as cosmetics. This has had a positive influence on profit margins.

Company Performance The Walgreen Co.'s profit margin has shown consistent improvement because of a change in corporate structure and sales mix. The outlook for profit margins is good because the firm has developed a strong position in the pharmacy business and has invested in service (including mail-order prescriptions) and inventory-control technology that will help the firm experience strong margins on this business. The firm also has emphasized high-profit-margin items, such as greeting cards, photofinishing, and cosmetics.

Specific estimates for Walgreen Co.'s future margins typically would begin with an analysis of the firm's relationship with retail store margins using time-series plots, such as those in Exhibit 14.9.[10] This time-series plot for the period 1993–2006 showed inconsistent results for Walgreens versus its industry. While Walgreens showed a slow but steady increase in its margin, the retail stores margin was very volatile with a sharp decline in 2000–2001 followed by a spectacular increase in 2002–2003. It is unclear if this was due to a change in the index sample. In any case, it is clear that one cannot depend on this relationship.

Following the analysis of the company-industry profit margin relationship, you should analyze the firm's common-size income statement for the period 2004–2007 contained in Exhibit 14.10. An analysis of the main items of interest—cost of goods sold and SG&A expense—was encouraging. The cost-of-sales percentage declined slightly more than 1 percent while there was almost a matching increase in the percentage of SG&A expense. As a result, the operating profit margin experienced a minimal increase from 5.71 percent to 5.86 percent. Finally, the tax rate declined from almost 38 percent to 36 percent in 2007.

Net Profit Margin Estimate The overall industry outlook is encouraging because of stable prices, an increase in mechanization within the industry, and the inclusion of more

[9] For a more complete discussion, see "Retail Stores" in *Standard & Poor's Industry Surveys* (New York: Standard & Poor's, 2007).
[10] Both the operating margin and the net before tax margin were analyzed; the results indicated that the net profit margins yielded the best relationships.

Exhibit 14.8 Profit Margins and Component Expenses for Walgreens, the Retail Store Industry, and the S&P Industrials: 1993–2006

Year	Walgreen Co.			Retail Drugstores			S&P Industrials		
	Operating Margin (%)	NBT Margin (%)	Net Profit Margin (%)	Operating Margin (%)	NBT Margin (%)	Net Profit Margin (%)	Operating Margin (%)	NBT Margin (%)	Net Profit Margin (%)
1993	4.90	4.82	2.67	5.00	4.70	3.13	9.10	6.95	4.99
1994	4.93	4.96	3.05	5.46	4.88	3.14	10.64	8.38	5.60
1995	5.00	5.04	3.09	5.40	4.00	2.43	11.18	8.94	6.14
1996	5.13	5.15	3.16	5.82	4.61	2.86	11.14	9.13	5.73
1997	5.30	5.33	3.26	5.91	4.87	3.01	11.21	9.36	5.92
1998	5.46	5.73	3.34	6.25	5.42	3.45	10.84	8.86	4.93
1999	5.69	5.76	3.50	6.82	5.85	3.61	11.44	9.51	5.70
2000	5.77	5.96	3.66	6.11	4.73	2.86	12.02	9.96	6.27
2001	5.68	5.78	3.60	5.89	4.34	2.57	9.45	7.42	4.61
2002	5.66	5.71	3.55	6.71	5.89	3.71	10.46	8.51	7.23
2003	5.69	5.81	3.62	8.19	7.95	5.02	11.02	9.07	5.84
2004	5.71	5.80	3.63	7.83	7.26	4.63	11.83	10.04	6.91
2005	5.74	5.82	3.70	8.65	8.03	5.18	12.16	10.30	6.94
2006	5.70	5.81	3.69	8.48	7.69	4.85	12.58	10.62	7.04

Exhibit 14.9 Time-Series Plot of Net Profit Margin for Walgreens and the Retail Store Industry: 1993–2006

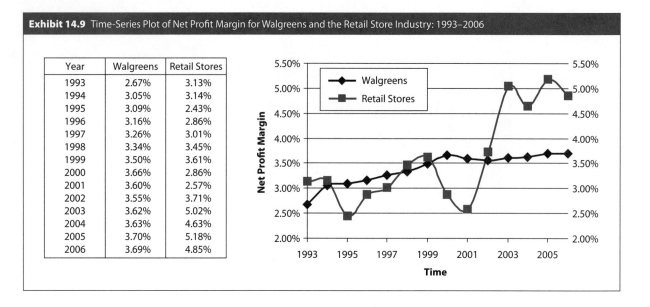

Year	Walgreens	Retail Stores
1993	2.67%	3.13%
1994	3.05%	3.14%
1995	3.09%	2.43%
1996	3.16%	2.86%
1997	3.26%	3.01%
1998	3.34%	3.45%
1999	3.50%	3.61%
2000	3.66%	2.86%
2001	3.60%	2.57%
2002	3.55%	3.71%
2003	3.62%	5.02%
2004	3.63%	4.63%
2005	3.70%	5.18%
2006	3.69%	4.85%

high-profit- margin items. Although Walgreen has experienced small increases in its margin as shown in Exhibit 14.10, it is estimated that the firm will experience a slight decline in 2008 to 3.75 percent (from 3.80 percent in 2007) due to the economic recession and the cost of several new programs intended to help it become a broad health care provider as discussed by Merrick (2008).

Computing Earnings per Share This margin estimate, combined with the prior sales estimate of $59 billion, indicates net income of $2,213 million. Assuming about 1,006 million common shares outstanding, earnings should be about $2.20 per share for 2008, which is an increase of almost 8 percent over the earnings of $2.04 per share in 2007. This is considered a fairly conservative estimate because we used our low estimate of sales, assumed a decline in the profit margin, and employed current shares outstanding although the firm has been repurchasing shares in recent years.

Our next step is to estimate an earnings multiplier for Walgreens.

14.6.2 Importance of Quarterly Estimates

Once we have derived an estimate of next year's sales and net earnings, it is essential that we also derive an estimate of each of the quarterly results for two important reasons. First, this is a way to confirm our annual estimate—that is, do the quarterly estimates required to arrive at the annual estimate seem reasonable? If not, we need to reevaluate the annual forecast. Second, unless we have quarterly forecasts that confirm our annual forecast, we will not be in a position to determine whether the subsequent *actual* quarterly results are a positive surprise, negative surprise, or no surprise. Further, if the actual quarterly results are a surprise relative to our estimate, we will want to understand the reason for the surprise—for example, did we under- or overestimate sales growth and/or was it due to differences in the profit margin from our estimates? This understanding is needed for an estimated *earnings revision* that reflects the new information from the company. Typically, an analyst would revise each of his or her future quarterly estimates to arrive at a new annual estimate.

14.7 Estimating Company Earnings Multipliers

As in our analysis of industry multipliers in Chapter 13, we use two approaches to estimate a company multiplier. First, we estimate the *P/E* ratio from the relationships between Walgreens,

Exhibit 14.10 Walgreen Co. and Subsidiaries Consolidated Statement of Income (Dollars in Millions, Except per Share Data): Years Ended August 31, 2004, 2005, 2006, and 2007

	2007		2006		2005		2004	
Net sales	53,762,000	100.00%	47,409,000	100.00%	42,201,600	100.00%	37,508,200	100.00%
Cost of sales	38,518,100	71.65%	34,240,400	72.22%	30,413,800	72.07%	27,310,400	72.81%
Gross profit	15,243,900	28.35%	13,168,600	27.78%	11,787,800	27.93%	10,197,800	27.19%
Selling, occupancy & administration expense	12,093,200	22.49%	10,467,100	22.08%	9,363,800	22.19%	8,055,100	21.48%
Operating Profit (EBIT)	3,150,700	5.86%	2,701,500	5.70%	2,424,000	5.74%	2,142,700	5.71%
Interest income	38,400	0.07%	52,600	0.11%	31,600	0.07%	17,300	0.05%
Interest expense	0	0.00%	0	0.00%	0	0.00%	0	0.00%
Other Income	0	0.00%	0	0.00%	0	0.00%	16,300	0.04%
Operating income before taxes (EBT)	3,189,100	5.93%	2,754,100	5.81%	2,455,600	5.82%	2,176,300	5.80%
Provisions for taxes	1,147,800	2.13%	1,003,500	2.12%	896,100	2.12%	816,100	2.18%
Reported net income	2,041,300	3.80%	1,750,600	3.69%	1,559,500	3.70%	1,360,200	3.63%
Reported net income available for common shares	2,041,300	3.80%	1,750,600	3.69%	1,559,500	3.70%	1,360,200	3.63%

its industry, and the market. This is the macroanalysis. Second, we estimate a multiplier based on its three components: the dividend-payout ratio, the required rate of return, and the rate of growth. We then resolve the estimates derived from each approach and settle on a set of estimates.

14.7.1 Macroanalysis of the Earnings Multiple

Exhibit 14.11 shows the mean future earnings multiple for the company, the RS industry, and the aggregate market for the period 1993–2006. As shown in Exhibit 14.4, the Walgreen Co.'s multiplier has generally followed the industry multipliers with a company/industry ratio between 0.84 and 1.63, an average of 1.30 but recent values closer to 1.50. The Walgreen Co.'s earnings multiplier has always been higher than the market multiplier by an average of 26 percent.

This pattern raises the question: Are the higher P/E ratios for Walgreens relative to both its industry and the market justified? The microanalyses should provide some insights regarding this question.

14.7.2 Microanalysis of the Earnings Multiplier

Again, the relevant question is, Why has the earnings multiplier for Walgreens been higher than for the market and industry? As before, we are looking for estimates of D/E, k, and g to find an earnings multiplier. We will use the historical data in Exhibit 14.12 to determine patterns for the data and to develop future projections.[11]

Comparing Dividend-Payout Ratios The dividend-payout ratio for Walgreens typically has been lower than its industry and the aggregate market in recent years. This consistent lower payout by itself would imply a lower P/E ratio for Walgreens than for its industry and the market.

Estimating the Required Rate of Return To find Walgreen Co.'s required rate of return (k), we recall the analysis of the firm's fundamental risk characteristics (BR, FR, LR, ERR, and CR) and also our estimate based on Walgreen Co.'s systematic risk (i.e., its beta).

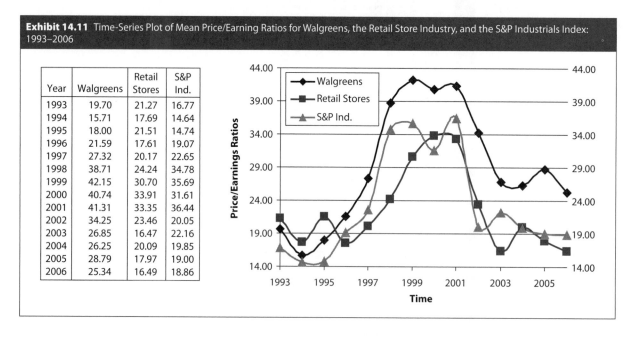

Exhibit 14.11 Time-Series Plot of Mean Price/Earning Ratios for Walgreens, the Retail Store Industry, and the S&P Industrials Index: 1993–2006

Year	Walgreens	Retail Stores	S&P Ind.
1993	19.70	21.27	16.77
1994	15.71	17.69	14.64
1995	18.00	21.51	14.74
1996	21.59	17.61	19.07
1997	27.32	20.17	22.65
1998	38.71	24.24	34.78
1999	42.15	30.70	35.69
2000	40.74	33.91	31.61
2001	41.31	33.35	36.44
2002	34.25	23.46	20.05
2003	26.85	16.47	22.16
2004	26.25	20.09	19.85
2005	28.79	17.97	19.00
2006	25.34	16.49	18.86

[11] Although some prior tables included data through 2007 using estimates for specific ratios, it is not possible to do this for industry and market variables in Exhibit 14.12 as of mid-2008.

Exhibit 14.12 Variables that Influence the Earnings Multiplier for Walgreens, the Retail Store Industry, and the S&P Industrials: 1993–2006

Year	Walgreens						Retail Stores						S&P Industrials					
	D/E	NPM	TAT	ROA	TAE	ROE	D/E	NPM	TAT	ROA	TAE	ROE	D/E	NPM	TAT	ROA	TAE	ROE
1993	33.52	2.67	3.27	8.74	1.84	16.08	28.26	3.13	1.32	4.07	3.35	13.86	52.04	4.99	0.87	3.27	3.59	15.65
1994	30.87	3.05	3.17	9.69	1.85	17.92	28.87	3.14	1.44	4.35	3.34	14.70	42.49	5.60	0.89	4.91	3.37	16.88
1995	31.75	3.09	3.20	9.86	1.81	17.90	32.09	2.43	1.58	4.08	2.76	11.43	38.05	6.14	0.94	5.19	3.25	18.68
1996	32.61	3.16	3.24	10.23	1.78	18.20	22.52	2.86	1.83	5.02	2.77	14.04	40.70	5.73	0.95	5.62	3.14	17.17
1997	31.24	3.26	3.18	10.36	1.77	18.37	21.80	3.01	1.85	5.38	2.70	14.60	39.12	5.92	0.95	5.33	3.14	17.55
1998	24.27	3.34	3.12	10.42	1.72	17.94	16.76	3.45	1.96	6.66	2.66	17.86	49.37	4.93	0.88	4.9	3.16	13.61
1999	20.85	3.50	3.02	10.57	1.70	17.91	16.30	3.61	2.02	6.91	2.60	18.07	39.02	5.70	0.84	5.22	3.11	14.96
2000	17.52	3.66	2.99	10.94	1.68	18.35	17.57	2.86	2.02	5.60	2.57	14.46	31.46	6.27	0.86	5.45	2.89	15.57
2001	16.09	3.60	2.79	10.03	1.70	17.01	17.32	2.57	2.00	4.92	2.61	12.86	44.40	4.61	0.79	1.79	3.00	10.90
2002	14.56	3.55	2.90	10.32	1.59	16.36	13.85	3.71	1.88	6.81	2.46	16.83	28.40	7.23	0.76	1.92	3.26	17.98
2003	13.57	3.62	2.85	10.31	1.59	16.34	14.88	5.02	1.67	7.27	2.23	16.22	35.48	5.84	0.76	4.29	3.02	13.46
2004	13.70	3.63	2.81	10.19	1.62	16.53	14.35	4.63	1.66	7.61	1.99	15.17	37.00	6.91	0.80	5.09	2.84	15.64
2005	20.19	3.70	2.89	10.68	1.64	17.54	16.34	5.18	1.70	8.53	2.15	18.34	30.05	6.94	0.84	6.06	2.77	16.12
2006	15.72	3.69	2.77	10.22	1.69	17.31	16.58	4.85	1.83	8.15	2.09	17.06	31.48	7.04	0.85	6.47	2.64	15.84
mean	22.60	3.39	3.01	10.18	1.71	17.41	19.82	3.60	1.77	6.10	2.59	15.39	38.50	5.99	0.86	4.68	3.08	15.71

Walgreens should have relatively low business risk due to its stable sales growth compared to its industry and the economy. As noted in Chapter 10, for a growth company like Walgreens it is necessary to adjust for both the growth and size factor by measuring variability around the growth trend and relating this volatility to the mean as in Exhibit 14.13. As shown in the appendix in Chapter 10, after adjusting for size and trend, the results indicated that Walgreen Co.'s sales and EBIT experienced *very stable growth*, which indicates low business risk.

Several financial risk variables for Walgreens, its industry, and the aggregate market are shown in Exhibit 14.14. Notably, except for Walgreens interest coverage these do not consider fairly large leases of stores. Without considering these financial leases, these financial risk ratios indicate that Walgreens has comparable financial risk to its industry and substantially lower financial risk than the aggregate stock market. In contrast, as shown in Chapter 10, when the leases are considered as they should be, the firm's financial risk is probably comparable to its industry where most firms lease their stroes, but it is somewhat higher than the market.

The firm's liquidity risk is low compared to its industry and the average firm in the market. Indicators of market liquidity are (1) the number of stockholders, (2) the number and market value of shares outstanding, (3) the number of shares traded, and (4) institutional interest in the stock. As of January 1, 2008, Walgreen had 30,000 holders of common stock—a relatively large number. At mid-2008, there were over 1 billion common shares outstanding with a market value of almost $40 billion. Clearly, Walgreens would qualify as an investment for institutions that require firms with large market value. Walgreen Co.'s stock has an annual trading turnover of about 80 percent, which is a little below average. Financial institutions own about 460 million shares of Walgreens, which is about 45 percent of the outstanding shares. Therefore, Walgreen Co.'s large number of stockholders, very large market capitalization, fairly active trading of its stock, and strong institutional interest indicate that Walgreens has very little liquidity risk.

The exchange rate risk for companies depends on what proportion of sales and earnings are generated outside the United States and the volatility of the exchange rates in the specific countries. Walgreens has very little exchange rate risk or country risk because the firm has virtually no non-U.S. sales.

In summary, Walgreens has below-average business risk, above average financial risk when we consider leases, low market liquidity risk, and virtually no exchange rate and country risk. This implies that the overall fundamental risk for Walgreens should be lower than the market.

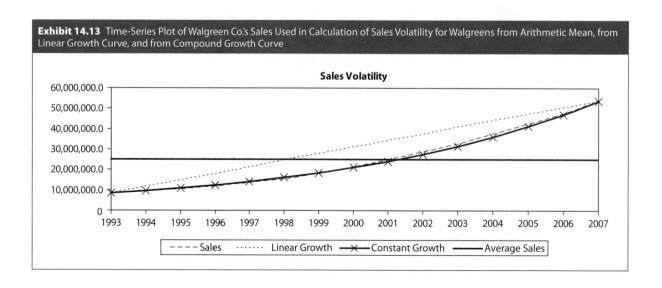

Exhibit 14.13 Time-Series Plot of Walgreen Co.'s Sales Used in Calculation of Sales Volatility for Walgreens from Arithmetic Mean, from Linear Growth Curve, and from Compound Growth Curve

Exhibit 14.14 Financial Risk Ratios for Walgreens, the Retail Store Industry, and the S&P Industrials: 1993–2006

	Walgreens				Retail Stores				S&P Industrials			
Year	Total Assets / Equity	Interest Coverage*	Cash Flow / Long-Term Debt	Cash Flow / Total Debt	Total Assets / Equity	Interest Coverage	Cash Flow / Long-Term Debt	Cash Flow / Total Debt	Total Assets / Equity	Interest Coverage	Cash Flow / Long-Term Debt	Cash Flow / Total Debt
1993	1.84	4.88	0.287	0.226	3.35	3.58	0.348	0.255	3.59	4.37	0.362	0.223
1994	1.85	4.61	0.265	0.222	3.34	5.67	0.241	0.176	3.37	4.89	0.496	0.332
1995	1.81	4.56	0.226	0.189	2.76	4.00	0.220	0.165	3.25	5.24	0.312	0.208
1996	1.78	4.54	0.235	0.197	2.77	4.50	0.346	0.268	3.14	5.84	0.505	0.338
1997	1.77	4.67	0.357	0.300	2.70	5.72	0.373	0.298	3.14	6.40	0.438	0.287
1998	1.72	4.12	0.230	0.197	2.66	5.77	0.599	0.499	3.16	5.74	0.406	0.270
1999	1.70	4.02	0.201	0.173	2.60	7.48	0.490	0.395	3.11	6.25	0.250	0.166
2000	1.68	3.74	0.240	0.208	2.57	6.52	0.437	0.340	2.89	6.19	0.348	0.233
2001	1.70	3.65	0.152	0.131	2.61	6.53	0.355	0.299	3.00	4.88	0.219	0.157
2002	1.59	3.59	0.262	0.228	2.46	8.78	0.397	0.324	3.26	5.75	0.354	0.270
2003	1.59	3.22	0.211	0.182	2.23	9.44	0.768	0.624	3.02	6.06	0.235	0.180
2004	1.62	3.26	0.203	0.176	1.99	12.79	0.658	0.556	2.84	7.25	0.274	0.205
2005	1.64	3.32	0.150	0.132	2.15	15.49	0.934	0.808	2.77	7.20	0.367	0.270
2006	1.69	3.37	0.242	0.213	2.09	15.10	0.676	0.595	2.64	7.08	0.518	0.393

*Includes implied interest expense from capitalized leases.

Analysts should also consider market-determined risk (beta) based on the CAPM. As noted in connection with the cash flow models, the stock's beta derived from five years of monthly data relative to the S&P Industrials for the period 2003–2007 was 0.90.

These results are consistent with those derived from an analysis of the fundamental factors—both indicate that Walgreen Co.'s risk is below the aggregate market. This means that the required rate of return *(k)* of 8 percent for Walgreen Co.'s stock estimated earlier using the CAPM is reasonable. By itself, this lower *k* would suggest an earnings multiplier above the market multiplier.

Estimating the Expected Growth Rate Recall that the expected growth rate *(g)* is determined by the firm's retention rate and its expected return on equity *(ROE)*. We have already noted Walgreen Co.'s dividend payout is similar to its industry and clearly lower than the aggregate market, which implies a higher retention rate than the market.

As discussed, a firm's *ROE* can be estimated in terms of the three ratios: (1) net profit margin (NPM), (2) total asset turnover (TAT), and (3) the financial leverage multiplier.[12] We also know that NPM × TAT = Return on Assets *(ROA)*. It is important to compare the *ROA* of alternative firms as a measure of operating performance—that is, profitability and asset efficiency. As shown in Exhibit 14.12 Walgreens has experienced a small decline in TAT, but this has been offset by an increase in NPM, causing the firm's *ROA* to be relatively stable and substantially above its industry and the market.

Finally, the firm's *ROE* equals the *ROA* times the financial leverage multiplier (total assets/equity). Notably, since 1993, Walgreens has reduced its leverage multiplier from 1.84 to 1.69 while the industry and market have experienced similar declines.

As a result, Walgreens has a higher *ROE* but equal financial risk relative to the industry and lower risk compared to the market using the ratios in Exhibit 14.12.

Using the results for the last three years (2004–2007), the *ROE*s would be approximately as follows:

	NPM	TAT	ROA	Total Assets/ Equity	ROE
Walgreens	3.67	2.82	10.36	1.65	17.13
Retail drugstores	4.89	1.73	8.10	2.08	16.86
S&P Industrials	6.96	0.83	5.87	2.75	15.87

The foregoing highlights the difference among the three units based on recent history. An analyst would need to *estimate* future components and derive an expected *ROE* that reflects the firm's expected *future* performance.

The demonstration can be extended by combining the average annual *ROE*s derived in the table above and the average of recent retention rates from Exhibit 14.15 to derive potential growth rates assuming you felt these recent results would continue in the future.

	Retention Rate	ROE	Potential Growth Rate
Walgreens	0.83	17.13	0.142
Retail drugstores	0.84	16.86	0.142
S&P Industrials	0.67	15.87	0.106

Taken alone, these potential growth rates for Walgreens would indicate that it should have a multiple about equal to its industry and clearly above the market.

---

[12] Notably, all of this analysis of *ROE* employs the data from Exhibit 14.12, which does not consider the capitalization of leases because we do not have comparable data for the industry and market.

Exhibit 14.15 Expected Growth Rate Components for Walgreens, the Retail Store Industry, and the S&P Industrials: 1993–2006

	Walgreens			Retail Stores			S&P Industrials		
Year	Retention Rate	ROE	Expected Growth Rate	Retention Rate	ROE	Expected Growth Rate	Retention Rate	ROE	Expected Growth Rate
1993	0.66	16.08	10.61	0.72	13.86	9.94	0.48	15.65	7.51
1994	0.69	17.92	12.38	0.71	14.70	10.45	0.58	16.88	9.70
1995	0.68	17.90	12.21	0.68	11.43	7.76	0.62	18.68	11.57
1996	0.67	18.20	12.26	0.77	14.04	10.88	0.59	17.17	10.18
1997	0.69	18.37	12.63	0.78	14.60	11.42	0.61	17.55	10.68
1998	0.76	17.94	13.58	0.83	17.86	14.86	0.51	13.61	6.89
1999	0.79	17.91	14.18	0.84	18.07	15.13	0.61	14.96	9.12
2000	0.82	18.35	15.13	0.82	14.46	11.92	0.69	15.57	10.67
2001	0.84	17.01	14.27	0.83	12.86	10.64	0.56	10.90	6.06
2002	0.85	16.36	13.98	0.86	16.83	14.50	0.72	17.98	12.87
2003	0.86	16.34	14.12	0.85	16.22	13.81	0.65	13.46	8.68
2004	0.86	16.53	14.27	0.86	15.17	12.99	0.63	15.64	9.85
2005	0.80	17.54	14.00	0.84	18.34	15.34	0.70	16.12	11.27
2006	0.84	17.31	14.59	0.83	17.06	14.23	0.69	15.84	10.85

Computing the Earnings Multiplier Comparing our estimates of D/E, k, and g to comparable values for the industry and the market, we find that the Walgreen Co.'s earnings multiplier based on the microanalysis should be greater than the multiplier for its industry and the market. Specifically, the dividend-payout ratio points toward a lower multiplier for Walgreens, whereas both the lower risk analysis and the higher expected growth rate would indicate a multiplier for Walgreens above that of its industry and the market.

The macroanalysis indicated that the Walgreen Co.'s multiplier typically has been above its industry and the market, and the microanalysis supported this relationship. Assuming a market multiple of about 16 and a retail drugstore multiplier of about 18 times, the multiplier of Walgreens should be between 18 and 22 with a tendency toward the upper end of the range and beyond (18–20–22 times). Alternatively, if we inserted some earlier estimated values for D/E, k, and g into the P/E ratio formula, we would not be able to derive an estimated multiplier for Walgreens because g is greater than k. As noted in Chapter 11, because Walgreens is a true growth company, we cannot use the standard DDM formula to estimate a specific multiple. We would need to estimate an intrinsic value based on the direction of change and the macroanalysis estimates of 18–20–22 times.

Estimates of Intrinsic Value for Walgreens Earlier, we estimated 2008 earnings per share for Walgreens of about $2.20 per share. Assuming multipliers of 18–20–22 implies the following estimated intrinsic values:

$$18 \times \$2.20 = \$39.60$$
$$20 \times \$2.20 = \$44.00$$
$$22 \times \$2.20 = \$48.40$$

14.7.3 Making the Investment Decision

In our prior discussions of valuation, we set forth the following investment decision rule: Compute the estimated intrinsic value for an investment using your required rate of return as the discount rate. If this intrinsic value is equal to or greater than the current market price of the investment, buy it. If the estimated intrinsic value is less than the market price, do not buy it, and if you own it, sell it.

Therefore, the required comparisons are the estimated values derived using the present value of cash flow models and the values estimated using the earnings multiple model to the current market price of Walgreens of about $37.00 a share. The following is a summary of these estimated values. Recall that we could not calculate constant-growth models because Walgreens has consistently experienced growth rates above its required rates of return (it is a true growth company).

Present Value of Cash Flow Models	
Three-stage DDM	$54.35
Three-stage FCFE	$61.76
Three-stage FCFF (OFCF)	$55.14

Earnings Multiple Models	
18 times estimated earnings	$39.60
20 times estimated earnings	$44.00
22 times estimated earnings	$48.40

Because all of the computed values are equal to or larger than the current market price of $37.00, you would recommend a purchase of the stock. Stated in terms of our earlier discussion, Walgreens is obviously a true growth company, and based on several valuations the firm's stock is expected to be a growth stock assuming that it is acquired at its current price.

14.8 Additional Measures of Relative Value

Beyond the well-known price/earnings ratio, analysts also calculate three additional measures of relative value—the price/book value ratio, the price/cash flow ratio, and the price/sales ratio, which were discussed in Chapter 11.

14.8.1 Price/Book Value (*P/BV*) Ratio

The price-to-book-value ratio (*P/BV*) has gained prominence because of the studies by Fama and French (1992); Rosenberg, Reid, and Lanstein (1985); and Fairfield (1994). Book value is a reasonable measure of value for firms that have consistent accounting practice (for example, firms in the same industry) and can apply to firms with negative earnings or cash flows. You should not attempt to use this ratio to compare firms with different levels of hard assets—for example, a heavy industrial firm and a service firm.

The annual *P/BV* ratios for Walgreens, its industry, and the market are in Exhibit 14.4, along with the ratio of the company *P/BV* ratio relative to its industry and relative to the market ratio. In this instance, the major variable that should cause a difference in the *P/BV* ratio is the firm's return on investment *(ROI)* relative to its cost of capital (its WACC). Assuming that most firms in an industry have comparable WACCs, the major differential should be the firm's *ROI* because the larger the *ROI*-WACC difference, the greater the justified *P/BV* ratio.

As shown in Exhibit 14.16, the *P/BV* ratios for the industry and market components have increased from about 2.5–3.5 to a peak of 5 and ended at 3.0. In contrast, WAG started at about 3.0, peaked at 7.5, and ended at 4.4. As shown in Exhibit 14.17, which contains a plot of relative valuation ratios, Walgreens has consistently sold at a higher *P/BV* ratio than its industry and the market. Since the late 1990s the relative ratio has ranged from about 1.40 to 1.60. A higher *P/BV* ratio for WAG is clearly justified relative to the market due to its higher *ROE*. It is less clear that WAG should have a higher *P/BV* ratio than its industry given the similar *ROE* values.

14.8.2 Price/Cash Flow (*P/CF*) Ratio

As noted in Chapter 10, the price/cash flow ratio has grown in prominence and use because many observers contend that a firm's cash flow is less subject to manipulation than its earnings per share and because cash flows are widely used in the present value of cash flow models discussed earlier. An important question is, which of the several cash flow specifications should an analyst employ? In this analysis, we use the EBITDA cash flow measure equal to net income

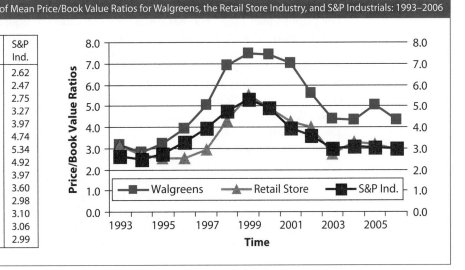

Exhibit 14.16 Time-Series Plot of Mean Price/Book Value Ratios for Walgreens, the Retail Store Industry, and S&P Industrials: 1993–2006

Year	Walgreens	Retail Store	S&P Ind.
1993	3.17	3.12	2.62
1994	2.81	2.71	2.47
1995	3.23	2.52	2.75
1996	3.94	2.51	3.27
1997	5.05	2.95	3.97
1998	6.94	4.33	4.74
1999	7.50	5.52	5.34
2000	7.46	4.89	4.92
2001	7.01	4.27	3.97
2002	5.62	3.99	3.60
2003	4.40	2.73	2.98
2004	4.35	3.31	3.10
2005	5.05	3.18	3.06
2006	4.38	2.92	2.99

Exhibit 14.17 Time-Series Plot of Relative Price/Book Value Ratios for Walgreens/Industry and Walgreens/Market: 1993–2006

Year	Ratio Co/Ind.	Ratio Co/Mkt
1993	1.02	1.21
1994	1.04	1.14
1995	1.28	1.17
1996	1.57	1.20
1997	1.71	1.27
1998	1.60	1.47
1999	1.36	1.41
2000	1.53	1.52
2001	1.64	1.77
2002	1.41	1.56
2003	1.61	1.47
2004	1.31	1.40
2005	1.59	1.65
2006	1.50	1.47

plus interest, depreciation, and taxes because this cash flow measure can be derived for both the RS industry and the market. Although it is certainly legitimate to have a preference for one of the other cash flow measures discussed in chapter 10, a demonstration using this measure should provide a valid comparison for learning purposes.

The time series graph of the P/CF ratios in Exhibit 14.18 shows that the industry and market ratios were highly correlated and ranged from about 10 in 1993 to a high of about 20 in 1999–2000 and ended in 2006 at 10 times. In contrast, the Walgreens ratio was very volatile, ranging from about 10 at the beginning to a high of 50 in 2001 and ended at 18 times in 2006. This ratio is similar to the P/E ratio because it is driven by the growth and volatility of cash flow, which means that Walgreens should have a higher ratio. Specifically, as shown in Exhibit 14.3, WAG's growth rate of cash flow is much higher than both the industry and market (19 percent versus 14 percent for the industry and only 5 percent for the market). Further its growth rate is quite stable compared to the industry and market. Therefore, since WAG's cash flow growth rate is higher and risk is lower its P/CF ratio should be larger—the question is whether it should be 50 percent higher as shown in Exhibit 14.19.

14.8.3 Price/Sales (P/S) Ratio

The price-to-sales ratio (P/S) has had a long but generally neglected existence followed by a recent reawakening. Phillip Fisher (1958), in his classic book, suggested this ratio as a valuable tool when considering investments, including growth stocks. Subsequently, his son Kenneth Fisher (1984) used the ratio as a major stock selection variable in his book. In the late 1990s, P/S was suggested as a valuable tool by Leibowitz (1997), and this ratio was espoused by O'Shaughnessy (1997), in his book that compared several stock selection techniques. Leibowitz makes the point that sales growth drives the growth of all subsequent earnings and cash flow. Those who are concerned with accounting manipulation point out that sales is one of the purest numbers available. Notably, this ratio is equal to the P/E ratio times the net profit margin (earnings/sales), which implies that it is heavily influenced by the profit margin of the entity being analyzed in addition to sales growth and sales volatility (risk).

As shown in Exhibit 14.4 and Exhibit 14.20, the P/S ratio for Walgreens has experienced an overall increase from 0.53 to a peak of 1.49, and finished at 0.93, compared to a small increase by its industry (0.67 to 0.80) and a healthy increase by the market (from 0.84 to 1.33). This substantial relative performance by Walgreens is reflected in Exhibit 14.21, which shows the plot of relative ratios wherein the company-to-industry ratio increased notably from 0.79 to 1.17,

Exhibit 14.18 Time-Series Plot of Price/Cash Flow Ratios for Walgreens, the Retail Store Industry, and S&P Industrials: 1993–2006

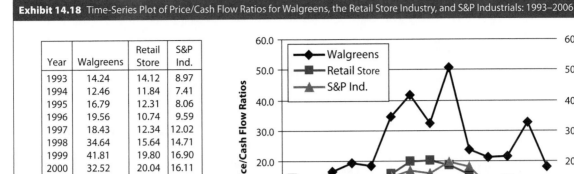

Year	Walgreens	Retail Store	S&P Ind.
1993	14.24	14.12	8.97
1994	12.46	11.84	7.41
1995	16.79	12.31	8.06
1996	19.56	10.74	9.59
1997	18.43	12.34	12.02
1998	34.64	15.64	14.71
1999	41.81	19.80	16.90
2000	32.52	20.04	16.11
2001	50.79	18.51	19.88
2002	23.77	15.33	18.40
2003	21.22	11.18	12.07
2004	21.64	13.27	12.36
2005	32.76	12.30	11.33
2006	18.16	11.27	11.12

Exhibit 14.19 Time-Series Plot of Relative Price/Cash Flow Ratios for Walgreens/Industry and Walgreens/Market: 1993–2006

Year	Ratio Co/Ind.	Ratio Co/Mkt
1993	1.01	1.59
1994	1.05	1.68
1995	1.36	2.08
1996	1.82	2.04
1997	1.49	1.53
1998	2.22	2.35
1999	2.11	2.47
2000	1.62	2.02
2001	2.74	2.55
2002	1.55	1.29
2003	1.90	1.76
2004	1.63	1.75
2005	2.66	2.89
2006	1.61	1.63

while the company-to-market ratio went from 0.63 to 0.70. Recall that three variables should impact the *P/S* ratio: sales growth rate, volatility of sales growth, and the profit margin. An overall analysis of the three variables justifies a higher *P/S* ratio for WAG relative to its industry but not relative to the market. Specifically, as shown in Exhibit 14.3, the 10 year growth rate of sales for WAG was clearly higher at 14.75 percent versus 9.57 percent and 4.44 percent for the industry and market. In addition, the volatility of sales growth for WAG was close to zero compared to the industry that experience a slowdown in 2002, while the market experienced a sales decline in both 2001 and 2002. Finally, the offset for WAG was a lower PM in Exhibit 14.8 than both the industry and market. Given the small difference in the Co/Ind profit margin the sales growth and risk dominates and justifies the higher *P/S* ratio for WAG compared to the industry. In contrast, the large Co/Mkt profit margin difference in favor of the market (3.69 percent versus 7.04 percent) dominates the sales growth and calls for the consistently higher *P/S* ratio for the market relative to WAG. Thus, the differences are expected as shown.

Exhibit 14.20 Time-Series Plot of Relative Price/Sales Ratios for Walgreens, the Retail Drugstore Industry, and S&P Indusrials: 1993–2006

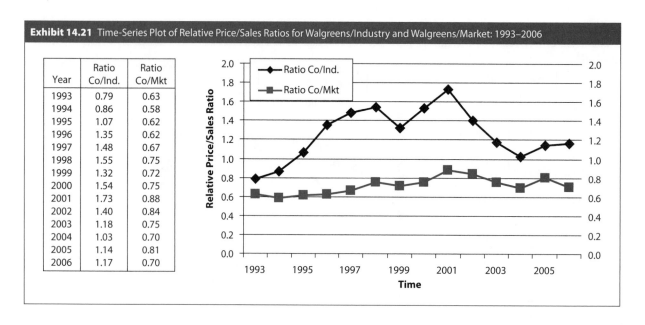

Year	Walgreens	Retail Store	S&P Ind.
1993	0.53	0.67	0.84
1994	0.48	0.56	0.82
1995	0.56	0.52	0.90
1996	0.68	0.50	1.09
1997	0.90	0.61	1.34
1998	1.29	0.84	1.71
1999	1.47	1.11	2.03
2000	1.49	0.97	1.98
2001	1.48	0.86	1.68
2002	1.22	0.87	1.45
2003	0.97	0.83	1.29
2004	0.95	0.93	1.37
2005	1.06	0.93	1.32
2006	0.93	0.80	1.33

Exhibit 14.21 Time-Series Plot of Relative Price/Sales Ratios for Walgreens/Industry and Walgreens/Market: 1993–2006

Year	Ratio Co/Ind.	Ratio Co/Mkt
1993	0.79	0.63
1994	0.86	0.58
1995	1.07	0.62
1996	1.35	0.62
1997	1.48	0.67
1998	1.55	0.75
1999	1.32	0.72
2000	1.54	0.75
2001	1.73	0.88
2002	1.40	0.84
2003	1.18	0.75
2004	1.03	0.70
2005	1.14	0.81
2006	1.17	0.70

14.8.4 Summary of Relative Valuation Ratios

The first observation related to these four ratios is that all of them experienced a cyclical change over the 14 years—they started at a low point in 1993, increased dramatically to a peak prior to the 2000–2001 crash, then typically declined back to the original values by 2006. The performance of the Walgreens ratios relative to its industry and the market varied between the specific ratios.

Regarding the *P/E* ratios, WAG should have a larger *P/E* than its industry and market because its earnings experienced higher growth and lower risk than both. Notably, the current differential appears to be less than expected implying undervaluation. WAG's *P/BV* ratio should also be relatively larger because of its higher *ROE*—the question is whether this ratio deserves to be about 1.50 times larger than its industry and the market. The evaluation of the *P/CF* ratio is similar. Based on WAG's stable high growth rates of CF relative to its industry and market, it should have a higher *P/CF* ratio, but should it be 50 to 60 percent higher? Finally, the results for the *P/S* ratio were consistent with expectations based on sales growth, volatility of growth, and the profit margin—WAG's *P/S* ratio was larger than its industry but lower than the market due to the profit margin.

In conclusion, virtually all the ratios for Walgreens were in the expected direction relative to its industry and the market—the only questions were the extent of difference. The *P/E* pointed toward an undervaluation of WAG, while the relative *P/BV* and *P/CF* ratios for WAG appeared high given the fundamentals.

The following section considers some techniques used to analyze and derive values for growth companies.

14.9 Analysis of Growth Companies

Investment literature contains numerous accounts of the rapid growth of such companies as Wal-Mart, Cisco Systems, Apple, Pfizer, and Google, along with stories about investors who became wealthy because of the timely acquisition of these stocks. These very high rates of return indicate that the early and proper valuation of true growth companies can be extremely rewarding. At the same time, for every successful Wal-Mart or Google, numerous firms did not survive. In addition, there are many instances where the stock price of a true growth company overcompensated for the firm's expected growth, and subsequent returns on the company's stock were below expectations. As noted in Solt and Statman (1989), the common stock of a growth company is *not* always a growth stock.

You are familiar with the DDM assumptions—that is, that dividends are expected to grow at a *constant rate* for an *infinite time period*. As explained in Chapter 11, although these assumptions are reasonable when evaluating the aggregate market and some large mature industries, they can be very tenuous when analyzing individual securities. *These assumptions are extremely questionable for a true growth company.*

14.9.1 Growth Company Defined

Recall that a growth company has the opportunities and ability to invest capital in projects that generate rates of return greater than the firm's cost of capital. Such a condition is considered to be *temporary* because, in a competitive economy, if the rates of return for a given industry or company exceed the rates of return expected based on the risk involved, other companies will enter the industry, increase the supply, and eventually drive prices down until the rates of return earned on capital invested are consistent with the risk involved.

14.9.2 Actual Returns above Required Returns

The notion of a firm consistently earning rates of return above its required rate of return needs elaboration. Firms are engaged in business ventures that offer opportunities for investment of corporate capital, and these investments entail some risk. Investors determine their required return for owning a firm based on the risk of its investments compared to the risk of other firms. This required rate of return is referred to as the firm's *cost of equity*. In a state of equilibrium, the rates of return earned on risky investments by the firm should equal the rates of return required by investors. Rates of return above those required for the risk involved are referred to as *pure profits* or *excess profits*.

Excess profits are possible only in a noncompetitive environment. Assume that a medical equipment firm is able to earn 20 percent on its capital, while investors require only 15 percent from the firm because of its risk. The extra 5 percent is defined as pure profit, and numerous companies would enter the medical equipment field to enjoy these excess profits. These competitors would increase the supply of equipment and reduce the price that producers could charge for the equipment until the marginal returns equaled the required return due to risk.

Because many firms have derived excess profits for a number of years, these excess returns are probably not due to a temporary disequilibrium but rather because of some noncompetitive factors that exist, such as patents or copyrights that provide monopoly rights to a process or a manuscript for a specified period. During this period of protection from competition, the firm can derive above-normal returns. Also, a firm could possess strategies, discussed by Porter, that provide added profits (e.g., a unique marketing technique or other organizational characteristics). Finally, there may be significant barriers to entry, such as capital requirements.

In a purely competitive economy, true growth companies would not exist because competition would not allow continuing excess return investments. The fact is, our economy is not perfectly competitive (although this typically is the best model to use) because there are a number of frictions that restrict competition. Therefore, it is possible for *temporary* true growth companies to exist in our economy. The significant question is, How long can these growth companies earn these excess profits?

14.9.3 Growth Companies and Growth Stocks

Recall that a growth stock is expected to experience above-average risk-adjusted rates of return during some future period. This means that any undervalued stock can be a growth stock, regardless of the type of company. Alternatively, the stock of a growth company that is substantially overvalued could be a speculative stock because the probability of below-normal returns on the stock would be very high even if the company fulfilled expectations.

In this section, we discuss models that are meant to help you evaluate the unique earnings stream of a growth company. As a result, you should derive a better estimate of the firm's value and be able to judge whether the stock of a growth company is (1) a growth stock, (2) a properly valued stock, or (3) a speculative overvalued stock.

14.9.4 Alternative Growth Models[13]

In this section, we consider the full range of growth models, from no growth and negative growth to dynamic true growth. Knowledge of the full range will help you understand the life cycle of true growth companies. We assume the company is an all-equity firm to simplify the computations.

14.9.5 No-Growth Firm

The no-growth firm is a mythical company that is established with a specified portfolio of investments that generate a constant stream of earnings (E) equal to r (equal to the rate of return on assets) times the value of assets. Earnings are calculated after allowing for depreciation expense used to maintain the assets at their original value. Therefore,

14.10
$$E = r \times \text{Assets}$$

It also is assumed that all earnings of the firm are paid out in dividends; if b is the rate of retention, $b = 0$. Hence,

14.11
$$E = r \times \text{Assets} = \text{Dividends}$$

Under these assumptions, the value of the firm is the discounted value of the perpetual stream of earnings (E). The discount rate (the investor's required rate of return) is specified as k. In this case, it is assumed that $r = k$. The firm's rate of return on assets equals its required rate of return. Therefore, the value of the firm is

14.12
$$V = \frac{E}{k} = \frac{(1-b)E}{k}$$

---

[13] The discussion in this section draws heavily from Salomon (1963), and Miller and Modigliani (1961).

In the no-growth case, the earnings stream never changes because the asset base never changes, and the rate of return *(r)* on the assets never changes. Therefore, the value of the firm never changes, and investors continue to receive *k* on their investment.

14.13
$$k = E/V$$

14.9.6 Long-Run Growth Models

Long-run models differ from the no-growth models because *they assume some of the earnings are reinvested.* In all cases, it is postulated that the market value *(V)* of an all-equity firm is the capitalized value of three component forms of returns discounted at the rate *k*.

- *E* = the level of (constant) net earnings expected from existing assets, without further net investments.
- *G* = the growth component that equals the present value of capital gains expected from reinvested funds. The return on reinvested funds is equal to *r*, which equals *mk* (*m* is the relative rate of return operator). If *m* is equal to 1, then *r = k*. If *m* is greater than 1, the projects that generate these returns are considered true growth investments *(r > k)*. If *m* is less than 1, the investments are generating returns *(r)* below the cost of capital *(r < k)*.
- *R* = the reinvestment of net earnings *(E)* and is equal to *bE*, where *b* is a percent of retention which is between zero (no reinvestment) and unity (total reinvestment; no dividends).

Simple Growth Model This model assumes the firm has growth investment opportunities that provide rates of return equal to *r*, where *r* is greater than *k* (*m* is above 1). Further, it is assumed that the firm can invest *R* dollars a year at these rates and that *R = bE*; *R* is a *constant dollar amount* because *E* is the constant earnings at the beginning of the period.

The value of *G*, the capital gain component, is computed as follows: the first investment of *bE* dollars yields a stream of earnings equal to *bEr* dollars, and this is repeated every year. Each of these earnings streams has a present value, as of the year it begins, of *bEr/k*, which is the present value of a constant perpetual stream discounted at a rate consistent with the risk involved. Assuming the firm does this every year, it has a series of investments, each of which has a present value of *bEr/k*. The present value of all these series is *(bEr/k)/k*, which equals *bEr/k²*. But because *r = mk*, this becomes

14.14
$$\frac{bEmk}{k^2} = \frac{bEm}{k} \quad \text{(Gross Present Value of Growth Investments)}$$

To derive these flows, the firm must invest *bE* dollars each year. The present value of these annual investments is equal to *bE/k*. Therefore, the *net* present value of growth investments is equal to

14.15
$$\frac{bEm}{k} - \frac{bE}{k} \quad \text{(Net Present Value of Growth Investments)}$$

The important variable is the value of *m*, which indicates the relationship of *r* to *k*. Combining this growth component with the capitalized value of the constant earnings stream indicates that the value of the firm is

14.16
$$V = \frac{E}{k} + \left[\frac{bEm}{k} - \frac{bE}{k} \right]$$

This equation indicates that the value of the firm is equal to the capitalized value of the constant earnings stream plus a growth component equal to the *net* present value of reinvestment in growth projects. By combining the first and third terms in Equation 14.16, it becomes

14.17
$$V = \frac{E(1 - b)}{k} + \frac{bEm}{k}$$

Because $E(1 - b)$ is the dividend (D), this model becomes

14.18 $$V = \frac{D}{k} + \frac{bEm}{k}$$ (Present Value of Constant Dividend plus the Gross Present Value of Growth Investments)

It can be stated as earnings only by rearranging equation 14.16:

14.19 $$V = \frac{E}{k} + \frac{bE(m - 1)}{k}$$ (Present Value of Constant Earnings plus the Present Value of Excess Earnings from Growth Investments)

Expansion Model The expansion model assumes a firm retains earnings to reinvest but receives a rate of return on its investments that is equal to its cost of capital ($m = 1$, so $r = k$). The effect of such a change can be seen in equation 14.15, where the net present value of growth investments would be zero. Therefore, equation 14.16 would become

14.20 $$V = \frac{E}{k}$$

Equation 14.17 would become

14.21 $$V = \frac{E(1 - b)}{k} + \frac{bE}{k} = \frac{E}{k}$$

Equation 14.18 is still valid, but the present value of the growth investment component would be smaller because m would be equal to 1. Finally, the last term in equation 14.19 would disappear.

This discussion indicates that simply because a firm retains earnings and reinvests them, it is not necessarily beneficial to the stockholder *unless the reinvestment rate is above the required rate* ($r > k$). Otherwise, the investor in a tax-free world would be as well off with all earnings paid out in dividends. Either way, your return is k.

Negative Growth Model The negative growth model applies to a firm that retains earnings ($b > 0$) and reinvests these funds in projects that generate rates of return *below* the firm's cost of capital ($r < k$ or $m < 1$). The impact of this on the value of the firm can be seen from equation 14.15, which indicates that with $m < 1$, the net present value of the growth investments would be *negative*. Therefore, the value of the firm in equation 14.16 would be *less* than the value of a no-growth firm or an expansion firm. This also can be seen by examining the effect of $m < 1$ in equation 14.19. The firm is withholding funds from the investor and investing them in projects that generate returns less than those available from comparable risk investments.

Such poor performance may be difficult to uncover because the firm's asset base will grow since it is retaining earnings and acquiring assets. Notably, the earnings of the firm will increase if it earns *any* positive rate of return on the new assets. The important point is, *the earnings will not grow by as much as they should,* so the value of the firm will decline over time when investors discount the below required cash flows from this reinvestment stream at the firm's cost of capital.

What Determines the Capital Gain Component? These equations highlight the factors that influence the capital gain component. Beginning with equation 14.14, all the equations suggest that the gross present value of growth investments is equal to

$$bEm/k$$

Therefore, three factors influence the size of this capital gain term. The first is *b,* the percentage of earnings retained for reinvestment. The greater the proportion of earnings retained, the larger the capital gain component. The second factor is *m,* which is the most critical variable because it indicates the relationship between the firm's rate of return on investments and the firm's required rate of return (i.e., its cost of capital). A value of 1 indicates the firm is earning only its required return. A firm with an *m* greater than 1 is a true growth company. The important question is, how much greater than *k* is the return? The final factor is the time period for the superior investments. How long can the firm make these superior return investments? This critical time factor often is overlooked because we have assumed an infinite horizon to simplify the computations. However, *when analyzing growth companies, this time estimate is clearly a major consideration.* In summary, the three factors that influence the capital gain component are

1. The amount of capital invested in growth investments *(b)*
2. The relative rate of return earned on the funds retained *(m)*
3. The time period for these growth investments

Dynamic True Growth Model A dynamic true growth model applies to a firm that invests a constant *percentage of current* earnings in projects that generate rates of return above the firm's required rate ($r > k$, $m > 1$). In contrast to the simple growth model where the firm invests a *constant* dollar amount each year, in this model the amount invested is *growing* each year as earnings increase. As a result, the firm's earnings and dividends will grow at a *constant rate* that is equal to *br* (the percentage of earnings retained times the return on investments). In the current model, this would equal *bmk,* where *m* is greater than 1. Given these assumptions, the dynamic growth model for an infinite time period is the dividend discount model derived in the appendix to Chapter 11:

14.22
$$V = \frac{D_1}{k - g}$$

Applying this model to a true growth company means that earnings and dividends are growing at a constant rate and *the firm is investing larger and larger dollar amounts in projects that generate returns greater than* k. Moreover, the DDM model implicitly assumes that the firm can continue to do this for *an infinite time period.* If the growth rate *(g)* is greater than *k,* the model blows up and indicates that the firm should have an infinite value. Durand (1957) considered this possibility and concluded that, although many firms had current growth rates above the normal required rates of return, very few of their stocks were selling for infinite values. He explained this by contending that investors expected the reinvestment rate to decline or they felt that the growing set of investment opportunities would not be available for an infinite time period. Exhibit 14.22 contains a summary of the alternative company characteristics.

14.9.7 The Real World

Because these models are simplified to allow us to develop a range of alternatives, several of them are extremely unrealistic. In the real world, companies generally would combine these models. Unfortunately, most firms have made some investments where $r < k$, and many firms invest in projects that generate returns about equal to their cost of capital. Finally, most firms invest in *some* projects that provide rates of return above the firm's cost of capital ($r > k$). The crucial questions are (1) how much is invested in these true growth projects? and (2) how long do these true growth opportunities last?

Given this understanding of growth companies and what creates their value, the rest of the chapter considers various models that help you understand how to identify a true growth company and estimate specific values for these growth companies. We begin with models that

---

Exhibit 14.22 Summary of Company Descriptions

	Retention	Return on Investments
No-growth company	$b = 0$	$r = k$
Long-run growth (assumes reinvestment)		
Negative growth	$b > 0$	$r < k$
Expansion	$b > 0$	$r = k$
Simple long-run growth	$b > 0$	
	(constant \$)	$r > k$
Dynamic long-run growth	$b > 0$	
	(constant %)	$r > k$

---

are intended to identify growth companies in terms of providing excess economic value, which some contend is due to franchise value. Subsequently, we consider several models that are intended to provide a valuation of these companies by concentrating on how long the superior growth can continue and, alternatively, the extent and length of the superior growth. This final model has some similarities to the three-stage cash flow models.

14.10 Measures of Value Added[14]

In addition to the DDM, which feeds into the *P/E* ratio valuation technique and the supplementary *P/BV* and *P/CF*, ratios, there is also interest in a set of performance measures referred to as "value added" measures. Notably, these value-added measures of performance are directly related to the capital budgeting techniques used in corporation finance. Specifically, they consider *economic profit,* which is analogous to the net present value (NPV) technique used in corporate capital budgeting. These value-added measures examine management performance based on the ability of managers to add value to the firm. They are also being considered by security analysts as possible indicators of future equity returns, based on the logic that superior management performance should be reflected in a company's stock returns. In the subsequent discussion, we concentrate on three measures of value added: **economic value added (EVA)** and **market value added (MVA)**, pioneered by Stern and Stewart, and discussed in Stewart (1991), and the **franchise factor** developed by Leibowitz and Kogelman (1994).

14.10.1 Economic Value Added (EVA)[15]

As noted, EVA is closely related to the net present value (NPV) technique wherein you evaluate the expected performance of an investment by discounting its future cash flows at the firm's weighted average cost of capital (WACC) and compare this sum of discounted future cash flows to the cost of the project. If the discounted cash flows are greater than its cost, the project is expected to generate a positive NPV, which implies that it will add to the value of the firm and, therefore, it should be undertaken. EVA extends this concept to evaluate the annual performance of management by comparing the firm's net operating profit less adjusted taxes (NOPLAT) to the firm's total cost of capital in dollar terms, including the cost of equity. In this analysis, if the firm's NOPLAT during a specific year exceeds its dollar cost of capital, it has a positive EVA for the year and has added value for its stockholders. In contrast, if the EVA is negative, the firm has not earned enough during the year to cover its total cost of capital and the value of the firm has declined. Specifically, NOPLAT indicates what the firm has earned

---

[14] This section benefited from Peterson and Peterson (1996).
[15] EVA is a registered trademark of Stern, Stewart, & Co.

for all capital suppliers and the dollar cost of capital is what all the capital suppliers required—including the firm's equity holders. The following summarizes the major calculations[16]:

EVA =

(A) Adjusted Operating Profits before Taxes
Minus (B) Cash Operating Taxes
Equals (C) Net Operating Profits Less Adjusted Taxes (NOPLAT)
Minus (D) The Dollar Cost of Capital
Equals (E) Economic Value Added (EVA)

In turn, these items are calculated as follows:

Operating Profit (After Depreciation and Amortization)

Add:	Implied Interest on Operating Leases
Add:	An Increase in the LIFO Reserve
Add:	Goodwill Amortization
Equals:	*(A) Adjusted Operating Profits before Taxes*

Income Tax Expense

Add:	Decrease in Deferred Taxes
Add:	Tax Benefit from Interest Expenses
Add:	Tax Benefit from Interest on Leases
Less:	Taxes on Nonoperating Income
Equals:	*(B) Cash Operating Taxes*

(A) minus (B) equals: (C) Net Operating Profits Less Adjusted Taxes (NOPLAT)

Capital =

	Net Working Capital (current assets less non-interest-bearing liabilities)
Add:	LIFO Reserve
Add:	Net Plant, Property, and Equipment
Add:	Other Assets
Add:	Goodwill
Add:	Accumulated Goodwill Amortized
Add:	Present Value of Operating Leases
Equals:	*Capital*

Weighted Average Cost of Capital (WACC) =

(Book Value of Debt/Total Book Value) × (the Market Cost of Debt)
(1 − Tax Rate)
(Book Value of Equity/Total Book Value) × (Cost of Equity)
(Cost of equity is based on the CAPM using the prevailing 10-year Treasury bond as the *RFR,* a calculated beta, and a market risk premium between 3 and 6 percent.)

(D)	Dollar Cost of Capital = Capital × WACC[17]
(E)	Economic Value Added (EVA) =
(C)	Net Operating Profits Less Adjusted Taxes (NOPLAT) Minus (D) Dollar Cost of Capital

EVA Return on Capital   The preceding calculations provide a positive or negative dollar value, which indicates whether the firm earned an excess above its cost of capital during the year analyzed. There are two problems with this annual dollar value for EVA. First, how does one judge

[16] For a detailed discussion, see Stewart (1991), or Peterson and Peterson (1996). For summary discussions, see Jones (1995).
[17] Recall that during the discussion earlier in this chapter when we calculated the WACC for Walgreens we made the point that using book value weights typically resulted in a lower WACC than using market value weights—for WAG the difference was 6.90 percent using book values versus 7.65 percent for market weights. A lower WACC means a higher EVA.

over time if the firm is prospering relative to its past performance? Although you would want the absolute EVA to grow over time, the question is whether the rate of growth of EVA is adequate for the additional capital provided. Second, how does one compare alternative firms of different sizes? Both of these concerns can be met by calculating an *EVA return on capital* equal to

$$\text{EVA Return on Capital} = \text{EVA/Capital}$$

You would want this EVA rate of return on capital for a firm to remain constant over time, or, ideally, to grow. Using this ratio you can compare firms of different sizes and determine which firm has the largest *economic profit per dollar of capital*.

An Alternative Measure of EVA An alternative but equal way to measure and think about EVA is to compare directly the firm's return on capital employed to the firm's average cost of capital (i.e., its WACC). As noted previously, it is this difference in the actual rate of return earned compared to the firm's required rate of return that identifies a company as a true growth company. Another way to measure EVA is to multiply this EVA spread (return on capital minus WACC) by the amount of capital employed. The appeal of this EVA spread approach is that it concentrates on the factors that create a growth company. Also, it helps the management and analysts recognize that true growth can be created by either (1) increasing the firm's return on capital, or (2) reducing its cost of capital.

14.10.2 Market Value Added (MVA)

In contrast to EVA, which generally is an evaluation of internal performance, MVA is a measure of external performance—how the market has evaluated the firm's performance in terms of the market value of debt and market value of equity compared to the capital invested in the firm.

$$\begin{aligned}\text{Market Value Added (MVA)} = &\ (\text{Market Value of Firm}) - \text{Capital}\\ & - \text{Market Value of Debt}\\ & - \text{Market Value of Equity}\end{aligned}$$

Again, to properly analyze this performance, it is necessary to look for positive changes over time—that is, the percent change each year. Subsequently, you need to compare these annual changes in MVA with those for the aggregate stock and bond markets, because these market values can be impacted by interest rate changes and general economic conditions.

14.10.3 Relationships between EVA and MVA

Although EVA is used primarily for evaluating management performance, it also is being used by external analysts to evaluate management with the belief that superior internal performance should be reflected in a company's stock performance. Several studies have attempted to determine the relationship between the two variables (EVA and MVA), and the results have not been encouraging. Although the stock of firms with positive EVAs has tended to outperform the stocks of negative EVA firms, the differences are typically insignificant and the relationship does not occur every year. This poor relationship may be due to the timing of the analysis (how fast EVA is reflected in stocks) or because the market values (MVAs) are affected by factors other than EVA—for example, MVA can be impacted by market interest rates and by changes in *future* expectations for a firm not considered by EVA. The point is, EVA does an outstanding job of evaluating management's *past* performance in terms of adding value. While one would certainly hope that superior past performance will continue, there is nothing certain about this relationship.

14.10.4 The Franchise Factor

The franchise factor concept is similar to EVA since it recognizes that, to add value to a firm, it is necessary to invest in projects that provide excess NPV—that is, the firm must generate rates of return above its WACC. This technique is directly related to the valuation approach we have been using since the franchise value approach breaks a firm's observed *P/E* ratio down into two components: (1) the *P/E* that is based on the company's ongoing business (its base *P/E*), plus (2) a franchise *P/E* that the market assigns to *the expected value of new and profitable business opportunities.* This can be visualized as:

14.23   Franchise *P/E* = Observed *P/E* − Base *P/E*

The base *P/E* is the reciprocal of the market discount rate *k* (it is 1/*k*). For example, if the stock's market discount rate is 8 percent, the base *P/E* would be about 12.5 times.

What determines the franchise *P/E*? Not surprising, it is a function of the relative rate of return on new business opportunities compared to the firm's cost of equity (the franchise factor) and the size of the superior return opportunities (the growth factor).

14.24   Incremental Franchise *P/E* = Franchise Factor × Growth Factor = $\dfrac{R - k}{rk} \times G$

where:

  R = the expected return on the new opportunities
  k = the current cost of equity
  r = the current *ROE* on investment
  G = the present value of the new growth projects relative to the current value of the firm

The critical factors determining the franchise *P/E* are the difference between *R* and *k* and the size of these growth opportunities relative to the firm's current size (i.e., *G*).[18]

14.10.5 Growth Duration Model

The purpose of the growth duration model is to help you *evaluate* the high *P/E* ratio for the stock of a growth company by relating its *P/E* ratio to the firm's *rate* of growth and *duration* of growth. As discussed previously, a stock's *P/E* ratio is a function of (1) the firm's expected rate of growth of earnings per share, (2) the stock's required rate of return, and (3) the firm's dividend-payout ratio. Assuming equal risk and no significant difference in the payout ratio for different firms, the principal variable affecting differences in the earnings multiple for two firms *is the difference in expected growth.* It has been noted earlier that the growth estimate must consider both the *rate* of growth and how long this growth rate can be sustained—that is, the *duration* of the expected growth rate. As noted earlier, no company can grow indefinitely at a rate substantially above normal. For example, Wal-Mart cannot continue to grow at 20 percent a year for an extended period, or it will eventually become the entire economy. In fact, Wal-Mart or any similar growth firm will eventually run out of excess profit investment projects. Recall that continued growth at a constant rate requires that larger amounts of money be invested in high-return projects because the constant growth model requires that you invest a constant *percentage* of current earnings. Eventually, competition will encroach on these high-return investments and the firm's growth rate will decline to a rate consistent with the rate for the overall economy. Therefore, a reasonable and accurate estimate of the implied duration of a firm's high-growth period becomes significant.

Computation of Growth Duration   The growth duration concept was suggested by Holt (1962), who showed that if you assume equal risk between a given security and a market security, such as the S&P Industrials (i.e., a beta close to one), you can concentrate on the differential expected growth rates for the market and the growth firm as a factor causing the alternative *P/E* ratios. This allows you to compute the market's *implied growth duration* for the growth firm.

---

[18] For further detail and examples of the application, see Leibowitz and Kogelman (1994).

If $E'(0)$ is the firm's current earnings, then $E'(t)$ is earnings in Period t according to the expression

14.25
$$E'(t) = E(0)(1 + G)^t$$

where G is the expected annual percentage growth rate for earnings. To adjust for dividend payments, it was assumed that all dividend payments are used to purchase further shares of the stock. This means the number of shares (N) will grow at the dividend yield rate (D). Therefore

14.26
$$N(t) = N(0)(1 + D)^t$$

To derive the total earnings for a firm, $E(t)$, the growth rate in per-share earnings and the growth rate in shares are combined as follows:

14.27
$$E(t) = E'(t)N(t) = E'(0)[(1 + G)(1 + D)]^t$$

Because G and D are small, this expression can be approximated by

14.28
$$E(t) \simeq E'(0)(1 + G + D)^t$$

Assuming the growth stock (g) and the nongrowth stock (a) have similar risk and payout, the market should value the two stocks in direct proportion to their earnings in year T (i.e., they will have the same P/E ratio), where T is the time when the growth company will begin to grow at the same rate as the market (i.e., the non-growth stock). Put another way, T is the number of years the growth stock is expected to grow at the high rate. In other words, *current prices should be in direct proportion to the expected future earnings ratio that will prevail in year T.* This relationship can be stated

14.29
$$\left(\frac{P_g(0)}{P_a(0)}\right) \simeq \left(\frac{E_g(0)(1 + G_g + D_g)^T}{E_a(0)(1 + G_a + D_a)^T}\right)$$

or

14.30
$$\left(\frac{P_g(0)/E_g(0)}{P_a(0)/E_a(0)}\right) \simeq \left(\frac{1 + G_g + D_g}{1 + G_a + D_a}\right)^T$$

Equation 14.30 implies that the *P/E ratios of the two stocks are in direct proportion to the ratio of composite growth rates raised to the Tth power.* You can solve for T by taking the log of both sides as follows:

14.31
$$\ln\left(\frac{P_g(0)/E_g(0)}{P_a(0)/E_a(0)}\right) \simeq T \ln\left(\frac{1 + G_g + D_g}{1 + G_a + D_a}\right)$$

The growth duration model answers the question: How long must the earnings of the growth stock grow at this expected high rate, relative to the nongrowth stock, to justify its prevailing above-average P/E ratio? You must then determine whether this *implied* growth duration estimate is reasonable in terms of the company's potential.

Consider the following example. The stock of Walgreens is selling for $37 a share with expected per-share earnings of $2.20 (its future earnings multiple is about 17 times). The expected EPS growth rate for Walgreens is estimated to be 13 percent a year, and its dividend yield has been 1 percent and is expected to remain at this level. In contrast, the S&P Industrials

Index has a future *P/E* ratio of about 15, an average dividend yield of 2 percent, and an expected growth rate of 6 percent. Therefore, the comparison is as follows:

	S&P Industrials	Walgreens
P/E ratio	15.00	17.00
Expected growth rate	0.06	0.13
Dividend yield	0.02	0.01

Inserting these values into equation 14.31 yields the following:

$$\ln\left(\frac{17.00}{15.00}\right) = T\ln\left(\frac{1 + 0.13 + 0.01}{1 + 0.06 + 0.02}\right)$$

$$\ln(1.14) = T\ln\left(\frac{1.14}{1.08}\right)$$

$$\ln(1.14) = T\ln(1.055)$$

$$T = \ln(1.14)/\ln(1.055) \text{ (log base 10)}$$

$$= 0.0569/0.02325$$

$$= 2.45 \text{ years}$$

These results indicate the market is implicitly assuming that Walgreens can continue to grow at this composite rate (14 percent) for only about 2.5 more years, after which it is assumed Walgreens will grow at the same total rate (8 percent) as the aggregate market (i.e., the S&P Industrials). You must now ask, can this superior growth rate be sustained by Walgreens for at least this period? If the implied growth duration is greater than you believe is reasonable, you would advise against buying Walgreens stock. If the implied duration is below your expectations, you would recommend buying the stock.

Intraindustry Analysis Besides comparing a company to a market series, you can directly compare two firms. For an intercompany analysis, you should compare firms in the same industry because the equal risk assumptions of this model are probably more reasonable.

Consider the following example from the computer software industry:

	Company A	Company B
P/E ratios	31.00	25.00
Expected annual growth rate	0.1700	0.1200
Dividend yield	0.0100	0.0150
Growth rate plus dividend yield	0.1800	0.1350
Estimate of *T*[a]		5.53 years

[a]Readers should check to see that they get the same answer.

These results imply that the market expects Company A to grow at an annual total rate of 18 percent for about 5.5 years, after which it will grow at Company B's rate of 13.5 percent. If you believe the implied duration for growth at 18 percent is too long, you will prefer Company B; if you believe it is reasonable or low, you will recommend Company A.

An Alternative Use of *T* Instead of solving for *T* and then deciding whether the figure derived is reasonable, you can use this formulation to compute a reasonable *P/E* ratio for a security relative to the aggregate market (or another stock) if the implicit assumptions are reasonable for the stock involved. Again, using Walgreens as an example, you estimate its expected composite growth to be 14 percent a year compared to the expected total market growth of 8 percent. Further, you believe that Walgreens can continue to grow at this above-normal rate for about 5 years. Using Equation 14.31, this becomes

$$\ln(X) = 5 \times \ln\frac{1.14}{1.08}$$
$$= 5 \times \ln(1.055)$$
$$= 5 \times (0.02325)$$
$$= 0.11625$$

To determine what the *P/E* ratio for Walgreens should be given these assumptions, you must derive the antilog of 0.11625, which is approximately 1.3069. Therefore, assuming the market multiple is 15, the earnings multiple for Walgreens should be about 1.3069 times the market *P/E* ratio, or about 20 times.

Alternatively, if you estimate that Walgreens can maintain a lower growth rate of 12 percent for a longer period (e.g., 10 years), you would derive the antilog for 1.5794 (10 × 0.01579). The answer is 1.4386, which implies a *P/E* ratio of about 21.6 times for Walgreen Co.'s stock. Notably, both of these estimates are above the current forward *P/E* for Walgreens of 17 times.

Factors to Consider When using the growth duration technique, remember the following factors: First, the technique assumes equal risk, which may be acceptable when comparing two large, well-established firms in the same industry (e.g., Merck and Pfizer) to each other. It is also reasonable for a large conglomerate, like General Electric, with a beta close to one. In the case of Walgreens, which has a beta of about 0.90, the result is conservative, meaning that the duration would be slightly lower than the estimated years. It is probably *not* a valid assumption when comparing a small growth company with a beta of 1.50 to the aggregate market. In this case, the growth duration generated would be an underestimate of what is required.

Second, which growth estimate should be used? We prefer to use the *expected* rate of growth based on the factors that affect *g* (i.e., the retention rate and the components of *ROE*).

Third, the growth duration technique assumes that stocks with higher *P/E* ratios have the higher growth rates. However, there are cases in which the stock with the higher *P/E* ratio does not have a higher expected growth rate or the stock with a higher expected growth rate has a lower *P/E* ratio. Either of the cases generates a useless negative growth duration value. Inconsistency between the expected growth and the *P/E* ratio could be attributed to one of four factors:

1. A major difference in the risk involved (the low *P/E* high growth company is much riskier).
2. Inaccurate growth rate estimates. You may want to reexamine your growth rate estimate for the firm with the higher *P/E* ratio, that is, could it be higher or should the growth estimate for the low *P/E* stock be lower?
3. The stock with a low *P/E* ratio relative to its expected growth rate is undervalued. (Before you accept this possibility, consider the first two factors.)
4. The stock with a high *P/E* and a low expected growth rate is overvalued. (Before this is accepted, consider both its risk and your estimated growth rate.)

The growth duration concept is valid, *given the assumptions made,* and can help you evaluate growth investments. It is not universally valid, though, because its answers are only as good as the data inputs (expected growth rates) and the applicability of the assumptions. The answer must be evaluated based on the analyst's knowledge.

The technique probably is most useful for helping spot overvalued growth companies with very high multiples. In such a case, the technique will highlight that the company must continue to grow at some very high rate for an extended period of time to justify its high *P/E* ratio (e.g., 15 to 20 years). Also, it can help you decide between two growth companies in the same industry by comparing each to the market, the industry, or directly to each other. Such a comparison has provided interesting insights wherein the new firms in an industry were growing faster than the large competitor but their *P/E* ratios were *substantially* higher and implied that these new firms had to maintain this large growth rate superiority for over *10 years* to justify the much higher *P/E* ratio.

14.11 Site Visits and the Art of the Interview

Brokerage house analysts and portfolio managers have access to persons that the typical small investor does not. Analysts frequently have contact with corporate personnel by telephone (conference calls), at formal presentations, or during plant site visits. Though insider trading laws restrict the analyst's ability to obtain material nonpublic information, these visits facilitate dialog between the corporation and the investor community. The analyst can gather information about the firm's plans and strategies, which helps the analyst understand the firm's prospects as an investment.

Interviewing is an art. The analyst wants information about the firm, and top management wants to put the firm in the best light possible. Thus, the analyst must be prepared to focus the interview on management's plans, strategies, and concerns. Analysts try to gauge the sensitivity of the firm's revenues, costs, and earnings to different scenarios by asking "what if" questions.

Analysts have frequent telephone contact with the firm's investor relations (IR) department regarding company pronouncements. The chief financial officer and chief executive officer of the firm also meet with security analysts and discuss the firm's planning process and major issues confronting the industry.

The analyst should talk with people other than top managers. Talking with middle managers or factory workers during a plant tour, visiting stores, and talking with customers provide insights beyond those of management. The firm's major customers can provide information regarding product quality and customer satisfaction. The firm's suppliers can furnish information about rising or falling supply orders and the timeliness of payments. Finally, an outstanding source of information is the firm's competitors who will be happy to point out the firm's weaknesses or possible problems. They may even be willing to admit which firm is its toughest competitor (if you could eliminate one competitor, who would it be?).

The idea was always that analysts were able to create a mosaic regarding future expectations for the firm from numerous sources (including the company) and transmit this information to the market by sending research reports to brokerage clients and portfolio managers of pensions and mutual funds. This traditional way of doing research was changed by the SEC in 2000 when they issued the Fair Disclosure (FD) guidelines that required all disclosure of "material information" to be made public to all interested parties at the same time. The intent was to level the playing field by ensuring that professional analysts did not have a competitive advantage over nonprofessional investors. The result of this law is that many firms will not agree to interviews with analysts and will only provide information during large public presentations over the Internet.

The long-run impact of this FD requirement is not clear in terms of how firms will relate to the professional analyst community. One benefit is that analysts will spend more time with information sources beyond the firm such as trade shows, customers, suppliers, and competitors to build the mosaic.

14.12 When to Sell

Our analysis has focused on determining if a stock should be purchased. In fact, when we make a purchase, a subsequent question gains prominence: When should the stock be sold? Many times holding on to a stock too long leads to a return below expectations or less than what was available earlier. When a stock's price declines immediately following an analyst's valuation and recommendation, is this a further buying opportunity, or does the decline indicate information that is new or was overlooked has significantly decreased the valuation?

The answer to the question of when to sell a stock is contained in the research that convinced the analyst to purchase the stock in the first place. The analyst should have identified the key assumptions and variables driving the expectations for the stock. Analysis of the stock doesn't end when intrinsic value is computed and the research report is written. Once the key value drivers are identified, the analyst must *continually monitor and update* his or her knowledge base about the firm. Notably, if the key value drivers appear to have weakened or there is a major change in management, it is time to reevaluate, and possibly sell, the stock.

The stock should also be closely evaluated when the current price approaches its intrinsic value estimate. When the stock becomes fairly priced (the undervaluation has been corrected), it may be time to sell it and reinvest the funds in other underpriced stocks. In short, if the "story" for buying the stock still appears to be true, continue to hold it if it has not become fully priced (i.e., market price equal to intrinsic value). If the "story" changes, it may be time to sell the stock. If you know why you bought the stock, and constantly update your valuation to reflect new information, you'll be able to recognize when to sell it.

14.13 Influences on Analysts

Stock analysts and portfolio managers are, for the most part, highly trained individuals who possess expertise in financial analysis and background in their industry. A computer hardware analyst knows as much about industry trends and new product offerings as any industry insider. A pharmaceutical analyst is able to independently determine the market potential of drugs undergoing testing and the FDA approval process. So why don't more brokerage house customers and portfolio managers who receive the analysts' expert advice achieve investment success? The following subsections discuss several factors that make it difficult to "beat the market."

14.13.1 Efficient Markets

As noted in Chapter 6, the efficient market is difficult to outsmart, especially if you are considering actively traded and frequently analyzed companies. Information about the economy, a firm's industry, and the firm itself is reviewed by numerous bright analysts, investors, and portfolio managers. Investors look for situations where stocks may not be fairly valued. Notably, because there are numerous bright, hardworking analysts, it is difficult to successfully, frequently, and consistently find undervalued shares. Put another way, in most instances, the value estimated for a stock will be very close to its market price, which indicates that it is properly valued. The analyst's best place to seek attractive stocks is not among well known companies and actively traded stocks, because they are analyzed by dozens of Wall Street analysts. Stocks with smaller market capitalizations, those not covered by many analysts, or those whose shares are mainly held by individual investors may be the best places to search for inefficiencies. Smaller capitalization stocks sometimes are too small for time-constrained analysts or too small for purchase by institutional investors.[19] The price of stocks not researched by many analysts ("neglected stocks") may not reflect all relevant information.[20]

14.13.2 Paralysis of Analysis

Analysts spend most of their time in a relentless search for one more contact or one more piece of information that will ensure the correct stock recommendation. Analysts need to develop a systematic approach for gathering, monitoring, and reviewing relevant information about economic trends, industry competitive forces, and company strategy. Analysts must evaluate the

---

[19] According to SEC regulations, mutual funds cannot own more than 10 percent of a firm's shares. For some large funds, this constraint will make the resulting investment too small to have any significant impact on fund returns, so analysts do not bother to consider such stocks for purchase.
[20] Information on the number of analysts covering a stock is available from research firms, such as IBES and Zacks.

information as a whole to discern patterns that indicate the intrinsic value of the stock rather than searching for one more piece of information.

Because markets are generally efficient, the consensus view about the firm is already reflected in its stock price. As noted previously, to earn above-average returns, there are two requirements; (1) the analyst must have expectations that differ from the consensus, *and* (2) the analyst must be correct. Thus, the analyst should concentrate on identifying what is wrong with the market consensus (i.e., why do you differ from the consensus?), or what surprises may upset the market consensus—that is, work at *estimating earning surprises*.

14.13.3 Analyst Conflicts of Interest

A potential conflict can arise if communication occurs between a firm's investment banking and equity research division. If the investment bankers assist a firm in a stock or bond offering, it will be difficult for an analyst to issue a negative evaluation of the company. Advisory fees have been lost because of a negative stock recommendation. Despite attempts to ensure the independence of stock analysts, firm politics may get in the way.

The analyst is in frequent contact with the top officers of the company he or she analyzes. Although there are guidelines about receiving gifts and favors, it is sometimes difficult to separate personal friendship and impersonal corporate relationships. Corporate officials may try to convince the analyst that his or her pessimistic report is in error or suggest that it glosses over recent positive developments. To mitigate these problems, an analyst should call the company's investor relations department immediately *after* changing a recommendation to explain his or her perspective. The analyst needs to maintain independence and be objective in his or her analysis. Unfortunately, there are also instances where firms have ostracized analysts who have issued "negative" reports on firms (i.e., not returning calls, not being available for visits, or not calling on them during conference calls.)

14.14 Global Company and Stock Analysis

As indicated on numerous occasions, a major goal of this text is to demonstrate investment techniques that can be applied globally to markets, industries, and companies around the world. This chapter has been heavily concerned with presenting and demonstrating these techniques to U.S. firms. While space constraints do not allow a full demonstration to international firms, it is important to point out some of the major factors and constraints that analysts and portfolio managers need to acknowledge and adjust for when investing globally.

14.14.1 Availability of Data

In the United States, we suffer from information (data) overload, which is a blessing and a curse since we have more information than anywhere else in the world (which is good), but, as a result, there is a lot of information to digest and analyze. When you start analyzing international markets, industries, and stocks and cannot get the necessary data for valuation, you come to appreciate what is available in the United States. Beyond the limited amount of information, there is also the problem of timeliness (how long before you get the data?) and the reliability (can you believe and depend upon the data published in some countries and by some global industries?).

14.14.2 Differential Accounting Conventions

Even when the financial data for an industry and a firm are timely and reliable, it is necessary to recognize that the accounting rules and practices differ dramatically around the world. Not only are the financial statements very different in general presentation, but the accounting practices differ related to sales and expense recognition. The fact is, identical transactions in different countries can generate significant differences in income and cash flow. As a result, stocks in different countries will have very different *P/E* and *P/CF* ratios, not because investors differ in valuation but because the accounting numbers used are not the same. Because of these accounting problems, many investors advocate using the price-to-sales ratio in valuations across countries since sales revenue is the least contaminated accounting figure. The good news is the movement toward using global accounting standards. For an overview of this transition, see Sandagaran (2001).

14.14.3 Currency Differences (Exchange Rate Risk)

A significant factor that must be considered by global investors is currency risk caused by changes in exchange rates among countries. While these rate changes can work for or against you, the point is that it creates a major uncertainty that must be considered when analyzing a company and valuing its stock.

14.14.4 Political (Country) Risk

In the United States, we are blessed with the most stable political and economic environment in the world. Therefore, by definition, every other country will have greater political/country risk, which in some cases (e.g., Russia, Indonesia, North Korea) can be substantial. Therefore, you must acknowledge this factor and estimate its effect on the cost of equity for firms in these countries.

14.14.5 Transaction Costs and Liquidity

Higher transaction costs result from less-liquid markets—where it takes longer to trade and there is more price volatility connected to a trade—or from a trade that costs more (e.g., higher commissions). Again, these costs vary dramatically among countries.

14.14.6 Valuation Differences

These individual country differences combine to cause a clear differential in the stock valuation for an international stock. Specifically, the earnings or cash flow numbers will differ and the required rate of return (the discount rate) for a non-U.S. stock will differ substantially because there are additional risks noted such as exchange rate risk, political risk, and higher liquidity costs.

14.14.7 Summary

In summary, the good news when investing globally is that the valuation process is the same around the world, and the investment decision in terms of the ultimate comparison of intrinsic value and price is similar. The negative news is that the practice of valuation requires attention to several additional factors that must be considered when valuing an international stock. Therefore, everything you have learned about analysis and valuation is relevant, but it must be applied differently (i.e., the inputs differ), depending on the country.

· · · · **SUMMARY** · · · ·

- This chapter demonstrates how to complete the fundamental analysis process by analyzing a company and deciding whether you should buy its stock. This requires a separate analysis of a company followed by the valuation of its stock. A wonderful company can have an overpriced stock, or a mediocre firm can have an underpriced stock.

- The chapter is mainly concerned with discussing and demonstrating alternative valuation techniques. The initial section contained a discussion of the strategic alternatives available to firms in response to different competitive pressures in their industries. The alternative corporate

strategies include low-cost leadership or differentiation which if properly implemented, should help the company attain above-average rates of return. In addition, we discussed applying SWOT analysis to a firm. This strategic analysis of the firm's goals, objectives, and strategy should put you in a position to properly estimate the intrinsic value of the stock.

- When estimating a stock's intrinsic value, we considered two approaches—the present value of cash flow, or the analysis of relative valuation ratios. We reviewed how to estimate the major inputs to the techniques and demonstrated these techniques on Walgreens.

- We derived several estimated values for Walgreens using the two approaches and compared the relative valuation ratios for the company to comparable ratios for both the retail store industry and the aggregate market.
- The investment decision compares a stock's intrinsic value to its prevailing market price. If the stock's intrinsic value exceeds the market price, we would buy the stock. If the intrinsic value is less than the market price, we would not buy the stock and would sell it if we owned it.
- Because of the difficulty in estimating the intrinsic value of growth firms, we considered alternative specifications for growth companies and several techniques that provide insights on valuing these firms. These techniques include economic value added, the franchise factor models, and a growth duration model. These models help the analyst concentrate attention on the relevant factors that determine true growth. The critical question is, is the stock of the growth company going to be a growth stock?
- We concluded with a discussion of several unique considerations an analyst must consider when analyzing and valuing global industries or firms.

• • • • SUGGESTED READINGS • • • •

Damodaran, Aswath. *Damodaran on Valuation,* 2nd ed. New York: Wiley, 2006.

Hackel, Kenneth S., and Joshua Livnat. *Cash Flow and Security Analysis,* 2nd ed. Burr Ridge, IL: Irwin Professional Publishing, 1996.

Koller, Tim, Marc Goedhart, and David Wessels. *Valuation: Measuring and Managing the Value of Companies,* 4th ed. New York: Wiley, 2005.

Palepu, Krishna, Paul Healy, and Victor Bernard. *Business Analysis and Valuation,* 3rd ed. Cincinnati, OH: South-Western Publishing, 2004.

Squires, Jan R., ed. *Practical Issues in Equity Analysis.* Charlottesville, VA: AIMR, 2000.

Stowe, John D., Thomas Robinson, Jerald Pinto, and Dennis McLeavey. *Analysis of Equity Investments: Valuation.* Charlottesville, VA: AIMR, 2002.

Sullivan, Rodney N., ed. *Equity Analysis Issues, Lessons and Techniques.* Charlottesville, VA: AIMR, 2003.

• • • • QUESTIONS • • • •

1. Give an example of a growth company and discuss why you identify it as such. Based on its *P/E,* do you think it is a growth stock? Explain.
2. Give an example of a cyclical stock and discuss why you have designated it as such. Is it issued by a cyclical company?
3. A biotechnology firm is growing at a compound rate of more than 21 percent a year. (Its *ROE* is over 30 percent, and it retains about 70 percent of its earnings.) The stock of this company is priced at about 65 times next year's earnings. Discuss whether you consider this a growth company and/or a growth stock.
4. Select a company outside the retail drugstore industry and indicate what economic series you would use for a sales projection. Discuss why this is a relevant series.
5. Select a company outside the retail drugstore industry and indicate what industry series you would use in an industry analysis. (Use one of the industry groups designated by Standard & Poor's.) Discuss why this industry series is appropriate. Were there other possible alternatives?
6. Select a company outside the retail drugstore industry and, based on reading its annual report and other public information, discuss what you perceive to be its competitive strategy (i.e., low-cost producer or differentiation).
7. Discuss a company that is known to be a low-cost producer in its industry and consider why it is a cost leader. Do the same for a firm known for differentiating.
8. Under what conditions would you use a two- or three-stage cash flow model rather than the constant-growth model?
9. What is the rationale for using the price/book value ratio as a measure of relative value?

10. What would you look for to justify a price/book value ratio of 3.0? What would you expect to be the characteristics of a firm with a *P/BV* ratio of 0.6?

11. Why has the price/cash flow ratio become a popular measure of relative value during the recent past? What factors would help explain a difference in this ratio for two firms?

12. Assume that you uncover two stocks with substantially different price/sales ratios (e.g., 0.5 versus 2.5). Discuss the factors that might explain the difference.

13. Specify the major components for the calculation of economic value added. Describe what a positive EVA signifies.

14. Discuss why you would want to use EVA return on capital rather than absolute EVA to compare two companies or to evaluate a firm's performance over time.

15. Differentiate between EVA and MVA and discuss the relatively weak relationship between these two measures of performance. Is this relationship surprising to you? Explain.

16. Discuss the two factors that determine the franchise value of a firm. Assuming a firm has a base cost of equity of 11 percent and does not have a franchise value, what will be its *P/E*?

17. You are told that a company retains 80 percent of its earnings, and its earnings are growing at a rate of about 8 percent a year versus an average growth rate of 6 percent for all firms. Discuss whether you would consider this a growth company.

18. Discuss the reasoning behind the contention that in a completely competitive economy, there would never be a true growth company.

19. Why is it not feasible to use the dividend discount model in the valuation of true growth companies?

20. Discuss the major assumptions of the growth duration model. Why could these assumptions present a problem?

21. You are told that a growth company has a *P/E* ratio of 13 times and a growth rate of 15 percent compared to the aggregate market, which has a growth rate of 8 percent and a *P/E* ratio of 16 times. What does this comparison imply regarding the growth company? What else do you need to know to properly compare the growth company to the aggregate market?

22. Given the alternative companies described in the chapter (negative growth, simple growth, dynamic growth), indicate what your label would be for Walgreens. Justify your label.

23. Indicate and justify a growth label for General Motors.

24. **CFA EXAMINATION LEVEL I** Using book value to measure profitability and to value a company's stock has limitations. Discuss *five* such limitations from an accounting perspective. Be specific. [10 minutes]

25. **CFA EXAMINATION LEVEL II** On your visit to Litchfield Chemical Corp. (LCC), you learned that the board of directors has periodically debated the company's dividend-payout policy.
    a. Briefly discuss *two* arguments *for* and *two* arguments *against* a high dividend-payout policy. [8 minutes]

        A director of LCC said that the use of dividend discount models by investors is "proof" that "the higher the dividend, the higher the stock price."
    b. Using a constant-growth dividend discount model as a basis of reference, evaluate the director's statement. [8 minutes]
    c. Explain how an increase in dividend payout would affect *each* of the following (holding all other factors constant):
        (1) Internal (implied, normalized, or sustainable) growth rate; and
        (2) Growth in book value. [8 minutes]

26. **CFA EXAMINATION LEVEL II** The Soft Corporation (SC) is planning to acquire a slower-growth competitor, which will materially increase SC's sales volume. The company to be acquired has pretax margins that are approximately the same as those of SC. SC plans to issue $300 million in long-term debt to finance the entire cost of the acquisition.
    a. Discuss how SC's potential acquisition might *decrease* its valuation based on a constant-growth dividend discount model. Be sure to comment on *each* of the three factors in such a model. [9 minutes]
    b. Discuss *two* reasons why SC's potential acquisition might *increase* the *P/E* multiple investors are willing to pay for SC. [4 minutes]

27. **CFA EXAMINATION LEVEL II** A generalized model for the value of any asset is the present value of the expected cash flows:

$$\text{Value} = \sum_{t=1}^{N} \frac{CF_t}{(1 + k)^t}$$

where:

N = life of the asset
CF_t = cash flow in Period t
k = appropriate discount rate

Both stock and bond valuation models use a discounted cash flow approach, which includes the estimation of three factors (N, CF_t, k).

Explain why *each* of these *three* factors is generally more difficult to estimate for common stocks than for traditional corporate bonds. [12 minutes]

• • • • **PROBLEMS** • • • •

1. Select two stocks in an industry of your choice, and perform a common-size income statement analysis over a two-year period.
   a. Discuss which firm is more cost-effective.
   b. Discuss the relative year-to-year changes in gross profit margin, operating profit margin, and net profit margin for each company.
2. Select a company outside the retail drugstore industry, and examine its operating profit margin relative to the operating margin for its industry during the most recent 10-year period. Discuss the annual results in terms of levels and percentage changes.
3. Given Cara's beta of 1.75 and a risk-free rate of 7 percent, what is the expected rate of return for Cara assuming
   a. a 15 percent market return?
   b. a 10 percent market return?
4. Select three companies from any industry except retail drugstores.
   a. Compute their P/E ratios using last year's average price [(high plus low)/2] and earnings.
   b. Compute their growth rate of earnings over the last five years.
   c. Look up the most recent beta reported in Value Line.
   d. Discuss the relationships between P/E, growth, and risk.
5. What is the implied growth duration of Kayleigh Industries given the following:

	S&P Industrials	Kayleigh Industries
P/E ratios	16	24
Expected growth	0.06	0.14
Dividend yield	0.04	0.02

6. Lauren Industries has an 18 percent annual growth rate compared to the market rate of 8 percent. If the market multiple is 18, determine P/E ratios for Lauren Industries, assuming its beta is 1.0 and you feel it can maintain its superior growth rate for
   a. the next 10 years.
   b. the next 5 years.
7. You are given the following information about two computer software firms and the S&P Industrials:

	Company A	Company B	S&P Industrials
P/E ratio	30.0	27.0	18.0
Expected annual growth rate	0.18	0.15	0.07
Dividend yield	0.00	0.01	0.02

    a. Compute the growth duration of each company stock relative to the S&P Industrials.

    b. Compute the growth duration of Company A relative to Company B.

    c. Given these growth durations, what determines your investment decision?

8. **CFA EXAMINATION LEVEL II** The value of an asset is the present value of the expected returns from the asset during the holding period. An investment will provide a stream of returns during this period, and it is necessary to discount this stream of returns at an appropriate rate to determine the asset's present value. A dividend valuation model such as the following is frequently used:

$$P_i = \frac{D_1}{(k_i - g_i)}$$

where:

P_i = the current price of Common Stock i
D_1 = the expected dividend in Period 1
k_i = the required rate of return on Stock i
g_i = the expected constant growth rate of dividends for Stock i

    a. *Identify* the three factors that must be estimated for any valuation model, and *explain* why these estimates are more difficult to derive for common stocks than for bonds. [9 minutes]

    b. *Explain* the principal problem involved in using a dividend valuation model to value

        (1) companies whose operations are closely correlated with economic cycles.

        (2) companies that are of giant size and are maturing.

        (3) companies that are of small size and are growing rapidly.

        Assume that all companies pay dividends. [6 minutes]

9. **CFA EXAMINATION LEVEL I** Your client is considering the purchase of $100,000 in common stock, which pays no dividends and will appreciate in market value by 10 percent per year. At the same time, the client is considering an opportunity to invest $100,000 in a lease obligation that will provide the annual year-end cash flows listed in Exhibit 14.23 below. Assume that each investment will be sold at the end of three years and that you are given no additional information.

    Calculate the present value of each of the two investments assuming a 10 percent discount rate, and state which one will provide the higher return over the three-year period. Use the data in Exhibit 14.23, and show your calculations. [10 minutes]

10. **CFA EXAMINATION LEVEL I** The constant-growth dividend discount model can be used both for the valuation of companies and for the estimation of the long-term total return of a stock.

    Assume: $20 = Price of a Stock Today
              8% = Expected Growth Rate of Dividends
          $0.60 = Annual Dividend One Year Forward

    a. Using *only* the preceding data, compute the expected long-term total return on the stock using the constant-growth dividend discount model. Show calculations.

Exhibit 14.23 Annual Cash Flow from Lease

End of Year

1	$ -0-
2 Lease receipts	15,000
3 Lease receipts	25,000
4 Sale proceeds	$100,000

Present Value of $1

Period	6%	8%	10%	12%
1	0.943	0.926	0.909	0.893
2	0.890	0.857	0.826	0.797
3	0.840	0.794	0.751	0.712
4	0.792	0.735	0.683	0.636
5	0.747	0.681	0.621	0.567

    b. Briefly discuss *three* disadvantages of the constant-growth dividend discount model in its application to investment analysis.

    c. Identify *three* alternative methods to the dividend discount model for the valuation of companies. [10 minutes]

11. **CFA EXAMINATION LEVEL II** An analyst expects a risk-free return of 4.5 percent, a market return of 14.5 percent, and the returns for Stocks A and B that are shown in Exhibit 14.24.

    a. Show on a graph

        (1) where Stocks A and B would plot on the security market line (SML) if they were fairly valued using the capital asset pricing model (CAPM).

        (2) where Stocks A and B actually plot on the same graph according to the returns estimated by the analyst and shown in Exhibit 14.24. [6 minutes]

    b. State whether Stocks A and B are undervalued or overvalued if the analyst uses the SML for strategic investment decisions. [4 minutes]

12. **CFA EXAMINATION LEVEL II** Scott Kelly is reviewing MasterToy's financial statements in order to estimate its sustainable growth rate. Using the information presented in Exhibit 14.25,

    a. (1) identify and calculate the *three* components of the DuPont formula.

        (2) calculate the *ROE* for 1999, using the three components of the DuPont formula.

        (3) calculate the sustainable-growth rate for 1999. [13 minutes]

Exhibit 14.24 Stock Information

Stock	Beta	Analyst's Estimated Return
A	1.2	16%
B	0.8	14%

Exhibit 14.25 MasterToy, Inc.: Actual 1998 and Estimated 1999 Financial Statements for Fiscal Year Ending December 31 ($ Millions, Except per-Share Data)

	1998	1999e	Change (%)
Income Statement			
Revenue	$4,750	$5,140	7.6
Cost of goods sold	$2,400	$2,540	
Selling, general, and administrative	1,400	1,550	
Depreciation	180	210	
Goodwill amortization	10	10	
Operating income	$ 760	$ 830	8.4
Interest expense	20	25	
Income before taxes	$ 740	$ 805	
Income taxes	265	295	
Net income	$ 475	$ 510	
Earnings per share	$ 1.79	$ 1.96	8.6
Average shares outstanding (millions)	265	260	
Balance Sheet			
Cash	$ 400	$400	
Accounts receivable	$ 680	$700	
Inventories	$ 570	$600	
Net property, plant, and equipment	$ 800	$870	
Intangibles	$ 500	$530	
Total assets	$2,950	$3,100	
Current liabilities	$ 550	$ 600	
Long-term debt	$ 300	$ 300	
Total liabilities	$ 850	$ 900	
Stockholders' equity	$2,100	$2,200	
Total liabilities and equity	$2,950	$3,100	
Book value per share	$ 7.92	$ 8.46	
Annual dividend per share	$ 0.55	$ 0.60	

b. Kelly has calculated actual and sustainable growth for each of the past four years and finds in each year that its calculated sustainable-growth rate substantially exceeds its actual growth rate. Cite *two* courses of action (other than ignoring the problem) that Kelly should encourage MasterToy to take, assuming the calculated sustainable-growth rate continues to exceed the actual growth rate. [6 minutes]

> **Note: Questions 13 through 17 relate to Telluride and its subsidiaries.**

13. **CFA EXAMINATION LEVEL II** The management of Telluride, an international diversified conglomerate based in the United States, believes that the recent strong performance of its wholly owned medical supply subsidiary, Sundanci, has gone unnoticed. In order to realize Sundanci's full value, Telluride has announced that it will divest Sundanci in a tax-free spin-off.

Sue Carroll, CFA, is Director of Research at Kesson and Associates. In developing an investment recommendation for Sundanci, Carroll has directed four of her analysts to determine a valuation of Sundanci using various valuation disciplines. To assist her analysts, Carroll has gathered the information shown in Exhibits 14.26 and 14.27.

Prior to determining Sundanci's valuation, Carroll analyzes Sundanci's return on equity (*ROE*) and sustainable growth.

a. (1) Calculate the *three* components of *ROE* in the DuPont formula for the year 2000.

(2) Calculate *ROE* for the year 2000.

(3) Calculate the sustainable-growth rate. Show your work. [12 minutes]

Carroll learns that Sundanci's Board of Directors is considering the following policy changes that will affect Sundanci's sustainable-growth rate:

- Director A proposes an increase in the quarterly dividend to $0.15 per share.
- Director B proposes a bond issue of $25 million, the proceeds of which would be used to increase production capacity.
- Director C proposes a 2-for-1 stock split.

Exhibit 14.26 Sundanci Actual 1999 and 2000 Financial Statements for Fiscal Years Ending May 31 ($ Million, Except per-Share Data)

	1999	2000
Income Statement		
Revenue	$474	$598
Depreciation	20	23
Other operating costs	368	460
Income before taxes	86	115
Taxes	26	35
Net income	60	80
Dividends	18	24
Earnings per share	$0.714	$0.952
Dividend per share	$0.214	$0.286
Common shares outstanding (millions)	84.0	84.0
Balance Sheet		
Current assets	$201	$326
Net property, plant and equipment	474	489
Total assets	675	815
Current liabilities	57	141
Long-term debt	0	0
Total liabilities	57	141
Shareholders' equity	618	674
Total liabilities and equity	675	815
Capital expenditures	34	38

Exhibit 14.27 Selected Financial Information for Sundanci

Required rate of return on equity	14%
Growth rate of industry	13%
Industry *P/E* ratio	26

b. Indicate the effect of *each* of these proposals on Sundanci's sustainable rate of growth, given that other factors remain unchanged. Identify which component of the sustainable-growth model, if any, is directly affected by *each* proposal. [9 minutes]

Note: Answer Question 13b using the following template.

TEMPLATE FOR QUESTION 13b

Proposal	Effect on Sustainable-Growth Rate (circle one)	Component Directly Affected (If Any)
Increase in quarterly dividend	Increase Decrease No effect	
Bond issue	Increase Decrease No effect	
Stock split	Increase Decrease No effect	

 14. **CFA EXAMINATION LEVEL II** Helen Morgan, CFA, has been asked by Carroll to determine the potential valuation for Sundanci, Inc., using the dividend discount model. Morgan anticipates that Sundanci's earnings and dividends will grow at 32 percent for two years and 13 percent thereafter.

Calculate the current value of a share of Sundanci stock using a two-stage dividend discount model and the data from Exhibits 14.26 and 14.27. Show your work. [8 minutes]

 15. **CFA EXAMINATION LEVEL II** Abbey Naylor, CFA, has been directed by Carroll to determine the value of Sundanci's stock using the free cash flow to equity model. Naylor believes that Sundanci's FCFE will grow at 27 percent for two years and 13 percent thereafter. Capital expenditures, depreciation, and working capital are all expected to increase proportionately with FCFE.

a. Calculate the amount of FCFE per share for the year 2000, using the data from Exhibit 14.26. Show your work. [6 minutes]

b. Calculate the current value of a share of Sundanci stock based on the two-stage FCFE model. Show your work. [8 minutes]

c. (1) Describe *one* limitation of the two-stage DDM model that is addressed by using the two-stage FCFE model. [6 minutes]

(2) Describe *one* limitation of the two-stage DDM model that is *not* addressed by using the two-stage FCFE model. [6 minutes]

 16. **CFA EXAMINATION LEVEL II** Christie Johnson, CFA, has been assigned by Carroll to analyze Sundanci using the constant-growth dividend price/earnings (*P/E*) ratio model. Johnson assumes that Sundanci's earnings and dividends will grow at a constant rate of 13 percent.

a. Calculate the *P/E* ratio based on information in Exhibits 14.26 and 14.27 and on Johnson's assumptions for Sundanci. Show your work. [4 minutes]

b. Identify, within the context of the constant-growth dividend model, how *each* of the fundamental factors shown in the following template would affect the *P/E* ratio. [4 minutes]

Note: A change in a fundamental factor is assumed to happen in isolation, and interactive effects between factors are ignored. Every other element of the firm is unchanged.

Note: Answer Question 16b using the following template.

TEMPLATE FOR QUESTION 16B

Fundamental Factor	Effect on *P/E* Ratio (circle one)
The riskiness (beta) of Sundanci increases substantially.	Increase Decrease May increase or decrease
The estimated growth rate of Sundanci's earnings and dividends increases.	Increase Decrease May increase or decrease
The dividend-payout ratio of Sundanci increases.	Increase Decrease May increase or decrease
The market risk premium increases.	Increase Decrease May increase or decrease

c. Explain why an increase in the dividend-payout ratio may not have the effect that the constant-growth dividend *P/E* ratio model suggests. [4 minutes]

17. **CFA EXAMINATION LEVEL II** One week after the spin-off of Sundanci, Carroll asks analyst Jim Martin to use economic value added and market value added to measure the performance of Sundanci. In addition to the information provided in Exhibits 14.26 and 14.27, Martin uses the following information in his analysis:
- Adjusted net operating profit after tax is $100 million.
- Total adjusted capital is $700 million.
- Closing stock price is $26.

a. Calculate the following for Sundanci. Show your work. [6 minutes]
(1) EVA for fiscal 2000
(2) MVA as of fiscal year-end 2000

b. Discuss the *two* primary differences in calculating economic profit (as used in EVA) versus accounting profit. [6 minutes]

18. **CFA EXAMINATION LEVEL II** Peninsular has another client who has inquired about the valuation method best suited for comparison of companies in an industry that has the following characteristics:
- Principal competitors within the industry are located in the United States, France, Japan, and Brazil.
- The industry is currently operating at a cyclical low, with many firms reporting losses.
- The industry is subjected to rapid technological change.

Jones recommends that the client consider the following valuation ratios:
1. Price to earnings
2. Price to book value
3. Price to sales

a. Determine which *one* of the three valuation ratios is most appropriate for comparing companies in this industry. Support your answer with *two* reasons that make that ratio superior to *either* of the other two ratios. [5 minutes]

The client also has expressed interest in economic value added as a measure of company performance. Jones asks his assistant to prepare a presentation about EVA for the client. The assistant's presentation includes the following statements:
1. EVA is a measure of a firm's excess shareholder value generated over a long period of time.
2. In calculating EVA, the cost of capital is the weighted average of the after-tax yield on long-term bonds with similar risk and the cost of equity as calculated by the capital asset pricing model.
3. EVA provides a consistent measure of performance across firms.

b. Determine whether *each* of the statements is correct or incorrect and, if *incorrect,* explain why. [6 minutes]

Note: Explanations cannot repeat the statement in negative form but must indicate what is needed to make the statement correct.

> **Note: Answer Question 18b using the following template.**

TEMPLATE FOR QUESTION 18B

Statement	Determine Whether Correct or Incorrect (circle one)	If Incorrect, Explain Why
1. EVA is a measure of a firm's excess shareholder value generated over a long period of time.	Correct Incorrect	
2. In calculating EVA, the cost of capital is the weighted average of the after-tax yield on long-term bonds with similar risk and the cost of equity as calculated by the capital asset pricing model.	Correct Incorrect	
3. EVA provides a consistent measure of performance across firms.	Correct Incorrect	

THOMSON ONE | Business School Edition

1. Identify two firms in an industry, one of which seems to follow a "cost leadership" strategy and one of which tries to be a "differentiator." How do their common-size financial statements differ? Examine their trends in *ROE* using DuPont analysis. Comment on the differences and/or similarities you find.

2. Update the analysis of Walgreens in this chapter by computing the following:
   a. average compound dividend growth rate from 1993 until the most recent year
   b. sustainable growth rate
   c. expected returns, based on Thomson One: Business School Edition's beta estimate and estimates you obtain of the current risk-free rate (the 10-year Treasury bond yield) and a market risk premium of 3 percent, 5 percent, 7 percent.
   d. present value of dividends, using the growth assumptions in the chapter. Compare your estimated value to the current market price of WAG and indicate if you would buy the stock.

3. Estimate Walgreen Co.'s free cash flow to equity and its operating free cash flow for the most recent year.

4. Using peer analysis, compare Walgreen Co.'s relative valuation ratios with those of its peers (click on the "peers" tab, then click on "overviews" and "valuation comparison").

5. Compute the current growth duration for WAG using the growth rate from Question 2b and assuming a divident yield of 1 percent. For the market assume a *P/E* of 18 times, growth of 6 percent and dividend yield of 2 percent.

CHAPTER 15

Technical Analysis*

After you read this chapter, you should be able to answer the following questions:

- How does technical analysis differ from fundamental analysis?
- What are the underlying assumptions of technical analysis?
- What major assumption causes a difference between technical analysis and the efficient market hypothesis?
- What are the major advantages of technical analysis?
- What are the major challenges to technical analysis?
- What is the logic for the major contrary-opinion rules used by technicians?
- What rules are used by technicians who want to "follow the smart money"?
- What is the breadth of market measures, and what are they intended to indicate?
- What are the three types of price movements postulated in the Dow Theory, and how are they used?
- Why is trading volume important and how do technicians use it?
- What are support and resistance levels and how are they used?
- How do technicians use moving-average lines to detect changes in trends?
- What is the rationale behind a relative-strength line?
- How are bar charts different from point-and-figure charts?
- What are some uses of technical analysis in foreign security markets?
- How is technical analysis used when analyzing bonds?

> *The market reacted yesterday to the report of a large increase in the short interest on the NYSE.*
>
> *Although the market declined today, it was not considered bearish because of the light volume.*
>
> *The market declined today after three days of increases due to profit taking by investors.*

These and similar statements appear daily in the financial news. All of them have as their rationale one of numerous technical trading rules. *Technical analysts,* or *technicians,* develop technical trading rules from observations of past price movements of the stock market and individual stocks. The philosophy behind technical analysis is in sharp contrast to the efficient market hypothesis that we studied, which contends that past performance has no influence on future performance or market values. It also differs from what we learned about fundamental analysis, which involves making investment decisions based on the examination of the economy, an industry, and company variables that lead to an estimate of intrinsic value for an investment, which is then compared to its prevailing market price. In contrast to the efficient market hypothesis or fundamental analysis, **technical analysis** involves the examination of past market data such as prices and the volume of trading, which leads to an estimate of future price trends and,

---

*Walter G. Murphy and Richard T. McCabe, from Merrill Lynch Capital Markets, provided helpful comments and material for this chapter.

therefore, an investment decision. Whereas fundamental analysts use economic data that are usually separate from the stock or bond market, the technical analyst uses data *from the market itself* because they contend that the market is its own best predictor. Therefore, technical analysis is an alternative method of making the investment decision and answering the questions: What securities should an investor buy or sell? When should these investments be made?

Technical analysts see no need to study the multitude of economic, industry, and company variables to arrive at an estimate of future value because they believe that past price movements will signal future price movements. Technicians also believe that a change in the price trend may predict a forthcoming change in the fundamental variables such as earnings and risk before the change is perceived by most fundamental analysts. Are technicians correct? Many investors using these techniques claim to have experienced superior rates of return on many investments. In addition, many newsletter writers base their recommendations on technical analysis. Finally, even the major investment firms that employ many fundamental analysts also employ technical analysts to provide investment advice. Numerous investment professionals and individual investors believe in and use technical trading rules to make their investment decisions. Therefore, whether a fan of fundamental analysis or an advocate of the efficient market hypothesis, investors should still have an understanding of the basic philosophy and reasoning behind technical approaches. Thus, we begin this chapter with an examination of the basic philosophy underlying technical analysis. Subsequently, we consider the advantages and potential problems with the technical approach. Finally, we present alternative technical trading rules applicable to both the U.S. and foreign securities markets.

15.1 Underlying Assumptions of Technical Analysis

Technical analysts base trading decisions on examinations of prior price and volume data to determine past market trends from which they predict future behavior for the market as a whole and for individual securities. Several assumptions summarized in Levy (1966) lead to this view of price movements. Certain aspects of these assumptions are controversial, leading fundamental analysts and advocates of efficient markets to question their validity. We have italicized those aspects in our list.

1. The market value of any good or service is determined solely by the interaction of supply and demand.
2. Supply and demand are governed by numerous rational and irrational factors. Included in these factors are those economic variables relied on by the fundamental analyst as well as opinions, moods, and guesses. The market weighs all these factors continually and automatically.
3. Disregarding minor fluctuations, *the prices for individual securities and the overall value of the market tend to move in trends, which persist for appreciable lengths of time.*
4. Prevailing trends change in reaction to shifts in supply and demand relationships. These shifts, no matter why they occur, *can be detected sooner or later in the action of the market itself.*

The first two assumptions are almost universally accepted by technicians and nontechnicians alike. Almost anyone who has had a basic course in economics would agree that, at any point in time, the price of a security (or any good or service) is determined by the interaction of supply and demand. In addition, most observers would acknowledge that supply and demand are governed by many variables. The only difference in opinion might concern the influence of the irrational factors. Certainly, everyone would agree that the market continually weighs all these factors.

In contrast, there is a significant difference of opinion regarding the assumption about the *speed of adjustment* of stock prices to changes in supply and demand. Technical analysts expect stock prices to move in trends that persist for long periods because they believe that new information does *not* come to the market at one point in time but rather enters the market *over a period*

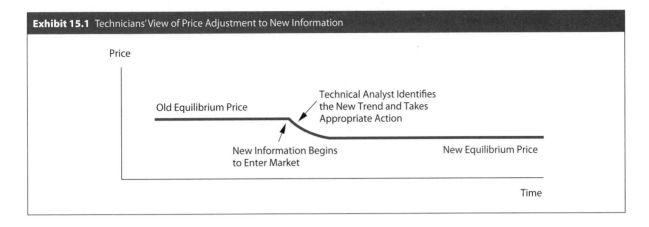

Exhibit 15.1 Technicians' View of Price Adjustment to New Information

of time. This pattern of information access occurs because of different sources of information or because certain investors receive the information or perceive fundamental changes earlier than others. As various groups—ranging from insiders to well-informed professionals to the average investor—receive the information and buy or sell a security accordingly, its price moves gradually toward the new equilibrium. Therefore, technicians do not expect the price adjustment to be as abrupt as fundamental analysts and efficient market supporters do; rather, they expect a *gradual price adjustment* to reflect the gradual dissemination of information.

Exhibit 15.1 shows this process wherein new information causes a decrease in the equilibrium price for a security but the price adjustment is not rapid. It occurs as a trend that persists until the stock reaches its new equilibrium. Technical analysts look for the beginning of a movement from one equilibrium value to a new equilibrium value but do not attempt to predict the new equilibrium value. They look for the start of a change so that they can get on the bandwagon early and benefit from the move to the new equilibrium price by buying if the trend is up or selling if the trend is down. Obviously, if there is a rapid adjustment of prices to the new information (as expected by those who espouse an efficient market), the ride on the bandwagon would be so short that investors could not benefit.

15.2 Advantages of Technical Analysis

Although technicians understand the logic of fundamental analysis, they see several benefits in their approach. Most technical analysts admit that a fundamental analyst with good information, good analytical ability, and a keen sense of information's impact on the market should achieve above-average returns. However, this statement requires qualification. According to technical analysts, it is important to recognize that the fundamental analysts can experience superior returns *only* if they obtain new information before other investors and process it *correctly* and *quickly.* Technical analysts do not believe the majority of investors can consistently get new information before other investors and consistently process it correctly and quickly.

In addition, technical analysts claim that a major advantage of their method is that *it is not heavily dependent on financial accounting statements*—the major source of information about the past performance of a firm or industry. As we know from Chapters 13 and 14, the fundamental analyst evaluates such statements to help project future return and risk characteristics for industries and individual securities. The technician contends that there are several major problems with accounting statements:

1. They lack a great deal of information needed by security analysts, such as information related to sales, earnings, and capital utilized by product line and customers.
2. According to GAAP (Generally Accepted Accounting Principles), corporations may choose among several procedures for reporting expenses, assets, or liabilities. Notably,

these alternative procedures can produce vastly different values for expenses, income, return on assets, and return on equity, depending on whether the firm is conservative or aggressive. As a result, an investor can have trouble comparing the statements of two firms within the same industry, much less firms across industries.

3. Many psychological factors and other nonquantifiable variables do not appear in financial statements. Examples include employee training and loyalty, customer goodwill, and general investor attitude toward an industry. Investor attitudes could be important when investors become concerned about the risk from restrictions or taxes on products such as tobacco or alcohol or when firms do business in countries that have significant political risk.

Therefore, because technicians are suspicious of financial statements, they consider it advantageous not to depend on them. As we will show, most of the data used by technicians, such as security prices, volume of trading, and other trading information, are derived from the stock market itself.

Also, a fundamental analyst must process new information correctly and *quickly* to derive a new intrinsic value for the stock or bond before other investors. Technicians, on the other hand, only need to quickly recognize a movement to a new equilibrium value *for whatever reason*—that is, they do not need to know about a specific event and determine the effect of the event on the value of the firm and its stock.

Finally, assume a fundamental analyst determines that a given security is under- or overvalued a long time before other investors. He or she still must determine when to make the purchase or sale. Ideally, the highest rate of return would come from making the transaction just before the change in market value occurs. For example, assume that based on your analysis in February, you expect a firm to report substantially higher earnings in June. Although you could buy the stock in February, you would be better off waiting until about May to buy the stock so your funds would not be tied up for an extra three months, but you may be reticent to wait that long. Because most technicians do not invest until the move to the new equilibrium is under way, they contend that they are more likely than a fundamental analyst to experience ideal timing.

· ·

15.3 Challenges to Technical Analysis

Those who doubt the value of technical analysis for investment decisions question the usefulness of this technique in two areas. First, they challenge some of its basic assumptions. Second, they challenge some specific technical trading rules and their long-run usefulness. In this section we consider these challenges.

15.3.1 Challenges to Technical Analysis Assumptions

The major challenge to technical analysis is based on the results of empirical tests of the efficient market hypothesis (EMH). As discussed in Chapter 6, for technical trading rules to generate superior risk-adjusted returns after taking account of transaction costs, the market would have to be slow to adjust prices to the arrival of new information; that is, it would have to be inefficient. This is referred to as the weak-form efficient market hypothesis. The two sets of tests of the weak-form EMH are (1) the statistical analysis of prices to determine if prices moved in trends or were a random walk, and (2) the analysis of specific trading rules to determine if their use could beat a buy-and-hold policy after considering transactions costs and risk. Almost all the studies testing the weak-form EMH using statistical analysis have found that prices do not move in trends based on statistical tests of autocorrelation and runs. These results support the EMH.

Regarding the analysis of specific trading rules, as discussed in Chapter 6, numerous technical trading rules exist that have not been or cannot be tested. Still, the vast majority of the results for the trading rules that have been tested support the EMH.

15.3.2 Challenges to Technical Trading Rules

An obvious challenge to technical analysis is that the past price patterns or relationships between specific market variables and stock prices may not be repeated. As a result, a technique that previously worked might miss subsequent market turns. This possibility leads most technicians to follow several trading rules and to seek a consensus of all of them to predict the future market pattern.

Other critics contend that many price patterns become self-fulfilling prophecies. For example, assume that many analysts expect a stock selling at $40 a share to go to $50 or more if it should rise above its current pattern and break through its channel at $45. As soon as it reaches $45, enough technicians will buy to cause the price to rise to $50, exactly as predicted. In fact, some technicians may place a limit order to buy the stock at such a breakout point. Under such conditions, the increase will probably be only temporary and the price will return to its true equilibrium.

Another problem with technical analysis is that the success of a particular trading rule will encourage many investors to adopt it. It is contended that this popularity and the resulting competition will eventually neutralize the technique. If numerous investors focus on a specific technical trading rule, some of them will attempt to anticipate the price pattern and either ruin the expected historical price pattern or eliminate profits for most traders by causing the price to change faster than expected. For example, suppose it becomes known that technicians who employ short-selling data have been enjoying high rates of return. Based on this knowledge, other technicians will likely start using these data and thus accelerate the stock price pattern following changes in short selling. As a result, this profitable trading rule may no longer be profitable after the first few investors react.

Further, as we will see when we examine specific trading rules, *they all require a great deal of subjective judgment.* Two technical analysts looking at the same price pattern may arrive at widely different interpretations of what has happened and, therefore, will come to different investment decisions. This implies that the use of various techniques is neither completely mechanical nor obvious. Finally, as we will discuss in connection with several trading rules, *the standard values that signal investment decisions can change over time.* Therefore, in some instances technical analysts adjust the specified values that trigger investment decisions to conform to the new environment. In other cases, trading rules have been abandoned because they no longer work.

15.4 Technical Trading Rules and Indicators

To illustrate the specific technical trading rules, Exhibit 15.2 shows a typical stock price cycle that could be an example for the overall stock market or for an individual stock. The graph shows a peak and trough, along with a rising trend channel, a flat trend channel, a declining trend channel, and indications of when a technical analyst would ideally want to trade.

The graph begins with the end of a declining (bear) market that finishes in a **trough**, followed by an upward trend that breaks through the **declining trend channel**. Confirmation that the declining trend has reversed would be a buy signal. The technical analyst would buy stocks that showed this pattern.

The analyst would then expect the development of a **rising trend channel**. As long as the stock price stayed in this rising channel, the technician would hold the stock(s). Ideally, they want to sell at the **peak** of the cycle, but they cannot identify a peak until after the trend changes.

If the stock (or the market) begins trading in a flat pattern, it will necessarily break out of its rising trend channel. At this point, some technical analysts would sell, but most would hold to see if the stock experiences a period of consolidation and then breaks out of the **flat trend channel** on the upside and begins rising again. Alternatively, if the stock were to break out of the channel on the downside, the technician would take this as a sell signal and would expect

Exhibit 15.2 Typical Stock-Market Cycle

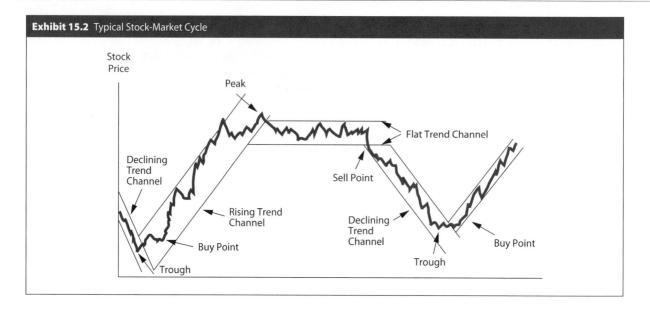

a declining trend channel. The next buy signal would come after the trough when the price breaks out of the declining channel and establishes a rising trend. We will consider strategies to detect these changes in trend and the importance of volume in this analysis shortly.

There are numerous technical trading rules and a range of interpretations for each of them. Almost all technical analysts watch many alternative rules and decide on a buy or sell decision based on a *consensus* of the signals because complete agreement of all the rules is rare. In the following discussion of several well-known techniques, we have divided the rules into four groups based on the attitudes of technical analysts. The first group includes trading rules used by analysts who like to trade against the crowd using contrary-opinion signals. The second group attempts to emulate astute investors, that is, the smart money. The third group includes popular technical indicators that are not easily classified. Finally, the fourth group contains pure price and volume techniques, including the famous Dow Theory.

15.4.1 Contrary-Opinion Rules

Many technical analysts rely on technical trading rules that assume that the majority of investors are wrong as the market approaches peaks and troughs. Therefore, these technicians try to determine when the majority of investors is either strongly bullish or bearish and then trade in the opposite direction.

Mutual Fund Cash Positions Mutual funds hold some part of their portfolio in cash for one of several reasons. One is that they need cash to liquidate shares submitted by fundholders. Another is that new investments in the mutual fund may not have been invested. Third, the portfolio manager might be bearish on the market and want to increase the fund's defensive cash position.

Mutual funds' ratios of cash as a percentage of the total assets in their portfolios (the *cash ratio* or *liquid asset ratio*) are reported in the press, including monthly figures in *Barron's*.[1] This percentage of cash has varied in recent years from a low point of about 4 percent to a high point near 11 percent, although there appears to be a declining trend to the series.

Contrary-opinion technicians believe that mutual funds usually are wrong at peaks and troughs. Thus, they expect mutual funds to have a high percentage of cash near a market

[1] *Barron's* is a prime source for numerous technical indicators. For a readable discussion of relevant data and their use, see Martin E. Zweig (1987).

trough—the time when they should be fully invested to take advantage of the impending market rise. At the market peak, these technicians expect mutual funds to be almost fully invested with a low percentage of cash when they should be selling stocks and realizing gains. Therefore, contrary-opinion technicians watch for the mutual fund cash position to approach one of the extremes and act contrary to the mutual funds. Specifically, they would tend to buy when the cash ratio approaches 11 percent and to sell when the cash ratio approaches 4 percent.

An alternative rationale for this buy-sell decision is that a high cash position is a bullish indicator because of potential buying power. Irrespective of the reason for a large cash balance, these technicians believe the large cash balance will eventually be invested and will cause stock prices to increase. Alternatively, a low cash ratio would mean that the institutions have bought heavily and are left with little potential buying power. As of January 2008, this ratio was at 4.1 percent which would be a bearish signal.

Credit Balances in Brokerage Accounts Credit balances result when investors sell stocks and leave the proceeds with their brokers, expecting to reinvest them shortly. The amounts are reported by the SEC and the NYSE in *Barron's*. Because technical analysts view these credit balances as potential purchasing power, a decline in these balances is considered bearish because it indicates lower purchasing power as the market approaches a peak. Alternatively, a buildup of credit balances indicates an increase in buying power and is a bullish signal.

Investment Advisory Opinions Many technicians believe that if a large proportion of investment advisory services are bearish, this signals the approach of a market trough and the onset of a bull market. Because most advisory services tend to be trend followers, the number of bears usually is greatest when market bottoms are approaching. This trading rule is specified in terms of the percent of advisory services that are bearish/bullish given the number of services expressing an opinion.[2] A 40 percent bearish or 25 percent bullish reading indicates a major market bottom (a bullish indicator), while a 40 percent bullish or 25 percent bearish reading suggests a major market top (a bearish signal). Exhibit 15.3 shows a time-series plot of the DJIA and the bearish sentiment index. As of March 2008, the index was at about 34 percent, which is a neutral rating.

NASDAQ versus NYSE Volume This ratio of trading volume is considered a measure of speculative activity. Speculative trading typically peaks at market peaks. Notably, the

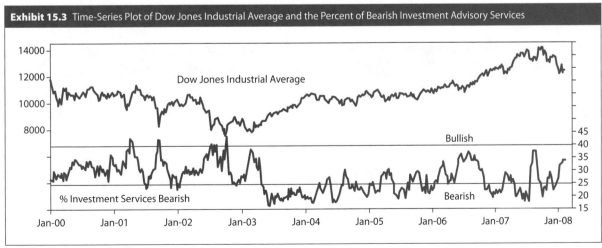

Exhibit 15.3 Time-Series Plot of Dow Jones Industrial Average and the Percent of Bearish Investment Advisory Services

Source: Investors Intelligence Chartcraft.

[2] This ratio is compiled by Investors Intelligence, Larchmont, NY 10538. The technicians at Merrill Lynch use this series as one of their "Investor Sentiment Indicators." Notably, the percentage signals have changed over time.

interpretation of the ratio has changed—that is, the decision rules have changed. Specifically, during the mid-1990s, the decision rule was in terms of specific percentages—112 percent was considered heavy speculative trading and an overbought market while 87 percent was considered low speculative trading and an oversold market. The problem was that the percentages kept increasing because of faster growth in NASDAQ trading volume and dominance of the NASDAQ market by a few large-cap stocks. It was subsequently decided to detect excess speculative activity by using the *direction* of the volume ratio as a guide. For example, if this ratio is increasing, it indicates a bearish speculative environment.

Chicago Board Options Exchange (CBOE) Put–Call Ratio Contrary-opinion technicians use put options, which give the holder the right to sell stock at a specified price for a given time period, as signals of a bearish attitude. A higher put–call ratio indicates a pervasive bearish attitude for investors, which technicians consider a bullish indicator.

This ratio historically fluctuated between 0.60 and 0.40 and was typically substantially less than 1 because investors tend to be bullish and avoid selling short or buying puts. Beginning in 2006, the series experienced a rising trend and has been in the range of 0.80 to 1.20. As of March 2008 the ratio was about 1.14, implying that investors are quite bearish, which would be a strong bullish sign for contrary opinion technicians.

Futures Traders Bullish on Stock-Index Futures Another relatively popular contrary-opinion measure is the percentage of speculators in stock-index futures who are bullish regarding stocks based on a survey of individual futures traders. These technicians would consider it a bearish sign when more than 70 percent of the speculators are bullish, and a bullish sign when this ratio declines to 30 percent or lower. The plot in Exhibit 15.4 shows that as of March 2008 this indicator was about 43 percent, which would be a neutral rating.

As we have shown, contrary-opinion technicians have several measures of how the majority of investors are investing that prompt them to take the opposite action. They generally employ several of these series to provide a consensus regarding investors' sentiment.

15.4.2 Follow the Smart Money

Some technical analysts have created a set of indicators and corresponding rules that they believe indicate the behavior of smart, sophisticated investors. We discuss three such indicators in this section.

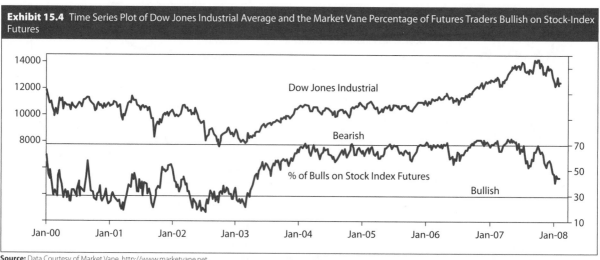

Exhibit 15.4 Time Series Plot of Dow Jones Industrial Average and the Market Vane Percentage of Futures Traders Bullish on Stock-Index Futures

Source: Data Courtesy of Market Vane, http://www.marketvane.net.

Confidence Index Published by *Barron's,* the Confidence Index is the ratio of *Barron's* average yield on 10 top-grade corporate bonds to the yield on the Dow Jones average of 40 bonds.[3] This index measures the change in yield spread over time between high-grade bonds and a large cross-section of bonds. Because the yields on high-grade bonds always should be lower than those on a large cross-section of bonds, this ratio should approach 100 as the spread between the two sets of bonds gets smaller.

Technicians believe the ratio is a bullish indicator because, during periods of high confidence, investors are willing to invest in lower-quality bonds for the added yield, which causes a decrease in the yield spread between the large cross-section of bonds relative to the yield on high-grade bonds. Therefore, this ratio of yields—the Confidence Index—will increase. In contrast, when investors are pessimistic, they avoid low-quality bonds, which increases the yield spread between high-grade and average bonds, and there is a decline in the Confidence Index.

Unfortunately, this interpretation assumes that changes in the yield spread are caused almost exclusively by changes in investor demand for different quality bonds. In fact, the yield differences have frequently changed because of changes in the supply of bonds. For example, a large issue of high-grade AT&T bonds could cause a temporary increase in yields on all high-grade bonds, which would reduce the yield spread, and increase the Confidence Index without any change in investors' attitudes. Therefore, this change in supply generates a false signal of a change in confidence.

T-Bill–Eurodollar Yield Spread A popular measure of investor attitude or confidence on a global basis is the spread between T-bill yields and Eurodollar rates measured as the ratio of T-bill/Eurodollar yields. It is reasoned that, at times of international crisis, this spread widens as the smart money flows to safe-haven U.S. T-bills, which causes a decline in this ratio. It is contended that the stock market typically experiences a trough shortly thereafter.

Debit Balances in Brokerage Accounts (Margin Debt) Debit balances in brokerage accounts represent borrowing (margin debt) by knowledgeable investors from their brokers. Hence, these balances indicate the attitude of sophisticated investors who engage in margin transactions. Therefore, an increase in debit balances implies buying by these sophisticated investors and is considered a bullish sign, while a decline in debit balances would indicate selling and would be a bearish indicator.

Monthly data on margin debt is reported in *Barron's.* Unfortunately, this index does not include borrowing by investors from other sources such as banks. Also, because it is an absolute value, technicians can only look for changes in the trend of borrowing—that is, increases are bullish, declines are bearish.

15.4.3 Momentum Indicators

In addition to contrary-opinion and smart-money signals, several indicators of overall market momentum are used to make aggregate market decisions.

Breadth of Market Breadth of market measures the number of issues that have increased each day and the number of issues that have declined. It helps explain the cause of a change of direction in a composite market index such as the S&P 500 Index. As we discussed in Chapter 5, most stock-market indexes are heavily influenced by the stocks of large firms because they are value weighted. Therefore, a stock-market index can experience an overall increase while the majority of the individual issues do not, which means that most stocks are not participating in the rising market. Such a divergence can be detected by examining the advance–decline figures for all stocks on the exchange, along with the overall market index.

---

[3] Historical data for this index are contained in the *Dow Jones Investor's Handbook,* Princeton, NJ (Dow Jones Books, annual). Current figures appear in *Barron's.*

Exhibit 15.5 Daily Advances and Declines on the New York Stock Exchange

Day	1	2	3	4	5
Issues traded	3,608	3,641	3,659	3,651	3,612
Advances	2,310	2,350	1,558	2,261	2,325
Declines	909	912	1,649	933	894
Unchanged	389	379	452	457	393
Net advances (advances minus declines)	+1,401	+1,438	−91	+1,328	+1,431
Cumulative net advances	+1,401	+2,839	+2,748	+4,076	+5,507
Changes in DJIA	+40.47	+95.75	−15.25	+108.42	+140.63

Sources: New York Stock Exchange and *Barron's.*

The advance–decline index is typically a cumulative index of net advances or net declines. Specifically, each day major newspapers publish figures on the number of issues on the NYSE that advanced, declined, or were unchanged. The figures for a five-day sample, as would be reported in *Barron's,* are shown in Exhibit 15.5. These figures, along with changes in the DJIA at the bottom of the table, indicate a strong market advance because the DJIA was increasing and the net advance figure was strong, indicating that the market increase was broadly based. Even the results on Day 3, when the market declined 15 points, were encouraging since it was a small overall decline and the individual stock issues were split just about 50–50, which points toward a fairly even environment.

Stocks above Their 200-Day Moving Average Technicians often compute moving averages of an index to determine its general trend. To examine individual stocks, the 200-day **moving average** of prices has been fairly popular. From these moving-average indexes for numerous stocks, Media General Financial Services calculates how many stocks currently are trading above their 200-day moving-average index, and this is used as an indicator of general investor sentiment. The market is considered to be *overbought* and subject to a negative correction when more than 80 percent of the stocks are trading above their 200-day moving average. In contrast, if less than 20 percent of the stocks are selling above their 200-day moving average, the market is considered to be *oversold,* which means investors should expect a positive correction. As shown in Exhibit 15.6, as of March 2008 the percent of stocks selling above their 200-day moving average has been about 20 percent, which indicates an oversold, bullish signal.

15.4.4 Stock Price and Volume Techniques

In the introduction to this chapter, we examined a hypothetical stock price chart that demonstrated market peaks and troughs along with rising and declining trend channels and breakouts from channels that signal new price trends or reversals of the price trends. While price patterns alone are important, most technical trading rules consider both stock price and corresponding volume movements.

Dow Theory Any discussion of technical analysis using price and volume data should begin with a consideration of the Dow Theory because it was among the earliest work on this topic and remains the basis for many technical indicators.[4] Dow described stock prices as moving in trends analogous to the movement of water. He postulated three types of price movements over time: (1) major trends that are like tides in the ocean, (2) intermediate trends that resemble waves, and (3) short-run movements that are like ripples. Followers of the Dow Theory attempt to detect the direction of the major price trend (tide), recognizing that intermediate

---

[4] A study that discusses and provides support for the Dow Theory is David A. Glickstein and Rolf E. Wubbels (1983).

Exhibit 15.6 Percentage of NYSE Common Stocks Trading above Their 200-Day Moving-Average Price

Source: Merrill Lynch Market Analysis.

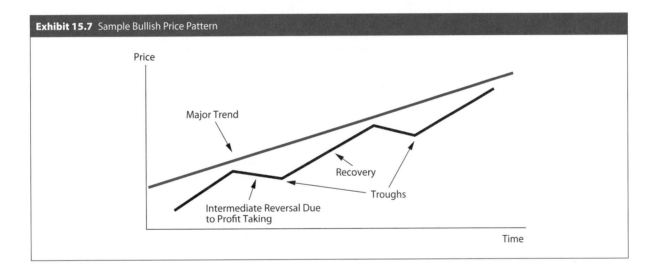

Exhibit 15.7 Sample Bullish Price Pattern

movements (waves) may occasionally move in the opposite direction. They recognize that a major market advance does not go straight up, but rather includes small price declines as some investors decide to take profits.

Exhibit 15.7 shows the typical bullish pattern. The technician would look for every recovery to reach a new peak above the prior peak, and this price rise should be accompanied by heavy trading volume. Alternatively, each profit-taking reversal that follows an increase to a new peak should have a trough above the prior trough, with relatively light trading volume during the profit-taking reversals. When this pattern of price and volume movements changes, the major trend may be entering a period of consolidation (a flat trend) or a major reversal.

Importance of Volume As noted, technicians watch volume changes along with price movements as an indicator of changes in supply and demand. A price movement in one direction means that the net effect on price is in that direction, but the price change alone does not indicate the breadth of the excess demand or supply. Therefore, the technician looks for a price increase on heavy volume relative to the stock's normal trading volume as an indication of bullish activity. Conversely, a price decline with heavy volume is considered bearish. A generally bullish pattern would be when price increases are accompanied by heavy volume and small price reversals occur with light trading volume.

Technicians also use a ratio of upside–downside volume as an indicator of short-term momentum for the aggregate stock market. Each day the stock exchanges announce the volume of trading in stocks that experienced an increase divided by the volume of trading in stocks that declined. These data are reported daily in the *Wall Street Journal* and weekly in *Barron's*. This ratio is used as an indicator of market momentum. Specifically, technicians believe that an upside–downside volume value of 1.75 or more indicates an overbought position that is bearish. Alternatively, a value of 0.75 and lower supposedly reflects an oversold position and is considered bullish. The value as of March 2008 is clearly below 1.00 and is providing a bullish signal.

Support and Resistance Levels A **support level** is the price range at which the technician would expect a substantial increase in the demand for a stock. Generally, a support level will develop after a stock has enjoyed a meaningful price increase and the stock experiences profit taking. Technicians reason that at some price below the recent peak other investors who did not buy during the first price increase (waiting for a small reversal) will get into the stock. When the price reaches this support price, demand surges and price and volume begin to increase again.

A **resistance level** is the price range at which the technician would expect an increase in the supply of stock and a price reversal. A resistance level develops after a significant decline from a higher price level. After the decline, the stock begins to recover, but the prior decline in price leads some investors who acquired the stock at a higher price to look for an opportunity to sell it near their breakeven points. Therefore, the supply of stock owned by these nervous investors is *overhanging* the market. When the price rebounds to the target price set by these investors, this overhanging supply of stock comes to the market and there is a price decline on heavy volume. It is also possible to envision a rising trend of support and resistance levels for a stock. For example, the rising support prices would be a set of higher prices where investors over time would see the price increase and would take the opportunity to buy when there is a "pull back" due to profit taking. In this latter case, there would be a succession of higher support and resistance levels over time.

Exhibit 15.8 contains the daily stock prices for Potash (POT), with support and resistance lines. The graphs show a rising pattern since Potash has experienced strong price increases during this period. At present, the resistance level is at about $195 and is rising, while the support level is about $150 and is also rising. The bullish technician would look for future prices to rise in line with this channel. If prices fell significantly below the rising support line on strong volume, it would signal a possible trend reversal and would be considered a bearish signal. In contrast, an increase above the resistance price line would be bullish.

Moving-Average Lines Earlier, we discussed how technicians use a moving average of past stock prices as an indicator of the long-run trend and how they examine current prices relative to this trend for signals of a change. We also noted that a 200-day moving average is a relatively popular measure for individual stocks and the aggregate market. In this discussion, we add a 50-day moving-average price line (short-term trend) and consider large volume.

Exhibit 15.9 is a daily stock price chart from Yahoo! Inc. for Dell, Inc. (DELL) for the year ending April 4, 2008. It also contains 50-day and 200-day moving-average (MA) lines. As noted, MA lines are meant to reflect the overall trend for the price series with the shorter MA line (the 50-day versus 200-day) reflecting shorter trends. Two comparisons involving the MA lines are considered important. The first comparison is the specific prices to the shorter-run 50-day MA line. If the overall price trend of a stock or the market has been down, the moving-average price line generally would lie above current prices. If prices reverse and break through the moving-average line *from below* accompanied by heavy trading volume, most technicians would consider this a *positive* change and speculate that this breakthrough could be a preliminary signal of a reversal of the declining trend. In contrast, if the price of a stock had

Exhibit 15.8 Daily Stock Prices and Volume for Potash with Indications of Support and Resistance Levels

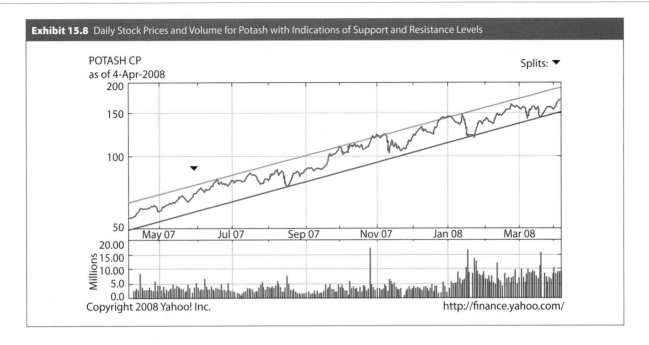

POTASH CP
as of 4-Apr-2008

Splits: ▼

Copyright 2008 Yahoo! Inc.   http://finance.yahoo.com/

Exhibit 15.9 Daily Stock Prices for Dell with 50-Day and 200-Day Moving-Average Lines

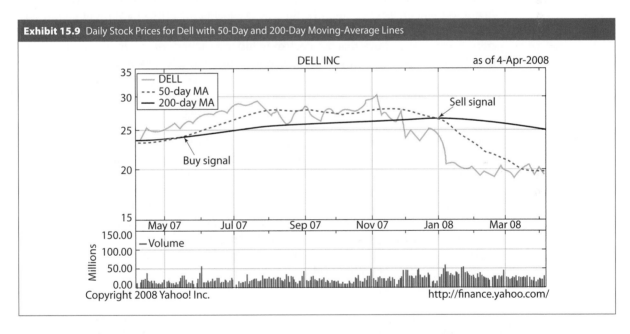

DELL INC   as of 4-Apr-2008

Copyright 2008 Yahoo! Inc.   http://finance.yahoo.com/

been rising, the moving-average line would also be rising, but it would be below current prices. If current prices declined and broke through the moving-average line *from above* accompanied by heavy trading volume, this would be considered a preliminary bearish pattern that would possibly signal a reversal of the long-run rising trend.

The second comparison is between the 50- and 200-day MA lines. Specifically, when these two lines cross, it confirms a change in the overall trend. Specifically, if the 50-day MA line crosses the 200-day MA line from below on good volume, this would be a bullish indicator (buy signal) because it confirms a reversal in trend from negative to positive. In contrast, when the 50-day line crosses the 200-day line from above, it confirms a change to a negative trend and would be a sell signal. As shown in Exhibit 15.9, in the case of DELL. Following the buy signal in May 2007, there were several negative changes in August and September when the price line went below the 50-day MA line. A strong negative change occurred in November 2007 when the price line broke through both the 50-day line and then the 200-day line on strong volume. This bearish sell signal was confirmed in early January 2008 when the 50-day MA line crossed the 200-day MA line from above.

The price line continued to decline after the sell signal to about $20 where it has been fluctuating. At the end of the period the stock has been "building a base" around the current 50-day MA line. A technician would look for the price to move above the 50-day line and eventually break above the 200-day line on strong volume for a preliminary buy signal.

Overall, for a *bullish* trend the 50-day MA line should be above the 200-day MA line. Notably, if this positive gap between the 50-day and 200-day lines gets too large (which happens with a fast run-up in price), a technician might consider this an indication that the stock is temporarily overbought, which is bearish in the short run. A *bearish* trend is when the 50-day MA line is always below the 200-day MA line. Still, if the gap gets very large on the downside, it might be considered a signal of an oversold stock, which is bullish for the short run.

Relative Strength   Technicians believe that once a trend begins, it will continue until some major event causes a change in direction. They believe this is also true of *relative* performance. If an individual stock or an industry group is outperforming the market, technicians believe it will continue to do so.

Therefore, technicians compute weekly or monthly **relative-strength (RS) ratios** for individual stocks and industry groups. The RS ratio is equal to the price of a stock or an industry index divided by the value for some stock-market index such as the S&P 500.[5] If this ratio increases over time, it shows that the stock or industry is outperforming the overall stock market, and a technician would expect this superior performance to continue. Relative-strength ratios work during declining as well as rising markets. In a declining market, if a stock's price declines less than the market does, the stock's relative-strength ratio will continue to rise. Technicians believe that if this ratio is stable or increases during a bear market, the stock should do well during the subsequent bull market.

Merrill Lynch publishes relative-strength charts for industry groups. Exhibit 15.10 describes how to read the charts. Further, some technicians construct graphs of stocks relative to the stock's industry index in addition to the comparison relative to the market.

Bar Charting   Technicians use charts that show daily, weekly, or monthly time series of stock prices. For a given interval, the technical analyst plots the high and low prices and connects the two points vertically to form a bar. Typically, he or she will also draw a small horizontal line across this vertical bar to indicate the closing price. Finally, almost all bar charts include the volume of trading at the bottom of the chart so that the technical analyst can relate the price and volume movements.

Candlestick Charts   Candlestick charts are basically an extension of the bar chart discussed above. In addition to high, low, and closing price for each trading day, they also include the opening price and indicate the change from open to close by shading whether the market or individual stock went down (dark shading) or up (white bar) for the day. The result for the Dow Jones Industrial Average shown in Exhibit 15.11 is additional information and insight regarding the stock market movements over time.

Multiple-Indicator Charts   Thus far we have presented charts that deal with only one trading technique such as moving-average lines or relative-strength rules. In the real world, it

---

[5] In contrast to these relative to market or industry ratios, there are ratios that are relative to the stock itself, which is fundamentally a momentum indicator. These are not the same.

Exhibit 15.10 How to Read Industry Group Charts

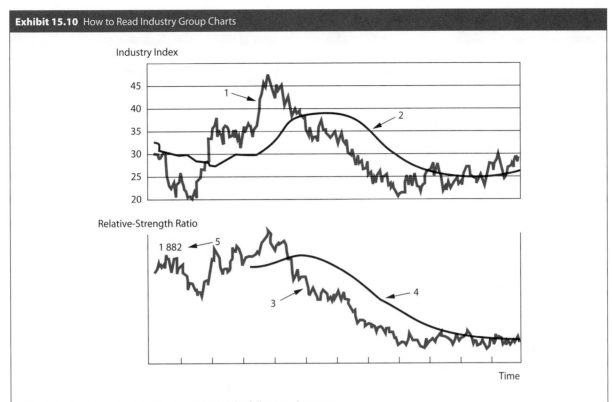

The industry group charts in this report display the following elements:

1. A line chart of the weekly close of the Standard & Poor's Industry Group Index for the past nine and one-half years, with the index range indicated to the left.
2. A line of the seventy-five-week moving average of the Standard & Poor's Industry Group Index.
3. A relative-strength line of the Standard & Poor's Industry Group Index compared with the New York Stock Exchange Composite Index.
4. A seventy-five-week moving average of relative strength.
5. A volatility reading that measures the maximum amount by which the index has outperformed (or underperformed) the NYSE Composite Index during the time period displayed.

Source: Richard T. McCabe and Walter G. Murphy, Analysts, Merrill Lynch, "Technical Analysis of Industry Groups," November 2002. Reprinted by permission. Copyright © 2002 Merrill Lynch, Pierce, Fenner & Smith Incorporated.

is fairly typical for technical charts to contain several indicators that can be used together like the two MA lines (50- and 200-day) and the RS line, because they can provide added support to the analysis. Technicians include as many price and volume indicators as are reasonable on one chart and then, based on the performance of *several* technical indicators, try to arrive at a consensus about the future movement for the stock.

Point-and-Figure Charts Another popular graph is the point-and-figure chart. Unlike the bar chart, which typically includes all ending prices and volumes to show a trend, the point-and-figure chart includes only significant price changes, regardless of their timing. The technician determines what price interval to record as significant (one point, two points, and so on) and when to note price reversals.

To demonstrate how a technical analyst would use such a chart, suppose we want to chart a volatile stock that is currently selling for $40 a share. Because of its volatility, we believe that anything less than a two-point price change is not significant. Also, we consider anything less than a four-point reversal, meaning a movement in the opposite direction, quite minor. Therefore, we would set up a chart similar to the one in Exhibit 15.12, but our new chart would start at 40; it would also progress in two-point increments. If the stock

Exhibit 15.11 A Typical Candlestick Chart Lists the Daily High, Low, Open, and Close for the Dow Jones Industrial Average and NYSE Volume for Three Months Ending April 3, 2008

Dow Jones Industrial Average

12626.03 ▲ 20.20, or 0.16%
High, low, open and close for each
trading day of the past three
months.

	Last	Year ago
Trailing P/E ratio	*53.11	16.98
P/E estimate*	13.54	14.69
Dividend yield	2.47	2.22
Current divisor	0.122820114	

All-time high: 14164.53, 10/09/2007

65-day moving average

Session high

Down | **UP**

Session open ▶

Close

13600

Close ▶

Open

Session low

13000

12400

11800

Bars measure the point change from session's open

11200

Jan.
2008

Feb.

Mar.

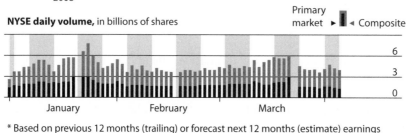

NYSE daily volume, in billions of shares

Primary
market ▶ ◀ Composite

6

3

0

January

February

March

* Based on previous 12 months (trailing) or forecast next 12 months (estimate) earnings

Sources: The *Wall Street Journal*, April 4, 2008, pC4. Copyright 2008 by DOW JONES & CO.

moved to $42, we would place an X in the box above 40 and do nothing else until the stock rose to $44 or dropped to $38 (a four-point reversal from its high of $42). If it dropped to $38, we would move a column to the right, which indicates a reversal in direction, and begin again at 38 (fill in boxes at 42 and 40). If the stock price dropped to $34, we would enter an X at 36 and another at 34. If the stock then rose to $38 (another four-point reversal), we would move to the next column and begin at 38, going up (fill in 34 and 36). If the stock then went to $46, we would fill in more Xs as shown and wait for further increases or a reversal.

Exhibit 15.12 Sample Point-and-Figure Chart

Price								
50								
48								
46			X					
44			X					
42	X	X	X					
40	X	X	X					
38		X	X					
36		X	X					
34		X	X					
32								
30								

Depending on how fast the prices rise and fall, this process might take anywhere from two to six months. Given these figures, the technician would attempt to determine trends just as with the bar chart. As always, the technician would look for breakouts to either higher or lower price levels. A long horizontal movement with many reversals but no major trends up or down would be considered a *period of consolidation* wherein the stock is moving from buyers to sellers and back again with no strong consensus about its direction. Once the stock breaks out and moves up or down after a period of consolidation, technical analysts anticipate a major move because previous trading set the stage for it. In other words, the longer the period of consolidation, the larger the expected subsequent move (up or down) when there is finally a breakout.

Point-and-figure charts provide a compact record of movements because they only consider significant price changes for the stock being analyzed. Therefore, some technicians contend they are easier to work with and give more vivid pictures of price movements.

15.5 Technical Analysis of Foreign Markets

Our discussion thus far has concentrated on U.S. markets, but analysts have discovered that these techniques apply to foreign markets as well. Merrill Lynch, for instance, prepares separate technical analysis publications for individual countries such as Japan, Germany, and the United Kingdom as well as a summary of all world markets. The examples that follow show that when analyzing non-U.S. markets, many techniques are limited to price and volume data rather than the more detailed U.S. market information. The reason is that the detailed information available on the U.S. market through the SEC, the several stock exchanges, and various investment services is not always available for other countries.

15.5.1 Foreign Stock Market Indexes

Exhibit 15.13 contains the daily time-series plot for the Japanese TOPIX Index. This chart shows a choppy flat performance from early 2006 to about July 2007 followed by a clear downtrend through March 2008 that is confirmed by the momentum series. The market analyst at Merrill Lynch commented that given the strong decline, it would be necessary to have a period of "base building" before a recovery could begin. Merrill Lynch publishes similar charts for several other countries and currencies.

15.5.2 Technical Analysis of Foreign Exchange Rates

On numerous occasions, we have discussed the importance of changes in foreign exchange rates on the rates of return on foreign securities. Because of the importance of these relationships,

Exhibit 15.13 Time-Series Plot of Japanese TOPIX Stock Index with the Medium Term Momentum Series

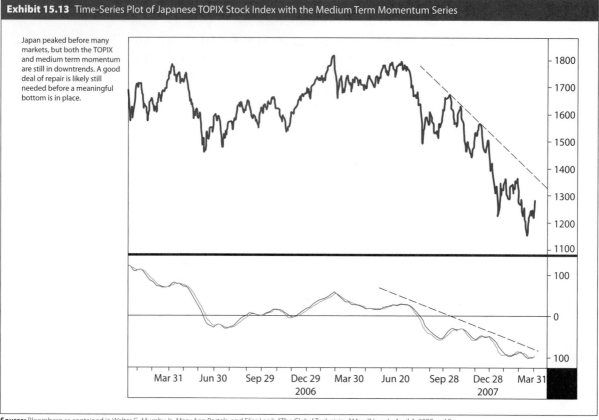

Japan peaked before many markets, but both the TOPIX and medium term momentum are still in downtrends. A good deal of repair is likely still needed before a meaningful bottom is in place.

Source: Bloomberg as contained in Walter G. Murphy Jr., Mary Ann Bartels, and Elias Lanik, "The Global Technician," Merrill Lynch, April 3, 2008, p. 10.

bond-and-stock traders in world markets examine the time-series data of various currencies such as the British pound and the Euro. They also analyze the spread between currencies, such as the difference between the Japanese yen and the British pound. Finally, they would typically examine the time series for the U.S. dollar trade-weighted exchange rate that experienced a peak in early 2002 and has declined steadily through 2007 and into 2008.

15.6 Technical Analysis of Bond Markets

Thus far, we have emphasized the use of technical analysis in stock markets. These techniques can also be applied to the bond market. The theory and rationale for technical analysis of bonds is the same as for stocks, and many of the same trading rules are used. A major difference is that it was generally not possible to consider the volume of trading of bonds because most bonds are traded OTC, where volume was not reported until 2004.

Exhibit 15.14 demonstrates the use of technical analysis techniques applied to bond-yield series. Specifically, the graph contains a time-series plot of yields for the U.S. 10-year note with a medium term momentum series. As shown, yields have declined from a peak of about 5.20 percent in June 2007 to about 3.55 percent in March 2008 where the analyst feels the series is bottoming and could experience a rally up to about 4 percent. Such a technical graph provides important insights to a bond-portfolio manager interested in adjusting his or her bond portfolio.

Exhibit 15.14 Time-Series Plot of Yields for the U.S. 10-Year Note with the Medium Term Momentum Series for the Yields

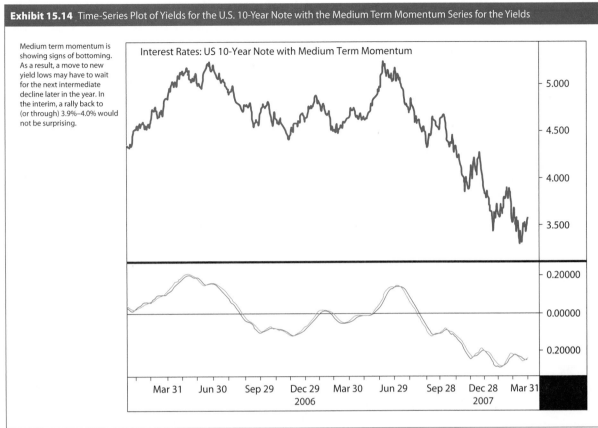

Medium term momentum is showing signs of bottoming. As a result, a move to new yield lows may have to wait for the next intermediate decline later in the year. In the interim, a rally back to (or through) 3.9%–4.0% would not be surprising.

Interest Rates: US 10-Year Note with Medium Term Momentum

Source: Bloomberg as contained in Walter G. Murphy, Jr., Mary Ann Bartels, and Elias Lanik, "The Global Technician" Merrill Lynch, April 3, 2008, p. 15.

• • • • SUMMARY • • • •

- Numerous investors believe in and use the principles of technical analysis. The fact is, the large investment houses provide extensive support for technical analysis, and a large proportion of the discussion related to securities markets in the media is based on a technical view of the market.

- Their answers to two main questions separate technical analysts and efficient market advocates. First, in the information dissemination process does everybody get the information at about the same time? Second, how quickly do investors adjust security prices to reflect new information? Technical analysts believe that news takes time to travel from the insider and expert to the individual investor. They also believe that price adjustments are not instantaneous.

As a result, they contend that security prices move in trends that persist and, therefore, they can use past price trends and volume information along with other market indicators to determine future price trends.

- Technical trading rules fall into four general categories: contrary-opinion rules, follow-the-smart-money tactics, momentum indicators, and stock price and volume techniques. These techniques and trading rules can be applied to both domestic and foreign markets. They can also be used to analyze currency exchange rates and determine the prevailing sentiment in the bond market.

- Most technicians employ several indicators and attempt to derive a consensus to guide their decision to buy, sell, or do nothing.[6]

[6] An analysis using numerous indicators is the study by Jerome Baesel, George Shows, and Edward Thorp (1982).

• • • • SUGGESTED READINGS • • • •

Benning, Carl J. "Prediction Skills of Real-World Market Timers." *Journal of Portfolio Management* 23, no. 2 (Winter 1997).

Brown, David P., and Robert H. Jennings. "On Technical Analysis." *Review of Financial Studies* 2, no. 4 (October 1989).

Colby, Robert W., and Thomas A. Mayers. *The Encyclopedia of Technical Market Indicators.* Homewood, IL: Dow Jones–Irwin, 1988.

DeMark, Thomas R. *The New Science of Technical Analysis.* New York: Wiley, 1994.

Edwards, R. D., and John Magee, Jr. *Technical Analysis of Stock Trends,* 6th ed. Boston: New York Institute of Finance, 1992.

Jagadeesh, Narasimhan. "Evidence of Predictable Behavior of Security Returns." *Journal of Finance* 45, no. 3 (July 1990).

Lo, Andrew W., and A. Craig MacKinley. *A Non-Random Walk Down Wall Street.* Princeton, NJ: Princeton University Press, 1999.

Meyers, Thomas A. *The Technical Analysis Course.* Chicago: Probus, 1989.

Pring, Martin J. *Technical Analysis Explained,* 3rd ed. New York: McGraw-Hill, 1991.

Shaw, Alan R. "Market Timing and Technical Analysis." In *The Financial Analysts Handbook,* 2nd ed., ed. Sumner N. Levine. Homewood, IL: Dow Jones–Irwin, 1988.

Zweig, Martin E. *Winning on Wall Street.* New York: Warner Books, 1986.

• • • • QUESTIONS • • • •

1. Technical analysts believe that one can use past price changes to predict future price changes. How do they justify this belief?

2. Technicians contend that stock prices move in trends that persist for long periods of time. What do technicians believe happens in the real world to cause these trends?

3. Briefly discuss the problems related to fundamental analysis that are considered advantages for technical analysis.

4. Discuss some disadvantages of technical analysis.

5. If the mutual fund cash position were to increase close to 10 percent, would a technician consider this cash position bullish or bearish? Give two reasons why the technical analyst would think this way.

6. Assume a significant decline in credit balances at brokerage firms. Discuss why a technician would consider this bearish.

7. If the bearish sentiment index of advisory service opinions were to increase to 61 percent, discuss why a technician would consider this bullish or bearish.

8. Discuss why an increase in debit balances is considered bullish or bearish.

9. Describe the Dow Theory and its three components. Which component is most important? What is the reason for an intermediate reversal?

10. Describe a bearish price and volume pattern, and discuss why it is considered bearish.

11. Discuss the logic behind the breadth of market index. How is it used to identify a peak in stock prices?

12. During a 10-day trading period, the cumulative net advance index goes from 1,572 to 1,053. During this same period of time, the DJIA goes from 11,200 to 12,100. As a technician, discuss what this set of events would mean to you.

13. Explain the reasoning behind a support level and a resistance level.

14. What is the purpose of computing a moving-average line for a stock? Describe a bullish pattern using a 50-day moving-average line and the stock volume of trading. Discuss why this pattern is considered bullish.

15. Assuming a stock price and volume chart that also contains a 50-day and a 200-day MA line, describe a bearish pattern with the two MA lines and discuss why it is bearish.

16. Explain how you would construct a relative-strength ratio for an individual stock or an industry group. What would it mean to say a stock experienced good relative strength during a bear market?

17. Discuss why most technicians follow several technical rules and attempt to derive a consensus.

• • • • PROBLEMS • • • •

1. Select a stock on the NYSE and construct a daily high, low, and close bar chart for it that includes its volume of trading for 10 trading days.

2. Compute the relative-strength ratio for the stock in Problem 1 relative to the S&P 500 index. Prepare a table that includes all the data and indicates the computations as follows:

	Closing Price		Relative-Strength Ratio
Day	Stock	S&P 500	Stock Price/S&P 500

3. Plot the relative-strength ratio computed in Problem 2 on your bar chart. Discuss whether the stock's relative strength is bullish or bearish.

4. Currently, Charlotte Art Importers is selling at $23 per share. Although you are somewhat dubious about technical analysis, you want to know how technicians who use point-and-figure charts would view this stock. You decide to note one-point movements and three-point reversals. You gather the following historical price information:

Date	Price	Date	Price	Date	Price
4/1	$23\frac{1}{2}$	4/18	33	5/3	27
4/4	$28\frac{1}{2}$	4/19	$35\frac{3}{8}$	5/4	$26\frac{1}{2}$
4/5	28	4/20	37	5/5	28
4/6	28	4/21	$38\frac{1}{2}$	5/6	$28\frac{1}{4}$
4/7	$29\frac{3}{4}$	4/22	36	5/9	$28\frac{1}{8}$
4/8	$30\frac{1}{2}$	4/25	35	5/10	$28\frac{1}{4}$
4/11	$30\frac{1}{2}$	4/26	$34\frac{1}{4}$	5/11	$29\frac{1}{8}$
4/12	$32\frac{1}{8}$	4/27	$33\frac{1}{8}$	5/12	$30\frac{1}{4}$
4/13	32	4/28	$32\frac{7}{8}$	5/13	$29\frac{7}{8}$

Plot the point-and-figure chart, using Xs for uptrends and Os for downtrends. How would a technician evaluate these movements? Discuss why you would expect a technician to buy, sell, or hold the stock based on this chart.

5. Assume the following daily closings for the Dow Jones Industrial Average:

Day	DJIA	Day	DJIA
1	14,010	7	14,220
2	14,100	8	14,130
3	14,165	9	14,250
4	14,080	10	14,315
5	14,070	11	14,240
6	14,150	12	14,310

a. Calculate a four-day moving average for Days 4 through 12.
b. Assume that the index on Day 13 closes at 14,300. Would this signal a buy or sell decision?

6. The cumulative advance–decline line reported in *Barron's* at the end of the month is 21,240. During the first week of the following month, the daily report for the *Exchange* is as follows:

Day	1	2	3	4	5
Issues traded	3,544	3,533	3,540	3,531	3,521
Advances	1,737	1,579	1,759	1,217	1,326
Declines	1,289	1,484	1,240	1,716	1,519
Unchanged	518	470	541	598	596

a. Compute the daily net advance–decline line for each of the five days.
b. Compute the cumulative advance–decline line for each day and the final value at the end of the week.

THOMSON ONE | Business School Edition

1. Examine the recent (past six months) price charts for Walgreens, Intel, and Merck (or any three firms of your choosing). What channels, buy/sell points, and patterns do you see in them?
2. What does the daily price and volume chart of the Dow Jones Industrial and S&P 500 for the past year imply for future price trends in the overall market?
3. For a stock of your choice, obtain daily price data for the past three years and download it into a spreadsheet. Compute and graph 5-day and 10-day moving averages of the price data along with the daily price data. How successful were the signals generated by the moving average lines?
4. Compute a table of relative strength for Walgreen's over the past 6 months. What does the daily relative strength measure indicate for trends in Walgreen Co.'s stock?
5. Using daily data for the most recent two months, construct a point-and-figure chart for Walgreens.

CHAPTER 16

Equity Portfolio Management Strategies

After you read this chapter, you should be able to answer the following questions:

- What are the two generic equity portfolio management styles?
- What are three techniques for constructing a passive index portfolio?
- How does the goal of a passive equity portfolio manager differ from the goal of an active manager?
- What is a portfolio's tracking error and how is it useful in the construction of a passive equity investment?
- What is the difference between an index mutual fund and an exchange-traded fund?
- What are the three themes that active equity portfolio managers can use?
- What stock characteristics do momentum-oriented investors look for?
- How can an investor measure the tax efficiency of an actively managed portfolio?
- What stock characteristics differentiate value-oriented and growth-oriented investment styles?
- What is style analysis and what does it indicate about a manager's investment performance?
- What techniques do active managers use in an attempt to outperform their benchmarks?
- What are the differences between the integrated, strategic, tactical, and insured approaches to asset allocation?

Recent chapters have reviewed how to analyze industries and companies, how to estimate a stock's intrinsic value, and how technical analysis can assist in stockpicking. Some equity portfolios are constructed one stock at a time. Research staffs analyze the economy, industries, and companies; evaluate firms' strategies and competitive advantages; and recommend individual stocks for purchase or for sale.

Other equity portfolios are constructed using quantitative, rather than analyst-intensive, methods. Computers analyze relationships between stocks and market sectors to identify undervalued stocks. Quantitative screens and factor models are used to construct portfolios of stocks with such attributes as low P/E ratios, low price/book ratios, small capitalization, or high dividend yield; those neglected by analysts; or stocks whose returns are strongly correlated with economic variables, such as interest rates.

Managers of equity portfolios do not need to focus on the security selection process to produce superior investment returns. They can also increase an investor's wealth through their sector and asset allocation decisions. For example, a manager acting as a market timer might split his funds into two index portfolios—one containing stocks and the other containing bonds—and then shift the allocation between these portfolios depending on which asset class he believes will perform the best during the coming period. This strategy, which is formally known as *tactical* asset allocation, benefits from correctly predicting broad market movements rather than trends for individual companies. Similarly, *insured* asset allocation attempts to limit investment losses by shifting funds between an existing equity portfolio and a risk-free security depending on changing market conditions.

16.1 Passive versus Active Management

Equity portfolio management strategies can be placed into either a passive or an active category. One way to distinguish between these strategies is to decompose the total actual return that the portfolio manager attempts to produce:

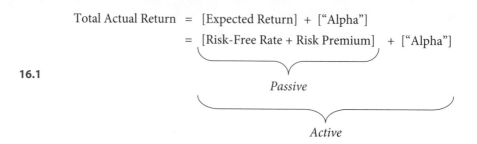

16.1

Passive portfolio managers just try to capture the expected return consistent with the risk level of their portfolios. In contrast, active managers attempt to "beat the market" by forming portfolios capable of producing actual returns that exceed risk-adjusted expected returns. The difference between the actual and expected return is often called the portfolio's *alpha* and it represents the amount of value that the active manager has added (if positive) or subtracted (if negative) to the investment process.

Passive equity portfolio management typically holds stocks so the portfolio's returns will track those of a benchmark index over time. Accordingly, this approach to investing is generally referred to as *indexing* and there is no attempt on the manager's part to generate an alpha return component. While indexing is often thought to be a long-term buy-and-hold strategy, occasional rebalancing of the portfolio is necessary as the composition of the underlying benchmark changes and cash distributions must be reinvested. However, since the purpose of the passive portfolio is to mimic an index, the passive manager is judged by how well he or she tracks the target—that is, minimizes the deviation between stock portfolio and index returns.

Conversely, *active equity portfolio management* is an attempt by the manager to outperform an equity benchmark on a risk-adjusted basis. The active manager can employ any of several specific investment strategies to do this, but broadly speaking there are two main ways to try to add alpha: *tactical adjustments* (e.g., equity style or sector timing) or *security selection* (i.e., stockpicking) skills. Notice that so-called hybrid investment strategies that may appear to fall into the middle ground between the passive and active categories (e.g., enhanced indexing) are really just more modest variations of an active approach to equity portfolio management. Further, *hedge funds* are actively managed portfolios that often pursue a "pure alpha" (i.e., absolute return) strategy in which the manager seeks to isolate the alpha component of return; these strategies are discussed in Chapter 24.

When deciding to follow either an active or a passive strategy (or some combination of the two), an investor must assess the trade-off between the low-cost but less-exciting alternative of indexing versus the potentially more lucrative alternative of active investing, which almost certainly will have higher management fees and trading costs. Sharpe (1991) argued that these higher expenses will *always* make active management the inferior alternative. Sorensen, Miller, and Samak (1998) noted that the critical factor in this evaluation is the stockpicking skill of the portfolio manager. Using pension fund performance data, they showed that the optimal allocation to indexing declines as managerial skill increases. However, they also concluded that some indexing is appropriate for most risk objective classes. Alford, Jones, and Winkelmann (2003) support this position by arguing that a disciplined approach to active

Exhibit 16.1 Active and Passive Investment in U.S. Equity and Fixed-Income Markets

Strategy	2005 (Billions)	2004 (Billions)	% Change
Active Equity	$1,979.5	$1,905.1	3.9
Passive Equity	1,098.5	983.1	11.7
Active Fixed Income	1,780.8	1,628.5	9.4
Passive Fixed Income	225.8	207.4	9.9

Source: *Pensions & Investment Money Manager Directory*, May 29, 2006, and May 30, 2005.

management—which they term structured portfolio management—is likely to be the most effective method for investors. Finally, Harlow and Brown (2006) showed that the active versus passive management decision for many investors comes down to their ability to identify superior managers in advance.

Exhibit 16.1 reports the amount of money in the U.S. equity and fixed-income markets using active and passive strategies for two recent years. The data are compiled from a survey of almost 1,000 professional managers on behalf of their clients. The main conclusion is that both active and passive funds play a prominent role with investors. Further, while active management strategies control the largest percentage of investor wealth, passively managed investment products are growing in importance at a rapid pace, particularly in the equity market.

16.2 An Overview of Passive Equity Portfolio Management Strategies

Passive equity portfolio management attempts to design a set of stock holdings that *replicates* the performance of a specific benchmark. As discussed in Chapter 2, the portfolio manager who earns higher returns by violating the client's policy statement should be fired. Similarly, a passive manager who is not really passive should also be dismissed. A passive manager earns a fee by constructing a portfolio that closely tracks the returns to a particular equity index meeting the client's needs and objectives. If the manager tries to outperform the benchmark, he or she clearly violates the passive premise of the portfolio.

Chapter 5 contained a summary of many of the different market indexes that a passive manager can attempt to replicate. Domestic equity indexes include the S&P 500, the Major Market index, the NASDAQ Composite index, and the Wilshire 5000. Benchmarks also exist for various sectors of the stock market, such as those for small capitalization stocks (Russell 2000), for value- or growth-oriented stocks (Russell Growth index and the Russell Value index), for numerous developed world regions (such as the EAFE index), and for collections of smaller countries (emerging markets). Fernholz, Garvy, and Hannon (1998), as well as Khorana, Nelling, and Trester (1998), have noted that as passive investing has grown in popularity, money managers have created an index fund for virtually every broad market category.

In Chapter 6, we presented several reasons for investing in a passive equity portfolio. Consistent evidence indicates that stock markets throughout the world are often fairly efficient. For many active managers, the annual costs of trying to beat the market (1 to 2 percent of the portfolio's assets) are difficult to overcome. However, it should also be noted that passive strategies are not costless to employ. Because of cash flows into and out of an index fund, as well as events that change the composition of the benchmark itself (e.g., mergers, bankruptcies, index rebalancing), the passive manager will inevitably need to buy and sell securities over time. These transactions mean that the passive portfolio will inevitably underperform its index over time, even if the manager minimizes turnover in the portfolio for every other reason. The extent of this underperformance can range from 0.05 to 0.25 percent in developed stock markets to 3 percent for portfolios mimicking less liquid indexes (e.g., emerging markets).

16.2.1 Index Portfolio Construction Techniques

There are three basic techniques for constructing a passive index portfolio: full replication, sampling, and quadratic optimization or programming. The most obvious technique is **full replication**, wherein all the securities in the index are purchased in proportion to their weights in the index. This technique helps ensure close tracking, but it may be suboptimal for two reasons. First, the need to buy many securities will increase transaction costs that will detract from performance. Second, the reinvestment of dividends will also result in high commissions when many firms pay small dividends at different times in the year.

The second technique, **sampling**, addresses the problem of having to buy numerous stock issues. With sampling, a portfolio manager would only need to buy a representative sample of stocks that comprise the benchmark index. Stocks with larger index weights are purchased according to their weight in the index; smaller issues are purchased so their aggregate characteristics (e.g., beta, industry distribution, and dividend yield) approximate the underlying benchmark. With fewer stocks to purchase, larger positions can be taken in the issues acquired, which should lead to proportionately lower commissions. Further, the reinvestment of dividend cash flows will be less problematic because fewer securities need to be purchased to rebalance the portfolio. The disadvantage of sampling is that portfolio returns will almost certainly not track the returns for the benchmark index as closely as with full replication.

Rather than obtaining a sample based on industry or security characteristics, **quadratic optimization** or programming techniques can be used to construct a passive portfolio. Historical information on price changes and correlations between securities are input to a computer program that determines the composition of a portfolio that will minimize return deviations from the benchmark. A problem with this technique is that it relies on *historical* price changes and correlations and, if these factors change over time, the portfolio may experience very large differences from the benchmark.

Sometimes customized passive portfolios, called **completeness funds**, are constructed to complement active portfolios that do not cover the entire market. For example, a large pension fund may allocate some of its holdings to active managers expected to outperform the market. Many times, these active portfolios are overweighted in certain market sectors or stock types. In this case, the pension fund sponsor may want the remaining funds to be invested passively to "fill the holes" left vacant by the active managers. The performance of the completeness fund will be compared to a customized benchmark that incorporates the characteristics of the stocks not covered by the active managers.

For example, suppose a pension fund hires three active managers to invest part of the fund's money. One manager emphasizes small-capitalization U.S. stocks, the second invests only in Pacific Rim countries, and the third invests in U.S. stocks with low *P/E* ratios. To ensure adequate diversification, the pension fund may want to passively invest the remaining assets in a completeness fund that will have a customized benchmark that includes large- and mid-capitalization U.S. stocks, U.S. stocks with normal to high *P/E* ratios, and international stocks outside the Pacific Rim.

Still other passive portfolios and benchmarks exist for investors with certain unique needs and preferences. Some investors may want their funds to be invested only in stocks that pay dividends or in a company that produces a product or service that the investor deems socially responsible. Mossavar-Rahmani (1988) and Dialynas (2001) show that benchmarks can be produced that reflect these desired attributes, and passive portfolios can be constructed to track the performance of the customized benchmark over time so investors' special needs can be satisfied.

16.2.2 Tracking Error and Index Portfolio Construction

If the goal of forming a passive portfolio is to replicate a particular equity index, the success of such a fund lies not in the absolute returns it produces but in how closely its returns match those of the benchmark. That is, the goal of the passive manager should be to minimize the portfolio's return volatility relative to the index. Said differently, the manager should try to minimize **tracking error**.

Tracking error can be defined as the extent to which return fluctuations in the managed portfolio are *not correlated* with return fluctuations in the benchmark. A flexible and straight-forward way of measuring tracking error can be developed as follows. Recalling the notation from Chapter 7, let

w_i = investment weight of Asset i in the managed portfolio
R_{it} = return to Asset i in Period t
R_{bt} = return to the benchmark portfolio in Period t

We can define the Period t return to managed portfolio as

$$R_{pt} = \sum_{i=1}^{N} w_i R_{it}$$

where:

N = number of assets in the managed portfolio

With these definitions, the Period t *return differential* between the managed portfolio and the benchmark is

16.2
$$\Delta_t = \sum_{i=1}^{N} w_i R_{it} - R_{bt} = R_{pt} - R_{bt}$$

Given the returns to the N assets in the managed portfolio and the benchmark, Δ is a function of the investment weights that the manager selects. Also, not all of the assets in the benchmark need be included in the managed portfolio (i.e., $w = 0$ for some assets).

For a sample of T return observations, the variance of Δ can be calculated as follows:

16.3
$$\sigma_\Delta^2 = \frac{\sum_{t=1}^{T} (\Delta_t - \overline{\Delta})^2}{(T-1)}$$

Finally, the standard deviation of the return differential is

$$\sigma_\Delta = \sqrt{\sigma_\Delta^2} = \text{periodic tracking error}$$

so that *annualized tracking error (TE)* can be calculated as

16.4
$$TE = \sigma_\Delta \sqrt{P}$$

where P is the number of return periods in a year (e.g., $P = 12$ for monthly returns, $P = 252$ for daily returns).

Suppose an investor has formed a portfolio designed to track a particular benchmark. Over the last eight quarters, the returns to this portfolio, as well as the index returns and the return difference between the two, were:

Period	Manager	Index	Difference (Δ)
1	2.3%	2.7%	−0.4%
2	−3.6	−4.6	1.0
3	11.2	10.1	1.1
4	1.2	2.2	−1.0
5	1.5	0.4	1.1
6	3.2	2.8	0.4
7	8.9	8.1	0.8
8	−0.8	0.6	−1.4

The periodic average and standard deviation of the manager's return differential (i.e., "delta") relative to the benchmark are

$$\text{Average } \Delta = [-0.4 + 1.0 + \cdots + 0.8 - 1.4] \div 8 = 0.2\%$$

$$\sigma = \sqrt{(-0.4 - 0.2)^2 + (1.0 - 0.2)^2 + \cdots + (-1.4 - 0.2)^2} \div \sqrt{(8 - 1)} = 1.0\%$$

Thus, the manager's annualized tracking error for this 2-year period is 2.0 percent ($= 1.0$ percent $\times \sqrt{4}$).

Generally speaking, there is an inverse relationship between a passive portfolio's tracking error relative to its index and the time and expense necessary to create and maintain the portfolio. For example, full replication of the S&P 500 would have virtually no tracking error but would involve positions in 500 different stocks and require frequent rebalancing. As smaller samples are used to replicate the S&P index's return performance, the expense of forming the managed portfolio would decline but the potential tracking error is likely to increase. Thus, the art of being a manager of a passive equity portfolio lies in balancing the costs (larger tracking error) and the benefits (easier management, lower trading commissions) of using smaller samples. Exhibit 16.2 estimates the tracking error that occurs from such sampling.

Alford, Jones, and Winkelmann (2003) have also shown that tracking error can be a useful way to categorize a fund's investment style. They argue that money managers can be classified

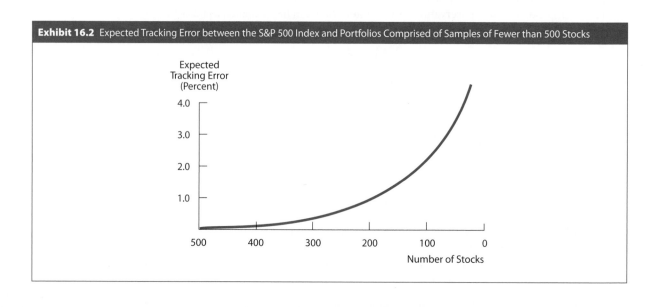

Exhibit 16.2 Expected Tracking Error between the S&P 500 Index and Portfolios Comprised of Samples of Fewer than 500 Stocks

using the following chart with regard to the tracking errors of their portfolios compared to the relevant benchmark:

Investment Style	Tracking Error Range
Passive	Less than 1.0% (0.5% or lower is normal)
Structured	Between 1.0% and 3.0%
Active	Over 3.0% (5.0% to 15.0% is normal)

Source: Andrew Alford, Robert Jones, Kurt Winkelmann, *A Spectrum Approach to Active Risk Budgeting, Journal of Portfolio Management* 30, no. 1 (September 2003): 49–60.

They also document that structured portfolio managers, who can be viewed as active managers with the tightest controls on the permissible level of their tracking errors, tend to produce superior risk-adjusted returns to those active managers whose investment mandates allow them to stray farther from their indexes.

16.2.3 Methods of Index Portfolio Investing

Although investors can construct their own passive investment portfolios that mimic a particular equity index, there are at least two prepackaged ways of accomplishing this goal that are typically more convenient and less expensive for the small investor. These are (1) buying shares in an *index mutual fund* or (2) buying shares in an *exchange-traded fund* (ETF).

Index Funds As we discuss in Chapter 24, mutual funds represent established security portfolios managed by professional investment companies (e.g., Fidelity, Vanguard, Putnam, AIM) in which investors can participate. The investment company is responsible for deciding how the fund is managed. For an indexed portfolio, the fund manager will typically attempt to replicate the composition of the particular index exactly, meaning that he or she will buy the exact securities comprising the index in their exact weights and then alter those positions anytime the composition of the index itself is changed. Since changes to most equity indexes occur sporadically index funds tend to generate low trading and management expense ratios. A prominent example of an index fund is Vanguard's 500 Index Fund (VFINX), which is designed to mimic the S&P 500 index. Exhibit 16.3 provides a descriptive overview of this fund and indicates that its historical return performance is virtually indistinguishable from that of the benchmark.

The advantage of index mutual funds is that they provide an inexpensive way for investors to acquire a diversified portfolio that emphasizes the desired market or industry within the context of a traditional money management product. As with any mutual fund, the disadvantages are that investors can only liquidate their positions at the end of the trading day (i.e., no intraday trading), usually cannot short sell, and may have unwanted tax repercussions if the fund has an unforeseen need to sell a portion of its holdings, thereby realizing capital gains.

Exchange-Traded Funds ETFs are a more recent development in the world of indexed investment products than index mutual funds. Essentially, ETFs are depository receipts that give investors a pro rata claim on the capital gains and cash flows of the securities that are held in deposit by the financial institution that issued the certificates. That is, a portfolio of securities is placed on deposit at a financial institution or into a unit trust, which then issues a single type of certificate representing ownership of the underlying portfolio. In that way, ETFs are similar to the American depository receipts (ADRs) described in Chapter 3.

There are several notable example of ETFs, including (1) Standard & Poor's 500 Depository Receipts (SPDRs or "spider" as they are sometimes called), which are based on a basket of all the securities held in that index; (2) iShares, which recreate indexed positions in several global developed and emerging equity markets, including countries such as Australia, Mexico, Malaysia, the United Kingdom, France, Germany, Japan, and China; and (3) sector ETFs, which invest in baskets of stocks from specific industry sectors, including consumer services, industrial, technology, financial services, energy, utilities, and cyclicals/transportation. Exhibit 16.4 shows descriptive and return data for the SPDR Trust certificates. Notice, however, that the returns to these shares do not track the index quite as closely as did the VFINX fund.

Exhibit 16.3 Details of the Vanguard 500 Index Trust Mutual Fund

A. Description

VFINX US $ SNAV **134.36 − 2.31**   Purch Prc **134.36**   As of Sep 7

VFINX US   **DESCRIPTION**   Page 1/4

VANGUARD 500 INDEX FUND-INV   Objective - Index Fund-Large Cap

Vanguard 500 Index Fund is an open-end fund incorporated in the USA. The Fund's objective is to track the performance of the Standard & Poor's 500 Index, which is dominated by the stocks of large U.S. companies. The Fund invests substantially all of its assets in the stocks that make up the Index.

Bloomberg Classification Data	
Asset Class	Equity
Style	Index Fund
Market Cap Focus	Large-cap
Geographic Focus	U. S.

Current/Operational Data			
1) GP NAV		$	134.36
Assets (mil)	8/31/07	$	123845
Inception Date		8/31/76	

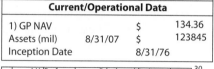

Performance/Percentile Ranking		
as of 9/ 7/07	Return	Rank in Obj.
3) TRA 1 Month	−1.34	71
YTD	3.74	79
1 Year	14.33	78
2006	15.64	80
5 Year	12.08	80

1 Yr Performance vs. Benchmark Indices

VFINX
SPX

29 SEP 06 30 NOV 31 JAN 07 30 MAR 31 MAY 31 JUL

{ FPC<GO> } FOR FUND PERFORMANCE CHARTS AND { FSRC<GO> } FOR FUND SEARCH

B. Historical Return Performance

Page

VFINX US   **DESCRIPTION**   Page 3/4

VANGUARD 500 INDEX FUND-INV   Currency - USD
Objective - Index Fund-Large Cap   Fund Type - Open-End Fund

Total Returns %	1 Month	3 Month	YTD	1 Year	3 Year	5 Year	2004	2005	2006
VFINX US	−1.34	−2.05	3.74	14.33	10.95	12.08	10.74	4.78	15.64
Index (SPX)	−1.34	−2.04	3.81	14.44	11.08	12.23	10.88	4.91	15.79
Peers Avg	−.75	−2.62	3.60	13.92	11.69	11.55	9.17	10.71	14.32

Absolute Measures % (1yr)	Fund	Index	Peers Avg	Relative Measures % (1yr)	vIndex
Maximum Return	3.54	3.55	3.77	Excess Return	−.11
Minimum Return	−4.89	−4.88	−5.16	Tracking Error	.03
Sharpe Ratio	.85	.86	.79	Information Ratio	−3.28
Volatility	11.24	11.25	12.24	Alpha	.00
Sortino Ratio	.74	.75	.69	Beta	1.00
Downside Risk	8.88	8.88	9.59	Correlation	1.00
Semivariance	12.94	12.94	14.32	**Peers Info (1yr)**	**Return %** · **Vol. %**
% Periods up	59.62	59.62	60.98	Average	13.92 · 12.24
% Periods down	40.38	40.38	39.02	Std Dev	4.80 · 1.80
Skewness	−1.00	−1.00	−.90	Median	13.90 · 11.26
Kurtosis	1.68	1.67	1.50	Number of funds	302

Max Drawdown (1yr)	Length	Recovery	Peak	Valley
−9.28	19.00	n.a.	07/19/2007	08/15/2007

13) HRH Hist. Return Histogram   15) HVG Hist. Price Volatility   17) FREP Fund Report
14) COMP Comparative Returns   16) HFA Hist. Fund Analysis

Exhibit 16.4 Details of the SPDR Exchange-Traded Fund

A. Description

SPY US $ S↓ **145.59** - .48 P   – –x– –   SHO   Equity**DES**
DELAY 15:10   Vol 185914572 0p 146.52 D Hi 146.72 D Lo 144.33 T   As of Sep 7
SPY US   **DESCRIPTION**   Page 1/4
SPDR TRUST SERIES 1   Objective - Growth-Large Cap

SPDR Trust Series 1 issues exchange-traded funds called Standard & Poor's Depository Reciepts or "SPDRS". The SPDR Trust holds all of the common stocks of the Standard & Poors 500 Composite Stock Price Index and intends to provide investment results that, before expenses, correspond to the price and yield of the S&P Index. Initial Index ration upon inception was 1/10 of SPX.

Bloomberg Classification Data

Asset Class	Equity	Style	Growth
Market Cap Focus	Large-cap		
		Graphics Focus	U.S.

Current Data		
Underlying Index	12)	SPX
1) GP Price	$	145.59
52Wk Hi	7/17 $	156.000
52Wk Lo	9/11 $	129.480
NAV	9/10 $	145.78
INAV	$	145.60
% Premium	n.a.	
Shares Out (x000)	9/10/97	457730.3
Market cap (mil)	$	66640.95

Intraday { SXV <index> }; NAV { SXVNV <index> }; Shs Out { SXVSO <index> }
Est Cash { SXVEU <index> }; Total Cash { SXVTC <index> }

B. Historical Return Performance

Equity**DES**

SPY US   **DESCRIPTION**   Page 3/4
SPDR TRUST SERIES 1   Currency - USD
Objective - Growth-Large Cap   Fund Type - ETF

Total Returns %	1 Month	3 Month	YTD	1 Year	3 Year	5 Year	2004	2005	2006
SPY US	−1.15	−1.61	4.00	14.50	11.03	12.12	10.70	4.82	15.85
Index (SPX)	−1.34	−2.04	3.81	14.44	11.08	12.23	10.88	4.91	15.79
Peers Avg	.18	−2.98	4.83	15.91	12.80	11.13	7.07	14.94	14.18

Absolute Measures % (1yr)	Fund	Index	Peers Avg	Relative Measures % (1yr)	vIndex
Maximum Return	3.51	3.55	1.47	Excess Return	.17
Minimum Return	−5.47	−4.88	−5.28	Tracking Error	1.78
Sharpe Ratio	.86	.86	.95	Information Ratio	.10
Volatility	11.48	11.25	13.68	Alpha	.00
Sortino Ratio	.74	.75	.85	Beta	1.01
Downside Risk	9.13	8.88	10.22	Correlation	.99

Semivariance	13.31	12.94	15.20	Peers Info (1yr)	Return %	Vol. %
% Periods up	55.77	59.62	60.98	Average	15.91	13.68
% Periods down	44.23	40.38	61.38	Std Dev	7.86	3.00
Skewness	−1.19	−1.00	−.64	Median	15.52	12.96
Kurtosis	2.65	1.67	1.42	Number of funds	185	

Max Drawdown (1yr)	Length	Recovery	Peak	Valley
−9.05	19.00	n.a.	07/19/2007	08/15/2007

13) HRH Hist. Return Histogram   15) HVG Hist. Price Volatility   17) FREP Fund Report
14) COMP Comparative Returns   16) HFA Hist. Fund Analysis

Exhibit 16.5 Performance of Active Mutual Funds vs. S&P 500: January 1980–June 2004

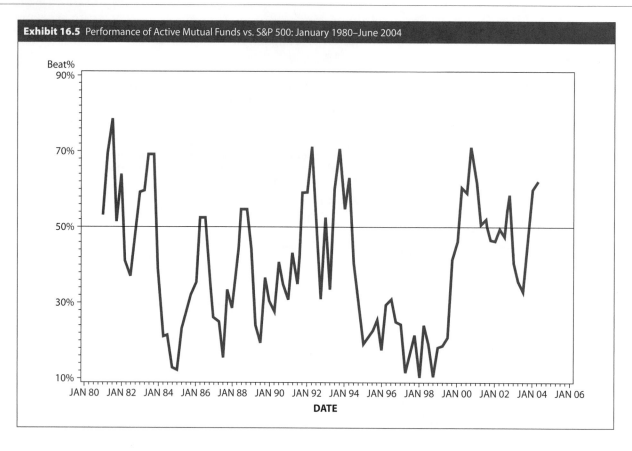

A significant advantage of ETFs over index mutual funds is that they can be bought and sold (and short sold) like common stock through an organized exchange or in an over-the-counter market. Further, they are backed by a sponsoring organization (e.g., for SPDRs, the sponsor is PDR Services LLC, a limited liability company whose sole member is the American Stock Exchange where SPDR shares trade) who can alter the composition of the underlying portfolio to reflect changes in the composition of the index. Other advantages relative to index funds include an often smaller management fee, the ability for continuous trading while markets are open, and the ability to time capital gain tax realizations. ETF disadvantages include the brokerage commission and the inability to reinvest dividends except on a quarterly basis.

16.3 An Overview of Active Equity Portfolio Management Strategies

The goal of active equity management is to earn a return that exceeds the return of a passive benchmark portfolio, net of transaction costs, on a risk-adjusted basis. The job of an active equity manager is not easy. If transaction costs and fees total 1.5 percent of the portfolio's assets annually, the portfolio has to earn a return 1.5 percentage points above the passive benchmark just to keep pace with it. Further, if the manager's strategy involves overweighting specific market sectors in anticipation of price increases, the risk of the active portfolio may exceed that of the passive benchmark, so the active portfolio's return will have to exceed the benchmark by an even wider margin to compensate for its higher risk.

Exhibit 16.5 shows the percentage of U.S.-domiciled mutual funds that were able to produce annual returns in excess of the S&P 500 index over a period of about a quarter century. Notice that for the majority of this period, the average fund manager was not able to

---

Exhibit 16.6 Equity Portfolio Investment Philosophies and Strategies

Passive Management Strategies

1. EFFICIENT MARKETS HYPOTHESIS
   Buy and hold
   Indexing

Active Management Strategies

2. FUNDAMENTAL ANALYSIS

   "Top down" (e.g., asset class rotation, sector rotation)
   "Bottom up" (e.g., stock undervaluation/overvaluation)

3. TECHNICAL ANALYSIS

   Contrarian (e.g., overreaction)
   Continuation (e.g., price momentum)

4. ANOMALIES AND ATTRIBUTES

   Calendar effects (e.g., weekend, January)
   Information effects (e.g., neglect)
   Security characteristics (e.g., *P/E*, *P/B*, earnings momentum, firm size)
   Investment style (e.g., value, growth)

---

outperform the broad index; the percentage of active funds whose return exceeded that of the index was less than 50 percent in 64 of the 98 quarters represented in the sample. However, the display also indicates that the percentage of active managers beating the market was never zero and occasionally rises as high as 70 percent, which is impressive given that there were more than 5,600 domestic equity funds by the end of 2003. Indeed, evidence provided by Brown and Goetzmann (1995) and Chen, Jegadeesh, and Wermers (2000) show that fund managers possess significant stockpicking skills that can translate into superior and persistent investment returns.

Exhibit 16.6 provides a broad overview of the different strategies that investment managers might adopt in forming their portfolios, as well as the investment philosophy that underlies each strategy. Notice that the passive strategies we just considered are based (at least implicitly) on the notion that capital markets are efficient and so equity portfolios should be invested to mimic broad indexes and not be traded actively. The realm of active management, however, is one in which managers are effectively betting against markets being perfectly efficient. For convenience, Exhibit 16.6 characterizes these bets as falling into three general categories: (1) fundamental, (2) technical, and (3) market anomalies and security attributes.

16.3.1 Fundamental Strategies

As we saw in Chapter 11, the top-down investment process begins with an analysis of broad country and asset class allocations and progresses down through sector allocation decisions to the bottom level where individual securities are selected. Alternatively, a bottom-up process simply emphasizes the selection of securities without any initial market or sector analysis. Active equity management based on fundamental analysis can start from either direction, depending on what the manager thinks is mispriced relative to his or her valuation models. Generally, active managers use three generic themes. First, they can try to time the equity market by shifting funds into and out of stocks, bonds, and T-bills depending on broad market forecasts and estimated risk premiums. Second, they can shift funds among different equity sectors and industries (e.g., financial stocks, technology stocks, consumer cyclicals, durable goods) or among investment styles (e.g., large capitalization, small capitalization, value, growth) to catch the next hot concept before the rest of the market. Third, equity managers can do stockpicking, looking at individual issues in an attempt to find undervalued stocks.

An asset class rotation strategy shifts funds in and out of the stock market depending on the manager's perception of how the stock market is valued compared to the various alternative

Exhibit 16.7 The Stock Market and the Business Cycle

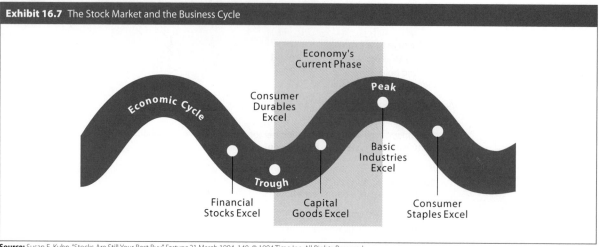

asset classes. Formally, such a strategy is called **tactical asset allocation** and will be described in more detail later in the chapter. A **sector rotation strategy** positions the portfolio to take advantage of the market's next move. Often, this means emphasizing or overweighting (relative to the benchmark portfolio) certain economic sectors or industries in response to the next expected phase of the business cycle. Exhibit 16.7 suggests how sector rotators may position their portfolios to take advantage of stock market trends during the economic cycle.

In general, asset and sector rotation strategies can be extremely profitable but also very risky for a manager to follow. This is shown in Exhibit 16.8, which lists the annual returns in each of several asset and sector classes from 1991 to 2006. The chart documents the tremendous volatility that existed during this period. For instance, bonds, which comprised the best-performing asset class in 2002, made up the worst class in the following four years. Conversely, large-cap growth stocks were one of the best places to invest for six years (i.e., 1994–1999), but this period was bracketed by years when this sector performed quite poorly. The message from this display is clear: While there are impressive gains to be made by correctly timing the hottest (or the coldest) market sectors, a manager must be right substantially more than he or she is wrong. Because this is an extremely difficult thing to do consistently, many investors choose to interpret Exhibit 16.8 as ultimately extolling the virtue of asset and sector class diversification.

A fundamental stockpicker operating on a pure bottom-up basis will form a portfolio of equities that can be purchased at a substantial discount to what his or her valuation model indicates they are worth. As we discussed in Chapter 14, these valuation models might be based on absolute judgments about the future of the company (i.e., discounted cash flow) or relative assessments of how attractive the stock is compared with shares in otherwise similar firms (i.e., relative price multiples). In either case, it is usually true that the active manager will find stockpicking to be a more reliable, although less profitable, way to invest than market timing.

Finally, a recent trend in fundamental equity management is the development of the so-called **130/30 strategy**. Fowler (2007) explains that funds based on this approach are allowed to take long positions up to 130 percent of the portfolio's original capital and have short positions up to 30 percent. Relative to "long only" portfolios, these *enhanced active* funds let managers exploit their expertise in two ways. First, as Jacobs and Levy (2007) note, the use of the short positions creates the leverage needed to extend the long holdings beyond the original capital limit, potentially increasing both risk and expected returns compared to the fund's benchmark. Second, and more importantly, 130/30 strategies enable managers to make full use of their fundamental research to buy stocks they identify as undervalued as well as short those that are overvalued. Thus, these strategies expand the ways in which investors can capture available alpha opportunities.

Exhibit 16.8 Asset and Sector Class Return Performance: 1991–2006

1991	1992	1993	1994	1995	1996	1997	1998	1999	2000	2001	2002	2003	2004	2005	2006
SG 48.2%	SV 26.52%	F 32.57%	F 7.78%	LV 33.04%	LG 21.72%	LV 31.35%	LG 35.84%	SG 39.03%	SV 21.54%	SV 14.54%	B 10.25%	SG 41.54%	SV 21.04%	F 14.02%	F 26.86%
S 39.94%	S 18.02%	SV 21.84%	LG 3.12%	L 32.60%	L 20.95%	L 29.85%	L 26.53%	LG 30.33%	B 11.63%	B 8.44%	SV −9.81%	S 40.49%	F 20.25%	LV 7.13%	SV 21.90%
SV 36.59%	LV 13.28%	S 17.86%	L 0.85%	LG 32.18%	LV 20.19%	SV 28.50%	F 20.00%	F 26.96%	LV 8.32%	S 5.15%	LV −14.84%	SV 39.54%	S 17.93%	LG 6.42%	LV 20.50%
LG 36.44%	SG 9.04%	LV 16.97%	SV −1.11%	SG 28.01%	SV 19.95%	LG 28.37%	LV 16.80%	S 21.01%	S 0.52%	SG −4.14%	F −15.56%	F 39.17%	LV 15.60%	L 5.56%	S 17.87%
L 29.99%	L 8.94%	SG 13.34%	S −1.31%	S 25.73%	S 16.41%	S 21.51%	SG 6.79%	L 19.92%	L −6.66%	LV −4.95%	S −20.21%	LV 27.30%	SG 14.74%	SV 5.51%	L 14.96%
LV 23.06%	B 7.40%	L 9.91%	LV −1.53%	SV 23.43%	SG 12.78%	SG 14.44%	B 8.70%	LV 7.92%	F −13.96%	L −11.32%	L −22.26%	L 27.00%	L 11.12%	S 5.49%	SG 13.77%
B 16.00%	LG 5.19%	B 9.75%	SG −1.72%	B 18.46%	F 6.05%	B 9.64%	S 1.14%	SV −0.54%	SG −17.29%	LG −18.09%	LG −30.16%	LG 26.76%	LG 8.96%	SG 5.31%	LG 9.00%
F 12.14%	F −12.18%	LG 3.17%	B −2.92%	F 11.21%	B 3.64%	F 1.78%	SV −4.35%	B −0.82%	LG −22.07%	F −21.21%	SG −32.39%	B 4.10%	B 4.34%	B 2.43%	B 4.33%

Legend:

L	=	Large Stocks (Russell 1000 Index)
LG	=	Large Growth Stocks (Russell 1000 Growth Index)
LV	=	Large Value Stocks (Russell 1000 Value Index)
S	=	Small Stocks (Russell 2000 Index)
SG	=	Small Growth Stocks (Russell 2000 Growth Index)
SV	=	Small Value Stocks (Russell 2000 Value Index)
F	=	Foreign Stocks (MSCI EAFE Index)
B	=	Bonds (Lehman Brothers Aggregate Bond Index)

Source: Frank Russell Company

16.3.2 Technical Strategies

Earlier, we discussed the role that technical analysis plays in the stock evaluation process. As we saw, assessing past stock price trends to surmise what information they imply about future price movements was one of the primary tools of this analytical approach. Active managers can form equity portfolios on the basis of past stock price trends by assuming that one of two things will happen: (1) past stock price trends will continue in the same direction, or (2) they will reverse themselves.

A **contrarian** investment strategy is based on the belief that the best time to buy (sell) a stock is when the majority of other investors are the most bearish (bullish) about it. The contrarian investor will attempt to always purchase the stock when it is near its lowest price and sell it (or even short sell it) when it nears its peak. Implicit in this approach is the belief that stock returns are *mean reverting,* indicating that, over time, stocks will be priced so as to produce returns consistent with their risk-adjusted expected (i.e., mean) returns. DeBondt and Thaler (1985) demonstrated the potential benefits of forming active portfolios based on this notion. They showed that investing on an *overreaction hypothesis* could provide consistently superior returns. Exhibit 16.9 illustrates a summary of their experiment in which they measured returns to a portfolio of stocks that had had the worst market performance over the prior three years (i.e., losers) and a portfolio of stocks with the best past performance (i.e., winners). If investors overreacted to either bad news or good news about companies, as DeBondt and Thaler contended, we should see subsequent abnormal returns move in the opposite direction. The cumulative abnormal returns (CARs) shown in the display appear to support this notion, although the evidence is stronger for losers than for winners.

At the other extreme, active portfolios can also be formed on the assumptions that recent trends in past prices will continue. A **price momentum** strategy, as it is more commonly called, assumes that stocks that have been hot will stay hot, while cold stocks will also remain so. Although there may well be sound economic reasons for these trends to continue (e.g., company revenues and earnings that continue to grow faster than expected), it may also be the case that investors periodically *underreact* to the arrival of new information. Thus, a pure price

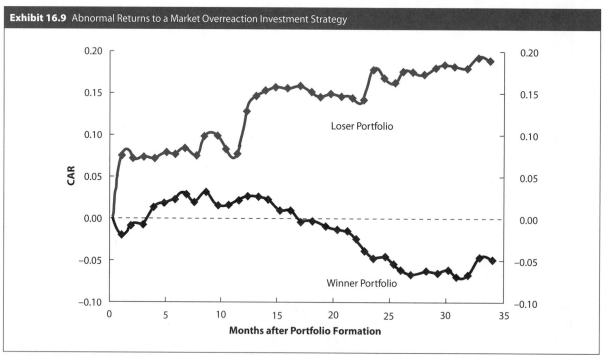

Exhibit 16.9 Abnormal Returns to a Market Overreaction Investment Strategy

Source: Werner F. M. DeBondt and Richard Thaler, "Does the Stock Market Overreact?" *Journal of Finance* 40, no. 3 (July 1985): 793–805. Reprinted with permission of Blackwell Publishing.

momentum strategy focuses on the trend of past prices alone and makes purchase and sale decisions accordingly. Chan, Jegadeesh, and Lakonishok (1999) investigated the profitability of this approach. They divided all of the stocks traded in U.S. markets over a 5-year period into 10 different portfolios based on their past six-month price movements and calculated returns over the following year. Panel A of Exhibit 16.10 shows these returns for each of the portfolios, from the one with the most positive past price trend (#10) to the worst price trend (#1). The data appear to justify the price momentum strategy in that the portfolios with the highest (lowest) level of price momentum generated the highest (lowest) subsequent returns. Also, the last column shows that a momentum-based hedge fund long in the best-trend portfolio and short in the worst-trend one would also have been quite profitable.

16.3.3 Anomalies and Attributes

The price momentum strategies just discussed could either be based on pure price trend analysis or supported by the underlying economic fundamentals of the company. An **earnings momentum** strategy is a somewhat more formal active portfolio approach that purchases and holds stocks that have accelerating earnings and sells (or short sells) stocks with disappointing earnings. The notion behind this strategy is that, ultimately, a company's share price will follow the direction of its earnings, which is one measure of the firm's economic success. In judging the degree of momentum in a firm's earnings, it is often the case in practice that investors will compare the company's actual EPS to some level of what was expected. Two types of expected earnings are used most frequently: (1) those generated by a statistical model and (2) the consensus forecast of professional stock analysts. Panel B of Exhibit 16.10 shows that earnings momentum strategies were generally successful, although not to the same degree as price momentum strategies.

In our examination of market efficiency in Chapter 6, we saw several anomalies that suggested a role for active equity management. Two of these—the weekend effect and the January effect—involved investing during particular times of the year. While conceptually viable, the limitations inherent in these anomalies do not produce particularly effective portfolio strategies. That is, managers investing in stocks only in January are not likely to be able to justify their annual fees, while the number of transactions implied by the weekend effect (i.e., buy every Monday, sell every Friday) generally makes for a cost-ineffective portfolio. However, whether or not these calendar-related anomalies produce successful active portfolios, they still are useful rules for trades that an investor plans to make anyway.

A more promising approach to active anomaly investing involves forming portfolios based on various characteristics of the companies themselves. Two characteristics we have seen to matter in the stock market are the total capitalization of the firm's outstanding equity (i.e., firm size) and the financial position of the firm, as indicated by its various financial ratios (e.g., *P/E, P/BV*). Two general conclusions can be made about these firm characteristics. First, over time, firms with smaller market capitalizations produce bigger risk-adjusted returns than those with large market capitalizations. Second, over time, firms with lower *P/E* and *P/BV* ratios produce bigger risk-adjusted returns than those with higher levels of those ratios. In fact, we saw in Chapter 9 that low and high levels of these ratios are used in practice to define value and growth stocks, respectively.

Another reason why these firm-specific attributes may be important to active investors is that the term *sector* considered earlier in the context of rotation strategies also can be defined by different stock attributes. Because the market seems to favor some attributes more than others, sector rotation may involve overweighting stocks with certain characteristics, such as small- or large-capitalization stocks, high or low *P/E* stocks, or stocks classified more generally as value or growth stocks. For example, Panel A of Exhibit 16.11 shows the difference in returns to portfolios invested in small- and large-cap stocks on a monthly basis from 1991–2007. The graph shows the large-cap portfolio return minus the small-cap return, so any net return above the horizontal axis indicates a period when the former outperformed the latter. Notice the consistent firm size rotation and spread in returns that occurred in this period; in given months, both

Exhibit 16.10 Profitability of Momentum Strategies: 1994–1998

	1 (Low)	2	3	4	5	6	7	8	9	10 (High)	10–1 (PPS)
A. Classification Based on Prior Six-Month Return											
1994	-12.00	-6.10	0.40	2.10	0.50	-0.90	-1.80	3.10	-4.50	-6.40	5.40
1995	35.70	27.40	32.30	35.00	32.30	32.20	30.30	36.70	35.30	42.10	6.40
1996	11.90	15.60	17.90	20.20	27.90	22.50	22.00	21.90	20.40	15.30	3.40
1997	7.20	05.70	14.80	20.80	26.60	32.80	35.60	37.30	37.50	23.80	16.60
1998	-2.30	-4.40	-7.00	-3.30	-0.40	0.00	04.50	0.10	-0.80	04.40	6.70
1994–1998 average	8.10	7.64	11.68	14.96	17.38	17.32	18.12	19.82	17.58	15.84	7.74
B. Classification Based on Standardized Unexpected Earnings											
1994	-2.30	-2.40	-6.80	-1.00	-4.60	-1.20	-0.10	-3.30	0.90	-2.00	0.30
1995	36.70	25.40	27.80	31.00	33.40	27.50	36.10	36.90	38.60	40.60	3.90
1996	16.30	17.90	19.20	16.30	21.90	19.60	23.10	22.70	24.70	18.40	2.10
1997	25.50	21.70	23.50	22.80	24.10	24.50	25.20	28.40	29.60	28.10	2.60
1998	-3.20	-5.20	-1.30	04.40	-0.60	5.00	-0.10	-0.60	0.00	-6.20	-3.00
1994–1998 average	14.60	11.48	12.48	14.70	14.84	15.08	16.84	16.82	18.76	15.78	1.18

Source: Copyright © 1999, Association for Investment Management and Research. Reproduced and republished from "The Profitability of Momentum Strategies," from the November/December 1999 issue of the *Financial Analyst's Journal*, with permission from the CFA Institute. All Rights Reserved.

Exhibit 16.11 Performance of Large- and Small-Cap Portfolios: 1991–2007

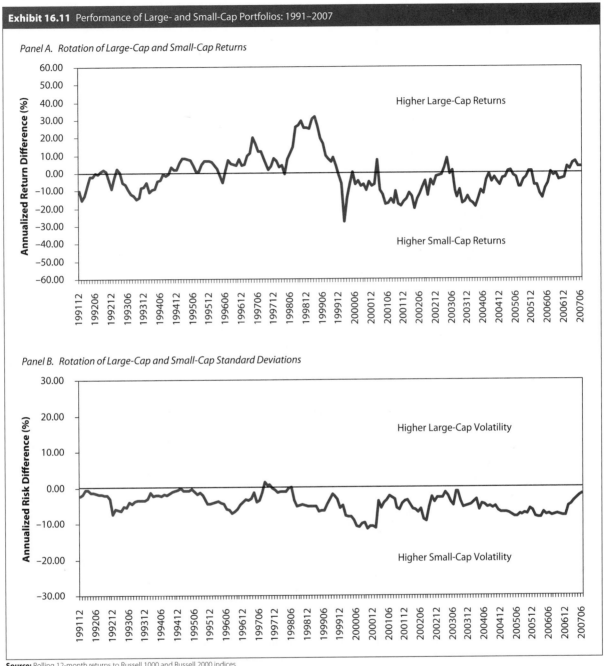

Panel A. Rotation of Large-Cap and Small-Cap Returns

Panel B. Rotation of Large-Cap and Small-Cap Standard Deviations

Source: Rolling 12-month returns to Russell 1000 and Russell 2000 indices.

large- and small-cap stocks outperformed the other by over 30 percent. Keep in mind, however, that small-cap stocks are almost always riskier than large-cap stocks. This is shown in Panel B of Exhibit 16.11 as the difference in the standard deviations of the large- and small-cap portfolios.

Similar analysis reveals the potential benefits of forming active global portfolios around financial ratios. Over a 20-year period, Fama and French (1998) divided the stocks in 13 world markets using several different ratios, including *P/E* and *P/BV*. They formed portfolios of stocks based on the highest and lowest 30 percent of each ratio and measured returns and standard deviations. Exhibit 16.12 summarizes their findings. For each country and each ratio, the display reports the average annual return differential between the lowest-ratio portfolio

Exhibit 16.12 Performance of Ratio-Based Stock Portfolios: 1975–1995

Country	P/E RATIO		P/BV RATIO	
	(Low–High) Return %	(Low–High) Std Dev %	(Low–High) Return %	(Low–High) Std Dev %
United States	6.71	2.87	6.79	1.13
Japan	7.47	−1.52	9.85	−2.75
United Kingdom	2.65	5.32	4.62	2.09
France	6.98	4.70	7.64	5.72
Germany	0.55	−10.20	2.75	−2.40
Italy	−5.37	−12.32	−5.99	−15.12
The Netherlands	5.11	0.59	2.30	12.06
Belgium	2.22	2.59	4.39	0.99
Switzerland	1.54	2.63	3.49	1.43
Sweden	8.19	17.67	8.02	12.05
Australia	9.67	−0.70	12.32	3.71
Hong Kong	4.99	4.02	7.16	8.47
Singapore	2.09	−5.13	9.67	9.18

Source: Eugene F. Fama and Kenneth R. French, "Value versus Growth: The International Evidence," *Journal of Finance* 53, no.6 (December 1998): 1975–1999. Reprinted with permission of Blackwell Publishing.

and the highest-ratio portfolio, as well as difference in standard deviation for those two portfolios. Two facts are clear from these results. First, over time, portfolios with the lowest *P/E* and *P/BV* ratios produced the highest returns everywhere in the world except Italy. Second, those low-ratio portfolios also tended to be more volatile, although this finding was far less uniform across countries. As we will see shortly, these results are important for understanding the differences between the value and growth investment styles.

16.3.4 Forming Momentum-Based Stock Portfolios: Two Examples

As we have just seen, in the world of active equity portfolio management the concept of momentum investing can mean two things: *price momentum* and *earnings momentum*. However, the justifications for these strategies are very different—price momentum is a technical strategy while earnings momentum is ultimately a fundamental approach to investing—so it should not be surprising that they can lead to forming very different types of portfolios. That is, a price momentum investor might be attracted to a stock with consistently strong, positive returns regardless of why they occurred. In contrast, the earnings momentum investor is likely to be attracted to stocks for companies that generate earnings in excess of market expectations, even if the past returns for those stocks have been negative.

To examine these differences in more specific terms, two separate computer screens of the stocks in the Russell 1000 index on March 31, 2007, were performed. In the first, the stocks were ranked from highest to lowest in terms of their returns over the past six months, which is a characteristic likely to be appealing to a price momentum investor. In the second screen, the stocks were ranked from highest to lowest by their *earnings surprise* (i.e., the percentage difference between the firm's actual earnings and the consensus forecast of professional stock analysts) over the prior year, which is what an earnings momentum investor would be interested in knowing. Financial data for 10 of the top-ranked stocks from each screening are shown in Exhibit 16.13.

Notice that the stocks most likely to be included in a price momentum-based portfolio all share the feature that they have had strong positive price increases over the prior three-month, six-month, and 1-year periods. However, there appear to be few other similarities between these securities. In particular, the earnings surprise component is actually negative for half of the stocks listed, even though the average earnings per share for these companies is forecast to rise from $3.03 to $4.41. Thus, the price momentum investor is making a bet on the *continuation* of

Exhibit 16.13 Financial Data for 20 Selected Momentum-Oriented Stocks from the Russell 1000 Index

Company	Ticker	Current EPS	Forecast Next Yr EPS	Current P/E	3-mo Total Return	6-mo Total Return	12-mo Total Return	1-yr EPS Surprise [Act–Est]	Est PEG
Price Momentum Stocks:									
AMR	AMR	$1.17	$5.82	29.46	6.07%	65.34%	32.95%	−23.56%	0.74
COACH	COH	1.54	2.10	31.08	13.02	55.87	34.28	0.79	1.06
HASBRO	HAS	1.24	1.60	23.42	10.07	44.16	44.59	−3.01	1.73
DEERE & CO	DE	6.46	8.30	16.53	15.07	38.10	43.08	2.28	1.49
AUTOZONE	AZO	8.02	9.49	15.45	10.07	36.77	24.44	0.92	1.44
HEWITT ASSOCIATES	HEW	1.31	1.60	22.53	18.15	32.89	9.43	−432.24	1.39
AVON PRODUCTS	AVP	1.39	2.09	26.60	14.90	29.19	21.11	8.59	1.64
ENTERGY CORP	ETR	4.71	6.75	20.74	9.11	28.61	40.56	1.44	1.87
COGNIZANT TECH SOLUTIONS	CTSH	1.55	2.91	57.03	11.13	28.15	52.02	−4.26	0.86
DU PONT	DD	2.88	3.46	17.57	10.31	27.56	29.41	−0.28	1.76
Average:		3.03	4.41	26.04	11.79	38.66	33.19	−44.93	1.40
Earnings Momentum Stocks:									
ANNALY CAPITAL MGMT	NLY	$0.73	$1.31	19.25	2.09%	15.06%	25.03%	79.91%	2.14
FOREST OIL	FST	2.18	2.80	14.44	−10.62	−8.10	−4.89	41.50	1.32
CBL & ASSOCIATES PROPERTIES	CBL	1.24	1.39	37.06	8.99	17.92	13.26	39.23	4.72
BOSTON SCIENTIFIC CORP	BSX	0.94	0.97	17.23	2.86	−6.68	−32.46	25.45	1.57
BEA SYSTEMS	BEAS	0.48	0.61	24.31	−13.47	−15.21	5.16	22.75	1.57
DOLLAR GENERAL	DG	0.74	0.84	22.51	6.47	31.01	−4.73	18.29	1.65
BEAR STEARNS	BSC	14.28	14.60	10.52	0.34	17.71	13.53	14.11	0.95
ELECTRONIC DATA SYSTEMS	EDS	0.97	1.74	28.59	4.22	16.19	2.80	13.66	1.65
BARNES & NOBLE	BKS	2.21	2.46	18.58	3.82	12.62	−3.87	8.96	1.43
AVON PRODUCTS	AVP	1.39	2.09	26.60	14.90	29.19	21.11	8.59	1.64
Average:		2.52	2.88	21.91	1.96	10.97	3.50	27.24	1.86

Source: Author calculations.

past price trends, perhaps for reasons that have more to do with the psychology of other investors in the market than with the underlying economic position of the companies themselves.

On the other hand, the earnings momentum–based manager will be attracted to stocks for companies that consistently produce earnings that surpass investor expectations. The 10 positions shown at the bottom of Exhibit 16.13 all have demonstrated that ability over the past year. Additionally, each of these stocks has a forecasted future level of earnings that is higher than current earnings. However, many of these stocks have also experienced negligible or negative returns at some point over the prior 12 months, which could mean that the stock disappointed investors in some other way in the past. Despite this, the belief of the earnings momentum investor is that firms whose fundamental economic position allows them to beat expectations will eventually see their stock prices increase to reflect that performance. Thus, the trading strategy in an earnings momentum portfolio is simple: Buy (and hold) stocks with positive earnings momentum, and sell those stocks when that momentum deteriorates or turns negative.

Two final points should be mentioned. First, notice that only one stock (AVP) was ranked at the top of both the price momentum and earnings momentum screens. This supports the earlier observation that these two active strategies tend to produce different collections of stocks. Second, the stocks listed in Exhibit 16.13 were selected in a purely mechanical manner without any additional insight from a professional money manager who might override the computer screen for any of several reasons. For instance, an earnings momentum manager following a "Growth at a Reasonable Price" (i.e., GARP) discipline might be more attracted to positive earnings surprise stocks that also sell at lower PEG ratios (FST, BSX) than to those that appear to be more expensive by that measure (NLY, CBL).

16.3.5 Tax Efficiency and Active Equity Management

We saw earlier that the primary intention of an actively managed equity portfolio is to produce a return that exceeds that of its passive benchmark. Of course, to accomplish that goal the active manager must form a portfolio that differs from the index itself, which usually requires trading stocks into and out of the fund on a frequent basis. Compared to a passively managed portfolio, there are two potential costs associated with these additional stock trades. First, the active fund will incur additional transaction costs, which will reduce the net return to the portfolio. Second, selling stocks that have appreciated in price will create a capital gain on which investors may have to pay taxes.

While the negative effect on returns due to high transaction fees are shared by all investors, the tax consequences of active equity management are a concern only for those investors who hold their portfolio in a taxable account. Many investors—institutions such as pension funds and university endowment funds or individuals with tax-deferred retirement plans—do not have to worry about paying additional taxes on the trades of an active portfolio manager. Reichenstein (2006) notes, though, that many other investors—particularly individuals not investing through a retirement plan—do need to worry about the **tax efficiency** of the active portfolio because this is an expense that they will ultimately bear.

The fund's **portfolio turnover** is an indirect measure of the amount of trading that could lead to a higher tax bill for a taxable investor. The portfolio turnover ratio is typically measured as the total dollar value of the securities sold from the portfolio in a year divided by the average dollar value of the assets managed by the fund. For instance, an active manager that sold $75 million worth of stocks in a year from a portfolio that averaged $100 million in assets under management would have a turnover ratio of 75 percent. In essence, the manager has replaced three out of every four stocks in the portfolio at some point during the year. While the turnover ratio is a good indicator of overall trading activity, it does not necessarily indicate that the majority of those trades generated capital gains that in turn created taxable events. Many of those trades might have been transacted at losses that actually *offset* the gains created by other sales.

A more direct measure of how well portfolio managers balance the capital gains and losses resulting from their trades is the **tax cost ratio**. As developed by Morningstar, Inc., a leading provider of investment analysis in the mutual fund industry, this statistic compares a fund's pretax return (PTR) with this same return adjusted for taxes (TAR), assuming that investors pay taxes on net short-term and long-term capital gains at the highest rate.

16.5 $$\text{Tax Cost Ratio} = [1 - \{(1 + \text{TAR})/(1 + \text{PTR})\}] \times 100$$

Ptak (2002) explains that the tax cost ratio represents the percentage of an investor's assets that are lost to taxes on a yearly basis due to the trading strategy employed by the fund manager. Notice that even if there is high turnover in a portfolio, TAR need not be significantly below PTR if the manager was able to "harvest" enough capital losses to balance out the capital gains associated by other trades.

For example, Exhibit 16.14 lists tax efficiency statistics for both a passive (the Vanguard 500 Index Fund we saw earlier) and an active (MFS Research Fund) mutual fund. Compared to the index fund, the active fund had both a higher **expense ratio** (which includes all management, operating, and administrative fees as a percentage of the fund's assets) as well as a higher turnover ratio (99 versus 5 percent). Thus, MFRFX was clearly a more expensive fund to investors with substantially more stock trading than VFINX. Despite those additional expenses, it outperformed the benchmark on a pretax basis (13.46 versus 12.03 percent) over the 3-year period shown. However, once the tax efficiency of the trades in the two funds is considered, the story changes. Specifically, notice that there is very little difference between the pretax and tax-adjusted returns for VFINX, meaning that what little trading there was in the index fund was fairly balanced in the creation of capital gains and losses. This leads to a tax cost ratio for VFINX of just 0.33 percent $(=[1-(1.1166/1.1203)]\times100)$. Conversely, the trades in MFRFX were far less tax efficient; its tax cost ratio was 2.02 percent, meaning that taxable investors in the fund saw their positions reduced by more than 2 percent per year due to taxes.

16.4 Value versus Growth Investing: A Closer Look

An important development in active equity management during the last several years has been the creation of portfolio strategies based on value- and growth-oriented investment styles. Indeed, it is now common for money management firms to define themselves as "value stock managers" or "growth stock managers" when selling their services to clients. Exhibit 16.15 indicates how pervasive these styles have become. Using the classifications of Morningstar, Inc., the number of available growth- and value-oriented funds grew dramatically, particularly toward the end of the reporting period. The chart shows that the available number of growth fund products expanded by more than 18 percent per year over this period, with large-cap

Exhibit 16.14 Tax Efficiency of Passive and Active Stock Funds: Example

	Vanguard 500 Index Fund (VFINX)	MFS Research Fund (MFRFX)
Management Approach	Passive	Active
Expense Ratio	0.18%	1.02%
Portfolio Turnover	5%	99%
3-yr Avg. Pretax Return	12.03%	13.46%
Tax-Adjusted Return	11.66%	11.17%
Tax Cost Ratio	0.33%	2.02%

Exhibit 16.15 Number of Growth and Value Mutual Funds: 1991–2007

	2007	2003	2000	1995	1991
Growth-Oriented Funds					
Large-cap	1,751	1,245	651	174	117
Mid-cap	985	784	415	106	79
Small-cap	843	672	383	77	42
Total	3,579	2,701	1,449	357	238
Annual % Increase (1991–2007)	18.5%				
Value-Oriented Funds					
Large-cap	1,405	946	615	211	133
Mid-cap	407	301	212	69	60
Small-cap	427	270	193	47	25
Total	2,239	1,517	1,020	327	218
Annual % Increase (1991–2007)	15.7%				

Source: Fidelity Management and Research. Adapted from Table 1 in Keith C. Brown, W.V. Harlow, and Hanjiang Zhang, "Staying the Course: Performance Persistence and the Role of Investment Style Consistency in Professional Asset Management," Working Paper, June 23, 2008.

portfolios being the most prevalent. Value fund availability did not increase quite as much but still expanded by almost 16 percent annually.

The distinction between value and growth investing can be best appreciated by considering the thought process of a representative manager for each style.[1] In Chapter 11, we saw that the price-earnings ratio for any company can be expressed as:

16.6
$$P/E \text{ Ratio} = \frac{(\text{Current Price per Share})}{(\text{Earnings per Share})}$$

where the earnings per share *(EPS)* measure can be based on either current or forecasted firm performance. Value and growth managers will focus on different aspects of this equation when evaluating stocks. Specifically, a growth-oriented investor will

- Focus on the *EPS* component (i.e., the denominator) of the *P/E* ratio and its economic determinants;
- Look for companies that he or she expects to exhibit rapid *EPS* growth in the future; and
- Often implicitly assume that the *P/E* ratio will remain constant over the near term, meaning that the stock price will rise as forecasted earnings growth is realized.

On the other hand, a value-oriented investor will

- Focus on the price component (i.e., the numerator) of the *P/E* ratio; he or she must be convinced that the price of the stock is "cheap" by some means of comparison;
- Not care a great deal about current earnings or the fundamental drivers of earnings growth; and
- Often implicitly assume that the *P/E* ratio is below its natural level and that the market will soon "correct" this situation by increasing the stock price with little or no change in earnings.

In summary, a growth investor focuses on the current and future economic "story" of a company, with less regard to share valuation. The value investor, on the other hand, focuses on share price in anticipation of a market correction and, possibly, improving company fundamentals.

[1] This motivation is based on an excellent overview of value- and growth-oriented investment styles that can be found in Christopherson and Williams (1995).

The conceptual difference between value and growth investing may be reasonably straightforward, but classifying individual stocks into the appropriate style is not always simple in practice. Since detailed company valuations are time-consuming to produce, most analysts rely on more easily obtained financial indicators—such as *P/E* and *P/B* ratios, dividend yields, and *EPS* growth rates—to define both individual equity holdings and style benchmark portfolios. Exhibit 16.16 shows one approach for classifying firms according to style and market capitalization. Notice that value stocks are relatively cheap (e.g., low *P/B*, high yield) and with modest growth opportunities (e.g., regulated firms) while growth stocks tend to be more expensive, reflecting their superior earnings potential (e.g., technology firms).

To get a better feel for the types of stock portfolios these two investment styles might produce, Exhibit 16.17 lists representative samples of the top holdings for the Harbor Capital Appreciation (HACAX) growth-oriented mutual fund and the T. Rowe Price Value (TRVLX) mutual fund as of June 30, 2007. Both funds feature large-cap companies but they differ in their investment approach in other important ways. Notably, HACAX's biggest holdings emphasize technology (GOOG, AAPL, CSCO) firms while TRVLX invests more on the industrial (TYC, IP) and consumer (HD, KO) side. On average, the stocks in the HACAX portfolio tend to have higher *P/E* and *P/BK* ratios and greater future growth potential than those in TRVLX. Also, the HACAX fund appears to hold riskier (i.e., higher beta) stocks, as well as ones that pay lower dividends. Interestingly, both portfolios hold General Electric and Microsoft among their top holdings, which underscores the room for investor judgment involved in classifying stocks along the value-growth dimension.

Although investors appear to pay somewhat more attention to growth-oriented strategies, research has shown that a value approach to portfolio management tends to provide superior returns. In particular, Capaul, Rowley, and Sharpe (1993) studied the long-term performance of value and growth portfolios (defined by relative *P/B* ratios) in six countries: the United States, the United Kingdom, Japan, France, Germany, and Switzerland. They demonstrated that global value stocks outperformed global growth stocks by an average of 3.3 percent per year. Further, value stocks outperformed growth stocks in each of the six countries considered separately. More recent evidence provided by Chan and Lakonishok (2004) supports this conclusion. Exhibit 16.18, which shows the cumulative performance of a large-cap growth index

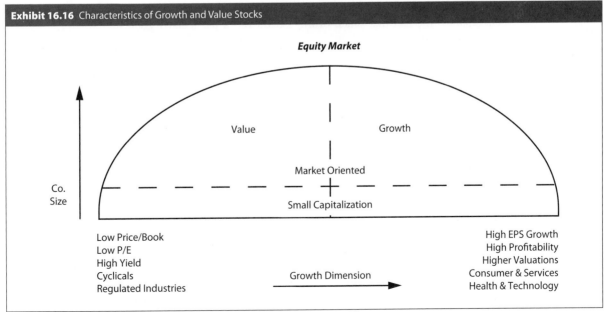

Exhibit 16.16 Characteristics of Growth and Value Stocks

Equity Market

Value   Growth

Market Oriented

Co. Size

Small Capitalization

Low Price/Book
Low P/E
High Yield
Cyclicals
Regulated Industries

Growth Dimension

High EPS Growth
High Profitability
Higher Valuations
Consumer & Services
Health & Technology

Exhibit 16.17 Top Stock Holdings of Growth and Value Mutual Funds

A. Harbor Capital Appreciation Fund (HACAX)

Company	Ticker	Market Cap ($ Bil)	P/E	P/BV	Est Growth EPS (%)	Div. Yld. (%)	Beta
Google	GOOG	163.1	45.13	8.28	31.68	0.00	1.22
Gilead Sciences	GILD	35.4	24.44	14.22	18.29	0.00	1.19
Adobe Systems	ADBE	25.8	38.62	4.96	14.80	0.00	1.17
Apple	AAPL	119.0	38.66	8.87	20.28	0.00	1.21
Walt Disney	DIS	65.4	18.13	2.15	14.64	0.92	0.85
Microsoft	MSFT	271.2	19.29	8.73	12.32	1.38	1.03
General Electric	GE	408.8	19.00	3.49	10.90	2.73	0.78
Cisco Systems	CSCO	192.9	25.18	6.12	14.92	0.00	1.10
Coach	COH	17.1	26.14	3.20	17.65	0.00	0.89
Intel	INTC	148.7	28.61	3.73	12.18	1.72	1.39
Total Fund Average:		*80.4*	*24.82*	*4.91*	*17.43*	*1.07*	*1.06*

B. T. Rowe Price Value Fund (TRVLX)

Company	Ticker	Market Cap ($ Bil)	P/E	P/BV	Est. Growth EPS (%)	Div. Yld. (%)	Beta
General Electric	GE	408.8	19.00	3.49	10.90	2.73	0.78
Tyco International	TYC	21.2	6.73	1.39	15.43	3.74	1.03
Microsoft	MSFT	271.2	19.29	8.73	12.32	1.38	1.03
Home Depot	HD	69.4	13.87	2.55	12.01	2.57	1.10
Coca-Cola	KO	129.2	21.90	6.80	9.72	2.94	0.73
International Paper	IP	14.9	19.04	2.25	6.75	2.89	1.19
Citigroup	C	227.6	10.15	1.79	9.77	4.61	1.03
Johnson & Johnson	JNJ	180.9	15.63	4.19	7.65	2.53	0.64
Wal-Mart Stores	WMT	173.8	14.28	2.79	11.95	1.94	0.87
Southwest Airlines	LUV	10.8	24.12	1.68	12.24	0.12	0.83
Total Fund Average:		*74.6*	*17.48*	*2.85*	*11.13*	*2.87*	*0.99*

Source: Author calculations.

(Russell 1000 Growth) and a large-cap value index (Russell 1000 Value), indicates that this performance advantage persisted in the U.S. market through June 2007. This is all the more notable for the fact that much of this period was a particularly good time for the large-cap growth investment style.

It is tempting to conclude that value is unambiguously superior to growth as an investment style. However, although value investing produces higher average returns than growth investing, this does not occur with much consistency from one investment period to another. Panel A of Exhibit 16.19 shows that there are significant differences in the value-growth return spread (based on the rolling annual performance of the Russell 1000 Value and Growth indexes) over time. The spread ranged from over 50 percent in favor of value investing to more than 30 percent to the advantage of the growth style. Conversely, Panel B indicates that the spread between value and growth return standard deviations, while itself volatile, is consistently negative, meaning that the growth strategy is consistently riskier than the value approach.

16.5 An Overview of Style Analysis

As we have seen, there are many equity investment styles, including forming portfolios around stock characteristics such as market capitalization, leverage, industry sector, relative valuation, and growth potential. Returns-based **style analysis** attempts to explain the variability in the observed returns to a security portfolio in terms of the movements in the returns to a series of benchmark portfolios capturing the essence of a particular security characteristic. Effectively,

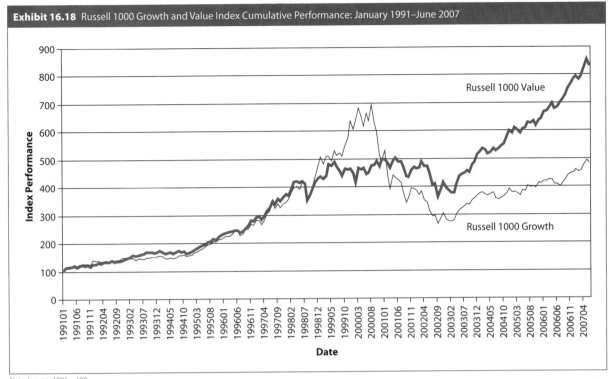

Exhibit 16.18 Russell 1000 Growth and Value Index Cumulative Performance: January 1991–June 2007

Note: January 1991 = 100

Source: Frank Russell Company

style analysis determines the combination of long positions in a collection of passive indexes that best mimics the past performance of a security portfolio.

The process of returns-based style analysis compares the past returns to a manager's portfolio with those to a series of indexes representing different investment styles to determine the relationship between the fund and those specific styles. The more highly correlated a fund's returns are with a given style index, the greater the weighting that style is given in the statistical assessment. The goals of the analysis are to better understand the underlying influences responsible for the portfolio's performance and to properly classify the manager's strategy when comparing him or her with other managers. Thus, regardless of whatever investment objective a manager might profess to follow, style analysis allows the portfolio to speak for itself.

Exhibit 16.20 shows a simple **style grid** that could be used to classify a manager's performance along two dimensions: firm size (large cap, mid cap, small cap) and relative value (value, blend, growth) characteristics. An investor whose portfolio produced returns best mimicked by the returns to indexes representing a small-cap value style (such as Manager A) would be plotted in the lower left quadrant of the grid. These grids are also useful to establish the implicit investment style for any of the popular stock market indicators described in Chapter 5. For example, Exhibit 16.21 shows the style plot points for the S&P 500, S&P Midcap, Wilshire 5000, NASDAQ Composite, Russell 3000 (R3), Russell 2000 (R2), and Russell 1000 (R1), among others.[2] Notice that the S&P 500 can be characterized as a large-cap, blend (i.e., between value and growth) fund. As such, it may not be the appropriate performance benchmark for someone managing a mid-cap, growth-oriented portfolio.

Formally, style analysis relies on the *constrained least squares* procedure, with the returns to the manager's portfolio as the dependent variable and the returns to the style index portfolios as the independent variables. There are often three constraints employed: (1) no intercept

---

[2] Exhibit 16.21 also plots the investment style for various subsets of the Russell indexes. For example, R1V and R1G are, respectively, the value and growth components of the Russell 1000. They are created by ranking the 1,000 companies in the index by their price-to-book ratios and assigning those with the lowest (highest) ratios to the (growth) subindex.

Exhibit 16.19 Performance of Value and Growth Portfolios: 1991–2007

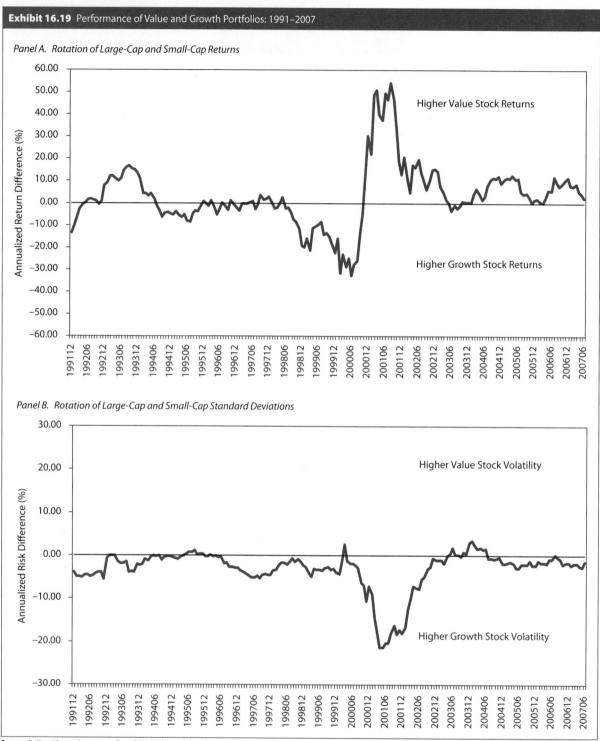

Panel A. Rotation of Large-Cap and Small-Cap Returns

Panel B. Rotation of Large-Cap and Small-Cap Standard Deviations

Source: Rolling 12-month returns to Russell 1000 Value and Growth indices.

term is specified, (2) the coefficients must sum to one, and (3) all the coefficients must be non-negative. As developed by Sharpe (1992), returns-based style analysis is simply an application of an asset class factor model:

16.7
$$R_{pt} = [b_{p1}F_{1t} + b_{p2}F_{2t} + \cdots + b_{pn}F_{nt}] + e_{pt}$$

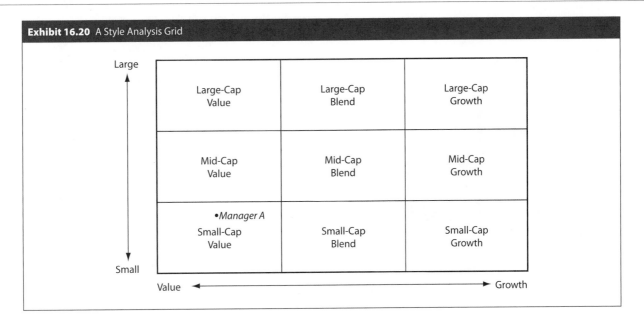

Exhibit 16.20 A Style Analysis Grid

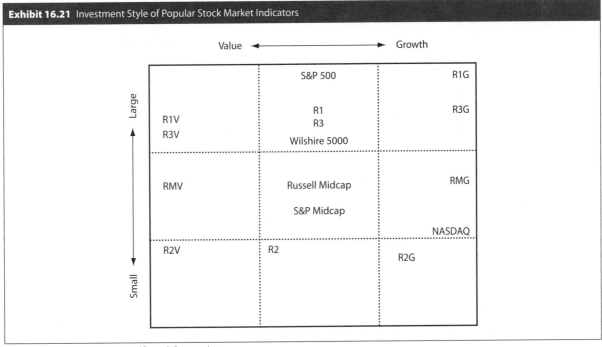

Exhibit 16.21 Investment Style of Popular Stock Market Indicators

Source: Based on Fidelity Management and Research Company data.

where:

R_{pt} = the tth period return to the portfolio of Manager p
F_{jt} = the tth period return to the jth style factor
b_{pj} = the sensitivity of Portfolio p to Style Factor j
e_{pt} = the portion of the return variability in Portfolio p not explained by variability in the set of factors

As with any regression equation, the coefficient of determination can be defined as

Exhibit 16.22 Style Analysis for Two Mutual Funds

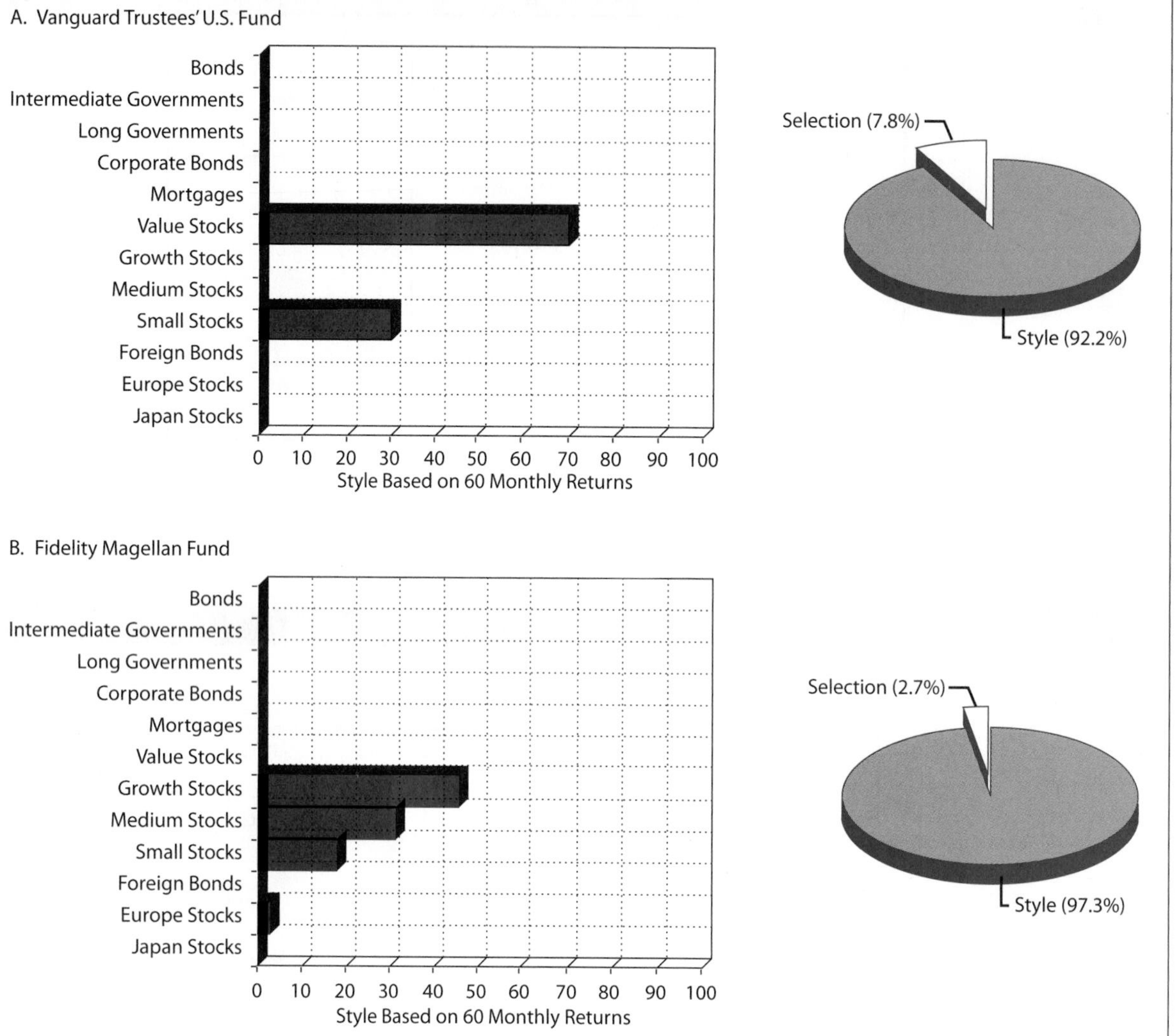

A. Vanguard Trustees' U.S. Fund

B. Fidelity Magellan Fund

Source: William F. Sharpe, "Asset Allocation: Management Style and Performance Measurement," *Journal of Portfolio Management* 18, no. 2 (Winter 1992): 7–19.

16.8

$$R^2 = 1 - [\sigma^2 (e_p)/\sigma^2 (R_p)]$$

Because of the way the factor model is designed, R^2 can be interpreted as the percentage of Manager p's return variability due to the portfolio's *style*, with $(1 - R^2)$ due to his or her *selection* skills.

The benchmark portfolios selected as style analysis factors should be consistent with the manager's pronounced style. This suggests that a different set of indexes might be specified for a domestic equity fund than for a global bond fund. Also, an effective benchmark portfolio should be easy be measure, have an investable proxy, and be as uncorrelated as possible with other style indexes.

To illustrate how this process can be implemented, Sharpe measured the investment styles of two large institutional equity portfolios—Vanguard Trustees' U.S. Fund and Fidelity Magellan Fund—over a five-year interval. Both portfolios performed well during the period, generating respective average annual returns of 15.5 percent and 20.6 percent. However, Exhibit 16.22 shows that the managers of these portfolios followed very different styles. The bar charts indicate the extent to which each portfolio's returns were correlated with the underlying style factors.

Exhibit 16.23 Mutual Fund Styles over Time

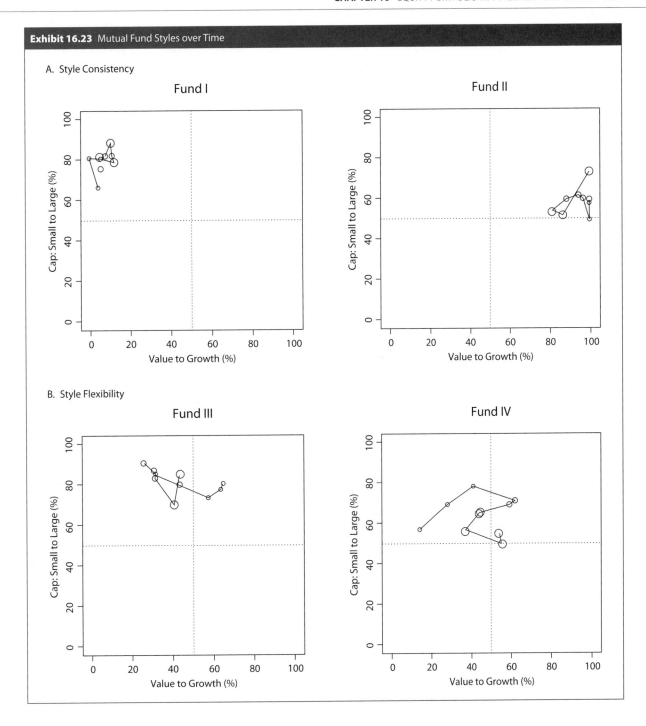

A. Style Consistency

B. Style Flexibility

Accordingly, the Trustees' Fund is best thought of as being a small-cap value fund over this period while the Magellan Fund was a small-to-mid-cap growth portfolio with some global exposure. Also, security selection accounted for a relatively small amount of Magellan's return variability (2.7 percent) but was more of a consideration (7.8 percent) in the Trustees' portfolio.

Finally, style analysis can also show whether a manager maintains a consistent investment style over time. This can be accomplished by reestimating the optimal combination of mimicking style indexes as additional performance data become available and then overlaying the plot points on the same grid. Exhibit 16.23 shows the connected sequence of plot points—or "snail trails" as they are sometimes called—for four different mutual funds managed by a leading investment company. Two of these funds (I and II) have well-defined style mandates and have been able to achieve relatively stable investment policies. The other two—III and IV—have exhibited considerable *style drift,* which in both cases is consistent with their flexible investment missions. Of course, an investor needs to be cautious about a manager whose portfolio exhibits unintentional style drift.

16.6 Asset Allocation Strategies

An equity portfolio does not stand in isolation; rather, it is part of an investor's overall investment portfolio. Many times the equity portfolio is part of a balanced portfolio that contains holdings in various long- and short-term debt securities (such as bonds and Treasury bills) in addition to equities.

In such situations, the portfolio manager must consider more than just the composition of the equity or the bond component of the portfolio. The manager also must determine the appropriate mix of asset categories in the entire portfolio. There are four general strategies for determining the asset mix of a portfolio: integrated, strategic, tactical, and insured asset allocation methods.

16.6.1 Integrated Asset Allocation

The integrated asset allocation strategy separately examines (1) capital market conditions and (2) the investor's objectives and constraints. These factors are combined to establish the portfolio asset mix that offers the best opportunity for meeting the investor's needs given the capital market forecast. The actual portfolio returns are used as inputs to an iterative process in which changes in the investor's objectives, constraints, and capital market expectations are noted. The optimal portfolio is then revised based on this update.

This integrated approach to portfolio formation is illustrated in Exhibit 16.24. Sharpe (1987, 1990) describes three key steps to integrated asset allocation. First, both capital market conditions and investor-specific objectives and constraints (e.g., risk tolerance, investment horizon, tax status) are summarized before the asset mix is determined. These processes are summarized in boxes C2 and I2, respectively, with the outcomes of those processes in boxes C3 and I3. An example of C3 might be the Markowitz efficient frontier containing portfolios of optimal risk–expected return combinations; the end product of I3 might be captured in an investment policy statement.

The second step in the integrated asset allocation process combines the information from the first step to select the single best portfolio for the investor in question. This is captured by the optimizer box in M1, with the resulting asset mix being shown in M2. One simple way of seeing how M1 might work is to calculate the *expected utility (EU)* of each prospective asset mix using the following formula:

16.8
$$EU_{pk} = ER_p - \left(\frac{\sigma_p^2}{RT_k} \right) = ER_p - (\text{Risk Penalty})$$

where ER_p and σ_p^2 are the expected return and variance for Portfolio p (which come from C3) and RT_k is the risk-tolerance factor for Investor k (which comes from I3). The risk-tolerance factor is an estimate intended to capture the essence of an investor's attitude toward risk bearing. Notice that the higher this number, the more risk tolerant the investor is and, hence, the less Portfolio p has its expected return "penalized" by its risk level. The optimal asset mix for any particular investor is then the one that generates the highest level of expected utility.

As an example, Panel A of Exhibit 16.25 shows the expected returns and variances for three different potential asset mixes (C3), while Panel B lists risk-tolerance factors for two investors (I3). Panel C shows the result of the expected utility calculations that combine this information (M2). For instance, the expected utility generated by Portfolio A for Investor 1 is 5.6 (= 7 − 7/5), which is the largest value of the three potential allocations and therefore his

Exhibit 16.24 Integrated Asset Allocation

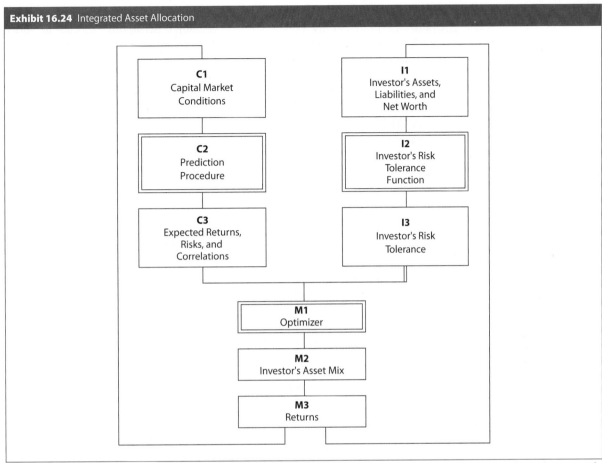

Exhibit 16.25 Optimal Portfolio Selection: An Example

A. Prospective Efficient Portfolios (C3)

Portfolio	ASSET MIX		ER	σ²
	Stock	Bond		
A	20%	80%	7%	7%
B	50	50	8	13
C	80	20	9	20

B. Risk-Tolerance Factors (I3)

Investor	RT	
1	5	(i.e., *less* tolerant)
2	40	(i.e., *more* tolerant)

C. Expected Utility Results (M2)

	A	B	C
Investor #1 *EU*	**5.6**	5.4	5.0
Investor #2 *EU*	6.8	7.8	**8.5**

optimal asset mix. By contrast, Investor 2 is more tolerant of risk and finds that Portfolio 3, which generates an expected utility level of 8.5 (= 9 − 20/40), is her optimal allocation. Notice that the risk-tolerance factor effectively deflates the risk penalty, allowing more risk-tolerant investors to pursue more volatile portfolios with higher expected returns.

The third stage of the integrated portfolio process occurs after enough time has passed that the optimal portfolio's actual performance can be compared with the manager's original expectations. This evaluation process is represented by Box M3 in Exhibit 16.24. Following this assessment, the manager can then make adjustments to the portfolio by including any new information into the optimization process. Adjustments to the initial asset mix can result from either a fundamental change in capital market conditions (e.g., increased inflation) or a change in the investor's circumstances (e.g., increased risk tolerance). It is this feedback loop that makes portfolio management a *dynamic* process.

16.6.2 Strategic Asset Allocation

Strategic asset allocation is used to determine the long-term policy asset weights in a portfolio. Typically, long-term average asset returns, risk, and covariances are used as estimates of future capital market results. Efficient frontiers are generated using this historical return information, and the investor decides which asset mix is appropriate for his or her needs during the planning horizon. This results in a *constant-mix* asset allocation with periodic rebalancing to adjust the portfolio to the specified asset weights.

One way to think of the strategic allocation process is as being equivalent to the integrated asset allocation process shown in Exhibit 16.24 but without the feedback loops. That is, the manager will determine the long-term asset allocation that is best suited for a particular investor by optimizing information from both the capital market and that investor. However, once this asset mix is established, the manager does not constantly attempt to adjust the allocation according to temporary changes in market and investor circumstances. Thus, as Ezra (1998) points out, the strategic allocation should define the basic nature of the trade-off between opportunity and safety that confronts the investor.

As an example, Brown, Garlappi, and Tiu (2008) examined the asset allocation patterns of college and university endowment funds in the United States and Canada. Exhibit 16.26 shows both the average actual and strategic (i.e., target) investment proportions for their fund sample in 2002 and 2005. There are several interesting things to note. First, endowment fund managers made some dramatic adjustments in the targeted investment proportions over these years; for instance, the strategic allocations to both U.S. equity (49.6% to 44.7%) and U.S. fixed-income (25.1% to 21.5%) *declined* significantly. Second, at the same time, managers apparently made an explicit decision to shift these assets to investments in the non-U.S. equity and hedge fund categories. Finally, planned investments in the rest of the asset classes listed remained relatively stable, which is consistent with the idea of a strategic allocation as a long-term view.

16.6.3 Tactical Asset Allocation

Unlike an investor's strategic allocation, which is set with a long-term focus and modified infrequently, tactical asset allocation frequently adjusts the asset class mix in the portfolio to take advantage of changing market conditions. With tactical asset allocation, these adjustments are driven solely by perceived changes in the relative values of the various asset classes; the investor's risk tolerance and investment constraints are assumed to be constant over time. In Exhibit 16.24, this is equivalent to an integrated approach to asset allocation that removes the feedback loop involving investor-specific information (i.e., I2).

Tactical asset allocation is often based on the premise of *mean reversion*: whatever a security's return has been in the recent past, it will eventually revert to its long-term average (mean) value. This assessment is usually done on a comparative basis. For instance, suppose that the ratio of stock and bond returns is normally 1.2, reflecting the greater degree of risk in the equity market. If stock returns were suddenly double those of bond returns, the tactical investor might

Exhibit 16.26 Strategic and Tactical Asset Allocations for University Endowment Funds

A. 2005 Year-End Data (709 Funds)

Asset Class	Actual Allocation	Strategic Allocation	Tactical Adjustment
U.S. Equity	45.7%	44.7%	+1.0%
Non-U.S. Equity	12.7	12.8	−0.1
U.S. Fixed Income	20.5	21.5	−1.0
Non-U.S. Fixed Income	0.9	1.0	−0.1
Real Estate—Public	1.2	1.3	−0.1
Real Estate—Private	2.0	2.2	−0.2
Hedge Funds	8.9	9.0	−0.1
Private Equity—Venture Capital	0.8	1.5	−0.7
Private Equity—Buyout	1.6	2.5	−0.9
Natural Resources	1.0	1.2	−0.2
Cash	3.4	1.6	+1.8
Other	1.4	0.8	+0.6

B. 2002 Year-End Data (535 Funds)

Asset Class	Actual Allocation	Strategic Allocation	Tactical Adjustment
U.S. Equity	46.4%	49.6%	−3.2%
Non-U.S. Equity	10.2	10.6	−0.4
U.S. Fixed Income	25.9	25.1	+0.8
Non-U.S. Fixed Income	1.1	0.7	+0.4
Real Estate—Public	1.2	1.0	+0.2
Real Estate—Private	1.4	1.2	+0.2
Hedge Funds	5.6	4.9	+0.7
Private Equity—Venture Capital	1.0	1.9	−0.9
Private Equity—Buyout	1.2	1.9	−0.7
Natural Resources	0.4	0.3	+0.1
Cash	4.0	1.6	+2.4
Other	1.6	1.2	+0.4

Source: Adapted from Keith C. Brown, Lorenzo Garlappi, and Cristian Tiu, "Does Asset Allocation Determine Portfolio Performance? Evidence From University Endownment Funds," Working Paper, June 11, 2008.

determine that bonds were now undervalued relative to stock. Accordingly, he should then overweight the fixed-income component of his portfolio, shifting, say, from a 60–40 percent initial mix of stocks and bonds to a 50–50 percent split.

Notice that tactical asset allocation is an inherently *contrarian* method of investing. That is, the investor adopting this approach will always be buying the asset class that is currently out of favor—on a relative basis, at least—and selling the asset class with the highest market value. In the preceding example, this was the case when the investor underweighted his stock allocation after stock prices rose substantially compared to bond prices. DuBois (1992) notes that how frequently the investor chooses to adjust the asset class mix in the portfolio will depend on several factors, such as the general level of volatility in the capital markets, relative equity and fixed-income risk premiums, and changes in the fundamental macroeconomic environment.

The endowment fund example in Exhibit 16.26 also shows the tactical adjustments made by managers. These adjustments can be measured as the difference between the actual and strategic (i.e., planned) allocation proportions and are listed in the last column. Notice that endowment fund managers went from being *underweighted* in the U.S. equity category in 2002 to being slightly *overinvested* by 2005 (−3.2% to +1.0%). This pattern was mirrored by an opposite movement for U.S. fixed income, which saw its tactical position fall from an overweight of +0.8% to an underweight of −1.0%. This means that endowment managers not only reduced their strategic allocations to fixed income between 2002 and 2005, but their actual investments in this category fell short of those targets as well. Obviously, this is a strong view against fixed-income investments. Finally, not all of the tactical adjustments shown in Exhibit 16.26 were probably intentional. The underweight positions in the private equity categories are likely due to managers not being able to get invested all of the money they had planned, which would also explain the overweight positions in their cash accounts. This reality of allocating assets to private equity investments will be discussed in Chapter 24.

16.6.4 Insured Asset Allocation

Insured asset allocation likewise results in continual adjustments in the portfolio allocation, assuming that expected market returns and risks are constant over time, while the investor's objectives and constraints change as his or her wealth position changes. For example, rising portfolio values increase the investor's wealth and consequently his or her ability to handle risk, which means the investor can increase his or her exposure to risky assets. Declines in the portfolio's value lower wealth, consequently decreasing his or her ability to handle risk, which means the portfolio's exposure to risky assets must decline. Often, insured asset allocation involves only two assets, such as common stocks and T-bills. As stock prices rise, the asset allocation increases the stock component. As stock prices fall, the stock component of the mix falls while the T-bill component increases. This is opposite of what would happen under tactical asset allocation. Insured asset allocation is like the integrated approach without the feedback loop on the capital market side (i.e., C2 in Exhibit 16.24). It is sometimes called a *constant proportion* strategy because of the shifts that occur as wealth changes.

16.6.5 Selecting an Active Allocation Method

Which asset allocation strategy is used depends on the perceptions of the variability in the client's objectives and constraints and the perceived relationship between past and future capital market conditions. If you believe that capital market conditions are relatively constant over time, you might use insured asset allocation. If you believe that the client's goals, risk preferences, and constraints are constant, you might use tactical asset allocation. Integrated asset allocation assumes that both the investor's needs and capital market conditions are variable and therefore must be constantly monitored. Under these conditions, the portfolio mix must be updated constantly to reflect current changes in these parameters.

• • • • SUMMARY • • • •

- Passive equity portfolios attempt to track the returns of an established benchmark, such as the S&P 500, or some other benchmark that meets the investor's needs. Active portfolios attempt to add value relative to their benchmark by market timing and/or by seeking to buy undervalued stocks. Index mutual funds and exchange-traded funds are popular ways for small investors to make passive investments.
- Tracking error, which is defined as the standard deviation of the difference between the returns to a managed fund and a benchmark, is a convenient way to categorize various management styles. Portfolios with tracking errors of less than 1 percent are generally considered to be passive, while active equity strategies often have tracking errors in excess of 5 percent.
- There are several methods for constructing and managing a passive portfolio, including full replication of a benchmark or sampling. Also, several active management approaches

exist, including sector rotation and price and earnings momentum strategies. Value- and growth-oriented strategies have become particularly popular in recent years, and style analysis helps the investor determine the exact investment style the manager is using. Investors should also consider the tax efficiency of an actively managed portfolio.

- Since equity portfolios typically are used with other assets in an investor's overall portfolio, we reviewed several common asset allocation strategies, including integrated asset allocation, strategic asset allocation, tactical asset allocation, and insured asset allocation. The basic difference between these strategies is whether they rely on current market expectations or long-run projections, as well as whether the investor's objectives and constraints remain constant over the planning horizon or change with market conditions.

• • • • SUGGESTED READINGS • • • •

Ammann, Manuel, and Heinz Zimmermann. "Tracking Error and Tactical Asset Allocation." *Financial Analysts Journal* 57, no. 2 (March/April 2001): 32–43.

Bernstein, Richard. *Style Investing: Unique Insight into Equity Management.* New York: Wiley, 1995.

Burns, Terrence E. *Asset Allocation in a Changing World.* Charlottesville, VA: AIMR, 1998.

Dreman, David M. *Contrarian Investment Strategies: The Next Generation.* New York: Simon & Schuster, 1998.

Hopkins, Peter J. B., and C. Hayes Miller. *Country, Sector, and Company Factors in Global Equity Portfolios.* Charlottesville, VA: Research Foundation of AIMR, 2001.

Sharpe, William F. "Expected Utility Asset Allocation," *Financial Analysts Journal* 63, no. 5 (September/October 2007): 18–30.

• • • • QUESTIONS • • • •

1. Why have passive portfolio management strategies increased in use over time?
2. What is meant by an indexing portfolio strategy and what is the justification for this strategy? How might it differ from another passive portfolio?
3. Briefly describe four techniques considered active equity portfolio management strategies.
4. Describe several techniques for constructing a passive portfolio.
5. Discuss three strategies active managers can use to add value to their portfolios.
6. How do trading costs and market efficiencies affect the active manager? How may an active manager try to overcome these obstacles to success?
7. Discuss how the four asset allocation strategies differ from one another.
8. **CFA EXAMINATION LEVEL III** Recent empirical research has suggested that holding portfolios of stocks classified as value (low price/book ratio) as opposed to growth (high price/book ratio) stocks in both U.S. and international markets has resulted in enhanced risk-adjusted returns. Critique the efficient market hypothesis in light of these findings.
9. Describe the difference between a price momentum strategy and an earnings momentum strategy. Under what conditions would you expect the two approaches to produce similar portfolios?
10. What are the trade-offs involved when constructing a portfolio using a full replication versus a sampling method?
11. Because of inflationary expectations, you expect natural resource stocks, such as mining companies and oil firms, to perform well over the next three to six months. As an active portfolio manager, describe the various methods available to take advantage of this forecast.

• • • • PROBLEMS • • • •

1. Given the monthly returns that follow, how well did the passive portfolio track the S&P 500 benchmark? Find the R^2, alpha, and beta of the portfolio. Compute the average return differential with and without sign.

Month	Portfolio Return	S&P 500 Return
January	5.0%	5.2%
February	−2.3	−3.0
March	−1.8	−1.6
April	2.2	1.9
May	0.4	0.1
June	−0.8	−0.5
July	0.0	0.2
August	1.5	1.6
September	−0.3	−0.1
October	−3.7	−4.0
November	2.4	2.0
December	0.3	0.2

CFA

2. **CFA EXAMINATION LEVEL III** Beth Stewart is an investment analyst for the U.S.-based Empire Pension Fund. Empire is considering the addition of two recently established U.S. large-capitalization equity mutual funds to its asset mix. Stewart utilizes return-based-style analysis to compare the performance of the Foreman Fund and the Copeland Fund for the past year.

	S&P 500 Index	Foreman Fund	Copeland Fund
R^2	—	68.5%	99.4%
Annual Return (gross)*	6.8%	9.2%	7.0%
Portfolio Turnover	—	45%	15%

* Management fees and administrative charges have not been deducted

Based on this data, Stewart concludes that Foreman is an actively managed fund, that Copeland is an index fund, and that Foreman outperformed Copeland for the year. A colleague tells Stewart that her conclusions may not be accurate and makes the following statements:
- Even though Foreman has a low R^2 with the S&P 500 Index, Foreman may not be an actively managed fund.
- Copeland may be an actively managed fund even though Copeland has low portfolio turnover.
- Foreman may not have had superior risk-adjusted performance compared with Copeland for the year.

For each of these three statements, describe one circumstance in which statement could be correct.

3. Consider the following trading and performance data for four different equity mutual funds:

	Fund W	Fund X	Fund Y	Fund Z
Assets Under Management, Avg for Past 12 months (mil)	$289.4	$653.7	$1,298.4	$5,567.3
Security Sales, Past 12 months (mil)	$37.2	$569.3	$1,453.8	$437.1
Expense Ratio	0.33%	0.71%	1.13%	0.21%
Pretax Return, 3-yr avg	9.98%	10.65%	10.12%	9.83%
Tax-adjusted return, 3-yr avg	9.43%	8.87%	9.34%	9.54%

a. Calculate the portfolio turnover ratio for each fund.
b. Which two funds are most likely to be actively managed and which two are most likely passive funds? Explain.
c. Calculate the tax cost ratio for each fund.
d. Which funds were the most and least tax efficient in the operations? Why?

CFA

4. **CFA EXAMINATION LEVEL III** Global Advisers Company (GAC) is an SEC-registered investment counseling firm solely involved in managing international securities portfolios. After much research on the developing economy and capital markets of the country of Otunia, GAC has decided to include an investment in the Otunia stock market in its Emerging Market Commingled Fund. However, GAC has not yet decided whether to invest actively or by indexing. Your opinion on the active versus indexing decision has been solicited. A summary of the research findings follows.

Otunia's economy is fairly well diversified across agricultural and natural resources, manufacturing (both consumer and durable goods), and a growing finance sector. Transaction costs in securities markets are relatively large in Otunia because of high commissions and government "stamp taxes" on securities trades. Accounting standards and disclosure regulations are quite detailed, resulting in wide public availability of reliable information about companies' financial performance.

Capital flows into and out of Otunia and foreign ownership of Otunia securities are strictly regulated by an agency of the national government. The settlement procedures under these ownership rules often cause long delays in settling trades made by nonresidents. Senior finance officials in the government are working to deregulate capital flows and foreign ownership, but GAC's political consultant believes that isolationist sentiment may prevent much real progress in the short run.

a. Briefly discuss four aspects of the Otunia environment that favor investing actively and four aspects that favor indexing.
b. Recommend whether GAC should invest in Otunia actively or by indexing and justify your recommendation based on the factors identified in Part a.

5. **CFA EXAMINATION LEVEL III** Betty Black's investment club wants to buy the stock of either NewSoft Inc. or Capital Corp. In this connection, Black has prepared the following table. You have been asked to help her interpret the data, based on your forecast for a healthy economy and a strong market over the next 12 months.

	NewSoft Inc.	Capital Corp.	S&P 500 Index
Current price	$30	$32	n/a
Industry	Computer Software	Capital Goods	n/a
P/E ratio (current)	25×	14×	16×
P/E ratio (5-yr avg)	27×	16×	16×
P/B ratio (current)	10×	3×	3×
P/B ratio (5-yr avg)	12×	4×	2×
Beta	1.5	1.1	1.0
Dividend yield	0.3%	2.7%	2.8%

NewSoft's shares have higher price/earnings (*P/E*) and price/book (*P/B*) ratios than those of Capital Corp. Identify and briefly discuss three reasons why the disparity in ratios may not indicate that NewSoft's shares are overvalued relative to the shares of Capital Corp. Answer the question in terms of the two ratios, and assume that there have been no extraordinary events affecting either company.

6. As the chief investment officer for a money management firm specializing in taxable individual investors, you are trying to establish a strategic asset allocation for two different clients. You have established that Ms. A has a risk-tolerance factor of 8 while Mr. B's risk-tolerance factor is 27. The characteristics for four model portfolios follow:

ASSET MIX

Portfolio	Stock	Bond	ER	σ^2
1	5%	95%	8%	5%
2	25	75	9	10
3	70	30	10	16
4	90	10	11	25

a. Calculate the expected utility of each prospective portfolio for each of the two clients.
b. Which portfolio represents the optimal strategic allocation for Ms. A? Which portfolio is optimal for Mr. B? Explain why there is a difference in these two outcomes.
c. For Ms. A, what level of risk tolerance would leave her indifferent between having Portfolio 1 or Portfolio 2 as her strategic allocation? Demonstrate.

7. **CFA EXAMINATION LEVEL II** Briefly discuss whether active asset allocation among countries could consistently outperform a world market index. Include a discussion of the implications of *integration versus segmentation* of international financial markets as it pertains to portfolio diversification, but ignore the issue of stock selection.

8. Consider the annual returns produced by two different active equity portfolio managers (A and B) as well as those to the stock index with which they are both compared:

Period	Manager A	Manager B	Index
1	12.8%	13.9%	11.8%
2	−2.1	−4.2	−2.2
3	15.6	13.5	18.9
4	0.8	2.9	−0.5
5	−7.9	−5.9	−3.9
6	23.2	26.3	21.7
7	−10.4	−11.2	−13.2
8	5.6	5.5	5.3
9	2.3	4.2	2.4
10	19.0	18.8	19.7

a. Did either manager outperform the index, based on the average annual return differential that he or she produced relative to the benchmark? Demonstrate.
b. Calculate the tracking error for each manager relative to the index. Which manager did a better job of limiting his or her client's unsystematic risk exposure? Explain.

THOMSON ONE | Business School Edition

1. Consider four different stock market indexes representing different equity investment styles:

   Large-cap, Value: Russell 1000-Value (FRUS1VA)
   Large-cap, Growth: Russell 1000-Growth (FRUS1GR)
   Small-cap, Value: Russell 2000-Value (FRUS2VA)
   Small-cap, Growth: Russell 2000-Growth (FRUS2GR).

   Which of these investment styles would have been the most profitable to invest in over the following periods ending December 29, 2006: (a) the past three months, (b) the past year, and (c) the past five years? [Hint: You can calculate the growth of a one dollar investment in all four strategies by taking the ratio of the beginning and ending index values for each of the respective investment periods.] Which strategy appears to have been the riskiest? Why?

2. Using the same companies represented in Panels A and B of Exhibit 16.17, update the financial information using the most recent data available. Given your analysis, would all of the various firms shown in the exhibit still qualify to be included in the same portfolio? In particular, should MSFT now be classified as a value stock or a growth stock? (Note: Use the longest-term EPS growth forecast available in constructing your display.)

3. Use the "Search for Companies" function to create your own portfolio according to a specific investment style mandate (e.g., large-cap growth, high-return momentum, industry-specific) of your own choosing. Once you have established this portfolio, use the "Save Set" command to name and save the identity of the portfolio companies you have selected. Analyze your portfolio's recent valuation, financial, and performance characteristics by accessing the various summary reports available under the "Portfolios" tab. [Note: You should experiment with the various search commands available in the company search menu in order to get acquainted with the multitude of portfolios that you can form as well as the scope of the financial reports that can be created for those portfolios.]

PART 5
Analysis and Management of Bonds

CHAPTER 17
Bond Fundamentals

CHAPTER 18
The Analysis and Valuation of Bonds

CHAPTER 19
Bond Portfolio Management Strategies

For most investors, bonds receive limited attention and very little respect. This is surprising when one considers that the total market value of the bond market in the United States and in most other countries is substantially larger than the market value of the stock market. For example, by the end of 2007 the U.S. market value of all publicly issued bonds was more than $22 trillion, while the market value of all stocks was about $19 trillion. On a global basis, the values are about $44 trillion for bonds versus $41 trillion for stocks. Beyond the size factor, bonds have a reputation for low, unexciting rates of return. Although this may have been true 40 or 50 years ago, it certainly has not been true during the past 25 years. Specifically, the average annual compound rate of return on government/corporate bonds for the period 1980–2007 was slightly over 10 percent versus about 14 percent for common stocks. These rates of return along with corresponding standard deviations (6 percent for bonds versus 15 percent for stocks) and the relatively low correlation between stocks and bonds (about 0.25) indicate that there are substantial opportunities in bonds for individual and institutional investors to enhance their risk–return performance.

The chapters in this section are intended to provide (1) a basic understanding of bonds and the bond markets around the world, (2) background on analyzing returns and risks in the bond market, (3) insights regarding the valuation of bonds, including numerous new fixed-income securities with very unusual cash flow characteristics, and (4) an understanding of either active or passive bond portfolio management.

Chapter 17 describes the global bond market in terms of country participation and the makeup of the bond market in major countries. Also, we examine characteristics of bonds in alternative categories, such as government, corporate, and municipal. We also discuss the many new corporate bond instruments developed in the United States, such as asset-backed securities, zero coupon bonds, high-yield bonds, and inflation protection securities. While the use of these securities globally has generally been limited to the large developed markets, it is certain that they will eventually be used around the world. Finally, we consider sources of price information needed by bond investors.

Chapter 18 is concerned with the analysis and valuation of bonds. This includes a detailed discussion of how one values a bond using a single discount rate or using spot rates. We also evaluate alternative rate of return measures for bonds. Subsequently, we consider what factors affect yields on bonds and what characteristics influence the volatility of bond returns including the very important concept of bond duration, which is a measure of bond price volatility that is important in active and passive bond portfolio management. We also consider bond convexity and the impact it has on bond price volatility. Notably, these concepts are examined for option-free securities. We also consider how they apply to a growing set of securities with embedded options.

Chapter 19 considers how to use the background provided in Chapter 17 and Chapter 18 to create and manage a bond portfolio. We consider three major categories of portfolio strategies in detail. The first is passive portfolio management strategies, which include either a simple buy-and-hold strategy or indexing to one of the major benchmarks. The second category includes active management strategies that can involve one of five alternatives: interest rate anticipation, valuation analysis, credit analysis, yield spread analysis, or bond swaps. The third category includes matched funding strategies, which include constructing dedicated portfolios, constructing classical or contingent immunization portfolios, or horizon matching.

The fact that three fairly long chapters are devoted to the study of bonds attests to the importance of the topic and the extensive research done in this area. During the past 20 years, there have been more developments related to the valuation and portfolio management of bonds than of stocks. This growth of the fixed-income sector does not detract from the importance of equities but certainly enhances the significance of fixed-income securities. Finally, readers should keep in mind that this growth in size, sophistication, and specialization of the bond market implies numerous and varied career opportunities in the bond area, including trading these securities, valuation, credit analysis, and domestic and global portfolio management.

CHAPTER 17

Bond Fundamentals

After you read this chapter, you should be able to answer the following questions:

- What are some of the basic features of bonds that affect their risk, return, and value?
- What is the current country structure of the world bond market and how has the makeup of the global bond market changed in recent years?
- What are the major components of the world bond market and the international bond market?
- How does the makeup of the bond market differ in major countries?
- What are bond ratings and what is their purpose? What is the difference between investment-grade bonds and high-yield (junk) bonds?
- What are the characteristics of bonds in the major bond categories, such as governments (including TIPS), agencies, municipalities, and corporates?
- What are the important characteristics of corporate bond issues developed in the United States during the past decade, such as mortgage-backed securities, other asset-backed securities, zero coupon and deep discount bonds, high-yield bonds, and structured notes?
- How do you read the quotes available for the alternative bond categories (e.g., governments, municipalities, corporates)?

The global bond market is large and diverse and represents an important investment opportunity. This chapter is concerned with publicly issued, long-term, nonconvertible debt obligations of public and private issuers in the United States and major global markets. In later chapters, we consider preferred stock and convertible bonds. An understanding of bonds is helpful in an efficient market because the existence of U.S. and foreign bonds increases the universe of investments available for the creation of a diversified portfolio.

In this chapter, we review some basic features of bonds and examine the structure of the world bond market. The bulk of the chapter involves an in-depth discussion of the major fixed-income investments. The chapter ends with a brief review of the price information sources for bond investors.

17.1 Basic Features of a Bond

Public bonds are long-term, fixed-obligation debt securities packaged in convenient, affordable denominations for sale to individuals and financial institutions. They differ from other debt, such as individual mortgages and privately placed debt obligations, because they are sold to the public rather than channeled directly to a single lender. Bond issues are considered fixed-income securities because they impose fixed financial obligations on the issuers. Specifically, the issuer agrees to

1. Pay a fixed amount of *interest periodically* to the holder of record
2. Repay a fixed amount of *principal* at the date of maturity

Normally, interest on bonds is paid every six months, although some bond issues pay in intervals as short as a month or as long as a year. The principal is due at maturity; this *par value* of the issue is rarely less than $1,000. A bond has a specified term to maturity, which defines the life of the issue. The public debt market typically is divided into three time segments based on an issue's original maturity:

1. Short-term issues with maturities of one year or less. The market for these instruments is commonly known as the **money market**.
2. Intermediate-term issues with maturities in excess of 1 year but less than 10 years. These instruments are known as **notes**.
3. Long-term obligations with maturities in excess of 10 years, called *bonds*.

The lives of debt obligations change constantly as the issues progress toward maturity. Thus, issues that have been outstanding in the secondary market for any period of time eventually move from long-term to intermediate to short-term. This change in maturity is important because a major determinant of the price volatility of bonds is the remaining life (maturity) of the issue.

17.1.1 Bond Characteristics

A bond can be characterized based on (1) its intrinsic features, (2) its type, (3) its indenture provisions, or (4) the features that affect its cash flows and/or its maturity.

Intrinsic Features The coupon, maturity, principal value, and the type of ownership are important intrinsic features of a bond. The **coupon** of a bond indicates the income that the bond investor will receive over the life (or holding period) of the issue. This is known as *interest income, coupon income,* or *nominal yield.*

The **term to maturity** specifies the date or the number of years before a bond matures (or expires). There are two different types of maturity. The most common is a **term bond**, which has a single maturity date. Alternatively, a **serial obligation bond** issue has a series of maturity dates, perhaps 20 or 25. Each maturity, although a subset of the total issue, is really a small bond issue with generally a different coupon. Municipalities issue most serial bonds.

The **principal**, or **par value**, of an issue represents the original value of the obligation. This is generally stated in $1,000 increments from $1,000 to $25,000 or more. Principal value is *not* the same as the bond's market value. The market prices of many issues rise above or fall below their principal values because of differences between their coupons and the prevailing market rate of interest. If the market interest rate is above the coupon rate, the bond will sell at a discount to par. If the market rate is below the bond's coupon, it will sell at a premium above par. If the coupon is comparable to the prevailing market interest rate, the market value of the bond will be close to its original principal value.

Finally, bonds differ in terms of ownership. With a **bearer bond**, the holder, or bearer, is the owner, so the issuer keeps no record of ownership. Interest from a bearer bond is obtained by clipping coupons attached to the bonds and sending them to the issuer for payment. In contrast, the issuers of **registered bonds** maintain records of owners and pay the interest directly to them.

Types of Issues In contrast to common stock, companies can have many different bond issues outstanding at the same time. Bonds can have different types of collateral and be either senior, unsecured, or subordinated (junior) securities. **Secured (senior) bonds** are backed by a legal claim on some specified property of the issuer in the case of default. For example, mortgage bonds are secured by real estate assets; equipment trust certificates, which are used by railroads and airlines, provide a senior claim on the firm's equipment.

Unsecured bonds (debentures) are backed only by the promise of the issuer to pay interest and principal on a timely basis. As such, they are secured by the general credit of the issuer. **Subordinate (junior) debentures** possess a claim on income and assets that is subordinated to other debentures. Income issues are the most junior type because interest on them is paid only if it is earned. Although income bonds are unusual in the corporate sector, they are very popular municipal issues, where they are referred to as **revenue bonds**. Finally, **refunding issues** provide funds to prematurely retire another issue.

The type of issue has only a marginal effect on comparative yield because it is the creditworthiness of the issuer that determines bond quality. A study of corporate bond price behavior by Hickman (1958) found that whether the issuer pledged collateral did not become important until the bond issue approached default. The collateral and security characteristics of a bond influence yield differentials only when these factors affect the bond's quality ratings.

Indenture Provisions   The *indenture* is the contract between the issuer and the bondholder specifying the issuer's legal requirements. A trustee (usually a bank) acting on behalf of the bondholders ensures that all the indenture provisions are met, including the timely payment of interest and principal. All the factors that dictate a bond's features, its type, and its maturity are set forth in the indenture.

Features Affecting a Bond's Maturity   Investors should be aware of the three alternative call option features that can affect the life (maturity) of a bond. One extreme is a *freely callable* provision that allows the issuer to retire the bond at any time with a typical notification period of 30 to 60 days. The other extreme is a *noncallable* provision wherein the issuer cannot retire the bond prior to its maturity.[1] Intermediate between these is a *deferred call* provision, which means the issue cannot be called for a certain period of time after the date of issue (e.g., 5 to 10 years). At the end of the deferred call period, the issue becomes freely callable. Callable bonds have a **call premium**, which is the amount above maturity value that the issuer must pay to the bondholder for prematurely retiring the bond.

A *nonrefunding provision* prohibits a call and premature retirement of an issue from the proceeds of a lower-coupon refunding bond. This is meant to protect the bondholder from a typical refunding, but it is not foolproof. An issue with a nonrefunding provision can be called and retired prior to maturity using other sources of funds, such as excess cash from operations, the sale of assets, or proceeds from a sale of common stock. This occurred on several occasions during the 1980s and 1990s when many issuers retired nonrefundable high-coupon issues early because they could get the cash from one of these other sources and felt that this was a good financing decision.

Another important indenture provision that can affect a bond's maturity is the **sinking fund**, which specifies that a bond must be paid off systematically over its life rather than only at maturity. There are numerous sinking-fund arrangements, and the bondholder should recognize this as a feature that can change the stated maturity of a bond. The size of the sinking fund can be a percentage of a given issue or a percentage of the total debt outstanding, or it can be a fixed or variable sum stated on a dollar or percentage basis. Similar to a call feature, sinking fund payments may commence at the end of the first year or may be deferred for 5 or 10 years from date of the issue. The amount of the issue that must be repaid before maturity from a sinking fund can range from a nominal sum to 100 percent. Like a call, the sinking-fund feature typically carries a nominal premium but is generally smaller than the straight call premium (e.g., 1 percent). For example, a bond issue with a 20-year maturity might have a sinking fund that requires that 5 percent of the issue be retired every year beginning in year 10. By year 20, half of the issue has been retired and the rest is paid off at maturity. Sinking-fund provisions have a small effect on comparative yields at the time of issue but have little subsequent impact on price behavior.

---

[1] The main issuer of noncallable bonds between 1985 and 2008 was the U.S. Treasury. Corporate long-term bonds typically have contained some form of call provision, except during periods of relatively low interest rates (e.g., 1994–2001) when the probability of exercising the option was very low. We discuss this notion in more detail in Chapter 18 in connection with the analysis of embedded options.

A sinking-fund provision is an obligation and must be carried out regardless of market conditions. Although a sinking fund allows the issuer to call bonds on a random basis, most bonds are retired for sinking-fund purposes through direct negotiations with institutional holders. Essentially, the trustee negotiates with an institution to buy back the necessary amount of bonds at a price slightly above the current market price.

17.1.2 Rates of Return on Bonds

The rate of return on a bond is computed in the same way as the rate of return on stock or any asset. It is determined by the beginning and ending price and the cash flows during the holding period. The major difference between stocks and bonds is that the interim cash flow on bonds (i.e., the interest) is contractual and accrues over time as discussed subsequently, whereas the dividends on stock may vary. Therefore, the holding period return (HPR) for a bond will be

17.1
$$HPR_{i,t} = \frac{P_{i,t+1} + Int_{i,t}}{P_{i,t}}$$

where:

$HPR_{i,t}$ = the holding period return for bond i during Period t
$P_{i,t+1}$ = the market price of bond i at the end of Period t
$P_{i,t}$ = the market price of bond i at the beginning of Period t
$Int_{i,t}$ = the interest paid or accrued on bond i during Period t. Because the interest payment is contractual, it accrues over time and if a bond owner sells the bond between interest payments, the sale price includes accrued interest[2]

The holding period yield (HPY) is:

17.2
$$HPY = HPR - 1$$

Note that the only contractual factor is the amount of interest payments. The beginning and ending bond prices are determined by market forces, as discussed in Chapter 11. Notably, the ending price is determined by market forces unless the bond is held to maturity, in which case the investor will receive the par value. These price variations in bonds mean that investors in bonds can experience capital gains or losses. Interest rate volatility has increased substantially since the 1960s, and this has caused large price fluctuations in bonds.[3] As a result, capital gains or losses have become a major component of the rates of return on bonds.

· ·

17.2 The Global Bond Market Structure[4]

The market for fixed-income securities is substantially larger than the listed equity exchanges (NYSE, TSE, LSE) because corporations tend to issue bonds rather than common stock. Figures released by Securities Industry and Financial Markets Association (SIFMA) indicate that in the United States during 2007, less than 10 percent of all new security issues were equity, which included preferred as well as common stock. Corporations issue less common or preferred stock because firms derive most of their equity financing from internally generated funds (i.e., retained earnings). Also, although the equity market is strictly corporations, the bond market in most countries has four noncorporate sectors: the pure government sector (e.g., the Treasury in the United States), government agencies (e.g., FNMA), state and local government bonds (municipals), and international bonds (e.g., Yankees and Eurobonds in the United States).

[2] The concept of accrued interest will be discussed further in Chapter 18 when we consider the valuation of bonds.
[3] The analysis of bond price volatility is discussed in detail in Chapter 18.
[4] For a further discussion of global bond markets, see Steward (2005), "International Bond Markets and Instruments"; Steward, Lynch, and Fabozzi (2005), "International Bond Investing and Portfolio Management"; and Malvey (2005), "Global Credit Bond Portfolio Management," all in *The Handbook of Fixed-Income Securities*, 7th ed., ed. Frank J. Fabozzi (New York: McGraw-Hill, 2005).

Exhibit 17.1 Total Face Value and Percentage of Total for Index-Qualifying Fixed Income Securities by Year (USD terms in millions)

Currency	2004	Percent	2003	Percent	2002	Percent
US Dollars	10,615,955	42.77%	10,181,215	43.73%	9,712,596	44.86%
Euro	7,526,638	30.32%	7,071,654	30.37%	6,520,821	30.12%
Japanese Yen	3,992,936	16.09%	3,645,001	15.65%	3,283,443	15.16%
Pound Sterling	1,132,734	4.56%	994,104	4.27%	877,950	4.05%
Canadian Dollar	541,192	2.18%	500,263	2.15%	470,166	2.17%
Indian Rupee	154,546	0.62%	146,524	0.63%	127,511	0.59%
Australian Dollar	143,120	0.58%	127,661	0.55%	117,588	0.54%
Swedish Krone	111,616	0.45%	106,711	0.46%	97,348	0.45%
Korean Won	110,370	0.44%	69,408	0.30%	46,400	0.21%
Danish Krone	84,643	0.34%	86,314	0.37%	90,448	0.42%
Taiwanese Dollar	81,020	0.33%	71,387	0.31%	64,611	0.30%
Swiss Franc	79,663	0.32%	68,680	0.29%	58,550	0.27%
All Other	247,119	0.99%	215,201	0.92%	184,589	0.85%
Total	**24,821,550**	**100.00%**	**23,284,123**	**100.00%**	**21,652,020**	**100.00%**
Annual Growth Rate		*6.60%*		*7.54%*		*10.36%*

Source: Adapted from data in Phil Galdi, "Growth Trends in the World Bond Markets," Merrill Lynch, January 28, 2005.

The size of the global bond market and the distribution among countries can be gleaned from Exhibit 17.1, which lists the dollar value of debt outstanding and the percentage distribution for the major currencies for the years 2002–2004. There has been consistent overall growth, at the rate of 6 to 10 percent a year. Also, the currency trends are significant. Specifically, the U.S. dollar market went from 45 percent of the total world bond market in 2002 to about 43 percent in 2004. A significant change in 1999 was the creation of the Eurozone sector, which includes a large part of Europe (i.e., Germany, Italy, France) with the significant exception of the United Kingdom. Notably, this Euro currency sector has held at about 30 percent over the three-year period.

17.2.1 Participating Issuers

In the Merrill Lynch report, there are five different categories of bonds for each currency: (1) sovereign bonds (e.g., the U.S. Treasury), (2) quasi and foreign governments (including agency bonds), (3) securitized and collateralized bonds from governments or corporations, (4) directly issued corporate bonds, and (5) high-yield and/or emerging market bonds. The division of bonds among these five categories for three large currency markets and the Eurozone during 2004 is contained in Exhibit 17.2.

Sovereigns The market for government securities is the largest sector in Japan. It involves a variety of debt instruments issued to meet the growing needs of this government. It is generally a stable component for other currencies.

Quasi Governments (agencies) and Foreign Governments Agency issues have become a major segment in the U.S. dollar and pound sterling market (over 12 percent) but are a smaller proportion in other countries (e.g., about 8 percent in Japan). These agencies represent political subdivisions of the government, although the securities are *not* typically direct obligations of the government. The U.S. agency market has two types of issuers: government-sponsored enterprises and federal agencies. The proceeds of agency bond issues are used to finance many legislative programs. Foreign government issues are from a country but not in its own currency (e.g., a Japanese government issue in dollars and sold in the United States).

Securitized/Collateralized Issues These can be either government agencies or corporate issues that are backed by cash flow securities such as mortgages or car loans. Collateralized securities can include several different issues and structured cash flows. As shown in Exhibit 17.2,

Exhibit 17.2 Makeup of Bonds Outstanding by Currency: 31-December-2004 (USD terms in millions)

	2004	
	Total Value	Percent of Total
A. U.S. Dollars		
Sovereign	3,657,702	34.5
Quasi & Foreign Govt	1,338,726	12.6
Securitized/Collateralized	2,930,919	27.6
Corporate	1,937,052	18.2
High Yield/Emerging Mkt.	751,555	7.1
Total	10,615,955	100.0
B. Euros		
Sovereign	4,820,940	64.1
Quasi & Foreign Govt	594,973	7.9
Securitized/Collateralized	924,098	12.3
Corporate	1,088,349	14.5
High Yield/Emerging Mkt.	98,278	1.3
Total	7,526,638	100.0
C. Japanese Yen		
Sovereign	3,249,865	81.4
Quasi & Foreign Govt	297,666	7.5
Securitized/Collateralized	3,598	0.1
Corporate	441,807	11.1
High Yield/Emerging Mkt.	0	0.0
Total	3,992,936	100.0
D. Pound Sterling		
Sovereign	568,551	50.2
Quasi & Foreign Govt	144,675	12.8
Securitized/Collateralized	67,618	6.0
Corporate	339,153	29.9
High Yield/Emerging Mkt.	12,737	1.1
Total	1,132,734	100.0

Source: Adapted from data in Phil Galdi, "Growth Trends in the World Bond Markets," Merrill Lynch, January 28, 2005.

this has become a major sector in the United States and fairly strong in the Eurozone countries. Therefore, they will be discussed in detail in a subsequent section.

Corporations The major nongovernmental issuer of debt is the corporate sector. The importance of this sector differs dramatically among countries. It is a slow growth factor in the United States; a smaller sector in Japan and in the Euro currency coutries and a significant part of the pound sterling market.

The market for corporate bonds is commonly subdivided into several segments: industrials, public utilities, transportation, and financial issues. The specific makeup varies between countries.[5]

High Yield/Emerging Market This section includes both high-yield bonds (noninvestment grade) from corporations in developed countries, and both government and corporate issues from emerging market countries such as China and India where the bonds can be either

[5] This sector of the bond market is described in more detail later in this chapter. It is possible to distinguish another sector that exists in the United States but not in other countries—institutional bonds. These are corporate bonds issued by a variety of *private, nonprofit institutions,* such as schools, hospitals, and churches. They are not broken out because they are only a minute part of the U.S. market and do not exist elsewhere.

investment grade or high yield (noninvestment grade). Notably, the only currency where this sector is significant is the U.S. dollar market where it constitutes over 7 percent. The other currencies have only nominal amounts currently, but these sectors are expected to experience significant growth in the future.

17.2.2 Participating Investors

Numerous individual and institutional investors with diverse investment objectives participate in the bond market. Individual investors are a minor portion because of the market's complexity and the high minimum denominations of most issues. Institutional investors typically account for 90 to 95 percent of the trading, although different segments of the market are more institutionalized than others. For example, institutions are involved heavily in the agency market, but they are less active in the corporate sector.

A variety of institutions invest in the bond market. Life insurance companies invest in corporate bonds and, to a lesser extent, in Treasury and agency securities. Commercial banks invest in municipal bonds and government and agency issues. Property and liability insurance companies concentrate on municipal bonds and Treasuries. Private and government pension funds are heavily committed to corporates and invest in Treasuries and agencies. Finally, fixed-income mutual funds have grown substantially in size and their demand spans the full spectrum of the market as they develop bond funds that meet the needs of a variety of investors. As we will discuss in Chapter 24, municipal bond funds and corporate bond funds (including high-yield bonds) have experienced significant growth.

Alternative institutions tend to favor different sectors of the bond market based on two factors: (1) the tax code applicable to the institution and (2) the nature of the institution's liability structure. For example, because commercial banks are subject to normal taxation and have fairly short-term liability structures, they favor short- to intermediate-term municipals. Pension funds are virtually tax-free institutions with long-term commitments, so they prefer high-yielding, long-term government or corporate bonds. Such institutional investment preferences can affect the short-run supply and demand of loanable funds and impact interest rate changes.

17.2.3 Bond Ratings

Agency ratings are an integral part of the bond market because most corporate and municipal bonds are rated by one or more of the rating agencies. The exceptions are very small issues and bonds from certain industries, such as bank issues. These are known as *nonrated bonds*. There are three major rating agencies: (1) Fitch Investors Service, (2) Moody's, and (3) Standard and Poor's.

Bond ratings provide the fundamental analysis for thousands of issues. The rating agencies analyze the issuing organization and the specific issue to determine the probability of default and inform the market of their analyses through their ratings.[6]

The primary question in bond credit analysis is whether the firm can service its debt in a timely manner over the life of a given issue. Consequently, the rating agencies consider expectations over the life of the issue, along with the historical and current financial position of the company. We consider default estimation further when we discuss high-yield (junk) bonds.

Studies by authors such as Belkaoui (1980) and Gentry, Whitford, and Newbold (1988) have examined the relationship between bond ratings and issue quality as indicated by financial variables. The results clearly demonstrated that bond ratings were positively related to profitability, size, and cash flow coverage, and they were inversely related to financial leverage and earnings instability.

[6] For a detailed listing of rating classes and a listing of factors considered in assigning ratings, see "Bond Ratings" in Levine (1988a). For a study that examines the value of two bond ratings, see Hsueh and Kidwell (1988). An analysis of the bond-rating industry is contained in Cantor and Packer (1995).

Exhibit 17.3 Description of Bond Ratings

	Fitch	Moody's	Standard & Poor's	Definition
High grade	AAA	Aaa	AAA	The highest rating assigned to a debt instrument, indicating an extremely strong capacity to pay principal and interest. Bonds in this category are often referred to as *gilt edge securities.*
	AA	Aa	AA	High-quality bonds by all standards with a strong capacity to pay principal and interest. These bonds are rated lower primarily because the margins of protection are less strong than those for Aaa and AAA bonds.
Medium grade	A	A	A	These bonds possess many favorable investment attributes, but elements may suggest a susceptibility to impairment given adverse economic changes.
	BBB	Baa	BBB	Bonds that are regarded as having adequate capacity to pay principal and interest, but certain protective elements may be lacking in the event of adverse economic conditions that could lead to a weakened capacity for payment.
Speculative	BB	Ba	BB	These bonds are considered to have only moderate protection of principal and interest payments during both good and bad times.
	B	B	B	Bonds that generally lack characteristics of other desirable investments. Assurance of interest and principal payments over any long period of time may be small.
Default	CCC	Caa	CCC	Poor-quality issues that may be in default or in danger of default.
	CC	Ca	CC	Highly speculative issues that are often in default or possess other marked shortcomings.
	C			The lowest-rated class of bonds. These issues can be regarded as extremely poor in investment quality.
		C	C	Rating given to income bonds on which no interest is being paid.
	DDD, DD, D		D	Issues in default with principal or interest payments in arrears. Such bonds are extremely speculative and should be valued only on the basis of their value in liquidation or reorganization.

Sources: *Bond Guide* (New York: Standard & Poor's, monthly); *Bond Record* (New York: Moody's Investors Services, Inc., monthly); *Rating Register* (New York: Fitch Investors Service, Inc., monthly).

The original ratings assigned to bonds have an impact on their marketability and effective interest rate. Generally, the three agencies' ratings agree. When they do not, the issue is said to have a *split rating.*[7] Seasoned issues are regularly reviewed to ensure that the assigned rating is still valid. If not, revisions are made either upward or downward. Revisions are usually done in increments of one rating grade. The ratings are based on both the company and the issue. After an evaluation of the creditworthiness of the total company is completed, a company rating is assigned to the firm's most senior unsecured issue. All junior bonds receive lower ratings based on indenture specifications. Also, an issue could receive a higher rating than justified because of credit-enhancement devices, such as the attachment of bank letters of credit, surety, or indemnification bonds from insurance companies.

The agencies assign letter ratings depicting what they view as the risk of default of an obligation. The letter ratings range from AAA (Aaa) to D. Exhibit 17.3 describes the various

---

[7] Split ratings are discussed in Billingsley, Lamy, Marr, and Thompson (1985); Ederington (1985); and Liu and Moore (1987).

ratings assigned by the major services. Except for slight variations in designations, the meaning and interpretation are basically the same. The agencies modify the ratings with + and – signs for Fitch and S&P or with numbers (1-2-3) for Moody's. As an example, an A+ (A1) bond is at the top of the A-rated group, while A– (A3) is at the bottom of the A category.

The top four ratings—AAA (or Aaa), AA (or Aa), A, and BBB (or Baa)—are generally considered to be *investment-grade securities*. The next level of securities is known as *speculative bonds* and includes the BB- and B-rated obligations. The C categories are generally either income obligations or revenue bonds, many of which are trading flat. (Flat bonds are in arrears on their interest payments.) In the case of D-rated obligations, the issues are in outright default, and the ratings indicate the bonds' relative salvage values.[8]

17.3 Alternative Bond Issues

We have described the basic features available for all bonds and the overall structure of the global bond market in terms of the issuers of bonds and investors in bonds. In this section, we provide a detailed discussion of the bonds available from the major issuers of bonds. The presentation is longer than you would expect because when we discuss each issuing unit, such as governments, municipalities, or corporations, we briefly consider the bonds available in several world financial centers, such as Japan, the United Kingdom, and the several major countries in the Eurozone.

17.3.1 Domestic Government Bonds

United States As shown in Exhibit 17.2, a significant percent of the U.S. dollar fixed-income market is U.S. Treasury obligations. The U.S. government, backed by the full faith and credit of the U.S. Treasury, issues Treasury bills (T-bills), which mature in less than one year, and two forms of long-term obligations: government notes, which have maturities of 10 years or less, and Treasury bonds, with maturities of 10 to 30 years. Current Treasury obligations come in denominations of $1,000 and $10,000. The interest income from the U.S. government securities is subject to federal income tax but exempt from state and local levies. These bonds are popular because of their high credit quality, substantial liquidity, and noncallable feature.

Short-term T-bills differ from notes and bonds because they are sold at a discount from par to provide the desired yield. The return is the difference between the purchase price and the par at maturity. In contrast, government notes and bonds carry semiannual coupons that specify the nominal yield of the obligations.

Government notes and bonds have unusual call features. First, the period specified for the deferred call feature on Treasury issues is very long and is generally measured relative to the maturity date rather than from date of issue. They generally cannot be called until five years prior to their maturity date. Notably, *all* U.S. Treasury issues since 1989 have been noncallable.

Treasury Inflation-Protected Securities (TIPS)[9] The Treasury began issuing these inflation-indexed bonds in January 1997 to appeal to investors who wanted or needed a *real* default-free rate of return. To ensure the investors will receive the promised yield in real terms, the bond principal and interest payments are indexed to the *Consumer Price Index for All Urban Consumers (CPI-U)* published by the Bureau of Labor Statistics. Because inflation is generally not known until several months after the fact, the index value used has a three-month lag built in—for example, for a bond issued on June 30, 2008, the beginning base index value used would be the CPI value as of March 30, 2008. Following the issuance of a TIPS bond, its principal

---

[8] Bonds rated below investment grade are also referred to as "high-yield bonds" or "junk" bonds. These high-yield bonds are discussed in the subsequent section on corporate bonds.
[9] This section draws heavily from excellent articles by Shen (1998); Roll (2004); and Kothari and Shanken (2004).

Exhibit 17.4 Principal and Interest Payment for a Treasury Inflation Protected Security (TIPS)

Par Value—$1,000
Issued on July 15, 2005
Maturity on July 15, 2010
Coupon—3.50%
Original CPI Value—185.00

Date	Index Value[a]	Rate of Inflation	Accrued Principal	Interest Payment[b]
7/15/05	185.00	—	$1,000.00	—
1/15/06	187.78	0.015	1,015.00	$17.76
7/15/06	190.59	0.015	1,030.22	18.03
1/15/07	193.83	0.017	1,047.74	18.34
7/15/07	197.51	0.019	1,067.65	18.68
1/15/08	201.46	0.020	1,089.00	19.06
7/15/08	205.49	0.020	1,110.78	19.44
1/15/09	209.19	0.018	1,130.77	19.79
7/15/09	212.96	0.018	1,151.13	20.14
1/15/10	217.22	0.020	1,174.15	20.55
7/15/10	222.65	0.025	1,203.50	21.06

[a] The CPI index value is for the period three months prior to the date.
[b] Semiannual interest payment equals 0.0175 (accrued principal).

value is adjusted every six months to reflect the inflation since the base period. In turn, the interest payment is computed based on this adjusted principal—that is, the interest payments equal the original coupon times the adjusted principal. The example in Exhibit 17.4 demonstrates how the principal and interest payments are computed. As shown in this example, both the interest payments and the principal payments are adjusted over time to reflect the prevailing inflation, thereby ensuring that the investor receives a *real* rate of return on these bonds of 3.50 percent.

Notably, these bonds can also be used to derive the prevailing market estimate of the expected rate of inflation during the remaining maturity of the TIPS bond. For example, if we assume that when the bond is issued on July 15, 2005, it sells at par for a YTM of 3.50 percent, while a nominal Treasury note of equal maturity is sold at a YTM of 5.75 percent. This differential in promised YTM implies that investors expect an average annual rate of inflation of 2.25 percent during this five-year period. If, a year later, the spread increased to 2.45 percent, it would indicate that investors expect a higher inflation rate during the next four years.

Japan[10] The second-largest country government bond market in the world is Japan's. It is controlled by the Japanese government and the Bank of Japan (Japanese Central Bank). Japanese government bonds (JGBs) are an attractive investment vehicle for those favoring the Japanese yen because their quality is equal to that of U.S. Treasury securities (they are guaranteed by the government of Japan) and they are very liquid. There are three maturity segments: medium-term (2, 3, or 4 years), long-term (10 years), and super-long (private placements for 15 and 20 years). Bonds are issued in both registered and bearer form, although registered bonds can be converted to bearer bonds.

Medium-term bonds are issued monthly through a competitive auction system similar to that of U.S. Treasury bonds. Long-term bonds are authorized by the Ministry of Finance and issued monthly by the Bank of Japan through an underwriting syndicate consisting of major financial institutions. Most super-long bonds are sold through private placement to a few financial institutions. Very liquid federal government bonds account for over 50 percent of the Japanese bonds outstanding and over 80 percent of total bond trading volume in Japan.

---

[10] For additional discussion, see Viner (1988), Elton and Gruber (1990), and Fabozzi (1990a).

At least 50 percent of the trading in Japanese government bonds will be in the so-called *benchmark issue* of the time. The benchmark issue is selected from 10-year coupon bonds. (As of mid-2008, the benchmark issue was a 1.30 percent coupon bond maturing in 2018.) The designation of a benchmark issue is intended to assist smaller financial institutions in their trading of government bonds by ensuring these institutions that there is a liquid market in this particular security. Compared to the benchmark issue, the comparable most active U.S. bond within a class accounts for only about 10 percent of the volume.

The yield on this benchmark bond is typically about 30 basis points below other comparable Japanese government bonds, reflecting its superior marketability. The benchmark issue changes when a designated issue matures or because of a decision by the Bank of Japan.

United Kingdom[11] The U.K. pound sterling government bond market is made up of jobbers and brokers who act as principals or agents with negotiated commission structures. In addition, there are 27 primary dealers similar to the U.S. Treasury market.

Maturities in this market range from short gilts (maturities of less than 5 years) to medium gilts (5 to 15 years) to long gilts (15 years and longer). Government bonds either have a fixed redemption date or a range of dates with redemption at the option of the government after giving appropriate notice. Government bonds are normally registered, although bearer delivery is available.

Gilts are issued through the Bank of England (the British central bank) using the tender method, whereby prospective purchasers tender offering prices at which they hope to be allotted bonds. The price cannot be less than the minimum tender price stated in the prospectus. If the issue is oversubscribed, allotments are made first to those submitting the highest tenders and continue until a price is reached where only a partial allotment is required to fully subscribe the issue. All successful allottees pay the lowest allotment prices.

These issues are extremely liquid and are highly rated because they are guaranteed by the British government. All gilts are quoted and traded on the London Stock Exchange and pay interest semiannually.

Eurozone[12] The combined value of the Euro sovereign bond market is actually larger in U.S. dollar terms than the Japanese market because it includes several relatively significant markets including Germany, which was the third largest by itself, as well as France and Italy among others. Because the Eurozone includes numerous countries that were previously economically independent, the issuing process for alternative countries differs dramatically except that all of the bonds are denominated in Euros. It is likely that over time the issuing process will become more uniform, but there will always be differences.

17.3.2 Government Agency Issues

In addition to pure government bonds, the federal government in each country can establish agencies that have the authority to issue their own bonds. The size and importance of these agencies differ among countries. They are a large and growing sector of the U.S. bond market, a much smaller component of the bond markets in Japan and Germany, and nonexistent in the United Kingdom.

United States Agency securities are obligations issued by the U.S. government through either a government agency or a government-sponsored enterprise (GSE). Six government-sponsored enterprises and over two dozen federal agencies issue these bonds. Exhibit 17.5 lists selected characteristics of the more popular government-sponsored and federal agency obligations.[13]

[11] For further discussion, see European Bond Commission (1989).
[12] For additional information on the Eurobond market, see Molinas and Bales (2004).
[13] We will no longer distinguish between federal agency and government-sponsored obligations; instead, the term *agency* shall apply to either type of issue.

Exhibit 17.5 Agency Issues: Selected Characteristics

Type of Security	Minimum Denomination	Form	Life of Issue	Tax Status	How Interest Is Earned
Government Sponsored					
Federal farm credit banks	50,000	Book Entry	5 to 365 days	FT SE LE	Discount actual, 360-day year
Consolidated systemwide notes	5,000	Book Entry	6 and 9 months	FT SE LE	Interest payable at maturity, 360-day year
Consolidated systemwide bonds	1,000	Book Entry	13 months to 15 years	FT SE LE	Semiannual interest
Federal Home Loan Bank					
Consolidated discount notes	100,000	Book Entry	30 to 360 days	FT SE LE	Discount actual, 360-day year
Consolidated bonds	10,000	Book Entry	1 to 20 years	FT SE LE	Semiannual interest, 360-day year
Federal Home Loan Mortgage					
Corporation debentures	10,000	Book Entry	18 to 30 years	FT ST LT	Semiannual interest, 360-day year
Participation certificates	100,000	Registered	30 years	FT ST LT	Monthly interest and principal payments
Federal National Mortgage Association discount notes	50,000	Registered	30 to 360 days	FT ST LT	Discount actual, 360-day year
Debentures	10,000	Book Entry	1 to 30 years	FT ST LT	Semiannual interest, 360-day year
Government National Mortgage Association					
Mortgage-backed bonds	25,000	Registered	1 to 25 years	FT ST LT	Semiannual interest, 360-day year
Modified pass-throughs	25,000	Registered	12 to 40 years	FT ST LT	Monthly interest and principal payments
Student Loan Marketing Association discount note	100,000	Registered	Out to 1 year	FT SE LE	Discount actual, 360-day year
Notes	10,000	Registered	3 to 10 years	FT SE LE	Semiannual interest, 360-day year
Floating rate notes	10,000	Registered	6 months to 10 years	FT SE LE	Interest rate adjusted weekly to an increment over the average auction rate of 91-day Treasury bills and payable quarterly
Tennessee Valley Authority (TVA)	1,000	Registered	5 to 25 years	FT SE LE	Semiannual interest, 360-day year
U.S. Postal Service	10,000	Registered	25 years	FT SE LE	Semiannual interest, 360-day year

FT - Federal Taxable; SE - State Exempt; ST - State Taxable; LE - Local Exempt; LT - Local Taxable.

Source: Adapted from partially available and government supplied information provided to Merrill Lynch Government Securities and other authorized government securities brokers and dealers.

Agency issues usually pay interest semiannually, and the minimum denominations vary between $1,000 and $10,000. These obligations are not direct Treasury issues, yet they carry the full faith and credit of the U.S. government. Moreover, some of the issues are subject to state and local income tax, whereas others are exempt.[14]

One agency issue offers particularly attractive investment opportunities: GNMA ("Ginnie Mae") pass-through certificates, which are obligations of the Government National Mortgage Association.[15] These bonds represent an undivided interest in a pool of federally insured mortgages. The bondholders receive monthly payments from Ginnie Mae that include both principal and interest because the agency "passes through" mortgage payments made by the original borrower (the mortgagee) to Ginnie Mae.

The coupons on these pass-through securities are related to the interest charged on the pool of mortgages. The portion of the cash flow that represents the repayment of the principal is tax-free, but the interest income is subject to federal, state, and local taxes. The issues have minimum denominations of $25,000 with maturities of 25 to 30 years but an average life of only 12 years because, as mortgages in the pool are paid off, payments and prepayments are passed through to the investor. Therefore, the monthly payment is not fixed because the rate of prepayment can vary dramatically over time when interest rates change.

As we will note in Chapter 18 in connection with the valuation of bonds with embedded options, mortgages generally have a call option whereby the homeowner can prepay the mortgage for one of two reasons: (1) because homeowners pay off their mortgages when they sell their homes and (2) because owners refinance their homes when mortgage interest rates decline. Therefore, a major disadvantage of these issues is that their *maturities are very uncertain* (i.e., they have *high prepayment risk*).

In addition, two other entities also acquire morgages and create mortgage-backed securities—the Federal National Mortgage Association (Fannie Mae) and the Federal Home Loan Mortgage Corporation (Freddie Mac). In contrast to being agencies of the government, they are government-sponsored enterprises (GSEs), so the bonds they issue are not officially guaranteed by the government, but there is an implicit understanding that the government would not allow the GSEs to default on their bonds under extreme circumstances. Therefore, Fannie and Freddie are publicly traded corporations that are regulated by the government and the bonds they issue to fund the purchase of mortgages have historically sold at yields that are typically very close to Treasury issues although this changed in 2008 due to events discussed below.

Notably, the lending practices of these two GSEs came under scrutiny during 2006–2007 because they were issuing large amounts of debt at the low yields noted above and using the funds to acquire mortgages that paid higher rates for the benefit of their stockholders. Their credit risk was critically examined during 2007–2008 in connection with the credit/liquidity crises that engulfed the country. Because they used the low-cost funds to invest in sub-prime mortgages that experienced high default rates, they suffered substantial losses that seriously eroded their capital. In addition, new accounting rules forthcoming will also have a negative impact on their capital. As a result they will require a significant capital infusion from the sales of stock at low prices. As discussed by Hagerty and Ng (2008) and Eavis (2008), because of these capital requirements, their common stock could be seriously diluted or it could become virtually worthless if the Government has to bail out the firms' bonds.

Japan The agencies in Japan, referred to as *government associate organizations,* account for about 7 percent of the total Japanese yen bond market. This agency market includes public agency debt that is issued like government debt.

---

[14] Federal National Mortgage Association (Fannie Mae) debentures, for example, are subject to state and local income tax, whereas the interest income from Federal Home Loan Bank bonds is exempt. In fact, a few issues are exempt from federal income tax as well (e.g., public housing bonds).

[15] For a further discussion of mortgage-backed securities, see Davidson and Ching (2005); Crawford (2005); and McElravey (2005), all in *The Handbook of Fixed-Income Securities,* 7th ed., ed. Frank J. Fabozzi (New York: McGraw-Hill, 2005).

United Kingdom   As shown in Exhibit 17.2, about 13 percent of the pound sterling market is agency and foreign government debt.

Eurozone   As shown in Exhibit 17.2, agency bonds and foreign government bonds are less than 8 percent of the Euro bonds outstanding.

17.3.3 Municipal Bonds

Municipal bonds are issued by states, counties, cities, and other political subdivisions. Again, the size of the municipal bond market (referred to as *local authority* in the United Kingdom) varies substantially among countries. It is about 9 percent of the total U.S. market, compared to less than 3 percent in Japan, nonexistent in the United Kingdom, and not specifically identified in the Eurozone data. Therefore, it is not broken out as a category in Exhibit 17.2. Because of the size and popularity of this market in the United States, we will discuss only the U.S. municipal bond market.

Municipalities in the United States issue two distinct types of bonds: general obligation bonds and revenue issues. **General obligation bonds (GOs)** are essentially backed by the full faith and credit of the issuer and its entire taxing power. Revenue bonds, in turn, are serviced by the income generated from specific revenue-producing projects of the municipality, such as bridges, toll roads, hospitals, municipal coliseums, and waterworks. Revenue bonds generally provide higher returns than GOs because of their higher default risk. Should a municipality fail to generate sufficient income from a project designated to service a revenue bond, it has no legal debt service obligation until the income becomes sufficient.

GO municipal bonds tend to be issued on a serial basis so that the issuer's cash flow requirements will be steady over the life of the obligation. Therefore, the principal portion of the total debt service requirement generally begins at a fairly low level and builds up over the life of the obligation. In contrast, most municipal revenue bonds are term issues, so the principal value is not due until the final maturity date.[16]

The most important feature of municipal obligations is that the interest payments are exempt from federal income tax and from taxes in the locality and state in which the obligation was issued. This means that their attractiveness varies with the investor's tax bracket.

You can convert the tax-free yield of a municipal to an equivalent taxable yield (ETY) using the following equation:

17.3
$$ETY = \frac{i}{1 - t}$$

where:

ETY = equivalent taxable yield
i = coupon rate of the municipal obligations
t = marginal tax rate of the investor

An investor in the 35 percent marginal tax bracket would find that a 5 percent yield on a municipal bond selling close to its par value is equivalent to a 7.69 percent fully taxable yield according to the following calculation:

$$ETY = \frac{0.05}{(1 - 0.35)} = 0.0769$$

Because the tax-free yield is the major benefit of municipal bonds, an investor's marginal tax rate is a primary concern in evaluating them. As a rough rule of thumb, using the tax rates expected in 2009, an investor must be in the 28 to 30 percent tax bracket before the lower yields available in municipal bonds are competitive with those from fully taxable bonds. However, although the interest payment on municipals is tax-free, any capital gains are not (which is why the ETY formula is correct only for a bond selling close to its par value).

---

[16] For a more detailed discussion of the municipal bond market, see Feldstein, Fabozzi, Grant, and Kennedy (2005). For discussion of the credit analysis of these bonds, see Feldstein and Grant (2005).

Municipal Bond Insurance A significant feature of the U.S. municipal bond market is *municipal bond insurance,* wherein an insurance company will guarantee to make principal and interest payments in the event that the issuer of a bond defaults. The insurance is placed on the bond at date of issue and is *irrevocable* over the life of the issue. The issuer purchases the insurance for the benefit of the investor, and the municipality benefits from lower interest costs due to lower credit risk, which causes an increase in the rating on the bond and increased marketability because more institutions can invest in the highly rated bond (typically AAA). Those who would benefit from the insurance are small government units that are not widely known and bonds with a complex capital structure.

The following discussion of the bond insurance companies will have two components—the traditional history of bond insurance, and then a discussion of the major problems encountered during the 2007–2008 credit/liquidity crises.

As of 2008, approximately 40 percent of all new municipal bond issues were insured by six private bond insurance firms: the Municipal Bond Investors Assurance (MBIA), American Municipal Bond Assurance Corporation (AMBAC), the Financial Security Assurance (FSA), the Financial Guaranty Insurance Company (FGIC), Capital Guaranty Insurance Company (CGIC), and Connie Lee Insurance Company. These firms insured either general obligation or revenue bonds. To qualify for private bond insurance, the issue must initially carry an S&P rating of BBB or better. Traditionally, the rating agencies would give an AAA (Aaa) rating to bonds insured by these firms because all the insurance firms have had AAA ratings. Notably, if an insurance company was downgraded, all the bonds that it insured would be downgraded. Insured bond issues have enjoyed a more active secondary market and lower required yields.[17]

As alluded to previously, this traditional environment for municipal bond insurance changed dramatically in 2007–2008 as a consequence of the credit/liquidity crises that impacted all the insurance companies. Notably, the problems were not caused by credit events in the municipal bond market but by changes in the business model of the insurance companies. Specifically, these insurance firms got into the bond insurance business in the 1980s by insuring only municipal bonds and they charged premium rates that reflected the fairly low default rates experienced by municipal bonds over time. This business line was very profitable for the insurance companies due to the continuing low default rates. Subsequently the firms sold insurance on investment-grade corporate bonds at higher premiums due to their slightly higher historical default rates (about 2 percent cumulative default over 10 years for BBB-rated bonds). Again this was generally a profitable business with low defaults overall. Finally, in the early 2000s they took a very large step and began insuring structured finance products including collateralized debt obligations (CDOs) (to be described later) that contained a combination of many securities (including subprime mortgages). Unfortunately, the premiums charged for this insurance were relatively low given the much higher risk involved. More important, the defaults experienced during 2007-2008 were substantially higher than envisioned and the payments required by these firms to cover the defaults on these securities were very large compared to the capital available to these insurance firms. As a result of these losses and the resulting capital impairment, the rating agencies downgraded the smaller insurance firms in early 2008 and the largest firms were downgraded in July, 2008. As noted above, when these insurance companies are downgraded, all the bonds that got a AAA rating because of the bond insurance also are downgraded. Therefore, the impact on the municipal bond market has been enormous and for a period in 2008 the typical negative spread on municipals relative to Treasuries became positive.

17.3.4 Corporate Bonds

Again, the importance of corporate bonds varies across countries. The absolute dollar value of corporate bonds in the United States is substantial and has grown overall and as a percentage

---

[17] For a general discussion of municipal bond insurance, see Feldstein, Fabozzi, Grant, and Kennedy (2005). For an analysis of the specific benefits to the issuer, see Kidwell, Sorenson, and Wachowicz (1987).

of U.S. long-term capital. At the same time, corporate debt as a percentage of total U.S. debt has stabilized at about 30 percent because of the faster growth of agency debt. The pure corporate sector in Japan is small and declining and the ex-bank corporate sector in the Eurozone has grown to be over 14 percent. The proportion of corporate debt in the United Kingdom has increased to almost 30 percent.

U.S. Corporate Bond Market Utilities dominate the U.S. corporate bond market. Other important segments include industrials, rail and transportation issues, and financial issues. This market is very diverse and includes debentures, first-mortgage issues, convertible obligations, bonds with warrants, subordinated debentures, income bonds (similar to municipal revenue bonds), collateral trust bonds backed by financial assets, equipment trust certificates, and asset-backed securities (ABS) including mortgage-backed bonds.

If we ignore convertible bonds and bonds with warrants, the preceding list of obligations varies by the type of collateral behind the bond. Most bonds have semiannual interest payments, sinking funds, and a single maturity date. Maturities range from 25 to 40 years, with public utilities generally on the longer end and industrials preferring the 25- to 30-year range. Most corporate bonds provide for deferred calls after 5 to 10 years. The deferment period varies directly with the level of the interest rates. Specifically, during periods of higher interest rates, bond issues typically will carry a 7- to 10-year deferment, while during periods of lower interest rates, the deferment periods decline.

On the other hand, corporate notes—with maturities of five to seven years—are generally noncallable. Notes become popular when interest rates are high because issuing firms prefer to avoid long-term obligations during such periods. In contrast, during periods of very low interest rates, such as 1997 and 2001–2004, most corporate issues did not include a call provision because corporations did not believe that they would be able to exercise the call option because rates were already very low, and the firms did not want to pay the required higher yield.

Generally, the average yields for industrial bonds will be the lowest of the three major sectors, followed by utility returns. The difference in yield between utilities and industrials occurs because utilities have the largest supply of bonds, so yields on their bonds must be higher to increase the demand for these bonds.[18]

Mortgage Bonds The issuer of a mortgage bond has granted to the bondholder a first mortgage lien on some piece of property or possibly all the firm's property. Such a lien provides greater security to the bondholder and a lower interest rate for the issuing firm.

Equipment Trust Certificates Equipment trust certificates are issued by railroads (the biggest issuers), airlines, and other transportation firms with the proceeds used to purchase equipment (freight cars, railroad engines, and airplanes), which serves as the collateral for the debt. Maturities range from 1 to about 15 years. The fairly short maturities reflect the nature of the collateral, which is subject to substantial wear and tear and tends to deteriorate rapidly.

Equipment trust certificates are appealing to investors because of their attractive yields, low default record, and a fairly liquid secondary market.

Collateral Trust Bonds As an alternative to pledging fixed assets or property, a borrower can pledge financial assets, such as stocks, bonds, or notes, as collateral. These bonds are termed *collateral trust bonds*. These pledged assets are held by a trustee for the benefit of the bondholder.

Mortgage Pass-Through Securities Earlier we discussed mortgage bonds backed by pools of mortgages. You will recall that the pass-through monthly payments are necessarily both

[18] For a further discussion, see Fabozzi, Mann, and Wilson (2005).

interest and principal and that the bondholder is subject to early retirement if the mortgagees prepay because the house is sold or the mortgage refinanced. Therefore, when you acquire the typical mortgage pass-through bonds, you would be uncertain about the size and timing of the payments.

Collateralized mortgage obligations (CMOs)[19] were developed in the early 1980s to offset some of the problems with the traditional mortgage pass-throughs. The main innovation of the CMO instrument is the segmentation of irregular mortgage cash flows to create short-term, medium-term, and long-term securities. Specifically, CMO investors own bonds that are serviced with the cash flows from mortgages; but, rather than the straight pass-through arrangement, the CMO substitutes a *sequential distribution process* that creates a series of bonds with varying maturities to appeal to a wider range of investors.

The prioritized distribution process is as follows:

- Several classes of bonds (these are referred to as *tranches*) are issued against a pool of mortgages, which are the collateral. For example, assume a CMO issue with four classes (tranches) of bonds. In such a case, the first three (e.g., Classes A, B, C) would pay interest at their stated rates beginning at their issue date and the fourth class would be an accrual bond (referred to as a *Z bond*).
- The cash flows received from the underlying mortgages are applied first to pay the interest on the bonds and then to retire these bonds.
- The classes of bonds are retired sequentially. All principal payments are directed first to the shortest-maturity class A bonds until they are completely retired. Then all principal payments are directed to the next shortest-maturity bonds (i.e., the class B bonds). The process continues until all the classes have been paid off.
- During the early periods, the accrual bonds (the class Z bonds) pay no interest, but the interest accrues as additional principal, and the cash flow from the mortgages that collateralize these bonds is used to pay interest on and retire the bonds in the other classes. Subsequently, all remaining cash flows are used to pay off the accrued interest, pay any current interest, and then to retire the Z bonds.

This prioritized sequential pattern means that the A-class bonds are fairly short term and each subsequent class is a little longer term until the Z-class bond, which is a long-term bond that functions like a zero coupon or PIK bond for the initial years.

Besides creating bonds that pay interest in a more normal pattern (quarterly or semiannually) and that have more predictable maturities, these bonds are considered very high quality securities (AAA) because of the structure and quality of the collateral. To obtain an AAA rating, CMOs are structured to ensure that the underlying mortgages will always generate enough cash to support the bonds issued, even under the most conservative prepayment and reinvestment rates. In fact, most CMOs are overcollateralized.

Further, the credit risk of the collateral is minimal because most are backed by mortgages guaranteed by a federal agency (GNMA, FNMA) or by the FHLMC. Those mortgages that are not backed by agencies carry private insurance from one of the GSEs (Fannie Mae or Freddie Mac) for principal and interest and mortgage insurance. Notably, even with this AAA rating, the yield on these CMOs typically has been higher than the yields on AA industrials. This premium yield has, of course, contributed to their popularity and growth.

Asset-Backed Securities (ABSs)   A rapidly expanding segment of the securities market is that of *asset-backed securities*, which involve *securitizing debt* beyond the residential mortgages that we have discussed. This is an important concept because it substantially increases the liquidity of these individual debt instruments, whether they be commercial mortgages, car loans, credit card debt, student loans, or home equity loans. This general class of securities was introduced

[19] For a detailed discussion, see Crawford (2005).

in 1983. As of December 31, 2007, there was almost $2.5 trillion of asset-backed securities outstanding. Beyond the mortgage securities, this market is dominated by securities backed by automobile loans and credit card receivables.

Certificates for Automobile Receivables (CARs) As discussed by Roever (2005), CARs are securities collateralized by loans made to individuals to finance the purchase of cars. Auto loans are self-amortizing, with monthly payments and relatively short maturities (i.e., two to five years). These auto loans can either be direct loans from a lending institution or indirect loans that are originated by an auto dealer and sold to the ultimate lender. CARs typically have monthly or quarterly fixed interest and principal payments, and expected weighted average lives of one to three years. The expected actual life of the instrument typically is shorter than the specified maturity because of early payoffs when cars are sold or traded in. The cash flows of CARs are comparable to short-term corporate debt. They provide a significant yield premium over General Motors Acceptance Corporation (GMAC) commercial paper, which is the most liquid short-term corporate alternative. The popularity of these collateralized securities makes them important not only by themselves but also as an indication of the potential for issuing additional collateralized securities backed by other assets and/or other debt instruments.

Credit Card Receivables Recently, the fastest-growing segment of the ABS market has been securities supported by credit card loans. As described by McElravey (2005), credit card receivables are a revolving credit ABS, in contrast to auto loan receivables that are referred to as an installment contract ABS—because of the nature of the loan. Specifically, whereas the mortgaged-backed and auto loan securities amortize principal, the principal payments from credit card receivables are not paid to the investor but are retained by the trustee to reinvest in additional receivables. This allows the issuer to specify a maturity for the security that is consistent with the needs of the issuer and the demands of the investors.

When buying a credit card ABS, the indenture specifies (1) the intended maturity for the security; (2) the "lockout period" during which no principal will be paid; and (3) the structure for repaying the principal, which can be accomplished through a single-bullet payment, such as a bond, or distributed monthly with the interest payment over a specified amortization period. For example, a 5-year credit card ABS could have a lockout period of 4 years followed by a 12-month amortization of the principal.

Beyond this standard arrangement, revolving credit securities are protected by early amortization events that can force early repayment if specific payout events occur that are detrimental to the investor (e.g., if there is an increase in the loss rate or if the issuer goes into bankruptcy or receivership). Although this early amortization feature protects the investor from credit problems, it causes an early payment that may not be desirable for the investor.

Auction-Rate Securities are issued by municipalities, hospitals, museums, and student loan authorities in an attempt to pay short-term rates for long-term funds. These securities have stated long maturities such as 20 or 30 years, but they act like short-term securities because the coupon is set during frequent auctions every week to 35 days. At these auctions the original investors can hold the security and get the new rate set at the auction. Alternatively if they want to liquidate or don't think the yield is high enough, they can sell the security at the auction. Investors, such as treasurers and pension funds, like these securities because they are generally very liquid and provide yields that exceed what is available on T-bills.

This $360 billion market was very popular prior to 2008 when it became very illiquid because there was a massive "flight to quality" and numerous auctions "failed," meaning that there were not enough bids to sell all the bonds available, so investors could not liquidate their position, or the required yield increased dramatically (e.g., from 4 percent to 15 percent). For a discussion of what transpired during this period, see Rappaport and Karmin (2008) and Smith, McGinty, and Rappaport (2008).

Variable-Rate Notes Introduced in the United States in the mid-1970s, **variable-rate notes** became popular during periods of high interest rates. As discussed by Fabozzi and Mann (2005), the typical variable-rate note possesses two unique features:

1. After the first 6 to 18 months of the issue's life, during which a minimum rate is often guaranteed, the coupon rate floats, so that every six months it changes to follow some standard. Usually it is pegged 1 percent above a stipulated short-term rate. For example, the rate might be the preceding three weeks' average 90-day T-bill rate.
2. After the first year or two, the notes are redeemable at par, at the *holder's* option, usually at six-month intervals.

Such notes represent a long-term commitment on the part of the borrower yet provide the lender with all the characteristics of a short-term obligation. They typically are available to investors in minimum denominations of $1,000. However, although the six-month redemption feature provides liquidity, the variable rates can cause these issues to experience wide swings in semiannual coupons.

Collateralized Debt Obligations (CDOs) are considered part of the asset-backed security market because they are backed by cash-flow generating assets similar to mortgages, car loans, or credit card accounts. They deserve special attention for four reasons: (1) their rapid growth since 2000, (2) the substantial diversity of assets that are used to back the securities, (3) the diversity of credit quality within a CDO issue in terms of credit rating, and (4) the significant problems generated by these securities caused by credit problems for the tranches with low credit ratings, and liquidity problems for the tranches with high credit ratings.

As noted, in contrast to most ABSs that are backed by one specific type of asset (mortgages, car loans, etc.), the CDO is generally backed by a diversified pool of several assets including investment-grade or high-yield bonds, domestic bank loans, emerging market bonds, residential and commercial mortgages, and even other CDOs. The reason for creating many CDOs is to allow an institution to reduce its capital requirements by removing some high-risk loans from its balance sheet. Beyond a diverse set of assets, the CDO is typically structured into tranches similar to the CMOs, but in this case the tranches differ by credit quality—that is, the issuers use credit enhancement techniques to create tranches that are rated from AAA to BBB or lower. Similar to other ABSs, the issuer, in consultation with the rating agencies, determines what credit enhancements are required to attain a given rating for a tranche. Therefore, investors can benefit from higher returns but can also select their desired credit risk based on the ratings assigned.

The problems in these securities began in 2006 when during the real estate "boom," mortgage loans were made to numerous individuals with very low credit scores resulting in sub-prime mortgage loans that were subsequently put into CDOs. In 2007 and 2008, there were a high proportion of defaults on these sub-prime loans that reduced the value of these tranches. Even the highly rated tranches that were protected by the credit enhancements techniques could not be traded—they were very illiquid because of a general flight to Treasury securities and away from complicated securities with credit ratings that were being questioned. As a result, there were significant price declines because of either credit or liquidity problems.

Zero Coupon and Deep Discount Bonds The typical corporate bond has a coupon and maturity. In turn, the value of the bond is the present value of the stream of cash flows (interest and principal) discounted at the required yield to maturity (YTM). Alternatively, some bonds do not have any coupons or have coupons that are below the market rate at the time of issue. Such securities are referred to as *zero coupon* or *minicoupon bonds* or *original-issue discount (OID) bonds*. A zero coupon discount bond promises to pay a stipulated principal amount at a future maturity date, but it does not promise to make any interim interest payments. Therefore, the price of the bond is the present value of the principal payment at the maturity date using the required discount rate for this bond. The return on the bond is the difference between what the investor pays for the bond at the time of purchase and the principal payment at maturity.

Consider a zero coupon, $10,000 par value bond with a 20-year maturity. If the required rate of return on bonds of equal maturity and quality is 8 percent and we assume semiannual discounting, the initial selling price for this bond would be $2,082.89 because the present-value factor at 8 percent compounded semiannually for 20 years is 0.208289. From the time of purchase to the point of maturity, the investor would not receive any cash flow from the firm. Notably, the investor must pay taxes, however, on the implied interest on the bond, although no cash is received. Because an investor subject to taxes would experience severe negative cash flows during the life of these bonds, they are primarily of interest to investment accounts not subject to taxes, such as pensions, IRAs, or Keogh accounts.[20]

A modified form of zero coupon bond is the OID bond where the coupon is set substantially below the prevailing market rate, for example, a 5 percent coupon on a bond when market rates are 12 percent. As a result, the bond is issued at a deep discount from par value. Again, taxes must be paid on the implied 12 percent return rather than the nominal 5 percent, so the cash flow disadvantage of zero coupon bonds, though lessened, remains.

High-Yield Bonds

A segment of the corporate bond market that has grown in size, importance, and controversy is **high-yield bonds**, also referred to as *speculative-grade bonds* and *junk bonds*. These are corporate bonds that have been assigned a bond rating as noninvestment grade, that is, they have a rating below BBB or Baa. The title of speculative-grade bonds is probably the most objective because bonds that are not rated investment grade are speculative grade. The designation of *high-yield (HY) bonds* was coined as an indication of the returns available for these bonds relative to Treasury bonds and investment-grade corporate bonds. The *junk bond* designation is obviously somewhat derogatory and refers to the low credit quality of the issues.

Brief History of the High-Yield Bond Market Based on a specification that bonds rated below BBB make up the high-yield market, this segment has existed as long as there have been rating agencies. Prior to 1980, most of the HY bonds were referred to as *fallen angels*, which means they were bonds that were originally issued as investment-grade securities, but because of changes in the firm over time, the bonds were downgraded into the noninvestment grade sector (BB and below).

The market changed in the early 1980s when Drexel Burnham Lambert (DBL) began aggressively underwriting HY bonds for two groups of clients: (1) small firms that did not have the financial strength to receive an investment-grade rating by the rating agencies, and (2) large and small firms that issued HY bonds in connection with leveraged buyouts (LBOs). As a result, the HY bond market went from a residual market that included fallen angels to a new-issue market where bonds were underwritten and issued with below-investment-grade ratings.

The high-yield bond market exploded in size and activity beginning in the early 1980s (recent data in Exhibit 17.6.). Beginning in 1983, more large issues became common and the average size of an issue currently is over $435 million. Also, high-yield issues have become a significant percentage of the total new-issue bond market. As of 2008, the total outstanding high-yield debt constituted about 20 percent of outstanding corporate debt in the United States.[21]

Distribution of High-Yield Bond Ratings Exhibit 17.7 contains the distribution of ratings for all the bonds contained in the Lehman Brothers High-Yield Bond Index as of December 31,

---

[20] These bonds will be discussed further in Chapter 18 in the section on volatility and duration and in Chapter 19 when we consider immunization.

[21] Almost everyone would acknowledge that the development of the high-yield debt market has had a positive impact on the capital-raising ability of the economy. For an analysis of this impact, see Perry and Taggart (1988). Updates on its characteristics are contained in Fridson (1994), Altman (1992), and Reilly and Wright (2001b).

Exhibit 17.6 High-Yield Bonds—New-Issue Volume: 1992–2007

Year	Public Principal Amount ($ Millions)	144A Principal Amount ($ Millions)	TOTAL Number of Issues	TOTAL Principal Amount ($ Millions)	Average Issue Size ($ Millions)
1992	39,755	3,811	274	43,566	159.00
1993	57,164	15,097	436	72,261	165.74
1994	34,599	7,734	272	42,332	155.63
1995	30,139	14,242	246	44,381	180.41
1996	30,739	35,173	359	65,912	183.60
1997	19,822	98,885	679	118,707	174.83
1998	29,844	111,045	720	140,889	195.68
1999	16,520	83,157	417	99,677	239.00
2000	10,621	39,594	181	50,215	277.40
2001	14,386	69,110	309	83,495	270.20
2002	6,551	54,516	251	61,067	243.30
2003	14,223	126,892	515	141,116	274.01
2004	12,299	146,910	629	159,209	255.72
2005	4,555	112,224	429	116,779	272.21
2006	24,158	147,937	399	172,095	431.32
2007 (e)	27,500	148,000	403	175,500	435.48

Note: Includes nonconvertible, corporate debt rated below investment grade by Moody's or Standard & Poor's. Excludes mortgage- and asset-backed issues, as well as non-144a private placements. (e) estimate

Source: Merrill Lynch & Co.; Securities Data Company.

Exhibit 17.7 High Yield Index Composition by Credit Quality: 1994–2007 (Percentage of Market Value)

Year	BB	B	CCC/Unrated
1994	42.61	48.00	9.38
1995	48.32	44.60	7.08
1996	45.67	47.36	6.97
1997	38.19	51.07	10.74
1998	35.28	52.04	12.68
1999	33.83	55.82	10.34
2000	36.63	53.94	9.43
2001	46.04	42.35	11.61
2002	41.20	39.70	19.20
2003	35.20	46.40	18.40
2004	39.30	45.10	15.60
2005	41.97	42.77	15.26
2006	35.50	47.76	16.74
2007	36.10	43.06	20.84

Source: Lehman Brothers, *Global Family of Indices* (New York: Lehman Brothers, Annual).

1994–2007. As shown, the heavy concentration by market value is typically in the B class, which contains almost half of all value. There was an overall decline in the BB category that decreased from about 43 percent in 1994 to about 36 percent in 2007.

Ownership of High-Yield Bonds The major owners of high-yield bonds have been mutual funds, insurance companies, and pension funds. As of the end of 2007, over 100 mutual funds were either exclusively directed to invest in high-yield bonds or included such bonds in their portfolio. Notably, there has been a shift of ownership away from insurance companies and savings and loans toward mutual funds. This shift occurred during the late 1980s when regulators "encouraged" the insurance companies and S&Ls to reduce or eliminate high-yield bonds from their portfolios.

The purpose of this discussion has been to introduce you to high-yield bonds because of the growth in size and importance of this segment of the market for individual and institutional investors. We revisit this topic in Chapter 19 on bond portfolio management, where we review the historical rates of return and alternative risk factors, including the default experience for these bonds. As discussed by Altman (1990), Fabozzi (1990b), and Fridson (1989), all of this must be considered by potential investors in these securities.

Japanese Corporate Bond Market The corporate bond market in Japan is made up of two components: (1) bonds issued by industrial firms or utilities and (2) bonds issued by banks to finance loans to corporations. As noted in connection with Exhibit 17.2, the pure corporate bond sector has declined in relative size over time to about 11 percent of the total.

Japanese corporate bonds are regulated by the *Kisaikai,* a council composed of 22 bond-related banks and seven major securities companies. It operates under the authority of the Ministry of Finance (MOF) and the Bank of Japan (BOJ) to determine bond-issuing procedures, including specifying the coupons on corporate bonds in relation to coupons on long-term government bonds in order to prevent any competition with the government bond market.

Because of numerous bankruptcies during the 1930s depression, the government mandated that all corporate debt be secured. This requirement was abolished in 1988. The issuance of unsecured debt led to the birth of bond-rating agencies, which were not needed with completely secured debt. Currently, there are five major bond-rating agencies.

The Ministry of Finance specifies minimum issuing requirements and controls the issuance system that specifies who can issue bonds and when they can be issued. In addition, lead underwriting managers are predetermined in accordance with a lead manager rotating system that ensures balance among the major securities firms in Japan.

Bank Bonds The substantial issuance of bank bonds is because of the banking system in Japan, which is segmented into the following components:

- Commercial banks (13 big-city banks and 64 regional banks)
- Long-term credit banks (3)
- Mutual loan and savings banks (6)
- Specialized financial institutions

During the post–World War II reconstruction, several banks were permitted to obtain funding by issuing medium- and long-term debentures at rates above yields on government bonds. These funds were used to make mortgage loans to firms in the industrial sector to rebuild plants and equipment. Currently, these financial institutions sell five-year coupon debentures and one-year discount debentures directly to individual and institutional investors. The long-term credit banks are not allowed to take deposits and thus depend on the debentures to obtain funds. These bonds are traded in the OTC market.

Pound Sterling Corporate Bond Market Corporate bonds in the United Kingdom, denominated in pound sterling, are available in three forms: debentures, unsecured loans, and convertible bonds. The value of securities in each class are about equal. The maturity structure of the corporate bond market is fairly wide and the coupon structure of corporate bonds also is broad with high-coupon bonds in the 10 to 14 percent range. In contrast, convertible bonds have low coupons. Almost all U.K. corporate bonds are callable term bonds.

U.K. corporate bonds are issued through both public offerings and private placements. After issuance, primary dealers trade corporate bonds directly with each other. All corporate bonds are issued in registered form.

Eurozone Corporate Bond Market Corporate bonds in the Eurozone are divided between pure corporate bonds that include industrial and utility firms (about 15 percent) and securitized/collaterlized bonds that include indirect corporate borrowing (about 12 percent).

17.3.5 International Bonds

Each country's international bond market has two components. The first, *foreign bonds,* are issues sold primarily in one country and currency by a borrower of a different nationality. An example would be U.S. dollar–denominated bonds sold in the United States by a Japanese firm. (These are referred to as *Yankee bonds.*) Second are *Eurobonds,* which are bonds underwritten by international bond syndicates and sold in several national markets. An example would be Eurodollar bonds that are securities denominated in U.S. dollars, underwritten by an international syndicate, and sold to non-U.S. investors outside the United States. The relative size of these two markets (foreign bonds versus Eurobonds) varies by country.

United States The Eurodollar bond market in the U.S. has become much larger than the Yankee bond market. However, because the Eurodollar bond market is heavily affected by changes in the value of the U.S. dollar, it experiences slower growth during periods when the dollar is weak. Such periods create a desire for diversification by investors.

Yankee bonds are issued by foreign firms who register with the SEC and borrow U.S. dollars, using issues underwritten by a U.S. syndicate for delivery in the United States. These bonds are traded in the United States and pay interest semiannually. Over 60 percent of Yankee bonds are issued by Canadian corporations and typically have shorter maturities and longer call protection than U.S. domestic issues. These features increase their appeal.

The Eurodollar bond market is dominated by foreign investors, and the center of trading is in London. Eurodollar bonds pay interest annually. The Eurodollar bond market currently comprises almost 40 percent of the total Eurobond market.

Japan Historically, the Japanese yen international bond market was dominated (over 90 percent) by foreign bonds (Samurai bonds) with the balance in Euroyen bonds. After the issuance requirements for Euroyen bonds were liberalized in the mid-1980s, the ratio of issuance swung heavily in favor of Euroyen bonds.

Samurai bonds are yen-denominated bonds sold by non-Japanese issuers and mainly sold in Japan. The market is fairly small and has limited liquidity. Notably, the market has experienced slow growth in terms of yen but substantial growth in U.S. dollar terms because of changes in the exchange rate.

Euroyen bonds are yen-denominated bonds sold in markets outside Japan by international syndicates. This market has grown substantially because of the liberal issue requirements. Its appeal over time is determined by the strength or weakness of the yen relative to other currencies.

United Kingdom Pound sterling foreign bonds, referred to as *bulldog bonds,* are sterling-denominated bonds issued by non-English firms and sold in London. Eurosterling bonds are sold in markets outside London by international syndicates.

Similar to other countries, the U.K. international bond market has become dominated by the Eurosterling bonds. The procedure for issuing and trading Eurosterling bonds is similar to that of other Eurobonds.

Eurozone The growth of Eurobonds issued by nonresidents has been impressive in recent years. This growth confirmed the popularity of the Euro markets among foreign issuers including issuers domiciled in the United States that accounted for over 7 percent of the market.

17.4 Obtaining Information on Bond Prices

Historically, the price information available to bond investors has been substantially different from price information available to stock investors. Specifically, stock investors can receive up-to-the-minute transaction prices on all NYSE, AMEX, and NASDAQ national stocks as well as daily closing prices for most other NASDAQ stocks. In contrast, most bond trading has been done on the over-the-counter (OTC) market, and there was limited reporting of transactions, with the exception of the very liquid government bond market. Fortunately, this environment in the bond market changed dramatically beginning in 2004. As described by Lucchetti and Soloman (2004) and subsequently by Rappaport (2004b), the National Association of Securities Dealers (NASD), through its Trade Reporting and Compliance Engine (TRACE), began releasing more timely pricing data for a broad group of corporate bonds. Specifically, as of October 2004, NASD expanded the number of corporate bonds for which it reports pricing information, from 4,500 bonds within 45 minutes of the transaction to 17,000 bonds within 30 minutes of the transaction. The existence of more bond issues than stock issues is possible because companies can have more than one bond issue, but typically only one stock issue. In 2005 the NASD began reporting transactions on all 23,000 corporate bond issues with the goal to reduce the reporting interval to within 15 minutes of the transaction. Clearly, the price transparency in the corporate bond market has changed dramatically and the transaction cost savings for bond investors has been dramatic.

In addition to better pricing data, as discussed by Rappaport (2004a), the overall bond market (and especially the corporate bond market) has benefited from the introduction of electronic bond trading through Thomson Trade Web and Market Axess, the two leading trading platforms. In early 2004, there was electronic trading in government agency and mortgage-backed securities, but it was not until late 2004 that the volume of trading and the size of corporate bond trading brought transparency to this market. Observers contend that the next frontiers will be electronic trading in high-yield bonds, emerging market debt, and interest rate derivatives.

Given this background, the following discussion considers how investors read and interpret bond price information in newspapers and quote sheets.

17.4.1 Interpreting Bond Quotes

Essentially, all bonds are quoted on the basis of either yield or price. Price quotes are always interpreted as a *percentage of par*. For example, a quote of 98½ is interpreted not as $98.50 but 98½ percent of par. The dollar price is derived from the quote, given the par value. If the par value is $5,000 on a municipal bond, then the price of an issue quoted at 98½ would be $4,925. Actually, the market follows three systems of bond pricing: one system for corporates, another for governments (both Treasury and agency obligations), and a third for municipals.

Corporate Bond Quotes Exhibit 17.8 is a listing of corporate bond quotes for the 40 most active fixed-coupon corporate bonds that appeared in *Barron's* on March 3, 2008. The data pertain to trading activity on February 29, 2008. Several quotes have been designated for illustrative purposes.

The first issue designated is a Citigroup (trading symbol C) issue that is representative of most corporate prices. This is a 6.875 percent coupon, which means that the annual coupon payment for this $1,000 par value bond is $68.75 or $34.375 every six months. The bond matures on March 5, 2038, which is almost exactly 30 years from March 3, 2008. The last transaction price for a bond trade on February 29 was 99.647 of par or $996.47, which implies a yield to maturity (YTM) for this bond (to be explained in detail in Chapter 18) of 6.903 percent. The estimated spread in basis points (100 basis points is one percentage point) indicates how the YTM for this bond compares to the prevailing yield to maturity for a Treasury note or bond of equal maturity. The Treasury issues are limited to the following maturities: 2, 3, 5, 10, and 30 years, and they use the latest issue at that maturity (that is referred to as "on the run") as listed. As shown, the computed spread for the Citigroup bond is 250 basis points (2.50 percent), which implies that at this time, the 30-year Treasury bond (a 5.00 coupon bond that matures in May 2037) is yielding about 4.40 percent (6.903–2.50). As can be seen from the other bonds in the exhibit, the average spread for all the bonds is fairly large—ranging from 125 to 1,020

Exhibit 17.8 Sample Corporate Bond Quotations

CORPORATE BONDS

For the week ending Friday, February 29, 2008
Forty most active fixed-coupon corporate bonds

COMPANY (TICKER)	COUPON	MATURITY	LAST PRICE	LAST YIELD	*EST SPREAD	UST†	EST $ VOL (000's)
Sprint Capital (S)	8.750	Mar 15, 2032	80.000	11.158	671	30	676,234
Citigroup (C)	**6.875**	**Mar 05, 2038**	**99.647**	**6.903**	**250**	**30**	**539,450**
Sprint Capital (S)	6.875	Nov 15, 2028	70.000	10.438	602	30	478,219
Sprint Capital (S)	8.375	Mar 15, 2012	88.500	12.061	959	5	467,809
Mcdonalds (MCD)	5.350	Mar 01, 2018	102.031	5.088	157	10	443,322
Sprint Capital (S)	6.900	May 01, 2019	74.500	10.903	738	10	433,674
General Electric Capital (GE)	5.875	Jan 14, 2038	95.140	6.235	182	30	397,860
Mcdonalds (MCD)	6.300	Mar 01, 2038	102.055	6.149	172	30	364,305
At&T (T)	5.500	Feb 01, 2018	100.343	5.454	193	10	336,310
Bear Stearns Inc (BSC)	7.250	Feb 01, 2018	96.783	7.719	420	10	323,921
Honeywell International (HON)	5.300	Mar 01, 2018	102.320	5.002	141	10	309,212
Sprint Nextel (S)	7.375	Aug 01, 2015	78.270	11.862	833	10	287,102
General Electric Co (GE)	**5.250**	**Dec 06, 2017**	**100.057**	**5.241**	**172**	**10**	**284,623**
Fifth Third Ban (FITB)	8.250	Mar 01, 2038	99.539	8.292	388	30	280,681
Sprint Nextel (S)	6.000	Dec 01, 2016	74.000	10.639	711	10	275,909
Goldman Sachs Group (GS)	5.950	Jan 18, 2018	100.994	5.815	228	10	274,368
Vale Overseas Ltd (CVRD)	6.875	Nov 21, 2036	94.233	7.359	293	30	227,052
Pacific Gas And Electric Co (PCG)	5.625	Nov 30, 2017	103.803	5.123	160	10	219,920
Sprint Capital (S)	6.375	May 01, 2009	n.a.	n.a.	n.a.	2	199,318
Honeywell International (HON)	4.250	Mar 01, 2013	101.427	3.932	142	5	197,976
Merrill Lynch Inc (MER)	5.450	Feb 05, 2013	100.850	5.250	277	5	192,404
Wells Fargo (WFC)	5.625	Dec 11, 2017	102.612	5.278	169	10	190,808
Mcdonalds (MCD)	**4.300**	**Mar 01, 2013**	**101.493**	**3.967**	**148**	**5**	**185,645**
Merrill Lynch Inc (MER)	6.400	Aug 28, 2017	101.891	6.134	254	10	184,623
Wells Fargo (WFC)	4.375	Jan 31, 2013	100.990	4.149	164	5	182,529
Sprint Nextel (S)	5.950	Mar 15, 2014	75.000	11.873	835	5	181,223
Kraft Foods (KFT)	6.125	Feb 01, 2018	100.941	5.994	248	10	174,935
Citigroup (C)	5.000	Sep 15, 2014	96.538	5.641	212	5	172,143
Vale Overseas Ltd (CVRD)	6.250	Jan 23, 2017	99.803	6.277	274	10	166,067
Pemex Project Funding Master Trust (PEMEX)	6.625	Jun 15, 2035	103.350	6.364	195	30	164,870
	7.625	Jan 30, 2011	88.000	12.688	1020	3	163,812
Sprint Capital (S)	5.250	Oct 19, 2012	104.647	4.134	165	5	163,520
General Electric Capital (GE)	6.000	Jan 15, 2018	103.297	5.559	202	10	161,930
Jpmorgan Chase (JPM)	6.350	Feb 15, 2038	102.948	6.134	169	30	161,548
Pacific Gas And Electric Co (PCG)	5.750	Feb 01, 2018	99.784	5.778	224	10	161,060
Wachovia (WB)	5.050	Oct 22, 2012	104.516	3.972	125	5	158,347
Ibm International Group Capital Llc* (IBM)	5.350	Mar 01, 2018	101.898	5.105	151	10	152,500
Peco Energy Co (EXC)	5.875	May 29, 2037	89.270	6.717	217	30	152,093
Citigroup * (C)	5.950	Dec 28, 2017	99.645	5.997	246	10	148,052
Morgan Stanley (MS)	6.900	Dec 15, 2017	100.877	6.774	325	10	146,857
American General Finance (AIG)							

Volume represents total volume for each issue; price/yield data are for trades of $1 million and greater. * Denotes a security whose last round lot trade did not take place on the last business day prior to publication. ** Estimated spreads, in basis points (100 basis points is one percentage point), over the 2, 3, 5, 10 or 30-year hot run Treasury note/bond. 2-year: 2.125 01/10; 5-year: 2.875 01/13; 10-year: 3.500 02/18; 30-year: 5.000 05/37; . †Comparable U.S. Treasury issue.

Source: MarketAxess Corporate BondTicker - www.bondticker.com

Source: *Barron's*, March 3, 2008, M45. Copyright 2008 DOW JONES & Co., Inc.

basis points. These larger than normal spreads are caused by the "flight to quality" brought on by the credit/liquidity crisis of 2007–2008 that caused lower Treasury yields and an increase in yields for risky (non-Treasury) bonds.

The second issue designated is the General Electric Co. (GE) bonds for this major industrial-financial conglomerate. These bonds, which mature in about 10 years and 9 months, are compared to a 10-year Treasury security due to mature in February 2018. The spread of 172 points is relatively small and is caused by the very strong AAA bond rating that GE enjoys. The yield of 5.241 percent compares to the prevailing 10-year Treasury security yield of about 3.52 percent.

The third issue is the McDonalds (MCD) 4.30 percent bond due to mature in March 2013 (almost exactly 5 years from the date of this exhibit). Notably, it has one of the smallest spreads of 148 basis points relative to the 5-year Treasury note that was currently yielding about

2.49 percent. This can be explained mainly by its Aa bond rating, its significant cash flows, and its short maturity. These examples indicate that bond prices are determined by yields to maturity that, in turn, are driven by required spreads to Treasury securities. The estimated volume indicates that there is substantial trading in these corporate bonds.

All fixed-income obligations, with the exception of preferred stock, are traded on an *accrued interest basis*. The prices pertain to the value of all *future* cash flows from the bond and exclude interest that has accrued to the holder since the last interest payment date. The actual price of the bond will exceed the quote listed because accrued interest must be added. Assume a bond with a 6 percent coupon. If two months have elapsed since interest was paid, the current holder of the bond is entitled to two-sixths (one-third) of the bond's semiannual interest payment that will be paid in four months. More specifically, the 6 percent coupon provides semiannual interest income of $30. The investor who held the obligation for two months beyond the last interest payment date is entitled to one-third of that $30 in the form of accrued interest. Therefore, whatever the current price of the bond, an accrued interest value of $10 will be added. If a bond is trading "flat," interest is not being paid and accrued interest would not be added.

Treasury and Agency Bond Quotes Exhibit 17.9 illustrates the quote system for Treasury bonds, notes, and bills. These quotes resemble those used for OTC securities because they contain both bid and ask prices. For U.S. Treasury bond quotes, a small "n" behind the maturity date indicates that the obligation is a Treasury *note*. Securities with original maturities over 10 years are Treasury bonds. The security identification is different because it is not necessary to list the issuer. Instead, the usual listing indicates the coupon, the month and year of maturity, and information on a call feature of the obligation. Call features have not been relevent for several years since the Treasury has not issued a bond with a call option since 1985 and previously outstanding callable issues have matured. The bid-ask figures provided are stated as a percentage of par. The yield figure provided is yield to maturity, or *promised* yield based on the asking price. This system is used for Treasuries, agencies, and municipals.

Quote 1 is a 3.125 percent obligation, due in September 2008, that demonstrates the basic difference in the price system of government bonds (i.e., Treasuries and agencies). The bid quote is 100:14, and the ask is 100:15. Governments are traded in 32nds of a point (rather than 8ths), and the figures to the right of the colons indicate the number of 32nds in the fractional bid or ask. In this case, the bid price is actually 100.4375 percent of par. These quotes also are notable in terms of the bid-ask spread, which typically is one 32nd, or less than half the size of the spread for most stocks. This small spread reflects the outstanding liquidity and low transaction costs for Treasury securities.

The third column contains quotes for U.S. Treasury zero coupon securities that have been stripped. Specifically, the typical bond promises a series of coupon payments and its principal at maturity. A stripped security is created by dividing into separate units each coupon payment and principal payment, which are treated like a zero coupon bond that matures on that date. The security labeled ② was originally a coupon that was to be paid in August 2010. The asking yield (2.24) is referred to as the spot rate for this maturity (spot rate will be discussed in Chapter 18). The coupon interest payment with no principal is designated as *ci* (stripped coupon interest), while the other strips for August 2010 containing only the principal payment is designated "np" (Treasury note, stripped principal).

The securities listed in the Treasury strip and Treasury bill section only report dates and days to maturity and no coupons. This is because these are pure discount securities, that is, the return is the difference between the price you pay and par at maturity.[22]

The final section contains Treasury Inflation Indexed Securities (TIPS) discussed earlier. Notice the accrued principal in the last column that reflects the inflation since the bond was issued. The bond designated ③ has been outstanding the longest time, so it has the highest

---

[22] For a discussion of calculating yields, see Fielitz (1983).

Exhibit 17.9 Sample Quotes for Treasury Bonds, Notes, and Bills

Treasury Bonds, Notes and Bills

Explanatory Notes

Representative Over-the-Counter quotation based on transactions of $1 million or more. Treasury bond, note and bill quotes are as of mid-afternoon. Colons in bid-and-asked quotes represent 32nds; 101:01 means 101 1/32. Net changes in 32nds. n-Treasury note. i-Inflation-Indexed issue. Treasury bill quotes in hundredths, quoted on terms of a rate of discount. Days to maturity calculated from settlement date. All yields are to maturity and based on the asked quote. Latest 13-week and 26-week bits are boldfaced. For bonds callable prior to maturity, yields are computed to the earliest call date for issues quoted above par and to the maturity date for issues below par. *When issued.

U.S. Treasury strips as of 3 p.m. Eastern time, also based on transactions of $1 million or more. Colons in bid and asked quotes represent 32nds; 99:01 means 99 1/32. Net changes in 32nds. Yields calculated on the asked quotation, ci-stripped coupon interest, bp-Treasury bond, stripped principal, op-Treasury not, stripped principal. For bonds callable prior to maturity, yields are computed to the earliest call date for issues quoted above par and to the maturity date for issues below par.

U.S. Zero Coupons and Other Government Agencys Source: Bear Steams Pricing Direct Inc. via Street Software Technology, Inc. Treasury Bills, Notes and Bonds Source: BGCantor. TIPS Source; Reuters

US TREASURY BILLS

Maturity	Days to Mat.	Bid	Asked	Fri. Chg.	Ask Yld.
Jan 31 '08	3	2.00	1.99	−0.66	2.02
Feb 07 '08	10	1.93	1.92	−0.65	1.95
Feb 14 '08	17	1.91	1.90	−0.65	1.93
Feb 21 '08	24	2.05	2.04	−0.59	2.07
Feb 28 '08	31	2.11	2.10	−0.56	2.13
Mar 06 '08	38	2.09	2.08	−0.66	2.11
Mar 13 '08	45	2.06	2.05	−0.68	2.08
Mar 20 '08	52	2.10	2.09	−0.67	2.13
Mar 27 '08	59	2.10	2.09	−0.67	2.13
Apr 03 '08	66	2.12	2.11	−0.65	2.15
Apr 10 '08	73	2.16	2.15	−0.62	2.19
Apr 17 '08	80	2.18	2.17	−0.61	2.21
Apr 24 '08	87	2.20	2.19	−0.59	2.23
May 01 '08	94	2.24	2.23	−0.55	2.27
May 08 '08	101	2.21	2.20	−0.56	2.24
May 15 '08	108	2.26	2.25	−0.52	2.30
May 22 '08	115	2.26	2.25	−0.53	2.30
May 29 '08	122	2.26	2.25	−0.52	2.30
Jun 05 '08	129	2.29	2.28	−0.49	2.33
Jun 12 '08	136	2.35	2.34	−0.44	2.39
Jun 19 '08	143	2.35	2.34	−0.44	2.39
Jun 26 '08	150	2.31	2.30	−0.46	2.35
Jul 03 '08	157	2.34	2.33	−0.45	2.39
Jul 10 '08	164	2.34	2.33	−0.44	2.39
Jul 17 '08	171	2.34	2.33	−0.43	2.39
Jul 24 '08	178	2.33	2.32	n.a.	2.38

US NOTES AND BONDS

Rate	Mo/Yr	Bid	Asked	Fri. Chg.	Ask Yld.
4⅜	Jan 08n	100:00	100:00	−1	2.25
3	Feb 08n	100:00	100:01	+2	1.99
5½	Feb 08n	100:04	100:05	...	1.99
3⅜	Feb 08n	100:01	100:02	+2	1.99
4⅝	Feb 08n	100:05	100:06	+1	2.14
4⅝	Mar 08n	100:12	100:13	+4	2.11
4⅞	Apr 08n	100:20	100:21	+5	2.25
2⅝	May 08n	100:01	100:02	+4	2.31
3¾	May 08n	100:12	100:13	+7	2.25
5⅝	May 08n	100:30	100:31	+6	2.31
4⅞	May 08n	100:26	100:27	+5	2.34
5⅛	Jun 08n	101:03	101:04	+5	2.39
5	Jul 08n	101:09	101:10	+7	2.29
3¼	Aug 08n	100:14	100:15	+8	2.35
4⅛	Aug 08n	100:29	100:30	+7	2.29
4⅞	Aug 08n	101:14	101:15	+8	2.29
3⅛	Sep 08n	100:14	100:15	+9	2.35
4⅝	Sep 08n	101:15	101:16	+8	2.31
3⅛	Oct 08n	100:16	100:17	+9	2.35
4⅞	Oct 08n	101:27	101:28	+8	2.30
3⅜	Nov 08n	100:25	100:26	+8	2.31
4¾	Nov 08n	101:28	101:29	+8	2.31
4⅜	Nov 08n	101:18	101:19	+8	2.27
4⅝	Nov 08n	101:30	101:31	+8	2.17
3⅜	Dec 08n	100:30	100:31	+8	2.25
4¾	Dec 08n	102:07	102:08	+9	2.23
3¼	Jan 09n	100:29	100:30	+9	2.25
4⅞	Jan 09n	102:19	102:20	+8	2.18
4½	Feb 09n	102:10	102:11	+8	2.20
3	Feb 09n	100:24	100:25	+8	2.22
4¾	Feb 09n	102:21	102:22	+7	2.20
2⅝	Mar 09n	100:13	100:14	+8	2.21
4½	Mar 09n	102:20	102:21	+8	2.16
3⅛	Apr 09n	101:03	101:04	+7	2.14
4½	Apr 09n	102:26	102:27	+7	2.15
3⅞	May 09n	102:03	102:04	+8	2.17

US ZERO-COUPONS

Maturity	Type	Bid	Asked	Fri. Chg.	Ask Yld.
Feb 08	ci	99:29	99:29	+2	1.65
Feb 08	np	99:28	99:29	+3	2.10
Feb 08	np	99:28	99:29	+3	1.96
Feb 08	np	99:28	99:29	+2	1.91
May 08	ci	99:11	99:12	+6	2.16
May 08	bp	99:09	99:09	+6	2.41
May 08	np	99:09	99:09	+6	2.42
May 08	np	99:09	99:09	+6	2.42
Aug 08	ci	98:27	98:27	+4	2.12
Aug 08	np	98:24	98:24	+9	2.29
Aug 08	bp	98:23	98:24	+9	2.32
Nov 08	ci	98:06	98:07	+8	2.27
Nov 08	np	98:05	98:06	+10	2.32
Nov 08	np	98:07	98:07	+11	2.25
Nov 08	bp	98:05	98:06	+10	2.32
Feb 09	ci	97:26	97:27	+7	2.09
Feb 09	np	97:22	97:22	+8	2.24
Feb 09	np	97:21	97:22	+8	2.25
May 09	ci	97:10	97:10	+8	2.10
May 09	np	97:08	97:08	+9	2.16
May 09	np	97:07	97:08	+9	2.17
May 09	np	97:07	97:08	+9	2.17
Aug 09	ci	96:23	96:23	+9	2.16
Aug 09	np	96:22	96:22	+9	2.18
Aug 09	bp	96:21	96:22	+10	2.20
Aug 09	bp	96:22	96:23	+10	2.17
Nov 09	ci	96:07	96:08	+11	2.14
Nov 09	bp	96:05	96:06	+10	2.18
Nov 09	np	96:08	96:09	+10	2.12
Nov 09	np	96:08	96:09	+10	2.12
Feb 10	ci	95:20	95:21	+8	2.18
Feb 10	np	95:21	95:22	+10	2.17
Feb 10	np	95:21	95:22	+11	2.16
Feb 10	np	95:19	95:20	+10	2.20
May 10	ci	94:31	94:31	+11	2.26
May 10	np	95:05	95:05	+10	2.17
May 10	np	95:06	95:07	+9	2.14
Aug 10	ci	94:15	94:15	+12	2.24
Aug 10	np	94:17	94:18	+11	2.21
Aug 10	bp	94:17	94:17	+10	2.21

INFLATION-INDEXED TREASURY SECURITIES

Rate	Mat.	Bid/ Asked	Chg	*Yld	Accr. Prin.
3.875	01/09	103-15/17	.....	0.199	1280
4.250	01/10	107-24/26	.....	0.268	1248
0.875	04/10	100-30/00	.....	0.424	1108
3.500	01/11	108-29/31	.....	0.451	1206
2.375	04/11	105-21/23	.....	0.574	1058
3.375	01/12	110-25/27	.....	0.603	1182
2.000	04/12	105-16/18	.....	0.663	1034
3.000	07/12	110-07/09	.....	0.661	1168
1.875	07/13	105-15/17	.....	0.836	1143
2.000	01/14	106-03/05	.....	0.938	1136
2.000	07/14	106-01/03	.....	1.025	1114
1.625	01/15	103-14/16	.....	1.104	1099
1.875	07/15	105-03/05	.....	1.154	1079
2.000	01/16	105-29/01	.....	1.205	1058
2.500	07/16	110-03/07	.....	1.226	1039
2.375	01/17	109-03/07	.....	1.283	1041
2.625	07/17	111-16/20	.....	1.317	1013
2.375	01/25	109-08/12	.....	1.736	1114
2.000	01/26	103-27/31	.....	1.743	1058
2.375	01/27	110-06/10	.....	1.735	1041
3.625	04/28	131-25/29	.....	1.745	1298
3.875	04/29	137-19/23	.....	1.741	1277
3.375	04/32	133-31/03	.....	1.659	1183

*Yld to maturity on accrued principal.

accrued principal value of 1,298 and its yield to maturity is computed using this as the principal amount to be paid at maturity (obviously this will continue to increase until it matures).

Municipal Bond Quotes Exhibit 17.10 contains municipal bond quotes from *The Blue List of Current Municipal Offerings*. These are ordered according to states and then alphabetically within states. Each issue gives the amount of bonds being offered (in thousands of dollars), the name of the security, the purpose or description of the issue, the coupon rate, the maturity (which includes month, day, and year), the yield or price, and the dealer offering the bonds. Bond quote 1 is for $200,000 of Indiana State Office Building bonds. The letters MBIA indicate that the bonds are guaranteed by the Municipal Bond Insurance Association (MBIA). These are zero (0.000) coupon bonds due July 1, 2010. In this instance, the yield to maturity is given (5.60 percent). To determine the price, compute the discount value or look up in a yield book the price of a zero coupon bond, due in 2010 to yield 5.60 percent. The dealer offering the bonds is Bearster. A list in the back of the publication gives the name and phone number of the firm offering the bond.

The second bond is for $115,000 of Indiana State Toll Road bonds with a 9 percent coupon. These bonds have an M/S/F (mandatory sinking fund) that becomes effective in 2011, although the bond matures in 2015. The letters ETM mean that the sinking fund is put into escrow till maturity. The market yield on these bonds is 6.30 percent, which means the bond would be selling at a premium.

Bond quote 3 refers to $10,000 of Indianapolis, Indiana, Airport Authority revenue bonds that are backed by a contract with US Air. Although the bonds mature in 2009, they were callable beginning in 1997 (C97) at 102 of par. The coupon is 7.50 percent and, in this case, the price of the bond is listed (100), which means its market yield also is 7.50 percent. Such bonds are called *dollar bonds*.

Exhibit 17.10 Quotes for Municipals

INDIANA

	No. of Bonds Offered	Municipal Issuer	Special Characteristics	Coupon	Maturity	Price/ YTM	Broker
	45	INDIANA HEALTH FAC FING AUTH	P/R @ 102	7.750	08/15/20C00	5.25	EQUITSEC
	200	INDIANA PORT COMMN PORT REV		6.750	07/01/10	993/4	NOYESDAV
① →	200	INDIANA ST OFFICE BLDG COMMN	MBIA	0.000	07/01/10	5.60	BEARSTER
	335	INDIANA ST RECREATIONAL DEV		6.050	07/01/14	6.45	SMITHBCH
② →	115	INDIANA ST TOLL RD COMMN TOLL	M/S/F 11	9.000	01/01/15ETM	6.30	DRIZOS
	95	INDIANA ST TOLL RD COMMN TOLL		9.000	01/01/15ETM	6.30	EMMET
	1000	INDIANA ST TOLL RD COMMN TOLL	N/C S/F 11	9.000	01/01/15ETM	6.00	WILLIAMA
	100	FORT WAYNE IND HOSP AUTH HOSP	P/R @ 102	9.125	07/01/15C95	3.80	GABRIELE
③ →	10	INDIANAPOLIS IND ARPT AUTH REV (CA @ 102.01)	US AIR	7.500	07/01/09C97	100	HSH
	15	INDIANAPOLIS IND ARPT AUTH REV	US AIR	7.500	07/01/19	8.25	STERLING
	25	INDIANAPOLIS IND LOC PUB IMPT		6.750	02/01/20	100	COUGHLIN

Thursday May 28, 1994   PAGE 15.A

Source: *The Blue List of Current Municipal Offerings*, May 28, 1994, 15A. The Blue List Division of Standard & Poor's, New York. Reprinted with permission.

It is always necessary to call the dealer to determine the current yield/price because these quotes are at least one day old when they are published.

• • • • SUMMARY • • • •

- We considered the basic features of bonds: interest, principal, and maturity. Certain key relationships affect price behavior. Price is essentially a function of coupon, maturity, and prevailing market interest rates. Bond price volatility depends on coupon and maturity. As will be demonstrated in Chapter 18, bonds with longer maturities and/or lower coupons respond vigorously to a given change in market rates.
- Each bond has unique intrinsic characteristics and can be differentiated by type of issue and indenture provisions. Major benefits to bond investors include high returns for nominal risk, the potential for capital gains, certain tax advantages, and possibly additional returns from active trading of bonds. Aggressive bond investors must consider market liquidity, investment risks, and interest rate behavior. We considered high-yield (junk) bonds because of the growth in size and status of this segment of the bond market.
- The global bond market includes numerous countries. The non-U.S. markets have experienced strong relative growth, whereas the U.S. market constitutes a stable half of the world bond market. The four major bond markets (the United States, Japan, Euroland, and the United Kingdom)

have a different makeup in terms of the proportion of governments, agencies, municipals, corporates, and international issues. The various market sectors also are unique in terms of liquidity, yield spreads, tax implications, and operating features.
- To gauge default risk, most bond investors rely on agency ratings. For additional information on the bond market, prevailing economic conditions, and intrinsic bond features, individual and institutional investors rely on a host of readily available publications. Extensive up-to-date quotes are generally available on Treasury bonds and notes. In contrast, trading and price information for corporates has been relatively difficult to find, but this changed dramatically since 2004. Unfortunately, the information on municipals is still limited.
- The world bond market is large and is continuing to grow due to government deficits around the world and the need for capital by corporations. It is also very diverse in terms of country alternatives and issuers within countries. This chapter provides the fundamentals that will allow us to consider the valuation of individual bonds in Chapter 18 and the alternative bond portfolio techniques in Chapter 19.

• • • • SUGGESTED READINGS • • • •

Barnhill, Theodore M., William F. Maxwell, and Mark R. Shenkman, eds. *High-Yield Bonds.* New York: McGraw-Hill, 1999.

Fabozzi, Frank J., ed. *Advances and Innovations in the Bond and Mortgage Markets.* Chicago: Probus Publishing, 1989.

Fabozzi, Frank J., ed. *The Handbook of Fixed-Income Securities,* 7th ed. New York: McGraw-Hill, 2005.

Norton, Joseph, and Paul Spellman, eds. *Asset Securitization.* Cambridge, MA: Basil Blackwell, Inc., 1991.

Sundaresan, Suresh. *Fixed-Income Markets and Their Derivatives,* 2nd ed. Cincinnati: South-Western, 2002.

Van Horne, James C. *Financial Market Rates and Flows,* 6th ed. Englewood Cliffs, NJ: Prentice Hall, 2001.

Wilson, Richard S., and Frank J. Fabozzi. *The New Corporate Bond Market.* Chicago: Probus Publishing, 1990.

• • • • QUESTIONS • • • •

1. Explain the difference between calling a bond and a bond refunding.
2. Identify the three most important determinants of the price of a bond. Describe the effect of each.
3. Given a change in the level of interest rates, discuss how two major factors will influence the relative change in price for individual bonds.
4. Briefly describe two indenture provisions that can affect the maturity of a bond.
5. Explain the differences in taxation of income from municipal bonds, from U.S. Treasury bonds, and from corporate bonds.
6. For several institutional participants in the bond market, explain what type of bond each is likely to purchase and why.

7. Why should investors be aware of the trading volume for bonds in their portfolio?
8. What is the purpose of bond ratings?
9. Based on the data in Exhibit 17.1, which was the fastest-growing bond market in the world? Which markets were losing market share?
10. Based on the data in Exhibit 17.2, discuss the makeup of the Japanese bond market and how and why it differs from the U.S. market.
11. Discuss the positives and negatives of investing in a government agency issue rather than a straight Treasury bond.
12. Discuss the difference between a foreign bond (e.g., a Samurai) and a Eurobond (e.g., a Euroyen issue).

13. **CFA EXAMINATION LEVEL I** List *three* differences between Eurodollar and Yankee bonds.

• • • • PROBLEMS • • • •

1. An investor in the 28 percent tax bracket is trying to decide which of two bonds to purchase. One is a corporate bond carrying an 8 percent coupon and selling at par. The other is a municipal bond with a 5½ percent coupon, and it, too, sells at par. Assuming all other relevant factors are equal, which bond should the investor select?
2. What would be the initial offering price for the following (assume semiannual compounding):
   a. A 15-year zero coupon bond with a yield to maturity (YTM) of 12 percent.
   b. A 20-year zero coupon bond with a YTM of 10 percent.
3. An 8.4 percent coupon bond issued by the state of Indiana sells for $1,000. What coupon rate on a corporate bond selling at its $1,000 par value would produce the same after-tax return to the investor as the municipal bond if the investor is in
   a. the 15 percent marginal tax bracket?
   b. the 25 percent marginal tax bracket?
   c. the 35 percent marginal tax bracket?
4. The Shamrock Corporation has just issued a $1,000 par value zero coupon bond with an 8 percent yield to maturity, due to mature 15 years from today (assume semiannual compounding).
   a. What is the market price of the bond?
   b. If interest rates remain constant, what will be the price of the bond in three years?
   c. If interest rates rise to 10 percent, what will be the price of the bond in three years?
5. Complete the information requested for each of the following $1,000 face value, zero coupon bonds, assuming semiannual compounding.

Bond	Maturity (Years)	Yield (Percent)	Price ($)
A	20	12	?
B	?	8	601
C	9	?	350

CHAPTER 18
The Analysis and Valuation of Bonds

After you read this chapter, you should be able to answer the following questions:

- How do you determine the value of a bond based on the present value formula?
- What are the alternative bond yields that are important to investors?
- How do you compute the following yields on bonds: current yield, yield to maturity, yield to call, and compound realized (horizon) yield?
- What are spot rates and forward rates and how do you calculate these rates from a yield to maturity curve?
- What are the spot rate yield curve and the forward rate curve?
- How and why do you use the spot rate curve to determine the value of a bond?
- What are the alternative theories that attempt to explain the shape of the term structure of interest rates?
- What factors affect the level of bond yields at a point in time?
- What economic forces cause changes in bond yields over time?
- When yields change, what characteristics of a bond cause differential percentage price changes for individual bonds?
- What is meant by the duration of a bond, how do you compute it, and what factors affect it?
- What is modified duration and what is the relationship between a bond's modified duration and its price volatility?
- What is the convexity for a bond, how do you compute it, and what factors affect it?
- Under what conditions is it necessary to consider both modified duration and convexity when estimating a bond's price volatility?
- What happens to the duration and convexity of bonds that have embedded call options?
- What are effective duration and effective convexity and when are they useful?
- What is empirical duration and how is it used with common stocks and other assets?
- What are the static yield spread and the option-adjusted spread?

In this chapter, we apply the valuation principles that were introduced in Chapter 11 to the valuation of bonds. This chapter is concerned with how one goes about finding the value of bonds using the traditional single yield to maturity rate and using multiple spot rates. We will also come to understand the several measures of yields for bonds. It is important to understand why these bond values and yields change over time. To do this, we begin with a review of value estimation for bonds using the present value model introduced in Chapter 11. This background on valuation allows us to understand and compute the expected rates of return on bonds.

After mastering the measurement of bond yields, we consider what factors influence the level of bond yields and what economic forces cause changes in yields over time. Next, we consider the different shapes of the yield curve and the alternative theories that explain changes in its shape. We discuss the effects of various characteristics and indenture provisions that affect the required returns and, therefore, the value of specific bond issues. This includes such factors as time to maturity, coupon, callability, and sinking funds.

We return to bond valuation and acknowledge that, when yields change, all bond prices do not change in the same way. An understanding of what factors affect price changes for bonds is important because the price volatility of bonds has increased substantially. Before 1950, bonds yields were relatively low and both yields and prices were stable so bonds were considered very safe investments and most investors held them to maturity. During the last several decades, however, the level of interest rates has increased substantially because of inflation, and interest rates have become more volatile because of changes in the rate of inflation and in monetary policy. As a result, bond prices and rates of return on bonds have become more volatile and the rates of return on bond investments have increased. Although this increase in interest rate volatility has affected all bonds, we discuss why the impact is more significant on bonds with embedded options, such as call features.

18.1 The Fundamentals of Bond Valuation

The value of bonds can be described in terms of dollar values or the rates of return they promise under some set of assumptions. In this section, we describe both the present value model, which computes a specific value for the bond using a single discount value, and the yield model, which computes the promised rate of return based on the bond's current price and a set of assumptions.

18.1.1 The Present Value Model

In Chapter 11, we saw that the value of a bond (or any asset) equals the present value of its expected cash flows. The cash flows from a bond are the periodic interest payments to the bondholder and the repayment of principal at maturity. Therefore, the value of a bond is the present value of the semiannual interest payments plus the present value of the principal payment. Notably, the standard technique is to use a single interest rate discount factor, which is the required rate of return on the bond. We can express this in the following present value formula that assumes semiannual compounding.[1]

18.1
$$P_m = \sum_{t=1}^{2n} \frac{C_i/2}{(1 + i/2)^t} + \frac{P_p}{(1 + i/2)^{2n}}$$

where:

P_m = the current market price of the bond
 n = the number of years to maturity
 C_i = the annual coupon payment for Bond i
 i = the prevailing yield to maturity for this bond issue
 P_p = the par value of the bond

The value computed indicates what an investor would be willing to pay for this bond to realize a rate of return that takes into account expectations regarding the *RFR*, the expected rate of inflation, and the risk of the bond. The standard valuation technique assumes holding the bond to its maturity. In this case, the number of periods would be the number of years to the maturity of the bond (referred to as its *term to maturity*) and the cash flows include all the periodic interest payments and the payment of the bond's par value at maturity.

We can demonstrate this formula using an 8 percent coupon bond that matures in 20 years with a par value of $1,000. Therefore, an investor who holds this bond to maturity will receive $40 every 6 months (one half of the $80 coupon) for 20 years (40 periods) and $1,000 at the

---

[1] Almost all U.S. bonds pay interest semiannually, so it is appropriate to use semiannual compounding wherein you cut the annual coupon rate in half and double the number of periods. To be consistent, you should also use semiannual compounding when discounting the principal payment of a coupon bond or even a zero coupon bond. All our present value calculations assume semiannual compounding.

maturity of the bond in 20 years. If we assume a yield to maturity for this bond of 10 percent (the market's required rate of return on the bond), the bond's value using Equation 18.1 would be:

$$P_m = \sum_{t=1}^{40} \frac{80/2}{(1 + .10/2)^t} + \frac{\$1,000}{(1 + .10/2)^{40}}$$

The first term is the present value of an annuity of $40 every 6 months for 40 periods at 5 percent, while the second term is the present value of $1,000 to be received in 40 periods at 5 percent. This can be summarized as follows:

Present value of interest payments $40 × 17.1591	=	$686.36
Present value of principal payment $1,000 × 0.1420	=	142.00
Total value of bond at 10%		$828.36

As expected, the bond will be priced at a discount to its par value because the market's required rate of return of 10 percent is greater than the bond's coupon rate, that is $828.36 or 82.836 percent of par.

Alternatively, if the market's required rate was 6 percent, the value would be computed as the present value of the annuity at 3 percent for 40 periods and the present value of the principal at 3 percent for 40 periods as follows:

Present value of interest payments $40 × 23.1148	=	$ 924.59
Present value of principal payment $1,000 × 0.3066	=	306.60
Total value of bond at 6%		$1,231.19

Because the bond's discount rate is lower than its coupon, the bond would sell at a premium above par value—that is, $1,231.19 or 123.119 of par.

The Price-Yield Curve When you know the basic characteristics of a bond in terms of its coupon, maturity, and par value, the only factor that determines its value (price) is the market discount rate—its required rate of return. As shown, as we increase the required rate, the price declines. We can demonstrate the specific relationship between the price of a bond and its yield by computing the bond's price at a range of yields as shown in Exhibit 18.1.

A graph of this relationship is shown in Exhibit 18.2. Besides demonstrating that price moves inverse to yield, the graph shows three other important points:

1. When the yield is below the coupon rate, the bond will be priced at a **premium** to its par value.
2. When the yield is above the coupon rate, the bond will be priced at a **discount** to its par value.
3. The price-yield relationship is not a straight line; rather, it is *convex*. As yields decline, the price increases at an increasing rate; and, as the yield increases, the price declines at a declining rate. This concept of a convex price-yield curve is referred to as *convexity* and will be discussed further in a later section.

Exhibit 18.1 Price-Yield Relationship for a 20-Year, 8 Percent Coupon Bond ($1,000 Par Value)

Required Yield	Price of Bond
2	$1,985.09
4	1,547.12
6	1,231.19
8	1,000.00
10	828.36
12	699.05
14	600.07
16	522.98

Exhibit 18.2 The Price-Yield Curve for a 20-Year, 8 Percent Coupon Bond

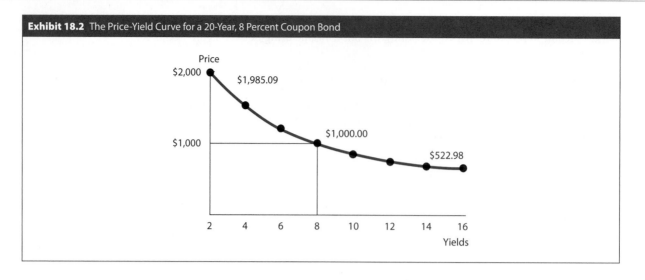

18.1.2 The Yield Model

Instead of determining the value of a bond in dollar terms, investors often price bonds in terms of **yields**—the promised rates of return on bonds under certain assumptions. Thus far, we have used cash flows and our required rate of return to compute an estimated value for the bond. To compute an expected yield, we use the current market price (P_m) and the expected cash flows to *compute the expected yield on the bond.* We can express this approach using the same present value model. The difference is that in Equation 18.1, it was assumed that we knew the appropriate discount rate (the required rate of return), and we computed the estimated value (price) of the bond. In this case, we still use Equation 18.1, but it is assumed that we know the price of the bond and we compute the discount rate (yield) that will give us the current market price (P_m).

$$P_m = \sum_{t=1}^{2n} \frac{C_i/2}{(1 + i/2)^t} + \frac{P_p}{(1 + i/2)^{2n}}$$

where the variables are the same as previously, except

> i = the discount rate that will discount the expected cash flows to equal the current market price of the bond

This i value gives the expected ("promised") yield of the bond under various assumptions to be noted, assuming you pay the price P_m. In the next section, we will discuss several types of bond yields that arise from the assumptions of the valuation model.

Approaching the investment decision stating the bond's value as a yield figure rather than a dollar amount, you consider the relationship of the computed bond yield to your required rate of return on this bond. If the computed promised bond yield is equal to or greater than your required rate of return, you should buy the bond; if the computed promised yield is less than your required rate of return, you should not buy the bond.

These approaches to pricing bonds and making investment decisions are similar to the two alternative approaches by which firms make investment decisions. We referred to one approach, the **net present value (NPV)** method, in Chapter 11. With the NPV approach, you compute the present value of the net cash flows from the proposed investment at your cost of capital and subtract the present value cost of the investment to get the net present value (NPV) of the project. If this NPV is positive, you consider accepting the investment; if it is negative, you reject it. This is basically the way we compared the intrinsic value of an equity investment to its market price.

The second approach is to compute the **internal rate of return (IRR)** on a proposed investment project. The IRR is the discount rate that equates the present value of cash outflows for an investment with the present value of its cash inflows. You compare this discount rate, or IRR (which is also the estimated rate of return on the project), to your cost of capital, and accept any investment proposal with an IRR equal to or greater than your cost of capital. We do the same thing when we price bonds on the basis of yield. If the estimated (promised) yield on the bond (yield to maturity, yield to call, or horizon yield) is equal to or exceeds your required rate of return on the bond, you should invest in it; if the estimated yield is less than your required rate of return on the bond, you should not invest in it.

18.2 Computing Bond Yields

Bond investors traditionally have used five yield measures for the following purposes:

Yield Measure	Purpose
Nominal yield	Measures the coupon rate.
Current yield	Measures the current income rate.
Promised yield to maturity	Measures the estimated rate of return for bond held to maturity.
Promised yield to call	Measures the estimated rate of return for bond held to first call date.
Realized (horizon) yield	Measures the estimated rate of return for a bond likely to be sold prior to maturity. It considers specific reinvestment assumptions and an estimated sales price. It also can measure the actual rate of return on a bond during some past period of time.

Nominal and current yields are mainly descriptive and contribute little to investment decision making. The last three yields are derived from the present value model described previously.

To measure an estimated realized yield (also referred to as the horizon yield or total return), a bond investor must estimate a bond's future selling price. Following our presentation of bond yields, we present the procedure for finding these prices. We conclude with a demonstration of valuing bonds using spot rates, which is becoming more prevalent.

18.2.1 Nominal Yield

Nominal yield is the coupon rate of a particular issue. A bond with an 8 percent coupon has an 8 percent nominal yield. This provides a convenient way of describing the coupon characteristics of an issue.

18.2.2 Current Yield

Current yield is to bonds what dividend yield is to stocks. It is computed as

18.2
$$CY = C_i / P_m$$

where:

CY = the current yield on a bond
C_i = the annual coupon payment of Bond i
P_m = the current market price of the bond

Because this yield measures the current income from the bond as a percentage of its price, it is important to income-oriented investors (e.g., retirees) who want current cash flow from their investment portfolios. Current yield has little use for investors who are interested in total return because it excludes the important capital gain or loss component.

18.2.3 Promised Yield to Maturity

Promised yield to maturity is the most widely used bond yield figure because it indicates the fully compounded rate of return promised to an investor who buys the bond at prevailing prices, *if two assumptions hold true.* Specifically, the *promised* yield to maturity will be equal to the investor's *realized* yield *if* these assumptions are met. The first assumption is that the investor holds the bond to maturity. This assumption gives this value its shortened name, *yield to maturity* (YTM). The second assumption is implicit in the present value method of computation. Referring to Equation 18.1, recall that it related the current market price of the bond to the present value of all cash flows as follows:

$$P_m = \sum_{t=1}^{2n} \frac{C_i/2}{(1 + i/2)^t} + \frac{P_p}{(1 + i/2)^{2n}}$$

To compute the YTM for a bond, we solve for the rate *i* that will equate the current price (P_m) to all cash flows from the bond to maturity. As noted, this resembles the computation of the internal rate of return (IRR) on an investment project. Because it is a present value–based computation, it implies a reinvestment rate assumption because it discounts the cash flows. That is, the equation assumes that *all interim cash flows (interest payments) are reinvested at the computed YTM.* This is referred to as a *promised* YTM because the bond will provide this computed YTM *only if* you meet its conditions:

1. You hold the bond to maturity.
2. You reinvest all the interim cash flows at the computed YTM rate.

If a bond promises an 8 percent YTM, you must reinvest coupon income at 8 percent to realize that promised return. If you spend (do not reinvest) the coupon payments or if you cannot find opportunities to reinvest these coupon payments at rates as high as its promised YTM, then the actual realized yield you earn will be less than the promised yield to maturity. As will be demonstrated in the section on realized return, if you can reinvest cash flows at rates above the YTM, your realized (horizon) return will be greater than the promised YTM. The income earned on this reinvestment of the interim interest payments is referred to as **interest-on-interest,** and is discussed in detail in Homer and Leibowitz (1972, Chapter 1).

The impact of the reinvestment assumption (i.e., the interest-on-interest earnings) on the actual return from a bond varies directly with the bond's coupon and maturity. A higher coupon and/or a longer term to maturity will increase the loss in value from failure to reinvest the coupon cash flow at the YTM. Put another way, a higher coupon or a longer maturity makes the reinvestment assumption more important—i.e., such bonds have greater reinvestment risk.

Exhibit 18.3 illustrates the impact of interest-on-interest for an 8 percent, 25-year bond bought at par to yield 8 percent. If you invested $1,000 today at 8 percent for 25 years and reinvested all the coupon payments at 8 percent, you would have approximately $7,100 at the end of 25 years. We will refer to this money that you have at the end of your investment horizon as your **ending-wealth value**. To prove that you would have an ending-wealth value of $7,100, look up the compound interest factor for 8 percent for 25 years (6.8493) or 4 percent for 50 periods (which assumes semiannual compounding and is 7.1073). In the case of U.S. bonds, the semiannual compounding is the appropriate procedure because almost all U.S. bonds pay interest every six months.

Exhibit 18.3 shows that this $7,100 is made up of $1,000 principal return, $2,000 of coupon payments over the 25 years ($80 a year for 25 years), and $4,100 in interest earned on the semiannual coupon payments reinvested at 4 percent semiannually. If you never reinvested any of the coupon payments, you would have an ending-wealth value of only $3,000. This ending-wealth value of $3,000 derived from the beginning investment of $1,000 gives you an actual (realized) yield to maturity of only 4.5 percent. That is, the rate that will discount $3,000 back

Exhibit 18.3 The Effect of Interest-on-Interest on Total Realized Return

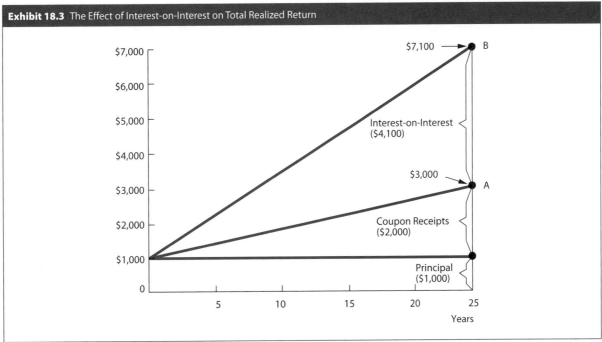

Promised yield at time of purchase: 8.00%

Realized yield over the 25-year investment horizon with no coupon reinvestment (A): 4.50%

Realized yield over the 25-year horizon with coupons reinvested at 8% (B): 8.00%

to $1,000 in 25 years is 4.5 percent. Reinvesting the coupon payments at some rate between 0 and 8 percent would cause your ending-wealth position to be above $3,000 and below $7,100; therefore, your actual realized rate of return would be somewhere between 4.5 percent and 8 percent. Alternatively, if you managed to reinvest the coupon payments at rates consistently above 8 percent, your ending-wealth position would be above $7,100, and your realized (horizon) rate of return would be above 8 percent.

Interestingly, during periods of very high interest rates, you often hear investors talk about "locking in" high yields. These people are subject to **yield illusion** because they do not realize that attaining the high *promised* yield requires that they reinvest all the coupon payments at the very high *promised* yields. For example, if you buy a 20-year bond with a promised yield to maturity of 15 percent, you will actually realize the promised 15 percent yield *only* if you are able to reinvest all the coupon payments at 15 percent over the next 20 years.

Computing the Promised Yield to Maturity   The promised yield to maturity can be computed by using the present value model with semiannual compounding. The present value model gives the investor an accurate result and is the technique used by investment professionals.

The present value model equation—Equation 18.1—shows the promised yield valuation model:

$$P_m = \sum_{t=1}^{2n} \frac{C_i/2}{(1 + i/2)^t} + \frac{P_p}{(1 + i/2)^{2n}}$$

All variables are as described previously. This model is somewhat complex because the solution requires iteration. As noted, the present value equation is a variation of the internal rate of return (IRR) calculation where we want to find the discount rate, i, that will equate the present value of the cash flows to the market price of the bond (P_m). Using the prior example of an

8 percent, 20-year bond, priced at $900, the equation gives us a semiannual promised yield to maturity of 4.545 percent, which implies an annual promised YTM of 9.09 percent.[2]

$$900 = 40 \sum_{t=1}^{40} \left(\frac{1}{(1.04545)^t} \right) + 1000 \left(\frac{1}{(1.04545)^{40}} \right)$$

$$= 40(18.2574) + 1,000(0.1702)$$

$$= 900$$

The values for $1/(1 + i)$ were taken from the present value interest factor tables in the appendix at the back of the book using interpolation. Fortunately, there are several handheld calculators that will do these calculations for you.

YTM for a Zero Coupon Bond In several instances, we have discussed the existence of zero coupon bonds that only have the one cash inflow at maturity. This single cash flow means that the calculation of YTM is substantially easier as shown by the following example.

Assume a zero coupon bond maturing in 10 years with a maturity value of $1,000 selling for $311.80. Because you are dealing with a zero coupon bond, there is only the one cash flow from the principal payment at maturity. Therefore, you simply need to determine what the discount rate is that will discount $1,000 to equal the current market price of $311.80 in 20 periods (10 years of semiannual payments). The equation is as follows:

$$\$311.80 = \frac{\$1,000}{(1 + i/2)^{20}}$$

You will see that $i = 6$ percent, which implies an annual rate of 12 percent. For future reference, this yield also is referred to as the 10-year spot rate, which is the discount rate for a single cash flow to be received in 10 years.

18.2.4 Promised Yield to Call

Although investors use promised YTM to value most bonds, they must estimate the return on certain callable bonds with a different measure—the **promised yield to call (YTC)**. Whenever a bond with a call feature is selling for a price above par (that is, at a premium) equal to or greater than its call price, a bond investor should consider valuing the bond in terms of YTC rather than YTM. This is because the marketplace uses the lowest, most conservative yield measure in pricing a bond. As discussed in Homer and Leibowitz (1972, Chapter 4), when bonds are trading at or above a specified **crossover price**, which is approximately the bond's call price plus a small premium that increases with time to call, the yield to call will provide the lowest yield measure. The crossover price is important because at this price the YTM and the YTC are equal—this is the *crossover yield*. When the bond rises to this price above par, the computed YTM becomes low enough that it would be profitable for the issuer to call the bond and finance the call by selling a new bond at this prevailing market interest rate.[3] Therefore, the YTC measures the promised rate of return the investor will receive from holding this bond until it is retired at the first available call date, that is, at the end of the deferred call period. Note that if an issue has multiple call dates at different prices (the call price will decline for later call dates), it will be necessary to compute which of these scenarios provides the *lowest* yield—this is referred to as computing **yield to worst**. Investors must consider computing the YTC for their bonds after a period when

---

[2] You will recall from your corporate finance course that you start with one rate (e.g., 9 percent or 4.5 percent semiannual) and compute the value of the stream. In this example, the value would exceed $900, so you would select a higher rate until you had a present value for the stream of cash flows of less than $900. Given the discount rates above and below the true rate, you would do further calculations or interpolate between the two rates to arrive at the correct discount rate that would give you a value of $900.

[3] An extensive literature on the refunding of bond issues includes studies by Boyce and Kalotay (1979), Harris (1980), Kalotay (1982a), and Finnerty (1983).

numerous high-yielding, high-coupon bonds have been issued. Following such a period, interest rates will decline, bond prices will rise, and the high-coupon bonds will subsequently have a high probability of being called—that is, their yields will fall below the crossover yield.

Computing Promised Yield to Call   Again, the present value method assumes that you hold the bond until the first call date and that you reinvest all coupon payments at the YTC rate.

Yield to call is calculated using a variation of Equation 18.1. To compute the YTC by the present value method, we would adjust the semiannual present value equation to give

18.3
$$P_m = \sum_{t=1}^{2nc} \frac{C_i/2}{(1 + i/2)^t} + \frac{P_c}{(1 + i/2)^{2nc}}$$

where:

P_m = the current market price of the bond
C_i = the annual coupon payment of Bond i
nc = the number of years to first call date
P_c = the call price of the bond

Following the present value method, we solve for i, which typically requires several computations or interpolations to get the exact yield. As before, this is a promised yield that requires the two assumptions noted earlier except that rather than holding to maturity, it is assumed that you hold until the first call date.

18.2.5 Realized (Horizon) Yield

The final measure of bond yield, **realized yield** or **horizon yield** (i.e., the actual return over a horizon period) measures the expected rate of return of a bond that you anticipate selling prior to its maturity. In terms of the equation, the investor has a holding period *(hp)* or investment horizon that is less than n. Realized (horizon) yield can be used to estimate rates of return attainable from various trading strategies. Although it is a very useful measure, it requires several additional estimates not required by the other yield measures. The investor must estimate the expected future selling price of the bond at the end of the holding period. This measure also requires a specific estimate of the reinvestment rate for the coupon flows prior to selling the bond. This technique also can be used by investors to measure their actual yields after selling bonds.

Computing Realized (Horizon) Yield   The realized yields over a horizon holding period are variations on the promised yield equations. The substitution of P_f (future selling price) and *hp* into the present value model (Equation 18.1) provides the following realized yield model:

18.4
$$P_m = \sum_{t=1}^{2hp} \frac{C_i/2}{(1 + i/2)^t} + \frac{P_f}{(1 + i/2)^{2hp}}$$

Again, this present value model requires you to solve for the i that equates the expected cash flows from coupon payments and the estimated selling price to the current market price.

You will note from the present value realized yield formula in Equation 18.4 that the coupon flows are implicitly discounted at the computed realized (horizon) yield. In many cases, this is an inappropriate assumption because available market rates might be very different from the computed realized (horizon) yield. Therefore, to derive a realistic estimate of the estimated realized yield, you also need to *estimate your expected reinvestment rate during the investment horizon.* We will demonstrate this in a subsequent subsection.

Therefore, to complete your understanding of computing estimated realized yield for alternative investment strategies, the next section considers the calculation of future bond prices. This is followed by a section on calculating a realized (horizon) return with different reinvestment rates.

18.3 Calculating Future Bond Prices

Dollar bond prices need to be calculated in two instances: (1) when computing realized (horizon) yield, you must determine the future selling price (P_f) of a bond if it is to be sold before maturity or first call, and (2) when issues are quoted on a promised yield basis, as with municipals. You can easily convert a yield-based quote to a dollar price by using Equation 18.1, which does not require iteration. (You need only solve for P_m.) The coupon (C_i) is given, as is par value (P_p) and the promised YTM, which is used as the discount rate.

Consider a 10 percent, 25-year bond with a promised YTM of 12 percent. You would compute the price of this issue as

$$P_m = 100/2 \sum_{t=1}^{50} \frac{1}{\left(1 + \frac{0.120}{2}\right)^t} + 1,000 \; \frac{1}{\left(1 + \frac{0.120}{2}\right)^{50}}$$

$$= 50(15.7619) + 1,000(0.0543)$$

$$= \$842.40$$

In this instance, we are determining the prevailing market price of the bond based on the current market YTM. These market yields indicate the consensus of all investors regarding the value of this bond. An investor with a required rate of return on this bond that differs from the market YTM would estimate a different value for the bond.

In contrast to the current market price, you will need to compute a future price (P_f) when estimating the expected realized (horizon) yield performance of alternative bonds. Investors or portfolio managers who consistently trade bonds for capital gains need to compute expected realized (horizon) yield rather than promised yield. They would compute P_f through the following variation of the realized yield equation:

18.5
$$P_f = \sum_{t=1}^{2n-2hp} \frac{C_i/2}{(1 + i/2)^t} + \frac{P_p}{(1 + i/2)^{2n-2hp}}$$

where:

P_f = the future selling price of the bond
P_p = the par value of the bond
n = the number of years to maturity
h_p = the holding period of the bond (in years)
C_i = the annual coupon payment of Bond i
i = the expected market YTM at the end of the holding period

This equation is a version of the present value model that is used to calculate the expected price of the bond at the end of the holding period *(hp)*. The term $2n - 2hp$ equals the bond's remaining term to maturity at the end of the investor's holding period, that is, the number of six-month periods remaining after the bond is sold. Therefore, the determination of P_f is based on four variables: two that are known and two that must be estimated by the investor.

Specifically, the coupon (C_i) and the par value (P_p) are given. The investor must forecast the length of the holding period and, therefore, the number of years remaining to maturity at the time the bond is sold $(n - hp)$. The investor also must forecast the expected market YTM at the time of sale *(i)*. With this information, you can calculate the future price of the bond. The real difficulty (and the potential source of error) in estimating P_f lies in predicting *hp* and *i*.

Assume you bought the 10 percent, 25-year bond just discussed at $842, giving it a promised YTM of 12 percent. Based on an analysis of the economy and the capital market, you expect this bond's market YTM to decline to 8 percent in 5 years. Therefore, you want to compute its future price (P_f) at the end of Year 5 to estimate your expected rate of return, assuming you are correct in your assessment of the decline in overall market interest rates. As noted, you estimate the holding period (5 years), which implies a remaining life of 20 years, and the estimated future market YTM of 8 percent. Using Equation 18.5 gives a future price:

$$P_f = 50 \sum_{t=1}^{40} \frac{1}{(1.04)^t} + 1{,}000\frac{1}{(1.04)^{40}}$$

$$= 50(19.7928) + 1{,}000(0.2083)$$

$$= 989.64 + 208.30$$

$$= \$1{,}197.94$$

18.3.1 Realized (Horizon) Yield with Differential Reinvestment Rates

The realized yield equation—Equation 18.4—is the standard present value formula with the changes in holding period and ending price. As such, it includes the implicit reinvestment rate assumption that all cash flows are reinvested at the computed i rate. There may be instances where such an implicit assumption is not appropriate, given your expectations for future interest rates. Assume that current market interest rates are very high and you invest in a long-term bond (e.g., a 20-year, 14 percent coupon) to take advantage of an expected decline in rates from 14 percent to 10 percent over a 2-year period. Computing the future price of a 19 percent 18-year bond yielding 10 percent (equal to $1,330.95) and using the realized yield equation to estimate the realized (horizon) yield, we will get the following fairly high realized rate of return:

$$P_m = \$1{,}000$$

$$hp = 2 \text{ Years}$$

$$P_f = \sum_{t=1}^{36} 70/(1 + 0.05)^t + \$1{,}000/(1.05)^{36}$$

$$= \$1{,}158.30 + \$172.65$$

$$= \$1{,}330.95$$

$$\$1{,}000 = \sum_{t=1}^{4} \frac{70}{(1 + i/2)^t} + \frac{1{,}330.95}{(1 + i/2)^4}$$

$$i = 27.5\%$$

As noted, this calculation assumes that all cash flows are reinvested at the computed i (27.5 percent). However, it is unlikely that during a period when market rates are going from 14 percent to 10 percent, you could reinvest the coupon at 27.5 percent. It is more appropriate and realistic to *explicitly estimate the reinvestment rates* and calculate the realized yields based on your *ending-wealth position*. This procedure is more precise and realistic, and it is easier because it does not require iteration.

The basic technique calculates the value of all cash flows at the end of the holding period, which is the investor's ending-wealth value. We compare this ending-wealth value to our *beginning-wealth value* to determine the *compound rate of return that equalizes these two values*. Adding to our prior example, assume we have the following cash flows:

$$P_m = \$1{,}000$$
$$i = \text{interest payments of } \$70 \text{ in 6, 12, 18, and 24 months}$$
$$P_f = \$1{,}330.95 \text{ (the ending market value of the bond)}$$

The ending value of the four interest payments is determined by our assumptions regarding specific reinvestment rates. Assume each payment is reinvested at a different declining rate that holds for its time period (that is, the first three interest payments are reinvested at progressively lower rates and the fourth interest payment is received at the end of the holding period).

$$
\begin{array}{llll}
i_1 \text{ at } 13\% \text{ for 18 months} & = \$70 \times (1 + 0.065)^3 & = \$ & 84.55 \\
i_2 \text{ at } 12\% \text{ for 12 months} & = \$70 \times (1 + 0.06)^2 & = & 78.65 \\
i_3 \text{ at } 11\% \text{ for 6 months} & = \$70 \times (1 + 0.055) & = & 73.85 \\
i_4 \text{ not reinvested} & = \$70 \times (1.0) & = & 70.00 \\
& \text{Future value of interest payments} & = & \overline{\$307.05}
\end{array}
$$

Therefore, our total ending-wealth value is

$$\$1,330.95 + \$307.05 = \$1,638.00$$

The compound realized (horizon) rate of return is calculated by comparing our ending-wealth value ($1,638) to our beginning-wealth value ($1,000) and determining what interest rate would equalize these two values over a two-year holding period. To find this, compute the ratio of ending wealth to beginning wealth (1.638). Find this ratio in a compound value table for four periods (assuming semiannual compounding). Table C.3 at the end of the book indicates that the realized rate is somewhere between 12 percent (1.5735) and 14 percent (1.6890). Interpolation gives an estimated semiannual rate of 13.16 percent, which indicates an annual rate of 26.32 percent. Using a calculator or computer, it is equal to $(1.638)^{1/4} - 1$. This compares to an estimate of 27.5 percent when we assume an implicit reinvestment rate of 27.5 percent.

This realized (horizon) yield computation specifically states the expected reinvestment rates as contrasted to assuming the reinvestment rate is equal to the computed realized yield. The actual assumption regarding the reinvestment rate can be very important.

The steps to calculate an expected realized (horizon) yield can be summarized as follows:

1. Calculate the future value at the horizon date of all coupon payments reinvested at estimated rates.
2. Calculate the expected sales price of the bond at your expected horizon date based on your estimate of the required yield to maturity at the horizon date.
3. Sum the values in Steps 1 and 2 to arrive at the total ending-wealth value.
4. Calculate the ratio of the ending-wealth value to the beginning value (the purchase price of the bond). Given this ratio and the time horizon, compute the compound rate of interest that will grow to this ratio over this time horizon.

$$\left[\frac{\text{Ending-wealth value}}{\text{Beginning value}} \right]^{\frac{1}{2n}} - 1$$

5. If all calculations assume semiannual compounding, double the interest rate derived from Step 4.

18.3.2 Price and Yield Determination on Noninterest Dates

So far, we have assumed that the investor buys (or sells) a bond precisely on the date that interest is due, so the measures are accurate only when the issues are traded on coupon payment dates.

However, when the semiannual model is used, and when more accuracy is necessary, another version of the price and yield model must be used for transactions on noninterest payment dates. Fortunately, the basic models need be extended only one more step because the value of an issue that trades X years, Y months, and so many days from maturity is found by extrapolating the bond value (price or yield) for the month before and the month after the day of transaction. Thus, the valuation process involves full months to maturity rather than years or semiannual periods.[4]

Accrued Interest   Having computed a value for the bond at a noninterest payment date, it is also necessary to consider the notion of *accrued interest*. Because the interest payment on a bond, which is paid every six months, is a contractual promise by the issuer, the bond investor has the right to receive a portion of the semiannual interest payment if he/she held the bond for some part of the six-month period. For example, assume an 8 percent, $1,000 par value bond that pays $40 every six months. If you sold the bond two months after the prior interest payment, you have held it for one-third of the six-month period and would have the right to one-third of the $40 ($13.33). This is referred to as the accrued interest on the bond. Therefore, when you sell the bond, there is a calculation of the bond's remaining value until maturity, that is, its price. What you receive is this price *plus* the accrued interest ($13.33).

18.3.3 Yield Adjustments for Tax-Exempt Bonds

Municipal bonds, Treasury issues, and many agency obligations possess one common characteristic: Their interest income is partially or fully tax-exempt. This tax-exempt status affects the valuation of taxable versus nontaxable bonds. Although you could adjust each present value equation for the tax effects, it is not necessary for our purposes. We can envision the approximate impact of such an adjustment, however, by computing the fully taxable equivalent yield, which is one of the most often cited measures of performance for municipal bonds.

The **fully taxable equivalent yield (FTEY)** adjusts the promised yield computation for the bond's tax-exempt status. To compute the FTEY, we determine the promised yield on a taxexempt bond using one of the yield formulas and then adjust the computed yield to reflect the rate of return that must be earned on a fully taxable issue. It is measured as

18.6
$$FTEY = \frac{i}{1 - T}$$

where:

  i = the promised yield on the tax-exempt bond
  T = the amount and type of tax exemption (i.e., the investor's marginal tax rate)

For example, if the promised yield on the tax-exempt bond is 6 percent and the investor's marginal tax rate is 30 percent, the taxable equivalent yield would be

$$FTEY = \frac{0.06}{1 - 0.30} = \frac{0.06}{0.70} = 0.0857$$
$$= 8.57\%$$

The FTEY equation has some limitations. It is applicable only to par bonds or current coupon obligations, such as new issues, because the measure considers only interest income, ignoring capital gains, which are not tax-exempt. Therefore, we cannot use it for issues trading at a significant variation from par value (premium or discount).

18.3.4 Bond Yield Books

Bond value tables, commonly known as *bond books* or *yield books*, can eliminate most of the calculations for bond valuation. A bond yield table is like a present value interest factor table in that it provides a matrix of bond prices for a stated coupon rate, various terms to maturity (on the horizontal axis), and promised yields (on the vertical axis). Such a table allows you to determine either the promised yield or the price of a bond.

---

[4] For a detailed discussion of these calculations, see "Bond Pricing and Return Measures" (Fabozzi, 2005, Chapter 4).

As might be expected, access to sophisticated calculators or computers has substantially reduced the need for and use of yield books. In addition, to truly understand alternative yield measures, you must master the present value model and its variations that generate values for promised YTM, promised YTC, realized (horizon) yield, and bond prices.

. . . .

18.4. Bond Valuation Using Spot Rates

Thus far, we have used the valuation model, which assumes that we discount all cash flows by one common yield, reflecting the overall required rate of return for the bond. Similarly, we compute the yield on the bond (YTM, YTC, horizon yield) as the single interest rate that would discount all the flows from the bond to equal the current market price of the bond. It was noted in the YTM calculations that this was a promised yield that depended on two assumptions: holding the bond to maturity and reinvesting all cash flows at the computed YTM (the IRR assumption). Notably, this second assumption often is very unrealistic because it requires a flat, constant yield curve. We know that it is extremely rare for the yield curve to be flat, much less remain constant for any period of time. The yield curve typically is upward sloping for several reasons, which we discuss in a later section. Investors at any point in time require *a different rate of return for flows at different times*. For example, if investors are buying alternative zero coupon bonds (promising a single cash flow at maturity), they will almost always require different rates of return if they are offered a bond that matures in 2 years, 5 years, or 10 years.

As mentioned earlier, the rates used to discount a cash flow at a certain point are called spot rates. It is possible to demonstrate the desire for different rates by examining the rates on government discount notes with different maturities (i.e., spot rates) as of April 2008, as shown in Exhibit 18.4. These rates indicate that investors require 1.79 percent for the cash flow in 2 years, 2.70 percent for the cash flow in 5 years, and 3.97 percent for the cash flow in 10 years. These differences in required rates for alternatives maturities are similar to historical differentials. The difference in yield between the 1-year bond (1.62 percent) and the 30-year bond (4.42 percent), referred to as the *maturity spread*, was 280 basis points in early 2008, which is a typical maturity spread historically.

Because of differences in spot rates across maturities, bond analysts and bond portfolio managers recognize that it is inappropriate to discount all the flows for a bond at one single rate where the rate used is often based on the yield to maturity for a government bond with a single

Exhibit 18.4 Yields on U.S. Treasury Strips with Alternative Maturities

Maturity	Yield
1 Year	1.62
2 Years	1.79
3 Years	1.94
4 Years	2.26
5 Years	2.70
6 Years	3.01
7 Years	3.24
8 Years	3.53
9 Years	3.81
10 Years	3.97
12 Years	4.27
14 Years	4.44
16 Years	4.53
18 Years	4.55
20 Years	4.59
25 Years	4.51
30 Years	4.42

Source: *Barron's*, April 14, 2008, p. M44. Dow Jones & Co.

maturity. For example, when asked about the value of a particular 20-year bond rated AA, a bond trader typically will respond that the bond should trade a certain number of basis points higher than comparable maturity Treasury bonds (e.g., plus 70 basis points). This means that if 20-year Treasury bonds are currently yielding 4.60 percent, this AA-rated bond should trade at about a 5.30 percent yield. Notably, this rate would determine the price for the bond with no consideration given to the specific cash flows of this security (i.e., high or low coupon). Therefore, there is a growing awareness that the valuation formula should be specified such that *all cash flows should be discounted at spot rates consistent with the timing of the flows* as follows:

18.7
$$P_m = \sum_{t=1}^{2n} \frac{C_t}{(1 + i_t/2)^t}$$

where:

P_m = the market price for the bond
C_t = the cash flow at Time t
n = the number of years
i_t = the spot rate for Treasury securities at maturity t

Note that this valuation model requires a different discount rate for each flow so it is not possible to use the annuity concept. Also, the principal payment at the end of the year n is no different from the interest coupon flow at year n.

To demonstrate the effect of this procedure, consider the following hypothetical spot rate curve for the next five years (in Exhibit 18.5) and three example bonds with equal maturities of five years, but with very different cash flows.

Beyond the differences in value because of the differences in cash flows and the rising spot rate curve, a significant comparison is the value that would be derived using a single discount rate based on the five-year maturity of all three bonds. If we assume two alternative yields to maturity of 6 percent and 6.5 percent for five-year bonds, the values for the three bonds are:

		6%			6.5%
Bond A	$ 60 × 8.5302 =	$ 511.81	$ 60 × 8.4254 =	$ 505.52
	$1,000 × 0.7441 =	744.10	$1,000 × 0.7270 =	727.00
	Total Value =	$1,255.91		= $1,232.52
Bond B	$ 30 × 8.5302 =	$ 255.90	$ 30 × 8.4254 =	$ 252.76
	$1,000 × 0.7441 =	744.10	$1,000 × 0.7270 =	727.00
	Total Value =	$1,000.00		= $ 979.76
Bond C	$1,000 × 0.7441 =	$ 744.10	$1,000 × 0.7270 =	$ 727.00
	Total Value =	$ 744.10		= $ 727.00

Because there is a rising spot-yield curve, we know the YTM would be somewhere between these two values. The point is, under these conditions valuing the bonds with a single high rate tends to generate a value that is lower than that derived from the spot rate curve. This implies that a single-rate valuation technique would typically misvalue these bonds relative to the more appropriate technique that considers each flow as a single bond discounted by its own spot rate.

18.5 What Determines Interest Rates?

Now that we have learned to calculate various yields on bonds and to determine the value of bonds using yields and spot rates, the question arises as to what causes differences and changes in yields over time. Market interest rates cause these effects because the interest rates reported in the media are simply the prevailing YTMs for the bonds being discussed. For example, when you hear that the interest rate on long-term government bonds declined from 5.80 percent to 5.70 percent, this means that the price of this particular bond increased such that the computed YTM

Exhibit 18.5 Demonstration of Different Valuation of Alternative Five-Year Maturity Bonds with Unique Cash Flows, Discounted Using the Spot Rate Curve

Maturity (Years)	Spot Rate	Discount Factor	BOND A $	BOND A PV	BOND B $	BOND B PV	BOND C $	BOND C PV
0.5	5.00	0.9756	60	$ 58.536	30	$ 29.268	—	—
1.0	5.20	0.9499	60	56.994	30	28.497	—	—
1.5	5.50	0.9218	60	55.308	30	27.654	—	—
2.0	5.70	0.8937	60	53.622	30	26.811	—	—
2.5	5.80	0.8668	60	52.008	30	26.004	—	—
3.0	5.90	0.8399	60	50.394	30	25.197	—	—
3.5	6.10	0.8103	60	48.618	30	24.309	—	—
4.0	6.30	0.7803	60	46.818	30	23.409	—	—
4.5	6.40	0.7532	60	45.192	30	22.596	—	—
5.0	6.50	0.7270	1,060	770.620	1,030	748.810	1,000	727.00
Total present value				$1,238.110		$982.555		$727.00

at the former price was 5.80 percent, but the computed YTM at the new, higher price is 5.70 percent. Yields and interest rates are the same. They are different terms for the same concept.

We have discussed the inverse relationship between bond prices and interest rates. When interest rates decline, the prices of bonds increase; when interest rates rise, there is a decline in bond prices. It is natural to ask which of these is the driving force—bond prices or bond interest rates? It is a simultaneous change, and you can envision either factor causing it. Most practitioners probably envision the changes in interest rates as the causes because they constantly use interest rates to describe changes. They use interest rates because they are comparable across bonds, whereas the price of a bond depends not only on the interest rate but also on the bond's specific characteristics, including its coupon and maturity. The point is, as demonstrated in Exhibit 18.1 and Exhibit 18.2, when you change the interest rate (yield) on a bond, you simultaneously change its price in the opposite direction. Later in the chapter we will discuss the specific price-yield relationship for individual bonds and demonstrate that this price-yield relationship differs among bonds based on their particular coupon and maturity.

Understanding interest rates and what makes them change is necessary for an investor who hopes to maximize returns from investing in bonds. Therefore, in this section we review our prior discussion of the following topics: what causes overall market interest rates to rise and fall, why alternative bonds have different interest rates, and why the difference in rates (i.e., the yield spread) between alternative bonds changes over time. To accomplish this, we begin with a general discussion of what influences interest rates and then consider the **term structure of interest rates** (shown by yield curves), which relates the interest rates on a set of comparable bonds to their terms to maturity. The term structure is important because it implies a set of spot rates that can be used in the valuation of bonds. In addition, the term structure reflects what investors expect to happen to interest rates in the future and it dictates their current risk attitude. In this section, we specifically consider the calculation of spot rates and forward rates from the reported yield curve. Finally, we consider *yield spreads*, which measure the differences in yields between alternative bonds. We describe various yield spreads and explore what causes changes in them over time.

18.5.1 Forecasting Interest Rates

As discussed, the ability to forecast interest rates and changes in these rates is critical to successful bond investing. Later, we consider the major determinants of interest rates, but for now you should keep in mind that interest rates *are the price for loanable funds*. Like any price, they are determined by the supply and demand for these funds. On the one side, investors are willing to provide funds (the supply) at prices based on their required rates of return for a particular borrower. On the other side, borrowers need funds (the demand) to support budget deficits (government), to invest in capital projects (corporations), or to acquire durable goods (cars, appliances) or homes (individuals).

Although lenders and borrowers have some fundamental factors that determine supply and demand curves, the prices for these funds (interest rates) also are affected for short periods by events that shift the curves. Examples include major government bond issues that affect demand for funds, or significant changes in Federal Reserve monetary policy that affect the supply of money.

Our treatment of interest rate forecasting recognizes that you must be aware of the basic determinants of interest rates and monitor these factors. We also recognize that detailed forecasting of interest rates is a very complex task that is best left to professional economists. Therefore, our goal as bond investors and bond portfolio managers is to continuously assess the major factors that affect interest rates but rely on others—such as economic consulting firms, banks, or investment banking firms—for detailed insights on such topics as the real *RFR* and the expected rate of inflation.[5] This is precisely the way most bond portfolio managers operate.

18.5.2 Fundamental Determinants of Interest Rates

As shown in Exhibit 18.6, average interest rates (yields) for long-term (10-year) U.S. government bonds during the period from 2004 to 2007, went from about 4.71 percent to 4.95 percent. These results were similar to those of the United Kingdom and the Euro area, while the rate on Japanese government bonds increased overall from about 1.31 percent to 1.57 percent. As a bond investor, you should understand why these differences exist and why interest rates within each country changed.

As you would expect, bond prices increased dramatically during periods when market interest rates dropped, and some bond investors experienced very attractive returns. In contrast, some investors experienced substantial losses during periods when interest rates increased. A casual analysis of this chart, which covers about four years, indicates the need for monitoring interest rates. Essentially, the factors causing interest rates *(i)* to rise or fall are described by the following model:

18.8
$$i = RFR + I + RP$$

where:

RFR = the real risk-free rate of interest
I = the expected rate of inflation
RP = the risk premium

This relationship should be familiar based on our presentations in Chapter 1 and Chapter 11. It is a simple but complete statement of interest rate behavior. The more difficult task is estimating the *future* behavior of such variables as real growth, expected inflation, and economic uncertainty. In this regard, interest rates, like stock prices, are extremely difficult to forecast with any degree of accuracy, as discussed by Fabozzi in "The Structure of Interest Rates" (2005, Chapter 6). Alternatively, we can visualize the source of changes in interest rates in terms of the economic conditions and issue characteristics as follows:

18.9
$$i = f \text{ (Economic Forces} + \text{Issue Characteristics)}$$

$$= (RFR + I) + RP.$$

---

[5] Sources of information on the bond market and interest rate forecasts would include Merrill Lynch's *Fixed Income Weekly* and *World Bond Market Monitor;* Goldman Sach's *Financial Market Perspectives* and *The Pocket Chartroom;* and the Federal Reserve Bank of St. Louis, *Monetary Trends.*

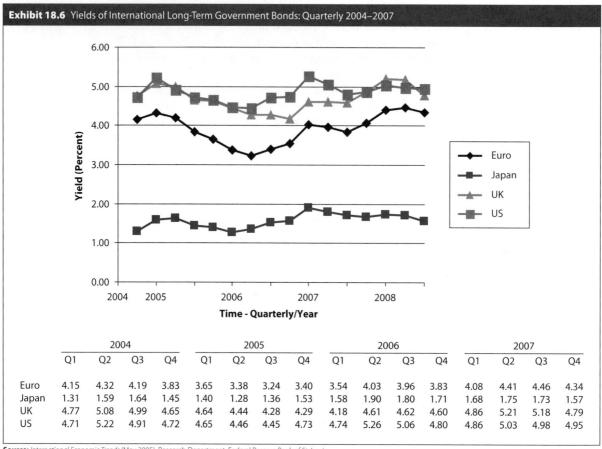

Exhibit 18.6 Yields of International Long-Term Government Bonds: Quarterly 2004–2007

	2004				2005				2006				2007			
	Q1	Q2	Q3	Q4	Q1	Q2	Q3	Q4	Q1	Q2	Q3	Q4	Q1	Q2	Q3	Q4
Euro	4.15	4.32	4.19	3.83	3.65	3.38	3.24	3.40	3.54	4.03	3.96	3.83	4.08	4.41	4.46	4.34
Japan	1.31	1.59	1.64	1.45	1.40	1.28	1.36	1.53	1.58	1.90	1.80	1.71	1.68	1.75	1.73	1.57
UK	4.77	5.08	4.99	4.65	4.64	4.44	4.28	4.29	4.18	4.61	4.62	4.60	4.86	5.21	5.18	4.79
US	4.71	5.22	4.91	4.72	4.65	4.46	4.45	4.73	4.74	5.26	5.06	4.80	4.86	5.03	4.98	4.95

Source: *International Economic Trends* (May 2005), Research Department, Federal Reserve Bank of St. Louis.

This rearranged version of the previous equation helps isolate the factors that determine interest rates; as discussed in Van Horne (2001).

Effect of Economic Factors The real risk-free rate of interest (RFR) is the economic cost of money, that is, the opportunity cost necessary to compensate individuals for forgoing consumption. As discussed previously, it is determined by the real growth rate of the economy with short-run effects due to ease or tightness in the capital market.

The expected rate of inflation is the other economic influence on interest rates. We add the expected level of inflation *(I)* to the real risk-free rate *(RFR)* to specify the nominal *RFR,* which is a market rate like the current rate on government T-bills. Given the stability of the real *RFR,* it is clear that the wide swings in nominal risk-free interest rates during the years covered by Exhibit 18.6 occurred because of the volatility of expected inflation. Besides the unique country and exchange rate risk that we discuss in the section on risk premiums, differences in the rates of inflation between countries have a major impact on their level of interest rates.

To sum up, one way to estimate the nominal *RFR* is to begin with the real growth rate of the economy, adjust for short-run ease or tightness in the capital market, and then adjust this real rate of interest for the expected rate of inflation.

Another approach to estimating changes in the nominal rate is the macroeconomic view, where the supply and demand for loanable funds are the fundamental economic determinants of *i.* As the supply of loanable funds increases, the level of interest rates declines, other things being equal. Several factors influence the supply of funds. Government monetary policies imposed by the Federal Reserve have a significant impact on the supply of money. The savings patterns of U.S. and non-U.S. investors also affect the supply of funds. Non-U.S. investors have become a stronger influence on the U.S. supply of loanable funds during recent years, as shown by the significant purchases of U.S. securities by non-U.S. investors. We know that this foreign supply of funds to the U.S. bond market has helped reduce our interest rates and the cost of capital.

Interest rates increase when the demand for loanable funds increases. The demand for loanable funds is affected by the capital and operating needs of the U.S. government, federal agencies, state and local governments, corporations, institutions, and individuals. Federal budget deficits increase the Treasury's demand for loanable funds. Likewise, the level of consumer demand for funds to buy houses, autos, and appliances affects rates, as does corporate demand for funds to pursue investment opportunities. The total of all groups determines the aggregate demand and supply of loanable funds and the level of the nominal *RFR*.

The Impact of Bond Characteristics   The interest rate of a specific bond issue is influenced by factors that affect the nominal *RFR* but also by the unique issue characteristics of the bond that influences the bond's risk premium (*RP*). The economic forces that determine the nominal *RFR* affect all securities, whereas issue characteristics are unique to individual securities, market sectors, or countries. Thus, the differences in the yields of corporate and Treasury bonds are not caused by economic factors but, rather, by different issue characteristics that affect the risk premiums.

Bond investors separate the risk premium into four components:

1. The quality of the issue as determined by its risk of default relative to other bonds
2. The term to maturity of the issue, which can affect price volatility
3. Indenture provisions, including collateral, call features, and sinking-fund provisions
4. Foreign bond risk, including exchange rate risk and country risk

Of the four factors, quality and maturity have the greatest impact on the risk premium for domestic bonds, while exchange rate risk and country risk are important components of risk for non-U.S. bonds.

The credit quality of a bond reflects the ability of the issuer to service its outstanding debt which is largely captured in the ratings issued by the bond rating firms. As a result, bonds with different ratings have different yields. For example, AAA-rated obligations possess lower risk of default than BBB obligations, so they have a lower required yield.

Notably, the risk premium differences between bonds of different quality levels change dramatically over time, depending on prevailing economic conditions. When the economy experiences a recession or a period of economic uncertainty, the desire for quality increases, and investors sell lower quality debt and bid up prices of higher rated bonds, which increases the difference in yield. This difference in yield is referred to as the *quality* or *credit spread*. Dialynas and Edington (1992) contend that this yield spread is also influenced by the volatility of interest rates. This variability in the credit risk premium over time was demonstrated and discussed in Chapter 1 and Chapter 11. The U.S. market experienced dramatic demonstrations of short-run risk premium explosions in August 1998 in response to Russia defaulting on its debt and following the terrorist attacks on September 11, 2001.

Term to maturity also influences the risk premium because it affects the price volatility of the bond. In the section on the term structure of interest rates, we will discuss the typical positive relationship between the term to maturity of a bond issue and its interest rate.

As discussed in Chapter 17, indenture provisions indicate the collateral pledged for a bond, its callability, and its sinking-fund provisions. Collateral gives protection to the investor if the issuer defaults on the bond because the investor has a specific claim on some assets in case of liquidation.

Call features indicate when an issuer can buy back the bond prior to its maturity. A bond is called by an issuer when interest rates have declined, so it is not to the advantage of the investor who must reinvest the proceeds at a lower interest rate. Obviously, an investor will charge the issuer for including the call option, and the cost of the option (which is a higher yield) will increase with the level of interest rates. Therefore, more protection against having the bond called reduces the risk premium. The significance (value) of call protection increases during periods of high interest rates. As noted by Marshall and Yawitz (1980) and Stanhouse and Stock (1999), when you buy a bond with a high coupon, you want protection from having it called away when rates decline.

As discussed by Kalotay (1981, 1982b), a sinking fund reduces the investor's risk and causes a lower yield for several reasons. First, a sinking fund reduces default risk because it requires the issuer to reduce the outstanding issue systematically. Second, purchases of the bond by the issuer to satisfy sinking-fund requirements provide price support for the bond. These purchases also contribute to a more liquid secondary market for the bond because of the increased trading. Finally, sinking-fund provisions require that the issuer retire a bond before its stated maturity, which reduces the issue's average maturity. The decline in average maturity tends to reduce the risk premium of the bond.

We know that foreign currency exchange rates change over time and that this increases the risk of global investing. The variability of exchange rates vary among countries because the trade balances and rates of inflation differ. Volatile trade balances and inflation rates make exchange rates more volatile, which adds to the uncertainty of future exchange rates and increases the exchange rate risk premium.

In addition to changes in exchange rates, investors also are concerned with the political and economic stability of a country. If investors are unsure about the political or economic environment in a country, they will increase the required risk premium to reflect this country risk.

18.5.3 The Term Structure of Interest Rates

The term structure of interest rates (or the *yield curve*, as it is more popularly known) is a static function that relates the term to maturity to the yield to maturity for a sample of bonds at *a given point in time*.[6] Thus, it represents a cross section of yields for a category of bonds that are comparable in all respects but maturity. Specifically, the quality of the issues should be constant, and ideally you should have issues with similar coupons and call features within a single industry category. You can construct different yield curves for Treasuries, government agencies, prime-grade municipals, AAA utilities, and so on. The accuracy of the yield curve will depend on the comparability of the bonds in the sample.

As an example, Exhibit 18.7 shows yield curves for a sample of U.S. Treasury obligations. It is based on the yield to maturity information for a set of comparable Treasury issues from a publication such as the *Federal Reserve Bulletin* or the *Wall Street Journal*. These promised yields were plotted on the graph, and a yield curve was drawn that represents the general configuration of rates. These data represent yield curves at three different points in time to demonstrate the changes in yield levels and in the shape of the yield curve over time.

All yield curves, of course, do not have the same shape as those in Exhibit 18.7. Although individual yield curves are static, their behavior over time is quite fluid. As shown, the yield curve was relatively flat during the period from April 2007 to October 2007. Subsequently, by April 2008 it had a strong positive slope due to significant reductions in short-term rates by the Federal Reserve. The point is, the shape of the yield curve can undergo dramatic alterations, following one of the four patterns shown in Exhibit 18.8. The rising yield curve is the most common and tends to prevail when interest rates are at low or modest levels. The declining yield curve tends to occur when rates are relatively high. The flat yield curve rarely exists for any period of time. The humped yield curve prevails when extremely high rates are expected to decline to more normal levels. Note that the slope of the yield curve tends to level off after 15 years.

---

[6] For a discussion of the theory and empirical evidence, see Sundaresan (2002).

Exhibit 18.7 Yields on U.S. Treasury Securities with Alternative Maturities at Different Times

Years	4/15/2008	10/15/2007	4/13/2007
0.25	1.21	4.42	5.06
0.5	1.36	4.55	5.09
1	1.72	4.35	5.03
2	1.82	4.19	4.75
3	2.04	4.24	4.69
4	2.48	4.30	4.66
5	2.68	4.38	4.67
7	3.17	4.54	4.71
8	3.47	4.61	4.74
9	3.65	4.68	4.77
10	3.77	4.75	4.78
15	4.35	5.03	5.02
20	4.47	4.99	5.03
25	4.43	4.94	4.98
30	4.45	4.92	4.93

Source: *International Economic Trends* (May 2005), Research Department, Federal Reserve Bank of St. Louis.

Why does the term structure assume different shapes? Three major theories attempt to explain this: the expectations hypothesis, the liquidity preference hypothesis, and the segmented market hypothesis.

Before we discuss these three alternative hypotheses, we must first discuss two previously noted rates that not only are an integral part of the term structure but also are important in the valuation of bonds. The next two subsections will deal with the specification and computation of *spot rates* and *forward rates*. Earlier, we discussed and used spot rates to value bonds with the idea that any coupon bond can be viewed as a collection of zero coupon securities.

Creating the Theoretical Spot Rate Curve[7] Earlier in the chapter, we discussed the notion that the yield on a zero coupon bond for a given maturity is the spot rate for the maturity. Specifically, the **spot rate** is defined as the discount rate for a cash flow at a specific maturity. At that time, we used the rates on a series of zero coupon government bonds created by stripping coupon government bonds.

In this case, we will construct a theoretical spot rate curve from the observable yield curve that is based on the existing yields of Treasury bills and the most recent Treasury coupon securities (referred to as *on-the-run* Treasury issues). One might expect the theoretical spot rate curve and the spot rate curve derived from the stripped zero coupon bonds used earlier to be the same. The fact is, while they are close, they will not be exactly the same because the stripped zero coupon bonds will not be as liquid as the on-the-run issues. In addition, there are instances where institutions will have a strong desire for a particular spot maturity and this preference will distort the term structure relationship. Therefore, while it is possible to use the stripped zero coupon curve for a general indication, if you are going to use the spot rates for significant valuation, you would want to use the theoretical spot rate curve.

The process of creating a theoretical spot rate curve from coupon securities is called *bootstrapping* wherein it is assumed that the value of the Treasury coupon security should be equal to the value of the package of zero coupon securities that duplicates the coupon bond's cash flow. Exhibit 18.9 lists the maturity and YTM for six hypothetical Treasury bonds that will be used to calculate the initial spot rates.

---

[7] This discussion of the theoretical spot rate curve and the subsequent presentation on calculating forward rates draw heavily from "The Structure of Interest Rates" by Fabozzi (2005, Chapter 6).

Exhibit 18.8 Types of Yield Curves

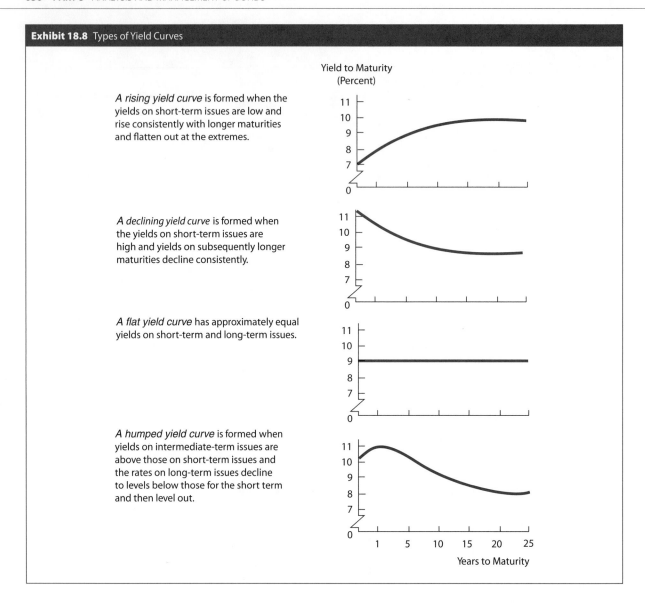

A rising yield curve is formed when the yields on short-term issues are low and rise consistently with longer maturities and flatten out at the extremes.

A declining yield curve is formed when the yields on short-term issues are high and yields on subsequently longer maturities decline consistently.

A flat yield curve has approximately equal yields on short-term and long-term issues.

A humped yield curve is formed when yields on intermediate-term issues are above those on short-term issues and the rates on long-term issues decline to levels below those for the short term and then level out.

Consider the six-month Treasury bill in Exhibit 18.9. As discussed earlier, a Treasury bill is a zero coupon instrument so its annualized yield of 8 percent is equal to the spot rate. Similarly, for the one-year Treasury bill, the cited yield of 8.3 percent is equal to the one-year spot rate. Given these two spot rates, we can compute the spot rate for a theoretical 1.5-year zero coupon Treasury. The price for this 1.5-year security should equal the present value of three cash flows from an actual 1.5-year coupon Treasury, where the yield used for discounting a specific coupon payment is the spot rate corresponding to the cash flow.

Using $100 as par, the *cash flow* for the 1.5-year, 8.50 percent coupon Treasury is as follows:

0.5 years	$0.085 \times \$100 \times 0.5$	=	$ 4.25
1.0 years	$0.085 \times \$100 \times 0.5$	=	$ 4.25
1.5 years	$0.085 \times \$100 \times 0.5 + \$100$	=	$104.25

Exhibit 18.9 Maturity and Yield to Maturity for Hypothetical Treasury Securities

Maturity (Years)	Coupon Rate	Price	Yield to Maturity
0.50	0.0000	96.15	0.0800
1.00	0.0000	92.19	0.0830
1.50	0.0850	99.45	0.0890
2.00	0.0900	99.64	0.0920
2.50	0.1100	103.49	0.0940
3.00	0.0950	99.49	0.0970

Sources: Federal Reserve Bulletin; Mergent Bond Record.

The present value of the cash flows discounted at the appropriate spot rates is then

$$\frac{4.25}{(1+z_1)^1} + \frac{4.25}{(1+z_2)^2} + \frac{104.25}{(1+z_3)^3}$$

where:

$z_1 = \frac{1}{2}$ the annualized six-month theoretical spot rate
$z_2 = \frac{1}{2}$ the one-year theoretical spot rate
$z_3 = \frac{1}{2}$ the 1.5-year theoretical spot rate

Because the six-month spot rate and one-year spot rate are 8.0 percent and 8.3 percent, respectively, we know that

$$z_1 = 0.04 \quad and \quad z_2 = 0.0415$$

We can compute the present value of the 1.5-year coupon Treasury security as

$$\frac{4.25}{(1.0400)^1} + \frac{4.25}{(1.0415)^2} + \frac{104.25}{(1+z_3)^3}$$

Because the price of the 1.5-year coupon Treasury security (from Exhibit 18.9) is $99.45, the following relationship must hold:

$$99.45 = \frac{4.25}{(1.0400)^1} + \frac{4.25}{(1.0415)^2} + \frac{104.25}{(1+z_3)^3}$$

We can solve for the theoretical 1.5-year spot rate as follows:

$$99.45 = 4.08654 + 3.91805 + \frac{104.25}{(1+z_3)^3}$$

$$91.44541 = \frac{104.25}{(1+z_3)^3}$$

$$\frac{104.25}{91.44541} = (1+z_3)^3$$

$$(1+z_3)^3 = 1.140024$$

$$z_3 = 0.04465$$

Doubling this yield, we obtain the bond-equivalent yield of 0.0893 or 8.93 percent, which is the theoretical 1.5-year spot rate. That rate is the rate that the market would apply to a 1.5-year zero coupon Treasury, if such a security existed.

Given the theoretical 1.5-year spot rate, we can obtain the theoretical 2-year spot rate. The cash flow for the 2-year, 9.0 percent coupon Treasury security in Exhibit 18.9 is

0.5 years	$0.090 \times \$100 \times 0.5$	=	$ 4.50
1.0 years	$0.090 \times \$100 \times 0.5$	=	$ 4.50
1.5 years	$0.090 \times \$100 \times 0.5$	=	$ 4.50
2.0 years	$0.090 \times \$100 \times 0.5 + 100$	=	$104.50

The present value of the cash flow is then

$$\frac{4.50}{(1 + z_1)^1} + \frac{4.50}{(1 + z_2)^2} + \frac{4.50}{(1 + z_3)^3} + \frac{104.50}{(1 + z_4)^4}$$

where:

$z_4 = \frac{1}{2}$ the two-year theoretical spot rate

Because the 6-month, 1-year, and 1.5-year spot rates are 8 percent, 8.3 percent, and 8.93 percent, respectively, then

$$z_1 = 0.04 \quad z_2 = 0.0415 \quad and \quad z_3 = 0.04465$$

Therefore, the present value of the two-year coupon Treasury security is

$$\frac{4.50}{(1.0400)^1} + \frac{4.50}{(1.0415)^2} + \frac{4.50}{(1.04465)^3} + \frac{104.50}{(1 + z_4)^4}$$

Because the price of the two-year, 9.0 percent coupon Treasury security is $99.64, the following relationship must hold:

$$99.64 = \frac{4.50}{(1.0400)^1} + \frac{4.50}{(1.0415)^2} + \frac{4.50}{(1.04465)^3} + \frac{104.50}{(1 + z_4)^4}$$

We can solve for the theoretical two-year spot rate as follows:

$$99.64 = 4.32692 + 4.14853 + 3.94730 + \frac{104,50}{(1 + z_4)^4}$$

$$87.21725 = \frac{104.50}{(1 + z_4)^4}$$

$$(1 + z_4)^4 = 1.198158$$

$$z_4 = 0.046235$$

Doubling this yield, we obtain the theoretical two-year spot rate bond-equivalent yield of 9.247 percent.

One can follow this approach sequentially to derive the theoretical 2.5-year spot rate from the calculated values of z_1, z_2, z_3, z_4 (the 6-month, 1-year, 1.5-year, and 2-year spot rates), and the price and the coupon of the bond with a maturity of 2.5 years. Subsequently, one could derive the theoretical spot rate for three years. The spot rates thus obtained are shown in Exhibit 18.10. They represent the term structure of spot interest rates for maturities up to three years, based on the prevailing bond price quotations.

As shown, with a rising YTM curve, the theoretical spot rate will increase at a faster rate such that the difference increases with maturity (i.e., the theoretical spot rate curve will be above a positively sloped YTM curve).

Exhibit 18.10 Theoretical Spot Rates

Maturity (Years)	Yield to Maturity	Theoretical Spot Rate
0.50	0.0800	0.08000
1.00	0.0830	0.08300
1.50	0.0890	0.08930
2.00	0.0920	0.09247
2.50	0.0940	0.09468
3.00	0.0970	0.09787

18.6 Calculating Forward Rates from the Spot Rate Curve

Now that we have derived the theoretical spot rate curve, it is possible to determine what this curve implies regarding the market's expectation of *future* short-term rates, which are referred to as *forward rates*. The following illustrates the process of extrapolating this information about expected future interest rates.

Consider an investor who has a one-year investment horizon and is faced with the following two alternatives:

Alternative 1: Buy a one-year Treasury bill.
Alternative 2: Buy a six-month Treasury bill and, when it matures in six months, buy another six-month Treasury bill.

The investor will be indifferent between the two alternatives *if* they produce the same return for the one-year investment horizon. The investor knows the spot rate on the six-month Treasury bill and the one-year Treasury bill. However, she does not know what yield will be available on a six-month Treasury bill six months from now. The yield on a six-month Treasury bill six months from now is called a **forward rate**. Given the spot rate for the six-month Treasury bill and the one-year bill, we can determine the forward rate on a six-month Treasury bill *that will make the investor indifferent between the two alternatives*.

At this point, however, we need to digress briefly and recall several present value and investment relationships. First, if you invested in a one-year Treasury bill, you would receive $100 at the end of one year. The price of the one-year Treasury bill would be

$$\frac{100}{(1 + z_2)^2}$$

where:

$z_2 = \frac{1}{2}$ the bond-equivalent yield of the theoretical one-year spot rate

Second, suppose you purchased a six-month Treasury bill for $X. At the end of six months, the value of this investment would be

$$\$X(1 + z_1)$$

where:

$z_1 = \frac{1}{2}$ the bond-equivalent yield of the theoretical six-month spot rate

Let $_{t+0.5}r_{0.5}$ represent one-half the forward rate (expressed as a bond-equivalent yield) on a six-month Treasury bill (0.5) available six months from now ($t + 0.5$). If the investor were to renew her investment by purchasing that bill at that time, then the future dollars available at the end of the year from the $X investment would be

$$X(1 + z_1)(1 + {}_{t+0.5}r_{0.5}) = 100$$

Third, it is easy to use that formula to find out how many dollars the investor must invest in order to get $100 one year from now. This can be found as follows:

$$X(1 + z_1)(1 + {}_{t+0.5}r_{0.5}) = 100$$

which gives us

$$X = \frac{100}{(1 + z_1)(1 + {}_{t+0.5}r_{0.5})}$$

We are now prepared to return to the investor's choices and analyze what that situation says about forward rates. The investor will be indifferent between the two alternatives confronting her if she makes the same dollar investment and receives $100 from both alternatives at the end of one year. That is, the investor will be indifferent if

$$\frac{100}{(1 + z_2)^2} = \frac{100}{(1 + z_1)(1 + {}_{t+0.5}r_{0.5})}$$

Solving for ${}_{t+0.5}r_{0.5}$ we get

$${}_{t+0.5}r_{0.5} = \frac{(1 + z_2)^2}{(1 + z_1)} - 1$$

Doubling r gives the bond-equivalent yield for the six-month forward rate six months from now.

We can illustrate the use of this formula with the theoretical spot rates shown in Exhibit 18.10. From that table, we know that

Six-month bill spot rate = 0.080 so $z_1 = 0.0400$
One-year bill spot rate = 0.083 so $z_2 = 0.0415$

Substituting into the formula, we have

$${}_{t+0.5}r_{0.5} = \frac{(1.0415)^2}{(1.0400)} - 1$$

$$= 0.043$$

Therefore, the forward rate six months from now ($t + 0.5$) on a six-month Treasury security, quoted annually, is 8.6 percent (0.043×2). Let us confirm our results. The price of a one-year Treasury bill with $100 maturity is

$$\frac{100}{(1.0415)^2} = 92.19$$

If $92.19 is invested for six months at the six-month spot rate of 8 percent, the amount at the end of six months would be

$$92.19(1.0400) = 95.8776$$

If $95.8776 is reinvested for another six months in a six-month Treasury bill offering 4.3 percent for six months (8.6 percent annually), the amount at the end of one year would be

$$95.8776(1.043) = 100$$

Both alternatives will have the same $100 payoff if the six-month Treasury bill yield six months from now is 4.3 percent (8.6 percent on a bond-equivalent basis). This means that, if an investor is guaranteed a 4.3 percent yield on a six-month Treasury bill six months from now, she will be indifferent between the two alternatives.

We used the theoretical spot rates to compute the forward rate. The resulting forward rate is called the *implied forward rate.*

It is possible to use the yield curve to calculate the implied forward rate for any time in the future for any investment horizon. This would include six-month or one-year forward rates for each year in the future. The one-year forward rates would be designated as follows:

$_{t+1}r_1$ = the 1-year forward rate, 1 year from now $(t + 1)$
$_{t+2}r_1$ = the 1-year forward rate, 2 years from now $(t + 2)$
$_{t+3}r_1$ = the 1-year forward rate, 3 years from now $(t + 3)$

Given the calculations, it is clear that with a rising spot rate curve, the forward rate curve would be above the spot rate curve. From Exhibit 18.10, we have the following one-year spot rates, which imply the following one-year forward rates:

$$_{t+1}r_1 = \frac{(1.09247)^2}{(1.08300)} - 1 = \frac{1.19349}{1.08300} - 1 = 0.1020$$

$$r_{t+2}r_1 = \frac{(1.09787)^3}{(1.00247)^2} - 1 = \frac{1.32328}{1.19349} - 1 = 0.1087$$

Therefore:

Maturity (Years)	Spot Rates	One–Year Forward Rates
1.0	0.08300	
2.0	0.09247	0.1020
3.0	0.09787	0.1087

Specifically, the one-year forward rate that is expected one year from now $(_{t+1}r_1)$ is 10.20 percent, while the one-year forward rate that is expected two years from now $(_{t+2}r_1)$ is 10.87 percent.

18.7 Term-Structure Theories

18.7.1 Expectations Hypothesis

According to the expectations hypothesis, the shape of the yield curve results from the interest rate expectations of market participants. More specifically, it holds that *any long-term interest rate simply represents the geometric mean of current and future one-year interest rates expected to prevail over the maturity of the issue.* In essence, the term structure involves a series of intermediate and long-term interest rates, each of which is a reflection of the geometric average of current and expected one-year interest rates. Under such conditions, the equilibrium long-term rate is the rate the long-term bond investor would expect to earn through successive investments in short-term bonds over the term to maturity of the long-term bond.

Generally, this relationship can be formalized as follows:

18.10 $$(1 + {_t}R_n) = \left[(1 + {_t}R_1)(1 + {_{t+1}}r_1) \cdots (1 + {_{t+n-1}}r_1)\right]^{1/N}$$

where:

R_n = the actual long-term rate
N = the term to maturity (in years) of the long issue
${_t}R_1$ = the current 1-year rate
${_{t+i}}r_1$ = the expected 1-year yield during some future period, $t + i$ (these future 1-year rates are referred to as *forward rates*)

Given the relationship set forth in this equation, the formula for computing the one-period forward rate beginning at time $t + n$ and implied in the term structure at time t is

18.11 $$1 + {}_{t+n}r_{1t} = \frac{(1 + {}_{t}R_{1t})(1 + {}_{t+1}r_{1t})(1 + {}_{t+2}r_{1t}) \cdots (1 + {}_{t+n}r_{1t})(1 + {}_{t+n}r_{1t})}{(1 + {}_{t}R_{1t})(1 + {}_{t+1}r_{1t}) \cdots (1 + {}_{t+n-1}r_{1t})}$$

$$= \frac{(1 + {}_{t}R_{n+1})^{n+1}}{(1 + {}_{t}R_{n})^{n}}$$

$${}_{t+n}r_{1t} = \frac{(1 + {}_{t}R_{n+1})^{n+1}}{(1 + {}_{t}R_{n})^{n}} - 1$$

where ${}_{t+n}r_{1t}$ is the one-year forward rate prevailing at $t + n$, using the term structure at time t.

Assume that the five-year spot rate is 10 percent (${}_{t}R_5 = 0.10$) and the four-year spot rate is 9 percent (${}_{t}R_4 = 0.09$). The forward one-year rate four years from now implied by these spot rates can be calculated as follows:

$${}_{t+4}r_{1t} = \frac{(1 + {}_{t}R_5)^5}{(1 + {}_{t}R_4)^4} - 1$$

$$= \frac{(1 + 0.10)^5}{(1 + 0.09)^4} - 1$$

$$= \frac{1.6105}{1.4116} - 1$$

$$= 1.1409 - 1 = 0.1409 = 14.09\%$$

The term structure at time t implies that the one-year spot rate four years from now (during Year 5) will be 14.09 percent. This concept and formula can be used to derive future rates for multiple years. Thus, the two-year spot rate that will prevail three years from now (which is a forward rate) could be calculated using the three-year spot rate and the five-year spot rate. The general formula for computing the j-period forward rate beginning at time $t + n$ as of time t is

18.12 $${}_{t+n}r_{jt} = \sqrt[j]{\frac{(1 + {}_{t}R_{n+j})^{n+j}}{(1 + {}_{t}R_{n})^{n}}} - 1$$

As a practical approximation of Equation 18.10, it is possible to use the *arithmetic* average of one-year rates to generate long-term yields.

The expectations theory can explain any shape of yield curve. Expectations for rising short-term rates in the future cause a rising yield curve; expectations for falling short-term rates in the future will cause long-term rates to lie below current short-term rates, and the yield curve will decline. Similar explanations account for flat and humped yield curves.

Consider the following explanation by the expectations hypothesis of the shape of the term structure of interest rates using arithmetic averages:

${}_{t}R_1$ = 5½ percent the 1-year rate of interest prevailing now (Period t)
${}_{t+1}r_1$ = 6 percent the 1-year rate of interest expected to prevail next year (Period $t + 1$)
${}_{t+2}r_1$ = 7½ percent the 1-year rate of interest expected to prevail 2 years from now (Period $t + 2$)
${}_{t+3}r_1$ = 8½ percent the 1-year rate of interest expected to prevail 3 years from now (Period $t + 3$)

Using these values and the known rate on a one-year bond, we compute rates on two-, three-, or four-year bonds (designated R_2, R_3, and R_4) as follows:

$_tR_1 = 5\frac{1}{2}$ percent
$_tR_2 = (0.055 + 0.06)/2 = 5.75$ percent
$_tR_3 = (0.055 + 0.06 + 0.075)/3 = 6.33$ percent
$_tR_4 = (0.055 + 0.06 + 0.075 + 0.085)/4 = 6.88$ percent

In this illustration (which uses the arithmetic average as an approximation of the geometric mean), the yield curve is upward sloping because, at present, investors expect future short-term rates to be above current short-term rates. This is not the formal method for constructing the yield curve. Rather, the yield curve is constructed on the basis of the prevailing promised yields for bonds with different maturities.

The expectations hypothesis attempts to explain *why* the yield curve is upward sloping, downward sloping, humped, or flat by explaining the expectations implicit in yield curves with different shapes. The evidence is fairly substantial and convincing that the expectations hypothesis is a workable explanation of the term structure. Because of the supporting evidence, its relative simplicity, and the intuitive appeal of the theory, the expectations hypothesis of the term structure of interest rates is rather widely accepted.

Consistent Investor Actions Besides the theory and empirical support, it is also possible to present a scenario wherein investor actions will cause the yield curve postulated by the theory. The expectations hypothesis predicts a declining yield curve when interest rates are expected to fall in the future rather than rise. In a case of expected falling rates, long-term bonds would be considered attractive investments because investors would want to buy them to lock in prevailing higher yields (which are not expected to be as high in the future) or they would buy them to capture the increase in bond prices (as capital gains) that will accompany a decline in rates. By the same reasoning, investors will sell short-term bonds and reinvest the funds in long-term bonds that will experience larger price increases if rates decline. The point is, investor transactions will reinforce the declining shape of the yield curve as they bid up the prices of long-maturity bonds (forcing yields to decline) while short-term bond issues are sold (so prices decline and yields rise). At the same time, there is confirming action by suppliers of bonds. Specifically, government or corporate issuers will avoid selling long bonds at the current high rates, waiting until the rates decline. In the meantime, they will issue short-term bonds, if needed, while waiting for lower rates. Therefore, in the long-term market, you will have an increase in demand and a decline in the supply and vice versa in the short-term market. These shifts between long- and short-term maturities will continue until equilibrium occurs or expectations change.

18.7.2 Liquidity Preference (Term Premium) Hypothesis

The theory of liquidity preference holds that long-term securities should provide higher returns than short-term obligations because investors are willing to accept lower yields for short-maturity obligations to avoid the higher price volatility of long-maturity bonds. Another way to interpret the liquidity preference hypothesis is to say that lenders prefer short-term loans, and, to induce them to invest in volatile long term bonds, it is necessary to offer higher yields.

The liquidity preference (also called term premium) theory contends that uncertainty and volatility cause investors to favor short-term issues over bonds with longer maturities because short-term bonds are less volatile and can easily be converted into predictable amounts of cash should unforeseen events occur. This theory argues that the yield curve should generally slope upward and that any other shape should be viewed as a temporary aberration.

This theory can be considered an extension of the expectations hypothesis because the formal liquidity preference position contends that the liquidity premium inherent in the yields for longer maturity bonds should be added to the *expected* future rate in arriving at long-term yields. Specifically, the liquidity (or term) premium *(L)* compensates the investor in long-term bonds for the added volatility inherent in long-term bonds compared to short-maturity securities. Because the liquidity premium *(L)* is provided to compensate the long-term investor, it is simply a variation of Equation 18.10 as follows:

$$(1 + {}_tR_N) = [(1 + {}_tR_1)(1 + {}_{t+1}r_1 + L_2) \cdots (1 + {}_{t+N-1}r_1 + L_N)]^{1/N}$$

In this specification, the *L*s are not the same but would be expected to increase with maturity because the price volatility increases with maturity. The liquidity preference theory has been found to possess some strong empirical support by Kessel (1965), Cagan (1969), and McCulloch (1975).

To see how the liquidity preference theory predicts future yields and how it compares with the pure expectations hypothesis, let us predict future long-term rates from a single set of one-year rates: 6 percent, 7.5 percent, and 8.5 percent. The liquidity preference theory suggests that investors add increasing liquidity premiums to successive rates to derive actual market rates. As an example, they might arrive at rates of 6.3 percent, 7.9 percent, and 9.0 percent.

As a matter of historical fact, the yield curve shows an upward bias, which implies that some combination of the expectations theory and the liquidity preference theory will more accurately explain the shape of the yield curve than either of them alone. Specifically, actual long-term rates consistently tend to be above what is envisioned from the price expectations hypothesis. This tendency implies the existence of a liquidity (term) premium.

18.7.3 Segmented Market Hypothesis

Despite meager empirical support, a third theory for the shape of the yield curve is the segmented market hypothesis, which enjoys wide acceptance among market practitioners. Also known as the *preferred habitat*, the *institutional theory*, or the *hedging pressure theory*, it asserts that different institutional investors have different maturity needs that lead them to confine their security selections to specific maturity segments. That is, investors supposedly focus on short-, intermediate-, or long-term securities. This theory contends that the shape of the yield curve ultimately is a function of these investment policies of major financial institutions.

As noted in Chapter 17, financial institutions tend to structure their investment policies in line with such factors as their tax liabilities, the types and maturity structure of their liabilities, and the level of earnings demanded by depositors. For example, because commercial banks are subject to normal corporate tax rates and their liabilities are generally short- to intermediate-term time and demand deposits, they consistently invest in short- to intermediate-term municipal bonds.

The segmented market theory contends that the business environment, along with legal and regulatory limitations, tends to direct each type of financial institution to allocate its resources to particular types of bonds with specific maturity characteristics. In its strongest form, the segmented market theory holds that the maturity preferences of investors and borrowers are so strong that investors never purchase securities outside their preferred maturity range to take advantage of yield differentials. As a result, the short- and long-maturity portions of the bond market are effectively segmented, and yields for a segment depend on the supply and demand *within* that maturity segment.

18.7.4 Trading Implications of the Term Structure

Information on maturity yields can help you formulate yield expectations by simply observing the shape of the yield curve. If the yield curve is declining sharply, historical evidence suggests that interest rates will probably decline. Expectations theorists would suggest that you need to examine only the prevailing yield curve to predict the direction of interest rates in the future.

Based on these theories, bond investors use the prevailing yield curve to predict the shapes of future yield curves. Using this prediction and knowledge of current interest rates, investors can determine expected yield volatility by maturity sector. As suggested by Hourdouvelis (1988), the maturity segments that are expected to experience the greatest yield changes give the investor the largest potential price change opportunities.

18.7.5 Yield Spreads

Another technique that helps bond investors make profitable trades is the analysis of *yield spreads*—the differences in promised yields between bond issues or segments of the market at any point in time. Such differences are specific to the particular issues or segments of the bond market. Thus yield spreads further shape the rates determined by the basic economic forces ($RFR + I$).

There are four major yield spreads:

1. Different *segments* of the bond market may have different yields. For example, pure government bonds will have lower yields than government agency bonds, and government bonds have much lower yields than corporate bonds.
2. Bonds in different *sectors* of the same market segment may have different yields. For example, prime-grade municipal bonds will have lower yields than good-grade municipal bonds; you will find spreads between AA utilities and BBB utilities, or between AAA industrial bonds and AAA public utility bonds.
3. Different *coupons* or *seasoning* within a given market segment or sector may cause yield spreads. Examples include current coupon government bonds versus deep-discount governments or recently issued AA industrials versus seasoned AA industrials.
4. Different *maturities* within a given market segment or sector also cause differences in yields. An example is the top line in Exhibit 18.11 that shows the spreads between long-term and short-term government bonds.

The differences among these bonds cause yield spreads that may be either positive or negative. More important, *the magnitude or the direction of a spread can change over time.* These changes in size or direction of yield spreads offer profit opportunities. We say that the spread narrows whenever the differences in yield become smaller; it widens as the differences increase. Exhibit 18.11 contains data on a variety of past yield spreads that have changed over time.

As a bond investor, you should evaluate yield spread changes because these changes influence bond price behavior and comparative return performance. You should attempt to identify (1) any normal yield spread that is expected to become abnormally wide or narrow in response to an anticipated swing in market interest rates, or (2) an abnormally wide or narrow yield spread that is expected to become normal.

Economic and market analyses will help you develop expectations regarding the potential for yield spreads to change. Taking advantage of these changes requires a knowledge of historical spreads, an ability to *predict* future total market changes, and an understanding of why and when specific spreads will change.[8]

Exhibit 18.11 Selected Mean Yield Spreads (Reported in Basis Points)

Comparisons	2002	2003	2004	2005	2006	2007
1. 10 Year Treasury–30 Day T-Bill	301	301	303	135	13	31
2. Aaa corporates–10 Year Treasury	188	166	136	95	78	93
3. Aaa corporates–Aaa municipals	163	115	145	95	143	142
4. Baa municipals–Aaa municipals	78	69	92	58	56	46
5. Utilities–industrials	60	50	25	10	7	8
6. Comp. HY Bond–10 Year Treasury	895	485	295	547	336	582

Note: Yield spreads are equal to the yield on the first bond minus the yield on the second bond—for example, the yield on long governments minus the yield on short governments.

Sources: Federal Reserve Bulletin, Mergent Bond Record.

[8]An article that identifies four determinants of relative market spreads and suggests scenarios when they will change is Dialynas and Edington (1992).

· ·
18.8 What Determines the Price Volatility for Bonds?

In this chapter, we have learned about alternative bond yields, how to calculate them, what determines bond yields (interest rates), and what causes them to change. Now that we understand why yields change, we can logically ask, What is the effect of these yield changes on the prices and rates of return for different bonds? We have discussed the inverse relationship between changes in yields and the price of bonds, so we can now discuss *the specific factors that affect the amount of price change for a yield change* in different bonds. This can also be referred to as the *interest rate sensitivity* of a bond. This section lists the specific factors that affect bond price changes for a given change in interest rates (i.e., the interest rate sensitivity of a bond) and demonstrates the effect for different bonds.

A given change in interest rates can cause vastly different percentage price changes for alternative bonds, which implies different interest rate sensitivity. This section will help you understand what causes these differences in interest rate sensitivity. To maximize your rate of return from an expected decline in interest rates, for example, you need to know which bonds will benefit the most from the yield change. This section helps you understand how to make this bond selection decision.

Throughout this section, we talk about bond price changes or bond price volatility interchangeably. **Bond price volatility** is measured as the percentage change in the price of the bond, computed as follows:

$$\frac{EPB}{BPB} - 1$$

where:

EPB = the ending price of the bond
BPB = the beginning price of the bond

A bond with high price volatility or high interest rate sensitivity is one that experiences a relatively large percentage price change for a given change in yields.

Bond price volatility is influenced by more than yield behavior alone. Malkiel (1962) used the bond valuation model to demonstrate that the market price of a bond is a function of four factors: (1) its par value, (2) its coupon, (3) the number of years to its maturity, and (4) the prevailing market interest rate. Malkiel's mathematical proofs showed the following relationships between yield (interest rate) changes and bond price behavior:

1. Bond prices move inversely to bond yields (interest rates).
2. For a given change in yields (interest rates), longer-maturity bonds experience larger price changes; thus, bond price volatility is *directly* related to term to maturity.
3. Bond price volatility increases at a diminishing rate as term to maturity increases.
4. Bond price movements resulting from equal absolute increases or decreases in yield are *not* symmetrical. A decrease in yield raises bond prices by more than an increase in yield of the same amount lowers prices.
5. Higher coupon issues show smaller percentage price fluctuation for a given change in yield; thus, bond price volatility is *inversely* related to coupon.

Homer and Leibowitz (1972) showed that the absolute level of market yields also affects bond price volatility. As the level of prevailing yields rises, the price volatility of bonds increases, *assuming a constant percentage change in market yields*. Note that, if you assume a constant percentage change in yield, the basis-point change will be greater when rates are high. For example, a 25 percent change in interest rates when rates are at 4 percent will be 100 basis points; the same 25 percent change when rates are at 8 percent will be a 200 basis-point change. In the discussion of bond duration, we will see that this difference in basis point change is important.

Exhibit 18.12 Effect of Maturity on Bond Price Volatility

| | PRESENT VALUE OF AN 8 PERCENT BOND ($1,000 PAR VALUE) | | | | | | | |
Term to Maturity	1 Year		10 Years		20 Years		30 Years	
Discount rate (YTM)	7%	10%	7%	10%	7%	10%	7%	10%
Present value of interest	$ 75	$ 73	$ 569	$498	$ 858	$686	$1,005	$757
Present value of principal	934	907	505	377	257	142	132	54
Total value of bond	$1,009	$980	$1,074	$875	$1,115	$828	$1,137	$811
Percentage change in total value	−2.9		−18.5		−25.7		−28.7	

Exhibit 18.13 Effect of Coupon on Bond Price Volatility

| | PRESENT VALUE OF 20-YEAR BOND ($1,000 PAR VALUE) | | | | | | | |
	0 Percent Coupon		3 Percent Coupon		8 Percent Coupon		12 Percent Coupon	
Discount rate (YTM)	7%	10%	7%	10%	7%	10%	7%	10%
Present value of interest	$ 0	$ 0	$322	$257	$ 858	$686	$1,287	$ 1030
Present value of principal	257	142	257	142	257	142	257	142
Total value of bond	$257	$142	$579	$399	$1,115	$828	$1,544	$1,172
Percentage change in total value	−44.7		−31.1		−25.7		−24.1	

Exhibit 18.14 Effect of Yield Level on Bond Price Volatility

| | PRESENT VALUE OF 20-YEAR, 4 PERCENT BOND ($1,000 PAR VALUE) | | | | | | | |
	(1) Low Yields		(2) Intermediate Yields		(3) High Yields		(4) 100 Basis-Point Change at High Yields	
Discount rate (YTM)	3%	4%	6%	8%	9%	12%	9%	10%
Present value of interest	$ 602	$ 547	$ 462	$396	$370	$301	$370	$343
Present value of principal	562	453	307	208	175	97	175	142
Total value of bond	$1,164	$1,000	$ 769	$604	$545	$398	$545	$485
Percentage change in total value	−14.1		−21.5		−27.0		−11.0	

Exhibits 18.12, 18.13, and 18.14 demonstrate these relationships assuming semiannual compounding. Exhibit 18.12 demonstrates the effect of maturity on price volatility. In all four maturity classes, we assume a bond with an 8 percent coupon and assume that the discount rate (YTM) changes from 7 percent to 10 percent. The only difference among the four cases is the maturities of the bonds. The demonstration involves computing the value of each bond at a 7 percent yield and at a 10 percent yield and noting the percentage change in price. As shown, this constant change in yield caused the price of the one-year bond to decline by only 2.9 percent; the 30-year bond declined by almost 29 percent. Clearly, the longer-maturity bond experienced the greater price volatility.

Also, price volatility increased at a decreasing rate with maturity. When maturity doubled from 10 years to 20 years, the percent change in price increased by less than 50 percent (from 18.5 percent to 25.7 percent). A much smaller change occurred when going from 20 years to 30 years. Therefore, Exhibit 18.12 demonstrates the first three of our price-yield relationships: (1) bond price is inversely related to yields, (2) bond price volatility is positively related to term to maturity, and (3) bond price volatility increases at a decreasing rate with maturity.

It also is possible to demonstrate the fourth relationship with this exhibit. Using the 20-year bond for demonstration purposes, if you computed the percentage change in price related to an *increase* in rates (e.g., from 7 percent to 10 percent), you would get the answer reported—a 25.7 percent decrease. In contrast, if you computed the effect on price of a *decrease* in yields from 10 percent to 7 percent, you would get a 34.7 percent increase in price (from $828 to $1,115). This demonstrates that prices change more in response to a decrease in rates (from 10 percent to 7 percent) than to a comparable increase in rates (from 7 percent to 10 percent).

Exhibit 18.13 demonstrates the coupon effect. In this set of examples, all the bonds have equal maturity (20 years) and experience the same change in YTM (from 7 percent to 10 percent). The exhibit shows the *inverse* relationship between coupon rate and price volatility: The smallest coupon bond (the zero) experienced the largest percentage price change (almost 45 percent) versus a 24 percent change for the 12 percent coupon bond.

Exhibit 18.14 demonstrates the yield level effect. In these examples, all the bonds have the same 20-year maturity and the same 4 percent coupon. In the first three cases, the YTM changed by a constant 33.3 percent (i.e., from 3 percent to 4 percent, from 6 percent to 8 percent, and from 9 percent to 12 percent). Note that the first change is 100 basis points, the second is 200 basis points, and the third is 300 basis points. The results in the first three columns confirm the statement that when rates change by a *constant percentage*, the change in the bond price is larger when the rates are at a higher level.

The fourth column shows that if you assume a *constant basis-point change in yields*, you get the opposite results. Specifically, a 100 basis-point change in yields from 3 percent to 4 percent provides a price change of 14.1 percent, while the same 100 basis-point change from 9 percent to 10 percent results in a price change of only 11 percent. Therefore, the yield level effect can differ, depending on whether the yield change is specified as a constant percentage change or a constant basis-point change.

Thus, the price volatility of a bond for a given change in yield (i.e., its interest rate sensitivity) is affected by the bond's coupon, its term to maturity, the level of yields (depending on what kind of change in yield), and the direction of the yield change. However, although both the level and direction of change in yields affect price volatility, they cannot be used for trading strategies. When yields change, the two variables that have a dramatic effect on a bond's interest rate sensitivity are coupon and maturity.

18.8.1 Trading Strategies

Knowing that coupon and maturity are the major variables that influence a bond's interest rate sensitivity, we can develop some strategies for maximizing rates of return when interest rates change. Specifically, if you expect a major *decline* in interest rates, you know that bond prices will increase, so you want a portfolio of bonds with the *maximum interest rate sensitivity* so that you will enjoy maximum price changes (capital gains) from the change in interest rates. In this situation, the previous discussion regarding the effect of maturity and coupon indicates that you should attempt to build a portfolio of long-maturity bonds with low coupons (ideally a long-term zero coupon bond). A portfolio of such bonds should experience the maximum price appreciation for a given decline in market interest rates.

In contrast, if you expect an *increase* in market interest rates, you know that bond prices will decline, and you want a portfolio with *minimum interest rate sensitivity* to minimize the capital losses caused by the increase in rates. Therefore, you would want to change your portfolio to short-maturity bonds with high coupons. This combination should provide minimal price volatility for a change in market interest rates.

18.8.2 Duration Measures

Because the price volatility (interest rate sensitivity) of a bond varies inversely with its coupon and directly with its term to maturity, it is necessary to determine the best combination of these two variables to achieve your objective. This effort would benefit from a composite measure that considered both coupon and maturity.

A composite measure of the interest rate sensitivity of a bond is referred to as **duration**. This concept and its development as a tool in bond analysis and portfolio management have existed for over 70 years. Notably, several specifications of duration have been derived over the past 20 years. First, **Macaulay duration**, developed over 70 years ago by Frederick Macaulay (1938), is a measure of the time flow of cash from a bond. A modified version of Macaulay duration can be used under certain conditions to indicate the price volatility of a bond in response to interest rate changes. Second, **modified duration** is derived by making a small adjustment (modification) to the Macaulay duration value. As already noted, under certain restrictive conditions (most important, there are no embedded options), modified duration can provide an approximation to the interest rate sensitivity of a bond (or any financial asset). Third, **effective duration** is a direct measure of the interest rate sensitivity of a bond (or any financial instrument) in cases where it is possible to estimate price changes following an interest rate change for an asset using a valuation model. Finally, **empirical duration** measures directly the percentage price change of an asset for an actual change in interest rates. This measure can be used as an estimate for an asset when there is no exact valuation model available. Because of the development of many new financial instruments, which have very unique cash flows *that change with interest rates*, effective duration and empirical duration have become widely used because of their flexibility and ability to provide a useful measure of interest rate sensitivity—the primary goal of duration. Therefore, in this section, we discuss and demonstrate these four duration measures, including their limitations.

Macaulay Duration   Macaulay showed that the duration of a bond was a more appropriate measure of time characteristics than the term to maturity of the bond because duration considers both the repayment of capital at maturity and the size and timing of coupon payments prior to final maturity. Using annual compounding, duration (**D**) is

18.13

$$D = \frac{\displaystyle\sum_{t=1}^{n} \frac{C_t(t)}{(1+i)^t}}{\displaystyle\sum_{t=1}^{n} \frac{C_t}{(1+i)^t}}$$

where:

t = the time period in which the coupon or principal payment occurs
C_t = the interest or principal payment that occurs in period t
i = the yield to maturity on the bond

The denominator in this equation is the price of a bond as determined by the present value model. The numerator is the present value of all cash flows *weighted according to the time to cash receipt*. The following example, which demonstrates the specific computations for two bonds, shows the procedure and highlights some of the properties of Macaulay duration. Consider the following two sample bonds:

	Bond A	Bond B
Face value	$1,000	$1,000
Maturity	10 years	10 years
Coupon	4%	8%

Assuming annual interest payments and an 8 percent yield to maturity on the bonds, duration is computed as shown in Exhibit 18.15.[9] If duration is computed by discounting flows using the yield to maturity of the bond, it is called *Macaulay duration.*

---

[9] We assume annual interest payments to reduce the space requirements and computations. In practice you would assume semiannual payments that would cause a slightly shorter duration since you receive half the payments earlier.

Exhibit 18.15 Computation of Macaulay Duration (Assuming 8 Percent Market Yield)

BOND A

(1) Year	(2) Cash Flow	(3) PV at 8%	(4) PV of Flow	(5) PV as % of Price	(6) (1) × (5)
1	$ 40	0.9259	$ 37.04	0.0506	0.0506
2	40	0.8573	34.29	0.0469	0.0938
3	40	0.7938	31.75	0.0434	0.1302
4	40	0.7350	29.40	0.0402	0.1608
5	40	0.6806	27.22	0.0372	0.1860
6	40	0.6302	25.21	0.0345	0.2070
7	40	0.5835	23.34	0.0319	0.2233
8	40	0.5403	21.61	0.0295	0.2360
9	40	0.5002	20.01	0.0274	0.2466
10	1,040	0.4632	481.73	0.6585	6.5850
Sum			$731.58	1.0000	8.1193

Duration = 8.12 Years

BOND B

(1) Year	(2) Cash Flow	(3) PV at 8%	(4) PV of Flow	(5) PV as % of Price	(6) (1) × (5)
1	$ 80	0.9259	$ 74.07	0.0741	0.0741
2	80	0.8573	68.59	0.0686	0.1372
3	80	0.7938	63.50	0.0635	0.1906
4	80	0.7350	58.80	0.0588	0.1906
5	80	0.6806	54.44	0.0544	0.2720
6	80	0.6302	50.42	0.0504	0.3024
7	80	0.5835	46.68	0.0467	0.3269
8	80	0.5403	43.22	0.0432	0.3456
9	80	0.5002	40.02	0.0400	0.3600
10	1,080	0.4632	500.26	0.5003	5.0030
Sum			$1,000.00	1.0000	7.2470

Duration = 7.25 Years

Characteristics of Macaulay Duration This example illustrates several characteristics of Macaulay duration. First, the Macaulay duration of a bond with coupon payments always will be less than its term to maturity because duration gives weight to these interim interest payments.

Second, there is *an inverse relationship between coupon and duration.* A bond with a larger coupon will have a shorter duration because more of the total cash flows come earlier in the form of interest payments. As shown in Exhibit 18.15, the 8 percent coupon bond has a shorter duration than the 4 percent coupon bond.

A zero coupon bond or a pure discount bond, such as a Treasury bill, will have *duration equal to its term to maturity.* In Exhibit 18.15, if you assume a single payment at maturity, duration will equal term to maturity because the only cash flow comes in the final (maturity) year—that is, you receive 100 percent of cash flows in year *n*.

Third, there is *generally a positive relationship between term to maturity and Macaulay duration,* but duration increases at a decreasing rate with maturity. Therefore, a bond with longer term to maturity almost always will have a higher duration. The relationship is not direct because as maturity increases the present value of the principal declines in value.

As shown in Exhibit 18.16, the shape of the duration-maturity curve depends on the coupon and the yield to maturity. The curve for a zero coupon bond is a straight line, indicating that duration equals term to maturity. In contrast, the curve for a low-coupon bond selling at a deep discount (due to a high YTM) will turn down at long maturities, which means that under these conditions, the longer-maturity bond will have lower duration because the discounted value of the principal payment becomes insignificant, which shifts the weight to the early interest payments, causing a decline in Macaulay duration.

Exhibit 18.16 Duration versus Maturity

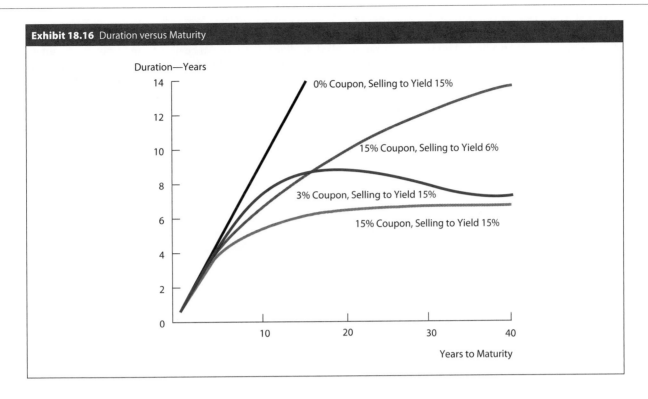

Fourth, all else the same, there is an *inverse relationship between YTM and duration*. A higher yield to maturity of a bond reduces its duration. As an example, in Exhibit 18.15, if the yield to maturity had been 12 percent rather than 8 percent, the duration for the 4 percent bond would have gone from 8.12 to 7.75, and the duration of the 8 percent bond would have gone from 7.25 to 6.80.[10] The combined effect of the inverse relationships between duration and both coupon and yield can be seen with the curve for the bond with a 15 percent coupon and yield where the duration tops out at about six years. The real-world example of such a bond would be a high-yield bond.

Finally, sinking funds and call provisions can have a dramatic effect on a bond's duration. They can change the total cash flows for a bond and, therefore, significantly change its duration. Between these two factors, the characteristic that causes the greatest uncertainty is the call feature—it is difficult to estimate when the call option will be exercised since it is a function of changes in interest rates. We consider this further when we discuss the effect of embedded options on the duration and convexity of a bond.

A summary of Macaulay duration characteristics is as follows:

- The duration of a zero coupon bond will equal its term to maturity.
- The duration of a coupon bond always will be less than its term to maturity.
- There is an *inverse* relationship between coupon and duration.
- There is generally a *positive* relationship between term to maturity and duration. Note that the duration of a coupon bond increases at a decreasing rate with maturity and the shape of the duration/maturity curve will depend on the coupon and YTM of the bond. Also, the duration of a deep discount bond will decline at very long maturities (over 20 years).
- There is an *inverse* relationship between yield to maturity and duration.
- Sinking funds and call provisions can cause a dramatic change in the duration of a bond. The effect of embedded options is discussed in a subsequent section.

[10] These properties are discussed and demonstrated in Reilly and Sidhu (1980) and Fabozzi, Buetow, and Johnson (2005).

18.8.3 Modified Duration and Bond Price Volatility

An adjusted measure of duration called *modified duration* can be used to approximate the interest rate sensitivity of an option-free (straight) bond. Modified duration equals Macaulay duration (computed in Exhibit 18.15) divided by 1 plus the current yield to maturity divided by the number of payments in a year. As an example, a bond with a Macaulay duration of 10 years, a yield to maturity *(i)* of 8 percent, and semiannual payments would have a modified duration of

$$D_{mod} = 10 / \left(1 + \frac{0.08}{2} \right)$$

$$= 10/(1.04) = 9.62$$

It has been shown, both theoretically and empirically by Hopewell and Kaufman (1973), that price movements of option-free bonds *will vary proportionally* with modified duration for *small changes in yields*.[11] Specifically, as shown in the following equation, an estimate of the percentage change in bond price equals the change in yield times modified duration:

18.14
$$\frac{\Delta P}{P} \times 100 = -D_{mod} \times \Delta i$$

where:

ΔP = the change in price for the bond
P = the beginning price for the bond
$-D_{mod}$ = the modified duration of the bond
Δi = the yield change in basis points divided by 100. For example, if interest rates go from 8.00 to 8.50 percent, $\Delta i = 50/100 = 0.50$.

Consider a bond with Macaulay $D = 8$ years and $i = 0.10$. Assume that you expect the bond's YTM to decline by 75 basis points (e.g., from 10 percent to 9.25 percent). The first step is to compute the bond's modified duration as follows:

$$D_{mod} = 8 / \left(1 + \frac{0.10}{2} \right)$$

$$= 8/(1.05) = 7.62$$

The estimated percentage change in the price of the bond using Equation 18.14 is:

$$\%\Delta P = -(7.62) \times \frac{-75}{100}$$

$$= (-7.62) \times (-0.75)$$

$$= 5.72$$

This indicates that the bond price should increase by approximately 5.72 percent in response to the 75 basis-point decline in YTM. If the price of the bond before the decline in interest rates was $900, the price after the decline in interest rates should be approximately $900 \times 1.0572 = $951.48.

The modified duration is always a negative value for a noncallable bond because of the inverse relationship between yield changes and bond price changes. Also, remember that this formulation provides an *estimate* or *approximation* of the percent change in the price of the

---

[11]The importance of the specification "for small changes in yields" will become clear when we discuss convexity in the next section. Because modified duration is an approximate measure of interest rate sensitivity, the "years" label is not appropriate.

bond. The following section on convexity shows that this formula that uses only modified duration provides an exact estimate of the percentage price change only for very small changes in yields of option-free securities.

Trading Strategies Using Modified Duration   We know that the longest duration security provides the maximum price variation. Exhibit 18.17 demonstrates that numerous ways exist to achieve a given level of duration. The following discussion indicates that an active bond investor who wants to adjust his/her portfolio for anticipated interest rate changes can use this measure of interest rate sensitivity to structure a portfolio to take advantage of changes in market yields.

If you expect a *decline* in interest rates, you should *increase* the average modified duration of your bond portfolio to experience maximum price volatility. If you expect an *increase* in interest rates, you should *reduce* the average modified duration of your portfolio to minimize your price decline. Note that the modified duration of your portfolio is the market-value-weighted average of the modified durations of the individual bonds in the portfolio.

18.8.4 Bond Convexity

Modified duration allows us to estimate bond price changes for a change in interest rates. However, the equation we used to make this calculation (Equation 18.14) is accurate only for *very small changes* in market yields. We will see that the accuracy of the estimate of the price change deteriorates with larger changes in yields because the modified duration calculation is a *linear* approximation of a bond price change that follows a *curvilinear* (convex) function. To understand the effect of this **convexity**, we must consider the price-yield relationship for alternative bonds.[12]

The Price-Yield Relationship for Bonds   Because the price of a bond is the present value of its cash flows at a particular discount rate, if you are given the coupon, maturity, and a yield for a bond, you can calculate its price at a point in time. The price-yield curve provides a set of prices for a specific maturity/coupon bond at a point in time using a range of yields to maturity (discount rates). As an example, Exhibit 18.18 lists the computed prices for a 12 percent, 20-year bond assuming yields from 1 percent to 12 percent. The exhibit shows that if you discount the flows from this bond at a yield of 1 percent, you would get a price of $2,989.47; discounting these same flows at 10 percent gives a price of $1,171.59. The graph of these prices relative to the yields that produced them (Exhibit 18.19) indicates that the price-yield relationship for this bond is not a straight line but a curvilinear relationship. That is, it is convex.

Exhibit 18.17   Bond Duration in Years for Bond Yielding 6 Percent under Different Terms

	COUPON RATES			
Years to Maturity	**0.02**	**0.04**	**0.06**	**0.08**
1	0.995	0.990	0.985	0.981
2	4.756	4.558	4.393	4.254
10	8.891	8.169	7.662	7.286
20	14.981	12.980	11.904	11.232
50	19.452	17.129	16.273	15.829
100	17.567	17.232	17.120	17.064
∞	17.167	17.167	17.167	17.167

Source: L. Fisher and R. L. Weil, "Coping with the Risk of Interest Rate Fluctuations: Returns to Bondholders from Naive and Final Strategies," *Journal of Business* 44, no. 4 (October 1971): University of Chicago Press. Reprinted by permission of the University of Chicago Press.

---

[12] For a further discussion of this topic, see Dunetz and Mahoney (1988) and Fabozzi, Buetow, and Johnson (2005).

Exhibit 18.18 Price-Yield Relationships for Alternative Bonds

A. 12 PERCENT, 20 YEAR		B. 12 PERCENT, 3 YEAR		C. ZERO COUPON, 30 YEAR	
Yield	Price	Yield	Price	Yield	Price
1.0%	$2,989.47	1.0%	$1,324.30	1.0%	$741.37
2.0	2,641.73	2.0	1,289.77	2.0	550.45
3.0	2,346.21	3.0	1,256.37	3.0	409.30
4.0	2,094.22	4.0	1,224.06	4.0	304.78
5.0	1,878.60	5.0	1,192.78	5.0	227.28
6.0	1,693.44	6.0	1,162.52	6.0	169.73
7.0	1,533.88	7.0	1,133.21	7.0	126.93
8.0	1,395.86	8.0	1,104.84	8.0	95.06
9.0	1,276.02	9.0	1,077.37	9.0	71.29
10.0	1,171.59	10.0	1,050.76	10.0	53.54
11.0	1,080.23	11.0	1,024.98	11.0	40.26
12.0	1,000.00	12.0	1,000.00	12.0	30.31

Exhibit 18.19 Price-Yield Relationship and Modified Duration at 4 Percent Yield

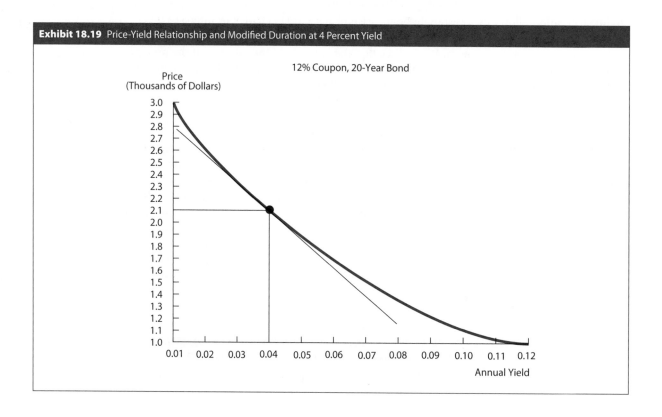

Two points are important about the price-yield relationship:

1. This relationship can be applied to a single bond, a portfolio of bonds, or any stream of future cash flows.
2. The convex price-yield relationship will differ among bonds or other cash flow streams, depending on the nature of the cash flow stream, that is, its coupon and maturity. For example, the price-yield relationship for a high-coupon, short-term security will be almost a straight line because the price does not change as much for a change in yields (e.g., the 12 percent, three-year bond in Exhibit 18.18). In contrast, the price-yield relationship for a low-coupon, long-term bond will curve radically (i.e., be very convex), as shown by the

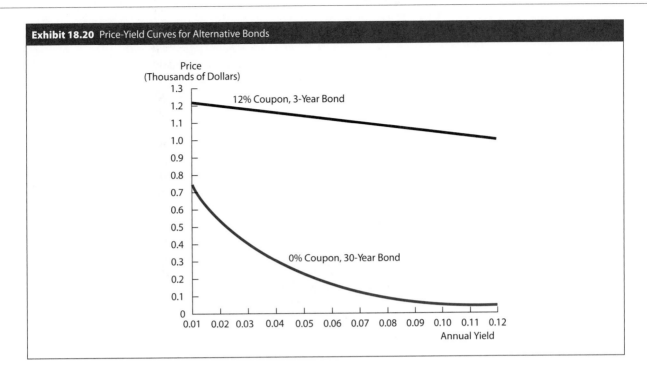

Exhibit 18.20 Price-Yield Curves for Alternative Bonds

zero coupon, 30-year bond in Exhibit 18.18. These differences in convexity are shown graphically in Exhibit 18.20. The curved nature of the price-yield relationship is referred to as the bond's *convexity*.

The Desirability of Convexity As shown by the graph in Exhibit 18.20, because of the convexity of the price-yield relationship (especially the long-term, zero coupon bond) as yield increases, the rate at which the price of the bond declines becomes slower. Similarly, when yields decline, the rate at which the price of the bond increases becomes faster. Therefore, convexity is considered a desirable trait. Specifically, if you have two bonds with equal duration but one has greater convexity, you would want the bond with greater convexity because it would have better price performance whether yields rise (the bond price declines less) or yields fall (the bond price increases more).

Given this price-yield curve, modified duration is the percentage change in price for a nominal change in yield as follows:[13]

18.15
$$D_{mod} = \frac{\dfrac{dP}{di}}{P}$$

Notice that the *dP/di* line is tangent to the price-yield curve *at a given yield* as shown in Exhibit 18.21. For *small* changes in yields (i.e., from y^* to either y_1 or y_2), this tangent straight line gives a good estimate of the actual price changes. In contrast, for larger changes in yields (i.e., from y^* to either y_3 or y_4), the straight line will estimate the new price of the bond at less than the actual price shown by the price-yield curve. This misestimate arises because the modified-duration line is a linear estimate of a curvilinear relationship. Specifically, the estimate using only modified duration will *underestimate* the actual price *increase* caused by

---

[13] In mathematical terms, modified duration is the first differential of this price-yield relationship with respect to yield.

Exhibit 18.21 Price Approximation Using Modified Duration

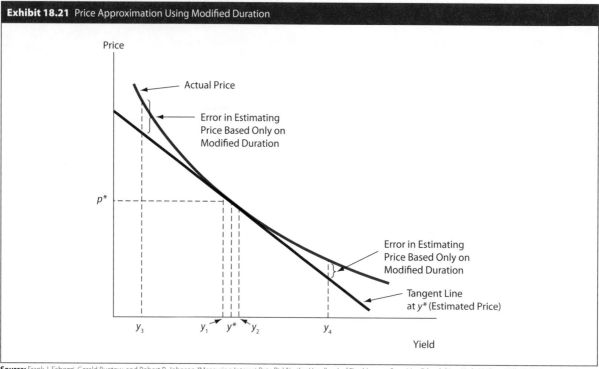

a yield decline and *overestimate* the actual price *decline* caused by an increase in yields. This graph, which demonstrates the convexity effect, also shows that price changes are *not* symmetric when yields increase or decrease. As shown, when rates decline, there is a larger price error than when rates increase because, due to convexity, when yields decline prices rise at an *increasing* rate, while prices decline at a *decreasing* rate when yields rise.

Determinants of Convexity   Convexity is a measure of the curvature of the price-yield relationship. In turn, because modified duration is the slope of the curve at a given yield, convexity indicates changes in duration. Mathematically, convexity is the second derivative of price with respect to yield (d^2P/di^2) divided by price. Specifically, convexity is the percentage change in dP/di for a given change in yield:

18.16
$$\text{Convexity} = \frac{\dfrac{d^2P}{di^2}}{P}$$

Convexity is a measure of how much a bond's price-yield curve deviates from the linear approximation of that curve. As indicated by Exhibit 18.19 and Exhibit 18.21 for *noncallable* bonds, convexity always is a positive number, implying that the price-yield curve lies above the modified-duration (tangent) line. Exhibit 18.20 illustrates the price-yield relationship for two bonds with very different coupons and maturities. (The yields and prices are contained in Exhibit 18.18.)

These graphs demonstrate the following relationship between these factors and the convexity of a bond:

•   There is an *inverse* relationship between coupon and convexity (yield and maturity constant)—that is, lower coupon, higher convexity.

- There is a *direct* relationship between maturity and convexity (yield and coupon constant)—that is, longer maturity, higher convexity.
- There is an *inverse* relationship between yield and convexity (coupon and maturity constant). This means that the price-yield curve is more convex at its lower-yield (upper left) segment.

Therefore, a short-term, high-coupon bond, such as the 12 percent coupon, three-year bond in Exhibit 18.20, has very low convexity—it is almost a straight line. In contrast, the zero-coupon, 30-year bond has high convexity.

Notably, the determinants of duration and convexity for option-free bonds are very similar. Specifically, the three factors are the same—maturity, coupon, and yield—and the direction of impact is the same—that is, maturity is positively related to both duration and convexity and both coupon and yield are inverse. Therefore, high-duration bonds have high convexity.

The Modified-Duration–Convexity Effects In summary, the change in a bond's price resulting from a change in yield can be attributed to two sources: the bond's modified duration and its convexity. The relative effect of these two factors on the price change will depend on the characteristics of the bond (i.e., its convexity) and the size of the yield change. For example, if you are estimating the price change for a 300 basis-point change in yield for a zero coupon, 30-year bond, the convexity effect would be fairly large because this bond would have high convexity, and a 300 basis-point change in yield is relatively large. In contrast, if you are dealing with only a 10 basis-point change in yields, the convexity effect would be minimal because it is a small change in yield. Similarly, the convexity effect would likewise be small even if you assume a larger yield change if you are dealing with a bond with small convexity (i.e., a high-coupon, short-maturity bond) because the price-yield curve for such a bond is almost a straight line.

In conclusion, modified duration can help you derive an *approximate* percentage bond price change for a given change in interest rates, but you must remember that it is only a good estimate when you are considering small yield changes. The point is, you must also consider the convexity effect on price change when you are dealing with large yield changes and/or when the securities or cash flows have high convexity.

Computation of Convexity Again, the formula for computing the convexity of a stream of cash flows looks fairly complex, but it can be broken down into manageable steps. You will recall from our convexity equation (18.16) that

$$\text{Convexity} = \frac{d^2 P / di^2}{P}$$

In turn,

18.17
$$\frac{d^2 P}{di^2} = \frac{1}{(1+i)^2}\left[\sum_{t=1}^{n}\frac{CF_t}{(1+i)}(t^2 + t)\right]$$

Exhibit 18.22 contains the computations related to this calculation for a three-year bond with a 12 percent coupon and 9 percent YTM assuming annual flows.

The convexity for this bond is very low because it has a short maturity, high coupon, and high yield. Note that the *convexity of a security will vary along the price-yield curve*. You will get a different convexity at a 3 percent yield than at a 12 percent yield. In terms of the computation, the maturity and coupon will be the same, but you will use a different discount rate that reflects where you are on the curve. This is similar to the earlier observation that *you will get a different modified duration at different points on the price-yield curve* because the slope varies along the curve. You also can see this mathematically because, depending on where you are on

Exhibit 18.22 Computation of Convexity

$$\text{Convexity} = \frac{d^2P/di^2}{PV \text{ of Cash Flows}} = \frac{d^2P/di^2}{\text{Price}}$$

$$\frac{d^2P}{di^2} = \frac{1}{(1+i)^2}\left[\sum_{t=1}^{n}(t^2+t)\frac{CF_t}{(1+i)^t}\right]$$

$$\text{Convexity} = \frac{d^2P/di^2}{\text{Price}}$$

Example: 3-Year Bond, 12% Coupon, 9% YTM

(1) Year	(2) CFt	(3) PV @ 9%	(4) PV CF	(5) t^2+t	(4)×(5)
1	120	0.9174	$ 110.09	2	$ 220.18
2	120	0.8417	101.00	6	606.00
3	120	0.7722	92.66	12	1,111.92
4	1,000	0.7722	772.20	12	9,266.40
			Price = $1,075.95		$11,204.50

$$\frac{1}{(1+i)^2} = \frac{1}{(1.09)^2} = \frac{1}{1.19} = 0.84$$

$$\$11,204.50 \times 0.84 = \$9,411.78$$

$$\text{Convexity} = \frac{9,411.78}{1,075.95} = 8.75$$

the curve, you will be using a different market yield, and the Macaulay and modified durations are inverse to the discount rate.[14]

To compute the price change attributable to the convexity effect after you know the bond's convexity, use this equation:

18.18   Price change due to convexity $= 1/2 \times \text{price} \times \text{convexity} \times (\Delta \text{ in yield})^2$

Exhibit 18.23 shows the change in bond price considering the duration effect and the convexity effect for an 18-year bond with a 12 percent coupon and 9 percent YTM. For demonstration purposes, we assumed a decline of 100 and 300 basis points (BP) in rates (i.e., 9 percent to 8 percent and 9 percent to 6 percent).

With the 300 BP change, if you considered only the modified-duration effect, you would have *estimated* that the bond went from 126.50 to 158.30 (a 25.14 percent increase), when, in fact, the actual price is closer to 164.41, which is about a *30 percent increase*.

18.8.5 Duration and Convexity for Callable Bonds

The discussion and presentation thus far regarding Macaulay and modified durations and convexity have been concerned with option-free bonds. A callable bond is different because it provides the issuer with an option to call the bond under certain conditions and pay it off with funds from a new issue sold at a lower yield. Observers refer to this as a bond with an *embedded option*. We noted earlier that the duration of a bond can be seriously affected

---

[14] Exhibit 18.31 in the appendix to this chapter is a table that combines the computation of Macaulay and modified duration and convexity using semiannual cash flows.

Exhibit 18.23 Analysis of Bond Price Change Considering Duration and Convexity

Example: 18-Year Bond, 12% Coupon, 9% YTM
Price: 126.50
Modified Duration: 8.38 (D^*)
Convexity: 107.70
Estimate of Price Change Using Duration:
   Percent Δ Price = D^* (Δ in YLD/100)
Estimate of Price Change from Convexity:
   Price Change = $1/2 \times$ Price $\times$ Convexity $\times$ (Δ in YLD)^2

A. Change in Yield: -100 BP

Duration Change: $-8.38 \times \left(\dfrac{-100}{100}\right) = +8.38\%$

$+8.38\% \times 126.50 = +10.60$

Convexity Change: $\dfrac{1}{2} \times (126.50) \times 107.70 \times (0.01)^2$

$= 63.25 \times 107.70 \times 0.0001$

$= 6,812.03 \times 0.0001 = 0.68$

Combined Effect: 126.50
$\underline{+10.60}$ (Duration)
137.10
$\underline{+0.68}$ (Convexity)
137.78

B. Change in Yield: -300 BP

Duration Change: $-8.38 \times \left(\dfrac{-300}{100}\right) = +25.14\%$

$126.50 \times 1.2514 = 158.30(+31.80)$

Convexity Effect: $\dfrac{1}{2} \times (126.50) \times 107.70 \times (0.03)^2$

$6,812.03 \times 0.0009 = 6.11$

Combined Effect: 126.50
$\underline{+31.80}$ (Duration)
158.30
$\underline{+6.11}$ (Convexity)
164.41

by an embedded call option if interest rates decline substantially below a bond's coupon rate. In such a case, the issuer will likely call the bond, which will dramatically change the maturity and the duration of the bond. For example, assume a firm issues a 30-year bond with a 9 percent coupon with a deferred call provision whereby the bond can be called in six years at 109 percent of par. If the bond is issued at par, its original *duration to maturity* will be about 11 years. A year later, if rates decline to about 7 percent, its duration to maturity will still be over *10 years* because duration is inversely related to yield and yields have declined. Notably, at a yield of 7 percent, this bond will probably trade at *yield to call* because at a 7 percent yield the firm will likely exercise its option and call the bond in five years. Notably, the bond's *duration to first call* would be about *four years*. Clearly, there is a significant difference between duration to maturity (over 10 years) and duration to first call (about 4 years).

To understand the impact of the call feature on the duration and convexity of a bond, it is important to consider what determines the price of a callable bond. A callable bond is a combination of a noncallable bond plus a *call option* that was *sold to the issuer*, which allows the issuer to call the bond under the conditions discussed earlier. Because the call option is owned by the issuer, it has negative value for the investor in the bond. Thus the bondholder's position is

18.19   Long a callable bond = Long a noncallable bond + A short position in a call option

Therefore, the value (price) of a callable bond is equal to

18.20   Callable bond price = Noncallable bond price − call option price

Given this valuation, anything that increases the value of the call option will reduce the value of the callable bond.[15] The point is, when interest rates decline, the right-hand side of this equation experiences a conflict between the value of the noncallable bond that increases in value, and the value of the call option that also increases but this has a negative effect on the bond price. Notably, if the value of the call option increases faster than the value of the noncallable bond, the overall value of the callable bond will *decline* when interest rates decline and this is referred to as *negative duration*—that is, in contrast to the usual inverse relationship between yield changes and bond price changes, in this case yield changes and price changes both decline.

Option-Adjusted Duration[16]   Given these two extreme values of (1) duration to maturity and (2) duration to first call, the investment community derives a duration estimate that is referred to as an option-adjusted or call-adjusted duration based on *the probability that the issuing firm will exercise its call option* for the bond when the bond becomes freely callable. This option-adjusted duration will be somewhere between these two extreme values. Specifically, when interest rates are substantially above the coupon rate, the probability of the bond being called is very small (i.e., the call option has very little value) and the option-adjusted duration will approach the duration to maturity. In contrast, if interest rates decline to levels substantially below the coupon rate, the probability of the bond being called at the first opportunity is very high (i.e., the call option is very valuable and will probably be exercised) and the option-adjusted duration will approach the duration to first call. In summary, the bond's option-adjusted duration will be somewhere between these two extremes with the exact option-adjusted duration depending on the level of interest rates relative to the bond's coupon rate.

The option-adjusted duration can also be envisioned or computed based on the duration of the two components, as follows:

18.21   Option-adjusted duration = Duration of the noncallable bond
                                        − duration of the call option

If one conceives of duration as interest rate sensitivity, we know that at high interest rates a change in yield will have little if any impact on the value of the option. Thus the duration (i.e., interest rate sensitivity) of the option would be close to zero and the option-adjusted duration would equal that of a noncallable bond. In contrast, when yields decline below the coupon yield, the call option will be very interest rate sensitive since the option will experience a large increase in value at low yields. Thus, the duration (i.e., the interest rate sensitivity) of the option will be fairly high and have a large impact on the callable bond's option-adjusted duration—it will drive the duration of the callable bond toward the duration to first call. In fact, it is possible to conceive of an option that is very leveraged such that it is extremely interest rate sensitive (i.e., has a very large duration that exceeds the duration of the noncallable bond) resulting in a *negative option-adjusted duration*. An example is a mortgage-backed security that might *decline* in price when there is a *decline* in interest rates.

---

[15] For a further discussion of the effect of these embedded options, see Fabozzi, Buetow, and Johnson (2005) and Fabozzi, Kalotay, and Williams (2005). Also see Winkelmann (1989).
[16] The discussion in this subsection will consider the option-adjusted duration on a conceptual and intuitive basis. For a detailed mathematical treatment, see Dunetz and Mahoney (1988).

Exhibit 18.24 Noncallable and Callable Bond Price-Yield Relationship

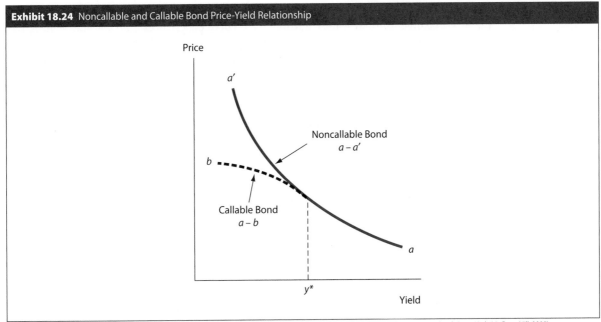

Source: Frank J. Fabozzi, Gerald W. Buetow, and Robert R. Johnson, "Measuring Interest Rate Risk" in the *Handbook of Fixed-Income Securities,* 7th ed., (New York: McGraw-Hill, 2005). Reproduced with permission from The McGraw-Hill companies.

Convexity of Callable Bonds Exhibit 18.24 shows what happens to the price of a callable bond versus the value of a noncallable bond when interest rates increase or decline. Starting from yield y^* (which is close to the par value yield), if interest *rates increase*, the value of the call option declines because, at market interest rates that are substantially above the coupon rate, it is unlikely the issuer will want to call the issue. Therefore, the call option has very little value and the price of the callable bond will be similar to the price of a non-callable bond. In contrast, when interest rates *decline below* y^*, there is an increase in the probability that the issuer will want to use the call option—that is, the value of the call option increases. As a result, the value of the callable bond will deviate from the value of the noncallable bond—that is, the price of the callable bond will initially not increase as fast as the noncallable bond price and eventually will not increase at all. This is what is shown in curve *a-b*.

In the case of the noncallable bond, we indicated that it had *positive convexity* because as yields declined, the price of the bond increased at a *faster* rate. With the callable bond, when rates decline, the price increases at a *slower* rate and eventually does not change at all. This pattern of price-yield change for a callable bond when yields decline is referred to as *negative convexity*.

Needless to say, this price pattern (negative convexity) is one of the risks of a callable bond versus a noncallable bond when interest rates decline.

18.8.6 Limitations of Macaulay and Modified Duration

It is important to understand Macaulay and modified duration because of the perspective they provide regarding factors that affect the volatility and interest rate sensitivity of bonds. However, it also is important for bond analysts and portfolio managers to recognize the serious limitations of these measures in the real world. The major limitations are as follows.

First, as noted in the discussion on convexity, the percent change estimates using modified duration are good only for small-yield changes. This was demonstrated in Exhibit 18.21. As a result, two bonds with equal duration may experience different price changes for large-yield changes—depending on *differences in the convexity* of the bonds.

Second, it is difficult to determine the interest rate sensitivity of a portfolio of bonds when there is a change in interest rates and the yield curve experiences a *nonparallel shift*. It was noted earlier that the duration of a portfolio is the weighted average of the durations of the bonds in the portfolio. Everything works well as long as all yields change by the same amount—that is, there is a parallel shift of the yield curve. However, when yields change, the yield curve *seldom* experiences a parallel shift. Assuming a nonparallel shift, which yield do you use to describe the change—the short-, intermediate-, or long-maturity yield? Two portfolios that begin the period with the same duration can have different ending durations and perform very differently, depending on how the yield curve changed (i.e., did it steepen or flatten?) and the composition of the portfolio (i.e., relative to its duration, was it a bullet or a barbell?). Consider the following simple example for two portfolios that have a duration of 4.50 years:

Bond	Coupon	Maturity (Years)	Yield	Modified Duration	Weights
Portfolio A					
A	7.00	4	7.00	2.70	0.555
B	9.00	20	9.00	6.75	0.445
Portfolio B					
C	8.00	10	8.00	4.50	1.000

As shown, the modified durations are equal at the initiation of the portfolio. Assume a nonparallel change in yields where the *yield curve steepens*. Specifically, 4-year yields decline to 6 percent, 10-year yields do not change, and 20-year yields rise to 10 percent. Portfolio B would experience a very small change in value because of stability in yield for 10-year bonds. In contrast, the price for 4-year bonds will experience a small increase (because of small duration) and the value of 20-year bonds will experience a large decline. Overall, the value of Portfolio A will decline because of the weight of Bond B in the portfolio and its large decline in value due to its large modified duration. Obviously, if the yield curve had flattened or inverted, the barbell portfolio would have benefited from the change. This differential performance because of the change in the shape of the yield curve (i.e., it did not experience a parallel shift) is referred to as *yield curve risk*, which cannot be captured by the traditional duration-convexity presentation.

The third limitation of Macaulay and modified durations involves our initial calculation. We assumed that cash flows from the bond *were not affected by yield changes*—that is, we assumed option-free bonds. Later, we saw the effect on the computed duration and convexity when we considered the effect of an embedded call option in Exhibit 18.24. Specifically, we saw that the option-adjusted duration would be some value between the duration to maturity and duration to first call and the specific value would depend on the current market yield relative to the bond's coupon. Further, we saw that when interest rates declined with an embedded call option, the convexity of the bond went from some positive value to *negative* convexity because the price of the callable bond increased at a slower rate or it did not change when the yields declined (i.e., there is *price compression*).

Because of these limitations, practitioners have developed a way to approximate the duration of a bond or any security that can be impacted by a change in interest rates. This is referred to as *effective duration*, which is discussed in the following section.

Effective Duration[17]   As noted previously, the purpose of duration is to indicate the price change of an asset to a change in yield—that is, it is *a measure of the interest rate sensitivity of an asset*. Because modified duration is based on Macaulay duration, it can provide a reasonable approximation of the interest rate sensitivity of a bond that experiences a small-yield change and one that is option free—if yield changes do not change the cash flows for the bond. Unfortunately, the Macaulay and modified-duration measures cannot be used (1) for

---

[17] This section benefited substantially from the thorough presentation in Fabozzi, Buetow, and Johnson (2005).

large-yield changes; (2) for assets with embedded options; or (3) for assets that are affected by variables other than interest rates, such as common stocks or real estate.

To overcome these limitations, practitioners use *effective duration*, a direct measure of the interest rate sensitivity of a bond or any asset where it is possible to use a pricing model to estimate the market prices surrounding a change in interest rates. As we will demonstrate, using this measure it is possible to derive negative durations (which is not mathematically possible with Macaulay) or durations that are longer than the maturity of the asset (likewise not possible with Macaulay). Specifically, effective duration measures the interest rate sensitivity of a bond taking into consideration that the cash flows of the bond can change when yields change due to the existence of embedded options (e.g., call or put options). It is also possible to calculate the effective duration for an option-free bond, in which case the computed duration value will be equal to what would be derived for small-yield changes using modified duration. Put another way, under those conditions the effective duration would equal the modified duration.

Notably, to implement the effective duration formula, it is necessary to use an interest rate model and a corresponding pricing model that will provide price estimates for the asset when interest rates and cash flows change. The formulas for calculating effective duration and effective convexity are:

18.22
$$\text{Effective Duration } (D_{Eff}) = \frac{(P_-) - (P_+)}{2PS}$$

18.23
$$\text{Effective Convexity } (C_{Eff}) = \frac{(P_-) - (P_+) - 2P}{PS^2}$$

where

P_- = the estimated price of the asset after a downward shift in interest rates
P_+ = the estimated price of the asset after an upward shift in interest rates
P = the current price of the asset (before any interest rate shifts)
S = the assumed shift in the term structure

The formulas are implemented by assuming small changes in yield (10 basis points) both down and up and using a pricing model to estimate the expected market prices (both P_- and P_+) at the new yields. Everything else in the formulas is given. Consider the following bond that we will initially assume is option free:

Par value	$1,000
Coupon	6%
Maturity	8 years
Initial YTM	6%
Initial price (P)	100

Given this initial scenario, we assume a change in yields of 10 basis points. The prices for the bond at yields to maturity of 5.90 percent (P_-) and 6.10 percent (P_+) are:

$$0.0590\,(P_-) = 100.42760054$$

$$0.0610\,(P_+) = 99.57457612$$
$$(P_-) - (P_+) = \overline{0.85302442}$$

$$2PS = (2)(100)(0.001) = 0.20$$

$$D_{Eff} = \frac{0.85302442}{0.20} = 4.265122$$

Because this is a noncallable bond (option free), we know that this effective duration equals the modified duration we would derive based upon the Macaulay duration of 4.39.

$$D_{mod} \frac{4.39}{\left(1 + \dfrac{0.06}{2}\right)} = \frac{4.39}{1.03} = 4.262$$

The difference is due to the rounding of the Macaulay duration.

The bond's effective convexity would equal

$$C_{Eff} = \frac{(P_-) + (P_+) - 2P}{PS^2}$$

$$= \frac{100.42760054 + 99.57457612 - 200}{(100)(0.001)^2}$$

$$= \frac{200.00217666 - 200}{0.0001}$$

$$= \frac{0.00217666}{0.0001} = 21.766$$

We know from our earlier discussion that, at a lower yield, the duration would be higher. Specifically, if we assumed a YTM of 4 percent, the effective and modified durations would be about 4.34 compared to about 4.26 at 6 percent.

Let us now assume that the bond is callable at 106 of par after 3 years. Using the Black, Derman, and Toy (1990) no-arbitrage binomial model to estimate prices for this bond beginning at a yield of 4 percent, we derive the following prices:

$$0.0390 \; (P_-) = 108.55626094$$

$$0.0410 \; (P_+) = 107.92318176$$

$$0.04 \; (P) = 108.24082177$$

$$D_{Eff} = \frac{108.55626094 - 107.92318176}{(2)(108.24082177)(0.001)}$$
$$= 2.92$$

As expected, because of the embedded call option that would have increased in value with a decline in yields, this duration value (2.92) would be lower than the duration for the option-free bond discussed earlier (4.34). In contrast, the effective durations for callable bonds at higher yields (e.g., 8 percent) would be equal to the durations for option-free bonds because the value of the option approaches zero.

The effective convexity of this callable bond at 4 percent would be

$$C_{Eff} = \frac{108.55626094 + 107.92318176 - [2(108.24082177)]}{(108.24082177)(0.001)^2}$$

$$= -20.33$$

As discussed, this is an example of negative convexity because the price increase is limited because of the increasing value of the call option. For comparison purposes, the convexity of the option-free bond at 4 percent is 23.76, which is, as expected, slightly higher than its convexity of 21.77 at 6 percent (recall that both duration and convexity are inversely related to yield).

Putable Bonds   Although it is not feasible to discuss in detail the properties of bonds with put options (putable bonds), it is possible to envision the effects if one considers the basic value of a putable bond as follows:

18.24   Value of putable bond = Value of nonputable bond + value of the put option

In this instance, the investor owns the option that allows him/her to sell the bond back to the issuer at a stated price. This option has a positive impact on the value of the bond and this option *increases* in value when interest rates *increase.* Therefore, when rates increase, the price of the bond does not decline as much as an option-free bond, but when rates decline, its price pattern is similar to that of an option-free bond because the value of the put option approaches zero.

A visual presentation of the effect of the call option on the price-yield curve was contained in Exhibit 18.24. Alternatively, Exhibit 18.25 and Exhibit 18.26 contain the effective duration-yield curves and the effective convexity–yield curves, which show the significant impact of embedded options on the effective duration and convexity of fixed-income securities.

Effective Duration Greater than Maturity   Because effective duration is simply interest rate sensitivity, it is possible to have an asset that is highly levered such that its interest rate sensitivity exceeds its maturity. For example, there are five-year, collateralized mortgage obligations (CMOs) that are highly levered and their prices will change by 15 percent to 20 percent when interest rates change by 100 basis points. Using the formula discussed (Equation 18.22), you would compute an effective duration of 15 or 20 for this five-year maturity security.

Negative Effective Duration   We know from the formula for Macaulay duration that it is not possible to compute a negative duration. Further, in the calculation for price volatility where we use modified duration, we use $-D^*$ to reflect the negative relationship between price changes and interest rate changes for *option-free bonds.* At the same time, we know that when we leave the world of option-free bonds and consider bonds with embedded options, it is possible to envision cases where bond prices move in the same direction as yields, which implies negative duration. A prime example would be mortgage-backed securities where a significant decline in interest rates will cause a substantial increase in refinancing prepayments by homeowners, which will reduce the value of these bonds to holders. Therefore, you would see a decline in interest rates and a decline in the price of these mortgage-backed bonds, which implies *negative duration.* Another way to explain a price decline with lower interest rates is the value formula (Equation 18.20)—that is, with lower interest rates, the value of the call option increases in value by more than the increase in value of the noncallable bond, which causes a decline in the value of the callable bond.

Empirical Duration[18]   In the preceding discussion of effective duration, the point was made that these computations required the use of an interest rate model and a bond pricing model that considered cash flow changes when yields changed and generated market price estimates that were inputs into the effective duration and effective convexity formulas. The question arises regarding what happens when you want to estimate interest rate sensitivity for an asset class where it is not possible to generate well-specified market price estimates in response to yield changes. The classic example would be common stocks where there is an impact on price when interest rates change, but the interest rate effect can be overpowered by the growth rate effect that is likewise unknown. The other obvious example would be bonds with exotic embedded options (including mortgage-backed bonds) where prices can change based upon the value of the exotic option that is difficult to price. In order to derive some estimate of interest rate sensitivity under such circumstances, analysts and portfolio managers employ empirical duration, which is the actual percentage price change for an asset in response to a change in yield

---

[18] The discussion in this section considered the analysis in Hayre and Chang (1997).

Exhibit 18.25 Effective Duration–Yield Curves

A. Effective Duration–Yield Curve for 8-Year, 6% Option-Free Bond

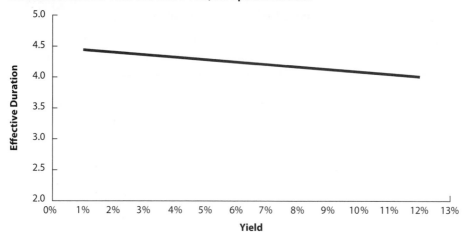

B. Effective Duration–Yield Curve for 8-Year, 6% Callable Bond after 3 Years

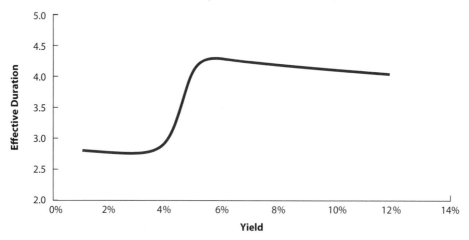

C. Effective Duration–Yield Curve for 8-Year, 6% Putable Bond after 3 Years

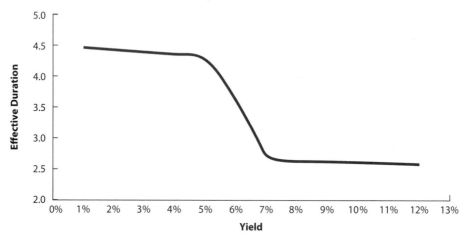

Exhibit 18.27 Effective Convexity—Yield Curves

A. Effective Convexity–Yield Curve for 8-Year, 6% Option-Free Bond

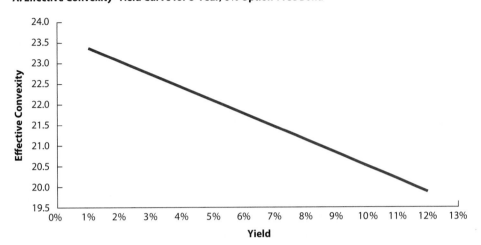

B. Effective Convexity–Yield Curve for 8-Year, 6% Callable Bond after 3 Years

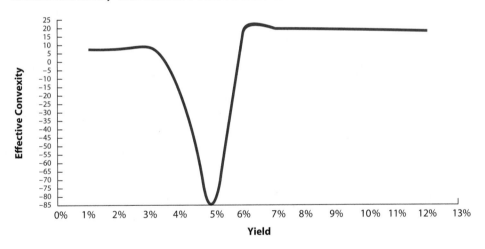

C. Effective Convexity–Yield Curve for 8-Year, 6% Putable Bond after 3 Years

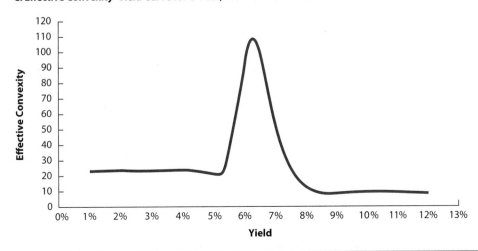

during a specified historical time period. The concept is best described by recalling the formula in Equation 18.14 used to determine the percentage price change for a bond using modified duration as follows:

$$\%\Delta Price = -D_{mod} \times (\Delta i)$$

where:

D_{mod} = the modified Macaulay duration
Δi = the change in interest rates in basis points divided by 100

The typical assumption is that we know D_{mod} and Δi and can solve for the approximate percentage price change. Alternatively, given this relationship, we can solve for D_{mod} as follows:

18.25
$$-D_{mod} = \frac{\%\Delta Price}{\Delta i}$$

When we solve for it this way, it is no longer D_{mod} (modified duration), but D_{emp}—empirical duration. Given this formulation, if you observe a change in interest rates (Δi) and the change in the price of an asset during the same time period, you can solve for the empirical duration of the asset. Consider the following simple example:

- Interest rates decline by 200 BP.
- The price of a bond increases by 10 percent.

$$D_{emp} = -\frac{10}{-200/100} = -\frac{10}{-2} = 5$$

Therefore, the change in price coincident with a change in interest rates indicates that this bond has an empirical duration (D_{emp}) of 5. This is a direct measure of the bond's interest rate sensitivity. You should think of it as *the approximate percentage change in price for a 100-basis-point change in interest rates.*

While this simple example indicates the concept of empirical duration, the technique that is generally suggested for estimating empirical duration is to employ the following regression model:

18.26
$$\frac{\Delta P}{P} = \alpha + D^{**}\Delta Y + u$$

where:

$\frac{\Delta P}{P}$ = percentage change in price
α = constant term
D^{**} = an estimate of D_{emp} (empirical duration)
ΔY = change in yield in basis points
u = random error term

The time interval for the data and the time period considered can vary based upon the asset and purpose of the analysis. When working with bonds, some analysts employ daily data for short time periods (months), while investigators using the concept for stocks or real estate (to be discussed) have employed weekly and monthly data for longer time periods (quarters or years).

Empirical Duration for Common Stock   If one considers the Macaulay duration of common stock, it is possible to envision a fairly high number because you are dealing with a perpetuity, and some growth stocks pay low dividends for many years. The values derived by Reilly and Sidhu (1980) using various assumptions of price and growth, ranged from 10 years to 20 years. In contrast, using empirical duration, one gets very different results.

Because we are dealing with the interest rate sensitivity of an asset, it is possible to compute an empirical duration for common stock that is much lower than what is implied by Macaulay duration and it is more variable. Observing a change in interest rates and the accompanying percentage change in stock prices would indicate the interest rate sensitivity of stocks. Leibowitz (1987) conducted such an analysis and derived a rolling, one-year effective duration for the S&P 500 that ranged *from about zero to almost seven.* When measuring the interest rate sensitivity of aggregate common stocks over time, you would expect changes because, as demonstrated by Reilly, Wright, and Chan (2000), the correlation between stock and bond returns varies substantially over time. In addition, you might anticipate significant differences in the effective duration for alternative stocks. For example, you would expect a large difference in the interest rate sensitivity (empirical duration) of a banking or utility stock (which is very interest rate sensitive) compared to the empirical duration of a small-cap or technology stock where its value is based more on changes in its specific growth expectations than interest rates. These differences in the interest rate sensitivity of common stocks are documented in Reilly, Wright, and Johnson (2005).

18.9 Yield Spreads with Embedded Options

Earlier in the chapter, we discussed the analysis of yield spread as a technique to enhance bond investments or bond trades. At this point, it is necessary to revisit the concept of yield spreads, keeping in mind the term structure of interest rates but, more important, with an awareness of the significant impact that interest rate volatility has on the value of embedded options in bonds. In this revisitation, we will consider two spreads: **(1) static yield spreads** that consider the total term structure and **(2) option-adjusted spreads** that consider changes in the term structure and alternative estimates of the volatility of interest rates.

18.9.1 Static Yield Spreads

You will recall that the traditional yield spread compares the yields between two bonds with similar coupons and equal maturities as follows:

8%—20-Year AA Corporate Bond	8.20%
8%—20-Year Treasury Bond	7.10%
Yield Spread	1.10%
	110 bp

There are three problems with this "traditional" yield spread:

- The two yields do not consider the prevailing term structures of interest rates but only consider the yield spread at the one point on the curve (at 20 years).
- The analysis does not consider the fact that the corporate bond could have an embedded option (put or call), whereby expected interest rate volatility may alter the cash flow for this bond.
- While not true in this example, it is possible that investors would compare two bonds with equal maturities but different coupon cash flow (e.g., a zero coupon bond versus a coupon bond or a 12 percent coupon versus a 4 percent coupon).

The first concern (neglect of the term structure) suggests the consideration of the *static spread.* It is contended that the proper way to compare non-Treasury bonds of the same maturity but with different coupon rates is to compare them to a portfolio of Treasury securities that have the same cash flow. The way to do this, if there is not an existing Treasury bond with the specified flows, is to discount the corporate bond's cash flow as if the flows were risk free. Specifically, discount them using the prevailing Treasury spot rates for the life of the corporate bond. Consider the following example:

Corporate bond—8%, five-year bond

Exhibit 18.27 Calculation of the Price of a Five-Year, 8 Percent Coupon Bond Using Treasury Spot Rates

Period	Cash Flow	Treasury Spot Rate	Present Value
1	$ 40	6.20	$ 38.80
2	40	6.30	37.60
3	40	6.40	36.40
4	40	6.50	35.20
5	40	6.60	34.00
6	40	6.70	32.84
7	40	6.80	31.64
8	40	6.90	30.48
9	40	7.00	29.36
10	1040	7.10	734.24
		Theoretical price	$1,040.56

Exhibit 18.28 Calculation of the Static Spread for a Five-Year, 8 Percent Coupon Corporate Bond

Period	Cash Flow	Treasury Spot Rate	80 BP Spread Spot Rate	Present Value
1	$ 40	6.20	7.00	$ 38.64
2	40	6.30	7.10	37.30
3	40	6.40	7.20	35.98
4	40	6.50	7.30	34.66
5	40	6.60	7.40	33.36
6	40	6.70	7.50	32.07
7	40	6.80	7.60	30.81
8	40	6.90	7.70	29.57
9	40	7.00	7.80	28.35
10	1040	7.10	7.90	705.95
			Present Value	$1,006.70

If we discount this bond's flows using the hypothetical Treasury spot rate curve contained in Exhibit 18.27, the price would be $1,040.56, which is what this bond would sell at if it were a Treasury bond. In fact, the bond is priced at $1,006.70. The *static spread* (also called the *zero volatility spread*) is the spread that will make the present value of the cash flows from the corporate bond when discounted at the Treasury spot rate plus the static spread, equal to the corporate bond's market price. To put it another way, how much of a static spread across all points on the Treasury spot rate curve is required to generate the current market price for this bond? Adding 70 basis points to every spot rate generates a price above $1,006.70, which indicates that we need to consider a larger spread. As shown in Exhibit 18.28, using a spread of 80 basis points generates a price of $1,006.70, which equals the current price of the corporate bond, which indicates that there is a static (zero volatility) spread for the bond of 80 basis points or 0.80 percent.

18.9.2 Option-Adjusted Spread

As noted, the traditional spread was a problem because it did not consider the full-term structure or the impact of interest rate volatility. The term structure problem was addressed by estimating the static (zero volatility) spread.

The interest rate volatility factor is considered by the option-adjusted spread (OAS) analysis. Why is interest rate volatility a problem? The point is, as discussed earlier in the chapter, if a bond has an embedded call option, this option can affect the bond's expected cash flow. The likelihood of the call being exercised will depend on future interest rates, the remaining maturity of the bond, the call price, and other costs of a call and new issue.

The goal of the OAS is similar to the static spread except that the technique allows for a *change in the term structure* over time based on some estimates of interest rate volatility.

The concept of OAS is best understood by a presentation of the steps involved in estimating the OAS for a specific bond as follows:

1. Based upon the prevailing Treasury yield curve, estimate the term structure of interest rates (i.e., the prevailing Treasury spot rate curve) and the implied short-term forward rates derived from the spot rates.
2. Select a probability distribution for short-term Treasury spot rates. This should be based on the current term structure and the historical behavior of interest rates. The significant estimate is the volatility of interest rates (i.e., the standard deviation of yields)—that is, how much will the forward rates change each period?
3. Using the probability distribution specified in Step 2 and Monte Carlo simulation, it is possible to randomly generate a large number of interest rate paths (e.g., 1,000).
4. For bonds with embedded options (such as callable bonds), develop rules for determining when the option will be exercised. For example, given the coupon, maturity, and call option, at what interest rate will the issue be called?
5. For each interest rate path generated in Step 3, determine the cash flows from the bond, given (a) the information about the bond (i.e., its call provision) and (b) the rules established in Step 4 for calling the bond.
6. For an assumed spread relative to the Treasury term structure of spot rates along a path, calculate a present value for all paths created in Step 3.
7. Calculate the *average* present value for all the interest rate paths.
8. Compare the average present value calculated in Step 7 to the market price of the bond. If they are equal, the assumed spread used in Step 6 is the option-adjusted spread. If they are not, try another spread and repeat Steps 6, 7, and 8.

The computed option-adjusted spread (OAS) is the average spread over the Treasury spot rate curve based on the potential paths that can be realized in the future for interest rates. The reason it is referred to as "option adjusted" is because the potential paths of cash flow are adjusted to reflect the effect of the options embedded in the bonds. Therefore, this option adjusted spread (OAS) is the spread *after* taking account of the spread required by the embedded option and, therefore, this OAS can be compared to a spread for an option-free bond. For example, the nominal spread for a callable corporate bond may be 300 basis points (3.00 percent) and look desirable relative to a noncallable corporate with a spread of only 125 basis points (1.25 percent). The fact is, the OAS for this callable bond might be only 140 basis points (which implies that the required extra yield for the embedded call option is 160 basis points). It is this 140 BP (1.40 percent) that needs to be compared to the 125 BP for the noncallable corporate bond.

The following are some technical issues that an analyst should be aware of when attempting to estimate the OAS and also factors that can cause differences in an estimate of the OAS for a bond by alternative dealers.

*   It is necessary to have a large number of paths for the simulation.
*   The estimate of the probability distribution, which includes your expected interest rate volatility, is crucial. Notably, if alternative firms differ in this estimate of expected interest rate volatility, it can cause differences in the OAS estimate.
*   It is necessary to determine the relationship between short-term rates and refinancing rates. Specifically, how much more does the firm have to pay above the short-term forward rate (i.e., the refinancing rate is a long-term rate)? Empirically, what is this relationship?
*   A call rule must be specified. This depends upon the coupon rate for the bond and other costs. It has been assumed to be almost 300 BP below the coupon rate (e.g., 5.0 percent with at least three years to maturity).

As noted, different assumptions regarding these technical issues can cause different estimates of the OAS by alternative dealers. The critical estimate is the expected interest rate volatility and this can vary between dealers; and, also, individual dealers can change their estimates over time.

• • • • SUMMARY • • • •

- The value of a bond equals the present value of all future cash flows accruing to the investor. Cash flows for the conservative bond investor include periodic interest payments and principal return; cash flows for the aggressive investor include periodic interest payments and the capital gain or loss when the bond is sold prior to its maturity. Bond investors can maximize their portfolio rates of return by accurately estimating the level of interest rates and, more importantly, by estimating changes in interest rates, yield spreads, and credit quality. Similarly, they must compare coupon rates, maturities, and call features of alternative bonds.

- There are five bond yield measures: nominal yield, current yield, promised yield to maturity, promised yield to call, and realized (horizon) yield. The promised YTM and promised YTC equations include the interest-on-interest (or coupon reinvestment) assumption. For the realized (horizon) yield computation, the investor estimates the reinvestment rate and the future selling price for the bond. The fundamental determinants of interest rates are a real risk-free rate, the expected rate of inflation, and a risk premium.

- The yield curve (or the term structure of interest rates) shows the relationship between the yields on a set of comparable bonds and the term to maturity. Based upon this yield curve, it is possible to derive a theoretical spot rate curve. In turn, these spot rates can be used to value bonds using an individual spot rate for each cash flow. This valuation approach is becoming more useful in a world where bonds have very different cash flows. In addition, these spot rates imply investor expectations about future rates referred to as forward rates. Yield curves exhibit four basic patterns. Three theories attempt to explain the shape of the yield curve: the expectations hypothesis, the liquidity preference (term premium) hypothesis, and the segmented market (preferred habitat) hypothesis.

- It is important to understand what causes changes in interest rates and how these changes in rates affect the prices of bonds. Differences in bond price volatility are mainly a function of differences in yield, coupon, and term to maturity. There are four duration measures that have been used as measures of bond price volatility or interest rate sensitivity. The Macaulay duration measure incorporates coupon, maturity, and yield in one measure. In turn, modified duration

(which is directly related to Macaulay duration) provides an estimate of the response of bond prices to changes in interest rates under certain assumptions. Because modified duration provides a straight-line estimate of the curvilinear price-yield function, you must consider modified duration together with the convexity of a bond for large changes in yields and/or when dealing with securities that have high convexity. Notably, an embedded call option feature on a bond can have a significant impact on its duration (the call feature can shorten it dramatically) and on its convexity (the call feature can change the convexity from a positive value to a negative value). Following a discussion of some of the limitations of Macaulay and modified durations as measures of interest rate sensitivity, effective duration is introduced as a direct measure of interest rate sensitivity—that is, it is the estimated percentage change in price for a 100-basis-point change in interest rates and allows for repricing due to changes in cash flow caused by changes in interest rates. Notably, with effective duration, it is necessary to have a valid bond pricing model and it is possible to have durations longer than maturity as well as negative duration.

- Finally, there are instances when it is very difficult to estimate the price when there is a change in interest rates as required for effective duration—such as with some mortgage-backed securities, common stock, and real estate. In these instances, analysts consider estimating empirical duration, which is based on the analysis of historical data on price changes that accompany interest rate changes. While it is possible to derive such estimates for a range of assets, it is important to remember that the duration values derived can vary dramatically and are notoriously unstable.

- We concluded the chapter with a revisitation to yield spreads for bonds with embedded options. To take account of the spread across the total term structure of interest rates, we described and demonstrated the static spread. In order to consider the impact of interest rate volatility on the embedded options, we discussed and described the steps to estimate the option-adjusted spread (OAS) for these bonds.

- Given the background in bond valuation and the factors that influence bond value and bond return volatility, we are ready to consider how to build a bond portfolio that is consistent with our goals and objectives. Bond portfolio analysis is the topic of Chapter 19.

• • • • SUGGESTED READINGS • • • •

Eavis, Peter. "Time for Fannie, Freddie?" *Wall Street Journal*, July 8, 2008, C14.

Fabozzi, Frank J. *Fixed-Income Mathematics*. Chicago: Probus, 1988.

Fabozzi, Frank J. *Bond Markets, Analysis and Strategies*, 5th ed. Upper Saddle River, NJ: 2004.

Fabozzi, Frank J. *Fixed-Income Analysis*, 2nd ed. Hoboken, NJ: John Wiley & Sons, 2007.

Fama, Eugene F. "Forward Rates as Predictors of Future Spot Rates." *Journal of Financial Economics* 3, no. 4 (October 1976).

Hagerty, James R., and Serena Ng, "Mortgage Giants Take Beating on Fears over Loan Defaults," *Wall Street Journal*, July 8, 2008, A1, A14.

Homer, Sidnay and Martin L. Leibowitz. *Inside the Yield Book*. New York: Bloomberg Publishing, 2004.

Tuckman, Bruce, *Fixed-Income Securities*, 2nd ed. New York: John Wiley & Sons, 2002.

Sundaresan, Suresh. *Fixed Income Markets and Their Derivates*, 2nd ed. Cincinnati, OH: South-Western, 2002.

• • • • QUESTIONS • • • •

1. Why does the present value equation appear to be more useful for the bond investor than for the common stock investor?

2. What are the important assumptions made when you calculate the promised yield to maturity? What are the assumptions when calculating promised YTC?

3. a. Define the variables included in the following model:

$$i = (RFR, I, RP)$$

   b. Assume that the firm whose bonds you are considering is not expected to break even this year.
   c. Discuss which factor will be affected by this information.

4. We discussed three alternative hypotheses to explain the term structure of interest rates. Briefly discuss the three hypotheses and indicate which one you think best explains the alternative shapes of a yield curve.

5. **CFA EXAMINATION LEVEL I**
   a. Explain what is meant by the *structure of interest rates.* Explain the theoretical basis of an upward-sloping yield curve. [8 minutes]
   b. Explain the economic circumstances under which you would expect to see the inverted yield curve prevail. [7 minutes]
   c. Define "real" rate of interest. [2 minutes]
   d. Discuss the characteristics of the market for U.S. Treasury securities. Compare it to the market for AAA corporate bonds. Discuss the opportunities that may exist in bond markets that are less than efficient. [8 minutes]
   e. Over the past several years, fairly wide yield spreads between AAA corporates and Treasuries have occasionally prevailed. Discuss the possible reasons for this. [5 minutes]

6. **CFA EXAMINATION LEVEL III** As the portfolio manager for a large pension fund, you are offered the following bonds:

	Coupon	Maturity	Price	Call Price	Yield to Maturity
Edgar Corp. (new issue)	14.00%	2012	$101.3/4	$114	13.75%
Edgar Corp. (new issue)	6.00	2012	48.1/8	103	13.60
Edgar Corp. (2000 issue)	6.00	2012	48.7/8	103	13.40

Assuming that you expect a decline in interest rates over the next three years, identify and justify which of these bonds you would select. [10 minutes]

7. You expect interest rates to decline over the next six months.
   a. Given your interest rate outlook, state what kinds of bonds you want in your portfolio in terms of duration and explain your reasoning for this choice.
   b. You must make a choice between the following three sets of noncallable bonds. For each set, select the bond that would be best for your portfolio given your interest rate outlook and the consequent strategy set forth in Part a. In each case briefly discuss why you selected the bond.

		Maturity	Coupon	Yield to Maturity
Set 1:	Bond A	15 years	10%	10%
	Bond B	15 years	6%	8%
Set 2:	Bond C	15 years	6%	10%
	Bond D	10 years	8%	10%
Set 3:	Bond E	12 years	12%	12%
	Bond F	15 years	12%	8%

8. At the present time, you expect a decline in interest rates and must choose between two portfolios of bonds with the following characteristics:

	Portfolio A	Portfolio B
Average maturity	10.5 years	10.0 years
Average YTM	7%	10%
Modified duration	5.7 years	4.9 years
Modified convexity	125.18	40.30
Call features	Noncallable	Deferred call features that range from 1 to 3 years

Select one of the portfolios and discuss three factors that would justify your selection.

9. The Francesca Finance Corporation has issued a bond with the following characteristics:

Maturity—25 years
Coupon—9%
Yield to maturity—9%
Callable—after 3 years @ 109
Duration to maturity—8.2 years
Duration to first call—2.1 years

a. Discuss the concept of call-adjusted duration and indicate the approximate value (range) for it at the present time.
b. Assuming interest rates increase substantially (i.e., to 13 percent), discuss what will happen to the call-adjusted duration and the reason for the change.
c. Assuming interest rates decline substantially (i.e., they decline to 4 percent), discuss what will happen to the bond's call-adjusted duration and the reason for the change.
d. Discuss the concept of negative convexity as it relates to this bond.

10. **CFA EXAMINATION LEVEL I** Duration may be calculated by *two* widely used methods. Identify these *two* methods, and briefly discuss the primary differences between them. [5 minutes]

11. **CFA EXAMINATION LEVEL II** *Option-adjusted duration and effective duration* are alternative measures used by analysts to evaluate fixed-income securities with embedded options.

Briefly describe *each* measure and how to apply *each* to the evaluation of fixed-income securities with embedded options. [8 minutes]

12. **CFA EXAMINATION LEVEL II** As a portfolio manager, during a discussion with a client, you explain that historical return and risk premia of the type presented in the following table are frequently used in forming estimates of future returns for various types of financial assets. Although such historical data are helpful in forecasting returns, most users know that history is an imperfect guide to the future. Thus, they recognize that there are reasons why these data should be adjusted if they are to be employed in the forecasting process.

U.S. HISTORICAL RETURN AND RISK PREMIA (1926–1994)

	Per Year
Inflation rate	3.0%
Real interest rate on Treasury bills	0.5%
Maturity premium of long Treasury bonds over Treasury bills	0.8%
Default premium of long corporate bonds over long Treasury bonds	0.6%
Risk premium on stock over long Treasury bonds	5.6%
Return on Treasury bills	3.5%
Return on long corporate bonds	4.9%
Return on large-capitalization stocks	9.9%

a. As shown in the table, the historical real interest rate for Treasury bills was 0.5 percent per year and the maturity premium on Treasury bonds over Treasury bills was 0.8 percent. Briefly describe and justify *one* adjustment to *each* of these two data items that should be made before they can be used to form expectations about future real interest rates and Treasury bond maturity premia. [6 minutes]

b. You recognize that even adjusted historical economic and capital markets data may be of limited use when estimating future returns. Independent of your Part a response, briefly describe *three* key circumstances that should be considered when forming expectations about future returns. [8 minutes]

13. **CFA EXAMINATION LEVEL I** A portfolio manager at Superior Trust Company is structuring a fixed-income portfolio to meet the objectives of a client. This client plans on retiring in 15 years and wants a substantial lump sum at that time. The client has specified the use of AAA-rated securities.

    The portfolio manager compares coupon U.S. Treasuries with zero coupon stripped U.S. Treasuries and observes a significant yield advantage for the stripped bonds.

Maturity	Coupon U.S. Treasuries	Zero Coupon Stripped U.S. Treasuries
3 year	5.50%	5.80%
5 year	6.00%	6.60%
7 year	6.75%	7.25%
10 year	7.25%	7.60%
15 year	7.40%	8.80%
30 year	7.75%	7.75%

Briefly discuss *two* reasons why zero coupon stripped U.S. Treasuries could yield more than coupon U.S. Treasuries with the same final maturity. [5 minutes]

14. **CFA EXAMINATION LEVEL II**

    a. In terms of option theory, explain the impact on the offering yield of adding a call feature to a proposed bond issue. [5 minutes]

    b. Explain the impact on *both* bond duration and convexity of adding a call feature to a proposed bond issue. [10 minutes]

    Assume that a portfolio of corporate bonds is managed to maintain targets for modified duration and convexity.

    c. Explain how the portfolio could include *both* callable and noncallable bonds while maintaining the targets. [5 minutes]

    d. Describe *one* advantage and *one* disadvantage of including callable bonds in this portfolio.

15. **CFA EXAMINATION LEVEL II** Beth Goetz, CFA, has decided to add some asset-backed securities (ABS) to her fixed-income portfolio. She has narrowed the choice to an automobile ABS and a fixed-rate home equity loan (second mortgage) ABS.

    Automobile ABS are available at a pricing spread of 75 basis points over comparable-maturity Treasuries, with a zero volatility spread of 67 basis points. Home equity loan ABS are available at a pricing spread of 85 basis points over comparable-maturity Treasuries, with an option-adjusted spread of 60 basis points.

    a. Explain why pricing spread is not an appropriate measure of yield advantage for ABS. [3 minutes]

    b. Describe the concepts of
       (1) Zero volatility spread
       (2) Option-adjusted spread [8 minutes]

    c. Explain why option-adjusted spread is the appropriate measure of yield for a second mortgage ABS. [4 minutes]

16. **CFA EXAMINATION LEVEL II** The asset-backed securities (ABS) market has grown in the past few years partly as a result of credit enhancements to ABS.

    a. Describe a "letter of credit" and the risk to the investor associated with relying exclusively on this type of credit enhancement. [6 minutes]

    b. Describe "early amortization" and the risk to the investor associated with relying exclusively on this type of credit enhancement. [6 minutes]

17. **CFA EXAMINATION LEVEL II** Rachel Morgan owns a newly issued U.S. government agency fixed-rate pass-through mortgagebacked security (MBS) and wants to evaluate the sensitivity of its principal cash flow to the following interest rate scenario:
    - Interest rates instantaneously decline by 250 basis points for all maturities, remain there for one year, and then,
    - Interest rates instantaneously increase 350 basis points for all maturities and remain there for the next year.

    Currently, the MBS is priced close to par and the yield curve is "flat." Morgan does not expect the shape of the yield curve to change during her interest rate scenario.

    a. (1) State whether, in the interest rate scenario described, the MBS principal cash flows
        - Increase or decrease in the first year
        - Increase or decrease in the second year
       (2) Discuss the reason why principal cash flows change. [6 minutes]

    Morgan also wants to evaluate the price sensitivity of her MBS to changes in interest rates. She knows that modified duration and effective duration are two possible measures she could use to evaluate price sensitivity.

    b. Select *and* justify with *one* reason which duration measure Morgan should use to evaluate the price sensitivity of her MBS. [6 minutes]

    Morgan also owns a newly issued U.S. government agency collateralized mortgage obligation interest-only (IO) security.

    c. State whether the IO security price increases or decreases in the first year of the interest rate scenario described. Justify your response. [6 minutes]

18. **CFA EXAMINATION LEVEL III** One common goal among fixed-income portfolio managers is to earn high incremental returns on corporate bonds versus government bonds of comparable durations. The approach of some corporate bond portfolio managers is to find and purchase those corporate bonds having the largest initial spreads over comparable-duration government bonds. John Ames, HFS's fixed-income manager, believes that a more rigorous approach is required if incremental returns are to be maximized.

    The following table presents data relating to one set of corporate/government spread relationships present in the market at a given date:

CURRENT AND EXPECTED SPREADS AND DURATIONS OF HIGH-GRADE CORPORATE BONDS (ONE-YEAR HORIZON)

Bond Rating	Initial Spread Over Governments	Expected Horizon Spread	Initial Duration	Expected Duration One Year from Now
Aaa	31 BP	31 BP	4 years	3.1 years
Aa	40 BP	50 BP	4 years	3.1 years

    a. Recommend purchase of *either* Aaa *or* Aa bonds for a one-year investment horizon given a goal of maximizing incremental returns. Show your calculations. (Base your decision *only* on the information presented in the preceding table.) [6 minutes]

    Ames chooses not to rely *solely* on initial spread relationships. His analytical framework considers a full range of other key variables likely to impact realized incremental returns, including
    - call provisions, and
    - potential changes in interest rates.

    b. Describe *two* variables, *in addition to those identified,* that Ames should include in his analysis *and* explain how *each* of these *two* variables could cause realized incremental returns to differ from those indicated by initial spread relationships. [10 minutes]

19. **CFA EXAMINATION LEVEL II** On May 30, 1999, Janice Kerr is considering purchasing one of the following newly issued 10-year AAA corporate bonds shown in the following exhibit. Kerr notes that the yield curve is currently flat and assumes that the yield curve shifts in an instantaneous and parallel manner.

BOND CHARACTERISTICS

Description	Coupon	Price	Callable	Call Price
Sentinel due May 30, 2009	6.00%	100.00	Noncallable	Not applicable
Colina due May 30, 2009	6.20%	100.00	Currently callable	102.00

a. Contrast the effect on the price of *both* bonds if yields decline more than 100 basis points. (No calculation is required). [6 minutes]

b. State and explain under which *two* interest rate forecasts Kerr would prefer the Colina bond over the Sentinel bond. [6 minutes]

c. State the directional price change, if any, assuming interest rate volatility increases, for *each* of the following: [6 minutes]
   (1) The Sentinel bond
   (2) The Colina bond

• • • • PROBLEMS • • • •

1. Four years ago, your firm issued $1,000 par, 25-year bonds, with a 7 percent coupon rate and a 10 percent call premium.
   a. If these bonds are now called, what is the *approximate* yield to call for the investors who originally purchased them?
   b. If these bonds are now called, what is the *actual* yield to call for the investors who originally purchased them at par?
   c. If the current interest rate is 5 percent and the bonds were not callable, at what price would each bond sell?

2. Assume that you purchased an 8 percent, 20-year, $1,000 par, semiannual payment bond priced at $1,012.50 when it has 12 years remaining until maturity. Compute:
   a. Its promised yield to maturity
   b. Its yield to call if the bond is callable in three years with an 8 percent premium

3. Calculate the duration of an 8 percent, $1,000 par bond that matures in three years if the bond's YTM is 10 percent and interest is paid semiannually.
   a. Calculate this bond's modified duration.
   b. Assuming the bond's YTM goes from 10 percent to 9.5 percent, calculate an estimate of the price change.

4. Two years ago, you acquired a 10-year zero coupon, $1,000 par value bond at a 12 percent YTM. Recently you sold this bond at an 8 percent YTM. Using semiannual compounding, compute the annualized horizon return for this investment.

5. A bond for the Chelle Corporation has the following characteristics:

   Maturity—12 years
   Coupon—10%
   Yield to maturity—9.50%
   Macaulay duration—5.7 years
   Convexity—48
   Noncallable

   a. Calculate the approximate price change for this bond using only its duration assuming its yield to maturity increased by 150 basis points. Discuss the impact of the calculation, including the convexity effect.
   b. Calculate the approximate price change for this bond (using only its duration) if its yield to maturity declined by 300 basis points. Discuss (without calculations) what would happen to your estimate of the price change if this was a callable bond.

6. **CFA EXAMINATION LEVEL I** The following table shows selected data on a German government bond (payable in Deutschmarks) and a U.S. government bond. Identify the components of return and calculate the total return in U.S. dollars for both of these bonds for the year 1991. Show the calculations for *each* component. (Ignore interest on interest in view of the short time period.) [8 minutes]

| | | MARKET YIELD | | | EXCHANGE RATE (DM/$U.S.) | |
	Coupon	1/1/91	1/1/92	Modified Duration	1/1/91	1/1/92
German government bond	8.50%	8.50%	8.00%	7.0	1.55	1.50
U.S. government bond	8.00%	8.00%	6.75%	6.5	—	—

7. **CFA EXAMINATION LEVEL I** Philip Morris has issued bonds that pay semiannually with the following characteristics:

Coupon	Yield to Maturity	Maturity	Macaulay Duration
8%	8%	15 years	10 years

a. Calculate modified duration using the preceding information. [5 minutes]
b. Explain why modified duration is a better measure than maturity when calculating the bond's sensitivity to changes in interest rates. [5 minutes]
c. Identify the direction of change in modified duration if
   (1) the coupon of the bond were 4 percent, not 8 percent.
   (2) the maturity of the bond were 7 years, not 15 years [5 minutes]
d. Define convexity and explain how modified duration *and* convexity are used to approximate the bond's percentage change in price, given a change in interest rates. [5 minutes]

8. **CFA EXAMINATION LEVEL I** You are a U.S. investor considering purchase of one of the following securities. Assume that the currency risk of the German government bond will be hedged, and the six-month discount on Deutschemark forward contracts is –0.75 percent versus the U.S. dollar.

Bond	Maturity	Coupon	Price
U.S. government	June 1, 2003	6.50%	100.00
German government	June 1, 2003	7.50%	100.00

Calculate the expected price change required in the German government bond that would result in the two bonds having equal total returns in U.S. dollars over a six-month horizon. [8 minutes]

9. **CFA EXAMINATION LEVEL II**
a. Using the information in the following table, calculate the projected price change for Bond B if the yield to maturity for this bond falls by 75 basis points. [7 minutes]
b. Describe the shortcoming of analyzing Bond A strictly to call or to maturity. Explain an approach to remedy this shortcoming. [6 minutes]

MONTICELLO CORPORATION BOND INFORMATION

	Bond A (Callable)	Bond B (Noncallable)
Maturity	2012	2012
Coupon	11.50%	7.25%
Current price	125.75	100.00
Yield to maturity	7.70%	7.25%
Modified duration to maturity	6.20	6.80
Convexity to maturity	0.50	0.60
Call date	2006	—
Call price	105	—
Yield to call	5.10%	—
Modified duration to call	3.10	—
Convexity to call	0.10	—

10. **CFA EXAMINATION LEVEL II** U.S. Treasuries represent a significant holding in Monticello's pension portfolio. You decide to analyze the yield curve for U.S. Treasury Notes.
a. Using the data in the following table, calculate the five-year spot and forward rates assuming annual compounding. Show calculations. [8 minutes]

U.S. TREASURY NOTE YIELD CURVE DATA

Years to Maturity	Par Coupon Yield to Maturity	Calculated Spot Rates	Calculated Forward Rates
1	5.00	5.00	5.00
2	5.20	5.21	5.42
3	6.00	6.05	7.75
4	7.00	7.16	10.56
5	7.00	—	—

b. Define and describe *each* of the following *three* concepts:
- Yield to maturity
- Spot rate
- Forward rate

Explain how these *three* concepts are related. [9 minutes]

You are considering the purchase of a zero coupon U.S. Treasury Note with four years to maturity.

c. Based on the preceding yield curve analysis, calculate *both* the expected yield to maturity and the price for the security. Show calculations. [8 minutes]

 11. **CFA EXAMINATION LEVEL II** The following table shows yields to maturity on U.S. Treasury securities as of January 1, 1993:

Term to Maturity	Yield to Maturity
1 year	3.50%
2 years	4.50%
3 years	5.00%
4 years	5.50%
5 years	6.00%
10 years	6.60%

a. Based on the data in the table, calculate the implied forward one-year rate of interest at January 1, 1996. [5 minutes]
b. Describe the conditions under which the calculated forward rate would be an unbiased estimate of the one-year spot rate of interest at January 1, 1996. [5 minutes]

Assume that one year earlier, at January 1, 1992, the prevailing term structure for U.S. Treasury securities was such that the implied forward one-year rate of interest at January 1, 1996, was significantly higher than the corresponding rate implied by the term structure at January 1, 1993.

c. On the basis of the pure expectations theory of the term structure, briefly discuss two factors that could account for such a decline in the implied forward rate. [8 minutes]

Multiple scenario forecasting frequently makes use of information from the term structure of interest rates.

d. Briefly describe how the information conveyed by this observed decrease in the implied forward rate for 1996 could be used in making a multiple scenario forecast. [5 minutes]

12. **CFA EXAMINATION LEVEL I** Bonds of Zello Corporation with a par value of $1,000 sell for $960, mature in five years, and have a 7 percent annual coupon rate paid semiannually.
a. Calculate the
   (1) current yield;
   (2) yield to maturity (to the nearest whole percent, i.e., 3 percent, 4 percent, 5 percent, etc.); *and*

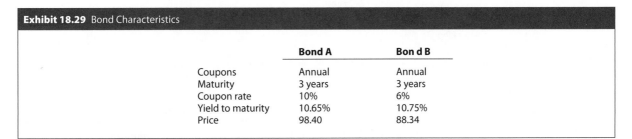

Exhibit 18.29 Bond Characteristics

	Bond A	Bond B
Coupons	Annual	Annual
Maturity	3 years	3 years
Coupon rate	10%	6%
Yield to maturity	10.65%	10.75%
Price	98.40	88.34

Exhibit 18.30 Spot Interest Rates

Term	Spot Rates (Zero Coupon)
1 year	5%
2 year	8%
3 year	11%

(3) horizon yield (also called realized or total return) for an investor with a three-year holding period and a reinvestment rate of 6 percent over the period. At the end of three years, the 7 percent coupon bonds with two years remaining will sell to yield 7 percent.
Show your work. [9 minutes]

b. Cite *one* major shortcoming for *each* of the following fixed-income yield measures:
(1) current yield;
(2) yield to maturity; *and*
(3) horizon yield (also called realized or total return). [6 minutes]

13. **CFA EXAMINATION LEVEL II** Exhibit 18.29 shows the characteristics of two annual pay bonds from the same issuer with the same priority in the event of default, and Exhibit 18.30 displays spot interest rates. Neither bond's price is consistent with the spot rates.

Using the information in Exhibits 18.29 and 18.30 recommend *either* Bond A *or* Bond B for purchase. Justify your choice. [10 minutes]

14. **CFA EXAMINATION LEVEL II** You ran a regression of the yield of KC Company's 10-year bond on the 10-year U.S. Treasury benchmark's yield using month-end data for the past year. You found the following result:

$$\text{Yield}_{KC} = 0.54 + 1.22 \ \text{Yield}_{Treasury}$$

where Yield_{KC} is the yield on the KC bond and $\text{Yield}_{Treasury}$ is the yield on the U.S. Treasury bond.
The modified duration on the 10-year U.S. Treasury is 7.0 years, and modified duration on the KC bond is 6.93 years.

a. Calculate the percentage change in the price of the 10-year U.S. Treasury, assuming a 50-basispoint change in the yield on the 10-year U.S. Treasury. [3 minutes]

b. Calculate the percentage change in the price of the KC bond, using the regression equation, assuming a 50-basis-point change in the yield on the 10-year U.S. Treasury. [6 minutes]

15. **CFA EXAMINATION LEVEL II** Patrick Wall is considering the purchase of one of the two bonds described in the following table. Wall realizes his decision will depend primarily on effective duration, and he believes that interest rates will decline by 50 basis points at all maturities over the next six months.

BOND DESCRIPTIONS

Characteristic	CIC	PTR
Market price	101.75	101.75
Maturity date	June 1, 2008	June 1, 2008
Call date	Noncallable	June 1, 2003
Annual coupon	6.25%	7.35%
Interest payment	Semiannual	Semiannual
Effective duration	7.35	5.40
Yield to maturity	6.02%	7.10%
Credit rating	A	A

a. Calculate the percentage price change forecasted by effective duration for *both* the CIC and PTR bonds if interest rates decline by 50 basis points over the next six months. Show your work. [6 minutes]

b. Calculate the six-month horizon return (in percent) for *each* bond, if the actual CIC bond price equals 105.55 and the actual PTR bond price equals 104.15 at the end of six months. Assume you purchased the bonds to settle on June 1, 1998. Show your work. [6 minutes]

Wall is surprised by the fact that although interest rates fell by 50 basis points, the actual price change for the CIC bond was greater than the price change forecasted by effective duration, whereas the actual price change for the PTR bond was less than the price change forecasted by effective duration.

c. Explain why the actual price change would be greater for the CIC bond and the actual price change would be less for the PTR bond. [6 minutes]

16. **CFA EXAMINATION LEVEL II**
   a. Discuss how *each* of the following theories for the term structure of interest rates could explain an upward slope of the yield curve:
      (1) Pure expectations (unbiased)
      (2) Uncertainty and term premiums (liquidity preference)
      (3) Market segmentation [9 minutes]

The following are the current coupon yields to maturity and spot rates of interest for six U.S. Treasury securities. Assume all securities pay interest annually.

YIELDS TO MATURITY AND SPOT RATES OF INTEREST

Term to Maturity	Current Coupon Yield to Maturity	Spot Rate of Interest
1-year Treasury	5.25%	5.25%
2-year Treasury	5.75	5.79
3-year Treasury	6.15	6.19
5-year Treasury	6.45	6.51
10-year Treasury	6.95	7.10
30-year Treasury	7.25	7.67

   b. Compute, under the pure expectations theory, the two-year implied forward rate three years from now, given the information provided in the preceding table. State the assumption underlying the calculation of the implied forward rate. [6 minutes]

· · · · · **APPENDIX: CHAPTER 18** · · · · ·

APPENDIX

Exhibit 18A.1 Calculation of Duration and Convexity for an 8 Percent Five-Year Bond Selling to Yield 6 Percent

Period	Cash Flow	Discount Factor	PV	PV × t	PV × t × (t + 1)
1	40.00	0.9709	38.83	38.83	77.67
2	40.00	0.9426	37.70	75.41	226.22
3	40.00	0.9151	36.61	109.82	439.27
4	40.00	0.8885	35.54	142.16	710.79
5	40.00	0.8626	34.50	172.52	1,035.13
6	40.00	0.8375	33.50	201.00	1,406.97
7	40.00	0.8131	32.52	227.67	1,821.32
8	40.00	0.7894	31.58	252.61	2,273.50
9	40.00	0.7664	30.66	275.91	2,759.10
10	1,040.00	0.7441	773.86	7,738.58	85,124.34
		Total	1,085.30	9,234.50	95,874.32

$$\text{Macaulay Duration} = \frac{9234.50}{2 \times 1,085.30} = 4.25$$

$$\text{Modified Duration} = \frac{4.25}{1.03} = 4.13$$

$$\text{Convexity} = \frac{95,874.32}{(1.03)^2 \times 2^2 \times 1,085.30} = 20.82$$

· APPENDIX ·

CHAPTER 19

Bond Portfolio Management Strategies

After you read this chapter, you should be able to answer the following questions:

- What are the five major classes of bond portfolio management strategies?
- How is the investment style box defined for fixed-income portfolios?
- What are the two main types of passive bond portfolio management strategies?
- What are the main active bond portfolio management strategies?
- How do active bond portfolio strategies differ from one another in terms of scope, scalability, and risk-adjusted return potential?
- What is meant by core-plus bond portfolio management?
- What are the primary "plus" strategies in a core-plus approach to management?
- How does a matched-funding approach to bond portfolio management differ from an active or passive approach?
- How does bond immunization work and how does that strategy differ from a cash-matching approach to managing a bond portfolio?
- What other dedicated management strategies are available to bond managers?
- What is meant by a contingent immunization approach to bond portfolio management?

In this chapter, we shift attention from bond valuation and analysis to an examination of the most widely used bond portfolio management strategies. After a brief discussion of how bonds have performed as an asset class in recent years and how fixed-income investment styles are typically classified, we will see that these strategies can be classified into one of five broad approaches: passive management, active management, core-plus management, matched-funding management, and contingent and structured active management. In the following sections, we describe these approaches in more detail and give examples of how each is used in practice.

19.1 Bond Portfolio Performance, Style, and Strategy

The volatile pattern of interest rates that has prevailed during recent decades has provided increasingly attractive returns to bond investors of all types. Active bond portfolio managers in particular have found the frequent opportunities to realize capital gains that resulted from those rates shifts to be especially attractive. However, despite the generally favorable economic climate that has prevailed for most of the last quarter century, it remains the case that fixed-income portfolios generally produce both less return and less volatility than found in other asset classes (e.g., domestic equity, foreign equity). Reilly and Wright (2004) confirmed this in their examination of the investment performance of 36 classes of long-term securities over the 21-year time horizon that began in 1980. Exhibit 19.1, which summarizes their findings, shows that bond portfolios—as represented by the Lehman Brothers U.S. Government Bond (LBG), U.S. Corporate Bond (LBC), and U.S. Aggregate Bond (LBA) indexes—fall at the lower end of the risk–return spectrum measured by the capital market line, making them a conservative choice within an investor's overall asset allocation strategy. On the other hand,

Exhibit 19.1 Risk–Return Comparison between Bond Portfolios and Other Asset Classes

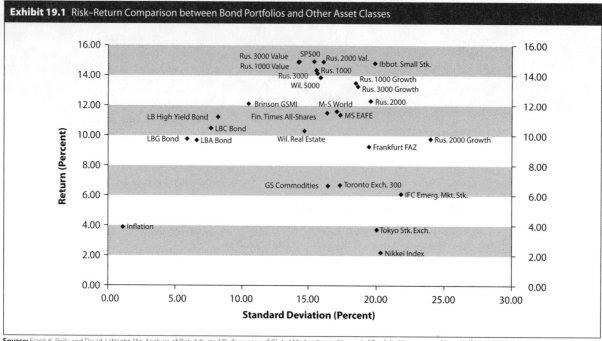

Source: Frank K. Reily and David J. Wright, "An Analysis of Risk-Adjusted Performance of Global Market Assets," *Journal of Portfolio Management* 30, no. 3 (Spring 2004); 63–77.

the relatively low historical correlation between fixed-income and equity securities—Reilly and Wright (2004) calculated this to be 0.27—have made bond portfolios an excellent tool for diversifying risk as well.

In Chapter 16, we saw that it was useful to classify the investment **style** of equity portfolios along two dimensions: market capitalization and relative valuation (i.e., value vs. growth). Similarly, the investment style of a bond portfolio can be summarized by its two most important characteristics: *credit quality* and *interest rate sensitivity*. Exhibit 19.2 shows how the 3 × 3 style grid can be adjusted to accommodate these dimensions. Specifically, the average credit quality of the portfolio can be classified as *high grade* (e.g., government, agency, AAA-rated or AA-rated corporate bonds), *medium grade* (e.g., A-rated or BBB-rated), or *low grade* (e.g., below BBB-rated), based on the profile of the composite holding. On the other hand, we established in the last chapter that average duration is an effective way to measure the portfolio's price sensitivity to interest rate changes. Accordingly, the second dimension of the bond portfolio's investment style can be separated as *short-term* (e.g., duration less than 3.0 years), *intermediate-term* (e.g., duration between 3.0 and 6.5 years), or *long-term* (e.g., duration above 6.5 years). For example, the Lehman Brothers U.S. Aggregate Bond index is purposely constructed to mimic the profile of the investment grade fixed-income security market in the United States, which typically consists of 70 to 80 percent government, agency, or AAA-rated bonds. Also, the LBA index is structured to maintain an average duration of between 4.0 and 5.0 years. Thus, it would plot in the middle cell of the top row of the style grid in Exhibit 19.2 and would be classified as a high-grade/intermediate-term portfolio.

Just as the inherent investment style of one bond portfolio compared to another can vary widely, so too can the underlying strategic approach adopted by the managers who formed those portfolios. As is often the case in investment management, the nature of the investor's problem usually dictates the way in which the manager will think about designing the bond portfolio that solves that problem. Consequently, an investor who desires a specific amount of cash to fund a financial obligation in the near future will likely have a very different strategy for assembling a fixed-income portfolio compared to someone whose goal is to maximize capital gains resulting from an anticipated shift in interest rates. Exhibit 19.3, which is based in part on

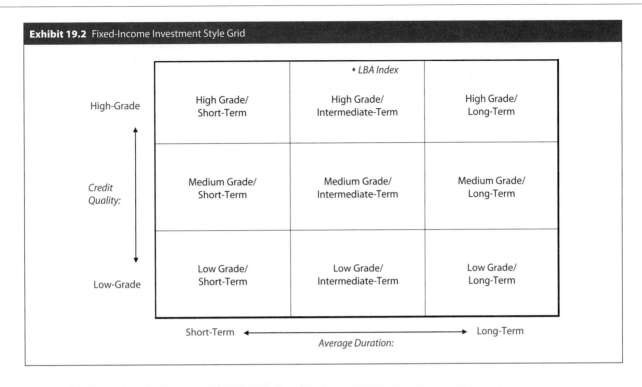

Exhibit 19.2 Fixed-Income Investment Style Grid

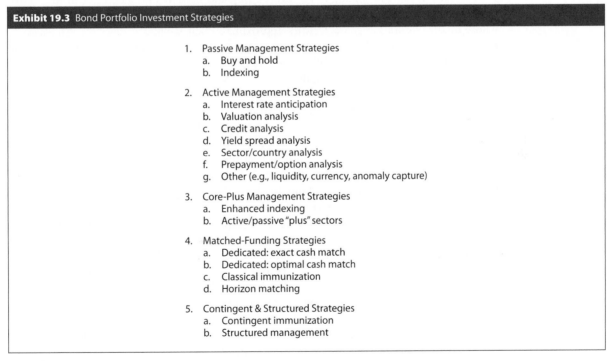

Exhibit 19.3 Bond Portfolio Investment Strategies

1. Passive Management Strategies
   a. Buy and hold
   b. Indexing

2. Active Management Strategies
   a. Interest rate anticipation
   b. Valuation analysis
   c. Credit analysis
   d. Yield spread analysis
   e. Sector/country analysis
   f. Prepayment/option analysis
   g. Other (e.g., liquidity, currency, anomaly capture)

3. Core-Plus Management Strategies
   a. Enhanced indexing
   b. Active/passive "plus" sectors

4. Matched-Funding Strategies
   a. Dedicated: exact cash match
   b. Dedicated: optimal cash match
   c. Classical immunization
   d. Horizon matching

5. Contingent & Structured Strategies
   a. Contingent immunization
   b. Structured management

the development in Leibowitz (1986a), indicates that bond portfolio strategies can be divided into the five broad groups mentioned above.

Prior to the 1960s, only the first two strategic approaches—passive and active—were widely available and most bond portfolios were managed on a buy-and-hold basis with the intention of producing a steady stream of cash flow for the investor. The early 1970s saw a growing level of curiosity with alternative active bond portfolio management approaches, while the late 1970s and early 1980s were characterized by record-breaking inflation and interest rates as well as extremely volatile yields across all spectrums of the bond market. This, in turn, led to the introduction of many new financial instruments in response to the increase in rate volatility (e.g., adjustable-rate bonds and mortgages). Since the mid-1980s, matched-funding techniques, core-plus strategies, and contingent bond management approaches have been developed to meet the increased needs of institutional investors, such as pension funds and insurance companies. Finally, beginning in the mid-1990s, it has become increasingly common to see bonds combined with positions in derivative securities in the management of sophisticated fixed-income portfolios; this topic will be explored in later chapters.

19.2 Passive Management Strategies

Two specific passive portfolio management strategies exist. First is a **buy-and-hold** strategy in which a manager selects a portfolio of bonds based on the objectives and constraints of the client with the intent of holding these bonds to maturity. In the second passive strategy—**indexing**—the objective is to construct a portfolio of bonds that will be matched as closely as possible to the performance of a specified bond index, such as the Lehman Brothers U.S. Aggregate Bond Index described earlier.

19.2.1 Buy-and-Hold Strategy

The simplest portfolio management strategy is to buy and hold. While obviously not unique to bond investors, this approach involves finding fixed-income securities with the desired levels of credit quality, coupon rate, term to maturity or duration, and other important indenture provisions, such as call and sinking fund features. Buy-and-hold investors do not consider active trading as a viable alternative to achieve abnormal returns but, rather, look for bond issue whose maturity/duration characteristics approximate their stipulated investment horizon in order to reduce price and reinvestment risk. Many successful bond investors and institutional portfolio managers follow a modified buy-and-hold strategy wherein they invest in an issue with the intention of holding it to maturity, but still look for opportunities to trade into a more desirable position should the occasion to do so arise. Of course, if the buy-and-hold approach is modified too much, it becomes an active strategy.

Whether the manager follows a strict or modified buy-and-hold approach, the critical concept is finding investment vehicles that possess the appropriate maturity, yield, and credit quality attributes. The strategy does not restrict the investor to accept whatever the market has to offer, nor does it imply that selectivity is unimportant. Attractive high-yielding issues with desirable features and quality standards are actively sought. For example, these investors recognize that agency issues or asset-backed securities generally provide attractive incremental returns relative to Treasuries with little sacrifice in quality, or that various call and put features can materially impact the risk and realized yield of an issue. Thus, successful buy-and-hold investors use their knowledge of market and issue characteristics to seek out attractive realized yields. Aggressive buy-and-hold investors also incorporate timing considerations into their strategy by using their knowledge of market rates, yield spreads, and expectations.

Finally, recognize that there is an important fundamental difference between managing a bond portfolio and a stock portfolio on a buy-and-hold basis. Since bonds eventually mature with the passing of time whereas stock shares do not, the bond manager is faced with the need to periodically reinvest the funds from a matured issue. However, it is possible for the stock manager to employ a "pure" buy-and-hold strategy in which he never adjusts the portfolio's composition once it is formed. Fixed-income portfolio managers often address this concern by forming a **bond ladder** in which they divide their investment funds evenly across the portfolio into instruments that mature at regular intervals. For instance, for a manager with an intermediate-term investment focus, instead of investing all of her funds in a five-year zero-coupon security—which would become a four-year security after one year had passed—she could follow a laddered approach and buy equal amounts of bonds maturing in annual intervals between one and nine years. The idea would then be to hold each bond to maturity, but to reinvest the proceeds from a maturing bond into a new instrument with a maturity at the far end of the ladder (that is, to reinvest a maturing bond in a brand-new nine-year issue). In this way, the desired maturity/duration target for the portfolio can be maintained over time without having to continually adjust the investment weights for the remaining positions.

19.2.2 Indexing Strategy

In the discussion of efficient capital markets earlier in the text, numerous empirical studies were cited that have demonstrated that the majority of money managers have not been able to match the risk-adjusted return performance of common stock and bond indexes. As a result, many investors have chosen to invest at least some of the funds dedicated to these asset classes on a passive basis. Rather than forming their own buy-and-hold portfolios, however, in many cases investors prefer to hold a bond portfolio designed to mimic a selected fixed-income index. In such a case, the bond index manager is judged not on the basis of his ability to produce abnormal returns relative to the index, but by how closely his portfolio produces returns that match those of the index. When describing similar concepts for stock index managers in Chapter 16, we saw that **tracking error** was a useful tool to judge how closely the returns of a managed portfolio match (i.e., "track") those of the targeted index. Recall that tracking error is measured as the standard deviation of the *difference* in returns produced by the managed portfolio and the index over time. An annualized tracking error statistic of 1 percent or less usually indicates that an index fund manager is doing a good job matching the performance of the index.

As with stock index funds, when designing an actual bond portfolio that attempts to mimic a hypothetical index, managers can follow two different paths: *full replication* or *stratified sampling*. While it is quite common when constructing stock index funds to fully replicate the underlying index, it is more likely that the bond index fund manager will follow a sampling approach, wherein a smaller number of instruments are held in the actual portfolio than appear in the index. One reason for this is that bond indexes often contain several thousand specific issues and are adjusted frequently, making them both impractical and expensive to replicate precisely in practice. The goal of the stratified sampling approach is to create a bond portfolio that matches the important characteristics of the underlying index—such as credit quality, industry composition, maturity/duration, or coupon rate—while maintaining a portfolio that is more cost effective to manage. To the extent that the manager is not able to match these characteristics over time, the tracking error of the indexed portfolio will typically increase.

When initiating an indexing strategy, the selection of an appropriate market index is clearly a very important decision, chiefly because it directly determines the client's risk–return results. Consequently, it is important for investors to be acquainted with the main characteristics (e.g., maturity/duration, credit quality) of their selected index. Reilly and Wright (1994, 1997, 2005) have examined many aspects of the major bond indexes, such as their risk–return characteristics and the correlation between them over time. Also, Dialynas and Murata (2006) and Volpert (2001) discuss how the characteristics of indexes affect their performance in different interest rate environments. For bond indexes, it is also important to be aware of how the aggregate bond market and the indexes change over time. Reilly, Kao, and Wright (1992) demonstrated that the market experienced significant shifts in composition, maturity, and duration since 1975, which can significantly impact the tracking error performance of an indexed portfolio.[1]

19.2.3 Bond Indexing in Practice: An Example

To see how two actual managers have responded to the challenge of forming a bond portfolio designed to track one of the leading indexes, we consider the several aspects of the Vanguard

---

[1] For further discussion on how bond market dynamics change over time, see Van Horne (2001) and Zhon (2001). For more on how these changes impact the management of an indexed portfolio, see Mossavar-Rahmani (1991) and Fabozzi (2007, Chapter 23).

Exhibit 19.4 Indexed Bond Investing: Index Fund vs. ETF, January 2008

Style Classification (Credit Grade/Duration)	Lehman U.S. Aggregate Index (LBUSTRUU) High Grade/ Intermediate-Term	Vanguard Total Bond Index Fund (VBMFX) High Grade/ Intermediate-Term	iShare Lehman U.S. Aggregate ETF (AGG) High Grade/ Intermediate-Term
# of Holdings	9,195	2,300	166
Annual Turnover (%)	—	64	483
Annual Yield (%)	4.6	4.9	4.8
Avg. Duration (yrs)	4.4	4.4	4.6
Avg. Maturity (yrs)	7.0	7.0	7.1
Credit Quality (% of Port.):			
Govt/Agency/AAA	79.3	79.8	74.4
AA	5.3	5.5	7.7
A	8.4	7.9	9.6
BBB	7.1	6.8	7.7
Other/Not Rated	0.0	0.0	0.7
Tracking Error (%/yr):			
(1/04 – 12/07)	—	0.19	0.61
Expense Ratio (%)	—	0.20	0.20

Source: Prepared by the authors using data from Morningstar, Inc. and Fidelity Investments.

Total Bond Index Fund (ticker: VBMFX) and the iShare Lehman U.S. Aggregate (ticker: AGG) exchange-traded fund over a recent investment period. Both of these portfolios were specifically created to mimic the performance of the Lehman Brothers U.S. Aggregate Index—whose formal ticker symbol is LBUSTRUU—and represent the two methods widely used in practice to create indexed portfolios for retail investors (i.e., index mutual funds and ETFs).

Exhibit 19.4 summarizes many of the most important structural characteristics for these funds, as well as for the underlying index. Notice that both managers have adopted a stratified sampling approach to replicating the index, which contains over 9,000 separate bond issues and would be difficult to recreate exactly. However, there is a wide disparity in how these managers implemented their sampling methods, which can be seen by the fact that the VBMFX holds 2,300 names while AGG attempts to mimic the index by holding only 166 distinct security positions. Not surprisingly, AGG also has a substantially higher portfolio turnover statistic than VBMFX—483 percent versus 64 percent—which is undoubtedly a by-product of trying to keep the ETF's portfolio composition aligned with that of the much larger index.

This difference in sampling approaches also leads to slight differences in the relevant investment characteristics of the portfolios. Generally speaking, the index mutual fund maintains a bond portfolio that is closer to the index in terms of average duration (Index: 4.4, VBMFX: 4.4, AGG: 4.6) and credit quality, as measured by the percentage of the portfolio carrying a rating of AAA or higher (Index: 79.3, VBMFX: 79.8, AGG: 74.4). These discrepancies lead, in turn, to a small difference in the tracking error statistic produced by each manager, with VBMFX and AGG having annualized values of 0.19 and 0.61 percent, respectively. Thus, although the exchange-traded fund's tracking error was roughly three times greater than that for the index mutual fund, both statistics fall well within the range of what is considered normal for a passive approach to investing. Finally, the expense ratios for both indexed vehicles are identical (i.e., 20 basis points) and much smaller than what would be typical for an actively managed bond portfolio.

19.3 Active Management Strategies

As we have seen with active equity portfolio management, the active fixed-income manager attempts to form a portfolio of securities that will outperform her designated benchmark over time. That is, she will attempt to hold a collection of bonds that produce superior risk-adjusted returns (i.e., alpha) compared to the index against which her investment performance is measured. Of course, to beat a benchmark, the active manager must form a portfolio that differs

Exhibit 19.5 Characteristics of Active Bond Portfolio Strategies

Source	Scalability	Sustainability	Risk-Adjusted Performance*	Extreme Values
Interest Rate Anticipation:				
Duration	High	Very Weak	1	Yes
Yield Curve Shape	Low	Very Weak	3	No
Valuation Analysis:				
Security Selection	Low	Medium	5	No
Anomaly Capture	Low	Weak	7	Yes
Credit Risk:	High	Strong	8	Yes
Yield Spread Analysis:				
Optionality	Medium	Medium	7	Yes
Prepayment	Medium	Medium	6	Yes
Liquidity	Low	Strong	3	Yes
Global & Tactical:				
Sector Allocation	High	Strong	6	No
Country Allocation	High	Strong	5	No
Currency	High	Medium	2	Yes

* 1 = Low, 10 = High (Note: This list is subjective; investors should make their own assessment of these criteria.)

Source: Adapted from Ronald Layard-Liesching, "Exploiting Opportunities in Global Bond Markets," in *Core-Plus Bond Management* (Charlottesville, VA: AIMR), 2001.

from the holdings comprising the index in a meaningful way. Thus, active bond management strategies are closely tied to the manager's view of what factors or market conditions will be the source of the incremental alpha returns she seeks.

Layard-Liesching (2001) has analyzed the investment attributes of several potential sources of alpha for the active bond portfolio manager, all of which depend on some structural barrier that prevents the bond market from being fully efficient. These characteristics are summarized in Exhibit 19.5. He compares each active strategy on four dimensions: (1) scalability (i.e., how large a position can be taken); (2) sustainability (i.e., how far into the future the strategy can be successfully employed); (3) risk-adjusted performance; and (4) extreme values (i.e., how exposed the strategy is to the chance of a large loss). For instance, in the interest rate anticipation category, he argues that duration-based active bets—in which the manager increases or decreases the average duration level of the active portfolio on the belief that the yield curve will either shift down or up, respectively—are highly scalable since they can be implemented with virtually any securities available in the market. However, they also offer the lowest chance of sustainable performance as well as the worst risk-adjusted returns. By contrast, credit risk bets—where the manager takes a position in a bond that she thinks has a substantially different default potential than has been priced in by the market—are a much more sustainable and reliable source of potential alpha. Finally, notice that while valuation analysis offers the active manager reasonable alpha potential, it is a more limited strategy from a scalability standpoint since it relies on identifying pricing errors in specific bond issues.[2]

In the remainder of this section, we will explore four categories of active bond strategies—interest rate anticipation, valuation analysis, credit risk, and yield spread analysis—in more detail, as well as describe bond swaps as a means to implement a specific active strategic view.

19.3.1 Interest Rate Anticipation

Interest rate anticipation is perhaps the riskiest active management strategy because it involves relying on uncertain forecasts of future interest rates. The idea is to preserve capital when an increase in interest rates is anticipated and achieve attractive capital gains when interest rates are expected to decline. Such objectives usually are attained by altering the duration structure of the portfolio (i.e., reducing portfolio duration when interest rates are expected to increase and increasing the portfolio duration when a decline in yields is anticipated). Thus, the risk in

---

[2] Additional discussions of active bond portfolio strategies can be found in Malvey (2005), Fong (2001), Squires (1997a), and Churchill (1994).

such portfolio restructuring is largely a function of these duration alterations. When durations are shortened, substantial income could be sacrificed and the opportunity for capital gains could be lost if interest rates decline rather than rise. Similarly, the portfolio shifts prompted by anticipation of a decline in rates are very risky. Assuming that we are at a peak in interest rates, it is likely that the yield curve is downward sloping, which means that bond coupons will decline with maturity. Therefore, the investor is sacrificing current income by shifting from high-coupon short bonds to longer-duration bonds. At the same time, the portfolio is purposely exposed to greater price volatility that could work against the portfolio if an unexpected increase in yields occurs. Note that the portfolio adjustments prompted by anticipation of an increase in rates involve less risk of an absolute capital loss. When you reduce the maturity, the worst that can happen is that interest income is reduced and/or capital gains are forgone (opportunity cost).

Once future (expected) interest rates have been determined, the procedure relies largely on technical matters. Assume that you expect an increase in interest rates and want to preserve your capital by reducing the duration of your portfolio. A popular choice would be high-yielding, short-term obligations, such as Treasury bills. Although your primary concern is to preserve capital, you would nevertheless look for the best return possible given the maturity constraint. Liquidity also is important because, after interest rates increase, yields may experience a period of stability before they decline, and you would want to shift positions quickly to benefit from the higher income and/or capital gains.

To illustrate this process, suppose that the yield curve for U.S. Treasury bonds is currently flat across all maturities at 4.75 percent. You have observed the following "paired" transaction by an active bond portfolio manager:

Bond	Transaction	Type	Maturity (yrs)	Coupon Rate (%)	Modified Duration
1	Buy	U.S. Govt.	7	8	5.438
2	Sell	U.S. Govt.	13	0	12.698

What does this trade suggest about the manager's view as to how the yield curve is likely to change in the future? First, and foremost, by switching out of a long-maturity, zero-coupon bond into an intermediate-maturity, high-coupon bond, the manager has significantly shortened the modified duration of the position and, presumably, of the entire portfolio. Thus, this trade is consistent with a view that the yields will rise in the future (i.e., the yield curve will shift up). Further, the manager will also benefit if the shape of the yield curve either stays flat or becomes upward sloping since he has replaced a bond whose future cash flow is paid out at one point in the future (i.e., 13 years) with a shorter-term instrument that makes payments every six months for the next seven years. Finally, notice that by using one Treasury security to replace another, the manager has not introduced any credit risk into the portfolio that might conflict with his interest rate anticipation view.

An alternative way to shorten maturities is to use a *cushion bond*—a high-yielding, long-term obligation that carries a coupon substantially above the current market rate and that, due to its current call feature and call price, has a market price lower than what it should be given current market yields. As a result, its yield is higher than normal. An example would be a 10-year bond with a 12 percent coupon, currently callable at 110. If current market rates are 8 percent, this bond (if it were noncallable) would have a price of about 127; because of its call price, however, it will stay close to 110, and its yield will be about 10 percent rather than 8 percent. Bond portfolio managers look for cushion bonds when they expect a modest increase in rates because such issues provide attractive current income *and* protection against capital loss. Because these bonds are trading at an abnormally high yield, market rates would have to rise to that abnormal level before their price would react.

The portfolio manager who anticipates higher interest rates, therefore, has two simple strategies available: shorten the duration of the portfolio or look for an attractive cushion bond as described by Homer and Leibowitz (2004, Chapter 5). In either case, you would want to invest in very liquid issues.

A totally different posture is assumed by investors who anticipate a decline in interest rates. The significant risk involved in restructuring a portfolio to take advantage of a decline in interest rates is balanced by the potential for substantial capital gains and holding period returns. When you expect lower interest rates, you should increase the duration of the portfolio because the longer the duration, the greater the positive price volatility. Also, liquidity is important because you want to be able to close out the position quickly when the drop in rates has been completed.

Notably, because interest rate sensitivity is critical, it is important to recall that the higher the quality of an obligation, the more sensitive it is to interest rate changes. Therefore, high-grade securities should be used, such as Treasuries, agencies, or corporates rated AAA through BBB. Finally, you want to concentrate on noncallable issues or those with strong call protection because of the substantial call risk discussed in Chapter 18 in connection with the analysis of duration and convexity.

19.3.2 Valuation Analysis

With **valuation analysis**, the portfolio manager attempts to select bonds based on their intrinsic value, which is determined based on their characteristics and the average value of these characteristics in the marketplace. As an example, a bond's rating will dictate a certain spread relative to comparable Treasury bonds: Long maturity might be worth an added 60 basis points relative to short maturity (i.e., the maturity spread); a given deferred call feature might require a higher or lower yield; a specified sinking fund would likewise mean higher or lower required yields. Given all the characteristics of the bond and the normal cost of the characteristics in terms of yield, you would determine the bond's required yield and, therefore, its implied intrinsic value. After you have done this for a number of bonds, you would compare these derived bond values to the prevailing market prices to determine which bonds are undervalued or overvalued. Based on your confidence in the characteristic costs, you would buy the undervalued issues and ignore or sell the overvalued issues.

Success in valuation analysis is based on understanding the characteristics that are important in valuation and being able to accurately *estimate* the yield cost of these characteristics with the understanding that these yield costs change over time.

19.3.3 Credit Analysis

A **credit analysis** strategy involves detailed analysis of the bond issuer to determine expected changes in its default risk. This involves attempting to project changes in the credit ratings assigned to bonds by the various rating agencies discussed in Chapter 17.[3] These rating changes are affected by internal changes in the entity (e.g., changes in important financial ratios) and by changes in the external environment (i.e., changes in the firm's industry and the economy). During periods of strong economic expansion, even financially weak firms may survive and prosper. In contrast, during severe economic contractions, normally strong firms may find it very difficult to meet financial obligations. Therefore, historically there has been a strong cyclical pattern to rating changes: typically, downgrades increase during economic contractions and decline during economic expansions.

To use credit analysis as a portfolio management strategy, it is necessary to project rating changes prior to the announcement by the rating agencies. This can be quite challenging because the market adjusts rather quickly to bond rating changes, especially to downgrades. Therefore, you want to acquire bond issues expected to experience an upgrade and sell or avoid those bond issues expected to be downgraded.

Credit Analysis of High-Yield (Junk) Bonds One of the most obvious opportunities for credit analysis is the analysis of high-yield (junk) bonds. As demonstrated by several studies,

---

[3] For a discussion of changes in the aggregate financial risk of U.S. corporations and the opportunities this has created, see Reilly and Gentry (2004). For a presentation on credit analysis that emphasizes changes in credit ratings, see Fabozzi (2005a, Chapter 32). For a set of readings on global credit analysis, see Squires (1998b).

Exhibit 19.6 Monthly Yield Spread History, Merrill Lynch High-Yield Master Index versus 10-Year Treasury

Source: M. Christopher Garman and Oleg Melentyev, Analysts, Merrill Lynch, "U.S. High Yield Market Update–1Q 2005," p. 25. Reprinted by permission. Copyright © 2005 Merrill Lynch, Pierce, Fenner & Smith Incorporated.

the yield differential between junk bonds that are rated below BBB and Treasury securities ranges from about 200 basis points to almost 1,000 basis points. Notably, these yield differentials vary substantially over time as shown by a time-series plot in Exhibit 19.6. Specifically, the average yield spread ranged from a low of less than 300 basis points in 1985 and 1997 to a high of over 950 basis points during early 1991 and late 2002.

Although the spreads have changed, a study by Mody and Taylor (2003) indicated that the average credit quality of high-yield bonds also changed over time as indicated by interest coverage changes over the business cycle. Also, the credit quality of bonds *within* rating categories changed over the business cycle as demonstrated by Reilly and Gentry (2004).

These changes in credit quality will make credit analysis of high-yield bonds more important, but also more difficult. This means that bond analysts and portfolio managers need to engage in detailed credit analysis to select bonds that will survive. Given the spread in promised yields, if a portfolio manager can—through rigorous credit analysis—avoid bonds with a high probability of default or downgrade, high-yield bonds will provide substantial rates of return for the investor; see Vine (2001) and Fabozzi (2005a).

In summary, substantial opportunity for generating high risk-adjusted returns can be derived by investing in high-yield bonds if you do the credit analysis required to avoid defaults, which occur with these bonds at substantially higher rates than the overall bond market, as shown by Altman (1989); Asquith, Mullins, and Wolff (1989); and Altman (1992).

Exhibit 19.7 lists the cumulative default rates for bonds with different ratings and for various time periods after issue. Over 10 years—the holding period that is widely used in practice for comparative purposes—the default rate for BBB investment-grade bonds is only 4.44 percent, but the default rate increases to almost 15 percent for BB-rated bonds, to over 30 percent for B-rated bonds, and to almost 50 percent for CCC-rated bonds. These default rates do not mean that investors should avoid high-yield bonds, but they do indicate that extensive credit analysis is a critical component for success within this risky sector of the fixed-income market.

Exhibit 19.7 Cumulative Average Default Rates by Bond Rating: 1981-2007 (%)

Rating	\u2014Time horizon (years)\u2014														
	1	**2**	**3**	**4**	**5**	**6**	**7**	**8**	**9**	**10**	**11**	**12**	**13**	**14**	**15**
AAA	0.00	0.00	0.09	0.18	0.28	0.41	0.48	0.59	0.63	0.67	0.67	0.67	0.67	0.73	0.79
AA+	0.00	0.06	0.06	0.13	0.20	0.28	0.35	0.35	0.35	0.35	0.35	0.35	0.35	0.35	0.35
AA	0.00	0.00	0.00	0.09	0.18	0.25	0.35	0.48	0.60	0.72	0.81	0.88	1.03	1.10	1.14
AA\u2212	0.02	0.09	0.20	0.32	0.45	0.61	0.76	0.86	0.96	1.08	1.21	1.35	1.41	1.53	1.60
A+	0.05	0.10	0.25	0.45	0.61	0.77	0.95	1.10	1.29	1.46	1.66	1.88	2.08	2.31	2.51
A	0.07	0.18	0.30	0.42	0.60	0.80	1.00	1.21	1.42	1.73	1.98	2.12	2.26	2.35	2.61
A\u2212	0.06	0.20	0.32	0.49	0.73	1.02	1.44	1.71	1.95	2.12	2.19	2.32	2.42	2.53	2.65
BBB+	0.15	0.46	0.91	1.30	1.74	2.22	2.58	2.91	3.36	3.71	4.07	4.27	4.62	5.14	5.72
BBB	0.23	0.54	0.85	1.39	1.95	2.47	2.95	3.48	3.93	4.44	5.00	5.44	5.93	6.12	6.50
BBB\u2212	0.31	1.02	1.78	2.78	3.74	4.60	5.25	5.87	6.33	6.91	7.42	7.94	8.54	9.37	10.03
BB+	0.52	1.41	2.85	4.20	5.41	6.71	7.88	8.41	9.36	10.21	10.82	11.41	11.85	12.35	13.07
BB	0.81	2.50	4.62	6.53	8.38	10.13	11.52	12.79	13.82	14.62	15.71	16.63	17.10	17.19	17.28
BB\u2212	1.44	4.16	7.04	9.90	12.32	14.66	16.52	18.35	19.87	21.03	21.93	22.62	23.51	24.22	24.87
B+	2.53	6.97	11.22	14.92	17.65	19.74	21.64	23.29	24.70	26.11	27.32	28.29	29.29	30.31	31.19
B	6.27	12.74	17.75	21.27	23.84	26.03	27.44	28.52	29.43	30.43	31.40	32.36	33.42	34.20	35.04
B\u2212	9.06	16.94	22.75	26.66	29.44	31.56	33.38	34.53	35.25	35.73	36.26	36.64	36.84	37.07	37.32
CCC/C	25.59	34.06	39.04	41.86	44.50	45.62	46.67	47.25	48.86	49.76	50.50	51.26	51.87	52.50	52.50
Investment grade	0.10	0.30	0.52	0.81	1.11	1.42	1.69	1.95	2.19	2.44	2.66	2.85	3.05	3.24	3.47
Speculative grade	2.81	6.54	10.00	12.92	15.23	17.23	18.87	20.25	21.46	22.54	23.52	24.34	25.12	25.79	26.43
All rated	0.98	2.30	3.53	4.62	5.52	6.32	6.98	7.56	8.06	8.53	8.96	9.31	9.66	9.98	10.32

Source: *2007 Annual Global Corporate Default Study and Rating Transitions* (New York: Standard & Poor's, February 2008): p. 11 (Table 8). Reprinted with permission.

Investing in Defaulted Debt Beyond high-yield bonds that have high credit risk and high default rates, a new set of investment opportunities has evolved—investing in defaulted debt. While this sector requires an understanding of legal procedures surrounding bankruptcy as well as economic analysis, as noted by Altman (1993a), the returns have generally been consistent with the risk, as demonstrated by Altman (1993b); Altman and Simon (2001); Ward and Griepentrog (1993); and Reilly, Wright, and Altman (1998).

Credit Analysis Models The credit analysis of high-yield bonds can use a statistical model or basic fundamental analysis that recognizes some of the unique characteristics of these bonds. Altman-Nammacher (1987) suggest that a modified *Z-score model* used to predict the probability of bankruptcy within two years can also be used to predict default for these high-yield bonds or as a gauge of changes in credit quality. The Z-score model combines traditional financial measures with a multivariate technique known as *multiple discriminant analysis* to derive a set of weights for the specified variables. The result is an overall credit score (zeta score) for each firm. The model is of the form

$$\text{Zeta} = a_0 + a_1 X_1 + a_2 X_2 + a_3 X_3 + \cdots + a_n X_n$$

where:

$\text{Zeta} = $ the overall credit score
$X_1 \ldots X_n = $ the explanatory variables (ratios and market measures)
$a_0 \ldots a_n = $ the weightings or coefficients

The final model used in this analysis included the following seven financial measures:

$X_1 = $ profitability: earnings before interest and taxes (EBIT)/total assets (TA)
$X_2 = $ stability of profitability measure: the standard error of estimate of EBIT/TA (normalized for 10 years)
$X_3 = $ debt service capabilities (interest coverage): EBIT/interest charges
$X_4 = $ cumulative profitability: retained earnings/total assets
$X_5 = $ liquidity: current assets/current liabilities
$X_6 = $ capitalization levels: market value of equity/total capital (five-year average)
$X_7 = $ size: total tangible assets (normalized)

Exhibit 19.8 Altman's Z-Score Analysis

A. *Amazon.com Inc.*

<HELP> for explanation, <MENU> for similar functions.   Corp **AZS**

ALTMAN'S Z - SCORE MODEL

AMZN US   Amazon.Com Inc

Total Assets	6485.00
Working Capital	1450.00
Retained Earnings	−1870.00
Earn Before Int & Taxes	655.00
Market Value of Equity	39927.84
Total Liabilities	5288.00
Sales to Total Assets	2.29
Total Shareholders' Equity	1197.00

Financial Health Assessment and Outlook

Reference Date	12/2007	Calculate: **A**	
Credit Rating	BB	Altman's Zscore	7.02
		Health Grade	C+

Australia 61 2 9777 8600 Brazil 5511 3048 4500 Europe 44 20 7330 7500 Germany 49 69 9204 1210 Hong Kong 852 2977 6000
Japan 81 3 3201 8900   Singapore 65 6212 1000   U.S. 1 212 318 2000   Copyright 2008 Bloomberg Finance L.P.
H464-414-0 02-Mar-2008 13:03:27

B. *General Motors Corp.*

<HELP> for explanation, <MENU> for similar functions.   Corp **AZS**

ALTMAN'S Z - SCORE MODEL

GM US   General Motors Corp

Total Assets	148883.00
Working Capital	-9720.00
Retained Earnings	−53356.00
Earn Before Int & Taxes	−4390.00
Market Value of Equity	14089.22
Total Liabilities	184363.00
Sales to Total Assets	1.22
Total Shareholders' Equity	−35480.00

Financial Health Assessment and Outlook

Reference Date	12/2007	Calculate: **A**	
Credit Rating	B	Altman's Zscore	0.59
		Health Grade	F

Australia 61 2 9777 8600 Brazil 5511 3048 4500 Europe 44 20 7330 7500 Germany 49 69 9204 1210 Hong Kong 852 2977 6000
Japan 81 3 3201 8900   Singapore 65 6212 1000   U.S. 1 212 318 2000   Copyright 2008 Bloomberg Finance L.P.
H464-414-0 02-Mar-2008 13:02:52

As an example of this process, Exhibit 19.8 illustrates the Z-score calculations for two companies whose bonds were rated below investment grade as of December 2007: Amazon.com (BB rating) and General Motors (B rating). Z-scores typically range from −5.0 to +20.0, with higher scores (i.e., above +3.0) indicating that bankruptcy over the next two years is unlikely while lower scores (i.e., below +1.8) suggest an increased potential for business failure. In this case, Amazon.com's Z-score shows that it is in a relatively strong financial position given its credit rating, while General Motors' Z-score indicates the opposite. It is important to note, however, that these scores are best interpreted as they change over time, rather than as a single observation. Thus, the active bond manager following a credit analysis strategy might use this as a tool to help predict rating upgrades and downgrades before they occur.[4]

In contrast to using a model that provides a composite credit score, many analysts simply adapt their basic corporate bond analysis techniques *to the unique needs of high-yield bonds,* which have characteristics of common stock as shown by Reilly and Wright (1994, 2001). Fabozzi (2005a, Chapter 32) claims that the analysis of high-yield bonds is the same as with any bond except that the following areas of analysis should be expanded:

1. What is the firm's *competitive position* in terms of cost and pricing? This can be critical to a small firm.
2. What is the firm's *cash flow* relative to cash requirements for interest, research, growth, and periods of economic decline? Also, what is the firm's *borrowing capacity* that can serve as a safety net and provide flexibility?
3. What is the *liquidity value of the firm's assets?* Are these assets available for liquidation (are there any claims against them)? In many cases, asset sales are a critical part of the strategy for a leveraged buyout.
4. How good is the *total management team?* Is the management team committed to and capable of operating in the high-risk environment of this firm?
5. What is the firm's *financial leverage* on an absolute basis and on a market-adjusted basis (using market value of equity and debt)?

In addition to the potentially higher financial risks, Sondhi (1995) and Squires (1998b) point out several factors that can also impact business risk. An increase in business risk may exist if the firm sells off some operations that have favorable risk characteristics with the remaining operations—that is, business risk would increase if the firm sells a division or a company that has low correlation of earnings with other units of the firm. Further, a change in management operating philosophy could have a negative impact on operating earnings. The managements of leveraged buyout (LBO) firms are known for making optimistic growth estimates related to sales and earnings, so the analyst should evaluate these estimates very critically. Asset divestiture plans often are a major element of an LBO because they provide necessary capital that is used to reduce the substantial debt taken on as part of the buyout. Therefore, it is important to examine the liquidity of the assets, their estimated selling values, and the timing of these programs. If the divestiture program is successful wherein the prices received are above normal expectations and the assets are sold ahead of schedule, this can be grounds for upgrading the debt. Finally, it is necessary to constantly monitor the firm's refinancing flexibility. Specifically, what refinancing will be necessary, what does the schedule look like, and will the capital suppliers be receptive to the refinancing?

The substantial increase in high-yield bonds issued and outstanding has been matched by an increase in research on credit analysis available to investors. The credit analysis of these bonds is similar to that of investment-grade bonds with an emphasis on the following factors: (1) *the use of cash flows* compared to debt obligations under very conservative assumptions; (2) the detailed analysis of *potential asset sales,* including a conservative estimate of sales prices, the asset's true liquidity, the availability of the assets, and a consideration of the timing of the sales; and (3) the recognition that high-yield bonds have many characteristics of common stock, which means that many equity analysis techniques are appropriate. An in-depth analysis of high-yield bonds is critical because of the number of issues, the wide diversity of quality within the high-yield bond universe, and the growing complexity of high-yield bond issues.[5]

19.3.4 Yield Spread Analysis

As discussed in Chapter 18, spread analysis assumes normal relationships exist between the yields for bonds in alternative sectors (e.g., the spread between high-grade versus low-grade

---

[4] For more on the analysis of default rates for high-yield bonds, see Jonsson and Fridson (1996), Helwege and Kleinman (1997), and Fridson, Garman, and Wu (1997).

[5] Examples of regularly published analysis on high-yield bonds include *High-Yield Prospects* (Standard & Poor's), *High-Yield Weekly* (Citi Smith Barney), and *High-Yield Report* (SourceMedia).

industrial or between industrial versus utility bonds). A bond portfolio manager would monitor these relationships and, when an abnormal relationship occurs, execute various sector swaps. The crucial factor is developing the background to know the normal yield relationship and to evaluate the liquidity necessary to buy or sell the required issues quickly enough to take advantage of the temporary yield abnormality.

Dialynas and Edington (1992) consider several specific factors that affect the aggregate spread. The generally accepted explanation of changes in the yield spread is that it is related to the economic environment. Specifically, the spread widens during periods of economic uncertainty and recession because investors require larger risk premiums (i.e., larger spreads). In contrast, the spread will decline during periods of economic confidence and expansion. Although not denying the existence of such a relationship, the authors contend that a more encompassing factor is the impact of interest rate (yield) volatility. They contend that yield volatility will affect the spread via three effects: (1) yield volatility and the behavior of embedded options, (2) yield volatility and transactional liquidity, and (3) the effect of yield volatility on the business cycle.

Recall that the value of callable bonds is equal to the value of a noncallable bond minus the value of the call option. Therefore, if the value of the option goes up, the value of the callable bond will decline and its yield will increase. When yield volatility increases, the value of the call option increases, which causes a decline in the price of the callable bond and a rise in the bond's yield and its yield spread relative to Treasury bonds. Similarly, an increase in yield volatility will raise the uncertainty facing bond dealers and cause them to increase their bid-ask spreads that reflect the transactional liquidity for these bonds. This liquidity will have a bigger effect on nongovernment bonds, so their yield spread relative to Treasury bonds will increase. Finally, interest rate volatility causes uncertainty for business executives and consumers regarding their cost of funds. This typically will precede an economic decline that will, in turn, lead to an increase in the yield spread.

It is possible to have a change in yield spread for reasons other than economic uncertainty. If there is a period of greater yield volatility that is not a period of economic uncertainty, the yield spread will increase due to the embedded option effect and the transactional liquidity effect. This analysis implies that when examining yield spreads, you should pay particular attention to interest rate (yield) volatility.

19.3.5 Implementing an Active Bond Transaction

Once a bond manager has decided on the specifics of an active strategy, the next step is to create a portfolio (or alter an existing one) to take advantage of that view. A popular approach for implementing these adjustments involves the use of **bond swaps**, which entail liquidating a current position and simultaneously buying a different issue in its place with similar attributes and a better chance for improved return. These trades can be executed to increase current yield, to increase yield to maturity, to take advantage of shifts in interest rates or the realignment of yield spreads, to improve the quality of a portfolio, or for tax purposes. Some swaps are highly sophisticated and require a computer for calculation. However, most are fairly simple transactions with obvious goals and risk. They go by such names as *profit takeouts, substitution swaps, intermarket spread swaps,* or *tax swaps.* Although many of these transactions involve low risk (such as the pure yield pickup swap), others entail substantial risk (the rate anticipation swap). Regardless of the risk involved, all trades have one basic purpose: portfolio improvement. In fact, Boyd and Mercer (2005) demonstrate that these swaps lead to a substantial improvement in risk-adjusted performance relative to standard bond benchmarks.

Most bond swaps involve several different types of risk. One obvious risk is that the market will move against you while the transaction is in progress. Interest rates may move up over the holding period and cause you to incur a loss. Alternatively, yield spreads may fail to respond as anticipated. Possibly the new bond may not be a true substitute and so, even if your expectations and interest rate formulations are correct, the swap may be unsatisfactory because the wrong issue was selected. Finally, if the work-out time is longer than anticipated, the realized yield might be less than expected. As noted by Homer and Leibowitz (2004) and Fabozzi,

Exhibit 19.9 A Pure Yield Pickup Swap

Pure yield pickup swap: A bond swap involving a switch—from a low-coupon bond to a higher-coupon bond of similar quality and maturity—in order to pick up a higher current yield and a better yield to maturity.

Example: Currently hold: 30-year, 10.0% coupon priced at 874.12 to yield 11.5%
Swap candidate: 30-year, Aa 12% coupon priced at $1,000 to yield 12.0%

	Current Bond	Candidate Bond
Dollar investment	$874.12	$1,000.00[a]
Coupon	100.00	120.00
i on one coupon (12.0% for 6 months)	3.000	3.600
Principal value at year end	874.66	1,000.00
Total accrued	977.66	1,123.60
Realized compound yield	11.514%	12.0%

Value of swap: 48.6 basis points in one year (assuming a 12.0% reinvestment rate).

The rewards for a pure yield pickup swap are automatic and instantaneous in that both a higher-coupon yield and a higher yield to maturity are realized from the swap. Other advantages include:

1. No specific work-out period needed because the investor is assumed to hold the new bond to maturity
2. No need for interest rate speculation
3. No need to analyze prices for overvaluation or undervaluation

A major disadvantage of the pure yield pickup swap is the book loss involved in the swap. In this example, if the current bond were bought at par, the book loss would be $125.88 ($1,000 – 874.12). Other risks involved in the pure yield pickup swap include:

1. Increased risk of call in the event interest rates decline
2. Reinvestment risk is greater with higher-coupon bonds

[a] Obviously, the investor can invest $874.12—the amount obtained from the sale of the bond currently held—and still obtain a realized compound yield of 12.0%.
Swap evaluation procedure is patterned after a technique suggested by Sidney Homer and Martin L. Leibowitz.
Source: Adapted from the book *Inside the Yield Book* by Sidney Homer and Martin L. Leibowitz, Ph.D. (Englewood Cliffs, NJ: Prentice Hall, 1972).

Mann, and Choudhry (2005, Chapter 55), you must be willing to accept such risks to improve your portfolio. The following subsections consider three of the more popular bond swaps.

Pure Yield Pickup Swap The pure yield pickup swap involves trading out of a low-coupon bond into a comparable higher-coupon bond to realize an automatic and instantaneous increase in current yield and yield to maturity. An example of such a trade would be an investor who currently holds a 30-year, Aa-rated 10 percent issue that is trading at an 11.50 percent yield. Assume that a comparable 30-year, Aa-rated obligation bearing a 12 percent coupon priced to yield 12 percent becomes available. The investor would report (and realize) some book loss if the original issue was bought at par but is able to improve current yield and yield to maturity simultaneously if the new obligation is held to maturity as shown in Exhibit 19.9.

The investor need not predict rate changes, and the swap is not based on any imbalance in yield spread. The object simply is to seek higher yields. Quality and maturity stay the same as do all other factors *except coupon*. The major risk is that future reinvestment rates may not be as high as expected, and, therefore, the total terminal value of the investment (capital recovery, coupon receipts, and interest-on-interest) may not be as high as expected or comparable to the original obligation. This reinvestment risk can be evaluated by analyzing the results with a number of reinvestment rates to determine the minimum reinvestment rate that would make the swap viable.

Substitution Swap The substitution swap generally is short term and relies heavily on interest rate expectations. Consequently, it is subject to considerably more risk than pure yield pickup swaps. The procedure assumes a short-term imbalance in yield spreads between issues that are perfect substitutes. The imbalance in yield spread is expected to be corrected in the near future. For example, the investor might hold a 30-year, 12 percent issue that is yielding

12 percent and be offered a comparable 30-year, 12 percent bond that is yielding 12.20 percent. Because the issue offered will trade at a price less than $1,000 for every issue sold, the investor can buy more than one of the offered obligations.

You would expect the yield spread imbalance to be corrected by having the yield on the offering bond decline to the level of your current issue. Thus, you would realize capital gains by switching out of your current position into the higher-yielding obligation. This swap is described in Exhibit 19.10.

Although a modest increase in current income occurs as the yield imbalance is corrected, attractive capital gains are possible, causing a differential in *realized yield*. The work-out time will have an important effect on the differential realized return. Even if the yield is not corrected until maturity, 30 years later, you will still experience a small increase in realized yield (about 10 basis points). In contrast, if the correction takes place in one year (as shown in Exhibit 19.10), the differential realized return is much greater. After the correction has occurred, you would have additional capital for a subsequent swap or other investment. Several risks are involved in this swap. In addition to the pressure of the work-out time, market interest rates could move against you, the yield spread may not be temporary, and the issue may not be a viable swap candidate (i.e., the spread may be due to the issue's lower quality).

Tax Swap   The tax swap is popular with individual investors because it is a relatively simple procedure that involves no interest rate projections and few risks. Investors enter into tax swaps due to tax laws and realized capital gains in their portfolios. Assume you acquired $100,000 worth of corporate bonds and after two years sold the securities for $150,000, implying a capital gain of $50,000. One way to eliminate the tax liability of that capital gain is to sell an issue that has a comparable long-term capital loss. If you had a long-term investment of $100,000 with a current

---

Exhibit 19.10 A Substitution Swap

Substitution swap: A swap executed to take advantage of temporary market anomalies in yield spreads between issues that are equivalent with respect to coupon, quality, and maturity.

Example: Currently hold: 30-year, Aa 12.0% coupon priced at $1,000 to yield 12.0%
Swap candidate: 30-year, Aa 12.0% coupon priced at $984.08 to yield 12.2%
Assumed work-out period: 1 year
Reinvested at 12.0%

	Current Bond	Candidate Bond
Dollar investment	$1,000.00	$ 984.08
Coupon	120.00	120.00
i on one coupon (12.0% for 6 months)	3.60	3.60
Principal value at year end (12.0% YTM)	1,000.00	1,000.00
Total accrued	1,123.60	1,123.60
Total gain	123.60	139.52
Gain per invested dollar	0.1236	0.1418
Realized compound yield	12.00%	13.71%
Value of swap: 171 basis points in one year		

The rewards for the substitution swap are additional basis-point pickups for YTM, additional realized compound yield, and capital gains that accrue when the anomaly in yield corrects itself. In the substitution swap, any basis-point pickup (171 points in this example) will be realized only during the work-out period. Thus, in our example, to obtain the 171 basis-point increase in realized compound yield, you must swap an average of once a year and pick up an average of 20 basis points in yield to maturity on each swap.

Potential risks associated with the substitution swap include:

1. A yield spread thought to be temporary may, in fact, be permanent, thus reducing capital gains advantages
2. The market rate may change adversely

Swap evaluation procedure is patterned after a technique suggested by Sidney Homer and Martin L. Leibowitz.

Source: Adapted from the book *Inside the Yield Book* by Sidney Homer and Martin L. Leibowitz, Ph.D. (Englewood Cliffs, NJ: Prentice Hall, 1972).

market value of $50,000, you could execute a tax swap to establish the $50,000 capital loss. By off-setting this capital loss and the comparable capital gain, you would reduce your income taxes.

Municipal bonds are considered particularly attractive tax swap candidates because you can increase your tax-free income and use the capital loss (subject to normal federal and state taxation) to reduce capital gains tax liability. To continue our illustration, assume you own $100,000 worth of New York City, 20-year, 7 percent bonds that you bought at par, but they have a current market value of $50,000. Given this tax loss, you need a comparable bond swap candidate. Suppose you find a 20-year New York City bond with a 7.1 percent coupon and a market value of 50. By selling your New York 7s and instantaneously reinvesting in the New York 7.1s, you would eliminate the capital gains tax from the corporate bond transaction. In effect, you have $50,000 of tax-free capital gains, and you have increased your current tax-free yield. The money saved by avoiding the tax liability can then be used to increase the portfolio's yield, as shown in Exhibit 19.11.

An important caveat is that *you cannot swap identical issues* (such as selling the New York 7s to establish a loss and then buying back the same New York 7s). If it is not a different issue, the IRS considers the transaction a *wash sale* and does not allow the loss. It is easier to avoid wash sales in the bond market than it is in the stock market because every bond issue, even with identical coupons and maturities, is considered distinct. Likewise, it is easier to find comparable bond issues with only modest differences in coupon, maturity, and quality. Tax swaps are common at year end as investors establish capital losses because the capital loss must occur in the same taxable year as the capital gain. This procedure differs from other bond swap transactions because it exists due to tax statutes rather than temporary market anomalies.

19.3.6 Active Global Bond Investing: An Example

An active approach to global fixed-income management must consider three interrelated factors: (1) the local economy in each country that includes the effect of domestic and international demand, (2) the impact of this total demand and domestic monetary policy on inflation and interest rates, and (3) the effect of the economy, inflation, and interest rates on the exchange

---

Exhibit 19.11 A Tax Swap

Tax swap: A swap undertaken when you wish to offset capital gains in other securities through the sale of a bond currently held and selling at a discount from the price paid at purchase. By swapping into a bond with as nearly identical features as possible, you can use the capital loss on the sale of the bond for tax purposes and still maintain your current position in the market.

Example: Currently hold: $100,000 worth of corporate bonds with current market value of $150,000 *and* $100,000 in NY, 20-year, 7% bonds with current market value of $50,000
Swap candidate: $50,000 in NY, 20-year, 7.1% bonds

A. Corporate bonds sold and long-term capital gains profit established	$50,000	
Capital gains tax liability (assume you have 20% capital gains tax rate) ($50,000 × 0.20)		$10,000
B. NY 7s sold and long-term capital *loss* established	$50,000	
Reduction in capital gains tax liability ($50,000 × 0.20)		($10,000)
Net capital gains tax liability		0
Tax *savings* realized		$10,000
C. Complete tax swap by buying NY 7.1s from proceeds of NY 7s		
Sale (therefore, amount invested remains largely the *same*)[a]		
Annual tax-free interest income—NY 7s	$ 7,000	
Annual tax-free interest income—NY 7.1s	$ 7,100	
Net *increase* in *annual* tax-free interest income	$ 100	

[a] NY 7.1s will result in substantial capital gains when liquidated at maturity (because they were bought at deep discounts) and, therefore, will be subject to future capital gains tax liability. The swap is designed to use the capital loss resulting from the swap to offset capital gains from other investments. At the same time, your funds remain in a security almost identical to your previous holding while you receive a slight increase in both current income and YTM. Because the tax swap involved no projections in terms of work-out period, interest rate changes, etc., the risks involved are minimal. Your major concern should be to avoid potential wash sales.

rates among countries.[6] Based on the evaluation of these factors, a portfolio manager must decide on the relative weight for each country. In addition, one might consider an allocation within each country among government, municipal, and corporate bonds. In the example that follows, most portfolio recommendations concentrate on the country allocation and do not become more specific except in the case of the United States.

Exhibit 19.12 is from the March 31, 2005, *Quarterly Investment Strategy* by UBS Global Asset Management, a global institutional asset manager. The table's "Benchmark" column indicates what the asset allocation would be if UBS had no opinion regarding the expected bond market performance in the alternative countries. In most cases, the normal allocation is based on the country's relative market value. Specifically, the normal allocation is 20.1 percent for the United States, 29.0 percent for Japan, and the remaining 50.9 percent for the other countries, including 40.0 percent for the combined EMU countries. Clearly, UBS *does* have an opinion regarding these countries (as shown in its implied *market strategy*, which equals the benchmark percentage plus or minus the over/underweight percentage). For example, it

Exhibit 19.12 UBS Global Bond Portfolio Strategy

Market Allocation as of March 31, 2005

	GLOBAL		GLOBAL (EX-US)	
	Benchmark	Over/Under Weight	Benchmark	Over/Under Weight
North America	**22.0%**	**−0.3%**	**2.4%**	**0.0%**
Canada	1.9	0.0	2.4	0.0
US	20.1	−0.3	0.0	0.0
EMU	**40.0**	**2.9**	**50.1**	**3.5**
Other Europe (Ex-UK)	**3.3**	**−2.4**	**4.2**	**−3.1**
Denmark	0.8	−0.8	1.0	−1.0
Norway	0.2	−0.2	0.3	−0.3
Poland	0.6	−0.6	0.7	−0.7
Sweden	0.9	0.0	1.1	0.0
Switzerland	0.8	−0.8	1.0	−1.0
UK	**5.0**	**−2.0**	**6.2**	**−2.2**
Japan	**29.0**	**0.0**	**36.3**	**0.0**
Australia	**0.3**	**2.0**	**0.4**	**2.0**
Singapore	**0.2**	**−0.2**	**0.3**	**−0.3**
	100.0%		100.0%	

	Europe (EMU)	
	Benchmark	Over/Under Weight
Austria	3.6%	6.7%
Belgium	7.0	−3.3
Finland	1.5	5.6
France	20.7	1.2
Germany	23.0	18.2
Greece	4.6	−4.6
Ireland	1.0	−1.0
Italy	22.7	−11.5
Netherlands	5.6	−0.8
Portugal	1.8	−1.9
Spain	8.5	−8.5
	100.0%	

(Continued)

[6] For a detailed discussion of the benefits of international bond investing as well as what is involved in the analysis, see Steward (2005), Munves (2005), Malvey (2005), and Steward, Lynch, and Fabozzi (2005a). Also see Churchill (1994), Squires (1996; 1997a, b; 2000a), and Jost (2002).

Exhibit 19.12 UBS Global Bond Portfolio Strategy (continued)

Currency Allocation

	GLOBAL		GLOBAL (EX-US)	
	Benchmark	Over/Under Weight	Benchmark	Over/Under Weight
North America	**22.0%**	**0.0%**	**2.4%**	**0.0%**
Canada	1.9	0.0	2.4	0.0
US	20.1	0.0	0.0	0.0
EMU	**40.0**	**0.0**	**50.1**	**0.0**
Other Europe (Ex-UK)	3.3	0.0	4.2	0.0
Denmark	0.8	0.0	1.0	0.0
Norway	0.2	0.0	0.3	0.0
Poland	0.6	0.0	0.7	0.0
Sweden	0.9	0.0	1.1	0.0
Switzerland	0.8	0.0	1.0	0.0
UK	**5.0**	**−4.0**	**6.2**	**−4.0**
Japan	**29.0**	**2.0**	**36.3**	**2.0**
Australia	**0.3**	**0.0**	**0.4**	**0.0**
Singapore	**0.2**	**2.0**	**0.3**	**2.0**
	100.0%		100.0%	

Totals may not add to 100% due to rounding.

Source: UBS Global Asset Management, *Quarterly Investment Strategy*, March 31, 2005 (Chicago, IL: UBS Global Asset Management).

has overweighted the EMU block of countries bond markets with a market strategy allocation of 42.9 percent (versus the benchmark allocation of 40.0 percent) and underweighted the
UK bond market with a market strategy allocation of only 3 percent (versus the benchmark
of 5 percent). Another country overweighted was Australia, while several are underweighted,
including Denmark, Norway, Poland, and Switzerland. In addition, UBS does a specific currency allocation between countries, which would likewise be based on the normal policy weight
unless the firm had an opinion on currencies. Again, UBS has an opinion: It heavily underweighted the U.K. pound and overweighted the currencies of Japan and Singapore.

In making your own allocations based on these specific expectations, you would look for
U.S. securities in which yields were expected to decline relative to Treasury securities and for
bond markets in foreign countries that likewise had bullish interest rate expectations. Finally,
you would look for countries in which the currency was expected to be strong relative to the
United States.

19.4 Core-Plus Management Strategies

Beyond a pure passive strategy designed to mimic an index or any of the several active management strategies we have just seen, recently there has been increased interest among professional
bond investors in a management approach that combines the two styles. Specifically, **core-plus**
bond portfolio management places a significant part (i.e., 70 to 80 percent) of the available
funds in a passively managed portfolio of high-grade securities reflecting a broad representation of the overall bond market; this is the "core" of the strategy. The remainder of the funds
would then be managed actively in the "plus" portion of the portfolio, where it is felt that the
manager's selection skills offer a higher probability of achieving positive abnormal rates of
return.

Typically, the core portion of a portfolio following this combination approach is effectively
managed as an index fund based on the belief that the designated core sectors of the bond
market are efficient to the point where it is not worth the time and cost to attempt to derive
substantial excess returns from them. Examples of market sectors that are often included in
this definition include the U.S. broad market sector or the U.S. government/corporate sector,

both of which are dominated by issues that carry a credit rating of AAA or higher. (The difference between these two core sectors is that the former includes the rapidly growing markets for mortgage-backed and asset-backed bonds.) Not surprisingly, then, the plus sectors included in the portfolio consist of those segments of the global bond market that are regarded as being less efficient and therefore more likely to be sources of alpha in the managed portfolio. This would include high-yield bonds, non-U.S. bonds from developed countries, and emerging market debt.

From the preceding description, it should be clear that a core-plus approach to bond management can also be considered a form of **enhanced indexing**, depending on how much of the portfolio is placed in the core portion and how actively the plus sectors are managed. As Davidson (2001) points out, the core-plus bond manager attempts to combine a substantial *beta* investment—that is, the funds invested to mimic the systematic risk exposure of the benchmark index—with the *alpha* potential associated with selecting bonds from the actively managed sectors. Thus, an important feature of a potential security position coming from the plus sectors is that it has the possibility of delivering high risk-adjusted returns over time that are not driven by systematic movements in the general bond market. This means that plus sector investments often have *high total risk*, as measured by their standard deviation of returns, but also *low correlations* with the other fixed-income sectors that represent the core of the portfolio. As we have seen, high-yield bonds are a good example of a plus sector since they tend to have very high standard deviations that make them equivalent to equity investments in many respects, but have very low correlations (e.g., 0.30 or lower) with the investment-grade bond sector.

Relative to a passive index strategy, a core-plus approach to managing a bond portfolio offers three potential advantages: (1) higher returns that occur from exploiting market inefficiencies outside the traditional core sectors, (2) increased opportunities for exploiting the manager's security selection skills, and (3) the ability to alter the composition of the fixed-income asset class in a manner consistent with the insights and views of the manager. Of course, these additional sources of alpha come at the expense of additional sources of risk. The incremental risk that the core-plus approach introduces into the passive portfolio can be particularly significant in no-growth or declining-growth economic scenarios given that much of the plus investing is likely to be done in lower credit grade instruments whose market values will be affected the most under those circumstances. Further, there may be a number of other risks associated with investments in the plus sectors—such as prepayment and liquidity risks—that are not as prevalent in the core portion of the portfolio. Finally, Dopfel (2003) cautions asset managers against the risks associated with changing correlations between stock and bond markets.

Hersey (2001) analyzed the composition and investment mandates for a broad sample of core and core-plus portfolios managed by leading U.S.-based fixed-income investment organizations. Exhibit 19.13 summarizes these findings. Notice that while both core and core-plus managers are given some investment latitude relative to the index—the Lehman Brothers U.S. Aggregate was the benchmark for the majority of these managers—the plus sectors were given substantially more. For instance, while core portfolios are allowed to hold an average of 5 percent of its positions in non-benchmark exposures, core-plus managers can maintain 15 to 40 percent. Specifically, although the index contained no high-yield positions, the typical core and core-plus portfolio invested 1 and 7 percent in this bond market segment, respectively. Both types of portfolios also contained larger allocations in asset-backed bonds than the index. Thus, to the extent that these sectors outperform—and that the managers exhibit good selection skills in these areas—the managed portfolios will be able to produce superior risk-adjusted returns. However, it is also important to note that core-plus managers face strict constraints on their ability to take on additional risk in the pursuit of these abnormal returns. In fact, the lower panel of Exhibit 19.13 shows that core-plus portfolios are expected to produce excess returns of 100 to 125 basis points while maintaining tracking errors that do not exceed 1.50 percent. Given Alford, Jones, and Winkelmann's (2003) description of the portfolio risk budgeting process, which suggests that passive portfolios have tracking errors of less than 1 percent, while

Exhibit 19.13 Characteristics of Core and Core-Plus Investments

A. *Typical Portfolio Composition*

Sector	Core	Core-Plus	Lehman U.S. Aggregate
Treasury/Agency	22%	19%	42%
Mortgage backed	37	36	36
Asset backed	10	8	1
Investment grade	27	21	21
Corporate			
High yield	1	7	na
Eurodollar	1	5	na
Other	2	3	na

na = not applicable

B. *Investment Mandates*

Characteristic	Core	Core-Plus
Benchmark excess return target	35–70 bps	100–125 bps
Tracking error	75–100 bps	125–150 bps
Consensus benchmark	Lehman U.S. Aggregate	Lehman U.S. Aggregate
Nonbenchmark exposures	0% (5% common)	15–40%
Management-fee differential	—	About a 10% premium over core

Note: bps = basis points

Source: Adapted from Brian E. Hersey, "Core-Plus: Prospects and Implications," in *Core-Plus Bond Management* (Charlottesville, VA: AIMR), 2001.

pure active portfolios have tracking errors greater than 3 percent, this mandate is consistent with the view that core-plus portfolio management is a combination strategy.

19.5 Matched-Funding Management Strategies

The goal for many participants in the bond market is simply to increase the wealth of their overall portfolios while providing risk diversification benefits across asset classes. For these investors, the passive, active, and core-plus strategies we have just seen are all potentially appropriate management styles, depending on their underlying beliefs about how efficient the bond market is. Other investors, however, face a more precise investment problem in which a specific set of liabilities needs to be met. For instance, life insurance companies have a series of future cash flow payments they are obligated to make, which they can predict in advance with a reasonable degree of accuracy given their actuarial forecasts. Further, defined-benefit pension funds can also predict fairly precisely the future retirement benefits they will be required to pay—in both amount and timing—to their constituents. For investors in these situations, the bond portfolios they form clearly should take into account the nature of the liabilities that those assets are intended to fund.

Matched-funding strategies are a form of **asset-liability management** whereby the characteristics of the bonds that are held in the portfolio are coordinated with those of the liabilities the investor is obligated to pay. As we will see, these matching techniques can range from an attempt to exactly match the levels and timing of the required cash payments to more general approaches that focus on other investment characteristics, such as setting the average duration or investment horizon of the bond portfolio equal to that of the underlying liabilities. An important assumption underlying all of the matched-funding techniques we will examine is that the investor's *liabilities are predictable* with some degree of precision. Said differently, as long as the fixed-income manager knows the obligations he faces, he can create a portfolio specifically designed to meet those needs in an optimal way.[7]

19.5.1 Dedicated Portfolios

Dedication refers to bond portfolio management techniques that are used to service a prescribed set of liabilities. Such a "dedicated" portfolio can be created in several ways. We will discuss two alternatives. A **pure cash-matched dedicated portfolio** is the most conservative strategy. Specifically, the objective of pure cash matching is to develop a portfolio of bonds that will provide a stream of payments from coupons, sinking funds, and maturing principal payments that will exactly match the specified liability schedules. An example of typical liability stream for a retired-lives component of a person system is shown in Exhibit 19.14. The goal is to build a portfolio that will generate sufficient funds in advance of each scheduled payment to ensure that the payment will be met. One alternative is to find a number of zero-coupon Treasury securities that will exactly cash match each liability. Such an exact cash match portfolio is referred to as a *total passive* portfolio because it is designed so that any prior receipts would not be reinvested (i.e., it assumes a zero reinvestment rate).

Dedication with reinvestment is similar to the pure cash-matched technique except it is assumed that the bonds and other cash flows do not have to exactly match the liability stream. Any inflows that precede liability claims can be reinvested at some reasonably conservative rate. This assumption allows the portfolio manager to consider a substantially wider set of bonds that may have higher return characteristics. In addition, the assumption of reinvestment within each period and between periods also will generate a higher return for the asset portfolio. As a result, the net cost of the portfolio will be lower, with almost equal safety, assuming the reinvestment rate assumption is conservative. An example would be to assume a reinvestment rate of 4 percent in an environment where market interest rates are currently ranging from 5 percent to 8 percent.

Potential problems exist with both of these approaches to a dedicated portfolio. When selecting potential bonds for these portfolios, it is critical to be aware of call/prepayment possibilities (refundings, calls, sinking funds) with specific bonds or mortgage-backed securities. These prepayment possibilities become very important following periods of historically

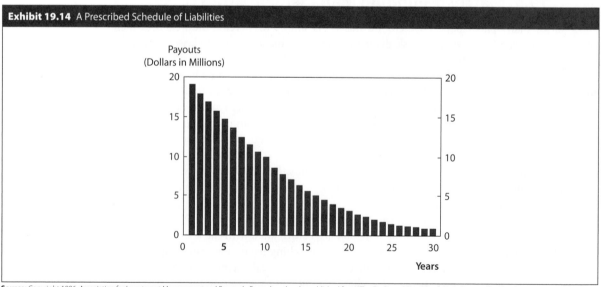

Exhibit 19.14   A Prescribed Schedule of Liabilities

Source: Copyright 1986, Association for Investment Management and Research. Reproduced and republished from "The Dedicated Bond Portfolio in Pension Funds—Part I: Motivations and Basics," in the *Financial Analysts Journal*, January/February 1986, with permission from the CFA Institute. All Rights Reserved.

[7] Additional discussion of the matched-funding approach to bond portfolio management can be found in Leibowitz (1986a) and Fabozzi (2005).

high rates. A prime example was the period 1982 to 1986, when interest rates went from over 18 percent to under 8 percent. Because of this substantial change in rates, many dedicated portfolios constructed without adequate concern for complete call protection were negatively affected when numerous bonds were called that were not expected to be called under normal conditions. For example, bonds selling at deep discounts (which typically provide implicit call protection), when rates were 16 percent to 18 percent, went to par and above when rates declined to under 10 percent and were then called. Obviously, the reinvestment of these proceeds at the lower rates caused many dedicated portfolios to be underfunded. Therefore, it is necessary to find bonds with complete call protection or to consider deep discount bonds under conservative interest rate conditions.

Although quality also is a legitimate concern, it is probably not necessary to invest only in Treasury bonds if the portfolio manager diversifies across industries and sectors. A diversified portfolio of AA or A industrial bonds can provide a current and total annual return of 40 to 60 basis points above Treasuries. This differential over a 30-year period can have a significant impact on the net cost of funding a liability stream.

19.5.2 Immunization Strategies

Instead of using a dedicated portfolio technique, a portfolio manager may decide that the optimal strategy is to immunize the portfolio from interest rate changes. *Immunization techniques* attempt to derive a specified rate of return (generally quite close to the current market rate) during a given investment horizon regardless of what happens to the future level of interest rates.

Components of Interest Rate Risk A major problem encountered in bond portfolio management is deriving a given rate of return to satisfy an ending-wealth requirement at a future specific date—that is, the **investment horizon**. If the term structure of interest rates were flat and market rates never changed between the time of purchase and the horizon date when funds were required, you could acquire a bond with a term to maturity equal to the desired investment horizon, and the ending wealth from the bond would equal the promised wealth position implied by the promised yield to maturity. Specifically, the ending-wealth position would be the beginning wealth times the compound value of a dollar at the promised yield to maturity. For example, assume you acquire a 10-year, $1 million bond with an 8 percent coupon at its par value. If the yield curve was flat and there were no changes in the curve, your wealth position at the end of your 10-year investment horizon (assuming semiannual compounding) would be

$$\$1,000,000 \times (1.04)^{20} = \$2,191,123$$

You can get the same answer by taking the $40,000 interest payment every six months and compounding it semiannually to the end of the period at 4 percent and adding the $1,000,000 principal at maturity. Unfortunately, in the real world, the term structure of interest rates typically is not flat and the level of interest rates is constantly changing. Consequently, the bond portfolio manager faces **interest rate risk** between the time of investment and the future target date. Interest rate risk is the uncertainty regarding the ending-wealth value of the portfolio due to changes in market interest rates between the time of purchase and the investor's horizon date. Notably, interest rate risk involves two component risks: **price risk** and **coupon reinvestment risk**.

The price risk occurs because if interest rates change before the horizon date and the bond is sold before maturity, the realized market price for the bond will differ from the *expected* price, assuming there had been no change in rates. If rates increased after the time of purchase, the realized price for the bond in the secondary market would be below expectations, whereas if rates declined, the realized price for the bond would be above expectations. Because you do not know whether interest rates will increase or decrease, you are uncertain about the bond's future price.

The coupon reinvestment risk arises because the yield to maturity computation implicitly assumes that all coupon cash flows will be reinvested at the promised yield to maturity. If, after the purchase of the bond, interest rates decline, the coupon cash flows will be reinvested at rates below the initial promised yield, and the ending wealth will be below expectations. In contrast, if interest rates increase, the coupon cash flows will be reinvested at rates above expectations, and the ending wealth will be above expectations. Again, because you are uncertain about future rates, you are uncertain about these reinvestment rates.

Classical Immunization and Interest Rate Risk Fisher and Weil (1971), as well as Bierwag and Kaufman (1977) and Bierwag (1977), showed that price risk and reinvestment risk are affected inversely by a change in market rates and that duration is the time period when these two risks are of equal magnitude, but in opposite directions. An increase in interest rates will cause an ending price below expectations, but the reinvestment rate for interim cash flows will be above expectations. A decline in market interest rates will cause the reverse situation. Clearly, a bond portfolio manager with a specific target date (investment horizon) will attempt to eliminate these two components of interest rate risk. The process intended to eliminate interest rate risk is referred to as **immunization** and was discussed by Redington (1952). It has been specified in detail by Fisher and Weil (1971) as follows:

> *A portfolio of investments in bonds is* immunized *for a holding period if its value at the end of the holding period, regardless of the course of interest rates during the holding period, must be at least as large as it would have been had the interest-rate function been constant throughout the holding period.*
>
> *If the realized return on an investment in bonds is sure to be at least as large as the appropriately computed yield to the horizon, then that investment is immunized* [p. 411].

Fisher and Weil found a significant difference between the *promised* yields and the *realized* returns on bonds for the period 1925 to 1968, indicating the importance of immunizing a bond portfolio. They showed that it is possible to immunize a bond portfolio if you can assume that any change in interest rates will be the same for all maturities—that is, if forward interest rates change, all rates will change by the same amount (there is a parallel shift of the yield curve). Given this assumption, Fisher and Weil proved that *a portfolio of bonds is immunized from interest rate risk if the duration of the portfolio is always equal to the desired investment horizon.*

The authors simulated the effects of applying the immunization concept (a duration-matched strategy) compared to a naive portfolio strategy where the portfolio's maturity was equal to the investment horizon. They compared the ending-wealth ratio for the duration-matched and for the naive strategy portfolios to a wealth ratio that assumed no change in the interest rate structure. In a perfectly immunized portfolio, the actual ending wealth should equal the expected ending wealth implied by the promised yield, so these comparisons should indicate which portfolio strategy does a superior job of immunization. The duration-matched strategy results were consistently closer to the promised yield results; however, the results were not perfect. The duration portfolio was not perfectly immunized because the basic assumption did not always hold; that is, when interest rates changed, all interest rates did not change by the same amount.

The Mechanics of Bond Immunization: A Simple Illustration[8] Suppose that an investor has a liability that she needs to pay off in exactly three years. Thus, her desired investment horizon is three years, which can also be considered as the duration of the liability she faces. Suppose further that the yield curve is currently flat at 10 percent but that it declines to

---

[8] The authors gratefully acknowledge Professor Robert Radcliffe's contribution to this example.

8 percent as soon as her initial investment is made. She considers four alternative bond investments to fund this liability:

(A)   Purchase a 10-year bond paying a 9 percent annual coupon and sell it in three years
(B)   Purchase three consecutive one-year "pure discount" (i.e., zero-coupon) bonds
(C)   Purchase a three-year, pure discount bond
(D)   Purchase a four-year bond paying a 34.85 precent annual coupon and sell it in three years

Under these assumptions, the promised yield for each of these prospective investments is 10 percent at the time she makes her initial decision. So, the relevant question to consider is: What will be the realized yields (RY) for all four positions at the end of her three-year investment horizon?

For *Bond A*, the initial investment (per $1,000 of face value) is:

$$P_0 = \sum_{t=1}^{10} \frac{90}{(1 + .10)^t} + \frac{1000}{(1 + .10)^{10}} = \$938.55$$

Since this position will not have matured by Year 3, it will have to be sold at the prevailing market rate (assumed to then be 8 percent). Also, she will be able to reinvest the coupons she receives prior to her planning horizon. Thus, the ending-wealth in this position is the combination of:

(i)   Sale of Bond:

$$P_3 = \sum_{t=1}^{7} \frac{90}{(1 + .08)^t} + \frac{1000}{(1 + .08)^7} = \$1052.06, \text{ and}$$

(ii)   Reinvested Coupon Payments:

$$90(1 + .08)^2 + 90(1 + .08) + 90 = \$292.18$$

or $1344.24. This means the investor's realized yield in Bond A would be:

$$RY_A = \sqrt[3]{\frac{1344.24}{938.55}} - 1 = 12.72 \text{ percent}$$

For *Bond B*, assume for simplicity that the bondholder invests $1,000 initially at 10 percent and then reinvests the total annual proceeds for two more years at 8 percent:

$$\text{Year 1: } (1000.00)(1 + .10) = \$1100.00$$
$$\text{Year 2: } (1100.00)(1 + .08) = \$1188.00$$
$$\text{Year 3: } (1188.00)(1 + .08) = \$1283.04$$

Thus, her realized yield from this "rollover" strategy would be:

$$RY_B = \sqrt[3]{\frac{1283.04}{1000.00}} - 1 = 8.66 \text{ percent}$$

The initial purchase price of *Bond C* (per $1,000 face value) is:

$$P_0 = (1000) \div (1 + .10)^3 = \$751.31$$

so, the realized yield would be:

$$RY_C = \sqrt[3]{\frac{1000.00}{751.31}} - 1 = 10.00 \text{ percent}$$

Finally, *Bond D* is similar to Bond A in that it must be sold prior to maturity and its coupons must be reinvested. The initial price for this security is:

$$P_0 = \sum_{t=1}^{4} \frac{348.50}{(1 + .10)^t} + \frac{1000}{(1 + .10)^4} = \$1787.71$$

The ending-wealth level in Year 3 combines:

(i) Sale of Bond:

$$P_3 = (1000 + 348.50) \div (1 + .08) = \$1248.61, \text{ and}$$

(ii) Coupon Payments:

$$348.50(1 + .08)^2 + 348.50(1 + .08) + 348.50 = \$1131.37$$

or $2379.98 and, thus, the realized yield would be:

$$RY_D = \sqrt[3]{\frac{2379.98}{1787.71}} - 1 = 10.00 \text{ percent}$$

Notice that only for Bonds C and D does the yield to maturity prevailing at the time of the original investment decision (i.e., the *promised* or *expected* return) equal the *actual* rate of return over the three-year investment horizon. To see why this is the case, it is easy to confirm that the duration statistics for each of these bonds are:

> Bond A: 6.89 years
> Bond B: 1.00 year (per bond)
> Bond C: 3.00 years
> Bond D: 3.00 years

Because the investor's planning horizon was three years, the only bonds that actually produced the expected yield of 10 percent were the two that have durations of three years. Put another way, by investing in a bond that pays out the "average" cash flow at precisely the time it is desired, it is possible to completely offset the effects of a subsequent change in interest rates. If interest rates fall (rise) after purchase, the bond price will rise (fall) by exactly enough to offset the decline (increase) in income from reinvested coupons. Once again, this selection process is known as *immunization*.

On the other hand, when the investor tried to fund a three-year liability with a longer-duration bond (i.e., Bond A), she had to sell the bond to get the majority of her cash out of the position. This resulted in a situation where the price risk component dominated the reinvestment risk component (i.e., *net price risk*). This produced a higher actual return than she was promised (12.72 versus 10 percent) because rates in the market fell, which benefited the bond's price more than it hurt coupon reinvestment potential. Conversely, when she tried to fund the three-year liability with a series of shorter-duration positions (i.e., Bond B), she received her cash back sooner than she needed it and therefore faced a *net reinvestment risk* problem, which in this case led to a lower realized yield as rates fell. However, the important point here is that with either Bond A or Bond B, the investor faces uncertainty over the outcome of her investment, as can be seen from the fact that her realized yield differed from her promised yield.

In summary, given that bond risk caused by changing interest rates can be split into price risk and reinvestment risk, the following general statements can be made:

> If *Duration > Investment Horizon*, the investor faces *Net Price Risk* (Bond A)
> If *Duration < Investment Horizon*, the investor faces *Net Reinvestment Risk* (Bond B)
> If *Duration = Investment Horizon*, the investor is *immunized* (Bonds C and D)

Finally, it should be noted that setting the duration of an asset equal to the duration of the liability (i.e., investment horizon) will just immunize an investment against the *next* interest rate movement. However, the position will remain immunized to subsequent yield changes *as long as it is rebalanced promptly*; this is demonstrated in the Appendix.

Another View of Immunization The previous example assumed that bond positions were acquired and held to the end of the desired investment horizon. An alternative way to envision what will happen with an immunized portfolio would be to examine the specific growth path that converts the beginning-wealth position into the ending-wealth position and then consider what happens when interest rates change.

Suppose you have the following conditions to begin with: an initial-wealth position of $1 million, your investment horizon is 10 years, and the coupon and current YTM are both 8 percent. We know from an earlier computation that this implies an ending-wealth position (assuming semiannual compounding) of $2,191,123; Exhibit 19.15A illustrates this compound growth path. In Exhibit 19.15B, it is assumed that at the end of Year 2, interest rates increase by 200 basis points from 8 percent to 10 percent. We know that, with no prior rate changes, at the end of Year 2 the value of the portfolio would have grown at an 8 percent compound rate to $1,169,859 ($[1.04]^4 \times \$1$ million). We also know that the rate change in Year 2 will impact the portfolio in two ways: (1) the market value (i.e., price) will decline to reflect the higher interest rates, and (2) the reinvestment potential, which is the future growth rate of the portfolio, will increase. The important question therefore is: What will be the new ending-wealth position of the portfolio? As we have seen, the answer depends on the duration of the position when rates change. Fisher and Weil (1971) showed that if portfolio duration is equal to the remaining investment horizon, the price decline will be such that, at the new reinvestment (i.e., growth) rate of 10 percent, the new portfolio value will still grow to the original expected ending-wealth position. In this example, the actual Year 2 value of the portfolio after the rate increase will be $1,003,779. Notice that if this new portfolio value grows at 10 percent a year for eight years, the projected ending-wealth value will be:

$$\$1,003,779 \times (1.05)^{16} = \$2,191,123$$

Thus, the price decline is exactly offset by the higher reinvestment rate, assuming that the duration of the portfolio at the time of the yield movement was equal to the remaining investment horizon.

What happens if the duration of the portfolio is not properly matched to the desired investment horizon? If, for instance, duration is greater than eight years, the price change will exceed the impact of a new reinvestment rate as you face net price risk. Thus, if interest rates increase, the value of the portfolio after the rate change will be less than $1,003,779. In this case, even if the new value of the portfolio grew at the higher growth rate of 10 percent a year, it would not reach the original expected ending-wealth value. This scenario is shown in Exhibit 19.15C, where it is assumed that the value of the portfolio with a duration greater than eight years declined to $950,000. Assuming that this new portfolio value then grew at the higher growth rate for the rest of the investment horizon, its ending value would be:

$$\$950,000 \times (1.05)^{16} = \$2,073,731$$

Therefore, the shortfall of $117,392 between the original expected ending-wealth level and the realized position is due to the fact that the portfolio was not properly duration matched (i.e., immunized) when the interest rate change occurred.

Alternatively, assume that at Year 2 interest rates had *declined* at a time when portfolio duration was greater than eight years. The value of the position would have increased to the point that, even when reinvested at a lower growth rate, the ending-wealth level would exceed $2,191,123. Exhibit 19.15D shows what can happen if the portfolio is not properly matched and interest rates decline by 200 basis points to 6 percent. First, assuming that the portfolio is

Exhibit 19.15 The Growth Path to the Expected Ending-Wealth Value and the Effect of Immunization

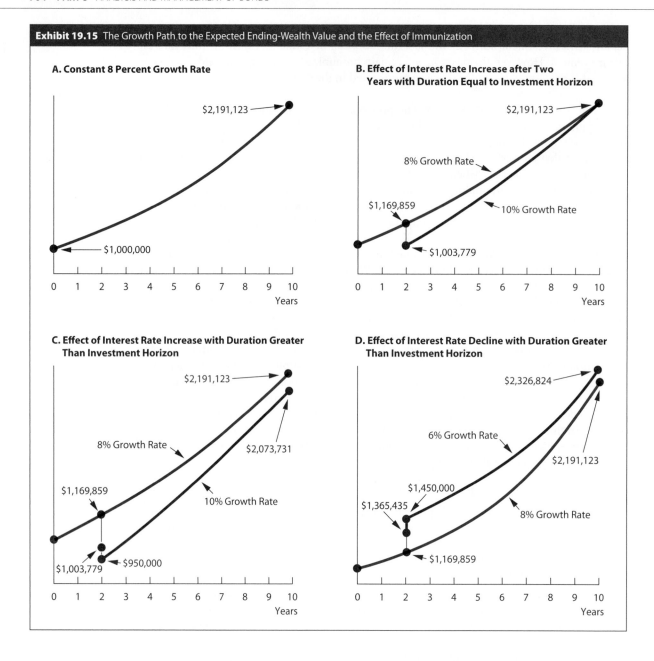

A. Constant 8 Percent Growth Rate

B. Effect of Interest Rate Increase after Two Years with Duration Equal to Investment Horizon

C. Effect of Interest Rate Increase with Duration Greater Than Investment Horizon

D. Effect of Interest Rate Decline with Duration Greater Than Investment Horizon

properly duration matched, its Year 2 value will increase to $1,365,435. If this amount subsequently grows at 6 percent for eight years, its ending value will be:

$$\$1,365,435 \times (1.03)^{16} = \$2,191,123$$

Instead, if duration exceeds eight years, the Year 2 portfolio value would be greater than the required value of $1,365,435. Supposing this amount to be $1,450,000, the revised ending-wealth position would be:

$$\$1,450,000 \times (1.03)^{16} = \$2,326,824$$

In this scenario, the projected ending-wealth value is greater than the original expected level because your portfolio was mismatched to your intended investment horizon and interest rates moved in your favor. The important point here is that *when you are not duration matched, you are effectively speculating on interest rate changes* and the result can be either very good or very bad. The purpose of immunization is to avoid this uncertainty and to lock in the expected ending-wealth level (i.e., $2,191,123), regardless of interest rate changes.

Application of Classical Immunization Stonewall Insurance Ltd. (a pseudonym for a real company) is a property and casualty insurance firm that operates as an offshore subsidiary of a construction firm based in the United States. Stonewall's primary function is to provide worker's compensation insurance benefits to the employees of the parent firm. Although the construction firm has an excellent safety record, there are nevertheless occasional worksite accidents that require the subsequent payment of compensation benefits. These benefit payments can continue for anywhere from a few months to several years; the parent firm conservatively plans for payments to continue an average of 3.50 to 4.50 years. Thus, they consider this to be the duration range of the potential liabilities (i.e., planning horizon) they face.

The uncertainty of both the size and length of the benefit claims that Stonewall is liable for makes the implementation of a cash-matched portfolio solution impractical. (It is typically the case that property and casualty insurance firms have less predictable liabilities than life insurance companies.) Instead, the insurance firm's solution to this asset-liability management problem is to assemble a bond portfolio that has a duration statistic (expressed in modified form, in this case) of around 4.00 years. Details of the specific securities they held as of January 2008 are shown in Exhibit 19.16. Notice in particular that the portfolio holds 27 separate positions—mostly corporate bonds—with an aggregate market value of $23 million and an average credit grade of between A1 (Moody's) and AA- (Standard & Poor's). More importantly, however, the portfolio has been assembled to have a modified duration of 3.91 years, which closely matches the target horizon period implied by their projected liabilities. Thus, the position is effectively immunized; an unexpected increase or decrease in interest rates at this point in time would have approximately equal and offsetting effects on the value of both Stonewall's assets and liabilities, leaving the firm's net worth unaffected by the rate movement.

This example also helps highlight some practical challenges an investor must face when designing an immunization strategy. First of all, except for the special case of a zero-coupon bond, an immunized portfolio will require frequent rebalancing. As shown in the Appendix to this chapter, such rebalancing will be necessary with every significant shift in the yield curve, but it will also be required by the passing time. For instance, even if market rates do not change, after a year has passed (i.e., January 2009) the modified duration of the bond portfolio will be substantially lower than 3.91 years. (Because duration declines more slowly than maturity as time passes, the January 2009 modified duration level for the firm will be somewhat higher than 2.91 years.) Of course, since the target investment horizon would still be 4.00 years, this decay in the duration of the portfolio would leave the firm in a position of net reinvestment risk and therefore adversely exposed to a subsequent downward movement in the yield curve. Thus, to remain immunized over time, the bond manager for Stonewall will periodically need to rebalance the portfolio to maintain the original duration target.

Second, in Chapter 18 we discussed the fact that duration changes inversely with changes in interest rates. In fact, it is this property that makes the relationship between a bond's price and its yield a curved (i.e., convex) function rather than a straight line. Consequently, the manager of an immunized bond portfolio should also pay attention to the convexity statistic of the position. Specifically, in addition to duration matching the company's assets and liabilities, the manager should attempt to construct a bond portfolio that has *greater convexity* than the firm's liabilities. When the convexity of the assets exceeds that of the liabilities at a time when the durations are matched, it will be the case that the *actual* decline in value for an upward rate movement will be less severe for the assets than for the liabilities. While it is difficult to know if the convexity level of 21.69 for Stonewall's portfolio accomplishes that goal without knowing more about the precise characteristics of its projected obligations, Kritzman (1992) demonstrates that for two portfolios with the same duration, the one with cash flows that are more

Exhibit 19.16 Immunized Bond Portfolio of Stonewall Insurance Ltd., January 2008

Category	Sector	Issuer	Ticker Symbol	CUSIP	Maturity	Coupon	Call Date (Price)	Par Value (000s)	Bid Yield	Bid Price	Total Bond Value	Accrued Interest	Total Pos. Value	% of Ttl Position	Mod. Dur.	Convex	Moody Rating	S&P Rating
Agency: 4.40%	—	Federal Home Loan Bank	FHLB	3133XD7E5	9/21/2012	5.250%	3/21/08 (100.000)	1000	5.237%	100.0454	$1,000,453.89	1.458	$1,015,037.22	4.395%	4.078	19.988	Aaa	AAA
Corporate: 95.60%	Aerospace:	McDonnell Douglas	BA	580169AM2	4/1/2012	9.750%	Not Callable	1000	5.097%	117.5649	$1,175,648.71	2.438	$1,200,023.71	5.196%	3.480	15.230	A2	A+
	Conglomerates:	Emerson Electric	EMR	EC9551796	5/1/2013	4.500%	MW (+10)	584	5.142%	97.0320	$566,666.79	0.750	$571,046.79	2.473%	4.636	25.403	A2	A
		General Dynamics	GD	369550AK4	5/15/2013	4.250%	MW (+25)	1000	4.870%	97.0952	$970,952.10	0.543	$976,382.66	4.228%	4.710	26.058	A2	A
	Consumer-Products:	Procter & Gamble	PG	742718DA4	8/15/2014	4.950%	MW (+10)	500	4.480%	102.6626	$513,312.85	1.870	$522,662.85	2.263%	5.516	36.530	Aa3	AA-
		Anheuser Busch	BUD	035229CY7	1/15/2015	5.000%	MW (+20)	500	4.979%	100.1212	$500,606.01	2.306	$512,133.79	2.218%	5.742	39.969	A2	A
	Consumer-Restaurants:	McDonald's	MCD	58013MDU5	6/1/2013	4.125%	MW (+15)	1000	4.538%	98.0330	$980,330.29	0.344	$983,767.79	4.260%	4.778	26.708	A3	A
	Consumer-Retail:	Target	TGT	87612EAH9	3/1/2012	5.875%	MW (+20)	500	4.857%	103.7907	$518,953.59	1.958	$528,745.25	2.290%	3.609	15.869	A2	A+
		Target	TGT	87612EAM8	6/15/2013	4.000%	MW (+15)	500	5.305%	93.8903	$469,451.51	2.178	$480,340.40	2.080%	4.698	26.340	A2	A+
		Wal-Mart Stores	WMT	931142BT9	5/1/2013	4.550%	Not Callable	1000	4.480%	100.3232	$1,003,232.41	0.758	$1,010,815.74	4.377%	4.658	25.607	Aa2	AA
	Energy:	Seariver Maritime	XOM	812293AB4	9/1/2012	0.000%	1/11/08 (88.708)	1000	4.520%	81.1732	$811,731.95	0.000	$811,731.95	3.515%	4.564	23.057	Aaa	AAA
		MidAmerican Energy	BRK	S95620AD7	10/1/2014	4.650%	MW (+15)	1000	4.968%	98.1880	$981,879.94	1.163	$993,504.94	4.302%	5.653	38.053	A2	A-
	Financial-Diversified:	General Electric Capital	GE	36962GV50	11/15/2010	6.875%	Not Callable	1000	4.135%	107.3425	$1,073,425.27	0.878	$1,082,209.99	4.686%	2.590	8.334	Aaa	AAA
	Financial-Global:	Merrill Lynch	MER	590188ES3	4/27/2008	7.000%	Not Callable	1000	5.533%	100.4513	$1,004,512.75	1.244	$1,016,957.20	4.404%	0.314	0.251	A1	A+
		Goldman Sachs	GS	38141GDQ4	10/15/2013	5.250%	Not Callable	500	5.120%	100.6361	$503,180.67	1.108	$508,722.34	2.203%	4.891	28.618	Aa3	AA-
		Morgan Stanley	MS	61748AAE6	4/1/2014	4.750%	Not Callable	500	5.855%	94.2768	$471,383.79	1.188	$477,321.29	2.067%	5.233	32.721	A1	A+
	Financial-Regional:	BankBoston	BAC	06606HD87	4/15/2008	6.375%	Not Callable	1000	5.072%	100.3593	$1,003,593.21	1.346	$1,017,051.55	4.404%	0.282	0.217	Aa1	AA
		Bank of America	BAC	060505BM5	6/15/2014	5.375%	Not Callable	1000	5.138%	101.2915	$1,012,915.24	2.926	$1,042,179.13	4.513%	5.255	33.778	Aa1	AA
	Healthcare:	AstraZeneca	AZN	046353AA6	6/1/2014	5.400%	MW (+15)	1000	4.925%	102.5818	$1,025,817.60	0.450	$1,030,317.60	4.462%	5.366	34.345	A1	AA-
		Bristol-Myers Squibb	BMY	110122AL2	8/15/2013	5.250%	MW (+15)	1000	4.622%	103.0727	$1,030,727.10	1.983	$1,050,560.43	4.549%	4.751	27.189	Aa3	A+
		Merck	MRK	589331AK3	3/1/2015	4.750%	MW (+15)	1000	4.865%	99.3048	$993,047.96	1.583	$1,008,881.29	4.369%	5.914	41.945	Aa3	AA-
	Industrial Equipment:	Caterpillar	CAT	149123BG5	9/15/2009	7.250%	MW (+10)	1000	4.146%	105.0517	$1,050,517.44	2.135	$1,071,864.67	4.642%	1.574	3.350	A2	A
	Office Equipment:	Pitney Bowes	PBI	72447WAU3	8/15/2014	4.875%	MW (+15)	1000	5.125%	98.6053	$986,053.02	1.842	$1,004,469.69	4.350%	5.487	36.212	A1	A+
	Mortgage:	Federal Natl. Mort. Assn.	FNMA	31360QP2	4/25/2019	10.450%	Serial Calls	23	4.571%	117.7500	$26,564.44	1.074	$26,806.74	0.116%	2.940	5.041	Aaa	AAA
	Technology:	Intl. Business Machines	IBM	45920QBZ6	1/26/2009	5.400%	Not Callable	1000	4.651%	100.7690	$1,007,689.68	2.325	$1,030,939.68	4.464%	1.007	1.536	A1	A+
	Telecommunications:	Verizon NJ	VZ	92344UAA3	1/17/2012	5.875%	MW (+30)	1000	4.716%	104.2198	$1,042,197.95	2.676	$1,068,961.84	4.629%	3.494	14.992	A3	A
		BellSouth Corp.	BLS	07986OAB8	10/15/2011	6.000%	MW (+20)	1000	4.918%	103.6902	$1,036,901.92	1.267	$1,049,568.59	4.545%	3.331	13.494	A2	A

Portfolio Summary

Number of Bond Issues	27
Total Portfolio Market Value	$23,093,005.12
Total Portfolio Par Value	$22,606,560.04
Wght. Avg. Bond Yield to Maturity	4.863%
Wght. Avg. Bond Coupon	5.445%
Portfolio Modified Duration	3.905
Portfolio Convexity	21.687
Wght. Avg. Moody's Rating	A1
Wght. Avg. S&P Rating	AA-

spread out (i.e., less concentrated around the duration date) will have greater convexity. Thus, the bond ladder approach adopted by Stonewall's managers (e.g., maturity dates ranging from 2009 to 2015) is likely to produce a more successful outcome that a portfolio that concentrated its cash flow payments around January 2012 (i.e., the current date plus 4.00 years).

Finally, because certain segments of the fixed-income market can be illiquid, there sometimes is a problem acquiring the bonds you have identified as optimal positions for your portfolio. For example, can you purchase the long-duration bonds you have targeted at a price that you consider to be acceptable? Further, bonds possessing the particular characteristics you need to match the target horizon exactly may not be available. Thus, Stonewall's modified duration statistic of 3.91 is likely as close as the manager could get to the target horizon of 4.00 given the nature of the bond market at the time of the example. In summary, it is important to recognize that classical immunization is generally *not* a passive strategy because it is subject to all of these practical issues that demand the attention of the manager.

19.5.3 Horizon Matching

Horizon matching is a combination of two of the techniques just discussed: cash-matching dedication and immunization. As shown in Exhibit 19.17, the liability stream is divided into two segments. In the first segment, the portfolio is constructed to provide a cash match for the liabilities during this horizon period (e.g., the first five years). The second segment is the remaining liability stream following the end of the horizon period—in the example, it is the 25 years following 2015. During this second time period, the liabilities are covered by a duration-matched strategy based on immunization principles. As a result, Leibowitz (1986b) contends that the client receives the certainty of cash matching during the early years and the cost saving and flexibility of duration-matched flows thereafter.

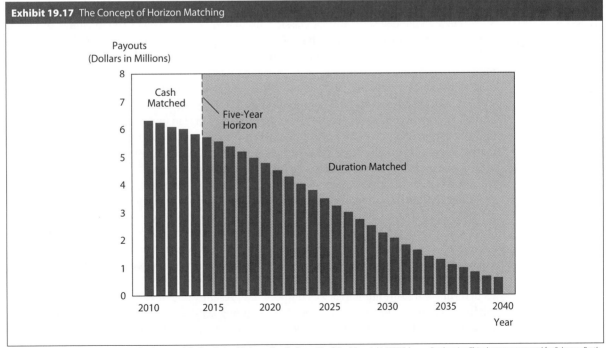

Exhibit 19.17 The Concept of Horizon Matching

Source: "Horizon Matching: A New Generalized Approach for Developing Minimum Cost Dedicated Portfolios." Copyright 1983 Salomon Brothers Inc. This chart was prepared for Salomon Brothers Inc. by Martin Leibowitz, a former Managing Director; Thomas E. Klaffky, Managing Director; Steven Mandel, a former Managing Director; and Alfred Weinberger, a former Director. Although the information in this chart has been obtained from sources that Salomon Brothers Inc. believed to be reliable, SSB does not guarantee their accuracy, and such information may be incomplete or condensed. All figures included in this chart constitute SSB's judgment as of the original publication date. Reprinted with permission from SalomonSmithBarney.

The combination technique also helps alleviate one of the problems with classical immunization: the potential for nonparallel shifts in the yield curve. Most of the problems related to non-parallel shifts are concentrated in the short end of the yield curve because this is where the most severe curve reshaping typically occurs. Because the near-term horizon is cash-matched, however, these irregular rate changes are not of concern. Further, we know that the long end of the yield curve tends toward parallel shifts.

An important decision when using horizon matching is the length of the horizon period. The trade-off when making this decision is between the safety and certainty of cash matching and the lower cost and flexibility of duration-based immunization. The portfolio manager should provide the client with a set of horizon alternatives and the costs and benefits of each of them and allow the client to make the decision.

As part of their discussion on horizon matching, Leibowitz, Klaffky, Mandel, and Weinberger (1983) point out that it also is possible to consider *rolling out* the cash-matched segment over time. Specifically, after the first year the portfolio manager would restructure the portfolio to provide a cash match during the original Year 6, which means that you would still have a five-year horizon. The ability and cost of rolling out depends on movements in interest rates; ideally you would still want to see parallel shifts in the yield curve.

19.6 Contingent and Structured Management Strategies

Contingent procedures for managing bond portfolios are a form of what has come to be called structured active management. The specific contingent procedure we discuss here is contingent immunization, which is a strategy that allows the bond manager flexibility to actively manage the portfolio subject to an overriding constraint that the portfolio remains immunized at some predetermined yield level. Other structured strategies, which typically involve supplementing the bonds held in the portfolio with positions in derivative securities (e.g., futures or option contracts), will be discussed in Chapters 20 to 23.

19.6.1 Contingent Immunization

Subsequent to the developments of classical immunization, Leibowitz and Weinberger (1982, 1983) suggest a portfolio strategy that allows a bond portfolio manager to pursue the highest returns available through active strategies while relying on classical bond immunization techniques to ensure a given minimal return over the investment horizon. That is, their new procedure allows active portfolio management with a safety net provided by classical immunization.

To understand contingent immunization, recall from our earlier discussion that when the portfolio duration is equal to the investment horizon, a change in interest rates will cause a change in the dollar value of the portfolio such that when the new asset value is compounded at the new market interest rate, it will equal the expected (desired) ending wealth value. This required change in value occurs *only* when the modified duration of the portfolio is equal to the remaining time horizon, which is why the modified duration of the portfolio must be maintained at the horizon value.

Consider the following example of this process. Assume that your desired ending-wealth value is $206.3 million. Given this specific ending value and the number of years to your horizon value, it is possible to determine how much you must invest today to attain that ending value if you assume a rate of return on the portfolio. Obviously, this is just the reverse of the price compounding exercise—that is, you compute the present value of the ending value at the expected yield for the horizon period.[9] In this case, we assume a five-year horizon and a 15 percent return, meaning that we compute the present value of $206.3 million at 15 percent for five years or 7.5 percent for 10 periods assuming semiannual compounding. The present value factor of 0.48473 times the $206.3 million ending value equals $100 million—this is

---

[9] The article on this topic was written when interest rates were at historically high levels of about 14–16 percent, which explains the high example rates. The concepts would be the same with lower rates.

the required initial investment under these assumptions to attain the desired ending value. Assuming the five-year horizon, we can do it for other interest rates as follows:

Percent	Present Value Factor[a]	Required Investment ($ Mil.)	Percent	Present Value Factor[a]	Required Investment ($ Mil.)
10	0.6139	$126.65	16	0.4632	$95.56
12	0.5584	115.20	18	0.4224	87.14
14	0.5083	104.86	20	0.3855	79.53
15	0.48473	100.00			

[a]Present value for 10 periods (5 years) at one-half the annual percentage rate.

Exhibit 19.18 reflects these calculations—that is, the dark line indicates the required initial amount that must be invested at every yield level to attain $206.3 million in five years. Clearly, at lower yields you need a larger initial investment (e.g., $126 million at 10 percent), and it declines with higher yields (e.g., it is less than $80 million at 20 percent). The dotted line in Exhibit 19.18 indicates that the price sensitivity of a portfolio with a modified duration of five years will have almost exactly the price sensitivity required.

Contingent immunization requires that the client be willing to accept a potential return below the current market return. This is referred to as a *cushion spread,* or the difference between the current market return and some floor rate. This cushion spread in required yield provides flexibility for the portfolio manager to engage in active portfolio strategies. For example, if current market rates are 15 percent, the client might be willing to accept a floor rate of 14 percent. If we assume the client initiated the fund with $100 million, the acceptance of this lower rate will mean that the portfolio manager does not have the same ending-asset requirements. Specifically, at 14 percent the required ending-wealth value would be $196.72 million (7 percent for 10 periods) compared to the $206.3 million at 15 percent. Because of this lower floor rate (and lower ending-wealth value), it is possible to experience some declines

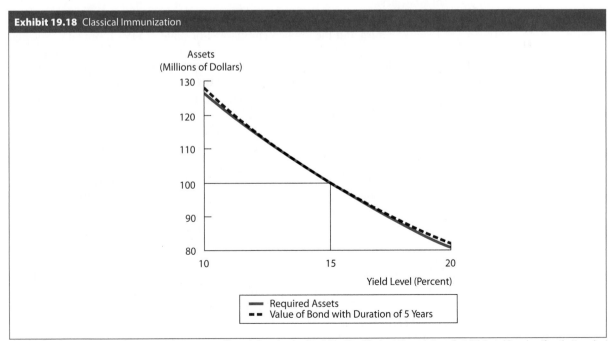

Exhibit 19.18 Classical Immunization

Source: Copyright 1982, Association for Investment Management and Research. Reproduced and republished from "Contingent Immunization—Part I: Risk Control Procedures" from the November/December 1982 issue of the *Financial Analysts Journal,* with permission from the CFA Institute. All Rights Reserved.

Exhibit 19.19 Price Behavior Required for Floor Return

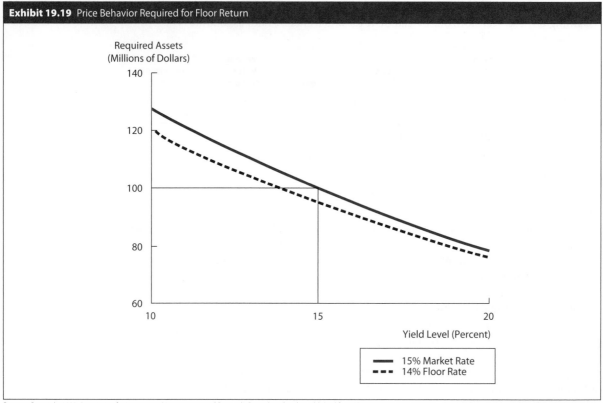

in the value of the portfolio while attempting to do better than the market through active management strategies.

Exhibit 19.19 shows the value of assets that are required at the beginning assuming a 14 percent required return and the implied ending-wealth value of $196.72 million. Notably, assuming current market rates of 15 percent, the required value of assets at the beginning would be $95.56 million, which is the present value of $196.72 million at 15 percent for five years. The difference between the client's initial fund of $100 million and the required assets of $95.56 million is the dollar cushion available to the portfolio manager. As noted, this dollar cushion arises because the client has agreed to a lower investment rate and, therefore, a lower ending-wealth value. Therefore, the manager effectively now has a $4.44 million (=100 – 95.56) "side fund" with which to pursue active management strategies in an attempt to add alpha to the overall portfolio.

At this point, the portfolio manager can engage in various active portfolio management strategies to increase the ending-wealth value of the portfolio above that required at 14 percent. As an example, assume that the portfolio manager believes that market rates will decline. Under such conditions, the portfolio manager might consider acquiring a 30-year bond that has a modified duration greater than the investment horizon of five years and, therefore, has greater price sensitivity to changes in market rates. Hence, if rates decline as expected, the value of the long-duration portfolio will experience a rapid increase above the initial value. In contrast, if rates increase, the value of the portfolio will decline rapidly. In this case, depending on how high rates go, the value of the portfolio could decline to a value below that needed to reach the desired ending-wealth value of $196.72 million.

Exhibit 19.20 shows what happens to the value of this portfolio if we assume an instantaneous change in interest rates when the fund is established. Specifically, if rates decline from

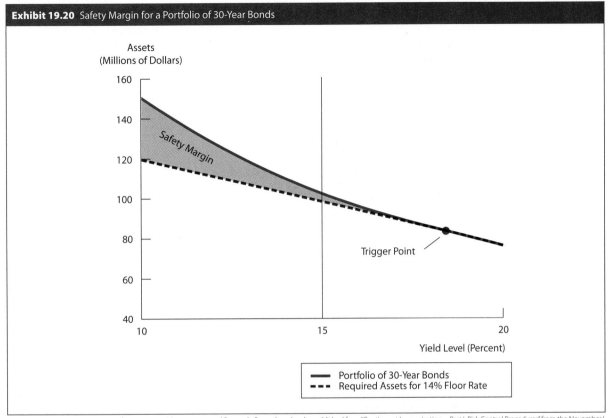

Exhibit 19.20 Safety Margin for a Portfolio of 30-Year Bonds

Assets
(Millions of Dollars)

Safety Margin

Trigger Point

Yield Level (Percent)

—— Portfolio of 30-Year Bonds
- - - Required Assets for 14% Floor Rate

15 percent, the portfolio of long-duration, 30-year bonds would experience a large increase in value and develop a *safety margin*—a portfolio value above the required value. In contrast, if rates increase, the value of the portfolio will decline until it reaches the asset value required at 14 percent. When the value of the portfolio reaches this point of minimum return (referred to as a *trigger point*), it is necessary to stop active portfolio management and use classical immunization with the remaining assets to ensure that you attain the desired ending-wealth value (i.e., $196.72 million).

Potential Return The concept of potential return is helpful in understanding the objective of contingent immunization. This is the return the portfolio would achieve over the entire investment horizon if, at any point, the assets on hand were immunized at the prevailing market rate. Exhibit 19.21 contains the various potential rates of return based on dollar asset values shown in Exhibit 19.20. If the portfolio were immediately immunized when market rates were 15 percent, its potential return would naturally be 15 percent. Alternatively, if yields declined instantaneously to 10 percent, the portfolio's asset value would increase to $147 million (see Exhibit 19.20). If this $147 million portfolio were immunized at the market rate of 10 percent over the remaining five-year period, the portfolio would grow to a total value of $239.45 million ($147 million × 1.6289, which is the compound growth factor for 5 percent and 10 periods). This ending value of $239.45 million represents an 18.25 percent realized (horizon) rate of return on the original $100 million portfolio.

In contrast, if interest rates increase, the value of the portfolio will decline substantially and the potential return will decline. For example, if market rates rise to 17 percent (i.e., a yield change of 2 percent), the asset value of the 30-year bond portfolio will decline to $88 million

Exhibit 19.21 The Potential Return Concept

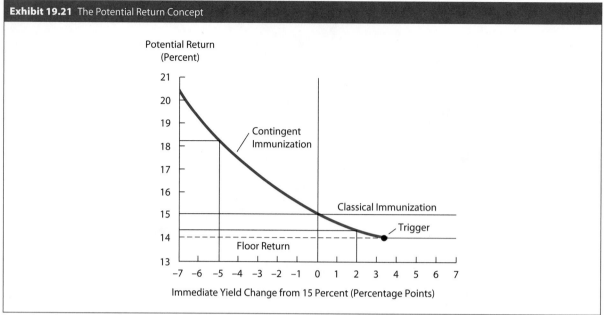

(see Exhibit 19.20). If this portfolio of $88 million were immunized for the remaining five years at the prevailing market rate of 17 percent, the ending value would be $199 million. This ending value implies a potential return of 14.32 percent for the total period.

As Exhibit 19.20 shows, if interest rates rose to 18.50 percent, the 30-year bonds would decline to a value of $81.16 million (the trigger point) and the portfolio would have to be immunized. At this point, if the remaining assets of $81.16 million were immunized at this current market rate of 18.50 percent, the value of the portfolio would grow to $196.73 million ($81.16 × 2.424, which is the compound value factor for 9.25 percent for 10 periods). This ending value implies that the potential return for the portfolio would be exactly 14 percent as shown in Exhibit 19.21. Regardless of what happens to subsequent market rates, the portfolio has been immunized at the floor rate of 14 percent. That is a major characteristic of the contingent immunized portfolio; if there is proper monitoring you will always know the trigger point where you must immunize to be assured of receiving a return no less than the minimum rate of return specified.

Monitoring the Immunized Portfolio   Clearly, monitoring the contingent immunized portfolio is crucial to ensure that, if the asset value falls to the trigger point, the appropriate action is taken to ensure that the portfolio is immunized at the floor-level rate. This can be done using a chart as in Exhibit 19.22. The top line is the current market value of the portfolio over time. The bottom line is the required value of the immunized floor portfolio. Specifically, the bottom line is *the required value of the portfolio* if we were to immunize at *today's rates* to attain the necessary ending-wealth value. This required minimum value for the portfolio is calculated by *computing the present value of the promised ending-wealth value at the prevailing market rate.*

To demonstrate how this floor portfolio would be constructed, consider again our example where we derived a promised ending-wealth value in five years of $196.72 million based on an initial investment of $100 million and an acceptable floor rate of 14 percent. If one year after the initiation of the portfolio, market rates were 10 percent, you would need a minimum portfolio value of approximately $133.14 million to get to $196.72 million in four years. To compute

Exhibit 19.22 Contingent Immunization Floor Portfolio over Time

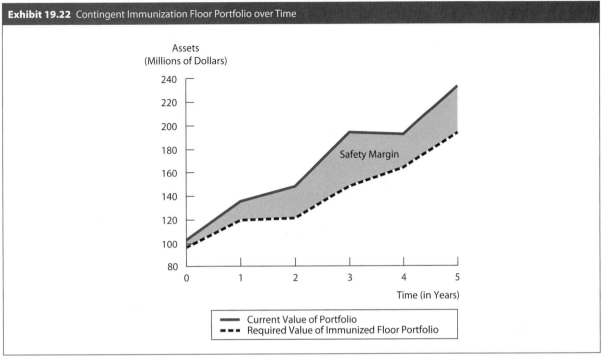

this minimum required value, you multiply the $196.72 million (promised ending-wealth value) times the present value factor for 5 percent for eight periods, assuming semiannual compounding (0.6768). The logic is that $133.14 million ($196.72 × .6768) invested at 10 percent for four years will equal $196.72 million.

If the active manager had originally predicted correctly that market rates would decline and had structured a long-duration portfolio under these conditions, the *actual* value of the portfolio would be much higher than this *minimum required* value, and there would be a safety margin. A year later (after Year 2), you would determine the assets needed at the rate prevailing at that point in time. Assuming interest rates had by then increased to 12 percent, you could determine that you would need a floor portfolio of about $138.69 million. Specifically, this is the present value of the $196.72 million for three years at 12 percent, assuming semiannual compounding (0.7050). Again, you would expect the actual value of the portfolio to be greater than this required floor portfolio, so you still have a safety margin. If you ever reached the point where the actual value of the portfolio was equal to the required floor value, you would stop the active management and immunize what was left *at the current market rate* to ensure that the ending value of the portfolio would be $196.72 million.

In summary, the contingent immunization strategy encompasses the opportunity for a bond portfolio manager to engage in various active portfolio strategies if the client is willing to accept a floor return (and ending-wealth value) that is below what is currently available. The graph in Exhibit 19.23 describes the trade-offs involved in contingent immunization. Specifically, by allowing for a slightly lower minimum target rate, the client is making it possible to experience a much higher potential return from active management by the portfolio manager.

Exhibit 19.23 Comparison of Return Distributions

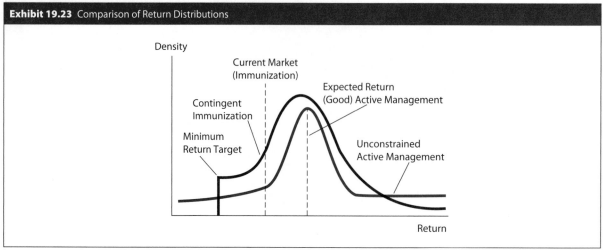

• • • • SUMMARY • • • •

- During the past few decades, there has been a significant increase in the number and variety of bond portfolio strategies available to individual investors and professional managers. These strategies, which can range from being quite simple to quite complex to implement and maintain, can be classified into five separate categories: passive management techniques, active management techniques, core-plus management techniques, matched-funding techniques, and contingent and structured techniques.

- Passive approaches to managing a bond portfolio can take two forms. Buy-and-hold investors simply choose a selection of bonds with the desired set of characteristics (e.g., duration, coupon rate, credit quality) and replace them when they mature. By contrast, an investor following an indexed approach constructs a portfolio that mimics the contents of a particular bond index. The construction of an indexed portfolio can either fully replicate the underlying benchmark or follow a stratified sampling approach that attempts to reproduce the index characteristics with a smaller number of instruments.

- Active bond management strategies attempt to exceed the risk–return performance produced by a bond index over time. The active manager does this by assembling a collection of bonds that differs from those in the benchmark in a manner consistent with his view of future bond market conditions. The number of active strategies available is numerous and includes interest rate anticipation, credit analysis, valuation analysis, yield spread analysis, and global and tactical techniques. Core-plus bond management can be viewed as type of enhanced indexing that combines passive and active techniques.

- Many institutional investors (e.g., pension funds, insurance companies) employ matched-funding strategies when the investment problem they confront involves forming a portfolio of assets designed to pay off a specific set of liabilities. Immunization techniques based on matching the durations of the organization's assets and liabilities are particularly useful in providing protection against adverse interest rate movements. Finally, contingent immunization is a form of structured active management that combines a classical immunization approach with some active management techniques.

• • • • SUGGESTED READINGS • • • •

Dattatreya, Ravi E., and Frank J. Fabozzi. 1995. *Active Total Return Management of Fixed-Income Portfolios*, rev. ed. Burr Ridge, IL: Irwin Professional.

Fabozzi, Frank J., ed. 2004. *Fixed-Income Readings for the Chartered Financial Analysts Program, 2nd ed.* New Hope, PA: Frank J. Fabozzi Associates.

Fabozzi, Frank J., Lionel Martellini, and Philippe Priaulet, eds., 2006. *Advanced Bond Portfolio Management.* Hoboken, NJ: John Wiley.

Fridson, Martin. 1989. *High-Yield Bonds: Assessing Risk and Identifying Value in Speculative Grade Securities.* Chicago: Probus.

Liebowitz, Martin L., William S. Krasker, and Ardavan Nozari. 1990. "Spread Duration: A New Tool for Bond Portfolio Management," *Journal of Portfolio Management* 16, no. 3 (Spring).

Sherrerd, Katrina F., ed., 2002. *Fixed-Income Management for the 21st Century.* Charlottesville, VA: Association for Investment Management and Research.

• • • • QUESTIONS • • • •

1. **CFA EXAMINATION LEVEL III** The use of bond index funds has grown dramatically in recent years.
   a. Discuss the reasons you would expect it to be easier or more difficult to construct a bond market index than a stock market index.
   b. It is contended that the *operational process* of managing a corporate bond index fund is more difficult than managing an equity index fund. Discuss three examples that support this contention. [15 minutes]

2. **CFA EXAMINATION LEVEL III** After determining the appropriate asset allocation to meet Lucinda Kennedy's needs, Richard Bulloch, CFA, invests a portion of Kennedy's assets in two fixed-income investment funds.
   Trinity Index Fund: A passively managed portfolio of global bonds designed to track the Lehman Brothers Global Aggregate Bond (LGAB) Index using a pure bond indexing strategy. The management fee is 15 basis points annually.
   Montego Global Bond Fund: An actively managed portfolio of global bonds designed to outperform the LGAB net of fees. The management fee is 50 basis points annually.
   Six months after investing in these funds, Kennedy and Bulloch review the performance data shown in the following exhibit:

   Total Returns on Index and Funds
   Index or Fund Six-Month Return
   LGAB Index 3.21%
   Trinity Index Fund* 3.66%
   Montego Global Bond Fund* 3.02%
   * *Net of Fees*

   Kennedy makes the following statements regarding her fixed-income investments:
   a. "The Trinity Index Fund is being managed well."
   b. "I expected that, as an active manager, Montego would outperform the index; therefore, the fund should be sold."
   Determine whether you agree or disagree with *each* of Kennedy's statements. Justify your response with *one* reason for *each* statement. [6 minutes]

3. How would you explain to a casual observer why high-yield bond returns are more correlated to common stock returns than to investment-grade bond returns?

4. **CFA EXAMINATION LEVEL III** The investment committee of the money management firm of Gentry, Inc., has typically been very conservative and has avoided investing in high-yield (junk) bonds, although they have had major positions in investment-grade corporate bonds. Recently, Pete Squire, a member of the committee, suggested that they should review their policy regarding junk bonds because they currently constitute over 25 percent of the total corporate bond market.
   As part of this policy review, you are asked to respond to the following questions:
   a. Briefly discuss the liquidity *and* pricing characteristics of junk bonds relative to *each* of the following types of fixed-income securities:
      • Treasuries
      • High-grade corporate bonds
      • Corporate loans
      • Private placements
   Briefly discuss the implications of these differences for Gentry's bond portfolio managers. The committee has learned that the correlation of rates of return between Treasuries and high-grade corporate bonds is approximately 0.98, while the correlation between Treasury/high-grade corporate bonds and junk bonds is approximately 0.45.
   b. Briefly explain the reason for this difference in correlations, and briefly discuss its implications for bond portfolios.
   The committee has also heard that durations at the times of issue for junk bonds are typically much shorter than for newly issued high-grade corporate bonds.
   c. Briefly explain the reason for this difference in duration, and briefly discuss its implication for the volatility of high-yield bond portfolios. [15 minutes]

5. **CFA EXAMINATION LEVEL II** Greg Kemp, CFA, Chief Investment Officer of Anchor Advisors, has received the following recommendation from his bond management group.

   > "We believe the current environment has focused excessive pessimism on high-grade corporate bonds. Fears of 'event risk' and weakness in the junk bond market have widened yield spreads to attractive levels.
   >
   > "It is recommended that our employee benefit bond accounts reduce their current U.S. Treasury weightings from 75 percent to 25 percent, with this money to be invested in callable Single-A and AA utility bonds with coupon rates between 9 percent and 11 percent. The durations of the bonds purchased will be equal to those sold."

   Kemp accepts the idea that yield spreads are wider than normal between U.S. Treasury bonds and corporate issues. Interest rates on long-term U.S. Treasury issues are currently 9 percent. He expects a significant (more than 100 basis points) drop in interest rates.

   a. Kemp has some concerns about the volatility implications of the proposed trade in light of his understanding of the concepts of duration, convexity, and option-adjusted spreads. Given his interest rate expectations, identify and explain *two* key questions that Kemp should raise about the proposed trade. [10 minutes]

   b. Recommend *two* modifications to the proposed trade that would address Kemp's concerns mentioned in Part a. [5 minutes]

6. You begin with an investment horizon of four years and a portfolio with a duration of four years with a market interest rate of 10 percent. A year later, what is your investment horizon? Assuming no change in interest rates, what is the duration of your portfolio relative to your investment horizon? What does this imply about your ability to immunize your portfolio?

7. During a conference with a client, the subject of classical immunization is introduced. The client questions the fee charged for developing and managing an immunized portfolio. The client believes it is basically a passive investment strategy, so the management fee should be substantially lower. What would you tell the client to show that it is not a passive policy?

8. **CFA EXAMINATION LEVEL III** The ability to *immunize* a bond portfolio is very desirable for bond portfolio managers in some instances.

   a. Discuss the components of interest rate risk. Assuming a change in interest rates over time, explain the two risks faced by the holder of a bond.

   b. Define immunization and discuss why a bond manager would immunize a portfolio.

   c. Explain why a duration-matching strategy is a superior technique to a maturity-matching strategy for the minimization of interest rate risk.

   d. Explain in specific terms how you would use a zero-coupon bond to immunize a bond portfolio. Discuss why a zero-coupon bond is an ideal instrument in this regard.

   e. Explain how *contingent immunization,* another bond portfolio management technique, differs from *classical immunization.* Discuss why a bond portfolio manager would engage in contingent immunization. [35 minutes]

9. **CFA EXAMINATION LEVEL III** During the past several years, there has been substantial growth in the dollar amount of portfolios managed using *immunization* and *dedication* techniques. Assume a client wants to know the basic differences between (1) classical immunization, (2) contingent immunization, (3) cash-matched dedication, and (4) duration-matched dedication.

   a. Briefly describe each of these four techniques.

   b. Briefly discuss the ongoing investment action you would have to carry out if managing an *immunized portfolio.*

   c. Briefly discuss three of the major considerations involved with creating a *cash-matched dedicated* portfolio.

   d. Describe two parameters that should be specified when using *contingent immunization.*

   e. Select one of the four alternative techniques that you believe requires the least degree of active management and justify your selection. [20 minutes]

10. **CFA EXAMINATION LEVEL III** After you have constructed a structured fixed-income portfolio (i.e., one that is dedicated, indexed, or immunized), it may be possible over time to improve on the initial optimal portfolio while continuing to meet the primary goal. Discuss three conditions that would be considered favorable for a restructuring—assuming no change in objectives for the investor—and cite an example of each condition. [10 minutes]

11. **CFA EXAMINATION LEVEL I** Robert Devlin and Neil Parish are portfolio managers at the Broward Investment Group. At their regular Monday strategy meeting, the topic of adding international bonds to one of their portfolios came up. The portfolio, an ERISA-qualified pension account for a U.S. client, was currently 90 percent invested in U.S. Treasury bonds and 10 percent invested in 10-year Canadian government bonds.

Devlin suggested buying a position in 10-year German government bonds, while Parish argued for a position in 10-year Australian government bonds.

a. Briefly discuss the *three* major issues that Devlin and Parish should address in their analysis of the return prospects for German and Australian bonds relative to those of U.S. bonds. [6 minutes]

Having made no changes to the original portfolio, Devlin and Parish hold a subsequent strategy meeting and decide to add positions in the government bonds of Japan, the United Kingdom, France, Germany, and Australia.

b. Identify and discuss *two* reasons for adding a broader mix of international bonds to the pension portfolio. [9 minutes]

12. **CFA EXAMINATON LEVEL III** A consultant suggests that the weighted-average portfolio duration calculation for a global bond portfolio is the same as for a domestic bond portfolio.

a. State whether the use of portfolio duration in international bond portfolio management is more limiting than in domestic bond portfolio management. Support your conclusion with *two* reasons. [8 minutes]

The consultant recognizes that currency, duration, and investing outside the benchmark are possible sources of excess return in global bond management. He is also curious about additional methods of adding value through global bond management.

b. List and discuss *two* additional potential sources of excess return. [6 minutes]

• • • • PROBLEMS • • • •

1. The par yield curve for U.S. Treasury bonds is currently flat across all maturities at 5.50 percent. You have observed following "paired" transaction by your bond portfolio manager:

Bond	Transaction	Type	Credit Spread (bp)	Maturity (yrs)	Coupon Rate (%)	Modified Duration
G	Buy	U.S. Govt.	—	15	0	14.599
H	Sell	Corporate	100	7	8	5.386

Briefly discuss what this paired trade suggests to you about the manager's implied view as to: (i) the general direction of future interest rate movement, (ii) the future shape of the par yield curve, and (iii) the future level of corporate bond credit spreads.

2. Answer the following questions assuming that at the initiation of an investment account, the market value of your portfolio is $200 million, and you immunize the portfolio at 12 percent for six years. During the first year, interest rates are constant at 12 percent.

a. What is the market value of the portfolio at the end of Year 1?

b. Immediately after the end of the year, interest rates *decline* to 10 percent. Estimate the new value of the portfolio, assuming you did the required rebalancing (use only modified duration).

3. Compute the Macaulay duration under the following conditions:

a. A bond with a five-year term to maturity, a 12 percent coupon (annual payments), and a market yield of 10 percent.

b. A bond with a four-year term to maturity, a 12 percent coupon (annual payments), and a market yield of 10 percent.

c. Compare your answers to Parts a and b, and discuss the implications of this for classical immunization.

4. Compute the Macaulay duration under the following conditions:

a. A bond with a four-year term to maturity, a 10 percent coupon (annual payments), and a market yield of 8 percent.

b. A bond with a four-year term to maturity, a 10 percent coupon (annual payments), and a market yield of 12 percent.

c. Compare your answers to Parts a and b. Assuming it was an immediate shift in yields, discuss the implications of this for classical immunization.

5. Evaluate the following pure-yield pickup swap: You currently hold a 20-year, Aa-rated, 9.0 percent coupon bond priced to yield 11.0 percent. As a swap candidate, you are considering a 20-year, Aa-rated, 11 percent coupon bond priced to yield 11.5 percent. (Assume reinvestment at 11.5 percent.)

	Current Bond	Candidate Bond
Dollar investment	_____	_____
Coupon	_____	_____
i on one coupon	_____	_____
Principal value at year end	_____	_____
Total accrued	_____	_____
Realized compound yield	_____	_____
Value of swap: _____ basis points in one year		

6. Evaluate the following substitution swap: You currently hold a 25-year, 9.0 percent coupon bond priced to yield 10.5 percent. As a swap candidate, you are considering a 25-year, Aa-rated, 9.0 percent coupon bond priced to yield 10.75 percent. (Assume a one-year work-out period and reinvestment at 10.5 percent.)

	Current Bond	Candidate Bond
Dollar investment	_____	_____
Coupon	_____	_____
i on one coupon	_____	_____
Principal value at year end	_____	_____
Total accrued	_____	_____
Realized compound yield	_____	_____
Value of swap: _____ basis points in one year		

7. A university endowment fund has sought your advice on its fixed-income portfolio strategy. The characteristics of the portfolio's current holdings are listed below:

Bond	Credit Rating	Maturity (yrs)	Coupon Rate (%)	Modified Duration	Convexity	Market Value of Position (000's)
A	U.S. Govt	3	0	2.727	9.9	$30,000
B	A1	10	8	6.404	56.1	30,000
C	Aa2	5	12	3.704	18.7	30,000
D	Agency	7	10	4.868	32.1	30,000
E	Aa3	12	0	10.909	128.9	30,000
						$150,000

a. Calculate the modified duration for this portfolio (i.e., Mod D_p).
b. Suppose you learn that the implied sensitivity (i.e., modified duration) of the endowment's liabilities is about 6.50 years. Identify whether the bond portfolio is: (i) immunized against interest rate risk, (ii) exposed to net price risk, or (iii) exposed to net reinvestment risk. Briefly explain what will happen to the net position of the endowment fund if in the future there is a significant parallel upward shift in the yield curve.
c. Briefly describe how you could increase the convexity of the portfolio while keeping the modified duration at the same level.
d. Your current active view for the fixed-income market over the coming months is that Treasury yields will decline and corporate credit spreads will also decrease. Briefly discuss how you could restructure the existing portfolio to take advantage of this view.

8. **CFA EXAMINATION LEVEL III** A major requirement in managing a fixed-income portfolio using a contingent immunization policy is monitoring the relationship between the current market value of the portfolio and the required value of the floor portfolio. This difference is defined as the *margin of error*. In this regard, assume a $300 million portfolio with a time horizon of five years. The available market rate at the initiation of the portfolio is 12 percent, but the client is willing to accept 10 percent as a

floor rate to allow use of active management strategies. The current market values and current market rates at the end of Years 1, 2, and 3 are as follows:

End of Year	Market Value ($ Mil)	Market Yield	Required Floor Portfolio ($ Mil)	Margin of Error ($ Mil)
1	$340.9	10%		
2	405.5	8		
3	395.2	12		

Assuming semiannual compounding:
a. Calculate the required ending-wealth value for this portfolio.
b. Calculate the value of the required floor portfolios at the end of Years 1, 2, and 3.
c. Compute the margin of error at the end of Years 1, 2, and 3.
d. Indicate the action that a portfolio manager utilizing a *contingent immunization* policy would take if the margin of error at the end of any year had been zero or negative.

 9. **CFA EXAMINATION LEVEL II** PowerTool is the largest U.S. manufacturer of industrial hand tools. Its sales force is strong, but clients have complained that marketing is weak. The industrial tool business is mature, with little or no future expected growth.

PowerTool has acquired Fenton Manufacturing, a small, innovative company whose sales are entirely in the retail tool market. The retail tool market is expected to grow at a 5 percent annual rate.

Fenton recently developed a patented line of rechargeable home power tools that displayed strong potential in test markets. Fenton expects this line to generate 50 percent of its sales within five years but lacks a sales force to market this product line. Jerry Fenton, the company's founder, recently retired.

PowerTool management is highly respected and the company has experienced little management turnover. However, the Chief Executive Officer has announced her retirement after 18 years of service and will be replaced by the current Chief Operating Officer.

You are a private investor with a large investment in PowerTool bonds and wish to determine the effect of the acquisition of Fenton on PowerTool's bonds.

Exhibit 19.24 presents financial ratios and debt ratings of PowerTool and Fenton prior to the merger and pro forma ratios of the combined company following the acquisition.

Exhibit 19.24 Financial Ratios and Debt Ratings: June 1, 1996

Company	Total Debt to Total Capital	Pretax Interest Coverage	Operating Cash Flow to Total Debt	Debt Rating
PowerTool	30%	6.2 times	50%	A+
Fenton	72	2.1 times	8	Not rated
Combined	42	5.4 times	40	To be determined

Exhibit 19.25 Bond Rating Criteria: June 1, 1996

Debt Rating	Total Debt to Total Capital	Pretax Interest Coverage	Operating Cash Flow to Total Debt
AA	26%	8.8 times	75%
A	37	4.6 times	44
BBB	48	2.5 times	29

a. Explain how *each* of the following *three* ratios should be used to evaluate a firm's financial risk:
   (1) Total debt to total capital
   (2) Pretax interest coverage
   (3) Operating cash flow to total debt [9 minutes]

PowerTool has issued debt with the following covenants, which continue in force after its acquisition of Fenton.

Dividend Test Covenant

PowerTool may not pay any cash dividend or repurchase shares if such payment would result in a total debt-to-capital ratio in excess of 50 percent.

Put Option Covenant

If PowerTool's debt rating falls below A, bondholders have the right to redeem the bonds at a price of 105 plus accrued interest within 60 days following the change in rating.

b. Discuss the impact of *each* of the *two* debt covenants as just described on PowerTool's financial flexibility following its acquisition of Fenton:
   (1) Dividend Test covenant
   (2) Put Option Covenant [8 minutes]

Use only the information provided in the introduction in answering the following question.

c. Discuss, *from the PowerTool bondholders' point of view, two* advantages and *two* disadvantages to PowerTool of the acquisition of Fenton, with regard to the following product lines:
   • Industrial tool business
   • Retail tool business [12 minutes]

   PowerTool debt has not yet been re-rated following the acquisition of Fenton. PowerTool bonds are currently trading at a price comparable to A-rated bonds.

Exhibit 19.25 displays financial ratios used to determine bond ratings.

d. Recommend whether you should *hold* or *sell* the PowerTool bonds. Support your recommendations with *four* reasons drawn from the Introduction, Exhibits 19.24 and 19.25, and your answers to Parts a through c. [13 minutes]

10. **CFA EXAMINATION LEVEL II** Mike Smith, CFA, an analyst with Blue River Investments, is considering buying a Montrose Cable Company Corporate bond. He has collected the following balance sheet and income statement information for Montrose as shown in Exhibit 19.26. He has also calculated the three ratios shown in Exhibit 19.27, which indicate that the bond is currently rated "A" according to the firm's internal bond-rating criteria shown in Exhibit 19.29.

Exhibit 19.26 Montrose Cable Company: Year Ended March 31, 1999 (US$ Thousand)

Balance Sheet	
Current assets	$ 4,735
Fixed assets	43,225
Total assets	$47,960
Current liabilities	$ 4,500
Long-term debt	10,000
Total liabilities	$14,500
Shareholder's equity	33,460
Total liabilities and shareholder's equity	$47,960
Income Statement	
Revenue	$18,500
Operating and administrative expenses	14,050
Operating income	$ 4,450
Depreciation and amortization	1,675
Interest expense	942
Income before income taxes	$ 1,833
Taxes	641
Net income	$ 1,192

Exhibit 19.27 Selected Ratios and Credit Yield Premium Data for Montrose

EBITDA/interest expense	4.72
Long-term debt/equity	0.30
Current assets/current liabilities	1.05
Credit yield premium over U.S. Treasuries	55 basis points

Exhibit 19.28 Montrose Off-Balance-Sheet Items

- Montrose has guaranteed the long-term debt (principal only) of an unconsolidated affiliate. This obligation has a present value of $995,000.
- Montrose has sold $500,000 of accounts receivable with recourse at a yield of 8 percent.
- Montrose is a lessee in a new noncancelable operating leasing agreement to finance transmission equipment. The discounted present value of the lease payments is $6,144,000 using an interest rate of 10 percent. The annual payment will be $1,000,000.

Exhibit 19.29 Blue River Investments: Internal Bond-Rating Criteria and Credit Yield Premium Data

Bond Rating	Interest Coverage (EBITDA/ Interest Expense)	Leverage (Long-Term Debt/Equity)	Current Ratio (Current Assets/ Current Liabilities)	Credit Yield Premium over U.S. Treasuries (in Basis Points)
AA	5.00 to 6.00	0.25 to 0.30	1.15 to 1.25	30 BPs
A	4.00 to 5.00	0.30 to 0.40	1.00 to 1.15	50 BPs
BBB	3.00 to 4.00	0.40 to 0.50	0.90 to 1.00	100 BPs
BB	2.00 to 3.00	0.50 to 0.60	0.75 to 0.90	125 BPs

Smith has decided to consider some off-balance-sheet items in his credit analysis, as shown in Exhibit 19.28. Specifically, Smith wishes to evaluate the impact of each of the off-balance-sheet items on each of the ratios found in Exhibit 19.27.

a. Calculate the combined effect of the *three* off-balance-sheet items in Exhibit 19.28 on *each* of the following *three* financial ratios shown in Exhibit 19.27. [9 minutes]

(1) EBITDA/interest expense
(2) Long-term debt/equity
(3) Current assets/current liabilities

The bond is currently trading at a credit premium of 55 basis points. Using the internal bond-rating criteria in Exhibit 19.29, Smith wants to evaluate whether or not the credit yield premium incorporates the effect of the off-balance-sheet items.

b. State and justify whether or not the current credit yield premium compensates Smith for the credit risk of the bond based on the internal bond-rating criteria found in Exhibit 19.29. [6 minutes]

• • • • • **APPENDIX: CHAPTER 19** • • • •

Bond Immunization and Portfolio Rebalancing

Suppose that you have decided to fund a three-year liability with a *portfolio* of bonds and that the only individual securities that you have to choose from are a two-year zero-coupon bond and a four-year zero-coupon bond. The current interest rate is 10 percent. Therefore:

$$\text{Price of 2-year bond (i.e., Bond 2)} = (1000) \div (1.1)^2 = \$826.45$$
$$\text{Price of 4-year bond (i.e., Bond 4)} = (1000) \div (1.1)^4 = \$683.01$$

In order to form a portfolio with duration of three years, you must purchase identical amounts of Bond 2 and Bond 4 since each of these zero-coupon instruments will have duration equal to its maturity. Consequently, you will need to buy 1.0 units of Bond 2 and $(826.45 \div 683.01) = 1.21$ units of Bond 4 for a total initial investment of $1652.89 [826.45 + (1.21)(683.01)]. The duration of your bond portfolio can then be calculated:

$$D_p = (826.45 \div 1652.89)(D_2) + (826.45 \div 1652.89)(D_4)$$
$$= (.5)(2.00) + (.5)(4.00) = 3.00$$

Assume now that immediately after you make your initial purchases, interest rates fall to 8 percent. If you do not rebalance your portfolio, what is your realized yield after three years? To establish this, compute:

Terminal Value of Portfolio:

(i) Allow two-year bond to mature and reinvest for one year: $(1000)(1.08) = \$1080.00$
(ii) Sell 1.21 four-year bonds: $(1.21)(1000 \div 1.08) = \$1120.37$

so that your total terminal value is $2200.37, and the realized yield is:

$$\sqrt[3]{\frac{2200.37}{1652.89}} - 1 = 10.00 \text{ percent}$$

Therefore, your actual return is equal to the original promised return (i.e., the yield to maturity) of 10 percent. By investing so that the duration of the portfolio was equal to your horizon date, you have immunized yourself against the *first* interest rate change and locked in the initial promised yield of 10 percent.

Now, continuing with the assumption that interest rates decline immediately after your initial purchases, suppose that you decide to *rebalance* your portfolio. To understand how you can do this, you need to first establish the new bond prices:

$$\text{Price of Bond 2} = (1000) \div (1.08)^2 = \$857.34$$
$$\text{Price of Bond 4} = (1000) \div (1.08)^4 = \$735.03$$

To see why you need to rebalance, calculate the new duration of your portfolio:

Value of Investment in Bond 2 =	857.34
Value of Investment in Bond 4 = (1.21)(735.03) =	889.39
Value of Total Investment =	$1746.73

so:

$$D_p = (857.34 \div 1746.73)(D_2) + (889.39 \div 1746.73)(D_4)$$
$$= (.4908)(2.00) + (.5092)(4.00) = 3.02$$

Notice that even though the change in interest rates didn't change the duration of the individual bonds it did *increase* the duration of the portfolio slightly since it altered the relative market values of Bond 2 and Bond 4. To correct the problem (i.e., to rebalance the portfolio), you need to *shorten* the overall duration by selling some of Bond 4 and purchasing some more of Bond 2. To accomplish this, you must once again invest equal dollar amounts in each security, or $873.365 [(.5)(1746.73)]. This in turn means that you must own the following number of each instrument:

$$\text{Number of Bond 2 to be held} = (873.365 \div 857.39) = 1.0186$$
$$\text{Number of Bond 4 to be held} = (873.365 \div 735.03) = 1.1882$$

After completing this step, you have rebalanced your portfolio to immunize against future changes in interest rate movements. By once again holding equal amounts of each bond, you have reset the duration of the portfolio to your original investment horizon of three years. An important assumption here is that this rebalancing can be done costlessly. If you must pay brokerage fees, the total dollar value of your portfolio, and hence your actual return, will be reduced accordingly.

By rebalancing your portfolio you have tampered with the composition of your initial investment. However, by doing so, have you also changed the realized yield that you will receive? Put another way, when you rebalance your portfolio at the new yield to maturity of 8 percent, will you still end up with the original yield of 10 percent? To answer this, calculate the terminal value of the rebalanced portfolio: (i) Allow 1.0182 two-year bonds to mature and reinvest for one year: (1.0182)(1000)(1.08) = $1100.12; and (ii) sell 1.1882 four-year bonds: (1.1882)(1000÷1.08) = $1100.19. Thus, your total terminal value of the rebalanced investment is $2200.31, and the realized yield is:

$$\sqrt[3]{\frac{2200.31}{1652.89}} - 1 = 10.00 \text{ percent}$$

Therefore, rebalancing your portfolio when interest rates change has *two effects*: (i) you immunize yourself against the next interest rate change, and (ii) your actual return is still equal to the yield to maturity that prevailed at the time of your original investment. Finally, it should be noted that although we assumed that the interest rate changed immediately after the initial purchase, the fundamentals of rebalancing also apply to yield curve shifts that occur at any point in the duration of the investment.

PART 6
Derivative Security Analysis

CHAPTER 20
An Introduction to Derivative Markets and Securities

CHAPTER 21
Forward and Futures Contracts

CHAPTER 22
Option Contracts

CHAPTER 23
Swap Contracts, Convertible Securities, and Other Embedded Derivatives

In recent years, it has been difficult to read the financial press without encountering at least a passing reference to an economic scandal attributed to trading in derivative securities. Procter & Gamble's ill-fated swap transactions and the equity index futures trades that brought down Barings Bank give the casual reader the impression that derivatives are highly volatile instruments used only by those investors interested in placing speculative "bets." Of course, nothing could be further from the truth. Although it is true that the companies in these examples either miscalculated or misunderstood the nature of their investment positions, the vast majority of derivative transactions are used by individuals and institutions seeking to reduce the risk exposures generated by their other business ventures.

Derivatives, in their many forms, have become a vital part of modern security markets, trailing only stocks and bonds in terms of importance. Unlike stocks and bonds, however, their widespread use is a relatively recent phenomenon; and misconceptions still exist about how derivatives work and the proper way for investors to trade them. The chapters in this section address this concern by providing the investor with a framework for understanding how derivatives are valued and used in practice. Chapter 20 begins this process by detailing the mechanics of the two basic forms of derivative contract—**forwards** and **options.** After providing an initial description of these instruments and the markets in which they trade, we present the fundamental principles that determine their prices. The chapter concludes with several specific examples of how investors use derivatives to adjust the risk-return characteristics of their stock and bond portfolios.

Chapter 21 analyzes forward and futures contracts—the most prevalent form of derivative instrument. The similarities and differences between forward and futures contracts are described, with particular emphasis on the creation of (and subsequent adjustments to) margin accounts and the concept of basis risk. In addition, the calculation of the optimal hedge ratio and the arbitrage-free approach to determining the contract delivery price are discussed. The chapter concludes with an examination of the features of forward and futures contracts that are designed to offset financial (as opposed to commodity) risk exposures, including interest rate, equity, and currency price movements. Applications and investment strategies involving each of these contract types illustrate this discussion.

In Chapter 22, the focus turns to option contracting. The discussion begins with a consideration of how option markets are organized and how both puts and calls—the two basic types of option contracts—are quoted and traded. Several different option-based investment and hedging strategies are described, as well as how these contracts can be used in conjunction with other securities to create customized payoff distributions. The chapter also includes a formal treatment of how option contracts are valued in an efficient market. Starting with the simple two-state option pricing model, which contains the essence of the basic valuation argument, the discussion progresses to include state-of-the-art approaches such as the binomial and the Black-Scholes models. In this development, special attention is paid to the role that price volatility plays in the valuation process.

Chapter 23, the last chapter of this section, considers four additional classes of derivative products. First, the rapidly developing market for swap, cap, and floor agreements is examined. After describing how these instruments are related to typical forward and option contracts, the discussion concentrates on the many ways in which investors and corporate risk managers use these products in practice. In particular, applications involving three different exposures—interest rates, equity prices, and credit risk—are developed. Second, the fundamentals of warrants and convertible securities are described. The emphasis of this discussion is on the option-like features of these instruments and how they alter the risk–return dynamics of traditional debt and equity products. Third, we examine the market for structured notes—instruments that can be viewed as "straight" bond issues into which derivatives have been embedded. Finally, the chapter concludes with a brief discussion of how understanding **real options** can help investors value certain types of complex investments that have embedded derivative-like features, such as oil fields or gold mines.

CHAPTER 20

An Introduction to Derivative Markets and Securities

After you read this chapter, you should be able to answer the following questions:

- What distinguishes a derivative security, such as a forward, futures, or option contract, from more fundamental securities, such as stocks and bonds?
- What are the important characteristics of forward, futures, and option contracts, and in what sense can they be interpreted as insurance policies?
- How are the markets for derivative securities organized and how do they differ from other security markets?
- What teminology is used to describe derivative market transactions?
- How are prices for derivative securities quoted and how should this information be interpreted?
- What are the similarities and differences between forward and futures contracts?
- What do the payoff and profit diagrams look like for forward and futures contracts?
- What do the payoff and profit diagrams look like for put and call option contracts?
- How are forward contracts, put options, and call options related to one another?
- How can derivatives be used in conjunction with stock and Treasury bills to replicate the payoffs to other securities and create arbitrage opportunities for an investor?
- How can derivative contracts be used to restructure cash flow patterns and modify the risks in existing investment portfolios?

So far, we have seen several ways in which individuals and institutions can design their investments to take advantage of future market conditions. We have also seen how investors can control the volatility associated with their stock and bond positions—at least in part—by forming well-diversified portfolios of securities, thereby reducing or eliminating the unsystematic component of a security's risk.

In this chapter, we begin our investigation of the role played by **derivative securities** in modern investment portfolios. A derivative instrument is one for which the ultimate payoff to the investor depends directly on the value of another security or commodity. Earlier in the text, we briefly described two basic types of derivatives: (1) forward and futures contracts and (2) option contracts. A call option, for example, gives its owner the right to purchase an underlying security, such as a stock or a bond, at a fixed price within a certain amount of time. In this manner, the option's ultimate value can be said to depend on—and thus derive from—that of the other asset. Similarly, a forward contract to sell a bond for a fixed price at a future date will see its value to the investor rise or fall with decreases or increases in the market price of the underlying bond.

The growth of the markets in which derivative securities are created and exchanged has been nothing short of phenomenal. The last few decades have seen the emergence of contracts to trade such fundamental products as agricultural commodities, energy, precious metals, currencies, common stock, and bonds. There are even derivatives to trade hypothetical underlying assets (e.g., options and futures contracts on the Standard & Poor's stock indexes) as well as combination derivatives, such as option contracts that allow the investor to decide at a later date to enter into a futures contract involving another security or commodity. Interest rate swaps, which will be shown in Chapter 23 to be forward contracts on a short-term borrowing or lending rate, are a good example of the prodigious growth of these markets. Starting with the first swap in 1981, the volume of swap market activity had grown in size to almost $200 trillion by the year 2006.

As we will see, derivative securities can be used by investors in the same way as the underlying assets; an investor believing that a certain common stock will increase in value can benefit from either a purchase of the stock directly or with an option to purchase that stock at a predetermined price. The exact returns will not be equal for these two alternatives, but both will gain from an upward movement in the stock's price. Ultimately, however, the real key to understanding how and why derivatives are used lies in their ability to modify the risk and expected return characteristics of existing investment portfolios. That is, options and futures allow investors to **hedge** (or even increase) the risk of a collection of stocks in ways that go far beyond the diversification results presented in the preceding chapters. We will see that derivative securities also allow for the duplication of cash flow patterns that already exist in other forms, thereby creating the possibility of **arbitrage** if two otherwise identical series of cash flows do not carry the same current price.

The balance of this chapter describes the fundamental nature and uses of forward, futures, and option contracts on common stock and bonds. (Subsequent chapters deal with more advanced forms of these products and valuation issues.) In the next section, we describe the basic terminology associated with these markets while the second section explains the payoff structures created by each of these instruments. The third section develops the formal relationship between forwards and options, a series of conditions collectively known as **put-call parity**. In the final section, we briefly introduce three popular ways in which derivatives are used to manage stock and bond portfolios, with an emphasis on how derivatives can adjust risk to better suit the needs of the investor.

· ·

20.1 Overview of Derivative Markets

As with any financial product, derivative transactions have a specific terminology that must be understood in order to use these instruments effectively. Unlike many other securities, however, the language used to describe forward, futures, and option contracts is often a confusing blend of jargon drawn from the equity, debt, and insurance markets with some unique expressions thrown in for good measure. Thus, we begin by summarizing the most important aspects of these products and the markets in which they trade.

It is useful to first consider the basic types of positions that an investor can hold in these markets. Exhibit 20.1 illustrates the possibilities. The chart reinforces the point made earlier that, at the broadest level, there are only two kinds of derivatives available: (1) forward and futures contracts, and (2) option contracts. Further, as we will explain shortly, while only one forward contract is needed for any particular maturity date and underlying asset, there must be two types of options—calls and puts—in order to offer investors a full range of choices. Finally, for each of these three general derivative arrangements (i.e., the forward contract, the call option, and the put option), an investor can enter into a transaction as either the long position (i.e., the buyer) or the short position (i.e., the seller). This leads to the six possible basic positions shown in the display.

Recognize that every derivative arrangement that investors might hold in their portfolios can be viewed in terms of one of these six positions, or as a combination of these positions. For instance, later in the chapter, we consider how an equity investor can use derivatives to protect himself or herself against general declines in the stock market. Two such strategies involve (1) shorting an equity index forward contract, and (2) buying an equity index "collar" agreement. In terms of Exhibit 20.1, we will see that the forward-based strategy represents Position 2, while the collar strategy involves a combination of the purchase of a put option (Position 5) and the sale of a call option (Position 4).

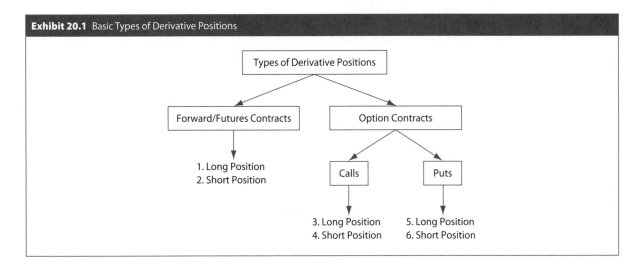

Exhibit 20.1 Basic Types of Derivative Positions

20.1.1 The Language and Structure of Forward and Futures Markets

To most investors, the **forward contract** is the most basic derivative product available. A forward contract gives its holder both the *right and the full obligation* to conduct a transaction involving another security or commodity—the underlying asset—at a predetermined future date and at a predetermined price. The future date on which the transaction is to be consummated is called the contract's *maturity* (or expiration) *date,* while the predetermined price at which the trade takes place is the forward **contract price**. Notice there must always be two parties (sometimes called **counterparties**) to a forward transaction: the eventual buyer (or **long position**), who pays the contract price and receives the underlying security, and the eventual seller (or **short position**), who delivers the security for the fixed price.

Forward and Spot Markets Forward contracts are not securities in the traditional sense; they are more appropriately viewed as *trade agreements* negotiated directly between two parties for a transaction that is scheduled to take place in the future. Suppose that two investors agree at Date 0 (the present) to transfer a bond from one party to the other at the future Date T. The two parties must agree on which bond and how much of it is to be exchanged, the date and location at which this exchange will take place, and the price at which the bond will be bought and sold. So, the terms that must be considered in forming a forward contract are the same as those necessary for a bond transaction that settled immediately (i.e., a *spot market* transaction) with two exceptions. First, the settlement date agreed to in the contract is purposefully set to be in the future. Second, the contract price—which we will represent as $F_{0,T}$, meaning a forward price set at Date 0 for a contract that matures at Date T—is usually different from the prevailing spot price (S_0) because of the different time frames involved.

One important way in which spot and forward market transactions are similar is the conditions under which the long and short positions will profit. Assume that at Date T, the long position in a bond forward contract is obligated to pay \$1,000 ($= F_{0,T}$) for a bond that is worth $S_T = \$1,050$ (i.e., the spot price at Date T). Since $F_{0,T} < S_T$, this will result in a profitable settlement for the long position in the contract since he will be able to acquire the bond for \$50 less than its current market value. On the other hand, the short position must deliver the bond at Date T and will lose \$50 on her forward position; she would have profited if S_T had been below the contract price of \$1,000. Thus, just as if the bond had been purchased at Date 0, the long position benefits when bond prices rise, at least relative to the contract price $F_{0,T}$. Conversely, the short position to the forward contract will gain from falling bond prices, just as if she had short sold the bond at Date 0. Even though the timing of the trade's settlement has shifted, "buy low, sell high" is still the way to make a profit in the forward market.

Forward and Futures Markets   Forward contracts are negotiated in the over-the-counter market. This means that forward contracts are agreements between two private parties—one of which is often a derivatives intermediary, such as a bank—rather than traded through a formal security or commodity exchange. One advantage of this private arrangement is that the terms of the contract are completely flexible; they can be whatever any two mutually consenting counterparties agree to. Another desirable feature to many counterparties is that these arrangements may not require *collateral*; instead, the long and short positions sometimes trust each other to honor their respective commitments at Date *T*. This lack of collateral means that forward contracts involve *credit* (or *default*) *risk,* which is one reason why banks are often market makers in these instruments.

One disadvantage of a forward contract is that it is quite often *illiquid,* meaning that it might be difficult or costly for a counterparty to exit the contract before it matures. Illiquidity is really a by-product of the contract's flexibility because the more specifically tailored an agreement is to the needs of a particular individual, the less marketable it will be to someone else. **Futures contracts** try to solve this problem by standardizing the terms of the agreement (e.g., expiration date, identity and amount of the underlying asset). In contrast to the forward market, both parties in a futures contract trade through a centralized market, called a *futures exchange.* Although the standardization of contracts reduces the ability of the ultimate end users to select the most desirable terms, it does create contract *homogeneity,* whereby the counterparties can always *unwind* a previous commitment prior to expiration by simply trading their existing position back to the exchange at the prevailing market price.

The *futures price* is analogous to the forward contract price and, at any time during the life of a contract, is set at a level such that a brand-new long or short position would not have to pay an initial premium. However, the futures exchange will require both counterparties to post collateral, or *margin,* to protect itself against the possibility of default. (A futures exchange is not a credit-granting institution.) These margin accounts are held by the exchange's *clearinghouse* and are *marked to market* (i.e., adjusted for contract price movements) on a daily basis to ensure that both end users always maintain sufficient collateral to guarantee their eventual participation. A list of some popular futures contracts, along with the markets where they trade, is shown in Exhibit 20.2. Although generally quite diverse, all of these underlying assets have two things in common: *volatile price movements* and *strong interest* from both buyers and sellers.

20.1.2 Interpreting Futures Price Quotations: An Example

To illustrate how futures prices are typically quoted in financial markets, consider Exhibit 20.3, which lists spot and futures prices for contracts on the Standard & Poor's 500 index as of September 17, 2007. Recall from Chapter 5 that the S&P 500 is a value-weighted index of a broad collection of industrial, financial, utility, and transportation companies representative of the entire United States stock market. At the close of trading on this particular day, the index level stood at 1,476.65, which can be considered as the spot price of one "share" of the S&P index (i.e., S_0).[1] Exhibit 20.3 also gives futures contract prices for eight different expiration dates falling in the months of March, June, September, and December for the years 2007, 2008, and 2009.

Consider the futures contract that expires in December 2007. The closing (or last) contract price is listed as 1,489.80 (i.e., $F_{0,T}$). This means that an investor taking a long position in this contract would be committing in September to buy a certain number of shares in the S&P 500 index—250 shares in the case of this contract—at a price of 1,489.80 per share on the expiration date in December. Conversely, the short position in this contract would be committing to sell 250 S&P shares under the same conditions. Note that, except for the margin posted with the

---

[1] In reality, actually purchasing the portfolio of 500 stocks comprising the S&P index would cost considerably more than $1,476.65. However, as the eventual profit or loss from a stock index futures contract is simply determined by the difference between the futures contract price and the spot price prevailing at contract expiration, this interpretation is nevertheless valid. The trading mechanics of these contracts will be described in greater detail in Chapter 21.

Exhibit 20.2 Popular Futures Contracts and Exchanges

Underlying Asset	Exchange
A. Physical Commodities	

Corn, soybeans, soybean meal, soybean oil, wheat
   Ethanol
	CME Group
	   (Chicago Board of Trade)

Cattle-feeder, Cattle-live, hogs, pork bellies
   Lumber
   Dairy
	CME Group
	   (Chicago Mercantile Exchange)

Cocoa, coffee, sugar-world, sugar-domestic
   Orange juice, cotton
	Intercontinental Exchange
	   (New York Board of Trade)

Copper, gold, silver, platinum Crude oil, heating oil, gasoline, natural gas	New York Mercantile Exchange
B. Financial Securities	

Yen, Euro, Canadian dollar, Swiss franc
   British pound, Mexican peso, Australian dollar,
   Treasury bills, Eurodollar (LIBOR), S&P 500
   Index, Nikkei 225 Index, Russell 2000 Index
	CME Group
	   (International Monetary Market)

Treasury bonds, Treasury notes, Interest rate
   Swap, Federal funds
   Dow Jones Industrials Average
	CME Group
	   (Chicago Board of Trade)

Euro LIBOR, British gilt, Japanese government bond, FT-SE 100 index	Euronext.liffe
Euro stock index, Euro stock volatility, credit default	Eurex

Exhibit 20.3 Standard & Poor's 500 Index Futures Contract Price Quotations

<HELP> for explanation, <MENU> for similar functions.   P233 Index **CT**
Screen saved as F:\spx CT.gif

Session: **PIT**   **Contract Table**

S&P 500 INDEX   Delayed monitoring enabled
Exchange Web page   Pricing Date: **9/17/07**
Chicago Mercantile Exchange   Delayed prices   --LATEST AVAILABLE--   **2**
Gery date = options trading

		Last	**1**Change	Time	Bid **1**	Ask	735200 OpenInt	141965 TotVol	Previous Close
1)SPX	spot	1476.65	−7.60	15:54	1476.07	1477.28	0	0	1480.25
2)SPU7	Sep 07	1476.90ds	−8.10	Close		1477.50	318525	67896	1485.00
3)SPZ7	Dec 07	1489.80ds	−8.20	Close	1489.80		405413	73741	1498.00
4)SPH8	Mar 08	1500.60 s	−8.20	Close	1503.80	1501.80	7792	328	1508.80
5)SPM8	Jun 08	1511.60 s	−8.20	Close	1514.80	1512.80	297	0	1519.80
6)SPU8	Sep 08	1521.60 s	−8.20	Close	1524.80	1522.80	25	0	1529.80
7)SPZ8	Dec 08	1530.80 s	−8.20	Close	1534.00	1532.00	3144	0	1539.00
8)SPH9	Mar 09	1540.00 s	−8.20	Close	1543.20	1541.20	1	0	1548.20
9)SPM9	Jun 09	1549.20 s	−8.20	Close	1552.40	1550.40	3	0	1557.40

Australia 61 2 9777 8600   Brazil 5511 3048 4500   Europe 44 20 7330 7500   Germany 49 69 920410
Hong Kong 852 2977 6000   Japan 81 3 3201 8900   Singapore 65 6212 1000   U.S. 1 212 318 2000   Copyright 2007 Bloomberg L.P.
H426–565–0 17–Sep–2007 15:54:35

future exchange (i.e., the Chicago Mercantile Exchange for this contract), no money changes hands between the long and short positions at the origination of the contract in September.

Exhibit 20.4 summarizes the payoff and net profit for this contract from the long position's point of view, assuming a hypothetical set of S&P index levels in the December expiration date (i.e., S_T). The most important thing to note is that the payoff to the long position is positive when the S&P index level rises (relative to the contract price of 1,489.80), while a loss is incurred when the S&P falls. For instance, if the expiration data level of the index is 1,520.00, the long position will receive a profit of $30.20 per share (=1,520−1,489.80). In that case, the profit is

Exhibit 20.4 Contract Payoff and Net Profit at Expiration from a Long Position in an S&P 500 Futures Contract

December S&P 500 Index Level	Futures Payoff at Expiration	Initial Futures Premium	Net Profit
1,370.00	(1,370 − 1,489.80) = −119.80	0.00	−119.80
1,400.00	(1,400 − 1,489.80) = −89.80	0.00	−89.80
1,430.00	(1,430 − 1,489.80) = −59.80	0.00	−59.80
1,460.00	(1,460 − 1,489.80) = −29.80	0.00	−29.80
1,489.80	(1,489.80 − 1,489.80) = 0.00	0.00	0.00
1,520.00	(1,520 − 1,489.80) = 30.20	0.00	30.20
1,550.00	(1,550 − 1,489.80) = 60.20	0.00	60.20
1,580.00	(1,580 − 1,489.80) = 90.20	0.00	90.20
1,610.00	(1,610 − 1,489.80) = 120.20	0.00	120.20

owed to the fact that the contract allows the investor to buy stock that is worth 1,520.00 for the predetermined price of only 1,489.80. On the other hand, if the December index level turns out to be 1,460.00, the futures contract still obligates the investor to purchase stock for the contract price, thus resulting in a loss of $29.80. This reinforces the fact that, as the buyer, the long position benefits when stock prices rise and suffers when prices fall, just as would be the case for an investor purchasing stock directly in the spot market. Of course, the short position to the contract, as the seller, would have payoffs exactly the opposite of those shown in Exhibit 20.4. Finally, notice that because entering the futures contract required no upfront premium payment, the net profit to the counterparty is the same as the expiration date payoff.

The data displayed in Exhibit 20.3 contain other information useful to investors as well. First, recognize that the spot and all of the futures contract prices listed finished lower than they had been the day before; this can be seen from the negative entries in the "Change" column in comparison with the "Last" and "Previous Close" prices. This suggests that futures contract prices are strongly linked to the prevailing level of the underlying spot index. Second, notice that the contract prices increase the farther into the future the expiration date occurs. That is, although all nine closing prices listed (i.e., the spot and the eight futures contracts) were set on the same day and correspond to the same S&P index share, the cost of that share gets increasingly more expensive, the further forward in time the delivery date is set. We will see later that this relationship is common for some securities but not for others. Third, the display also lists the *open interest* and *trading volume* for each contract. Open interest is the number of outstanding contracts while trading volume is the number of those contracts that changed hands that day. Thus, it appears in this case that the nearest-term contracts (i.e., September and December 2007) are the most abundant and that about 19 percent (= 141,965 ÷ 735,200) of the total number of S&P contracts in existence were traded on September 17, 2007.

20.1.3 The Language and Structure of Option Markets

An **option contract** gives its holder the right—but not the obligation—to conduct a transaction involving an underlying security or commodity at a predetermined future date and at a predetermined price. Unlike the forward contract, the option gives the long position the right to decide whether the trade will eventually take place. On the other hand, the seller (or *writer*) of the option must perform on his side of the agreement if the buyer chooses to exercise the option. Thus, the obligation in the option market is inherently one-sided; buyers can do as they please, but sellers are obligated to the buyers under the terms of the agreement. As a consequence, two different types of options are needed to cover all potential transactions: a **call option**—the right to buy the underlying security—and a **put option**—the right to sell that same asset.

Option Contract Terms Two prices are important in evaluating an option position. The **exercise,** or striking, **price** is the price the call buyer will pay to—or the put buyer will receive from—the option seller if the option is exercised. The exercise price (represented here as X) is to an option what the contract price (i.e., $F_{0,T}$) is to a forward agreement. The second price of interest is the price that the option buyer must pay to the seller at Date 0 to acquire the contract itself. To avoid confusion, this second price is typically referred to as the **option premium**. A basic difference between options and forwards is that an option requires this upfront premium payment from buyer to seller while the forward ordinarily does not. This is because the forward contract allowed both the long and short positions to "win" at Date T (depending on where S_T settled, relative to $F_{0,T}$), but the option agreement will only be exercised in the buyer's favor; hence the seller must be compensated at Date 0, or she would never agree to the deal. Notice also that although both puts and calls require premium payments, it is quite likely that these two prices will differ. In the analysis that follows, we will define the Date 0 premium to acquire an option expiring at Date T as $C_{0,T}$ for a call and $P_{0,T}$ for a put. For example, in lieu of a long position in a bond forward contract, the investor in an earlier example could have paid \$20 ($= C_{0,T}$) at Date 0 for a call option that would have given him the right to buy the bond for \$1,000 (=X) at Date T, but would not require him to do so if $S_T <$ \$1,000.

Options can be designed to provide a choice of when the contract can be exercised. **European options** can only be exercised at maturity (Date T), while **American options** can be executed any time up to expiration. For a European-style call option, the buyer will only exercise when the expiration date market value of the underlying asset is greater than the exercise price. On the other hand, a European-style put option will only be rationally exercised when the Date T price of the asset is lower than X. (The decision to exercise an American-style contract is more complex and will be considered in a later chapter.)

Option Valuation Basics The Date 0 premium for an option can be divided into two components: **intrinsic value** and **time premium**. Intrinsic value represents the value that the buyer could extract from the option if she exercised it immediately. For a call, this is the greater of either zero or the difference between the price of the underlying asset and the exercise price (i.e., $\max[0, S_0 - X]$). For a put, intrinsic value would be $\max[0, X - S_0]$ as X would now represent the proceeds generated from the asset's sale. An option with positive intrinsic value is said to be **in the money**, while one with zero intrinsic value is **out of the money**. For the special case where $S_0 = X$, the option is **at the money**. The time premium component is then simply the difference between the whole option premium and the intrinsic component: $(C_{0,T} - \max[0, S_0 - X])$ for a call and $(P_{0,T} - \max[0, X - S_0])$ for a put. The buyer is willing to pay this amount in excess of the option's immediate exercise value because of her ability to complete the transaction at a price of X that will remain in force until Date T. Thus, the time premium is connected to the likelihood that the underlying asset's price will move in the anticipated direction by the contract's maturity.

Although a more complete discussion of valuing option premiums will be deferred until Chapter 22, several basic relationships can be seen now. First, because the buyer of a call option is never obligated to exercise, the contract should always at least be worth its intrinsic value. (The situation for put option prices or when the underlying asset pays a dividend can be more complicated and will be discussed later.) In any event, neither a call nor a put option can be worth less than zero. Second, for call options having the same maturity and the same underlying asset, the lower the exercise price, the higher will be the contract's intrinsic value and, hence, the greater its overall premium. Conversely, put options with higher exercise prices are more valuable than those with lower striking prices for the same reason. Third, increasing the amount of time until any option expires will increase the contract's time premium because it allows the price of the underlying security more opportunity to move in the direction anticipated by the investor (i.e., up for a call option, down for a put option). Finally, because they provide investors with more choices about exercising the agreement, American-style options are at least as valuable as otherwise comparable European-style contracts.

Option Trading Markets Like forwards and futures, options trade both in over-the-counter markets and on exchanges. When exchange-traded, just the seller of the contract is required

Exhibit 20.5 Popular Option Contracts and Exchanges

Underlying Asset	Exchange
A. Financial Securities	
Individual Equities	Chicago Board Options Exchange
S&P 100 Index, Dow Jones Industrial Average	
S&P 500 volatility index	
Yen, Euro, Canadian dollar, Swiss franc	Philadelphia Stock Exchange
British pound, Australian dollar	
Russell 2000 Index, Equity Sector Index	
EuroStoxx ETF, DAX index, SMI index	Eurex
B. Futures Options	
Cattle-feeder, Cattle-live, hogs, dairy	CME Group
Yen, Euro, Canadian dollar, Swiss franc British pound	(Chicago Mercantile Exchange)
Eurodollar (LIBOR), Treasury bill	
S&P 500 Index, NASDAQ 100 Index	
Corn, soybeans, soybean meal, soybean oil, wheat	CME Group
Treasury bonds, Treasury notes, Federal Funds	(Chicago Board of Trade)
Dow Jones Industrials Average	
British gilt, GermanEuro government bonds	Euronext.liffe
Wheat, sugar	
Crude oil, heating oil, gasoline, natural gas	New York Mercantile Exchange
Copper, gold, silver, aluminum	

to post a margin account because he is the only one obligated to perform on the contract at a later date. Also, options can be based on a wide variety of underlying securities, including futures contracts or other options. Exhibit 20.5 lists the underlying assets and exchanges where a number of popular option contracts trade.

20.1.4 Interpreting Option Price Quotations: An Example

Exhibit 20.6 shows data for a variety of call and put options on the S&P 500 index as of September 17, 2007. All of the contracts listed expire in December 2007, making them comparable to the S&P 500 futures contracts considered above. However, unlike the futures contracts, for which there was a single contract price for a given expiration month, Exhibit 20.6 indicates that there are several December 2007 options with different exercise prices. The display lists bid and ask premium quotes for both puts and calls, with striking prices ranging from 1,430 to 1,520.[2] Consistent with our earlier observation, calls become more valuable (e.g., higher ask premiums) as the exercise price declines, with the opposite holding true for put options.

Consider the fortunes of two different investors, one of whom purchases a December S&P call struck at 1,475 (i.e., X) and the other who buys a December 1,475 put. At the origination of the transaction in September, these investors will pay their sellers the ask prices of $76.20 (i.e., $C_{0,T}$) and $61.70 (i.e., $P_{0,T}$), respectively. In return, the investor holding the call option has the right, but not the obligation, to buy one S&P share for $1,475 at the expiration date in December. Since the current (i.e., spot) price of the index is 1,476.65, this call option is in the money. Thus, the total put premium of $76.20 can be divided into an intrinsic value component of $1.65 (= 1,476.65 − 1,475) and a time premium of $74.55 (= 76.20 − 1.65). Similarly, the investor holding the put option has the right, but not the obligation, to sell one S&P share for $1,475 at the expiration date in December. The put is out of the money, however, as this exercise price is lower than the current index level. Thus, the put option has no intrinsic value, so that the $61.70 ask price is a time premium.

---

[2] Recall that an investor buys a security from a dealer—in this case, the options exchange—at the ask price, and sells securities to the dealer at the bid price. The difference in these prices, which is the *bid-ask spread*, represents part of the compensation to the exchange for making a market in these contracts.

Exhibit 20.6 Standard & Poor's 500 Index Option Contract Price Quotations

SPX	↑**1476.65 – 7.60**							1476.07/1477.28			P266		Index **OMON**
At 15:58	0p	1484.24 Hi		1484.24 Lo		1472.82							

SPX Index ▼	Templates	Edit	Actions	Expiry	Option Monitor

S&P 500 INDEX	1476.65 –7.60	1476.07/1477.28	Hi 1484.24	Lo 1471.82	Vol

Center 1476.65 ▼   Number of Strikes ▼ 18 or ▮▮▮ % from Center   Exchange Composite ▼

	51) Calls							52) Puts				
	Ticker	Strike	Bid	Ask	Last	Volm		Ticker	Strike	Bid	Ask	Last	Volm

	Ticker	Strike	Bid	Ask	Last	Volm		Ticker	Strike	Bid	Ask	Last	Volm
SPX 22 DEC 2007 (Contract Size 100)							SPX 22 DEC 2007 (Contract Size 100)						
1)	SXZ+LF	1430	103.40	106.40	92.00 y		21)	SXZ+XF	1430	44.60	47.60	47.50 y	
2)	SXZ+LG	1435	99.90	102.90	85.00 y		22)	SXZ+XG	1435	46.00	49.00	60.00 y	
3)	SXZ+LH	1440	96.40	99.40	67.50 y		23)	SXZ+XH	1440	47.40	50.40	45.50 y	
4)	SXZ+LJ	1450	89.50	91.40	92.60	4400	24)	SXZ+XJ	1450	50.40	52.40	51.00	7336
5)	SXZ+LK	1455	86.20	89.20			25)	SXZ+XK	1455	51.90	54.90	59.50 y	
6)	SXZ+LL	1460	82.90	85.90	87.00 y		26)	SXZ+XL	1460	53.60	56.60	55.00	80
7)	SXZ+LM	1465	79.60	82.60			27)	SXZ+XM	1465	55.20	58.20		
8)	SXZ+LN	1470	76.40	79.40			28)	SXZ+XN	1470	56.90	59.90		
9)	SXZ+LO	1475	73.20	76.20	76.00	2442	29)	SXZ+XO	1475	58.70	61.70	59.00	2913
10)	SXZ+LP	1480	70.10	73.10	72.00	106	30)	SXZ+XP	1480	60.50	63.50	61.00	1407
11)	SXZ+LQ	1485	67.00	70.00	67.00	1133	31)	SXZ+XQ	1485	62.40	65.40	65.00	1133
12)	SXZ+LR	1490	65.00	67.00	66.00	19541	32)	SXZ+XR	1490	64.30	67.30	66.00	19286
13)	SXZ+LS	1495	61.10	64.10	65.00	5492	33)	SXZ+XS	1495	66.30	69.30	66.00	5102
14)	SXM+LT	1500	58.20	61.20	59.00	5698	34)	SXM+XT	1500	68.30	71.30	69.00	4295
15)	SXM+LA	1505	55.40	58.40			35)	SXM+XA	1505	70.40	73.40		
16)	SXM+LB	1510	52.60	55.60			36)	SXM+XB	1510	72.60	75.60		
17)	SXM+LC	1515	50.00	53.00			37)	SXM+XC	1515	74.80	77.80		
18)	SXM+LD	1520	47.30	50.30			38)	SXM+XD	1520	77.10	80.10		
SPX 22 MAR 2008 (Contract Size 100)							SPX 22 MAR 2008 (Contract Size 100)						
19)	SXY+CE	1325	206.60	210.60			39)	SXY+OE	1325	35.80	39.80		
20)	SXY+CJ	1350	187.20	191.20	192.00 y		40)	SXY+OJ	1350	40.80	44.80	40.00 y	

Australia 61 2 9777 8600		Brazil 5511 3048 4500		Europe 44 20 7330 7500		Germany 49 69 92040
Hong Kong 852 2977 6000	Japan 81 3 3201 8900	Singapore 65 6212 1000	U.S. 1 212 318 2000	Copyright 2007 Bloomberg L.P.		

H426-565-0 17-Sep-2007 15:58:27

The expiration date payoffs and net profits to these long option positions are listed in Exhibit 20.7 for a variety of possible S&P index levels. Looking first at the call option payoffs in Panel A, notice that the investor will only exercise the contract to buy a share of the S&P index when the December S&P level is above 1,475; at index levels at or below 1,475, the option expires worthless and the investor will simply lose his initial investment. Recognize, though, that while the call is in the money at index levels above 1,475, the investor will not realize a net profit until the December index level rises above 1,551.20, an amount equal to the exercise price plus the call premium (i.e., $X + C_{0,T}$). For the put option payoffs shown in Panel B, the holder will exercise the contract at December index levels below the exercise price, using the contract to sell for $1,475 an S&P share that is worth less than that. However, the display also documents that the put investor will not realize a positive net profit until the index level falls below 1,413.30 (i.e., $X - P_{0,T}$). For December S&P values above $1,475, the put option expires out of the money.

20.2 Investing with Derivative Securities

Although the preceding section highlighted many of the differences between forward and option agreements, the two types of derivatives are quite similar in terms of the benefits they produce for investors. The ultimate difference between forwards and options lies in the way

---

Exhibit 20.7 Contract Payoff and Net Profit at Expiration from Long Positions in S&P 500 Call and Put Option Contracts

A. Long Call with Exercise Price of 1,475:

December S&P 500 Index Level	Call Payoff at Expiration		Initial Call Premium	Net Profit
1,370.00	0.00		−76.20	−76.20
1,400.00	0.00		−76.20	−76.20
1,430.00	0.00		−76.20	−76.20
1,460.00	0.00		−76.20	−76.20
1,490.00	(1,490 − 1,475)	= 15.00	−76.20	−61.20
1,520.00	(1,520 − 1,475)	= 45.00	−76.20	−31.20
1,551.20	(1,551.20 − 1,475)	= 76.20	−76.20	0.00
1,580.00	(1,580 − 1,475)	= 105.00	−76.20	28.80
1,610.00	(1,610 − 1,475)	= 135.00	−76.20	58.80

B. Long Put with Exercise Price of 1,475:

December S&P 500 Index Level	Put Payoff at Expiration		Initial Put Premium	Net Profit
1,370.00	(1,475 − 1,370)	= 105.00	−61.70	43.30
1,400.00	(1,475 − 1,400)	= 75.00	−61.70	13.30
1,413.30	(1,475 − 1,413.30)	= 61.70	−61.70	0.00
1,460.00	(1,475 − 1,460)	= 15.00	−61.70	−46.70
1,490.00	0.00		−61.70	−61.70
1,520.00	0.00		−61.70	−61.70
1,550.00	0.00		−61.70	−61.70
1,580.00	0.00		−61.70	−61.70
1,610.00	0.00		−61.70	−61.70

---

the investor must pay to acquire those benefits. This concept, along with an examination of the basic payoff and net profit structures that exist in these markets, is described below.

20.2.1 The Basic Nature of Derivative Investing

Consider Investor 1 who has decided to purchase a share of stock in SAS Corporation six months from now, coinciding with an anticipated receipt of funds. We assume that both SAS stock forward contracts and call options are available with the market prices of $F_{0,T}$ and $C_{0,T}$ (where $T = 0.50$ year) and that the exercise price of the call option, X, is equal to $F_{0,T}$. Thus, if the investor wants to lock in the price now at which the stock purchase will eventually take place, he has two alternatives: a long position in the forward or the purchase of the call option. Exhibit 20.8 compares the Date 0 and Date T cash flow exchanges for both possibilities.

The clear difference between these strategies at the time of origination is that the forward position requires no payment or receipt by either party to the transaction whereas the investor (i.e., the call buyer) must pay a cash premium to the seller of the option. As noted, this front-end option payment releases the investor from the obligation to purchase SAS stock at Date T if the terms of the contract turn out to be unfavorable (i.e., $S_T < X$). This is shown in Panel B of Exhibit 20.8. When the expiration date price of SAS stock exceeds the exercise price, the investor will exercise the call and purchase the share of stock. However, this leads to exactly the same exchange as the long forward contract. It is only when the stock price falls below X (and $F_{0,T}$) on Date T that there is a difference between the two positions; under this condition, the right provided by the option *not* to purchase SAS stock is valuable since the investor in the forward contract will be required to execute that position at a loss. Thus, the call option can be viewed as the "good half" of the long forward position because it allows for the future acquisition of SAS stock at a fixed price but doesn't require the transaction to take place.

This is the critical distinction between forward and option contracts. Both the long forward and the long call positions have been structured to provide the investor with exactly the

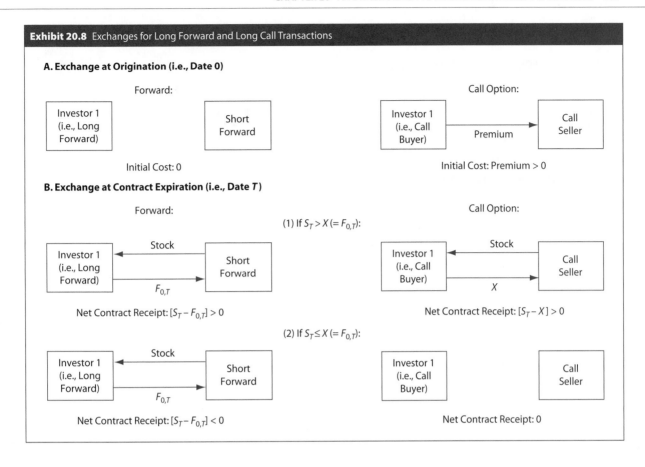

Exhibit 20.8 Exchanges for Long Forward and Long Call Transactions

A. Exchange at Origination (i.e., Date 0)

Forward:

Investor 1 (i.e., Long Forward)   →   Short Forward

Initial Cost: 0

Call Option:

Investor 1 (i.e., Call Buyer)   —Premium→   Call Seller

Initial Cost: Premium > 0

B. Exchange at Contract Expiration (i.e., Date T)

Forward:

(1) If $S_T > X (= F_{0,T})$:

Investor 1 (i.e., Long Forward)   ←Stock—   Short Forward
$F_{0,T}$ →

Net Contract Receipt: $[S_T - F_{0,T}] > 0$

Call Option:

Investor 1 (i.e., Call Buyer)   ←Stock—   Call Seller
X →

Net Contract Receipt: $[S_T - X] > 0$

(2) If $S_T \leq X (= F_{0,T})$:

Investor 1 (i.e., Long Forward)   ←Stock—   Short Forward
$F_{0,T}$ →

Net Contract Receipt: $[S_T - F_{0,T}] < 0$

Investor 1 (i.e., Call Buyer)   Call Seller

Net Contract Receipt: 0

same amount of "insurance" against the price of SAS stock rising over the next six months. That is, both contracts provide a payoff of $[S_T - X] = [S_T - F_{0,T}]$ whenever S_T exceeds X, which reduces the effective purchase price for the stock back to X. The difference in contract design is how the investor is required to pay for that price insurance. With a forward contract, no money is paid up front, but the investor will have to complete the purchase at the expiration date, even if the stock price falls below $F_{0,T}$. Conversely, the call option will never require a future settlement payment, but the investor will have to pay the premium at origination. Thus, for the same Date T benefit, the investor's decision between these two "insurance policies" comes down to choosing the certainty of a present premium payment (i.e., long call) versus the possibility of a future payment (i.e., long forward) that could potentially be much larger.

To see this distinction more clearly, suppose that Investor 1 plans to buy SAS stock in six months when some of the bonds in his portfolio mature. He is concerned that share values could rise substantially between now and the time he receives his investment funds, and so to hedge that risk he considers two insurance strategies to lock in the eventual purchase price: (1) pay nothing now to take the long position in a six-month SAS stock forward contract with a contract price of $F_{0,T} = \$45$, or (2) pay a premium of $C_{0,T} = \$3.24$ for a six-month, European-style call option with an exercise price of $X = \$45$. If at the time of his decision the price of SAS stock is $S_0 = \$40$, the call option is out of the money, meaning that its intrinsic value is zero and the entire \$3.24 is time premium.

As mentioned earlier, an obvious difference between these two strategies is that the option entails a front-end expense while the forward position does not. The other difference occurs at the expiration date, depending on whether the SAS stock price is above or below \$45. If, for instance, $S_T = \$51$, both the long forward position and the call option will be worth \$6 (i.e., $51 - 45$) to the investor, reducing his net purchase price for SAS shares to \$45 (= $51 - 6$).

Exhibit 20.9 Exchanges for Short Forward and Long Put Transactions

A. Exchange at Origination (i.e., Date 0)

Forward:

| Investor 2 (i.e., Short Forward) | → | Long Forward |

Initial Cost: 0

Put Option:

| Investor 2 (i.e., Put Buyer) | → Premium → | Put Seller |

Initial Cost: Premium > 0

B. Exchange at Contract Expiration (i.e., Date T)

Forward:

(1) If $S_T > X (= F_{0,T})$:

Investor 2 (i.e., Short Forward) — Stock → Long Forward; ← $F_{0,T}$

Net Contract Receipt: $[F_{0,T} - S_T] < 0$

Put Option:

Investor 2 (i.e., Put Buyer) | Put Seller

Net Contract Receipt: 0

(2) If $S_T \leq X (= F_{0,T})$:

Investor 2 (i.e., Short Forward) — Stock → Long Forward; ← $F_{0,T}$

Net Contract Receipt: $[F_{0,T} - S_T] > 0$

Investor 2 (i.e., Put Buyer) — Stock → Put Seller; ← X

Net Contract Receipt: $[X - S_T] > 0$

That is, when the stock settled above $45 (i.e., the common value for $F_{0,T}$ and X), both the long forward and long call positions provided the same protection against rising prices. On the other hand, if $S_T = \$40.75$, the forward contract would have required that the investor pay $4.25 (= 40.75 − 45) to his counterparty, which would have once again raised the net cost of his shares to $45. With the call option, however, he could have let the contract expire without exercising it and purchased his SAS shares in the market for only $40.75. Thus, in exchange for the option's front-end expense of $3.24, the investor retains the possibility of paying less than $45 for his eventual stock purchase.

The connection between forward contracts and put options can be made in a similar fashion. Suppose a different investor—call her Investor 2—has decided to liquidate a share of SAS stock from her portfolio in six months' time. Rather than risk a falling stock price over that period, she could arrange now to sell the share at that future date for a predetermined fixed price in one of two ways: a short forward position or the purchase of a put option. Exhibit 20.9 illustrates the exchanges for these alternatives. Once again, for the same insurance against SAS stock price declines, the choice comes down to the certainty of paying the put option premium versus the possibility of making a potentially larger payment with the forward contract by having to sell her stock for $X (= F_{0,T})$ when that value is considerably less than the stock's Date T market price. Notice once again that the put option allows the investor to walk away from her obligation under the short forward position to sell her stock on the expiration date under disadvantageous conditions. Thus, in exchange for a front-end premium payment, the put option enables the investor to acquire the "good half" of the short position in a forward contract.

20.2.2 Basic Payoff and Profit Diagrams for Forward Contracts

Exhibit 20.8 and Exhibit 20.9 show that the respective expiration date payoffs for long and short positions in a forward contract are $[S_T − F_{0,T}]$ and $[F_{0,T} − S_T]$ and that these values could

Exhibit 20.10 Expiration Date Payoffs and Profits to Long and Short Forward Positions

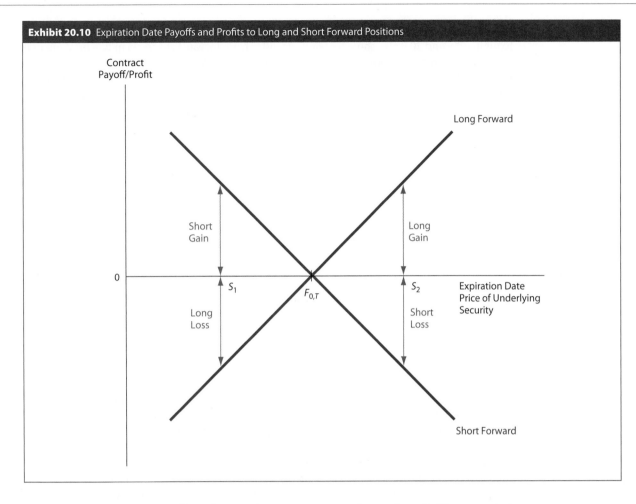

be either positive or negative depending on the spot price prevailing at Date T. These terminal payoffs are plotted against the possible expiration date values of the underlying security price in Exhibit 20.10. There are two interesting items in this display.

First, the payoffs to both long and short positions in the forward contract are *symmetric,* or two-sided, around the contract price. This is a direct result of a contract that fully obligates each party to complete the agreed-upon transaction—even at a financial loss. For instance, in the last example, the investor holding a long position in a SAS stock forward contract with a contract price of $45 lost $4.25 when the Date T price of SAS stock was $40.75 but gained $6 when S_T = $51. Also, since no front-end premiums were paid, the contract payoffs shown in Exhibit 20.10 are also the net profits to the investors.

Second, the Date T payoffs to the short and long positions are mirror images of each other; in market jargon, forward contracts are *zero-sum games* because the long position gains must be paid by the short position and vice versa. This illustration shows that when the Date T spot price is lower than the contract price (i.e., S_1), the short position will receive the net payoff of $[F_{0,T} - S_1]$ from the long position while the settlement is reversed at S_2, where the security price is above $F_{0,T}$. Thus, forward markets reinforce the fundamental financial tenet that long positions benefit from rising prices while short positions benefit from falling prices. Finally, notice that these gains and losses can be quite large. In fact, the short forward position has the potential for unlimited loss while the long forward position has the potential for unlimited gain since there is no theoretical limit on how high the price for the underlying security can rise. Conversely, the loss potential for the long position (and the gain potential for the short position) is limited because the price of the underlying security cannot fall below zero.

20.2.3 Basic Payoff and Profit Diagrams for Call and Put Options

Exhibits 20.8 and 20.9 also show that options differ from forward contracts in two fundamental ways: (1) the expense of purchasing either a put or a call represents a sunk cost to the investor, reducing the upside return relative to the comparable forward position, and (2) the investor receives expiration date payoffs that are decidedly *asymmetric,* or one-sided. Exhibit 20.11 shows the net effect these differences have on the terminal payoffs and net profits to both long and short positions in call options, while Exhibit 20.12 provides a similar illustration for put option traders. This analysis assumes that both options are European-style and reach expiration without having been exercised prematurely.

For call option positions, notice again that the buyer of the contract receives a payoff whenever the terminal security price (i.e., S_T) exceeds the contract purchase (i.e., exercise) price of X. However, given that the holder had to pay an initial premium of $C_{0,T}$, the position doesn't generate a positive profit until S_T is greater than X by the amount of the premium paid. Put another way, although the call option is in the money (and hence will be exercised) when $S_T > X$, it will not produce a capital gain for the buyer until $S_T > (X + C_{0,T})$.[3] (Recall that this result was shown for the S&P 500 index option example in Exhibit 20.7.) When $X < S_T < (X + C_{0,T})$, the option is exercised at a loss, but this loss will be less than the full cost of the option, which is what the long position would incur if the call were not exercised. In fact, when $S_T < X$, the option is out of the money and the buyer who makes the rational decision to let the contract expire will lose $C_{0,T}$.

Notice, then, that the buyer of the call option has unlimited gain potential as the security price could rise indefinitely with losses limited to the option premium no matter how far prices fall. On the other hand, the short position benefits when the terminal price of the underlying asset is lower than X but only to the extent that he gets to keep the full amount of the option premium. When $S_T > X$, the seller of the call has unlimited liability. Like forward contracts, the call option is a zero-sum game between the long and short positions.

For the put option positions shown in Exhibit 20.12, the buyer benefits whenever $X > S_T$ and receives a positive profit when the Date T price of the underlying security falls below the contractual selling price, less the cost of the option. In this case, the put buyer's maximum capital gain is limited to $X - P_{0,T}$ as the underlying security itself is limited to a minimum price of zero; the best the put holder can hope for is to force the seller of the contract to buy worthless stock for X at the expiration date. As with the call option, the owner of an out-of-the-money put can only lose his initial investment of $P_{0,T}$, which will occur when $S_T > X$. Not surprisingly, the profit and loss opportunities for the put seller are exactly opposite of those for the put buyer. The contract seller will gain when $S_T > (X - P_{0,T})$, but this gain is limited to the amount of the option premium. A short position in a put also has limited loss potential; but, at a maximum of $X - P_{0,T}$, this can still be a large amount.

In summary, when held as investments, options are *directional views* on movements in the price of the underlying security. Call buyers and put sellers count on S_T to rise (or remain) above X, while put buyers and call sellers hope for S_T to fall (or remain) below the exercise price at the expiration date. Importantly, option buyers—whether a put or a call—always have limited liability since they do not have to exercise an out-of-the-money position. This limited liability feature for option holders also means that the gain potential for the seller is limited as the two positions are mirror images of each other. For adverse price movements, though, option sellers face large potential losses, with the liability of the call writer being theoretically infinite just as if she had sold short the underlying security.

---

[3] The expiration date profits shown in Exhibits 20.11 and 20.12 are somewhat inaccurate in that they show the net of the Date T value of the option and its initial cost, which was paid at Date 0. Thus, although this is an accurate way of portraying capital gains and losses from an accounting standpoint, it ignores the difference in the timing of the two payments.

Exhibit 20.11 Expiration Date Payoffs and Profits to Long and Short Call Positions

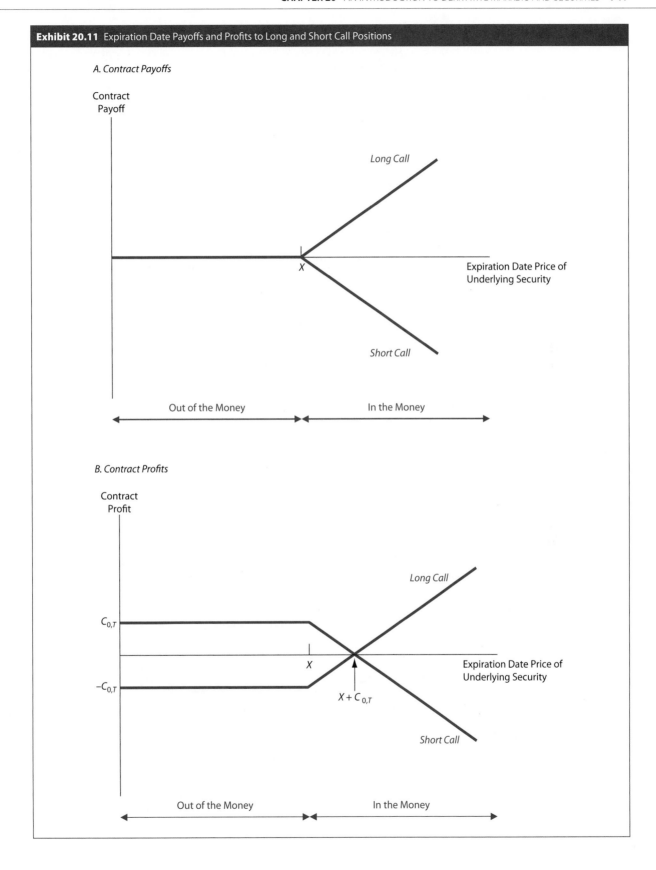

A. Contract Payoffs

Contract Payoff

Long Call

X

Expiration Date Price of Underlying Security

Short Call

Out of the Money

In the Money

B. Contract Profits

Contract Profit

Long Call

$C_{0,T}$

$-C_{0,T}$

X

$X + C_{0,T}$

Expiration Date Price of Underlying Security

Short Call

Out of the Money

In the Money

Exhibit 20.12 Expiration Date Payoffs and Profits to Long and Short Put Positions

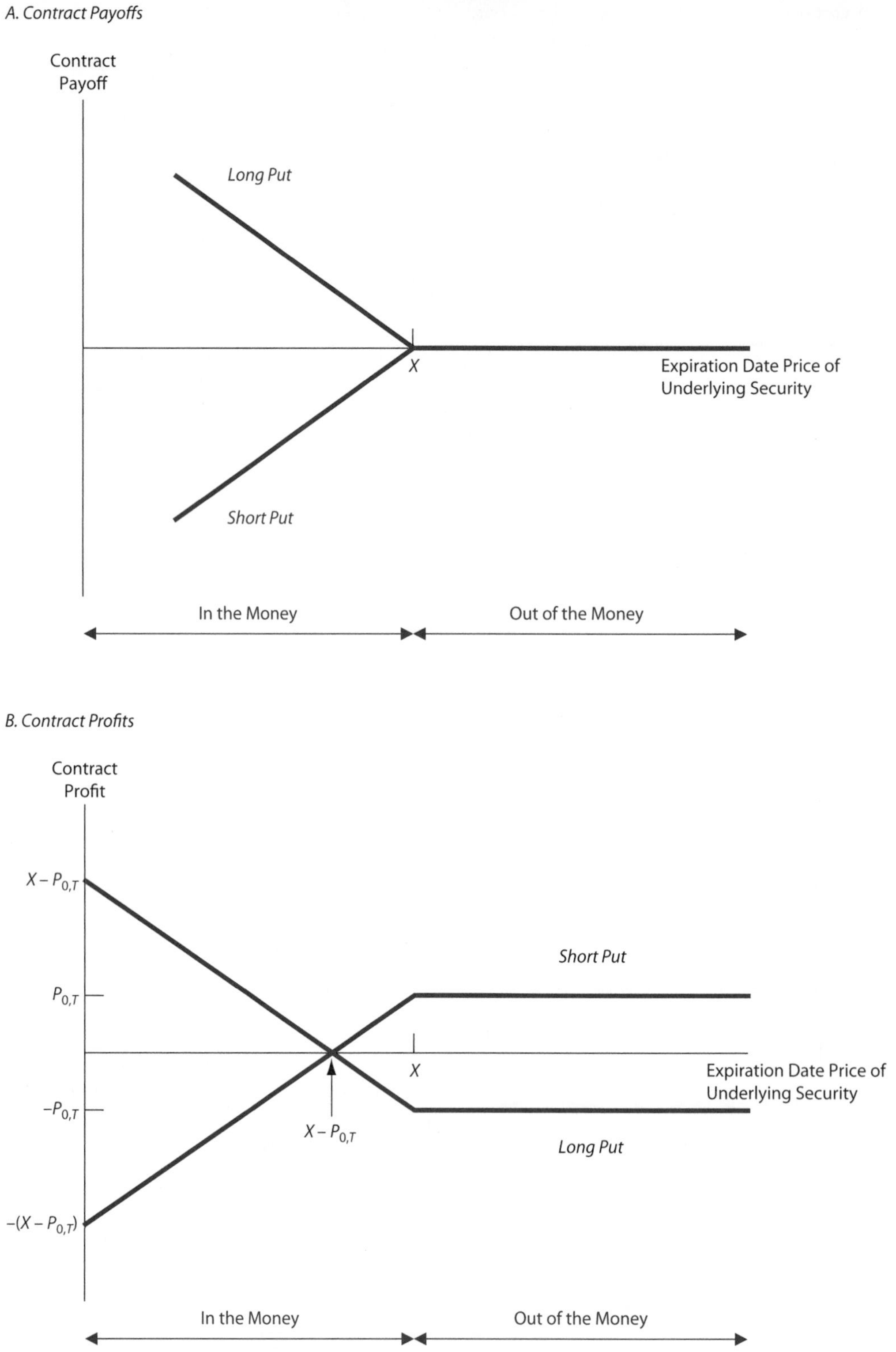

A. Contract Payoffs

Contract Payoff

Long Put

Short Put

X

Expiration Date Price of Underlying Security

In the Money | Out of the Money

B. Contract Profits

Contract Profit

$X - P_{0,T}$

$P_{0,T}$

$-P_{0,T}$

$-(X - P_{0,T})$

$X - P_{0,T}$

Short Put

Long Put

X

Expiration Date Price of Underlying Security

In the Money | Out of the Money

20.2.4 Option Profit Diagrams: An Example

Although there will only be one value of $F_{0,T}$ for any given futures contract maturing at Date T, we have seen that option contracts can be designed with several different values for the exercise price. We now consider how the choice of the exercise price affects the investor's expiration date profit. Extending the last example, suppose that a share of SAS stock currently sells for $40 and six different SAS options—three calls and three puts—are available to investors. The options all expire on the same date in the future and have exercise prices of either $35, $40, or $45. Current market prices for these contracts, which are assumed to be European-style, are shown in Exhibit 20.13, where they are broken down into their intrinsic value and time premium components.

Given that S_0 = $40, Call 1 (with X = 35) and Put 3 (with X = 45) are both $5 in the money, which leaves $3.07 and $1.47, respectively, of time premium. Call 3 and Put 1 are both currently $5 out of the money and so their market prices are purely time premium; someone buying either of these two contracts anticipates that stock prices will move in the desired direction by at least the option price *plus* $5. Notice that neither of the two at-the-money options, Call 2 and Put 2, have any intrinsic value, but they still sell in the market for different prices. Specifically, the call with X = $40 is more valuable than the comparable put option. As we will see shortly, this occurs because of **put-call parity**, which is the formal relationship that must exist between put and call options in efficient capital markets. (In fact, for options on a stock that does not pay a dividend, this situation should always hold. However, the value of an at-the-money put can exceed that of an at-the-money call if the underlying security is a stock, a bond, or currency that does pay a cash flow.) Finally, the last column of Exhibit 20.13 shows that the time premium is largest for the at-the-money options because, at this point, the greatest amount of uncertainty exists as to whether the option will be in or out of the money (and hence valuable, or not) at expiration.

Exhibit 20.14 compares the expiration date profit diagrams for options on the same security with varying exercise prices but similar in every other respect. For simplicity, only the profits for the long positions in these contracts are shown. The call option profits portrayed in Panel A indicate that, although it is the most expensive, the deepest in-the-money contract (Call 1) becomes profitable the quickest, requiring only that S_T rise to $43.07 (= 35 + 8.07). Call 3 is the least expensive to purchase but requires the greatest movement in the price of the underlying stock—to $48.24 in this example—before it provides a positive profit to the investor. The put options illustrated in Panel B tell the same story, with Put 1 (the out-of-the-money contract) costing the least but needing the largest price decline to be profitable at expiration. In general, by varying the exercise price on a series of options with otherwise identical contract terms, an investor can create just as many different risk-reward trade-offs for herself. This is one of several ways in which derivatives can be used to modify investment risk and to customize a desired payoff structure.

Exhibit 20.13 Hypothetical Stock and Option Prices

Instrument	Exercise Price	Market Price	Intrinsic Value	Time Premium
SAS Stock	—	$40.00	—	—
Call: 1	$35.00	8.07	$5.00	$3.07
2	40.00	5.24	0.00	5.24
3	45.00	3.24	0.00	3.24
Put: 1	35.00	1.70	0.00	1.70
2	40.00	3.67	0.00	3.67
3	45.00	6.47	5.00	1.47

Exhibit 20.14 Terminal Profits to Options with Different Exercise Prices

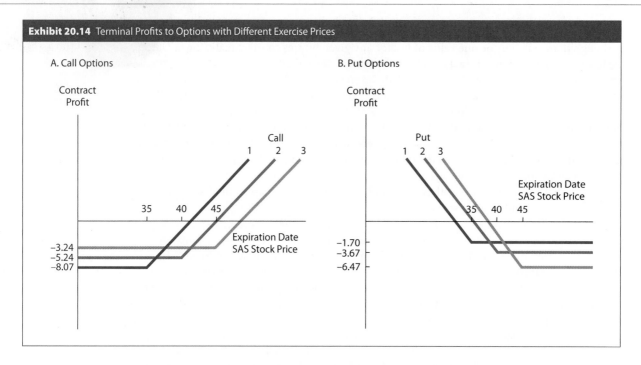

Exhibit 20.15 Stock and Option Investment Returns

A. Long Stock versus Long Call

Terminal Stock Price	Long Stock	Long Call
30	$\frac{30}{40} - 1 = -25.0\%$	$\frac{0}{5.24} - 1 = -100.0\%$
40	$\frac{40}{40} - 1 = 0.0\%$	$\frac{0}{5.24} - 1 = -100.0\%$
50	$\frac{50}{40} - 1 = 25.0\%$	$\frac{10}{5.24} - 1 = -90.8\%$

B. Short Stock versus Long Put

Terminal Stock Price	Short Stock	Long Put
30	$1 - \frac{30}{40} = 25.0\%$	$\frac{10}{3.67} - 1 = -172.5\%$
40	$1 - \frac{40}{40} = 0.0\%$	$\frac{0}{3.67} - 1 = -100.0\%$
50	$1 - \frac{50}{40} = -25.0\%$	$\frac{0}{3.67} - 1 = -100.0\%$

Options and Leverage As a final extension of this example, we compare the returns to an investment in either a put or a call option with a direct investment (or short sale) in a share of the underlying SAS stock. We will limit the analysis to Call 2 and Put 2, the two at-the-money contracts. Exhibit 20.15 summarizes the holding period returns for various positions assuming three different expiration date stock prices: $30, $40, and $50. Two different comparisons are made: (1) long stock versus long call and (2) short stock versus long put. In calculating the returns to the stock positions, we have measured the change in value of the SAS share as a percentage of the initial price of $40. For the option positions, the terminal payoffs of max $[0, S_T - 40]$ for the call and max $[0, 40 - S_T]$ for the put are listed relative to the contract's purchase price.

Notice that both put and call options magnify the possible positive and negative returns of investing in the underlying security. In the case of the long call option position, for an initial cost of $5.24, the investor can retain the right to obtain the price appreciation of a share of SAS stock without spending $40 to own the share outright. This degree of financial *leverage* manifests itself in a 100 percent loss when the stock price falls by a quarter of that amount and a 91 percent gain when SAS shares increase in value from $40 to $50. Notably, if the stock price remains at $40, the owner of the share would not have lost anything while the call holder would have lost his entire investment in the at-the-money contract. This suggests that in addition to anticipating the *direction* of the subsequent underlying stock price movement, the option investor also is taking a view on the *timing* of that movement. If the price of SAS stock had stayed at $40 through Date T and then rose to $50 on the following day, the stockholder would have experienced a 25 percent gain, while the buyer of the call option would have seen the instrument expire worthless.

· ·

20.3 The Relationship between Forward and Option Contracts

The preceding discussion highlighted the fact that positions in forward and option contracts can lead to similar investment payoffs if the price of the underlying security moves in the anticipated direction. This similarity in payoff structures suggests that there is a tractable set of relationships between these instruments. In fact, we will see that the values of five different securities can be linked: a risk-free bond, an underlying asset, a forward contract for the future purchase or sale of that asset, a call option, and a put option. These relationships, known as put-call parity, specify how the put and call premiums should be set relative to one another. Further, these conditions can be expressed in terms of the connection between these two option types and either the spot or forward market price for the underlying asset. They depend on the assumption that financial markets are free from arbitrage opportunities, meaning that securities (or portfolios of securities) offering identical payoffs with identical risks must sell for the same current price. As such, put-call parity represents a crucial first step in understanding how derivatives are valued in an efficient capital market.[4]

20.3.1 Put-Call-Spot Parity

Suppose that at Date 0 (the present) an investor forms the following portfolio involving three securities related to Company WYZ:

- Long in a share of WYZ common stock at a purchase price of S_0,
- Long in a put option to deliver one share of WYZ stock at an exercise price of X on the Expiration Date T. This put could be purchased for the price of $P_{0,T}$,
- Short in a call option allowing the purchase of one share of WYZ stock at an exercise price of X on the Expiration Date T. This call could be sold for the price of $C_{0,T}$.

In this example, both of the WYZ options are European-style and have the same expiration date and exercise price. However, the specific values of the expiration date and exercise price do not affect the conclusion of the analysis that follows. Further, we will assume initially that WYZ stock does not pay a dividend during the life of the options.

Panel A of Exhibit 20.16 lists the Date 0 investment necessary to acquire this portfolio as $(S_0 + P_{0,T} - C_{0,T})$, which is the cost of the long positions in the stock and the put option less

---

[4] The development of the relationships linking put and call option prices is commonly attributed to Stoll (1969). Others have embellished Stoll's findings in many interesting ways; those subsequent studies include Merton (1973a), Klemkosky and Resnick (1979), and Bharadwaj and Wiggins (2001).

Exhibit 20.16 Put-Call-Spot Parity

A. Net Portfolio Investment at Initiation (Date 0)

Portfolio	
Long 1 WYZ stock	S_0
Long 1 put option	$P_{0,T}$
Short 1 call option	$-C_{0,T}$
Net investment:	$S_0 + P_{0,T} - C_{0,T}$

B. Portfolio Value at Option Expiration (Date T)

Portfolio	(1) If $S_T \leq X$:	(2) If $S_T > X$:
Long 1 WYZ stock	S_T	S_T
Long 1 put option	$(X - S_T)$	0
Short 1 call option	0	$-(S_T - X)$
Net position:	X	X

the proceeds generated by the sale of the call option.[5] Consider also the value that this portfolio will have at the expiration date of the two options. Given that the stock's value at Date T (i.e., S_T) is unknown when the investment is made at Period 0, two general outcomes are possible: (1) $S_T \leq X$ and (2) $S_T > X$. Panel B shows the value of each position as well as the net value of the whole portfolio at Date T.

Whenever the Date T value of WYZ stock is less than the exercise price common to the put and call options, it is best for the investor to exercise the long position in the put and sell the WYZ share for X instead of its lower market value. In that case, it will not be rational for the holder of the call to pay X for a share that is worth less so the call will expire out of the money. On the other hand, when S_T exceeds X, the holder of the call will exercise the option to purchase WYZ stock for X while the put would be out of the money. In either scenario, the net expiration date value of the portfolio is X because the combination of options guarantees that the investor will sell the share of WYZ stock at Date T for the fixed price X. That is, at stock prices lower than X, the investor will choose to sell the share at a profit, although he will be forced to sell at a loss when WYZ trades at a market price higher than X. The investor has, in effect, a guaranteed contract to sell the share of stock when the long put and short call positions are held jointly.

The consequence of this result is that when the investor commits $(S_0 + P_{0,T} - C_{0,T})$ to acquire the position at Date 0, he knows that it will be worth X at Date T. Thus, this particular portfolio has a comparable payoff structure to a U.S. Treasury bill, another risk-free, zero coupon security that can be designed to have a face value of X and a maturity date T. In an arbitrage-free capital market, this means that the Date 0 value of the portfolio must be equal to that of the T-bill, which is just the face value X discounted to the present using the risk-free rate. This "no arbitrage" condition can be formalized as follows:

20.1
$$S_0 + P_{0,T} - C_{0,T} = \frac{X}{(1 + RFR)^T}$$

where:

RFR = the annualized risk-free rate
T = the time to maturity (expressed in years)

---

[5] In the "arithmetic" of engineering financial portfolios, a plus (+) sign can be interpreted as a long position, and a minus (−) sign represents a short position. Thus the portfolio investment represented by $(S_0 + P_{0,T} - C_{0,T})$ can also be expressed as (long stock) + (long put) + (short call). Smith (1989a) explains this approach in more detail.

Defining $[X(1 + RFR)^{-T}]$ as the present value of a T-bill, this equation can be expressed on Date 0 in financial arithmetic terms as:

$$\text{(Long Stock)} + \text{(Long Put)} + \text{(Short Call)} = \text{(Long T-Bill)}$$

In either form, this condition—known as the *put-call-spot* parity condition—indicates the efficient market linkages between prices for stock, T-bills, put options, and call options.

20.3.2 Put-Call Parity: An Example

Suppose that WYZ stock is currently valued at $53 and that call and put options on WYZ stock with an exercise price of $50 sell for $6.74 and $2.51, respectively. Assuming that both options can only be exercised in exactly six months, Equation 20.1 suggests that we can create a synthetic T-bill by purchasing the stock, purchasing the put, and selling the call for a net price of $48.77 (= 53.00 + 2.51 − 6.74). At the options' expiration date, this portfolio would have a terminal value of $50. Thus, the risk-free rate implied by this investment can be established by solving the following equation for *RFR*:

$$48.77 = 50(1 + RFR)^{-0.5}$$

or

$$RFR = [(50 \div 48.77)^2 - 1] = 5.11\%$$

If the rate of return on an actual six-month T-bill with a face value of $50 is not 5.11 percent, then an investor could exploit the difference. Suppose, for instance, that the actual T-bill rate is 6.25 percent and that there are no restrictions against using the proceeds from the short sale of any security. In such a situation, an investor wanting a risk-free investment would clearly choose the actual T-bill to lock in the higher return, while someone seeking a loan might attempt to secure a 5.11 percent borrowing rate by short-selling the synthetic T-bill. With an arithmetic rearrangement of Equation 20.1, such an artificial short position can be obtained as

$$\text{(Short Stock)} + \text{(Short Put)} + \text{(Long Call)} = \text{(Short T-Bill)}$$

With no transaction costs, a financial arbitrage could be constructed by combining a long position in the actual T-bill with a short sale of the synthetic portfolio. Given that the current value of the actual T-bill is $48.51 [= $50 (1.0625)$^{-0.5}$], this set of transactions would generate the cash flows shown in Exhibit 20.17 and produce a $0.26 profit per each T-bill pair created. As the arbitrage trade did not require the investor to bear any risk (i.e., both the Date 0 and Date *T* values of the net position were known at inception) nor commit any capital, there is nothing in this example to prevent the investor from expanding the size of the trade to increasingly larger levels. However, as additional transactions take place, the price discrepancy will disappear. In this case, the purchase of the actual T-bill and sale of the synthetic (short stock, short put, and long call) will continue until rates are equalized. This is how the markets remain efficient through arbitrage trading.

Another way of seeing this trade is

$$C_{0,T} - P_{0,T} = S_0 - X(1 + RFR)^{-T}$$

That is, the "no arbitrage" difference between the call and put prices should equal the difference between the stock price and the present value of the joint exercise price. The market-determined risk-free rate of 6.25 percent implies that the correct difference between the two derivatives should be $4.49 (= 53 − 48.51), which is $0.26 greater than the $4.23 (= 6.74 − 2.51) actual difference. This discrepancy suggests that if you assume the actual T-bill is priced correctly, the call price is undervalued relative to the put option. Not surprisingly, then, the arbitrage transaction requires the purchase of the call option while shorting the put option.

Exhibit 20.17 A Put-Call Parity Arbitrage Example

A. Net Initial Investment (Date 0)

Transaction	
1. Long actual T-bill at 6.25%	−48.51
2. Short synthetic T-bill at 5.11%:	
Short WYZ stock	53.00
Short put option	2.51
Long call option	−6.74
Net receipt:	0.26

B. Position Value at Option Expiration (Date T)

Transaction	(1) If $S_T \leq 50$:	(2) If $S_T > 50$:
1. Long actual T-bill at 6.25%	50	50
2. Short synthetic T-bill at 5.11%:		
Short WYZ stock	$-S_T$	$-S_T$
Short put option	$-(50 - S_T)$	0
Long call option	0	$(S_T - 50)$
Net position:	0	0

20.3.3 Creating Synthetic Securities Using Put-Call Parity

The preceding example demonstrates that a risk-free portfolio could be created by combining three risky securities: stock, a put option, and a call option. The parity condition developed in the example can be expressed in other useful ways as well. In particular, one of the four assets represented in Equation 20.1 is always *redundant* because it can be defined in terms of the others. Three additional ways of manipulating this result are:

20.2
$$P_{0,T} = \frac{X}{(1 + RFR)^T} - S_0 + C_{0,T}$$

20.3
$$C_{0,T} = S_0 + P_{0,T} - \frac{X}{(1 + RFR)^T}$$

20.4
$$S_0 = \frac{X}{(1 + RFR)^T} - P_{0,T} + C_{0,T}$$

Equation 20.2 and Equation 20.3 indicate, respectively, that (1) the payoffs to a long position in a put option can be replicated by a portfolio consisting of a long position in a T-bill, a short stock position, and the purchase of a call option; and (2) a synthetic call option can be mimicked by a portfolio that is long in the stock and the put option and short in the T-bill. Equation 20.4 indicates that the payoff to the stock itself can be created with its derivative securities and the T-bill.

These results are useful in two ways. First, if actual put or call options do not exist, these equations indicate how investors can obtain the desired, but unavailable, pattern of cash flows through the appropriate "packaging" of the other three assets. Suppose, for example, that a put option on WYZ stock did not exist but a call option does. Exhibit 20.18 shows the Date 0 and Date T cash flows associated with the portfolio replicating the terminal payoff. Combining both panels of the display, an initial investment of $[X (1 + RFR)^{-T} - S_0 + C_{0,T}]$ leads to a final cash flow that is no less than zero and as large as $X - S_T$ whenever $X > S_T$. Expressed in a more traditional manner, the expiration date payoff to the synthetic put is max$[0, X - S_T]$.

A second way these alternative put-call parity expressions are used in practice is the identification of arbitrage opportunities. Even when a particular derivative instrument trades actively in the market, if its cash flows and risks can be duplicated, this leads to the possibility that the

Exhibit 20.18 Replicating a Put Option

A. Net Portfolio Investment at Initiation (Date 0)

Portfolio	
Long 1 T-bill	$X(1 + RFR)^{-T}$
Short 1 WYZ stock	$-S_0$
Long 1 call option	$C_{0,T}$
Net investment:	$X(1 + RFR)^{-T} - S_0 + C_{0,T}$

B. Portfolio Value at Option Expiration (Date *T*)

Portfolio	(1) If $S_T \leq X$:	(2) If $S_T > X$:
Long 1 T-bill	X	X
Short 1 WYZ stock	$-S_T$	$-S_T$
Long 1 call option	0	$(S_T - X)$
Net position:	$X - S_T$	0

price of the actual instrument and the net cost of the replicating portfolio will differ. From the previous example, the Date *T* distribution of $\max[0, 50 - S_T]$ could be acquired through the synthetic strategy at a cost of \$2.25 (= 48.51 − 53 + 6.74) or through the purchase of the actual put for \$2.51.

This is the same \$0.26 price differential we saw earlier when designing an arbitrage transaction involving the actual and synthetic T-bill. The put option arbitrage would be to short the actual put while buying the replicating portfolio (i.e., long T-bill, short stock, and long call), which is the same set of transactions we used in the T-bill arbitrage. This underscores the important point that the put-call parity model only allows us to make *relative*—rather than absolute—statements about security values. Although we can change our perspective about the misvalued instrument (e.g., T-bill versus put option), the real source of the market inefficiency came from examining the *difference* between the put and call prices in relation to the stock and T-bill prices. Consequently, all four securities need to be included in the arbitrage trade.

20.3.4 Adjusting Put-Call-Spot Parity for Dividends

Another extension of the put-call-spot parity model involves the payment of dividends to the shareholders of WYZ stock. Suppose that in the basic portfolio listed in Exhibit 20.16, WYZ stock pays a dividend of D_T immediately prior to the expiration of the options at Date *T*. Assume further that the amount of this distribution is known when the investment is initiated, a condition that is almost certainly met for values of $T \leq 0.25$ year because U.S.-based companies typically pay quarterly dividends. With these modifications the terminal value of the long stock position will be $(S_T + D_T)$ while the terminal payoffs to the put and call options remain $\max[0, X - S_T]$ and $\max[0, S_T - X]$, respectively, as the holders of the two derivative contracts will not participate directly in the payment of dividends to the stockholder.[6] Thus, the net Date *T* value of the portfolio acquired originally for $(S_0 + P_{0,T} - C_{0,T})$ is $(X + D_T)$.

With the critical assumption that the dividend payment is known at Date 0, the portfolio long in WYZ stock, long in the put, and short in the call once again can be viewed as equivalent to a T-bill, now having a face value of $(X + D_T)$. This allows Equation 20.1 to be adapted as follows:

$$S_0 + P_{0,T} - C_{0,T} = \frac{X + D_T}{(1 + RFR)^T} = \frac{X}{(1 + RFR)^T} + \frac{D_T}{(1 + RFR)^T}$$

---

[6] The fact that the expiration date payoff to a call option on both a dividend- and nondividend-paying stock can be expressed as $\max[0, S_T - X]$ does not mean that the two will generate the same dollar amount of cash flow. This is because the stock's value will be reduced by the payment of the dividend in the former case but not in the latter. Thus, with the lower terminal payout, the call on the dividend-paying stock will be less valuable than an otherwise comparable contract on a nondividend-paying equity. We will explore this topic more fully in Chapter 22.

which can be interpreted as:

(Long Stock) + (Long Put) + (Short Call) = (Long T-Bill) + (Long Present Value of Dividends)

Alternatively, it is often more useful to rearrange this Equation as follows:

$$\left\{ S_0 - \frac{D_T}{(1 + RFR)^T} \right\} + P_{0,T} - C_{0,T} = \frac{X}{(1 + RFR)^T}$$

This form of the equation can be compared directly with the no-dividend put-call-spot parity result and shows that the current stock price must be *adjusted downward* by the present value of the dividend. With an initial stock price of $53 and an annualized risk-free rate on a six-month T-bill of 6.25 percent, a $1 dividend paid just before the expiration of a call and a put option with an exercise price of $50 would result in a theoretical price differential of:

$$C_{0.05} - P_{0.05} = \left\{ 53 - \frac{1}{(1 + 0.0625)^{0.5}} \right\} - \frac{50}{(1 + 0.0625)^{0.5}} = \$3.52$$

This value differs from the parity differential for options on the nondividend-paying stock, which was shown earlier to be $4.49. Thus, the payment of the dividend has reduced the price of the call relative to the put by $0.97, which is the discounted amount of the $1 cash distribution.

20.3.5 Put-Call-Forward Parity

Suppose that instead of buying the stock in the spot market at Date 0, we took a long position in a forward contract allowing us to purchase one share of WYZ stock at Date T. The price of this acquisition, $F_{0,T}$, would be established at Date 0. As before, we assume that this transaction is supplemented by the purchase of a put option and the sale of a call option, each having the same exercise price and expiration date. Exhibit 20.19 summarizes both the initial and terminal cash flows to this position.

Panel B reveals that this is once again a risk-free portfolio. There are, however, two important differences in its cash flow patterns. First, the net initial investment of $(P_{0,T} - C_{0,T})$ is substantially smaller than when the stock was purchased in the spot market. Second, the riskless terminal payoff of $(X - F_{0,T})$ also is smaller than before as the stock now must be purchased at Date T rather than at Date 0. This intuition leads directly to the *put-call-forward* parity condition:

20.5
$$P_{0,T} - C_{0,T} = \frac{X - F_{0,T}}{(1 + RFR)^T} = \frac{X}{(1 + RFR)^T} - \frac{F_{0,T}}{(1 + RFR)^T}$$

Exhibit 20.19 Put-Call-Forward Parity

A. Net Portfolio Investment at Initiation (Date 0)

Portfolio	
Long 1 forward contract	0
Long 1 put option	$P_{0,T}$
Short 1 call option	$-C_{0,T}$
Net investment:	$P_{0,T} - C_{0,T}$

B. Portfolio Value at Option Expiration (Date *T*)

Portfolio	(1) If $S_T \le X$:	(2) If $S_T > X$:
Long 1 forward contract	$(S_T - F_{0,T})$	$(S_T - F_{0,T})$
Long 1 put option	$(X - S_T)$	0
Short 1 call option	0	$-(S_T - X)$
Net position:	$(X - F_{0,T})$	$(X - F_{0,T})$

which says that for markets to be free from arbitrage, the difference between put and call prices must equal the discounted difference between the option exercise price and the forward contract price. Just as $F_{0,T}$ did not appear in the spot market version of the parity condition, the current stock price does not appear in Equation 20.5.

This result implies that the only time that put and call prices should be equal to one another in an efficient market is when $X = F_{0,T}$. That is, although the put-call parity result holds for any common exercise price, there is only one value of X for which there would be no net cost to the option combination and that is the prevailing forward price. Recall, for example, that when WYZ stock did not pay a dividend, the theoretical difference between $C_{0,0.5}$ and $P_{0,0.5}$ was $4.49 (= 53 − 48.51). This meant that an investor long in the call and short in the put with a joint $50 exercise price would have what amounted to a forward contract to buy WYZ stock in six months at a price of $50.[7] However, she would have to pay $4.49 for this arrangement, suggesting that $50 is a below-market forward price. How much below the prevailing forward contract price is $50? By the future value of $4.49, invested at the prevailing risk-free rate of 6.25 percent. Thus, the no-arbitrage forward price under these circumstances should be $54.63 [= 50 + 4.49 (1 + 0.0625)^{0.5}].

Another way to see this result comes from combining the put-call-forward parity condition with the put-call-spot condition. Specifically, inserting the expression for $(P_{0,T} − C_{0,T})$ from the put-call-forward parity condition into the put-call-spot condition leaves

$$S_0 + \left\{ \frac{X}{(1 + RFR)^T} - \frac{F_{0,T}}{(1 + RFR)^T} \right\} = \frac{X}{(1 + RFR)^T}$$

which simplifies to

$$S_0 = \frac{F_{0,T}}{(1 + RFR)^T}$$

In the absence of dividend payments, notice that the spot price for the share of stock should simply be the discounted value of purchasing the same security in the forward market. Equivalently, this equation can be rewritten so that $F_{0,T} = S_0 (1 + RFR)^T$. In the preceding example, the market-clearing (i.e., no net initial cost) contract price for a WYZ stock forward agreement should be $F_{0,0.5} = (53)(1 + 0.0625)^{0.5} = \$54.63$. Finally, when dividends are paid, the equation for the put-call-forward parity condition can be inserted into the dividend-adjusted spot parity condition to produce

$$\left\{ S_0 - \frac{D_T}{(1 + RFR)^T} \right\} = \frac{F_{0,T}}{(1 + RFR)^T}$$

Thus, if a $1 dividend were paid on WYZ stock just prior to the maturity of the contract in six months, the forward price would be adjusted down to $F_{0,0.5} = (53)(1 + 0.0625)^{0.5} − 1 = \$53.63$ to account for the payment to the actual shareholders but not the derivative holder.

. . . .

20.4 An Introduction to the Use of Derivatives in Portfolio Management

Beyond the unique risk–reward profiles they offer as standalone investments, derivatives also are used widely to restructure the fundamental nature of an existing portfolio of assets.

---

[7] This interpretation follows by noting that the long call position will be exercised when $S_T > 50$ and the short put will be exercised against the investor when $S_T \leq 50$. Therefore, the investor's net option position produces an identical result to holding a long position in a forward contract with a contract price of $50. Generalizing this result, any time we have a call and a put option on the same underlying stock with a common exercise price and expiration date, the following is true: (long call at X) + (short put at X) = (long forward at X). Similarly, shorting the call and buying the put produces a synthetic short forward position.

Typically, the intent of this restructuring is to modify the portfolio's risk. In this section, we review three prominent derivative applications in the management of equity positions: shorting forward contracts, purchasing **protective puts**, and purchasing **equity collars**.

20.4.1 Restructuring Asset Portfolios with Forward Contracts

Suppose the manager of a small corporate pension fund currently has all of her investable funds committed to a well-diversified portfolio of equity securities designed to reflect the movements of the Standard & Poor's 500 index. Implicit in this investment approach is the manager's belief that she cannot add value by trying to select superior individual securities. She does, however, feel that it is possible to take advantage of perceived trends at a macroeconomic level by switching her funds on a tactical basis between her current equity holding and any of several other portfolios mimicking different asset classes (e.g., fixed-income, cash equivalents).

The stock market has increased steadily over the past several months, and the pension fund has a present market value of $100 million. The manager has now become concerned about the possibility that inflationary pressures will dampen corporate earnings and drive stock prices down. She also feels confident that the uncertainty will be resolved in the coming quarter. Accordingly, she would like to shift her allocation from 100 percent equity to 100 percent T-bills for the next three months. There are two ways she can make this change. The most direct method would be to sell her stock portfolio and buy $100 million (less the transaction costs) of 90-day T-bills. When the T-bills mature in three months, she could then repurchase her original equity holdings.

The second approach would be to maintain her current stock holdings but convert them into a synthetic risk-free position with a three-month forward contract specifying $100 million of the stock index as the underlying asset. This is a classic example of a *hedge position,* wherein the price risk of the underlying asset is offset (rather than eliminated) by a supplementary derivative transaction. The following table captures the dynamics of this hedge at a basic level.

Economic Event	Actual Stock Exposure	Desired Forward Exposure
Stock prices fall	Loss	Gain
Stock prices rise	Gain	Loss

To neutralize the risk of falling stock prices, the fund manager will need to adopt a forward position that benefits from that potential movement. Said differently, the manager requires a hedge position with payoffs that are *negatively correlated* with those of the existing exposure. As we saw in Exhibit 20.10, this requires committing to the short side of the contract. This hedging argument is identical to the point we made in the portfolio formation analysis of Chapter 7 that it is always possible to combine two perfectly negatively correlated assets to create a risk-free position.

The primary benefit of converting the pension fund's asset allocation using this approach is that it is far quicker and more cost-effective than the physical transformations demanded by the first solution. For instance, Exhibit 20.20 shows that when all of the costs of transaction are considered (e.g., trading commissions, market impact, taxes), the average expense of actually rebalancing a U.S. equity portfolio is about 42 basis points of the position's value, while the same trade with an equity forward contract would cost just 6 basis points. Trading expenses in other countries, though different in absolute level, reflect this same general trend.

This synthetic restructuring is best understood through the effect that it has had on the systematic risk—or beta—of the portfolio. Assume that the original stock holding had a beta of one, matching the volatility of a proxy for the market portfolio. The combination of being long $100 million of stock and short a forward covering $100 million of a stock index converts the systematic portion of the portfolio into a synthetic T-bill, which by definition has a beta of zero. Once the contract matures in three months, however, the position will revert to its original risk

Exhibit 20.20 Comparative Stock and Stock Futures Trading Costs

Cost Factor	United States (S&P 500)	Japan (NIKKEI 225)	United Kingdom (FT-SE 100)	France (CAC 40)	Germany (DAX)	Hong Kong (Hang Seng)
A. Stocks						
Commissions	0.12%	0.20%	0.20%	0.25%	0.25%	0.50%
Market impact	0.30	0.70	0.70	0.50	0.50	0.50
Taxes	0.00	0.21	0.50	0.00	0.00	0.34
Total	0.42%	1.11%	1.40%	0.75%	0.75%	1.34%
B. Futures						
Commissions	0.01%	0.05%	0.02%	0.03%	0.02%	0.05%
Market impact	0.05	0.10	0.10	0.10	0.10	0.10
Taxes	0.00	0.00	0.00	0.00	0.00	0.00
Total	0.06%	0.15%	0.12%	0.13%	0.12%	0.15%

profile. This is illustrated in Exhibit 20.21. More generally, the short forward position can be designed to allow for intermediate combinations of stock and T-bills as well. To see this, let w_s be the stock allocation so that $(1 - w_s)$ is the allocation to the risk-free asset created synthetically. The net beta for the converted portfolio is simply a weighted average of the systematic risks of its equity and T-bill portions or

20.6 $$\beta_P = (w_S)\,\beta_S + (1 - w_S)\,\beta_{RFR}$$

Thus, if the manager had wished to change the original allocation from 100 percent stock to a "60–40" mix of stock and T-bills, she would have shorted only $40 million of the index forward to leave her with an unhedged equity position totaling $60 million (i.e., $w_s = 0.60$ and $(1 - w_s) = 0.40$). This in turn would leave her with an adjusted portfolio beta of $[(0.6)(1) + (0.4)(0)] = 0.6$.

20.4.2 Protecting Portfolio Value with Put Options

Although the manager's concern in the previous example was to protect her stock portfolio against possible share price declines over the next three months, by shorting the stock index forward contract, she has effectively committed to "selling" her equity position—even if stock prices rise. That is, by using a derivative with a symmetric payoff structure to hedge her risk, the manager also has surrendered the upside potential of her original holding. Suppose instead that she designed a hedge position correlated to her stock portfolio as follows:

Economic Event	Actual Stock Exposure	Desired Forward Exposure
Stock prices fall	Loss	Gain
Stock prices rise	Gain	*No loss*

In seeking an asymmetric hedge, this manager wants a derivative contract that allows her to sell stock when prices fall but keep her shares when prices rise. As we have seen, she must purchase a put option to obtain this exposure.

The purchase of a put option to hedge the downside risk of an underlying security holding is called a *protective put* position and is the most straightforward example of a more general set of derivative-based strategies known as *portfolio insurance*.[8] In lieu of the short forward position, suppose the manager purchased a three-month, at-the-money put option on her

---

[8] The concept and use of portfolio insurance has received a great deal of scrutiny in the research literature. See, for example, the studies by Rubinstein (1985), Kritzman (1986), and Basak (2002).

Exhibit 20.21 Altering the Systematic Risk of a Stock Portfolio Synthetically

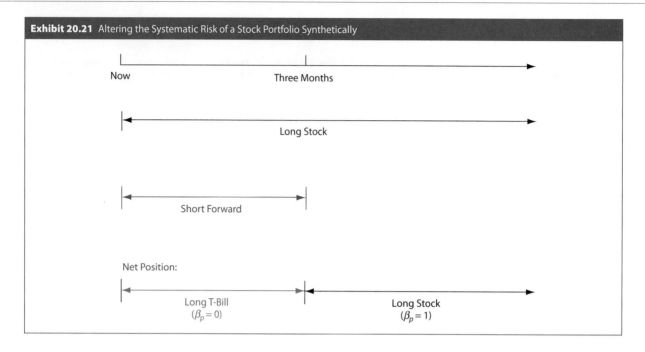

$100 million stock portfolio for an up-front premium of $1.324 million. The value of the protective put position (net of the initial cost of the hedge) is calculated in Exhibit 20.22 for several different expiration date prices for the underlying stock portfolio. In particular, notice that with the exercise price set equal to the current portfolio value of $100 million, the put contract exactly offsets any expiration date share price decline while allowing the position to increase in value as stock prices increase. Thus, the put provides the manager with insurance against falling prices with no *deductible*.[9]

The terminal value of the combined stock and put option portfolio shown in the last column of Exhibit 20.22 resembles the payoff diagram of the long call option position illustrated earlier in Exhibit 20.11. This is shown in Exhibit 20.23, which indicates that being long in the stock and long in the put generates the same net payoff as an at-the-money long call option holding "elevated" by $100 million. Given the put-call-spot parity results of the previous section, this should come as no surprise. Indeed, the no-arbitrage equation (Equation 20.1) can be rewritten:

$$S_0 + P_{0,T} = C_{0,T} + \frac{X}{(1 + RFR)^T}$$

This expression says that the protective put method of providing portfolio insurance generates the same expiration date payoff as a long position in a call option with equivalent characteristics as the put and a long position in a T-bill with a face value equal to the options' exercise price. It is this final term that provides the elevation to the call payoff diagram in Exhibit 20.23. Thus, the manager has two ways of providing price insurance for her current stock holding: (1) continue to hold her shares and purchase a put option, or (2) sell her shares and buy both a T-bill and a call option. Her choice between them will undoubtedly come down to considerations such as relative option prices and transaction costs.

---

[9] In general, the deductible portion of the portfolio insurance contract can be defined as $[S_0 - X]$. For instance, with an exercise price of only 95, the manager would not receive compensation from the hedge until the portfolio value fell below $95 million; she would effectively be self-insuring the first $5 million of losses. Naturally, the larger this deductible amount, the lower the cost of the put option.

Exhibit 20.22 Expiration Date Value of a Protective Put Position

Potential Portfolio Value	Value of Put Option	Cost of Put Option	Net Protective Put Position
60	$(100 - 60) = 40$	-1.324	$(60 + 40) - 1.324 = 98.676$
70	$(100 - 70) = 30$	-1.324	$(70 + 30) - 1.324 = 98.676$
80	$(100 - 80) = 20$	-1.324	$(80 + 20) - 1.324 = 98.676$
90	$(100 - 90) = 10$	-1.324	$(90 + 10) - 1.324 = 98.676$
100	0	-1.324	$(100 + 0) - 1.324 = 98.676$
110	0	-1.324	$(110 + 0) - 1.324 = 108.676$
120	0	-1.324	$(120 + 0) - 1.324 = 118.676$
130	0	-1.324	$(130 + 0) - 1.324 = 128.676$
140	0	-1.324	$(140 + 0) - 1.324 = 138.676$

Exhibit 20.23 Terminal Payoff to an Insured Stock Position

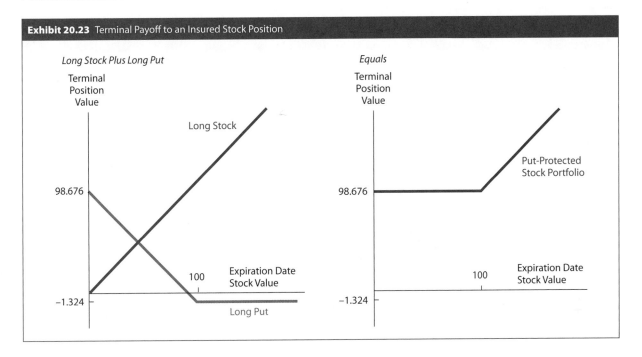

20.4.3 An Alternative Way to Pay for a Protective Put

There is a third alternative for protecting against potential stock price declines, which fits between paying nothing for a hedge but surrendering future stock gains for the next three months (i.e., the short forward position) and keeping those potential gains in exchange for a considerable initial payment (i.e., the protective put position). Specifically, suppose that the manager makes two simultaneous decisions. First, she decides to purchase a three-month, out-of-the-money protective put option with an exercise price of $97 million and a commensurately lower initial cost of $0.560 million. (Notice that in purchasing an out-of-the-money contract, the manager is creating a $3 million deductible compared to her current portfolio value.) Second, she decides not to pay cash for the put option; instead, she sells back to the option dealer a call option with a three-month expiration and an exercise price of $108 million that also carries an initial premium of $0.560 million. The simultaneous purchase of an out-of-the-money put and sale of an out-of-the-money call on the same underlying asset and with the same expiration date and market price is a strategy known as a **collar agreement**.

Exhibit 20.24 shows the expiration date outcomes of the manager's equity collar-protected portfolio for several different terminal stock portfolio values. Notice that, like the forward

Exhibit 20.24 Expiration Date Value of an Equity Collar-Protected Portfolio

Potential Portfolio Value	Net Option Expense	Value of Put Option	Value of Call Option	Net Collar-Protected Position
60	(0.56 − 0.56) = 0	(97 − 60) = 37	0	60 + 37 = 97
70	(0.56 − 0.56) = 0	(97 − 70) = 27	0	70 + 27 = 97
80	(0.56 − 0.56) = 0	(97 − 80) = 17	0	80 + 17 = 97
90	(0.56 − 0.56) = 0	(97 − 90) = 7	0	90 + 7 = 97
97	(0.56 − 0.56) = 0	0	0	97 + 0 = 97
100	(0.56 − 0.56) = 0	0	0	100 + 0 = 100
108	(0.56 − 0.56) = 0	0	0	108 − 0 = 108
110	(0.56 − 0.56) = 0	0	(108 − 110) = − 2	110 − 2 = 108
120	(0.56 − 0.56) = 0	0	(108 − 120) = −12	120 − 12 = 108
130	(0.56 − 0.56) = 0	0	(108 − 130) = −22	130 − 22 = 108
140	(0.56 − 0.56) = 0	0	(108 − 140) = −32	140 − 32 = 108

Exhibit 20.25 Expiration Date Value of a Collar-Protected Portfolio

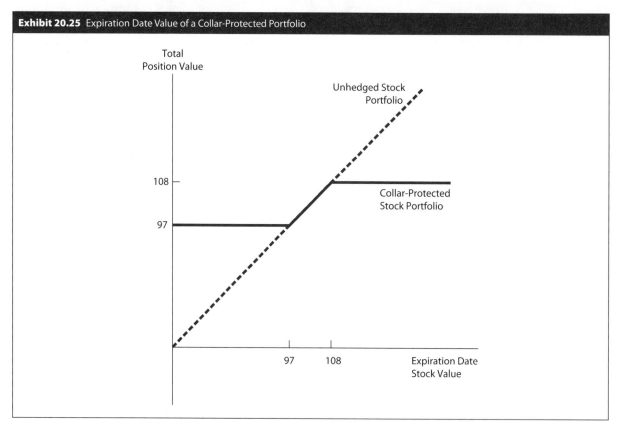

contract hedge, there is no initial out-of-pocket expense associated with this derivative combination. Instead, the manager effectively pays for her desired portfolio insurance by surrendering an equivalent amount of the portfolio's future upside potential. That is, in exchange for being "made whole" for any stock decline below $97 million, she agrees to give up any stock price appreciation beyond $108 million. Another thing to notice is that, like the protective put (and unlike the short forward position), she does retain some of the benefit of a rising stock market. However, this upside gain potential stops at the exercise price of the call option. As shown in Exhibit 20.25, the manager has placed a collar around her portfolio for the next three months—its net value will not fall below $97 million and will not rise above $108 million. At any terminal value for the stock portfolio between these extreme levels, both of the options expire out of the money and no contract settlement payment will be required of either the manager or the dealer.

• • • • SUMMARY • • • •

- As their popularity in financial markets has increased over the past few decades, derivative securities have become an indispensable part of the investment manager's toolkit. Although forward, futures, and option contracts play important roles as stand-alone investments, the real advantage of derivatives is their ability to modify the risk–return characteristics of a collection of existing securities in a cost-effective manner. This use of forwards and options to restructure a portfolio synthetically has two dimensions: (1) it is possible to combine derivatives with the underlying position to replicate the cash flows of another traded instrument, and (2) derivatives can be used with the original portfolio to create a payoff structure that is otherwise unavailable.

- Forward and option contracts can be viewed as insurance policies that an investor can hold against adverse price movements in his underlying position. The basic difference between these contracts lies in how the investor must pay for the desired insurance. Forwards, with symmetrical terminal payoffs, typically do not require any initial payment but do obligate the investor to the possibility of an unfavorable transaction at a future date. Conversely, options provide asymmetrical terminal payoffs, but the investor must pay an up-front premium.

- There are well-defined relationships that must exist in an efficient capital market between the prices of forward and option contracts. The put-call parity conditions delineate the linkages between five different securities: the underlying asset (e.g., stock), T-bills, forward contracts, call options, and put options. An important consequence of these relationships is that one of these securities is always redundant because its cash flow patterns can be replicated by the remaining instruments. This leads to another important use for derivatives: arbitrage investing. Through their ability to help create synthetic replicas of existing securities, derivatives provide investors with the possibility of riskless excess returns when the synthetic and actual instruments sell for different prices.

- There are several issues related to the use and management of derivative securities that remain to be addressed, such as how individual positions in forwards, futures, and options are valued and the adjustments that investors need to make when using derivatives on an underlying asset other than common stock. These topics will be considered in subsequent chapters. For now, though, it is important to appreciate these instruments for their ability to assist investors in repackaging the risks and cash flows of their portfolios.

• • • • SUGGESTED READINGS • • • •

Bookstaber, Richard M., and Roger G. Clarke. "Options Can Alter Portfolio Return Distributions," *Journal of Portfolio Management* 7, no. 3 (Spring 1981): 63–70.

Brown, Keith C., ed. *Derivative Strategies for Managing Portfolio Risk.* Charlottesville, VA: AIMR, 1993.

Burns, Terrence E., ed. *Derivatives in Portfolio Management.* Charlottesville, VA: AIMR, 1998.

Chance, Don M., and Rober Brooks. *An Introduction to Derivatives and Risk Management,* 7th ed. Mason, OH: Southwestern Publishing, 2007.

Moriarty, Eugene, Susan Phillips, and Paula Tosini. "A Comparison of Options and Futures in the Management of Portfolio Risk," *Financial Analysts Journal* 37, no. 1 (January–February 1981).

• • • • QUESTIONS • • • •

1. Explain why the difference between put and call prices depends on whether or not the underlying security pays a dividend during the life of the contracts.

2. When comparing futures and forward contracts, it has been said that futures are more liquid but forwards are more flexible. Explain what this statement means and comment on how differences in contract liquidity and design flexibility might influence an investor's preference in choosing one instrument over the other.

3. Compare and contrast the gain and loss potential for investors holding the following positions: long forward, short forward, long call, short call, long put, and short put. Indicate what the terms *symmetric* and *asymmetric* mean in this context.

4. **CFA EXAMINATION LEVEL III** The Franklin Medical Research Foundation is to be established with a gift from Mr. John Franklin in memory of his deceased wife. The foundation's grant-making and investment policy issues have been finalized. Receipt of the expected $45 million Franklin cash gift will not

occur for 90 days, yet the committee believes current stock and bond prices are unusually attractive and wishes to take advantage of this perceived opportunity.

   a. Briefly describe two strategies that utilize derivative financial instruments and could be implemented to take advantage of the committee's market expectations.

   b. Evaluate whether or not it is appropriate for the foundation to undertake a derivatives-based hedge to bridge the expected 90-day time gap, considering both positive and negative factors.

 5. **CFA EXAMINATION LEVEL II** Robert Chen, CFA, is reviewing the characteristics of derivative securities and their use in portfolios. Chen is considering the addition of either a short position in stock index futures or a long position in stock index options to an existing well-diversified portfolio of equity securities. Contrast the way in which each of these two alternatives would affect the risk and return of the resulting combined portfolios.

6. Explain how call and put options can represent a leveraged way of investing in the stock market and also enable investors to hedge their risk completely. Specifically, under what circumstances will the addition of an option increase the risk of an existing portfolio and under what circumstances will it decrease portfolio risk?

7. It has been said that, from an investor's perspective, a long position in a call option represents the "good half" of a long position in a forward contract. Explain what is meant by this statement. Also, describe what the "bad half" of the long forward position would have to be for this statement to be true.

8. Discuss the difficulties that having options in a security portfolio create for the measurement of portfolio risk. Specifically, explain why standard deviation is a deficient statistic for capturing the essence of risk in a put-protected portfolio. How could the standard deviation statistic be modified to account for this concern?

9. If the current price of a non-dividend-paying stock is $32 and a one-year futures contract on that stock has a contract price of $35, explain how an investor could create an "off-market" long position in a forward contract at an exercise price of $25. Would this synthetic contract require a cash payment from either the long or short position? If so, explain which party would have to make the payment and how that payment should be calculated.

• • • • PROBLEMS • • • •

1. The common stock of Sophia Enterprises serves as the underlying asset for the following derivative securities: (1) forward contracts, (2) European-style call options, and (3) European-style put options.

   a. Assuming that all Sophia derivatives expire at the same date in the future, complete a table similar to the following for each of the following contract positions:

     (1) A long position in a forward with a contract price of $50

     (2) A long position in a call option with an exercise price of $50 and a front-end premium expense of $5.20

Expiration Date Sophia Stock Price	Expiration Date Derivative Payoff	Initial Derivative Premium	Net Profit
25			
30			
35			
40			
45			
50			
55			
60			
65			
70			
75			

(3) A short position in a call option with an exercise price of $50 and a front-end premium receipt of $5.20

In calculating net profit, ignore the time differential between the initial derivative expense or receipt and the terminal payoff.

b. Graph the net profit for each of the three derivative positions, using net profit on the vertical axis and Sophia's expiration date stock price on the horizontal axis. Label the breakeven (i.e., zero profit) point(s) on each graph.

c. Briefly describe the belief about the expiration date price of Sophia stock that an investor using each of these three positions implicitly holds.

2. Refer once again to the derivative securities using Sophia common stock as an underyling asset discussed in Problem 1.

a. Assuming that all Sophia derivatives expire at the same date in the future, complete a table similar to the following for each of the following contract positions:

(1) A short position in a forward with a contract price of $50

(2) A long position in a put option with an exercise price of $50 and a front-end premium expense of $3.23

(3) A short position in a put option with an exercise price of $50 and a front-end premium receipt of $3.23

Expiration Date Sophia Stock Price	Expiration Date Derivative Payoff	Initial Derivative Premium	Net Profit
25			
30			
35			
40			
45			
50			
55			
60			
65			
70			
75			

In calculating net profit, ignore the time differential between the initial derivative expense or receipt and the terminal payoff.

b. Graph the net profit for each of the three derivative positions, using net profit on the vertical axis and Sophia's expiration date stock price on the horizontal axis. Label the breakeven (i.e., zero profit) point(s) on each graph.

c. Briefly describe the belief about the expiration date price of Sophia stock that an investor using each of these three positions implicitly holds.

3. Suppose that an investor holds a share of Sophia common stock, currently valued at $50. She is concerned that over the next few months the value of her holding might decline and she would like to hedge that risk by supplementing her holding with one of three different derivative positions, all of which expire at the same point in the future:

(1) A short position in a forward with a contract price of $50

(2) A long position in a put option with an exercise price of $50 and a front-end premium expense of $3.23

(3) A short position in a call option with an exercise price of $50 and a front-end premium receipt of $5.20

a. Using a table similar to the following, calculate the expiration date value of the investor's combined (i.e., stock and derivative) position. In calculating net portfolio value, ignore the time differential between the initial derivative expense or receipt and the terminal payoff.

b. For each of the three hedge portfolios, graph the expiration date value of her combined position on the vertical axis, with potential expiration date share prices of Sophia stock on the horizontal axis.

c. Assuming that the options are priced fairly, use the concept of put-call parity to calculate the zero-value contract price (i.e., $F_{0,T}$) for a forward agreement on Sophia stock. Explain why this value differs from the $50 contract price used in Part a and Part b.

Expiration Date Sophia Stock Price	Expiration Date Derivative Payoff	Initial Derivative Premium	Combined Terminal Position Value
25	_____	_____	_____
30	_____	_____	_____
35	_____	_____	_____
40	_____	_____	_____
45	_____	_____	_____
50	_____	_____	_____
55	_____	_____	_____
60	_____	_____	_____
65	_____	_____	_____
70	_____	_____	_____
75	_____	_____	_____

4. You strongly believe that the price of Breener Inc. stock will rise substantially from its current level of $137, and you are considering buying shares in the company. You currently have $13,700 to invest. As an alternative to purchasing the stock itself, you are also considering buying call options on Breener stock that expire in three months and have an exercise price of $140. These call options cost $10 each.

    a. Compare and contrast the size of the potential payoff and the risk involved in each of these alternatives.

    b. Calculate the three-month rate of return on both strategies assuming that at the option expiration date Breener's stock price has (1) increased to $155 or (2) decreased to $135.

    c. At what stock price level will the person who sells you the Breener call option break even? Can you determine the maximum loss that the call option seller may suffer, assuming that he does not already own Breener stock?

5. The common stock of Company XYZ is currently trading at a price of $42. Both a put and a call option are available for XYZ stock, each having an exercise price of $40 and an expiration date in exactly six months. The current market prices for the put and call are $1.45 and $3.90, respectively. The risk-free holding period return for the next six months is 4 percent, which corresponds to an 8 percent annual rate.

    a. For each possible stock price in the following sequence, calculate the expiration date payoffs (net of the initial purchase price) for the following positions: (1) buy one XYZ call option, and (2) short one XYZ call option:

    20, 25, 30, 35, 40, 45, 50, 55, 60

    Draw a graph of these payoff relationships, using net profit on the vertical axis and potential expiration date stock price on the horizontal axis. Be sure to specify the prices at which these respective positions will break even (i.e., produce a net profit of zero).

    b. Using the same potential stock prices as in Part a, calculate the expiration date payoffs and profits (net of the initial purchase price) for the following positions: (1) buy one XYZ put option, and (2) short one XYZ put option. Draw a graph of these relationships, labeling the prices at which these investments will break even.

    c. Determine whether the $2.45 difference in the market prices between the call and put options is consistent with the put-call parity relationship for European-style contracts.

6. Consider Commodity Z, which has both exchange-traded futures and option contracts associated with it. As you look in today's paper, you find the following put and call prices for options that expire exactly six months from now:

Exercise Price	Put Price	Call Price
40	$0.59	$8.73
45	1.93	—
50	—	2.47

    a. Assuming that the futures price of a six-month contract on Commodity Z is $48, what must be the price of a put with an exercise price of $50 in order to avoid arbitrage across markets? Similarly, calculate the "no arbitrage" price of a call with an exercise price of $45. In both calculations, assume that the yield curve is flat and the annual risk-free rate is 6 percent.

    b. What is the "no arbitrage" price differential that should exist between the put and call options having an exercise price of $40? Is this differential satisfied by current market prices? If not, demonstrate an arbitrage trade to take advantage of the mispricing.

7. **CFA EXAMINATION LEVEL III** Industrial Products Corp. (IPC), a publicly held company, is considering going private. It is extremely important to IPC's management that the pension fund's present surplus level be preserved pending completion of buyout financing. For the next three months (until September 1, 1990), management's goal is to sustain no loss of value in the pension fund portfolio. Today (June 1, 1990), this value is $300 million. Of this total, $150 million is invested in equities in the form of an S&P 500 Index fund, producing an annual dividend yield of 4 percent; the balance is invested in a single U.S. government bond issue, having a coupon of 8 percent and a maturity of 6/01/2005. Since the "no-loss strategy" has only a three-month time horizon, management does not wish to sell any of the present security holdings.

   Assume that sufficient cash is available to satisfy margin requirements, transaction costs, and so on, and that the following market conditions exist as of June 1, 1990:
   - The S&P 500 Index is at the 350 level, with a yield of 4.0 percent.
   - The U.S. government 8.0 percent bonds due 6/1/2005 are selling at 100.
   - U.S. Treasury bills due on 9/1/90 are priced to yield 1.5 percent for the three-month period (i.e., 6 percent annually).

   Available investment instruments are the following:

Contract	Expiration	Current Contract Price	Strike Price	Contract Size
S&P 500 Index future	9/1/90	$355.00	—	$175,000
Future on U.S. government 8% bonds due 6/1/2005	9/1/90	101.00	—	100,000
S&P 500 call option	9/1/90	8.00	350	35,000
S&P 500 put option	9/1/90	7.00	350	35,000
U.S. government 8% due 6/1/2005 call option	9/1/90	2.50	100	100,000
U.S. government 8% due 6/1/2005 put option	9/1/90	4.50	100	100,000

   a. Assume that the management wishes to protect the portfolio against any losses (ignoring the costs of purchasing options or futures contracts) but wishes also to participate in any stock or bond market advances over the next three months. Using the preceding instruments, design two strategies to accomplish this goal, and calculate the number of contracts needed to implement each strategy.
   b. Using the put-call parity relationship and the fair value formula for futures (both follow), recommend which one of the two strategies designed in Part a should be implemented. Justify your choice.

   > Put Price = Call Price Minus Security Price Plus Present Value of (Exercise Price Plus Income on the Underlying Security)
   >
   > Futures Price = Underlying Security Price Plus (Treasury Bill Income Minus Income on the Underlying Security)

8. As an option trader, you are constantly looking for opportunities to make an arbitrage transaction (i.e., a trade in which you do not need to commit your own capital or take any risk but can still make a profit). Suppose you observe the following prices for options on DRKC Co. stock: $3.18 for a call with an exercise price of $60, and $3.38 for a put with an exercise price of $60. Both options expire in exactly six months, and the price of a six-month T-bill is $97.00 (for face value of $100).
   a. Using the put-call-spot parity condition, demonstrate graphically how you could synthetically recreate the payoff structure of a share of DRKC stock in six months using a combination of puts, calls, and T-bills transacted today.
   b. Given the current market prices for the two options and the T-bill, calculate the no-arbitrage price of a share of DRKC stock.
   c. If the actual market price of DRKC stock is $60, demonstrate the arbitrage transaction you could create to take advantage of the discrepancy. Be specific as to the positions you would need to take in each security and the dollar amount of your profit.

9. You are currently managing a stock portfolio worth $55 million and you are concerned that, over the next four months, equity values will be flat and may even fall. Consequently, you are considering two different strategies for hedging against possible stock declines: (1) buying a protective put, and (2) selling a *covered call* (i.e., selling a call option based on the same underlying stock position you

hold). An over-the-counter derivatives dealer has expressed interest in your business and has quoted the following bid and offer prices (in millions) for at-the-money call and put options that expire in four months and match the characteristics of your portfolio:

	Bid	Ask
Call	$2.553	$2.573
Put	1.297	1.317

a. For each of the following expiration date values for the unhedged equity position, calculate the terminal values (net of initial expense) for a protective put strategy.

$$35, 40, 45, 50, 55, 60, 65, 70, 75$$

b. Draw a graph of the protective put net profit structure in Part a and demonstrate how this position could have been constructed by using call options and T-bills, assuming a risk-free rate of 7 percent.

c. For each of these same expiration date stock values, calculate the terminal net profit values for a covered call strategy.

d. Draw a graph of the covered call net profit structure in Part c and demonstrate how this position could have been constructed by using put options and T-bills, again assuming a risk-free rate of 7 percent.

10. **CFA EXAMINATION LEVEL III** A stock currently sells for $77.50. Call options on the stock have an exercise price of $75 and sell for $7.75, and put options have an exercise price of $75 and sell for $4. These options will expire in three months. The three-month U.S. Treasury bill annualized yield is 5 percent. There are no transaction costs and no restrictions against using the proceeds from the short sale of any security.

a. A synthetic Treasury bill can be constructed by investing in a combination of the securities identified.
   (1) Identify the three transactions needed to construct a synthetic Treasury bill.
   (2) Calculate the synthetic Treasury bill's annualized yield.

b. An arbitrage strategy can be constructed with 75 actual and 100 synthetic Treasury bills, producing a face amount of $750,000.
   (1) State the arbitrage strategy.
   (2) Calculate the immediate incoming net cash flow.

c. Determine the net cash flow of the arbitrage strategy at the six-month expiration date if the stock price at expiration is $80. (Ignore any cash flows stemming from the original arbitrage profit.)

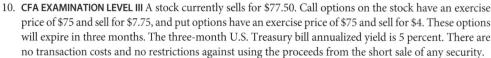

THOMSON ONE Business School Edition

1. The *put/call ratio* calculates the trading volume of put contracts outstanding for a particular stock or stock index divided by trading volume for the total number of outstanding call options. The ratio is sometimes viewed as an investor sentiment indicator: When the ratio is relatively high, investors are bearish about market conditions; when the ratio is relatively low, investors are bullish.

a. Under the "Indices" tab, download monthly data over the most recent five years for the level of the Eurex Index Option Put Call Ratio (EUXDIPC).

b. Calculate the average value for this ratio for: (i) the full five-year period; and (ii) each of the past five one-year periods. Explain what you think the trend this ratio has exhibited over time implies about investor expectations for the European stock market.

c. Download monthly price data over the most recent five years for the Dow Jones Euro Stoxx 50 index (DJEURST), Europe's leading indicator of blue-chip companies. Use these price data to calculate monthly returns (i.e., price changes without dividends) for the five-year period. (Note: You will lose one month from the sample period when you convert prices to returns.)

d. Calculate the correlation coefficient between two series: the EUXDIPC ratio and the DJEURST for the same month (i.e., both from month *t* for a given pair of observations).

e. Repeat your calculation of the correlation coefficient with the following adjustment: use the EUXDIPC ratio *lagged by one month* (month *t*-1) paired with the DJEURST from month *t* (i.e., you observe the put/call ratio one month before you observe the DJ Euro stock index return). You will lose another observation when you lag the put/call ratio data series.

f. Interpret the correlation coefficients that you have calculated in Parts d and e and explain whether either of them support the view of the put/call ratio as an effective indicator of market sentiment.

CHAPTER 21
Forward and Futures Contracts

After you read this chapter, you should be able to answer the following questions:

- What are the differences in the way forward and futures contracts are structured and traded?
- How are the margin accounts on a futures contract adjusted for daily changes in market conditions?
- How can an investor use forward and futures contracts to hedge an existing risk exposure?
- What is a hedge ratio and how should it be calculated?
- What economic functions do the forward and futures markets serve?
- How are forward and futures contracts valued after origination?
- What is the relationship between futures contract prices and the current and expected spot price for the underlying commodity or security?
- How can an investor use forward and futures contracts to speculate on a particular view about changing market conditions?
- How can forward and futures contracts be designed to hedge interest rate risk?
- What is stock index arbitrage and how is it related to program trading?
- How can forward and futures contracts be designed to hedge foreign exchange rate risk?
- What is interest rate parity and how would you construct a covered interest arbitrage transaction?

As we saw in Chapter 20, forward and futures contracts are the most straightforward form of *derivative instrument* because they allow an investor to lock in the purchase or sales price of a transaction that will not be completed until a later date. In this chapter we continue our discussion of these contracts along several lines. First, we take a closer look at the contract terms and trading mechanics of forwards and futures. We examine important differences that exist between the two markets and describe the process by which futures contracts are **marked to market** on a daily basis. Further, we discuss how these contracts are used to hedge the price risk inherent in an existing or anticipated position and how **hedge ratios** are computed.

Second, we consider how forward and futures contracts are priced in an efficient capital market. Given that these instruments are not really securities in the same sense that stocks and bonds are, the notion of traditional security valuation is not quite appropriate. Instead, valuation involves specifying the proper relationship between the forward contract price and the spot price for the underlying position. We develop the "no arbitrage" result that the forward contract price should be equal to the spot price plus the cumulative costs of transporting the underlying security or commodity from the present to the future delivery date. These carrying costs can be either positive or negative; therefore, the correct forward contract price can be either higher or lower than the spot price.

Finally, we demonstrate several applications for using forward and futures contracts. We concentrate on a class of contracts—*financial forwards and futures*—that are particularly useful to investors. The underlying securities in financial futures include stock indexes, Treasury bonds, bank deposits, and foreign currencies. The use of these financial futures will be illustrated in a series of examples demonstrating the connections between cash and futures markets.

21.1 An Overview of Forward and Futures Trading

Forward contracts are agreements negotiated directly between two parties in the OTC (i.e., nonexchange-traded) markets. A typical participant in a forward contract is a commercial or investment bank that, serving the role of the market maker, is contacted directly by the customer. Forward contracts are individually designed agreements and can be tailored to the specific needs of the ultimate end user. Futures contracting, on the other hand, is somewhat more complicated. An investor wishing either to buy or to sell in the futures market gives his order to a broker (a *futures commission merchant*), who then passes it to a trader on the floor of an exchange (the *trading pit*) or through an electronic trading network. After a trade has been agreed on, details of the deal are passed to the **exchange clearinghouse**, which catalogs the transaction. The ultimate end users in a futures contract never deal with each other directly, but transact with the clearinghouse, which is also responsible for overseeing the delivery process, settling daily gains and losses, and guaranteeing the overall transaction. Exhibit 21.1 highlights the differences in how these contracts are created.[1]

As an example, consider the traditional agricultural commodity futures that have been traded for more than 150 years beginning with the creation of the Chicago Board of Trade (CBT), the world's oldest and largest derivatives exchange. Futures contracts based on a wide array of commodities and securities have been created and now trade on almost 100 exchanges worldwide. Exhibit 21.2 lists the leading futures exchanges in the United States and the world, ranked by trading volume. Notice that two of the top four and three of the top nine exchanges in the world are located in the United States. Additionally, Exhibit 21.3 shows price and trade activity data for a representative sample of commodity futures contracts; financial futures will be described in detail later in the chapter. Each of these commodity contracts is standardized

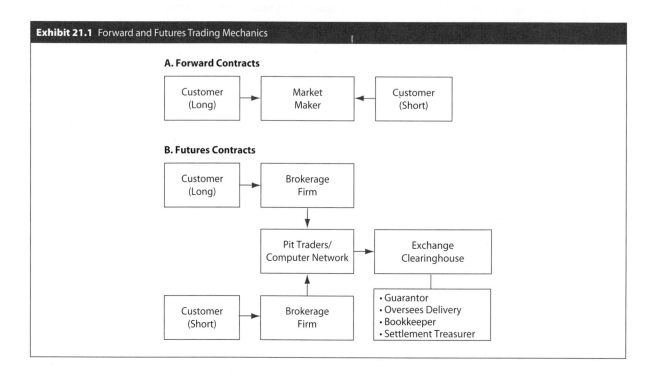

Exhibit 21.1 Forward and Futures Trading Mechanics

A. Forward Contracts

Customer (Long) → Market Maker ← Customer (Short)

B. Futures Contracts

Customer (Long) → Brokerage Firm

Pit Traders/ Computer Network → Exchange Clearinghouse

Customer (Short) → Brokerage Firm

- Guarantor
- Oversees Delivery
- Bookkeeper
- Settlement Treasurer

---

[1] For a more detailed discussion of the historical futures trading process, see Clarke (1992); some of this discussion is based on his book.

Exhibit 21.2 Leading Futures Exchanges Ranked by Relative Trading Volume

A. U.S. Futures Exchanges (2007 Data)

Exchange Name & Abbreviation	Trading Volume
CME Group: Chicago Mercantile (CME)	1,775.4
CME Group: Chicago Board of Trade (CBT)	1,029.6
New York Mercantile Exchange (NYM)	353.4
ICE Futures U.S. (ICE)	53.8

B. International Futures Exchanges & Groups (2007 Data)

Exchange & Country	Trading Volume
Korea Exchange, Korea	2,709.1
EUREX, Germany & Switzerland	1,899.9
LIFFE, Belgium, France, Netherlands, UK, Portugal	949.0
BM&F, Brazil	426.4
National Stock Exchange, India	379.9
Bolsa de Valores, Brazil	367.7
JSE, South Africa	329.6
Mexican Derivatives Exchange, Mexico	229.0
Dalian Commodity Exchange, China	185.6
OMX Nordic Exchange, Denmark, Finland, Norway	142.5
ICE Futures Europe	138.5

Source: Futures Industry Association. Reprinted with permission.

in terms of the amount and type of the commodity involved and the available dates on which it can be delivered. As we will see, this standardization can lead to an important source of risk that may not exist in forward contracts.

21.1.1 Futures Contract Mechanics

To interpret the display in Exhibit 21.3, consider the gold futures contract traded on the Commodity Exchange (CMX), a division of the New York Mercantile Exchange (NYM), on October 5, 2007. Each contract calls for the long position to buy, and the short position to sell, 100 troy ounces of gold in the appointed months. With commodity futures, it usually is the case that delivery can take place any time during the month at the discretion of the short position. Contracts are available with settlement dates every other month for the next five years, although only contracts for the next year are shown. An investor committing on this particular date to a long position in the February 2008 contract is obligated to buy 100 ounces of gold four months later for the contract price of $750.10 per ounce. Open interest—the total number of outstanding contracts—was 27,330 for this expiration date.[2]

Another important difference between forward and futures contracts is how the two types of agreements account for the possibility that a counterparty will fail to honor its obligation. Forward contracts may not require either counterparty to post collateral, in which case each is exposed to the potential default of the other during the entire life of the contract. In contrast, the futures exchange requires each customer to post an *initial* **margin account** in the form of cash or government securities when the contract is originated. (The futures exchange, as a well-capitalized corporation, does not post collateral to protect customers from its potential default.) This margin account is then adjusted, or marked to market, at the end of each trading

---

[2] New contracts are created when a new customer comes to the exchange at a time when no existing contract holder wishes to liquidate his position. On the other hand, if an existing customer wants to close out her short position and there is not a new customer to take her place, the contract price will be raised until an existing long position is enticed to sell back his agreement, thereby canceling the contract and reducing open interest by one.

Exhibit 21.3 Commodity Futures Quotations

Metal & Petroleum Futures

	Open	High hi lo	Low	Settle	Chg	Open Interest
Copper-High(CMX)- 25,000 lbs.; cents per lb						
Oct	374.00	374.00	368.90	**371.50**	−3.45	1,040
Dec	374.90	375.85	370.20	**373.80**	−2.55	60,743
Gold (CMX)-100 troy oz.; $ per troy oz.						
Oct	725.10	736.80	724.30	**737.80**	8.50	613
Dec	734.80	744.70	726.30	**743.80**	8.10	294,720
Feb'08	740.80	750.60	733.30	**750.10**	8.10	27,330
April	747.20	756.10	738.50	**756.00**	8.20	22,289
June	752.40	761.00	746.50	**761.90**	8.30	19,309
Aug	758.00	758.20	755.70	**767.60**	8.40	17,481
Platinum(NYM)-50 troy oz.; $ per troy oz.						
Oct	1379.50	1379.90	1376.00	**1377.40**	13.50	216
Jan'08	1366.80	1380.00	1352.50	**1378.40**	9.50	14,280
Silver (CMX)-5,000 troy oz.; cnts per troy oz.						
Oct	1321.0	1339.5	1320.5	**1338.9**	4.0	16
Dec	1343.0	1353.0	1315.0	**1350.0**	3.0	77,533
Crude Oil, Light Sweet(NYM)-1,000 bbls.; $ per bbl.						
Nov	79.68	81.75	78.91	**81.44**	1.50	312,071
Dec	78.70	80.91	78.10	**80.64**	1.62	252,757
Jan'08	77.83	80.09	77.36	**79.83**	1.73	96,096
Dec	73.83	76.00	73.56	**75.65**	1.75	155,503
Dec'09	71.80	73.80	71.80	**73.65**	1.71	58,563
Dec'10	71.73	72.70	71.73	**72.76**	1.71	56,242
Heating Oil No. 2 (NYM) -42,000 gal.; $ per gal.						
Nov	2.1690	2.2425	2.1552	**2.2313**	.0526	83,940
Dec	2.1875	2.2570	2.1746	**2.2463**	.0501	56,073
Gasoline-NY RBOB (NYM)- 42,000 gal.; $ per gal.						
Nov	1.9945	2.0599	1.9825	**2.0522**	.0563	87,318
Dec	1.9915	2.0624	1.9825	**2.0572**	.0548	31,525
Natural Gas (NYM) -10,000 MMBtu.; $ per MMBtu.						
Nov	7.240	7.431	7.150	**7.412**	.135	124,442
Dec	7.880	8.046	7.800	**8.027**	.112	59,870
Jan'08	8.220	8.370	8.160	**8.355**	.100	59,642
March	8.074	8.207	8.016	**8.193**	.096	43,977
April	7.690	7.785	7.655	**7.773**	.076	37,784
Oct	8.003	8.090	8.000	**8.075**	.061	34,866

Agriculture Future

	Open	High hi lo	Low	Settle	Chg	Open Interest
Corn (CBT)-5,000 bu.; cents per bu.						
Dec	346.00	349.75	341.00	**342.25**	−2.25	599,600
March'08	362.00	366.25	357.50	**359.00**	−2.00	170,597
Ethanol (CBT)-29,000 gal.; $ per gal.						
Nov	...	...	...	**1.572**	.002	71
July'08	1.610	1.610	1.610	**1.600**	.020	79
Oats (CBT)-5,000 bu.; cents per bu.						
Dec	278.50	282.00	274.25	**274.25**	−5.25	11,473
March'08	290.00	292.00	285.50	**285.50**	−4.00	2,221
Soybeans (CBT)-5,000 bu.; cents per bu.						
Nov	951.25	958.50	946.00	**954.25**	3.25	262.008
Jan'08	969.00	976.25	963.75	**972.25**	2.75	112,710
Soybean Meal (CBT)-100 tons.; $ per tons.						
Oct	265.20	266.20	263.90	**265.70**	−.40	4,918
Dec	272.20	273.50	269.90	**270.80**	−1.00	103,392
Soybean Oil (CBT)-60,000 lbs.; cents per lb.						
Oct	38.08	38.60	38.06	**38.55**	.44	5,066
Dec	38.70	39.29	38.53	**39.18**	.48	152,299
Rough Rice (CBT)-2,000 cwt.; cents per cwt.						
Nov	1163.50	1178.00	1160.00	**1167.00**	4.00	10,518
Jan'08	1198.50	1208.00	1193.00	**1200.00**	4.00	3,612

	Open	High hi lo	Low	Settle	Chg	Open Interest
Coffee (ICE-US)-37,500 lbs.; cents per lb.						
Dec	135.85	137.40	134.10	**135.20**	−.65	106,550
March'08	139.00	140.90	137.80	**138.80**	−.70	31,576
Sugar-World (ICE-US)-112,000 lbs.; cents per lb.						
March	9.81	9.94	9.77	**9.79**	−.05	386,938
May	9.87	9.97	9.83	**9.84**	−.04	63,204
Sugar-Domestic (ICE-US)-112,000 lbs.; cens per lb.						
Nov	...	...	...	**21.20**	.05	363
Jan'08	...	...	...	**20.65**	−.10	3,863
Cotton (ICE-US)-50,000 lbs.; cents per lb.						
Oct	...	...	...	**60.49**	.06	27
Dec	63.43	63.96	63.15	**63.49**	.06	142,819
Orange Juice (ICE-US)-15,000 lbs.; cents per lb.						
Nov	133.60	139.20	133.60	**137.15**	2.85	12,496
Jan'08	135.00	139.95	134.35	**137.25**	3.10	10,004
Wheat (CBT)-5,000 bu.; cents per bu.						
Dec	939.00	948.00	904.00	**906.00**	−21.00	233,311
July'08	670.00	687.00	663.25	**679.00**	6.50	62,181
Wheat (KC)-5,000 bu.; cents per bu.						
Dec	928.75	944.00	905.75	**910.00**	−17.00	93,845
March'08	934.50	941.50	907.00	**911.00**	−12.00	21,515
Wheat (MPLS)-5,000 bu.; cents per bu.						
Dec	908.75	935.75	899.75	**903.50**	−5.75	41,690
March'08	910.00	925.00	897.00	**901.00**	−1.00	19,690
Cattle-Feeder (CME)-50,000 lbs.; cents per lb.						
Oct	114.750	115.075	114.450	**115.000**	.100	5,215
Dec	114.500	115.200	114.250	**115.050**	.350	11,687
Cattle-Live (CME)-40,000 lbs.; cents per lb.						
Oct	95.050	95.450	94.775	**95.350**	.250	24,662
Dec	97.400	98.000	96.900	**97.850**	.450	122,087
Hogs-Lean (CME)-40,000 lbs.; cents per lb.						
Oct	58.750	59.000	57.800	**58.650**	−.025	13,584
Dec	60.550	61.025	59.550	**60.075**	−.525	95,916
Pork Bellies (CME)-40,000 lbs.; cents per lb.						
Feb	87.000	87.500	86.250	**87.325**	−.575	1,039
May	89.350	89.350	89.150	**89.150**	−.750	76
Lumber (CME)-110,000 bd. ft., $ per 1,000 bd. ft.						
Nov	243.10	246.50	240.60	**242.50**	−.90	5,003
Jan'08	265.20	268.20	262.10	**262.20**	−3.20	4,164
Milk (CME)-200,000 lbs.; cents per lb.						
Sept	20.17	20.17	20.11	**20.14**	.02	4,805
Oct	18.39	18.57	18.26	**18.56**	.06	4,100
Cocoa (ICE-US)-10 metric tons; $ per ton.						
Dec	1,881	1,904	1,866	**1,875**	−1	64,217
March'08	1,880	1,897	1,866	**1,877**	2	34,298

day according to that day's price movements. All outstanding positions are adjusted to the **settlement price**, which is set by the exchange after trading ends to reflect the midpoint of the closing price range.

The marked-to-market process effectively credits or debits each customer's margin account for daily trading gains or losses as if the customer had closed out her position, even though the contract remains open. For example, Exhibit 21.3 indicates that the settlement price of the February 2008 gold contract increased by $8.10 per ounce from the previous trading day. This price increase benefits the holder of a long position by $810 (= 8.10 per ounce × 100 ounces). Specifically, if she had entered into the contract yesterday, she would have a commitment to buy gold for $742.00, which she could now sell for $750.10. Accordingly, her margin account will be increased by $810. Conversely, any party who is short February gold futures will have his margin account reduced by $810 per contract. To ensure that the exchange always has enough protection, collateral accounts are not allowed to fall below a predetermined *maintenance level*, typically about 75 percent of the initial level. If this $810 adjustment reduced the short position's account beneath the maintenance margin, he would receive a **margin call** and be required to restore the account to its full initial level or face involuntary liquidation.

21.1.2 Comparing Forward and Futures Contracts

To summarize, the main trade-off between forward and futures contracts is *design flexibility* versus *credit and liquidity risks*, as highlighted by the following comparison.

	Futures	Forwards
Design flexibility:	Standardized	Can be customized
Credit risk:	Clearinghouse risk	Counterparty risk
Liquidity risk:	Depends on trading	Negotiated exit

These differences represent extremes; some forward contracts, particularly in foreign exchange, are quite standard and liquid while some futures contracts now allow for greater flexibility in the terms of the agreement. Also, forwards require less managerial oversight and intervention—especially on a daily basis—because of the lump-sum settlement at delivery (i.e., no margin accounts or marked-to-market settlement), a feature that is often important to unsophisticated or infrequent users of these products.

21.2 Hedging with Forwards and Futures

21.2.1 Hedging and the Basis

The goal of a *hedge* transaction is to create a position that, once added to an investor's portfolio, will offset the price risk of another, more fundamental holding. The word "offset" is used here rather than "eliminate" because the hedge transaction attempts to neutralize an exposure that remains on the balance sheet. In Chapter 20, we expressed this concept with the following chart, which assumes that the underlying exposure results from a long commodity position:

Economic Event	Actual Commodity Exposure	Desired Hedge Exposure
Commodity prices fall	Loss	Gain
Commodity prices rise	Gain	Loss

In this case, a short position in a forward contract based on the same commodity would provide the desired negative price correlation. By virtue of holding a short forward position against the long position in the commodity, the investor has entered into a **short hedge**. A **long hedge** is created by supplementing a short commodity holding with a long forward position.

The basic premise behind any hedge is that as the price of the underlying commodity changes, so too will the price of a forward contract based on that commodity. The hope of the hedger is that the spot and forward prices change in a predictable way relative to one another. For instance, the short hedger in the preceding example is hoping that if commodity prices fall and reduce the value of her underlying asset, the forward contract price also will fall by the same amount to create an offsetting gain on the derivative. Thus, a critical feature that affects the quality of a hedge transaction is how spot and forward prices change over time.

Defining the Basis To understand better the relationship between spot and forward price movements, it is useful to develop the concept of the **basis**. At any Date t, the basis is the spot price minus the forward price for a contract maturing at Date T:

21.1
$$B_{t,T} = S_t - F_{t,T}$$

where:

> S_t = the Date t spot price
> $F_{t,T}$ = the Date t forward price for a contract maturing at Date T

Potentially, a different level of the basis may exist on each trading Date t. Two facts always are true, however. First, the *initial basis* at Date 0 ($B_{0,T}$) always will be known since both the current spot and forward contract prices can be observed. Second, the *maturity basis* at Date T ($B_{T,T}$) always is zero whenever the commodity underlying the forward contract matches the asset held exactly. For this to occur, the forward price must *converge* to the spot price as the contract expires ($F_{T,T} = S_T$).

Consider again the investor who hedged her long position in a commodity by agreeing to sell it at Date T through a short position in a forward contract. The value of the combined position is ($F_{0,T} - S_0$). If the investor decides to liquidate her entire position (including the hedge) prior to maturity, she will have to (1) sell her commodity position on the open market for S_t, and (2) buy back her short forward position for the new contract price of $F_{t,T}$.[3] The profit from the short hedge liquidated at Date t is

21.2
$$B_{t,T} - B_{0,T} = (S_t - F_{t,T}) - (S_0 - F_{0,T})$$

The term $B_{t,T}$ often is called the *cover basis* because that is when the forward contract is closed out, or covered.

21.2.2 Understanding Basis Risk

Equation 21.2 highlights an important fact about hedging. Once the hedge position is formed, the investor no longer is exposed to the absolute price movement of the underlying asset alone. Instead, she is exposed to **basis risk** because the terminal value of her combined position is defined as the cover basis minus the initial basis. Notice that only the cover basis is unknown at Date 0, and so her real exposure is to the **correlation** between subsequent changes in the spot and forward contract prices. If these movements are highly correlated, the basis risk will be quite small. In fact, it is usually possible to design a forward contract that reduces basis risk to zero, since $F_{T,T} = S_T$. However, basis risk is a possibility when contract terms are standardized and is most likely to occur in the futures market where standardization is the norm.

To illustrate the concept of basis risk, suppose the investor wishes in October to hedge a long position of 75,000 pounds of coffee she is planning to sell in February. Exhibit 21.3 shows that coffee futures contracts do exist, but with delivery months in either December or March.

---

[3] The mechanics of liquidating a forward or futures contract prior to maturity are described in the next section.

With each contract requiring the delivery of 37,500 pounds of coffee, she decides to short two of the March contracts, specifically intending to liquidate her position a month early. Suppose that on the date she initiates her short hedge, the spot coffee price was $1.3162 per pound and the March futures contract price was $1.3880 per pound. This means that her initial basis was −7.18 cents, which she hopes will move toward zero in a smooth and predictable manner. Suppose, in fact, that when she closes out her combined position in February, coffee prices have declined so that S_t = $1.2978 and $F_{t,T}$ = $1.3092, leaving a cover basis of −1.14 cents. This means the basis has increased in value, or *strengthened*, which is to the short hedger's advantage. The net February selling price for her coffee is $1.3766 per pound, which is equal to the spot price of $1.2978 plus the net futures profit of $0.0788 = (1.3880 − 1.3092). Notice that this is lower than the original futures price but considerably higher than the February spot price. Thus, the short hedger has benefited by exchanging pure price risk for basis risk.

Although it is difficult to generalize, substantial indirect evidence exists that minimizing basis risk is the primary goal of most hedgers. For example, Brown and Smith (1995a) noted that the phenomenal growth of OTC products to manage interest rate risk—despite the existence of exchange-traded contracts—is a response to the desire to create customized solutions. Further, a survey by Jesswein, Kwok, and Folks (1995) showed that corporate risk managers preferred to hedge their firms' foreign exchange exposure with forward contracts rather than with futures by a ratio of about five to one. However, Bali, Hume, and Martell (2007) showed that hedging with futures does not necessarily reduce a firm's rate of return.

21.2.3 Calculating the Optimal Hedge Ratio

In the preceding example, the decision to short two coffee futures contracts was a simple one because the investor held exactly twice as much of the same commodity as was covered by a single contract. In most cases, calculating the appropriate hedge ratio, or the number of futures contracts per unit of the spot asset, is not that straightforward. The approach suggested by Johnson (1960), Stein (1961), and Castelino (2000) is to choose the number of contracts that minimizes the variance of net profit from a hedged commodity position.

Consider the position of a short hedger who is long one unit of a particular commodity and short N forward contracts on that commodity. Rewriting Equation 21.2 for the profit from a short hedge and allowing for a variable number of contracts, the net profit (Π_t) of this position at Date t can be written

$$\Pi_t = (S_t - S_0) - (F_{t,T} - F_{0,T})\,(N) = (\Delta S) - (\Delta F)(N)$$

The variance of this value is then given as

$$\sigma_\Pi^2 = \sigma_{\Delta S}^2 + (N^2)\sigma_{\Delta F}^2 - 2(N)\mathrm{COV}_{\Delta S,\Delta F}$$

where:

COV = the covariance of changes in the spot and forward prices

Minimizing this expression and solving for N leaves

21.3
$$N^* = \frac{\mathrm{COV}_{\Delta S,\Delta F}}{\sigma_{\Delta F}^2} = \left(\frac{\sigma_{\Delta S}}{\sigma_{\Delta F}}\right)\rho$$

where:

ρ = the correlation coefficient between the spot and forward price changes[4]

---

[4] Given data for spot and forward prices, σ_Π^2 in the variance equation is a function of just one variable, N. Thus differentiating this equation with respect to N leaves $[d\sigma_\Pi^2/dN] = 2(N)\sigma_{\Delta F}^2 - 2\mathrm{COV}_{\Delta S,\Delta F}$, which can be set equal to zero and solved for N^*. It is easily confirmed that the second derivative of this function is positive and so N^* is a minimizing value.

The optimal hedge ratio (N^*) can be interpreted as the ratio of the spot and forward price standard deviations multiplied by the correlation coefficient between the two series. That is, the optimal number of contracts is determined by the ratio of total volatilities deflated by ρ to account for the *systematic* relationship between the spot and forward prices. (It is directly comparable to the beta coefficient of a common stock.) An important implication of this is that the best contract to use in hedging an underlying spot position is the one that has the highest value of ρ. What if, for instance, a clothing manufacturer wanted to hedge the eventual purchase of a large quantity of wool, a commodity for which no exchange-traded futures contract exists? The expression for N^* suggests that it may be possible to form an effective **cross hedge** if prices for a contract based on a related commodity (e.g., cotton) are highly correlated with wool prices. In fact, the expected basis risk of such a cross hedge can be measured as $(1 - \rho^2)$. Finally, note that the value for N^* also can be calculated as the slope coefficient of a regression using ΔS and ΔF as the dependent and independent variables, respectively.[5] In the regression context, ρ^2 is called the coefficient of determination or, more commonly, R^2. Some examples of these calculations are presented in subsequent sections.

· ·

21.3 Forward and Futures Contracts: Basic Valuation Concepts

Forward and futures contracts are not securities but *trade agreements* that enable both buyers and sellers of an underlying commodity or security to lock in the eventual price of their transaction. They typically require no front-end payment from either the long or short position to motivate the other's participation and, consequently, the contract's initial market value usually is zero. Once the terms of the agreement are set, however, any change in market conditions will likely increase the value of the contract to one of the participants. For example, an obligation made in May to purchase soybeans in September for $9.50 per bushel is surely quite valuable in July if soybean prices in the spot market are already $9.95 and no additional harvest is anticipated in the next two months. A description of the valuation of these agreements, which is different for futures and forward contracts, follows.

21.3.1 Valuing Forwards and Futures

Suppose that at Date 0 you contracted in the forward market to buy Q ounces of gold at Date T for $F_{0,T}$. At Date t, prior to the maturity Date T, you decide that this long position is no longer necessary for your portfolio. Accordingly, you want to **unwind** your original obligation. One way to do this is to take a short position in a Date t forward contract designed to offset the terms of the first. That is, at Date t you would agree to sell Q ounces of gold at Date T for the price of $F_{t,T}$. This is shown in Panel A of Exhibit 21.4. Because you now have contracts to buy and sell Q ounces of gold, you have no exposure to gold price movements between Dates t and T. The profit or loss on this pair of forward contracts is $(Q)[F_{t,T} - F_{0,T}]$, or the difference between the selling and purchase prices multiplied by the quantity involved. However, this amount would not be received (if $F_{t,T} > F_{0,T}$) or paid until Date T, meaning that the value of the original long forward position when it is sold on Date t (i.e., its unwind value) would be the *present value* of $(Q)[F_{t,T} - F_{0,T}]$, or

21.4
$$V_{t,T} = (Q)[F_{t,T} - F_{0,T}] \div (1 + i)^{(T-t)}$$

where:

   i = the appropriate annualized discount rate

---

[5] Some have questioned whether regression-based hedge ratios are stable enough to be useful in practice. Recent researchers, however, have concluded that they are stationary; see Ferguson and Leistikow (1998).

Exhibit 21.4 Unwind Values for Forward and Futures Contracts

Date 0 (Origination)	Date t (Unwind)	Date T (Maturity)

A. Forward Contract
- Long Forward ($F_{0,T}$)

- Short Forward ($F_{t,T}$)
- Contract Unwind Value: $V_{t,T} = (Q)\,[F_{t,T} - F_{0,T}] \div (1 + i)^{(T - t)}$

B. Futures Contract
- Long Futures ($F^*_{0,T}$)

- Short Futures ($F^*_{t,T}$)
- Contract Unwind Value: $V^*_{t,T} = (Q)\,[F^*_{t,T} - F^*_{0,T}]$

Equation 21.4 expresses the Date t value of a long forward contract maturing at Date t. The value $V_{t,T}$ can be positive or negative depending on whether $F_{t,T}$ is greater or less than the original contract price, $F_{0,T}$. Also, the value of the short side of the same contract is just (Q) $[F_{0,T} - F_{t,T}] \div (1 + i)^{(T - t)}$, reinforcing the fact that forward contracts are *zero-sum games* since whatever the long position gains, the short position loses, and vice versa. For example, if you had originally agreed to a long position in a six-month gold forward at $F_{0,\,0.5} = \$700$, and after three months the new forward contract price is $F_{0.25,\,0.5} = \$715$, the value of your position would be $\$1,464.68\ [=(100)\,(715 - 700) \div (1.1)^{0.25}]$, assuming a 10 percent discount rate. Conversely, the value of the original short position would then have to be $-\$1,464.68$. Finally, notice that as Date t approaches Date T, the value of the contract simply becomes $(Q)(F_{T,T} - F_{0,T})$.

Valuing a futures contract is conceptually similar to valuing a forward contract with one important difference. As we saw earlier, futures contracts are marked to market on a daily basis, and this settlement amount was not discounted to account for the difference between Dates t and T. That is, the Date t value of the futures contract is simply the undiscounted difference between the futures prices at the origination and unwind (or cover) dates, multiplied by the contract quantity, as shown in Panel B of Exhibit 21.4 and

21.5
$$V^*_{t,T} = (Q)(F^*_{t,T} - F^*_{0,T})$$

where:

- $*$ = the possibility that forward and futures prices for the same commodity at the same point in time might be different

Cox, Ingersoll, and Ross (1981) showed that $F^*_{0,T}$ and $F_{0,T}$ would be equal if short-term interest rates (i in Equation 21.4) are known but need not be the same under other circumstances.

Typically, for commodities and securities that support both forward and futures markets, differences between $F^*_{0,T}$ and $F_{0,T}$ exist but are relatively small. Cornell and Reinganum (1981) found few economically meaningful differences between forward and futures prices in the foreign exchange market, while Park and Chen (1985) showed that certain agricultural and precious metal futures prices were significantly higher than the analogous forward prices. Grinblatt and Jegadeesh (1996) documented that differences in prices for Eurodollar forward and futures contracts are due to a mispricing of the latter, although this mispricing has been eliminated over time. Finally, note once again that $V^*_{t,T}$ can be either positive or negative depending on how contract prices have changed since inception.

21.3.2 The Relationship between Spot and Forward Prices

In many respects, the relationship between the spot and forward prices at any moment in time is a more challenging question than how the contract is valued. We can understand the intuition for this relationship with an example: You have agreed at Date 0 to deliver 5,000 bushels of corn to your counterparty at Date T. What is a fair price ($F_{0,T}$) to charge? One way to look at this question is to consider how much it will cost you to fulfill your obligation. If you wait until Date T to purchase the corn on the spot market, you have a *speculative* position, since your purchase price (S_T) will be unknown when you commit to a selling price.

Alternatively, suppose you buy the corn now for the current cash price of S_0 per bushel and store it until you have to deliver it at Date T. Under this scheme, the forward contract price you would be willing to commit to would have to be high enough to cover (1) the present cost of the corn and (2) the cost of storing the corn until contract maturity. In general, these storage costs, denoted here as $SC_{0,T}$ can involve several things, including commissions paid for the physical warehousing of the commodity ($PC_{0,T}$) and the cost of financing the initial purchase of the underlying asset ($i_{0,T}$) but less any cash flows received ($D_{0,T}$) by owning the asset between Dates 0 and T. Thus, in the absence of arbitrage opportunities, the forward contract price should be equal to the current spot price plus the **cost of carry** necessary to transport the asset to the future delivery date:

21.6
$$F_{0,T} = S_0 + SC_{0,T} = S_0 + (PC_{0,T} + i_{0,T} - D_{0,T})$$

Notice that even if the funds needed to purchase the commodity at Date 0 are not borrowed, $i_{0,T}$ accounts for the opportunity cost of committing one's own financial capital to the transaction.

This cost of carry model is useful in practice because it applies in a wide variety of cases. For some commodities, such as corn or cattle, physical storage is possible but the costs are enormous. Also, neither of these assets pays periodic cash flows. In such situations, it is quite likely that $F_{0,T} > S_0$ and the market is said to be in **contango**. On the other hand, common stock is costless to store but often pays a dividend. This cash flow sometimes makes it possible for the basis to be positive (i.e., $F_{0,T} < S_0$), meaning that $SC_{0,T}$ can be negative. There is another reason why $SC_{0,T}$ might be less than zero. For certain storable commodities that do not pay a dividend, $F_{0,T} < S_0$ can occur when there is a premium placed on currently owning the commodity. This premium, called a **convenience yield**, results from a small supply of the commodity at Date 0 relative to what is expected at Date T after, say, a crop harvest. (Wheat is a commodity that sometimes satisfies this condition, as indicated in Exhibit 21.3.) Although it is extremely difficult to quantify, the convenience yield can be viewed as a potential negative storage cost component that works in a manner similar to $D_{0,T}$. A futures market in which $F_{0,T} < S_0$ is said to be **backwardated**.

Equation 21.6 implies that there should be a direct relationship between contemporaneous forward and spot prices; indeed, this positive correlation is the objective of any well-designed hedging strategy. A related question involves the relationship between $F_{0,T}$ and the spot price expected to prevail at the time the contract matures (i.e., $E(S_T)$). There are three possibilities. First, the *pure expectations* hypothesis holds that, on average, $F_{0,T} = E(S_T)$, so that futures prices serve as unbiased forecasts of future spot prices. When this is true, futures prices serve an important *price discovery* function for participants in the applicable market. Conversely, $F_{0,T}$ could be less than $E(S_T)$, a situation that Keynes (1930) and Hicks (1939) argued would arise whenever short hedgers outnumber long hedgers. In that case, a risk premium in the form of a lower contract price would be necessary to attract a sufficient number of long speculators. For reasons that are not entirely clear, this situation is termed *normal backwardation*. Finally, a *normal contango* market occurs when the opposite is true, specifically, when $F_{0,T} > E(S_T)$.

The existence of a risk premium in the futures market is widely debated. Kamara (1984) surveyed the early literature on the subject and found the evidence from the commodity markets to be mixed. He concluded that although the normal backwardation hypothesis was supported, futures markets are mainly driven by risk-averse hedgers who have been able to acquire "cheap" insurance. Krehbiel and Collier (1996) examined the price behavior in the Eurodollar and Treasury bill futures markets and found evidence consistent with the existence of risk premia that were necessary to balance net hedging and net speculative positions. Finally, Brooks (1997) documented that the risk premia priced into Eurodollar futures contracts have a substantial impact on the pricing of interest rate swaps, which can be viewed as portfolios of Eurodollar contracts.

21.4 Financial Forwards and Futures: Applications and Strategies

Originally, forward and futures markets were organized largely around trading agricultural commodities, such as corn and wheat. Although markets for these products remain strong, the most significant recent developments involve the use of financial securities as the asset underlying the contract. Exhibit 21.5 shows that the top three most heavily traded derivative contracts globally are based on financial securities. In this section, we take a detailed look at three different types of financial forwards and futures: interest rate, equity index, and foreign exchange.

21.4.1 Interest Rate Forwards and Futures

Interest rate forwards and futures were among the first derivatives to specify a financial security as the underlying asset. The earliest versions of these contracts were designed to lock in the forward price of a particular fixed-coupon bond, which in turn locks in its yield. As we will see in Chapter 23, this market has progressed to where such contracts as *forward rate agreements* and *interest rate swaps* now fix the desired interest rate directly without reference to any specific underlying security. To understand the nuances of the most popular exchange-traded instruments, it is useful to separate them according to whether they involve long- or short-term rates.

21.4.2 Long-Term Interest Rate Futures

Treasury Bond and Note Contract Mechanics The U.S. Treasury bond and note contracts at the Chicago Board of Trade (CBT) are among the most popular of all the financial futures contracts. Delivery dates for both note and bond futures fall in March, June, September, and December. Exhibit 21.6 shows a representative set of quotes for these contracts.

Both the T-bond and the longer-term T-note contracts traded at the CBT call for the delivery of $100,000 face value of the respective instruments. For the T-bond contract, any Treasury bond that has at least 15 years to the nearest call date or to maturity (if noncallable) can be used for delivery. Bonds with maturities ranging from 6.5 to 10 years and 4.17 to 5.25 years can be used to satisfy the 10-year and 5-year T-note contracts, respectively. Delivery can take place on any day during the month of maturity, with the last trading day of the contract falling seven business days prior to the end of the month.

Mechanically, the quotation process for T-bond and T-note contracts work the same way. For example, the settlement price of 112-01, for the March 2008 T-bond contract on the CBT represents $112\frac{1}{32}$ percent of the face amount, or $112,031.25. The contract price went up by 8 ticks from the previous day's settlement, meaning that the long side had its margin account increased by $\frac{8}{32}$ percent of $100,000—or $250—where each $\frac{1}{32}$ movement in the bond's price equals $31.25 (i.e., $1,000 \div 32$).

Exhibit 21.5 Leading Global Derivative Contract Categories Ranked by Trading Volume

Underlying Asset of Contract	Jan–Apr 2007 Volume (mil)	Jan–Apr 2006 Volume (mil)
Equity Indexes	1,751.96	1,478.36
Individual Equities	1,177.90	942.06
Interest Rate	1,120.38	1,043.29
Agricultural Commodities	173.87	147.49
Energy Products	161.47	111.43
Foreign Currency	97.07	71.43
Non-Precious Metals	46.09	39.55
Precious Metals	33.40	34.06
Other	1.28	1.69

Source: Futures Industry Association. Reprinted with permission.

Exhibit 21.6 Treasury Bond and Note Futures Quotations

	Open	High	Contact hi lo Low	Settle	Chg	Open Interest
Treasury Bonds (CBT)-$100,000; pts 32nds of 100%						
Dec	111-20	111-07	112-15	**112-03**	8	914,980
March'08	111-25	111-01	111-23	**112-01**	8	1,785
Treasury Notes (CBT)-$100,000; pts 32nds of 100%						
Dec	109-105	109-225	109-070	**109-200**	5.0	2,307,596
March'08	109-000	109-070	109-000	**109-060**	5.5	95,543
5 Yr. Treasury Notes (CBT)-$100,000; pts 32nds of 100%						
Dec	106-285	107-055	106-265	**107-035**	3.0	1,634,048
March'08	106-235	106-235	106-235	**106-310**	3.0	760
2 Yr. Treasury Notes (CBT)-$200,000; pts 32nds of 100%						
Dec	103-127	103-165	103-115	**103-150**	.5	914,679

Source: From the *Wall Street Journal*, October 5, 2007. Copyright 2007 by DOW JONES & CO INC. Reproduced with permission of DOW JONES & CO INC in the format Other Book via Copyright Clearance Center.

Although T-bond and T-note futures contracts are called interest rate futures, what the long and short positions actually agree to is the price of the underlying bond. Once that price is set, however, the yield will be locked in. When a yield is quoted, it is for reference only and historically has assumed a coupon rate of 6 percent and 20 years to maturity. For the March 2008 bond contract, the settlement yield would be 5.038 percent, which can be established by solving for the internal rate of return in the following bond math problem

$$\$1,120.3125 = \sum_{t=1}^{40} \frac{\$30}{(1 + i/2)^t} + \frac{\$1,000}{(1 + i/2)^{40}}$$

This pricing formula takes into account the fact that Treasury bonds pay semiannual interest. So, a 20-year, 6 percent bond makes 40 coupon payments of 3 percent each. Thus, the long position in this contract has effectively agreed in October to buy a 20-year T-bond in March priced to yield 5.04 percent. If, in March, the actual yield on the 20-year bond is below 5.04 percent (i.e., the bond's price is greater than $112,031.25), the long position will have made a wise decision. Thus, the long position in this contract gains as prices rise and rates decrease and loses as increasing rates lead to lower bond prices.

Because the bond and note futures contracts allow so many different instruments to qualify for delivery, the seller would naturally choose to deliver the least expensive bond if no adjustments were made for varying coupon rates and maturity dates. To account for this, the CBT uses **conversion factors** to correct for the differences in the deliverable bonds. The conversion factor is based on the price of a given bond if its yield is 6 percent at the time of delivery and the face value is $1. For example, the October 2007 conversion factor for the 6.5 percent T-bond maturing in November 2026 would be 1.0562, calculated as

$$1.0562 = \sum_{t=1}^{38} \frac{0.0325}{(1 + 0.03)^t} + \frac{1}{(1 + 0.03)^{38}}$$

The actual delivery price, or invoice price, for that Treasury bond would be the quoted futures price, $112,031.25, times the conversion factor, 1.0562, for a total of $118,327.41 (plus accrued interest). The buyer must pay more than $112,031.25 because the seller is delivering more valuable bonds, since their coupon rate exceeds 6 percent.

The conversion factors used by the CBT are technically correct only when the Treasury yield curve is flat at 6 percent. Therefore, there usually will be a *cheapest to deliver* bond that maximizes the difference between the invoice price (the amount received by the short) and the cash market price (the amount paid by the short to acquire the delivery bond). Market participants always know which bond is the cheapest to deliver. Therefore, the T-bond futures contract trades as if this particular security were the actual underlying delivery bond. In fact, the cheapest to deliver security usually is the T-bond with the longest duration when yields are above 6 percent, and the one with the shortest duration for yields less than 6 percent.

A Duration-Based Approach to Hedging In Chapter 18, we stressed that the main benefit of calculating the duration statistic was its ability to link interest rate changes to bond price changes by the formula

$$\left(\frac{\Delta P}{P}\right) \approx -D\left(\frac{\Delta(1 + i/n)}{(1 + i/n)}\right)$$

We also saw that a more convenient way to write this expression is:

$$\left(\frac{\Delta P}{P}\right) \approx -\left(\frac{D}{(1 + i/n)}\right)\Delta(1+i/n) = -D_{mod}\Delta(i/n)$$

where:

D_{mod} = the bond's modified duration, combining the Macaulay duration and its periodic yield into a single measure

Earlier in this chapter, we noted that the objective of hedging was to select a hedge ratio (N) such that $\Delta S - \Delta F(N) = 0$, where S is the current spot price of the underlying asset and F is the current futures contract price. Rewriting this leaves

$$N^* = \frac{\Delta S}{\Delta F}$$

Using the modified duration relationship, this optimal hedge ratio can now be expanded as follows:

$$N^* = \frac{\Delta S}{\Delta F} = \frac{\left(\frac{\Delta S}{S}\right)}{\left(\frac{\Delta F}{F}\right)} \times \frac{S}{F} = \frac{-D_{mod S} \times \Delta(i_S/n)}{-D_{mod F} \times \Delta(i_F/n)} \times \frac{S}{F}$$

or

21.7
$$N^* = \frac{D_{mod S}}{D_{mod F}} \times \beta_i \times \frac{S}{F}$$

where:

β_i = the "yield beta"

The yield beta is also called the ratio of changes in the yields applicable to the two instruments where n is the number of payment periods per year (e.g., $n = 2$ for semiannual coupon bonds). For example, consider the following fixed-income securities, each making annual payments (i.e., $n = 1$):

Instrument	Coupon	Maturity	Yield
A	8%	10 years	10%
B	10%	15 years	8%

How much of Instrument B is necessary to hedge A? This question can be answered in three steps. First, using the method shown in Chapter 18 (and summarized in Appendix 21A), the duration statistics for each position are:

$$D_A = 7.0439 \text{ so } D_{modA} = (7.0439) \div (1.10) = 6.4036 \text{ years}$$
$$D_B = 8.8569 \text{ so } D_{modB} = (8.8569) \div (1.08) = 8.2009 \text{ years}$$

Second, we will assume that yield beta is unity (i.e., $\beta_i = 1$). In general, this is calculated by observing historical yield curve movements across the 10- and 15-year maturities. Finally, current prices are easily confirmed to be 87.71 for Security A and 117.12 for Security B assuming par value of 100. Thus, the duration-based hedge ratio is

$$N^* = \left(\frac{6.4036}{8.2009}\right)(1)\left(\frac{87.71}{117.12}\right) = 0.5847$$

or 0.5847 unit of B short for every one unit of A held long.

Treasury Futures Applications

Hedging a Future Funding Commitment In late July, the treasurer of a U.S.-based company is arranging a 15-year, $100 million funding. The company will be ready to launch its new debt issue in late September but he is concerned that, between July and September, interest rates may rise, thereby increasing the company's funding cost. He decides to hedge this exposure in the T-bond futures market. In this case, he will need to take a *short* position in the futures market, which will appreciate in value if interest rates increase, offsetting the higher payments required on the underlying debt.

If the bond issue was placed today, the credit standing of the firm would lead to a funding cost of 8.25 percent for the 15-year period. He knows that a September T-bond futures contract is trading at a price of 83–16 to yield 7.62 percent. He knows that bond yields beyond 10 years to maturity tend to move in a parallel fashion so he is comfortable that a yield beta of 1.0 is appropriate. Further, the treasurer is aware that T-bond futures cannot hedge for changes in the firm's risk premium over the risk-free rate; he will have to live with this source of basis risk.

If he plans to launch his new issue at par value, how many T-bond futures contracts would he need to short today? Assuming semiannual coupons for both the Treasury and corporate issues, their durations can be calculated using the closed-form equation shown in Appendix 21A:

$$D_{corp} = \frac{1.04125}{0.04125} - \frac{1.04125 + [30(0.04125 - 0.04125)]}{0.04125[(1.04125)^{30} - 1] + 0.04125} = 17.74 \text{ periods}$$

and

$$D_{trsy} = \frac{1.0381}{0.0381} - \frac{1.0381 + [40(0.03 - 0.0381)]}{0.03[(1.0381)^{40} - 1] + 0.0381} = 22.22 \text{ periods}$$

These statistics are denominated in half years so that the hedge ratio will be expressed in the same terms used to price the bonds. With these statistics, we can calculate the modified durations as follows: $D_{modC} = 17.04 (= 17.74 \div 1.04125)$ and $D_{modT} = 21.40 (= 22.22 \div 1.0381)$. Finally, since each T-bond futures contract is standardized to a denomination of $100,000, the treasurer can calculate the optimal number of contracts to short as

$$(\text{Number of Contracts}) = \frac{(17.04)}{(21.40)} \times (1.0) \times \frac{(\$100,000,000)}{(\$83,500)} = 953.6, \text{ or } 954 \text{ Contracts}$$

A T-Bond/T-Note (NOB) Futures Spread Frequently, speculators in the bond market have a clear view on a change in the overall shape of the yield curve but can be less certain as to the actual direction in future rate movements. Suppose you think the yield curve—which is currently upward sloping across all maturities—will flatten, but you're not sure how this might occur:

- Short-term rates rise and long-term rates fall.
- Short- and long-term rates both rise, but short-term rates rise by more.
- Short- and long-term rates both fall, but short-term rates fall by less.

Clearly, taking a long or short position in a single futures contract linked to a single point on the yield curve is too risky, given your view; you could be right about the shape shift but guess wrong about direction. One way to mitigate this unwanted risk is to go both long and short in contracts representing different points on the yield curve. This is known as the Treasury "Notes over Bond" **spread** (or "NOB" spread) strategy.

Suppose in mid-February you observe the following price quotes (along with their implied yields to maturity) for T-bond and T-note futures contracts maturing in June:

Contract	Settle Price	Implied Yield
20-yr, 6% T-bond	103–02	5.74%
10-yr, 6% T-note	104–02	5.47%

Notice that your expectation of a flattening yield curve is identical to the view that the 27 basis point yield gap (= 0.0574 − 0.0547) between the longer- and shorter-term contracts will shrink. If you also feel this will occur by mid-June, the appropriate strategy would be:

- Go long in one Treasury bond futures.
- Go short in one Treasury note futures.

The net profit from this joint position when you close out the two contracts is calculated as the sum of the profits on the short T-note position and the long T-bond contract, or

$$\left[\frac{104.0625 - \text{June T-Note Price}}{100} + \frac{\text{June T-Bond Price} - 103.0625}{100} \right](\$100,000)$$

To see how this combined position would pay off if your view is correct, consider two scenarios in which the yield curve flattens to where there is no difference between 10- and 20-year rates by the time you close your positions in June:

1. *Rates increase to 6.00 percent by June.*
   In this case, both futures contracts will sell at par and so your net profit will be

   $$\text{Net Profit} = [0.040625 - 0.030625](\$100,000) = \$1,000$$

   Notice that this same calculation can be done on a "price tick" basis:

   $$\text{Net Profit} = \{[(104\text{–}02) - (103\text{–}02)] - [(100\text{–}00) - (100\text{–}00)]\}(\$31.25)$$
   $$= (32 \text{ Ticks})(\$31.25) = \$1,000$$

   which is equivalent to the change in the number of ticks in the NOB spread multiplied by the dollar value of a tick (i.e., $31.25).
2. *Rates decrease to 5.00 percent by June.*
   In this scenario, the settlement prices on the two futures contracts will be

   $$P_{\text{T-note}} = \sum_{t=1}^{20} \frac{\$3}{(1 + 0.025)^t} + \frac{\$100}{(1 + 0.025)^{20}} = \$107.79 \approx 107\text{–}25$$

   and

   $$P_{\text{T-bond}} = \sum_{t=1}^{40} \frac{\$3}{(1 + 0.025)^t} + \frac{\$100}{(1 + 0.025)^{40}} = \$112.55 \approx 112\text{–}18$$

so that net profit from the NOB spread will be

$$\text{Net Profit} = \{[(104\text{--}02) - (103\text{--}02)] - [(107\text{--}25) - (112\text{--}18)]\} \ (\$31.25)$$
$$= (32 + 153) \ (\$31.25) = \$5,781.25$$

Interpreting this outcome differently, you made $9,500.00 on your long position in the T-bond contract ($= [(112\text{--}18) - (103\text{--}02)](31.25)$), but you lost $3,718.75 on your short T-note position ($= [(104\text{--}02) - (107\text{--}25)](31.25)$) for a net gain of $5,781.25.

These results show that the futures spread allows speculators to separate their views on yield curve shape from an explicit forecast of a change in the curve's position. However, the investor must be careful to recognize that, because the duration of the T-bond is greater than that of the T-note, the former will be more sensitive to a given rate change.

21.4.3 Short-Term Interest Rate Futures

Short-term interest rate futures have become a rapidly expanding segment of the exchange-traded market. Currently, investors can hedge their exposures to several different money market rates (e.g., T-bill, LIBOR, Banker's Acceptance, Federal Funds) denominated in a multitude of currencies (e.g., U.S. dollar, Japanese yen, Euro). In the following analysis, we concentrate on one of these contracts: Eurodollar futures.

Eurodollar Contract Mechanics The Eurodollar contract traded on the Chicago Mercantile Exchange (CME) has become enormously successful since it was launched in the early 1980s. Delivery dates occur monthly for a brief period before following the March, June, September, December cycle and now extend 10 years into the future. The final trading and settlement date is the second London business day before the third Wednesday of the delivery month. A representative set of quotes is shown in Exhibit 21.7.

Hypothetically, the Eurodollar contract requires the long position to make a $1,000,000, 90-day bank deposit with the short position at the maturity date. Unlike the Treasury bond and note futures just described, this contract requires all outstanding obligations to be settled in cash. This provision is necessary because the contract nominally requires the long position to make, and the short position to receive, a 90-day Euro-time deposit. However, that is something that the short position can't legally do unless it is a bank. The underlying interest rate is the 3-month (i.e., 90-day) LIBOR that is quoted on a 360-day bank add-on basis. As we will see, arbitrage trading should drive the sequence of Eurodollar (or LIBOR) futures rates to equal the forward rates implied by the yield curve for interbank lending in the cash market. That is, in an efficient market, the futures rates should be close to the comparable implied forward rates.

In Exhibit 21.7, the quoted contract price for the March 2008 contract is 95.375, which is not an actual purchase price but merely an index calculated as 100 minus the effective settlement yield of 4.625 percent. Eurodollar futures use this settlement price index because it conveniently

Exhibit 21.7 Eurodollar (LIBOR) Futures Quotations

	Open	High	Contact hi lo	Low	Settle	Chg	Open Interest
Eurodollar (CME)-$100,000; pts of 100%							
Oct	94.7600	94.7850		94.7600	**94.7725**	...	181,813
Dec	95.0300	95.0600		95.0100	**95.0450**	...	1,543,488
March'08	95.3500	95.3900		95.3300	**95.3750**	-.0050	1,452,115
June	95.5250	95.5700		95.4950	**95.5550**	...	1,336,326

preserves the inverse relation between price and yield. Thus, a long position in this contract can still be thought to "win" when prices rise—and the short position wins with falling prices—even though it is the opposite movement in the underlying interest rate that matters.

If the price index for this contract moved by one "tick" (i.e., 0.01), the contract itself would change by $25 (=$1,000,000 × 0.0001 × 90/360), which is called the *basis point value* of the position. Thus, the one-half tick (−0.005) decline in the price of the March 2008 contract—which is the minimum price change allowed—means that LIBOR increased by one-half basis point from the prior day's settlement. This would benefit a person who acquired a short position at the close of the prior day, inasmuch as he would have a locked-in borrowing cost for the 90-day period from March to June 2008 that is now one-half basis point lower than the market level. In fact, all sellers of this contract gained $12.50 per contract (i.e., $25 per tick times one-half tick) in their margin accounts.

Finally, notice that Eurodollar open interest is spread over the various delivery dates to a greater extent than for the T-bond contract (shown in Exhibit 21.6). Brown and Smith (1988) interpreted these trading patterns as suggesting that T-bond futures are used in the market more as a speculative trading contract and that Eurodollar futures are used more frequently as a buy-and-hold hedging instrument.

Short-Term Interest Rate Future Applications

Creating a Synthetic Fixed-Rate Funding with a Eurodollar Strip Suppose that on March 15 a bank loan officer is considering an investment scheme for lending $2,000,000 to a large-cap manufacturing firm. The plan would last for one year and have the payment rate reset on a quarterly basis at LIBOR. At the planning stage, the LIBOR yield curve appears as follows:

90-day LIBOR	5.00%
180-day LIBOR	5.10
270-day LIBOR	5.20
360-day LIBOR	5.30

Given the debt market convention that yields on floating-rate deal structures always are determined in advance and paid in arrears, she knows that her loan receipt for the first three months would be based on the prevailing 5.00 percent rate and be receivable in 90 days. Her concern is the level of her receipts in the subsequent three quarters; she is worried that they may fall to an unacceptable level. Accordingly, she considers using the Eurodollar futures market to hedge her exposure.

As a prelude to checking futures contract price quotes, she calculates the forward rates implied by the current yield curve. Using the money-market implied forward rate formula shown in Appendix 21B, these computations generate:

$$_{180}IFR_{90} = \left[\frac{(0.051)(180) - (0.050)(90)}{(180 - 90)} \right] \left[\frac{1}{1 + \left(\frac{(90)(0.050)}{360} \right)} \right] = 5.14\%$$

$$_{270}IFR_{180} = \left[\frac{(0.052)(270) - (0.051)(180)}{(270 - 180)} \right] \left[\frac{1}{1 + \left(\frac{(180)(0.051)}{360} \right)} \right] = 5.27\%$$

$$_{360}IFR_{270} = \left[\frac{(0.053)(360) - (0.052)(270)}{(360 - 270)} \right] \left[\frac{1}{1 + \left(\frac{(270)(0.052)}{360} \right)} \right] = 5.39\%$$

She checks with her trading desk for quotes on the relevant Eurodollar futures contracts and receives the following information:

Contract Expiration	Settlement Price
June	94.86
September	94.73
December	94.61

The futures settlement prices indicate LIBOR contract rates that are identical to the implied forward rates, suggesting there is no arbitrage potential between the cash and futures markets on this date.

To lock in her receipts for the $2,000,000 loan, the banker would go long a *strip* of Eurodollar futures contracts. That is, she takes long positions in two June contracts, two September contracts, and two December contracts. (Recall that the long position in a Eurodollar contract gains when the price index rises with a falling LIBOR; this is the protection she is seeking.) With these positions, her quarterly interest receipts will be fixed at the following levels:

$$\text{June Receipt} = (\$2,000,000)\left[\frac{(0.0500)(90)}{360}\right] = \$25,000$$

$$\text{September Receipt} = (\$2,000,000)\left[\frac{(0.0514)(90)}{360}\right] = \$25,700$$

$$\text{December Receipt} = (\$2,000,000)\left[\frac{(0.0527)(90)}{360}\right] = \$26,350$$

$$\text{March (Next Year) Receipt} = (\$2,000,000)\left[\frac{(0.0539)(90)}{360}\right] = \$26,950$$

Although these cash inflows are fixed in advance, they clearly differ in amount from quarter to quarter. The banker then asks herself the following question: What quarterly annuity payment does this sequence of receipts imply? This amount can be calculated as the solution to:

$$\frac{\$25,000}{\left[1 + \frac{(0.050)(90)}{360}\right]} + \frac{\$25,700}{\left[1 + \frac{(0.051)(180)}{360}\right]} + \frac{\$26,350}{\left[1 + \frac{(0.052)(270)}{360}\right]} + \frac{\$26,950}{\left[1 + \frac{(0.053)(360)}{360}\right]}$$

$$= \frac{\text{Annuity}}{\left[1 + \frac{(0.050)(90)}{360}\right]} + \frac{\text{Annuity}}{\left[1 + \frac{(0.051)(180)}{360}\right]} + \frac{\text{Annuity}}{\left[1 + \frac{(0.052)(270)}{360}\right]} + \frac{\text{Annuity}}{\left[1 + \frac{(0.053)(360)}{360}\right]}$$

Solving this formula for annuity gives a value of $25,989.38, where the discount rates are from the prevailing cash market LIBOR curve. Finally, notice that this annuity payment, when expressed on a full 360-day percentage basis, is

$$\left[\frac{\$25,989.38}{\$2,000,000}\right]\left[\frac{360}{90}\right] = 5.198\%$$

which is a time-weighted average of the 90-day spot LIBOR and the series of three implied forward rates.

Creating a TED Spread One of the features that makes the Eurodollar futures contract such a popular hedging vehicle is the rate it is based on—three-month LIBOR. This rate can be thought of as equivalent to the three-month T-bill yield *plus* a risk premium (i.e., credit spread). Sometimes, bond traders will have a view on future movements in this credit spread; for example, a trader might believe the current difference between the LIBOR and T-bill yield is too narrow and that it will soon widen. The problem with trying to play this view with a short position in the Eurodollar contract alone is, even if the trader is right about the spread, the general level of interest rates could still decline by more than enough to offset any spread gains.

The solution is to isolate the credit spread component in LIBOR through a strategy known as the *TED* (Treasury/EuroDollar) *spread*. The TED spread is created by taking simultaneous, but opposite, positions in both a Eurodollar and T-bill futures contract having the same maturity. In the parlance of the market, we have the following definitions.

$$\text{Long TED Spread} = (\text{Long T-Bill Futures}) + (\text{Short Eurodollar Futures})$$
$$\text{Short TED Spread} = (\text{Short T-Bill Futures}) + (\text{Long Eurodollar Futures})$$

Notice that a long position in a TED spread will gain when the credit spread increases; the short TED spread benefits from a narrowing of the credit spread. Exhibit 21.8 shows how volatile the three-month TED spread has been over time.

Suppose that in early August you observe the following prices in the Eurodollar and T-bill futures markets:

	T-Bill	Eurodollar	Spread
September contracts	95.24	94.80	44 BP
December contracts	94.68	94.11	57 BP
March contracts	94.42	93.86	56 BP

Recall that the difference between the T-bill and Eurodollar price indexes is the spread built into the Eurodollar contract for a particular maturity.

If you believe the economy will remain sluggish for an extended period of time and that credit spreads currently are too narrow in the short-term contract, you would want to take a long TED spread position (i.e., short the Eurodollar futures and buy the T-bill contract). After you establish this position using the September contracts, the Federal Reserve Board tightens rates again so that by mid-September the following prices prevail when you unwind the strategy:

New September T-bill contract	94.55
New September Eurodollar contract	93.95
New spread	0.60

This new spread is more closely aligned with the December and March contracts. The profit on your transaction is calculated as

$$(\text{New TED Spread}) - (\text{Original TED Spread})$$

or

$$(94.55 - 93.95) - (95.24 - 94.80) = 16 \text{ Basis Points}$$

With each contract standardized so that a basis point is worth $25, the profit per contract pair from this trade would be $(16 \times \$25) = \$400$. Another way to see this profit is that you made an 85-basis-point profit on the short position in the Eurodollar contract ($= 94.80 - 93.95$) but lost 69 basis points on the long T-bill contract ($= 94.55 - 95.24$). However, if both rates had declined, you still would have made money if the T-bill yield had fallen by more than LIBOR.

21.4.4 Stock Index Futures

In this section, we consider the basics of stock index futures trading and discuss two applications for these instruments, including a popular form of computer-assisted trading known as stock index arbitrage.

Exhibit 21.8 TED Spread for Three-Month Contracts

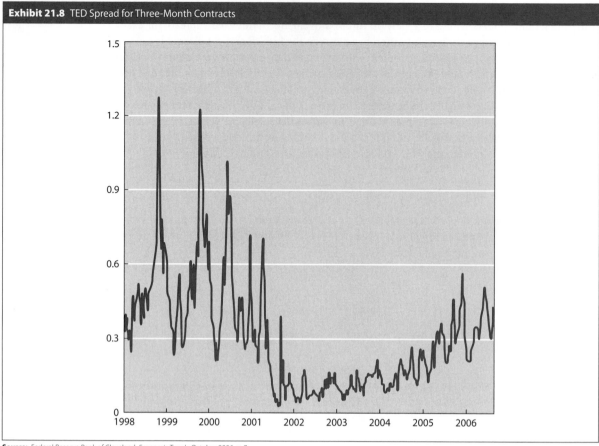

Source: Federal Reserve Bank of Cleveland. *Economic Trends*, October 2006, p. 7.

Stock Index Futures Contract Fundamentals Like interest rate futures, stock index futures were originally intended to provide a hedge against movements in an underlying financial asset. As detailed in Chapter 5 and the introductory example in Chapter 20, the underlying financial asset for a stock index futures contract is a hypothetical creation that does not exist in practice and therefore cannot be delivered to settle a contract. Thus, stock index futures can only be settled in cash, similar to the Eurodollar (i.e., LIBOR) contract.

Stock index futures are intended to provide general hedges against stock market movements and can be applied to either whole (i.e., diversified) portfolios or individual stocks. Hedging an individual stock with an index futures contract is done in an attempt to isolate the unsystematic portion of that security's risk. Additionally, stock index futures often are used to convert entire stock portfolios into synthetic riskless positions to exploit an apparent mispricing between stock in the cash and futures markets. This strategy, commonly called **stock index arbitrage**, is the most prominent example of a wider class of computer-assisted trading schemes known as *program trading*.

Exhibit 21.9 lists quotes for futures contracts on several U.S. stock indexes, including the Dow Jones Industrial Average, Standard & Poor's 500, NASDAQ 100, and Russell 1000. Contracts for indexes representing global markets [e.g., Nikkei 225 (Japan), DAX 30 (Germany), Euro Stoxx 50] are traded actively but not shown in the display. For example, an investor planning in October to buy stock the following June can hedge against the risk of his eventual purchase price increasing by entering into the long position in the June 2008 S&P 500 contract. Given the settlement price of 1,573.90, he has obligated himself to the theoretical purchase of 250 shares of the S&P 500 on the day before the third Friday of June for $393,475 (= 1,573.90 × 250).

Exhibit 21.9 Stock Index Futures Quotations

	Open	High	Contact hi lo	Low	Settle	Chg	Open Interest
DJ Industrial Average (CBT)-$10 x index							
Dec	14059	14090		14025	**14041**	−11	27,586
Mini DJ Industrial Average (CBT)-$5 x index							
Dec	14057	14090		14026	**14041**	−11	90,300
March'08	14150	14153		14125	**14139**	−11	34
S&P 500 Index (CME)-$250 x index							
Dec	1550.80	1554.70		1548.10	**1552.20**	1.50	573,448
June'08	1574.50	1575.30		1571.30	**1573.90**	1.60	874
Mini S&P 500 (CME)-$50 x index							
Dec	1550.75	1554.75		1548.00	**1552.25**	1.50	1,864,257
March'08	1562.75	1565.75		1559.50	**1563.50**	1.75	2,706
Nasdaq 100 (CME)-$100 x index							
Dec	2121.00	2129.00		2109.00	**2123.0**	2.25	45,983
Mini Nasdaq 100 (CME)-$20 x index							
Dec	2121.3	2128.8		2108.5	**2123.0**	2.3	380,611
March'08	2140.0	2151.3		2132.5	**2146.0**	2.8	64
Russell 1000 (ICE-US)-$500 x index							
Dec	844.00	845.00		844.00	**845.20**	1.00	7,668
U.S. Dollar Index (ICE-US)-$1,000 x index							
Dec	78.56	78.65		78.22	**78.38**	−0.8	37,188
March'08	78.50	78.36		78.36	**78.31**	−0.8	2,824

The minimum contract price movement is 0.10 index points, which equals $25. Thus, if the actual level of the index on the contract settlement date turned out to be 1,576.10, the long position would gain $550, or $25 times 22 ticks [i.e., $(1,576.10 − 1,573.90) ÷ 0.10$], thereby reducing the net purchase price for his desired equity position. Finally, notice that a "mini" version of the S&P 500 futures contract requiring the hypothetical purchase or sale of only 50 shares is also available.

Stock Index Futures Valuation and Index Arbitrage   Earlier, we established that the key to understanding the pricing of futures contracts is the concept of arbitrage. To see how this works for index contracts, suppose that at Date 0 an investor (1) purchases a portfolio of stock representing the underlying stock index for S_0, and (2) goes short a stock index future (with an expiration date of T) for $F_{0,T}$. Assume further that the funds for the long position are borrowed at the risk-free rate of *RFR*. On unwinding this position at Date t, the net profit (Π) is given by

$$\Pi = (F_{0,T} - F_{t,T}) + (S_t - S_0 - S_0 RFR_t + S_0 d_t) = (F_{0,T} - F_{t,T}) + [S_t - S_0(1 + RFR_t - d_t)]$$

where:

d_t = the dividend yield accruing to the stocks comprising the index between Dates 0 and t

In other words, the profit you make on this short hedge in stock index futures will consist of two components: the net difference in the futures position and the net difference in the underlying index position (after adding borrowing costs and subtracting dividends received from the initial purchase).

Now assume the long position in the stock portfolio is held until the expiration of the futures contract (i.e., Date $t = T$) so that the futures price and index level will converge. That is, at Date T, we will have $F_{T,T} = S_T$, which means that the short hedge profit (Π) equation can be written

$$\Pi = [F_{0,T} - S_0 - S_0(RFR_t - d_T)]$$

As before, $RFR_t - d_T$ is called the net cost of carry and represents the difference between the borrowing cost paid and the dividend received.

If the dividend yield is known at Date 0, this position is riskless and requires no initial investment. Thus, buying and selling among arbitrageurs trading in both markets should ensure that $\Pi = 0$. The futures price set at Date 0 will be

21.8
$$F_{0,T} = S_0 + S_0(RFR_t - d_T)$$

As discussed earlier, the futures price could be set below the spot level of the index (i.e., a backwardated market) if $(RFR_t - d_T) < 0$. That is, the index futures contract will be priced lower than the current level of the stock index whenever the dividends received by holding stock exceed the borrowing cost.

To see how this parity relationship helps establish the appropriate futures price, assume that one share of the S&P 500 index can be purchased for $1,250.00 and that the dividend yield and risk-free rate over the holding period are 1.5 percent and 2.5 percent, respectively. Under these conditions, the contract price on a six-month S&P 500 futures should be

$$F_{0,0.5} = 1,250 + 1,250(0.025 - 0.015) = 1,262.50$$

Now suppose that you construct a short hedge position by (1) purchasing the index at 1,250.00 and (2) shorting the futures at 1,262.50. If the position is held to expiration, your profit at various expiration date levels of the S&P will be as shown in Exhibit 21.10. Notice that your net profit remains constant no matter the level of the index at the expiration date. This net profit can be expressed as

$$(31.25) \div (1,250) = 2.5 \text{ percent}$$

which is the assumed cost of borrowing.

Implementing an Index Arbitrage Strategy What if the parity condition between the stock index and the stock index futures price does not hold? Could you design a portfolio to take advantage of the situation? Suppose that in the preceding example the actual contract price on a six-month S&P 500 futures was 1,265.50 [i.e., $F_{0,T} > S_0 + S_0(RFR_t - d_T)$]. You could then implement the following arbitrage transaction: (1) short the stock index future at a price of 1,265.50; (2) borrow money at 2.5 percent to purchase the stock index at 1,250.00; and (3) hold the position until maturity, collecting 18.75 in dividends and then selling the stock to repay your loan. Your net profit at maturity would be

$$1,265.50 - 1,250 - 1,250 (0.025 - 0.015) = \$3.00$$

However, since this strategy was riskless (i.e., the sales price of the stock and the dividends were known in advance) and none of your own capital was used, it is an arbitrage profit.

This is *stock index arbitrage,* which is possible whenever the index futures price is set at a level sufficiently different from the theoretical value for $F_{0,T}$ to account for trading costs. If the actual level of $F_{0,T} < S_0 + S_0(RFR_t - d_T)$, the previous strategy could be reversed: (1) buy the stock index future at a price of $F_{0,T}$, (2) lend money at RFR_t and short the stock index at S_0, and (3) cover the position at the expiration date of the futures contract. Indeed, index arbitrage is a popular form of trading. Exhibit 21.11 reports that about 3.1 percent of all computer-assisted program trading used this strategy. Further program trading accounted for about 36 percent of trading volume on the New York Stock Exchange.

Exhibit 21.10 Stock Index Futures Valuation Example

	S&P AT EXPIRATION IS:				
	1,220	**1,240**	**1,260**	**1,280**	**1,300**
Net futures profit	42.50	22.50	2.50	(17.50)	(37.50)
Net index profit	(30.00)	(10.00)	10.00	30.00	50.00
Dividend	18.75	18.75	18.75	18.75	18.75
Net profit	31.25	31.25	31.25	31.25	31.25

One important side effect of this trading activity is that stock index futures prices tend to stay close to their theoretical levels. This is because the arbitrage prescription for a futures settlement price that is too low (too high) is to go long (short) in the contract, which, when done in sufficient volume, adjusts the price in the proper direction. Panel A of Exhibit 21.12 compares the actual and theoretical levels of the nearest-term future contract for several stock indexes throughout the world, including the S&P 500 (SPX), Dow Jones Industrial (INDU), and the Nikkei 225 (NKY). The pricing errors on this particular day never exceeded $\frac{4}{10}$ of 1 percent for any contract and was much lower than that in most markets. Panel B of Exhibit 21.12 details the calculation of the theoretical level of the December 2007 S&P 500 futures price (SPZ7). The display shows that the actual contract price (1,572.30) was virtually identical to its theoretical value (1,573.36), which can be computed as the spot price (1,562.47) plus the net cost of carry $[1,562.47 \times (0.0525 - 0.0184) \times (73/365)]$. These values support the notion that the market for stock index futures is an efficient one.

The empirical evidence tends to support this view, particularly after transaction costs and other trading realities are considered. Cornell (1985), found that stock index futures prices tracked their model values more closely as the market matured, although Keim and Smirlock (1989) detected some temporal (i.e., day-of-the-week, January) pricing patterns. In response

---

Exhibit 21.11 Program Trading and Stock Index Arbitrage

Program Trading

NEW YORK—Program trading in the week ended Sept. 28 amounted to 35.7% of New York Stock Exchange average daily volume of 2,72 billion shares, or 971.2 million program shares traded per day.

Program trading encompasses a range of portfolio-trading strategies involving the purchase or sale of a basket of at least 15 stocks with a total value of $1 million or more. The program-trading level is buying-and-selling volume as a percent of all NYSE reported volume.

In all markets program trading by member firms averaged 2.31 billion shares a day during the past week. About 42% of program trading took place on the NYSE, 1% in non-U.S. markets and 57% in other domestic markets, including Nasdaq, the American Stock Exchange and regional markets.

NYSE PROGRAM TRADING
Volume in million of shares in the week ennded Sept. 28, 2007

Top 15 FIRMS	INDEX ARB.	DERIV.- RELATED*	OTHER STRAT.	TOTAL
Lehman Brothers	15.1	....	763.6	778.7
Goldman Sachs Group	....	....	692.1	692.1
Morgan Stanley	1.8	....	541.5	543.3
Merrill Lynch	....	....	514.6	514.6
Credit Suisse	9.1	....	391.0	400.1
Deutsche Bank	30.7	....	338.4	369.1
UBS Securities	....	....	231.6	231.6
Bear Stearns	13.5	....	183.1	196.6
RBC Capital Market	52.8	....	136.9	189.7
Citigroup Global	....	....	171.5	171.5
Banc of America Sec.	3.0	....	143.1	146.1
BNP Paribas	....	....	114.4	114.4
Interactive Brokers	....	....	103.0	103.0
JP Morgan	....	....	80.5	80.5
Calyon Securities	0.1	....	43.9	44.0
OVERALL TOTAL	**150.6**	**......**	**4705.6**	**4856.2**

*Other derivative-related strategies besides index arbitrage

Exhibit 21.12   Actual and Theoretical Stock Index Futures Prices

Panel A. Mispricing in Stock Index Futures Contracts throughout the World

<Help> for explanation, <MENU> for similar functions.   Index **FV**
Hit (#) Go to monitor the intra-day spread of cash and futures (basis)

EQUITY INDEX FUTURE ANALYSIS
FAIR VALUE

	Cash	Future	Theo. Future	Fair Value	Spread Basis	Percent Misprice
1) Americas						
4) SPZ7vsSPX	1562.47	1572.30	1573.36	10.89	9.83	−.068%
5) YUZ7vsNYA	10264.49	10345.00	10334.85	70.36	80.51	+.098%
6) DJZ7vsINDU	14078.69	14140.00	14154.69	76.00	61.31	−.104%
7) MDZ7vsMID	916.50	922.50	924.03	7.53	6.00	−.166%
8) NDZ7vsNDX	2176.98	2195.50	2198.39	21.41	18.52	−.131%
9) PTZ7vsSPTSX60	827.69	832.10	831.45	3.76	4.41	+.078%
2) Europe						
10) Q Z7vsE100	3316.38	3333.00	3337.95	21.57	16.62	−.148%
11) Z Z7vsUKX	6633.00	6683.50	6687.42	54.42	50.50	−.059%
12) CFV7vsCAC	5838.49	5846.00	5844.29	5.80	7.51	+.029%
13) GXZ7vsDAX	7986.57	8042.00	8068.10	81.53	55.43	−.324%
14) SMZ7vsSMI	9182.30	9230.00	9234.80	52.50	47.70	−.052%
15) EOV7vsAEX	554.57	554.70	555.18	.61	.13	−.087%
3) Asia/Pacific						
16) NKZ7vsNKY	17177.89	17200.00	17195.84	17.95	22.11	+.024%
17) NIV7vsNKY	17177.89	17180.00	17178.18	.29	2.11	+.011%
18) TPZ7vsTPX	1658.18	1661.50	1659.87	1.69	3.32	+.098%
19) XPV7vsAS51	6738.30	6724.00	6747.23	8.93	−14.30	−.344%

Hit <#> <Index> **FVD** Go for detail Fair Value analysis.

Australia 61 2 9777 8600   Brazil 5511 3048 4500   Europe 44 20 7330 7500   Germany 49 69 920410

Hong Kong 852 2977 6000 Japan 81 3 3201 8900 Singapore   65 6212 1000 U.S.   1 212 318 2000 Copyright 2007 Bloomberg L.P.
H445-95-0 10–Oct–2007 15 : 08 : 45

Panel B. Calculating the December 2007 S&P 500 Futures Contract Price

<Help> for explanation, <MENU> for similar functions.   Index **FVD**
ENTER ALL VALUES AND HIT <GO>

EQUITY INDEX FAIR VALUE (DETAIL)

S&P 500 INDEX	Cash	Future	Theo. Future	Fair Value	Spread (Basis)	Upper Bound	Lower Bound
1) SPZ7vsSPX	1562.47	1572.30	1573.36	10.89	9.83	12.07	9.72
Risk Free:	5.25%	Expire:	12/21/07	Dividend:	5.82	Dvd Yld:	1.84%
Imlied Rate:	4.91%	Days:	73	Precent of Gross Dividend:		100.0%	
2) SPH8vsSPX	1562.47	1588.10	1586.33	23.86	25.63	25.05	22.68
Risk Free:	5.23%	Expire:	3/20/08	Dividend:	13.55	Dvd Yld:	1.84%
Implied Rate:	5.47%	Days:	163	Percent of Gross Dividend:		100.0%	

Note: use RDFL<go> for the risk free rate default.

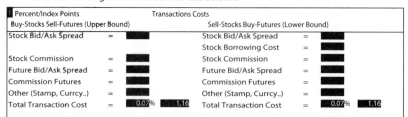

Percent/Index Points		Transactions Costs		
Buy-Stocks Sell-Futures (Upper Bound)			Sell-Stocks Buy-Futures (Lower Bound)	
Stock Bid/Ask Spread	=		Stock Bid/Ask Spread	=
			Stock Borrowing Cost	=
Stock Commission	=		Stock Commission	=
Future Bid/Ask Spread	=		Future Bid/Ask Spread	=
Commission Futures	=		Commission Futures	=
Other (Stamp, Currcy..)	=		Other (Stamp, Currcy..)	=
Total Transaction Cost	=	0.07% 1.16	Total Transaction Cost	= 0.07% 1.16

Hit <#> Go to monitor the intra-day spread of cash & futures (Basis)

Australia 61 2 9777 8600   Brazil 5511 3048 4500   Europe 44 20 7330 7500   Germany 49 69 920410

Hong Kong 852 2977 6000 Japan   81 3 3201 8900   Singapore   65 6212 1000 U.S.   1 212 318 2000 Copyright 2007 Bloomberg L.P.
H445-95-0 10–Oct–2007 15 : 09 : 01

to the allegation that index arbitrage caused the worldwide stock market crash of October 1987, Roll (1988) documented that countries with the greatest level of program trading activity experienced less pronounced price declines. This finding is consistent with the notion that index arbitrage reduces volatility by stabilizing cash and futures prices.

A Stock Index Futures Application

Isolating the Unsystematic Risk of an Individual Stock In Chapter 20, we demonstrated how stock index futures could alter the systematic risk of an otherwise well-diversified portfolio. When the holding is an individual stock, this process can isolate the unique attributes of the company. Recall that:

$$\text{Total Stock Risk} = \text{Systematic Risk} + \text{Unsystematic Risk}$$

with the systematic component representing about 25–40 percent of the total risk for the typical firm. Thus, using stock index futures to adjust the stock's beta to zero effectively isolates the unsystematic portion of risk.

To see how this might work, suppose that in mid-February you own 75,000 shares of Pharmco Inc., a multinational pharmaceutical firm. The current price of Pharmco stock is $46.75, and you calculate the company's beta at 0.99. You like the stock as an investment because of the quality of its management and some other unique attributes of the firm, but you are concerned that over the next few months the aggregate stock market might undergo a sizable correction that could more than offset any firm-specific gains.

To protect yourself, you decide to sell June S&P 500 futures contracts, which are currently trading at a settlement price of 1,271.10. At this price, we have seen that the implied dollar value of a single contract is $317,775. The current value of your Pharmco stock is $3,506,250. Since the stock's beta can be defined as $\rho \; [\sigma_{\Delta S} \div \sigma_{\Delta F}]$ the optimal hedge ratio formula developed earlier leaves:

$$N^* = \left[\frac{\text{Market Value of Spot Position}}{\text{Value Implied by Futures Contract}} \right] \beta$$

$$= [(\$3,506,250) \div (\$317,775)](0.99) = 10.92$$

so you decide to short 11 contracts.

Now suppose that by mid-June when your futures position expires, the S&P 500 index settles at a level of 1,251.10 while the price of Pharmco stock has increased to $47.50. Although you have made a modest profit on your common stock holding (i.e., $56,250, or 1.60 percent), you will also benefit from a trading profit on the futures position of $55,000 (= (11) [1,271.10 − 1,251.10](250)). Your total return is $111,250, which, expressed as a percentage of your original investment of $3,506,250 is equivalent to an unsystematic appreciation in Pharmco's stock of 3.17 percent. Notice that the difference between this amount and the gross increase of 1.60 percent in Pharmco stock is equal to the 1.57 percent (= [1,251.1 ÷ 1,271.1] − 1) that the stock index future position fell.

21.4.5 Currency Forwards and Futures

Whether in the spot or forward markets, foreign exchange (FX) transactions often involve a confusing blend of unique terminology and market conventions. These conventions represent an initial barrier to understanding how FX deals work. Thus, we begin our analysis of currency derivatives with a brief overview of some of the fundamental features of these products.

The Mechanics of Currency Transactions The market for foreign currency is no different than any other market, in that buyer and seller negotiate for the exchange of a certain amount of a predetermined commodity at a fixed cash price. The challenge in FX transactions is that the "commodity" involved is someone else's currency. This means that the transaction can be viewed in two ways. For example, suppose that Company A agrees to pay 100 U.S. dollars to Company B in exchange for 50 British pounds. In this case, is Company A buying sterling (GBP) or selling dollars (USD)?[6] Similarly, is Company B selling pounds or buying dollars? Both are correct, depending on one's point of view.

Because of this dual interpretation, the price for all FX transactions also can be quoted in two ways. Assuming that Company A is a U.S.-based firm, it would probably think of the transaction as the purchase of 50 pounds at a cost of 100 dollars, which would yield the price of USD 2.0000/GBP ($= 100/50$). This method of quoting FX prices is called the *direct,* or *American,* convention. Under this convention, the pound (i.e., the foreign currency from the U.S. firm's perspective) is treated as the commodity, and its price per unit is expressed in terms of dollars. On the other hand, if Company B is a British corporation, its managers would likely think of prices in terms of the amount of sterling they have to pay to acquire dollars. Here, that amount translates into a price of GBP 0.5000/USD. Treating the dollar as the commodity yields the *indirect,* or *European,* quotation method. Of course, the direct and indirect quotes are just *reciprocals* of one another, as they describe the same transaction from two different perspectives.

Exhibit 21.13 shows a representative set of FX quotes. Two prices are listed beside each currency. The first column reports the current days' dollar price for trading one unit of that currency (i.e., direct quote). For instance, the prevailing price of a Norwegian krone on that date was USD 0.1839. The next column expresses this same price in indirect terms (e.g., NOK 5.4377/USD = $1 \div$ USD 0.1839/NOK). Thus, the terms of a spot FX transaction can be structured to meet the particular needs of the counterparties involved.

Another important aspect of the FX markets highlighted by this display is that although many currencies trade in the spot market, relatively few also quote prices for forward transactions. In this list, only the British, Canadian, Japanese, and Swiss currencies have forward contracts. These contracts, which are negotiated in the over-the-counter market with a currency dealer (such as a multinational bank), carry maturities one, three, and six months into the future. For example, an investor wishing to buy Swiss francs would pay USD 0.8515 per franc if the transaction were completed immediately, 0.8534 if the transaction were negotiated now but consummated in 30 days, and USD 0.8569 or USD 0.8614 for exchanges completed in 90 or 180 days, respectively.

In the situation where it costs increasingly more dollars to buy the same franc the farther out in the future it is delivered, the dollar is said to be trading at a **forward discount** to the franc. Conversely, the franc is at a **forward premium** to the dollar. This relationship depends on the currencies being compared. In this set of quotes, the U.S. dollar is trading at a forward discount to the Swiss franc, Canadian dollar, and the Japanese yen, while it is at a forward premium to the British pound. We will see shortly that whether a particular currency trades at a discount or a premium to another depends on the relative level of the investment rates in the two countries.

Exhibit 21.14 lists quotes for a sample of exchange-traded currency futures contracts. These specific instruments are traded at the CME. Each contract involving U.S. dollars follows the convention that the U.S. dollar is the native monetary unit and the foreign currency is the commodity, meaning that all prices are quoted using the direct method. These contracts are also standardized to deliver a set number of units of the foreign currency on a specific date in the future. For instance, the March 2008 Euro contract negotiated on that date required the long position to purchase—and the short position to deliver—125,000 euros at the price of USD 1.4149 per euro. By convention, all currency futures on the CME mature on the third Wednesday of the stated delivery month and can be settled with a wire transfer of the foreign currency. Notice that the dollar traded at a forward discount to the euro at this time.

---

[6] Currency traders often use three-letter abbreviations to denote a particular currency. Some of the more common abbreviations include USD (U.S. dollars), CAD (Canadian dollars), GBP (British pounds), JPY (Japanese yen), CHF (Swiss franc), and EUR (the Euro currency). For a more complete listing, see Gastineau and Kritzman (2001).

Exhibit 21.13 Spot and Forward Currency Quotations

U.S.-dollar foreign-exchange rates in late New York trading

Country/currency	Thurs in US$	Thurs per US$	US$vs, YTD chg (%)	Country/currency	Thurs in US$	Thurs per US$	US$vs, YTD chg (%)
Americas				**Europe**			
Argentina peso*	.3170	3.1546	**3.1**	**Czech Rep.** koruna**	.05125	19.512	**−6.3**
Brazil real	.5487	1.8225	**−14.7**	**Denmark** krone	.1897	5.2715	**−6.7**
Canada dollar	1.0027	.9973	**−14.5**	**Euro area** euro	1.4136	.7074	**−6.6**
1-mos forward	1.0029	.9971	**−14.4**	**Hungary** forint	.005604	178.44	**−6.3**
3-mos forward	1.0036	.9964	**−14.3**	**Malta** lira	3.2927	.3037	**−6.6**
6-mos forward	1.0038	.9962	**−14.1**	**Norway** krone	.1839	5.4377	**−12.8**
Chile peso	.001976	506.07	**−4.9**	**Poland** zloty	.3752	2.6652	**−8.2**
Colombia peso	.0004959	2016.54	**−9.9**	**Russia** ruble‡	.04004	24.975	**−5.1**
Ecuador US dollar	1	1	**unch**	**Slovak Rep** koruna	.04135	24.184	**−7.4**
Mexico peso*	.0919	10.8767	**0.7**	**Sweden** krona	.1537	6.5062	**−4.9**
Peru new sol	.3311	3.020	**−5.5**	**Switzerland** franc	.8515	1.1744	**−3.7**
Uruguay peso†	.04420	22.62	**−7.2**	1-mos forward	.8534	1.1718	**−3.6**
Venezuela bolivar	.000466	2145.92	**unch**	3-mos forward	.8569	1.1670	**−3.5**
Asia-Pacific				6-mos forward	.8614	1.1609	**−3.3**
				Turkey lira**	.8335	1.1998	**−15.2**
Australian dollar	.8875	1.1268	**−11.0**	**UK pound**	2.0383	.4906	**−3.9**
China yuan	.1332	7.5060	**−3.9**	1-mos forward	2.0368	.4910	**−3.8**
Hong Kong dollar	.1289	7.7598	**−0.2**	3-mos forward	2.0340	.4916	**−3.7**
India rupee	.02535	39.448	**−10.6**	6-mos forward	2.0287	.4929	**−3.5**
Indonesia rupiah	.0001096	9124	**1.5**	**Middle East/Africa**			
Japan yen	.008583	116.51	**−2.1**				
1-mos forward	.008616	116.06	**−2.1**	**Bahrain** dinar	2.6533	.3769	**unch**
3-mos forward	.008677	115.25	**−2.0**	**Egypt** pound*	.1803	5.5475	**−2.9**
6-mos forward	.008761	114.14	**−1.8**	**Israel** shekel	.2494	4.0096	**−4.9**
Malaysia ringgit§	.2933	3.4095	**−3.4**	**Jordan** dinar	1.4125	.7080	**−0.1**
New Zealand dollar	.7555	1.3236	**−6.7**	**Kuwait** dinar	3.5700	.2801	**−3.1**
Pakistan rupee	.01647	60.717	**−0.1**	**Lebanon** pound	.0006612	1512.40	**unch**
Philippines peso	.0222	44.984	**−8.3**	**Saudi Arabia** riyal	.2671	3.7439	**−0.2**
Singapore dollar	.6750	1.4815	**−3.4**	**South Africa** rand	.1446	6.9156	**−1.1**
South Korea won	.0010911	916.51	**−1.4**	**UAE** dirham	.2723	3.6724	**unch**
Taiwan dollar	.03067	35.605	**0.1**				
Thailand baht	.03155	31.696	**−10.6**	**SDR**††	1.5515	.6445	**−3.0**

*Floating rate   †Financial.   §Government rate   ‡Russian Central Bank rate   ** Rebased as of Jan 1, 2005
††Special Drawing Rights (SDR); from the International Monetary Fund; based on exchange rates for U.S., British and Japanese currencies.
Note: Based on trading among banks of $1 million and more, as quoted at 4 p.m. ET by Reuters.

Interest Rate Parity and Covered Interest Arbitrage   A key concept in FX risk management is **interest rate parity**, a condition that specifies the "no arbitrage" relationship between spot and forward FX rates and the level of interest rates in each currency. This connection is best seen through an example. Suppose that an institutional investor has USD 100,000 to invest for one year and is considering two different riskless alternatives. The first strategy entails the purchase of a U.S. Treasury bill. Assume that under current market conditions, the effective U.S. dollar risk-free interest rate is 4.50 percent per annum for a one-year maturity, so that a direct T-bill investment would return USD 104,500 at the end of the 12 months.

For the second strategy, suppose that the investor also can sell the USD 100,000 in the spot market at the current exchange rate of AUD 1.20/USD (or, equivalently, USD 0.8333/AUD) to obtain a total of 120,000 Australian dollars. We assume that that amount can then be invested in a Australian risk-free security at an annualized rate of 7.00 percent, returning AUD 128,400 at the end of the year. Of course, to make this return comparable to the USD-denominated

Exhibit 21.14 Currency Futures Quotations

	Open	High	Contact hi lo Low	Settle	Chg	Open interest
Japanese Yen (CME)-¥12,500,000; $ per 100¥						
Dec	.8638	.8675	.8636	**.8657**	.0011	198,186
March'08	.8725	.8759	.8725	**.8743**	.0012	8,620
Canadian Dollar (CME)-CAD 100,000; $ per CAD						
Dec	1.0025	1.0044	.9990	**1.0040**	.0004	145,472
March'08	1.0019	1.0047	.9999	**1.0045**	.0004	1,726
British Pound (CME)-£62,500; $ per £						
Dec	2.0289	2.0400	2.0247	**2.0346**	.0058	104,514
March'08	2.0256	2.0345	2.0204	**2.0296**	.0058	833
Swiss Franc (CME)-CHF 125,000; $ per CHF						
Dec	.8517	.8562	.8505	**.8548**	.0024	77,045
March'08	.8563	.8608	.8556	**.8594**	.0024	152
Australian Dollar (CME)-AUD 100,000; $ per AUD						
Dec	.8797	.8873	.8768	**.8845**	.0049	101,524
March'08	.8741	.8828	.8737	**.8802**	.0049	194
Mexican Peso (CME)-MXN 500,000; $ per 10MXN						
Oct	....	....	....	**.91825**	.00275	69
Dec	.91150	.91550	.91100	**.91450**	.00225	73,494
Euro (CME)-€125,000; $ per €						
Dec	1.4111	1.4170	1.4087	**1.4137**	.0011	208,935
March'08	1.4136	1.4184	1.4102	**1.4149**	.0011	1,321

Source: From the *Wall Street Journal*, October 5, 2007. Copyright 2007 by DOW JONES & CO INC. Reproduced with permission of DOW JONES & CO INC in the format Other Book via Copyright Clearance Center.

proceeds from the first strategy, the Australian dollars will have to be converted back into U.S. currency. If this translation is negotiated at the end of the investment, however, the investor will be subjected to foreign exchange risk in that he will not know at Date 0 what the AUD/USD exchange rate will be at Date T. Thus, to make the second strategy riskless, the investor must enter into a forward contract to exchange AUD back into USD at the end of the year. The question then is, What would the exchange rate priced into a one-year forward contract have to be at Date 0 to leave the investor indifferent between these two strategies?

These investments are depicted in Exhibit 21.15. The essence of the arbitrage argument is that the one-year forward FX rate must be such that USD 104,500 equals AUD 128,400. Otherwise there would be an arbitrage opportunity, or at least a dominating investment choice. The forward contract rate consistent with interest rate parity is AUD 1.2287/USD (= 128,400 ÷ 104,500) on an indirect basis, or USD 0.8139/AUD quoted directly. This is a breakeven value in the sense that it allows the 4.50 percent investment return in the United States to be equal to the 7.00 percent available in Australia when the two are converted to the same currency. That is, the Australian return must be "deflated" by 250 basis points to leave the investor indifferent between the two strategies. This reduction occurs because, to invest in the AUD-denominated security, the investor buys Australian dollars at a price of USD 0.8333/AUD but must sell them back in the forward market at the lower price of USD 0.8139/AUD. Thus, the loss on the roundtrip currency translation required in the second strategy adjusts its net return down to the 4.50% available on the direct dollar investment.[7]

If the actual one-year forward contract FX rate were *higher* than this breakeven level—say, for instance, AUD 1.25/USD—the currency translation loss would be greater than 250 basis points, leaving the USD-based strategy the most profitable choice. Given that there is now a difference between the returns to two otherwise comparable riskless investments, arbitrage is possible. In this case, an arbitrageur could enter the following transactions:

1. Borrow AUD 120,000 at 7.00%; agree to repay AUD 128,400 in one year.
2. Sell the foreign currency on the spot market at AUD 1.20/USD; receive USD 100,000.

---

[7] Under these conditions the actual currency loss is calculated as $(0.8139/0.8333 - 1) = -2.33\%$. This, in turn, means the dollar-denominated return to the second strategy is $[(1 + 0.07) \times (1 - 0.233) - 1] = 4.50\%$.

Exhibit 21.15 Interest Rate Parity

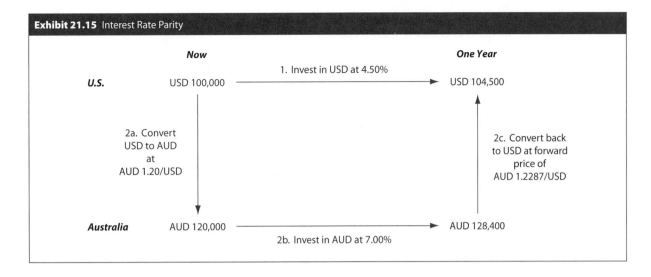

3. Invest the USD 100,000 at 4.50%; receive USD 104,500 in one year.
4. Sell USD 104,500 forward at AUD 1.25/USD; agree to receive AUD 130,625.
5. Repay the CAD loan; collect net profit of AUD 2,225.

If the actual one-year forward rate was *lower* than breakeven—for instance, AUD 1.21/USD—the arbitrageur would implement the opposite trade:

1. Borrow USD 100,000 at 4.50%; agree to repay USD 104,500 in one year.
2. Sell the dollars on the spot market at AUD 1.20/USD; receive AUD 120,000.
3. Invest the AUD 120,000 at 7.00%; receive AUD 128,400 in one year.
4. Buy USD 104,500 forward at AUD 1.21/USD; agree to pay AUD 126,445.
5. Repay the U.S. dollar loan; collect net profit of AUD 1,955.

These strategies are known as **covered interest arbitrage** because the arbitrageur will always hold the security denominated in the currency that is the least expensive to deliver in the forward market. In this sense, the arbitrage position is hedged, or covered, against adverse foreign exchange movements while receiving the largest amount of net interest income. In practice, traders involved in covered interest arbitrage strategies utilize bank rates (e.g., LIBOR) for borrowing and lending, which injects a slight amount of credit risk into the scheme. After surveying the empirical evidence, Solnik and McLeavey (2004) have concluded that the ability to take these arbitrage positions keeps interest rate parity a viable description of the way spot and forward prices are set for the world's major currencies.

   With exchange rates quoted on an *indirect basis* (i.e., foreign currency [FC] per U.S. dollar), the general formula for the forward rate implied by interest rate parity is

$$\text{Forward} = \text{Spot} \times \left(\frac{1 + (\text{Foreign Interest Rate})\left(\frac{T}{365}\right)}{1 + (\text{U.S. Interest Rate})\left(\frac{T}{365}\right)} \right)$$

where:

   T = the number of days from the joint settlement of the futures and cash positions until they mature

In the last example, $T = 365$ so that AUD 1.2287/USD = AUD 1.20/USD × (1.07/1.045). This formula also assumes that the rates in question are quoted on a 365-day basis. If U.S. money market rates such as LIBOR are used, then the equation should be adjusted to a 360-day year.

Letting S_0 and $F_{0,T}$ once again denote the current spot and forward prices for an instrument that matures at Date T, the preceding expression can be rewritten as

21.9
$$\frac{F_{0,T}}{S_0} = \left(\frac{1 + (RFR_{FC})\left(\dfrac{T}{365}\right)}{1 + (RFR_{USD})\left(\dfrac{T}{365}\right)} \right)$$

where:

RFR_{USD} = the annualized risk-free rate in the United States
RFR_{FC} = the annualized risk-free rate in the foreign market

Equation 21.9 defines the relationship between four different prices, all of which are determined at Date 0: spot foreign exchange rate, forward foreign exchange rate, U.S. investment rate, and foreign investment rate. Importantly, notice that, if the markets are aligned properly, $F_{0,T}$ will be greater than S_0 whenever RFR_{FC} is greater than RFR_{USD}, with the opposite holding when $RFR_{FC} < RFR_{USD}$. With indirect currency quotes, $F_{0,T} > S_0$ implies that the foreign currency is at a forward discount to the dollar. In other words, the country with the *lowest* investment rate should see its currency trade at a forward premium. The intuition behind this is that to keep investment capital from flowing to the country with the highest returns, the currency translation must adjust accordingly. Thus, the high-interest country will suffer from a weaker forward value for its currency.[8]

A Currency Futures Application

Calculating Implied World Investment Rates Suppose that you are the cash manager for a multinational company and you have $1,000,000 in short-term balances that you can invest in sovereign-issued paper for the next several months. On Thursday, October 4, 2007, you obtain the following quotes for both spot and futures exchange rates for several currencies:

Currency	Spot (USD/FC)	March 2008 Futures (USD/FC)
Australian dollar	0.8875	0.8802
Japanese yen	0.008583	0.008743
Swiss franc	0.8515	0.8594
Canadian dollar	1.0027	1.0045
British pound	2.0383	2.0296
Mexican peso	0.09190	0.09145

If you enter into any of these transactions, they will settle on Monday, October 8 (i.e., two business days later). The futures contracts mature on Wednesday, March 19, 2008, which leaves a 163-day investment window from settlement to maturity.

You also observe that a U.S. Treasury bill maturing at virtually the same time (i.e., March 20) pays a bond equivalent (i.e., 365-day) yield of 4.15 percent. Before checking the actual quotes for foreign-currency-denominated government paper from these other countries, you first calculate the investment rates implied by the interest rate parity relationship. Specifically, for the six countries listed, you compute:

$$\text{Implied Rate} = \left[\left(\frac{\text{Spot}}{\text{Futures}} \right)\left(1 + (\text{U.S. Interest Rate})\left(\frac{163}{365}\right)\right) - 1 \right]\left(\frac{365}{163}\right)$$

---

[8] When using direct quotes (i.e., USD/FC), the interest rate parity condition must be adjusted by taking the reciprocal of the ratio on the left-hand side: $[S_0 \div F_{0,T}] = [(1 + RFR_{FC} (T \div 365)) \div (1 + RFR_{USD} (T \div 365))]$. In the example given, with the direct quotes for the spot and forward being USD 0.8333/AUD (= 1/1.20) and USD 0.8139/AUD, respectively, we have $S_0 =$ USD 0.8333/AUD = USD 0.8139/AUD $\times$ (1.07/1.045).

which is just the parity relationship rearranged to use direct currency quotes and to isolate the foreign interest rate. The direct parity formulation is the correct one to use because of the convention prevailing in the U.S. currency futures market. For British sterling, this calculation yields an implied 163-day annualized investment rate of:

$$\left[\left(\frac{2.0383}{2.0296}\right)\left(1 + (0.0415)\left(\frac{163}{365}\right)\right) - 1\right]\left(\frac{365}{163}\right) = 5.13\%$$

This means that with the current spot and futures prices for exchanging dollars and pounds, you would be indifferent between receiving a 5.5-month investment rate of 4.15 percent in the United States or 5.13 percent in England.

Summarizing this calculation for all of the countries leaves:

Country	Implied 163-Day Rate
Australia	6.04%
Japan	−0.02
Switzerland	2.05
Canada	3.74
Great Britain	5.13
Mexico	5.27

You can now compare these figures to the actual investment rates in each of the countries to determine if a futures-based synthetic foreign bond strategy is warranted. If, for example, the actual British six-month gilt rate were 5.50 percent, you could exceed the 4.15 percent dollar-denominated T-bill return by (1) exchanging your dollars for pounds in the spot market at USD 2.0383/GBP, (2) investing for 163 days in the sterling-based security at 5.50 percent, and (3) translating your proceeds back into dollars at maturity using the futures rate of USD 2.0296/GBP.

Finally, notice that the countries with implied rates higher than 4.15 percent (i.e., Australia, Great Britain, and Mexico) are those whose currencies sold at a forward discount to the U.S. dollar over this 163-day window. Conversely, Japan, Switzerland, and Canada had currencies at a forward premium to the dollar and thus had implied investment rates less than 4.15 percent. One caution necessary in interpreting these yields properly is that it is imperative that the futures and spot FX quotes were obtained simultaneously and pertain to the same investment denomination. In this example, these conditions were more than likely violated to some extent. [This, in fact, is the likely explanation for Japan's implied investment rate being negative (i.e., −0.02 percent), although Japan's actual short-term government rates were virtually zero at this time.]

• • • • SUMMARY • • • •

- As the most fundamental type of derivative instruments available, forward and futures contracts greatly increase the alternatives that investors have to create and manage their portfolios and establish new trading opportunities. In this chapter, we discuss how these contracts work and the ways they are used in practice. Forwards and futures differ primarily in the areas of design flexibility and collateralization. Specifically, forward agreements generally are more flexible but carry more credit risk, while the process of marking margin accounts to market on a daily basis makes futures contracts more secure (to the exchange, at least) even as the standardization of contract terms makes them less adaptable to the end user.

- Hedging is key to understanding forward-based contracting and the basis is the most important concept in understanding hedging. The basis is defined as the difference between spot and forward prices at any point in time. It contains the essence of a short hedge position so that the hedger effectively trades the price risk of the underlying asset for the basis risk inherent in the spot-forward combination. This notion also leads to the calculation of an optimal hedge ratio, which specifies the appropriate number of contracts by minimizing the amount of basis (i.e., correlation) risk in the combined position.
- Although forward and futures contracts are not securities, their contract settlement prices still must follow certain regularities for these markets to remain efficient. The cost

of carry model suggests that in order to avoid arbitrage, the forward price should be equal to the spot price plus the cost of transporting the underlying asset to the future delivery date. These carrying costs can include commissions for physical storage, an opportunity cost for the net amount of invested capital, and a premium for the convenience of consuming the asset now. When forward prices are set in this manner, the market value of a new contract should be zero, although this value can become either positive or negative as the contract matures under changing market conditions.

These concepts were illustrated with detailed examinations of three types of financial futures contracts: interest rate, equity index, and foreign exchange. In addition to describing the dynamics of each of these markets, we discussed different applications, including those involving hedging, speculation, and arbitrage. These applications produced some useful adaptations of the basic concepts, such as duration, and beta-based hedge ratios for interest rate and stock index futures as well as the currency futures version of the cost of carry model known as interest rate parity.

· · · · SUGGESTED READINGS · · · ·

- McDonald, Robert L. *Derivatives Markets*, 2nd ed. Boston, MA: Addison-Wesley, 2006.
- Smithson, Charles W. *Managing Financial Risk*, 3rd ed. New York: McGraw-Hill, 1998.
- Stulz, Rene M. *Risk Management and Derivatives.* Mason, OH: South-Western Publishing, 2003.
- Telser, Lester G. "Futures Trading and the Storage of Cotton and Wheat." *Journal of Political Economy* 66 (June 1958).
- Working, Holbrook. "Economic Functions of Futures Markets." In *Selected Writings of Holbrook Working.* Chicago: Chicago Board of Trade, 1977.

· · · · QUESTIONS · · · ·

1. We have futures contracts on Treasury bonds, but we do not have futures contracts on individual corporate bonds. We have cattle and hog futures but no chicken futures. Explain why the market has developed in this manner. What do you think are the most important characteristics for the success of a new futures contract concept?

2. "Hedgers trade price risk for basis risk." What is meant by this statement? In particular, explain the concept of the basis in a hedge transaction and how forward and futures contracts can be selected to minimize risk.

3. Suppose you are a derivatives trader specializing in creating customized commodity forward contracts for clients and then hedging your position with exchange-traded futures contracts. Your latest position is an agreement to deliver 100,000 gallons of unleaded gasoline to a client in three months.
   a. Explain how you can hedge your position using gasoline futures contracts.
   b. In calculating your hedge ratio, how must you account for the different valuation procedures used for forward and futures contracts? That is, what difference does it make that forward contracts are valued on a discounted basis while futures contracts are marked to market without discounting?
   c. If the only available gasoline futures contracts call for the delivery of 42,000 gallons and mature in either two or four months, describe the nature of the basis risk involved in your hedge.

4. A multinational corporation is about to embark on a major financial restructuring program. One critical stage will be the issuance of seven-year Eurobonds sometime within the next month. The CFO is concerned with recent instability in capital markets and with the particular event that market yields rise prior to issuance, forcing the corporation to pay a higher coupon rate on the bonds. It is decided to hedge that risk by selling 10-year Treasury note futures contracts. Notice that this is a classic cross hedge wherein 10-year Treasury notes are used to manage the risk of 7-year Eurobonds.

   Describe the nature of the basis risk in the hedge. In particular what specific events with respect to the shape of the Treasury yield curve and the Eurobond spread over Treasuries could render the hedge ineffective? In other words, under what circumstances would the hedge fail and make the corporation worse off?

5. **CFA EXAMINATION LEVEL II** Mike Lane will have $5 million to invest in five-year U.S. Treasury bonds three months from now. Lane believes interest rates will fall during the next three months and wants to take advantage of prevailing interest rates by hedging against a decline in interest rates. Lane has sufficient bonds to pay the costs of entering into and maintaining a futures position.

   a. Describe what action Lane should take using five-year U.S. Treasury note futures contracts to protect against declining interest rates.

   Assume three months have gone by and, despite Lane's expectations, five-year cash and forward market interest rates have increased by 100 basis points compared with the five-year forward market interest rates of three months ago.

   b. Discuss the effect of higher interest rates on the value of the futures position that Lane entered into in Part a.

   c. Discuss how the return from Lane's hedged position differs from the return he could now earn if he had not hedged in Part a.

6. You own an equally weighted portfolio of 50 different stocks worth about $5,000,000. The stocks are from several different industries, and the portfolio is reasonably well diversified. Which do you think would provide you with the best overall hedge: a single position in an index futures or 50 different positions in futures contracts on the individual stocks? What are the most important factors to consider in making this decision?

7. **CFA EXAMINATION LEVEL II** Four factors affect the value of a futures contract on a stock index. Three of these factors are: the current price of the stock index, the time remaining until the contract maturity (delivery) date, and the dividends on the stock index. Identify the fourth factor and explain how and why changes in this factor affect the value of the futures contract.

8. It is often stated that a stock index arbitrage trade is easier to implement when the stock index futures contract price is above its theoretical level than when it is below that value. What institutional realities might make this statement true? Describe the steps involved in forming the arbitrage transaction in both circumstances. To the extent that the statement is valid, what does it suggest about the ability of the stock index futures market to remain efficient?

9. **CFA EXAMINATION LEVEL III** The World Ecosystem Consortium (WEC) pension trust holds $100 million in long-term U.S. Treasury bonds. To reduce interest rate risk, you, as an independent advisor to the WEC, suggest that the trust diversify by investing $30 million in German government bonds (bunds) for six months. You point out that a fixed-currency futures hedge (shorting a fixed number of contracts) could be used by WEC's pension trust to protect the $30 million in bonds against exchange rate losses over the six months.

   Explain how a fixed-currency futures hedge could be constructed for the WEC trust by shorting currency futures contracts to protect against exchange rate losses. Describe one characteristic of this hedge that WEC's investment committee might deem undesirable.

10. Explain why the currency of Country A, whose interest rates are twice as great as those in Country B, must trade at a forward discount. If there were no difference between the spot and forward exchange rates in this interest rate environment, what arbitrage trade could be constructed to take advantage of the situation?

• • • • PROBLEMS • • • •

1. It is March 9, and you have just entered into a short position in a soybean meal futures contract. The contract expires on July 9 and calls for the delivery of 100 tons of soybean meal. Further, because this is a futures position, it requires the posting of a $3,000 initial margin and a $1,500 maintenance margin; for simplicity, however, assume that the account is marked to market on a monthly basis. Assume the following represent the contract delivery prices (in dollars per ton) that prevail on each settlement date:

March 9 (initiation)	$173.00
April 9	179.75
May 9	189.00
June 9	182.50
July 9 (delivery)	174.25

   a. Calculate the equity value of your margin account on each settlement date, including any additional equity required to meet a margin call. Also compute the amount of cash that will be returned to you on July 9, and the gain or loss on your position, expressed as a percentage of your initial margin commitment.

b. Assuming that the underlying soybean meal investment pays no dividend and requires a storage cost of 1.5 percent (of current value), calculate the current (i.e., March 9) spot price for a ton of soybean meal and the implied May 9 price for the same ton. In your calculations, assume that an annual risk-free rate of 8 percent prevails over the entire contract life.

c. Now suppose that on March 9 you also entered into a long forward contract for the purchase of 100 tons of soybean meal on July 9. Assume further that the July forward and futures contract prices always are identical to one another at any point in time. Calculate the cash amount of your gain or loss if you unwind both positions in their respective markets on May 9 and June 9, taking into account the prevailing settlement conditions in the two markets.

2. You are a coffee dealer anticipating the purchase of 82,000 pounds of coffee in three months. You are concerned that the price of coffee will rise, so you take a long position in coffee futures. Each contract covers 37,500 pounds, and so, rounding to the nearest contract, you decide to go long in two contracts. The futures price at the time you initiate your hedge is 55.95 cents per pound. Three months later, the actual spot price of coffee turns out to be 58.56 cents per pound and the futures price is 59.20 cents per pound.

a. Determine the effective price at which you purchased your coffee. How do you account for the difference in amounts for the spot and hedge positions?

b. Describe the nature of the basis risk in this long hedge.

 3. **CFA Examination Level III** June Klein, CFA, manages a $100 million (market value) U.S. government bond portfolio for an institution. She anticipates a small parallel shift in the yield curve and wants to fully hedge the portfolio against any such change.

PORTFOLIO AND TREASURY BOND FUTURES CONTRACT CHARACTERISTICS

Security	Modified Duration	Basis Point Value	Conversion Factor for Cheapest to Deliver Bond	Portfolio Value/Future Contract Price
Portfolio	10 years	$100,000	Not Applicable	$100,000,000
U.S. Treasury bond futures contract	8 years	$75.32	1	94–05

a. Discuss two reasons for using futures rather than selling bonds to hedge a bond portfolio. No calculations required.

b. Formulate Klein's hedging strategy using only the futures contract shown. Calculate the number of futures contracts to implement the strategy. Show all calculations.

c. Determine how each of the following would change in value if interest rates increase by 10 basis points as anticipated. Show all calculations.
   (1) The original portfolio
   (2) The Treasury bond futures position
   (3) The newly hedged portfolio

d. State three reasons why Klein's hedging strategy might not fully protect the portfolio against interest rate risk.

e. Describe a zero-duration hedging strategy using only the government bond portfolio and options on U.S. Treasury bond futures contracts. No calculations required.

4. A bond speculator currently has positions in two separate corporate bond portfolios: a long holding in Portfolio 1 and a short holding in Portfolio 2. All the bonds have the same credit quality. Other relevant information on these positions includes:

Portfolio	Bond	Market Value (Mil.)	Coupon Rate	Compounding Frequency	Maturity	Yield to Maturity
1	A	$6.0	0%	Annual	3 yrs	7.31%
	B	4.0	0	Annual	14 yrs	7.31
2	C	11.5	4.6	Annual	9 yrs	7.31

Treasury bond futures (based on $100,000 face value of 20-year T-bonds having an 8 percent semiannual coupon) with a maturity exactly six months from now are currently priced at 109–24 with a corresponding yield to maturity of 7.081 percent. The "yield betas" between the futures contract and Bonds A, B, and C are 1.13, 1.03, and 1.01, respectively. Finally, the modified duration for the T-bond underlying the futures contract is 10.355 years.

   a. Calculate the modified duration (expressed in years) for each of the two bond portfolios. What will be the *approximate* percentage change in the value of each if all yields increase by 60 basis points on an annual basis?

   b. Without performing the calculations, explain which of the portfolios will *actually* have its value impacted to the greatest extent (in absolute terms) by the shift yields. (Hint: This explanation requires knowledge of the concept of *bond convexity*.)

   c. Assuming the bond speculator wants to hedge her *net* bond position, what is the optimal number of futures contracts that must be bought or sold? Start by calculating the optimal hedge ratio between the futures contract and the two bond portfolios separately and then combine them.

5. **CFA Examination Level II** Susan Baker is an investor who seeks to find arbitrage pricing discrepancies in the marketplace over the next six months. She has noted the following data:

Instrument	Spot Price	Futures Price for Contract Expiring In Six Months	Income from Treasury Note for Six Months	Finance Charge for Six Months
U.S. Treasury note deliverable on the futures contract	$101	$100 (invoice price)	$4.50	$2.50

List the components of the arbitrage transaction and calculate the arbitrage profits, if any, that are available to exploit a possible pricing discrepancy. Show your calculations.

6. As a relationship officer for a money-center commercial bank, one of your corporate accounts has just approached you about a one-year loan for $1,000,000. The customer would pay a quarterly interest expense based on the prevailing level of LIBOR at the beginning of each three-month period. As is the bank's convention on all such loans, the amount of the interest payment would then be paid at the end of the quarterly cycle when the new rate for the next cycle is determined. You observe the following LIBOR yield curve in the cash market.

90-day LIBOR	4.60%
180-day LIBOR	4.75
270-day LIBOR	5.00
360-day LIBOR	5.30

   a. If 90-day LIBOR rises to the levels "predicted" by the implied forward rates, what will the dollar level of the bank's interest receipt be at the end of each quarter during the one-year loan period?

   b. If the bank wanted to hedge its exposure to failing LIBOR on this loan commitment, describe the sequence of transactions in the futures markets it could undertake.

   c. Assuming the yields inferred from the Eurodollar futures contract prices for the next three settlement periods are equal to the implied forward rates, calculate the annuity value that would leave the bank indifferent between making the floating-rate loan and hedging it in the futures market, and making a one-year fixed-rate loan. Express this annuity value in both dollar and annual (360-day) percentage terms.

7. Suppose that one day in early April, you observe the following prices on futures contracts maturing in June: 93.35 for Eurodollar and 94.07 for T-bill. These prices imply three-month LIBOR and T-bill settlement yields of 6.65 percent and 5.93, respectively. You think that over the next quarter the general level of interest rates will rise while the credit spread built into LIBOR will narrow. Demonstrate how you can use a TED (Treasury/Eurodollar) spread, which is a simultaneous long (short) position in a Eurodollar contract and short (long) position in the T-bill contract, to create a position that will benefit from these views.

8. An investment bank engages in stock index arbitrage for its own and customer accounts. On a particular day, the S&P index at the New York Stock Exchange is 602.25 when the futures contract for delivery in 90 days is 614.75. If the annualized 90-day interest rate is 8.00 percent and the (annualized) dividend yield is 3 percent, would program trading involving stock index arbitrage possibly take place? If so, describe the transactions that should be undertaken and calculate the profit that would be made per each "share" of the S&P 500 index used in the trade.

9. **CFA Examination Level III** Alex Andrew, who manages a $95 million large-capitalization U.S. equity portfolio, currently forecasts that equity markets will decline soon. Andrew prefers to avoid the transaction costs of making sales but wants to hedge $15 million of the portfolio's current value using S&P 500 futures.

   Because Andrew realizes that his portfolio will not track the S&P 500 index exactly, he performs a regression analysis on his actual portfolio returns versus the S&P futures returns over the past year. The regression analysis indicates a risk-minimizing beta of 0.88 with an R^2 of 0.92.

   Futures Contract Data

S&P 500 futures price	1,000
S&P 500 index	999
S&P 500 index multiplier	250

   a. Calculate the number of futures contracts required to hedge $15 million of Andrew's portfolio, using the data shown. State whether the hedge is long or short. Show all calculations.

   b. Identify two alternative methods (other than selling securities from the portfolio or using futures) that replicate the strategy in Part a. Contract each of these methods with the futures strategy.

10. The treasurer of a middle market, import-export company has approached you for advice on how to best invest some of the firm's short-term cash balances. The company, which has been a client of the bank that employs you for a few years, has $250,000 that it is able to commit for a one-year holding period. The treasurer is currently considering two alternatives: (1) invest all the funds in a one-year U.S. Treasury bill offering a bond equivalent yield of 4.25 percent, and (2) invest all the funds in a Swiss government security over the same horizon, locking in the spot and forward currency exchanges in the FX market. A quick call to the bank's FX desk gives you the following two-way currency exchange quotes.

	Swiss Francs per U.S. Dollar	U.S. Dollar per Swiss Franc (CHF)
Spot	1.5035	0.6651
1-year CHF futures	—	0.6586

    a. Calculate the one-year bond equivalent yield for the Swiss government security that would support the interest rate parity condition.

    b. Assuming the actual yield on a one-year Swiss government bond is 5.50 percent, which strategy would leave the treasurer with the greatest return after one year?

    c. Describe the transactions that an arbitrageur could use to take advantage of this apparent mispricing and calculate what the profit would be for a $250,000 transaction.

11. **CFA Examination Level II** Donna Doni, CFA, wants to explore potential inefficiencies in the futures market. The TOBEC stock index has a spot value of 185.00 now. TOBEC futures contracts are settled in cash, and underlying contract values are determined by multiplying $100 times the index value. The current annual risk-free interest rate is 6.0 percent.

    a. Calculate the theoretical price of the futures contract expiring six months from now, using the cost-of-carry model. Show your calculations.

    The total (roundtrip) transaction cost for trading a futures contract is $15.00.

    b. Calculate the lower bound for the price of the futures contract expiring six months from now. Show your calculations.

· · · · · APPENDIX: CHAPTER 21 · · · ·

A. A Closed-Form Equation for Calculating Duration

To calculate the duration statistic, it helps to think of a bond that pays a fixed coupon for a finite maturity as being just a portfolio of zero coupon cash flows. Duration is then the weighted average of the payment (i.e., maturity) dates of those zero coupon cash flows. Thus, a bond's duration is its *zero coupon equivalent maturity*.

Consider a nonamortizing, five-year bond with a face value of $1,000 making annual coupon payments of $120 (i.e., 12 percent). Assuming a current yield to maturity of 10 percent, this bond will trade at a premium and its weighted average payment date (i.e., duration) is 4.074 years, as shown in Exhibit 21A.1. Interpreting the coupon bond as a portfolio of zero coupon cash flows, the duration of 4.0740 years is the weighted average maturity of that portfolio, where the weights are the respective shares of market value (e.g., the one-year zero coupon cash flow is 10.14 percent of the value of the portfolio, the five-year zero 64.64 percent).

This five-year coupon bond with a duration of 4.0740 years is equivalent in terms of price risk to a zero coupon bond having a maturity of 4.0740 years. This suggests that when the interest rate increases by 1 percent above its original level (i.e., $[\Delta (1 + i) \div (1 + i)] = 0.01$), then the price of this bond will decline by about 4.074 percent).

The Macaulay duration can be calculated with the following formula:

21.A1
$$D = \frac{1 + \dfrac{Y}{n}}{\dfrac{Y}{n}} - \frac{1 + \dfrac{Y}{n} + \left[(n \times T)\left(\dfrac{C}{F} - \dfrac{Y}{n}\right)\right]}{\dfrac{C}{F}\left[\left(1 + \dfrac{Y}{n}\right)^{n \times T} - 1\right] + \dfrac{Y}{n}}$$

where:

C = the periodic coupon payment
F = the face value at maturity
T = the number of years until maturity
n = the payments per year
Y = the yield to maturity

In the preceding numerical example, $Y = 0.10$, $n = 1$, $T = 5$, $C/F = 0.12$, and $Y/n = 0.10$. The bond's duration can therefore be solved as:

$$D = \frac{1 + 0.10}{0.10} - \frac{1 + 0.10 + 5(0.12 - 0.10)}{(0.12)[(1 + 0.10)^5 - 1] + 0.10} = 4.0740$$

As a second example of this formula, what is the duration of a 30-year Treasury bond with a 7⅝ percent coupon and a stated yield to maturity of 7.72 percent? Recall that T-bonds pay semiannual interest and so the appropriate definitions of the variables are: $C/F = 0.38125$, $T = 30$, $n = 2$, and $Y/n = 0.0386$. Therefore:

$$D = \frac{1 + 0.0386}{0.0386} - \frac{1 + 0.0386 + 60(0.038125 + 0.0386)}{(0.038125)[(1 + 0.0386)^{60} - 1] + 0.0386} = 24.18.$$

or 12.09 years. Although the method summarized by Exhibit 21A.1 always will work for any nonamortizing bond, the closed-form expression is considerably quicker when a large number of coupon payments are involved.

Exhibit 21A.1 A Duration Calculation

Year	Cash Flow	PV at 10%	PV ÷ Price	Year × (PV ÷ Price)
1	$120	$ 109.09	0.1014	0.1014
2	120	99.17	0.0922	0.1844
3	120	90.16	0.0838	0.2514
4	120	81.96	0.0762	0.3047
5	$1,120	695.43	0.6464	3.2321
		Price = $1,075.82		Duration = 4.0740 years

B. Calculating Money Market Implied Forward Rates

Implied forward rates are an essential factor in understanding how short-term interest rate futures contracts are priced. In our discussion of the expectations hypothesis of yield curve in Chapter 18, we saw that implied forward rates represented the sequence of future short-term rates that were built into the yield to maturity of a longer-term security. However, implied forward rates can have another interpretation. Consider an investor who is deciding between the following strategies for making a two-year investment: (1) buy a single two-year, zero coupon bond yielding 6 percent per annum; or (2) buy a one-year, zero coupon bond with a 5 percent yield and replace it at maturity with another one-year instrument. An implied forward rate is the answer to the following question: At what rate must the investor be able to reinvest the interim proceeds from the second strategy to exactly equal the total return from the first investment? In other words, the implied forward rate is a *breakeven* reinvestment rate. In the notation of Chapter 18, we want to solve for $_2r_1$ in the following equation:

$$(1 + 0.06)^2 = (1 + 0.05)(1 + {_2r_1})$$

or $_2r_1 = [(1 + 0.06)^2 \div (1 + 0.05)] - 1 = 7$ percent.

Implied forward money market rates can be interpreted in the same way as bond yields, but they must be calculated differently because of differences in the quotation methods for the various rates. We have seen that LIBOR is a bank *add-on yield* (AY) that is used to figure out how much money, F, an investor will have at maturity in T days given an initial investment of P (i.e., interest is "added on"):

$$F = P + \left[P \times AY \times \frac{T}{360}\right] = P\left[1 \times AY \times \frac{T}{360}\right]$$

Notice that LIBOR is based on a presumed 360-day year, the standard U.S. money market practice. Smith (1989) has shown that the implied forward rate between two money market instruments quoted on an add-on basis (e.g., LIBOR) can be calculated as

21B.1
$$_BAY_A = \left[\frac{(B \times AY_B) - (A \times AY_A)}{B - A}\right]\left[\frac{1}{1 + \left(\frac{A \times AY_A}{360}\right)}\right]$$

where AY_A and AY_B are add-on yields for A and B days from settlement to maturity, with $B > A$. The implied forward rate ($_BAY_A$) also is on an add-on basis and has maturity of $(B - A)$ days.

Consider the following short-term yield curve for LIBOR:

Maturity	LIBOR
30 days	4.15%
60 days	4.25
90 days	4.35

What is the implied forward LIBOR between Days 60 and 90? Using $AY_A = 0.0425$, $AY_B = 0.0435$, $A = 60$ days, and $B = 90$ days for LIBOR, we have:

$$_{90}AY_{60} = \left[\frac{(90 \times 0.0435) - (60 \times 0.0425)}{90 - 60}\right]\left[\frac{1}{1 + \left(\frac{60 \times 0.0425}{360}\right)}\right] = 4.52\%$$

That is, investing in a 60-day bank deposit at 4.25 percent and then a 30-day deposit at 4.52 percent would have the same total return (or cost of funds) as the 90-day deposit at 4.35 percent.

CHAPTER 22

Option Contracts

After you read this chapter, you should be able to answer the following questions:

- How are options traded on exchanges and in OTC markets?
- How are options for stock, stock indexes, foreign currency, and futures contracts quoted in the financial press?
- How can investors use option contracts to hedge an existing risk exposure?
- What are the three steps in establishing the fundamental no-arbitrage value of an option contract?
- What is the binomial (or two-state) option pricing model, and in what way is it an extension of the basic valuation approach?
- What is the Black-Scholes option pricing model, and how does it extend the binomial valuation approach?
- What is the relationship between the Black-Scholes and put-call parity valuation models?
- How can models for valuing stock options be adapted to other underlying assets such as stock indexes, foreign currency, and futures contracts?
- How do American- and European-style options differ from one another?
- What is implied volatility, and what is its role in the contract valuation process?
- How do investors use options with the underlying security or in combination with one another to create payoff structures tailored to a particular need or view of future market conditions?
- What differentiates a spread from a straddle, a strangle, or a range forward?

At the most basic level, only two kinds of derivative contracts exist: forwards, which fix the price or rate of an underlying asset; and options, which allow holders to decide at a later date whether such a fixing is in their best interest. Having examined forward and futures contracts, this chapter focuses on the trading and valuation of option contracts. We develop the discussion in four parts. First, we consider more closely the contract terms and trading mechanics for both call and put options. Options trade on exchanges as well as in the OTC dealer markets. To focus this discussion, we concentrate on options that have financial instruments as underlying securities, including options on individual stocks, stock indexes, foreign currency, and futures contracts.

The second topic we explore is how option contracts are valued in an efficient capital market. We show that, at least intuitively, this can be viewed as a simple, three-step process: (1) creating a riskless hedge portfolio combining options with the underlying security, (2) invoking a no-arbitrage assumption about the rate of return that such a portfolio should earn, and (3) solving for the option value consistent with the first two steps. We show that several of the most widely used valuation models, including the **binomial** and **Black-Scholes** models, are consistent with this approach. In this analysis, it is important to keep in mind that we will be *valuing* options and not *pricing* them. Prices are established through the actions of buyers and sellers; investors and analysts use valuation models to estimate what those prices should be.

Third, we consider several extensions and advanced topics in option valuation. We show how the Black-Scholes model for call options on stock can be adapted to value put options, as well as the other financial assets commonly used as underlying assets. We describe how the payment of dividends affects an option's value and how the model can be adjusted accordingly. We discuss the practical differences between the European and American styles of contracting, and we also examine price or return volatility—the role it plays in the valuation process and the ways an investor can estimate it in practice.

Finally, several option-based investment and hedging strategies are examined. After describing protective put and covered call strategies, we demonstrate how options can be used in combination with one another to create risk–reward trade-offs that do not otherwise exist in financial markets. We consider three broad classes of option combination strategies: **straddles**, which involve the purchase and sale of both puts and calls; **spreads**, in which the investor simultaneously buys one call (or put) while selling another; and **range forwards** (or collars), which require the purchase of a call and the concurrent sale of a put, or vice versa.

22.1 An Overview of Option Markets and Contracts

In Chapter 21, we discussed the primary difference between forward and futures contracts: Futures are standardized and trade on exchanges, while forward contracts have negotiable terms and therefore must be arranged in the OTC market. Option contracts offer investors similar trading alternatives. The most important features of how these contracts are traded and quoted in the financial press are highlighted in the following sections.

22.1.1 Option Market Conventions

Option contracts have been traded for centuries in the form of separate agreements or embedded in other securities. Malkiel (2007), for example, tells the story of how call options were used to speculate on flower prices during the tulip bulb frenzy in 17th-century Holland. Then, and for most of the time until now, options were arranged and executed in private transactions. Collectively, these private transactions represent the OTC market for options and agreements can be structured around any terms or underlying asset to which two parties can agree. This has been a particularly useful mechanism when the underlying asset is too illiquid to support a widely traded contract. Also, credit risk is a paramount concern in this market because OTC agreements typically are not collateralized. This credit risk is one-sided with an option agreement because the buyer worries about the seller's ability to honor his obligations, but the seller has received everything he will get up front and is not concerned about the buyer's creditworthiness.

As in all security markets, OTC options ultimately are created in response to the needs and desires of the corporations and individual investors who use them. Financial institutions, such as money-center banks and investment banks, serve as market makers by facilitating the arrangement and execution of these deals. Over the years, various trade associations of broker-dealers in OTC options have emerged (and, in some cases, faded), including the Put and Call Brokers and Dealers Association, which helped arrange private stock option transactions, and the International Swap and Derivatives Association, which monitors the activities of market makers for interest rate and foreign exchange derivatives. These trade groups create a common set of standards and language to govern industry transactions.

In April 1973, the Chicago Board of Trade opened the Chicago Board Options Exchange (CBOE). Specializing in stock and stock index options, the CBOE has introduced two important aspects of market uniformity. Foremost, contracts offered by the CBOE are standardized in terms of the underlying common stock, the number of shares covered, the delivery dates, and the range of available exercise prices. This standardization was meant to help develop a secondary market for the contracts. The rapid increase in trading volume on the CBOE and other options exchanges suggests that this feature is desirable compared to OTC contracts that must often be held to maturity due to a lack of liquidity.

The centralization of the trading function also necessitated the creation of the **Options Clearing Corporation (OCC)**, which acts as the guarantor of each CBOE-traded contract. Therefore, end users in option transactions ultimately bear the credit risk of the OCC. For this reason, even though the OCC is independent of the exchange, it demands that the option seller post margin to guarantee future performance. The option buyer will not have a margin account because a future obligation to the seller is nonexistent. Finally, this central market structure makes monitoring, regulation, and price reporting much easier than in the decentralized OTC markets.

22.1.2 Price Quotations for Exchange-Traded Options

Equity Options Options on the common stock of individual companies have traded on the CBOE since 1973. Several other markets, including the American (AMEX) and Philadelphia (PHLX) Exchanges, began trading their own contracts shortly afterward. The CBOE remains the largest exchange in terms of option market volume with a market share of 33 percent, with the AMEX second at around 10 percent. Options on each of these exchanges are traded similarly, with a typical contract for 100 shares of stock. Because exchange-traded contracts are not issued by the company whose common stock is the underlying asset, they require secondary transactions in the equity if exercised.[1]

Panel A of Exhibit 22.1 displays price and volume statistics for a sample of the most actively traded equity options on October 16, 2007. Options for both individual equities and exchange-traded funds are included in this list. Several of the names represented—Procter & Gamble (PG), Intel (INTC), Microsoft (MSFT), Russell 2000 iShares (IWM)—also rank among the most actively traded stocks and ETFs. To interpret this exhibit, suppose that an investor wanted to buy an option on Microsoft common stock. The highlighted entry indicates that on this day the MSFT call with an exercise price of 30 and an expiration date in January 2008 traded at a price of $1.72 per share of the underlying stock. By convention, stock options expire on the Saturday following the third Friday of the designated month. Panel B of Exhibit 22.1 provides more details for this contract, along with many other MSFT options available on this date.

To consider the dynamics of a specific option transaction in more detail, assume that on October 16, 2007, the investor did indeed buy the MSFT January 2008 30 call. Based on the last reported price, her contract would cost a total of $172.00, calculated as the stated per-share price of 1.72 multiplied by 100 shares. In exchange for that payment, the holder of this American-style call would then be able to exercise the option in mid-January—or any time before then—by paying $3,000 (= 30 × 100) and would receive 100 Microsoft shares from the option seller, who is obligated to make that exchange at the buyer's request. That request will only be rational if the mid-January price of MSFT is greater than $30. If that price closes below $30, the investor will simply let the call expire without acting on the option; that is her right as the derivative buyer. Finally, notice that with the prevailing Microsoft share price being $30.35 (which is shown in Panel B), the investor could immediately recover $0.35 of the $1.72 she paid for the contract. Her time premium of $1.37 (= 1.72 − 0.35) preserves her right to buy MSFT stock at a price of $30 for the next three months, even if the market value of those shares moves higher.[2]

Consider another investor who sells the January 30 Microsoft put, the details of which are also highlighted in Panel B of Exhibit 22.1. In return for an upfront receipt of $111 (= 1.11 × 100), he must stand ready to buy 100 shares of stock in mid-January for $3,000 if the option holder chooses to exercise his option to sell. The stock price will, of course, have to fall from its current level before this can occur. The investor in this case has sold an out-of-the-money contract and hopes that it will stay out of the money through expiration, letting the passing of time decay the time premium to zero. As we saw earlier, the front-end premium is all that sellers of put or call options ever receive, and they hope to retain as much of it possible. Like the long position in the call, the short put position benefits from an increase in MSFT share prices.

Finally, notice that most of the options listed in both panels of Exhibit 22.1 expire within a few months of the quotation date. In fact, the expiration dates available for these exchange-traded

---

[1] Call options issued directly by the firm whose common stock is the underlying asset are called *warrants*. We discuss the use and valuation of these contracts in Chapter 23.

[2] Recall from Chapter 20 that a call option's value can be divided into two components: the *intrinsic value*, which is the greater of either zero or the stock price minus the striking price, and the *time premium*. In this example, the Microsoft call is said to be *in the money* because it has positive intrinsic value, whereas an option with no intrinsic value is *out of the money*.

Exhibit 22.1 Stock Option Quotations

A. Most Active Individual Stock and ETF Options

<HELP> for explanation.   Msg: A. LOPEZ
Enter #<Equity><go> or #<Corp><go> for selection.

Most Actives by Volume

PAGES		Page	1/3

US Exchange: US Opt Comp   1 1–Today , 2–Previous   * Ex-Date
1 1–Name. 2–Ticker   1 1–Net, 2–Percent   * Split
                                 1 1–Equity, 2–Index   * Ex & Split

PAGES
1–Most Active
2–Most Up
3–Most Down

Options (Only US Index options avail)

Name				Last	Chng	vol		Name				Last	Chng	vol
1)	PG	Oct07	C65	PG+JM	5.93– .17	181852	15)	MO	Jan08	C70	MO+AN	3.21+ .16	25499
2)	INTC	Oct07	C27½	INQ+JY	.13– .01	42098	16)	YHOO	Jan09	P25	VYH+ME	2.57+ .35	25150
3)	IWM	Nov07	P82	IOW+WD	2.18+ 0.21	41669	17)	YHOO	Oct07	C27½	YHQ+JY	.95– .44	24164
4)	INTC	Oct07	P25	INQ+VE	.14+ .07	37354	18)	IWM	Oct07	P83	IOW+VE	1.21+ .22	22994
5)	AAPL	Oct07	C170	APU+JN	2.67+ .57	36250	19)	MSFT	Jan08	C30	MSQ+AK	1.72+ .19	22893
6)	YHOO	Oct07	P25	YHQ+VE	.37+ .05	35795	20)	XLF	Jan08	C39	XLF+AM	.25– .14	22600
7)	IWM	Oct07	P81	IOW+VC	.38+ .03	35712	21)	INTC	Nov07	C27½	INQ+KY	.39+ .01	22182
8)	YHOO	Oct07	C30	YHQ+JF	.27– .22	32374	22)	IMB	Nov07	P15	IMB+WC	.95+ .25	21809
9)	INTC	Oct07	C25	INQ+JE	1.02– .13	32251	23)	SMH	Nov07	P35	SMH+WG	.67– .08	21119
10)	PG	Oct07	C60	PG+JL	10.95– .05	31005	24)	IWM	Nov07	P76	IOW+WX	.74+ .04	20602
11)	SPY	Oct07	P153	SYH+VW	.70+ .15	28796	25)	SPY	Oct07	C156	SYH+JZ	.36– .38	20543
12)	NOK	Oct07	C35	NAY+JG	1.40– .35	28483	26)	F	Nov07	P8	F+WK	.20+ .07	20520
13)	IWM	Oct07	P82	IOW+VD	.65+ .05	28249	27)	IWM	Oct07	P75	IOW+VW	.02– .02	20036
14)	YHOO	Oct07	P25	YHO+PE	1.84+ .23	25661	28)	IWM	Oct07	P80	IOW+VB	.21+ .01	19183

Australia 61 2 9777 8600   Brazil 5511 3048 4500   Europe 44 20 7330 7500   Germany 49 69 920410
Hong Kong 852 2977 6000   Japan 81 3 3201 8900   Singapore 65 6212 1000   U.S. 1 212 318 2000   Copyright 2007 Bloomberg L.P.
                                                                                               H426–565–0 16–Oct–2007 13:22: 41

B. Stock Options for Microsoft (MSFT)

<HELP> for explanation, <MENU> for similar functions. 120x228 sMsg:A. LOPEZ
Enter #<Equity><GO> for selection. Note: All values in USD

Pages:
1 – Most Active
2 – Most Up
3 – Most Down

T T–today   or   P–previous
V Vvolume   O–open inter.

MOST ACTIVE OPTIONS ON   Page 1 of 3

MICROSOFT CORP

	Total	Call	Put
Volume	105,181	89,375	15,806
Open Int.	3686944	2178493	1508451

Underlying:	Last	Volume	1–Day Chg	Open	High	Low	Yest.	2–Day Ch
MSFT US	30.35	35607907	+.31	30.24	30.58	30.23	30.04	+.18

	Option		Symbol	Last	Chng	Vol		Option		Symbol	Last	Chng	Vol
1)	Jan08	30 Calls	AK	1.72	+ .19	22893	17)	Apr08	32.5 Calls	DZ	1.20	+ .09	990
2)	Oct07	30 Calls	JK	.52	+ .16	17363	18)	Jan08	35 Calls	AL	.19	+ .04	693
3)	Jan08	25 Calls	AJ	5.80	+ .40	14982	19)	Jan09	25 Calls	AE	7.20	+ .20	540
4)	Jan08	27.5 Calls	AY	3.55	+ .30	10192	20)	Jan09	27.5 Calls	AY	5.50	+ .25	534
5)	Oct07	30 Puts	VK	.14	– .11	4132	21)	Jan08	32.5 Puts	MZ	2.50	– .24	521
6)	Nov07	30 Puts	WK	.72	– .14	3982	22)	Jan08	40 Calls	AH	.03	– .01	491
7)	Nov07	30 Calls	KK	1.14	+ .17	3867	23)	Oct07	27.5 Puts	VY	.01	unch	402
8)	Jan08	32.5 Calls	AZ	.60	+ .07	3334	24)	Nov07	27.5 Calls	KY	3.15	+ .35	329
9)	Jan09	32.5 Calls	AZ	2.75	+ .17	3195	25)	Oct07	32.5 Calls	JZ	.01	– .01	286
10)	Jan10	35 Calls	AL	3.15	+ .16	3001	26)	Apr08	32.5 Puts	PZ	2.86	– .24	259
11)	Nov07	32.5 Puts	WZ	2.35	– .28	2397	27)	Oct07	27.5 Calls	JY	2.90	+ .33	189
12)	Apr08	35 Calls	DL	.55	+ .08	2058	28)	Nov07	35 Calls	KL	.05	– .01	156
13)	Nov07	32.5 Calls	KZ	.25	+ .03	1904	29)	Jan10	30 Puts	MK	3.25	– .20	139
14)	Apr08	30 Puts	PK	1.51	– .20	1770	30)	Nov07	27.5 Puts	WY	.15	– .02	114
15)	Jan08	30 Puts	MK	1.11	– .15	1594	31)	Apr08	22.5 Calls	DX	8.50	+ .40	110
16)	Apr08	30 Calls	DK	2.44	+ .23	1529	32)	Apr08	37.5 Calls	DU	.23	+ .02	108

Australia 61 2 9777 8600   Brazil 5511 3048 4500   Europe 44 20 7330 7500   Germany 49 69 920410
Hong Kong 852 2977 6000   Japan 81 3 3201 8900   Singapore 65 6212 1000   U.S. 1 212 318 2000   Copyright 2007 Bloomberg L.P.
                                                                                               H426–565–0 16–Oct–2007 13: 24: 42

Exhibit 22.2 Long-Term Equity Anticipation Securities (LEAPS) Quotations for MSFT

Calls	Last Sale	Net	Bid	Ask	Vol	Open Int	Puts	Last Sale	Net	Bid	Ask	Vol	Open Int
09 Jan 20.00 (VMF AD-E)	11.30	0.0	11.25	11.45	0	16996	09 Jan 20.00 (VMF MD-E)	0.35	0.0	0.37	0.39	0	40936
09 Jan 22.50 (VMF AX-E)	9.00	0.0	9.15	9.30	0	7656	09 Jan 22.50 (VMF MX-E)	0.75	0.0	0.64	0.68	0	51145
09 Jan 25.00 (VMF AE-E)	7.20	−0.15	7.20	7.30	420	49868	09 Jan 25.00 (VMF ME-E)	1.06	0.0	1.04	1.08	0	85265
09 Jan 27.50 (VMF AY-E)	5.46	0.0	5.45	5.60	0	37927	09 Jan 27.50 (VMF MY-E)	1.85	0.0	1.64	1.69	0	60892
09 Jan 30.00 (VMF AF-E)	3.90	0.0	3.90	4.00	0	160002	09 Jan 30.00 (VMF MF-E)	2.53	0.0	2.52	2.56	0	104238
09 Jan 32.50 (VMF AZ-E)	2.73	+0.08	2.68	2.74	108	33312	09 Jan 32.50 (VMF MZ-E)	3.95	0.0	3.70	3.80	0	19663
09 Jan 35.00 (VMF AG-E)	1.76	+0.11	1.73	1.80	10	57738	09 Jan 35.00 (VMF MG-E)	6.50	0.0	5.30	5.40	0	10574
09 Jan 40.00 (VMF AH-E)	0.65	+0.08	0.63	0.68	60	71701	09 Jan 40.00 (VMF MH-E)	10.60	0.0	9.45	9.75	0	25
10 Jan 20.00 (WMF AD-E)	12.00	0.0	11.90	12.20	0	1242	10 Jan 20.00 (VMF MD-E)	0.66	0.0	0.67	0.75	0	1465
10 Jan 25.00 (WMF AJ-E)	7.75	0.0	8.30	8.55	0	1543	10 Jan 25.00 (WMF MJ-E)	1.72	0.0	1.59	1.79	0	7359
10 Jan 30.00 (WMF AK-E)	5.20	0.0	5.25	5.55	0	23695	10 Jan 30.00 (WMF MK-E)	3.50	0.0	3.15	3.30	0	21327
10 Jan 35.00 (WMF AL-E)	3.00	0.0	3.00	3.20	0	3245	10 Jan 35.00 (WMF ML-E)	5.35	0.0	5.70	6.00	0	143
10 Jan 40.00 (WMF AH-E)	1.64	0.0	1.62	1.70	0	2468	10 Jan 40.00 (WMF MH-E)	10.74	0.0	9.50	9.90	0	120

Source: Chicago Board Options Exchange (www.cboe.com); October 16, 2007. Provided as a courtesy by Chicago Board Options Exchange, Incorporated.

contracts are the two nearest term months (October and November for Microsoft) and up to three additional months from a quarterly cycle beginning in either January, February, or March. In the case of Microsoft options, January 2008 and April 2008 (which is part of the quarterly cycle beginning in January) are the additional months most frequently listed. Exhibit 22.2 gives quotations for Long-Term Equity Anticipation Securities (LEAPS), which are simply regular call and put options with longer expiration dates. Like the contracts just described, LEAPS are also traded on the CBOE and have comparable terms.

The LEAPS quotes allow us to see the effect that time to expiration has on the value of an option. The highlighted entries in the display show prices for four different calls and puts for MSFT. Each contract has an exercise price of 30, but the expiration dates are either 1.25 years (January 2009) or 2.25 years (January 2010) in the future. For both calls and puts, the value of the contract increases as the expiration date is pushed farther out (e.g., $3.90 for the January 2009 call versus $5.20 for the January 2010). Of course, since these contracts have the same exercise price ($30) and underlying stock price ($30.35), the intrinsic value is the same as discussed earlier. Thus, the difference in the contract prices is purely because of additional time premium.

Stock Index Options   As we saw in Chapter 20, options on stock indexes, such as Standard and Poor's 100 or 500, are patterned closely after equity options. However, they differ in one important way: Index options can only be settled in cash. This is because of the underlying index, which is a hypothetical portfolio that would be quite costly to duplicate in practice. First traded on the CBOE in 1983, index options are popular with investors for the same reason as stock index futures: They provide a relatively inexpensive and convenient way to take an investment or hedging position in a broad-based indicator of market performance. Index puts are particularly useful in portfolio insurance applications, such as the protective put strategy described earlier and again at the end of this chapter.

Prices for two widely traded contracts—the S&P 500 and Russell 2000 index options—are listed in Exhibit 22.3. They are interpreted the same way as individual equity option prices, with each contract specifying the transfer of 100 "shares" of the underlying index. For example, the November 2007 SPX index call option with an exercise price of 1,540 is out of the money, given that the index level on October 16, 2007, was 1,538.53. This contract could be purchased at the ask price for $3,460 (= 34.60 × 100) and would only be exercised to acquire $154,000 worth of the index if the S&P rises above 1,540 by the expiration date. In contrast, a November 2007 RUT index put option with an exercise price of 830 is in the money given the current index level of 823.35. In exchange for an upfront payment of $2,570 (= 25.70 × 100), the owner of

Exhibit 22.3 Stock Index Option Quotations for SPX and RVT

Panel A. Standard & Poor's 500 Index (SPX)

Calls	Last Sale	Net	Bid	Ask	Vol	Open Int	Puts	Last Sale	Net	Bid	Ask	Vol	Open Int
07 Oct 1530.00 (SXM JF-E)	16.00	−4.00	15.20	17.20	148	21354	07 Oct 1530.00 (SXM VF-E)	7.50	+3.20	5.70	7.70	8120	19974
07 Oct 1535.00 (SXM JG-E)	12.20	−5.30	11.50	13.50	12596	22052	07 Oct 1535.00 (SXM VG-E)	8.80	+1.80	7.80	8.80	8166	11786
07 Oct 1540.00 (SXM JH-E)	9.50	−7.50	8.70	10.70	1194	11174	07 Oct 1540.00 (SXM VH-E)	10.20	+2.20	10.20	11.00	7006	21385
07 Oct 1545.00 (SXM JI-E)	7.00	−6.00	6.30	8.30	1183	10047	07 Oct 1545.00 (SXM VI-E)	13.50	+4.70	12.50	14.00	3044	6731
07 Nov 1530.00 (SXM KF-E)	41.80	−6.20	39.30	41.30	1560	990	07 Nov 1530.00 (SXM WF-E)	28.00	+4.30	26.40	28.40	6174	4583
07 Nov 1535.00 (SXM KG-E)	41.60	−9.00	36.20	38.20	2	32	07 Nov 1535.00 (SXM WG-E)	28.20	+2.80	28.30	30.20	620	16656
07 Nov 1540.00 (SXM KH-E)	33.80	−7.60	32.60	34.60	98	791	07 Nov 1540.00 (SXM WH-E)	31.00	+0.50	30.20	32.20	481	14958
07 Nov 1545.00 (SXM KI-E)	30.30	−5.90	30.10	32.10	4463	2172	07 Nov 1545.00 (SXM WI-E)	33.40	+1.40	32.70	34.70	5892	1340

Panel B. Russell 2000 Index (RUT)

Calls	Last Sale	Net	Bid	Ask	Vol	Open Int	Puts	Last Sale	Net	Bid	Ask	Vol	Open Int
07 Oct 810.00 (RUZ JB-E)	17.60	−1.85	16.40	17.00	76	3436	07 Oct 810.00 (RUZ VB-E)	3.20	+0.90	3.10	3.40	348	9736
07 Oct 820.00 (RUZ JD-E)	10.45	−1.60	9.60	10.10	291	8973	07 Oct 820.00 (RUZ VD-E)	5.90	+1.70	6.00	6.40	564	13292
07 Oct 830.00 (RUZ JF-E)	5.00	−2.05	4.80	5.20	2664	8384	07 Oct 830.00 (RUZ VF-E)	11.20	+3.70	11.20	11.70	2280	6912
07 Oct 840.00 (RUZ JH-E)	2.20	−2.50	2.10	2.45	3757	8907	07 Oct 840.00 (RUZ VH-E)	17.30	+3.30	18.40	19.00	186	9572
07 Nov 810.00 (RUZ KB-E)	33.95	−0.80	32.60	33.20	18	3034	07 Nov 810.00 (RUZ WB-E)	17.80	+1.80	17.40	18.00	83	3562
07 Nov 820.00 (RUZ KD-E)	27.00	−1.80	26.20	26.80	141	1456	07 Nov 820.00 (RUZ WD-E)	19.25	−0.35	20.90	21.50	50	13731
07 Nov 830.00 (RUZ KF-E)	21.65	−0.70	20.40	21.00	43	2820	07 Nov 830.00 (RUZ WF-E)	25.30	+0.30	25.10	25.70	346	5897
07 Nov 840.00 (RUZ KH-E)	15.60	−3.90	15.40	15.90	55	7152	07 Nov 840.00 (RUZ WH-E)	30.40	+0.80	30.00	30.50	284	9923

Source: Chicago Board Options Exchange (www.cboe.com); October 16, 2007. Provided as a courtesy by Chicago Board Options Exchange, Incorporated.

this put contract would be able to sell $83,000 worth of the index, assuming the Russell 2000 index remained below 830 at the expiration date.

Foreign Currency Options Foreign currency options are structurally parallel to the currency futures contracts discussed in Chapter 21. Each contract allows for the sale or purchase of a set amount of foreign (i.e., non-U.S. dollar) currency at a fixed exchange (FX) rate. A currency call option is like the long position in the currency futures since it permits the contract holder to buy the currency at a later date. (Of course, unlike futures, options do not require that this exchange be made.) A currency put is therefore the option analog to being short in the futures market. These contracts exist for several major currencies, including the euro, Australian dollars, Japanese yen, Canadian dollars, British pounds, and Swiss francs. The majority of currency options trading, which began in 1982, occurs on the PHLX. Exhibit 22.4 shows quotes from a sample of the available British pound contracts, along with the spot foreign exchange rates for the same trading day.

Like the FX furutes market, all the prices are quoted from the perspective of U.S.-based investors. Consider an investor who lives in New York and holds British pound–denominated government bonds in her portfolio. It is October and, when the bonds come due in two months, she will need to convert the proceeds back into U.S. dollars. This exposes the investor to the risk that the British currency will weaken by December. To hedge this risk, she buys the December put on the British pound with an exercise price of USD 203/GBP, which is expressed in U.S. cents per pound. Thus, her initial cost to purchase a put option to sell 31,250 pounds is USD 671.88 (= 0.0215 × 31,250), using the listed ask price of the contract. This option would allow the holder to sell GBP 31,250 in December for USD 63,437.50 (= 31,250 × 2.03). The investor will only exercise the contract if the spot USD/GBP rate prevailing in December is less than 2.03 (i.e., the British pound weakened relative to the U.S. dollar). Finally, because the spot rate at the time the put is sold in October is USD 2.0328/GBP, this contract is out of the money and the entire purchase price represents a time premium.

Exhibit 22.4 Foreign Currency Option Quotations

<HELP> for explanation.   Curncy**FXC**

09:53
Wed 10/17

AS OF CLOSE : Tue 10/16
KEY CROSS CURRENCY RATES

	USD	EUR	JPY	GBP	CHF	CAD	AUD	NZD	HKD	NOK	SEK
SEK	6.4537	9.1465	5.5195	13.119	5.4570	6.5915	5.7328	4.8153	.83201	1.1927	....
NOK	5.4110	7.6687	4.6277	10.999	4.5753	5.5265	4.8065	4.0372	.69758	....	.83843
HKD	7.7568	10.993	6.6340	15.768	6.5588	7.9224	6.8904	5.7875	....	1.4335	1.2019
NZD	1.3403	1.8995	1.1463	2.7245	1.1333	1.3689	1.1906	....	.17278	.24769	.20767
AUD	1.1257	1.5955	.96279	2.2884	.95188	1.1498	....	.83995	.14513	.20805	.17443
CAD	.97910	1.3876	.83737	1.9903	.82789	....	.86973	.73053	.12622	.18095	.15171
CHF	1.1827	1.6761	1.0115	2.4041	....	1.2079	1.0505	.88240	.15247	.21857	.18325
GBP	.49193	.69719	.42072	....	.41596	.50243	.43698	.36704	.06342	.09091	.07622
JPY	116.93	165.71	....	237.69	98.867	119.42	103.86	87.241	15.074	21.609	18.118
EUR	.70559	....	.60346	1.4343	.59662	.72065	.62678	.52646	.09096	.13040	.10933
USD	....	1.4173	.85525	2.0328	.84556	1.0213	.88830	.74613	.12892	.18481	.15495

(×100)

Spot   Enter 1M,2M etc. for forward rates   **E** EURO   **D** Default Currencies
       Hit –1,–2…<Page> for previous days   **A** Show all

BLOOMBERG COMPOSITE
Australia 61 2 9777 8600   Brazil 5511 3048 4500   Europe 44 20 7330 7500   Germany 49 69 920410
Hong Kong 852 2977 6000   Japan 81 3 3201 89000   Singapore 65 6212 1000   U.S. 1 212 318 2000   Copyright 2007 Bloomberg L.P.
H463–263–0 17–Oct–2007 09:53:59

BPC   203.80   + .64   Curncy**OMON**

At DELAYED Vol n.a. Op 203.57 Hi 204.04 Lo 203.44 OpInt n.a.   Option Monitor

| BPC Currency ▾ | Templates ▾ | Edit ▾ | Actions ▾ | Expiry ▾ |

BRITISH £ SPOT EURO STD   203.80 +0.64   Hi 204.04   Lo 203.44   Vol

Center 203.28 ▾   Number of Strikes ▾   18   or   % from Center   Exchange Composite ▾

				51) Calls						52) Puts		
	Ticker	Strike	Bid	Ask	Last	Volm		Ticker	Strike	Bid	Ask	Last	Volm
BPC 07 DEC 2007 (Contract Size 31250)							BPC 07 DEC 2007 (Contract Size 31250)						
1)	BPZ7C C	194			5.58 y		20)	BPZ7P C	194			1.74y	
2)	BPZ7C C	198			3.98 y		21)	BPZ7P C	198	.61	.76		
3)	BPZ7C C	199					22)	BPZ7P C	199	.75	.90		
4)	BPZ7C C	200					23)	BPZ7P C	200	.98	1.13		
5)	BPZ7C C	201					24)	BPZ7P C	201	1.27	1.42		
6)	BPZ7C C	202	3.03	3.28			25)	BPZ7P C	202	1.62	1.77		
7)	BPZ7C C	203	2.51	2.73			26)	BPZ7P C	203	2.00	2.15		
8)	BPZ7C C	204	2.03	2.18			27)	BPZ7P C	204	2.51	2.70		
9)	BPZ7C C	205	1.61	1.76			28)	BPZ7P C	205	3.02	3.27		
10)	BPZ7C C	206	1.20	1.35	1.27 y		29)	BPZ7P C	206				
11)	BPZ7C C	207	.95	1.10			30)	BPZ7P C	207				
12)	BPZ7C C	208	.71	.86			31)	BPZ7P C	208				
13)	BPZ7C C	209	.54	.69			32)	BPZ7P C	209				
BPC 09 NOV 2007 (Contract Size 31250)							BPC 09 NOV 2007 (Contract Size 31250)						
14)	BPX7C C	198					33)	BPX7P C	198	.27	.42		
15)	BPX7C C	199					34)	BPX7P C	199	.39	.54		
16)	BPX7C C	200					35)	BPX7P C	200	.54	.69		
17)	BPX7C C	201					36)	BPX7P C	201	.72	.87		
18)	BPX7C C	202	2.56	2.81			37)	BPX7P C	202	1.02	1.17		
19)	BPX7C C	203	2.01	2.16			38)	BPX7P C	203	1.39	1.54		

Australia 61 2 9777 8600   Brazil 5511 3048 4500   Europe 44 20 7330 7500   Germany 49 69 920410
Hong Kong 852 2977 6000   Japan 81 3 3201 8900   Singapore 65 6212 1000   U.S. 1 212 318 2000   Copyright 2007 Bloomberg L.P.
H464–158–1 17–Oct–2007 10:03:09

Exhibit 22.5 Futures Option Quotations

Strike Price	Calls			Puts		
	Nov07	Dec07	Mar08	Nov07	Dec07	Mar08

US TREASURY BONDS (CBOT)
$100,000, pts & 64ths of 100 pct

Strike Price	Nov07	Dec07	Mar08	Nov07	Dec07	Mar08
11200	0-07	0-27	1-17	1-44	2-00	2-55
11300	0-02	0-14	0-61	2-40	2-51	3-34
11400	0-01	0-08	0-45	3-38	3-45	4-17
Volume	Calls	45,788		Puts	23,004	
Open Interest	Calls	382,266		Puts	496,896	

HI GRADE COPPER (COMX)
25,000 lbs., cents per lb.

Strike Price	Nov07	Dec07	Mar08	Nov07	Dec07	Mar08
355	11.65	19.20	23.20	3.55	10.15	14.15
360	8.55	16.45	20.55	5.50	12.35	16.45
365	6.05	13.95	18.15	7.95	14.85	19.00
Volume	Calls	34		Puts	61	
Open Interest	Calls	803		Puts	1,318	

CORN (CBOT)
5,000 bu, cents per bushel

Strike Price	Nov07	Dec07	Mar08	Nov07	Dec07	Mar08
360	7.250	13.375	33	6.750	12.625	16
365	–	11.125	-	9.625	15.375	-
370	3.500	9.125	27.750	13	18.375	20.750
Volume	Calls	16,922		Puts	25,481	
Open Interest	Calls	879,667		Puts	647,429	

LIGHT SWEET CRUDE (NYMX)
1,000 bbl., dollars per bbl.

Strike Price	Nov07	Dec07	Mar08	Nov07	Dec07	Mar08
8450	3.14	3.97	4.22	0.04	1.90	3.14
8500	2.67	3.66	3.96	0.06	2.08	3.39
8550	2.22	3.36	3.72	0.11	2.29	3.64
Volume	Calls	115,844		Puts	97,802	
Open Interest	Calls	1,257,866		Puts	1,717,242	

Options on Futures Contracts Although they have existed for decades in the OTC markets, options on futures contracts have only been exchange-traded since 1982. Also known as futures options, they give the holder the right, but not the obligation, to enter into a futures contract on an underlying security or commodity at a later date and at a predetermined price. Purchasing a call on a futures contract allows for the acquisition of a long position in the futures market, while exercising a put would create a short futures position. On the other hand, the seller of the call would be obligated to enter into the short side of the futures contract if the option holder decided to exercise the contract, while the seller of the put might be forced into a long futures position. Futures options exist for a wide variety of underlying assets, including agricultural, metal, and energy commodities; Treasury bonds and notes; foreign currencies; and stock indexes. Exhibit 22.5 lists prices quotations for a representative set of contracts.

To understand how these contracts work, consider the December call option on copper with an exercise price of $3.65 (i.e., 365 cents) per pound. This contract would cost the buyer 13.95 cents per pound of copper covered by the futures position. As each copper futures contract on the Commodity Exchange (COMX) specifies 25,000 pounds of the metal, the total purchase price for this futures call is $3,487.50 (= 25,000 × 0.1395). Because the December copper futures price on this day in October settled at $3.641, this option was out of the money.

As with any call option, the holder will only exercise at the expiration date if the prevailing price of the underlying asset exceeds the exercise price. This arrangement might fit the needs of an electronics manufacturer exposed to higher copper prices as a factor of production or a speculator bullish on copper prices. Suppose that on the expiration date, the contract price of the December futures has risen to \$3.80. The holder will exercise her option and assume a long position in the December futures with a contract price of \$3.65 per pound. Her new position will immediately be marked to market and \$3,875 ($= (3.80 - 3.65) \times 25,000$) will be added to her margin account. Alternatively, she may decide to unwind her below-market futures contract and take the \$3,875 in cash.

Leverage is the primary attraction of this derivative. The call buyer has been able to control 25,000 pounds of copper for two months for an investment of \$3,487.50. Had she purchased the copper outright, it would have cost her \$91,025 ($= 25,000 \times 3.641$), assuming that spot and futures prices were the same on this date. Further, the cost of the futures call is less than margin required for a direct long position in the December copper futures contract, which was set by the exchange at \$6,413 for non-member customers. Because leverage—and not acquiring the underlying future position—is the driving force behind this market, in most cases the option expires at virtually the same time as the futures contract.

22.2 The Fundamentals of Option Valuation

Although options can be used by investors to anticipate future security prices, the key to understanding how they are valued is that they also are risk-reduction tools. In this section we show that an option's theoretical value depends on combining it with its underlying security to create a *synthetic risk-free portfolio*. That is, it always is theoretically possible to use the option as a perfect *hedge* against fluctuations in the value of the asset on which it is based.

Recall that this was essentially the same approach we used in Chapter 20 to establish the put-call parity relationships. The primary differences between put-call parity and what follows are twofold. First, the hedge portfolio implied by the put-call parity transaction did not require special calibration or adjustment; it simply consisted of one stock long, one put long, and one call short held until the expiration date. However, hedging an underlying asset position's risk with a single option position—whether it is a put or a call—often involves using multiple contracts and frequent changes in the requisite number to maintain the riskless portfolio. Second, the put-call parity paradigm did not demand a forecast of the underlying asset's future price level whereas the following analysis will. We will see that *forecasting the volatility of future asset prices* is the most important input the investor must provide in determining option values.

22.2.1 The Basic Approach

While the mathematics associated with option valuation can be complex, the fundamental intuition behind the process is straightforward and can be illustrated quite simply. Suppose you have just purchased a share of stock in WYZ Corp. for \$50. The stock is not expected to pay a dividend during the time you plan to hold it, and you have forecast that in one year the stock price will either rise to \$65 or fall to \$40. This can be summarized as follows:

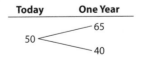

Suppose further that you can either buy or sell a call option on WYZ stock with an exercise price of \$52.50. If this is a European-style contract that expires in exactly one year, it will have the following possible expiration date values:

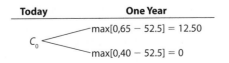

Given your forecast of future WYZ stock prices, you know what the option is worth at expiration. The dilemma is establishing what the contract should sell for today (i.e., C_0).

This question can be answered in three steps. First, design a hedge portfolio consisting of one share of WYZ stock held long and some number of call options (i.e., h), so that the combined position will be riskless. The number of call options needed can be established by ensuring that the portfolio has the same value at expiration no matter which of the two forecasted stock values occurs, or

$$65 + (h)(12.50) = 40 + (h)(0)$$

leaving

$$h = \frac{(65 - 40)}{(0 - 12.5)} = -2.00$$

There are both *direction* and *magnitude* dimensions to this number. The negative sign indicates that, in order to create negative correlation between two assets that are naturally positively correlated, call options must be *sold* to hedge a long stock position. Further, given that the range of possible expiration date option outcomes (i.e., 12.5 – 0) is only half as large as the range for WYZ stock (i.e., 65 – 40), twice as many options must be sold as there is stock in the hedge portfolio. The value h is known as the *hedge ratio*.[3] Thus, the risk-free hedge portfolio can be created by purchasing one share of stock and selling two call options.

The second step in the option valuation process assumes capital markets that are free from arbitrage, so that all riskless investments are priced to earn the risk-free rate over the time until expiration. The hedge portfolio costing $[50 – (2)(C_0)]$ today would grow to the certain value of \$40 by the following formula:

$$[50 - (2.00)(C_0)](1 + RFR)^T = 40$$

where:

RFR = the annualized risk-free rate
T = the time to expiration (i.e., one year)

Two unknown values exist in this formula: C_0 and RFR. Finding a suitable estimate for RFR seldom is a problem because the investor can use as a proxy the yield to maturity on a U.S. Treasury security of appropriate length. For example, if the one-year T-bill yield is 8 percent, the formula for C_0 can be solved as follows:

$$C_0 = \frac{50 - 40/1.08}{2.00} = \$6.48$$

This bit of algebraic manipulation is the third and final step in establishing the call's fair market value. That is, \$6.48 represents the fundamental value of a one-year call option on WYZ stock, given both the prevailing market prices for two other securities (i.e., stock and T-bills) and the investor's forecast of future share values. Because the security prices are observable, the investor's forecast of future share values becomes the critical element in determining if this present value is a reasonable estimate. Finally, because the call option is currently out of the money, this amount is purely a time premium.

22.2.2 Improving Forecast Accuracy

Because it is unrealistic to assume only two possible outcomes for future WYZ share prices, the quality of the preceding valuation is highly suspect. To improve accuracy, the expiration date forecast of stock prices can be expanded to allow for numerous possibilities. To see the

---

[3] In some valuation models (e.g., Black-Scholes), the hedge ratio is expressed as the option's potential volatility divided by that of the stock. In this example, that would be $(0 - 12.5) \div (65 - 40) = -0.5$, meaning that the option is half as volatile in dollar terms as the share of stock. Of course, this alternative calculation is just the reciprocal of the value of $h = -2.00$.

consequences of this expansion in the simplest terms possible, consider a revised forecast that includes only one additional potential price falling between the previous values:

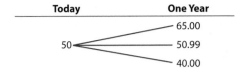

Although the three-step riskless hedge approach to calculating C_0 is still conceptually valid, the exact methodology must be modified because it is now impossible to calculate a hedge ratio that simultaneously accounts for all three Date T possibilities. There will be several different hedge ratios defined by each distinct pair of future share prices, which means that it is impossible for the preceding valuation process to consider all three possible stock outcomes at once.

Creating a Stock Price Tree   The solution to this problem involves dividing the time to expiration into as many *subintervals* as necessary so that at any point in time the subsequent price can only move up or down. In this example, only one additional subinterval is needed. Exhibit 22.6 shows how the WYZ stock price forecast might be embellished. This illustration, which is sometimes called a *stock price tree,* indicates that for the stock price to reach, say, $65 in one year, it must first move up to $57.01 in Subperiod S1 before moving up a second time to its final value. Similarly, the lower extreme of $40 can only be reached by two consecutive "down" price changes. On the other hand, there are two different paths to the terminal outcome in the middle: (i) one "up" followed by one "down" or (ii) a down movement followed by an up movement—both reach $50.99.

Once the investor fills in this price tree, the call option's value can be solved by working backward on each pair of possible outcomes from the future. If, for instance, an initial up movement left the price of WYZ stock at $57.01, a price change over the remaining subperiod could be characterized as:

The corresponding change in the value of the call option (i.e., C_{11}) can then be shown as

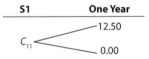

With $X = 52.50$, the call option will be in the money at expiration only if WYZ stock moves up in price again. This suggests a hedge ratio of:

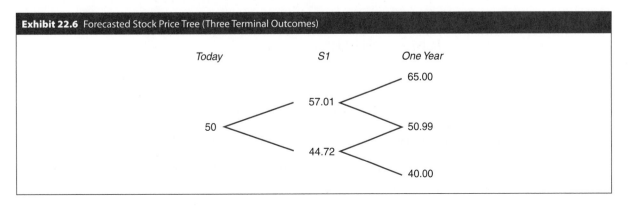

Exhibit 22.6 Forecasted Stock Price Tree (Three Terminal Outcomes)

$$h = \frac{(65.00 - 50.99)}{(0.00 - 12.50)} = -1.12$$

meaning that the riskless hedge portfolio at this point would contain one share of stock long and 1.12 calls short. The intermediate option value is then found by solving:

$$[57.01 - (1.12)(C_{11})](1.08)^{0.5} = [65 - (1.12)(12.50)] = 50.99$$

or

$$C_{11} = \frac{57.01 - 50.99/1.0392}{1.12} = \$7.09$$

Here the factor 1.0392 $[= (1.08)^{0.5}]$ is roughly one-half the annual risk-free rate (plus one) since the original holding period was divided into two six-month subintervals.

Valuing in Other Subintervals Having established the value for C_{11}, the value for the option corresponding to an S1 share price of $44.72 (i.e., C_{12}) can be established by the same three-step procedure with the stock and option price trees truncated as follows:

S1	**One Year**
44.72	50.99
	40.00

and

S1	**One Year**
C_{12}	0.00
	0.00

In this case the call option is certain to be out of the money at the expiration date one subinterval hence since even a subsequent increase to $50.99 (i.e., an up move in the second subperiod) would leave the share price below the $52.50 exercise price. Thus, it is clear that C_{12} must be $0.00; any security that is certain to be worthless in the future must also be worthless today. Further, the concept of forming a riskless hedge portfolio under such circumstances is meaningless.

These intermediate calculations have little importance to the investor who only cares about the current value of the option. They are, however, a necessary evil as C_0 cannot be established before determining C_{11} and C_{12}. With these values in hand, the relevant part of the stock price tree is

Today	**S1**
50.00	57.01
	44.72

with the corresponding call option tree being given by

Today	**S1**
C_0	7.09
	0.00

Once again applying the three-step valuation process, the initial (i.e., Date 0) hedge ratio is

$$h = \frac{(57.01 - 44.72)}{(0.00 - 7.09)} = -1.73$$

so that the riskless hedge portfolio at inception would short 1.73 calls for every share held long. The current option value is then found by solving

$$[50.00 - (1.73)(C_0)](1.08)^{0.5} = [44.72 - (1.73)(0.00)] = 44.72$$

or

$$C_{11} = \frac{50.00 - 44.72/1.0392}{1.73} = \$4.02$$

These initial, intermediate, and terminal option values are summarized in Exhibit 22.7.

Two interesting things resulted from this expansion from two to three possible stock price outcomes. First, the addition of a third potential terminal stock price had the effect of reducing the Date 0 option value from $6.48 to $4.02. Although this reduction was a consequence of choosing a third stock price (i.e., $50.99) that caused the option to be out of the money—selecting a value closer to $65.00 would have increased C_0—it does underscore once again that the option valuation process critically depends on the investor's stock price forecast. Second, notice also that the hedge ratio changes with stock price changes prior to the expiration date. That is, the composition of the riskless hedge portfolio must be rebalanced after each share price movement. From the initial position of being short 1.73 calls against one share held long, an upward movement in WYZ stock from $50.00 to $57.01 would require buying back 0.61 (= 1.73 – 1.12) options. Thus, replicating a risk-free position with stock and call options is a *dynamic* process.

Expanding the Stock Price Tree This valuation process can become even more precise as more terminal share price outcomes are included in the forecast. Of course, as this happens, the number of pairwise calculations and the number of necessary subperiods will also increase. Consequently, there is a trade-off between realism and the volume of required calculations. To see how even seemingly minor expansions of the stock price forecast can dramatically increase the computational burden, consider the implications of including four potential expiration date stock prices:

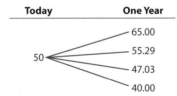

Today	One Year
	65.00
	55.29
50	47.03
	40.00

Valuing the option in this case will require the creation of two subintervals (S1 and S2) and five intermediate stock price forecasts. These are illustrated in Exhibit 22.8.

To compute C_0, the investor must now work recursively backward through calculations for the five intermediate option values: C_{21}, C_{22}, and C_{23} in Subperiod S2 and C_{11} and C_{12} in

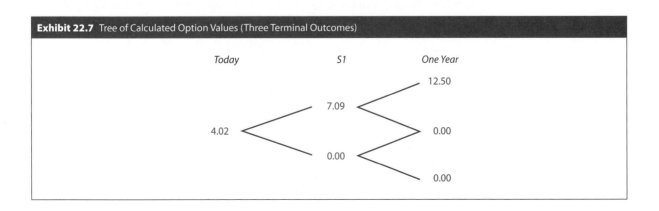

Exhibit 22.7 Tree of Calculated Option Values (Three Terminal Outcomes)

Exhibit 22.8 Forecasted Stock Price Tree (Four Terminal Outcomes)

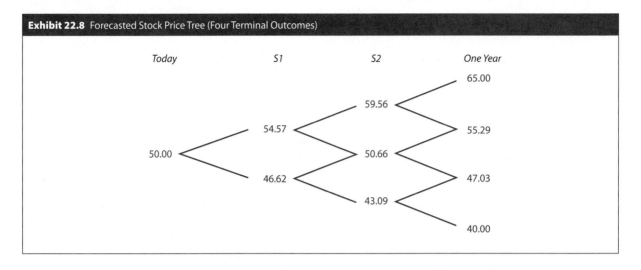

Subperiod 1. Of course, each of these calculations applies the same three-step riskless hedge process outlined earlier, appropriately modified for the new length of a subperiod (i.e., one-third of a year instead of six months). If, for instance, two consecutive up movements took the price of WYZ stock from $50.00 to $54.57 to $59.56, a price change over the remaining subperiod could be characterized as

S2	One Year
	65.00
59.56	
	55.29

The change in the value of the call option from this uppermost state of Subinterval S2 (i.e., C_{21}) can then be shown as

S2	One Year
	12.50
C_{21}	
	2.79

Given its exercise price of $52.50, the call option would be certain to be in the money for both expiration date stock values. This suggests a hedge ratio of

$$h = \frac{65.00 - 55.29}{2.79 - 12.50} = -1.00$$

so that the riskless hedge portfolio at this point would contain one share of stock long and one call short. C_{21} can then be found by solving

$$[59.56 - (1.00)(C_{21})](1.08)^{0.33} = [65 - (1.00)(12.50)] = 52.50$$

or

$$C_{21} = \frac{59.56 - 52.50/1.026}{1.00} = \$8.39$$

The discount factor of 1.026 ($= (1.08)^{0.33}$) is now based on roughly one-third of the annual risk-free rate since the one-year option expiration period was adjusted to accommodate three sub-intervals. Solving for the remaining values leaves the option value tree shown in Exhibit 22.9. Once again, the net effect of these particular forecast improvements has been to change the current value of the derivative to $3.60.

Exhibit 22.9 Tree of Calculated Option Values (Four Terminal Outcomes)

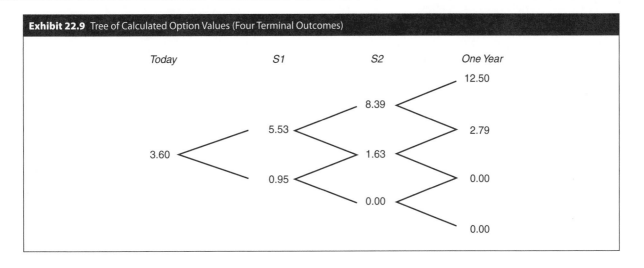

22.2.3 The Binomial Option Pricing Model

A crucial element of this basic approach to option valuation is that future changes in the underlying asset's price always can be simplified to one of two possibilities: an up movement or a down movement. As shown by Rendleman and Bartter (1979) and Cox, Ross, and Rubinstein (1979), this analytical development is part of a more general valuation methodology known as the *two-state option pricing model*. One difficulty with the preceding examples is that they required the investor to specify cash amounts for each of the future potential stock prices in all the subperiods demanded by the forecast. This can be a daunting task as the number of terminal outcomes is allowed to grow larger with the time to expiration of the contract.

Forecasting Price Changes To simplify this process, suppose an investor focuses her estimates on how stock prices change between subperiods, rather than on the dollar levels. That is, beginning with today's known stock price, for the next subperiod she forecasts: (1) one plus the percentage change for an up *(u)* movement, and (2) one plus the percentage change for a down *(d)* movement. Further, to limit the number of required forecasts, suppose she also assumes that the same values for *u* and *d* apply to every up and down price change in all subsequent subperiods. With these assumptions, the investor need only forecast three things: *u, d,* and *N*—the total number of subperiods.

Exhibit 22.10 shows the effect that these modifications—which represent the essence of the **binomial option pricing model**—have on the forecasted stock price and option value trees. Consistent with the four-outcome version of the preceding example, this illustration allows for three subperiods (i.e., *N* = 3). The upper panel of the display shows that after an up and a down movement during the first two subperiods, the initial stock price of *S* will have changed to *(ud)S*. Of course, the values *(ud)S* and *(du)S* are equal, meaning that the forecast does not depend on whether the stock price begins its journey by rising or falling. As before, once *u, d,* and *N* are determined, the expiration date payoffs to the option (i.e., C_{uuu}, C_{uud}, C_{udd} and C_{ddd}) are established.

As before, the initial value for the call, C_0, can be solved by working backward through the tree and solving for each of the remaining intermediate option values. However, another distinct advantage of the binomial model is that these intermediate values are much easier to compute. In fact, in the *j*th state in any subperiod, the value of the option can be calculated by

22.1
$$C_j = \frac{(p)C_{ju} + (1-p)C_{jd}}{r}$$

Exhibit 22.10 Binomial Model Forecast Trees

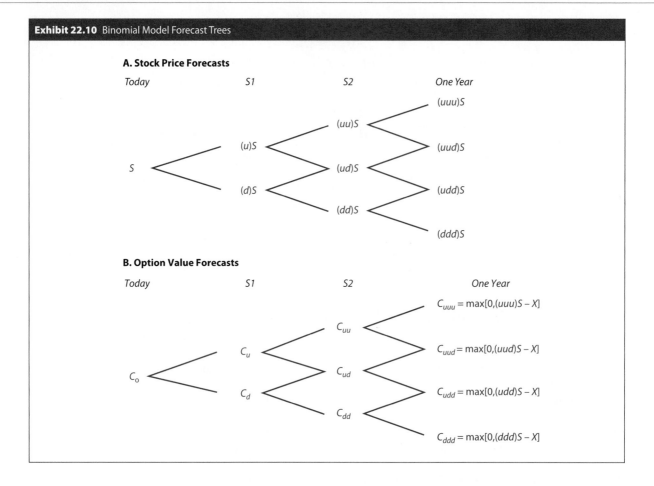

where

$$p = \frac{r - d}{u - d}$$

and

r = one plus the risk-free rate over the subperiod.

If p is interpreted as the probability of an up movement in the security's price, which would mean that $(1 - p)$ is the probability of a down move, then the formula for C_j has an intuitively appealing interpretation. The option's value at any point is simply its expected value one sub-period hence discounted back to the current time. Further, although p was not an explicit part of the investor's forecast, it is nevertheless generated by the model. In this sense, p is referred to as the *implied probability* of an upward price movement. To ensure that this interpretation holds, the binomial model requires that $d < r < u,$ a condition that is quite reasonable in practice.

Generalizing the Model Equation 22.1 can be extended by recognizing that the value for C_j it generates is one of the inputs for valuing the option in the preceding subperiod. Thus, the formula for an option in Subperiod t can be inserted into the right-hand side of the formula for Subperiod $t - 1$. Carrying this logic all the way back to Date 0, the binomial option valuation model becomes

22.2 $$C_0 = \left\{ \sum_{j=0}^{N} \frac{N!}{(N-j)!j!} p^j (1-p)^{N-j} \max \left[0, \left(u^j d^{N-j} \right) S - X \right] \right\} \div r^N$$

where

$$N! = [(N)(N-1)(N-2) \ldots (2)(1)]$$

To interpret Equation 22.2, the ratio $[N! \div (N-j)!j!]$ is the "combinatorial" way of stating how many distinct paths lead to a particular terminal outcome, $p^j(1-p)^{N-j}$ is the probability of getting to that outcome, and $\max[0, (u^j d^{N-j})S - X]$ is the payoff associated with that outcome. Letting m be the smallest integer number of up moves guaranteeing that the option will be in the money at expiration (i.e., $u^m d^{N-m})S > X$), this formula can be reduced further to

22.3
$$C_0 = \left\{ \sum_{j=m}^{N} \frac{N!}{(N-j)!j!} p^j(1-p)^{N-j}[(u^j d^{N-j})S - X] \right\} \div r^N$$

As an example of how this model works, assume the investor has gathered contract terms and price data and has made her forecasts as follows: $S = 50.00$, $X = 52.50$, $T = $ one year, $RFR = $ 8 percent (through expiration), $u = 1.09139$, $d = 0.92832$, and $N = 3$. By these forecasts, the investor has divided the one-year life of the option into three subperiods and estimated up and down moves during any subperiod as slightly greater than 9 and 7 percent, respectively. Also, the values for r and p implied by these forecasts are 1.026 [$= (1.08)^{0.33}$] and 0.599 [$= (1.026 - 0.92832) \div (1.09139 - 0.92832)$]. By Equation 22.3, which ignores the two terminal option outcomes that are equal to zero, the value of a one-year European-style call option with an exercise price of $52.50 is

$$C_0 = \frac{(3)(0.599)^2(0.401)(2.79) + (1)(0.599)^3(12.50)}{(1.026)^3} = \$3.60$$

This is the same value the three-step approach produced in the previous example because the forecasted stock price tree in Exhibit 22.8 was generated with these same values of u and d (e.g., $(uu)S = (1.09139)^2(50) = \$59.56$). We also can confirm that the tree of forecasted option values illustrated in Exhibit 22.9 may be replicated through repeatedly calculating the "State j" equation.[4] Finally, with this notation, the hedge ratio for any state j becomes

$$h_j = \frac{(u-d)S_j}{(C_{jd} - C_{ju})}$$

Thus, a share of stock held long could be hedged initially by shorting 1.78 call options [$= (1.09139 - 0.92832)(50) \div (0.95 - 5.53)$], a position that would be rebalanced to 1.32 calls after one subperiod if the first price change was positive.

22.2.4 The Black-Scholes Valuation Model

The binomial model is a *discrete* method for valuing options because it allows security price changes to occur in distinct upward or downward movements. Prices can also change *continuously* throughout time. This was the approach taken by Black and Scholes (1973) in developing their celebrated equation for valuing European-style options. This is not a more realistic assumption because it presumes that security prices change when markets are closed (e.g., at night, on weekends). The advantage of the Black-Scholes approach—identical in spirit to the basic three-step, riskless hedge method outlined earlier—is that it leads to a relatively simple, closed-form equation capable of valuing options accurately under a wide array of circumstances.

The Black-Scholes model assumes that stock price movements can be described by a statistical process known as *geometric Brownian motion*. This process is summarized by a volatility

---

[4] For example, $C_{uu} = [(0.599)(12.50) + (0.401)(2.79)] \div (1.026) = \$8.39$.

factor, σ, which is analogous to the investor's stock price forecasts in the previous models. Formally, the stock price process assumed by Black and Scholes is

$$\frac{\Delta S}{S} = \mu[\Delta T] + \sigma\epsilon[\Delta T]^{1/2}$$

so that a stock's return ($\Delta S/S$) from the present through any future Period T has both an expected component ($\mu[\Delta T]$) and a "noise" component ($\sigma\epsilon[\Delta T]^{1/2}$), where μ is the mean return and ϵ is the standard normally distributed random error term.[5]

Assuming the continuously compounded risk-free rate and the stock's variance (i.e., (σ^2) remain constant until the expiration date T, Black and Scholes used the riskless hedge intuition to derive the following formula for valuing a call option on a nondividend-paying stock:

22.4
$$C_0 = SN(d_1) - X(e^{-(RFR)T})N(d_2)$$

where $e^{-(RFR)T}$ is the discount function for continuously compounded variables,

$$d_1 = [(\ln(S/X) + (RFR + 0.5\sigma^2)[T])] \div (\sigma[T]^{1/2})$$

and

$$d_2 = d_1 - \sigma[T]^{1/2}$$

with $\ln(\cdot)$ being the natural logarithm function. The variable $N(d)$ represents the cumulative probability of observing a value drawn from the standard normal distribution (i.e., one with a mean of zero and a standard deviation of one) equal to or less than d. As the standard normal distribution is symmetric around zero, a value of $d = 0$ would lead to $N(d) = 0.5000$; positive values of d would then have cumulative probabilities greater than 50 percent, with negative values of d leading to cumulative probabilities of less than one-half.

Values for $N(d)$ can be established in two ways. First, an investor can use a table of calculated values for the standard normal distribution, such as the one shown in Appendix D at the end of the book. For example, if the value of d_1 is 0.65, $N(d_1)$ could be established by finding the entry corresponding to the 0.6 row and the 0.05 column, or 0.7422. This means that 74.22 percent of the observations in the standard normal distribution have a value of 0.65 or less. If d_1 had been −0.65, the value of $N(-d_1) = 1 - N(d_1) = 1 - 0.7422 = 0.2578$, which must be the case since the distribution is symmetric.

A second approach to calculating cumulative normal probabilities is approximating them with the following formula.[6]

$$N(d) \approx \begin{cases} 0.5e^{-(d^2)/2 - 281/(83 - 351/d)} & \text{if } d < 0 \\ 1 - 0.5e^{-(d^2)/2 - 281/(83 + 351/d)} & \text{if } d \geq 0 \end{cases}$$

For example, with $d = 0.65$, we have an approximate probability of

$$N(0.65) \approx 1 - 0.5e^{-(0.65^2)/2-281/(83 + 351/0.65)} = 0.7422$$

Properties of the Model The **Black-Scholes valuation model** reveals that the option's value is a function of five variables:

1. Current security price
2. Exercise price
3. Time to expiration
4. Risk-free rate
5. Security price volatility

---

[5] For a detailed analysis of the mathematics underlying the Black-Scholes model, see Hull (2009).
[6] For more on this approximation method, see Carr (1988).

Exhibit 22.11 Factors Affecting Black-Scholes Option Values

| | WILL CAUSE AN INCREASE/DECREASE IN: | |
An Increase In:	Call Value	Put Value
Security price (S)	Increase	Decrease
Exercise price (X)	Decrease	Increase
Time to expiration (T)	Increase	Increase or decrease
Risk-free rate (RFR)	Increase	Decrease
Security volatility (σ)	Increase	Increase

Functionally, the Black-Scholes model holds that $C = f(S, X, T, RFR, \sigma)$. The first and fourth factors are observable market prices, and the second and third variables are defined by the contract itself. Thus, the only variable an investor must provide is the volatility factor. As noted earlier, the estimate of σ embeds the investor's forecast of future stock prices.

The value of the call option will rise with increases in each of the five factors *except* the exercise price. Exhibit 22.11 summarizes these relationships. The middle column of the exhibit shows what will happen to the value of the call when one of the five factors increases. The intuition behind the first three of these relationships is straightforward: An increase in the underlying asset's price (i.e., S) will increase the call's intrinsic value; a larger exercise price (i.e., X) will reduce the intrinsic value. Also, the longer the option has until it expires, the more valuable the time premium component. This is because a greater opportunity exists for the contract to finish in the money. On the other hand, the relationships between C, RFR, and σ are less obvious. An increase in RFR will increase the call's value because this reduces the present value of X, an expense that the call holder must pay at expiration to exercise the contract. Similarly, when the volatility of the underlying asset's price increases, the call becomes more valuable since this increases the probability that the option will be deeper in the money at expiration.[7]

Another useful facet of the Black-Scholes model is that the hedge ratio at any moment is simply $N(d_1)$, the partial derivative of the call's value with respect to the stock price (i.e., $\delta C/\delta S$). Under this interpretation, $N(d_1)$ is the change in the option's value given a one dollar change in the underlying security's price. For this reason, $N(d_1)$ often is called the option's **delta**, and it indicates the number of stock shares that can be hedged by a single call—the exact reciprocal of the previous interpretation of the hedge ratio, h. Finally, although the Black-Scholes model was developed several years before the binomial framework, the former is actually an extension of the latter. As the number of subperiods (i.e., N) approaches infinity, the up or down price movements begin to occur on a continuous basis. If the values of u and d are then set equal to $e^{\sigma[\Delta T]^{1/2}}$ and $e^{-\sigma[\Delta T]^{1/2}}$, respectively, the binomial model collapses to become the Black-Scholes formula.

An Example Consider the following values for the five input variables: $S = 40$, $X = 40$, $T =$ one year, $RFR = 9$ percent, and $\sigma = 0.30$. To calculate the Black-Scholes value of a European-style call option under these conditions, first calculate:

$$d_1 = (\ln(40/40) + (0.09 + 0.5(0.3)^2)[1]) \div (0.3[1]^{1/2}) = 0.45$$

and

$$d_2 = 0.45 - 0.3[1]^{1/2} = 0.15$$

[7] In more technical terms, these relationships can be summarized as $\delta C/\delta S > 0$, $\delta C/\delta RFR > 0$, $\delta C/\delta T > 0$, $\delta C/\delta\sigma > 0$, and $\delta C/\delta X < 0$.

Exhibit 22.12 Example of Black-Scholes Valuation

Stock Price ($)	Call Value ($)	Hedge Ratio
25	0.44	0.1321
30	1.51	0.3054
35	3.53	0.5020
40	6.49	0.6736
45	10.19	0.8003
50	14.42	0.8837
55	18.98	0.9347

Note: Assumes $X = 40$, $T = 1$ year, $RFR = 9\%$, and $\sigma = 0.30$.

so that

$$N(d_1) = 1 - 0.5e^{-(0.45^2)/2 - 281/(83 + 351/0.45)} = 0.6736$$

and

$$N(d_2) = 1 - 0.5e^{-(0.15^2)/2 - 281/(83 + 351/0.15)} = 0.5596$$

Thus,

$$C_0 = (40)(0.6736) - 40(e^{-.09})(0.5596) = \$6.49$$

$N(d_1)$ says that the call option will change in value by about 67 cents for every dollar of a change in the underlying asset, which suggests a hedge ratio of one-and-a-half calls short for every stock share held long. Exhibit 22.12 shows how both the option's value and N(d1) change as the security's value changes—with the other factors held constant. Notably, the hedge ratios range in value from 0 to 1, and increase as stock prices increase. Therefore, the deeper in the money the option is, the closer its price movements will come to duplicating those of the stock itself. The relationship between stock prices and call option prices for this example is shown in Exhibit 22.13. The delta, or hedge ratio, associated with a given stock price is simply the slope of a line tangent to the call option price curve.

Exhibit 22.13 Black-Scholes Values

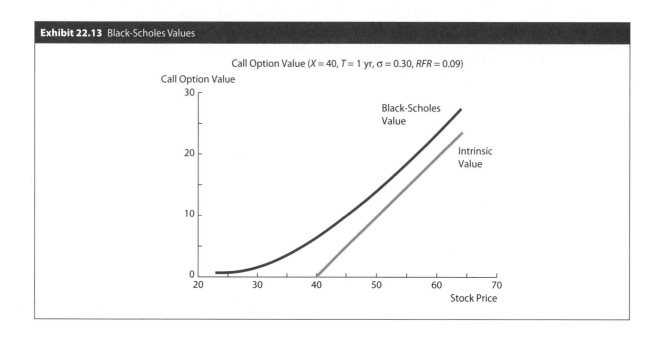

Call Option Value ($X = 40$, $T = 1$ yr, $\sigma = 0.30$, $RFR = 0.09$)

22.2.5 Estimating Volatility

Just as the growth rate of dividends (i.e., *g*) was a crucial element in establishing the fundamental value of common stock using the dividend discount model, option valuation depends critically on an accurate forecast of the underlying asset's future price level. In the Black-Scholes framework, this means selecting the proper σ, which is equivalent to the standard deviation of returns to the underlying asset. This value can be estimated in two ways. First, it can be calculated in the traditional manner using historical returns. Specifically, calculate the Day *t price relative* as $R_t = \ln(P_t \div P_{t-1})$. If a series of price relatives are calculated for a sequence of *N* days in the recent past, the mean and standard deviation of this series can be established as

$$\overline{R} = \left(\frac{1}{N}\right)\sum_{t=1}^{N} R_t \text{ and } \sigma^2 = \left(\frac{1}{N-1}\right)\sum_{t=1}^{N}(R_t - \overline{R})^2$$

The factor σ is expressed in terms of daily price movements. To annualize this value, σ can be multiplied by the square root of the number of trading days in the year (usually assumed to be 250), which then becomes the estimate of volatility employed in the Black-Scholes formula. The advantage of historical volatility is that it is easy to compute and requires no prior assumption about stock market efficiency; its disadvantage is its presumption that stock price behavior in the future will continue as it has in the past, a sometimes dubious assumption. Exhibit 22.14 lists 30-day historical volatilities for a representative sample of optionable stocks during November 2004 and May 2007.

An alternative to relying on historical price movements is a second volatility estimation approach that involves the Black-Scholes equation. Recall that if we know all five input factors—*S, X, T, RFR,* and σ—we can solve for the value of the call option. However, if we know the current price of the option (call it *C**) and the four other variables, we can calculate the level of σ that forces the Black-Scholes value to equal *C**. That is, the volatility implied by current market prices is established by finding σ* such that $C^* = f(S, X, T, RFR, \sigma^*)$. Accordingly, the value σ* is known as the **implied volatility**. No simple closed-form solution exists for performing this calculation; it must be done by trial and error.

Exhibit 22.14 Historical Volatility Estimates

Company	Ticker	30-day Volatility Estimate (%)	
		November 2004	May 2007
Altria	MO	36.96	11.30
Amazon.com	AMZN	32.66	36.57
Applied Materials	AMAT	27.98	30.76
Bank of America	BAC	12.44	8.58
Continental Airlines	CAL	18.95	33.01
Cisco Systems	CSCO	32.82	31.71
Citigroup	C	14.87	16.63
Coca-Cola	KO	9.16	12.65
Dell Computer	DELL	31.97	41.13
Duke Energy	DUK	20.97	15.93
eBay	EBAY	25.81	21.15
General Electric	GE	14.27	10.07
Halliburton	HAL	28.23	23.74
Intel	INTC	26.23	21.41
Merck	MRK	34.18	14.46
Oracle	ORCL	20.91	18.52
Pfizer	PFE	22.00	9.65
Tivo	TIVO	69.25	41.20
Wal-Mart	WMT	23.22	9.61
Xerox	XRX	26.10	20.34

Source: Chicago Board Options Exchange, October 16, 2007. Provided as a courtesy by Chicago Board Options Exchange, Incorporated.

Implied volatility is advantageous because it calculates the same volatility forecast investors use to set option prices. The disadvantage of implied volatility is its presumption that markets are efficient in that the option price set in the market corresponds directly to that generated by the Black-Scholes equation. Beckers (1981) has shown that implied volatilities do a better job than historical volatilities of predicting future stock price movements; however, Figlewski (1989b) and Szakmary, Ors, Kim, and Davidson (2003) caution that σ^* can be "noisy" because it picks up not only the true level of volatility but also any misestimate inherent in the valuation process.

Brown, Harlow, and Tinic (1989) estimated the volatilities implied by the S&P 500 index call option contract for the 121-day period surrounding the stock market crash in October 1987. These calculations are reproduced in Exhibit 22.15. The time variable is denominated relative to "Black Monday" (i.e., Day 0), which occurred on October 19, 1987. To see how much market risk changed with the crash, the *average* implied volatility measure for the period Day -60 to Day -5 (i.e., the period beginning approximately two and a half months before the crash) was 18.9 percent. The comparable statistic for the period from Day $+5$ to Day $+60$ was 43.3 percent. Moreover, on Black Monday itself, the implied volatility rose to 145 percent, more than seven and a half times its precrash level!

The concept of implied volatility is also the foundation of a popular measure of stock market sentiment. Introduced by Whaley (1993), the **Volatility Index (VIX)** is calculated as a weighted average of the implied volatility estimates from options on the Standard & Poor's 500 index using a wide range of exercise prices. VIX purports to measure investor expectations of near-term (i.e., 30-day) volatility in the stock market, with higher levels of the index indicating greater investor wariness about future economic conditions. In a typical year, the VIX can range between 10.00 and 45.00 percent. Futures and options contracts using the VIX as the underlying asset have traded on the CBOE since 2004 and 2006, respectively.

22.2.6 Problems with Black-Scholes Valuation

The Black-Scholes option valuation model is popular with investors for at least two reasons: It is computationally convenient and it produces reasonable values under a wide variety of conditions. There are, however, circumstances in which the model is less than desirable. In one of the earliest empirical tests of the Black-Scholes equation, MacBeth and Merville (1979) showed that implied volatilities tended to be overly large when the associated call options were in the money and too small for out-of-the-money contracts. Assuming that at-the-money options are priced fairly by the market, this suggested that in-the-money options were priced higher by investors than their Black-Scholes values, with the opposite being true for the out-of-the-money contracts.

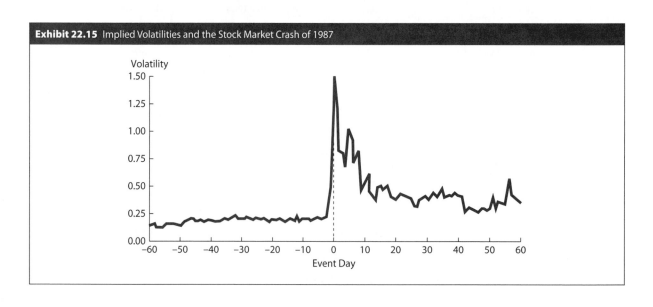

Exhibit 22.15 Implied Volatilities and the Stock Market Crash of 1987

Thus, for the authors' sample of stocks, the Black-Scholes model overvalued out-of-the-money call options and undervalued in-the-money contracts. Interestingly, in two different studies, Rubinstein (1985b, 1994) found evidence that both supported and contradicted these results.

In general, any violation of the assumptions upon which the Black-Scholes model is based could lead to a misvaluation of the option contract. For instance, because stock prices do not change continuously, less actively traded stocks might have options that are priced differently in the market than those stocks that trade frequently. Figlewski (1989a) has noted how such market imperfections as brokerage fees, bid-ask spreads, and inflexible position sizes can create arbitrageable differences between option values and prices. He cautioned that Black-Scholes values should be viewed as approximations, best suited for comparing prices of different contracts. Further, Black (1989a) has observed that other conditions of the model are almost certain to be violated in practice, such as the assumption that the risk-free rate and volatility level remain constant until the expiration date.

· ·
22.3 Option Valuation: Extensions and Advanced Topics

The preceding discussion has concentrated on the valuation of European-style call options having a nondividend-paying stock as the underlying asset. Many other conditions and underlying assets exist for which options need to be valued. This section explores several extensions of the basic approach.

22.3.1 Valuing European-Style Put Options

The put-call-spot parity model of Chapter 20 held that, in an efficient market, the value of a European-style put on a nondividend-paying security should be equivalent to a portfolio short in the security while long in both a call option and a Treasury bill having a face value equal to the common exercise price X. Using a continuous discounting process for the T-bill, this relationship can be expressed

$$P_0 = C_0 + X(e^{-(RFT)T}) - S$$

This formula implies that if we know the prices of the security, the call option, and the T-bill, we can solve for the value of the put option. If the Black-Scholes value for C is inserted into this expression, we have

$$P_0 = [SN(d_1) - X(e^{-(RFR)T})N(d_2)] + X(e^{-(RFR)T}) - S$$

which can be manipulated to equal

22.5 $$P_0 = X(e^{-(RFR)T})N(-d_2) - SN(-d_1)$$

where all the notation is the same as before. Equation 22.5 is the Black-Scholes put option valuation model.

The comparative statics of put option valuation were shown in the final column of Exhibit 22.11. The value of the put will increase with higher levels of X but decline with an increase in S because of the effect these movements have on the contract's intrinsic value. Like the call option, the put's value benefits from an increase in σ since this increases the likelihood that the contract will finish deep in the money. Also, an increase in the risk-free rate reduces the present value of X, which hurts the holder of the put who receives the exercise price if the contract is executed. Finally, the sign of $\delta P/\delta T$ could be either positive or negative depending on the trade-off between the longer time over which the security price could move in the desired direction and the reduced present value of the exercise price received by the seller at expiration.

In the preceding valuation example, we had the following inputs: $S = 40$, $X = 40$, $T = $ one year, $RFR = 9$ percent, and $\sigma = 0.30$. With these assumptions, d_1 and d_2 still are 0.45

and 0.15, respectively, but now we need to compute $N(-0.45) = 1 - 0.6736 = 0.3264$ and $N(-0.15) = 1 - 0.5596 = 0.4404$. Thus:

$$P_0 = 40(e^{-.09})(0.4404) - 40(0.3264) = \$3.04$$

Finally, the hedge ratio for the put option in this model is $[N(d_1) - 1]$, which in this case is -0.3264 and indicates that the put option's value will *decrease* by approximately 33 cents for every dollar *increase* in S.

22.3.2 Valuing Options on Dividend-Bearing Securities

We learned earlier that the put-call parity relationship required an adjustment when the underlying asset common to the put and call options paid a dividend. This adjustment is needed because the payment of the dividend reduces the asset's market value, converting the investor's return from capital appreciation to cash flow. Other than the tax implications of this conversion, the underlying asset's owner should not lose any overall net worth with the payment of the dividend. However, the prospective call option owner will not receive the dividend; therefore, the reduction in the present value of the stock will reduce the value of his derivative contract. Being rational, he will reduce the price he is willing to pay for the call option on the dividend-bearing security. Consequently, dividends become a sixth factor in the option valuation process.

The original Black-Scholes valuation model can be modified to incorporate dividend payments in two ways. The most straightforward approach is reducing the current share price by the present value of the dividends paid during the option's life and then using this amount in place of the actual stock price, that is, replace S in the model with $S' = S - PV$ (dividends). For the case of the one-year, at-the-money call option with an exercise price of $40 that we saw earlier, assume that a dividend payment of $1 is made in six months, with another $1 paid just prior to expiration. The continuously compounded risk-free rate and volatility factors were 9 percent and 30 percent, respectively, so

$$S' = 40 - (1)e^{-(0.09)(0.5)} - (1)e^{-(0.09)(1.0)} = 38.13$$

When inserted into the formulas for d_1 and d_2, S' generates values of 0.29 and -0.01, respectively.

With these inputs, the Black-Scholes valuation then becomes

$$C_0 = (38.13)N(0.29) - (40)e^{-0.09}N(-0.01) = (38.13)(0.6141) - (36.56)(0.4960) = \$5.28$$

This amount can be compared to the $6.49 contract value for an otherwise identical call on a nondividend-paying share that we estimated earlier. The reduction in option value (i.e., $1.21) is not as great as the present value of the dividends (i.e., $1.87). This is due to the possibility that the option would have expired out of the money even without the dividend payment, meaning that the dividend-induced stock price reduction will not always affect the contract's terminal payoff. Also, the hedge ratio in the formula is reduced from its original level of 0.6736 to 0.6141.

The second approach to adjusting the option valuation process for dividend payments involves modifying the model itself rather than the stock price input. This requires expressing the dividend in *yield* form, defined as the annual payment divided by the current stock price, and assuming that this yield is paid continuously. Merton (1973) first showed that the Black-Scholes model can be rewritten as

$$C_0 = (e^{-(D)T})SN(d_1) - X(e^{-(RFR)T})N(d_2)$$

with

$$d_1 = [\ln((e^{-(D)T})S/X) + (RFR + 0.5\sigma^2)[T]] \div (\sigma[T]^{1/2})$$

and

$$d_2 = d_1 - \sigma[T]^{1/2}$$

where:

D = the annualized dividend yield

The yield appears as a "discount" factor to the current stock value in two places in these equations. If we set $S' = (e^{-(D)T})S$, this second dividend adjustment is just a continuous version of the first.

Extending the original example, we now have six factors to include: $S = 40$, $X = 40$, T = one year, RFR = 9 percent, σ = 30 percent, and $D = (2/40) = 5$ percent. Plugging these into the model, we get values of 0.28 for d_1 and -0.02 for d_2 so that

$$C_0 = (e^{-0.05})(40)N(0.28) - (e^{-0.09})(40)N(-0.02)$$

$$= (38.05)(0.6103) - (36.56)(0.4920) = \$5.23$$

This amount differs from the first adjustment process amount because the assumption of a continuous dividend stream does not match the reality of how these payments are made. However, modifying the model's structure is often much more convenient than adjusting the stock input level for a specific payment structure.

22.3.3 Valuing American-Style Options

The preceding valuation discussion assumed European-style options. If the contract had been American-style—that is, its exercise is not limited to the expiration date—how would the valuation process change? The possibility of early exercise makes the derivation of an exact closed-form analog to the Black-Scholes equation an elusive goal. Instead Roll (1977b), Geske (1979), and Whaley (1981) have designed elaborate approximation procedures for estimating the value of American-style calls. Further, Johnson (1983) and Barone-Adesi and Whaley (1986), among others, have taken different approaches to address the issue of American put valuation.

A formal summary of these models is beyond the scope of this discussion; however, we can consider several fundamental properties. Most important is that an American put or call has to be at least as valuable as its European-style counterpart because, by definition, the American option gives the holder more choices than the simpler contract. The American contract holder can exercise at the same time as the European option owner (i.e., at expiration) as well as any point prior to that terminal date. Since we have seen that an option's value ultimately derives from the choice to exercise the agreement or not, superior terms for that decision means a more valuable contract. Letting C_a and C_e represent the values of American and European calls, this relationship can be expressed as

$$S \geq C_a(S,T,X) \geq C_e(S,T,X) \geq \max[0, S - Xe^{-(RFR)T}] \geq \max[0, S - X] \geq 0$$

This expression says that (1) the American call is at least as valuable as the European contract, (2) neither call can be more valuable than the underlying stock, and (3) both contracts are at least as valuable as their intrinsic values, expressed on both a nominal and discounted basis. For puts, a similar boundary condition would be

$$X \geq P_a(S,T,X) \geq P_e(S,T,X) \geq \max[0, Xe^{-(RFR)T} - S] \geq 0$$

For a stock that does not pay dividends, C_a and C_e will be equal to one another. At any point prior to expiration, the preceding relationship shows that $C_a(S,T,X) - \max[0, S - X] > 0$, with $\max[0, S - X]$ being the value the investor would extract from the option's exercise. Therefore, without the reduction in the stock's price caused by the dividend payment, an investor wishing to liquidate his American call position would sell it rather than exercise it so as not to surrender the contract's time premium. Thus, in the absence of dividends, the American call offers choices that the investor neither wants nor is willing to pay for. Thus, the Black-Scholes model for C_e can be used to value C_a as well.[8]

When the stock pays dividends, this situation changes. Suppose an investor holds an American call option on a stock just prior to its ex-dividend date. On the ex-date—call it Date t—the value of the stock will decline by about the dividend amount, leaving $S_t = S_{t-1} -$ (dividend)$_t$ assuming no other new information impacted the share's value from the previous day. The value of the option will decline as well, from $C(S_{t-1})$ to $C(S_t)$. Selling the contract on the day prior to the ex-date will not be possible since rational buyers know what will happen the following day. Therefore, the investor must decide on Date $t - 1$ whether he should exercise his contract and receive only the intrinsic value of max$[0, S_{t-1} - X]$. This is the proper choice if the loss of the option's time premium is less than $C(S_{t-1}) - C(S_t)$, which will likely occur when the option is (1) close to maturity (and, hence, the time premium is low) and (2) the stock's dividend is large. Because the American option allows the investor the possibility of preserving value when the European contract cannot, we must have $C_a > C_e$ for almost all cases.

Deciding to exercise a put prior to maturity does not depend on the presence of dividends. Indeed, dividend payments increase a put's value because they reduce the underlying common stock's value without an offset in the exercise price. Instead, the relevant issue is the limited liability of the stock itself. Suppose an investor holds an American put on a nearly bankrupt company. The contract, which is struck at $50, has three more months before it expires, and the stock is currently selling for $1. In this case, the option holder would evaluate the trade-off between exercising the contract today to capture the $49 intrinsic value or waiting three months and hoping the stock becomes worthless. That is, she must decide whether she would rather have $49 now or the present value of the possibility of receiving $50. Depending on the discount rate and the estimated recovery probability, it is likely that she will exercise now.

On the other hand, the European put does not offer the investor this choice. Because the stock's expected return is positive, an efficient capital market would predict that the price of the nondividend-paying stock will be higher in three months, thereby reducing the expiration date value of the contract below $49. Without the ability to exercise the put prior to expiration, the European put sometimes can be worth less than its intrinsic value, which always is a lower bound for the American contract. Thus, P_e can be either greater or less than max$[0, X - S]$, with the latter situation most likely to occur at extremely low values of S and large values of T. The preceding boundary condition shows that P_e must only be greater than the discounted version of the intrinsic value formula, or max$[0, Xe^{-(RFR)T} - S]$. These relationships are illustrated in Exhibit 22.16.

22.3.4 Other Extensions of the Black-Scholes Model

The dividend-adjusted Black-Scholes model is also quite useful in valuing options for underlying assets other than common stock. Three of the more important applications along these lines follow.

Stock Index Options Stock index options are fundamentally no different than regular stock options. However, as a hypothetical creation, the stock index cannot be delivered to settle the contract and so it must be settled in cash. Beyond that, because it is a well-diversified portfolio, the volatility of the stock index's price usually is quite a bit lower than the typical stock. Finally, the applicable dividend yield is the average annualized yield on the index during the option's life, which is likely to be known to investors at least one calendar quarter into the future.

Suppose the Standard and Poor's 100 currently is at a level of 601.40 and a call option on the index with an exercise price of 600 is being offered at a price of $17.75. An investor wants to determine whether the fair value of this contract is above or below the market price. The option

[8] For a complete development of these boundary conditions, see Chance and Brooks (2007).

Exhibit 22.16 Comparing American and European Put Values

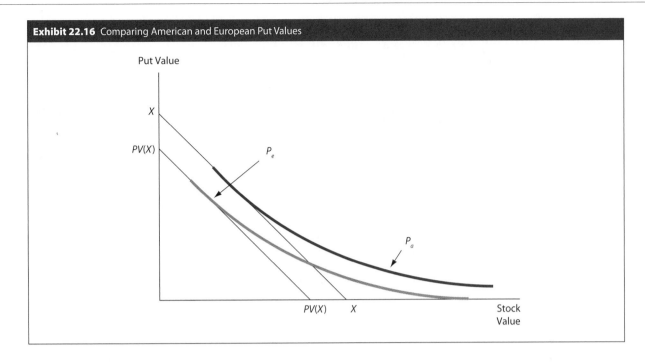

is set to expire in exactly 61 days, which translates to 0.1671 (= 61/365) year. The dividend yield on the S&P 100 is 2.00 percent, and the annualized yield on a 61-day Treasury bill is 5.70 percent. The investor forecasts the index's volatility to be 18 percent, and establishes that

$$d_1 = [\ln(601.40e^{-(0.02)0.1671}/600) + (0.057 + 0.5(0.18)^2)[0.1671]] \div (0.18[0.1671]^{1/2}) = 0.1525$$

and

$$d_2 = 0.1525 - 0.18[0.1671]^{1/2} = 0.0789$$

leading to $N(d_1) = 0.5607$ and $N(d_2) = 0.5315$. Thus, she estimates the call's value to be

$$C_0 = (599.39)(0.5607) - (600)(e^{-(0.057)0.1671})(0.5315) = \$20.20$$

Since this is higher than the market price of the option (i.e., $17.75), the contract appears undervalued. This is not necessarily an arbitrage opportunity, however, as the investor's valuation was based on two assumptions that may not match the consensus view of other market participants: (1) the Black-Scholes framework is appropriate, and (2) the index's volatility is 18 percent and not something lower.

Foreign Currency Options   Recall that prices for exchange-traded currency options are quoted in U.S. cents per unit of foreign currency, reflecting that a call option is the right to buy a fixed amount of foreign currency with U.S. dollars. Let RFR_f and RFR_d be the risk-free rates in the foreign and U.S. domestic markets, respectively. Further, let σ be the volatility of the exchange rate between the United States and the foreign country, denominated in USD per unit of FC. Garman and Kohlhagen (1983) and Biger and Hull (1983) showed that the Black-Scholes model for European-style calls and puts under these conditions can be written as

$$C_0 = \left(e^{-(RFR_f)T}\right) SN(d_1) - X\left(e^{-(RFR_d)T}\right) N(-d_2)$$
$$P_0 = X\left(e^{-(RFF_d)T}\right) N(d_2) - \left(e^{-(RFR_f)T}\right) SN(-d_1)$$

where:

$$d_1 = [\text{In } (e^{-(RFRf)T})S/X + (RFR_d + 0.5\sigma^2)[T]] \div (\sigma[T]^{1/2})$$

$$d_2 = d_1 - \sigma[T]^{1/2}$$

S = the spot exchange rate quoted on a direct (i.e., USD/FC) basis

Again, this formula is equivalent to the dividend-adjusted Black-Scholes model for stock options when RFR_f is interpreted as the "dividend yield" on the foreign currency. As an example, suppose the spot exchange rate between the U.S. dollar and the British pound is USD 1.50/GBP. The risk-free rates in the United States and England are 4.5 percent and 9 percent, respectively, so interest rate parity holds that the dollar should trade at a forward premium relative to the pound. To the extent that forward FX rates "predict" future spot rates, this suggests that the dollar price of sterling will fall. Thus, an at-the-money put option should be more valuable to an investor than an at-the-money sterling call. To see if this is the case, consider the valuation of six-month contracts where $S = 1.50$, $X = 1.50$, $RFR_d = 4.5$ percent, $RFR_f = 9$ percent, $\sigma = 13$ percent, and $T = 0.5$. With these inputs, $S' = S(e^{-(.09)0.5}) = 1.434$ so that

$$d_1 = [\ln(1.434/1.50) + (0.045 + 0.5(0.13)^2)[0.5]] \div (0.13[0.5]^{1/2}) = -0.20$$

and

$$d_2 = -0.20 - 0.13[0.5]^{1/2} = -0.29$$

Therefore, the option values are

$$C_0 = (1.434)(0.4207) - (1.50)(e^{-(0.045)0.5})(0.3859) = \$0.037$$

and

$$P_0 = (1.50)(e^{-(0.045)0.5})(0.6141) - (1.434)(0.5793) = \$0.070$$

as expected.

Futures Options   In the preceding chapter, we showed that in the absence of physical storage costs or dividends, the futures contract price (F) should simply be the spot price (S) of the underlying asset carried forward to date T at the risk-free rate. With continuous yields, this can be written as $F = Se^{(RFR)T}$. Black (1976) showed that substituting F for S in the Black-Scholes formula for call options leaves

$$C_0 = [e^{-(RFR)T}F]N(d_1) - (e^{-(RFR)T})XN(d_2)$$

$$= (e^{-(RFR)T})[FN(d_1) - XN(d_2)]$$

where:

$$d_1 = (\ln(F/X) + 0.5\sigma^2[T]^{1/2})$$

$$d_2 = d_1 - \sigma[T]^{1/2}$$

In the expressions for d_1 and d_2, the risk-free rate factor drops out because a risk-free hedge portfolio with futures and call options requires no initial investment since futures contracts require no front-end payment. Also, here σ represents the futures price volatility, which normally is assumed to be equal to the underlying asset volatility.

· ·

22.4 Option Trading Strategies

The introductory analysis in Chapter 20 highlighted two ways in which investors use options. First, we saw that the asymmetrical payoff structures they possess as stand-alone positions allowed investors to isolate the benefits of an anticipated change in the value of an underlying security while limiting the downside risk of an adverse price movement. Options are a leveraged

Exhibit 22.17 Hypothetical SAS Corporation Stock and Option Prices

Instrument		Exercise Price ($)	Market Price ($)	Intrinsic Value ($)	Time Premium ($)
Stock:		—	40.00	—	—
Call:	#1	35.00	8.07	5.00	3.07
	#2	40.00	5.24	0.00	5.24
	#3	45.00	3.24	0.00	3.24
Put:	#1	35.00	1.70	0.00	1.70
	#2	40.00	3.67	0.00	3.67
	#3	45.00	6.47	5.00	1.47

alternative to making a direct investment in the asset on which the contract is based. Second, we also saw that put options could be used in conjunction with an existing portfolio to limit the portfolio's loss potential. After revisiting this protective put application in the context of individual stock holdings, in this section we will consider a **covered call** option strategy as another method for modifying the risk or enhancing the return of an existing equity position.

This section also emphasizes a third way in which options are used: in *combination* with one another to create customized payoff distributions that do not exist in more fundamental securities, like stocks or bonds. The equity collar example that concluded Chapter 20 is a good example of this type of option strategy. In designing such combinations, the investor usually attempts to exploit a very specific view about future economic conditions. For example, he may feel that a particular company's stock returns will be extraordinarily volatile but have no clear impression about the price movement direction. Or, he may feel that another company's shares will trade within a very narrow range around their current price during the next few months. In developing all these strategies, we will return to the hypothetical example of SAS Corporation, which has exchange-traded common stock, as well as call and put options. Current prices for SAS stock and six different derivatives, all of which expire at the same time, are reproduced in Exhibit 22.17.

22.4.1 Protective Put Options

Although the protective put strategy is most often used to provide insurance for price declines in entire portfolios, Brown and Statman (1987) have noted that the technique can also be employed with individual equity positions. To see how this "insured stock" concept works, consider an investor who holds SAS stock in her portfolio but is concerned that an unexpected downturn in the company's product sales may lead to a decline in the value of her position in the coming months. To hedge against this firm-specific exposure, she decides to purchase an at-the-money put option on SAS shares, meaning that she would spend $3.67 to buy Put #2 with an exercise price of $40. If at expiration the price of SAS had declined below $40, the put option would pay her the difference.

The effect of this acquisition is shown in Exhibit 22.18, which lists the expiration date value of the combined protective put position for a range of possible SAS prices. As noted earlier, the primary benefit of the insured stock strategy is that it creates a profile equivalent to holding a call option on SAS stock. That is, the protective put holding preserves the investor's upside potential from rising share prices but limits her losses when share prices fall. In this case, the at-the-money put insures her against any losses beyond the $3.67 initial put premium. This is the same outcome the investor would have if, instead of the put-protected SAS shares, she had held an at-the-money SAS call option and a T-bill; the risk-free security provides the safety and the call option provides the potential for price appreciation. Recall from the put-call parity model of Chapter 20 that this result was shown as $S_0 + P_{0,T} = C_{0,T} + PV(X)$ or

$$(\text{Long Stock}) + (\text{Long Put}) = (\text{Long Call}) + (\text{Long T-bill})$$

Exhibit 22.18 Expiration Date Value of a Protective Put Position

Potential SAS Stock Value	Value of Put Option	Cost of Put Option	Net Protective Put Position
20	(40 − 20) = 20	−3.67	(20 + 20) − 3.67 = 36.33
25	(40 − 25) = 15	−3.67	(25 + 15) − 3.67 = 36.33
30	(40 − 30) = 10	−3.67	(30 + 10) − 3.67 = 36.33
35	(40 − 35) = 5	−3.67	(35 + 5) − 3.67 = 36.33
40	0	−3.67	(40 + 0) − 3.67 = 36.33
45	0	−3.67	(45 + 0) − 3.67 = 41.33
50	0	−3.67	(50 + 0) − 3.67 = 46.33
55	0	−3.67	(55 + 0) − 3.67 = 51.33
60	0	−3.67	(60 + 0) − 3.67 = 56.33

To extend the insurance interpretation of the protective put, Exhibit 22.19 shows the expiration date profits (net of the initial $40 purchase price for the investor's SAS shares) for using each of three put options available to her. To interpret this display, if SAS shares are priced at $40 on the expiration date, for Protective Put #2 (i.e., the at-the-money contract), the investor's combined position will be worth $36.33, giving her a net loss of $3.67. The main thing about this illustration is the trade-off it shows between the risk and reward potential of the various positions. Put #1 has the smallest front-end expense, but its $35 exercise price forces the investor to bear the first $5 of SAS stock price declines; this $5 "deductible" leads to the largest potential loss of three positions at $6.70 (= 1.70 + 5.00). However, for this degree of self-insuring on the part of the investor, Protective Put #1 has, at $41.70 (= 35.00 + 6.70), the smallest breakeven price. Conversely, Put #3, with an exercise price above the current share

Exhibit 22.19 Terminal Net Profits to Three Protective Put Positions

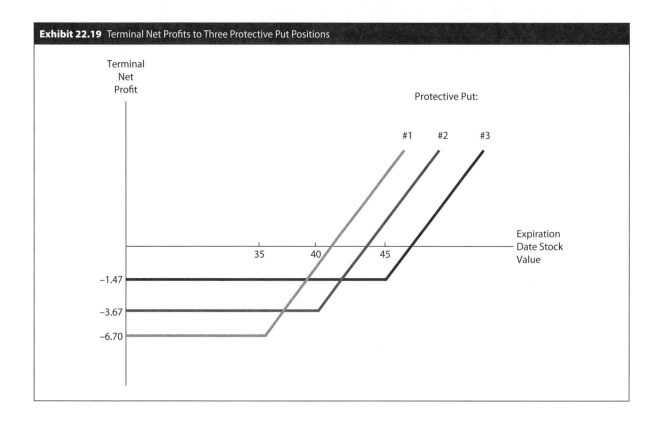

value, does not break even until SAS prices reach $46.47 but has a maximum possible loss of only $1.47 and therefore provides the best downside protection.

22.4.2 Covered Call Options

Another popular way in which derivatives are used to alter the payoff structure of an equity position involves the sale of call options. When investors sell call options based on an underlying position they own, they are said to be *writing* covered calls. Usually, the purpose of this strategy is to generate additional income for a stock holding that is not expected to change in value much over the near term. By selling a call, an investor receives the premium from the option contract to bolster an otherwise small (or negative) return. As Yates and Kopprasch (1980) explain, however, the danger is that the value of the stock position rises above the exercise price by the end of the contract's life causing the shares to be called away.

Suppose now that our investor believes that over the next few months the value of her SAS stock will neither rise nor fall by an appreciable amount. She decides not to insure her position against losses but, instead, to increase the cash flow of the investment by selling an at-the-money call option (Call #2). In exchange for granting the contract buyer the right to purchase her stock for $40 at the expiration date, she receives an immediate payment of $5.24. The expiration date values for the covered call position are listed in Exhibit 22.20. The construction of the terminal profit diagram—once again net of the current SAS share price—is depicted in Exhibit 22.21.

Both of these displays indicate that the expiration date payoff to the covered call position is comparable in form to that of a short position in a put option. Once again, this can be seen directly by adjusting the put-call parity condition as follows:

$$(\text{Long Stock}) + (\text{Short Call}) = (\text{Long T-bill}) + (\text{Short Put})$$

Notice in Exhibit 22.21 that there are two dimensions to the price risk inherent in this strategy. First, if by the option expiration date, SAS stock has risen above $40, the investor will be forced to sell her shares for less than they are actually worth. However, this will represent a lost opportunity only at prices above $45.24, or the exercise price plus the initial call premium. Second, if SAS stock experiences a decline in value, her potential loss is not hedged beyond the $5.24 in premium income that she received for selling the call; after prices fall beyond $31.09 (= 40 − 5.24 − 3.67), she would have been better off purchasing the at-the-money protective put option. Thus, to be profitable, the covered call strategy requires that the investor guess correctly that share values remain in a reasonably narrow band around their present levels.

22.4.3 Straddles, Strips, and Straps

A *straddle* is the simultaneous purchase (or sale) of a call and a put option with the same underlying asset, exercise price, and expiration date. A long straddle requires the purchase of the put and the call, while a short straddle sells both contracts. The long straddle gives the investor a

Exhibit 22.20 Expiration Date Value of a Covered Call Position

Potential SAS Stock Value	Value of Call Option	Proceeds from Call Option	Net Covered Call Position
20	0	5.24	(20 − 0) + 5.24 = 25.24
25	0	5.24	(25 − 0) + 5.24 = 30.24
30	0	5.24	(30 − 0) + 5.24 = 35.24
35	0	5.24	(35 − 0) + 5.24 = 40.24
40	0	5.24	(40 − 0) + 5.24 = 45.24
45	−(45 − 40) = −5	5.24	(45 − 5) + 5.24 = 45.24
50	−(50 − 40) = −10	5.24	(50 − 10) + 5.24 = 45.24
55	−(55 − 40) = −15	5.24	(55 − 15) + 5.24 = 45.24
60	−(60 − 40) = −20	5.24	(60 − 20) + 5.24 = 45.24

Exhibit 22.21 Terminal Net Profit to a Covered Call Position

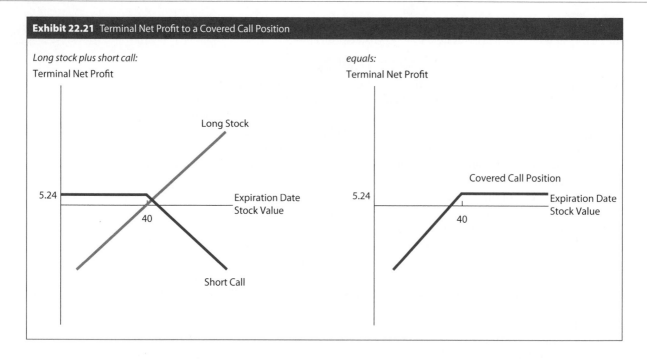

Long stock plus short call:
Terminal Net Profit

equals:
Terminal Net Profit

combination that will appreciate in value whether stock prices rise or fall in the future. Buying two options increases the initial cost; that is, to profit from this investment, stock price movements must be more pronounced than if the investor had predicted changes in a single direction. In this sense, a straddle is a *volatility* play; the buyer expects stock prices to move strongly one way or the other, while the seller hopes for lower-than-normal volatility.

Assume that an investor who does not hold SAS stock purchases a put and a call, each with an exercise price of $40. The cost of this purchase will be the combined prices of Call #2 and Put #2, or $8.91 (= 5.24 + 3.67). Recalling that the terminal values of the options are $\max[0, S_T - 40]$ and $\max[0, 40 - S_T]$, respectively, the potential expiration date profits to the straddle position (net of the initial cost, unadjusted for the time value differential) are shown in Exhibit 22.22. These are illustrated in Exhibit 22.23, which also depicts the profit to the seller of the straddle. The breakeven points on this graph occur at $31.09 (= 40 – 8.91) and $48.91 (= 40 + 8.91).

The expiration date values to the long and short positions are mirror images of each other; if the individual options themselves are zero-sum games, so too must be any combination of contracts. The buyer of the straddle is hoping for a dramatic event—such as a company-specific technological breakthrough or the impending judgment in a major lawsuit—that will either

Exhibit 22.22 Expiration Date Profits to a Long Straddle Position

SAS Stock Price at Expiration	Value of Calls	Value of Puts	Cost of Options	Net Profit
20.00	0.00	20.00	−8.91	11.09
25.00	0.00	15.00	−8.91	6.09
30.00	0.00	10.00	−8.91	1.09
35.00	0.00	5.00	−8.91	−3.91
40.00	0.00	0.00	−8.91	−8.91
45.00	5.00	0.00	−8.91	−3.09
50.00	10.00	0.00	−8.91	1.09
55.00	15.00	0.00	−8.91	6.09
60.00	20.00	0.00	−8.91	11.09

Exhibit 22.23 The Straddle Illustrated

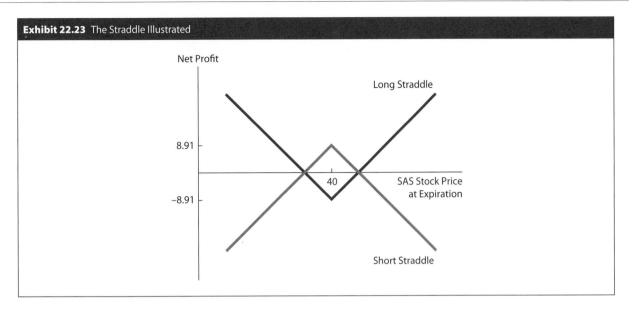

increase or decrease the stock price from its present $40 by at least $8.91. Conversely, the best result for the straddle seller is for SAS stock to continue to trade at its current price through the expiration date (i.e., no volatility at all) so that both options expire worthless. The seller's position demonstrates that it is possible to make money in the stock market even when prices do not change.

The long straddle position assumes implicitly that the investor has no intuition about the likely direction of future stock price movements. A slight modification is overweighting either the put or call position to emphasize a directional belief while maintaining a contract that would profit from a price movement the other way. A long *strap* position is the purchase of two calls and one put with the same exercise price, suggesting an investor who thinks stock prices are more likely to increase. An investor with a more bearish view could create a long *strip* position by purchasing two puts and only one call. The terminal profits to both of these combinations are listed in Exhibit 22.24, which again assumes the use of the two at-the-money SAS contracts.

Panel A of the exhibit shows that for the higher up-front payment of $14.15 [= (2 × 5.24) + 3.67], the strap will accelerate the profit in a rising market relative to the straddle. The settlement payment when SAS stock finishes above $40 on the expiration date is twice as great because the strap has doubled the investor's number of calls. The gross payoff when the price falls below $40 remains the same; however, the net amount received is considerably lower because the extra contract the investor purchased would then be out of the money. The net terminal value of the strip position tells a similar story, only with the acceleration of the profit generated by falling stock prices. The strap is more expensive than the strip under these conditions because SAS is a nondividend-paying common stock that is expected to increase in price to provide the investor with a positive expected return.

22.4.4 Strangles

One final variation on the straddle is an option combination known as a *strangle*, which also involves the simultaneous purchase or sale of a call and a put on the same underlying security with the same expiration date. Unlike the straddle, however, the options used in the strangle do not have the same exercise price; instead, they are selected so that both are out of the money. By buying two out-of-the-money contracts, the investor reduces the original straddle position's initial cost. Offsetting this reduced cost, though, is that stock prices will have to change by a greater amount before the strangle becomes profitable. Thus, the strangle offers a more modest risk–reward structure than the straddle.

Exhibit 22.24 Expiration Date Profits to Long Strap and Long Strip Positions

A. Strap Position (Two Calls and One Put)

SAS Stock Price at Expiration	Value of Calls	Value of Puts	Cost of Options	Net Profit
20.00	0.00	20.00	−14.15	5.85
25.00	0.00	15.00	−14.15	0.85
30.00	0.00	10.00	−14.15	−4.15
35.00	0.00	5.00	−14.15	−9.15
40.00	0.00	0.00	−14.15	−14.15
45.00	10.00	0.00	−14.15	−4.15
50.00	20.00	0.00	−14.15	5.85
55.00	30.00	0.00	−14.15	15.85
60.00	40.00	0.00	−14.15	25.85

B. Strip Position (Two Puts and One Call)

SAS Stock Price at Expiration	Value of Calls	Value of Puts	Cost of Options	Net Profit
20.00	0.00	40.00	−12.58	27.42
25.00	0.00	30.00	−12.58	17.42
30.00	0.00	20.00	−12.58	7.42
35.00	0.00	10.00	−12.58	−2.58
40.00	0.00	0.00	−12.58	−12.58
45.00	5.00	0.00	−12.58	−7.58
50.00	10.00	0.00	−12.58	−2.58
55.00	15.00	0.00	−12.58	2.42
60.00	20.00	0.00	−12.58	7.42

Suppose the investor purchased Call #3 and Put #1 for a combined price of $4.94 (= 3.24 + 1.70). If the price of SAS stock remained between the put exercise price of $35 and the call exercise price of $45, both contracts would expire worthless and the investor would lose his entire initial investment. Prices would have to decline to $30.06 (= 35 − 4.94) or increase to $49.94 (= 45 + 4.94) before the investor would break even on the position. Exhibit 22.25 shows that these breakeven points for the strangle are outside those for the straddle described earlier. Thus, among the set of "volatility bets," the strangle costs less to implement than the straddle but requires greater movement in the underlying security's price before it generates a positive return. Finally, by varying the exercise prices on the two options, the investor can create a strangle position that offers the exact trade-off between initial cost and future expected profit that he desires.

22.4.5 Chooser Options

The straddle is a special case of a wider class of option contracts sometimes called *chooser* options. With a chooser option, the investor selects an exercise price and expiration date but doesn't have to decide if the option should be a put or a call until after the contract is purchased. That is, the straddle is just a chooser option for which the decision can be deferred until the expiration date. Rubinstein (1992) has shown that the value of a chooser option will depend on when the investor has to make the put or call choice.

At one extreme, if the decision has to be made immediately, the buyer will select the option most likely to be in the money at expiration. In the previous example, with $X = 40$, we have seen that this will be the call. Thus, a chooser option in this case is worth $5.24. At the other extreme, a chooser option that allows the holder to defer the decision until expiration is, as already noted, equivalent to holding both a put and a call for the entire time to expiration. Consequently, the straddle price of $8.91 is the upper bound of the chooser option value struck at $40. The usual design for the chooser contract requires the holder to make a choice after

Exhibit 22.25 Comparing the Long Strangle and Long Straddle Positions

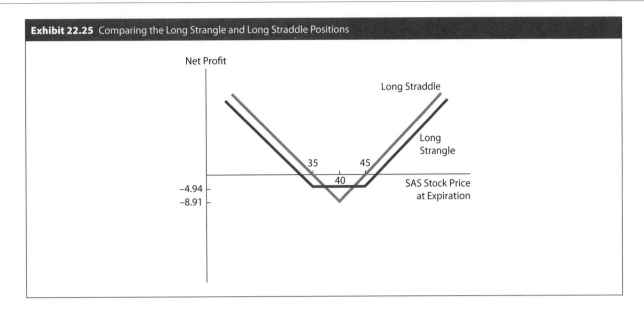

the initial purchase but before expiration, which would create a position worth somewhere between $5.24 and $8.91.

22.4.6 Spreads

As described by Black (1975), option spreads are the purchase of one contract and the sale of another, where the options are alike in all respects except for one distinguishing characteristic. In a *money* spread, the investor would sell an out-of-the-money call and purchase an in-the-money call on the same stock and expiration date. Alternatively, a *calendar* (or time) spread requires the purchase and sale of two calls—or two puts—with the same exercise price but different expiration dates. Option spreads are often used when one contract is perceived to be misvalued relative to the other. For instance, if an investor determines that a call option with an exercise price of X_1 and an expiration date T is selling at too high a price in the market, he can short it, thereby speculating on an eventual correction. However, if a broad-based increase in the stock market occurs before this contract-specific correction, he stands to lose a great deal because the short call position has unlimited liability. Thus, when he sells the first option, he can hedge some or all of the risk by buying a call with an exercise price of X_2 expiring at T.

Returning to the data for SAS options, assume the investor purchases the in-the-money call (Call #1) and sells the contract that is out of the money (Call #3). This requires a net cash outlay of $4.83 (= 8.07 – 3.24). At the common expiration date, three price ranges should be considered. If SAS stock settles below $35, both options will expire worthless and the investor will lose all of his initial investment. With an SAS price above $45, both contracts will be exercised, meaning that the investor must sell at $45 the share he bought for $35, leaving a $10 gross payoff. Finally, if SAS prices fall between the two exercise prices, the option the investor owns will be in the money while the contract he sold will not. This situation is summarized by the net profit calculations shown in Exhibit 22.26.

This combination is sometimes called a *bull* money spread because it will be profitable when stock prices rise. With the initial cost of $4.83, the investor's breakeven point occurs when the stock price rises to $39.83 (= 35 + 4.83). His benefit stops increasing if SAS shares reach $45, since this is where the short position in Call #3 becomes a liability. Exhibit 22.27 contrasts this situation with the outright purchase of the in-the-money call. This contract costs $8.07 initially, leading to the higher breakeven price of $43.07. It would not have a constraint on the upside profit potential, however, so once a share price of $48.24 is reached [= 45 + (8.07 – 4.83)], it would become the preferable alternative. Thus, in exchange for a lower initial purchase price,

Exhibit 22.26 Expiration Date Profits to a Bull Money Spread Position

SAS Stock Price at Expiration	Value of Call #1	Value of Call #3	Cost of Options	Net Profit
20.00	0.00	0.00	−4.83	−4.83
25.00	0.00	0.00	−4.83	−4.83
30.00	0.00	0.00	−4.83	−4.83
35.00	0.00	0.00	−4.83	−4.83
40.00	5.00	0.00	−4.83	0.17
45.00	10.00	0.00	−4.83	5.17
50.00	15.00	−5.00	−4.83	5.17
55.00	20.00	−10.00	−4.83	5.17
60.00	25.00	−15.00	−4.83	5.17

Exhibit 22.27 Comparing the Bull Money Spread and Long Call Positions

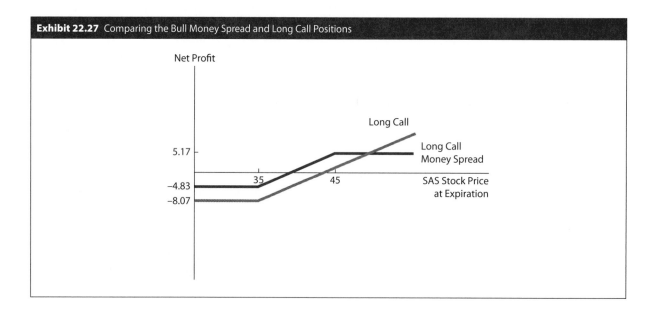

the bull spread investor is giving up the benefits of rising SAS prices after some point—a strategy that makes sense only if he expects the share price to settle within a fairly narrow range.

The profit for a *bear* money spread (the purchase of Call #3 and the sale of Call #1) is the opposite of that for the bull money spread. That is, buying a bear spread is equivalent to selling a bull spread. Consequently, a long bear spread position could be used by an investor who believed stock prices might decline but did not want to be short in the stock. A spread transaction also can be created using put options. For instance, suppose a new investor undertakes the simultaneous purchase of Put #3 and sale of Put #1. Her net cost to acquire the position would be $4.77 (= 6.47 − 1.70), which would then generate the terminal profits displayed in Exhibit 22.28. If SAS stock settled at $45 or higher, both puts would be worthless and the investor would lose all of her initial investment. If the expiration date share price was $35 or less, both options would be in the money, leaving the investor with a net position of $5.23 (= 45 − 35 − 4.77). Thus, this is the put option version of a bear money spread.

A final extension of this concept is the *butterfly* spread. Suppose an investor designed the following portfolio of SAS options: long one Call #1, short two Calls #2, and long one Call #3. This position is equivalent to holding

- a bull money spread (i.e., buy Call #1 and sell Call #2), *and*
- a bear money spread (i.e., buy Call #3 and sell Call #2)

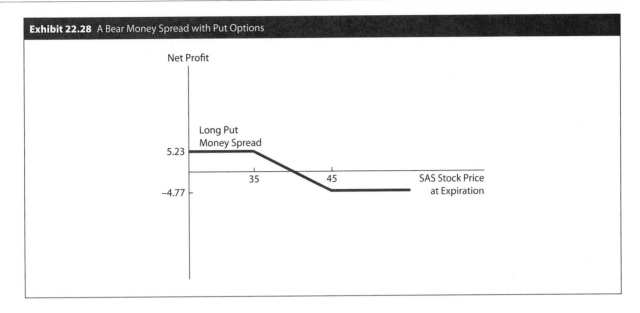

Exhibit 22.28 A Bear Money Spread with Put Options

The net purchase price for these transactions is $0.83 [= (8.07 − 5.24) + (3.24 − 5.24)]. The expiration date profits are listed in Exhibit 22.29 and show that the value of the position peaks at a stock price of $40 and that the investor can lose, at most, her initial investment. The breakeven stock prices are $35.83 and $44.17. This form of the butterfly spread is equivalent to a hedged version of a short straddle position. That is, in exchange for receiving a smaller potential payoff (i.e., $4.17 vs. $8.91) from a view on low volatility, the investor has limited her losses if SAS's stock price is more explosive than she expected. This trade-off is shown in Exhibit 22.30.

22.4.7 Range Forwards

In Chapter 20, we discussed an *equity collar* as a way that an investor could protect her stock portfolio from adverse movements while allowing for some upside gain potential. We saw that although the equity collar had some of the same attributes as a forward contract (e.g., no upfront premium expense), it was actually a combination of two options—the purchase of an out-of-the money put and sale of an out-of-the-money call. Equity collars are an example of a wider class of option combinations known as **range** (or flexible) **forwards**, and they are used to manage the risk of underlying assets other than equity as well.

To see how range forward positions might be used in a different context, assume that the treasurer of a U.S. multinational corporation knows today that he will have a bill for imported goods that must be paid in three months. This bill, denominated in Swiss francs and requiring payment of CHF 1,000,000, presents a challenge for a dollar-based company, which must buy

Exhibit 22.29 Expiration Date Profits to a Butterfly Spread

SAS Stock Price at Expiration	Value Bull Spread	Value Bear Spread	Cost of Options	Net Profit
20.00	0.00	0.00	−0.83	−0.83
25.00	0.00	0.00	−0.83	−0.83
30.00	0.00	0.00	−0.83	−0.83
35.00	0.00	0.00	−0.83	−0.83
40.00	5.00	0.00	−0.83	4.17
45.00	5.00	−5.00	−0.83	−0.83
50.00	5.00	−5.00	−0.83	−0.83
55.00	5.00	−5.00	−0.83	−0.83
60.00	5.00	−5.00	−0.83	−0.83

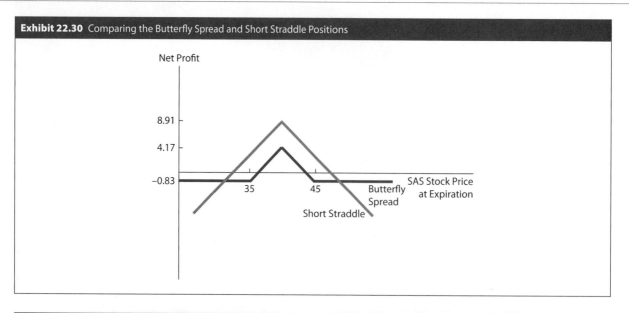

Exhibit 22.30 Comparing the Butterfly Spread and Short Straddle Positions

Exhibit 22.31 Hypothetical CHF Derivative Prices and Terms

Derivative	Contract/Exercise Price (USD/CHF)	Expiration	CHF Amount	Price (USD/CHF)
Forward:	0.67	3 months	1,000,000	—
Calls:	0.64	3 months	1,000,000	0.034
	0.67	3 months	1,000,000	0.015
	0.70	3 months	1,000,000	0.004
Puts:	0.64	3 months	1,000,000	0.004
	0.67	3 months	1,000,000	0.015
	0.70	3 months	1,000,000	0.034

the francs it needs, since it does not generate them in the natural flow of business. This is a classic opportunity to use derivatives to hedge the firm's FX exposure.

After contacting dealers in the OTC market, the treasurer establishes prices and terms for several CHF forward and option contracts. These are listed in Exhibit 22.31, which states prices on a direct (i.e., USD/CHF) basis. The treasurer could lock in a three-month forward rate of USD 0.67/CHF without cost in two ways. First, he could commit to a long position in the CHF forward with a contract amount of CHF 1,000,000. Second, he could buy the CHF call option struck at USD 0.67/CHF and pay for it by selling the CHF put at the same exercise rate. As shown in Chapter 20, the put-call parity model indicates that buying a call and selling a put with the same exercise rate is equivalent to a long forward position. Further, this second strategy would generate a zero-cost forward (i.e., $C_0 = P_0$) only when the common exercise rate is set equal to the prevailing forward rate.

As a third alternative, what if the treasurer (1) bought the 0.70 call for USD $0.004 per franc and (2) sold the 0.64 put for the same price? Once again, this would be a costless combination of options; however, since the two options do not have a common exercise price, this combination is not equivalent to the actual forward—it is a range forward. At the expiration date, one of three things will happen: (1) if the spot FX rate is greater than USD 0.70/CHF, the treasurer will exercise his call and buy francs at that level; (2) if the spot FX rate is less than USD 0.64/CHF, the dealer to whom the treasurer sold the put will force him to buy francs for USD 0.64 per franc, and (3) if the spot FX rate is between these extremes, both options will finish out of the money and the treasurer will buy the required currency at the regular market price. This payoff scheme is contrasted with the regular forward contract in Exhibit 22.32.

Exhibit 22.32 Comparing Long Positions in Regular and Range Forwards

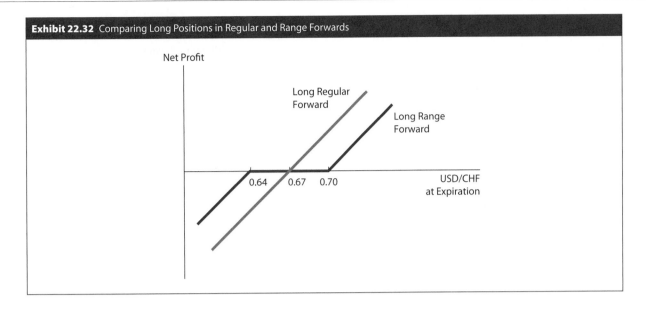

If the treasurer takes a long position in the regular forward contract, he will buy his francs at USD 0.67/CHF, whether or not the prevailing exchange rate in three months is above or below this level. Thus, although he is protected against a weakening dollar, he cannot benefit if the domestic currency strengthens. With a long position in the range forward, though, in exchange for worse FX insurance—namely, a maximum purchase USD 0.70/CHF—he could pay as little as USD 0.64/CHF if the dollar gets stronger. Finally, many zero-cost range forwards could be created; for any desired out-of-the-money call option, there will be an out-of-the-money put at some exercise price that has the same premium. In fact, the actual forward contract can be viewed as a zero-cost range forward for which the put and the call options are both struck at USD 0.67/CHF.

• • • • SUMMARY • • • •

- Along with forwards and futures, options represent another basic form of derivative contracting. Puts and calls are used as either standalone investments or as supplements to an existing collection of assets. In the latter application, they provide investors with a convenient way to restructure the risk–reward trade-off in a portfolio and create unique payoff structures by combining different options in various ways. Option straddles, for instance, allow the holder to take advantage of a view on the underlying asset's volatility while remaining neutral about the direction of future price movements. Forward contracts can be viewed as a specifically chosen pair of options and are special cases of option combinations known as range forwards (or collars).

- We consider how option contracts are valued in an efficient market. Although the mathematics of some valuation models can be formidable, the intuition behind the process is not. Each of three models we discuss— the two-state, the binomial, and the Black-Scholes—is based on the same three-step evolution. The first step is

combining options with the underlying asset in order to create a riskless position. This usually requires the sale (purchase) of multiple calls (puts) to offset to the full cash exposure of a single share of stock held long. This hedge ratio changes with movements in the underlying asset's price and the passage of time; therefore, the riskless hedge portfolio needs to be rebalanced frequently. Once it is formed, however, the option's value can be established by assuming that the hedge portfolio should earn the risk-free rate (i.e., the no-arbitrage condition) and solving for the option value that makes this assumption true.

- The Black-Scholes model is extremely flexible. Although originally created for European-style call options on non-dividend-bearing stock, this model extends easily to valuing put options and options on dividend-paying stocks. We also consider how volatility, the only user-provided variable in the valuation model, is either estimated directly from a historical series of asset prices or implied from option prices themselves.

• We discuss the process for valuing American-style puts and calls and how this differs from the valuation of their European counterparts. Further, we explain how the Black-Scholes model could be adapted to value options on other underlying assets, such as stock indexes, foreign currency, or commodity futures contracts.

• • • • SUGGESTED READINGS • • • •

Black, Fisher. "How We Came Up with the Option Formula," *Journal of Portfolio Management* 15, no. 2 (Winter 1989): 4–8.

Clarke, Roger G., and Mark P. Kritzman. *Currency Management: Concepts and Practices.* Charlottesville, VA: Research Foundation of AIMR, 1996.

Chance, Don M. *Analysis of Derivatives for the CFA Program.* Charlottesville, VA: AIMR, 2003.

Cox, John C., and Mark Rubinstein. *Option Markets.* Englewood Cliffs, NJ: Prentice Hall, 1985.

Dubofsky, David A., and Thomas W. Miller. *Derivatives: Valuation and Risk Management.* New York: Oxford University Press, 2003.

• • • • QUESTIONS • • • •

1. Straddles have been described as "volatility plays." Explain what this means for both long and short straddle positions. Given the fact that volatility is a primary factor in how options are priced, under what conditions might an investor who believes that markets are efficient ever want to create a straddle?

2. Put-call-forward parity and range forward positions both involve the purchase of a call option and the sale of a put option (or vice versa) on the same underlying asset. Describe the relationship between these two trading strategies. Is one a special case of the other?

 3. **CFA EXAMINATION LEVEL II** Michelle Industries issued a Swiss-franc denominated five-year discount note for CHF 200 million. The proceeds were converted to U.S. dollars to purchase capital equipment in the United States. The company wants to hedge this currency exposure and is considering the following alternatives:
   (a) At-the-money Swiss franc call options
   (b) Swiss franc forwards
   (c) Swiss franc futures
   Contrast the essential characteristics of each of these three derivative instruments. Evaluate the suitability of each in relation to Michelle's hedging objective, including both advantages and disadvantages.

 4. **CFA EXAMINATION LEVEL III** Six factors affect the value of call options on stocks. Three of these factors are: the current price of the stock, the time remaining until the option expires, and the dividend on the stock. Identify the other three factors and explain how and why changes in each of these three factors affect the value of call options.

5. "Although options are risky investments, they are valued by virtue of their ability to convert the underlying asset into a synthetic risk-free security." Explain what this statement means, being sure to describe the basic three-step process for valuing option contracts.

6. In valuing currency options with the Black-Scholes model, we saw that the risk-free rate on the foreign currency was equivalent to the dividend yield when an individual stock or stock index was the underlying asset. Discuss the appropriateness of this analogy. What sort of transaction involving foreign currency would be required to make this parallel exact?

7. Describe the condition under which it would be rational to exercise both an American-style put and call stock option before the expiration date. In both cases, comment specifically on the role that dividends play.

8. Explain why a change in the time to expiration (i.e., T) can have either a positive or negative impact on the value of a European-style put option. In this explanation, it will be useful to contrast the put's reaction with that of a European-style call, for which an increase in T has an unambiguously positive effect.

9. Currency option traders often speak of "buying low volatility (or 'vol') and selling high vol" rather than buying or selling the option itself. What does this mean exactly? From this perspective, what is the real underlying asset: volatility or foreign currency?

10. On October 19, 1987, the stock market (as measured by the Dow Jones Industrial Average) lost almost one-quarter of its value in a single day. Nevertheless, some traders made a profit buying call options on the stock index and then liquidating their positions before the market closed. Explain how this is possible, assuming that it was not a case of the traders taking advantage of spurious upward ticks in stock prices.

• • • • PROBLEMS • • • •

1. **CFA EXAMINATION LEVEL III** You are considering the sale of a call option with an exercise price of $100 and one year to expiration. The underlying stock pays no dividends, its current price is $100, and you believe it will either increase to $120 or decrease to $80. The risk-free rate of interest is 10 percent.
   a. Describe the specific steps involved in applying the binomial option pricing model to calculate the option's value.
   b. Compare the binomial option pricing model to the Black-Scholes option pricing model.

2. **CFA EXAMINATION LEVEL II** Joel Franklin is a portfolio manager responsible for derivatives. Franklin observes an American-style option and a European-style option with the same strike price, expiration, and underlying stock. Franklin believes that the European-style option will have a higher premium than the American-style option.
   a. Critique Franklin's belief that the European-style option will have a higher premium. Franklin is asked to value a one-year European-style call option for Abaco Ltd. common stock, which last traded at $43.00. He has collected the following information:

Closing stock price	$43.00
Call and put option exercise price	$45.00
One-year put option price	$ 4.00
One-year Treasury bill rate	5.50%
Time to expiration	One year

   b. Calculate, using put-call parity and the information provided, the European-style call option value.
   c. State the effect, if any, of each of the following three variables on the value of a call option: (1) an increase in short-term interest rate, (2) an increase in stock price volatility, and (3) a decrease in time to option expiration.

3. Assuming that a one-year call option with an exercise price of $38 is available for the stock of the DEW Corp., consider the following price tree for DEW stock over the next year:

Now	S1	S2	One Year
			46.31
		44.10	
	42.00		42.34
40		40.32	
	38.40		38.71
		36.86	
			35.39

   a. If the sequence of stock prices that DEW stock follows over the year is $40.00, $42.00, $40.32, and $38.71, describe the composition of the initial riskless portfolio of stock and options you would form and all the subsequent adjustments you would have to make to keep this portfolio riskless. Assume the one-year risk-free rate is 6 percent.
   b. Given the initial DEW price of $40, what are the probabilities of observing each of the four terminal stock prices in one year? (Hint: In arriving at your answer, it will be useful to consider (1) the

number of different ways that a particular terminal price could be achieved and (2) the probability of an up or down movement.)

c. Use the binomial option model to calculate the present value of this call option.

d. Calculate the value of a one-year put option on DEW stock having an exercise price of $38; be sure your answer is consistent with the correct response to Part c.

4. Following is a two-period price tree for a share of stock in SAB Corp.:

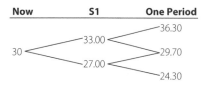

Using the binomial model, calculate the current fair value of a regular call option on SAB stock with the following characteristics: $X = 28$, $RFR = 5$ percent (per subperiod). You should also indicate the composition of the implied riskless hedge portfolio at the valuation date.

5. Consider the following questions on the pricing of options on the stock of ARB Inc.:

a. A share of ARB stock sells for $75 and has a standard deviation of returns equal to 20 percent per year. The current risk-free rate is 9 percent and the stock pays two dividends: (1) a $2 dividend just prior to the option's expiration day, which is 91 days from now (i.e., exactly one-quarter of a year); and (2) a $2 dividend 182 days from now (i.e., exactly one-half year). Calculate the Black-Scholes value for a European-style call option with an exercise price of $70.

b. What would be the price of a 91-day European-style put option on ARB stock having the same exercise price?

c. Calculate the change in the call option's value that would occur if ARB's management suddenly decided to suspend dividend payments and this action had no effect on the price of the company's stock.

d. Briefly describe (without calculations) how your answer in Part a would differ under the following separate circumstances: (1) the volatility of ARB stock increases to 30 percent, and (2) the risk-free rate decreases to 8 percent.

6. Consider the following data relevant to valuing a European-style call option on a non-dividend-paying stock: X = 40, RFR = 9 percent, T = six months (i.e., 0.5), and σ = 0.25.

a. Compute the Black-Scholes option and hedge ratio values for the series of hypothetical current stock price levels shown in Exhibit 22.12.

b. Explain why the values in Part a differ from those shown in Exhibit 22.12.

c. For $S = 40$, calculate the Black-Scholes value for a European-style put option. How much of this value represents time premium?

7. Suppose the current value of a popular stock index is 653.50 and the dividend yield on the index is 2.8 percent. Also, the yield curve is flat at a continuously compounded rate of 5.5 percent.

a. If you estimate the volatility factor for the index to be 16 percent, calculate the value of an index call option with an exercise price of 670 and an expiration date in exactly three months.

b. If the actual market price of this option is $17.40, calculate its implied volatility coefficient.

c. Besides volatility estimation error, explain why your valuation and the option's traded price might differ from one another.

8. Consider the following price data for TanCo stock in two different subperiods:

Subperiod A: 168.375; 162.875; 162.5; 161.625; 160.75; 157.75; 157.25; 157.75; 161.125; 162.5; 157.5; 156.625; 157.875; 155.375; 150.5; 155.75; 154.25; 155.875; 156; 152.75; 150.5; 150.75

Subperiod B: 122.5; 124.5; 121.875; 120.625; 119.5; 118.125; 117.75; 119.25; 122.25; 121.625; 120; 117.75; 118.375; 115.625; 117.75; 117.5; 118.5; 117.625; 114.625; 110.75

a. For each subperiod, calculate the annualized historical measure of stock volatility that could be used in pricing an option for TanCo. In your calculations, you may assume that there are 250 trading days in a year.

b. Suppose now that you decide to gather additional data for each subperiod. Specifically, you obtain information for a call option with a current price of $12.25 and the following characteristics: X = 115; S = 120.625; time to expiration = 62 days; RFR = 7.42 percent; and dividend yield = 3.65 percent. Here the risk-free rate and dividend yields are stated on an annual basis. Use the volatility measure from Subperiod B and the Black-Scholes model to obtain the "fair value" for this call option. Based on your calculations, is the option currently priced as it should be? Explain.

9. In March, a derivatives dealer offers you the following quotes for June British pound option contracts (expressed in U.S. dollars per GBP):

		MARKET PRICE OF CONTRACT	
Contract	Strike Price	Bid	Offer
Call	USD 1.40	0.0642	0.0647
Put		0.0255	0.0260
Call	USD 1.44	0.0417	0.0422
Put		0.0422	0.0427
Call	USD 1.48	0.0255	0.0260
Put		0.0642	0.0647

a. Assuming each of these contracts specifies the delivery of GBP 31,250 and expires in exactly three months, complete a table similar to the following (expressed in dollars) for a portfolio consisting of the following positions:
   (1) Long one 1.44 call
   (2) Short one 1.48 call
   (3) Long one 1.40 put
   (4) Short one 1.44 put

June USD/GBP	Net Initial Cost	Call 1.44 Profit	Call 1.48 Profit	Put 1.40 Profit	Put 1.44 Profit	Net Profit
1.36	—	—	—	—	—	—
1.40	—	—	—	—	—	—
1.44	—	—	—	—	—	—
1.48	—	—	—	—	—	—
1.52	—	—	—	—	—	—

b. Graph the total net profit (i.e., cumulative profit less net initial cost, ignoring time value considerations) relationship using the June USD/GBP rate on the horizontal axis (be sure to label the breakeven point(s)). Also, comment briefly on the nature of the currency speculation represented by this portfolio.

c. If in exactly one month (i.e., in April) the spot USD/GBP rate falls to 1.385 and the effective annual risk-free rates in the United States and England are 5 percent and 7 percent, respectively, calculate the equilibrium price differential that should exist between a long 1.44 call and a short 1.44 put position. (Hint: Consider what sort of forward contract this option combination is equivalent to and treat the British interest rate as a dividend yield.)

10. **CFA EXAMINATION LEVEL II** Linda Morgan is evaluating option strategies that will allow her to profit from large moves in a stock's price, either up or down. She believes that a combination of a long put and a long call option with the same expiration and exercise price (straddle) would meet her objective.

Price information on APEX stock and options follows. (Assume it is June 1999.)

APEX Stock and Option Current Market Prices

APEX stock: $50
Call option with an exercise price of $50 expiring December 1999: $4
Put option with an exercise price of $50 expiring December 1999: $3
No transactions costs or taxes exist

a. Draw a net-profit-and-loss diagram at expiration for the straddle, using the preceding information. Calculate and label the following on a graph:
   • Maximum loss
   • The breakeven points of the position
Morgan is considering a lower-cost strategy that would allow her to profit from large changes in the stock's price.

APEX Stock and Option Current Market Prices

APEX stock: $50
Call option with an exercise price of $55 expiring December 1999: $2.50
Put option with an exercise price of $45 expiring December 1999: $2.00
No transactions costs or taxes exist

    b. Draw a net-profit-and-loss diagram at expiration for the alternative option strategy, using this additional information. Calculate and label the following on a graph:
- Maximum loss
- The breakeven points of the position.

11. In mid-May, there are two outstanding call option contracts available on the stock of ARB Co.:

Call #	Exercise Price	Expiration Date	Market Price
1	$50	August 19	$8.40
2	60	August 19	3.34

    a. Assuming that you form a portfolio consisting of *one* Call #1 held long and *two* Calls #2 held short, complete the following table showing your intermediate steps. In calculating net profit, be sure to include the net initial cost of the options.

Price of ARB Stock at Expiration ($)	Profit on Call #1 Position	Profit on Call #2 Position	Net Profit on Total Position
40	—	—	—
45	—	—	—
50	—	—	—
55	—	—	—
60	—	—	—
65	—	—	—
70	—	—	—
75	—	—	—

    b. Graph the net profit relationship in Part a, using stock price on the horizontal axis. What is (are) the breakeven stock price(s)? What is the point of maximum profit?

    c. Under what market conditions will this strategy (which is known as a *call ratio spread*) generally make sense? Does the holder of this position have limited or unlimited liability?

12. In developing the butterfly spread position, we showed that it could be broken down into two call option money spreads. Using the price data for SAS stock options from Exhibit 22.17, demonstrate how a butterfly profit structure similar to that shown in Exhibit 22.30 could be created using put options. Be specific as to the contract positions involved in the trade and show the expiration date net payoffs for the combined transaction.

13. **CFA EXAMINATION LEVEL II** Donna Donie, CFA, has a client who believes the common stock price of TRT Materials (currently $58 per share) could move substantially in either direction in reaction to an expected court decision involving the company. The client currently owns no TRT shares but asks Donie for advice about implementing a strangle strategy to capitalize on the possible stock price movement. Donie gathers the TRT option pricing data shown in the following table:

TRT MATERIALS OPTION PRICING DATA (USD)

Characteristic	Call Option	Put Option
Price	5	4
Strike Price	60	55
Time to Expiration	90 days from now	90 days from now

    a. Recommend whether Donie should choose a long strangle strategy or a short strangle strategy to achieve the client's objective. Justify your recommendation with *one* reason.

b. Indicate, at expiration for the appropriate strangle strategy in Part a, the:
   - Maximum possible loss per share
   - Maximum possible gain per share
   - Breakeven stock price(s)

   Note: Your responses should ignore taxes and transaction costs.

   The delta of the call option is 0.625 and TRT common stock does not pay any dividends.

c. Calculate the appropriate change in price for the call option if TRT's stock price immediately increases to $59.

CHAPTER 23

Swap Contracts, Convertible Securities, and Other Embedded Derivatives

After you read this chapter, you should be able to answer the following questions:

- What are forward rate agreements and how can they be used to reduce the interest rate exposure of a borrower or an investor?
- What are interest rate swaps and how can they transform the cash flows of a fixed or floating rate security?
- How does the swap market operate and how are swap contracts quoted and priced?
- How are interest rate swaps valued?
- What are interest rate caps and floors and how are they related to interest rate swaps?
- How can the swap contracting concept be adapted to manage equity price risk and credit risk?
- How do the derivatives in convertible securities and warrant issues differ from traditional exchange-traded products?
- What are the similarities and differences between convertible preferred stock and convertible bonds?
- What are structured notes and what factors make their existence possible?
- How can securities with embedded derivatives reduce the funding cost of a corporate borrower?
- What are real options and how can an investor use them to value company flexibility?

Although derivatives only come in two basic "flavors"—forwards and options—the preceding chapters have shown that they can be used in a virtually unlimited number of situations by simply changing the contract terms or the nature of the underlying asset. In this chapter, we discuss several more ways in which these instruments can be modified. Invariably, these modifications involve combining derivatives with other assets or liabilities to create the most highly valued cash flow pattern. We look at two general approaches to forming these combinations: "packages" of derivatives, such as **interest rate swaps**, caps, and floors; and derivatives that have been "embedded" in more fundamental assets, such as equity or debt issues.

To begin, we consider the market for OTC interest rate agreements—one of the fastest-growing segments of the derivatives industry in the past 30 years. We once again focus on the differences between forward-based and option-based agreements while exploring the connection between the two. We then extend our discussion of swap contracting to include agreements based on equity price movements and credit risk events. Next, we provide an overview of the myriad ways in which forwards and options are incorporated into other financial instruments, including convertible securities, warrants, and **structured notes**. These innovations allow investors to acquire various exposures (e.g., interest rate, currency, equity, or commodity price risk) in a creative and cost-effective manner. We conclude with a discussion of how investors can value the options embedded in real assets.

$\cdots\cdots\cdots\cdots\cdots\cdots\cdots\cdots\cdots\cdots\cdots\cdots\cdots\cdots\cdots$

23.1 OTC Interest Rate Agreements

An extremely active OTC market exists for products designed to manage an investor's or an issuer's interest rate risk. In describing strategies involving these instruments, it is useful to classify them as either forward-based or option-based contracts.[1]

23.1.1 Forward-Based Interest Rate Contracts

Forward Rate Agreements The **forward rate agreement (FRA)** is the most basic of the OTC interest rate contracts. In an FRA, two parties agree today to a future exchange of cash flows based on two different interest rates. One of the cash flows is tied to a yield that is fixed at the deal's origination (the fixed rate); the other is determined at some later date (the floating rate). On the contract's settlement date, the difference between the two interest rates is multiplied by the FRA's **notional principal** and prorated to the length of the holding period. The London Interbank Offer Rate (LIBOR) is frequently used as the floating rate index, making FRAs the OTC equivalent of the Eurodollar futures contracts with two important exceptions: (1) FRAs typically require no collateral account, and (2) they are not marked to market on a daily basis.

An FRA's settlement date and maturity are defined by its name: a 3×6 FRA allows the investor to lock in three-month LIBOR, three months forward; a 12×18 FRA locks in six-month LIBOR, one year forward. FRA market makers quote a bid-offer spread on a rate basis. Suppose the FRA rates for three-month LIBOR shown in Exhibit 23.1 prevail in the market at Date 0, with current three-month LIBOR assumed to be 4.50 percent. This means that on a 3×6 FRA, the market maker is prepared to pay a fixed rate of 4.81 percent for receipt of three-month LIBOR and to receive a fixed rate of 4.83 percent for payment of LIBOR. In either case, there will be no payment until LIBOR is revealed in Month 3. Settlement can then be made in arrears at Month 6 or in advance at Month 3. If in arrears, the settlement flow will be adjusted to the actual number of days in the holding period and calculated by the following formula:

23.1 $$[\text{LIBOR} - \text{Fixed Rate}] \times [\text{Notional Principal}] \times \left[\frac{\text{Number of Days}}{360} \right]$$

recalling that, in the U.S. market, LIBOR is based on a 360-day year. The advance settlement amount is calculated as the present value of the in-arrears amount, using the prorated level of the realized LIBOR as the discount rate. This settlement occurs on a net basis, with only a single check for the rate differential being written.

To see how FRAs are used, assume that Company Z decides to borrow financial capital for a six-month period, in two three-month installments. With the "set in advance, pay in arrears" convention used in most debt markets, the firm finds itself exposed to rising interest rates over

Exhibit 23.1 Indicative Bid-Offer Quotes on Three-Month Forward Rate Agreements		
Period	**Bid (%)**	**Offer (%)**
3×6	4.81	4.83
6×9	5.20	5.22
9×12	5.64	5.66
12×15	6.37	6.39
15×18	6.78	6.80
18×21	7.10	7.12
21×24	7.36	7.38

[1] Some of the discussion in this section is based on work by Brown and Smith (1995a).

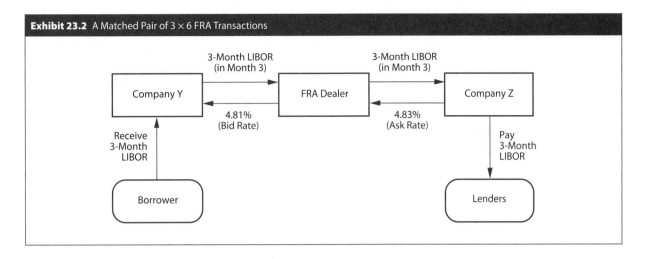

Exhibit 23.2 A Matched Pair of 3 × 6 FRA Transactions

the next three months because the level of its second interest payment will not be established until the end of that period. (The amount of Company Z's first three-month payment would be known at origination.) The firm can acquire a 3 × 6 FRA whereby it pays the dealer's quoted fixed rate of 4.83 percent in exchange for receiving three-month LIBOR at the settlement date. This is illustrated on the right-hand side of Exhibit 23.2, which depicts both the borrowing and derivative transactions.

Once the dealer has committed to the FRA with Company Z, two things occur. First, Company Z no longer is exposed to a rising funding cost because it now has a forward contract that obligates the dealer to "sell" the LIBOR it needs in Month 3 at a "price" of 4.83 percent. Second, the dealer now is exposed to rising LIBOR because it will be obligated to make the net settlement payment if LIBOR exceeds 4.83 percent three months from now. Company Z has effectively used the FRA to transfer its interest rate exposure to the dealer. Unless the dealer wishes to speculate that rates will subsequently fall, the exposure can be hedged by "buying" LIBOR from another counterparty for its bid rate of 4.81 percent. This is shown on the left-hand side of Exhibit 23.2 as a second FRA with Company Y, which is assumed to be an investor in a variable-rate asset who is naturally concerned about falling rates.

Now suppose that three-month LIBOR is 5.00 percent on the rate-determination date in Month 3 and that the agreements with Companies Y and Z were negotiated to have a notional principal of $10 million. If its contract specified settlement in arrears at Month 6, Company Y would be obligated to pay the market maker $4,750, calculated as

$$[0.0500 - 0.0481] \times [10,000,000] \times \left[\frac{90}{360}\right]$$

aassuming there are 90 days between Months 3 and 6. If settled in advance, the Month 3 payment would be

$$4,750 \div \left(1 + \frac{90 \times 0.0500}{360}\right) = \$4,691.36$$

Similarly, the payment from the dealer to Company Z would be $4,250 [= (0.0500 − 0.0483) × 10,000,000 × (90/360)] in Month 6, or $4,197.53 if accelerated to Month 3. By matching the FRAs, the market maker is fully hedged from interest rate risk. Its spread of two basis points, which translates into $500, compensates for the costs (e.g., transaction costs, credit risk) of making a market in these contracts.

Finally, although the terms *buy* and *sell* are awkward, they are commonly used when describing FRA transactions. Since the FRA has an initial value of zero and therefore is neither an asset nor a liability, a counterparty doesn't really buy or sell anything. Instead, the parties to the transaction enter into a contract that may obtain a positive or a negative value, depending on the direction of future interest rate changes. Nevertheless, this language is consistent with interpreting LIBOR as the commodity involved in the deal. In that case, the fixed rate is then the price paid or received in exchange for LIBOR, so that the payer of the fixed rate (Company Z) is said to be buying LIBOR, with the fixed-rate receiver (Company Y) selling LIBOR.

Interest Rate Swaps   FRAs represent a one-time-only solution to an interest rate risk management problem since they have a single settlement date. In fact, both investors and borrowers are routinely exposed to interest rate movements at regular intervals over an extended period of time, such as with a **floating-rate note (FRN)** that resets its coupon rate twice annually for several years according to movements in six-month LIBOR.[2] In that case, several exposure dates would need to be hedged, which could be accomplished with a series of FRAs. For example, suppose that an investor holding a one-year FRN paying quarterly coupons of three-month LIBOR becomes concerned that rates may fall in the future, thereby depressing the level of her last three coupons. By convention her first coupon, payable in three months, is based on current LIBOR, which was assumed to be 4.50 percent. She offsets this exposure by agreeing to receive the fixed rate on three separate FRA contracts: the 3×6, the 6×9, and the 9×12. Given the bid rates quoted in Exhibit 23.1, these positions transform the cash flows on the floating-rate asset as shown in Exhibit 23.3.

This series of FRAs locks in the coupon levels, but they are at different fixed rates and require three separate contracts. This may be inconvenient to the investor, who might prefer a single contract that covers all the future coupon dates using the same fixed rate. This is exactly what an interest rate swap does. Specifically, the swap contract can be viewed as a prepackaged series of forward contracts to buy or sell LIBOR (i.e., FRAs) at the same fixed rate. For the swap and FRA markets to remain efficient, the single fixed rate on the swap would have to be the appropriate average of 4.50 percent, 4.81 percent, 5.20 percent, and 5.64 percent. For simplicity, assume that each quarterly settlement period is exactly 0.25 year. This average can be approximated by solving for the internal rate of return on the hedged FRN:

$$100 = \frac{4.50 \times 0.25}{(1 + IRR)^1} + \frac{4.81 \times 0.25}{(1 + IRR)^2} + \frac{5.20 \times 0.25}{(1 + IRR)^3} + \frac{100 + [5.64 \times 0.25]}{(1 \times IRR)^4}$$

or $IRR = 1.258$ percent. Thus, 5.03 percent (1.258×4) would be the fixed rate on a one-year, receive-fixed swap consistent with the forward rate agreements listed in Exhibit 23.1. This IRR calculation is a very accurate approximation for the forward rate annuitization process we saw in Chapter 21. A more general way to determine the swap fixed rate (SFR) that represents the appropriate average of this sequence of spot and forward LIBOR would be to solve the following equation:

$$\frac{(4.50)(0.25)(NP)}{\left[1 + \frac{i_{0.3}}{4}\right]^1} + \frac{(4.81)(0.25)(NP)}{\left[1 + \frac{i_{0.6}}{4}\right]^2} + \frac{(5.20)(0.25)(NP)}{\left[1 + \frac{i_{0.9}}{4}\right]^3} + \frac{(5.64)(0.25)(NP)}{\left[1 + \frac{i_{0.12}}{4}\right]^4}$$

$$= \frac{(SFR)(0.25)(NP)}{\left[1 + \frac{i_{0.3}}{4}\right]^1} + \frac{(SFR)(0.25)(NP)}{\left[1 + \frac{i_{0.6}}{4}\right]^2} + \frac{(SFR)(0.25)(NP)}{\left[1 + \frac{i_{0.9}}{4}\right]^3} + \frac{(SFR)(0.25)(NP)}{\left[1 + \frac{i_{0.12}}{4}\right]^4}$$

[2] As we discussed briefly in Chapter 17, a floating (or variable) rate note is a debt instrument that is similar to a fixed-income bond in that it pays coupons at regular (e.g., semiannual) dates during its life. The difference is that the floating-rate note, or FRN, pays a coupon that is adjusted with changes in some reference rate (e.g., reset the coupon every six months at LIBOR + 0.50 percent). Do not confuse the two acronyms FRA and FRN: The former is an over-the-counter forward contract; the latter is a bond.

Exhibit 23.3 Converting A Floating-Rate Note with a Series of FRAs

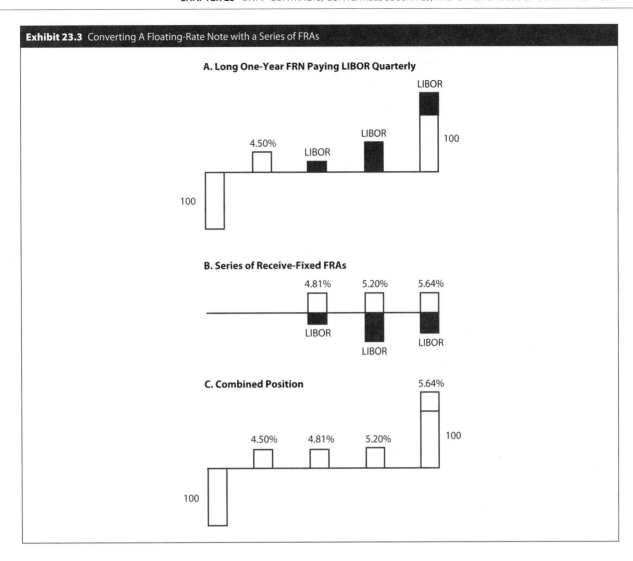

where *NP* is the swap's notional principal and $i_{0,t}$ is the spot discount rate for a cash flow received or paid at a date *t* months in the future. For a given interest rate term structure and contract notional principal, *SFR* is the only unknown element in this equation and can be solved for accordingly; see Bansal, Ellis, and Marshall (1993) and Brooks (1997).

Interest rate swaps are priced using the LIBOR forward yield curve, but they are quoted using the Treasury bond yield curve. That is, the fixed rate side of a U.S. dollar–based swap generally is broken down to two components for trading purposes: (1) the yield of a Treasury bond with a maturity comparable to that of the swap; and (2) a risk premium term known as the **swap spread**. Exhibit 23.4 lists a representative set of fixed-rate quotes for U.S. dollar swaps, both in absolute and swap spread terms. Each of the swaps represented in this exhibit assumes semiannual settlement dates with six-month LIBOR as the floating rate. For example, the swap dealer would be willing to receive the fixed rate of 4.720 percent on a five-year contract, a rate that is 65.90 basis points greater than the five-year T-bond yield. Swaps with maturities as long as 30 years are quoted, although most contracts are transacted with maturities of 10 years or less.

With the fixed rate on the swap linked to a bond (i.e., 30/360 day count) yield and the floating rate as a money market (i.e., actual/360 day count in the U.S. market) yield, the swap settlement cash flows are calculated in a slightly different manner than for FRAs. While the swap is still a net settlement contract, the Date *t* fixed- and floating-rate payments are determined separately as

Exhibit 23.4 Interest Rate Swap and Swap Spread Quotes

<HELP> for explanation, <MENU> for similar functions.　　　　　　　　　　　Curncy**NWAX**
Screen saved as F:\irsb.gif

USD INTEREST RATE SWAPS

12:49	Cheel#1				Cheel#2				
Ticker	**Bid**	**Ask**	**Mid**	**Chng**	**Ticker**	**Bid**	**Ask**	**Mid**	**Chng**
US Semi 30/360									
2) 1 YR	4.6560	4.6640	4.6600	–.0290	**US SPREADS**				
3) 2 YR	4.4870	4.4920	4.4895	–.0490	23) 2 YR	66.80	67.20	66.66	–1.14
4) 3 YR	4.5310	4.5460	4.5410	–.0460	24) 3 YR	70.38	70.70	70.54	–.59
5) 4 YR	4.6270	4.6320	4.6295	–.0365	25) 4 YR	67.50	68.00	67.69	–.96
6) 5 YR	4.7170	4.7200	4.7185	–.0345	26) 5 YR	65.50	65.90	65.70	–1.00
7) 6 YR	4.8040	4.8040	4.8040	–.0235	27) 6 YR	66.80	67.20	66.66	–1.24
8) 7 YR	4.8770	4.8770	4.8770	–.0185	28) 7 YR	67.10	67.50	67.30	–.80
9) 8 YR	4.9400	4.9400	4.9400	–.0140	29) 8 YR	66.40	66.80	66.60	–.80
10) 9 YR	4.9940	4.9990	4.9975	–.0075	30) 9 YR	64.90	66.00	65.45	–.55
11) 10 YR	5.0410	5.0460	5.0435	–.0055	31) 10 YR	61.63	62.90	62.26	–1.44
12) 15 YR	5.1940	5.1990	5.1975	+.0030	32) 15 YR	70.70	71.10	70.90	–.40
13) 20 YR	5.2690	5.2690	5.2690	+.0075	33) 20 YR	70.50	70.90	70.70	–.30
14) 25 YR	5.2900	5.2960	5.2930	+.0100	34) 25 YR	65.60	66.00	65.80	–.50
15) 30 YR	5.2980	5.3030	5.3005	+.0130	35) 30 YR	59.00	59.40	58.76	–1.24
Change on day					Change on day				
IYC4 152<GO>					IYC4 148<GO>				
Change on Month					Change on Month				
IYC6 152<GO>					For US Govt Yield Curve, type {IYC1 125 <GO>}				
Pricing based on XDF<GO> settings					For US swap Curve, type {IYC1 152 <GO>}				

Page 1　　　　　　　　　　　　　　　Page 2　　　　　　　　　　　　　　　Page 3

Australia 61 2 9777 8600　　　　　Brazil 5511 3048 4500　　　　　Europe 44 20 7330 7500　　　　　Germany 49 69 920410
Hong Kong 852 2977 6000　　Japan 81 3 3201 8900　　Singapore 65 6212 1000　　U.S. 1 212 318 2000　　Copyright 2007 Bloomberg L.P.
　　　　　　　　　　　　　　　　　　　　　　　　　　　　　　　　　　　　G469–83–0 23–Oct–2007 12:49:39

$$(\text{Fixed-Rate Payment})_t = (\text{Swap Fixed Rate}) \times \left(\frac{\text{Number of "30/360" Days}}{360} \right) \times (\text{Notional Principal})$$

and

$$(\text{Floating-Rate Payment})_t = (\text{Reference Rate})_{t-1} \times \left(\frac{\text{Number of Days}}{360} \right) \times (\text{Notional Principal})$$

In these equations, the fixed rate never changes and the floating-rate reference rate (i.e., LIBOR) always is determined at the beginning of a given settlement period.

Assume that Counterparty A is an institutional investor who currently holds a three-year bond paying a semiannual coupon of 4.80 percent. He feels that interest rates are likely to rise in the near term and, although he does not want to sell this position, he is concerned about a reduction in the bond's value. Instead, the investor decides to convert his investment into a synthetic floating-rate note whose coupons will rise with future LIBOR increases. He accomplishes this by agreeing to pay the fixed rate on a three-year interest rate swap contract with Counterparty B (i.e., the swap dealer). The terms of this agreement can be summarized as follows:

- Origination date: October 23, 2007
- Maturity date: October 23, 2010
- Notional principal: $30 million
- Fixed-rate payer: Counterparty A (i.e., the investor)
- Swap fixed rate: 4.546 percent (semiannual, 30/360 bond basis)

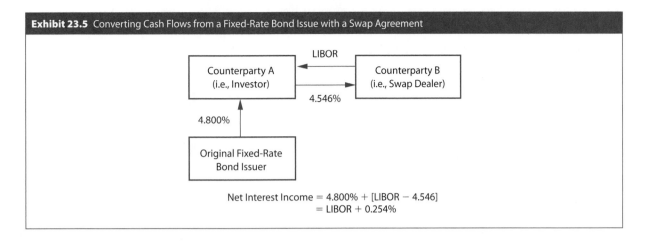

Exhibit 23.5 Converting Cash Flows from a Fixed-Rate Bond Issue with a Swap Agreement

- Fixed-rate receiver: Counterparty B (i.e., the swap dealer)
- Floating rate: Six-month LIBOR (money market basis)
- Settlement dates: October 23 and April 23
- LIBOR determination: Set in advance, paid in arrears

This "fixed-for-floating" transaction—the most basic form of a swap—is often called a *plain vanilla* agreement. Exhibit 23.5 illustrates the approximate effect (ignoring slight day count differentials) of combining the swap with the underlying bond position, while Exhibit 23.6 lists the precise settlement cash flows from the investor's perspective for a hypothetical time series of six-month LIBOR. In this agreement, the fixed-rate payer makes the net settlement payment when the day count-adjusted level of LIBOR is less than 4.546 percent; the fixed-rate receiver makes the settlement payment when LIBOR exceeds 4.546 percent.

Plain vanilla swaps are generally used for the same reason as FRAs: namely, to restructure the cash flows of an interest-sensitive asset or liability. In this example, the investor has reduced the price sensitivity (i.e., duration) of his asset by converting the fixed-rate coupon into one that adjusts to shifting market conditions without having to actually sell what might be a highly illiquid bond. Given A's original coupon rate of 4.8 percent, the net annualized cash flow he will receive after accounting for the swap position will be (again ignoring day count differentials):

Fixed-Rate Bond Coupon Receipt	= 4.800%
Swap: (1) LIBOR Receipt	= LIBOR
(2) Fixed Payment	= (4.546%)
Net Interest Income:	= LIBOR + 0.254%

Thus, the net impact of combining the swap with the fixed-rate bond is to convert that security into a variable-rate asset paying a coupon of LIBOR plus 25.4 basis points.

Exhibit 23.6 Settlement Cash Flows for a Three-Year Plain Vanilla Interest Rate Swap (Fixed-Payer's Perspective)

Settlement Date	Number of Actual Days	Number of 30/360 Days	Current LIBOR	Fixed-Rate Payment	Floating-Rate Receipt	Net Payment (Receipt)
10/23/2007	—	—	4.25%	—	—	—
4/23/2008	183	180	4.40%	681,900	648,125	33,775
10/23/2008	183	180	4.90%	681,900	671,000	10,900
4/23/2009	182	180	5.05%	681,900	743,167	(61,267)
10/23/2009	183	180	4.60%	681,900	770,125	(88,225)
4/23/2010	182	180	4.35%	681,900	697,667	(15,767)
10/23/2010	183	180	4.20%	681,900	663,375	18,525

Exhibit 23.7 A Capital Market Interpretation of an Interest Rate Swap

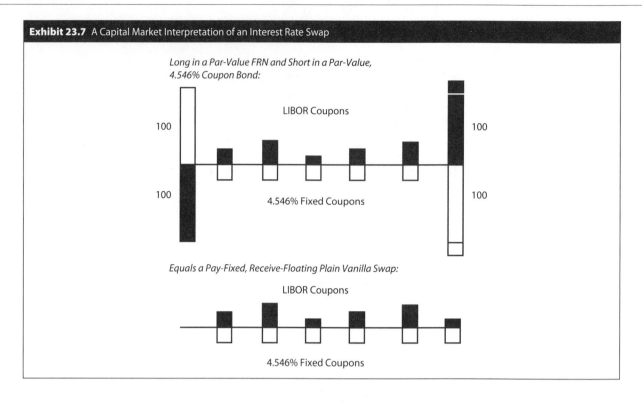

Long in a Par-Value FRN and Short in a Par-Value, 4.546% Coupon Bond:

LIBOR Coupons

100   100

100   4.546% Fixed Coupons   100

Equals a Pay-Fixed, Receive-Floating Plain Vanilla Swap:

LIBOR Coupons

4.546% Fixed Coupons

There is another important way of viewing this swap transaction. Counterparty A is effectively paying the fixed-rate coupons he receives from his bond in exchange for receiving floating-rate coupons. That is, the pay-fixed swap position is equivalent to holding a portfolio consisting of (1) a long position in a par-value FRN paying semiannual coupons of LIBOR, and (2) a short position in a par-value fixed-rate note paying semiannual coupons of 4.546 percent. This capital market interpretation is illustrated in Exhibit 23.7. By essentially buying and selling two different par-value instruments, no net principal amount exists at origination or maturity; this is what allows the swap's principal to be notional (i.e., not actually exchanged). Thus, all the swap agreement really does is transform the nature of the coupon payments.

With this interpretation, at any point in time, the value of the pay-fixed swap position can be calculated as the present value of the floating-rate cash flows held as an asset minus the present value of the fixed-rate bond cash flow that is a liability, or

$$(\textit{PV} \text{ of Pay-Fixed Swap}) = (\textit{PV} \text{ of } \textit{FRN} \text{ Paying LIBOR}) - (\textit{PV} \text{ of Fixed-Rate Bond Paying 4.546\%}).$$

Suppose that one year after this swap was originated, yields have generally risen so that the fixed rate on a new two-year swap (i.e., the remaining time until the original maturity) is 5.546 percent. The contract's value under these conditions can be established in two steps. First, on any settlement date, the FRN will be valued at par, since its coupon always is reset according to current market conditions. Second, the market value of a bond paying a coupon of only 4.546 percent will fall, which benefits Counterparty A to whom this is a liability. Using the new swap rate as a discount factor, A's position in the agreement (which had no value at origination) is now worth

$$100 - \left[\sum_{t=1}^{4} \frac{(4.546/2)}{(1 + 0.05546/2)^t} + \frac{100}{(1 + 0.05546/2)^4} \right] = 1.8687$$

or 1.8687 percent of notional principal. Therefore, if Counterparty A chose to unwind his contract at this time, the dealer would be willing to pay as much as $560,610 (= 0.018687 ×

$30 million) and then find a new swap counterparty who would pay the now current fixed rate of 5.546 percent. The $560,610 is considered to be the *marked-to-market value* of the swap. Given that interest rates have risen since inception, the original contract is now an asset to the fixed-rate payer (i.e., Counterparty A) and a liability to the fixed-rate receiver (i.e., the dealer).

The fact that the swap agreement becomes an *asset* to one participant and a *liability* to the other as soon as market conditions change means that swaps entail credit risk. To see why, consider what would happen to Counterparty A if, on a particular settlement date when LIBOR was 8 percent, the swap dealer was unable to make the net settlement payment. In that case, the investor would receive only the 4.8 percent coupon from his bond rather than the 8.254 percent (= LIBOR + 0.254 percent) coupon he expected from his synthetic FRN. The possibility that the swap counterparty either cannot or will not honor its obligation means that the synthetic floating-rate note carries more credit risk than the original fixed-rate bond. Conversely, the swap dealer will be concerned about Counterparty A's performance when LIBOR is less than 4.546 percent. Thus, like any forward arrangement, the credit risk on a swap runs two ways.

What would it cost Counterparty A if, with exactly two years remaining on the contract described, the swap dealer suffered bankruptcy and defaulted on the remainder of the agreement? The investor would have to find a new swap dealer to replace the old contract. Unfortunately, with the change in market conditions, Counterparty A will now have to pay 5.546 percent to receive LIBOR over the next two years, implying an additional cost of 50 basis points (times 30 million) each settlement period. Thus, the economic consequence to A of the dealer's default can be measured as

$$\sum_{t=1}^{4} \frac{\left[(0.05546/2) - (0.04546/2)\right] \times (30,000,000)}{(1 + 0.05546/2)^t} = \$560,610$$

which, of course, is the same amount as the marked-to-market value of the swap and represents the current potential default loss for the counterparty to whom the swap is an asset.[3]

Interest rate swaps have been in existence since 1981, and some empirical evidence exists on how they are priced in the marketplace. The available evidence includes Kim and Koppenhaver's (1993) investigation of commercial bank activity in the swap market; results from a study by Sun, Sundaresan, and Wang (1993), who examined the consistency of bid-ask quotes issued by two swap dealers with different credit grades; and findings by Brown, Harlow, and Smith (1994), Minton (1997), and Liu, Longstaff, and Mandell (2006), who tested several theoretical relationships designed to explain the historical pattern of variation in the swap spread component. Although each of the studies examined a different aspect of the swap contracting process, the collective evidence is consistent with the notion that this market works in an efficient manner and seems to be integrated with other affiliated securities, such as Treasury notes and bills and Eurodollar futures contracts.

23.1.2 Option-Based Interest Rate Contracts

In this section, we discuss two types of OTC interest rate option arrangements as well as their relationship with interest rate swaps: (1) caps and floors, the two most basic option-based products; and (2) collars, special combinations of caps and floors.

Caps and Floors   Interest rate cap and floor agreements are equivalent to portfolios of interest rate option contracts, each corresponding to a different settlement period. A **cap agreement** is a series of cash settlement interest rate options, typically based on LIBOR. The seller of the cap, in return for the option premium, is obliged to pay the difference between LIBOR and the exercise, or cap, rate (times the fraction of the year, times the notional principal) whenever that difference is positive. The seller of a **floor agreement** makes settlement payments

---

[3] For interesting discussions of default risk in the swap market, see Sorensen and Bollier (1994) and Bomfim (2003).

only when LIBOR is below the floor rate. No payment is made if LIBOR is above the floor or below the cap rate. As with swaps and FRAs, settlement can be either in advance or in arrears. Payment in arrears is more common because these contracts usually are used to hedge exposure to floating-rate loans and notes, which typically settle in arrears.

The Date t settlement payments on cap and floor agreements can be written as follows:

23.2 *Cap Settlement:* $(\text{Notional Principal}) \times \left(\dfrac{\text{Number of Days}}{360}\right) \times \max[\text{LIBOR}_{t-1} - X_c, 0]$

and

23.3 *Floor Settlement:* $(\text{Notional Principal}) \times \left(\dfrac{\text{Number of Days}}{360}\right) \times \max[X_f - \text{LIBOR}_{t-1}, 0]$

where:

X_c = the cap exercise rate
X_f = the floor exercise rate.

Consider a three-year, semiannual settlement, 8 percent cap on six-month LIBOR. The buyer of the cap pays the writer an up-front premium, quoted as a percentage of the notional principal. Assuming the cost is 120 basis points and the notional principal is $100 million, the cost of the cap is $1,200,000.[4] Suppose that settlement dates are on the 15th of May and November of each year and that LIBOR on one particular May 15th is 9.125 percent. The holder of the cap will receive settlement in arrears the following November in the amount of $575,000, calculated as (9.125 percent − 8 percent) × $100 million × (184/360).

The payoff relationships for caps and floors can be illustrated using traditional, option-style diagrams. Exhibit 23.8 portrays an 8 percent cap and a 4 percent floor on LIBOR. Notice that the payoff diagram for the cap looks like a typical call option on a commodity and the floor takes the form of a put option. Indeed, following the convention where LIBOR is the commodity, caps are referred to as "calls on LIBOR," and floors as "puts on LIBOR." Alternatively, a cap agreement on LIBOR is a series of put options on an underlying Eurodollar time deposit. In effect, the owner of the option has the right, but not the obligation, to sell to the cap writer a time deposit having a coupon rate equal to the cap rate in the amount of the notional principal of the contract. The owner exercises that option if current LIBOR exceeds the cap rate, thus selling a relatively low coupon deposit at par value. Whether one interprets a cap as a call on LIBOR or a put on a time deposit (and, similarly, a floor as a put on LIBOR or a call on a time deposit) is purely a matter of semantic preference.

Collars   In Chapter 20, we saw that an equity collar arrangement consisted of a long position in an equity put option that was paid for with a short position in a call option on the same stock. Similarly, an **interest rate collar** is a combination of a cap and a floor, a long position in one and a short position in the other. Acquiring a 4 percent–8 percent collar on LIBOR is to buy an 8 percent cap and to write a 4 percent floor. The buyer will receive cash payments when LIBOR exceeds 8 percent, make payments when LIBOR is below 4 percent, and neither receive nor pay if LIBOR is between 4 percent and 8 percent. Often the motive for a firm to acquire a collar is to reduce the initial cost of obtaining the protection against rising LIBOR, as the upfront receipt from selling the floor can be used to offset the cost of buying the cap.

---

[4] In practice, interest rate caps and floors are quoted by market makers on a volatility basis, for instance, 18.5 percent bid and 19.5 percent offered. That measure of volatility (stated as a standard deviation), plus the exercise rate, the current term structure of interest rates, and the time frame for the contract, are then entered into an option pricing model to obtain the actual amount of the premium. Hull (2009) has shown that this amount can be established by adapting Black's model for valuing futures options to price each separate option in the contract and then summing them across all settlement dates.

Exhibit 23.8 Payoff Diagrams for Buying and Writing an Interest Rate Cap and Floor

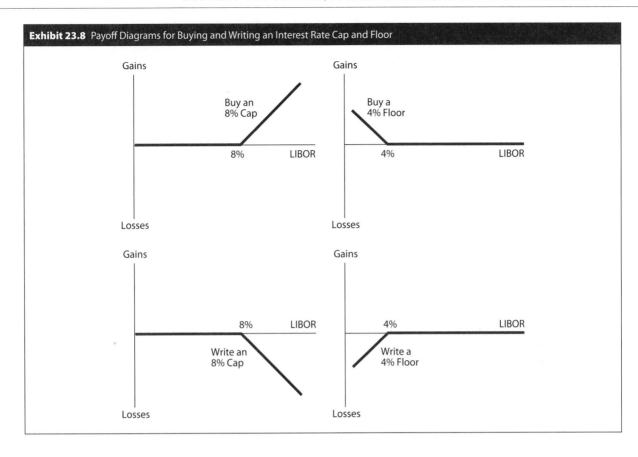

A special interest rate collar occurs when the initial premiums on the cap and the floor are equal and therefore offset each other. Suppose that the premium on a three-year, 4 percent floor is 120 basis points, which matches the premium on the 8 percent cap. The combination is known as a *zero-cost*, or zero-premium, collar. An interest rate swap is just a special case of a zero-cost interest rate collar. To see this, consider again the agreement that was constructed from buying the 8 percent cap and selling the 4 percent floor. Now tighten the collar by lowering the cap rate to 7 percent. The upfront premium paid by the buyer must go up; an insurance policy providing protection whenever LIBOR exceeds 7 percent has to cost more than a policy that pays off only when LIBOR moves above 8 percent. Assume that premium is 200 basis points (times the notional principal). To keep the collar at a zero initial cost, the written floor must then generate additional premium for the seller as well. This requires a higher floor rate because a contract in which the seller makes settlement payments whenever LIBOR is less than 5 percent is worth more than one with a floor rate of 4 percent. If we keep tightening the collar at some exercise rate common to both the cap and the floor, say 6 percent, the combination will be zero cost. That will be the pay-fixed swap fixed rate that prevails in the market. This is illustrated in Exhibit 23.9.

To summarize, buying a 6 percent cap and writing a 6 percent floor on LIBOR are equivalent in terms of settlement cash flows to an interest rate swap paying a fixed rate of 6 percent and receiving LIBOR. When LIBOR is above 6 percent, the net settlement receipt on the swap is the same as the receipt on the in-the-money cap that is owned. When LIBOR is below 6 percent, the net settlement payment on the swap is the same as the payment on the in-the-money floor that has been sold. Similarly, writing a cap and buying a floor at the same exercise rate are identical to a receive-fixed interest rate swap. A cap-floor combination at the same exercise rate always has the same payoffs as a swap contract. However, only when the combination also nets to a zero initial cost does that common rate match the prevailing swap fixed rate.

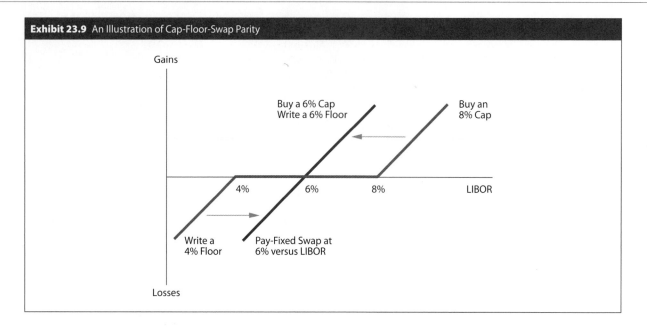

Exhibit 23.9 An Illustration of Cap-Floor-Swap Parity

This relationship is known as *cap-floor-swap parity* and is equivalent to the put-call-forward parity formula first discussed in Chapter 20 and extended to the range forward strategy in Chapter 22.

Along with the "portfolio of FRAs" and "pair of bonds" ways of viewing a swap contract, cap-floor-swap parity shows that a third interpretation exists: The swap can be viewed as a pair of option positions. This can be used to test the internal consistency of credit risk and valuation models for swaps. For example, because selling a cap and buying a floor at the same exercise rate amounts to a receive-fixed swap, the projected credit risk on the swap must be comparable to the credit risk on the floor agreement. (A firm bears the counterparty's credit risk on purchased options and not on written options, because only with purchased options is the firm relying on the other party's future performance.) Yaksick (1992) explains how this parity relationship allows the option valuation models discussed in Chapter 22 to be used in the valuation of swap contracts.

23.2 Swap Contracting Extensions

Although interest rate swaps are by far the most prevalent OTC rate contract, other extensions of this concept that are important for portfolio managers have been developed as well. All these variations preserve the essential feature of a swap contract by exchanging cash flows based on two different rates or prices. We will examine two such agreements in detail.

23.2.1 Equity Index-Linked Swaps

Similar in form to interest rate swaps, equity-index-linked swaps or **equity swaps** are equivalent to portfolios of forward contracts calling for the exchange of cash flows based on two different investment rates: (1) a variable-debt rate (e.g., three-month LIBOR) and (2) the return to an equity index (e.g., Standard and Poor's 500). The index-linked payment is based on either the total return (i.e., dividends plus capital gain or loss) or just the percentage index change for the settlement period plus a fixed spread adjustment. The floating-rate payments typically are based on LIBOR "flat" (i.e., no adjustment). Equity swaps are traded in the OTC markets and can have maturities out to 10 years or beyond.

In addition to the S&P 500, equity swaps can be structured around foreign indexes, such as TOPIX (Japan), FT-SE 100 (Great Britain), DAX (Germany), CAC 40 (France), TSE 35 (Canada), and Hang Seng (Hong Kong). These agreements also can be designed so that the cash flows are denominated in the same currency or in two different currencies. The equity-index-based cash flow typically is denominated in the currency of the index's country of origination, but this payment can be automatically hedged into a different currency. Further, these agreements specify a notional principal that is not exchanged at origination but serves the purpose of converting percentage returns into cash flows. This notional principal can either be variable or fixed during the life of the agreement, but the same notional principal applies to both sides of the transaction.

The equity swap market has developed for several reasons. First, these agreements allow investors to take advantage of overall price movements in a specific country's stock market without having to purchase the equity securities directly.[5] This has the advantage of reducing both the transaction costs and tracking errors associated with assembling a portfolio that mimics the index as well as avoiding dividend withholding taxes normally associated with cross-border investing. Second, creating a direct equity investment in a foreign country may be difficult for some investors where prohibited by law or policy. Finally, an investment fund wanting to accumulate foreign index returns denominated in their domestic currency may not be able or legally permitted to obtain sufficient exchange-traded derivative contracts to hedge a direct equity investment. The equity swap can be structured so that there is no need for separate hedging transactions.

The most common application for an equity swap involves a counterparty that receives the index-based payment in exchange for making the floating-rate payment. Consider a pension fund that currently has a substantial portion of its asset portfolio invested in floating-rate notes paying quarterly coupons based on LIBOR. If the fund manager wants to alter her existing asset allocation by converting some of this debt into equity, she has two ways to do so. First, she can sell the existing floating-rate notes and purchase a portfolio of stock directly in the market. Alternatively, the manager can enter into an equity swap with an initial notional principal equal to the amount of the existing debt holdings she wants to convert. As we have seen, from the standpoint of reducing transaction costs, the second alternative is clearly preferable. The mechanics of this arrangement are illustrated in Exhibit 23.10.

The net return to the fund in this example is simply the return on the equity index plus the spread adjustment. Further, if the floating-rate notes yield more than LIBOR, this would increase the overall net return. Assuming both cash flows are denominated in the same

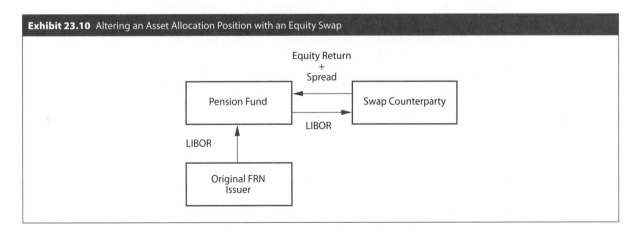

Exhibit 23.10 Altering an Asset Allocation Position with an Equity Swap

[5] For a more detailed analysis of the uses and development of this product, see Allen and Showers (1991) and Chance (2004).

currency, the net settlement payment on the equity swap from the company's standpoint can be calculated as the difference between the variable-rate outflow and the equity-linked inflow, where

23.4 $$\text{Payment} = \left[\text{LIBOR} - \text{Spread}\right] \times \left[\text{Notional Principal}\right] \times \left[\frac{\left(\text{Number of Days}\right)}{360}\right]$$

and

$$\text{Receipt} = \left[\frac{\text{Index}_{\text{new}} - \text{Index}_{\text{old}}}{\text{Index}_{\text{old}}}\right] \times \left[\text{Notional Principal}\right]$$

where $\text{Index}_{\text{new}}$ and $\text{Index}_{\text{old}}$ represent the index levels occurring on the current and immediate past settlement dates, assuming all dividends are reinvested. Notice that to minimize calculations, the settlement payment is computed using LIBOR – Spread rather than adding a separate inflow for the equity spread itself. Gastineau (1993) and Chance and Rich (1998) investigated indicative spread quotes for various indexes throughout the world and found that, while some were positive (e.g., 90 BP for DAX, 25 BP for FT-SE), others were negative (e.g., –10 BP for S&P 500, –60 BP for Hang Seng). However, equity swap quotations methods are not standardized across all dealers; therefore, the quoted values may not be directly comparable.

Another way to view this swap-based cash flow transformation is shown in Exhibit 23.11. It should be clear that equity swaps differ from interest rate swaps in one important way. Specifically, because there is no guarantee that the equity index will appreciate in value from one settlement period to the next, it is possible that the company receiving the equity index will have to make a double payment. First, the usual debt-related cash flow, based on LIBOR, will have to be paid. Second, whenever $\text{Index}_{\text{new}}$ is less than $\text{Index}_{\text{old}}$, the company will make an equity-index-based payment to (i.e., "receive" a negative payment from) its counterparty. Rather than netting one cash flow against the other, the company will pay both when the value of the equity index declines. (Examples of this situation are represented by the third and fifth payments in the exhibit.)

23.2.2 Credit-Related Swaps

One of the newest swap contracting extensions has been the development of agreements designed to help investors manage their credit risk exposures. From their introduction in the late 1990s, credit-related swaps have grown in popularity to where the International Swap and Derivatives Association reported that by mid-2007 contracts exceeding $45 trillion in notional value were in place. These contracts cover exposures to credit markets throughout the world and include as end-users institutions ranging from banks and corporations to traditional asset managers and hedge funds. Hull (2009) provides a detailed examination of how these products are structured and valued.

One of the first attempts to provide credit risk protection in the derivatives market was the **total return swap**. As with equity swaps, total return swaps provide for the periodic exchange of cash flows based on (1) a variable-debt rate (e.g., LIBOR) and (2) the total return (i.e., periodic interest and any capital gain or loss) to a *reference entity* specified by the agreement. The reference entity can be either a specific bond obligation or a portfolio (index) of bonds. When an individual security is designated as the reference entity, it is possible to design the total return swap to allow for physical delivery of the bond at maturity in exchange for a payment of the bond's initial value. However, neither party in the swap transaction is required to own the reference entity, nor does the maturity or notional principal in the agreement need to match those of the underlying security.

The top panel of Exhibit 23.12 illustrates how this agreement might be used to hedge credit risk. Suppose a fixed-income portfolio manager holds a bond issued by Company BAB in his portfolio but he is concerned that the firm's credit rating might be downgraded. In lieu

Exhibit 23.11 Converting a Bond with an Equity Swap

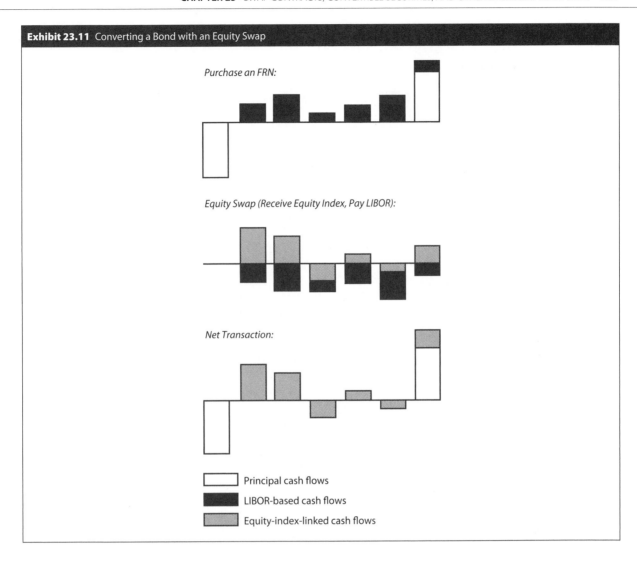

Purchase an FRN:

Equity Swap (Receive Equity Index, Pay LIBOR):

Net Transaction:

☐ Principal cash flows

■ LIBOR-based cash flows

▨ Equity-index-linked cash flows

of trying to sell what might be an illiquid position outright, he arranges an agreement with a counterparty whereby every quarter for the next five years (i.e., the remaining maturity of the BAB bond) he pays the interest received on the bond plus any gain or loss of principal and receives a cash flow based on LIBOR times the notional principal, which here is set equal to the face value of the reference bond. If BAB's credit does not deteriorate during a given settlement period and interest rates in the market fall, the bond will appreciate in value but the manager will have to pay this capital gain, along with the interest from the bond, to the swap dealer in exchange for the LIBOR-based receipt.

On the other hand, if BAB is downgraded—or if market rates increase for any other reason—the reference bond will experience a capital loss which will reduce the manager's swap payment. If the loss in value is severe enough, it could more than offset any interest income (i.e., a negative total return), which would lead to the swap dealer making a double payment, similar to what happened with the equity swap when stock prices declined. Of course, the additional swap payment linked to a decline in value for the BAB reference bond simply offsets the loss that the manager experiences in his actual portfolio. Thus, the total return swap enables the manager to transfer the credit risk of holding the BAB bond to the counterparty by essentially

Exhibit 23.12 Credit Related Swap Agreements

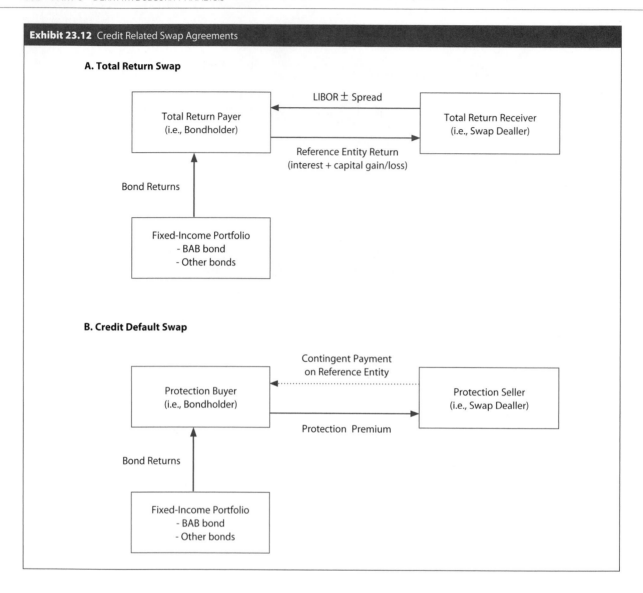

A. Total Return Swap

B. Credit Default Swap

"selling" that total exposure to the dealer via the swap agreement in exchange for "buying" a floating-rate note paying LIBOR.

One drawback of using total return swaps to manage credit risk is that they require cash flow exchanges for events—such as general interest rate movements—that have nothing to do with the default potential of the reference entity. A **credit default swap** (CDS) addresses this shortcoming by making the payment of any compensation for loss *contingent on the actual occurrence of a credit-related event*. This contingent payment makes the credit default contract closer in form to an insurance policy than a traditional swap agreement. As illustrated in the bottom panel of Exhibit 23.12, the *protection buyer* pays an annual premium in exchange for the *protection seller's* obligation to make a settlement payment if a credit-related event occurs to the reference entity during the life of the swap. The range of credit-related events covered by a CDS agreement can be wide, but typically includes bankruptcy, failure to pay in a timely fashion, and a default-rating downgrade resulting from a corporate restructuring.

Suppose that the portfolio manager holding the BAB bond decides to hedge his credit exposure with a CDS agreement. Assume further that he owns $5 million in par value of a security that matures in five years and that the swap premium is 160 basis points. This means he will pay an annual protection premium to the swap dealer of \$80,000 (= 0.016 × 5,000,000), usually in quarterly installments of \$20,000. These payments continue until the expiration of the contract—assumed here to match the maturity of the reference bond—or until a credit event occurs. If, for instance, Company BAB does default after two years, the swap dealer will be obligated to either purchase the BAB bond from the portfolio manager at par value (i.e., physical settlement) or pay him the difference between par value and the post-default market value of the bond (i.e., cash settlement), depending on how the swap contract is structured. If BAB bonds trade at 31 percent of their par value after default, the settlement payment would be \$3,450,000 (= [1.00 − 0.31] × 5,000,000). This credit-event contingent payment then cancels the remainder of the agreement. On the other hand, if no credit event occurs, the portfolio manager continues to make premium payments to the swap dealer and receives his invested principal back from Company BAB when the bond matures.

The bondholder in this example used the CDS contract the hedge his credit exposure to a specific bond by effectively paying the swap dealer to bear that risk for him. From the protection seller's perspective, in the absence of any other offsetting agreements, the swap dealer is effectively speculating that Company BAB will not suffer a credit event before the expiration of the contract, allowing them to continue to collect the protection premium without having to make a contingency payment. In fact, if BAB's credit quality actually improves during the life of the agreement, it is likely that the market value of the swap premium will decline in price—say, to 110 basis points—and the swap dealer can "sell" (i.e., unwind or transfer) the remainder of its existing contract at a profit.

Since any risky bond yield can be decomposed into (1) the yield for a risk-free bond with the same maturity, and (2) a credit spread (i.e., risk premium), it is easy to see that protection payer is using the CDS contract to transfer just the credit spread to the protection seller. That is, if the BAB bond does not default before maturity, the bond manager's net return on that position should be the risk-free rate. This means that the CDS premium should be approximately equal to the difference between the par yield on the risk bond and the par yield on Treasury bond with comparable maturity. Duffie (1999) and Hull and White (2000) demonstrate that this amount can be calculated from default probability estimates that allow for the estimation of the value of the cash flows expected to be paid by the risky bond. Exhibit 23.13 lists five-year CDS premium prices for a number of U.S. corporations as of October 2007. These data emphasize the wide range of spreads that can occur for firms with credit ratings ranging from A (e.g., 18.0 basis points for Bell South) to BB (e.g., 288.3 basis points for American Axle). As in other credit markets, CDS spreads increase dramatically for credit ratings that fall below investment grade status.

23.3 Warrants and Convertible Securities

A popular investment strategy in recent years has involved the creation of security "packages" in which derivatives are combined with, or embedded into, more basic instruments, such as stock shares or bonds. In this section, we examine two important variations on this theme: (1) bonds with warrants that give the investor the right to buy additional shares of the company's common stock; and (2) securities, such as debt or preferred stock, that the investor can convert into other securities.

23.3.1 Warrants

A **warrant** is an equity call option issued directly by the company whose stock serves as the underlying asset. The key feature that distinguishes it from an ordinary call option is that, if exercised, the company will create new shares of stock to give to the warrantholder. Thus, the exercise of a warrant will increase the total number of outstanding shares, which reduces the value of each individual share. Because of this dilutive effect, the warrant is not as valuable as an otherwise comparable option contract. Indeed, the valuation of warrants is complicated by

Exhibit 23.13 CDS Premiums for Various U.S. Corporations

<HELP> for explanation.   Curncy**WCDS**
Enter # <GO> to view in CDSD.

WORLD CDS PRICING   Page 1/7

Source **CMAN** ▾   CMA NY EOD Mid/Last Spreads (New York)

Select **Single Name CDS** ▾ **Fitch Rating** **20) Edit** **AAA,A...** **Sector** **All** ▾

Search **Corporate Ticker** ▾ **Go** Country **UNITED STATES** ▾ Currency **USD** ▾

Reference Name	**5** ▾	Year	Fitch	Spread	**Abs** ▾	Chg	Time	**A** ▾	Ann
1) AT&T Corp	CATT1U5		A	18.500		0.300	10/26		−2.000
2 AT&T Inc	CSBC1U5		A	27.500		−1.200	10/26		2.500
3) AT&T Mobility LLC	CCNG1U5		A	20.500		−1.000	10/26		2.500
4) Aetna Inc	CAET1U5		A	37.000		−1.000	10/26		19.085
5) Affiliated Computer..	CT375016		BB	247.400		4.300	10/26		13.650
6) Allegheny Energy Sup..	CAYE1U5		BB	105.000		0.000	10/26		32.500
7) American Axle & Manu..	CT370292		BB	288.300		5.000	10/26		−87.325
8) American Electric Po..	CAEP1U5		BBB	35.100		0.100	10/26		10.185
9) AmerisourceBergen Co..	CABC1U5		BBB	43.500		−1.300	10/26		−3.000
10) Anheuser–Busch Cos I..	CBUD1U5		A	19.500		0.000	10/26		3.250
11) Apache Corp	CAPA1U5		A	22.500		−0.300	10/26		1.625
12) Avis Budget Car Rent..	CT376680		BB	212.500		2.500	10/26		−45.000
13) Avis Budget Group In..	CCD1U5		BB	205.000		0.400	10/26		89.500
14) Avon Products Inc	CAVP1U5		A	18.500		0.300	10/26		3.000
15) BRE Properties Inc	CT367092		BBB	91.000		−3.800	10/26		56.500
16) Ball Corp	CT356919		BB	102.700		2.700	10/26		−7.300
17) Baxter International..	CBAX1U5		A	17.500		0.000	10/26		7.750
18) BellSouth Corp	CBLS1U5		A	18.000		−0.200	10/26		−3.500

Australia 61 2 9777 8600   Brazil 5511 3048 4500   Europe 44 20 7330 7500   Germany 49 69 920410
Hong Kong 852 2977 6000   Japan 81 3 3201 8900   Singapore 62 6212 1000   U.S. 1 212 318 2000   Copyright 2007 Bloomberg L.P.
                                                                                                                   G257–123–2 29–Oct–2007 12:40:40

many factors, such as how and when the number of outstanding warrants will be exercised, what the company's current capital structure looks like, and what the company plans to do with the new funds if and when the warrant is exercised.

Galai and Schneller (1978) proposed a simple warrant valuation model in which a firm is presently financed with all equity and the warrants it issues are European-style. On its expiration date T, the warrant will be worth

$$W_T = \max\left[\frac{V_T + N_w X}{N + N_w} - X, 0\right]$$

where:

N = the current number of outstanding shares
N_W = the number of new shares created if the warrants are exercised
V_T = the value of the firm before the warrants are exercised
X = the exercise price.

They show that this terminal value can be rewritten as

23.5
$$W_T = \left[\frac{1}{1 + (N_w/N)}\right] C_T$$

where:

C_T = the expiration date value of a regular call option with otherwise identical terms as the warrant

Consequently, at any point prior to expiration, the value of the warrant should be equal to the value of the call deflated (i.e., diluted) by the factor $[1 + (N_w/N)]^{-1}$.

Although warrants can be issued as standalone instruments, more frequently a company will attach them to a bond issue to lower its initial funding cost. Warrants created in this manner usually can be detached from the debt instrument by the buyer and traded separately. Suppose a firm with 1,000,000 shares of common stock outstanding at a current share price of $100 attempts to raise an additional $10 million by issuing a 10-year bond paying annual coupons. Assume further that the yield it would have to pay for a straight debt issue is 8.50 percent. The firm could lower this borrowing cost by attaching to the bond European-style equity warrants that mature in exactly one year and have an exercise price of $115 per share. If the firm eventually hopes to raise an additional $5.75 million with these warrants, it will have to create new derivative contracts to cover 50,000 shares ($5.75 million ÷ $115).

Assuming that the one-year risk-free rate is 7 percent and the volatility of the firm's stock is 25 percent, the Black-Scholes value for a one-year call option to buy one share at $X = \$115$ can be calculated as $7.09, meaning the warrants are worth $6.75 ($= 7.09 \div [1 + (50,000/1,000,000)]$) per share. If each warrant allows for the purchase of one share and the face value of a single bond is $1,000, the firm will issue 10,000 bonds with five warrants attached to each. With an 8.50 percent coupon, the total proceeds it would generate from the sale of each bond with the warrants attached would be $1,033.75, or $1,000 for the bond and $33.75 ($= 5 \times \$6.75$) for the warrants. Thus, the firm can reduce its funding cost to 8.00 percent—the solution to the yield to maturity in the following bond calculation:

$$1033.75 = \sum_{t=1}^{10} \frac{85}{(1+y)^t} + \frac{1000}{(1+y)^{10}}$$

Packaging warrants with bonds to reduce debt expenses for the issuer and enhance return potential for the investor can be done in a variety of ways. A recent trend in financial markets is for a firm to attach to its bonds an option that is based on an underlying asset other than the company's own stock such as foreign exchange and stock index transactions. For instance, Rogalski and Seward (1991) detail the development of the market for *foreign currency exchange warrants,* which give the holder the right, but not the obligation, to purchase a fixed number of U.S. dollars for a price denominated in a foreign currency. Although called warrants, these contracts are closer in form to traditional call options on the dollar (or, equivalently, put options on the foreign currency) because they do not result in any direct change to the issuing firm's capital structure. That is, no dilutive valuation effect exists for these derivatives since there are no new shares of stock issued. Beyond that, these instruments generally can be settled only in cash but can be detached and traded separately from the original bond.[6]

23.3.2 Convertible Securities

A convertible security gives its owner the right, but not the obligation, to convert the existing investment into another form. Typically, the original security is either a bond or a share of preferred stock, which can be exchanged into common stock according to a predetermined formula. A convertible security is a hybrid issue consisting of a regular bond or preferred stock holding and a call option that allows for the conversion. Similar to warrants, they have been popular with issuers because they generally lead to a lower initial borrowing cost and represent a future supply of equity capital. In fact, McGuire (1991) and Schmidt (2003) have noted that these securities often are used in connection with mergers and venture capital deals, because they help align managerial incentives and generate capital without immediately diluting the equity base of the acquiring firm. On the other hand, investors in convertibles gain the upside potential of common stock while actually holding a less-risky asset.

---

[6] For additional information about how warrants are used in capital markets, see Francis, Toy, and Whittaker (2000) and Howe and Su (2001).

23.3.3 Convertible Preferred Stock

To see how convertible securities work, consider the dynamics of convertible preferred stock. As previously suggested, owning a share of convertible preferred is equivalent to holding a portfolio long in a normal share of preferred stock and long in a call option on the firm's common stock that can be exercised by surrendering the preferred stock. There generally is no waiting period before the conversion can be made, and the conversion privilege usually never expires. This means that the *minimum value of the convertible* issue must be:

$$\max[\text{Preferred Stock Value, Conversion Value}]$$

where the **conversion value** is the value of the common stock into which the preferred issue can be exchanged.

Suppose that for a $1,000,000 investment, an institutional investor could purchase 25,000 shares of a convertible preferred issue with the following terms (per share):

- Current convertible share price: $40.00
- Annual convertible dividend: $ 3.00
- Convertible yield: 7.50% (= $3 ÷ $40)
- Regular preferred yield: 10.00%
- Current common stock price: $20.00
- Conversion ratio: 1.75

With these conditions, the share value of a regular preferred stock issue paying a $3 dividend would be $30.00 (= 3 ÷ 0.10), or the perpetual dividend amount divided by the prevailing regular yield. This means that the convertible issue sells at a 33 percent premium to the regular preferred. Also, given the **conversion ratio** of 1.75 shares of common to each share of preferred, the conversion value of the convertible issue is $35 (= 1.75 × 20). Thus, the minimum price of the convertible security would be $35, the greater of the regular preferred price and the conversion value. Since the market price of the convertible still is above this level, this implies a **conversion premium** of 14.29 percent [= (40 − 35) ÷ 35], meaning that the convertible currently is selling based on its option value.

The future value of the convertible issue will depend on two events: (1) interest rate movements, which directly affect the yield on the regular preferred stock component, and (2) changes in common stock prices, given the 1.75 conversion ratio. Consider the matrix of minimum values for various levels of these two variables shown in Exhibit 23.14. In this situation, the value of the convertible preferred stock will likely be driven by its conversion value when interest rates and common stock prices are high and by its preferred stock value when rates and share prices are low.

23.3.4 Convertible Bonds

Like convertible preferred stock, a convertible bond can be viewed as a prepackaged portfolio containing two distinct securities: a regular bond and an option to exchange the bond for a prespecified number of shares of the issuing firm's common stock. Thus, a convertible bond represents a hybrid investment involving elements of both the debt and equity markets.

Exhibit 23.14 Minimum Convertible Preferred Stock Values as a Function of Regular Preferred Yields and Common Stock Prices

		COMMON STOCK PRICES		
		15	20	25
Yield	8%:	37.50	37.50	43.75
	10%:	30.00	35.00	43.75
	12%:	26.25	35.00	43.75

From the investor's standpoint, there are both advantages and disadvantages to this packaging. Although the buyer receives equity-like returns with a "guaranteed" terminal payoff equal to the bond's face value, he must also pay the option premium, which is embedded in the price of the security. Lummer and Riepe (1993) argue that the risk–return dynamics convertible bonds offer are sufficiently unique as to merit their own asset class. On the other side, the issuer of a convertible bond increases the company's leverage while providing a potential source of equity financing in the future. Exhibit 23.15 shows a page from *Standard & Poor's Bond Guide* summarizing details for a sample of these instruments.

As a specific example, consider the 3.375 percent coupon convertible bonds issued by Eastman Kodak (EK), the imaging products manufacturer whose stock trades on the NYSE. The listing for this issue, which is scheduled to mature in October 2033, is shown on the eighth line from the top. The second and third columns indicate that this bond pays interest semi-annually on April 15 and October 15 and has a default rating of B. The bond issue has $575 million outstanding and is convertible until maturity. At the time of this report (i.e., April 2007), the listed price of the bond was 100.25 percent of par and the price of EK common stock was $22.56. Additional details of this security are shown in Exhibit 23.16.

As spelled out at the top of Exhibit 23.16—and approximated in the seventh column of Exhibit 23.15—each $1,000 face value of this bond can be converted into 32.2373 shares of Kodak common stock. As before, this statistic is called the instrument's **conversion ratio**. At the listed share price of $22.56, an investor exercising her conversion option would have received $727.27 (= 22.56 × 32.2373) worth of stock, an amount less than the bond's current market value. In fact, the **conversion parity price** (i.e., the common stock price at which immediate conversion would make sense) is equal to $31.09, which is the bond price of $1,002.50 divided by the conversion ratio of 32.2373. The prevailing market price of 22.56 is below this parity level, meaning that the conversion option is currently out of the money. Of course, if the conversion parity price ever fell below the market price for the common stock, an astute investor could buy the bond and immediately exchange it into stock with a greater market value.

As indicated in the "Security Information" and "Redemption Information" boxes of Exhibit 23.16, this EK convertible bond is also putable by the investor and callable by the issuer at par value any time after October 2010. A company will never call a bond selling for less than its call price and firms often wait until the bond is selling for significantly more than its call price before calling it.[7] If the company calls the bond under these conditions, investors will have an incentive to convert the bond into stock that is worth more than they would receive from the call price, a situation known as *forcing conversion*. Two other factors also increase the investors' incentive to convert their bonds. First, some instruments have conversion prices that step up over time according to a predetermined schedule. Since a stepped-up conversion price leads to a lower number of shares received, it becomes more likely that investors will exercise their option just before the conversion price increases. Second, a firm can encourage conversion by increasing the dividends on the stock, making the income generated by the shares more attractive relative to the income from the bond.

The **payback** or *breakeven time*, measures how long the higher interest income from the convertible bond (compared to the dividend income from the common stock) must persist to make up for the difference between the price of the bond and its conversion value (i.e., the conversion premium). The calculation is as follows:

$$\text{Payback} = \frac{\text{Bond Price} - \text{Conversion Value}}{\text{Bond Income} - \text{Income from Equal Investment in Common Stock}}$$

For instance, the annual coupon yield payment on the Kodak convertible bond is $33.75, while the firm's annual dividend is $0.50 per share, or $16.12 per converted bond. Thus, assuming you

[7] In an empirical study of this issue, Ingersoll (1977) showed that almost all of the convertible securities studied were called later than the theoretically optimal time. This topic was also investigated by Asquith and Mullins (1991).

Exhibit 23.15 Convertible Bond Information Summary

Exchange ↓ Issue, Rate, Interest Dates and Maturity	S&P Rating	Bond Form	Outstdg. Mil-$	Conv. Ex-pires	Shares per $1,000 Bond	Price per Share	Div. Income per Bond	2007 Price Range High	2007 Price Range Low	Curr Bid Sales(s) Ask(A)	Curr. Yield	Yield to Mat	Stock Value of Bond	Conv Parity	Stock Data Month End	Stock Data P/E Ratio	Earnings Per Share Yr. End	2005	2006	Last 12 Mos
Dick's[1]Sporting[2](Sr-V/R[3]).......... Fa18 2024	NR	BE	254	2024	[4]17.20	....	....	105.50	89.87	104.62	....	....	100.51	61.04	•58.26	25	Ja	v1.35	v2.03	2.03
Disney[5](Walt)[5](Sr)................ 2½s Ao15 2023	A–	BE	1322	2023	[7]33.94	29.46	10.52	126.25	117.12	120.87	1.74	0.67	118.75	35.94	•34.43	18	Sp	v1.24	v1.64	[12]2.06
Dixie Group[8]........................... 7s Mn15 2012	B–	R	19.7	2012	31.06	32.20	....	94.50	91.62	92.37	7.58	8.96	37.86	29.74	12.02	21	Dc	Pv0.79	v0.59	0.59
Dobson[9]Communic[10](Sr)......... 1½s aO 2025	NR	BE	160	2025	[11]97.07	10.30	....	115.62	105.37	108.00	1.38	0.99	87.16	11.19	8.59	d	Dc	vd0.90	v0.02	0.02
DST[12]Systems[12](Sr)[14]......... 4⅛s [15]fA15 2023	NR	BE	540	2023	[16]20.37	....	....	167.12	139.00	164.25	2.49	0.02	156.68	81.36	•75.20	16	Dc	v5.39	v3.78	3.78
DST[17]Systems[10](Sr)[14]......... 3¾s [19]fA15 2023	NR	BE	300	2023	[16]20.37	....	....	162.87	133.75	159.62	2.25	0.02	156.68	79.09	•75.20	16	Dc	v5.39	v3.78	3.78
Duke[20]Energy[21](Sr)[10]........ 1¾s Mn15 2023	BBB	BE	131	2023	[22]42.74	23.40	54.71	145.00	98.25	98.87	1.77	1.82	125.34	23.16	•20.29	21	Dc	v1.88	v1.57	1.57
Eastman[23]Kodak[10](Sr)......... 3⅜s aO15 2033	B	BE	575	2033	[22]32.24	31.02	16.12	107.00	99.87	100.25	3.37	3.36	75.18	31.09	•22.56	d	Dc	vd4.53	vd2.09	d2.09
El Paso[24]Corp[25](Sr-Zero)................ [25] 2021	BB–	BE	[27]21.9	2021	4.78	....	0.76	55.50	54.62	54.87	....	Flat	7.31	114.80	•14.47	23	Dc	Pvd0.97	v0.64	0.64
Elan Fin Corp Ltd[28](Zero).................... 2018	NR	BE	1644	2018	[29]13.75	....	....	....	....	....	....	Flat	19.97	....	•13.29	d	Dc	vd0.93	Pvd0.62	d0.62
Electronic[30] Data[31]Sys[32](Sr-Zero)... [33] 2021	BBB–	BE	[27]5.15	2021	[22]9.73	....	1.95	81.25	79.25	79.62	....	Flat	27.04	81.83	•27.68	30	Dc	v0.28	v0.89	0.89
Encysive Pharma[10](Sr)........ 2½s Ms15 2012	NR	BE	130	2012	71.71	13.95	....	71.87	67.50	69.37	3.59	10.65	25.74	–9.70	•2.71	d	Dc	vd1.29	vd1.86	d1.86
[10]Enzon Inc[34]........................... 4½ lJ 2008	NR	BE	123	2008	14.09	70.98	....	97.62	95.75	97.37	4.62	7.32	11.66	69.10	8.15	18	Dc	vd6.69	v0.46	0.46
Equinix[35]Inc[10]...................... 2½s Fa15 2024	NR	BE	75.0	2024	[4]25.32	39.50	....	231.12	195.87	226.12	1.09	0.02	226.10	90.59	85.63	d	Dc	vd1.78	Pvd0.23	d0.23
Euronet[36]Worldwide[37](Sr)[38]... 1½s lD15 2024	B+	BE	140	2024	[39]29.74	33.63	....	109.87	100.75	103.00	1.57	1.41	80.08	34.71	26.86	25	Dc	v0.74	v1.17	1.17
Euronet[40]Worldwide[41](Sr)[38]..... 3½s aO15 2025	B+	BE	175	2025	[39]24.70	40.48	....	107.87	98.75	100.25	3.49	3.48	66.51	40.58	26.86	25	Dc	v0.74	v1.17	1.17
Fair[42]Isaac[43]Corp[25](Sr)........ 1½s [44]fA15 2023	NR	BE	0.33	2023	[4]22.75	43.95	1.82	107.12	102.37	105.12	1.44	1.20	89.74	45.87	•38.68	23	Dc	v1.86	v1.59	[12]1.68
[45]Fairchild Semiconductor[38]..... 5s mN 2008	B	BE	200	2008	[46]33.33	30.00	....	99.37	98.62	98.87	5.06	5.61	56.96	29.66	•16.72	25	Dc	vd2.01	v0.67	0.67
FEI Co[31].. 5½s fA15 2008	NR	BE	50.1	2008	20.19	49.52	....	100.00	98.00	99.12	5.56	6.56	73.71	49.03	36.06	49	Dc	vd2.33	v0.53	0.53
FEI Co[47](Zero)[30] .... [48] 2023	NR	BE	150	2023	[49]36.86	....	....	141.00	104.37	136.37	....	Flat	134.57	37.26	36.06	49	Dc	vd2.33	v0.53	0.53
Finisar Corp[38]............................ 5¼s aO15 2008	NR	BE	100	2008	181.00	5.52	....	100.37	99.12	99.62	5.27	5.45	66.60	5.50	3.50	NA	Ap	vd0.49	v0.09	[7]d0.02
Finisar[60]Corp[36]......................... 2½s aO15 2010	NR	BE	150	2010	269.91	3.71	....	126.00	115.25	127.75	1.99	0.02	99.32	4.65	3.50	NA	Ap	vd0.49	v0.09	[7]d0.02
Fisher[8]Scientific[39](Sr) .... 2½s aO 2023	BBB+	BE	300	2023	[39]21.07	47.46	....	216.12	192.87	210.37	1.19	0.02	182.42	99.60	....	20	Dc	v3.05	....	[9]3.77
Flextronics Intl[30]............................. 1s fA 2010	BB–	BE	500	2010	[39]64.41	15.55	....	99.25	95.12	95.62	1.04	2.49	70.33	14.86	10.94	43	Mr	v0.24	E0.77	[12]0.74
FLIR[51]Systems[10](Sr) .... 3s Jd 2023	NR	BE	210	2023	[39]45.06	22.19	....	174.12	146.75	173.50	1.72	0.02	167.53	38.64	35.67	24	Dc	v1.16	v1.32	1.32
Fluor[35]Corp[10](Sr) 1½s Fa15 2024	BBB+	BE	330	2024	Cv fr 2-17-05[52]			169.12	140.75	167.50	0.90	0.02	165.02	93.59	•89.72	27	Dc	v2.62	v2.95	2.95
Four[53]Seasons[10]Hotels[54](Sr). 1½s jJ30 2024	BBB–	BE	250	2024	[55]13.96	71.64	1.32	125.62	120.25	122.25	1.53	0.50	114.17	87.57	•80.30	61	Dc	vd0.77	v1.33	1.33
Gasco Energy[38](Sr) 5½s aO5 2011	NR	BE	65.0	2011	250.00	4.00	....	....	....	136.12	4.04	0.02	49.00	5.44	♦2.44	d	Dc	NIL	vd0.65	d0.65
Gateway Inc[56](Sr) .... 1½s [57] 2009	NR	BE	150	2009	[39]115.87	8.63	....	88.00	86.12	87.62	1.71	6.14	25.25	7.56	•2.19	67	Dc	v0.02	v0.03	0.03
Gateway Inc[56](Sr) .... 2s [58] 2011	NR	BE	150	2011	[39]115.87	8.63	....	82.75	80.12	80.75	2.47	6.62	25.25	6.97	•2.19	67	Dc	v0.02	v0.03	0.03
GATX[44]Corp[59](Sr)[10] .... 5s fA 15 2023	BBB+	BE	125	2023	[39]40.75	24.54	39.12	201.75	175.12	198.62	2.49	0.02	200.44	49.20	•47.80	21	Dc	vd0.29	v2.00	2.00
GenCorp[38]Inc 5¾s Ao15 2007	B–	BE	20.0	04-14-07	54.29	18.42	....	105.00	102.37	100.00	5.56	....	76.71	19.06	•13.84	NA	Nv	vd4.21	Pvd0.66	[2]0.13
General[50]Mills[61](Sr-Zero)[62]............. [63] 2022	BBB+	BE	[27]371	2022	[22]13.03	....	19.28	77.00	72.87	76.37	....	Flat	76.69	58.71	•58.22	17	My	v3.08	v2.90	[2]3.16
Genesis HealthCare Corp 2½s 2025	B		0.02		....	....	....	130.00	105.25	129.25	1.93	0.73	....	....	....	..		....	....	....
Genesis[64] HealthCare[55] Corp 2½s Ms15 2025	NR	BE	180	2025	[39]18.45	54.20	....	130.00	105.25	129.25	1.93	0.73	116.23	70.25	63.11	NA	Sp	v2.11	v1.90	[12]1.86

Uniform Footnote Explanations—See Page 1. Other: [1]Int at 1.6081% pd in cash to 2-18-09, then zero cpn. [2] (HRO)On2-18-09(14&19) at $676.25 & accr OID. [3] (HRO)On Chge of Ctrl at: $676.25 & accr OID. [4] Not cv unless min com price met or called for red. [5] (HRO)On 4-15-08 (13&18) at 100. [6] (HRO)For Fundamental Chge at 100 to 4-14-08. [7] Not conv unless com price met or called for red. [8] Was Dixie Yams. [9] (HRO)On 10-1-10(15&20) at 100. [10] (HRO)For Fundamental Chge at 100. [11] Into Cl A Com:Co may pay cash val of stk. [12] Int at 4.125% pd in cash to 8-15-10 then accretes as prin. [13] (HRO)On 8-15-10 (15&20) at 100 (accreted amt). [14] (HRO) For Fundamental Chge at 100 (accreted amt). [15] Contingent int pay fr 8-20-10 based on secur price. [16] Co may pay cash val of stk:Not conv unless min com price met or called for red. [17] Int at 3.625% pd in cash to 8-15-08, then accretes as prin. [18] (HRO)On 8-15-08(13&18) at 100(accreted amt). [19] Contingent int pay fr 8-20-08 based on secur price. [20] Contigent int pay fr 5-15-07 based on secur price. [21] (HRO)On 5-15-07 (12&17)at 100. [22] Not conv unless min com price met or called for red. [23] (HRO)On 10-15-10(13,18,23&28) at 100. [24] (HRO)On 2-28-06(11&16) at $452.89 & accr OID. [25] (HRO)For Fundamental Chge at $452.89 & accr OID. [26] Due 2-28-21. [27] Incl disc. [28] (HRO)On 12-14-03(08&13)at $524.78 & accr OID. [29] Into ADSs of Elan Corp . [30] Contingent int pay fr 10-10-04 based on secur price. [31] (HRO)On 10-10-03(04,06,11&16) at $779.41 & accr OID. [32] (HRO)For Fundamental Chge at $779.41 & accr OID to 10-9-03. [33] Due 10-10-21. [34] Now Enzon Pharmaceuticals. [35] (HRO)On 2-15-09(14&19) at 100. [36] Contingent int pay fr 12-20-09 based on secur price. [37] (HRO)On 12-15-09(14&19) at 100. [38] (HRO)On Chge of Ctrl at 100. [39] Co may pay cash val of stk. [40] Contingent int pay fr 10-15-12 based on secur price. [41](HRO)On 10-15-12(15&20) at 100. [42] Int at 1.50% pd in cash to 8-15-08, then accrues to mat. [43] (HRO)On 8-15-07(08,13&18) at 100. [44] Contingent int pay fr 8-15-08 based on secur price. [45] Subsid of & gtd by Fairchild Semiconductor Intl. [46] Into Fairchild Semi Intl com. [47] (HRO)On 6-15-08 at 100.25 & 6-15-13(&18) at 100. [48] Due 6-15-23. [49] Co may pay cash val of stk: Not cv unless min com price met or called for red. [50] (HRO)On 10-15-07 at 100. [51] (HRO)On 6-1-10(&18) at 100. [52] Cv into 17.87 com shs/cash val if min com price met or called. [53] (HRO)On 7-30-09(14&19) at 100. [54] Co may red in whole, at 100, for tax low chge. [55] Into Limited Vtg shs:Co may pay cash val of stk. [56] (HRO) For Designated Event at 100. [57] Due 12-31-09:Int paid Jun 30 & Dec 31. [58] Due 12-31-11:Int paid Jun 30 & Dec 31. [59] (HRO)On 8-15-08(13&18) at 100. [60] Contingent int pay fr 10-28-05 based on secur price. [61] (HRO)On Chge of Ctrl at $671.65 & accr OID. [62] (HRO)On 10-28-05 (07,12 & 17) at $671.65 & accr OID. [63] Due 10-28-22. [64] (HRO)On 3-15-12(15&20) at 100.

Source: *Standard & Poor's Bond Guide*, April 2007, p. 218.

Exhibit 23.16 Details of Eastman Kodak's Convertible Bond Issue

Page	Corp **ODES**

Enter 10 <GO> for News, 11 <Go> for Involved Parties

SECURITY DISPLAY　　　　　PAGE   1/ 6

EASTMAN KODAK CO EK 3 $^3/_8$ 10/15/33　　　N O T   P R I C E D

CONV TO　　　　32.2373　SHRS(PER　　1000 .0) EK　　(NY) $27.51　(　0.50)

CONVERTIBLE UNTIL 10/15/33

SECURITY INFORMATION		ISSUER INFORMATION	
		SERIES: 144A	NAME EASTMAN KODAK CO
CPN FREQ	SEMI– AN		TYPE Industrial
CPN TYPE	Fixed	IDENTIFICATION # 's	REDEMPTION INFO
MTY/REFUND TYP	Conv/Put/Call	CUSIP 2774618X0	MATURITY DT 10/15/33
CALC TYP (49)	CONVERTIBLE	MLNUM A0PH2	REFUNDING DT
DAY COUNT (5)	30/360		NEXT CALL DT 10/15/10
MARKET ISS	Priv Placement		WORKOUT DT 10/15/33
COUNTRY/CURR	US /USD		RISK FACTOR 17.1992
COLLATERAL TYP	Senior Notes	ISSUANCE INFO	
AGGR AMT ISS	575,000(M)*	ANNOUNCE DT 10/ 8/03	RATINGS
AGGR AMT OUT	575,000(M)*	1ST SETTLE DT 10/10/03	MOODY B2
MIN PC/INC	1,000/ 1,000	1ST CPN DT 4/15/04	S & P B
PAR AMT	1,000.00	INT ACCRUE DT 10/10/03	COMP B
LEADMGR/UWRTR	CITI, LEH	PRICE @ ISSUE 100	
EXCHANGE	TRACE		FI B

NOTES   HAVE PROSPECTUS, *AGGREGATE AMT FOR ALL FORMS, DTC, BOOKENTRY

PRX/SHR=US$31.02. CVT PREM=47.01%. SUBJ TO CONTINGENT CVR. POSION PUT. GREENSHOE
EXER FOR $75MM EFF 10/09/03. REG'D EFF 2/26/04, SEE CUSIP# 277461BE8.

Australia 61 2 9777 8600　　　　Brazil 5511 3048 4500　　　Europe 44 20 7330 7500　　　　Germany 49 69 920410
Hong Kong 852 2977 6000　Japan 81 3 3201 8900　Singapore 65 6212 1000　U.S. 1 212 318 2000　Copyright 2007 Bloomberg L.P.
　　　　　　　　　　　　　　　　　　　　　　　　　　　　　　H464–158–0 26–Oct–2007 13:17:18

sold the bond for $1,002.50 and used the proceeds to purchase 44.44 shares (= 1,002.50/22.56) of EK stock, the payback period would be:

$$\frac{\$1,002.50 - \$727.27}{\$33.75 - \$16.12} = 15.61 \text{ years}$$

This implies a point in the future somewhat sooner than when the bond matures (i.e., 26.50 years), suggesting that investors are likely to make back the conversion premium with the incremental cash flow from the bond alone.

It is also possible to calculate the combined value of the investor's conversion option, put option, and the issuer's call feature that are embedded in the security. With a market price of $1,002.50, the EK convertible's yield-to-maturity can be calculated as the solution to:

$$\$1,002.50 = \sum_{t=1}^{53} \frac{16.875}{(1 + y/2)^t} + \frac{1000}{(1 + y/2)^{53}}$$

or $y = 3.361$ percent (reported as 3.36 percent in the fourteenth column of Exhibit 23.15). This computation assumes 53 semiannual coupon payments of $16.875 (= 33.75 ÷ 2). Since the indicative yield on a Kodak debt issue with no embedded options and the same (B) credit rating and maturity was 8.24 percent, the present value of a "straight" fixed-income security with the same cash flows would be:

$$\$479.07 = \sum_{t=1}^{53} \frac{16.875}{(1 + 0.0412)^t} + \frac{1000}{(1 + 0.0412)^{53}}$$

Exhibit 23.17 Illustrating the Value of a Convertible Bond

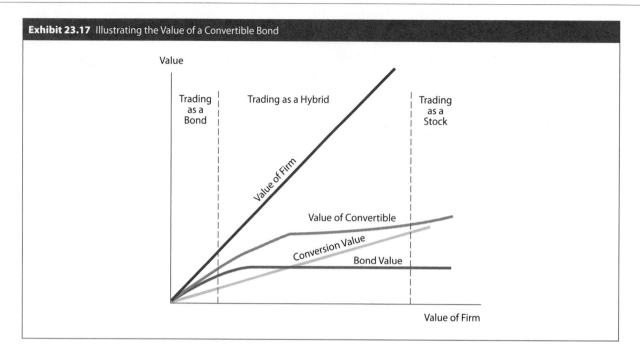

This means that the net value of the combined options is $523.43, or $1,002.50 −$479.07. Using the Black-Scholes valuation model, it is easily confirmed that a 26.5-year call option to buy *one* share of Kodak stock at an exercise price of $31.09 (i.e., the conversion parity value) is equal to $8.555.[8] Thus, the value of the investor's conversion option must be $275.80 (= 32.2373 × $8.555). The joint consequence of the bond's other embedded options (i.e., long put, short call) is therefore costing the bondholder an additional $247.63 (= 523.43 − 275.80).

Exhibit 23.17 illustrates the value of a convertible bond in a more general way. Since it cannot sell for more than the company's assets, the value of the firm is an upper bound for the value of a convertible. The "straight" bond value component is relatively flat for a wide range of firm values because, at some point, higher firm values do not benefit bondholders who receive only their promised payments. However, at fairly low firm values, the value of the bond drops off as bankruptcy becomes more likely. Conversion value rises directly with the value of the firm. The value of the convertible shows that when firm value is low, the convertible will act more like a bond, trading for only a slight premium over the bond value. Alternatively, when firm values are high, the convertible will act more like a stock, selling for only a slight premium over the conversion value. In the middle range—which is where the EK bond falls—the convertible will trade as the hybrid security that acts somewhat like a bond and somewhat like a stock.

23.4 Other Embedded Derivatives

For many years, the nature of borrowing and lending in securitized capital markets remained quite stable, with companies typically issuing bonds at par value and paying either a fixed or floating rate of interest in the same currency in which the money was borrowed. With few exceptions, the choice of maturity or coupon structure was driven by the economic situation faced by the borrower, rather than the investor. This scenario has greatly changed with the development of the *structured note* market. Structured notes are debt issues that have their principal or coupon payments linked to some other underlying variable. Examples include

---

[8] This calculation assumes the following input values: $S = 22.56$, $X = 31.09$, $T = 26.5$, $RFR = 0.0498$, $\sigma = 0.33$, and $D = 0.0222$.

bonds whose coupons are tied to the appreciation of an equity index, such as the S&P 500, or a zero coupon bond with a principal amount tied to the appreciation of an oil price index.

Crabbe and Argilagos (1994) and Das (2005) point out several common features that distinguish structured notes from regular fixed-income securities, two of which are important here. First, structured notes are designed for a specific investor with a very particular need. That is, these are not generic instruments but products tailored to address an investor's special constraints, which often result from tax, regulatory, or institutional policy restrictions. Second, after structuring the financing to meet the investor's needs, the issuer typically will hedge any unwanted exposure with swaps or exchange-traded derivatives. Since the structured note likely required an embedded derivative to create the investor's desired payoff structure, unwinding of the derivative position by the issuer generates an additional profit opportunity for the bond underwriter.

The growth of this market has been quite rapid. From its ostensible origin in the mid-1980s, by 2007 about $150 billion of these notes were issued annually. Equally impressive is the wide variety of economic risks that have been embedded and the maze of new acronyms that has accompanied these innovations (e.g., FLAG, LYON, SPEL, STEER, PERCS, and ICON). We take a detailed look at four structures representative of the major exposures an investor might desire: currency, equity, commodity, and interest rates.

23.4.1 Dual Currency Bonds

A dual currency bond is a debt instrument that has coupons denominated in a different currency than its principal amount. They have been popular funding instruments, particularly in the Euromarkets, for several years and have been designed to include virtually all the world's major currencies. These bonds can be viewed as a combination of two simpler financial instruments: (1) a single-currency fixed-coupon bond, and (2) a forward contract to exchange the bond's principal into a predetermined amount of a foreign currency. They often are sold to investors who are willing to take a long-term view in the foreign exchange markets. By attaching the currency forward to the bond, fixed-income portfolio managers who might otherwise be restricted from trading in FX have the potential to enhance their performance if their beliefs about future market conditions prove correct.

As an example, consider a five-year bond paying an annual coupon of 9 percent in U.S. dollars and redemption amount of JPY 110,000. The initial price of the bond is USD 1,020, relative to a par value of USD 1,000. If a regular five-year, dollar-denominated bond of comparable risk yielding 9 percent could have been issued at par, this means that the forward contract portion of the dual currency instrument is off market because it carries a present value of USD 20. Exhibit 23.18 shows the cash flows for this structure from the investor's point of view. It also demonstrates how it can be assembled from its more basic component parts.

Exhibit 23.18 Cash Flows for a Dual Currency Bond from the Investor's Perspective

	YEAR					
	0	**1**	**2**	**3**	**4**	**5**
Transaction						
1. Long 9% USD bond	−USD 1,000	+ USD 90	+ USD 90	+ USD 90	+ USD 90	+ USD 1,090
2. Long yen forward (pay USD, receive JPY)	−USD 20	—	—	—	—	+JPY 110,000 and −USD 1,000
3. Long dual currency bond (Transaction 1 + Transaction 2)	−USD 1,020	− USD 90	+ USD 90	+ USD 90	+ USD 90	+ JPY 110,000 and +USD 90

The embedded forward contract allows the bondholder to exchange the USD 1,000 for JPY 110,000, generating an implied *nominal* exchange rate of JPY 110/USD (or, equivalently, USD 0.0091/JPY). However, given that the investor has to pay an additional USD 20 today for this future transaction, this is not the *effective* exchange rate that the investor faces. Indeed, the fact that the investor is willing to pay the additional USD 20 suggests that JPY 110/USD is a favorable price to purchase yen forward. The effective exchange rate built into this transaction can be established by dividing JPY 110,000 by the sum of USD 1,000 and the future value (in Year 5) of USD 20. Calculating this latter amount as 30.77 [$= 20 \times (1.09)^5$], the effective exchange rate becomes JPY 106.72/USD [$= 110,000 \div (1,000 + 30.77)$].

There are at least two reasons why this dual currency bond might trade at a premium over a comparable single-currency 9 percent coupon bond. First, it is possible that the five-year forward exchange rate between yen and dollars is JPY 106.72/USD, meaning that at USD 1,020, the bond is priced properly. More likely, though, the five-year forward rate actually is JPY 110/USD and investors are paying up for a desirable FX exposure that they cannot acquire in any other way. If this is true, the issuer—who is effectively short the regular dollar bond and short in the yen forward—can unwind its derivative position at a profit, thereby reducing its funding cost below 9 percent. That is, the issuer's commitment to sell JPY 110,000 to the investor in Year 5 can be offset by a long position in a separate yen forward (usually done with the bond's underwriter as the counterparty) at the market forward exchange rate of JPY 110/JSD. Thus, the issuer's net borrowing cost can be calculated by solving for the yield as follows:

$$1,020 = \sum_{t=1}^{5} \frac{90}{(1 + y)^t} + \frac{1,000}{(1 + y)^5}$$

or $y = 8.49$ percent. This 51-basis-point differential from the plain vanilla borrowing rate of 9 percent represents the issuer's compensation for creating an investment vehicle that is tailored to the needs of the investor.

23.4.2 Equity-Index Linked Notes

In February 2000, Deutsche Bank AG, through its Bankers Trust Company unit, raised capital by issuing a class of unsecured senior debt securities called S&P 500 Market-Linked Deposits. These instruments are an example of a wider class of structured notes known as *variable principal redemption* (VPR) securities because the amount of the bond's principal refunded at maturity is not fixed but depends on the returns to an equity index. These particular VPR bonds mature on February 18, 2010, and, as their name implies, have their redemption amount tied to movements in the S&P 500 index between the origination and maturity dates. Other VPR notes that have traded in the market in recent years have tied the principal redemption to a wide variety of global stock indexes, including the Dow Jones Industrial Average, the Russell 1000, the FT-SE 100, and the Nikkei 225, as well as to "baskets" of those indexes.

This VPR note pays no coupons prior to maturity. At maturity, the bondholder receives the original issue price (stated here as 100 percent of minimum face value) plus a "supplemental redemption amount," which depends on where the S&P 500 index settles relative to a predetermined initial level. This supplemental amount cannot be less than zero, so the total payout to the investor at maturity is:

$$100 + \max\left[0, \left\{100 \times \left(\frac{\text{Final SPX Value} - \text{Initial SPX Value}}{\text{Initial SPX Value}}\right) \times 1.00\right\}\right]$$

where the initial S&P 500 (i.e., SPX) index value was specified as 1346.09. The "market participation" factor of 1.00 indicates that the investor receives 100 percent of the return to the SPX over the 10-year period, provided that return is positive.

Recognize that the VPR structure combines a 10-year, zero-coupon bond with a SPX index call option, both of which were issued by Deutsche Bank. Thus, the structured note investor essentially owns a "portfolio" that is: (1) long in a bond, and (2) long in an index call option position. This particular security might have been designed for investors who wanted to participate in the equity market but, for regulatory or taxation reasons, were not permitted to do so directly. For example, the manager of a fixed-income mutual fund might be able to enhance her return performance by purchasing this "bond" and then hoping for an appreciating stock market. The use of the call option in this design makes it easy for Deutsche Bank to market to its institutional customers as a "no lose" proposition; the worst-case scenario for the investor is that she simply gets her money back without interest in 10 years. (Of course, the customer does carry the bank's credit risk for this period.) Thus, unlike the dual currency bond where the investor could either gain or lose from changing FX rates, at origination this VPR issue had no downside exposure to stock price declines.

The call option embedded in this structure is actually a partial position. To see this, we can rewrite the option portion of the note's redemption value as:

$$\max\left[0, \left\{100 \times 1.00 \times \left(\frac{\text{Final SPX} - 1346.09}{1346.09}\right)\right\}\right] = \max\left[0, \left\{\left(\frac{100}{1346.09}\right)(\text{Final SPX} - 1346.09)\right\}\right]$$

or

$$(0.0743)\{\max[0, (\text{Final SPX} - 1346.09)]\}$$

Thus, given that a regular index option would have a terminal payoff of $\max[0, (\text{Final SPX} - X]$, where X is the exercise price, the derivative in the VPR represents 7.43 percent of this amount. The terminal payoffs to the VPR embedded option are shown in Exhibit 23.19, along with those to a regular index call option, for several potential February 2010 levels of the S&P 500 index. Although both the VPR and regular options become in the money at the same point (i.e., 1346.09), only the latter produces a "dollar-for-dollar" payoff with increasing values of the index beyond this level. The payoff to the call feature in the structured note still rises for any S&P 500 level exceeding the exercise price, but gains only $0.0743 for every one point gained by the index.

Exhibit 23.20 provides a different way to visualize the VPR investment structure. For the initial (i.e., February 2000) payment of $100, the investor has purchased the equivalent of a 10-year zero-coupon bond maturing in February 2010 plus a partial call option on the index on the S&P 500 index. Thus, the $100 initial payment can be split into the value of the zero-coupon bond—which is simply $100 discounted to the present at Deutsche Bank's 10-year bond yield—and the remainder, which must be the value of the embedded SPX call option at the origination date. This also makes valuing the VPR at any point in its life a more transparent process since it must always be that the value of the entire structure is just the value of the bond portion plus the value of the option component.

To see how this might work, consider that on August 18, 2007, the closing level for the S&P 500 was 1445.94. Further, the semiannually compounded yield of a zero-coupon (i.e., "stripped") Treasury bond on this date was 4.21 percent while a Deutsche Bank bond maturing at about the same time as the VPR issue carried a yield of 4.54 percent. (This 33 basis point credit spread was appropriate for Deutsche Bank's credit rating of Aa1 and AA- by Moody's and Standard & Poor's, respectively.) Given the remaining time to maturity (i.e., two years and six months, or five half-years), the bond portion of the VPR issue should be worth:

$$\text{VPR Bond Value} = \frac{100}{\left(1 + \dfrac{.0454}{2}\right)^5} = \$89.384$$

The value of a regular call option on a stock index can be calculated with the dividend yield-adjusted version of the Black-Scholes model. To perform this computation, three additional

Exhibit 23.19 Terminal Payoffs to VPR Embedded Call Option and Regular Index Call Option (X = 1346.09)

Final SPX Value	Regular Index Call	VPR Call
1225	0.00	0.00
1250	0.00	0.00
1275	0.00	0.00
1300	0.00	0.00
1325	0.00	0.00
1350	3.91	0.29
1375	28.91	2.15
1400	53.91	4.00
1425	78.91	5.86
1450	103.91	7.72
1475	128.91	9.58
1500	153.91	11.43
1525	178.91	13.29
1550	203.91	15.15
1575	228.91	17.01
1600	253.91	18.86
1625	278.91	20.72
1650	303.91	22.58
1675	328.91	24.43
1700	353.91	26.29
1725	378.91	28.15
1750	403.91	30.01

inputs are needed. First, the S&P 500 dividend yield on August 18, 2007, was 1.84 percent. Second, the continuously compounded equivalent of the quoted risk-free rate is 4.17 percent.[9] Finally, the volatility of SPX index returns over the time to VPR issue's maturity is assumed to be 19.92 percent, based on prevailing implied volatilities for traded index options on that date.

The value of an index call option with an exercise price of 1346.09 can now be generated by the Black-Scholes formula using the following inputs: $S = 1445.94$, $X = 1346.09$, $T = 2.50$, $RFR = 0.0417$, $D = 0.0184$, and $\sigma = 0.1992$. Under these conditions:

$$d_1 = [\ln(1445.94e^{-(.0184)\,2.50}/1346.09) + (.0417 + 0.5(.1992)^2)(2.50)] \div (.1992[2.50]^{1/2}) = 0.5696$$

and

$$d_2 = 0.5696 - .1992[2.50]^{1/2} = 0.2546$$

so that $N(d_1) = 0.7156$ and $N(d_2) = 0.6006$. Thus, the index call's Black-Scholes value is:

$$C_0 = (1445.94)(e^{-(.0184)2.50})(0.7156) - (1346.09)(e^{-(.0417)2.50})(0.6006) = 259.696$$

The value of the embedded VPR call is then established by multiplying 259.696 by 0.0743, which leaves a value of $19.295. As shown in Exhibit 23.20, on this particular date the VPR

---

[9] This value can be established by solving for r in the following equation:

$e^r = (1 + (.0421/2))^2$

or

$r = \ln[(1 + (.0421/2))^2] = 0.0417$.

Exhibit 23.20 Illustrating the VPR Transaction

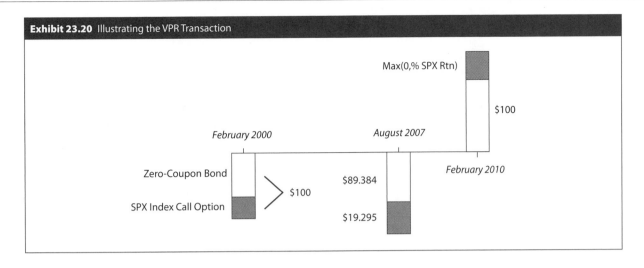

issue was valued at \$108.679 (= 89.384 + 19.295). Finally, notice that since the August 18, 2007, index value (i.e., 1445.94) was already greater than the initial (i.e., exercise) level, the VPR call feature is in the money and the value of the embedded option can be further broken down into \$7.419 (= (.0743)[1445.94 − 1346.09]) of intrinsic value and \$11.876 (= 19.295 − 7.419) of time premium.

23.4.3 Commodity-Linked Bull and Bear Bonds

Fixed-income securities can be designed to give an investor exposure to commodity price movements as well. The commodities involved in these structures are seldom exchanged but instead represented in the form of "cash settlement only" derivatives. Thus, virtually no limit exists to the number of different underlying assets that can be embedded into a bond issue. However, innovation in the structured note market is dictated by investor demands, which to date have tended to concentrate on either oil or precious metals. As in the previous examples, the primary attractions to the investor of gaining the desired exposure through the purchase of structured notes are their convenience and their ability to avoid restrictions on taking commodity positions directly.

A particularly interesting form of the commodity-linked bond is the so-called bull-and-bear note. This structure gets its name from a bond that is issued in two portions: a bull tranche, whose principal redemption amount increases directly with the price of the designated commodity; and a bear tranche, whose principal declines with increasing commodity prices. One of the first issues of this kind occurred in October 1986 when the Kingdom of Denmark raised \$120 million in two separate \$60 million tranches, each having a payoff structure tied to an index of gold prices.[10] Both of these gold-linked note tranches had a seven-year maturity, paid an annual coupon of 3 percent, and were issued at a price of 100.125 percent of par value. The principal redemptions for each \$1,000 of face value for the two tranches were:

> *Bull Redemption:* \$1,000 × [1.158 × (Index at Redemption ÷ Initial Index)]

and

> *Bear Redemption:* \$1,000 × {2.78 − [1.158 × (Index at Redemption ÷ Initial Index)]}

For both tranches, maximum and minimum redemption levels of \$2,280 and \$500, respectively, were set.

[10] Additional details of this bull-and-bear structure are explained in Walmsley (1998), who also provides descriptions of an exhaustive set of such deals.

Exhibit 23.21 Redemption Values for the Bull-and-Bear Gold-Linked Note (in U.S. Dollars)

Terminal Gold Index	Bull Tranche	BearTranche	Average
100	500	2,280	1,390
150	500	2,280	1,390
200	543	2,237	1,390
250	679	2,101	1,390
300	815	1,965	1,390
350	950	1,830	1,390
400	1,086	1,694	1,390
450	1,222	1,558	1,390
500	1,358	1,422	1,390
550	1,493	1,287	1,390
600	1,629	1,151	1,390
650	1,765	1,015	1,390
700	1,901	879	1,390
750	2,036	744	1,390
800	2,172	608	1,390
850	2,280	500	1,390
900	2,280	500	1,390

Exhibit 23.21 shows the redemption amount that the Kingdom of Denmark is obligated to pay on each tranche for a series of gold index levels relative to the initial level, which was set at 426.50. The final column of this display shows what the average redemption value is when the two tranches are considered together. This average amount does not vary, so *the issuer has no net exposure to gold price movements.* Unlike the dual currency bond considered earlier, which required the issuer to adopt an additional derivative position to offset the instrument's FX exposure, the virtue of this two-tranche approach is that the commodity exposure is neutralized internally. That is, the Kingdom of Denmark is effectively both long and short gold in equal amounts across the bear and bull segments, respectively. This leaves a fixed funding cost for the full $120 million issue of:

$$1,001.25 = \sum_{t=1}^{7} \frac{30}{(1 + y)^t} + \frac{1,390}{(1 + y)^7}$$

or $y = 7.42$ percent. At the time this deal was launched, a regular seven-year, par-value debt issue would have required a yield of about 8 percent, which underscores the Kingdom of Denmark's incentive to create this structure in the first place.

The attraction for the investors, of course, is the ability to purchase a fixed-income security that also allows for participation in gold price movements. In exchange for accepting a lower-than-market coupon, buyers of the bull (bear) tranche receive a redemption value that exceeds their purchase price if the gold index increases (declines). Exhibit 23.22, which graphs the redemption values for the two tranches, suggests that the commodity derivatives embedded in this transaction are not simple forward or option positions. Rather, the minimum and maximum principal payoffs effectively convert the gold exposure into a call option money spread—a bull spread for the bull tranche, a bear for the bear—as described in Chapter 22. The investors, undoubtedly different people for the two positions, pay for this spread position through a reduction in their average yield to maturity relative to the regular bond.

Exhibit 23.22 Redemption Values for the Bull-and-Bear Gold-Linked Note

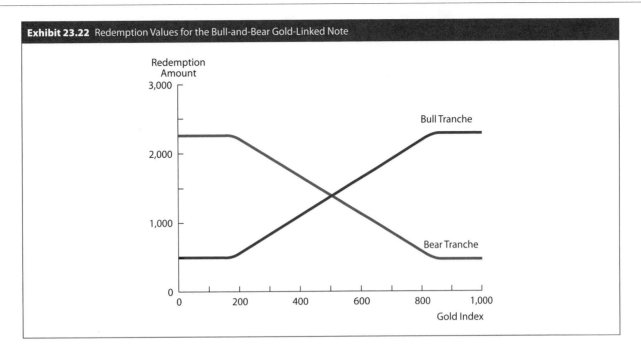

23.4.4 Swap-Linked Notes

As we have seen, interest rate swaps are efficient mechanisms for transforming the cash flows of existing debt issues. They also are quite useful in the new-issue market when the desired rate exposures of the borrower and lender do not coincide naturally. Imagine, for example, that Company LMN wishes to raise $50 million by issuing a fixed-rate note with semiannual coupon payments over a three-year period. A large institutional investor is willing to accept LMN's credit risk on a privately placed loan, providing that the deal can be structured to its satisfaction. In particular, the fund manager thinks interest rates are going to decline substantially over the next few years and wants to take advantage of that possibility. Accordingly, she wants the semiannual coupon on the note to move inversely with the level of some variable interest rate index, such as LIBOR. This sort of arrangement is known as a *reverse floating-rate* contract; the coupon rate changes as the general level of interest rates moves but in the opposite direction.

Suppose the specific structure that LMN and the investor agree on resets the coupon on a semiannual basis at a level equal to 12 percent minus LIBOR. If six-month LIBOR on a particular settlement date is 7.5 percent, the coupon payment will be 4.5 percent ($\times$ .5 $\times$ $50,000,000). Conversely, a LIBOR of only 3.75 percent would generate a coupon of 8.25 percent. In this way, the investor gains the desired benefit from falling rates and does so in a convenient form that entails less credit risk than if she had transformed a regular bond issue with a derivative on her own. In addition, the reverse floater will actually benefit more from a rate decline than would a fixed-rate note of identical maturity; while the price of a fixed-rate bond paying constant coupons will appreciate when yields fall, the reverse floater will increase its coupons as well.

Although this design satisfies the investor's requirements, it does not do the same for the issuer. This shortcoming can be easily remedied, though, by combining Company LMN's debt position with a swap in which it receives the fixed rate and pays LIBOR. This is illustrated in Exhibit 23.23, assuming a three-year fixed swap rate of 6.5 percent against sixmonth LIBOR. To see how a swap must be written to fix the coupon on a reverse rate structure, notice that paying a coupon of 12 percent minus LIBOR is equivalent to paying a coupon of 12 percent and receiving one of LIBOR. Thus, to neutralize LMN's floating-rate exposure, it must pay out LIBOR on the swap.

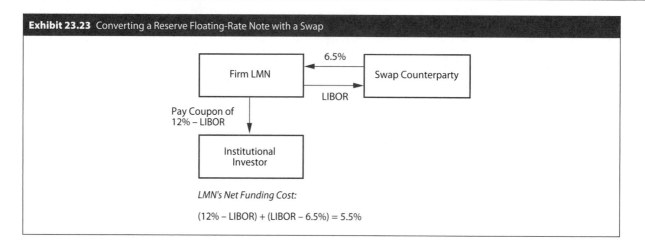

Exhibit 23.23 Converting a Reserve Floating-Rate Note with a Swap

LMN's Net Funding Cost:

(12% − LIBOR) + (LIBOR − 6.5%) = 5.5%

Exhibit 23.23 also shows that the net synthetic fixed-rate funding cost to Company LMN is 5.5 percent. This will only be true, however, whenever LIBOR does not exceed 12 percent. If LIBOR is greater than 12 percent, the benefit from paying lower coupons to the investor will stop—the coupon rate can never go negative—but LMN will continue having to make the higher net settlement payment on the swap, which raises the effective borrowing cost above 5.5 percent. Consequently, because there is an implicit cap on LIBOR built into the reverse floating-rate loan, Company LMN will need to offset this by purchasing an actual cap agreement with an exercise rate of 12 percent and a notional principal of $50 million. This option will not be expensive because it is quite far out of the money but it will not be free, so the net funding cost will be somewhat greater than 5.5 percent.

Recall that an interest rate swap can be interpreted as a pair of capital market transactions. In this particular case, a "receive 6.5 percent fixed, pay LIBOR" swap can be viewed as a portfolio long in a fixed-rate note paying 6.5 percent and short in a LIBOR-based floating-rate note. Recalling also that "+" represents a long position and "−" represents a short position, the synthetic fixed-rate issue from Company LMN's perspective can be written:

$$
\begin{aligned}
- (\text{Synthetic Fixed Rate Bond at 5.5\%}) = {} & - (\text{Reverse Floater at 12\%} - \text{LIBOR}) \\
& + (\text{Receive 6.5\%, Pay LIBOR Swap}) \\
& + (\text{Cap at 12\% Exercise Rate}) \\
= {} & - (\text{Reverse Floater at 12\%} - \text{LIBOR}) \\
& - (\text{FRN at LIBOR}) + (\text{Fixed Rate Bond at 6.5\%}) \\
& + (\text{Cap at 12\% Exercise Rate})
\end{aligned}
$$

Brown and Smith (1995b) argue that this structured solution would only make sense to the issuer if it led to a funding cost that was lower than a direct fixed-rate loan. The biggest reason for this is that while a direct fixed-rate loan would carry no credit risk for the borrower, the structured loan would because of the swap and cap positions. Thus, the swap-based borrowing requires a lower cost to entice the issuer.

· ·

23.5 Valuing Flexibility: An Introduction to Real Options

Recently, energy companies have begun to open gas-fired power plants that generate electricity at an expense 50 percent to 70 percent greater than those of other, more cost-effective plants. McGrath and MacMillan (2005) note that these new, "inefficient" plants are intended to operate only when the price of electricity is high enough to justify the cost. The energy firms hope to make a profit on the new plants because power prices have become increasingly volatile and the new plants—although they cost more to run—are much less costly than traditional plants to fire up and shut down on short notice. Although these "peaking" plants are also cheaper to build, their main attraction lies in their *flexibility:* They allow energy companies to supply more electricity when prices are high and to cease production almost immediately when electricity prices have dropped.

How should investors value companies that possess this sort of operational flexibility? Conventional net present value calculations ignore the benefits of flexibility and may therefore undervalue projects that allow companies to react rapidly to changing circumstances. For instance, that these new power plants are expected to run only part of the year is easily incorporated into a standard value calculation. However, predicting future cash flows based on factors like expected running time, expected electricity prices, or expected production costs will fail to capture the most valuable feature of these plants: namely, that they will only be generating electricity when the price of a megawatt-hour of electricity exceeds the cost of producing it. This is in contrast to conventional plants that produce electricity more cheaply overall but are sometimes forced to sell below-cost power because shutting down and then restarting the facility would be prohibitively expensive.

So far, the derivative contracts we have discussed are exchanged in financial markets and the asset underlying the derivative contract is often another financial instrument (such as a share of common stock, a government bond, or a futures contract). However, options are also embedded in real assets owned by firms; these are known as **real options**. A pharmaceutical company, for example, owns valuable options in the form of its collection of drug patents. The firm has the right, but not the obligation, to develop marketable drugs based on its patents and will do so if the discounted present value of those drugs exceeds the cost of development and regulatory approval. In the language of derivative contracting, these costs can be considered as the strike price for the development option. In the energy example, the peaking plant in effect gives the firm the right but not the obligation to buy Y megawatt-hours of electricity at an exercise price X, where Y is the total capacity of the plant and X is the generating cost per megawatt-hour.

Although real options have existed ever since humans first walked the earth—for instance, storing food and other necessities gave people a valuable option, allowing them to consume more (or less) than the amount produced in a given time period—a number of recent changes have made understanding them more important than ever. These factors include (1) the *pace of technological innovation,* which has made a company's long-term planning more difficult to assess for managers and investors alike; (2) *deregulation and privatization,* which have created new incentives for firms to analyze real options to gain a competitive advantage; and (3) *advances in derivatives pricing theory* and *decreases in the computing costs,* making it easier to interpret and value real options.

23.5.1 Company Valuation with Real Options

To highlight the advantages of the real options approach over traditional company valuation methods, we present the case of the fictional GoldFlex Corporation.[11] One of GoldFlex's assets is a lease on a gold mine, which expires exactly one year from now (i.e, Year 1). GoldFlex geologists estimate that the mine—which is currently idle—holds 100,000 Troy ounces of gold and that extraction costs are $260/ounce. The current (i.e, Year 0) spot price of an ounce of gold is $264.40, while the Year 1 forward contract price equals $268.40. For simplicity, assume that all the gold is extracted at the end of the year. To be able to mine gold in a year, the company must spend $1,000,000 today to restore the mining facilities to working order. Suppose further that the spot price of gold in one year will be either $290 or $240 and that the one-year risk-free rate is 5 percent. How should an investor establish the value of GoldFlex's mining lease?

---

[11] This example follows a greatly simplified approach based on the valuation method first introduced by Brennan and Schwartz (1985).

Recognize that GoldFlex could sell all of its gold at the current forward price. Since the resulting sales proceeds a year from now would then be known, assuming that extraction costs and the quantity of gold are known with certainty, the appropriate discount rate is the one-year T-bill (i.e., risk-free) yield. Thus, the value of the mine calculated using a traditional net present value approach would be

$$NPV = \{[(268.40 - 260) \div 100,000] \div 1.05\} - 1,000,000 = -\$200,000$$

Of course, this implies that the lease has no value because opening the mine would be a money-losing project. However, the traditional approach ignores the value of flexibility: If gold prices decline in the future, management can shut down production and leave the gold in the ground. Once we consider the possibility of shutting down, the cash flows from the mine can be viewed in a different and more realistic manner.

The main premise behind the derivatives-based approach to valuing a real asset with embedded timing options (such as the mine) is that it is possible for an investor to assemble a portfolio of financial securities that has the same pattern of future cash flows with the same level of risk. Specifically, such an investor could value the potential future cash flows by creating a hypothetical portfolio consisting of risk-free, one-year T-bills and gold forward contracts that would exactly mimic the mining operation. This *replicating portfolio* will have the same possible cash flows as the gold mine, so its value in an efficient capital market should also be the same. We can use a two-state framework to view the valuation question as follows:

TODAY (YEAR 0)	IN ONE YEAR (YEAR 1)	
	Gold Price	**Cash Flow**
	$290	$3,000,000
Spend $1 Million to Reopen Mine?		[= (290 – 260) × 100,000]
	$240	$0 (No Production)

How many forward contracts are necessary to build a security position that duplicates these cash flows? Since the other asset involved in this process is risk free, all the variation in the cash flows of the replicating portfolio must come from the payoff to the forward contract. With the assumed Year 1 gold price forecasts, a long position in a one-year gold forward contract will leave the investor with either a profit of $21.60 (= 290 – 268.40) or a loss of –$28.40 (= 240 – 268.40) per ounce. The difference between these two payoffs equals $50 [= $21.6 – (–$28.4)], while the difference between the two possible cash flows from the mine is $3,000,000. Therefore, the number of forward contracts necessary to form a replicating portfolio (where each contract stipulates the delivery of one ounce of gold) is

$$(3,000,000) \div (50) = 60,000$$

To find the amount of the T-bill investment needed in the replicating portfolio, notice that if the price of gold drops to $240 in one year, the holder of 60,000 forward contracts will lose $1,704,000 (= 28.4 × 60,000), while the cash flow from the mine would be zero. The payoff from the risk-free investment must make up for the difference, so the amount that must be invested in one-year T-bills to form a "synthetic mine" is

$$1,704,000 \div 1.05 = \$1,622,857$$

Exhibit 23.24 summarizes the process of creating this replicating portfolio.

Given that this portfolio of securities has the same future cash flows as the mine with the same level of volatility, the replicating portfolio and the mine should have the same present value. This can be expressed as

Exhibit 23.24 Creating a "Real Options" Replicating Portfolio

Step 1: *Design a portfolio containing F forward contracts and T invested in a risk-free security that has the same future payoffs as the mine:*

"Up" State (Gold Price = $290): $[F \times (290 - 268.4)] + [(1.05) \times (T)] = \$3,000,000$

"Down" State (Gold Price = $240): $[F \times (240 - 268.4)] + [(1.05) \times (T)] = \$0$

Step 2: *Solve for F and T simultaneously:*

a. Rewrite the "down" state cash flow equation:

$$T = F \times [(-28.4) \div (-1.05)] = F \times [(28.4) \div (1.05)]$$

b. Insert the "down" state T value into the "up" state cash flow equation:

$$[F \times (21.6)] + [(1.05) \times F \times [(28.4) \div (1.05)]] = 50 \times F = 3,000,000$$

c. Solve for F:

$$F = (3,000,000) \div 50 = 60,000$$

d. Solve for T from 2(a):

$$T = (60,000) \times [(28.4) \div (1.05)] = \$1,622,857$$

(*Note:* This is the "real options" value of the mine lease cash flows, before netting out the initial reopening expense.)

Step 3: *Confirm the equality of replicating portfolio and mine future cash flows:*

"Up" State: $[(60,000) \times (21.6)] + (1.05)(1,622,857) = \$3,000,000$

"Down" State: $[(60,000) \times (-28.4)] + (1.05)(1,622,857) = 0$

(Value of Gold Forward Position) + (Value of T-bill Position) = (Value of Mine Lease)

Since the present value of an "at-market" forward contract is zero, the replicating portfolio (and therefore the lease on the mine) is worth $1,622,857, which is greater than the $1,000,000 required to restore the facilities. Investors using traditional discounted cash flow analysis will consider the lease worthless and ignore an important asset when valuing GoldFlex. Also, increased volatility in future gold prices will have no effect on the traditional valuation estimate, but would increase the value of the lease when using the real options methodology since greater uncertainty generally leads to higher option values.

In practice, real options are much more complex than this example. For instance, gold production typically takes place steadily during the year, so the analysis may require either a continuous-time (e.g., Black-Scholes) option valuation model or an expansion of the prior binomial tree approach to include a large number of subintervals. Also, extraction costs and the exact amount of the gold deposits are rarely known with certainty. The problem of having uncertain extraction costs can be solved by realizing that the lease on the mine in effect becomes an *exchange option,* a problem that was first considered by Margrabe (1978). In this example, the leaseholder effectively has an option to exchange the gold in the mine for the extraction costs (e.g., the cost of the required equipment, material and manpower).[12]

---

[12] We would like to thank Professor Andras Marosi for his contributions to this section.

• • • • SUMMARY • • • •

- The genius of modern financial markets is that they continuously provide new products and strategies to meet the constantly changing needs of anyone willing to pay the required price. In this chapter, we explore several ways in which derivatives can aid in that development process. We see that innovation sometimes takes the form of creating a new set of instruments, such as interest rate swaps, while at other times it involves packaging existing securities in a creative way. Structured notes, which combine bonds with a derivative position based on a different sort of underlying asset, are a good example of this latter approach. Ultimately, the purpose of financial engineering is to help borrowers and lenders manage one of four types of potential exposures: interest rate, currency, equity, or commodity price risk.

- We began our discussion with an examination of the market for OTC interest rate agreements. Although forward rate agreements are the most basic product, interest rate swaps are the most popular. Swap contracts can be interpreted in three ways: as a series of FRAs, as a portfolio of bond positions, or as a zero-cost collar, which consists of a pair of cap and floor agreements. We then extended the plain vanilla swap concept to include contracts designed to handle other exposures, such as credit and equity swaps.

- We conclude with an analysis of several ways in which derivatives can be embedded into other securities to create customized payoff distributions. Warrants, which are call options on common stock issued directly by the company itself, can be attached to a debt issue to offer investors the upside potential of equity with the safety of a bond. Further, bonds and preferred stock issues can be set up to allow for conversion into common stock at the investor's option. Finally, a class of instruments known as structured notes carries this concept even further by embedding into bonds derivatives that often are based on exposures that may not appear on the issuer's balance sheet. These instruments epitomize how much value derivatives can add when they are used properly, and are indicative of the ways in which investors are likely to see them appear in the market for years to come. Finally, we discuss how the derivative features embedded in physical assets (i.e., real options) can be used by investors to value companies.

• • • • SUGGESTED READINGS • • • •

Buetow, Gerald W., Jr., and Frank J. Fabozzi. *Valuation of Interest Rate Swaps and Swaptions*. New York: John Wiley, 2000.

Chance, Don M., and Pamela P. Peterson. *Real Options and Investment Valuation*. Charlottesville, VA: Research Foundation of AIMR, 2002.

Finnerty, John D. "An Overview of Corporate Securities Innovation," *Journal of Applied Corporate Finance* 4, no. 4 (Winter 1992).

Kat, Harry M. *Structured Equity Derivatives: The Definitive Guide to Exotic Options and Structured Notes*. London: Wiley, 2001.

• • • • QUESTIONS • • • •

1. **CFA EXAMINATION LEVEL III** Several Investment Committee members for the pension fund you work for have asked about interest rate swap agreements and how they are used in the management of domestic fixed-income portfolios.
    a. Define an interest rate swap and briefly describe the obligation of each party involved.
    b. Cite and explain two examples of how interest rate swaps could be used by a fixed-income portfolio manager to control risk or improve return.

2. Explain how an interest rate swap can be viewed as either a series of forward rate agreements, a pair of bond transactions, or a pair of option agreements. To make your description more precise, take the point of view of the fixed-rate receiver in the swap.

3. "When the yield curve is upward sloping, the fixed rate on a multiyear swap must be higher than the current level of LIBOR. With a downward-sloping yield curve, the opposite will occur." Explain what is meant by this statement and why it must be true.

4. Total return swaps and credit default swaps were both developed as tools to help investors manage credit risk. In practice, however, credit default swaps are used far more widely. Compare the relevant features of both derivative agreements and explain the reason for this difference in popularity.

5. **CFA EXAMINATION LEVEL III** The manager of the Bontemps International (BI) defined-benefit pension plan's fixed-income portfolio has shown exceptional security selection skills and has produced returns consistently above those on BI's fixed-income benchmark portfolio. The Board wants to allocate more money to this manager to enhance further the fund's alpha. This action would increase the proportion allocated to fixed income and decrease the proportion in equities. However, the Board wants to keep the present fixed-income/equity proportions unchanged.

   a. Identify two distinct strategies using derivative financial instruments that the Board could use to increase the fund's allocation to the fixed-income manager without changing the present fixed-income/equity proportions. Briefly explain how each of these two strategies would work. (Note: Make sure that equity swaps are one of the two strategies that you choose.)

   b. Briefly discuss one advantage and one disadvantage of each of the strategies you identified in Part a. Present your discussion in terms of the effect(s) of these advantages and disadvantages on the portfolio's
      (1) risk characteristics and
      (2) return characteristics.

6. **CFA EXAMINATION LEVEL III** The Board of Bontemps International (BI) will substantially increase the company's defined-benefit pension fund's allocation to international equities in the future. However, the board wants to retain the ability to reduce temporarily this exposure without making the necessary transactions in the cash markets. You develop a way to meet the board's condition:

   BI enters into a swap arrangement with Bank A for a given notional amount and agrees to pay the EAFE (Europe, Australia, and Far East) Index return (in U.S. dollars) in exchange for receiving the LIBOR interest rate plus 0.2 percent (20 basis points).

   On the same notional amount, BI arranges another swap with Bank B under which BI receives the return on the S&P 500 Index (in U.S. dollars) in exchange for paying the interest rate on the U.S. Treasury bill plus 0.1 percent (10 basis points).

   Both swaps would be for a one-year term.

   From BI's perspective, identify and briefly describe
   (a) the major risk that this transaction would eliminate,
   (b) the major risk that this transaction would not eliminate (i.e., retain), and
   (c) three risks that this transaction would create.

7. **CFA EXAMINATION LEVEL III** A pension plan is currently underfunded by about $400 million. This situation will be resolved soon when the plan sponsor issues a $400 million private placement two-year floater bond that will be placed into the plan under a stipulation that it will be held to maturity. This bond will carry an interest rate of 50 basis points (or 0.5 percent) above the rate of U.S. Treasury bills.

   The actual, as well as desired, asset allocation is 50 percent bonds and 50 percent domestic equities. When the bond is added, the portfolio will become significantly overweighted in fixed-income instruments. In addition, the overall duration will be decreased for the next two years. When the bond matures, the proceeds can be used to buy equities and liquid bonds with longer maturities. One Board member has suggested that futures or swaps could be used to keep the portfolio allocation in line with the desired asset allocation during the two-year period before the floater's maturity.

   a. Describe the transactions needed to restore the desired 50 percent/50 percent portfolio allocation using each of the following two derivative instruments: (1) futures, and (2) swaps.

   b. Discuss one advantage and one disadvantage of using futures instead of swaps to implement this strategy.

8. We have seen that equity warrants are not as valuable as an otherwise identical call option on the stock of the same company. Explain why this must be the case. Also, what is the incentive for a firm to issue a warrant rather than issuing stock directly?

9. Bonds and preferred stock that are convertible into common stock are said to provide investors with both upside potential and downside protection. Explain how one security can possess both attributes. What implications do these features have for the way a convertible security is priced?

10. **CFA EXAMINATION LEVEL II** Martin Bowman is preparing a report distinguishing traditional debt securities from structured note securities.

    a. Discuss how the following structured note securities differ from a traditional debt security with respect to coupon and principal payments:
       (1) Equity-index-linked notes
       (2) Commodity-linked bear bond

Bowman is also analyzing a dual currency bond (USD/CHF) as a possible addition to his bond portfolio. Bowman is a USD-based investor and believes the CHF will appreciate against the USD over the life of the bond.

b. (1) Describe the principal and coupon components of a dual currency bond.

(2) State one reason why a dual currency bond might trade at a premium over an otherwise identical single currency bond.

(3) Discuss whether there is an impact on a dual currency bond's interest payments and principal payments if the CHF appreciates against the USD over the life of the bond.

• • • • PROBLEMS • • • •

1. With the interest rate swap quotations shown in Exhibit 23.4, calculate the swap cash flows from the point of view of the fixed-rate receiver on a two-year swap with a notional principal of $22.5 million. You may assume the relevant part of the settlement date pattern and the realized LIBOR path shown in Exhibit 23.6 for the three-year agreement. Also, calculate the fixed-rate payment on a 30/360-day count and the floating-rate payments on an actual/360-day basis.

2. **CFA EXAMINATION LEVEL II** To protect the value of the Star Hospital Pension Plan's bond portfolio against the rising interest rates that she expects, Sandra Kapple enters into a one-year pay fixed, receive floating U.S. LIBOR interest rate swap, as described in the following table.

U.S. LIBOR Interest Rate Swap Terms

1-year Fixed Rate (annualized)	1.5%
90-day U.S. LIBOR Rate [$L_0(90)$] (annualized)	1.1%
Notional Principal	$1
Day Count Convention	90/360

Note: $L_i(m)$ is the m-day LIBOR on Day i.

Sixty days have passed since initiation of the swap, and interest rates have changed. Kapple is concerned that the value of her swap has also changed. The U.S. LIBOR term structure and present value factors of interest rates are described in this table:

U.S. LIBOR TERM STRUCTURE AND PRESENT VALUE FACTORS (60 DAYS AFTER SWAP INITIATION)

U.S. LIBOR Term Structure (annualized)	Present Value Factors
$L_{60}(30) = 1.25$ percent	0.9990
$L_{60}(120) = 1.50$ percent	0.9950
$L_{60}(210) = 1.75$ percent	0.9899
$L_{60}(300) = 2.00$ percent	0.9836

Note: $L_i(m)$ is the m-day LIBOR on Day i

Calculate the dollar market value of the interest rate swap entered into by Kapple, at 60 days after the initiation of the swap and using a $1 notional principal. Show your calculations.

Note: Your calculations should be rounded to 4 decimal places.

3. The treasurer of a British brewery is planning to enter a plain vanilla, three-year, quarterly settlement interest rate swap to pay a fixed rate of 8 percent and to receive three-month sterling LIBOR. But first he decides to check various cap-floor combinations to see if any might be preferable. A market maker in British pound sterling OTC options presents the treasurer with the following price list for three-year, quarterly settlement caps and floors:

	INTEREST RATE CAPS		INTEREST RATE FLOORS	
Strike Rate	Buy	Sell	Buy	Sell
7%	582 GBP	597 GBP	320 GBP	335 GBP
8%	398	413	401	416
9%	205	220	502	517

The prices are in basis points, which when multiplied by the notional principal give the actual purchase or sale price in pounds sterling. These quotes are from the perspective of the market maker, not the firm. That is, the treasurer could buy a 9 percent cap from the market maker for 220 BP, or sell one for 205 BP. The strike rates are quoted on a 365-day basis, as is sterling LIBOR.

In financial analysis of this sort, the treasurer assumes that the three-year cost of funds on fully amortizing debt would be about 8.20 percent (for quarterly payments). Should another structure be considered in lieu of the plain vanilla swap?

4. **CFA EXAMINATION LEVEL II** Takeda Development Corporation has issued a $100 million floating rate note (FRN) that will mature in three years. The FRN has quarterly coupons equal to three-month LIBOR, payable in arrears and due on the first business day of each quarter. Anne Yelland, Takeda Development's Treasurer, wants to hedge against an increase in three-month LIBOR during the remaining term to maturity of the FRN. To implement the hedge, she realizes she can use either of two alternatives: An interest rate cap or a package of over-the-counter (OTC) call options on interest rates.

   a. State whether, to correctly implement the hedge using *each* of the two alternatives, Yelland should:
      i. buy or sell an interest rate cap
      ii. buy or sell a package of over-the-counter (OTC) call options on interest rates
      Discuss *one* requirement that *both* alternatives must meet for Yelland's hedge to be effective.

   Yelland decides to implement the hedge using an interest rate cap with the following characteristics:
   - The reference rate on the interest rate cap is three-month LIBOR.
   - The cap rate (strike rate) is 5.50 percent.
   - The length of the agreement is for the remaining three-year life of the FRN.
   - The notional principal of the cap is $100 million.
   - There is quarterly settlement of the cap, payable in arrears.

   The following table shows the three-month annualized LIBOR observed on the first business day of each quarter during the first year of the cap.

   THREE-MONTH ANNUALIZED LIBOR BEGINNING OF EACH QUARTER

Quarter	Three-month Annualized LIBOR
1	4.50%
2	6.50%
3	7.50%
4	7.00%

   b. Compute the payoff (in dollars) to the interest rate cap at the beginning of *each* of the following two quarters:
      (1) Quarter 2
      (2) Quarter 3

5. On December 2, the manager of a tactical asset allocation fund that is currently invested entirely in floating-rate debt securities decides to shift a portion of her portfolio to equities. To effect this change, she has chosen to enter into the "receive equity index" side of a one-year equity swap based on movements in the S&P 500 index plus a spread of 10 basis points. The swap is to have quarterly settlement payments with the floating-rate side of the agreement pegged to three-month LIBOR denominated in U.S. dollars. At the origination of the swap, the value of the S&P 500 index was 463.11 and three-month LIBOR was 3.50 percent. The notional principal of the swap is set for the life of the agreement at $50 million, which matches the amount of debt holdings in the fund that she would like to convert to equity.

   a. Calculate the net cash receipt or payment—from the fund manager's perspective—on each future settlement date, assuming the value for the S&P 500 index (with all dividends reinvested) and LIBOR are as follows:

Settlement Date	Number of Days	S&P Level	LIBOR Level
December 2 (initial year)	—	463.11	3.50%
March 2 (following year)	90	477.51	3.25
June 2	92	464.74	3.75
September 2	92	480.86	4.00
December 2	91	482.59	—.

    b. Explain why the fund manager might want the notional principal on this swap to vary over time and what the most logical pattern for this variation would be.

6. You are considering the purchase of a convertible bond issued by Bildon Enterprises, a non-investment-grade medical service firm. The issue has seven years to maturity and pays a semiannual coupon rate of 7.625 percent (i.e., 3.8125 percent per period). The issue is callable by the company at par and can be converted into 48.852 shares of Bildon common stock. The bond currently sells for $965 (relative to par value of $1,000), and Bildon stock trades at $12.125 a share.

    a. Calculate the current conversion value for the bond. Is the conversion option embedded in this bond in the money or out of the money? Explain.

    b. Calculate the conversion parity price for Bildon stock that would make conversion of the bond profitable.

    c. Bildon does not currently pay its shareholders a dividend, having suspended these distributions six months ago. What is the payback (i.e., breakeven time) for this convertible security and how should it be interpreted?

    d. Calculate the convertible's current yield to maturity. If a "straight" Bildon fixed-income issue with the same cash flows would yield 9.25 percent, calculate the net value of the combined options (i.e., the issuer's call and the investor's conversion) embedded in the bond.

 7. **CFA EXAMINATION LEVEL II** Rajiv Singh, a bond analyst, is analyzing a convertible bond. The characteristics of the bond and the underlying common stock follow.

CONVERTIBLE BOND AND UNDERLYING STOCK CHARACTERISTICS

Convertible Bond Characteristics

Par Value	$1,000
Annual coupon rate (annual pay)	6.5%
Conversion ratio	22
Market price	105% of par value
Straight value	99% of par share

Underlying Stock Characteristics

Current market price	$40 per share
Annual cash dividend	$1.20 per share

    a. Compute the bond's

       (1) Conversion value

       (2) Market conversion price

       (3) Premium payback period

    b. Determine whether the value of a callable convertible bond will increase, decrease, or remain unchanged in response to each of the following changes, and justify each of your responses with one reason:

       (1) An increase in stock price volatility

       (2) An increase in interest rate volatility

8. On May 26, 1991, Svensk Exportkredit (SEK), the Swedish export credit corporation, issued a Bull Indexed Silver Opportunity Note (BISON). Consider an extended version of this BISON issue that has the following terms:

Maturity	May 26, 1993
Coupon	6.50%, paid annually in arrears
Face value	USD 30 million
Purchase price	100,125% of par value

Additionally, this BISON includes a redemption feature that, for each USD 1,000 of face value held at maturity, repays the investor's principal according to the following formula:

$$USD\ 1,000 + [(Spot\ Silver\ Price\ per\ Ounce - USD\ 4.46) \times (USD\ 224.21525)]$$

a. Demonstrate that, from SEK's perspective, the BISON represents a combination of a straight debt issue priced at a small premium and a derivative contract. Be explicit as to the type of derivative contract and the underlying asset on which it is based. What implicit speculative position are the investors who buy these bonds taking?

b. Calculate the yield to maturity for an investor holding USD 10,000 in face value of these BISON if the May 1993 spot price for silver is (1) USD 4.96 per ounce, or (2) USD 3.96 per ounce.

c. In May 1991 (i.e., when the BISON were used), the prevailing delivery price on a two-year silver futures contract was USD 4.35 per ounce. If SEK wanted to hedge its BISON-related exposure to silver prices with an offsetting futures position at this price, what type of position would need to be entered? Ignoring margin accounts and underwriting fees, calculate SEK's average annualized borrowing cost of funds for the resulting synthetic straight bond.

9. In July 1986, Guinness Finance B.V. placed a three-year, $100 million Eurobond issue known as *Stock Performance Exchange Linked* (SPEL) bonds. The concept of the SPEL is that the bond has its principal redemption amount tied to the level of the NYSE composite index at maturity (i.e., NY_3) by the following formula:

$$Variable\ Redemption\ Amount = \max \{100, 100 \times (1 + [(NY_3 - 166) \div 166])\}$$

Notice that the investor is guaranteed redemption at par as a minimum. The bond also pays an annual coupon of 3 percent, which is 0.5 percent below the average annual dividend yield of shares on the NYSE. At the time the SPEL was launched, the NYSE composite index stood at 134.

a. Demonstrate that the SPEL is a combination of a regular debt issue and an equity option by analyzing the pattern of annual cash flows generated by the issue. In your work, assume a par value of 100.

b. The SPEL bonds were issued at a price of 100.625. Assuming that Guinness would ordinarily have to pay a borrowing cost of 7.65 percent on a three-year "straight" bond (i.e., one with no attached options), calculate the implicit dollar price of the equity index option embedded in this issue. How much of this amount represents intrinsic value and how much is time premium?

10. A firm has 100,000 shares of stock outstanding priced at $35 per share. The firm has no debt and does not pay a dividend. To raise more capital, it plans to issue 10,000 warrants, each allowing for the purchase of one share of stock at a price of $50. The warrants are European-style and expire in five years. The standard deviation of the firm's common stock is 34 percent and the continuously compounded, five-year risk-free rate is 5.2 percent.

a. Estimate the fair value of the warrants, first using the relevant information to calculate the Black-Scholes value of an analogous call option.

b. Determine the stock price at expiration, assuming the warrants are exercised if the value of the firm is at least $5,200,000.

c. Using the information in Parts a and b about initial and terminal warrant and stock prices, discuss the relative merits of these two ways of making an equity investment in the firm.

11. You are an investor trying to value a gold mining company's lease on a gold mine that is currently not operating. It would cost $1,000,000 for the company to reopen the mine, and it is expected to produce 100,000 ounces of gold at the end of next year. The forward contract price on a one-year gold forward contract is $268.40/ounce and the current one-year risk-free rate is 5 percent. Extraction costs are estimated to be $260/ounce.

a. Assuming the per-ounce gold price in the spot market one year from now is forecasted to be either $300 or $230, calculate (1) the composition of a portfolio of T-bills and gold forward contracts that would replicate the cash flows from the mine and (2) the "real options" value of the mine lease.

b. Assuming the per-ounce gold price in the spot market one year from now is forecasted to be either $280 or $250, calculate (1) the composition of a portfolio of T-bills and gold forward contracts that would replicate the cash flows from the mine, and (2) the real options value of the mine lease.

c. What do your answers in Parts a and b tell you about the effect that the volatility of future gold prices has on the current value of the mine lease?

PART 7
Specification and Evaluation of Asset Management

CHAPTER 24
Professional Money Management, Alternative Assets, and Industry Ethics

CHAPTER 25
Evaluation of Portfolio Performance

This final section of the book contains two chapters: the first deals with professional asset management, and the second is concerned with the evaluation of portfolio performance. The discussions of both of these topics are designed to address the needs of individual and institutional investors alike; both individual and institutional investors periodically need the services of a professional money manager and both types of investors also need to be aware of how one evaluates the performance of a portfolio.

Because many investors employ professional asset managers to manage their assets, Chapter 24 is an important wrap-up to their asset allocation and portfolio construction process. After a broad overview of the different ways that professional asset management firms can be organized, the chapter describes how the asset management industry has changed over time and how professional managers are compensated for their expertise. Particular emphasis is paid to the role of *investment companies* (also more commonly called mutual funds), which manage the majority of assets held by individual investors. The discussion includes a description of the major forms of investment companies and the general types of funds available, such as money market, growth, aggressive growth, income, balanced, and bond funds. It is argued that almost any investment objective can be met by investing in one or several investment companies. The chapter also provides a detailed examination of how *alternative asset* investments—hedge funds and private equity—are structured and managed. These investments are among the fastest showing segments of the money management industry.

We conclude Chapter 24 with a discussion of ethical and regulatory issues that arise when hiring a professional asset manager. We argue that most of these issues arise from the classical *principal-agent problem* that defines many economic relationships. After first examining the myriad regulations that govern the behavior of professional portfolio managers, we then describe the set of standards that the industry has adopted voluntarily in an effort to foster an atmosphere of trust and responsibility. The chapter ends with several examples of ethical conflicts that can arise when investors employ professional money managers. Two issues that are of special concern are designing compensation contracts to provide managers with the proper incentives to act in the investor's best interest and the proper use of trading commission fees.

We conclude the book with Chapter 25, which deals with the evaluation of portfolio performance. Perhaps the most important concept to understand from this discussion is that any meaningful evaluation of an investment manager's performance must consider both the return and the riskiness of the portfolio. Thus, after a discussion of what is required of a portfolio manager, we review in detail the major *risk-adjusted* portfolio performance models including a recent performance attribution model that, in turn, is capable of evaluating a global portfolio that necessarily includes the effect of currency allocation. We also consider how the alternative models relate to each other. This is followed by a demonstration of their use with a sample of mutual funds.

As always, it is important to understand potential problems with a technique or model. Therefore, we discuss *holdings-based* measures, which evaluate a manager's performance by examining the contents of the portfolio rather than relying on a statistical model to measure expected returns (e.g., CAPM). We also consider potential problems with the traditional performance measures including a review of Roll's benchmark problem and its effect on these performance models. It is demonstrated that this benchmark problem has become more significant with the growth of global investing. Also, because the factors that determine success in bonds differ from what is important in equities, we review alternative models used to evaluate the performance of bond portfolio managers. The chapter finishes with a consideration of how investment performance results should be presented so as to be consistent with industry practice.

CHAPTER 24

Professional Money Management, Alternative Assets, and Industry Ethics

After you read this chapter, you should be able to answer the following questions:

- What are the different ways that professional money management firms can be organized and how has the structure of the industry changed over time?
- Who manages the portfolios at investment advisory firms and investment companies and how are those managers compensated?
- How do you compute the net asset value (NAV) for investment companies?
- What is the difference between closed-end and open-end investment companies?
- What are load fees, 12b-1 fees, and management fees and how do they influence investment company performance?
- How are funds classified by investment objective and which groups have experienced relative growth or decline?
- What are hedge funds and how do they differ from other professionally managed investment products?
- What investment strategies do hedge funds employ and what has been the performance of those fund types over time?
- What attributes do private equity investments possess that make them a unique asset class?
- How do venture capital and buyout-oriented private equity investments differ from one another and what has been their historical performance?
- What are some of the ethical dilemmas involved in the professional money management industry?
- What functions should investors expect professional asset managers to perform for them?

So far, we have discussed how investors can analyze the aggregate market, different industry sectors, and individual companies when deciding upon which stocks and bonds to include in their investment portfolios. We have also considered how those portfolio positions can be augmented with various derivative positions in order to create additional risk–return possibilities. This chapter introduces another possibility to the investor: entrusting one's money to a professional portfolio manager. Using a professional money manager can entail establishing a private account with an investment advisor, purchasing shares of an established security portfolio managed by an investment company, or becoming a limited partner in an organization managed by a general partner. In any form, professionally managed investments often represent a substantial portion of an individual's total holdings.

Both individual and institutional (e.g., corporate pension plans, university endowments) investors alike seek the services of professional money managers for several reasons. First and foremost, it is often presumed that these managers may possess superior investment skills that will lead to higher returns than investors could obtain on their own. Beyond that, there are a number of additional benefits professional managers supply, such as offering access to asset classes and investment strategies that might otherwise be unavailable or providing a cost-effective way to choose among a wide variety of diversified portfolios spanning the risk–return spectrum. However, these relationships also create potential conflicts of interest between the goals of the investor and those of the manager that need to be considered.

After explaining the various ways in which asset management firms are typically organized and charge for their services, we explore three different types of professional money management firms: traditional private management firms, investment (i.e., fund) companies, and "alternative asset" companies (i.e., hedge funds, private equity firms) created through limited partnership vehicles. We pay particular attention to the contrast between investment companies, which are the most prevalent way in which investors employ professional counsel, and alternative asset vehicles, which represent the most rapidly growing segment of the industry. We conclude with a description of the legal and regulatory environment that governs professional investors, as well as some of the ethical implications of the investor-manager relationship.

24.1 The Asset Management Industry: Structure and Evolution

There are two basic ways that traditional professional asset management firms are organized. In the most straightforward structure, individuals as well as institutional investors make contracts directly with a **management and advisory firm** for its services. These services can range from providing standard banking transactions (savings accounts, personal loans) to advising clients on structuring their own portfolios to actually managing the investment funds themselves. Although banking and financial advice were once the main services these firms offered, there has recently been a dramatic shift toward the *assets under management* (AUM) approach. In that arrangement, the management firm becomes the custodian of the investor's capital, usually with full discretion as to how those funds are invested. An important feature of this structure is that each client of the management firm has a *separate account.* Even if investors select the firm because of its expertise in a particular niche—say, selecting small-cap growth stocks—the assets of each client will be accounted for separately regardless of whether the firm employs a single "model" portfolio. This situation is illustrated in Panel A of Exhibit 24.1.

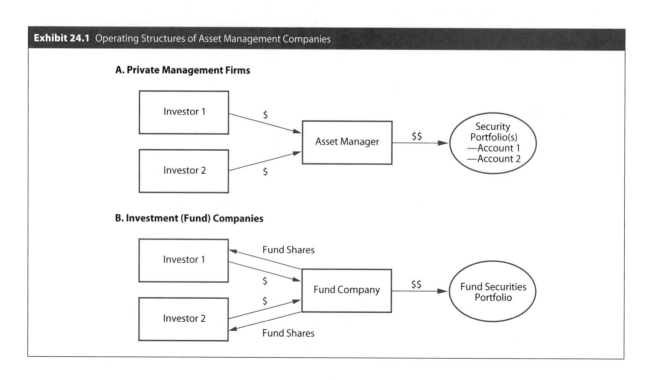

Exhibit 24.1 Operating Structures of Asset Management Companies

A second general approach to asset management involves the *commingling* of investment capital from several clients. An **investment company** invests a pool of funds belonging to many individuals in a single portfolio of securities. In exchange for this capital, the investment company issues to each investor new shares representing his or her proportional ownership of the mutually held securities portfolio, which is commonly known as a *fund.* For example, assume an investment company sells 10 million shares to the public at $10 a share, thereby raising $100 million. If the fund's purpose is to emphasize large-cap common stocks, the manager would invest the proceeds of the fund share sale ($100 million less any brokerage fees) in the stock of such companies as Merck, IBM, Xerox, and General Electric. Each investor who bought shares of the investment company would then own the appropriate percentage of the overall fund, rather than any portion of the shares in the portfolio themselves. Panel B of Exhibit 24.1 shows how this structure might work.

There are important differences between these two organizational forms. Private management and advisory firms typically develop a personal relationship with their clients, getting to know the specific investment objectives and constraints of each. The collection of assets held in the various separate accounts can then be tailored to these special needs, even if a general blueprint portfolio is used for all clients. Of course, special attention comes at a cost, and for this reason private management firms are used mainly by investors with substantial levels of capital, such as pension fund sponsors and high net worth individuals. Conversely, a mutual fund offered by an investment company is formed as a general solution to an investment problem and then marketed to investors who might fit that profile. The primary clients who seek professional asset management through investment companies are individual investors with relatively small pools of capital. The Investment Company Institute (a nonprofit industry trade association) reported that in 2006, 87 percent of mutual fund shares were held by households, with only 13 percent being held by business organizations.[1]

It is not unusual for professional asset management firms to combine these two structures by offering private advisory services as well as publicly traded funds. For instance, consider T. Rowe Price Associates, a multi-asset, independent advisory firm located in Baltimore, Maryland. Founded in 1937, T. Rowe Price has seen its business grow to the point where it managed almost $335 billion by the end of 2006, compared with less than $54 billion AUM just 12 years earlier. The majority of this capital is invested in the firm's various public mutual fund port-folios, but T. Rowe Price also has several hundred private clients, including corporate retirement funds, public funds and unions, foundations and endowments, and individual investors.[2]

The AUM growth that T. Rowe Price has experienced during the past few years has been typical for the entire industry. Exhibit 24.2 charts the top 50 asset management companies as of the end of 1994 and 2006. A striking feature of these lists is the rapid increase in the number of large asset management firms, defined as those organizations with AUM of more than $100 billion. In 1994, there were only 10 such firms; by 2006, there were 74, including all 50 listed on the left side of Exhibit 24.2. Much of this asset growth can be explained by the strong performance of global equity markets during this period, but another important contributing factor was the consolidation trend that marked the industry. Typical of this phenomenon was the merger of the asset management groups Union Bank of Switzerland and Brinson Partners (ranked 36th and 39th on the 1994 list, respectively) to become UBS Global Asset Management (ranked 13th on the 2006 list). This consolidation trend is likely to continue, because the competition among existing asset management firms for the flow of new investment capital is expected to increase significantly.[3]

---

[1] See Chapter 6 of 2007 *Investment Company Fact Book* (Washington, DC: Investment Company Institute).

[2] This, and much more, information is available from T. Rowe Price's public home page at http://www.troweprice.com.

[3] Good economic analysis of the professional asset management business can be found in Hurley et al. (1995) and Brinson (2005).

Exhibit 24.2 Asset Under Management (AUM) for Leading Firms

	December 31, 2006		December 31, 1994	
Rank	Firm	AUM ($MM)	Firm	AUM ($MM)
1	Barclays Global	1,813,820	Fidelity Management & Research	314,543
2	State Street Global	1,746,920	Bankers Trust Company	186,797
3	Fidelity Investments	1,635,128	Merrill Lynch Asset Management Group	163,822
4	Vanguard Group	1,167,414	Capital Group	162,634
5	BlackRock	1,124,627	Wells Fargo/BMZ	158,392
6	Capital Research	1,081,486	State Street Global Advisors	140,413
7	JPMorgan Asset Management	1,007,523	Alliance Capital Management	121,290
8	Mellon Financial	995,237	Franklin/Templeton Group	114,100
9	Legg Mason	957,558	J.P. Morgan Investment Management	111,983
10	AIG Global Investment	730,921	American Express Financial/IDS	102,128
11	AllianceBernstein Inst'l	716,895	Putnam Investments	95,182
12	Deutsche Asset Management	715,880	INVESCO	94,066
13	UBS Global Asset Management	702,879	Scudder Stevens & Clark	91,253
14	Northern Trust Global	697,166	The Northern Trust Company	82,353
15	Goldman Sachs Group	693,049	Wellington Management Company	81,970
16	PIMCO	667,776	The Vanguard Group	81,743
17	Prudential Financial	616,047	Citibank Global Asset Management	73,999
18	Morgan Stanley	606,476	Pacific Investment Management Company (PIMCO)	72,175
19	Wellington Mgmt.	575,492	Smith Barney Capital	69,114
20	Franklin Templeton	552,905	Kemper Financial Services	62,748
21	Credit Suisse Asset Management	548,700	Dreyfus Corp.	62,055
22	MetLife	527,700	New England Investment Cos.	56,609
23	ING	490,847	PNC Asset Management Group	56,422
24	Columbia Management	433,426	T. Rowe Price Associates	53,705
25	TIAA-CREF	405,647	Dean Witter InterCapital	51,197
26	BNP Paribas Asset	391,091	Federated Investors	50,743
27	MassMutual Financial	366,105	Van Kampen American Capital	46,699
28	T. Rowe Price	334,698	John Nuveen Co.	46,497
29	Pioneer Investment	294,357	Chase Manhattan Corp.	44,839
30	Hartford Financial	291,876	Bank of New York	42,599
31	RiverSource Investments	289,381	TCW Group	41,981
32	Evergreen Investments	273,215	SunTrust Banks	41,811
33	INVESCO	257,350	Chemical Bank Portfolio Group	41,725
34	Schroder Investment	251,542	Bank of America Investment Mgmt Services	41,328
35	ABN AMRO Asset Management	251,184	NationsBank	40,771
36	Federated Investors	236,817	Union Bank of Switzerland	38,685
37	Lehman Brothers Holdings	228,775	GE Investments	38,230
38	New York Life Inv. Management	223,647	Goldman Sachs Asset Management	37,400
39	MFC Global Investment	215,942	Brinson Partners	36,540
40	Dodge & Cox	212,313	Boatmen's Trust Co.	36,420
41	Nomura Asset Management	203,619	Morgan Stanley Asset Management	35,678
42	Principal Global Investors	201,361	National Bank of Detroit	35,590
43	GE Asset Management	196,477	Mitchell Hutchins Asset Management	34,394
44	Russell Investment Group	195,400	Harris Bankcorp.	33,827
45	Putnam Investments	192,075	Massachusetts Financial Services	33,432
46	Charles Schwab Investment	190,484	U.S. Trust Company of New York	33,032
47	Wells Capital	189,110	Mellon Capital Management	31,910
48	MFS Investment	187,150	Banc One Investment Corp.	31,537
49	SEI Investments	181,500	HSBC Asset Management	30,488
50	General Motors Asset Management	170,501	Fiduciary Trust Co. Int'l	29,903

Source: *Pensions & Investments* and Goldman, Sachs.

24.2 Private Management and Advisory Firms

While larger management companies offer a broader range of services and products, the majority of private management and advisory firms are still much smaller and more narrowly focused on a particular niche of the market. To examine one typical organization in greater detail, consider Prudent Capital Management (PCM),[4] a growth-oriented equity and fixed-income manager located in Southern California. PCM utilizes a "bottom-up" security selection process, with its portfolio managers looking for companies that have exceptional profitability, market share, return on equity, and earnings growth. PCM's clients include both institutional investors and high-net-worth individuals (with between $2 million and $5 million in assets) in both separate and commingled accounts. The firm offers management of both taxed and nontaxed products. Exhibit 24.3 shows the myriad investment products that PCM offers, along with the minimum investment accepted in each.

Like the industry as a whole, PCM saw the assets under its management increase steadily over the past several years. Panel A of Exhibit 24.4 reports that over a recent five-year period, the firm's AUM grew by almost 80 percent, from $11.8 billion to $21.2 billion. During the same period, the median separate account size jumped from $24.8 million to over $39 million. This suggests that PCM's clients tend to be institutional investors, and the client profile summarized in Panel B of Exhibit 24.4 confirms this. The company offers services to more than 350 clients, but the majority of these are—and the vast majority of the assets come from—institutional investors. Perhaps because of the minimum investment restrictions, relatively few of the clients are individual investors and the assets they represent are slightly less than 3 percent (535 ÷ 21,165) of PCM's business.

Panel C of Exhibit 24.4 shows fee schedules representative of both the equity and fixed-income management services that PCM offers. Typical of the entire industry, these fees are not flat amounts but are expressed as percentages of invested capital on an annual basis. They are

Exhibit 24.3 Representative Private Management Firm Investment Products

	Large-Cap	Mid-Cap	Small-Cap
Equity:	$5 million	$5 million	
	$2 million	$5 million	$10 million
	Commingled fund (Delaware Business Trust)	Commingled fund (Delaware Business Trust)	Commingled fund (closed)
	$2 million for sponsored program affiliates	$2 million for sponsored program affiliates	
Balanced:	$5 million		
	$2 million for sponsored program affiliates		
Concentrated:	$5 million		
	$2 million for sponsored program affiliates		
Tax-Sensitive Management:	$5 million Equity, balanced, fixed		
	$2 million for sponsored program affiliates		
Concentrated:	$5 million		
Tax-Sensitive Management:	$2 million for sponsored program affiliates		
Active Fixed Income:	$5 million Separately managed		
	$2 million for sponsored program affiliates		

[4] Prudent Capital Management is a pseudonym for a real firm whose name has been changed by request. However, all of the subsequent information reported is real.

Exhibit 24.4 Representative Private Management Firm: AUM, Clients, and Fees

A. AUM

Date	Assets Managed ($ Mil.)	No. of Institutional Clients	ACCOUNT SIZE	
			Average ($ Mil.)	Median ($ Mil.)
Year 5	21,165.0	207	97.5	39.3
Year 4	18,441.0	206	85.1	34.9
Year 3	17,608.0	226	74.2	30.6
Year 2	17,808.0	233	72.3	30.4
Year 1	14,578.0	237	61.5	27.8
Year 0	11,833.0	230	51.4	24.8

B. Clients

	No. of Clients	Assets ($ Mil.)
Corporate retirement funds	126	7,937.0
Public funds	35	3,881.0
Unions (Taft-Hartley)	18	1,442.0
Foundations, endowments, associations	66	1,656.0
Commingled funds	4	1,682.0
General insurance accounts	N/A	N/A
Limited partnership	N/A	N/A
Mutual funds	18	3,411.0
Individuals: IRAs and other	75	535.0
Other	5	186.0
Taxable corporate	17	435.0

C. Fee Schedule

Large-Cap Growth Equity Accounts	Fixed-Income Accounts
• 1.00% on the first $10,000,000 • 0.75% on the next $10,000,000 • 0.50% above $20,000,000	• 0.375% on the first $25,000,000 • 0.30% over $25,000,000

Source: Data adapted from *Nelson's Directory of Investment Managers.*

also graduated on a declining scale so that the more capital an investor commits to the firm, the lower his or her average cost would be. An individual with $15 million would pay annual fees of $137,500 (10,000,000 × 0.01 + 5,000,000 × 0.0075), or 0.92 percent of total invested capital. On the other hand, the fee paid by a pension fund with $115 million under management would be $650,000 (10,000,000 × 0.01 + 10,000,000 × 0.0075 + 95,000,000 × 0.005), or 0.57 percent. One advantage to the investor of having the fee schedule tied directly to AUM is that, as the management firm performs better for the client, its fees will increase. This reward system helps to align the incentives of the investor and the manager.

24.2.1 Investment Strategy at a Private Money Management Firm

The representation of a private money management firm shown in Panel A of Exhibit 24.1 indicated that each client's assets were held in a separate account. It was also noted that the security portfolios formed for each client are likely to be guided by the firm's overall investment philosophy. It is this investment philosophy—along with the returns it produces—that attracts clients to a particular money manager in the first place. Exhibit 24.5 reproduces the investment strategy and major holdings for two of PCM's model portfolios, one in equities and one in fixed-income securities.

The investment approach expressed in Panel A of Exhibit 24.5 makes it clear that clients choosing to invest in PCM's large-cap growth stock product will have their money invested

---

Exhibit 24.5 Investment Strategy at a Representative Private Management Firm

A. Large-Cap Growth Equity Portfolio

Investment Approach:

Our focused, fundamental research process is primarily based on the ideas from our in-house analysts. Our analysts operate as specialists. They direct their expertise on specific industries and sectors covering seven key growth sectors: technology/ components, technology/systems, telecom, healthcare, retail, consumer, and finance.

Our investment process seeks out companies that have at least one or more catalysts for growth. The catalysts may be identified as: new products, exploitation of demographic trends, proprietary products, gaining market share, and/or changing cost structure, in order to attain or maintain very strong earnings per share growth.

We search for companies that have: significant management ownership, well-thought-out management goals and growth plans supported by stringent controls, and a commitment to enhancing shareholder value. We also seek out companies with a proven track record (at least three to five years) of superior revenue and earnings growth, strong pretax margins, low levels of debt, exceptional profitability, market share, high return on equity, high reinvestment rates, and attractive valuations relative to their industry and the market in general.

Largest Holdings:
1. Microsoft
2. Nokia
3. Cisco Systems
4. Qualcomm
5. Genentech
6. Motorola
7. Sun Microsystems
8. EMC
9. Amgen
10. Flextronics

Benchmark Used: Russell 1000 Growth index

B. Active Fixed Income

Investment Approach:
We believe that superior risk-adjusted returns can be achieved by capturing changes in relative value through active yield curve management, sector rotation and prudent security selection. We follow a disciplined process designed to add incremental value over long periods of time by taking advantage of relative value opportunities without accepting excessive interest rate risk. Our process is not dependent on forecasts of future interest rates or economic events. Rather our decisions are based on current conditions, analyzed in the context of historical relationships. Our performance record has been built employing this process. We expect that in the future market conditions will offer similar opportunities. While markets will change our process will not.

Largest Holdings:
1. A–Baa rated corporates (56.9%)
2. Treasury/agencies (33.6%)
3. Aaa–Aa rated corporates (9.5%)

Benchmark Used: Lehman Government/Corporate index

Source: Data adapted from *Nelson's Directory of Investment Managers.*

primarily in technology companies. While the specific stock allocations might vary from one client to another, the same fundamental orientation toward stock selection will be applied to all accounts. Similarly, a client choosing to invest in PCM's core fixed-income product will end up holding a portfolio of bonds split between government and investment-grade corporate names. The stated investment process at PCM requires extensive interaction between the firm's portfolio managers and security analysts. At the time in question, PCM employed 11 equity portfolio managers, 10 equity analysts, 3 equity traders, and 6 additional manager/analysts.

24.3 Organization and Management of Investment Companies

An investment company typically is a corporation that has as its major assets the portfolio of marketable securities referred to as a fund. The management of the portfolio of securities and most of the other administrative duties are handled by a separate **investment management company** hired by the board of directors of the investment company. This legal description oversimplifies the typical arrangement. The actual management usually begins with an investment advisory firm that starts an investment company and selects a board of directors for the fund. Subsequently, this board of directors hires the investment advisory firm as the fund's portfolio manager.

The contract between the investment company (the portfolio of securities) and the investment management company details the duties and compensation of the management company. The major duties of the investment management company include investment research, the management of the portfolio, and administrative duties, such as issuing securities and handling redemptions and dividends. The management fee is generally stated as a percentage of the total value of the fund and typically ranges from ¼ to ½ of 1 percent, with a sliding scale as the size of the fund increases.

To achieve economies of scale, many management companies launch numerous funds with different characteristics. The variety of funds allows the management group to appeal to many investors with different risk–return preferences. In addition, it allows investors to switch among funds as economic or personal conditions change. This "family of funds" promotes flexibility and increases the total capital managed by the investment firm.

24.3.1 Valuing Investment Company Shares

When clients have their invested capital held in separate accounts, the value of any given account can be calculated by simply totaling the market value of the securities held in the portfolio, less fees. When the securities are held jointly, as they are in an investment company, the appropriate way to value a client's investment is to multiply the number of shares in the fund owned by the per-share value of the entire security fund. This per-share value is known as the **net asset value (NAV)** of the investment company. It equals the total market value of all the firm's assets divided by the total number of fund shares outstanding, or

$$\text{Fund NAV} = \frac{(\text{Total Market Value of Fund Portfolio}) - (\text{Fund Expenses})}{(\text{Total Fund Shares Outstanding})}$$

The NAV for an investment company is analogous to the share price of a corporation's common stock; like common stock, the NAV of the fund shares will increase as the value of the underlying assets (the fund security portfolio) increases.

In an earlier example, we saw that an investment company with a $100 million large-cap stock portfolio and 10 million outstanding shares would have an NAV of $10. What would happen if during a holding period the value of the stock portfolio increased to $112.5 million while the fund incurred $0.1 million in trading expenses and management fees? If no new shares were sold during the period, the net value of the total investment company is $112.4 million, which leaves a net asset value for each existing fund share of $11.24 ([112,500,000 − 100,000] ÷ 10,000,000). Thus, the NAV provides an immediate reflection of the investment company's market value net of operating expenses. Had the investment company made any capital gain or dividend distributions to its investors, these too would be reflected in the NAV calculation because they would reduce the value of the fund portfolio. For publicly traded funds, NAVs are calculated and reported on a daily basis.

24.3.2 Closed-End Versus Open-End Investment Companies

Investment companies begin like any other company by selling common stock to a group of investors. However, it uses the proceeds to purchase the securities of other publicly held companies rather than buildings and equipment. An open-end investment company (often referred to as a **mutual fund**) differs from a closed-end investment company (typically referred to as a *closed-end fund*) in the way each operates *after* the initial public offering.

A **closed-end investment company** functions like any other public firm. Its stock trades on the regular secondary market, and the market price of its shares is determined by supply and demand conditions. Thus, if you want to buy or sell shares in a closed-end fund, you must make transactions in the market where its shares are listed (e.g., NYSE, AMEX). No new investment dollars are available for the investment company unless it makes another public sale of securities. Similarly, no funds can be withdrawn unless the investment company decides to repurchase its stock, which is quite unusual. Exihibit 24.6 lists the number of closed-end funds

Exhibit 24.6 Closed-End Funds: Categories and AUM

STATISTIC			VALUE
Total Number of Closed-End Funds:			701
Total Assets:			$286,070.7

ASSETS BY CLASSIFICATION

Classifications	Code	Funds	Assets
CA Ins Muni Debt Funds	FLX	13	$2,574.4
CA Muni Debt Funds	GIM	24	5,167.3
Convertible Sec Funds	GB	12	6,330.7
Core Funds	GML	27	14,271.3
Corp Debt BBB Rated Fds	GUS	15	5,441.6
Emerging Markets Funds	GL	8	6,165.3
Emerging Mkts Debt Funds	GLI	12	5,037.3
FL Muni Debt Funds	GE	15	2,193.7
Flexible Income Funds	HM	7	3,977.3
Gen & Ins Unleveraged	HYL	9	3,181.9
General Bond Funds	HY	13	3,307.4
General Muni Leveraged	PS	54	22,352.2
General US Govt Funds	MIL	6	4,060.5
Global Funds	IMD	24	20,226.3
Global Income Funds	LT	15	6,742.3
Growth Funds	LP	8	1,236.6
Hi Yld Muni Debt Funds	MI	15	3,136.8
High Yield Fds Leveraged	SF	40	12,303.8
High Yield Funds	NJ	6	1,153.9
Income & Pref Stock Fds	NYI	32	20,436.1
Insured Muni Leveraged	NY	23	9,370.2
Intmdt Muni Debt Funds	OS	8	1,456.4
Latin American Funds	OTH	6	2,160.0
Loan Participation Funds	PA	46	27,042.1
MI Muni Debt Funds	XJ	7	818.4
Misc Country/Region Fds	PC	7	1,304.3
NJ Muni Debt Funds	RE	13	1,687.8
NY Ins Muni Debt Funds	SE	12	2,796.9
NY Muni Debt Funds	USM	17	1,894.5
Opt Arbitrage/Opt Strat	VE	33	24,047.1
Other States Muni Debt	WE	46	2,776.6
PA Muni Debt Funds	FLX	9	1,227.6
Pacific Ex Japan Funds	GIM	16	7,529.9
Pacific Region Funds	GB	5	3,337.2
Real Estate Funds	GML	29	14,706.9
Sector Equity Funds	GUS	39	16,648.8
US Mortgage Funds	GL	11	1,756.4
Value Funds	GLI	14	14,548.5
Western European Funds	GE	5	1,664.4

Assets are net assets after deductions of all operating costs, expressed in $ millions.

Source: Closed-End Fund Association, November 29, 2007. Reprinted with permission.

traded on U.S. exchanges, broken down by investment objective and category AUM. More than 700 funds are represented in over three dozen categories, including general domestic equity and bond funds, global equity funds, loan participation funds, flexible income funds, national municipal bond funds, and single state municipal bond funds.

The closed-end investment company's NAV is computed throughout the day based on prevailing market prices for the portfolio securities, but the *market price* of the shares is determined by how they trade on the exchange. When buying or selling shares of a closed-end fund, investors pay or receive this market price plus or minus a regular trading commission. Recognize that *the NAV and the market price of a closed-end fund are almost never the same!* Over the long run, the market price of these shares has historically been from 5 to 20 percent below the NAV (i.e., closed-end funds typically sell at a discount to NAV).

This relationship has prompted questions from investors: Why do these funds sell at a discount? Why do the discounts differ between funds? What are the returns available to investors from funds that sell at large discounts? This final question arises because an investor who acquires a portfolio at a price below market value (i.e., below NAV) expects an above-average dividend yield. Still, the total rate of return on the fund depends on what happens to the discount during the holding period. If the discount relative to the NAV declines, the investment should generate positive excess returns. If the discount increases, the investor will likely experience negative excess returns. The analysis of these discounts remains a major question of modern finance.[5]

The interest in closed-end funds has led Thomas J. Herzfeld Advisors, a firm that specializes in closed-end funds, to create an index that tracks the market price performance of a sample of U.S. closed-end funds that invest principally in U.S. equities. The price-weighted series is based on fund market values rather than on NAVs. In addition to its market price index, Herzfeld also computes the average discount from NAV. The lower right-hand graph in Exhibit 24.7 indicates that the average discount from NAV changes over time and has a major impact on the market performance of the index. For example, during 2006–2007, this value changed from a discount of 4 percent to a premium of about 5 percent. Despite this, the performance of the Herzfeld closed-end average at the end of this period was ahead of the DJIA.

Open-end investment companies, or mutual funds, continue to sell and repurchase shares after their initial public offerings. They stand ready to sell additional shares of the fund at the NAV, with or without sales charge, or to buy back (redeem) shares of the fund at the NAV, with or without redemption fees.

Open-end investment companies have enjoyed substantial growth since World War II, as shown by the figures in Exhibit 24.8. Clearly, open-end funds account for a substantial portion of invested assets, and they provide a very important service for almost 300 million accounts.

Exhibit 24.7   Closed-End Funds: Discount/Premium to NAV

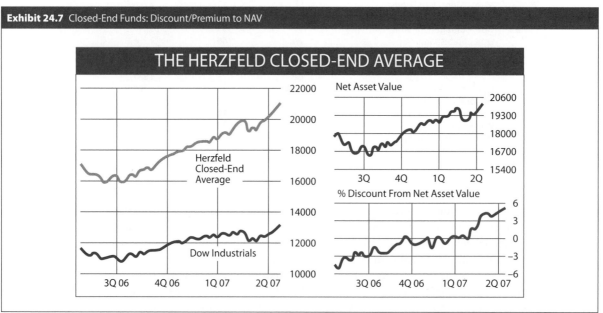

Source: *Investor's Guide to Closed-End Funds*, May 2007, Thomas Herzfeld Advisors, Inc. Reprinted with permission.

[5] Studies over the years include research by Lee, Shleifer, and Thaler (1991); Barclay, Holderness, and Pontiff (1993); Klibanoff, Lamont, and Wizman (1998); and Berk and Stanton (2007).

Exhibit 24.8   Open-End Investment Companies: Number and Value of Assets: 1945–2006

	Number of Reporting Funds	Assets ($ Billions)		Number of Reporting Funds	Assets ($ Billions)
1945	73	1.3	1994	5,325	2,155.3
1950	98	2.5	1995	5,725	2,811.3
1955	125	7.8	1996	6,248	3,525.8
1960	161	17.0	1997	6,684	4,468.2
1965	170	35.2	1998	7,314	5,525.2
1970	361	47.6	1999	7,791	6,846.3
1975	426	45.6	2000	8,155	6,964.6
1980	564	134.8	2001	8,305	6,974.9
1985	1,528	495.4	2002	8,244	6,390.4
1990	3,079	1,065.2	2003	8,126	7,414.4
1991	3,403	1,393.2	2004	8,041	8,106.9
1992	3,824	1,642.5	2005	7,975	8,904.8
1993	4,534	2,070.0	2006	8,120	10,413.6

Note: Does not include money market and short-term bond funds.
Source: Adapted from data in Investment Company Institute, *2007 Investment Company Fact Book.*

Load Versus No-Load Open-End Funds   One distinction of open-end funds is that some charge a sales fee for share sales. The offering price for a share of a *load fund* equals the NAV of the share plus a sales charge, which can be as large as 7.5 to 8.0 percent of the NAV. A fund with an 8 percent sales charge (load) would give an individual who invested $1,000 in the fund shares that are worth only $920. Such funds generally charge no redemption fee, which means the shares can be redeemed at their NAV. These funds typically are quoted with an NAV and an offering price. The NAV price is the redemption (bid) price, and the offering (ask) price equals the NAV divided by 1.0 minus the percent load. For example, if the NAV of a fund with an 8 percent load is $8.50 a share, the offering price would be $9.24 ($8.50/0.92). The 74-cent differential is really 8.7 percent of the NAV. The load percentage typically declines with the size of the order.

A **no-load fund** imposes no initial sales charge so it sells shares at their NAV. Some of these funds charge a small redemption fee of about one-half of 1 percent. In the financial press, quotes for these no-load funds list bid prices as the NAV with the designation "NL" (no load) for the offering price—that is, the bid and offer are the same. The number of no-load funds has increased substantially in recent years. In fact, the Investment Company Institute noted that in 2003, the number of no-load equity funds exceeded the number of load funds for the first time.

Between the full-load fund and the pure no-load fund, several important variations exist. The first is the **low-load fund**, which imposes a front-end sales charge when the fund is bought, but it is typically in the 3 percent range rather than 7 to 8 percent. Generally, low-load funds are used for bond funds or equity funds offered by management companies that also offer no-load funds. For example, most Fidelity Investments funds were no load prior to 1985, but several of their newer funds have carried a low load of 3 percent. Alternatively, some funds—previously charging full loads—have reduced their loads.

The second major innovation is the **12b-1 plan**, named after a 1980 SEC ruling. This plan permits funds to deduct as much as 0.75 percent of average net assets *per year* to cover distribution costs, such as advertising, brokers' commissions, and general marketing expenses. A large and growing number of no-load funds are adopting these plans, as are a few low-load funds. You can determine if a fund has a 12b-1 plan by reading the prospectus or using an investment service that reports charges in substantial detail.

Finally, some funds have instituted **contingent, deferred sales loads** in which a sales fee is charged when the fund is sold if it is held for less than some time period, perhaps three or four years.

24.3.3 Fund Management Fees

In addition to selling charges (loads or 12b-1 charges), all investment firms charge annual **management fees** to compensate professional managers of the fund. Similar to the compensation structure for private management firms, such a fee typically is a percentage of the average net assets of the fund varying from about 0.25 to 1.00 percent. Most of these management fees are on sliding scales that decline with the size of the fund. A fund with assets under $1 billion might charge 1 percent, funds with assets between $1 billion and $5 billion might charge 0.50 percent, and those over $5 billion would charge 0.25 percent.

These management fees are a major factor driving the creation of new funds. More assets under management generate more fees, but the costs of management do not increase at the same rate as the managed assets because substantial economies of scale exist in managing financial assets. Once the research staff and management structure are established, the incremental costs do not rise in line with the assets under management. The cost of managing $1 billion of assets is *not* twice the cost of managing $500 million. Finally, one consequence of the industry consolidation we discussed earlier is that mutual fund fees have been declining. The Investment Company Institute reported that between 1980 and 2006, total shareholder costs to equity fund investors decreased by over 50 percent, from 2.32 to 1.07 percent of average fund AUM.

24.3.4 Investment Company Portfolio Objectives

A mutual fund can be created around any portfolio of assets. As a practical matter, however, mutual funds tend to exist for only the more liquid asset classes, such as stocks and bonds. There are four broad fund objective categories recognized by the Investment Company Institute: common stock funds, bond funds, hybrid funds, and money market funds. Each of these strategies is described briefly here, while Exhibit 24.9 provides a more detailed list of many of the more popular subcategories within these objective classes.

Equity funds invest almost exclusively in common stocks. Within that broad mission, however, substantial differences can be found, including funds that focus on specific industries (e.g., Chemical Fund, Oceanography Fund), collection of industries (e.g., Technology Fund), security characteristics (e.g., Growth Fund, Large-Cap Fund), or even geographic areas (e.g., Global Funds, Northeast Fund). With several thousand to choose from, any investor can almost certainly find an existing equity fund that matches his or her desired investment strategy. Thus, the important thing that an investor must do is to decide what that preferred strategy happens to be.

Bond funds concentrate on various types of bonds to generate high current income with minimal risk. They are similar to common stock funds; however, their investment policies differ. Some funds concentrate on U.S. government or high-grade corporate bonds, others hold a mixture of investment-grade bonds, and some concentrate on high-yield (junk) bonds. Management strategies also can differ, ranging from buy and hold to extensive trading of the portfolio bonds.

In addition to government, mortgage, and corporate bond funds, a change in the tax law in 1976 caused the creation of numerous municipal bond funds. These funds provide investors with monthly interest payments that are exempt from federal income taxes, although some of the interest may be subject to state and local taxes. To avoid the state tax, some municipal bond funds concentrate on bonds from specific states, such as the New York Municipal Bond Fund, which allows New York residents to avoid most state taxes on the interest income.

Balanced funds diversify outside a single market by combining common stock with fixed-income securities, including government bonds, corporate bonds, convertible bonds, or preferred stock. The ratio of stocks to fixed-income securities will vary by fund, as stated in each fund's prospectus. **Flexible portfolio** (or *asset allocation*) **funds** seek high total returns by investing in a mix of stocks, bonds, and money-market securities.

Money market funds were initiated during 1973 when short-term interest rates were at record levels. These funds attempt to provide current income, safety of principal, and liquidity by investing in diversified portfolios of short-term securities, such as Treasury bills, banker

Exhibit 24.9 Mutual Fund Objectives

Stock Funds

- **Aggressive growth funds** invest primarily in common stock of small, growth companies with potential for capital appreciation.
- **Emerging market equity funds** invest primarily in equity securities of companies based in less-developed regions of the world.
- **Global equity funds** invest primarily in worldwide equity securities, including those of U.S. companies.
- **Growth and income funds** attempt to combine long-term capital growth with steady income dividends. These funds pursue this goal by investing primarily in common stocks of established companies with the potential for both growth and good dividends.
- **Growth funds** invest primarily in common stocks of well-established companies with the potential for capital appreciation. These funds' primary aim is to increase the value of their investments (capital gain) rather than generate a flow of dividends.
- **Income equity funds** seek income by investing primarily in equity securities of companies with good dividends. Capital appreciation is not an objective.
- **International equity funds** invest at least 80 percent of their portfolios in equity securities of companies located outside the United States.
- **Regional equity funds** invest in equity securities of companies based in specific world regions, such as Europe, Latin America, the Pacific Region, or individual countries.
- **Sector equity funds** seek capital appreciation by investing in companies in related fields or specific industries, such as financial services, health care, natural resources, technology, or utilities.

Bond Funds

- **Corporate bond–general funds** seek a high level of income by investing 80 percent or more of their portfolios in corporate bonds and have no explicit restrictions on average maturity.
- **Corporate bond–intermediate-term-funds** seek a high level of income with 80 percent or more of their portfolios invested at all times in corporate bonds. Their average maturity is five to 10 years.
- **Corporate bond–short-term funds** seek a high level of current income with 80 percent or more of their portfolios invested at all times in corporate bonds. Their average maturity is one to five years.
- **Global bond–general funds** invest in worldwide debt securities and have no

stated average maturity or an average maturity of more than five years. Up to 25 percent of their portfolios' securities (not including cash) may be invested in companies located in the United States.

- **Global bond–short-term funds** invest in worldwide debt securities and have an average maturity of one to five years. Up to 25 percent of their portfolios' securities (not including cash) may be invested in companies located in the United States.
- **Government bond–general funds** invest at least 80 percent of their portfolios in U.S. government securities and have no stated average maturity.
- **Government bond–intermediate-term funds** invest at least 80 percent of their portfolios in U.S. government securities and have an average maturity of five to 10 years.
- **Government bond–short-term funds** invest at least 80 percent of their portfolios in U.S. government securities and have an average maturity of one to five years.
- **High-Yield funds** seek a high level of current income by investing at least 80 percent of their portfolios in lower-rated corporate bonds (Baa or lower by Moody's and BBB or lower by Standard and Poor's rating services).
- **Mortgage-Backed funds** invest at least 80 percent of their portfolios in pooled mortgage-backed securities.
- **National municipal bond–general funds** invest predominantly in municipal bonds and have an average maturity of more than five years or no stated average maturity. The funds' bonds are usually exempt from federal income tax but may be taxed under state and local laws.
- **National municipal bond–short-term funds** invest predominantly in municipal bonds and have an average maturity of one to five years. The funds' bonds are usually exempt from federal income tax but may be taxed under state and local laws.
- **Other world bond funds** invest at least 80 percent of their portfolios in a combination of foreign government and corporate debt. Some funds in this category invest primarily in debt securities of emerging markets.
- **State municipal bond–general funds** invest primarily in municipal bonds of a single state and have an average maturity of more than five years or no stated average maturity. The funds' bonds are exempt from federal and state income taxes for residents of that state.

- **State municipal bond–short-term funds** invest predominantly in municipal bonds of a single state and have an average maturity of one to five years. The funds' bonds are exempt from federal and state income taxes for residents of that state.
- **Strategic income funds** invest in a combination of domestic fixed-income securities to provide high current income.

Hybrid Funds

- **Asset allocation funds** seek high total return by investing in a mix of equities, fixed-income securities and money market instruments. Unlike flexible portfolio funds (defined below), these funds are required to strictly maintain a precise weighting in asset classes.
- **Balanced funds** invest in a specific mix of equity securities and bonds with the three-part objective of conserving principal, providing income, and achieving long-term growth of both principal and income.
- **Flexible portfolio funds** seek high total return by investing in common stock, bonds and other debt securities, and money market securities. Portfolios may hold up to 100 percent of any one of these types of securities and may easily change, depending on market conditions.
- **Income mixed funds** seek a high level of current income by investing in a variety of income-producing securities, including equities and fixed-income securities. Capital appreciation is not a primary objective.

Money Market Funds

- **National tax-exempt money market funds** seek income not taxed by the federal government by investing in municipal securities with relatively short maturities.
- **State tax-exempt money market funds** invest predominantly in short-term municipal obligations of a single state, which are exempt from federal and state income taxes for residents of that state.
- **Taxable money market–government funds** invest principally in short-term U.S. Treasury obligations and other short-term financial instruments issued or guaranteed by the U.S. government, its agencies or instrumentalities.
- **Taxable money market–nongovernment funds** invest in a variety of money market instruments, including certificates of deposit of large banks, commercial paper, and banker's acceptances.

Source: Adapted from data in Investment Company Institute, *2007 Investment Company Fact Book.*

certificates of deposit, bank acceptances, and commercial paper. They typically are no-load funds that impose no penalty for early withdrawal and generally allow holders to write checks against their account. Exhibit 24.10 documents the significant growth of these funds, which often depend on investor attitudes toward the stock market. When investors are bullish toward stocks, they withdraw funds from their money market accounts to invest; when they are uncertain, they shift from stocks to the money funds.

24.3.5 Breakdown by Fund Characteristics

Exhibit 24.11 groups funds by their method of sale and by investment objectives. The two major means of distribution are (1) by a sales force and (2) by direct purchase from the fund or

Exhibit 24.10 Money Market Funds: 1975–2006

| | Number of Funds | | Total Accounts | Total Net |
	Taxable	Tax-Exempt	Outstanding (thousands)	Assets ($ Billions)
1975	36	—	209	3.7
1980	96	10	4,762	76.4
1985	348	112	14,935	243.8
1990	506	235	22,969	498.3
1995	674	323	30,137	753.0
2000	703	336	48,138	1,845.2
2001	689	326	47,236	2,285.3
2002	679	310	45,380	2,272.0
2003	662	312	41,214	2,052.0
2004	639	304	37,636	1,913.2
2005	595	276	36,838	2,040.5
2006	576	273	38,434	2,354.5

Note: Data for funds that invest primarily in other mutual funds were excluded from the series.
Source: Adapted from data in Investment Company Institute, *2007 Investment Company Fact Book.*

Exhibit 24.11 Total Net Assets by Fund Characteristics ($ Billions)

| | | 2006 | | 1995 | |
		Dollars	Percent	Dollars	Percent
Total Net Assets		$10,413.6	100.0%	$2,811.3	100.0%
Method of Sale:					
Sales Force		—	62.0%	—	59.0%
Direct Institutional Marketing		—	27.0%	—	20.0%
Direct Retail Sales		—	11.0%	—	21.0%
Investment Objective:					
Equity funds	Capital Appreciation	2,701.05	25.9%	572.34	20.4%
	World	1,314.14	12.6%	196.51	7.0%
	Total Return	1,896.46	18.2%	480.23	17.1%
Bond funds	Corporate	272.17	2.6%	84.75	3.0%
	High Yield	156.23	1.5%	59.70	2.1%
	World	59.42	0.6%	24.83	0.9%
	Government	193.04	1.9%	143.00	5.1%
	Strategic Income	448.61	4.3%	33.30	1.2%
	State Muni	154.87	1.5%	117.30	4.2%
	National Muni	210.03	2.0%	135.99	4.8%
Hybrid funds		653.15	6.3%	210.33	7.5%
Money market funds	Taxable	1,988.06	19.1%	629.99	22.4%
	Tax-Exempt	366.40	3.5%	123.03	4.4%

Source: Adapted from data in Investment Company Institute, *1996* and *2007 Investment Company Fact Book.*

direct marketing. Sales forces would include brokers, such as Merrill Lynch; commission-based financial planners; or dedicated sales forces, such as those of American Express Retirement Services. Almost all mutual funds acquired from these individuals charge sales fees (loads) from which salespeople are compensated.

Investors typically purchase shares of directly marketed funds through the mail, telephone, bankwire, or an office of the fund. These direct sales funds usually impose a low sales charge or none at all. In the past, because they had no sales fee, they had to be sold directly because a broker had no incentive to sell a no-load fund. This has changed recently because some brokerage firms, such as Charles Schwab & Co., have developed agreements with specific no-load funds whereby they will sell these funds to their clients and collect a fee from the fund. As of December 2007, Schwab had a list of thousands of no-load funds that it would sell through its OneSource service. As seen in the most recent figures available in Exhibit 24.11, the division between these two major distribution channels is currently about 60 to 40 percent in favor of the sales force method, although there has been a steady shift toward direct institutional marketing. Given the investor preference for no-load funds and the increasing availability through firms like Charles Schwab, this trend toward direct marketed funds should continue.

The breakdown by investment objective indicates the investment companies' response to a shift in investor emphasis toward equity funds and reflects not only the overall growth of the industry but also the creation of new funds in response to the evolving demands of investors. Capital appreciation and total return funds have continued to grow and generally increased their percentages. Finally, the growing desire for international diversification is reflected in the ongoing popularity of world equity funds, a trend discussed more thoroughly in the following.

24.3.6. Global Investment Companies

As discussed throughout this text, investors must give serious thought to global diversification of their investment portfolios. Funds that invest in non-U.S. securities are generally called either *international funds* or *global funds.* International funds often hold only non-U.S. stocks from such countries as Germany, Japan, Singapore, and Korea, while global funds contain both U.S. and non-U.S. securities. Both international and global funds fall into familiar categories: money funds, long-term government and corporate bond funds, and equity funds. In turn, an international equity fund might limit its focus to a segment of the non-U.S. market, such as the European Fund or Pacific Basin Fund, or to a single country. Given the need to invest in a diversified portfolio of emerging markets, an emerging market mutual fund that contains a number of them is an ideal vehicle for this asset allocation.

Although most global or international funds are open-end funds (either load or no load), a significant number are closed-end funds, including most of the single country and the emerging-market funds. These funds have opted to be closed end so that they are not subject to major investor liquidations that require the sale of stocks in the portfolio on an illiquid foreign stock exchange.

A final alternative that all investors—particularly those in the United States—should appreciate is the large number of non-U.S. investment companies that offer both domestic and global products in their local markets. In fact, the Investment Company Institute reported that of $21.76 trillion invested worldwide in open-end investment companies at the end of 2006, over 52 percent of these assets were controlled by firms located outside the United States. In order, the largest concentrations of these AUM occured in Luxembourg, France, Australia, Hong Kong, and Japan. Further, of the 61,506 investment companies in operation during 2006, slightly more than 8,000 were domiciled in the United States. From these statistics, it is reasonable to assume that no single region of the world has a monopoly on investment management skill.

24.3.7 Mutual Fund Organization and Strategy: An Example

The Dreyfus Corporation, established in 1951 and headquartered in New York City, is one of the leading mutual fund companies in the United States, managing more than $200 billion as of December 2007.[6] The Dreyfus Appreciation Fund (DGAGX) is a one of several equity-oriented portfolios that the company offers to its institutional and retail investors. The Appreciation Fund, which follows a large-cap blend investment style, is different than many of the other funds in the Dreyfus family in that it is not managed in house by portfolio managers that it employs directly. Rather, DGAGX is managed by Fayez Sarofim, a Houston, Texas, money manager who has run his own private management firm since 1958 and serves Dreyfus as a subinvestment advisor. A portion of Bloomberg's description of DGAGX is shown in Exhibit 24.12. Notice that DGAGX has about $4.6 billion (Panel A) of assets under management and is a no-load fund that also does not charge a 12b-1 fee (Panel B). However, investors do pay an annual management fee of 0.55 percent of the portfolio's assets and the expense ratio, which accounts for the total cost of running the fund, is 0.92 percent of AUM.

One of the reasons why Dreyfus chose to enter into this arrangement was to allow investors who would not otherwise have sufficient capital to gain access to a private manager with an outstanding long-term performance record. Fayez Sarofim's investment philosophy is somewhat unique among mutual fund managers, in that he preaches a patient approach to portfolio formation that seeks to keep turnover below 15 percent per annum. The firm describes its investment approach as follows:

> *Our investment philosophy leads us to construct a portfolio comprised predominantly of large capitalization, US-based, multinational companies. These companies are global leaders in structurally attractive industries. They benefit from increasing global market share, ongoing product introduction or innovation, and productivity enhancements— three key drivers of long-term earnings growth. In addition, their financial strength allows them to make profitable investments at any point in the economic cycle. We believe these businesses are most capable of generating superior growth in earnings, dividends, and cash flow over time, leading to greater capital appreciation. Investing in high quality companies at reasonable prices also produces two additional advantages for our clients—low portfolio turnover and a higher likelihood of preservation of capital.[7]*

One interesting concept implied in this statement of philosophy is that Fayez Sarofim can be considered a global portfolio manager, even though the majority of the stocks he selects are from companies domiciled in the United States. The equity holdings of DGAGX are designed to mimic the portfolios that Sarofim assembles for his own private clients, and thus follows the same philosophy. Panel A of Exhibit 24.13 shows the top 10 holdings of the fund as of December 2004. Not surprisingly, all of these stocks (e.g., Exxon Mobil, Procter & Gamble, General Electric) fit the profile of being large companies with dominant global franchises. Also, the DGAGX portfolio has a lower level of systematic risk than the market, with a beta coefficient of 0.90. Finally, Panel B of the exhibit shows that DGAGX underperformed the Standard & Poor's 500 index (which is a relevant comparison for a large-cap blend fund manager) by almost 15 percent during the five-year period ending in November 2007, a period marked by significant growth in global equity markets.

24.4 Investing in Alternative Asset Classes

The investment structures just described—private management firms and investment companies—are extremely efficient ways for investors to gain access to a number of different asset classes and strategies. This is particularly true when the desired asset class investments are in liquid markets, such as with stocks, bonds, or money market securities. Recently, however,

---

[6] Much of the information contained in this example is available from Dreyfus Corporation's Web site at http://www.dreyfus.com.
[7] The complete statement of the Fayez Sarofim investment philosophy can be found on the firm's Web site (http://www.sarofim.com).

Exhibit 24.12 Description of Dreyfus Appreciation Fund (DGAGX)

Panel A. Overview

Screen Printed

DGAGX US

DREYFUS APPRECIATION FD INC

DESCRIPTION
Objective - Blue Chip

Equity**DES**

Page 1/ 4

Dreyfus Appreciation Fund, Inc. is an open-end fund incorporated in the USA. The Fund's objective is long-term capital growth consistent with the preservation of capital. Its secondary goal is current income. The Fund invests at least 80% of its net assets in the common stock of U.S. and foreign blue-chip companies of market capitalization of more than $5 billion.

Bloomberg Classification Data	
Asset Class	Equity
Style	Blue Chip
Market Cap Focus	Multi-cap
Geographic Focus	Global

Performance/Percentile Ranking		
as of 12/3/07	Return	Rank
3) TRA 1 Month	.06	94
YTD	6.70	40
1 Year	9.40	41
2006	16.26	84
5 Year	9.82	30

Current / Operational Data		
1)GP NAV	$	46.70
Assets(mil) 10/31/07	S	4556.00
Inception Date	1/18/84	

1 Yr Performance vs. Benchmark Indices

DGAGX
SPX

29DEC06 28FEB07 30APR 29JUN 31AUG 31OCT

{ FPC<GO> } FOR FUND PERFORMANCE CHARTS AND   { FSRC<GO> } FOR FUND SEARCH

Subadvisor: Fayez Sarofim & Co.

Panel B. Management & Fee Structure

Page

DGAGX US

DREYFUS APPRECIATION FD INC

DESCRIPTION
Fund Type - Open-End Fund

Equity**DES**

Page 2/ 4

Contact Details
Fund Manager
11)FAYEZ SHALABY SAROFIM
Management Company
Dreyfus Corp/The
Address
Dreyfus Funds
200 Park Avenue
New York, NY 10166
USA
Telephone   1-800-645-6561 Domestic
1-516-794-5452 Intl
Web Site
7)www.dreyfus.com
Transfer Agent
Dreyfus Transfer Inc

Isin	US2619701079	Valor	N.A.
Cusip	261970107	Sicovam	N.A.
Sedol	2291244 US	WPK	N.A.

Fees & Expenses	
Front Load	.000 %
Back Load	.000 %
Early Withdraw	.000 %
Current Mgmt Fee	.550 %
Performance Fee	%
Expense Ratio	.920 %
12b1 fee	.000 %

Min	Investment	$	2500
Min	Subsequent	$	100
Min	IRA	$	750

Distributions – Irreg			
6)DVD		Income	Capital Gain
YTD	$	.02	.00
2006	$	.62	1.79
2005	$	.54	.00
2004	$	.52	.00
2003	$	.41	.00
2002	$	.30	.02

Pricing Source

   NASDAQ

Exhibit 24.13 DGAGX Portfolio Holdings and Performance

Panel A. Portfolio Composition

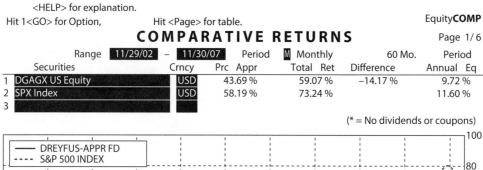

Page   Equity**DES**

DGAGX US   **DESCRIPTION**   Page 4/ 4
DREYFUS APPRECIATION FD INC   Objective - Blue Chip

Asset Allocation as of	9/30/07
Government	.00%
Corporate	.00%
Mortgage	.00%
Preferred	.00%
Municipal	.00%
Equity	99.73%
Cash and Other	.27%

Sector /Geo Allocation	9/30/07
Oil&Gas	21.01
Diversified Finan Serv	9.84
Retail	7.45
Beverages	7.29
Cosmetics/Personal Care	5.93
Agriculture	5.36
U.S.	88.61
Switzerland	4.27
France	3.59
U.K	2.38
Netherlands	1.14

Top 10 Holdings	9/30/07	Position	% Net
Exxon Mobil Corp		3393398	6.900
Altria Group Inc		3500700	5.347
General Electric Co		4878000	4.437
Chevron Corp		1974800	4.060
ConocoPhillips		1942000	3.745
Procter & Gamble Co		2389400	3.692
Citigroup Inc		3515933	3.605
PepsiCo Inc		2041600	3.286
Nestle SA		1244900	3.073
Coca-Cola Co/The		2396600	3.026
5) MHD			

Portfolio Statics		9/30/07	
Top 10 Hldgs % Port	41.17	Avg P/E	16.52
Median Market Cap	146.38BLN	Avg P/C	
Avg Wtd Mkt Cap	166.31BLN	Avg P/S	1.71
Avg Div Yield	2.12	Avg P/B	3.27

Australia 61 2 9777 8600   Brazil 5511 3048 4500   Europe 44 20 7330 7500   Germany 49 69 920410   Hong Kong 852 2977 6000
Japan 81 3 3201 8900   Singapore 65 6212 1000   U.S. 1 212 318 2000   Copyright 2007 Bloomberg Finance L.P.
                                                                                                                      H445–82–1 04–Dec–2007 10:43:53

Panel B. Returns Compared to S&P 500 Index

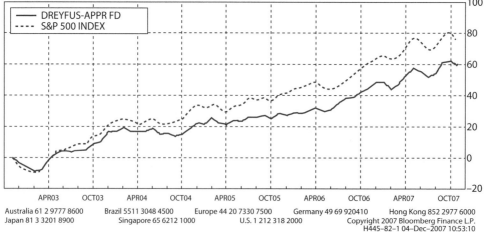

<HELP> for explanation.
Hit 1<GO> for Option,   Hit <Page> for table.   Equity**COMP**
                              COMPARATIVE RETURNS   Page 1/ 6

Range 11/29/02 – 11/30/07   Period   M Monthly   60 Mo.   Period

	Securities	Crncy	Prc Appr	Total Ret	Difference	Annual Eq
1	DGAGX US Equity	USD	43.69 %	59.07 %	–14.17 %	9.72 %
2	SPX Index	USD	58.19 %	73.24 %		11.60 %
3						

(* = No dividends or coupons)

DREYFUS-APPR FD
S&P 500 INDEX

APR03   OCT03   APR04   OCT04   APR05   OCT05   APR06   OCT06   APR07   OCT07

Australia 61 2 9777 8600   Brazil 5511 3048 4500   Europe 44 20 7330 7500   Germany 49 69 920410   Hong Kong 852 2977 6000
Japan 81 3 3201 8900   Singapore 65 6212 1000   U.S. 1 212 318 2000   Copyright 2007 Bloomberg Finance L.P.
                                                                                                                      H445–82–1 04–Dec–2007 10:53:10

individual and institutional investors alike have become interested in committing their financial capital in nontraditional asset classes. These **alternative asset** classes can include a wide variety of investment opportunities, but the most notable ones are hedge funds, private equity, real estate, or natural resources and commodities. In this section, we will take a detailed look at hedge funds and private equity investments.

Alternative asset investing can take place either through the creation of separate accounts for each investor or through the commingling of investor capital into a single pool of assets. Thus, these structures can appear as either Panel A or Panel B in Exhibit 24.1. Most often, though, an alternative asset investment is structured as a commingled collection of assets (i.e., Panel B), with the important difference that it is usually formed as a **limited partnership** rather than as a mutual fund. In a limited partnership, one or more *general partners* are responsible for running the organization and assuming its legal obligations, while the remaining *limited partners* are only liable to the extent of their investments. For example, in a hedge fund or private equity partnership, the general partner develops, implements, and maintains the investment portfolio around an initial strategy, while the limited partners (e.g., high-net-worth individuals, pension funds, endowment funds) provide the majority of the capital but have no direct involvement in the actual investment process.

Of course, one of the reasons that investors consider hiring professional asset managers is the belief that they will be able to deliver superior investment performance relative to simple indexed investments. In the parlance of the asset management industry, investors feel that professional managers can consistently add *alpha*, which is defined as the difference between a fund's actual and expected (e.g., CAPM, benchmark) return. In fact, one of the reasons for the impressive recent development of the alternative assets market is the growing belief that they are better able to produce superior returns than traditional investment structures, such as mutual funds. This argument is summarized in Exhibit 24.14, which illustrates an "excess returns" form of the Security Market Line (SML) for several different asset classes. Notice that standard "long only" positions in U.S. stocks and bonds plot virtually on the SML—indicating

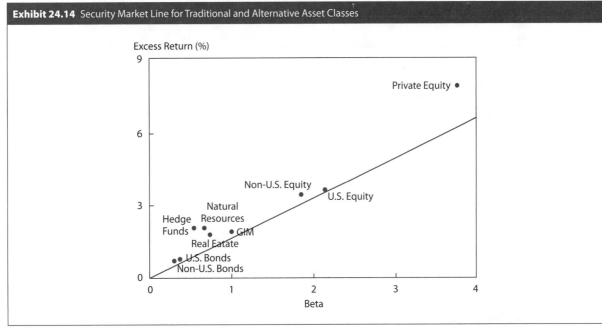

Exhibit 24.14 Security Market Line for Traditional and Alternative Asset Classes

Note: GIM = Global Investment Market.
Source: Brian D. Singer, Renato Staub, and Kevin Terhaar, "Determining the Appropriate Allocation to Alternative Investments," *Hedge Fund Management* (Charlottesville, VA: CFA Institute, 2002), 10. Copyright © 2002 CFA Institute. Reproduced and republished from *Financial Management Journal* with permission from the CFA Institute. All Rights Reseved.

very little possibility for adding alpha—while the alternative asset classes (i.e., hedge funds, private equity) have substantially more potential in that area.

24.4.1 Hedge Funds

One of the most significant developments in the professional asset management industry over the past 20 years has been the emergence of the global market for hedge fund investing. Exhibit 24.15 shows that the increase in both the number of hedge funds in existence, as well as the assets under management those funds control, has been nothing short of phenomenal. There were about 600 funds at the start of the 1990s controlling less than $40 billion in assets; by 2006 there were over 9,000 active funds controlling an estimated $1.34 trillion in assets. This represents AUM expansion of about 23 percent per annum over the past several years.

Despite this recent surge in growth, hedge fund investing is not new. In fact, Lhabitant (2002) notes that use of the term "hedge fund" originated in 1949, when Alfred Winslow Jones

Exhibit 24.15 Development of the Hedge Fund Industry

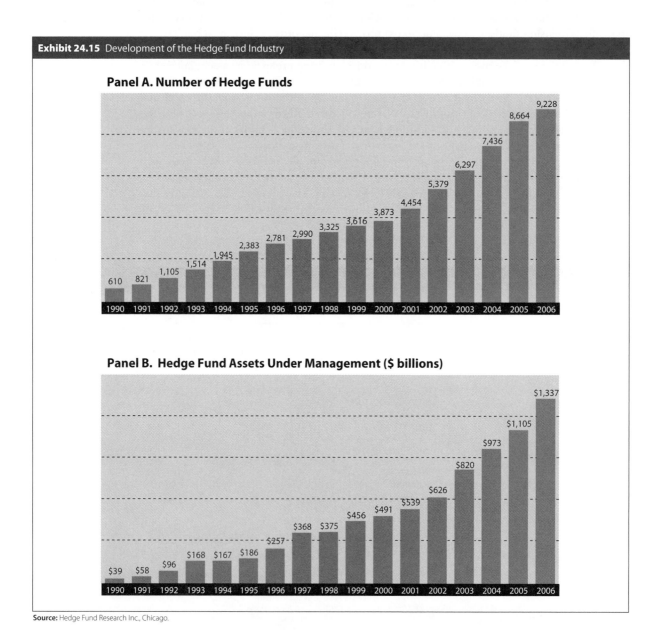

Panel A. Number of Hedge Funds

Panel B. Hedge Fund Assets Under Management ($ billions)

Source: Hedge Fund Research Inc., Chicago.

tested his security selection skills by forming a portfolio that combined both long and short position in the equity market with the use of financial leverage to enhance returns. Jones did this using a partnership structure that avoided Security and Exchange Commission restrictions and also included an incentive fee for superior performance. Despite the fact that the performance of this original hedge fund was indeed spectacular—it outperformed the best mutual fund of the era by almost 90 percent over a 10-year period—Jones's strategy was not widely imitated for several decades. However, as indicated in Exhibit 24.15, that situation has certainly changed.

24.4.2 Characteristics of a Hedge Fund

There are several immediate consequences to creating a hedge fund as a limited partnership. Most notably, hedge fund investments are far less liquid than mutual fund (or even closed-end fund) shares; there are severe limitations on when and how often investment capital can be contributed to or removed from a partnership. On the other hand, as a private partnership, hedge funds are generally less restricted in how and where they can make investments, which is perhaps the biggest reason why investors believe that these vehicles have the ability to deliver abnormally large returns on a consistent basis. They also tend to be less correlated with tradional asset class investments, providing investors with additional diversification benefits in their overall portfolios.

Exhibit 24.16 highlights several important features related to the way hedge funds are structured. As just mentioned, the average hedge fund only permits investors to enter or exit a few times a year (i.e., monthly and quarterly, respectively) compared to the daily ownership adjustments allowed by mutual funds. Also, most hedge funds allow managers to use leverage (71%), short sell (82%), and derivatives (69%). By contrast, Almazan et al. (2004) document that the vast majority of mutual fund managers cannot employ these investment tools. Further, as Fung and Hsieh (2006) note, it is typical for hedge fund managers to receive their compensation in two components: a regular management fee (e.g., 1 percent of AUM) and a performance

Exhibit 24.16 Characteristics of Hedge Fund Investments

	Mean	Median	Mode
Fund Size	$83 million	$26.5 million	$20 million
Fund Age	6.8 years	6.2 years	8.0 years
Minimum Investment Required	$649,000	$250,000	$1,000,000
Number of Entry Dates per Year	22	12	12
Number of Exit Dates per Year	17	4	4
Management Fee	1.4%	1.0%	1.0%
Performance Allocation ("Fee")	17.2%	20.0%	20.0%

	YES
Fund has hurdle rate (of those with a performance allocation)	14%
Fund has high water mark	93%
Fund has audited financial statements or audited performance	95%
Manager has $500,000 of own money in fund	78%
Fund can handle "hot issues"	56%
Fund is diversified	44%
Fund can short sell	82%
Fund can use leverage	71%
Fund uses derivatives for hedging only, or none	69%

Level of turnover	Low (0–25%) = 17%	Medium (26–75%) = 26%	High (>75%) = 58%	
Capitalization of underlying investments	Small ($1–$500m) = 12%	Medium ($500–$1,000m) = 4%	Large (>$1,000m) = 10%	Mixed = 73%

allocation fee, which normally amounts to 20 percent of the fund's profits beyond a certain pre-specified return level (i.e., hurdle rate). In calculating this performance fee, investors usually require that any past losses be recouped before managers receive the additional payout; this arrangement is known as a *high-water mark.* Finally, as a tangible signal to investors of belief in their abilities, most hedge fund managers put a substantial amount of their own capital into the fund.

24.4.3 Hedge Fund Strategies

Saying you are invested in a hedge fund is a little like saying you play a sport—it is a statement that conveys some information but could actually mean a great many different things. In fact, several investment strategies are often included under the hedge fund designation, and these vary greatly in the risk and expected return profiles they imply. Within a given strategic category, there can be as many interpretations of how the portfolio should be designed as there are fund managers. Nevertheless, some common features define the more popular hedge fund strategies, and we will now describe them.[8]

I. Equity-Based Strategies
- *Long-short equity:* The original and perhaps the most basic form of hedge fund investing. Managers attempt to identify misvalued stocks and take long positions in the undervalued ones and short positions in the overvalued ones. Since investors participate in both the long and the short side of the market, one major advantage of the long-short strategy is the ability to generate "double alpha" (i.e., profit from price corrections for both undervalued and overvalued securities), unlike the long-only possibilities in the mutual fund industry. The 130/30 funds discussed in Chapter 16 can be considered as a variation of this strategy.
- *Equity market neutral:* Like the long-short strategy, returns are generated by exploiting perceived pricing inefficiencies between securities. However, equity market neutral strategies also attempt to limit the overall volatility exposure of the fund by taking offsetting risk positions on the long and short side, an effort that might also involve adopting derivative positions. Absent leverage, these portfolios are expected to produce returns of 2 to 4 percent above the risk-free rate, which has led some investors to refer to them as *absolute return* strategies.

II. Arbitrage-Based Strategies
- *Fixed-income arbitrage:* Returns are generated by taking advantage of bond pricing disparities caused by changing market events, investor preferences, or fluctuations in the fixed-income market. Because the valuation disparities between related instruments (e.g., coupon-bearing Treasury bonds and zero-coupon Treasury strips) are typically small, managers usually employ leverage to enhance their overall returns. The ability to generate alpha is driven largely by the manager's skill at building quantitative models, as well as structuring and managing fixed-income portfolios.
- *Convertible arbitrage:* Seeks to profit from disparities in the relationship between prices for convertible bonds and the underlying common stock. A typical position involves purchasing the convertible bond and short selling the underlying stock, thereby isolating the conversion option embedded in the bond. Returns are generated in several ways, including interest income on the convertible bonds, interest on the proceeds of related equity short sales, and the price appreciation of the convertible

---

[8] The following list of hedge fund strategies, which draws from the discussion in Nicholas (1999), is intended to be representative rather than exhaustive. Alternative lists of strategies can be found at the following Web sites: http://www.greenwichai.com and http://www.thehfa.org.

bonds as they gradually assume the value of the equity into which they are exchangeable. Like fixed-income arbitrage, convertible arbitrage positions often utilize leverage to enhance returns.

- *Merger (risk) arbitrage:* Returns are dependent upon the magnitude of the spread on merger transactions, which are directly related to the likelihood of the deal not being completed due to regulatory, financial, or company-specific reasons. As the probability of the merger improves, the spread narrows, generating profits for the position. Merger arbitrage investors essentially bet that their subjective assessment of whether the proposed deal is ultimately completed is superior to that of the other investors in the market.

III. Opportunistic Strategies

- *High yield and distressed:* One advantage that bond investors enjoy relative to stock investors is that, if the issuer does not default, a bond's price will return to par at maturity. When companies are distressed, their securities can be purchased at deep discounts. If and when the turnaround materializes, security prices will approach their intrinsic value, generating profits for the distressed manager. *Emerging market* investing can be viewed as a global application of this strategy using sovereign securities instead of corporate instruments.

- *Global macro:* This broad class of strategies seeks to profit from changes in global economies, typically brought about by shifts in government policy that impact interest rates, in turn affecting currency, stock, and bond markets. Fund managers typically use a "top-down" global approach to identifying opportunities and often participate in all major markets—equities, bonds, currencies, and commodities—though not always at the same time. The strategy uses leverage and derivatives to enhance returns, but also might hedge exposures on a situational basis.

- *Managed futures:* This strategy entails using long and short positions in a variety of futures contracts, both to take "directional" positions on certain economic or company-specific events (e.g., changing conditions in stock or bond markets) and to exploit pricing discrepancies between various contracts. The assets underlying these futures positions may involve commodities, equities, interest rates, or foreign currencies. These strategies frequently employ a substantial degree of financial leverage.

- *Special situations*: Special situation returns occur due to the outcomes of significant events that occur during the normal life cycle of a corporation. These strategies may involve investing in companies around the time of bankruptcies, financial restructurings or recapitalizations, spinoffs, or carveouts. Given the underlying reason for the investment, positions are usually directional and not fully hedged. Depending on the manager's specific strategy, *event-driven* returns are realized when the catalyst necessary to generate the position's intrinsic value (e.g., the spinoff of an operating division) takes place.

IV. Multiple Strategies

- *Fund of funds:* Although not formally a separate strategic category, this investment vehicle acts like a mutual fund of hedge funds, giving investors access to managers that might otherwise be unavailable to them. The primary benefit to the investor of a fund of funds position is that it is a convenient method for achieving a well-diversified allocation to the hedge fund investment space. A fund of funds can offer either a concentration in a particular strategy (e.g., long-short equity) and then diversify across different hedge fund managers—this is a *multiple manager* approach—or it can diversify across strategies, which is the *multiple strategy* approach. The primary disadvantage to the fund of funds investor is that there will be an extra layer of fees necessary to compensate the fund of funds manager; this additional fee can be as high as 3 percent of the assets under management.

24.4.4 Risk Arbitrage Investing: A Closer Look

A popular hedge fund strategy involves taking equity positions in companies that are the target of a merger or takeover attempt. These risk arbitrage investments require managers to compare their own subjective judgment about the ultimate success of the proposed takeover with the success probability implied by the market price of the target firm's stock following the announcement of the prospective deal. If the manager thinks the takeover is more likely to occur than the market does, she will buy shares in the target firm. Conversely, the manager might short sell the target firm shares if she thinks the proposed deal is less likely to be completed.

To understand how a manager can establish the market's consensus forecast for the success of an announced takeover, consider the following hypothetical example. Suppose the shareholders of Company XYZ receive an unsolicited cash tender offer for $30 per share. At the time of the offer—which we assume was a complete surprise—XYZ's shares traded for $20. Suppose further that shortly after the takeover announcement—which still must be approved by regulatory authorities—the price of XYZ's shares rises to $28. Brown and Raymond (1986) showed that a simple estimate of the market's *implied probability* that the takeover bid will ultimately be successful is (28 − 20) ÷ (30 − 20), or 80 percent. In this situation, the risk arbitrage hedge fund manager must think the deal has better than a four-in-five chance of being completed in order to justify purchasing XYZ stock for $28 in the hope of selling at the tender offer price of $30; if the deal falls apart, the manager can assume that XYZ's shares will return to $20. Exhibit 24.17 compares the implied probabilities for a sample of proposed takeovers that were ultimately completed (both competing and noncompeting) to a sample of deals that failed. Investors in the market are very good at discriminating between "good" and "bad" deals as far as three months prior to the final resolution.

Panel A of Exhibit 24.18 summarizes the relevant aspects of JP Morgan Chase (JPM) Bank's takeover of Hambrecht & Quist (HQ), a San Francisco–based investment bank specializing in transactions involving technology firms. In an effort to bolster its equity business, JPM made a tender offer of $50 per share for all of the outstanding shares of HQ, which at the time

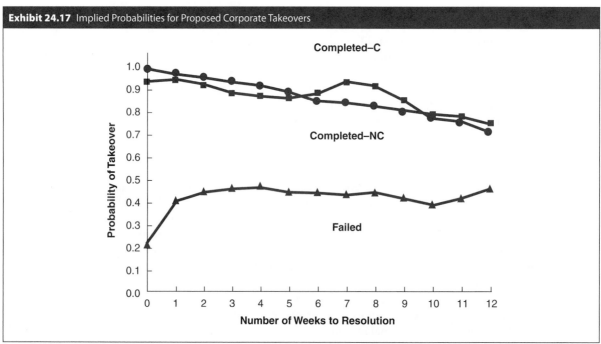

Exhibit 24.17 Implied Probabilities for Proposed Corporate Takeovers

Source: Keith C. Brown and Michael V. Raymond, "Risk Arbitrage and the Prediction of Successful Corporate Takeovers," *Financial Management* 15, no. 3 (August 1986), 54–63.

Exhibit 24.18 JP Morgan Chase's Takeover of Hambrecht & Quist

A. Tender Offer Details

<HELP> for explanation.
<MENU> to return

N090 **Equity CACS**

More Deal Info	Target Info	Acquirer Info	Acquisition Detail		
Target: JP Morgan H&Q			HQ US	Price:	
Industry: Finance–Invest Bnkr/Brkr				SIC Code: SEC BROKER/DLR	
Country: United States					
Acquirer: JPMorgan Chase & Co			JPM US	Price:	39.28 USD
Industry: Money Center Banks				SIC Code: NATL COML BANK	
Country: United States					
Announced Date: 9/28/99					
Completion Date: 12/10/99			% owned:		
Status: Completed			% acquired: 100.00		
Currency: USD					
Annd tot. value: 1222.2290 Mln			Announced premium: 22.35%		
Final tot. val: 1222.2290 Mln					
Paym't Type: Cash			Arbitrage profit:		
Cash Terms: 50.0000 /Sh.			Cash Value:		
Stock Terms:			Acct'g meth:		
Net Debt:					
Nature of Bid: Friendly			Action ID: 4845653		
TENDER OFFER EFF: 12/08/99 (94.5%). ACQ'R N/C FROM HAMBRECHT & QUIST GROUP UPON COMPLETION.					

Australia 61 2 9777 8600   Brazil 5511 3048 4500   Europe 44 20 7330 7500   Germany 49 69 920410
Hong Kong 852 2977 6000   Japan 81 3 3201 8900   Singapore 65 6212 1000   U.S. 1 212 318 2000   Copyright 2004 Bloomberg Finance L.P.
G469–10–0 08–Nov–04 16:36:43

B. HQ Share Price Movements

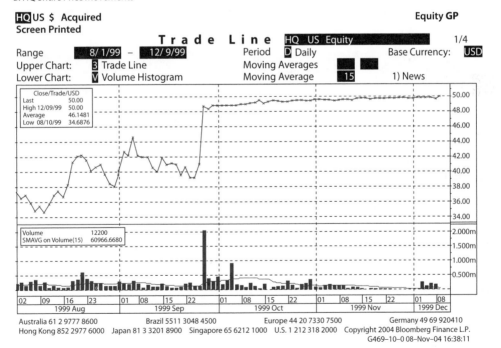

HQ US $ Acquired
Screen Printed

Equity GP

T r a d e   L i n e   HQ US Equity   1/4

Range   8/ 1/99 – 12/ 9/99   Period **D** Daily   Base Currency: **USD**
Upper Chart: **3** Trade Line   Moving Averages
Lower Chart: **V** Volume Histogram   Moving Average   **15**   1) News

Close/Trade/USD	
Last	50.00
High 12/09/99	50.00
Average	46.1481
Low 08/10/99	34.6876

Volume	12200
SMAVG on Volume(15)	60966.6680

02 09 16 23 | 01 08 15 22 | 01 08 15 22 | 01 08 15 22 | 01 08
1999 Aug | 1999 Sep | 1999 Oct | 1999 Nov | 1999 Dec

Australia 61 2 9777 8600   Brazil 5511 3048 4500   Europe 44 20 7330 7500   Germany 49 69 920410
Hong Kong 852 2977 6000   Japan 81 3 3201 8900   Singapore 65 6212 1000   U.S. 1 212 318 2000   Copyright 2004 Bloomberg Finance L.P.
G469–10–0 08–Nov–04 16:38:11

of the announcement were trading for $39.28. This represents a tender premium of $10.72, and capturing as much of this premium as possible is the goal of the risk arbitrage investor. However, Panel B indicates that within a day of the announcement, HQ shares were already trading for $48.69. This means that the market had already assessed the probability of this friendly takeover attempt to be 88 percent [= (48.69 – 39.28) ÷ (50 – 39.28)]. Thus, a hedge fund manager who did not already own HQ stock would have to be extremely confident that this deal would ultimately be completed to purchase shares at that point.

24.4.5 Hedge Fund Performance

Nicholas (2005) studied the performance of several of the strategies that defined the early hedge fund market. His findings are summarized in Exhibit 24.19, which plots a Capital Market Line (CML) comparing total risk and return characteristics over the period from 1990 to 2004. During this time, all of the indicated strategies plotted above the CML, demonstrating the ability of hedge fund managers to add a positive alpha to their investors over and above the returns that investments in traditional products such as Treasury bills or the S&P 500 equity index produced. There is also tremendous variation in the level of risk inherent in the myriad strategies; arbitrage-based strategies and those that take both long and short positions (e.g., equity market neutral) tend to exhibit far less volatility than those that adopt directional positions (e.g., macro and event-driven strategies). Clearly, not all hedge funds are the same when it comes to their risk and return profiles, a fact that participants in this market need to understand.

While these CML results are encouraging for potential hedge fund investors, keep in mind that they represent comparisons based on long-term averages over one specific time period. Investors should also be aware that the returns to these strategies show a high degree of variability on a year-to-year basis, in both an absolute and a relative sense. Exhibit 24.20, which lists the annual returns and rankings for 10 different broad hedge fund categories,

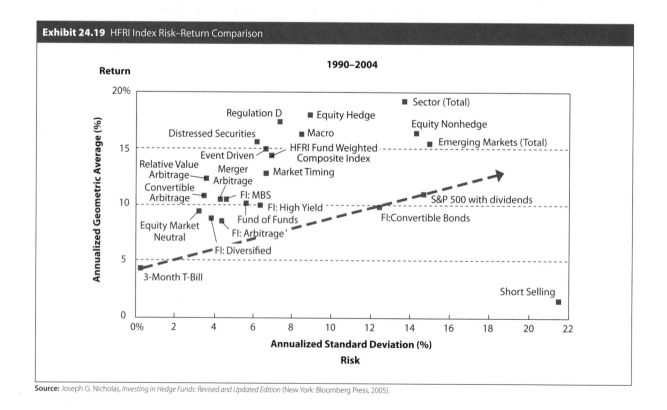

Exhibit 24.19 HFRI Index Risk–Return Comparison

Source: Joseph G. Nicholas, *Investing in Hedge Funds: Revised and Updated Edition* (New York: Bloomberg Press, 2005).

Exhibit 24.20 Hedge Fund Strategy Return Performance: 1994–2007

1994	1995	1996	1997	1998	1999	2000	2001	2002	2003	2004	2005	2006	2007
DS 14.9%	GM 30.7%	EM 34.5%	GM 37.1%	MF 20.6%	LS 47.2%	CA 25.6%	ED 20.0%	MF 18.3%	EM 28.8%	ED 15.6%	EM 17.4%	EM 20.5%	EM 20.6%
EM 12.5%	ED 26.1%	GM 25.6%	EM 26.6%	LS 17.2%	EM 44.8%	DS 15.8%	GM 18.4%	DS 18.1%	ED 25.1%	EM 12.5%	DS 17.0%	ED 15.6%	GM 17.2%
MF 12.0%	LS 23.0%	ED 25.6%	LS 21.5%	MN 13.3%	ED 22.2%	MN 15.0%	CA 14.6%	GM 14.7%	GM 18.0%	LS 11.6%	ED 11.7%	LS 14.4%	LS 14.5%
RA 5.3%	CA 16.6%	CA 17.9%	ED 20.7%	RA 5.6%	CA 16.0%	RA 14.7%	MN 9.3%	MN 7.4%	LS 17.3%	GM 8.5%	LS 9.7%	CA 14.3%	RA 10.4%
ED 0.7%	FI 12.5%	LS 17.1%	MN 14.8%	ED -1.7%	MN 15.3%	GM 11.7%	FI 8.0%	EM 7.4%	MF 14.1%	FI 6.9%	GM 9.3%	GM 13.5%	MN 9.6%
FI 0.3%	RA 11.9%	MN 16.6%	CA 14.5%	GM -3.6%	RA 13.2%	FI 6.3%	EM 5.8%	FI 5.8%	CA 12.9%	MN 6.5%	MN 6.1%	MN 11.2%	ED 9.1%
MN -2.0%	MN 11.0%	FI 15.9%	RA 9.8%	CA -4.4%	FI 12.1%	MF 4.2%	RA 5.7%	CA 4.1%	RA 9.0%	MF 6.0%	RA 3.1%	FI 8.7%	DS 6.5%
GM -5.7%	MF -7.1%	RA 13.8%	FI 9.3%	DS -6.0%	GM 5.8%	LS 2.1%	MF 1.9%	ED -0.7%	FI 8.0%	RA 5.5%	FI 0.6%	RA 8.2%	MF 6.2%
CA -8.1%	DS -7.4%	MF 12.0%	MF 3.1%	FI -8.2%	MF -4.7%	ED 2.0%	DS -3.6%	LS -1.6%	MN 7.1%	CA 2.0%	MF -0.1%	MF 8.1%	CA 6.1%
LS -8.1%	EM -16.9%	DS -5.5%	DS 0.4%	EM -37.7%	DS -14.2%	EM -5.5%	LS -3.7%	RA -3.5%	DS -32.6%	DS -7.7%	CA -2.6%	DS -6.6%	FI 4.0%

Legend:

CA	=	Convertible Arbitrage
DS	=	Dedicated Short Bias
ED	=	Event Driven—Distressed
EM	=	Emerging Markets
FI	=	Fixed-Income Arbitrage
GM	=	Global Macroeconomic
LS	=	Long/Short Equity
MF	=	Managed Futures
MN	=	Equity Market Neutral
RA	=	Event Driven—Risk Arbitrage

Source: © Credit Suisse Tremont Index LLC. All rights reserved.

documents this *strategy rotation* effect. Some of the swings represented in the display can be dramatic. For example, emerging markets (EM) was the worst performing strategy in 1995, posting a loss of 16.9 percent. However, it was the best performing strategy during the following year, returning 34.5 percent to investors. Similar patterns exist throughout the exhibit; for instance, the long/short equity (LS) strategy performed well in 2003 and 2004, but lost money in 2002. Finally, notice that there are only two (of 14) years in which every strategy class earned positive returns.

24.4.6 Private Equity

Like hedge funds, **private equity** can also include a wide variety of different investment vehicles and strategies. A private equity investment refers to any ownership interest in an asset (or collection of assets) that is not tradable in a public market. This non-tradeability feature has two immediate consequences. First, private equity transactions typically fund either new companies that do not have sufficient operating histories to issue common stock on a public exchange or established firms that are seeking to change their organizational structure or are experiencing financial distress. Second, private equity investments are generally far less liquid than public stock holdings and are therefore considered to be long-term positions within an investor's overall portfolio.

The security market dynamics illustrated in Exhibit 24.14 showed that, on average, private equity commitments are among the highest risk and highest reward investments available. This risk–return trade-off is one of things that distinguishes private equity as a separate asset class from other forms of ownership in the public markets. Another important aspect of private equity that defines it as a unique investment category is that it is not perfectly correlated with the other traditional asset classes (e.g., U.S. and non-U.S. stocks, U.S. bonds) or alternative asset classes (e.g., hedge funds, real estate). This is shown in Exhibit 24.21, which lists expected return, standard deviation, and correlation statistics for several different asset classes based on data from the 10-year period ending in 2005. While the private and public equity markets in the United States are highly correlated (i.e., a correlation coefficient of 0.50), the same is not as true for private equity with U.S. bonds (0.05) or real estate (0.15). Thus, in addition to their potential to deliver high returns, private equity investments also serve as an important source of diversification.

This combination of higher risk and less liquidity often precludes small investors from participating in the private equity market. It is not unusual for private equity funds to require minimum initial investment levels of several million dollars as well as capital "lock ups" (i.e., minimum time commitments) of one year or longer. Further, cash distributions from a fund may occur on a sporadic basis and only after an extended period of time. Thus, even when the investment risks are diversified across a well-designed collection of holdings, private equity deals are designed for those investors who can afford to have the funds committed for a lengthy

Exhibit 24.21 Asset Class Return, Risk, and Correlations Statistics

Asset Class	Expected Return	Standard Deviation	Correlations:					
			U.S. Equity	Non-U.S. Equity	U.S. Bonds	Hedge Funds	Real Estate	Private Equity
U.S. Stock	8.9%	16.4%	1.00					
Non-U.S. Stock	8.9	17.5	0.67	1.00				
U.S. Bonds	5.2	5.3	0.05	−0.13	1.00			
Hedge Funds	6.9	6.5	0.51	0.48	0.06	1.00		
Real Estate	7.9	13.6	0.53	0.47	−0.12	0.37	1.00	
Private Equity	*13.1*	*30.1*	*0.50*	*0.45*	*0.05*	*0.40*	*0.15*	*1.00*

Source: University of Texas Investment Management Company, *Asset Allocation Review 2005.*

period of time and be able to absorb the possibility that they may lose all of their initial capital. This best describes institutional investors, such as public and corporate pension funds or endowments, and high-net-worth individual investors.

Development and Organization of the Private Equity Market As Hsu and Kenney (2005) discuss, organized private equity investing began in the United States with the creation of the American Research & Development Corporation (ARD) in 1946. The ARD was formed in the immediate aftermath of World War II as a means of providing investment capital for new business ventures created by and for returning soldiers. Beyond this goal, the overriding premise of ARD that helped to shape the modern private equity industry was the belief that combining a pool of investment capital with skilled management could simultaneously benefit startup companies and produce superior returns for investors. Although it was ultimately disbanded, ARD did manage to raise about $7.5 million in capital and fund at least one firm (i.e., Digital Equipment Company) that produced significant profits. It also served as the model for the limited partnership format employed by most private equity funds today, a design that allows for a separation between the main sources of the investment capital and the source of the investment expertise (e.g., the company serving as general partner which organizes the fund). By the late 1950s, various agencies of the government had joined the effort to help startup companies by sponsoring Small Business Investment Companies (SBIC), in which private equity partnerships augment their capital by borrowing federal funds.

While private equity investments can be defined to include *any* non-public ownership interest, these transactions are typically classified into three different subcategories:[9]

I. *Venture Capital*: Focuses on investments in startup firms, early stage businesses, and new products and services created by established businesses. For the past two decades, venture investments have often been concentrated in the technology (e.g., Internet, telecommunications, software) and health care industries. Venture capital funds tend to specialize by stage of investing, as determined by the time frame in a company's development:

- *Seed*: An entrepreneur has a new idea or product, but no established organization or operating structure. Investors at this stage (who are sometimes called "angels") tend to provide limited financial capital and other physical resources to help the entrepreneur develop a coherent business plan.
- *Early Stage*: The business organization has moved beyond the planning stage and has now been formed. It has employees and products that are in the developmental stage. Early-stage investors commit capital once companies complete the business plan and have at least part of the management team in place.
- *Later Stage:* The firm now has an established infrastructure in place, as well as a viable product that is either ready for the market or already producing revenues. Later-stage investors usually provide financing for the expansion of a company that is already producing and shipping a product and increasing its sales volume.

II. *Buyouts*: Involves the acquisition of a product line, set of assets, or business from an established company. The company that is being acquired can be either a public or a private firm of virtually any size and payment for the transaction can involve both debt and equity. (A transaction that involves the uses of debt to fund the acquisition of a company is called a *leveraged buyout*, or LBO.) In a LBO, the assets of the acquired firm are used as collateral for the debt, which is then paid off using either the cash flow generated by the company or the sale of some of the assets. A change in the ownership control of the company being acquired is almost always a feature of a buyout transaction, which can also include recapitalizations,

---

[9] These descriptions of the various types of private equity investments are adapted from Ennis Knupp (2004), which also provides an excellent overview of the industry.

spin-offs, carve-outs, consolidations, and roll-ups. Firms seek buyout financing for several reasons, including a desire to expand their operations, divest themselves of a business unit that no longer fits the strategic plan, or to affect a change in management or ownership. When a public firm is bought out and taken private, there also may be less scrutiny of its operations by outside parties (e.g., regulators, financial analysts).

III. *Special Situations*: Includes investments in distressed companies or firms with unique opportunities that may be available on a one-time basis (e.g., an investment subsidy resulting from a change in a governmental regulation). Two important classes in this category are:

- *Distressed Debt*: Investors acquire multiple classes of the debt or equity of a publicly traded firm that is in or near bankruptcy. The goal of distressed investors is to create new value in the firm through an infusion of capital and a reorganization of its operations. In a reorganization, distressed investors often forgive the debt obligations of the company in exchange for enough equity to compensate them; this is why distressed debt funds are considered equity investors. However, these funds can also profit by liquidating a firm, which is why they are sometimes called "vulture capitalists."

- *Mezzanine Financing*: Investors provide a middle-level of funding that is subordinated to senior debt but ranks above the existing equity. A typical mezzanine investment includes a subordinated loan to the company—at an interest rate higher than the yield on the senior debt—along with the receipt of some form of equity participation (e.g., warrants, common stock, preferred stock). Thus, like distressed debt investors, mezzanine financiers are providing both private debt and private equity funding.

From the preceding descriptions, it should be clear that not all of these categories will produce investments with the same risk–return trade-offs. Venture capital commitments are generally considered to be the riskiest private equity transactions because they are often made before the organization in question has created a viable source of revenue. Buyout investments can also involve a considerable amount of risk—especially when a large amount of leverage is used in the transaction—but they have the advantage of involving companies with established product markets, which typically makes them somewhat more predictable than venture-related deals. Finally, special situation investments such as mezzanine transactions fall on the safer end of the private equity spectrum because they involve a commitment of capital with a senior claim on the firm's resources.

International Financial Services, a London-based trade support organization, estimated that commitments to private equity funds throughout the world totaled more than $230 billion in 2005, with more than half of that amount actually invested in the market. Roughly 40 percent of those funds came from investors in the United States. Exhibit 24.22 illustrates the extent of private equity investing in the United States, in terms of both the dollars committed and the number of available partnership funds. There has been a significant increase in private equity investments over the past 10–15 years, particularly in the amount of buyout activity. (Venture capital investing appears to have peaked during the technology-related boom in the equity market that occurred in the late 1990s.) As Acharya et al. (2007) point out, this trend reflects the simultaneous impact of several factors in place during this period: (i) the influx of a substantial amount of new investment capital as institutional investors shifted their strategic asset allocation policies toward alternative assets, (ii) the availability of relatively inexpensive credit, which made debt financing a cheap source of funds, and (iii) relatively high valuations in the equity market.

The Private Equity Investment Process To better understand the dynamics of private equity investing, consider the progression followed by the hypothetical company illustrated in Exhibit 24.23. Suppose initially that Bob and Susan, two young entrepreneurs who recently

Exhibit 24.22 Development of the Private Equity Industry in the United States

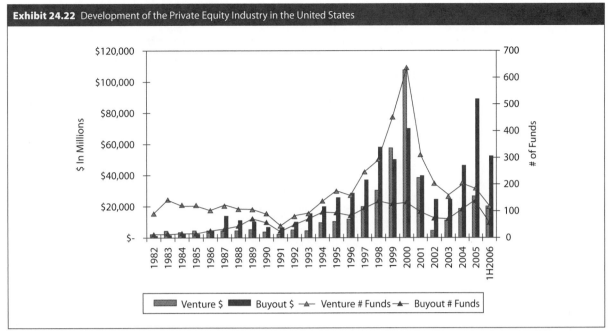

Source: Venture Economics.

graduated from college, have developed a better and more cost-effective way to search for Web sites on the Internet. After exhausting their personal savings and bank loans to develop the business—which is sometimes called *zero-stage capital*—they turn to a venture capital firm to provide the additional seed and early-stage funding they need to advance their idea to the next level. Following an evaluation of Bob and Susan's business plan, Venture Partners Fund agrees to provide financial capital and operating expertise to help launch the Internet Search Engine Company (i.e., Step 1a). In exchange for these resources, Venture Partners receives an equity stake in the new company.

As noted earlier, venture capital investing is extremely risky because the enterprise in question is unlikely to have an established stream of revenues or profits. Thus, investors like Venture Partners Fund must evaluate firms like Internet Search Engine Company on the basis of their *potential* for future success. Typically, only two or three out of 10 first-stage ventures become profitable and only one in 10 becomes a huge success (e.g., Apple Computer, Genentech, Federal Express). One consequence of this high failure rate is that venture capital firms usually mitigate their risk by diversifying their investments across a portfolio of startup companies. Another is that venture funds limit their exposure to a given startup by providing funding in stages as the company demonstrates its capacity for success. Thus, Venture Partners Fund will only provide later-stage equity capital to help Internet Search Engine Company expand its operations once the firm has established a viable product (i.e., Step 1b).

While venture capital funds help companies develop and grow, they will ultimately want to liquidate their equity holdings in order to create a return on their investment and provide capital to fund new ventures. A typical holding period for their successful investments is between three and seven years. Generally, there are two ways that a venture fund can "exit" one of the companies in their investment portfolio: (i) through a buyout arranged with another private equity investor, or (ii) through an initial public offering (IPO) of common stock to the public equity market. Assuming that Internet Search Engine Company has developed a solid support base for its product among users and advertisers, now suppose that it has attracted the interest of Buyout Partners Fund, a firm specializing in doing leveraged buyouts of privately

Exhibit 24.23 The Private Equity Investment Process

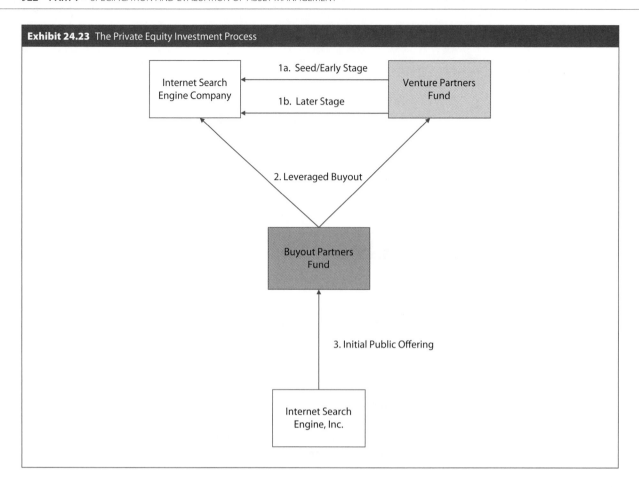

held companies. Using both debt and its own capital, Buyout Partners Fund purchases all of the existing equity from both Bob and Susan (i.e., the original entrepreneurs) and Venture Partners Fund (i.e., Step 2). Like the venture capitalists, buyout funds attempt to diversify their collection of investments across as many as two or three dozen companies.

Of course, a primary goal of all equity investors is to sell their holdings for more than they paid for them. Given the risk of private transactions compared to the public stock market, buyout capitalists typically attempt to receive an average return of two-to-three times their initial cost. To achieve this outcome, which can take 10 years or longer, these investors must be able to increase the value of their holdings in any of three ways. (i) First and foremost, buyout funds provide a considerable amount of expertise in how a particular business can be run more effectively. In fact, in addition to supplying financial capital, these investors often become very active participants in the day-to-day operations of the firms with the intention of increasing operating cash flows (i.e., EBITDA). (ii) Second, buyout firms can also unlock value in a company by adjusting its capital structure to a more optimal combination of debt and equity financing. (iii) Finally, value can also be created by expanding the cash flow multiple (i.e., price-earnings, price-EBITDA) that the market is willing to pay for a firm, which can be achieved by expanding growth opportunities or reducing the company's level of risk. Because of this need for operational expertise, it is not unusual for buyout funds to specialize in certain industries or market sectors.

Buyout funds can also liquidate their investments through either a private sale to another buyout investor or through an IPO in the public market. Assume that Internet Search Engine Company has continued to expand its operations under the new management team that Buyout Partners Fund put into place to replace the original entrepreneurs. After continuing to run the company with a combination of debt and private equity funds for a number of years, the buyout firm now feels the time is right to expand the capital base further by selling additional shares of stock to the general public (i.e., Step 3). As a result of the IPO event, the company now becomes Internet Search Engine, Inc., a publicly traded corporation. An immediate advantage to Buyout Partners Fund is that the IPO creates a broader and more liquid market for their ownership shares. However, it is frequently the case in an initial stock offering that the existing owners (i.e., Buyout Partners) are restricted from selling their positions for six months or more.

Returns to Private Equity Funds   As the preceding discussion emphasizes, private equity commitments should be viewed as long-term, highly illiquid investments, regardless of the stage of a company's development in which the partnership fund specializes. In fact, although average annual returns for these investments tend to be quite high over time, the initial years of a new private equity commitment usually produce negative returns. This is because the organizational expenses incurred by the fund's general partner are drawn from invested capital, as well as the fact that the less-successful investments in the portfolio tend to be recognized quickly and written down. However, as the better-performing investments increase in value over time and are sold at a profit, the returns to the private equity fund tend to increase dramatically. This return pattern is known as the **J-curve effect** and is illustrated in Exhibit 24.24. The performance measure in this exhibit is the internal rate of return (IRR), which is the most widely used statistic for private market investments. In the early years of a fund's operations, these IRR calculations are usually based on valuation estimates, since the portfolio companies are themselves illiquid assets that trade infrequently. As these assets are sold over time, the IRR statistics become based on the actual cash distributions to the investors.

Beyond the historical data summarized in Exhibit 24.14 and Exhibit 24.21, another way to think about the performance of private equity investments relative to other asset classes is to compare the *dispersion* of outcomes that investors experience over time. Exhibit 24.25 lists returns for several different asset class categories when the investment was made with (i) a "good" fund manager (i.e., a manager with performance in the top quartile of all available managers), (ii) an "average" manager (i.e., the median performer), and (iii) a "bad" manager (i.e.,

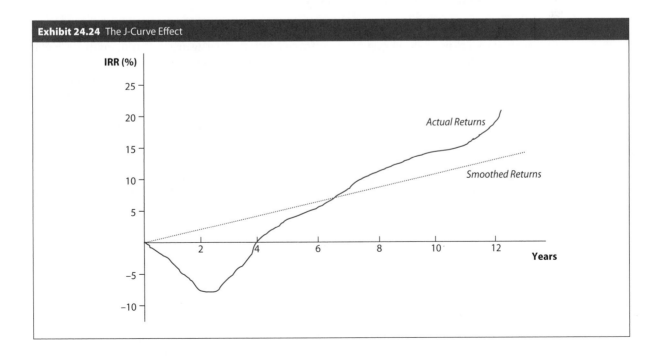

Exhibit 24.24 The J-Curve Effect

a bottom-quartile performer). The return data reflect historical performance over the 10-year period ending in 2006. The last row of the exhibit lists the *interquartile range* for each asset class, which is the difference in the returns between the top- and bottom-quartile managers. This statistic serves as a measure of the dispersion in returns for a given asset category because it reflects the opportunity cost of placing capital with a low-performing manager instead of a top performer. For instance, in large-cap U.S. public equities, the difference between the performance of a good and bad manager is only 1.26 percent. However, in private equity, this difference is 11.38 percent, almost 10 times as large! Thus, in addition to its higher overall risk level, investors also need to realize that the selection of the right private equity fund manager is critical to the success of the investment.

24.5 Ethics and Regulation in the Professional Asset Management Industry

The issue of ethical behavior arises any time one person is hired to perform a service for or look after the interests of another. Economists often refer to this potential conflict as the *principal-agent problem*, which can be summarized as follows: A principal (owner of the assets) hires an agent (manager) to manage her assets. She rightfully expects that the manager will make decisions that are in her best interest. Although he is being paid to protect the owner's assets, the manager also has the incentive to take actions that may be in his best interest rather than the client's. For instance, the manager might misuse the owner's assets in both subtle ways (e.g., generating unnecessary expenses for first-class travel or office furnishings) and more blatant ways (e.g., expropriation of resources).

This sort of **agency conflict** occurs frequently in financial relationships. The stockholders of a corporation (i.e., principals) are the owners of the firm's assets, but they usually hire professional managers (i.e., agents) to run the company. Thus, the stockholders face the constant challenge of how they can keep the managers' incentives aligned with theirs. This topic is particularly important for the investment management business because the entire industry is based on handling someone else's money, meaning that agency issues are always present. In this section, we consider how the industry addresses these conflicts, both from a legal (i.e., regulatory) and ethical standpoint.

24.5.1 Regulation in the Asset Management Industry

Professional portfolio managers are entrusted with the management of trillions of dollars. It is therefore not surprising that the investment industry is highly regulated to ensure a minimum level of acceptable practice. These regulations, which often involve a complex interaction between state and federal laws, are designed for the primary purpose of ensuring that portfolio managers act in the best interests of their investors. At their most basic level, these regulations are written to promote adequate disclosure of information related to the investment process

Exhibit 24.25 Dispersion of Asset Class Investment Returns: 1997–2006

Quartile Break	U.S. Equity Large Cap	U.S. Equity Small Cap	Non-U.S. Equity	Fixed Income U.S.	Fixed Income Non-U.S.	Private Equity
25th	9.87%	14.35%	11.79%	6.82%	7.45%	23.33%
Median	9.14	13.38	9.95	6.05	6.16	13.78
75th	8.61	11.21	8.03	5.88	5.30	11.95
Interquartile Range	1.26%	3.14%	3.76%	0.94%	2.15%	11.38%

Source: Data from a report to the Board of Trustees at Texas Teachers Retirement System.

and to provide various antifraud protections. Exhibit 24.26 describes the six principal securities laws that govern the investment management industry, including the Securities Act of 1933 (primary regulatory target: security issuers), the Securities Exchange Act of 1934 (security brokers), the Investment Company Act of 1940 (mutual funds), the Investment Advisers Act of 1940 (advisors and private managers), the Employee Retirement Income Security Act of 1974 (retirement asset managers and fiduciaries), and the Pension Protection Act of 2006 (pension fund sponsors and managers).

One of the main intentions of these regulations is to guarantee that investment professionals keep accurate and detailed transaction records and that account information is reported to investors in a fair and timely manner. As the Investment Company Institute notes, the U.S. Securities and Exchange Commission (SEC) is the main federal agency responsible for regulating professional asset management activities in the United States. In addition to monitoring compliance with existing statutes, the SEC performs the following functions:

- Maintains strict standards on the use of leverage so that funds do not take undue risk;
- Ensures that funds maintain effective governance systems;
- Requires understandable reporting and full disclosure to investors and works to eliminate fraud and abuse;
- Reviews required filings of investment companies; and
- Develops and revises rules to adapt regulations to new circumstances.

Other regulatory agencies that help to govern behavior in the investment industry include the U.S. Department of Labor (protection of pension plans, including 401(k) plans), NASDR (regulation of the securities industry under National Association for Securities Dealer rules), the U.S. Commodity and Futures Trading Commission (monitors futures and commodities trading activities), and the U.S. Internal Revenue Service (setting and enforcing of tax policies).

The main federal regulation governing the management of private pension funds is the Employee Retirement Income Security Act (ERISA), which was enacted in 1974 and primarily impacts the activities of private management companies as well as mutual funds.

Exhibit 24.26 Principal Securities Laws for the Asset Management Industry

The Securities Act of 1933 requires federal registration of all public offerings of securities, including investment company shares or units. The 1933 Act also requires that all investors receive a current prospectus describing the fund.

The Securities Exchange Act of 1934 regulates broker-dealers, including investment company principal underwriters and other entities that sell mutual fund shares, and requires them to register with the U.S. Securities and Exchange Commission (SEC). Among other things, the 1934 Act requires registered broker-dealers to maintain extensive books and records, segregate customer securities in adequate custodial accounts, and file detailed, annual financial reports.

The Investment Company Act of 1940 regulates the structure and operations of investment companies by imposing restrictions on investments and requiring investment companies, among other things, to maintain detailed books and records, safeguard their portfolio securities, and file semiannual reports with the SEC.

The Investment Advisers Act of 1940 requires federal registration of all investment advisers, including those to mutual funds and other investment companies. The Advisers Act contains provisions requiring fund advisors to meet recordkeeping, custodial, reporting, and other regulatory responsibilities.

The Employees Retirement Income Security Act of 1974 (ERISA) requires minimum standards for the organization, management, and disclosure of employee benefit plans, such as pension plans in private industry. ERISA also established standards of conduct for employee benefit plan fiduciaries and created the Individual Retirement Account (IRA) investment vehicle.

The Pension Protection Act of 2006 requires pension plan sponsors to more accurately calculate their plan obligations and gives employees greater control over how their accounts are invested. The 2006 Act also reforms regulations regarding the management and payout provisions for private foundations.

Source: Adapted in part from data in Investment Company Institute, *2007 Investment Company Fact Book.*

ERISA clearly states that pension funds are to be managed to the needs of the plan participants and their beneficiaries—as opposed to the corporation sponsoring the plan—and that managers should diversify plan assets so as to minimize the risk of large losses. As Del Guercio (1996) discusses, a key feature of ERISA is the *prudent man* statute, which outlines the level of fiduciary care that the manager must provide to the investor. This definition of the manager's required level of "care, skill, prudence, and diligence" was the first legal recognition of prudence involving the entire portfolio, rather than the individual securities on a case-by-case basis.

One of the appreciable advantages that the hedge fund industry enjoys is that it is relatively free from regulatory prohibitions that might otherwise impede the investment process. These funds tend to adopt a limited liability format (e.g., limited partnership, limited liability company) purposely to avoid having to register with the SEC. This freedom allows hedge fund managers to employ certain strategic tools (e.g., leverage, short selling) that are not available to traditional fund managers. A hedge fund qualifies for an exemption from the Investment Company Act if it has fewer than 100 investors, while hedge fund managers are exempt from the Investment Advisors Act if they manage less than $25 million in assets. Beyond this, the National Securities Markets Improvement Act of 1996 further increased the number of hedge funds and investors that are exempt from government regulation. On the other hand, if a quarter of a hedge fund's assets consist of retirement plan assets, the fund must comply with the restrictions set forth under ERISA.

24.5.2 Standards for Ethical Behavior

Many developed economies like that in the United States are founded on the notion of financial market discipline. In such a system, government intervention is necessary to remedy situations when market forces fail to adequately protect investor interests. Unfortunately, as Boatright (2008) points out, such failures do occur. Investors are well aware of the securities scandals of the 1980s that made Ivan Boesky and Michael Milken household names. Further, the market timing trading scandals that tainted the mutual fund industry in 2003 proved that lapses in ethical judgment could take place at the company level as well. Finally, the financial rescue of Long Term Capital Management that occurred in the 1990s created considerable interest in increasing governmental oversight of the hedge fund industry.

Transgressions of this nature attest to the fact that although regulations can punish those found in violation of the law, they cannot prevent all such abuses from occurring in the first place. Absolute prevention requires self-regulation on the part of the asset manager in the form of a strict set of personal ethical standards. Prentice (2007) and Jennings (2000) have stressed that the desire of individuals and firms in the investment management business to maintain their reputation with clients is a major motivating factor in the practice of self-regulation. Avera (1994) has outlined four general principles that should form the cornerstone of the standards of conduct in the profession. First, managers must conduct themselves with integrity and act in an ethical manner in all dealings. Second, they should perform financial analysis in a professional and ethical manner. Third, managers should act with competence and strive to maintain and improve their competence. Finally, they should always use proper care and exercise independent professional judgment.[10]

The CFA (i.e., Chartered Financial Analysts) Institute—which was formerly known as the Association for Investment Management and Research (AIMR)—has developed for its worldwide membership of security analysts and money managers a rigorous *Code of Ethics* and *Standards of Professional Conduct* based on these principals. (These are available online at

[10] For interesting discussions of the investing public's perception of ethics in the asset management industry, see Lummer (1994) and Ware (2000).

www.cfainstitute.org/centre/ethics/code/.) The *Code of Ethics* contains an expanded version of the four themes listed above and can be stated as follows:

Members of the CFA Institute must:

- Act with integrity, competence, diligence, respect, and in an ethical manner with the public, clients, prospective clients, employers, employees, colleagues in the investment profession, and other participants in the global capital markets.
- Place the integrity of the investment profession and the interests of clients above their own personal interests.
- Use reasonable care and exercise independent professional judgment when conducting investment analysis, making investment recommendations, taking investment actions, and engaging in other professional activities.
- Practice and encourage others to practice in a professional and ethical manner that will reflect credit on ourselves and the profession.
- Promote the integrity of, and uphold the rules governing, capital markets.
- Maintain and improve their professional competence and strive to maintain and improve the competence of other investment professionals.

The specific standards of practice suggested by these ethical mandates are summarized at the back of the book in Appendix B. These standards provide asset managers with precisely defined conduct and actions that are acceptable (or, more to the point, unacceptable) in daily practice. For example, the general principle that managers should use proper care becomes a specific requirement that they must be able to justify the suitability of any investment decision made on behalf of a particular client. The CFA Institute expects all of its members, which includes everyone holding the CFA designation, to uphold these standards on a voluntary basis. Violations deemed severe enough can result in the loss of a manager's charter.

To further promote ethical behavior in the asset management industry, the CFA Institute recently launched the Centre for Financial Market Integrity. The stated purpose in creating the Centre was "to develop timely, practical solutions to global capital market issues, while advancing investors' interests by promoting the highest standards of ethics and professionalism within the investment community worldwide."[11] The Centre's guiding principles—which stress the fact that investors should come first in all of the manager's activities, from investment decisions

---

Exhibit 24.27 Guiding Principles for Ethical Behavior in the Asset Management Industry

- Investors come first. The interests of the investing client must always take precedence over the interests of investment professionals and their employers.
- Investment professionals must act ethically and in accordance with the highest professional standards. They must:
  – Act with integrity in all their dealings
  – Maintain independence and objectivity.
  – Continuously strive to maintain and improve their professional knowledge and competence.
- Investors need complete, accurate, timely and transparent information from securities issuers.
- Financial statements should be reported from the perspective of the shareholder who bears the ultimate risk, and with the shareholder's best interests held paramount.
  – Financial statements should be fully transparent and report the fair values of all assets, liabilities, exchanges and transactions that could potentially impact the investor.
  – All assets and liabilities should be included in the balance sheet, with no hidden assets, hidden debt or hidden obligations.
- Markets should move toward one set of global, high-quality standards for reporting financial information.
- Self-regulation is generally the preferred method for promoting fair and efficient markets. However, we recognize that some circumstances require additional regulation in order to ensure adequate investor protection.

Source: *CFA* Centre for Financial Market Integrity.

---

[11] A more complete description of the Centre's goals and activities can be found at http://www.cfainstitute.org/centre.

to financial reporting—are listed in Exhibit 24.27. In recognition of the unique place of trust that portfolio managers enjoy, one recent initiative that the Centre has undertaken on behalf of the worldwide constituency of the CFA Institute has been the creation of a comprehensive *Asset Manager Code of Professional Conduct.* Established in 2005, the *Asset Manager Code* sets forth minimum standards for providing asset management services to clients. It seeks to extend the voluntary standards of practice governing individual conduct to a set of rules that pertains to entire investment management firms. Although many firms already have such standards in place, others (including both traditional managers and hedge funds) do not, and this is the niche the new *Code* is designed to fill.

24.5.3 Examples of Ethical Conflicts

Many ethical breaches, such as plagiarizing research reports or falsifying performance statements, are unambiguously wrong. Other lapses are not as clear-cut. We will conclude this section with a discussion of three examples of how possible conflicts between the manager and the investor can arise from accepted business practices.

Incentive Compensation Schemes The first example is related to the way in which managers are compensated for their services. We saw earlier in the chapter that traditional asset management companies—both public and private—typically receive fees based on AUM. Further, hedge fund managers also receive a performance allocation fee that is tied directly to the portfolio's performance. The managers at these companies, in turn, are often compensated with a base salary and bonus that depends on the performance of their portfolios relative to those of their peers. Brown, Harlow, and Starks (1996) argued that this arrangement is analogous to a golf or tennis tournament where the players with the best relative performance at the end of the competition receive the largest payoffs. They documented that mutual fund managers with the worst relative performance midway through a compensation period were more likely to increase the risk of the portfolio in an effort to increase their final standing. Of course, altering fund risk to enhance their own compensation suggests that some managers may not always act in their clients' best interests.

Soft Dollar Arrangements A second potential ethical dilemma for professional asset managers involves the use of **soft dollars.** Soft dollars are generated when a manager commits the investor to paying a brokerage commission that is higher than the simple cost of executing a security trade in exchange for the manager receiving additional bundled services from the broker. A typical example of this practice would be for a manager to route her equity trades through a nondiscount broker in order to receive security research reports that the brokerage firm produces. It may not be hard for the manager to justify how this additional research benefits the investor—who, of course, is ultimately paying for the service—but the story is quite different if, instead of research, the manager receives from the broker "perks," such as office equipment, secretarial services, or even payment for personal travel. Authors such as Blume (1993) have argued that this practice can result in a misallocation of resources or an expropriation of investor wealth by the manager, although Horan and Johnsen (2000) document that the use of soft dollars is actually a cost-effective way for investors to monitor a manager's behavior. In 1998, the CFA Institute adopted a comprehensive set of voluntary standards designed to give its members guidance on the permissible uses of soft dollar arrangements.

Marketing Investment Management Services A final example of an ethical dilemma that confronts professional asset management organizations is how and when to advertise their services. Conventional wisdom holds that it would be in the investors' best interests for any particular investment management company to build a steady awareness over time of its relative merits. However, in their consumer (i.e., investor) survey in the mutual fund market, Capon,

Fitzsimons, and Prince (1996) documented that the main factor in the decision of which fund's shares to buy was the immediate past total return performance of the portfolio. Zweig (2000) observed that a consequence of this tendency has been the development of a situation in which mutual funds time their advertisements around relative peaks in their performance. Further, firms that run a family of funds can choose which portfolio or manager they want to promote on a situational basis, while still maintaining continuous brand awareness for the entire complex. Despite the usual disclaimers to the effect that "past returns are not an indication of future performance," the decision to always promote the "hot hand" is likely to be effective, but it is also likely to result in a misallocation of investor capital.

In summary, it is important for investors to recognize that potential ethical conflicts will exist any time they hire professional investment managers. Investors are protected by the series of regulations that oversee the security industry as well as the strict standards imposed by trade associations such as the CFA Institute. Of course, perhaps the best protection that investors have is the vast majority of the thousands of investment advisors and managers throughout the world who are unwilling to do anything that would jeopardize their personal and professional reputations.

· ·

24.6 What Do You Want from a Professional Asset Manager?

What functions do you want your portfolio manager to perform for you? The list probably includes some or all of the following:

1. Help determine your investment objectives and constraints (e.g., return goals, risk tolerance) and develop a portfolio that is consistent with them.
2. Diversify your portfolio to eliminate unsystematic risk.
3. Maintain your portfolio diversification within your desired risk class while allowing flexibility so that you can shift between alternative investment instruments as desired.
4. Attempt to achieve a risk-adjusted performance level that is superior to that of your relevant benchmark; some investors may be willing to sacrifice diversification for superior returns in limited segments of their portfolios.
5. Administer the account, keep records of costs and transactions, provide timely information for tax purposes, and reinvest dividends if desired.
6. Maintain ethical standards of behavior at all times.

Not all of the types of asset management organizations we have discussed in this chapter address each of these goals. For instance, mutual funds do not determine your risk preference for you, while alternative asset investments are seldom well diversified. However, once you determine your risk-return preferences, you can choose a mutual fund from a large and growing variety of alternatives designed to meet almost any investment goal. In general, these types of managers are consistent in meeting their stated goals for investment strategies, risk, and returns. Private asset management companies are oriented toward providing similar services (including investment policy development) for clients who have larger amounts of investable capital.

Diversifying your portfolio to eliminate unsystematic risk is one of the major benefits of both private management companies and mutual funds. Many mutual funds provide *instant diversification,* which is especially beneficial to small investors who do not have the resources to form their own large-scale portfolios. Although diversification varies among funds, typically a large percentage of existing portfolios have a correlation with the market above 0.80. Therefore, most mutual funds provide excellent diversification, especially if they state this goal as an explicit objective.

The third function your portfolio manager might perform for you is to maintain the diversification of your portfolio within your desired risk class. It should not be too surprising that both types of traditional asset manager (i.e., private management companies and mutual funds) generally maintain the stability of their correlation with the market over time because few managers change the makeup of reasonably well-diversified portfolios very much. Strong evidence exists regarding the consistency of the risk class mandates for portfolios regardless of whether the overall performance is better or worse than average. On the other hand, hedge fund portfolios often vary significantly within the broad context of their designated strategy as managers attempt to add the maximum amount of alpha (i.e., the difference between actual and expected return).

Mutual funds have met the desire for flexibility to change investment instruments by creating numerous funds within a given management company. Typically, investment groups—such as T. Rowe Price, Vanguard, or Fidelity Investments—will allow you to shift between portfolios in their family of funds without a charge simply by calling the company. Therefore, you can shift between an aggressive stock fund, a money market fund, and a bond fund for much less than it would cost you in time and money to buy and sell numerous individual issues. By their nature, both private management companies and hedge funds tend to restrict an investor's ability to make these sorts of changes; accordingly, both of these management types are considered to be less liquid than mutual funds.

The fourth function of your portfolio manager is to provide risk-adjusted performance that is superior to your benchmark, which implies that it is superior to a naive buy-and-hold investment policy. The rapid development of the alternative asset industry over the past several years suggests two things in this regard. First, investors increasingly view these managers as being better suited to produce positive and consistent alphas than traditional managers. Second, it is becoming more and more difficult for many traditional asset managers to generate superior risk-adjusted returns because of the many constraints imposed on their investment process (e.g., short sale prohibitions, leverage restrictions).

The fifth function of a portfolio manager is account administration. All managers provide this service to some degree. However, private management companies are the most likely to see all (or substantially all) of a client's assets and so these firms are in the best position to administer the account most effectively. Conversely, most mutual funds also provide many valuable administrative services. For instance, they allow automatic reinvestment of dividends with no charge and supply annual statements of dividend income and capital gain distribution that can be used to prepare tax returns. Give their partnership format, hedge funds and private equity funds also provide investors with necessary tax information as well as periodic accounting of investment activity.

The final function that you should expect from your portfolio manager is ethical behavior that strictly follows the prevailing regulations and standards of conduct in the industry. For all investors, this is—and should be—a nonnegotiable requirement of any manager, regardless of the organizational form of the company. As we have seen, professional asset management is a fiduciary business, and those managers whose conduct violates the trust of those whose wealth they protect and grow will not last long. In extreme cases, they may even suffer legal consequences.

In summary, as an investor, you probably want your portfolio manager to perform a broad array of functions. Typically, however, no single manager is equipped to provide all of the services that you may require. Therefore, it is quite common for investors to form a "portfolio" of managers with different talents and capabilities (e.g., a hedge fund manager to provide superior risk-adjusted returns, an index mutual fund manager to provide diversification for the majority of your assets). Given what we know about the value of diversifying our financial capital across different asset classes and securities, it should come as no surprise that the same principle holds for portfolio management skills as well.

• • • • SUMMARY • • • •

- There are two primary types of professional asset management companies. Management and advisory firms hold the assets of individual and institutional investors in separate accounts. Investment companies are pools of assets that are managed collectively. Investors in these funds receive shares representing their proportional ownership in the underlying portfolio of stocks, bonds, or other securities. These fund shares can either be traded in the secondary market (closed-end) or sold directly back to the investment company (mutual fund) at the prevailing net asset value. A wide variety of funds are available, so you can find one to match almost any investment objective or combination of investment objectives.

- In recent years, the professional asset management industry has undergone considerable structural change. Among traditional "long-only" asset management firms, there has been a trend toward consolidating assets under management (AUM) in large, multiproduct companies. This trend has had a beneficial effect for investors of reducing management fees, which are usually charged on a declining percentage of AUM. Investment companies also often charge fees for marketing their shares, in the form of front-end fees, annual 12b-1 fees, or back-end load fees. A substantial amount of publicly available information exists on mutual fund investment practices and performance,

to help investors make decisions that are appropriate for their circumstances.

- A second trend that has marked the professional asset management industry in recent years has been the rapid development of vehicles to invest in alternative asset classes, such as hedge funds and private equity. One of the main advantages that these funds enjoy over traditional investment companies is that they are generally less restricted in what strategies they can follow and investment techniques they can employ. An example of this is the use of both leverage and short selling to supplement main portfolio formation strategy. As a consequence of this additional level of flexibility, many investors have come to regard hedge funds as being in a unique position to produce superior risk-adjusted returns.

- Issues of ethical behavior arise any time one person is hired to perform a service for another. The professional asset management industry protects investors through a series of government regulations and voluntary standards of practice imposed by trade associations on their members. The primary purpose of these regulations and standards is to ensure that managers deal with all investors fairly and equitably and that information about investment performance is accurately reported. Two areas of particular concern in the investment community involve manager compensation arrangements and the use of soft dollars.

• • • • SUGGESTED READINGS • • • •

CFA Institute. *Standards of Practice Handbook*, 9th ed. Charlottesville, VA: 2006.

CFA Institute. *Points of Inflection: New Directions for Portfolio Management*. Charlottesville, VA: 2004.

Lakonishok, Josef, Andrei Shleifer, and Robert W. Vishny. "The Structure and Performance of the Money Management Industry." In *Brookings Papers on Economic Activity*. Washington, DC: Brookings Institute, 1992.

Oberlechner, Thomas. *The Psychology of Ethics in the Finance and Investment Industry*. Charlottesville, VA: Research Foundation of CFA Institute, 2007.

Pozen, Robert C. *The Mutual Fund Business*, 2nd ed. Boston, MA: Houghton Mifflin, 2002.

• • • • QUESTIONS • • • •

1. What are the differences between a management and advisory firm and an investment company? Describe the approach toward portfolio management adopted by each organization.

2. It has been suggested that the professional asset management community is rapidly becoming dominated by a fairly small number of huge, multiproduct firms. Discuss whether the data presented in Exhibit 24.2 support that view.

3. Closed-end funds generally invest in securities and financial instruments that are relatively illiquid whereas most mutual funds invest in widely traded stocks and bonds. Explain the difference between closed-end and open-end funds and why this liquidity distinction matters.

4. What is the difference between a load fund and a no-load fund?

5. Should you care about how well a mutual fund is diversified? Why or why not?

6. As an investigator evaluating how well mutual fund managers select undervalued stocks or project market returns, discuss whether net or gross returns are more relevant.

7. You are told that Fund X experienced *above-average* performance over the past two years. Do you think it will continue over the next two years? Why or why not?

8. **CFA EXAMINATION LEVEL III** Catherine Marco is a portfolio manager with Mouton Investments, Inc., a regional money management firm. She is considering investments in alternative assets and decides to research the following three questions about long-short strategies and hedge funds:

   1. How can the alpha generated from a long-short strategy in one asset class be transported to another asset class?

   2. What are the *three* major quantifiable sources of risk that a fund of hedge funds manager must consider in risk monitoring?

   3. For a fund of hedge funds, how does risk-based leverage differ from accounting-based leverage?

   a. Formulate *one* correct response to *each* of Marco's three questions.

   Marco decides to explore various hedge fund investment strategies and reviews the following three strategy components:

   1. Buy stocks after positive earnings surprise announcements, anticipating that the stock price will rise in the short term.

   2. Establish appropriate long and short positions in stocks of companies that have announced a merger or acquisition or are rumored to be considering such a transaction.

   3. Use neural networks to detect patterns in historical data.

   b. Identify the hedge fund investment strategy that is best characterized by *each* of the three strategy components reviewed by Marco.

   Following her research, Marco applies her findings to the situation of an individual client. This client currently holds only traditional equity and fixed income investments and is willing to consider investing in alternative assets to lower the risk of his portfolio. Marco forms the following five conclusions about investing in alternative assets for this client:

   1. Investing in a fund of hedge funds is likely to increase the client's portfolio diversification and allow the client's portfolio to have exposure to a wide variety of hedge funds that may not otherwise be available to the client.

   2. A lack of transparency and the fund manager's inability to add value through portfolio construction are both disadvantages of investing in a fund of hedge funds.

   3. Because a directional hedge fund is expected to exhibit a lower dispersion of returns than a non-directional hedge fund, a directional hedge fund is a more appropriate investment for this client.

   4. One appropriate hedge fund investment strategy for this client is a macro hedge fund, which is likely to provide increased returns with a relatively low standard deviation of returns.

   5. Another approach that is consistent with the client's objectives is to use an equitized long-short strategy, which can be expected to neutralize market risk.

   c. Judge whether *each* of Marco's five conclusions is correct or incorrect. If incorrect, give *one* reason why the conclusion is incorrect.

9. Most money managers have a portion of their compensation tied to the performance of the portfolios they manage. Explain how this arrangement can create an ethical dilemma for the manager.

10. What are soft dollar arrangements? Describe one potential way they can be used to transfer wealth from the investor to the manager.

• • • • PROBLEMS • • • •

1. Suppose ABC Mutual Fund had no liabilities and owned only four stocks as follows:

Stock	Shares	Price	Market Value
W	1,000	$12	$12,000
X	1,200	15	18,000
Y	1,500	22	33,000
Z	800	16	12,800
			$75,800

The fund began by selling $50,000 of stock at $8.00 per share. What is its NAV?

2. Suppose you are considering investing $1,000 in a load fund that charges a fee of 8 percent, and you expect your investment to earn 15 percent over the next year. Alternatively, you could invest in a no-load fund with similar risk that charges a 1 percent redemption fee. You estimate that this no-load fund will earn 12 percent. Given your expectations, which is the better investment and by how much?

3. Consider the recent performance of the Closed Fund, a closed-end fund devoted to finding under-valued, thinly traded stocks:

Period	NAV	Premium/Discount
0	$10.00	0.0%
1	11.25	−5.0
2	9.85	+2.3
3	10.50	−3.2
4	12.30	−7.0

   Here price premiums and discounts are indicated by pluses and minuses, respectively, and Period 0 represents Closed Fund's initiation date.
   a. Calculate the average return per period for an investor who bought 100 shares of the Closed Fund at the initiation and then sold her position at the end of Period 4.
   b. What was the average periodic growth rate in NAV over that same period?
   c. Calculate the periodic return for another investor who bought 100 shares of Closed Fund at the end of Period 1 and sold his position at the end of Period 2.
   d. What was the periodic growth rate in NAV between Periods 1 and 2?

4. CMD Asset Management has the following fee structure for clients in its equity fund:

1.00% of first $5 million invested
0.75% of next $5 million invested
0.60% of next $10 million invested
0.40% above $20 million

   a. Calculate the annual dollar fees paid by Client 1, which has $27 million under management, and Client 2, which has $97 million under management.
   b. Calculate the fees paid by both clients as a percentage of their assets under management.
   c. What is the economic rationale for a fee schedule that declines (in percentage terms) with increases in assets under management?

5. **CFA EXAMINATION LEVEL II** Describe a potential conflict of interest in each of the following four situations:
   a. An investment advisor whose compensation is based on commissions from client trades
   b. An investment manager's use of client brokerage ("soft dollars") to purchase research or other services
   c. A portfolio manager of a mutual fund who purchases, for the fund, a substantial amount of stock in a small-capitalization company whose warrants the manager owns
   d. A research analyst who accepts reimbursement for food, lodging, and air transportation expenses for a site visit from the company on which she is writing a research report

> **Note:** In formulating your answers, you should consider AIMR's
> **Code of Ethics and Standards of Professional Conduct.**

6. Suppose that at the start of the year, a no-load mutual fund has a net asset value of $27.15 per share. During the year, it pays its shareholders a capital gain and dividend distribution of $1.12 per share and finishes the year with an NAV of $30.34.
   a. What is the return to an investor who holds 257.876 shares of this fund in his (nontaxable) retirement account?
   b. What is the after-tax return for the same investor if these shares were held in an ordinary savings account? Assume that the investor is in the 30 percent tax bracket.
   c. If the investment company allowed the investor to automatically reinvest his cash distribution in additional fund shares, how many additional shares could the investor acquire? Assume that the distribution occurred at year end and that the proceeds from the distribution can be reinvested at the year-end NAV.

7. The Focus Fund is a mutual fund that holds long-term positions in a small number of nondividend-paying stocks. Their holdings at the end of two recent years are as follows:

Stock	YEAR 1 Shares	YEAR 1 Price	YEAR 2 Shares	YEAR 2 Price
A	100,000	$45.25	100,000	$48.75
B	225,000	25.38	225,000	24.75
C	375,000	14.50	375,000	12.38
D	115,000	87.13	115,000	98.50
E	154,000	56.50	154,000	62.50
F	175,000	63.00	175,000	77.00
G	212,000	32.00	212,000	38.63
H	275,000	15.25	275,000	8.75
I	450,000	9.63	450,000	27.45
J	90,000	71.25	90,000	75.38
K	87,000	42.13	87,000	49.63
L	137,000	19.88	0	27.88
M	0	17.75	150,000	19.75
Cash		$3,542,000		$2,873,000
Expenses		$ 730,000		$ 830,000

8. At the end of both years, Focus Fund had 5,430,000 shares outstanding.
   a. Calculate the net asset value for a share of the Focus Fund at the end of Year 1, being sure to include the cash position in the net total portfolio value.
   b. Immediately after calculating its Year 1 NAV, Focus Fund sold its position in Stock L and purchased its position in Stock M (both transactions were done at Year 1 prices). Calculate the Year 2 NAV for Focus Fund and compute the growth rate in the fund share value on a percentage basis.
   c. At the end of Year 2, how many fund shares of the Focus Fund could the manager redeem without having to liquidate her stock positions (i.e., using only the cash account)?
   d. If immediately after calculating the Year 2 NAV, the manager received investor redemption requests for 500,000 shares, how many shares of each stock would she have to sell in order to maintain the same proportional ownership position in each stock? Assume that she liquidates the entire cash position before she sells any stock holdings.

8. Mutual funds can effectively charge sales fees in one of three ways: front-end load fees, 12b-1 (i.e., annual) fees, or deferred (i.e., back-end) load fees. Assume that the SAS Fund offers its investors the choice of the following sales fee arrangements: (1) a 3 percent front-end load, (2) a 0.50 percent annual deduction, or (3) a 2 percent back-end load, paid at the liquidation of the investor's position. Also, assume that SAS Fund averages NAV growth of 12 percent per year.
   a. If you start with $100,000 in investment capital, calculate what an investment in SAS would be worth in three years under each of the proposed sales fee schemes. Which scheme would you choose?
   b. If your investment horizon were 10 years, would your answer in Part a change? Demonstrate.
   c. Explain the relationship between the timing of the sales charge and your investment horizon. In general, if you intend to hold your position for a long time, which fee arrangement would you prefer?

9. **CFA EXAMINATION LEVEL II** Clark & Kerns (C&K), a U.S. pension fund manager for more than 20 years, plans to establish offices in a European and a Pacific Rim country in order to manage pension funds located in those countries and invest in their local stock markets. Tony Clark, CFA, managing partner, learns that investment organizations and their affiliates in the European country perform three functions:
   - consult with corporate pension sponsors on how the pension fund should be managed and by whom;
   - manage their portfolios; and
   - execute securities transactions as a broker for the funds.

   Common practice in this country is to withhold disclosure of the ownership of business organizations. Clark believes that C&K must provide all three functions to compete effectively. He therefore decides to establish offices in Europe to offer all three services to prospective pension fund clients, through local organizations owned by C&K. The pension consulting organization will be Europension Group; the portfolio management firm will be C&K International; and the broker-dealer operation will be Alps Securities.

a. Briefly describe two AIMR Standards of Professional Conduct that apply to Clark, if C&K provides all three functions on a combined basis. Describe the specific duty Clark is required to perform to comply with these Standards.

Clark learns that a customary practice in the European country is to allocate at least 80 percent of pension fund assets to fixed-income securities.

b. Identify and briefly explain two AIMR Standards of Professional Conduct that apply to this situation.

Clark observes that portfolio managers in the Pacific Rim country frequently use insider information in their investment decisions. Because the pension fund management industry is performance oriented, Clark decides to adopt local investment practices as the only way to attract and retain local corporate clients in that country.

c. Identify and briefly explain two AIMR Standards of Professional Conduct that apply to this situation.

10. **CFA EXAMINATION LEVEL II** Peter and Andrea Mueller have built up their $600,000 investment portfolio over many years through regular purchases of mutual funds holding only U.S. securities. Each purchase was based on personal research but without consideration of their other holdings. They would now like advice on their total portfolio, which follows:

	Type	Market Sector	Beta	Percent of Total
Andrea's company stock	Stock	Small-cap growth	1.40	35
Blue-chip growth fund	Stock	Large-cap growth	1.20	20
Super beta fund	Stock	Small-cap growth	1.60	10
Conservative fund	Stock	Large-cap value	1.05	2
Index fund	Stock	Large-cap index	1.00	3
No dividend fund	Stock	Large-cap growth	1.25	25
Long-term zero coupon fund	Bond	Government	—	5

Evaluate the Mueller's portfolio in terms of the following criteria:

a. Preference for "minimal volatility"

b. Equity diversification

c. Asset allocation (including cash flow needs)

After you read this chapter, you should be able to answer the following questions:

- What major requirements do clients expect from their portfolio managers?
- What is the peer group comparison method of evaluating an investor's performance?
- What is the Treynor portfolio performance measure?
- What is the Sharpe portfolio performance measure?
- What is the Jensen portfolio performance measure and how can it be adapted to include multifactor models of risk and expected return?
- What is the information ratio and how is it related to the other performance measures?
- When evaluating a sample of portfolios, how do you determine how well diversified they are?
- What are the Fama and Sortino portfolio performance measures and what information do they provide beyond other measures?
- How can investment performance be measured by analyzing the security holdings of a portfolio?
- What is attribution analysis and how can it be used to distinguish between a portfolio manager's market timing and security selection skills?
- What are customized benchmarks and what are the important characteristics that any benchmark should possess?
- How do bond portfolio performance measures differ from equity portfolio performance measures?
- What are time-weighted and dollar-weighted returns, and which should be reported under the CFA Institute's Performance Presentation Standards?

This chapter outlines the theory and practice of evaluating the performance of an investment portfolio. We begin this discussion by considering what an investor should require of his or her portfolio manager. We also briefly discuss how investment performance was evaluated before portfolio theory and the asset pricing models were developed and examine an assessment technique—called a *peer group comparison*—still widely used today that does not require an explicit adjustment for the risk exposure of the portfolio.

While comparing a portfolio's historical returns to those produced by other managers or indexes can be instructive, such comparisons do not produce a complete picture of the portfolio's performance. The central tenet of the modern approach to performance measurement is that it is impossible to make a thorough evaluation of an investment without explicitly controlling for the risk of the portfolio. Given the complexity of the issues involved, it should not be surprising to learn that there is not a single universally accepted procedure for risk-adjusting portfolio returns. Instead, there are several techniques that are commonly employed in practice and we will consider the most prominent of these in detail. There are four portfolio performance evaluation techniques (referred to as *composite performance measures*) that comprise the basic "toolkit" for measuring risk-adjusted performance. Although some redundancy exists

among the measures, each of them provides unique perspectives, so they are best viewed as a complementary set.

Following this discussion, we consider some additional techniques that measure different aspects of investment performance. We demonstrate how an investor can evaluate a manager's performance by looking at the underlying security holdings of the portfolio and examine attribution analysis, a measurement technique designed to establish the source of a portfolio manager's skill. We will also discuss how measuring the performance of a bond portfolio differs from that of a collection of stocks.

The chapter concludes with a discussion of a number of factors to consider when applying these various measures. We examine the controversy surrounding the selection of the proper benchmark to use in the risk-adjustment process and discuss why this *benchmark problem* becomes larger when you begin investing globally. The characteristics of a good benchmark are also described. Finally, we examine industry standards for calculating returns and reporting portfolio performance to investors.

25.1 What Is Required of a Portfolio Manager?

There are two desirable attributes of a portfolio manager's performance:

1. The ability to derive above-average returns for a given risk class.
2. The ability to diversify the portfolio completely to eliminate all unsystematic risk, relative to the portfolio's benchmark.

In terms of return, the first requirement is obvious, but the need to consider *risk* in this context was generally not apparent before the 1960s, when work in portfolio theory became widely accepted. As we have seen, superior risk-adjusted returns can be derived through *either* superior timing or superior security selection.

An equity portfolio manager who can do a superior job of predicting the peaks or troughs of the equity market can adjust the portfolio's composition to anticipate market trends, holding a completely diversified portfolio of high-beta stocks through rising markets and favoring low-beta stocks and money market instruments during declining markets. Bigger gains in rising markets and smaller losses in declining markets give the portfolio manager above-average risk-adjusted returns.

A fixed-income portfolio manager with superior timing ability changes the portfolio's duration in anticipation of interest rate changes by increasing the duration of the portfolio in anticipation of failing interest rates and reducing it when rates are expected to rise. If properly executed, this bond portfolio management strategy likewise provides superior risk-adjusted returns.

As an alternative strategy, a portfolio manager may try consistently to select undervalued stocks or bonds for a given risk class. Even without superior market timing, such a portfolio would likely experience above-average risk-adjusted returns.

The second factor to consider in evaluating a portfolio manager is the ability to diversify completely. We have seen that, on average, the market rewards investors only for bearing systematic (market) risk. Unsystematic risk is not considered when determining required returns because it can be eliminated in a diversified market portfolio. Because they can expect no reward for bearing this uncertainty, investors often want their portfolios completely to be diversified. The level of diversification can be judged on the basis of the correlation between the portfolio returns and the returns for a market portfolio or some other benchmark index. A completely diversified portfolio is perfectly correlated with the fully diversified benchmark portfolio.

These two requirements of a portfolio manager are important because some portfolio evaluation techniques take into account one requirement but not the other. Other techniques implicitly consider both factors but do not differentiate between them.

25.2 Early Performance Measurement Techniques

25.2.1 Portfolio Evaluation before 1960

At one time, investors evaluated portfolio performance almost entirely on the basis of the rate of return. They were aware of the concept of risk but did not know how to measure it, so they could not consider it explicitly. Developments in portfolio theory in the early 1960s showed investors how to quantify risk in terms of the variability of returns. Still, because no single measure combined both return and risk, the two factors had to be considered separately, as Friend, Blume, and Crockett (1970) did by grouping portfolios into similar risk classes based on return variance and then compared the rates of return for alternative portfolios directly within these risk classes.

25.2.2 Peer Group Comparisons

A **peer group comparison**, which Kritzman (1990) describes as the most common manner of evaluating portfolio managers, collects the returns produced by a representative universe of investors over a specific period of time and displays them in a simple boxplot format. The universe is typically divided into percentiles, showing the relative ranking of a given investor. For instance, a portfolio manager who produced a one-year return of 12.4 percent would be in the 10th percentile if only 9 other portfolios in a universe of 100 produced a higher return. Although these comparisons can get quite detailed, it is common for the boxplot graphic to include the maximum and minimum returns, as well as the returns falling at the 25th, 50th (i.e., the median), and 75th percentiles.

Exhibit 25.1 shows the returns from periods of varying length for a representative investor—labeled here as "U.S. Equity with Cash"—relative to its peer universe of other U.S. domestic equity managers.[1] Also included in the comparison are the periodic returns to three indexes of the overall market: Standard and Poor's 500, Russell 1000, and Russell 3000. The display shows return quartiles for investment periods ranging from 5 to 10 years. The investor in question (indicated by the large dot) performed admirably, finishing above the median in each of the comparison periods. The manager of this portfolio produced the largest 9-year return (16.5 percent), well above the median return of 13.0 percent. Notice, however, that although the investor's 10-year average return exceeds the 9-year level (16.6 percent), it falls below the fifth percentile, which is no longer the best.

There are several potential problems with the peer group comparison method of evaluating an investor's performance. First, the boxplots shown in Exhibit 25.1 do not make any explicit adjustment for the risk level of the portfolios in the universe. Investment risk is only *implicitly* considered to the extent that all the portfolios in the universe have essentially the same level of volatility. This is not likely to be the case for any sizable peer group, particularly if the universe mixes portfolios with different investment styles. Second, it is almost impossible to form a truly comparable peer group that is large enough to make the percentile rankings valid and meaningful. Finally, by focusing on nothing more than relative returns, such a comparison loses sight of whether the investor in question has accomplished his individual objectives and satisfied his investment constraints.

25.3 Composite Portfolio Performance Measures

This section describes in detail the four major composite equity portfolio performance measures that combine risk and return performance into a single value. We describe each measure and then demonstrate how to compute it and interpret the results. We also compare the measures and discuss how they differ and why they rank portfolios differently.

---

[1] This example comes from Singer (1996) and was based on data from the Frank Russell Company.

Exhibit 25.1 An Illustrative Peer Group Comparison

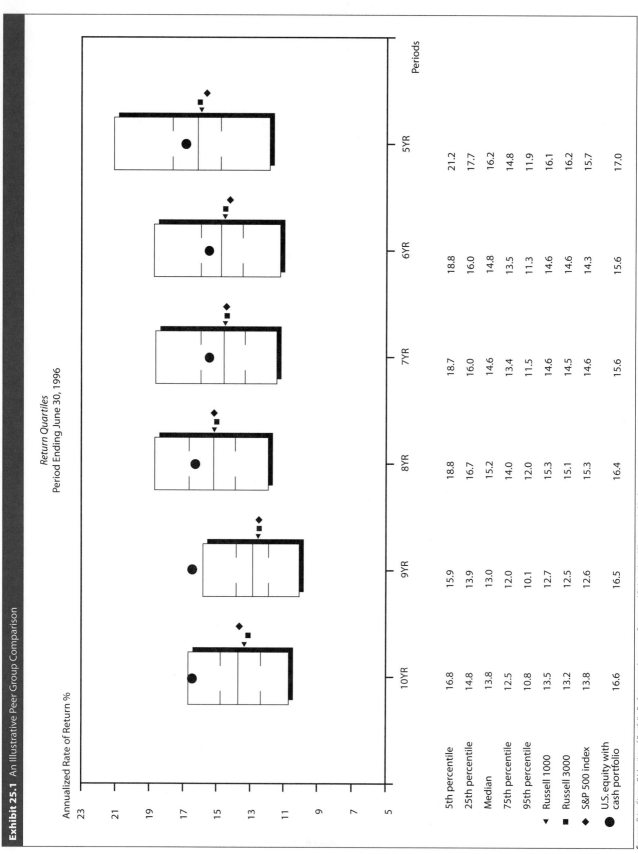

Return Quartiles
Period Ending June 30, 1996

Annualized Rate of Return %

	10YR	9YR	8YR	7YR	6YR	5YR
5th percentile	16.8	15.9	18.8	18.7	18.8	21.2
25th percentile	14.8	13.9	16.7	16.0	16.0	17.7
Median	13.8	13.0	15.2	14.6	14.8	16.2
75th percentile	12.5	12.0	14.0	13.4	13.5	14.8
95th percentile	10.8	10.1	12.0	11.5	11.3	11.9
▼ Russell 1000	13.5	12.7	15.3	14.6	14.6	16.1
■ Russell 3000	13.2	12.5	15.1	14.5	14.6	16.2
◆ S&P 500 index	13.8	12.6	15.3	14.6	14.3	15.7
● U.S. equity with cash portfolio	16.6	16.5	16.4	15.6	15.6	17.0

Periods

Source: Brian Singer, "Valuation of Portfolio Performance: Aggregate Return and Risk Analysis," *The Journal of Performance Measurement* 1, no. 1 (Fall 1996): 6–16.

25.3.1 Treynor Portfolio Performance Measure

Treynor (1965) developed the first **composite measure** of portfolio performance that included risk. He postulated two components of risk: (1) risk produced by general market fluctuations and (2) risk resulting from unique fluctuations in the portfolio securities. To identify risk due to market fluctuations, he introduced the *characteristic line,* which defines the relationship between the return for a portfolio over time and the return for the market portfolio. As we know from Chapter 8, the slope of this line is the portfolio's beta coefficient. A higher slope (beta) characterizes a portfolio that is more sensitive to market returns and has greater market risk.

Deviations from the characteristic line indicate unique return components for the portfolio relative to the market. In a completely diversified portfolio, these unique returns should cancel out. As the correlation of the portfolio with the market increases, unique risk declines and diversification improves. Because Treynor was not concerned about this aspect of portfolio performance, he gave no further consideration to the diversification measure.

Treynor's Composite Performance Measure   Treynor was interested in a measure of performance that would apply to all investors, regardless of their risk preferences. Building on developments in capital market theory, he introduced a risk-free asset that could be combined with different portfolios to form a portfolio possibility line. He showed that rational, risk-averse investors would always prefer the portfolio line with the largest slope because this would place them on the highest indifference curve. The slope of this portfolio possibility line (designated T) is equal to[2]

25.1
$$T_i = \frac{\overline{R_i} - \overline{RFR}}{\beta_i}$$

where:

$\overline{R_i}$ = the average rate of return for Portfolio i during a specified time period

$\overline{RFR}$ = the average rate of return on a risk-free investment during the same time period

β_i = the slope of the fund's characteristic line during that time period

As noted, a larger T value indicates a better portfolio for all investors, regardless of their risk preferences. Because the numerator of this ratio $(\overline{R_i} - \overline{RFR})$ is the *risk premium* and the denominator is a measure of risk, the total expression indicates the portfolio's *risk premium return per unit of risk.* All risk-averse investors would prefer to maximize this value. The risk variable beta measures systematic risk and tells us nothing about the diversification of the portfolio. It *implicitly assumes* a completely diversified portfolio.

Comparing a portfolio's T value to a similar measure for the market portfolio indicates whether the portfolio would plot above the SML. Calculate the T value for the aggregate market as follows:

$$T_M = \frac{\overline{R_M} - \overline{RFR}}{\beta_M}$$

In this expression, β_M equals 1.0 (the market's beta) and T_M indicates the slope of the SML. Therefore, a portfolio with a higher T value than the market portfolio plots above the SML, indicating superior risk-adjusted performance.

Demonstration of Comparative Treynor Measures   Suppose that during the most recent 10-year period, the average annual total rate of return (including dividends) on an aggregate market portfolio, such as the S&P 500, was 14 percent $(\overline{R_M} = 0.14)$ and the average nominal rate of return on government T-bills was 8 percent $(\overline{RFR} = 0.08)$. As administrator of

---

[2] The terms used in the formula differ from those used by Treynor but are consistent with our earlier discussion. Also, our discussion is concerned with general *portfolio* performance rather than being limited to mutual funds.

a large pension fund that has been divided among three money managers during the past 10 years, you must decide whether to renew their investment management contracts.

Assume you are given the following results:

Investment Manager	Average Annual Rate of Return	Beta
W	0.12	0.90
X	0.16	1.05
Y	0.18	1.20

You compute T values for the market portfolio and for each of the individual portfolio managers as follows:

$$T_M = \frac{0.14 - 0.08}{1.00} = 0.060$$

$$T_W = \frac{0.12 - 0.08}{0.90} = 0.044$$

$$T_X = \frac{0.16 - 0.08}{1.05} = 0.076$$

$$T_Y = \frac{0.18 - 0.08}{1.20} = 0.083$$

These results indicate that Investment Manager W not only ranked the lowest of the three managers but did not perform as well as the aggregate market on a risk-adjusted basis. In contrast, both X and Y beat the market portfolio, and Manager Y performed somewhat better than Manager X. Both of their portfolios plotted above the SML, as shown in Exhibit 25.2.

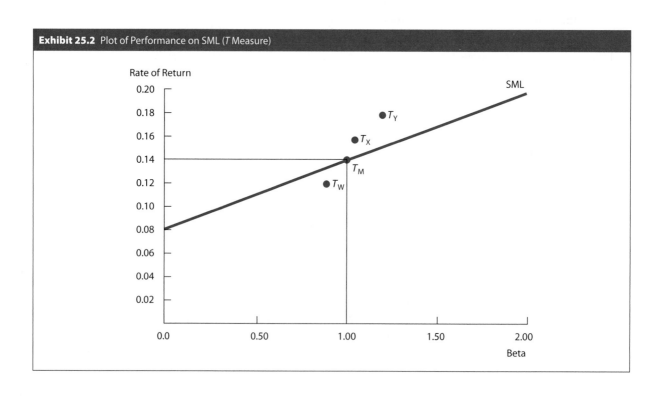

Exhibit 25.2 Plot of Performance on SML (T Measure)

Very poor return performance or very good performance with very low risk may yield negative T values. An example of poor performance is a portfolio with both an average rate of return below the risk-free rate and a positive beta. For instance, assume that a fourth portfolio manager, Z, had a portfolio beta of 0.50 but an average rate of return of only 0.07. The T value would be

$$T_Z = \frac{0.07 - 0.08}{0.50} = -0.02$$

Obviously, this performance would plot below the SML in Exhibit 25.2.

A portfolio with a *negative* beta and an average rate of return above the risk-free rate of return would likewise have a negative T value. In this case, however, it indicates exemplary performance. Suppose Portfolio Manager G invested heavily in gold mining stocks during a period of great political and economic uncertainty. Because gold often has a negative correlation with most stocks, this portfolio's beta could be negative. Assume that our gold portfolio G had a beta of –0.20 and yet experienced an average rate of return of 10 percent. The T value for this portfolio would then be

$$T_G = \frac{0.10 - 0.08}{-0.20} = -0.100$$

Although the T value is negative, if you plotted these results on a graph, it would indicate a position substantially above the SML in Exhibit 25.2.

Because negative betas can yield T values that give confusing results, it is preferable either to plot the portfolio on an SML graph or to compute the expected return for this portfolio using the SML equation and then compare this expected return to the actual return. For Portfolio G, the expected return would be

$$
\begin{aligned}
E(R_G) &= RFR + \beta_i(R_M - RFR) \\
&= 0.08 + (-0.20)(0.06) \\
&= 0.08 - 0.012 \\
&= 0.068
\end{aligned}
$$

Comparing this expected return of 6.8 percent to the actual return of 10 percent shows that Portfolio Manager G has done a superior job.

25.3.2 Sharpe Portfolio Performance Measure

Sharpe (1966) likewise conceived of a composite measure to evaluate the performance of mutual funds. The measure followed closely his earlier work on the capital asset pricing model (CAPM), dealing specifically with the capital market line (CML).

The **Sharpe measure** of portfolio performance (designated S) is stated as follows:

25.2
$$S_i = \frac{\overline{R_i} - \overline{RFR}}{\sigma_i}$$

where in addition to the earlier notation:

σ_i = the standard deviation of the rate of return for Portfolio i during the time period

This performance measure clearly is similar to the Treynor measure; however, it seeks to measure the *total risk* of the portfolio by using the standard deviation of returns rather than considering only the systematic risk summarized by beta. Because the numerator is the portfolio's risk premium, this measure indicates the *risk premium return earned per unit of total risk*. As such, this portfolio performance measure uses the CML to compare portfolios, whereas the Treynor measure examines portfolio performance in relation to the SML. Finally, the standard deviation in S_i can be calculated using either (1) total portfolio returns or (2) portfolio returns in excess of the risk-free rate.[3]

Demonstration of Comparative Sharpe Measures Again, assume that $\overline{R_M} = 0.14$ and $\overline{RFR} = 0.08$. Suppose you are told that the standard deviation of the annual rate of return for the market portfolio over past 10 years was 20 percent ($\sigma_M = 0.20$). You want to examine the risk-adjusted performance of the following portfolios:

Portfolio	Average Annual Rate of Return	Standard Deviation of Return
D	0.13	0.18
E	0.17	0.22
F	0.16	0.23

The Sharpe measures for these portfolios are as follows:

$$S_M = \frac{0.14 - 0.08}{0.20} = 0.300$$

$$S_D = \frac{0.13 - 0.08}{0.18} = 0.278$$

$$S_E = \frac{0.17 - 0.08}{0.22} = 0.409$$

$$S_F = \frac{0.16 - 0.08}{0.23} = 0.348$$

The D portfolio had the lowest risk premium return per unit of total risk, failing to perform as well as the market portfolio. In contrast, Portfolios E and F performed better than the aggregate market: Portfolio E did better than Portfolio F.

Given the market portfolio results during this period, it is possible to draw the CML. If we plot the results for Portfolios D, E, and F on this graph, as shown in Exhibit 25.3, we see that Portfolio D plots below the line, whereas the E and F portfolios are above the line, indicating superior risk-adjusted performance.

25.3.3 Jensen Portfolio Performance Measure

Like the T and S measures just discussed, the **Jensen measure** (Jensen, 1968) was originally based on the capital asset pricing model (CAPM), which calculates the expected one-period return on any security or portfolio by the following expression:

25.3 $$E(R_j) = RFR + \beta_j[E(R_M) - RFR]$$

where:

$E(R_j)$ = the expected return on security or Portfolio j

RFR = the one-period risk-free interest rate

β_j = the systematic risk (beta) for security or Portfolio j

$E(R_M)$ = the expected return on the market portfolio of risky assets

The expected return and the risk-free return vary for different periods. Consequently, we are concerned with the time series of expected rates of return for Security or Portfolio j. Moreover, assuming the asset pricing model is empirically valid, you can express Equation 25.3 in terms of *realized* rates of return as follows:

$$R_{jt} = RFR_t + \beta_j[R_{mt} - RFR_t] + e_{jt}$$

---

[3] The Sharpe measure was formulated using the total risk (i.e., σ) of a portfolio, but recently Sharpe (1994, 2007) and Lo (2002) have suggested using the standard deviation of the excess portfolio return (i.e., σ_{ER}) instead. With this adjustment, the measure becomes $S_i = [\overline{R_i} - \overline{RFR}] \div \sigma_{ER}$. The advantage of this approach will be clear shortly when we discuss the *information ratio* performance measure.

Exhibit 25.3 Plot of Performance on CML (*S* Measure)

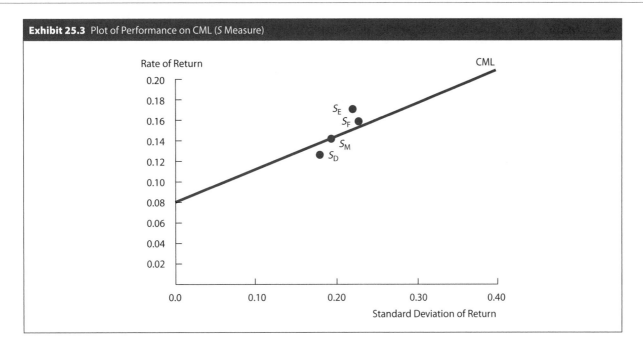

This equation states that the realized rate of return on a security or portfolio during a given time period should be a linear function of the risk-free rate of return during the period, plus a risk premium that depends on the systematic risk of the security or portfolio during the period plus a random error term (e_{jt}).

Subtracting the risk-free return from both sides, we have

$$R_{jt} - RFR_t = \beta_j[R_{mt} - RFR_t] + e_{jt}$$

so that the risk premium earned on the *j*th portfolio is equal to β_j times a market risk premium plus a random error term. An intercept for the regression is not expected if all assets and portfolios were in equilibrium.

Alternatively, superior portfolio managers who forecast market turns or consistently select undervalued securities earn higher risk premiums over time than those implied by this model. Such managers have consistently positive random error terms because the actual returns for their portfolios consistently exceed their expected returns. To detect this superior performance, you must allow for an intercept (a nonzero constant) that measures any positive or negative difference from the model. Consistent positive differences cause a positive intercept, whereas consistent negative differences (inferior performance) cause a negative intercept. With an intercept included, the earlier equation becomes

25.4 $$R_{jt} - RFR_t = \alpha_j + \beta_j[R_{mt} - RFR_t] + e_{jt}$$

In Equation 25.4, the α_j value indicates whether the portfolio manager is superior or inferior in her investment ability. A superior manager has a significant positive α (or "alpha") value because of the consistent positive residuals. In contrast, an inferior manager's returns consistently fall short of expectations based on the CAPM model giving consistently negative residuals. In such a case, α is a significant negative value.

The performance of a portfolio manager with no forecasting ability but not clearly inferior equals that of a naive buy-and-hold policy. Because returns on such a portfolio typically match the returns you expect, the residual returns generally are randomly positive and negative. This gives a constant term that differs insignificantly from zero, indicating that the portfolio manager basically matched the market on a risk-adjusted basis.

Therefore, the α coefficient represents how much of the managed portfolio's return is attributable to the manager's ability to derive above-average returns adjusted for risk. Superior risk-adjusted returns indicate that the manager is good at either predicting market turns or selecting undervalued issues for the portfolio, or both.

Applying the Jensen Measure The Jensen's alpha measure of performance requires using a different *RFR* for each time interval during the sample period. For example, to examine the performance of a fund manager over a 10-year period using yearly intervals, you must examine the fund's annual returns less the return on risk-free assets for each year and relate this to the annual return on the market portfolio less the same risk-free rate. This contrasts with the Treynor and Sharpe composite measures, which examine the *average* returns for the total period for all variables (the portfolio, the market, and the risk-free asset).

Also, like the Treynor measure, the Jensen measure does not directly consider the portfolio manager's ability to diversify because it calculates risk premiums in terms of systematic risk. As noted earlier, to evaluate the performance of a group of well-diversified portfolios such as mutual funds, this is likely to be a reasonable assumption, since such portfolios can be correlated with the market at rates above 0.90.

Finally, the Jensen performance measure is flexible enough to allow for alternative models of risk and expected return than the CAPM. Specifically, risk-adjusted performance (i.e., α) can be computed relative to any of the multifactor models discussed in Chapter 9 as follows:

25.5
$$R_{jt} - RFR_t = \alpha_j + [b_{j1} F_{1t} + b_{j2}F_{2t} + \cdots + b_{jk}F_{kt}] + e_{jt}$$

where F_{kt} represents the Period t return to the kth common risk factor

25.3.4 The Information Ratio Performance Measure

Closely related to the statistics just presented is a fourth widely used performance measure: the **information ratio**. This statistic measures a portfolio's average return in excess of that of a comparison or **benchmark portfolio** divided by the standard deviation of this excess return. Formally, the information ratio (*IR*) for portfolio *j* is calculated as:

25.6
$$IR_j = \frac{\overline{R}_j - \overline{R}_b}{\sigma_R} = \frac{\overline{ER}_j}{\sigma_{ER}}$$

where:

$\overline{R}_b$ = the average return for the benchmark portfolio during the period

σ_{ER} = the standard deviation of the excess return during the period

To interpret *IR,* the mean excess return in the numerator represents the investor's ability to use her talent and information to generate a portfolio return that differs from that of the benchmark against which her performance is being measured (e.g., the Standard and Poor's 500 index). Conversely, the denominator measures the amount of residual (unsystematic) risk that the investor incurred in pursuit of those excess returns. The coefficient σ_{ER} is sometimes called the *tracking error* of the investor's portfolio and it is a "cost" of active management in that fluctuations in the periodic ER_j values represent random noise, beyond an investor's control, that could hurt performance. Thus, the *IR* can be viewed as a benefit-to-cost ratio that assesses the quality of the investor's information deflated by unsystematic risk generated by the investment process.

Goodwin (1998) noted that the Sharpe ratio is a special case of the *IR* where the risk-free asset is the benchmark portfolio, although this interpretation violates the spirit of a statistic that should have a value of zero for any passively managed portfolio. He also showed that if excess portfolio returns are estimated with historical data using the same single-factor regression equation used to compute Jensen's alpha, the *IR* simplifies to

$$IR_j = \frac{\alpha_j}{\sigma_e}$$

where:

σ_e = the standard error of the regression[4]

---

[4] The development of this form of the information ratio is credited to Treynor and Black (1973).

Finally, he showed that an information ratio based on periodic returns measured T times per year could be annualized is as follows:

$$\text{Annualized } IR = \frac{(T)\alpha_j}{\sqrt{T}\sigma_e} = \sqrt{T}(IR)$$

For instance, an investor that generated a quarterly ratio of 0.25 would have an annualized IR of 0.50 $= (\sqrt{4} \times 0.25)$.

Grinold and Kahn (2000) argued that reasonable information ratio levels should range from 0.50 to 1.00, with an investor having an IR of 0.50 being good, and one with an IR of 1.00 being exceptional. These appear to be difficult hurdles to clear. Goodwin (1998) studied the performance of more than 200 professional equity and fixed-income portfolio managers with various investment styles over a 10-year period. He found that the IR of the median manager in each style group was positive but never exceeded 0.50. Thus, although the average manager added value to investors—α (and hence IR) is greater than zero—she doesn't qualify as "good." Further, no style group had more than 3 percent of its managers deliver an IR in excess of 1.00. Information ratio histograms summarizing this research are shown in Exhibit 25.4.

25.3.5 Comparing the Composite Performance Measures

Each of the portfolio performance statistics just described is widely used in practice and has its own strengths and weaknesses. The primary advantages and disadvantages of the T, S, α, and IR measures are listed in Exhibit 25.5. The important thing to recognize is that no one of these measures dominates the others and they all provide at least slightly different information useful to investors in the assessment of a portfolio's risk-adjusted performance. Consequently, it is generally advisable to compute all of them in order to provide a complete performance picture.

The Sharpe ratio is simplest measure to compute, requiring just a few straightforward calculations based on the portfolio returns themselves. In its original form, S uses the standard deviation of total returns, whereas the Treynor ratio uses the portfolio's systematic risk (i.e., beta) coefficient. As we demonstrated in Chapter 8, beta can also be calculated directly from the returns to the portfolio and the market index, but that is a somewhat more involved process. For a completely diversified portfolio, T and S give identical performance rankings because total risk and systematic risk are the same. However, a poorly diversified portfolio could have a high ranking based on the Treynor ratio, which ignores unsystematic risk, but a much lower ranking based on the Sharpe measure, which does not. Any difference in rankings produced by T and S comes directly from a difference in portfolio diversification levels.

A disadvantage of the Treynor and Sharpe measures is that they only produce *relative*, not absolute, performance rankings. For example, the Sharpe values for Portfolios E and F in Exhibit 25.3 show that both managers generated risk-adjusted returns above the market. Further, E's risk-adjusted performance measure (0.409) is larger than F's (0.348). What we cannot say with certainty, however, is whether any of these differences are statistically significant. The same dilemma exists when comparing the performance of Portfolio X and Y using the Treynor measures illustrated in Exhibit 25.2.

The Jensen's alpha measure is typically the most difficult to compute because it requires a formal regression analysis. Offsetting that drawback are three substantial advantages relative to the T and S measures. First, it is easier to understand: An alpha value of 0.02 indicates that the manager generated a return of 2 percent per period more than what was expected given the portfolio's risk level. On the other hand, a Sharpe ratio of 0.409 means that the portfolio manager generated *0.409 units of excess return per unit of total risk*, which is more challenging language to interpret. Second, because α is estimated from a formal statistical process, it is possible to make statements about the statistical significance of the manager's skill level, or the difference in skill between two different managers. Third, Jensen's alpha can be computed

Exhibit 25.4 Information Ratios for Six Investment Styles: 1986:Q1 to 1995:Q4

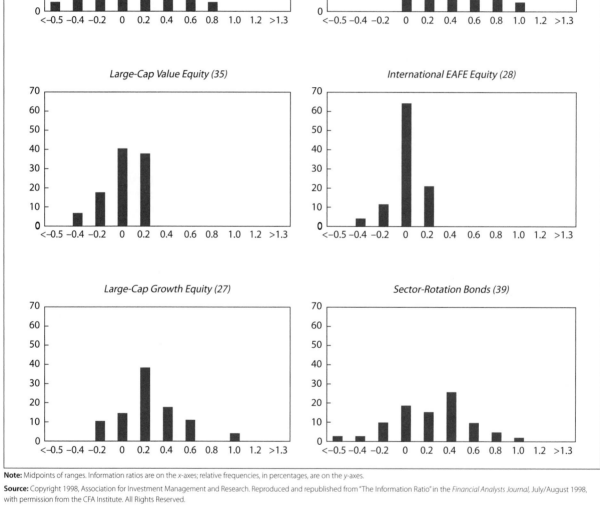

Note: Midpoints of ranges. Information ratios are on the *x*-axes; relative frequencies, in percentages, are on the *y*-axes.

relative to any of several different risk–return models, in contrast to *S*, which focuses on total risk and ignores the return-generating process altogether, and *T*, which is locked into beta as the specific estimate of systematic risk.

Finally, because the information ratio is similar in form to *T* and *S*, it shares many of the same strengths and weakness of those two ratios. The primary advantage that differentiates *IR* from the other composite measures is that it provides a direct comparison between the return performance of the portfolio manager and that of the specific benchmark index against

Exhibit 25.5 Comparing the Portfolio Performance Measures

Performance Measure	Risk-Adjustment Measure	Advantages	Disadvantages
Treynor Ratio (T)	Portfolio beta relative to market index proxy	• Simple and intuitive "benefit-cost" comparison of the risk–return trade-off • Linked conceptually to the SML and capital market theory • Relatively simple to calculate and widely used in practice	• Permits only relative assessments of performance for different portfolios • Difficult to interpret and assess statistical significance • Ignores unsystematic risk in a portfolio
Sharpe Ratio (S)	(i) Standard deviation of total portfolio return; *or* (ii) Standard deviation of portfolio return in excess of risk-free rate	• Simple and intuitive "benefit-cost" comparison of the risk–return trade-off • Linked conceptually to the CML and capital market theory • Simplest to calculate and widely used in practice	• Permits only relative assessments of performance for different portfolios • Difficult to interpret and assess statistical significance • Ignores diversification potential of portfolio
Jensen's Alpha (α)	(i) Portfolio beta relative to market index proxy; *or* (ii) Portfolio betas relative to multiple risk factors	• Most rigorous risk-adjustment process separating systematic and unsystematic risk components • Can be adapted to either CAPM or multifactor models of the risk–return trade-off • Intuitive interpretation of measure that permits statistical significance assessment	• More difficult computation requiring formal regression analysis • Diversification of portfolio assessed in separate measure from performance • Alpha level and significance can vary greatly depending on specification of return-generating model
Information Ratio (IR)	Standard deviation of portfolio return in excess of return to style-class benchmark index (i.e., tracking error)	• Direct comparison of portfolio performance compared to benchmark in investment style class • Simple and intuitive measure of the "benefit-cost" trade-off involved with active management • Flexible design permitting multiple benchmark comparisons	• Permits only relative assessments of performance for different portfolios in a style class • Difficult to interpret and assess statistical significance • Implicitly assumes that portfolio and benchmark have similar levels of systematic risk

which she is competing. Since investors can often own this benchmark portfolio directly—either through index mutual funds or exchange-traded funds—the *IR* measure calculates the risk-adjusted value added by the active portfolio manager relative to a passive investment alternative.

25.4 Application of Portfolio Performance Measures

To apply these measures, we selected 30 open-end mutual funds from the nine investment style classes described in Chapter 16 and used monthly data for the five-year period from April 2002 to March 2007. The monthly rates of return for one of these funds (Neuberger Berman Partners) and the S&P 500 are contained in Exhibit 25.6. The total rate of return for each month is computed as follows:

$$R_{it} = \frac{EP_{it} + Div_{it} + Cap.Dist._{it} - BP_{it}}{BP_{it}}$$

where

R_{it} = the total rate of return on Fund i during month t
EP_{it} = the ending price for Fund i during month t
Div_{it} = the dividend payments made by Fund i during month t
$Cap.Dist._{it}$ = the capital gain distributions made by Fund i during month t
BP_{it} = the beginning price for Fund i during month t

These return computations do not take into account any sales charges by the funds.

The arithmetic average annual rate of return for Neuberger Berman Fund was 10.72 percent versus 6.88 percent for the market, and the fund's beta was greater than 1.00 (1.157). Using the average annual rate of T-bills of 2.46 percent as the $\overline{RFR}$, the Treynor measure for the NPRTX(T_i) was substantially bigger than the comparable measure for the market T_M (7.132 vs. 4.420), primarily because the S&P index performed modestly over this five-year period. Likewise, the standard deviation of returns of the Neuberger Berman fund was greater than the market's (15.72 vs. 12.26), but the Sharpe measure for the fund (S_i) was still bigger than the measure for the market (S_M) (0.525 vs. 0.360).

Finally, a one-factor regression of the fund's annual risk premium ($R_{it} - RFR_t$) and the market's annual risk premium ($R_{Mt} - RFR_t$) indicated a positive intercept (constant) value of 0.261 but was not statistically significant. If this intercept value had been significant, NPRTX's risk-adjusted annual rate of return would have averaged about a quarter percent above the market on a reliable basis.

Total Sample Results The overall results in Exhibit 25.7 indicate that active fund managers performed much better than has been documented in earlier performance studies. A primary factor for this outcome was the abnormally poor performance of the index during the first part of the sample period. Also, our sample was rather casually selected because we intended it for demonstration purposes only. The mean annual return for all the funds was above the market return (10.95 vs. 6.88). Considering only the rate of return, 25 of the 30 funds outperformed the market.

The R^2 statistic comparing a portfolio with the market can serve as a measure of diversification. The closer the R^2 is to 1.00, the more completely diversified the portfolio. The average R^2 for our sample was fairly high at 0.736, although the range was quite large, from 0.407 to 0.938. This suggests that many of the funds were reasonably well diversified, with 24 of the 30 portfolios having R^2 values greater than 0.65. (Recall that a typical individual stock would have an R^2 value of around 20–30 percent.)

The two risk measures (standard deviation and beta) also show a wide degree of dispersion but generally are consistent with expectations. Specifically, 23 of the 30 funds had larger standard deviations than the market, and the mean standard deviation was larger (13.58 vs. 12.26). Only 10 of the funds had a beta of 1.00 or greater; the average beta was 0.946.

Exhibit 25.6 Example of Computing Portfolio Evaluation Measures Using Neuberger Berman Partners (NPRTX) Fund

	R_{it}	R_{mt}	RFR_t	$R_{it} - RFR_t$	$R_{mt} - RFR_t$
April 2002	−3.47	−6.10	0.15	−3.62	−6.25
May 2002	−1.16	−0.78	0.14	−1.30	−0.92
June 2002	−8.35	−7.13	0.13	−8.48	−7.26
July 2002	−11.19	−7.40	0.15	−11.34	−7.55
August 2002	0.54	0.70	0.14	0.40	0.56
September 2002	−11.88	−10.90	0.14	−12.02	−11.04
October 2002	5.51	8.86	0.14	5.37	8.72
November 2002	8.90	5.90	0.12	8.78	5.78
December 2002	−7.41	−5.88	0.11	−7.52	−5.99
January 2003	−1.28	−2.66	0.10	−1.38	−2.76
February 2003	−1.04	−1.52	0.09	−1.13	−1.61
March 2003	0.52	1.03	0.10	0.42	0.93
⋮	⋮	⋮	⋮	⋮	⋮
⋮	⋮	⋮	⋮	⋮	⋮
⋮	⋮	⋮	⋮	⋮	⋮
April 2006	2.31	1.21	0.36	1.95	0.85
May 2006	−4.48	−2.83	0.43	−4.91	−3.26
June 2006	−1.43	0.16	0.40	−1.83	−0.24
July 2006	−1.30	0.56	0.40	−1.70	0.16
August 2006	2.57	2.42	0.42	2.15	2.00
September 2006	−0.70	2.65	0.41	−1.11	2.24
October 2006	4.88	3.25	0.41	4.47	2.84
November 2006	5.92	1.84	0.42	5.50	1.42
December 2006	0.25	1.38	0.40	−0.15	0.98
January 2007	1.48	1.41	0.44	1.04	0.97
February 2007	−1.05	−2.19	0.38	−1.43	−2.57
March 2007	0.87	1.00	0.43	0.44	0.57
Average (annual)	10.72	6.88	2.46	8.25	4.42
Standard deviation	15.72	12.26	0.45		
Beta	1.157				
S_i	0.525				
S_m	0.360				
T_i	7.132				
T_m	4.420				
Jensen alpha (1 factor)	0.261				
R^2_{im}	0.813				

The various performance measures ranked the performance of individual funds consistently, if somewhat differently. (These rankings are listed in parentheses beside each measure.) Only four out of 30 funds had a lower Treynor ratio than that of the market; only six funds had a lower Sharpe as well. Also, 26 of the 30 Jensen's alpha values using the Single-Index Market Model were positive, with 11 of these being statistically significant. The mean Jensen alpha value of 0.359 indicates that the average manager in the sample was able to produce a return of about 36 basis points per month more than what would have been expected given the risk level of the fund. The mean values for the Sharpe and Treynor measures were considerably higher than the aggregate market figure. These results confirm that, overall, this sample of funds produced much better risk-adjusted performance than the market during this time period.

One might expect the best performance by funds with low diversification because they apparently are attempting to beat the market by being unique in their security selection or market timing. This seems to be true for some of the top-performing funds, such as RS Partners Fund, whereas portfolios that produced returns more closely aligned with overall market, such as the Fidelity Magellan Fund, were among the worst performing funds. It appears that during this period it was often better to *not* look like the market portfolio, although this is not always the case.

Exhibit 25.7 Performance Measures for 30 Selected Mutual Funds

Fund	Ticker	Style Class	Average Annual Rate of Return	Standard Deviation	Beta	R²	Treynor		Sharpe		Jensen (1 Factor)	
AllianceBerstein Growth	AGRYX	Large Growth	6.15	14.63	1.016	0.722	3.630	(27)	0.252	(27)	−0.067	(27)
American Century Sm Val	ASVIX	Small Value	12.25	13.46	0.898	0.666	10.898	(13)	0.727	(14)	0.485	(12)
Buffalo Small Cap	BUFSX	Small Growth	12.21	19.34	1.301	0.677	7.497	(19)	0.504	(19)	0.334	(15)
Aim Constellation	CSTGX	Large Growth	4.66	13.36	1.011	0.861	2.174	(30)	0.165	(30)	−0.189	(30)
Dreyfus Appreciation	DGAGX	Large Blend	4.69	10.63	0.813	0.883	2.734	(28)	0.209	(28)	−0.114	(28)
DFA Tax-Managed Value	DTMMX	Mid Value	10.94	14.33	1.090	0.869	7.782	(18)	0.592	(17)	0.305	(16)
Fidelity Magellan	FMAGX	Large Growth	4.64	12.67	1.001	0.938	2.176	(29)	0.172	(29)	−0.187	(29)
Goldman Sachs Mid Value	GCMAX	Mid Value	13.76	10.55	0.700	0.658	16.138	(2)	1.070	(2)	0.683[a]	(5)
Heartland Value	HRTVX	Small Blend	15.96	17.45	1.049	0.541	12.869	(6)	0.774	(12)	0.739	(2)
Hotchkis & Wiley Lrg Val	HWLIX	Large Value	13.23	13.21	0.971	0.806	11.080	(12)	0.815	(9)	0.539[a]	(10)
Janus Twenty	JAVLX	Large Growth	9.91	12.39	0.862	0.728	8.640	(15)	0.601	(16)	0.303	(17)
DWS Dreman High Rtn	KDHBX	Large Value	7.27	13.48	0.976	0.787	4.928	(25)	0.357	(25)	0.041	(25)
Columbia Acorn	LACAX	Mid Growth	14.21	13.47	0.933	0.717	12.591	(7)	0.872	(5)	0.635[a]	(6)
Lazard Mid Cap	LZMIX	Mid Value	11.46	11.82	0.880	0.831	10.228	(14)	0.761	(13)	0.426[a]	(14)
Morgan Stanley Small Value	MCVAX	Small Value	13.96	14.16	0.961	0.693	11.954	(8)	0.811	(10)	0.604[a]	(8)
Munder Mid Cap Select	MGOYX	Mid Growth	13.43	12.73	0.802	0.594	13.662	(5)	0.861	(6)	0.618[a]	(7)
Numeric Investors Mid Cap	NIGVX	Mid Blend	12.23	11.94	0.839	0.740	11.635	(9)	0.818	(8)	0.505[a]	(11)
Neuberger Berman Partners	NPRTX	Large Blend	10.72	15.72	1.157	0.813	7.132	(21)	0.525	(18)	0.261	(20)
Wells Fargo Small Cap Op	NVSOX	Small Growth	13.29	13.97	0.949	0.692	11.415	(11)	0.775	(11)	0.553	(9)
Allianz OCC Value	PDLIX	Large Value	9.42	17.89	1.374	0.885	5.067	(24)	0.389	(24)	0.074	(24)
JPMorgan Small Growth	PGSGX	Small Growth	10.17	15.75	0.984	0.585	7.835	(16)	0.489	(21)	0.280	(19)
T. Rowe Price Small Value	PRSVX	Small Value	14.78	13.31	0.796	0.534	15.476	(3)	0.925	(3)	0.733[a]	(3)
RS Partners	RSPFX	Small Blend	20.41	12.84	0.673	0.407	26.674	(1)	1.398	(1)	1.248[a]	(1)
Royce Premier	RYPRX	Mid Growth	14.82	13.45	0.856	0.606	14.425	(4)	0.919	(4)	0.714[a]	(4)
Wells Fargo Large Growth	SLGIX	Large Growth	7.62	11.98	0.866	0.783	5.955	(22)	0.431	(23)	0.111	(23)
TCW Diversified Value	TGDVX	Large Value	10.61	13.54	1.042	0.887	7.819	(17)	0.602	(15)	0.295	(18)
Tweedy, Browne American	TWEBX	Large Value	5.59	9.65	0.697	0.784	4.479	(26)	0.324	(26)	0.003	(26)
Van Kampen Mid Growth	VGRAX	Mid Growth	9.42	14.02	0.954	0.695	7.293	(20)	0.496	(20)	0.228	(21)
Vanguard Primecap	VPMCX	Large Growth	8.90	14.43	1.119	0.902	5.754	(23)	0.446	(22)	0.124	(22)
JPMorgan Mid Cap Equity	VSNGX	Mid Blend	11.77	11.22	0.814	0.789	11.430	(10)	0.830	(7)	0.476[a]	(13)
Average Fund			10.95	13.58	0.946	0.736	9.379		0.630		0.359	
S&P 500			6.88	12.26	1.000	1.000	4.420		0.360		0.000	
90-day T-bill rate			2.46	0.45								

[a] Significant at the 0.05 level.

Exhibit 25.8 reports information ratios for these 30 funds. To interpret the display, consider that the TCW Diversified Value Fund had a monthly *IR* value of 0.223, which was calculated by dividing its alpha (0.295) by its regression standard error (1.32). This statistic is then annualized to 0.772 by multiplying the monthly *IR* by the square root of 12. Notice that 26 of the 30 funds had positive *IR* levels, which follows directly from the number of funds that had a positive Jensen's alpha. The mean annualized *IR* for the sample was 0.563, which exceeded the Grinold-Kahn standard for "good" performance of 0.500. Thus, on average, even after accounting for tracking error costs, this collection of funds added substantial value to its investors.

Potential Bias of One-Parameter Measures Friend and Blume (1970) pointed out that the composite measures of performance should be independent of alternative measures of risk because they are *risk-adjusted* measures. However, their analysis of the relationship between the composite measures and two definitions of risk (standard deviation and beta) for 200 random stock portfolios indicated that the risk-adjusted performance of low-risk portfolios was better than the comparable performance for high-risk portfolios. Subsequently, Klemkosky (1973) examined the relationship between composite performance measures and risk measures using actual mutual fund data. The results showed a *positive* relationship between the composite performance measures and the risk involved. This was especially true for the Treynor and Jensen measures. He concluded that although a bias might exist, one could not be certain of its direction. More recently, Leland (1999) has shown that alpha can be biased downward for those portfolios designed to limit downside risk.

Exhibit 25.8 Information Ratios for 30 Funds

Fund	Alpha	Standard Error	IR	Annualized IR	Rank
AllianceBerstein Growth	−0.067	2.25	−0.030	−0.103	(27)
American Century Sm Val	0.485	2.27	0.214	0.741	(15)
Buffalo Small Cap	0.334	3.21	0.104	0.360	(19)
Aim Constellation	−0.189	1.45	−0.131	−0.452	(29)
Dreyfus Appreciation	−0.114	1.06	−0.108	−0.375	(28)
DFA Tax-Managed Value	0.305	1.51	0.202	0.701	(16)
Fidelity Magellan	−0.187	0.91	−0.205	−0.709	(30)
Goldman Sachs Mid Value	0.683	1.80	0.380	1.316	(2)
Heartland Value	0.739	3.44	0.214	0.743	(14)
Hotchkis & Wiley Lrg Val	0.539	1.70	0.318	1.100	(3)
Janus Twenty	0.303	1.88	0.161	0.559	(17)
DWS Dreman High Rtn	0.041	1.81	0.023	0.079	(25)
Columbia Acorn	0.635	2.09	0.304	1.053	(5)
Lazard Mid Cap	0.426	1.42	0.301	1.042	(6)
Morgan Stanley Small Value	0.604	2.28	0.264	0.916	(10)
Munder Mid Cap Select	0.618	2.37	0.261	0.905	(11)
Numeric Investors Mid Cap	0.505	1.78	0.284	0.985	(8)
Neuberger Berman Partners	0.261	1.98	0.132	0.457	(18)
Wells Fargo Small Cap Op	0.553	2.25	0.245	0.850	(12)
Allianz OCC Value	0.074	1.76	0.042	0.145	(24)
JPMorgan Small Growth	0.280	2.96	0.095	0.328	(21)
T. Rowe Price Small Value	0.733	2.65	0.277	0.958	(9)
RS Partners	1.248	2.90	0.430	1.491	(1)
Royce Premier	0.714	2.46	0.290	1.005	(7)
Wells Fargo Large Growth	0.111	1.62	0.068	0.236	(23)
TCW Diversified Value	0.295	1.32	0.223	0.772	(13)
Tweedy, Browne American	0.003	1.31	0.003	0.009	(26)
Van Kampen Mid Growth	0.228	2.25	0.101	0.351	(20)
Vanguard Primecap	0.124	1.32	0.095	0.328	(22)
JPMorgan Mid Cap Equity	0.476	1.50	0.317	1.098	(4)
Mean	0.359	1.98	0.163	0.563	
Median	0.319	1.84	0.208	0.721	

Measuring Performance with Multiple Risk Factors   Equation 25.5 showed in general terms how the Jensen's alpha measure could be estimated relative to multifactor models of risk and expected return. Exhibit 25.9 shows the Jensen measures calculated for the 30 mutual funds using two different versions of the Fama-French model discussed in Chapter 9:

$$R_{jt} - RFR_t = \alpha_j + \{[b_{j1}(R_{mt} - RFR_t) + b_{j2}SMB_t + b_{j3}HML_t] + b_{j4}MOM_t\} + e_{jt}$$

Specifically, alphas are computed relative to: (1) a three-factor model including the market ($R_m - RFR$), firm size (SMB), and relative valuation (HML) variables; and (2) a four-factor model that also includes the return momentum (MOM) variable.

The performance results in Exhibits 25.7 and 25.8 showed that the vast majority of the active mutual fund managers in the sample were able to outperform the market on a risk-adjusted basis over the April 2002–March 2007 period. However, it is possible that some of this superior performance was an illusion because the S&P 500 index was not the appropriate benchmark for many of the portfolios. In fact, the style classifications for the 30 funds in Exhibit 25.7 show that only two portfolios followed the large-cap blend style, the category for which the S&P 500 index applies. Thus, the advantage of measuring a fund's alpha using a multifactor approach is that it is designed to control for both market (i.e., R_m), style (i.e., SMB and HML), and momentum (i.e., MOM) risk influences.

Exhibit 25.9   Performance Measures for 30 Funds Using Multifactor Models

Fund	Style Class	$R_m - RFR$	SMB	HML	MOM	Jensen Alpha (3-Factor)	Rank	Jensen Alpha (4-Factor)	Rank
		Factor Betas							
AGRYX	Large Growth	1.132	0.197	−0.461	0.283	−0.154	(21)	−0.170	(23)
ASVIX	Small Value	0.841	0.588	0.396	−0.075	−0.129	(19)	−0.125	(19)
BUFSX	Small Growth	1.064	0.898	0.068	−0.209	−0.179	(23)	−0.167	(21)
CSTGX	Large Growth	1.088	0.108	−0.343	0.195	−0.274	(28)	−0.285[a]	(28)
DGAGX	Large Blend	0.889	−0.412	0.060	0.026	−0.150	(20)	−0.152	(20)
DTMMX	Mid Value	1.117	0.160	0.343	−0.025	−0.170	(22)	−0.168	(22)
FMAGX	Large Growth	1.025	−0.135	−0.215	0.049	−0.191	(25)	−0.193	(24)
GCMAX	Mid Value	0.824	0.217	0.350	0.120	0.175	(5)	0.168	(5)
HRTVX	Small Blend	0.920	1.020	0.528	−0.138	−0.126	(18)	−0.119	(18)
HWLIX	Large Value	0.907	0.214	0.326	−0.134	0.133	(9)	0.141	(8)
JAVLX	Large Growth	0.964	−0.100	−0.201	0.159	0.244	(3)	0.235	(3)
KDHBX	Large Value	1.058	−0.312	0.508	−0.065	−0.326	(30)	−0.322	(30)
LACAX	Mid Growth	0.952	0.531	0.115	0.081	0.148	(7)	0.143	(7)
LZMIX	Mid Value	0.857	0.258	0.102	−0.021	0.113	(10)	0.114	(10)
MCVAX	Small Value	0.908	0.560	0.305	−0.061	0.042	(15)	0.046	(15)
MGOYX	Mid Growth	0.920	0.488	−0.007	0.234	0.173	(6)	0.159	(6)
NIGVX	Mid Blend	0.886	0.330	0.166	0.067	0.079	(12)	0.076	(12)
NPRTX	Large Blend	1.185	0.244	0.249	0.000	−0.210	(26)	−0.210	(26)
NVSOX	Small Growth	0.920	0.562	0.131	0.008	0.075	(14)	0.074	(13)
PDLIX	Large Value	1.194	0.004	0.365	−0.335	−0.243	(27)	−0.224	(27)
PGSGX	Small Growth	1.015	0.754	−0.136	0.187	−0.186	(24)	−0.196	(25)
PRSVX	Small Value	0.808	0.735	0.292	0.073	0.077	(13)	0.073	(14)
RSPFX	Small Blend	0.731	0.604	0.583	0.030	0.479[a]	(1)	0.477	(1)
RYPRX	Mid Growth	0.849	0.589	0.041	0.057	0.276	(2)	0.272	(2)
SLGIX	Large Growth	0.917	0.075	−0.440	0.171	0.141	(8)	0.131	(9)
TGDVX	Large Value	0.989	0.131	0.244	−0.106	−0.046	(16)	−0.040	(16)
TWEBX	Large Value	0.708	0.042	0.309	−0.047	−0.320[a]	(29)	−0.317[a]	(29)
VGRAX	Mid Growth	1.048	0.344	−0.151	0.204	−0.076	(17)	−0.088	(17)
VPMCX	Large Growth	1.058	0.087	−0.254	−0.027	0.080	(11)	0.082	(11)
VSNGX	Mid Blend	0.853	0.271	0.000	0.085	0.183	(4)	0.178	(4)
	Mean	0.954	0.302	0.109	0.026	−0.012		−0.014	

[a] Significant at the 0.05 level.

Exhibit 25.10 Correlations between Alternative Portfolio Performance Measures

	Treynor	Sharpe	Jensen (1-Factor)	Jensen (3-Factor)	Jensen (4-Factor)	Information Ratio
Treynor	—					
Sharpe	0.978	—				
Jensen (1-factor)	0.976	0.979	—			
Jensen (3-factor)	0.773	0.795	0.734	—		
Jensen (4-factor)	0.780	0.803	0.743	0.997	—	
Information Ratio	0.879	0.953	0.919	0.744	0.754	—

Although not listed in Exhibit 25.9, the average annual returns (i.e., risk premia) for the *SMB, HML,* and *MOM* factors were 0.40 percent, 0.60 percent, and 0.18 percent, respectively. This indicates that in the stock market as a whole over this investment period, small stocks outperformed large stocks (i.e., a positive mean *SMB* return), value stocks outperformed growth stocks (i.e., a positive mean *HML* return), and high-momentum stocks outperformed low-momentum stocks (i.e., a positive mean *MOM* return). For this particular collection of 30 funds, the mean factor betas—0.954 for the market factor, 0.302 for the *SMB* factor, 0.109 for the *HML* factor, and 0.026 for the *MOM* factor—indicate that the average fund has less systematic market risk than average and is oriented toward holding smaller, more value-oriented stocks that exhibit positive return momentum.

The Jensen alpha results for both the three-factor and four-factor models show some important differences with the comparable findings from the one-factor model reported in Exhibit 25.7. In particular, the mean value for alpha is now slightly negative in each case (−0.012 and −0.014, respectively). Also, 15 (rather than 26) of the funds had positive alpha values, but only one (rather than 11) of the funds with positive alphas had statistically significant outperformance with the three-factor model. Further, two of the funds (CSTGX and TWEBX) exhibited statistically significant underperformance when measured against the four-factor model. For instance, HRTVX, a small-cap blend fund, had a large positive alpha of 0.739 when its performance was measured relative to a large-cap blend index (i.e., S&P 500), but relative to models that take investment style and momentum into account, its alpha was reduced to −0.126 (three-factor) and −0.119 (four factor). This highlights the fact that the one-factor and multifactor Jensen measures produce similar but distinct performance rankings and should therefore be considered as different from one another as the Sharpe and Treynor measures.

Relationship among Performance Measures Exhibit 25.10 contains the matrix of rank correlation coefficients among the Treynor, Sharpe, Jensen (one-factor, three-factor, and four-factor), and Information Ratio measures. The striking feature of the display is that all of these statistics are positively correlated with one another, but not perfectly so. (The two multifactor Jensen measures produced virtually identical rankings for this fund sample.) This suggests that, although the measures provide a generally consistent assessment of portfolio performance when taken as a whole, they remain distinct at an individual level. The exhibit reinforces our earlier point that it is best to consider these composites collectively and that the user must understand what each means.

· ·
25.5 Portfolio Performance Evaluation: Some Extensions

In this section, we will consider five extensions of the basics performance "toolkit" that we have just developed: (1) a composite measure that takes the portfolio's diversification level into account; (2) a composite measure that considers the portfolio's "downside" risk; (3) techniques that focus on the portfolio's holdings rather its returns; (4) attribution analysis, which attempts to establish why a portfolio manager's portfolio performed the way that it did; and (5) measures of market timing skills.

25.5.1 Components of Investment Performance

Following the work of Treynor, Sharpe, and Jensen, Fama (1972) suggested that the *overall performance* of a portfolio, in excess of the risk-free rate, can be decomposed into measures of risk-taking and security selection skill.

$$\text{Overall Performance} = \text{Excess Return} = \text{Portfolio Risk} + \text{Selectivity}$$

The *selectivity* component represents the portion of the portfolio's actual return beyond that available to an unmanaged portfolio with identical systematic risk and is used to assess the manager's investment prowess.

Evaluating Selectivity Formally, you can measure the return due to selectivity as follows:

$$\text{Selectivity} = R_a - R_x(\beta_a)$$

where:

R_a = the actual return on the portfolio being evaluated
$R_x(\beta_a)$ = the return on the combination of the riskless asset and the market portfolio M that has risk β_x equal to β_a, the risk of the portfolio being evaluated

As shown in Exhibit 25.11, selectivity measures the vertical distance between the actual return and the *ex post* market line and is quite similar to Treynor's measure.

Overall performance in terms of selectivity and the returns from assuming risk can be written:

25.7 $$\text{Overall Performance} = \text{Selectivity} + \text{Risk}$$
$$[R_a - RFR] = [R_a - R_x(\beta_a)] + [R_x(\beta_a) - RFR]$$

Exhibit 25.11 shows that overall performance is the total return above the risk-free return and includes the return that *should* have been received for accepting the portfolio risk (β_a), which is equal to $[R_x(\beta_a) - RFR]$. Any excess over this expected return is due to selectivity.

Exhibit 25.11 An Illustration of the Performance Measures

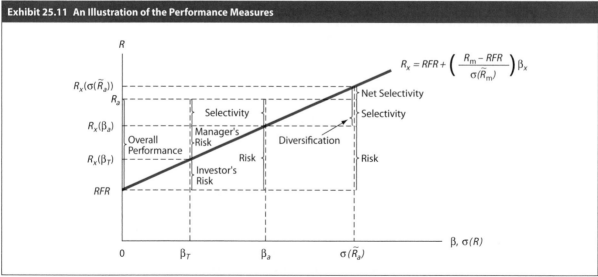

Source: Eugene F. Fama, "Components of Investment Performance," *Journal of Finance* 27, no. 3 (June 1972): 588. Reprinted with permission of Blackwell Publishing.

Evaluating Diversification The selectivity component in Equation 25.7 can also be broken down into two parts. If a portfolio manager attempts to select undervalued stocks and in the process gives up some diversification, it is possible to measure the added return necessary to justify this diversification decision. The portfolio's *gross selectivity* is made up of *net selectivity* plus *diversification* as follows:

$$\underset{\text{Selectivity}}{R_a - R_x(\beta_a)} = \text{Net Selectivity} + \underset{\text{Diversification}}{[R_x(\sigma\,(R_a)) - R_x(\beta_a)]}$$

or

25.8
$$\begin{aligned}\text{Net Selectivity} &= R_a - R_x(\beta_a) - [R_x(\sigma\,(R_a)) - R_x(\beta_a)]\\ &= R_a - R_x(\sigma\,(R_a))\end{aligned}$$

where:

$R_x(\sigma\,(R_a))$ = the return on the combination of the riskless asset and the market portfolio that has return volatility equivalent to that of the portfolio being evaluated

Therefore, the diversification measure in Equation 25.8 indicates the *added return* required to justify any loss of diversification in the portfolio. If the portfolio is completely diversified so that total risk (σ) is equal to systematic risk (β), then the $R_x(\sigma\,(R_a))$ would be the same as $R_x(\beta_a)$, and the diversification term would equal zero. Because the diversification measure always is nonnegative, net selectivity will always be equal to or less than gross selectivity.[5]

Example of Fama Performance Measure Suppose that over a recent five-year investment period you observed that the average annual return on the market portfolio and the risk-free security were 22.96 percent and 5.28 percent, respectively. Thus, an investment portfolio with a beta of 0.815 would be expected to deliver a return of 19.69 percent [= 5.28 + 0.815 (22.96 − 5.28)]. Suppose further that this portfolio actually returned 19.67 percent per annum. The return for *selectivity* is the difference between the actual excess performance (19.67 − 5.28 = 14.39) and the required excess return for risk of 14.41 (= 19.69 − 5.28) or −0.02, indicating the manager fell slightly short of matching expectations consistent with the actual risk level of the portfolio.

What if the manager also did not fully diversify the portfolio? Assume that the standard deviations on the market and the manager's portfolio were 14.95 percent and 13.41 percent, respectively. The ratio of total risk in the portfolio per unit of market total risk is 0.897 (= 13.41/14.95), but since the manager's beta (0.815) is less than this, it appears that the portfolio contained elements of unsystematic risk. Recalling that beta is defined as the total risk ratio multiplied by the correlation between the portfolio and the market [0.815 = (13.41/14.95) × $r_{p,m}$], the manager's level of diversification is captured by an R^2 coefficient of 0.82. Thus, the selectivity measure of −0.02 understates the true performance shortfall.

To adjust the selectivity measure for the lack of complete diversification, notice that the fund's required return given its standard deviation is 21.14 [= 5.28 + 0.897 (22.96 − 5.28)]. The difference of 1.45 (= 21.14 − 19.69) between the required returns using total versus systematic risk is the added return required because of less-than-perfect diversification. This is subtracted from the selectivity measure to create the manager's *net selectivity* performance of −1.47 (= −0.02 − 1.45). After accounting for the added cost of incomplete diversification, this manager's performance would plot substantially below the market line in Exhibit 25.11.

25.5.2 Performance Measurement with Downside Risk

The **Sortino measure** is a risk-adjusted investment performance statistic that differs from the Sharpe ratio in two ways. First, the Sortino ratio measures the portfolio's average return in excess of a user-selected *minimum acceptable return threshold*, which is often the risk-free

---

[5] Modigliani and Modigliani (1997) present a performance measure (dubbed M^2) that is a variation of both the Sharpe measure and Fama's $R_x[\sigma(R_a)]$ component.

rate used in the S statistic although it need not be. Second, the Sharpe measure focuses on total risk—effectively penalizing the manager for returns that are both too low *and* too high—while the Sortino ratio captures just the **downside risk** (DR) in the portfolio. Sortino and Price (1994) calculate this measure as follows:

25.9
$$ST_i = \frac{\overline{R}_i - \tau}{DR_i}$$

where

τ = the minimum acceptable return threshold specified for the time period

DR_i = the downside risk coefficient for Portfolio i during the specified time period

Like the Sharpe ratio, higher values of the ST measure indicate superior levels of portfolio management.

Downside risk is the volatility of the returns produced by a portfolio that *fall below some hurdle rate* that the investor chooses, such as the zero (i.e., negative returns) or the portfolio's expected return. Thus, downside risk attempts to measure the volatility associated with the *shortfall* that occurs if an investment produces a return that is lower than anticipated. Because of this focus on falling short of the return goal, DR comes closer than measures of total risk (e.g., σ) to capturing what investors truly consider risky. Harlow (1991) discusses a number of ways to calculate DR in practice. One of the most popular measures is the *semi-deviation*, which uses the portfolio's average (expected) return as the hurdle rate:

$$Semi\text{-}Deviation = \sqrt{\frac{1}{n} \sum_{R < \overline{R}} (R_{it} - \overline{R}_i)^2}$$

where

n = the number of portfolio returns falling below the expected return

It should be apparent that semi-deviation is closely related to the standard deviation measure of total risk, but does not include as "risky" those portfolio returns that exceed expectations.

Comparing the Sharpe and Sortino Ratios Suppose that over the past 10 years, two portfolio managers have produced the following returns:

Year	Portfolio A Return (%)	Portfolio B Return (%)
1	−5	−1
2	−3	−1
3	−2	−1
4	3	−1
5	3	0
6	6	4
7	7	4
8	8	7
9	10	13
10	13	16
Average:	4	4
Std. Dev.:	5.60	5.92

Both portfolios had an average annual return of 4 percent over this horizon, meaning that it will be how their risk is measured that determines which manager performed the best.

Based on the listed standard deviation coefficients, it appears that Portfolio A is the less volatile portfolio. Notice, however, that a substantial amount of the variation for Portfolio B came from two large positive returns, which are included in the computation of total risk. Assuming the average risk-free rate during this period was 2 percent, the Sharpe ratio calculations confirm that Portfolio A outperformed Portfolio B: $S_A = 0.357 \ (= [4 - 2]/5.60)$ and $S_B = 0.338 \ (= [4 - 2]/5.92)$.

The story changes when just the downside risk of the portfolios is considered. In addition to more extreme positive values, notice that Portfolio B also had losses that were limited to 1 percent in any given year, perhaps as a result of a portfolio insurance strategy the manager is using. Using semi-deviation to compute *DR* for both portfolios leaves:

$$DR_A = \sqrt{[(-5-4)^2 + (-3-4)^2 + (-2-4)^2 + (3-4)^2 + (3-4)^2] \div 5} = 5.80$$

and

$$DR_B = \sqrt{[(-1-4)^2 + (-1-4)^2 + (-1-4)^2 + (-1-4)^2 + (0-4)^2] \div 5} = 4.82$$

Thus, when only the possibility of receiving a less-than-average return is considered, Portfolio A now appears to be the risky alternative due to the fact it has more extreme negative returns than Portfolio B. Assuming a minimum return threshold of 2 percent to match the Sharpe measure, the Sortino ratios for both portfolios indicate that, by limiting the extent of his downside risk, the manager for Portfolio B was actually the superior performer: $ST_A = 0.345 (= [4-2]/5.80)$ and $ST_B = 0.415 (= [4-2]/4.82)$.

25.5.3 Holdings-Based Performance Measurement

Each of the conventional performance measures just discussed are based on the returns produced by the investment portfolios being compared. There are two distinct advantages to assessing performance based on investment returns. First, returns are usually easy for the investor to observe on a frequent (e.g., daily) basis. Second, they also represent the bottom line that the investor actually takes away from the portfolio manager's investing prowess. However, *returns-based* measures are indirect indications of the decision-making ability of a manager that do not reveal the underlying reasons why the portfolio produced the returns it did.

It is also possible to view investment performance in terms of which securities the manager buys or sells from the portfolio. By looking at how the portfolio's holdings change over time, the investor is able to establish precisely which stock or bond positions were responsible for creating that performance. Thus, when the portfolio's contents can be observed, using a **holdings-based measure** can provide additional insights about the quality of the portfolio manager. Two of the most popular holdings-based performance measures are described below.

Grinblatt-Titman (GT) Performance Measure Assuming that an investor knows the exact investment proportions of each security position in her portfolio on two consecutive reporting dates (e.g., quarterly reports for mutual funds), Grinblatt and Titman (1993) showed that the manager's security selection ability can be established by how he adjusted these weights. For a particular reporting period *t*, their performance measure is:

25.10
$$GT_t = \sum_j (w_{jt} - w_{jt-1}) R_{jt}$$

where:

(w_{jt}, w_{jt-1}) = the portfolio weights for the *j*th security at the beginning of Period *t* and Period *t* − 1, respectively,

R_{jt} = the return to the *j*th security during Period *t*, which begins on Date *t* − 1 and ends on Date *t*

A series of GT_t for a manager can be averaged over several periods to create a better indication of the ongoing quality of his decision-making ability.

$$\text{Average GT} = \frac{\sum_t \text{GT}_t}{T}$$

where T is the total number of investment periods used in the evaluation

Exhibit 25.12 illustrates how the GT performance measure is calculated for two different portfolios: (1) a passive value-weighted index of all the stocks in the market, and (2) an active portfolio manager. Panel A shows the share prices for five stocks representing the investable universe on six different dates relative to the current Date 0. No dividends are paid and the returns to each stock position are also shown for the four full holding periods starting at Date 0 (e.g., Period 1 begins at Date 0 and ends at Date 1).

Panel B shows the total shares outstanding for each stock on Date −1, Date 0, Date 1, Date 2, and Date 3, which are the beginning dates for Period 0, Period 1, Period 2, Period 3, and Period 4, respectively. Alongside the shares outstanding, which remain stable, Panel B lists the corresponding index weights that would apply at the beginning of each investment period. For instance, the index weight shown for Stock A at the beginning of Period 2 (i.e., w_2) is 28.0 percent, which is calculated by multiplying the share price at Date 1 (i.e., $14) by the shares outstanding at Date 1 (i.e., 200) and then dividing that product by the total market value of all five stocks at Date 1 (i.e., $[200 \times 14] + \cdots + [200 \times 10] = \$10,000$). Notice that as the share prices change over time, the value-based index weights will also change even though the number of shares outstanding do not.

Panel C provides similar data for a hypothetical active portfolio manager whose performance is to be assessed using the GT measure. This manager has made two explicit adjustments to his portfolio holdings. First, on Date 0 (i.e., the beginning of Period 1), he has sold half of his share positions in Stocks B and C in order to buy 10 shares of Stock A. Second, on Date 2 (i.e., the beginning of Period 3), he sells the remainder of his Stock B holding to repurchase five shares of Stock C. As a consequence, the portfolio weights of this active manager change because of both explicit stock trades and implicit adjustments due to changing market prices.

The last panel of Exhibit 25.12 calculates the GT measure for both the stock index and the active manager. For the index, the average GT across the four investment periods is virtually zero (i.e., −0.03 percent = [0.00 − 0.57 + 0.18 + 0.29]/4). This should be the case for any passive buy-and-hold portfolio, assuming that the stock returns are not correlated from one period to the next. That is, while index weights will vary with stock prices (e.g., $w_2 - w_1 = 0.280 - 0.200 = 0.080$, for Stock A), the product of these weight changes with the subsequent stock returns should net out over time if there is no momentum effect present in the returns. This is consistent with viewing the GT measure as the return to a zero-cost hedge portfolio that is long at the current investment weights and short at the previous weights.

In contrast, the GT measure for an active portfolio manager will likely not be zero. Here the manager's average GT value is 3.41 percent [= (15.00 − 0.71 − 0.97 + 0.34)/4], indicating that he added a substantial amount of value through his stock-picking prowess. In Period 1, the decision to buy Stock A at Date 0, whose price subsequently rose, contributed 10.00 percent [= (0.250 − 0.000) × 40%] whereas the decisions to sell some of Stocks B and C contributed 2.50 percent each [= (0.125 − 0.250) × −20%] since both stocks declined in value during Period 1. On the other hand, the decision to repurchase Stock C on Date 2 subtracted 1.19 percent of value [= (0.190 − 0.095) × −12.5%] since the price of these shares fell from $8 to $7 during Period 3.

This example demonstrates that it is possible to create a very detailed analysis of how each decision the manager made contributed to his overall performance. Additionally, the GT statistic can be computed without reference to any specific benchmark, which was not the case for returns-based measures such as the Information Ratio. However, the GT measure fails to reward or penalize the manager for portfolio adjustments where the share price change actually occurs in a later period. For instance, the manager received no credit in Period 3 for the decision to sell Stock B because the subsequent share price decline from $8 to $6 did not occur

Exhibit 25.12 Holdings-Based Performance Measurement with the GT Method

A. Stock Market Data

Stock	SHARE PRICE ($)						RETURN (%)			
	Date -1	Date 0	Date 1	Date 2	Date 3	Date 4	Period 1	Period 2	Period 3	Period 4
A	10	10	14	13	13	14	40.00	-7.14	0.00	7.69
B	10	10	8	8	8	6	-20.00	0.00	0.00	-25.00
C	10	10	8	8	7	6	-20.00	0.00	-12.50	-14.29
D	10	10	10	11	12	12	0.00	10.00	9.09	0.00
E	10	10	10	10	10	10	0.00	0.00	0.00	0.00

B. Value-Weighted Index Holding Data

Stock	SHARES OUTSTANDING ON						INDEX WEIGHT (w_{JT}) AT BEGINNING OF:				
	Date -1	Date 0	Date 1	Date 2	Date 3	Date 4	Period 0	Period 1	Period 2	Period 3	Period 4
A	200	200	200	200	200	200	0.200	0.200	0.280	0.260	0.260
B	200	200	200	200	200	200	0.200	0.200	0.160	0.160	0.160
C	200	200	200	200	200	200	0.200	0.200	0.160	0.160	0.140
D	200	200	200	200	200	200	0.200	0.200	0.200	0.220	0.240
E	200	200	200	200	200	200	0.200	0.200	0.200	0.200	0.200

C. Active Manager Holding Data

Stock	SHARES HELD ON						PORTFOLIO WEIGHT (w_{JT}) AT BEGINNING OF:				
	Date -1	Date 0	Date 1	Date 2	Date 3	Date 4	Period 0	Period 1	Period 2	Period 3	Period 4
A	0	10	10	10	10	10	0.000	0.250	0.333	0.310	0.310
B	10	5	5	0	0	0	0.250	0.125	0.095	0.000	0.000
C	10	5	5	10	10	10	0.250	0.125	0.095	0.190	0.167
D	10	10	10	10	10	10	0.250	0.250	0.238	0.262	0.286
E	10	10	10	10	10	10	0.250	0.250	0.238	0.238	0.238

D. Calculation of GT Measure

Stock	INDEX:				ACTIVE MANAGER:			
	$(w_1-w_0)\times R_1$	$(w_2-w_1)\times R_2$	$(w_3-w_2)\times R_3$	$(w_4-w_3)\times R_4$	$(w_1-w_0)\times R_1$	$(w_2-w_1)\times R_2$	$(w_3-w_2)\times R_3$	$(w_4-w_3)\times R_4$
A	0.00	-0.57	0.00	0.00	10.00	-0.59	0.00	0.00
B	0.00	0.00	0.00	0.00	2.50	0.00	0.00	0.00
C	0.00	0.00	0.00	0.29	2.50	0.00	-1.19	0.34
D	0.00	0.00	0.18	0.00	0.00	-0.12	0.22	0.00
E	0.00	0.00	0.00	0.00	0.00	0.00	0.00	0.00
GT_t:	0.00%	-0.57%	0.18%	0.29%	15.00%	-0.71%	-0.97%	0.34%
Average GT:	-0.03%				3.41%			

until Period 4. This deficiency can be overcome by calculating portfolio weight adjustments over longer holding periods (e.g., annual vs. quarterly).

Characteristic Selectivity (CS) Performance Measure A limitation of the GT measure is that it does not control directly for changes in either risk or investment style that result when a manager revises his portfolio holdings. If a manager sells a risky stock in order to buy a more risky one, he should be rewarded with higher gross returns over time but not necessarily higher risk-adjusted returns. Similarly, GT does not distinguish between stocks that perform well because of security-specific factors and those that merely benefit from broader trends, such as price momentum effects. Daniel et al. (1997) developed an alternative holdings-based measure that compares the returns of each stock held in an actively managed portfolio to the return of a benchmark portfolio that has the same aggregate investment characteristics. Their *characteristic selectivity* (CS) performance statistic is given by:

25.11
$$CS_t = \sum_j w_{jt}(R_{jt} - R_{Bjt})$$

where, in addition to the earlier notation, R_{Bjt} is the Period t (i.e., from Date $t - 1$ to Date t) return to a passive portfolio whose investment characteristics are matched at the beginning of Period t with those of Stock j. Like GT, a series of periodic CS_t values can be averaged to indicate the manager's ability to pick specific stocks within the context of a larger investment style mandate:

$$\text{Average CS} = \frac{\sum_t CS_t}{T}$$

The CS measure credits the active manager whenever he holds a stock that outperforms a style-matched index investment and penalizes him when the opposite is true. The implicit assumption underlying this calculation is that, in lieu of hiring the active manager, investors could always purchase an indexed product with equivalent investment characteristics. Thus, the true test of the active manager's skill is whether he can pick a sufficient number of specific stocks that outperform portfolios that investors could have formed for themselves.

The major obstacle to implementing CS is identifying a set of benchmark portfolios to match the risk and style characteristics of every stock that an active manager might want to hold. Daniel et al. (1997) proposed forming 125 different passive portfolios, based on three investment characteristics: (1) market capitalization (i.e., size), (2) book-to-market ratio, and (3) stock price momentum. They created their benchmarks by sorting every stock listed on the NYSE, AMEX, and NASDAQ exchanges into quintiles based first on size, then on book-to-market ratios, and finally on price momentum. The benchmark returns (i.e., R_{Bjt}) were then calculated as value-weighted averages of all of the stocks contained in that particular portfolio. The appropriate characteristic-matched benchmark for any given stock position is simply the one that contains that stock.

Exhibit 25.13 summarizes a performance evaluation of almost 2,000 mutual funds with a diverse set of investment objectives from 1975 to 1994. Four different measures are compared: (1) GT, (2) CS, (3) one-factor Jensen, and (4) four-factor Jensen. The display shows the average annualized values of each performance measure over the entire investment period as well as over several subperiods. The GT measure, which captures the net benefit of the broad range of trading strategies employed by active fund managers, shows that the average fund added 1.94 percent of value per year over the 20-year horizon. However, the CS measure—which controls for momentum, size, and value-versus-growth effects—shows that the benefit provided by just the manager's security selection skills accounted for less than half of this amount (i.e., 0.79 percent per year). Both of the returns-based Jensen performance measures were also positive, but they were statistically insignificant.

Exhibit 25.13 Comparison of GT, CS, and Jensen Performance Measures

Investment Period	Number of Funds	Gross Return (%)	GT Measure (%)	CS Measure (%)	1-Factor Jensen (%)	4-Factor Jensen (%)
1975–1979	214	21.33	2.06[a]	1.58[b]	2.78[b]	1.44
1980–1984	508	16.31	2.10[b]	0.79	0.62	0.98
1984–1989	786	20.07	1.79[b]	0.33	–0.80	0.83
1990–1994	1,973	10.26	1.86[b]	0.45	–0.16	–0.36
1975–1994	—	16.99	1.94[a]	0.79[b]	0.60	0.39

[a]Significant at the 0.01 level.

[b]Significant at the 0.05 level.

Source: Kent Daniel, Mark Grinblatt, Sheridan Titman, and Russ Wermers, "Measuring Mutual Fund Performance with Characteristic Benchmarks," *Journal of Finance* 52, no. 3 (July 1997). Reprinted with permission of Blackwell Publishing.

25.5.4 Performance Attribution Analysis

As we have seen, portfolio managers can add value for their investors in either of two ways: selecting superior securities or demonstrating superior timing skills by allocating funds to different asset or sector classes. **Attribution analysis** attempts to distinguish which of these factors is the source of the portfolio's overall performance. This method compares the manager's total return to the return for a predetermined benchmark policy portfolio and decomposes the difference into an *allocation effect* and a *selection effect*. The most straightforward way to measure these two effects is as follows:

25.12
$$\text{Allocation Effect} = \Sigma_i[(w_{ai} - w_{pi}) \times (R_{pi} - R_p)]$$
$$\text{Selection Effect} = \Sigma_i[(w_{ai}) \times (R_{ai} - R_{pi})]$$

where:

w_{ai}, w_{pi} = the investment proportions of the *i*th *market segment* (e.g., asset class, industry group) in the manager's portfolio and the policy portfolio, respectively

R_{ai}, R_{pi} = the investment return to the *i*th market segment in the manager's portfolio and the policy portfolio, respectively

R_p = the total return to the policy portfolio

The allocation effect measures the manager's decision to over- or underweight a particular market segment (i.e., $[w_{ai} - w_{pi}]$) in terms of that segment's return performance relative to the overall return to the benchmark (i.e., $[R_{pi} - R_p]$). Good timing skill is therefore a matter of investing more money in those market segments that end up producing greater than average returns. The selection effect measures the manager's ability to form specific market segment portfolios that generate superior returns relative to how the comparable market segment is defined in the benchmark portfolio (i.e., $[R_{ai} - R_{pi}]$), weighted by the manager's actual market segment investment proportions. The manager's total value-added performance is the sum of the allocation and selection effects.[6]

An Example Consider an investor whose top-down portfolio strategy consists of two dimensions. First, he decides on a broad allocation across three asset classes: U.S. stocks, U.S. long-term bonds, and cash equivalents, such as Treasury bills or certificates of deposit. Once this judgment is made, the investor's second general decision is choosing which specific

---

[6] Bailey, Richards, and Tierney (2007) argue that a better way to measure the selection effect is to multiply the market segment return differential by the benchmark for that segment, or $\Sigma_i[(w_{pi}) \times (R_{ai} - R_{pi})]$. A drawback of this approach is that the allocation and selection effects no longer sum to the total value-added return. To balance the equation, he calculates an *interaction effect* as $\Sigma_i[(w_{ai} - w_{pi}) \times (R_{ai} - R_{pi})]$ to measure residual performance.

stocks, bonds, and cash instruments to buy. As a policy benchmark, he selects a hypothetical portfolio with a 60 percent allocation to the Standard and Poor's 500 index, a 30 percent investment in the Lehman Corporate Long Bond index, and a 10 percent allocation to three-month Treasury bills.

Suppose that at the start of the investment period, the investor believes equity values are somewhat inflated relative to the fixed-income market. Compared to the benchmark, he therefore decides to underweight stocks and overweight bonds and cash. The investment proportions he chooses are 50 percent in equity, 38 percent in bonds, and 12 percent in cash. Further, he decides to concentrate on equities in the interest rate–sensitive sectors, such as utilities and financial companies, while deemphasizing the technology and consumer durables sectors. Finally, he resolves to buy shorter duration bonds of a higher credit quality than are contained in the benchmark bond index and to buy commercial paper rather than Treasury bills.

The manager has made active investment decisions involving both the allocation of assets and the selection of individual securities. To determine if either (or both) of these decisions proved to be wise ones, at the end of the investment period he can calculate his overall and segment-specific performance. Exhibit 25.14 summarizes these returns for the investor's actual and benchmark asset class portfolios, as well as the investment weightings for each. The overall returns can be computed as:

$$\text{Overall Manager Return} = (0.50 \times 0.097) + (0.38 \times 0.091) + (0.12 \times 0.056)$$
$$= 8.98\%$$

and

$$\text{Overall Benchmark Return} = (0.60 \times 0.086) + (0.30 \times 0.092) + (0.10 \times 0.054)$$
$$= 8.46\%$$

Thus, the manager beat the policy benchmark by 52 basis points (= 0.0898 − 0.0846) over this particular investment horizon.

The goal of attribution analysis is to isolate the reason for this value-added performance. The manager's allocation effect can be computed by multiplying the excess asset class weight by that class's relative investment performance:

$$[-0.10 \times (0.086 - 0.0846)] + [0.08 \times (0.092 - 0.0846)] + [0.02 \times (0.054 - 0.0846)] = -0.02\%$$

This shows that if the investor had made just his market timing decisions and not picked different securities than those in the benchmark, his performance would have lagged behind the policy return by two basis points. This total allocation effect can be broken down further into an equity allocation return of −2 basis points [= −0.10 × (0.086 − 0.0846)], a bond allocation return of 6 basis points [= 0.08 × (0.092 − 0.0846)], and a cash allocation return of −6 basis points [= 0.02 × (0.054 − 0.0846)]. Therefore, the decision to underweight stock and overweight cash (asset classes that generated returns above and below the benchmark, respectively) resulted in diminished performance that more than offset the benefit of overweighting bonds.

Exhibit 25.14 Asset Class Performance Attribution Analysis

Asset Class	INVESTMENT WEIGHTS			RETURNS		
	Actual	**Benchmark**	**Excess**	**Actual**	**Benchmarck**	**Excess**
Stock	0.50	0.60	−0.10	9.70%	8.60%	1.10%
Bonds	0.38	0.30	0.08	9.10	9.20	−0.10
Cash	0.12	0.10	0.02	5.60	5.40	0.20

Since the investor knows that he outperformed the benchmark overall, a negative allocation effect must mean that he exhibited positive security selection skills. His selection effect can be computed as:

$$[0.50 \times (0.097 - 0.086)] - [0.38 \times (0.091 - 0.092)] + [0.12 \times (0.056 - 0.054)] = 0.54\%$$

In this example, the investor formed superior stock and cash portfolios, although his bond selections did not perform quite as well as the Lehman index. One important caveat is that, because the returns are not risk-adjusted, it is possible that the asset class portfolios formed by the investor are riskier than their benchmark counterparts. This is almost certainly true for a cash portfolio that holds short-term corporate debt obligations instead of Treasury bills, so the investor should expect a somewhat higher return that has nothing to do with his skill. Finally, the investor's total incremental return of 52 basis points can be decomposed as:

$$\text{Total Value Added} = \text{Allocation Effect} + \text{Selection Effect}$$
$$= -0.02\% + 0.54\% = 0.52\%$$

Using a procedure similar to the one just described, Brinson, Hood, and Beebower (1986) examined the performance of a group of 91 large U.S. pension plans from 1974 to 1983. The mean annual return for this sample was 9.01 percent, compared to 10.11 percent for their benchmark. Thus, active management cost the average plan 110 basis points of return per year. This "value subtracted" return increment consisted of a −77-basis-point allocation effect and a −33-basis-point selection effect. They concluded that a plan's initial strategic asset allocation choice, rather than any of its active management decisions, was the primary determinant of portfolio performance. In a follow-up study, Brinson, Singer, and Beebower (1991) reached a similar conclusion for a different group of 82 pension plans over the 1977–1987 period. For this new sample, the total active return shortfall dropped to −7 basis points, which was divided into an 18-basis-point selection effect and a −25-basis-point allocation effect.

Performance Attribution Extensions In addition to assessing the ability to time broad asset class movements, the attribution methodology can be used to distinguish security selection skills from other decisions that an investor might make. For instance, the manager of an all-equity portfolio must decide which economic sectors (e.g., basic materials, consumer nondurables, transportation) to under- and overweight before she can choose her preferred companies in those sectors. Performance attribution analysis is still applicable, with a "sector rotation" effect replacing the market timing effect. Exhibit 25.15 summarizes the performance of the growth-oriented stock portfolio managed by The MBA Investment Fund, L.L.C., a privately funded investment management company run by a group of graduate students at the University of Texas. Because the Fund's investment mandate was to beat the return on the

Exhibit 25.15 MBA Investment Fund Sector Performance Attribution Analysis

| S&P 500 Sector | INVESTMENT WEIGHTS | | | EXCESS RETURNS |
	Actual	S&P 500	Excess	S&P Sector—Overall S&P
Basic materials	0.0331	0.0670	−0.0339	−15.15%
Capital equipment and technology	0.2544	0.1841	0.0703	−3.31
Consumer services	0.0208	0.0692	−0.0484	6.95
Consumer durables	0.0588	0.0353	0.0235	−21.34
Consumer nondurables	0.2752	0.2851	−0.0099	5.85
Energy	0.1170	0.0935	0.0235	−7.08
Financial	0.1619	0.1249	0.0370	7.15
Transportation	0.0199	0.0172	0.0027	−1.72
Utilities	0.0590	0.1000	−0.0410	1.91
Miscellaneous	0.0000	0.0242	−0.0242	−13.15

Standard and Poor's 500, the managers had two basic decisions to make: which sectors to emphasize and which individual stocks to buy within those sectors.

During the year shown here, the overall returns to the S&P 500 and the Fund were 29.63 percent and 29.54 percent, respectively. The second and third columns of Exhibit 25.15 document the actual and benchmark weights for the 10 economic sectors comprising the S&P 500 index, with the Fund's excess weightings (i.e., $[w_{ai} - w_{pi}]$) listed in the fourth column. The last column shows the benchmark sector return relative to the overall S&P return (i.e., $[R_{pi} - R_p]$). The sector allocation effect can be calculated by summing the product of the entries in the last two columns:

$$(-0.0339 \times -0.1515) + (0.0703 \times -0.0331) + \cdots + (-0.0242 \times -0.1315) = -0.28\%$$

With an overall return difference of -9 basis points ($= 0.2954 - 0.2963$), this means that the Fund's managers generated a security selection effect of 19 basis points $[= (-0.0009) - (-0.0028)]$. Consequently, while the student managers virtually matched the strong performance of the entire stock market, it appears they were better at picking stocks than forecasting broader economic trends.

This general attribution analysis methodology has been extended to other specific asset classes as well. Kuberek (1995) showed that producing fixed-income attributions for bond portfolio managers is quite straightforward once the relevant decision variables have been specified. He noted that these decision variables might include allocations to different countries, foreign exchange effects, individual bond selections, and other risk factors, such as the portfolio's term structure positioning. Karnosky and Singer (1994) and Ankrim and Hensel (1994) have developed a unified framework for attributing performance in a global asset management context. They have added both active and hedged currency allocation returns to the single-currency attribution model of Brinson, Hood, and Beebower to allow for the intricacies of cross-border investing. Comparing the performance of one of their global portfolios relative to the MSCI World Equity Index during 1989, they demonstrated that the combined effect of the currency selection decision accounted for 563 basis points of the 7.66 percent return advantage that the portfolio enjoyed.

25.5.5 Measuring Market Timing Skills

As we saw in Chapter 16, tactical asset allocation (TAA) attempts to produce active value-added returns solely through allocation decisions. Instead of trying to pick superior individual securities, TAA managers adjust their asset class exposures based on perceived changes in the relative valuations of those classes. This means that the relevant performance measurement criterion for a TAA manager is how well he is able to time broad market movements. There are two reasons why attribution analysis is ill-suited for this task. First, by design, a TAA manager indexes his actual asset class investments and so the selection effect is not relevant. Second, TAA might entail dozens of changes to asset class weightings during an investment period, which could render meaningless an attribution effect computed on the average holdings. Because of these problems, many analysts consider a regression-based method for measuring timing skills to be a superior approach.

Weigel (1991) tested the market timing skills of a group of 17 U.S.-based TAA managers. His methodology was motivated by the pioneering work of Merton (1981) and Hendriksson and Merton (1981) and assumed that perfect market timing ability was equivalent to owning a lookback call option that pays at expiration the return to the best-performing asset class among stocks, bonds, and cash. That is, in Period t, a manager with perfect market timing skills would have a return (R_{at}) equal to

$$R_{at} = RFR_t + \max[R_{st} - RFR_t, R_{bt} - RFR_t, 0]$$

where R_{st} and R_{bt} are the Period t returns to the stock and bond benchmark portfolios, respectively. Controlling for stock and bond price movements in a manner comparable to Jensen's method, the following regression equation can be calculated:

$$(R_{at} - RFR_t) = \alpha + \beta_b(R_{bt} - RFR_t) + \beta_s(R_{st} - RFR_t)$$
$$+ \gamma\{\max[R_{st} - RFR_t, R_{bt} - RFR_t, 0]\} + e_t$$

The average value for γ, which measures the proportion of the perfect timing option that the TAA managers were able to capture, was 0.30. This value was statistically significant, meaning that these managers had reliable, although not perfect, market timing skills. Also, the average alpha was -0.5 percent per quarter, indicating that these same managers had negative nonmarket timing skills (e.g., hedging strategies).

Many other studies have examined the market timing ability of portfolio managers who are not exclusively TAA practitioners. Kon (1983) and Chang and Lewellen (1984) concluded that mutual fund managers generally possess negative market timing skills, a position supported by Baver and Dahlquist (2001). Coggin, Fabozzi, and Rahman (1993) carried this analysis further by looking at both the timing and selectivity skills of a group of U.S. equity pension fund managers. They demonstrated that their sample of managers possessed positive, but small, selection skills and negative timing skills. From these studies, it is reasonable to conclude that only those managers explicitly trying to time market movements have a chance of doing so.

· ·

25.6 Factors That Affect Use of Performance Measures

All the performance measures just described are only as good as their data inputs. Of course, an analyst should use judgment and be patient in the evaluation process. It is not possible to evaluate a portfolio manager on the basis of a quarter or even a year. An evaluation should extend over several years and cover at least a full market cycle, which allows one to determine whether the manager's performance differs during rising and declining markets as Ferson and Schadt (1996) demonstrate.

Many of the equity portfolio performance measures we have discussed are derived from the CAPM and assume the existence of a market portfolio at the point of tangency on the Markowitz efficient frontier. Theoretically, the market portfolio is an efficient, completely diversified portfolio. As we discussed in Chapter 8, this market portfolio must contain all risky assets in the economy and all components must be market-value weighted. The problem arises in finding a realistic proxy for this theoretical market portfolio. Analysts typically use the Standard and Poor's 500 index as the proxy for the market portfolio because it contains a fairly diversified portfolio of stocks, and the sample is market-value weighted. Unfortunately, it does not represent the true composition of the market portfolio. Specifically, it includes only common stocks and most of them are listed on the NYSE. Notably, it excludes many other risky assets that theoretically should be considered, such as numerous domestic stocks, foreign stocks, foreign and domestic bonds, real estate, alternative assets, and collectibles.

This lack of completeness was highlighted in several articles by Roll (1977a, 1978, 1980, 1981), who detailed the problem with the market proxy and pointed out its implications for measuring portfolio performance. Although a detailed discussion of Roll's critique will not be repeated here, we need to consider his major problem with the measurement of the market portfolio, which he refers to as a **benchmark error**. He showed that if the proxy for the market portfolio is not a truly efficient portfolio, then the SML using this proxy may not be the true SML—the true SML could have a higher slope. In such a case, a portfolio plotted above the SML and derived using a poor benchmark could actually plot below the SML that uses the true market portfolio.

Another problem is that the beta could differ from that computed using the true market portfolio. For example, if the true beta were larger than the beta computed using the proxy, the true position of the portfolio would shift to the right. In an empirical test, Brown and Brown (1987) documented a considerable amount of ranking reversal when the definition of the market portfolio was changed in a Jensen's alpha analysis of a sample of well-established mutual funds. Terhaar (2001) also showed how the benchmark error problem can affect attribution analysis.

25.6.1 Demonstration of the Global Benchmark Problem

To illustrate the impact of the benchmark problem in global capital markets, consider what happens to the individual measures of risk when the world equity market is employed to estimate the beta coefficient from the SML. Exhibit 25.16 contains beta estimates for the 30 stocks in the Dow Jones Industrial Average (DJIA) using the S&P 500, which is the typical proxy for stocks of companies domiciled in the United States, and the Morgan Stanley Capital International (MSCI) World Stock Index, which is a market-value-weighted index that contains stocks from around the world. These findings were calculated using weekly returns from two different three-year periods: 2002–2004 and 2005–2007. The percentage difference between the U.S. beta and the World beta is also shown, using the higher of the two risk estimates as the base.

There are two major differences in the various beta statistics. First, for many stocks, the beta estimates change a great deal over time. For example, General Electric's U.S. and World betas during 2002–2004 were 1.14 and 1.17, respectively. However, during 2005–2007, both of these values substantially decreased (to 0.67 and 0.52, respectively). Second, although the mean and median values for the U.S. and World beta estimates appear to be somewhat similar during both time periods, the "% Difference" columns show that there are some substantial differences in betas estimated for the same stock over the same time period when two different definitions

Exhibit 25.16 Beta Estimates for Dow Jones Industrials Stock Using Domestic and World Stock Market Indices: 2002–2004 & 2005–2007

Stock	Ticker	2002–2004			2005–2007		
		Beta-US	Beta-World	% Diff	Beta-US	Beta-World	% Diff
3M Company	MMM	0.73	0.71	2.7%	0.83	0.73	12.0%
Alcoa	AA	1.35	1.53	11.8%	1.63	1.72	5.2%
Altria Group	MO	0.53	0.51	3.8%	0.73	0.60	17.8%
American Express	AXP	1.39	1.50	7.3%	1.30	1.05	19.2%
American Intl Group	AIG	1.34	1.38	2.9%	1.01	0.77	23.8%
AT&T	T	1.08	1.13	4.4%	0.79	0.68	13.9%
Boeing	BA	0.86	0.92	6.5%	0.87	0.78	10.3%
Caterpillar	CAT	1.20	1.26	4.8%	1.70	1.67	1.8%
Citigroup	C	1.29	1.45	11.0%	1.10	0.84	23.6%
Coca-Cola	KO	0.55	0.56	1.8%	0.61	0.49	19.7%
Du Pont	DD	0.96	0.93	3.1%	1.24	1.09	12.1%
ExxonMobil	XOM	0.74	0.72	2.7%	1.27	1.23	3.1%
General Electric	GE	1.14	1.17	2.6%	0.67	0.52	22.4%
General Motors	GM	1.02	1.12	8.9%	1.68	1.58	6.0%
Hewlett-Packard	HPQ	1.57	1.68	6.5%	1.02	0.84	17.6%
Home Depot	HD	1.06	1.06	0.0%	1.29	1.10	14.7%
Honeywell	HON	1.32	1.37	3.6%	1.34	1.24	7.5%
Intel	INTC	1.51	1.65	8.5%	1.31	1.16	11.5%
Intl Business Machines	IBM	1.23	1.36	9.6%	0.90	0.74	17.8%
Johnson & Johnson	JNJ	0.68	0.60	11.8%	0.47	0.40	14.9%
JPMorgan	JPM	1.67	1.89	11.6%	1.23	0.99	19.5%
McDonald's	MCD	0.84	0.94	10.6%	0.92	0.81	12.0%
Merck	MRK	0.90	0.86	4.4%	0.71	0.67	5.6%
Microsoft	MSFT	1.17	1.24	5.6%	0.86	0.79	8.1%
Pfizer	PFE	0.90	0.85	5.6%	1.04	1.00	3.8%
Procter & Gamble	PG	0.39	0.28	28.2%	0.43	0.33	23.3%
United Technologies	UTX	0.83	0.83	0.0%	0.99	0.96	3.0%
Verizon	VZ	0.80	0.83	3.6%	0.93	0.78	16.1%
Wal-Mart Stores	WMT	0.87	0.74	14.9%	0.85	0.71	16.5%
Walt Disney	DIS	1.19	1.25	4.8%	0.81	0.76	6.2%
Mean:		1.04	1.08	6.8%	1.02	0.90	13.0%
Median:		1.04	1.09	5.2%	0.96	0.80	13.0%

of the benchmark portfolio are employed. For instance, the U.S. and World beta estimates for Johnson & Johnson differed by almost 12 percent in 2002–2004 and then by almost 15 percent in 2005–2007. Overall, the median size of this discrepancy increased over time—from 5.2 percent to 13.0 percent—which is a sizable difference. It indicates that the specification of the proper benchmark remains a critical issue in the performance evaluation process.

Reilly and Akhtar (1995) examined the effect of the choice of a benchmark on global performance measurement by plotting SMLs for six different indexes over three time horizons: 1983–1988, 1989–1994, and 1983–1994. Four country-specific benchmarks—the S&P 500 (United States), the Nikkei (Japan), the FTAll Shares (England), and the FAZ (Germany)—and two aggregate benchmarks—M-S World and Brinson GSMI—were used in the analysis. The results indicate that using alternative market proxies for different countries generates SMLs that differ substantially during a given time period and that these SMLs tend to be very unstable over time. For instance, the Nikkei SML had the largest risk premium during 1983–1988 but a negative risk premium during 1989–1994, which clearly is contrary to capital market theory. Finally, the S&P 500 provided investors with the biggest performance hurdle over the whole sample period, which was mostly due to the high risk premiums in the United States during 1989–1994.

25.6.2 Implications of the Benchmark Problems

Several points are significant regarding this benchmark criticism. First, the problems noted by Roll, which are increased with global investing, do not negate the value of the CAPM as a *normative* model of equilibrium pricing; the theory is still viable. The problem is one of *measurement* when using the theory to evaluate portfolio performance. You need to find a better proxy for the market portfolio or to adjust measured performance for benchmark errors. Roll (1981) and Grinold (1992) have made several suggestions to help overcome this problem. Finally, the multiple markets index (MMI), developed by Brinson, Diermeier, and Schlarbaum (1986), is a major step toward a truly comprehensive world market portfolio.

Alternatively, the analyst might consider giving greater weight to the Sharpe and Sortino portfolio performance measures because they do not depend on the market portfolio. Although the evaluation process based on these statistics generally uses a benchmark portfolio as an example of an unmanaged portfolio for comparison purposes, the risk measure for the portfolio being evaluated does not directly depend on a market portfolio. Also, recall that the portfolio rank from the Sharpe measure typically correlates highly with the ranks derived from alternative performance measures.

25.6.3 Required Characteristics of Benchmarks

Concurrent with the search for a global market portfolio, there has also been a search for appropriate **normal portfolios**, which are customized benchmarks that reflect the specific styles of alternative managers. Bailey, Richards, and Tierney (2007) consider this a critical need of pension plans and endowments who hire multiple managers with widely divergent styles. They point out that if a broad market index is used rather than a specific benchmark portfolio, it is implicitly assumed that the portfolio manager does not have an investment style, which is quite unrealistic. Also, it does not allow the plan sponsors to determine if the money manager is consistent with his or her stated investment style. The authors contend that any useful benchmark should have the following characteristics:

- *Unambiguous.* The names and weights of securities comprising the benchmark are clearly delineated.
- *Investable.* The option is available to forgo active management and simply hold the benchmark.
- *Measurable.* It is possible to calculate the return on the benchmark on a reasonably frequent basis.

- *Appropriate.* The benchmark is consistent with the manager's investment style or biases.
- *Reflective of current investment opinions.* The manager has current investment knowledge (be it positive, negative, or neutral) of the securities that make up the benchmark.
- *Specified in advance.* The benchmark is constructed prior to the start of an evaluation period.
- *Owned.* The manager should accept accountability for benchmark performance.

If a benchmark does not possess all of these properties, it is considered flawed as an effective management tool. One example of a flawed benchmark is the use of the median manager from a broad universe of managers or even a limited universe of managers. This criticism is spelled out in detail by Bailey (1992), who argues that the manager universe is inadequate on almost every characteristic. Finally, Dialynas (2001) considers the special problems of creating benchmarks for fixed-income portfolios.

. . . .

25.7 Evaluation of Bond Portfolio Performance

The analysis of risk-adjusted performance for equity portfolios began in the late 1960s following the development of portfolio theory and the CAPM. No such development has simplified analysis for the bond market, where numerous and complex factors can influence portfolio returns. However, prior to the 1970s, most bond portfolio managers followed buy-and-hold strategies, so their performance probably did not differ much. In this era, interest rates were relatively stable, so one could gain little from the active management of bond portfolios.

The environment in the bond market changed considerably in the late 1970s when interest rates increased dramatically and became more volatile. This created an incentive to trade bonds activety and, in turn, substantially more diverse performance by bond portfolio managers. This trend also created demand for techniques that would help investors evaluate the performance of bond portfolio managers. Further, the historic decline in interest rates that began in the early 1990s and the attendant increase in the level of rate volatility fostered a renewed interest in measuring the risk-adjusted performance of bond portfolios as well as attempts to explain the causes of that performance.

As it was for stocks, bond performance measurement can also be divided into attempts to assess *how* portfolio managers performed relative to investor expectations and *why* the managers produced the performance they did. We now consider techniques that address both of these questions.[7]

25.7.1 Returns-Based Bond Performance Measurement

Early attempts to analyze fixed-income performance often involved peer group comparisons of the returns generated by bond portfolio managers with comparable investment styles. Kritzman (1983) examined the ranking for 32 bond managers over two five-year periods. He determined each manager's percentile ranking in each period, and correlated the rankings. The results revealed no relationship between levels of performance in the two periods and no relationship between past and future performance, even when comparing the best and worst performers. He concluded that it is necessary to look at something besides past performance to determine superior bond portfolio managers.

Of course, peer group comparisons are potentially flawed because they do not account for investment risk directly. In principle, the Jensen's alpha approach described in previous sections can be employed to measure the performance of *any* asset portfolio. In practice, however, when the assets in the portfolio change from stocks to bonds, it is likely that a straightforward application of the conventional risk models will not produce the most meaningful results. Fama and French (1993) addressed this issue by expanding their

---

[7] A good overview of this area and a discussion of the historical development of the various performance measures are contained in Fong (2001).

Exhibit 25.17 Risk Factor and Jensen's Alpha Estimates for Seven Bond Portfolios: 1963–1991

| | BOND PORTFOLIOS | | | | | | |
| | Government | | Corporate | | | | |
Risk Factor:	1–5FG	6–10G	Aaa	Aa	A	Baa	LG
$(R_m - RFR)$	−0.02[a]	−0.04[a]	−0.02[a]	0.00	0.00	0.02	0.18[a]
SMB	0.00	−0.02	−0.02[a]	−0.01[a]	0.00	0.05[a]	0.08[a]
HML	0.00	−0.02	−0.02[a]	−0.00	0.00	0.04[a]	0.12[a]
TERM	0.47[a]	0.75[a]	1.03[a]	0.99[a]	1.00[a]	0.99[a]	0.64[a]
DEF	0.27[a]	0.32[a]	0.97[a]	0.97[a]	1.02[a]	1.05[a]	0.80[a]
Portfolio Alpha:	0.09[a]	0.11[a]	−0.00	−0.00	−0.00	0.02	−0.07

[a]Significant at the 0.05 level.

Source: Eugene F. Fama and Kenneth R. French, "Common Risk Factors in the Returns on Stocks and Bonds," *Journal of Financial Economics* 33, no. 1 (January, 1993): 3–56.

three-factor equation to include two additional factors specifically related to how returns are generated for fixed-income securities:

25.13 $R_{jt} - RFR_t = \alpha_j + [b_{j1}(R_{mt} - RFR_t) + b_{j2}SMB_t + b_{j3}HML_t] + [b_{j4}TERM_t + b_{j4}DEF_t] + e_{jt}$

The two additional risk factors are defined as follows: (1) *TERM* is the term premium built into the slope of the Treasury yield curve and is calculated as the difference between the long-term and short-term government bond yields, and (2) *DEF* is the default premium and is calculated by the credit spread between the long-term corporate and government bond yields.

Fama and French (1993) tested this model using seven different bond portfolios over the 342-month period from July 1963 to December 1991. The seven bond portfolios were formed with the following securities: 1- to 5-year Treasuries (1–5G) 6- to 10-year Treasuries (6–10G), Aaa-rated corporates, Aa-rated corporates, A-rated corporates, Baa-rated corporates, and low-grade corporates rated below Baa (LG). Their findings are summarized in Exhibit 25.17.

Although both stock and bond risk factors were included, the two bond factors provide the dominant explanation for how these bond portfolio returns varied over time. While all of the portfolios groups had significant positive exposures to *TERM* and *DEF*, only a few of the categories also had significant loadings on the stock market variables. Further, the reported alpha coefficients in the last row are quite small and were insignificant for all of the corporate bond portfolios. Since these portfolios represent the performance of indexed fixed-income investments, these results are what you would expect. However, the same process can be used to assess the value added by active bond managers as well.

25.7.2 Bond Performance Attribution

In this section, we present one attempt to develop a bond portfolio performance attribution model that considers multiple risk factors.

The Bond Market Line Wagner and Tito (1977) applied asset pricing techniques to the evaluation of bond performance. The main factor necessary for a proper bond performance attribution is the development of an appropriate index and for this a measure of risk is necessary, similar to the beta coefficient for equities. As we have seen in Chapter 18, a bond's duration statistic captures the net effect of the volatility inherent in the underlying coupon and maturity structure.

Using this as a measure of risk, the authors derived a bond market line much like the security market line used to evaluate equity performance. Duration simply replaces beta as the risk variable. The bond market line in Exhibit 25.18 is drawn from points defined by returns on Treasury bills to the Lehman Brothers Government–Corporate Bond Index rather than the S&P 500 index. The Lehman Brothers Index gives the market's average annual rate of return during some common period, and the duration for the index is the value-weighted duration for the individual bonds in the index. Given the bond market line, this technique divides the portfolio

Exhibit 25.18 Bond Market Line and Performance Breakdown

Management effect is the improvement in investment performance of a passive strategy through active bond management. It is the difference between total bond portfolio return and the expected return at the long-term average duration.

Trading effect is the result of the current quarter's trading, either through effective trade-desk operation or short-term selection abilities. It is the difference between total management effect and the effects attributable to analysis and interest rate anticipation.

Policy effect is the difference between long-term duration of a bond portfolio and the duration of a bond market index resulting from long-term investment policy. Measured as the return at the long-term average less the return on the Lehman Brothers Index.

Analysis effect, attributable to the selection of issues with better-than-average long-term prospects, is the difference between the actual return of the buy-and-hold portfolio at the beginning of the quarter and the expected return of that buy-and-hold portfolio.

Bond market line is a straight line drawn through the return/duration of Treasury bills and the return/duration of the Lehman Brothers Index.

Interest rate anticipation effect is attributable to changes in portfolio duration resulting from attempts to profit from and ability to predict bond market movements. It is the difference between the expected return at the actual portfolio duration and the expected return at the long-term duration.

Buy-and-hold portfolio is the composition of the portfolio at the beginning of the quarter. Used to differentiate between trading gains secured within a quarter and long-term analysis gains.

Duration is a measure of the average time to receipt of cash flows from an investment. It is a measure of the sensitivity of a bond's price to changes in interest rates.

Source: Wayne H. Wagner and Dennis A. Tito, "Definitive New Measures of Bond Performance and Risk," *Pension World* (May 1977): 17–26.

return that differs from the return on the Lehman Brothers Index into four components: (1) a **policy effect**, (2) a **rate anticipation effect**, (3) an **analysis effect**, and (4) a **trading effect**. When the latter three effects are combined, they are referred to as the **management effect**.

The policy effect measures the difference in the expected return for a given portfolio because of a difference in policy regarding its duration compared to the duration of the index.[8] For example, assume the duration and return for the Lehman Brothers Index is 9.0 years and 8.25 percent, respectively. If the manager's policy portfolio has a duration of 9.5 years, according to the prevailing bond market line, the return should be about 8.60 percent. In this example, the policy effect is 0.5 year and 0.35 percent (35 basis points). The higher duration implies that the portfolio should have a higher average return of 0.35 percent (this positive relationship assumes the typical upward-sloping yield curve).

Given the expected return and duration for this long-term portfolio, all deviations from the index portfolio are attributable to the remaining management effect components. The interest rate anticipation effect captures the differential return from changing the duration during this period compared to the portfolio's long-term duration. Assume the policy duration for the long-term portfolio is 9.5 years, which implies an expected return of 8.60 percent, and that the actual prevailing duration for the portfolio being evaluated is 10.0 years, which implies an expected return of 9.00 percent using the bond market line. Therefore, the rate anticipation effect during this period is 0.40 percent (9.00 − 8.60).

[8] Notably, the duration of the various bond market indexes has changed over time (i.e., the duration of the corporate bond series has declined, whereas the duration of the government bond series has increased slightly). See Reilly and Wright (2001).

The difference between this expected return based on the portfolio's dursation and the actual return for the portfolio during this period is a combination of an analysis effect and a trading effect. The analysis effect is the differential return attributable to acquiring bonds that are temporarily mispriced relative to their risk level and is measured by the *expected* return for the portfolio held at the beginning of the period (using the bond market line) to the *actual* return of this same portfolio. An actual return greater than the expected return suggests that the portfolio manager acquired some underpriced issues that provided excess returns during the period. For example, if the portfolio at the beginning of the period had a duration of 10 years, this might indicate that the portfolio's expected return was 9.00 percent for the period. In turn, if the actual return for this buy-and-hold portfolio was 9.40 percent, it would indicate an analysis effect of 40 basis points.

Finally, the trading effect occurs because of short-run changes in the portfolio during the period. It is measured as the residual after taking account of the analysis effect from the total excess return based on duration. Suppose the total actual return is 10.50 percent with a duration of 10.0 years. The prevailing bond market line indicates an expected return of 9 percent for a portfolio with a 10-year duration. Thus, the combination of the analysis and trading effects is 1.50 percent (= 10.50 − 9.00). Since the analysis effect was 0.40 percent, the trading effect must be 1.10 percent. In summary, for this portfolio manager, the actual return was 10.50 percent, compared to a return for the Lehman Brothers Index of 8.25 percent. This total excess of 2.25 percent would be divided as follows:

- 0.35 percent policy effect due to higher long-term duration
- 0.40 percent interest rate anticipation effect due to increasing the duration of the current portfolio above the long-term portfolio duration
- 0.40 percent analysis effect—the impact of superior selection of individual issues in the beginning portfolio
- 1.10 percent trading effect—the impact of trading the issues *during* the period.

This technique breaks down the return based on the duration as a comprehensive risk measure. However, *it does not consider differences in the risk of default* (e.g., it does not differentiate between an Aaa bond with a duration of eight years and a Baa bond with the same duration). A portfolio manager who invested in Baa bonds, for example, could experience a very positive analysis effect simply because the bonds were lower quality than the average quality implicit in the Lehman Brothers Index. The only way to avoid this would be to construct differential market lines for alternative ratings or construct a benchmark line that matches the quality makeup of the portfolio being evaluated.

Layard-Liesching (2001) used the information ratio to assess the relative impact of each possible decision that a bond manager could make on the return to the overall portfolio. His analysis showed that while large-scale duration "bets" could certainly be taken, their payoffs were likely to be low once the high degree of tracking error they created was taken into account. He argued that credit quality bets were more likely to be fruitful, particularly as the global movement to privatizing companies that were previously under governmental control continues to create new investment opportunities.[9]

. . . .

25.8 Reporting Investment Performance

The performance measures described in this chapter represent the essential elements of how any investor's performance should be evaluated. However, before the various composite statistics can be calculated, a more fundamental question must be addressed: How should the returns used in the evaluation process be reported to the investor? We conclude our discussion

---

[9] Other attribution models that decompose bond returns in somewhat different ways can be found in Fong, Pearson, and Vasicek (1983) and Campisi (2000). For more detailed discussions of bond performance measurement, see Reilly and Sidhu (1980), Gudikunst and McCarthy (1992), and Kahle, Maxwell, and Xu (2007).

by exploring two dimensions of this problem. First, we consider the issue of how returns should be computed for a portfolio that experiences infusions and withdrawals of cash during the investment period. Second, we will briefly summarize the **performance presentation standards (PPS)** created by the CFA Institute, an international organization of over 90,000 investment practitioners and educators in more than 100 countries.

25.8.1 Time-Weighted and Dollar-Weighted Returns

As we saw in Chapter 1, the holding period yield (HPY) for any investment position was determined by that position's market value at the end of the period divided by its initial value:

$$\text{HPY} = \frac{\text{Ending Value of Investment}}{\text{Beginning Value of Investment}} - 1$$

For any security or portfolio, we also saw that there are two basic reasons why the ending and beginning values could differ: the receipt of cash payments (e.g., dividends) or a change in price (e.g., capital gains) during the period. Thus, for most investment positions, calculating returns during any given time frame is a reasonably straightforward matter.

For professional money managers and management companies, however, there is another reason why the beginning and ending value of a portfolio can differ, and it has nothing to do with the manager's investment prowess. If the investor either withdraws or adds to her initial investment capital during the period, the ending value of the position will reflect these changes. Of course, it would be unfair to credit the manager with having produced high returns that were due to additional capital commitments. Similarly, it would be equally unfair to penalize him for reductions in the ending value of the investment that were caused by the investor removing funds from her account. Consequently, an evaluation of the manager's true performance must take these contributions and withdrawals into account.

Consider two portfolio managers (A and B) who have exactly identical investment styles and stockpicking abilities. Indeed, we will assume that over a two-period investment horizon, they produce exactly the same capital gains with the investment capital entrusted to them: 25 percent in Period 1, and 5 percent in Period 2. Further, suppose that each manager receives from his respective investor $500,000 to invest. The difference is that Manager A receives all of these funds immediately whereas Manager B's investor commits only $250,000 initially and the remaining $250,000 at the end of the first period.

The immediate effect of this investment timing difference can be seen by calculating the terminal (Period 2) value of each portfolio:

$$\text{Portfolio A: } 500{,}000 \left[(1 + 0.25)(1 + (0.05)\right] = \$656{,}250$$

and

$$\text{Portfolio B: } 250{,}000[(1 + 0.25)(1 + 0.05)] + 250{,}000(1 + 0.05) = \$590{,}625$$

Obviously, Manager B's portfolio is worth less than Manager A's, but this is a result of the way the investment funds were committed rather than of any differences in the performance of the two managers. Accordingly, the managers' performance evaluation should not be affected by the investors' decisions concerning the timing of their capital commitments. In other words, Manager B should not be held accountable for the fact that Investor B did not have all of her funds invested during the high-return environment of the first period.

One common method of computing average returns that we have seen is to use a discounted cash flow approach to calculate an investment's internal rate of return. For the two managers in this example, these calculations generate the following returns:

$$\text{Manager A: } 500{,}000 = \frac{656{,}250}{(1 + r_{dA})^2}, \text{ or } r_{dA} = 14.56 \text{ percent}$$

and

$$\text{Manager B: } 250{,}000 = \frac{-250{,}000}{(a + r_{dB})^1} = \frac{590{,}625}{(1 + r_{dB})^2}, \text{ or } r_{dB} = 11.63 \text{ percent}$$

These returns (r_{dA} and r_{dB}) are sometimes called **money-weighted returns** because they are the discount rates that set the present value of future cash flows (including future investment contributions and withdrawals) equal to the level of the initial investment. Unfortunately, in this case, money-weighted returns give an inaccurate impression of Manager B's ability; he did not actually perform 2.93 percent (= 0.1456 − 0.1163) worse than Manager A. Thus, while this internal rate of return method gives an accurate assessment of *Investor* B's return, it is a misleading measure of *Manager* B's talent.

A better way of evaluating a manager's performance would be to consider how well he did regardless of the size or timing of the investment funds involved. For both managers in this example, the **time-weighted return** is simply the geometric average of (one plus) the periodic returns:

$$r_{tA} = r_{tB} = \sqrt[2]{(1 + 0.25)(1 + 0.05)} - 1 = 14.56 \text{ percent}$$

Money-weighted and time-weighted returns are only the same when there are no interim investment contributions within the evaluation period. This was the case for Manager A. For Manager B, the money-weighted return understates the true (time-weighted) performance because of the way the investor deployed her funds. When there are contributions, Dietz and Kirschman (1990) have suggested a method for adjusting holding period yields:

$$\text{Adjusted HPY} = \frac{\text{Ending Value of Investment} - (1 - DW)(\text{Contribution})}{\text{Beginning Value of Investment} + (DW)(\text{Contribution})} - 1$$

where the contribution can be either positive (a new commitment) or negative (a withdrawal). This adjustment process alters the initial and terminal values of the portfolios by the weighted amount of the contribution made during the holding period. In this calculation, the day-weight (DW) factor represents the portion of the period that the contribution is actually held in the account. For example, if a contribution were placed in the portfolio halfway through a 30-day month, DW would be 0.5 [= (30 − 15)/30].

25.8.2 Performance Presentation Standards

The preceding example underscores the fact that there may not always be a straightforward answer to a seemingly simple question. Although Portfolio B had a money-weighted return of 11.63 percent, its manager generated an average return of 14.56 percent. Which should be reported to the investor? The Securities and Exchange Commission has established regulations to guard against the publication of outright fraudulent claims, but Lawton and Remington (2007) point out that the following reporting practices have been historically permissible:

- Present returns only for the best-performing portfolios as though those returns were fully representative of the manager's expertise in a given strategy or style.
- Base portfolio market values on unsubstantiated estimates of asset prices or present simulated returns as though they had actually been earned.
- Inflate returns by annualizing partial-period returns.
- Select the most favorable measurement period, calculating returns from a low point to a high point.
- Choose as a benchmark the particular index the selected portfolios have outperformed by the greatest margin during the measurement period.
- Portray growth in AUM in a way that masks the difference between investment returns and client contributions.

Largely as a result of such abuses, the investment community has recently begun to demand the adoption of a more rigorous set of reporting guidelines.

In an effort to fulfill the call for uniform, accurate, and consistent performance reporting, CFA Institute (formerly known as the Association for Investment Management and Research, or AIMR) has developed a comprehensive set of performance presentation standards (PPS). Introduced in 1987, formally adopted in 1993, and modified in 1999, the AIMR-PPS quickly became the accepted practice within the investment management community. However, early versions of these standards tended to have country-specific elements that made them difficult to translate to a fully global platform. Consequently, in 1999 the CFA Institute also adopted a companion set of Global Investment Performance Standards (GIPS), which were intended to serve the following purpose:

> *A global investment performance standard leads to readily accepted presentations of investment performance that (1) present performance results that are readily comparable among investment management firms without regard to geographical location and (2) facilitate a dialogue between investment managers and their prospective clients about the critical issues of how the investment management firm achieved performance results and determines future investment strategies.*[10]

By 2005, the GIPS had been adopted by 25 countries throughout North America, Europe, Africa, and the Asia Pacific region. They have replaced the original AIMR-PPS and are now considered the definitive set of standards for reporting investment performance.

Although a detailed analysis of these standards (which are revised frequently) is beyond our current scope, it is worth noting several of the fundamental principles on which they are based:

- Total return, including realized and unrealized gains plus income, must be used when calculating investment performance.
- Time-weighted rates of return must be used.
- Portfolios must be valued at least monthly, and periodic returns must be geometrically linked.
- If composite return performance is presented, this composite must contain all actual fee-paying accounts, including all terminated accounts for periods up through the last full reporting period the account was under management. Composite results may not link simulated or model portfolios with actual performance.
- Performance must be calculated after the deduction of trading expenses (e.g., broker commissions and SEC fees), if any.
- For taxable clients, taxes on income and realized capital gains must be recognized in the same period they were incurred and must be subtracted from results regardless of whether taxes are paid from assets outside the account.
- Annual returns for all years must be presented. Performance of less than one year must not be annualized. A 10-year performance record (or a record for the period since firm inception if less than 10 years) must be presented.
- Performance presentation must disclose whether performance results are calculated gross or net of investment management fees and what the firm's fee schedule is. Presentation should also disclose any use of leverage (including derivatives) and any material change in personnel responsible for investment management.

In addition to the preceding requirements, CFA Institute also encourages managers to disclose the volatility of the aggregate composite return and to identify benchmarks that parallel the risk or investment style the composite is expected to track. Exhibit 25.19 shows a sample performance presentation that is in compliance with the Standards.

---

[10] See *Global Investment Performance Standards* (Charlottesville, VA: CFA Institute, February 2005).

Exhibit 25.19 A Sample Performance Presentation

SAMPLE 1 INVESTMENT FIRM
BALANCED COMPOSITE
1 JANUARY 1995 THROUGH 31 DECEMBER 2004

Year	Gross-of-Fees Return (percent)	Net-of-Fees Return (percent)	Benchmark Return (percent)	Number of Portfolios	Internal Dispersion (percent)	Total Composite Assets (CAD Million)	Total Firm Assets (CAD Million)
1995	16.0	15.0	14.1	26	4.5	165	236
1996	2.2	1.3	1.8	32	2.0	235	346
1997	22.4	21.5	24.1	38	5.7	344	529
1998	7.1	6.2	6.0	45	2.8	445	695
1999	8.5	7.5	8.0	48	3.1	520	839
2000	−8.0	−8.9	−8.4	49	2.8	505	1014
2001	−5.9	−6.8	−6.2	52	2.9	499	995
2002	2.4	1.6	2.2	58	3.1	525	1125
2003	6.7	5.9	6.8	55	3.5	549	1225
2004	9.4	8.6	9.1	59	2.5	575	1290

Sample 1 Investment Firm has prepared and presented this report in compliance with the Global Investment Performance Standards (GIPS*).

Notes:
1. Sample 1 Investment Firm is a balanced portfolio investment manager that invests solely in Canadian securities. Sample 1 Investment Firm is defined as an independent investment management firm that is not affiliated with any parent organization. For the periods from 2000 through 2004, Sample 1 Investment Firm has been verified by Verification Services Inc. A copy of the verification report is available upon request. Additional information regarding the firm's policies and procedures for calculating and reporting performance results is available upon request.
2. The composite includes all nontaxable balanced portfolios with an asset allocation of 30% S&P TSX and 70% Scotia Canadian Bond Index Fund, which allow up to a 10% deviation in asset allocation.
3. The benchmark: 30% S&P TSX; 70% Scotia Canadian Bond Index Fund rebalanced monthly.
4. Valuations are computed and performance reported in Canadian dollars.
5. Gross-of-fees performance returns are presented before management and custodial fees but after all trading expenses. Returns are presented net of nonreclaimable withholding taxes. Net-of-fees performance returns are calculated by deducting the highest fee of 0.25% from the quarterly gross composite return. The management fee schedule is as follows: 1.00% on first CAD25M; 0.60% thereafter.
6. This composite was created in February 1995. A complete list and description of firm composites is available upon request.
7. For the periods 1995 and 1996, Sample 1 Investment Firm was not in compliance with the GIPS standards because portfolios were valued annually.
8. Internal dispersion is calculated using the equal-weighted standard deviation of all portfolios that were included in the composite for the entire year.

• • • • SUMMARY • • • •

- The first major goal of portfolio management is to derive returns that equal or exceed the returns on a naively selected portfolio with equal risk. The second goal is to attain complete diversification relative to a suitable benchmark. Several techniques have been derived to evaluate equity portfolios in terms of both risk and return (composite measures). The Treynor measure considers the excess returns earned per unit of systematic risk. The Sharpe measure indicates the excess return per unit of total risk. The Jensen and Information Ratio measures likewise evaluate performance in terms of the systematic risk involved and show how to determine whether the difference in risk-adjusted performance (good or bad) is statistically

significant. Additional work in equity portfolio evaluation has been concerned with models that focus on downside risk, how a portfolio's security holdings change, and those that indicate what components of the management process contributed to the results. Finally, attribution analysis seeks to establish whether market timing or security selection skills (or both) are the source of a manager's performance.
- Richard Roll challenged the validity of all techniques which assume a market portfolio that theoretically includes all risky assets but which then use a proxy such as the S&P 500 that is limited to U.S. common stocks. This criticism does not invalidate the normative asset pricing model, only its application because of measurement problems related to the proxy for

the market portfolio. The measurement problem is increased in an environment where global investing is the norm.

- Although the techniques for evaluating equity portfolio performance have been in existence for almost 50 years, comparable techniques for examining bond portfolio performance were initiated more recently. While it is possible to adapt equity risk models for the evaluation of bond managers, it is often necessary to consider separately the several important decision variables related to bonds: the overall market factor, the impact of maturity-duration decisions, the influence of sector and quality factors, and the impact of individual bond selection.

- Investors need to evaluate their own performance and the performance of hired managers. The various techniques discussed provide theoretically justifiable measures that differ from one another. Although there is high rank correlation among the alternative measures, *all the measures should be used* because they provide different insights regarding the performance of managers. Finally, an evaluation of a portfolio manager should be done many times over different market environments before a final judgment is reached regarding the strengths and weaknesses of a manager.

· · · · SUGGESTED READINGS · · · ·

Amenc, Noel, and Veronique LeSourd. *Portfolio Theory and Performance Analysis.* West Sussex, England: Wiley, 2003.

Bacon, Carl. *Practical Portfolio Performance Measurement and Attribution.* West Sussex, England: Wiley, 2004.

DeFusco, Richard A., Dennis Mc Leavey, Jerald A. Pinto, and David E. Runkle. *Quantitative Methods for Investment Analysis*, 2nd ed. Charlottesville, VA: CFA Institute, 2004.

Feibel, Bruce J. *Investment Performance Measurement.* Hoboken, NJ: Wiley, 2003.

Sherrerd, Kartrina F., ed. *Benchmarks and Attribution Analysis.* Charlottesville, VA: Association for Investment Management and Research, 2001.

· · · · QUESTIONS · · · ·

1. Describe two major factors that a portfolio manager should consider before designing an investment strategy. What types of decisions can a manager make to achieve these goals?

2. Compare and contrast four prominent approaches to measuring investment performance on a risk-adjusted basis. In developing your answer, comment on the conditions under which each measure will be most useful.

3. The Sharpe and Treynor performance measures both calculate a portfolio's average excess return per unit of risk. Under what circumstances would it make sense to use both measures to compare the performance of a given set of portfolios? What additional information is provided by a comparison of the rankings achieved using the two measures?

4. Describe how the Jensen measure of performance is calculated. Under what conditions should it give a similar set of portfolio rankings as the Sharpe and Treynor measures? Is it possible to adjust the Jensen measure so that a portfolio's alpha value is measured relative to an empirical form of the arbitrage pricing theory rather than the capital asset pricing model? Explain.

5. The information ratio *(IR)* has been described as a benefit-cost ratio. Explain how the *IR* measures portfolio performance and whether this analogy is appropriate.

 6. **CFA EXAMINATION LEVEL I**
   a. Explain why the asset allocation decision is the primary determinant of total portfolio performance over time.
   b. Describe three reasons why successful implementation of asset allocation decisions is even more difficult in practice than in theory.

7. Performance attribution analysis is an attempt to divide a manager's "active" residual return into an allocation effect and a selection effect. Explain how these two effects are measured and why their sum must equal the total value-added return for the manager. Is this analysis valid if the actual portfolio in question is riskier than the benchmark portfolio to which it is being compared?

 8. **CFA EXAMINATION LEVEL III** During the annual review of Acme's pension plan, several trustees questioned Lucy Graham, a pension consultant, about various aspects of performance measurement and

risk assessment. In particular, one trustee asked about the appropriateness of using each of the following benchmarks:

- Market index
- Benchmark normal portfolio
- Median of the manager universe

a. Explain *two* different weaknesses of using each of the three benchmarks to measure the performance of a portfolio.

Another trustee asked how to distinguish among the following performance measures:

- The Sharpe ratio
- The Treynor measure
- Jensen's alpha

b. (1) Describe how *each* of the three performance measures is calculated.
   (2) State whether *each* measure assumes that the relevant risk is systematic, unsystematic, or total. Explain how each measure relates excess return and the relevant risk.

9. **CFA EXAMINATION LEVEL III** Richard Roll, in an article on using the capital asset pricing model (CAPM) to evaluate portfolio performance, indicated that it may not be possible to evaluate portfolio management ability if there is error in the benchmark used.

a. In evaluating portfolio performance, describe the general procedure, with emphasis on the benchmark employed.

b. Explain what Roll meant by the benchmark error and identify the specific problem with this benchmark.

c. Draw a graph that shows how a portfolio that has been judged as superior relative to a "measured" security market line (SML) can be inferior relative to the "true" SML.

d. Assume that you are informed that a given portfolio manager has been evaluated as superior when compared to the DJIA, the S&P 500, and the NYSE Composite Index. Explain whether this consensus would make you feel more comfortable regarding the portfolio manager's true ability.

e. While conceding the possible problem with benchmark errors as set forth by Roll, some contend this does not mean the CAPM is incorrect, but only that there is a measurement problem when implementing the theory. Others contend that because of benchmark errors, the whole technique should be scrapped. Take and defend one of these positions.

10. It has been contended that the derivation of an appropriate model for evaluating the performance of a bond manager is more difficult than an equity portfolio evaluation model because more decisions are required. Discuss some of the specific decisions that need to be considered when evaluating the performance of a bond portfolio manager.

• • • • PROBLEMS • • • •

1. The following portfolios are being considered for investment. During the period under consideration, $RFR = 0.07$.

Portfolio	Return	Beta	σ_i
P	0.15	1.0	0.05
Q	0.20	1.5	0.10
R	0.10	0.6	0.03
S	0.17	1.1	0.06
Market	0.13	1.0	0.04

a. Compute the Sharpe measure for each portfolio and the market portfolio.

b. Compute the Treynor measure for each portfolio and the market portfolio.

c. Rank the portfolios using each measure, explaining the cause for any differences you find in the rankings.

2. **CFA EXAMINATION LEVEL II** An analyst wants to evaluate Portfolio X, consisting entirely of U.S. common stocks, using both the Treynor and Sharpe measures of portfolio performance. The following

table provides the average annual rate of return for Portfolio X, the market portfolio (as measured by the Standard and Poor's 500 index), and U.S. Treasury bills (T-bills) during the past eight years.

	Annual Average Rate of Return	Standard Deviation of Return	Beta
Portfolio X	10%	18%	0.60
S&P 500	12	13	1.00
T-bills	6	n/a	n/a

n/a = not applicable

a. Calculate both the Treynor measure and the Sharpe measure for both Portfolio X and the S&P 500. Briefly explain whether Portfolio X underperformed, equaled, or outperformed the S&P 500 on a risk-adjusted basis using both the Treynor measure and the Sharpe measure.

b. Based on the performance of Portfolio X relative to the S&P 500 calculated in Part a, briefly explain the reason for the conflicting results when using the Treynor measure versus the Sharpe measure.

3. You have been assigned the task of comparing the investment performance of five different pension fund managers. After gathering 60 months of excess returns (i.e., returns in excess of the monthly risk-free rate) on each fund as well as the monthly excess returns on the entire stock market, you perform the regressions of the form:

$$(R_{fund} - RFR)_t = \alpha + \beta (R_{mkt} - RFR)_t + e_t$$

You have prepared the following summary of the data, with the standard errors for each of the coefficients listed in parentheses.

Portfolio	REGRESSION DATA			$(R_{FUND} - RFR)$	
	α	β	R^2	Mean	σ
ABC	0.192 (0.11)	1.048 (0.10)	94.1%	1.022%	1.193%
DEF	−0.053 (0.19)	0.662 (0.09)	91.6	0.473	0.764
GHI	0.463 (0.19)	0.594 (0.07)	68.6	0.935	0.793
JKL	0.355 (0.22)	0.757 (0.08)	64.1	0.955	1.044
MNO	0.296 (0.14)	0.785 (0.12)	94.8	0.890	0.890

a. Which fund had the highest degree of diversification over the sample period? How is diversification measured in this statistical framework?

b. Rank these funds' performance according to the Sharpe, Treynor, and Jensen measures.

c. Since you know that according to the CAPM the intercept of these regressions (i.e., alpha) should be zero, this coefficient can be used as a measure of the value added provided by the investment manager. Which funds have statistically outperformed and underperformed the market using a two-sided 95 percent confidence interval? (Note: The relevant t-statistic using 60 observations is 2.00.)

4. You have just gathered the following performance data for three different money managers, based on a regression of their excess returns relative to those for the S&P 500 index. Each manager's performance was measured over the same three-year period, but the return period for each was different.

Manager	Alpha	Beta	Std. Error of Regression	Return Period
A	0.058%	0.95	0.533%	Weekly
B	0.115	1.12	5.884	Biweekly
C	0.250	0.78	2.165	Monthly

a. Calculate the information ratio for each manager, ignoring the difference in return reporting periods.

b. Calculate the annualized information ratio for each manager.

c. Rank the managers' performance according to your answers in Parts a and b. Which manager performed the best? Explain.

5. Consider the following historical performance data for two different portfolios, the Standard and Poor's 500, and the 90-day T-bill.

Investment Vehicle	Average Rate of Return	Standard Deviation	Beta	R^2
Fund 1	26.40%	20.67%	1.351	0.751
Fund 2	13.22	14.20	0.905	0.713
S&P 500	15.71	13.25		
90-day T-bill	6.20	0.50		

   a. Calculate the Fama overall performance measure for both funds.
   b. What is the return to risk for both funds?
   c. For both funds, compute the measures of (1) selectivity, (2) diversification, and (3) net selectivity.
   d. Explain the meaning of the net selectivity measure and how it helps you evaluate investor performance. Which fund had the best performance?

6. You are evaluating the performance of two portfolio managers and you have gathered annual return data for the past decade:

Year	Manager X Return (%)	Manager Y Return (%)
1	−1.5	−6.5
2	−1.5	−3.5
3	−1.5	−1.5
4	−1.0	3.5
5	0.0	4.5
6	4.5	6.5
7	6.5	7.5
8	8.5	8.5
9	13.5	12.5
10	17.5	13.5

   a. For each manager, calculate: (i) the average annual return, (ii) the standard deviation of returns, and (iii) the semi-deviation of returns.
   b. Assuming that the average annual risk-free rate during the 10-year sample period was 1.5 percent, calculate the Sharpe ratio for each portfolio. Based on these computations, which manager appears to have performed the best?
   c. Calculate the Sortino ratio for each portfolio, using the average risk-free rate as the minimum acceptable return threshold. Based on these computations, which manager appears to have performed the best?
   d. When would you expect the Sharpe and Sortino measures to provide (i) the same performance ranking, or (ii) different performance rankings? Explain.

7. Consider the following performance data for two portfolio managers (A and B) and a common benchmark portfolio:

	BENCHMARK		MANAGER A		MANAGER B	
	Weight	Return	Weight	Return	Weight	Return
Stock	0.6	−5.0%	0.5	−4.0%	0.3	−5.0%
Bonds	0.3	−3.5	0.2	−2.5	0.4	−3.5
Cash	0.1	0.3	0.3	0.3	0.3	0.3

   a. Calculate: (1) the overall return to the benchmark portfolio; (2) the overall return to Manager A's actual portfolio; and (3) the overall return to Manager B's actual portfolio. Briefly comment on whether these managers have under- or outperformed the benchmark fund.
   b. Using attribution analysis, calculate (1) the *selection effect* for Manager A, and (3) the *allocation effect* for Manager B. Using these numbers in conjunction with your results from Part a, comment on whether these managers have added value through their selection skills, their allocation skills, or both.

8. **CFA EXAMINATION LEVEL III** A U.S. pension plan hired two off-shore firms to manage the non-U.S. equity portion of its total portfolio. Each firm was free to own stocks in any country market included in Morgan Stanley/Capital International's Europe, Australia, and Far East Index (EAFE) and free to use any form of dollar and/or nondollar cash or bonds as an equity substitute or reserve. After three years had elapsed, the records of the managers and the EAFE Index were as follows:

SUMMARY: CONTRIBUTIONS TO RETURN

	Currency	Country Selection	Stock Selection	Cash/Bond Allocation	Total Return Recorded
Manager A	(9.0%)	19.7%	3.1%	0.6%	14.4%
Manager B	(7.4)	14.2	6.0	2.81	5.6
Composite of A & B	(8.2)	16.9	4.5	1.71	5.0
EAFE Index	(12.9)	19.9	—	—	7.0

You are a member of the plan sponsor's Pension Committee, which will soon meet with the plan's consultant to review manager performance. In preparation for this meeting, you go through the following analysis:

a. Briefly describe the strengths and weaknesses of each manager, relative to the EAFE Index data.
b. Briefly explain the meaning of the data in the "Currency" column.

9. **CFA EXAMINATION LEVEL III** To illustrate for the Investment Committee of the profit-sharing plan to which you are a consultant on some of the issues that arise in measuring performance, you have identified three U.S. fixed-income management firms whose investment approaches are representative of general practice. Each firm's approach follows.

Firm A: An enhanced index fund manager that seeks to add value by superior security selection while maintaining portfolio duration and sector weights equal to the overall bond market.
Firm B: An active duration manager investing only in the government and corporate bond sectors. The firm uses futures to manage portfolio duration.
Firm C: An active manager seeking to add value by correctly anticipating changes in the shape of the yield curve, while maintaining portfolio duration and sector weights roughly equal to the overall bond market.

You have provided the Committee with the following additional information about these firms, derived from a consultant's database.

ANNUALIZED TOTAL RETURN DATA (PAST FIVE YEARS)

	Firm A	Firm B	Firm C
Reported Returns	9.2%	9.3%	9.0%

INDEX SECTORS

	Aggregate Index	Governments	Corporates	Government/ Corporate	Mortgages
Index Return	8.7%	9.0%	9.8%	9.5%	8.3%

CONSULTANT'S MANAGER UNIVERSE

	All Managers	Managers Using the Aggregate Index as Their Benchmark	Managers Using the Govt./Corp. Sector as Their Benchmark
Return 5th percentile	6.0%	7.7%	8.4%
25th percentile	7.1	8.1	8.9
50th percentile	8.0	8.6	9.4
75th percentile	8.6	9.1	9.9
95th percentile	9.3	13.1	13.9

a. Evaluate the performance of each of these three firms relative to its appropriate Index and to the manager universe. Use only the data from the descriptions and the preceding table, even though other information would be required for a more complete and accurate appraisal.

To provide additional guidance to the Committee, you decide to do an attribution analysis on the returns produced by Firm A and Firm C and have prepared the following table:

PERFORMANCE ATTRIBUTION ANALYSIS (PAST FIVE YEARS—ANNUALIZED TOTAL RETURNS)

	Total Return	=	Duration Decisions	+	Yield Curve Decisions	+	Sector Weighting Decisions	+	Security Selection Decisions & Residuals
Firm A									
Total return	9.20%		8.00%		0.80%		0.00%		0.40%
Benchmark index return	8.70		7.00		0.50		0.70		0.50
Difference	0.50		1.00		0.30		−0.70		−0.10
Firm C									
Total return	9.00%		7.03%		0.80%		0.71%		0.46%
Benchmark index return	8.70		7.00		0.50		0.70		0.50
Difference	0.30		0.03		0.30		0.01		−0.04

   b. Evaluate the performance of Firm A and of Firm C based on all the information previously provided and your interpretation of the data in this new table.
   c. Based solely on the attribution analysis you performed in Part b, state which firm produced the better result and justify your conclusion.
10. For each of the last six quarters, Managers L and M have provided you with the total dollar value of the funds they manage, along with the quarterly contributions or withdrawals made by their clients. (*Note:* Contributions are indicated by positive numbers, withdrawals by negative numbers.)

	MANAGER L		MANAGER M	
Quarter	Total Funds Under Management	Contributions/ Withdrawals	Total Funds Under Management	Contributions/ Withdrawals
Initial	$500,000	—	$700,000	—
1	527,000	12,000	692,000	−35,000
2	530,000	7,500	663,000	−35,000
3	555,000	13,500	621,000	−35,000
4	580,000	6,500	612,000	−35,000
5	625,000	10,000	625,000	−35,000

For each manager, calculate:
a. her money-weighted return;
b. her time-weighted return; and
c. estimates of her quarterly performance returns using the Dietz approximation method, assuming contributions/withdrawals are made exactly halfway through the quarter.

How to Become a CFA® Charterholder

As mentioned in the section on career opportunities, the professional designation of Chartered Financial Analyst (CFA) is becoming a significant requirement for a career in investment analysis and/or portfolio management. For that reason, this section presents the history and objectives of CFA Institute and general guidelines for acquiring the CFA designation. If you are interested in the program, you can write or email CFA Institute for more information.

The CFA examinations were first offered in 1963 by the Institute of Chartered Financial Analysts (ICFA), which was formed in 1959 to enhance the professionalism of those involved in various aspects of the investment decision-making process and to recognize those who achieve a high level of professionalism. The ICFA combined with the Financial Analysts Federation in 1990 to form the Association for Investment Management and Research, which became CFA Institute in early 2004.

The mission of CFA Institute is to lead the investment profession globally by setting the highest standards of ethics, education, and professional excellence. As applied to the CFA program, the focus of CFA Institute is:

- To develop and keep current a "body of knowledge" applicable to the investment decision-making process. The principal components of this knowledge are financial accounting, economics, both debt and equity securities analysis, portfolio management, ethical and professional standards, and quantitative techniques.
- To administer a study and examination program for eligible candidates, the primary objectives of which are to assist the candidate in mastering and applying the body of knowledge and to test the candidate's competency in the knowledge gained.
- To award the professional CFA designation to those candidates who have passed three examination levels (encompassing a total of 18 hours of testing over a minimum of two years), who meet stipulated standards of professional conduct, and who otherwise are eligible for membership in CFA Institute.
- CFA Institute also provides a useful and informative program of continuing education through seminars, publications, and other formats that enable members, candidates, and others in the investment constituency to be more aware of and to better utilize the changing and expanding body of knowledge.

- Importantly, CFA Institute also sponsors and enforces a Code of Ethics and Standards of Professional Conduct that apply to enrolled candidates and to all members.

To enter the CFA program an applicant must have a bachelor's degree (or the equivalent work experience). Students who confirm they are in their final year of a degree program may register and enroll for Level I of the CFA program. Student candidates can take the CFA Level I exam and receive results but will not be allowed to enroll for the Level II exam until confirmation of a degree has been provided. A candidate may sit for all three examinations without having had investment experience per se or having joined a member society or chapter of CFA Institute. However, after passing the three examination levels, the CFA Charter will not be awarded unless or until the candidate:

- has at least four years of acceptable work experience and
- has been accepted for regular membership in CFA Institute and has applied for regular membership in an affiliated society.

The curriculum of the CFA study program covers:

1. Ethical and Professional Standards
2. Quantitative Methods
3. Economics
4. Financial Statement Analysis
5. Corporate Finance
6. Analysis of Debt Investments
7. Analysis of Equity Investments
8. Analysis of Derivatives
9. Analysis of Alternative Investments
10. Portfolio Management and Wealth Planning

Members and candidates are typically employed in the investment field. From 1963 to July 2008, over 100,000 charters have been awarded. There were more than 175,000 candidate registrations for the 2008 CFA Program. If you are interested in learning more about the CFA Program, CFA Institute has a booklet that describes the program and includes an application form. The address is: CFA Institute, Attn: Information Central, PO Box 3668, Charlottesville, Virginia, 22903, USA. You may also find more information at the CFA Institute website, http://www.cfainstitute.org, or by requesting a booklet by email to info@cfainstitute.org.

APPENDIX B

Code of Ethics and Standards of Professional Conduct

Preamble

The CFA Institute Code of Ethics and Standards of Professional Conduct (Code and Standards) are fundamental to the values of CFA Institute and essential to achieving its mission to lead the investment profession globally by setting high standards of education, integrity, and professional excellence. High ethical standards are critical to maintaining the public's trust in financial markets and in the investment profession. Since their creation in the 1960s, the Code and Standards have promoted the integrity of CFA Institute members and served as a model for measuring the ethics of investment professionals globally, regardless of job function, cultural differences, or local laws and regulations. All CFA Institute members (including holders of the Chartered Financial Analyst® (CFA®) designation) and CFA candidates must abide by the Code and Standards and are encouraged to notify their employer of this responsibility. Violations may result in disciplinary sanctions by CFA Institute. Sanctions can include revocation of membership, candidacy in the CFA Program, and the right to use the CFA designation.

The Code of Ethics

Members of CFA Institute (including Chartered Financial Analyst® [CFA®] charterholders and candidates for the CFA designation ("Members and Candidates")) must:

- Act with integrity, competence, diligence, respect, and in an ethical manner with the public, clients, prospective clients, employers, employees, colleagues in the investment profession, and other participants in the global capital markets.
- Place the integrity of the investment profession and the interests of clients above their own personal interests.
- Use reasonable care and exercise independent professional judgment when conducting investment analysis, making investment recommendations, taking investment actions, and engaging in other professional activities.
- Practice and encourage others to practice in a professional and ethical manner that will reflect credit on themselves and the profession.
- Promote the integrity of, and uphold the rules governing, capital markets.
- Maintain and improve their professional competence and strive to maintain and improve the competence of other investment professionals.

Standards of Professional Conduct

I. Professionalism

A. **Knowledge of the Law.** Members and Candidates must understand and comply with all applicable laws, rules, and regulations (including the CFA Institute Code of Ethics and Standards of Professional Conduct) of any government, regulatory organization, licensing agency, or professional association governing their professional activities. In the event of conflict, Members and Candidates must comply with the more strict law, rule, or regulation. Members and Candidates must not knowingly participate or assist in and must dissociate from any violation of such laws, rules, or regulations.

B. **Independence and Objectivity.** Members and Candidates must use reasonable care and judgment to achieve and maintain independence and objectivity in their professional activities. Members and Candidates must not offer, solicit, or accept any gift, benefit, compensation, or consideration that reasonably could be expected to compromise their own or another's independence and objectivity.

C. **Misrepresentation.** Members and Candidates must not knowingly make any misrepresentations relating to investment analysis, recommendations, actions, or other professional activities.

D. **Misconduct.** Members and Candidates must not engage in any professional conduct involving dishonesty, fraud, or deceit or commit any act that reflects adversely on their professional reputation, integrity, or competence.

II. Integrity of Capital Markets

A. **Material Nonpublic Information.** Members and Candidates who possess material nonpublic information that could affect the value of an investment must not act or cause others to act on the information.

B. **Market Manipulation.** Members and Candidates must not engage in practices that distort prices or artificially inflate trading volume with the intent to mislead market participants.

III. Duties to Clients

A. **Loyalty, Prudence, and Care.** Members and Candidates have a duty of loyalty to their clients and must act with reasonable care and exercise prudent judgment. Members and Candidates must act for the benefit of their clients and place their clients' interests before their employer's or their own interests. In relationships with clients, Members and Candidates must determine applicable fiduciary duty and must comply with such duty to persons and interests to whom it is owed.

B. **Fair Dealing.** Members and Candidates must deal fairly and objectively with all clients when providing investment analysis, making investment recommendations, taking investment action, or engaging in other professional activities.

C. **Suitability.**
1. When Members and Candidates are in an advisory relationship with a client, they must:
   a. Make a reasonable inquiry into a client's or prospective clients' investment experience, risk and return objectives, and financial constraints prior to making any investment recommendation or taking investment action and must reassess and update this information regularly.
   b. Determine that an investment is suitable to the client's financial situation and consistent with the client's written objectives, mandates, and constraints before making an investment recommendation or taking investment action.
   c. Judge the suitability of investments in the context of the client's total portfolio.
2. When Members and Candidates are responsible for managing a portfolio to a specific mandate, strategy, or style, they must only make investment recommendations or take investment actions that are consistent with the stated objectives and constraints of the portfolio.

D. **Performance Presentation.** When communicating investment performance information, Members or Candidates must make reasonable efforts to ensure that it is fair, accurate, and complete.

E. **Preservation of Confidentiality.** Members and Candidates must keep information about current, former, and prospective clients confidential unless:
1. The information concerns illegal activities on the part of the client or prospective client.
2. Disclosure is required by law.
3. The client or prospective client permits disclosure of the information.

IV. Duties to Employers

A. **Loyalty.** In matters related to their employment, Members and Candidates must act for the benefit of their employer and not deprive their employer of the advantage of their skills and abilities, divulge confidential information, or otherwise cause harm to their employer.

B. **Additional Compensation Arrangements.** Members and Candidates must not accept gifts, benefits, compensation, or consideration that competes with, or might reasonably be expected to create a conflict of interest with, their employer's interest unless they obtain written consent from all parties involved.

C. **Responsibilities of Supervisors.** Members and Candidates must make reasonable efforts to detect and prevent violations of applicable laws, rules, regulations, and the Code and Standards by anyone subject to their supervision or authority.

V. Investment Analysis, Recommendations, and Action

A. **Diligence and Reasonable Basis.** Members and Candidates must:
1. Exercise diligence, independence, and thoroughness in analyzing investments, making investment recommendations, and taking investment actions.
2. Have a reasonable and adequate basis, supported by appropriate research and investigation, for any investment analysis, recommendation, or action.

B. **Communication with Clients and Prospective Clients.** Members and Candidates must:
1. Disclose to clients and prospective clients the basic format and general principles of the investment processes used to analyze investments, select securities, and construct portfolios and must promptly disclose any changes that might materially affect those processes.
2. Use reasonable judgment in identifying which factors are important to their investment analyses, recommendations, or actions and include those factors in communications with clients and prospective clients.
3. Distinguish between fact and opinion in the presentation of investment analysis and recommendations.

C. **Record Retention.** Members and Candidates must develop and maintain appropriate records to support their investment analysis, recommendations, actions, and other investment-related communications with clients and prospective clients.

VI. Conflicts of Interest

A. **Disclosure of Conflicts.** Members and Candidates must make full and fair disclosure of all matters that could reasonably be expected to impair their independence and objectivity or interfere with respective duties to their clients, prospective clients, and employer. Members and Candidates must ensure that such disclosures are prominent, are delivered in plain language, and communicate the relevant information effectively.

B. **Priority of Transactions.** Investment transactions for clients and employers must have priority over investment transactions in which a Member or Candidate is the beneficial owner.

C. **Referral Fees.** Members and Candidates must disclose to their employer, clients, and prospective clients, as appropriate, any compensation, consideration, or benefit received from, or paid to, others for the recommendation of products or services.

VII. Responsibilities as a CFA Institute Member or CFA Candidate

A. **Conduct as Members and Candidates in the CFA Program.** Members and Candidates must not engage in any conduct that compromises the reputation or integrity of CFA Institute or the CFA designation or the integrity, validity, or security of the CFA examinations.

B. **Reference to CFA Institute, the CFA designation, and the CFA Program.** When referring to CFA Institute, CFA Institute membership, the CFA designation, or candidacy in the CFA Program, Members and Candidates must not misrepresent or exaggerate the meaning or implications of membership in CFA Institute, holding the CFA designation, or candidacy in the CFA Program.

Interest Tables

TABLE C.1   Present Value of $1: PVIF $= 1/(1 + k)^t$

Period	1%	2%	3%	4%	5%	6%	7%	8%	9%	10%	12%	14%	15%	16%	18%	20%	24%	28%	32%	36%
1	.9901	.9804	.9709	.9615	.9524	.9434	.9346	.9259	.9174	.9091	.8929	.8772	.8696	.8621	.8475	.8333	.8065	.7813	.7576	.7353
2	.9803	.9612	.9426	.9246	.9070	.8900	.8734	.8573	.8417	.8264	.7972	.7695	.7561	.7432	.7182	.6944	.6504	.6104	.5739	.5407
3	.9706	.9423	.9151	.8890	.8638	.8396	.8163	.7938	.7722	.7513	.7118	.6750	.6575	.6407	.6086	.5787	.5245	.4768	.4348	.3975
4	.9610	.9238	.8885	.8548	.8227	.7921	.7629	.7350	.7084	.6830	.6355	.5921	.5718	.5523	.5158	.4823	.4230	.3725	.3294	.2923
5	.9515	.9057	.8626	.8219	.7835	.7473	.7130	.6806	.6499	.6209	.5674	.5194	.4972	.4761	.4371	.4019	.3411	.2910	.2495	.2149
6	.9420	.8880	.8375	.7903	.7462	.7050	.6663	.6302	.5963	.5645	.5066	.4556	.4323	.4104	.3704	.3349	.2751	.2274	.1890	.1580
7	.9327	.8706	.8131	.7599	.7107	.6651	.6227	.5835	.5470	.5132	.4523	.3996	.3759	.3538	.3139	.2791	.2218	.1776	.1432	.1162
8	.9235	.8535	.7894	.7307	.6768	.6274	.5820	.5403	.5019	.4665	.4039	.3506	.3269	.3050	.2660	.2326	.1789	.1388	.1085	.0854
9	.9143	.8368	.7664	.7026	.6446	.5919	.5439	.5002	.4604	.4241	.3606	.3075	.2843	.2630	.2255	.1938	.1443	.1084	.0822	.0628
10	.9053	.8203	.7441	.6756	.6139	.5584	.5083	.4632	.4224	.3855	.3220	.2697	.2472	.2267	.1911	.1615	.1164	.0847	.0623	.0462
11	.8963	.8043	.7224	.6496	.5847	.5268	.4751	.4289	.3875	.3505	.2875	.2366	.2149	.1954	.1619	.1346	.0938	.0662	.0472	.0340
12	.8874	.7885	.7014	.6246	.5568	.4970	.4440	.3971	.3555	.3186	.2567	.2076	.1869	.1685	.1372	.1122	.0757	.0517	.0357	.0250
13	.8787	.7730	.6810	.6006	.5303	.4688	.4150	.3677	.3262	.2897	.2292	.1821	.1625	.1452	.1163	.0935	.0610	.0404	.0271	.0184
14	.8700	.7579	.6611	.5775	.5051	.4423	.3878	.3405	.2992	.2633	.2046	.1597	.1413	.1252	.0985	.0779	.0492	.0316	.0205	.0135
15	.8613	.7430	.6419	.5553	.4810	.4173	.3624	.3152	.2745	.2394	.1827	.1401	.1229	.1079	.0835	.0649	.0397	.0247	.0155	.0099
16	.8528	.7284	.6232	.5339	.4581	.3936	.3387	.2919	.2519	.2176	.1631	.1229	.1069	.0930	.0708	.0541	.0320	.0193	.0118	.0073
17	.8444	.7142	.6050	.5134	.4363	.3714	.3166	.2703	.2311	.1978	.1456	.1078	.0929	.0802	.0600	.0451	.0258	.0150	.0089	.0054
18	.8360	.7002	.5874	.4936	.4155	.3503	.2959	.2502	.2120	.1799	.1300	.0946	.0808	.0691	.0508	.0376	.0208	.0118	.0068	.0039
19	.8277	.6864	.5703	.4746	.3957	.3305	.2765	.2317	.1945	.1635	.1161	.0829	.0703	.0596	.0431	.0313	.0168	.0092	.0051	.0029
20	.8195	.6730	.5537	.4564	.3769	.3118	.2584	.2145	.1784	.1486	.1037	.0728	.0611	.0514	.0365	.0261	.0135	.0072	.0039	.0021
25	.7798	.6095	.4776	.3751	.2953	.2330	.1842	.1460	.1160	.0923	.0588	.0378	.0304	.0245	.0160	.0105	.0046	.0021	.0010	.0005
30	.7419	.5521	.4120	.3083	.2314	.1741	.1314	.0994	.0754	.0573	.0334	.0196	.0151	.0116	.0070	.0042	.0016	.0006	.0002	.0001
40	.6717	.4529	.3066	.2083	.1420	.0972	.0668	.0460	.0318	.0221	.0107	.0053	.0037	.0026	.0013	.0007	.0002	.0001	*	*
50	.6080	.3715	.2281	.1407	.0872	.0543	.0339	.0213	.0134	.0085	.0035	.0014	.0009	.0006	.0003	.0001	*	*	*	*
60	.5504	.3048	.1697	.0951	.0535	.0303	.0173	.0099	.0057	.0033	.0011	.0004	.0002	.0001	*	*	*	*	*	*

*The factor is zero to four decimal places.

TABLE C.2 — Present Value of an Annuity of $1 Per Period for *n* Periods:

$$PVIFA = \sum_{t=1}^{n} \frac{1}{(1 + k)^t} = \frac{1 - \dfrac{1}{(1 + k)^n}}{k}$$

Number of Payments	1%	2%	3%	4%	5%	6%	7%	8%	9%	10%	12%	14%	15%	16%	18%	20%	24%	28%	32%
1	0.9901	0.9804	0.9709	0.9615	0.9524	0.9434	0.9346	0.9259	0.9174	0.9091	0.8929	0.8772	0.8696	0.8621	0.8475	0.8333	0.8065	0.7813	0.7576
2	1.9704	1.9416	1.9135	1.8861	1.8594	1.8334	1.8080	1.7833	1.7591	1.7355	1.6901	1.6467	1.6257	1.6052	1.5656	1.5278	1.4568	1.3916	1.3315
3	2.9410	2.8839	2.8286	2.7751	2.7232	2.6730	2.6243	2.5771	2.5313	2.4869	2.4018	2.3216	2.2832	2.2459	2.1743	2.1065	1.9813	1.8684	1.7663
4	3.9020	3.8077	3.7171	3.6299	3.5460	3.4651	3.3872	3.3121	3.2397	3.1699	3.0373	2.9137	2.8550	2.7982	2.6901	2.5887	2.4043	2.2410	2.0957
5	4.8534	4.7135	4.5797	4.4518	4.3295	4.2124	4.1002	3.9927	3.8897	3.7908	3.6048	3.4331	3.3522	3.2743	3.1272	2.9906	2.7454	2.5320	2.3452
6	5.7955	5.6014	5.4172	5.2421	5.0757	4.9173	4.7665	4.6229	4.4859	4.3553	4.1114	3.8887	3.7845	3.6847	3.4976	3.3255	3.0205	2.7594	2.5342
7	6.7282	6.4720	6.2303	6.0021	5.7864	5.5824	5.3893	5.2064	5.0330	4.8684	4.5638	4.2883	4.1604	4.0386	3.8115	3.6046	3.2423	2.9370	2.6775
8	7.6517	7.3255	7.0197	6.7327	6.4632	6.2098	5.9713	5.7466	5.5348	5.3349	4.9676	4.6389	4.4873	4.3436	4.0776	3.8372	3.4212	3.0758	2.7860
9	8.5660	8.1622	7.7861	7.4353	7.1078	6.8017	6.5152	6.2469	5.9952	5.7590	5.3282	4.9464	4.7716	4.6065	4.3030	4.0310	3.5655	3.1842	2.8681
10	9.4713	8.9826	8.5302	8.1109	7.7217	7.3601	7.0236	6.7101	6.4177	6.1446	5.6502	5.2161	5.0188	4.8332	4.4941	4.1925	3.6819	3.2689	2.9304
11	10.3676	9.7868	9.2526	8.7605	8.3064	7.8869	7.4987	7.1390	6.8052	6.4951	5.9377	5.4527	5.2337	5.0286	4.6560	4.3271	3.7757	3.3351	2.9776
12	11.2551	10.5753	9.9540	9.3851	8.8633	8.3838	7.9427	7.5361	7.1607	6.8137	6.1944	5.6603	5.4206	5.1971	4.7932	4.4392	3.8514	3.3868	3.0133
13	12.1337	11.3484	10.6350	9.9856	9.3936	8.8527	8.3577	7.9038	7.4869	7.1034	6.4235	5.8424	5.5831	5.3423	4.9095	4.5327	3.9124	3.4272	3.0404
14	13.0037	12.1062	11.2961	10.5631	9.8986	9.2950	8.7455	8.2442	7.7862	7.3667	6.6282	6.0021	5.7245	5.4675	5.0081	4.6106	3.9616	3.4587	3.0609
15	13.8651	12.8493	11.9379	11.1184	10.3797	9.7122	9.1079	8.5595	8.0607	7.6061	6.8109	6.1422	5.8474	5.5755	5.0916	4.6755	4.0013	3.4834	3.0764
16	14.7179	13.5777	12.5611	11.6523	10.8378	10.1059	9.4466	8.8514	8.3126	7.8237	6.9740	6.2651	5.9542	5.6685	5.1624	4.7296	4.0333	3.5026	3.0882
17	15.5623	14.2919	13.1661	12.1657	11.2741	10.4773	9.7632	9.1216	8.5436	8.0216	7.1196	6.3729	6.0472	5.7487	5.2223	4.7746	4.0591	3.5177	3.0971
18	16.3983	14.9920	13.7535	12.6593	11.6896	10.8276	10.0591	9.3719	8.7556	8.2014	7.2497	6.4674	6.1280	5.8178	5.2732	4.8122	4.0799	3.5294	3.1039
19	17.2260	15.6785	14.3238	13.1339	12.0853	11.1581	10.3356	9.6036	8.9501	8.3649	7.3658	6.5504	6.1982	5.8775	5.3162	4.8435	4.0967	3.5386	3.1090
20	18.0456	16.3514	14.8775	13.5903	12.4622	11.4699	10.5940	9.8181	9.1285	8.5136	7.4694	6.6231	6.2593	5.9288	5.3527	4.8696	4.1103	3.5458	3.1129
25	22.0232	19.5235	17.4131	15.6221	14.0939	12.7834	11.6536	10.6748	9.8226	9.0770	7.8431	6.8729	6.4641	6.0971	5.4669	4.9476	4.1474	3.5640	3.1220
30	25.8077	22.3965	19.6004	17.2920	15.3725	13.7648	12.4090	11.2578	10.2737	9.4269	8.0552	7.0027	6.5660	6.1772	5.5168	4.9789	4.1601	3.5693	3.1242
40	32.8347	27.3555	23.1148	19.7928	17.1591	15.0463	13.3317	11.9246	10.7574	9.7791	8.2438	7.1050	6.6418	6.2335	5.5482	4.9966	4.1659	3.5712	3.1250
50	39.1961	31.4236	25.7298	21.4822	18.2559	15.7619	13.8007	12.2335	10.9617	9.9148	8.3045	7.1327	6.6605	6.2463	5.5541	4.9995	4.1666	3.5714	3.1250
60	44.9550	34.7609	27.6756	22.6235	18.9293	16.1614	14.0392	12.3766	11.0480	9.9672	8.3240	7.1401	6.6651	6.2402	5.5553	4.9999	4.1667	3.5714	3.1250

TABLE C.3   Future Value of $1 at the End of n Periods: $FVIF_{k,n} = (1 + k)^n$

Period	1%	2%	3%	4%	5%	6%	7%	8%	9%	10%	12%	14%	15%	16%	18%	20%	24%	28%	32%	36%
1	1.0100	1.0200	1.0300	1.0400	1.0500	1.0600	1.0700	1.0800	1.0900	1.1000	1.1200	1.1400	1.1500	1.1600	1.1800	1.2000	1.2400	1.2800	1.3200	1.3600
2	1.0201	1.0404	1.0609	1.0816	1.1025	1.1236	1.1449	1.1664	1.1881	1.2100	1.2544	1.2996	1.3225	1.3456	1.3924	1.4400	1.5376	1.6384	1.7424	1.8496
3	1.0303	1.0612	1.0927	1.1249	1.1576	1.1910	1.2250	1.2597	1.2950	1.3310	1.4049	1.4815	1.5209	1.5609	1.6430	1.7280	1.9066	2.0972	2.3000	2.5155
4	1.0406	1.0824	1.1255	1.1699	1.2155	1.2625	1.3108	1.3605	1.4116	1.4641	1.5735	1.6890	1.7490	1.8106	1.9388	2.0736	2.3642	2.6844	3.0360	3.4210
5	1.0510	1.1041	1.1593	1.2167	1.2763	1.3382	1.4026	1.4693	1.5386	1.6105	1.7623	1.9254	2.0114	2.1003	2.2878	2.4883	2.9316	3.4360	4.0075	4.6526
6	1.0615	1.1262	1.1941	1.2653	1.3401	1.4185	1.5007	1.5869	1.6771	1.7716	1.9738	2.1950	2.3131	2.4364	2.6996	2.9860	3.6352	4.3980	5.2899	6.3275
7	1.0721	1.1487	1.2299	1.3159	1.4071	1.5036	1.6058	1.7138	1.8280	1.9487	2.2107	2.5023	2.6600	2.8262	3.1855	3.5832	4.5077	5.6295	6.9826	8.6054
8	1.0829	1.1717	1.2668	1.3686	1.4775	1.5938	1.7182	1.8509	1.9926	2.1436	2.4760	2.8526	3.0590	3.2784	3.7589	4.2998	5.5895	7.2058	9.2170	11.703
9	1.0937	1.1951	1.3048	1.4233	1.5513	1.6895	1.8385	1.9990	2.1719	2.3579	2.7731	3.2519	3.5179	3.8030	4.4355	5.1598	6.9310	9.2234	12.166	15.916
10	1.1046	1.2190	1.3439	1.4802	1.6289	1.7908	1.9672	2.1589	2.3674	2.5937	3.1058	3.7072	4.0456	4.4114	5.2338	6.1917	8.5944	11.805	16.059	21.646
11	1.1157	1.2434	1.3842	1.5395	1.7103	1.8983	2.1049	2.3316	2.5804	2.8531	3.4785	4.2262	4.6524	5.1173	6.1759	7.4301	10.657	15.111	21.198	29.439
12	1.1268	1.2682	1.4258	1.6010	1.7959	2.0122	2.2522	2.5182	2.8127	3.1384	3.8960	4.8179	5.3502	5.9360	7.2876	8.9161	13.214	19.342	27.982	40.037
13	1.1381	1.2936	1.4685	1.6651	1.8856	2.1329	2.4098	2.7196	3.0658	3.4523	4.3635	5.4924	6.1528	6.8858	8.5994	10.699	16.386	24.758	36.937	54.451
14	1.1495	1.3195	1.5126	1.7317	1.9799	2.2609	2.5785	2.9372	3.3417	3.7975	4.8871	6.2613	7.0757	7.9875	10.147	12.839	20.319	31.691	48.756	74.053
15	1.1610	1.3459	1.5580	1.8009	2.0789	2.3966	2.7590	3.1722	3.6425	4.1772	5.4736	7.1379	8.1371	9.2655	11.973	15.407	25.195	40.564	64.358	100.71
16	1.1726	1.3728	1.6047	1.8730	2.1829	2.5404	2.9522	3.4259	3.9703	4.5950	6.1304	8.1372	9.3576	10.748	14.129	18.488	31.242	51.923	84.953	136.96
17	1.1843	1.4002	1.6528	1.9479	2.2920	2.6928	3.1588	3.7000	4.3276	5.0545	6.8660	9.2765	10.761	12.467	16.672	22.186	38.740	66.461	112.13	186.27
18	1.1961	1.4282	1.7024	2.0258	2.4066	2.8543	3.3799	3.9960	4.7171	5.5599	7.6900	10.575	12.375	14.462	19.673	26.623	48.038	85.070	148.02	253.33
19	1.2081	1.4568	1.7535	2.1068	2.5270	3.0256	3.6165	4.3157	5.1417	6.1159	8.6128	12.055	14.231	16.776	23.214	31.948	59.567	108.89	195.39	344.53
20	1.2202	1.4859	1.8061	2.1911	2.6533	3.2071	3.8697	4.6610	5.6044	6.7275	9.6463	13.743	16.366	19.460	27.393	38.337	73.864	139.37	257.91	468.57
21	1.2324	1.5157	1.8603	2.2788	2.7860	3.3996	4.1406	5.0338	6.1088	7.4002	10.803	15.667	18.821	22.574	32.323	46.005	91.591	178.40	340.44	637.26
22	1.2447	1.5460	1.9161	2.3699	2.9253	3.6035	4.4304	5.4365	6.6586	8.1403	12.100	17.861	21.644	26.186	38.142	55.206	113.57	228.35	449.39	866.67
23	1.2572	1.5769	1.9736	2.4647	3.0715	3.8197	4.7405	5.8715	7.2579	8.9543	13.552	20.361	24.891	30.376	45.007	66.247	140.83	292.30	593.19	1178.6
24	1.2697	1.6084	2.0328	2.5633	3.2251	4.0489	5.0724	6.3412	7.9111	9.8497	15.178	23.212	28.625	35.236	53.108	79.496	174.63	374.14	783.02	1602.9
25	1.2824	1.6406	2.0938	2.6658	3.3864	4.2919	5.4274	6.8485	8.6231	10.834	17.000	26.461	32.918	40.874	62.668	95.396	216.54	478.90	1033.5	2180.0
26	1.2953	1.6734	2.1566	2.7725	3.5557	4.5494	5.8074	7.3964	9.3992	11.918	19.040	30.166	37.856	47.414	73.948	114.47	268.51	612.99	1364.3	2964.9
27	1.3082	1.7069	2.2213	2.8834	3.7335	4.8223	6.2139	7.9881	10.245	13.110	21.324	34.389	43.535	55.000	87.259	137.37	332.95	784.63	1800.9	4032.2
28	1.3213	1.7410	2.2879	2.9987	3.9201	5.1117	6.6488	8.6271	11.167	14.421	23.883	39.204	50.065	63.800	102.96	164.84	412.86	1004.3	2377.2	5483.8
29	1.3345	1.7758	2.3566	3.1187	4.1161	5.4184	7.1143	9.3173	12.172	15.863	26.749	44.693	57.575	74.008	121.50	197.81	511.95	1285.5	3137.9	7458.0
30	1.3478	1.8114	2.4273	3.2434	4.3219	5.7435	7.6123	10.062	13.267	17.449	29.959	50.950	66.211	85.849	143.37	237.37	634.81	1645.5	4142.0	10143.
40	1.4889	2.2080	3.2620	4.8010	7.0400	10.285	14.974	21.724	31.409	45.259	93.050	188.88	267.86	378.72	750.37	1469.7	5455.9	19426.	66520.	•
50	1.6446	2.6916	4.3839	7.1067	11.467	18.420	29.457	46.901	74.357	117.39	289.00	700.23	1083.6	1670.7	3927.3	9100.4	46890.	•	•	•
60	1.8167	3.2810	5.8916	10.519	18.679	32.987	57.946	101.25	176.03	304.48	897.59	2595.9	4383.9	7370.1	20555.	56347.	•	•	•	•

*FVIFA > 99,999

TABLE C.4

Sum of an Annuity of $1 Per Period for n Periods:

$$FVIFA_{k,n} = \sum_{t=1}^{n}(1+k)^{t-1} = \frac{(1+k)^n - 1}{k}$$

Number of Periods	1%	2%	3%	4%	5%	6%	7%	8%	9%	10%	12%	14%	15%	16%	18%	20%	24%	28%	32%	36%
1	1.0000	1.0000	1.0000	1.0000	1.0000	1.0000	1.0000	1.0000	1.0000	1.0000	1.0000	1.0000	1.0000	1.0000	1.0000	1.0000	1.0000	1.0000	1.0000	1.0000
2	2.0100	2.0200	2.0300	2.0400	2.0500	2.0600	2.0700	2.0800	2.0900	2.1000	2.1200	2.1400	2.1500	2.1600	2.1800	2.2000	2.2400	2.2800	2.3200	2.3600
3	3.0301	3.0604	3.0909	3.1216	3.1525	3.1836	3.2149	3.2464	3.2781	3.3100	3.3744	3.4396	3.4725	3.5056	3.5724	3.6400	3.7776	3.9184	4.0624	4.2096
4	4.0604	4.1216	4.1836	4.2465	4.3101	4.3746	4.4399	4.5061	4.5731	4.6410	4.7793	4.9211	4.9934	5.0665	5.2154	5.3680	5.6842	6.0156	6.3624	6.7251
5	5.1010	5.2040	5.3091	5.4163	5.5256	5.6371	5.7507	5.8666	5.9847	6.1051	6.3528	6.6101	6.7424	6.8771	7.1542	7.4416	8.0484	8.6999	9.3983	10.146
6	6.1520	6.3081	6.4684	6.6330	6.8019	6.9753	7.1533	7.3359	7.5233	7.7156	8.1152	8.5355	8.7537	8.9775	9.4420	9.9299	10.980	12.135	13.405	14.798
7	7.2135	7.4343	7.6625	7.8983	8.1420	8.3938	8.6540	8.9228	9.2004	9.4872	10.089	10.730	11.066	11.413	12.141	12.915	14.615	16.533	18.695	21.126
8	8.2857	8.5830	8.8923	9.2142	9.5491	9.8975	10.259	10.636	11.028	11.435	12.299	13.232	13.726	14.240	15.327	16.499	19.122	22.163	25.678	29.731
9	9.3685	9.7546	10.159	10.582	11.026	11.491	11.978	12.487	13.021	13.579	14.775	16.085	16.785	17.518	19.085	20.798	24.712	29.369	34.895	41.435
10	10.462	10.949	11.463	12.006	12.577	13.180	13.816	14.486	15.192	15.937	17.548	19.337	20.303	21.321	23.521	25.958	31.643	38.592	47.061	57.351
11	11.566	12.168	12.807	13.486	14.206	14.971	15.783	16.645	17.560	18.531	20.654	23.044	24.349	25.732	28.755	32.150	40.237	50.398	63.121	78.998
12	12.682	13.412	14.192	15.025	15.917	16.869	17.888	18.977	20.140	21.384	24.133	27.270	29.001	30.850	34.931	39.580	50.894	65.510	84.320	108.43
13	13.809	14.680	15.617	16.626	17.713	18.882	20.140	21.495	22.953	24.522	28.029	32.088	34.351	36.786	42.218	48.496	64.109	84.852	112.30	148.47
14	14.947	15.973	17.086	18.291	19.598	21.015	22.550	24.214	26.019	27.975	32.392	37.581	40.504	43.672	50.818	59.195	80.496	109.61	149.23	202.92
15	16.096	17.293	18.598	20.023	21.578	23.276	25.129	27.152	29.360	31.772	37.279	43.842	47.580	51.659	60.965	72.035	100.81	141.30	197.99	276.97
16	17.257	18.639	20.156	21.824	23.657	25.672	27.888	30.324	33.003	35.949	42.753	50.980	55.717	60.925	72.939	87.442	126.01	181.86	262.35	377.69
17	18.430	20.012	21.761	23.697	25.840	28.212	30.840	33.750	36.973	40.544	48.883	59.117	65.075	71.673	87.068	105.93	157.25	233.79	347.30	514.66
18	19.614	21.412	23.414	25.645	28.132	30.905	33.999	37.450	41.301	45.599	55.749	68.394	75.836	84.140	103.74	128.11	195.99	300.25	459.44	700.93
19	20.810	22.840	25.116	27.671	30.539	33.760	37.379	41.446	46.018	51.159	63.439	78.969	88.211	98.603	123.41	154.74	244.03	385.32	607.47	954.27
20	22.019	24.297	26.870	29.778	33.066	36.785	40.995	45.762	51.160	57.275	72.052	91.024	102.44	115.37	146.62	186.68	303.60	494.21	802.86	1298.8
21	23.239	25.783	28.676	31.969	35.719	39.992	44.865	50.422	56.764	64.002	81.698	104.76	118.81	134.84	174.02	225.02	377.46	633.59	1060.7	1767.3
22	24.471	27.299	30.536	34.248	38.505	43.392	49.005	55.456	62.873	71.402	92.502	120.43	137.63	157.41	206.34	271.03	469.05	811.99	1401.2	2404.6
23	25.716	28.845	32.452	36.617	41.430	46.995	53.436	60.893	69.531	79.543	104.60	138.29	159.27	183.60	244.48	326.23	582.62	1040.3	1850.6	3271.3
24	26.973	30.421	34.426	39.082	44.502	50.815	58.176	66.764	76.789	88.497	118.15	158.65	184.16	213.97	289.49	392.48	723.46	1332.6	2443.8	4449.9
25	28.243	32.030	36.459	41.645	47.727	54.864	63.249	73.105	84.700	98.347	133.33	181.87	212.79	249.21	342.60	471.98	898.09	1706.8	3226.8	6052.9
26	29.525	33.670	38.553	44.311	51.113	59.156	68.676	79.954	93.323	109.18	150.33	208.33	245.71	290.08	405.27	567.37	1114.6	2185.7	4260.4	8233.0
27	30.820	35.344	40.709	47.084	54.669	63.705	74.483	87.350	102.72	121.09	169.37	238.49	283.56	337.50	479.22	681.85	1383.1	2798.7	5624.7	11197.9
28	32.129	37.051	42.930	49.967	58.402	68.528	80.697	95.338	112.96	134.20	190.69	272.88	327.10	392.50	566.48	819.22	1716.0	3583.3	7425.6	15230.2
29	33.450	38.792	45.218	52.966	62.322	73.639	87.346	103.96	124.13	148.63	214.58	312.09	377.16	456.30	669.44	984.06	2128.9	4587.6	9802.9	20714.1
30	34.784	40.568	47.575	56.084	66.438	79.058	94.460	113.28	136.30	164.49	241.33	356.78	434.74	530.31	790.94	1181.8	2640.9	5873.2	12940.	28172.2
40	48.886	60.402	75.401	95.025	120.79	154.76	199.63	259.05	337.88	442.59	767.09	1342.0	1779.0	2360.7	4163.2	7343.8	22728.	69377.	•	•
50	64.463	84.579	112.79	152.66	209.34	290.33	406.52	573.76	815.08	1163.9	2400.0	4994.5	7217.7	10435.	21813.	45497.	•	•	•	•
60	81.669	114.05	163.05	237.99	353.58	533.12	813.52	1253.2	1944.7	3034.8	7471.6	18535.	29219.	46057.	•	•	•	•	•	•

*FVIF > 99.999

Standard Normal Probabilities

z	0.00	0.01	0.02	0.03	0.04	0.05	0.06	0.07	0.08	0.09
0.0	.5000	.5040	.5080	.5120	.5160	.5199	.5239	.5279	.5219	.5359
0.1	.5398	.5438	.5478	.5517	.5557	.5596	.5636	.5675	.5714	.5753
0.2	.5793	.5832	.5871	.5910	.5948	.5987	.6026	.6064	.6103	.6141
0.3	.6179	.6217	.6255	.6293	.6331	.6368	.6406	.6443	.6480	.6517
0.4	.6554	.6591	.6628	.6664	.6700	.6736	.6772	.6808	.6844	.6879
0.5	.6915	.6950	.6985	.7019	.7054	.7088	.7123	.7157	.7190	.7224
0.6	.7257	.7291	.7324	.7357	.7389	.7422	.7454	.7486	.7517	.7549
0.7	.7580	.7611	.7642	.7673	.7704	.7734	.7764	.7794	.7823	.7852
0.8	.7881	.7910	.7939	.7967	.7995	.8023	.8051	.8078	.8106	.8133
0.9	.8159	.8186	.8212	.8238	.8264	.8289	.8315	.8340	.8365	.8389
1.0	.8413	.8438	.8461	.8485	.8508	.8531	.8554	.8577	.8599	.8621
1.1	.8643	.8665	.8686	.8708	.8729	.8749	.8770	.8790	.8810	.8830
1.2	.8849	.8860	.8888	.8907	.8925	.8943	.8962	.8980	.8997	.9015
1.3	.9032	.9049	.9066	.9082	.9099	.9115	.9131	.9147	.9162	.9177
1.4	.9192	.9207	.9222	.9236	.9251	.9265	.9279	.9292	.9306	.9319
1.5	.9332	.9345	.9357	.9370	.9382	.9394	.9406	.9418	.9429	.9441
1.6	.9452	.9463	.9474	.9484	.9495	.9505	.9515	.9525	.9535	.9545
1.7	.9554	.9564	.9573	.9582	.9591	.9599	.9608	.9616	.9625	.9633
1.8	.9641	.9649	.9656	.9664	.9671	.9678	.9686	.9693	.9699	.9706
1.9	.9713	.9719	.9726	.9732	.9738	.9744	.9750	.9756	.9761	.9767
2.0	.9772	.9778	.9783	.9788	.9793	.9798	.9803	.9808	.9812	.9817
2.1	.9821	.9826	.9830	.9834	.9838	.9842	.9846	.9850	.9854	.9857
2.2	.9861	.9864	.9868	.9871	.9875	.9878	.9881	.9884	.9887	.9890
2.3	.9893	.9896	.9898	.9901	.9904	.9906	.9909	.9911	.9913	.9916
2.4	.9918	.9920	.9922	.9925	.9927	.9929	.9931	.9932	.9934	.9936
2.5	.9938	.9940	.9941	.9943	.9945	.9946	.9948	.9949	.9951	.9952
2.6	.9953	.9955	.9956	.9957	.9959	.9960	.9961	.9962	.9963	.9964
2.7	.9965	.9966	.9967	.9968	.9969	.9970	.9971	.9972	.9973	.9974
2.8	.9974	.9975	.9976	.9977	.9977	.9978	.9979	.9979	.9980	.9981
2.9	.9981	.9982	.9982	.9983	.9984	.9984	.9985	.9985	.9986	.9986
3.0	.9987	.9987	.9987	.9988	.9988	.9989	.9989	.9989	.9990	.9990

Acharya, Viral A., Julian Franks, and Henri Servaes. 2007. "Private Equity: Boom or Bust?" *Journal of Applied Corporate Finance* 19, no. 4 (Fall): pp. 44-53.

Albright, S. Christian. 1987. *Statistics for Business and Economics.* New York: Macmillan.

Alexander, Gordon J. 1980. "Applying the Market Model to Long-Term Corporate Bonds." *Journal of Financial and Quantitative Analysis* 15, no. 5 (December): 1063-1080.

Alford, A., R. Jones, and K. Winkelmann. 2003. "A Spectrum Approach to Active Risk Budgeting." *Journal of Portfolio Management* 30: 49-60.

Allen, Julie A., and Janet L. Showers. 1991. *Equity-Index-Linked Derivatives: A User's Guide.* New York: Salomon Brothers.

Almazan, Andres, Keith C. Brown, Murray Carlson, and David A. Chapman. 2004. "Why Constrain Your Mutual Fund Manager?" *Journal of Financial Economics* 73, no. 2 (August): 289-321.

Altman, Edward I. 1968. "Financial Ratios, Discriminant Analysis and the Prediction of Corporate Bankruptcy." *Journal of Finance* 23, no. 4 (September): 589-609.

Altman, Edward I. 1989. "Measuring Corporate Bond Mortality and Performance." *Journal of Finance* 44, no. 4 (September): 909-922.

Altman, Edward I. 1992. "Revisiting the High-Yield Bond Market." *Financial Management* 21, no. 2 (Summer): 78-92.

Altman, Edward I. 1993b. "Defaulted Bonds: Demand, Supply, and Performance, 1987-1992." *Financial Analysts Journal* 49, no. 3 (May-June): 55-60.

Altman, Edward I., Robert G. Haldeman, and P. Narayanan. 1997. "Zeta Analysis: A New Model to Identify Bankruptcy Risk of Corporations." *Journal of Banking and Finance* 1, no. 2 (June).

Altman, Edward I., and Edith Hotchleiss. 2006. *Corporate Financial Distress and Bankruptcy,* 3rd ed. New York: Wiley.

Altman, Edward I., and Scott A. Nammacher. 1987. *Investing in Junk Bonds.* New York: Wiley.

Altman, Edward I., and Babe E. Simon. 2001. "The Investment Performance of Defaulted Bonds for 2000 and 1987-2000." New York: New York University Salomon Center, February.

Amenc, Noel, and Veronique LeSourd. 2003. *Portfolio Theory and Performance Analysis.* West Sussex, England: Wiley.

Amihad, Y., and H. Mendelson. 1987. "Trading Mechanisms and Stock Returns. An Empirical Investigation." *Journal of Finance* 42, no. 3 (July): 533-553.

Ammann, Manuel, and Heinz Zimmermann. 2001. "Tracking Error and Tactical Asset Allocation." *Financial Analysts Journal* 57, no. 2 (March/April): 32-43.

Anderson, Jenny. 2005. "Cheap Seats Provide View of Troubles at Exchange." *New York Times,* January 10, pp. C1, C8.

Ang, Andrew, Robert J. Hodrick, Yuhang Xing, and Xiaoyan Zhang. 2006. "The Cross-Section of Volatility and Expected Returns." *Journal of Finance* 61, no. 1 (February): 259-299.

Ankrim, Ernest M., and Chris R. Hensel. 1994. "Multicurrency Performance Attribution." *Financial Analysts Journal* 50, no. 2 (March-April): 29-35.

Arbel, Avner, and Paul Strebel. 1983. "Pay Attention to Neglected Firms!" *Journal of Portfolio Management* 9, no. 2 (Winter): 37-42.

Arnott, Robert D., Jason C. Hsu, and John M. West. 2008. *The Fundamental Index,* New York: Wiley.

Ascarelli, Silvia, and Peter McKay. 2005. "European Exchanges Gobble Up Each Other." *Wall Street Journal,* January 20, pp. C1, C4.

Asquith, Paul, and David W. Mullins, Jr. 1991. "Convertible Debt: Corporate Call Policy and Voluntary Conversion." *Journal of Finance* 46, no. 4 (September): 1273-1289.

Asquith, Paul, David W. Mullins, Jr., and Eric D. Wolff. 1989. "Original-Issue High-Yield Bonds: Aging Analysis of Defaults, Exchanges, and Calls." *Journal of Finance* 44, no. 4 (September): 929-952.

Association for Investment Management and Research (AIMR). 1999. *Standards of Practice Handbook,* 8th ed. Charlottesville, VA: AIMR.

Atkinson, Thomas R. 1967. *Trends in Corporate Bond Quality.* New York: National Bureau of Economic Research.

Avera, William F. 1994. "Definition of Industry Ethics and Development of a Code." In *Good Ethics: The Essential Element of a Firm's Success,* ed. K. Baker. Charlottesville, VA: AIMR.

Aziz, A., and G. H. Lawson. 1989. "Cash Flow Reporting and Financial Distress Models: Testing of Hypothesis." *Financial Management* 18, no. 1 (Spring): 55-63.

Babcock, Guilford. 1970. "The Concept of Sustainable Growth." *Financial Analysts Journal* 26, no. 3 (May-June): 108-114.

Bacon, Carl. 2004. *Practical Portfolio Performance Measurement and Attribution.* West Sussex, England: Wiley.

Baesel, Jerome, George Shows, and Edward Thorp. 1982. "Can Joe Granville Time the Market?" *Journal of Portfolio Management* 8, no. 3 (Spring): 5-9.

Bailey, Jeffrey V. 1992. "Are Manager Universes Acceptable Performance Benchmarks?" *Journal of Portfolio Management* 18, no. 3 (Spring): 9-13.

Bailey, Jeffery V., Thomas M. Richards, and David E. Tierney. 2007. "Evaluating Portfolio Performance." In *Managing Investment Portfolio: A Dynamic Process,* 3rd ed., eds. John L. Maginn, Donald L. Tuttle, Jerald E. Pinto, and Dennis W. McLeavey. Hoboken, NJ: Wiley.

Bailey, Warren, and Joseph Lim. 1992. "Evaluating the Diversification Benefits of the New Country Funds." *Journal of Portfolio Management* 18, no. 3 (Spring): 74-80.

Bali, Turan G., Susan R. Hume, and Terrence F. Martell. 2007. "A New Look at Hedging With Derivatives: Will Firms Reduce Market Risk Exposure?" *Journal of Futures Markets* 27, no. 11 (November): 1053-1083.

Ball, Ray. 1995. "The Theory of Stock Market Efficiency: Accomplishments and Limitations." *Journal of Applied Corporate Finance* 8, no. 1 (Spring): 4-18.

Balog, James, ed. 1993. *The Health Care Industry.* Charlottesville, VA: AIMR.

Bansal, Vipul S., M. E. Ellis, and John F. Marshall. 1993. "The Pricing of Short-Dated and Forward Interest Rate Swaps." *Financial Analysts Journal* 49, no. 2 (March-April): 82-87.

Banz, R. W. 1981. "The Relationship between Return and Market Value of Common Stocks." *Journal of Financial Economics* 9, no. 1 (March): 3-18.

Barber, Brad, and Terrance Odean. "Online Investors: Do the Slow Die First?" *Review of Financial Studies* 15, no. 2 (2002): 455-489.

Barber, Brad, and Terrance Odean. 1999. "The Courage of Misguided Convictions: The Trading Behavior of Individual Investors." *Financial Analysts Journal* 55, no. 6 (November-December): 41-55.

Barber, Brad, and Terrance Odean. 2000. "Trading Is Hazardous to Your Wealth: The Common Stock Investment Performance of Individual Investors." *Journal of Finance* 55, no. 2 (April): 773–806.

Barber, Brad, and Terrance Odean. 2001. "Boys Will Be Boys: Gender, Overconfidence, and Common Stock Investment." *Quarterly Journal of Economics* 116, no. 1 (February): 261–292.

Barberis, Nicholas, and Richard Thalen. 2003. "A Survey of Behavioral Finance." *Handbook of the Economics of Finance,* ed. G.M. Constantianides, M. Harris, and Rene Stulz. New York: Elsevier Science.

Barclay, Michael J., William G. Christie, Jeffrey H. Harris, Eugene Kandel, and Paul Schultz. 1999. "The Effects of Market Reform on the Trading Costs and Depth of Nasdaq Stocks." *Journal of Finance* 54, no. 1 (March): 1–66.

Barclay, Michael, Clifford Holderness, and Jeffrey Pontiff. 1993. "Private Benefits from Block Ownership and Discounts on Closed-End Funds." *Journal of Financial Economics* 33, no. 3 (June): 263–292.

Barone-Adesi, Giovanni, and Robert E. Whaley. 1986. "The Valuation of American Call Options and the Expected Ex-Dividend Stock Price Declines." *Journal of Financial Economics* 17, no. 1 (September): 91–112.

Barry, Christopher B., and Stephen J. Brown. 1984. "Differential Information and the Small Firm Effect." *Journal of Financial Economics* 13, no. 2 (June): 283–294.

Baruch, Lev. 1989. "On the Usefulness of Earnings and Earnings Research: Lessons and Directions from Two Decades of Empirical Research." *Journal of Accounting Research* 27 (Supplement).

Basak, Suleyman. 2002. "A Comparative Study of Portfolio Insurance." *Journal of Economic Dynamics and Control* 26, no. 7-8 (July): 1217-1241.

Basu, Senjoy. 1977. "Investment Performance of Common Stocks in Relation to Their Price-Earnings Ratios: A Test of the Efficient Market Hypothesis." *Journal of Finance* 32, no. 3 (June): 663–682.

Battalio, Robert H. 1997. "Third Market Broker-Dealers: Cost Competitors or Cream Skimmers?" *Journal of Finance* 52, no. 1 (March): 341–352.

Battalio, Robert, Jason Greene, and Robert Jennings. 1997. "How Do Competing Specialists and Preferencing Dealers Affect Market Quality?" *Review of Financial Studies* 10: 969–993.

Bauer, Richard J., and Julie R. Dahlquist. 2001. "Market Timing and Roulette Wheels." *Financial Analysts Journal* 57, no. 1 (January/February): pp. 28-40.

Baumol, William J., and Burton Malkiel. 1993. "Redundant Regulation of Foreign Security Trading and U.S. Competitiveness." *Journal of Applied Corporate Finance* 5, no. 4 (Winter): 19–27.

Beard, Allison. 2001. "Short Selling Goes from Strength to Strength." *Financial Times,* March 16, p. 29.

Beard, Craig, and Richard Sias. 1997. "Is There a Neglected-Firm Effect?" *Financial Analysts Journal* 53, no. 5 (September–October): 19–23.

Beaver, William H. 1966. "Financial Ratios as Predictors of Failure." *Empirical Research in Accounting: Selected Studies,* supplement to vol. 4, *Journal of Accounting Research.*

Beaver, William H. 1968. "Market Prices, Financial Ratios, and the Prediction of Failure." *Journal of Accounting Research* 6, no. 2 (Autumn).

Beaver, William H. 1989. *Financial Reporting: An Accounting Revolution.* Englewood Cliffs, NJ: Prentice Hall.

Beaver, William H., Paul Kettler, and Myron Scholes. 1970. "The Association between Market-Determined and Accounting-Determined Risk Measures." *Accounting Review* 45, no. 4 (October): 654–672.

Beaver, William H., and Dale Morse. 1978. "What Determines Price-Earnings Ratios?" *Financial Analysts Journal* 34, no. 4 (July–August): 65–76.

Beckers, Stan. 1981. "Standard Deviations Implied in Option Prices as Predictors of Future Stock Price Variability." *Journal of Banking and Finance* 5, no. 3 (September): 363–381.

Beidleman, Carl R., ed. 1991. *Interest Rate Swaps.* Homewood, IL: Business One–Irwin.

Belfer, Nathan. 1988. "Economic Indicators and Their Significance." In *The Financial Analysts Handbook,* 2nd ed., ed. Sumner N. Levine. Homewood, IL: Dow Jones–Irwin.

Belkaoui, Ahmed. 1980. "Industrial Bond Ratings: A New Look." *Financial Management* 9, no. 3 (Fall): 44–52.

Benesh, Gary A., and Pamela P. Peterson. 1986. "On the Relation between Earning Changes, Analysts' Forecasts and Stock Price Fluctuations." *Financial Analysts Journal* 42, no. 6 (November/December): 29–39.

Benning, Carl J. 1997. "Prediction Skills of Real-World Market Timers." *The Journal of Portfolio Management* 23, no. 2 (Winter): 55–65.

Benveniste, L. M., A. J. Marcus, and W. J. Wilhelm. 1992. "What's Special about the Specialist?" *Journal of Financial Economics* 32, no. 1 (August): 61–86.

Berkman, Neil. 1977. "Institutional Investors and the Stock Market." *New England Economic Review* (November–December): 60–77.

Berk, Jonathan B., and Richard Stanton. 2007. "Managerial Ability, Compensation, and the Closed-End Fund Discount." *Journal of Finance* 62, no. 2 (April), pp. 529-556.

Berkowitz, Stephen A., Louis D. Finney, and Dennis Logue. 1988. *The Investment Performance of Corporate Pension Plans.* New York: Quorum Books.

Bernard, Victor. 1989. "Capital Markets Research in Accounting during the 1980s: A Critical Review." In *The State of Accounting Research as We Enter the 1990s,* ed. Thomas J. Frecka. Urbana: University of Illinois Press.

Bernard, Victor L., and Jacob K. Thomas. 1989. "Post-Earnings–Announcements Drift: Delayed Price Response or Risk Premium?" *Journal of Accounting Research* 27 (Supplement).

Bernard, Victor L., and Jacob K. Thomas. 1990. "Evidence That Stock Prices Do Not Fully Reflect the Implications of Current Earnings for Future Earnings." *Journal of Accounting and Economics* (December): 305–341.

Bernstein, Leopold A., and John J. Wild. 1998. *Financial Statement Analysis: Theory, Application, and Interpretation,* 6th ed. Homewood, IL: Irwin/McGraw-Hill.

Bernstein, Richard. 1995. *Style Investing: Unique Insight into Equity Management.* New York: Wiley.

Bhandari, Laxmi Chand. 1988. "Debt/Equity Ratio and Expected Common Stock Returns: Empirical Evidence." *Journal of Finance* 43, no. 2 (June): 507–528.

Bharadwaj, Anu, and James B. Wiggins. 2001. "Box Spread and Put-Call Parity Tests for the S&P 500 Index LEAPS Market." *Journal of Derivatives* 8, no. 4 (Summer): 62–71.

Bhatia, Sanjiv, ed. 1995. *The Consumer Staples Industry: Proceedings of the AIMR Seminar "Industry Analysis: Consumer Staples," March 28–29, 1995, St. Louis, Missouri.* Charlottesville, VA: AIMR.

Bhatia, Sanjiv, ed. 1996a. *Global Equity Investing: Proceedings of the AIMR Seminar "Exploring the Frontiers of Global Equity Investing," November 29–December 1, 1995, Singapore.* Charlottesville, VA: AIMR.

Bhatia, Sanjiv, ed. 1996b. *The Media Industry: Proceedings of the AIMR Seminar "The Media Industry," January 31–February 1, 1996, New York, New York.* Charlottesville, VA: AIMR.

Bierwag, G. O. 1977. "Immunization, Duration, and the Term Structure of Interest Rates." *Journal of Financial and Quantitative Analysis* 12, no. 5 (December): 725–742.

Bierwag, G. O., and George G. Kaufman. 1977. "Coping with the Risk of Interest Rate Fluctuations: A Note." *Journal of Business* 50, no. 3 (July): 364–370.

Biger, Nahum, and John Hull. 1983. "The Valuation of Currency Options." *Financial Management* 12, no. 1 (Spring): 24–28.

Billingsley, Randall S., ed. 1994. *The Telecommunications Industry: November 10–11, 1993, New York, New York.* Charlottesville, VA: AIMR.

Billingsley, Randall, ed. 1995. *Corporate Financial Decision Making and Equity Analysis: Proceedings of the AIMR Seminar "Equity Analysis: The Role of Corporate Financial Decision Making," January 18, 1995, Washington, DC.* Charlottesville, VA: AIMR.

Billingsley, Randall S., R. Lamy, M. Marr, and T. Thompson. 1985. "Split Ratings and Bond Reoffering Yields." *Financial Management* 14, no. 2 (Summer): 59–65.

Black, Fischer. 1972. "Capital Market Equilibrium with Restricted Borrowing." *Journal of Business* 45, no. 3 (July): 444–455.

Black, Fischer. 1975. "Fact and Fantasy in the Use of Options." *Financial Analysts Journal* 31, no. 4 (July–August): 36–41, 61–72.

Black, Fischer. 1976. "The Pricing of Commodity Contracts." *Journal of Financial Economics* 3, no. 1/2 (January–March): 167–179.

Black, Fischer. 1989a. "How to Use the Holes in Black-Scholes." *Journal of Applied Corporate Finance* 1, no. 4 (Winter): 67–73.

Black, Fischer. 1989b. "How We Came Up with the Option Formula." *Journal of Portfolio Management* 15, no. 2 (Winter): 4–8.

Black, Fischer, E. Derman, and Wo Toy. 1990. "A One-Factor Model of Interest Rates and Its Application to Treasury Bond Options." *Financial Analysts Journal* 46, no. 1 (January–February): 33–39.

Black, Fischer, Michael Jensen, and Myron Scholes. 1972. "The Capital Asset Pricing Model: Some Empirical Tests." In *Studies in the Theory of Capital Markets,* ed. Michael Jensen. New York: Praeger.

Black, Fischer, and Myron Scholes. 1973. "The Pricing of Options and Corporate Liabilities." *Journal of Political Economy* 81, no. 2 (May–June): 637–654.

Black, Fischer, and Myron Scholes. 1979. "The Effects of Dividend Yield and Dividend Policy on Common Stock Prices and Returns." *Journal of Financial Economics* 1, no. 1 (March): 1–22.

Blake, Christopher R., Edwin J. Elton, and Martin J. Gruber. 1993. "The Performance of Bond Mutual Funds." *Journal of Business* 66, no. 3 (July): 371–403.

Bleakley, Fred R. 1996. "Economy's Strength Is Seen Cooling in Second Half." *Wall Street Journal,* July 1, p. A2.

Blume, Lawrence, David Easley, and Maureen O'Hara. 1994. "Market Statistics and Technical Analysis: The Role of Volume." *Journal of Finance* 49, no. 1 (March): 153–181.

Blume, Marshall E. 1993. "Soft Dollars and the Brokerage Industry." *Financial Analysts Journal* 49, no. 2 (March–April): 36–44.

Blume, Marshall E., and Jeremy J. Siegel. 1992. "The Theory of Security Pricing and Market Structure." *Financial Markets, Institutions and Instruments* 1, no. 3. New York University Salomon Center.

Boatright, John R. 2008. *Ethics in Finance,* 2nd ed. Malden, MA: Blackwell Publishing.

Boland, Vincent. 2001. "Securing a Future." *Financial Times,* March 5.

Bomfim, Antulio N. 2003. "Counterparty Credit Risk in Interest Rate Swaps During Times of Market Stress." *Federal Reserve Board Discussion Series,* no. 9.

Bookstaber, Richard M., and Roger G. Clarke. 1981. "Options Can Alter Portfolio Return Distributions." *Journal of Portfolio Management* 7, no. 3 (Spring): 63–70.

Born, Jeffery, James Moses, and Dennis Officer. 1988. "Changes in Dividend Policy and Subsequent Earnings." *Journal of Portfolio Management* 14, no. 4 (Summer): 56–62.

Boyce, W. M., and A. J. Kalotay. 1979. "Optimum Bond Calling and Refunding." *Interfaces* (November): 36–49.

Boyd, Naomi E., and Jeffrey M. Mercer. 2005. "Gains from Bond Swap Strategies." Working Paper, George Washington University.

Bradford, R. W. 1989. "How to Lose a Mint." *Barron's,* March 6, pp. 54, 55.

Branch, Ben. 1977. "A Tax Loss Trading Rule." *Journal of Business* 50, no. 2 (April): 198–207.

Branch, Ben, and Kyun Chun Chang. 1985. "Tax-Loss Trading—Is the Game Over or Have the Rules Changed?" *Financial Review* 20, no. 1 (February): 55–69.

Brealey, Richard A., and Stewart C. Myers. 2004. *Principles of Corporate Finance,* 8th ed. New York: McGraw-Hill.

Brennan, Michael. 1969. "Capital Market Equilibrium with Divergent Borrowing and Lending Rules." *Journal of Financial and Quantitative Analysis* 4, no. 1 (March): 4–14.

Brennan, Michael J., and Eduardo S. Schwartz. 1985. "Evaluating Natural Resource Investments." *Journal of Business* 58, no. 2 (April): 135–158.

Brennan, Michael J., and A. Subramanyam. 1996. "Market Microstructure and Asset Pricing on the Compensation for Illiquidity in Stock Returns." *Journal of Financial Economics* 41, no. 3 (July): 341–344.

Brigham, Eugene. 2004. *Fundamentals of Financial Management,* 10th ed. Mason, OH: South-Western.

Brigham, Eugene, and Louis C. Gapenski. 2003. *Financial Management: Theory and Practice,* 10th ed. Cincinnati, OH: South-Western.

Brinson, Gary P. 2005. "The Future of Investment Management." *Financial Analysts Journal* 61, no. 4 (July/August), pp. 24-28.

Brinson, Gary P., Jeffrey J. Diermeier, and G. G. Schlarbaum. 1986. "A Composite Portfolio Benchmark for Pension Plans." *Financial Analysts Journal* 42, no. 2 (March–April): 15–24.

Brinson, Gary P., L. Randolph Hood, and Gilbert L. Beebower. 1986. "Determinants of Portfolio Performance." *Financial Analysts Journal* 42, no. 4 (July–August): 39–44.

Brinson, Gary P., Brian D. Singer, and Gilbert L. Beebower. 1991. "Determinants of Portfolio Performance II: An Update." *Financial Analysts Journal* 47, no. 3 (May–June): 40–48.

Brooks, Robert. 1997. *Interest Rate Modeling and the Risk Premiums in Interest Rate Swaps.* Charlottesville, VA: Research Foundation of the Institute of Chartered Financial Analysts.

Brown, David P., and Robert H. Jennings. 1989. "On Technical Analysis." *Review of Financial Studies* 2, no. 4 (October).

Brown, Gregory. 1999. "Volatility, Sentiment, and Noise Traders." *Financial Analysts Journal* 55, no. 2 (March–April): 82–90.

Brown, Gregory. 2001. "Managing Foreign Exchange Risk with Derivatives." *Journal of Financial Economics* 60, nos. 2–3 (May/June): 401–448.

Brown, Keith C., ed. 1993. *Derivative Strategies for Managing Portfolio Risk.* Charlottesville, VA: AIMR.

Brown, Keith C., and Gregory D. Brown. 1987. "Does the Composition of the Market Portfolio Really Matter?" *Journal of Portfolio Management* 13, no. 2 (Winter): 26–32.

Brown, Keith C., and W.V. Harlow, 2005. "Staying the Course: Performance Persistence and the Role of Investment Style Consistency in Professional Asset Management," Working Paper.

Brown, Keith C., W. V. Harlow, and Donald J. Smith. 1994. "An Empirical Analysis of Interest Rate Swap Spreads." *Journal of Fixed Income* 3, no. 3 (March): 61–78.

Brown, Keith C., W. V. Harlow, and Laura T. Starks. 1996. "Of Tournaments and Temptations: An Analysis of Managerial Incentives in the Mutual Fund Industry." *Journal of Finance* 51, no. 1 (March): 85–110.

Brown, Keith C., W. V. Harlow, and Seha M. Tinic. 1989. "How Rational Investors Deal with Uncertainty (or, Reports of the Death of Efficient Market Theory Are Greatly Exaggerated)." *Journal of Applied Corporate Finance* 2, no. 3 (Fall): 45–58.

Brown, Keith C., and Michael V. Raymond. 1986. "Risk Arbitrage and the Prediction of Successful Corporate Takeovers." *Financial Management* 15, no. 3 (August), 54–63.

Brown, Keith C., and Donald J. Smith. 1988. "Recent Innovations in Interest Rate Risk Management and the Reintermediation of Commercial Banking." *Financial Management* 17, no. 4 (Winter): 45–58.

Brown, Keith C., and Donald J. Smith. 1995a. *Interest Rate and Currency Swaps: A Tutorial.* Charlottesville, VA: Research Foundation of Institute of Chartered Financial Analysts.

Brown, Keith C., and Donald J. Smith. 1995b. "Structured Swaps." In *Yearbook of Fixed Income Investing,* ed. J. Finnerty and M. Fridson. Burr Ridge, IL: Irwin Professional.

Brown, Keith C., and Meir Statman. 1987. "The Benefits of Insured Stocks for Corporate Cash Management." *Advances in Futures and Options Research* 2: 243–261.

Brown, Keith C., Lorenzo Garlappi, and Cristian Tiu. 2007. "The Troves of Academe: Asset Allocation, Risk Budgeting and the Investment Performance of University Endowment Funds," Working Paper, August 8.

Brown, Ken. 2000. "Fund Diversification Dies a Not Very Slow Death." *Wall Street Journal,* February 7, pp. R1, R5.

Brown, Stephen J., and William Goetzmann. 1995. "Performance Persistence." *Journal of Finance* 50, no. 3 (June): 679–698.

Brown, Stephen J., William Goetzmann, Roger G. Ibbotson, and Stephen A. Ross. 1992. "Survivorship Bias in Performance Studies." *Review of Financial Studies* 5, no. 4 (December).

Brown, Stephen J., and Mark I. Weinstein. 1983. "A New Approach to Testing Asset Pricing Models: The Bilinear Paradigm." *Journal of Finance* 38, no. 3 (June): 711–743.

Buetow, Gerald W., Jr., and Frank J. Fabozzi. 2000. *Valuation of Interest Rate Swaps and Swaptions.* New York: Wiley.

Burmeister, Edwin, and Marjorie B. McElroy. 1988. "Joint Estimation of Factor Sensitivities and Risk Premia for the Arbitrage Pricing Theory." *Journal of Finance* 43, no. 3 (July): 721–733.

Burmeister, Edwin, Richard Roll, and Stephen A. Ross. 1994. "A Practitioner's Guide to Arbitrage Pricing Theory." In *A Practitioner's Guide to Factor Models,* ed. John Peavy. Charlottesville, VA: Research Foundation of the Institute of Chartered Financial Analysts.

Burns, Terence E., ed. 1998. *Derivatives in Portfolio Management.* Charlottesville, VA: AIMR.

Bush, Janet. 1990. "Hoping for a New Broom at the NYSE." *Financial Times,* August 16, p.13.

Byrnes, Nanette, and David Henry. 2001. "Confused about Earnings?" *BusinessWeek,* November 26, pp. 77–84.

Byrnes, Nanette, Mike McNamee, Diane Brady, Louis Lavelle, and Christopher Palmeri. 2002. "Accounting in Crisis." *BusinessWeek,* January 28, pp. 44–48.

Caccese, Michael S. 1997. "Ethics and the Financial Analyst." *Financial Analysts Journal* 53, no. 1 (January/February): 9–14.

Cagan, Phillip. 1969. *Essays on Interest Rates.* New York: Columbia University Press for the National Bureau of Economic Research.

Campbell, John Y., and John Ammer. 1993. "What Moves the Stock and Bond Markets? A Variance Decomposition for Long-Term Asset Returns." *Journal of Finance* 48, no. 1 (March): 3–38.

Campbell, John Y., Martin Lettau, Burton G. Malkiel, and Yexiao Xu. 2001. "Have Individual Stocks Become More Volatile?: An Empirical Exploration of Idiosyncratic Risk." *Journal of Finance* 56, no. 1 (February): 1-43.

Campisi, Stephen. 2000. "Primer on Fixed Income Performance Attribution." *Journal of Performance Measurement* 4, no. 4 (Summer): pp. 14-25.

Cantor, Richard, and Frank Packer. 1995. "The Credit Rating Industry." *Journal of Fixed Income* 5, no. 3 (December): 10–34.

Caouette, J. B., E. I. Altman, and P. Narayanan. 1998. *Managing Credit Risk.* New York: Wiley.

Capaul, Carlo, Ian Rowley, and William F. Sharpe. 1993. "International Value and Growth Stock Returns." *Financial Analysts Journal* 49, no.1 (January/February): 27–36.

Capon, N., G. Fitzsimons, and R. Prince. 1996. "An Individual Level Analysis of the Mutual Fund Investment Decision." *Journal of Financial Services Research* 10: 59–82.

Carhart, Mark M. 1997. "On Persistence in Mutual Fund Performance." *Journal of Finance* 52, no. 1 (March): 57–82.

Carpenter, Michael D., and David E. Upton. 1981. "Trading Volume and Beta Stability." *Journal of Portfolio Management* 7, no. 2 (Winter): 60–64.

Carr, Peter. 1988. "A Calculator Program for Option Values and Implied Standard Deviations." *Journal of Financial Education* 17, no. 1 (Fall): 89–93.

Carter, Richard B., Frederick Dark, and Asah Singh. 1998. "Underwriter Reputation, Initial Returns, and the Long-Run Performance of IPO Stocks." *Journal of Finance* 53, no. 1 (February): 285–311.

Case, Carl, and Robert Shiller. 1987. "Price of Single Family Homes since 1970: New Indexes for Four Cities." Working Paper no. 2393. New York: National Bureau of Economic Research.

Castelino, Mark G., 2000, "Hedging Effectiveness: Basis Risk and Minimum Variance Hedging." *Journal of Futures Markets* 20, no. 1 (January): 89-103.

Cavaglia, Stefano, Christopher Brightman, and Michael Aked. 2000. "The Increasing Importance of Industry Factors." *Financial Analysts Journal* 56, no. 5 (September–October): 41–54.

CFA Institute. 2004. *Points of Inflection: New Directions for Portfolio Management.* Charlottesville, VA: CFA Institute.

Chan, Louis, Narasimhan Jegadeesh, and Josef Lakonishok. 1999. "The Profitability of Momentum Strategies." *Financial Analysts Journal* 55, no. 6 (November/ December): 80–90.

Chan, Louis, and Josef Lakonishok. 2004. "Value and Growth Investing: Review and Update." *Financial Analysts Journal* 60, no. 1 (January/February): 71–86.

Chan, Wesley. 2003. "Stock Price Reaction to News and No-News: Drift and Reversal after Headlines." *Journal of Financial Economics* 70, no. 2 (November): 223–260.

Chance, Don M. 2003. *Analysis of Derivatives for the CFA Program.* Charlottesville, VA: AIMR.

Chance, Don M., and Rober Brooks. 2007. An Introduction to Derivatives and Risk Management, 7th ed. Mason, OH: Southwestern Publishing.

Chance, Don M. 2004. "Equity Swaps and Equity Investing." *Journal of Alternative Investing* 7 (Summer): 75–97.

Chance, Don M., and Pamela P. Peterson. 2002. *Real Options and Investment Valuation.* Charlottesville, VA: Research Foundation of AIMR.

Chance, Don M., and Don Rich. 1998. "The Pricing of Equity Swaps and Swaptions." *Journal of Derivatives* 5, no. 2 (Summer): 19–31.

Chang, Eric C., and Wilbur G. Lewellen. 1984. "Market Timing and Mutual Fund Investment Performance." *Journal of Business* 57, no. 1 (January): 57–72.

Charron, Terry Sylvester. 1999. "Tax Efficient Investing for Tax-Deferred and Taxable Accounts." *Journal of Private Portfolio Management* 2, no. 2 (Fall): 31–37.

Chemmanur, Thomas, and An Yan. 2004. "A Theory of Corporate Spin-offs." *Journal of Financial Economics* 72, no. 2 (May): 259–290.

Chen, H. L., N. Jegadeesh, and R. Wermers. 2000. "An Examination of the Stockholdings and Trades of Mutual Fund Managers." *Journal of Financial and Quantitative Analysis* 35 (September): 343–368.

Chen, Nai-fu. 1983. "Some Empirical Tests of the Theory of Arbitrage Pricing." *Journal of Finance* 38, no. 5 (December): 1393–1414.

Chen, Nai-fu, Richard Roll, and Stephen A. Ross. 1986. "Economic Forces and the Stock Market." *Journal of Business* 59, no. 3 (April): 383–404.

Chen, Sheng-Syan, Cheng-few Lee, and Keshab Shrestha. 2003. "Futures Hedge Ratios: A Review." *Quarterly Review of Economics and Finance* 43, no. 3 (Autumn): 433-465.

Chen, Son-Nan. 1981. "Beta Nonstationarity, Portfolio Residual Risk, and Diversification." *Journal of Financial and Quantitative Analysis* 16, no. 1 (March): 95–111.

Cherney, Elena, and Thom Beal. 2000. "As NYSE Plans for Global Market, Nasdaq Gets Left Out in the Cold." *Wall Street Journal,* June 8, p. C1.

Chernoff, Joel. 1996. "OECD Eyes Pension Rules." *Pensions and Investments,* December 23, pp. 2, 34.

Cho, D. Chinhyung. 1984. "On Testing the Arbitrage Pricing Theory: Inter-Battery Factor Analysis." *Journal of Finance* 39, no. 5 (December): 1485–1502.

Cho, D. Chinhyung, Edwin J. Elton, and Martin J. Gruber. 1984. "On the Robustness of the Roll and Ross Arbitrage Pricing Theory." *Journal of Financial and Quantitative Analysis* 19, no. 1 (March): 1–10.

Choi, Frederick D. S., Carol Ann Frost, and Gary Meek. 2000. *International Accounting.* Englewood Cliffs, NJ: Prentice Hall.

Choie, Kenneth S. 1990. "A Simplified Approach to Bond Portfolio Management: DDS." *Journal of Portfolio Management* 16, no. 3 (Spring): 40–45.

Chote, Robert. 1998. "Indonesia Risks Further Unrest as Debt Talks Falter." *Financial Times,* May 11, p. 1.

Chowdhury, M., J. S. Howe, and J. C. Lin. 1993. "The Relation between Aggregate Insider Transactions and Stock Market Returns." *Journal of Financial and Quantitative Analysis* 28, no. 3 (September): 431–437.

Christie, William. 1990. "Dividend Yield and Expected Returns." *Journal of Financial Economics* 28, no. 1 (November–December): 95–125.

Christopherson, Jon A., Wayne E. Ferson, and Debra A. Glassman. 1998. "Conditioning Manager Alphas on Economic Information: Another Look at the Persistence of Performance," *Review of Financial Studies* 11, no. 1 (Spring): 111–142.

Christopherson, Jon A., and C. Nola Williams. 1995. "Equity Style: What It Is and Why It Matters." In *The Handbook of Equity Style Management,* ed. T. Daniel Coggin and Frank J. Fabozzi. New Hope, PA: Frank J. Fabozzi Associates.

Churchhill, Dwight D., ed. 1994. *Fixed-Income Management: Techniques and Practices.* Charlottesville, VA: AIMR.

Clarke, Roger G. 1992. *Options and Futures: A Tutorial.* Charlottesville, VA: Research Foundation of the Institute of Chartered Financial Analysts.

Clarke, Roger G., and Mark P. Kritzman. 1996. *Currency Management: Concepts and Practices.* Charlottesville, VA: Research Foundation of the Institute of Chartered Financial Analysts.

Clarke, Roger G., and Meir Statman. 1998. "Bullish or Bearish." *Financial Analysts Journal* 54, no. 3 (May–June): 63–72.

Claus, James, and Jacob Thomas. 2001. "Equity Premium as Low as 3 Percent? Evidence from Analysts Earnings Forecasts for Domestic and International Stock Markets." *Journal of Finance* 56, no. 5 (October): 1629–1666.

Clayman, Michelle. 1987. "In Search of Excellence: The Investor's Viewpoint." *Financial Analysts Journal* 43, no. 3 (May–June): 54–63.

Clements, Jonathan. 1997a. "Retirement Honing: How Much Should You Have Saved for a Comfortable Life?" *Wall Street Journal,* January 28, p. C1.

Clements, Jonathan. 1997b. "Squeezing the Right Amount from a Retirement Stash." *Wall Street Journal,* February 25, p. C1.

Clements, Jonathan. 1997c. "Jam Today or Jam Tomorrow? Roth IRA Will Show Many Investors It Pays to Wait." *Wall Street Journal,* September 16, p. C1.

Coggin, Daniel T., Frank J. Fabozzi, and Shafiqur Rahman. 1993. "The Investment Performance of U.S. Equity Pension Fund Managers: An Empirical Investigation." *Journal of Finance* 48, no. 3 (July): 1039–1055.

Cohen, Abby J. 1996. "Economic Forecasts and the Asset Allocation Decision." In *Economic Analysis for Investment Professionals.* Charlottesville, VA: AIMR, November.

Cohen, Abby J., and Gabrielle Napolitano, eds. 2001. *Investment Strategy Chartbook.* New York: Goldman Sachs.

Colby, Robert W., and Thomas A. Mayers. 1988. *The Encyclopedia of Technical Market Indicators.* Homewood, IL: Dow Jones–Irwin.

Connor, Gregory. 1995. "The Three Types of Factor Models: A Comparison of Their Explanatory Power." *Financial Analysts Journal* 51, no. 3 (May/June): 42–46.

Connor, Gregory, and Robert A. Korajczyk. 1993. "A Test for the Number of Factors in an Approximate Factor Model." *Journal of Finance* 48, no. 4 (September): 1263–1291.

Cooper, Richard V. L. 1974. "Efficient Capital Markets and the Quantity Theory of Money." *Journal of Finance* 29, no. 3 (June): 887–908.

Cornell, Bradford. 1985. "Taxes and the Pricing of Stock Index Futures: Empirical Results." *Journal of Futures Markets* 5, no. 1: 89–101.

Cornell, Bradford. 1993. *Corporate Valuation.* Burr Ridge, IL: Irwin Professional.

Cornell, Bradford, and Marc R. Reinganum. 1981. "Forward and Futures Prices: Evidence from Foreign Exchange Markets." *Journal of Finance* 36, no. 5 (December): 1035–1045.

Corrado, Charles J., and Thomas W. Miller, Jr. 1996. "Efficient Option-Implied Volatility Estimators." *Journal of Futures Markets* 16, no. 3 (June): 247–272.

Cossin, Didier, and Hugues Pirotte. 2000. *Advanced Credit Risk Analysis.* Hoboken, NJ: Wiley.

Cox, John C., Jonathan Ingersoll, and Stephen Ross. 1981. "The Relation between Forward Prices and Futures Prices," *Journal of Financial Economics* 9, no. 4 (December): 321–346.

Cox, John C., Stephen A. Ross, and Mark Rubinstein. 1979. "Option Pricing: A Simplified Approach." *Journal of Financial Economics* 7, no. 3 (September): 229–264.

Cox, John C., and Mark Rubinstein. 1985. *Option Markets.* Englewood Cliffs, NJ: Prentice Hall.

Crabbe, Leland E., and Joseph D. Argilagos. 1994. "Anatomy of the Structured Note Market." *Journal of Applied Corporate Finance* 7, no. 3 (Fall): 85–98.

Craig, Susanne, and Kate Kelly. 2004. "NYSE Chief Has Balancing Act." *Wall Street Journal,* February 3, pp. C1, C4.

Damodaran, Aswath. 2002. *Investment Valuation,* 2nd ed. New York: Wiley.

Damodaran, Aswath. 2006. *Damodaran on Valuation,* 2nd ed. New York: Wiley.

Daniel, Kent, Mark Grinblatt, Sheridan Titman, and Russ Wermers. 1997. "Measuring Mutual Fund Performance with Characteristics-Based Portfolios." *Journal of Finance* 52, no. 3 (July): 1035–1058.

Danielson, M. G. 1998. "A Simple Valuation Model and Growth Expectations." *Financial Analysts Journal* 54, no. 3 (May–June): 50–57.

Das, Satyajit. 2005. *Structured Products Volume 2: Equity; Commodity; Credit & New Markets,* 3rd ed. New York: John Wiley.

Dattatreya, Ravi E., and Frank J. Fabozzi. 1995. *Active Total Return Management of Fixed-Income Portfolios,* rev. ed. Burr Ridge, IL: Irwin Professional.

Davidson, Lawrence S., and Richard T. Froyen. 1982. "Monetary Policy and Stock Returns: Are Stock Markets Efficient?" Federal Reserve Bank of St. Louis *Review* 64, no. 3 (March): 3–12.

Davidson, Steve. 2001 "Core Plus Bond Strategies: The Investor Search for Higher Returns." *Community Banker* 2, no. 7 (July).

DeBondt, Werner F. M., and Richard Thaler. 1985. "Does the Stock Market Overreact?" *Journal of Finance* 40, no. 3 (July): 793–805.

DeFusco, Richard A., Dennis W. McLeavey, Jerald E. Pinto, and David E. Runkle. 2004. *Quantitative Methods for Investment Analysis,* 2nd ed. Charlottesville, VA: CFA Institute.

Degennaro, Ramon P., and Cesare Robotti. 2007. "Financial Market Frictions." *Economic Review* 92, no. 3 (Third Quarter): 1–16.

Del Guercio, Diane, "The Distorting Effect of the Prudent-Man Laws on Institutional Equity Investments," *Journal of Financial Economics* 40, no. 1 (January 1996), 31–62

DeMark, Thomas R. 1999. *The New Science of Technical Analysis.* New York: Wiley.

Dennis, Patrick, Steven Perfect, Karl Snow, and Kenneth Wiles. 1995. "The Effects of Rebalancing on Size and Book-to-Market

Ratio Portfolio Returns." *Financial Analysts Journal* 51, no. 3 (May–June): 47–57.

Der Hovanesian, Mara. 2004. "Put the Big Board on the Big Board." *BusinessWeek,* September 13, pp. 90–91.

Desai, H., and P. Jain. 1999. "Firm Performance and Focus: Long-Run Stock Market Performance Following Spin-offs." *Journal of Financial Economics* 54, no. 1 (February): 75–102.

De Servigney, Arnaud, and Olivier Renault. 2004. *Measuring and Managing Credit Risk.* New York: McGraw-Hill.

Dhrymes, Phoebus J., Irwin Friend, Mustofa N. Gultekin, and N. Bulent Gultekin. 1985. "New Tests of the APT and Their Implications." *Journal of Finance* 40, no. 3 (July): 659–674.

Dhrymes, Phoebus J., Irwin Friend, and N. Bulent Gultekin. 1984. "A Critical Re-examination of the Empirical Evidence on the Arbitrage Pricing Theory." *Journal of Finance* 39, no. 2 (June): 323–346.

Dialynas, Chris P., and Alfred Murata. 2006. "The Active Decisions in the Selection of Passive Management and Performance Bogeys." In *Active Bond Portfolio Management,* eds. Frank J. Fabbozzi, Lionel Martellini, and Philippe Priaulet. Hoboken, NJ: John Wiley.

Dialynas, Chris P., and David H. Edington. 1992. "Bond Yield Spreads—A Postmodern View." *Journal of Portfolio Management* 19, no. 1 (Fall): 60–75.

Diermeier, Jeffrey J. 1990. "Capital Market Expectations: The Macro Factors." In *Managing Investment Portfolios: A Dynamic Process,* 2nd ed., eds. John L. Maginn and Donald L. Tuttle. Boston: Warren, Gorham, & Lamont.

Dietz, Peter O., and Jeannette R. Kirschman. 1990. "Evaluating Portfolio Performance." In *Managing Investment Portfolios,* 2nd ed., ed. J. Maginn and D. Tuttle. Boston: Warren, Gorham, & Lamont.

Dimson, E. 1979. "Risk Management When Shares Are Subject to Infrequent Trading." *Journal of Financial Economics* 7, no. 2 (June): 197–226.

Douglas, G. W. 1969. "Risk in the Equity Markets: An Empirical Appraisal of Market Efficiency." *Yale Economic Essays* 9, no. 1: 3–48.

Dopfel, Frederick E. 2003. "Asset Allocation in a Lower Stock-Bond Correlation Environment." *Journal of Portfolio Management* 30, no. 1 (Fall).

Dow Jones Investor's Handbook. Princeton, NJ: Dow Jones Books (annual).

Dreman, David M. 1998. *Contrarian Investment Strategies: The Next Generation.* New York: Simon & Schuster.

Droms, William G., ed. 1991. *Initiating and Managing a Global Investment Program.* Charlottesville, VA: AIMR.

Dubofsky, David A., and Thomas W. Miller. 2003. *Derivatives: Valuation and Risk Management.* New York: Oxford University Press.

DuBois, Charles H. 1992. "Tactical Asset Allocation: A Review of Current Techniques." In *Active Asset Allocation,* ed. R. Arnott and F. Fabozzi. Chicago: Probus.

Dudley, William C., and Jan Hatzius. 2000. "The Goldman Sachs Financial Conditions Index: The Right Tool for a New Monetary Policy Regime." *Goldman Sachs Global Economics Paper,* no. 44 (June 8). New York: Goldman Sachs Global Research.

Dudley, William C., and Edward F. McKelvey. January 1997. "The Brave New Business Cycle: No Recession in Sight." *U.S. Economics Research,* Goldman Sachs.

Duffie, Darrell. 1999. "Credit Swap Valuation." *Financial Analysts Journal* 55, no. 1 (January/February): pp. 73–87.

Dumbolena, I. G., and J. M. Shulman. 1988. "A Primary Rule of Detecting Bankruptcy: Watch the Cash." *Financial Analysts Journal* 44, no. 5 (September– October): 74–78.

Dunetz, Mark L., and James M. Mahoney. 1988. "Using Duration and Convexity in the Analysis of Callable Bonds." *Financial Analysts Journal* 44, no. 3 (May–June): 53–73.

Durand, David. 1957. "Growth Stocks and the Petersburg Paradox." *Journal of Finance* 12, no. 3 (September): 348–363.

Dutta, Prajit, and Ananth Madhaven. 1997. "Competition and Collusion in Dealer Markets." *Journal of Finance* 52, no. 1 (March): 245–276.

Dwyer, Paula, A. Osterland, K. Capell, and S. Reier. 1998. "The 21st Century Stock Market." *BusinessWeek,* August 10, pp. 66–72.

Dybvig, Philip H., and Stephen A. Ross. 1985. "Yes, The APT Is Testable." *Journal of Finance* 40, no. 4 (September): 1173–1188.

Easley, David, Nicholas Kiefer, and Maureen O'Hara. 1996. "Cream-Skimming or Profit Sharing? The Curious Role of Purchased Order Flow." *Journal of Finance* 51, no. 3 (July): 811–833.

Eavis, Peter. "Time for Fannie, Freddie?" 2008. *Wall Street Journal,* July 8, C14.

Economides, Nicholas, and Robert A. Schwartz. 1995. "Electronic Call Market Trading." *Journal of Portfolio Management* 21, no. 3 (Spring): 10–18.

Ederington, L. H. 1985. "Why Split Ratings Occur." *Financial Management* 14, no. 1 (Spring): 37–47.

Edwards, Franklin. 1993. "Listing of Foreign Securities on U.S. Exchanges." *Journal of Applied Corporate Finance* 5, no. 4 (Winter): 28–36.

Edwards, R. D., and John Magee, Jr. 1992. *Technical Analysis of Stock Trends,* 6th ed. Boston: New York Institute of Finance.

Eichholtz, A. 1996. "Does International Diversification Work Better for Real Estate than for Stocks and Bonds?" *Financial Analysts Journal* 52, no. 1 (January–February): 56–62.

Elton, Edwin J., and Martin J. Gruber, eds. 1990. *Japanese Capital Markets.* New York: Harper & Row.

Elton, Edwin J., Martin J. Gruber, and Christopher R. Blake. 1996. "The Persistence of Risk-Adjusted Mutual Fund Performance." *Journal of Business* 69, no. 2 (April): 133–157.

Elton, Edwin J., Martin J. Gruber, Stephen J. Brown, and William N. Goetzmann. 2006. *Modern Portfolio Theory and Investment Analysis,* 7th ed. New York: Wiley.

Elton, Edwin J., Martin J. Gruber, and Joel Rentzler. 1983. "A Single Examination of the Empirical Relationship between Dividend Yields and Deviations from the CAPM." *Journal of Banking and Finance* 7, no. 1 (March): 135–146.

Emmons, William R. 1997. "Indexed Bonds and Falling Inflation Expectations." Federal Reserve Bank of St. Louis *Monetary Trends* (September).

Emmons, William R. 1999. "What Can 'Buy-and-Hold' Stock Investors Expect?" Federal Reserve Bank of St. Louis *Monetary Trends* (June).

Ennis Knupp & Associates. 2004. *Private Equity Overview.* (January).

Evans, John, and Stephen Archer. 1968. "Diversification and the Reduction of Dispersion: An Empirical Analysis." *Journal of Finance* 23, no. 5 (December): 761–767.

Evans, Thomas G., Martin E. Taylor, and Oscar Holzmann. 1985. *International Accounting and Reporting.* New York: Macmillan.

Ewing, Terzah, and Silvia Ascarelli. 2000. "One World, How Many Stock Exchanges?" *Wall Street Journal,* May 15, p. C1.

Ezra, D. Don. 1998. "Strategic Asset Allocation and Total Portfolio Returns." In *Asset Allocation in a Changing World.* Charlottesville, VA: AIMR.

Fabozzi, Frank J. 1988. *Fixed-Income Mathematics.* Chicago: Probus.

Fabozzi, Frank J., ed. 1989. *Advances and Innovations in the Bond and Mortgage Markets.* Chicago: Probus.

Fabozzi, Frank J., ed. 1990a. *The Japanese Bond Markets.* Chicago: Probus.

Fabozzi, Frank J., ed. 1990b. *The New High-Yield Debt Market.* New York: Harper Business.

Fabozzi, Frank J. 2007. *Fixed-Income Analysis,* 2nd ed. Hoboken, NJ: Wiley.

Fabozzi, Frank J., ed. 2004. *Fixed-Income Readings,* 2nd ed. Hoboken, NJ: Wiley.

Fabozzi, Frank J. 2007. *Bond Markets, Analysis and Strategies,* 6th ed. Upper Saddle River, NJ: Pearson Prentice Hall.

Fabozzi, Frank J., Steven V. Mann, and Mourad Choudhry. "Interest Rate Swaps and Swaptions." In *The Handbook of Fixed-Income Securities,* 7th ed. New York: McGraw-Hill.

Fabozzi, Frank J., Gerald W. Buetow, and Robert R. Johnson. 2005. "Measuring Interest Rate Risk." In *The Handbook of Fixed-Income Securities,* 7th ed., ed. Frank J. Fabozzi. New York: McGraw-Hill.

Fabozzi, Frank J. 2005. "Bond Immunization: An Asset/Liability Optimization Strategy." In *The Handbook of Fixed-Income Securities,* 7th ed., ed. Frank J. Fabozzi. New York: McGraw-Hill.

Fabozzi, Frank J. 2005. "Dedicated Bond Portfolios." In *The Handbook of Fixed-Income Securities,* 7th ed., ed. Frank J. Fabozzi. New York: McGraw-Hill.

Fabozzi, Frank J., Andrew J. Kalotay, and George O. Williams. 2005. "Valuation of Bonds with Embedded Options." In *The Handbook of Fixed-Income Securities,* 7th ed., ed. Frank J. Fabozzi. New York: McGraw-Hill.

Fabozzi, Frank J., and Christopher K. Ma. 1988. "The Over-the-Counter Market and New York Stock Exchange Trading Halts." *Financial Review* 23, no. 4 (November): 427–437.

Fabozzi, Frank J., and Chuck Ramsey. 2005. "Mortgages and Overview of Mortgage-Backed Securities." In *The Handbook of Fixed-Income Securities,* 7th ed., ed. Frank J. Fabozzi. New York: McGraw-Hill.

Fabozzi, Frank J., Richard Wilson, and Richard Todd. 2005. "Corporate Bonds." In *The Handbook of Fixed-Income Securities,* 7th ed., ed. Frank J. Fabozzi. New York: McGraw-Hill.

Fairfield, Patricia. 1994. "P/E, P/B, and the Present Value of Future Dividends." *Financial Analysts Journal* 50, no. 4 (July–August): 23–31.

Fama, Eugene F. 1970. "Efficient Capital Markets: A Review of Theory and Empirical Work." *Journal of Finance* 25, no. 2 (May): 383–417.

Fama, Eugene F. 1972. "Components of Investment Performance." *Journal of Finance* 27, no. 3 (June): 551–567.

Fama, Eugene F. 1976. "Forward Rates as Predictors of Future Spot Rates." *Journal of Financial Economics* 3, no. 4 (October): 361–377.

Fama, Eugene F. 1981. "Stock Returns, Real Activity, Inflation, and Money." *American Economic Review* 71, no. 4 (September): 545–565.

Fama, Eugene F. 1991a. "Efficient Capital Markets: II." *Journal of Finance* 46, no. 5 (December): 1575–1617.

Fama, Eugene F. 1991b. "Stock Returns, Real Activity, Inflation and Money." *American Economic Review* 71, no. 2 (June): 545–565.

Fama, Eugene. 1998. "Market Efficiency, Long-Term Returns, and Behavioral Finance." *Journal of Financial Economics* 49, no. 3 (September): 283–306.

Fama, Eugene F., L. Fisher, M. Jensen, and R. Roll. 1969. "The Adjustment of Stock Prices to New Information." *International Economic Review* 10, no. 1 (February): 1–21.

Fama, Eugene F., and Kenneth French. 1989. "Business Conditions and Expected Returns on Stocks and Bonds." *Journal of Financial Economics* 25, no. 1 (November): 23–49.

Fama, Eugene F., and Kenneth French. 1992. "The Cross Section of Expected Stock Returns." *Journal of Finance* 47, no. 2 (June): 427–465.

Fama, Eugene F., and Kenneth R. French. 1993. "Common Risk Factors in the Returns on Stocks and Bonds." *Journal of Financial Economics* 33, no. 1 (January): 3–56.

Fama, Eugene F., and Kenneth French. 1995. "Size and Book-to-Market Factors in Earnings and Returns." *Journal of Finance* 50, no. 1 (March): 131–155.

Fama, Eugene F., and Kenneth French. 1996. "Multifactor Explanations of Asset Pricing Anomalies." *Journal of Finance* 51, no. 1 (March): 55–84.

Fama, Eugene F., and Kenneth R. French. 1998. "Value versus Growth: The International Evidence." *Journal of Finance* 53, no. 6 (December): 1975–1999.

Fama, Eugene F., and Merton H. Miller. 1972. *The Theory of Finance.* New York: Holt, Rinehart and Winston.

Farinella, Joseph A., Edward Graham, and Cynthia McDonald. 2001. "Does High Short Interest Lead Underperformance?" *Journal of Investing* 10, no. 2 (Summer).

Farrell, James L. 1985. "The Dividend Discount Model: A Primer." *Financial Analysts Journal* 41, no. 6 (November–December): 16–25.

Farrell, James L., Jr. 1997. *Portfolio Management Theory and Application,* 2nd ed. New York: McGraw-Hill.

Feibel, Bruce J. 2003. *Investment Performance Measurement.* Hoboken, NJ: Wiley.

Feldstein, Sylvan G. 2005. "Guidelines in the Credit Analysis of General Obligation and Revenue Municipal Bonds." In *The Handbook of Fixed-Income Securities,* 7th ed., ed. Frank J. Fabozzi. New York: McGraw-Hill.

Feldstein, Sylvan, Frank J. Fabozzi, and Patrick M. Kennedy. 2005. "Municipal Bonds." In *The Handbook of Fixed-Income Securities,* 7th ed., ed. Frank J. Fabozzi. New York: McGraw-Hill.

Ferguson, Robert, and Dean Leistikow. 1998. "Are Regression Approach Futures Hedge Ratios Stationary?" *Journal of Futures Markets* 18, no. 7 (October): 851–866.

Fernholz, Robert, Robert Garvy, and John Hannon. 1998. "Diversity-Weighted Indexing." *Journal of Portfolio Management* 24, no. 2 (Winter): 74–82.

Ferris, Stephen P., and Anil K. Makhija. 1987. "A Search for Common Stock Inflation Hedges." *Review of Business and Economic Research* 22, no. 2 (Spring): 27–36.

Ferson, Wayne E., and Rudi W. Schadt. 1996. "Measuring Fund Strategy and Performance in Changing Economic Conditions." *Journal of Finance* 52, no. 2 (June): 425–461.

Fielitz, Bruce D. 1983. "Calculating the Bond Equivalent Yield for T-Bills." *Journal of Portfolio Management* 9, no. 3 (Spring): 58–60.

Figlewski, Stephen. 1989a. "Options Arbitrage in Imperfect Markets." *Journal of Finance* 44, no. 5 (December): 1289–1311.

Figlewski, Stephen. 1989b. "What Does an Option Pricing Model Tell Us about Option Prices?" *Financial Analysts Journal* 45, no. 5 (September–October): 12–15.

Finkel, Sidney R., and Donald L. Tuttle. 1971. "Determinants of the Aggregate Profit Margin." *Journal of Finance* 26, no. 5 (December): 1067–1075.

Finnerty, John D. 1983. "Evaluating the Economics of Refunding High-Coupon Sinking-Fund Debt." *Financial Management* 12, no. 1 (Spring): 5–10.

Finnerty, John D. 1992. "An Overview of Corporate Securities Innovation." *Journal of Applied Corporate Finance* 4, no. 4 (Winter).

Finnerty, John D., and Dean Leistikow. 1993. "The Behavior of Equity and Debt Risk Premiums." *Journal of Portfolio Management* 19, no. 4 (Summer): 73–84.

Fisher, Irving. 1961. *The Theory of Interest.* New York: Augustus M. Kelley. (Orig. publ. Macmillan, 1930)

Fisher, Kenneth L. 1984. *SuperStocks.* Woodside, CA: Business Classics.

Fisher, Lawrence. 1959. "Determinants of Risk Premiums on Corporate Bonds." *Journal of Political Economy* 67, no. 3 (June): 217–237.

Fisher, Lawrence, and James H. Lorie. 1977. *A Half Century of Returns on Stocks and Bonds.* Chicago: University of Chicago Graduate School of Business.

Fisher, Lawrence, and Roman L. Weil. 1971. "Coping with the Risk of Interest-Rate Fluctuations: Returns to Bondholders from Naive and Optimal Strategies." *Journal of Business* 44, no. 4 (October): 408–431.

Fisher, Phillip A. 1984. *Common Stocks and Uncommon Profits.* Woodside, CA: PSR Publications. (Orig. publ. Harper, 1958)

Fogler, H. Russell. 1993. "A Modern Theory of Security Analysis." *Journal of Portfolio Management* 19, no. 3 (Spring): 6–14.

Fogler, H. Russell, ed. 1994. *Blending Quantitative and Traditional Equity Analysis: March 30–31, 1994, Boston, Massachusetts.* Charlottesville, VA: AIMR.

Fogler, H. Russell, ed. 2001. *Developments in Quantitative Investment Models.* Charlottesville, VA: AIMR.

Fong, Gifford, Charles Pearson, and Oldrich Vasicek. 1983. "Bond Performance: Analyzing Sources of Return." *Journal of Portfolio Management* 9, no. 3 (Spring): 46–50.

Fong, Gifford, Charles Pearson, Oldrich Vasicek, and Theresa Conroy. 1991. "Fixed-Income Portfolio Performance: Analyzing Sources of Returns." In *The Handbook of Fixed-Income Securities,* 3rd ed., ed. Frank J. Fabozzi. Homewood, IL: Business One-Irwin.

Fong, H. Gifford. 2001. "Bond Management: Past, Current, and Future." In *The Handbook of Fixed-Income Securities,* 6th ed., ed. Frank J. Fabozzi. New York: McGraw-Hill.

Fons, Jerome S. 1991. "An Approach to Forecasting Default Rates." New York: Moody's Investors Services, August.

Foster, F. D., and S. Viswanathan. 1993. "The Effects of Public Information and Competition on Trading Volume and Price Volatility." *Review of Financial Studies* 6, no. 1 (Spring): 23–56.

Fowler, Gordon B., Jr. 2007. "Understanding 130/30 Equity Strategies." *CFA Institute Conference Proceedings Quarterly* (September): 11-16.

Francis, Jack Clark, William W. Toy, and J. Gregg Whittaker. 2000. *The Handbook of Equity Derivatives.* New York: John Wiley.

Frecka, Thomas J., and Cheng F. Lee. 1983. "Generalized Financial Ratio Adjustment Processes and Their Implications." *Journal of Accounting Research* 27, no. 1 (Spring).

Fridson, Martin. 1989. *High-Yield Bonds: Assessing Risk and Identifying Value in Speculative Grade Securities.* Chicago: Probus.

Fridson, Martin S. 1994. "The State of the High-Yield Bond Market: Overshooting or Return to Normalcy." *Journal of Applied Corporate Finance* 7, no. 1 (Spring): 85–97.

Fridson, Martin S. 2002. "This Year in High Yield—2001." Merrill Lynch *Extra Credit* (January–February).

Friedman, Milton. 1969. *The Optimum Quantity of Money and Other Essays.* Chicago: Aldine.

Friedman, Milton, and Leonard J. Savage. 1948. "The Utility Analysis of Choices Involving Risk." *Journal of Political Economy* 56, no. 3 (August): 279–304.

Friedman, Milton, and Anna J. Schwartz. 1963. "Money and Business Cycles." *Review of Economics and Statistics* 45, no. 1, part 2, supplement (February): 32–78.

Friend, Irwin, and Marshall Blume. 1970. "Measurement of Portfolio Performance under Uncertainty." *American Economic Review* 60, no. 4 (September): 561–575.

Friend, Irwin, Marshall Blume, and Jean Crockett. 1970. *Mutual Funds and Other Institutional Investors.* New York: McGraw-Hill.

Fung, William, and David A Hsieh. 2006. "Hedge Funds: An Industry in its Adolescence." *Economic Review* 91, no. 4 (Fourth Quarter): pp. 1-33.

Galai, Dan, and Meir I. Schneller. 1978. "Pricing Warrants and the Value of the Firm." *Journal of Finance* 33, no. 5 (December): 1333–1342.

Gall, Carlotta. 1998. "Moscow Stock Market Falls by 11.8%." *Financial Times,* May 19, p. 1.

Garman, Mark B., and Steven W. Kohlhagen. 1983. "Foreign Currency Option Values." *Journal of International Money and Finance* 2, no. 3 (December): 231–237.

Gastineau, Gary. 1988. *The Options Manual,* 3rd ed. New York: McGraw-Hill.

Gastineau, Gary. 1993. "Using Swaps in Equity Portfolios." In *Derivative Strategies for Managing Portfolio Risk,* ed. K. Brown. Charlottesville, VA: AIMR.

Gastineau, Gary. 2001. "Exchange-Traded Funds: An Introduction." *Journal of Portfolio Management* 27, no. 3 (Spring): 88–96.

Gastineau, Gary L., and Sanjiv Bhatia, eds. 1995. *Risk Management.* Proceedings of a seminar by the Association for Investment Management and Research. Charlottesville, VA: AIMR.

Gastineau, Gary L., and Mark P. Kritzman. 2001. *Dictionary of Financial Risk Management,* 3rd ed. New York: Wiley.

Gentry, James A., Paul Newbold, and David T. Whitford. 1985a. "Classifying Bankrupt Firms with Funds Flow Components." *Journal of Accounting Research* 23, no. 1 (Spring).

Gentry, James A., Paul Newbold, and David T. Whitford. 1985b. "Predicting Bankruptcy: If Cash Flow's Not the Bottom Line, What Is?" *Financial Analysts Journal* 41, no. 5 (September–October): 47–56.

Gentry, James A., David T. Whitford, and Paul Newbold. 1988. "Predicting Industrial Bond Ratings with a Profit Model and Funds Flow Components." *Financial Review* 23, no. 3 (August): 269–286.

Gervais, S., and T. Odean. 2001. "Learning to be Overconfident," *Review of Financial Studies* 14:1–27.

Geske, Robert. 1979. "A Note on an Analytical Valuation Formula for Unprotected American Call Options on Stocks with Known Dividends." *Journal of Financial Economics* 7, no. 4 (June): 375–380.

Geweke, John, and Guofu Zhou. 1996. "Measuring the Price of the Arbitrage Pricing Theory." *Review of Financial Studies* 9, no. 2 (Summer): 557–587.

Gibbons, Michael. 1982. "Multivariate Tests of Financial Models: A New Approach." *Journal of Financial Economics* 10, no. 1 (March): 3–28.

Glickstein, David A., and Rolf E. Wubbels. 1983. "Dow Theory Is Alive and Well." *Journal of Portfolio Management* 9, no. 3 (Spring): 28–32.

Global Investment Performance Standards. 1999. Charlottesville, VA: AIMR.

Goetzmann, William N., and Roger G. Ibbotson. 1990. "The Performance of Real Estate as an Asset Class." *Journal of Applied Corporate Finance* 3, no. 1 (Spring): 65–76.

Gombola, M. F., M. E. Haskins, J. E. Katz, and D. D. Williams. 1987. "Cash Flow in Bankruptcy Prediction." *Financial Management* 16, no. 4 (Winter): 55–65.

Goodman, D. A., and John W. Peavy, III. 1983. "Industry Relative Price-Earnings Ratios as Indicators of Investment Returns." *Financial Analysts Journal* 39, no. 2 (March–April): 60–66.

Goodwin, Thomas H. 1998. "The Information Ratio." *Financial Analysts Journal* 54, no. 4 (July–August): 34–43.

Gordon, Myron J. 1962. *The Investment, Financing, and Valuation of the Corporation.* Homewood, IL: Irwin.

Grabbe, J. Orlin. 1986. *International Financial Markets.* New York: Elsevier Science.

Gray, H. Peter. 1976. "Determinants of the Aggregate Profit Margin: A Comment." *Journal of Finance* 31, no. 1 (March): 163–165.

Greenberg, Herb. 2000. "Alphabet Dupe: Why EBITDA Falls Short." *Fortune* 10 (July): 240–241.

Grinblatt, Mark, and Narasimhan Jegadeesh. 1996. "Relative Pricing of Eurodollar Futures and Forward Contracts." *Journal of Finance* 51, no. 4 (September): 1499–1522.

Grinblatt, Mark, and Sheridan Titman. 1992. "The Persistence of Mutual Fund Performance." *Journal of Finance* 47, no. 5 (June): 1977–1984.

Grinblatt, Mark, and Sheridan Titman. 1993. "Performance Measurement without Benchmarks: An Examination of Mutual Fund Returns." *Journal of Business* 66, no. 1 (January): 47–68.

Grinblatt, Mark, and Sheridan Titman. 1995. "Performance Evaluation." In *Handbook in Operations Research and Management Science,* ed. R. Jarrow et al. New York: Elsevier Science B.V.

Grinold, Richard C. 1992. "Are Benchmark Portfolios Efficient?" *Journal of Performance Management* 19, no. 1 (Fall): 34–40.

Grinold, Richard C., and Ronald N. Kahn. 1994. "Multiple-Factor Models for Portfolio Risk." In *A Practitioner's Guide to*

Factor Models, ed. John Peavy. Charlottesville, VA: Research Foundation of the Institute of Chartered Financial Analysts.

Grinold, Richard C., and Ronald N. Kahn. 2000. *Active Portfolio Management,* 2nd ed. New York: McGraw-Hill.

Grossman, Sanford J., and Merton H. Miller. 1988. "Liquidity and Market Structure." *Journal of Finance* 43, no. 3 (July): 617–633.

Grundy, Kevin, and Burton Malkiel. 1996. "Reports of Beta's Death Have Been Greatly Exaggerated." *Journal of Portfolio Management* 22, no. 3 (Spring): 36–44.

Gudikunst, Arthur, and Joseph McCarthy. 1992. "Determinants of Bond Mutual Fund Performance." *Journal of Fixed Income* 2, no. 1 (June): 95–101.

Guerico, Diane Del. 1996. "The Distorting Effect of the Prudent-Man Laws on Institutional Equity Investments." *Journal of Financial Economics* 40, no. 1 (January): 31–62.

Gultekin, Mustofa N., and N. Bulent Gultekin. 1987. "Stock Return Anomalies and the Tests of APT." *Journal of Finance* 42, no. 5 (December): 1213–1224.

Gumbel, Peter. 1995. "The Hard Sell: Getting Germans to Invest in Stocks." *Wall Street Journal,* August 4, p. A2.

Hackel, Kenneth S., and Joshua Livnat. 1996. *Cash Flow and Security Analysis,* 2nd ed. Burr Ridge, IL: Irwin Professional.

Hafer, R. W. 1985. "The Response of Stock Prices to Changes in Weekly Money and the Discount Rate." Federal Reserve Bank of St. Louis *Review* 64, no. 3 (March): 5–14.

Hagerty, James R., and Serena Ng. 2008. "Mortgage Giants Take Beating on Fears over Loan Defaults," *Wall Street Journal,* July 8, A1, A14.

Hagstrom, Robert G. 2001. *The Essential Buffett.* New York: Wiley.

Hamao, Yasushi. 1989. "Japanese Stocks, Bonds, Inflation, 1973–1987." *Journal of Portfolio Management* 16, no. 2 (Winter): 20–26.

Handa, Puneet, S. P. Kothari, and Charles Wasley. 1989. "The Relation between the Return Interval and Betas: Implications of the Size Effect." *Journal of Financial Economics* 23, no. 1 (June): 79–100.

Handa, Puneet, and Robert A. Schwartz. 1996. "How Best to Supply Liquidity to a Securities Market." *Journal of Portfolio Management* 22, no. 2 (Winter): 44–51.

Hanks, Sara. 1990. "SEC Ruling Creates a New Market." *Wall Street Journal,* May 16, p. A12.

Hardy, Eric S. 1995. "The Ground Floor." *Forbes,* August 14, p. 185.

Harlow, W. V. 1991. "Asset Allocation in a Downside Risk Framework." *Financial Analysts Journal* 47, no. 5 (September/October): pp. 28-40.

Harlow, W. V., and Keith C. Brown, 2006, "The Right Answer to the Wrong Question: Identifying Superior Active Portfolio Management." *Journal of Investment Management* 4, no. 4 (Fourth Quarter): 15-40.

Harrington, Diana R. 1987. *Modern Portfolio Theory, the Capital Asset Pricing Model, and Arbitrage Pricing Theory: A User's Guide,* 2nd ed. Englewood Cliffs, NJ: Prentice Hall.

Harris, Diane. 1984. "An Investment for Rent." *Money,* April, pp. 87–90.

Harris, Jeffrey, and Paul Schultz. 1998. "The Trading Profits of SOES Bandits." *Journal of Financial Economics* 50, no. 1 (October): 39–62.

Harris, Larry. 2003. *Trading and Exchanges.* New York: Oxford University Press.

Harris, R. S. 1980. "The Refunding of Discounted Debt: An Adjusted Present Value Analysis." *Financial Management* 9, no. 4 (Winter): 7–12.

Hasbrouck, Joel. 1993. "Assessing the Quality of a Security Market: A New Approach to Transaction-Cost Measurement." *Review of Financial Studies* 6, no. 1.

Hasbrouck, Joel. 1995. "One Security, Many Markets: Determining the Contribution to Price Discovery." *Journal of Finance* 50, no. 4 (September): 1175–1200.

Haugen, Robert A., and Nardin L. Baker. 1996. "Commonality in the Determinants of Expected Stock Returns." *Journal of Financial Economics* 41, no. 3 (July): 401–439.

Hawawini, Gabriel. 1983. "Why Beta Shifts as the Return Interval Changes." *Financial Analysts Journal* 39, no. 3 (May–June): 73–77.

Hawawini, Gabriel. 1984. *European Equity Markets: Price Behavior and Efficiency.* Monograph Series in Finance and Economics, monograph no. 1984-4/5. New York: Salomon Brothers Center for the Study of Financial Institutions, Graduate School of Business, New York University.

Hawthorne, Fran. 1986. "The Battle of the Bond Indexes." *Institutional Investor* 20, no. 4 (April).

Hayre, Lakhbir, and Hubert Chang. 1997. "Effective and Empirical Durations of Mortgage Securities." *Journal of Fixed Income* 6, no. 4 (March): 17–33.

Hayre, Lakhbir S., Cyrus Mohebbi, and Thomas A. Zimmerman. 2005. "Mortgage Pass-Throughs." In *The Handbook of Fixed-Income Securities,* 7th ed., ed. Frank J. Fabozzi. New York: McGraw-Hill.

Heckle, Kenneth S., and Joshua Livnat. 1996. *Cash Flow and Security Analysis,* 2nd ed. Burr Ridge, IL: Business One–Irwin.

Helfert, Erich A. 2002. *Techniques of Financial Analysis,* 11th ed. New York: McGraw-Hill/Irwin.

Hendershott, Terrence, and Haim Mendelson. 2000. "Crossing Networks and Dealer Markets: Competition and Performance." *Journal of Finance* 55, no. 5 (October): 2071–2115.

Hendriksson, Roy D., and Robert C. Merton. 1981. "On Market Timing and Investment Performance: Statistical Procedures for Evaluating Forecasting Skills." *Journal of Business* 54, no. 4 (October): 513–534.

Henriques, Diana. 1989. "Don't Take Any Wooden Nickels." *Barron's,* June 19, pp. 16, 18, 20, 32.

Henry, David. 2001. "The Numbers Game." *BusinessWeek,* May 14, pp. 100–110.

Hersey, Brian E. 2001. "Core-Plus: Prospects and Implications." In *Core-Plus Bond Management,* Association for Investment Management and Research. Charlottesville, VA: 11-20.

Hickman, Kent, and Glenn Petry. 1990. "A Comparison of Stock Price Predictions Using Court Accepted Formulas, Dividend Discount, and P/E Models." *Financial Management* (Summer): 76–87.

Hickman, W. Braddock. 1958. *Corporate Bond Quality and Investor Experience.* Princeton, NJ: Princeton University Press.

Hicks, John. 1939. *Value and Capital.* Oxford, UK: Clarendon Press.

Higgins, Robert C. 2005. *Analysis for Financial Management,* 8th ed. New York: McGraw-Hill/Irwin.

Hirschleifer, David. 2001. "Investor Psychology and Asset Pricing." *Journal of Finance* 56, no. 4 (August): 1533–1597.

Holt, Charles C. 1962. "The Influence of Growth Duration on Share Prices." *Journal of Finance* 7, no. 3 (September): 465–475.

Homa, Kenneth, and Dwight Jaffee. 1971. "The Study of Money and Stock Prices." *Journal of Finance* 26, no. 5 (December): 1015–1066.

Homer, Sidney, and Martin L. Leibowitz. 2004. *Inside the Yield Book: The Book that Changed Bond Analysis.* New York: Bloomberg.

Hopewell, Michael H., and George Kaufman. 1973. "Bond Price Volatility and Term to Maturity: A Generalized Respecification." *American Economic Review* 63, no. 4 (September): 749–753.

Hopewell, Michael H., and Arthur L. Schwartz, Jr. 1978. "Temporary Trading Suspensions in Individual NYSE Securities." *Journal of Finance* 33, no. 5 (December): 1355–1373.

Hopkins, Peter J. B., and C. Hayes Miller. 2001. *Country, Sector, and Company Factors in Global Equity Portfolios.* Charlottesville, VA: Research Foundation of AIMR.

Horan, Stephen M., and D. Bruce Johnsen. 2000. *The Welfare Effects of Soft Dollar Brokerage: Law and Economics.* Charlottesville,

VA: Research Foundation of the Institute of Chartered Financial Analysts.

Horowitz, Jed, and Kate Kelly. 2005. "NASD Completes Its Sale of Amex to Member Group." *Wall Street Journal,* January 4, p. C3.

Hourdouvelis, Gikas A. 1988. "The Predictive Power of the Term Structure during Recent Monetary Regimes." *Journal of Finance* 43, no. 2 (June): 339–356.

Howe, John S., and Tie Su. 2001. "Discretionary Reductions in Warrant Exercise Prices." *Journal of Financial Economics* 61, no. 2 (August): 227–252.

Hsu, David H., and Martin Kenney. 2005. "Organizing Venture Capital: The Rise and Demise of American Research & Development Corporation, 1946-1973." *Industrial and Corporate Change* 14, no. 4 (August), pp. 579-616.

Hsueh, L. Paul, and David S. Kidwell. 1988. "Bond Ratings: Are Two Better Than One?" *Financial Management* 17, no. 1 (Spring): 46–53.

Huberman, Gur, and Shmuel Kandel. 1990. "Market Efficiency and Value Line's Record." *Journal of Business* 63, no. 2 (April).

Hudson-Wilson, Susan, and Bernard L. Elbaum. 1995. "Diversification Benefits for Investors in Real Estate." *Journal of Portfolio Management* 21, no. 3 (Spring): 92–99.

Hull, John, and Alan White. 2000. "Valuing Credit Default Swaps I: No Counterparty Default Risk." *Journal of Derivatives* 8, no. 1 (Fall): pp. 29-40.

Hull, John. 2009. *Options, Futures, and Other Derivatives,* 7th ed. Upper Saddle River, NJ: Pearson Education.

Hurley, M., S. Meers, B. Bornstein, and N. Strumingher. 1995. *The Coming Evolution of the Investment Management Industry: Opportunities and Strategies.* New York: Goldman Sachs, October.

Ibbotson Associates. *Stocks, Bonds, Bills, and Inflation.* Chicago: Ibbotson Associates, annual.

Ibbotson, Roger G., and Gary P. Brinson. 1993. *Global Investing.* New York: McGraw-Hill.

Ibbotson, Roger G., and Paul D. Kaplan. 2000. "Does Asset Allocation Policy Explain 40, 90, or 100 Percent of Performance?" *Financial Analysts Journal* 56, no. 1 (January–February): 26–33.

Ibbotson, Roger G., Paul D. Kaplan, and James D. Peterson. 1997. "Estimates of Small-Stock Betas Are Much Too Low." *Journal of Portfolio Management* 23, no. 4 (Summer): 104–111.

Ibbotson, Roger G., Jody Sindelar, and Jay R. Ritter. 1988. "Initial Public Offerings." *Journal of Applied Corporate Finance* 1, no. 3 (Summer).

Ibbotson, Roger G., Jody L. Sindelar, and Jay R. Ritter. 1994. "The Market Problems with the Pricing of Initial Public Offerings." *Journal of Applied Corporate Finance* 7, no. 1 (Spring): 66–74.

Ibbotson, Roger G., and Rex A. Sinquefield. 1982. *Stocks, Bonds, Bills and Inflation: The Past and Future.* Charlottesville, VA: Financial Analysts Research Foundation.

Ibbotson, R. S., M. A. Milevsky, P. Chen, and K. X. Zhu. 2007. *Lifetime Financial Advice: Human Capital Asset Allocation and Insurance.* Charlottesville, VA: The Research Foundation of the CFA Institute.

Imhoff, Eugene, and G. Lobo. 1984. "Information Content of Analysts' Composite Forecast Revisions." *Journal of Accounting Research* 22, no. 3 (Autumn).

Implementing Global Equity Strategy: Spotlight on Asia. 1997. Charlottesville, VA: AIMR.

Ineichen, Alexander M. 2000. "Twentieth Century Volatility." *Journal of Portfolio Management* 27, no. 1 (Fall): 93–101.

Ingersoll, Jonathan E., Jr. 1977. "An Examination of Corporate Call Policies on Convertible Securities." *Journal of Finance* 32, no. 2 (May): 463–478.

Investing Worldwide. Annual conference (beginning 1990) sponsored by the Association for Investment Management and Research (AIMR), Charlottesville, VA.

Ip, Greg. 1998a. "Prices Soften for Exchange Seats." *Wall Street Journal,* May 27, pp. C1, C17.

Ip, Greg. 1998b. "What's Behind the Trailing Performance of the Dow Industrials vs. the S & P 500?" *Wall Street Journal,* August 20, pp. C1, C17.

Ip, Greg. 1999. "Instinet Expands Its Presence." *Wall Street Journal,* July 28, p. C1.

Ip, Greg. 2000. "Margin Debt Set a Record in January, Sparking Fresh Fears Over Speculation." *Wall Street Journal,* February 15, pp. C1, C2.

Ip, Greg. 2001a. "Big Board Specialists: A Profitable Anachronism." *Wall Street Journal,* March 12, p. A10.

Ip, Greg. 2001b. "If Big Board Specialists Are an Anachronism, They're a Profitable One." *Wall Street Journal,* March 12, pp. A1, A10.

Ip, Greg, and Randal Smith. 1999. "Big Board Members Face Off on the Issue of Automated Trading." *Wall Street Journal,* November 15, p. 1.

Iqbal, M. Zafar. 2002. *International Accounting: A Global Approach.* Cincinnati, OH: South-Western.

Ivkovic, A., and N. Jegadeesh. 2004. "The Timing and Value of Forecast and Recommendation Revisions." *Journal of Financial Economics* 73, no. 3 (September): 433–463.

Jacobs, Bruce I., and Kenneth N. Levy. 2007. "20 Myths About Enhanced Active 120-20 Strategies." *Financial Analysts Journal* 63, no. 4 (July-August): 19-26.

Jaffe, Jeffrey F., and Gershon Mandelker. 1976. "The 'Fisher Effect' for Risky Assets: An Empirical Analysis." *Journal of Finance* 31, no. 2 (May): 447–458.

Jaffee, Dwight M. 1975. "Cyclical Variations in the Risk Structure of Interest Rates." *Journal of Monetary Economics* 1, no. 2 (July): 309–325.

Jagannathan, Ravi, and Zhenyu Wang. 1996. "The Conditional CAPM and the Cross Section of Expected Returns." *Journal of Finance* 51, no. 1 (March): 3–53.

Jain, Prom C. 1988. "Response of Hourly Stock Prices and Trading Volume to Economic News." *Journal of Business* 61, no. 2 (April).

James, Christopher, and Robert Edmister. 1983. "The Relation between Common Stock Returns, Trading Activity, and Market Value." *Journal of Finance* 38, no. 4 (September): 1075–1086.

Jegadeesh, Narasimhan. 1990. "Evidence of Predictable Behavior of Security Returns." *Journal of Finance* 45, no. 3 (July): 881–898.

Jegadeesh, Narasimhan, J. Kim, S. Krische, and C. M. Lee. 2004. "Analyzing the Analysts: When Do Recommendations Add Value?" *Journal of Finance* 59, no. 3 (June): 1083–1124.

Jennings, Marianne M. 2000. "Professional Responsibilities, Ethics, and the Law." In *Ethical Issues for Today's Firm.* Charlottesville, VA: AIMR.

Jennings, Robert. 1984. *Reaction of Financial Analysts to Corporate Management Earnings per Share Forecasts.* Monograph no. 20. New York: Financial Analysts Research Foundation.

Jensen, Gerald R., Jeffrey Mercer, and Robert R. Johnson. 1996. "Business Conditions, Monetary Policy, and Expected Security Returns." *Journal of Financial Economics* 40, no. 2 (February): 213–237.

Jensen, Gerald R., Robert R. Johnson, and Jeffrey M. Mercer. 1997. "New Evidence on Size and Price-to-Book Effects in Stock Returns." *Financial Analysts Journal* 53, no. 6 (November–December): 34–42.

Jensen, Gerald R., Robert R. Johnson, and Jeffrey M. Mercer. 1998. "The Inconsistency of Small Firm and Value Stock Premiums." *Journal of Portflio Management* 24, no. 2 (Winter): 27–36.

Jensen, Gerald R., Robert R. Johnson, and Jeffrey M. Mercer. 2000. *The Role of Monetary Policy in Investment Management.* Charlottesville, VA: Research Foundation of AIMR.

Jensen, Michael C. 1968. "The Performance of Mutual Funds in the Period 1945-1964." *Journal of Finance* 23, no. 2 (May): 389–416.

Jensen, Michael C., and Clifford W. Smith, Jr., eds. 1986. "Symposium on Investment Banking and the Capital Acquisition Process." *Journal of Financial Economics* 15, no. 1/2 (January–February): 3–29.

Jensen, Michael C., and Jerald B. Warner. 1988. "The Distribution of Power among Corporate Managers, Shareholders, and Directors." *Journal of Financial Economics* 20, no. 1–2 (January–March): 3–24.

Jesswein, Kurt, Chuck C. Y. Kwok, and William R. Folks. 1995. "What New Currency Risk Products Are Companies Using and Why?" *Journal of Applied Corporate Finance* 8, no. 3 (Fall): 103–114.

Jobson, J. D. 1982. "A Multivariate Linear Regression Test for the Arbitrage Pricing Theory." *Journal of Finance* 37, no. 4 (September): 1037–1042.

Johnson, H. E. 1983. "An Analytic Approximation for the American Put Price." *Journal of Financial and Quantitative Analysis* 18, no. 1 (March): 143–151.

Johnson, Leland L. 1960. "The Theory of Hedging and Speculation in Commodity Futures." *Review of Economic Studies* 27: 139–160.

Johnson, R. S., Lyle Fiore, and Richard Zuber. "The Investment Performance of Common Stocks in Relation to Their Price-Earnings Ratios: An Update of the Basu Study." *Financial Review* 24, no. 3 (August 1989): 499–505.

Jones, Christopher S., 2001, "Extracting Factors From Heteroskedastic Asset Returns." *Journal of Financial Economics* 62, no. 2 (November): 293-325.

Jones, C. N., G. Kaul, and M. L. Lipson. 1994. "Information, Trading and Volatility." *Journal of Financial Economics* 36, no. 1 (August): 127–154.

Jones, C. P., R. J. Rendleman, Jr., and H. A. Latané. 1985. "Earnings Announcements: Pre- and Post-Responses." *Journal of Portfolio Management* 11, no. 3 (Spring): 28–32.

Jones, Thomas P. 1995. "The Economic Value-Added Approach to Corporate Investments." In *Corporate Financial Decision Making and Equity Analysis.* Charlottesville, VA: AIMR.

Jonsson, Jon G., and Martin S. Fridson. 1996. "Forecasting Default Rates on High-Yield Bonds." *Journal of Fixed Income* 6, no. 1 (June): 69–77.

Jorion, Philippe. 1991. "The Pricing of Exchange Rate Risk in the Stock Market." *Journal of Financial and Quantitative Analysis* 26, no. 3 (September): 363–376.

Jost, Kathryn Dixon, ed. 2001a. *Best Execution and Portfolio Performance.* Charlottesville, VA: AIMR.

Jost, Kathryn Dixon, ed. 2001b. *Evolution in Equity Markets: Focus on Asia.* Charlottesville, VA: AIMR.

Jost, Kathryn Dixon, ed. 2002. *Fixed-Income Management for the 21st Century.* Charlottesville, VA: AIMR.

Kahle, Kathleen M., William F. Maxwell, and Danielle Xu. 2007. "Measuring Abnormal Bond Performance." Working paper, University of Arizona, February.

Kalotay, A. J. 1981. "On the Management of Sinking Funds." *Financial Management* 10, no. 2 (Summer): 34–40.

Kalotay, A. J. 1982a. "On the Structure and Valuation of Debt Refundings." *Financial Management* 11, no. 1 (Spring): 41–42.

Kalotay, A. J. 1982b. "Sinking Funds and the Realized Cost of Debt." *Financial Management* 11, no. 1 (Spring): 43–54.

Kamara, Avraham. 1984. "The Behavior of Futures Prices: A Review of Theory and Evidence." *Financial Analysts Journal* 40, no. 4 (July–August): 68–75.

Kaplan, Robert S., and Gabrial Urwitz. 1979. "Statistical Models of Bond Ratings: A Methodological Inquiry." *Journal of Business* 52, no. 2 (April).

Kaplan, S. N., and R. S. Ruback. 1995. "The Valuation of Cash Flow Forecasts: An Empirical Analysis." *Journal of Finance* 50, no. 4 (September): 1059–1093.

Karnosky, Denis S., and Brian D. Singer. 1994. *Global Asset Management and Performance Measurement.* Charlottesville,

VA: Research Foundation of the Institute of Chartered Financial Analysts.

Kat, Harry M. 2001. *Structured Equity Derivatives: The Definitive Guide to Exotic Options and Structured Notes.* London: Wiley.

Kee, C. 1993. "Market Integration and Price Execution for NYSE-Listed Securities." *Journal of Finance* 48, no. 3 (June): 1009–1038.

Keim, Donald B. 1983. "Size-Related Anomalies and Stock Return Seasonality." *Journal of Financial Economics* 12, no. 1 (June): 13–32.

Keim, Donald B. 1986. "The CAPM and Equity Return Regularities." *Financial Analysts Journal* 42, no. 3 (May–June): 19–34.

Keim, Donald B., and Michael Smirlock. 1989. "Pricing Patterns in Stock Index Futures." In *The Handbook of Stock Index Futures and Options,* ed. F. Fabozzi and G. Kipnis. Homewood, IL: Dow Jones–Irwin.

Keim, Donald B., and Robert F. Stambaugh. 1986. "Predicting Returns in Stock and Bond Markets." *Journal of Financial Economics* 17, no. 2 (December): 357–390.

Kelly, Kate. 2004a. "A Little Scary: NYSE's Chief Seeks to Sell Electronic Trading to the Floor." *Wall Street Journal,* February 2, pp. C1, C6.

Kelly, Kate. 2004b. "NYSE's Automatic Transition." *Wall Street Journal,* June 22, pp. C1, C5.

Kelly, Kate, and Deborah Solomon. 2004. "NYSE May Receive 'Fast Market' Status, as SEC Forges Rules." *Wall Street Journal,* February 24, p. C3.

Keran, Michael W. 1971. "Expectations, Money, and the Stock Market." Federal Reserve Bank of St. Louis *Review* 53, no. 1 (January): 16–31.

Kessel, Reuben A. 1965. "The Cyclical Behavior of the Term Structure of Interest Rates." Occasional Paper 91. New York: National Bureau of Economic Research.

Keynes, John Maynard. 1930. *A Treatise on Money.* London: Macmillan.

Khorana, Ajay, Edward Nelling, and Jeffrey Trester. 1998. "The Emergence of Country Index Funds." *Journal of Portfolio Management* 24, no. 4 (Summer): 78–84.

Kidwell, D. S., E. H. Sorenson, and J. M. Wachowicz. 1987. "Estimating the Signaling Benefits of Debt Insurance: The Case of Municipal Bonds." *Journal of Financial and Quantitative Analysis* 22, no. 3 (September): 299–313.

Kim, Sung-Hwa, and Gary D. Koppenhaver. 1993. "An Empirical Analysis of Bank Interest Rate Swaps." *Journal of Financial Services Research* 7, no. 1 (January): 57–72.

Klemkosky, Robert C. 1973. "The Bias in Composite Performance Measures." *Journal of Financial and Quantitative Analysis* 8, no. 3 (June): 505–514.

Klemkosky, Robert C., and Bruce G. Resnick. 1979. "Put-Call Parity and Market Efficiency." *Journal of Finance* 34, no. 5 (December): 1141–1155.

Klibanoff, Peter, Owen Lamont, and Thierry A. Wizman. 1998. "Investor Reaction to Salient News in Closed-End Country Funds." *Journal of Finance* 53, no. 2 (April): 673–699.

Koenig, Evan, and Kenneth Emery. 1991. "Misleading Indicators? Using the Composite Leading Indicators to Predict Cyclical Turning Points." Federal Reserve Bank of Dallas *Economic Review* (July): 1–14.

Koller, Tim, Marc Goedhart, and David Wessels. 2005. *Valuation: Measuring and Managing the Value of Companies,* 4th ed. New York: Wiley.

Kon, Stanley J. 1983. "The Market-Timing Performance of Mutual Fund Managers." *Journal of Business* 56, no. 3 (July): 323–347.

Kostovetsky, Leonard. 2003. "Index Mutual Funds and Exchange-Traded Funds." *Journal of Portfolio Management* 29, no. 4 (Summer): 80–92.

Kothari, S. P., and Jay Shanken. 2004. "Asset Allocation with Inflation-Protected Bonds." *Financial Analysts Journal* 60, no. 1 (January/February): 54–70.

Kothari, S. P., Jay Shanken, and Richard G. Sloan. 1995. "Another Look at the Cross Section of Expected Stock Returns." *Journal of Finance* 50, no. 2 (March): 185–224.

Kramer, Charles. 1994. "Macroeconomic Seasonality and the January Effect." *Journal of Finance* 49, no. 5 (December): 1883–1891.

Kraus, Alan, and Robert Litzenberger. 1976. "Skewness Preference and the Valuation of Risky Assets." *Journal of Finance* 31, no. 4 (September): 1085–1094.

Krehbiel, Tim, and Roger Collier. 1996. "Normal Backwardation in Short-Term Interest Rate Markets." *Journal of Futures Markets* 16, no. 8 (December): 899–913.

Kritzman, Mark. 1983. "Can Bond Managers Perform Consistently?" *Journal of Portfolio Management* 9, no. 4 (Summer): 54–56.

Kritzman, Mark. 1986. "What's Wrong with Portfolio Insurance?" *Journal of Portfolio Management* 13, no. 1 (Fall): 13–17.

Kritzman, Mark P. 1990. "Quantitative Methods in Performance Measurement." In *Quantitative Methods for Financial Analysis*, 2nd ed., ed. S. Brown and M. P. Kritzman. Homewood, IL: Dow Jones–Irwin.

Kritzman, Mark. 1992. "What Investors Need to Know About Duration and Convexity." *Financial Analysts Journal* 48, no. 6 (November-December): 17-20.

Kuberek, Robert C. 1995. "Attribution Analysis for Fixed Income." In *Performance Evaluation, Benchmarks, and Attribution Analysis*, ed. J. Squires. Charlottesville, VA: AIMR.

Kuhn, Susan E. 1996. "Real Estate: A Smart Alternative to Stocks." *Fortune*, May 27, p. 186.

Laderman, Jeffrey M. 1996. "The Stampede to Index Funds." *Business Week*, April 1, pp. 78–79.

Lakonishok, Josef, Andrei Shleifer, and Robert W. Vishny. 1992. "The Structure and Performance of the Money Management Industry." In *Brookings Papers on Economic Activity*. Washington, DC: Brookings Institute.

Lascelles, David. 1989. "Calls to Bring Watchdogs into Line." *Financial Times*, August 14, p. 10.

Lawton, Philip, and W. Bruce Remington. 2007. "Global Investment Performance Standards." In *Managing Investment Portfolio: A Dynamic Process*, 3rd ed., eds. John L. Maginn, Donald L. Tuttle, Jerald E. Pinto, and Dennis W. McLeavey. Hoboken, NJ: Wiley.

Layard-Liesching, Ronald. 2001. "Exploiting Opportunities in Global Bond Markets." In *Core-Plus Bond Management*, Association for Investment Management and Research. Charlottesville, VA: 30-38.

Layard-Liesching, Ronald. 2001. "Exploiting Opportunities in Global Bond Markets." In *Core-Plus Bond Management*, ed. Katrina Sherrerd. Charlottesville, VA: AIMR.

Lee, C. F., Joseph Finnerty, and Edgar Norton. 2003. *Foundations of Financial Management*, 3rd ed. St. Paul, MN: West.

Lee, Charles. 2003. "Fusion Investing." In *Equity Valuation in a Global Context*. Charlottesville, VA: AIMR.

Lee, Charles, Andrei Shleifer, and Richard Thaler. 1991. "Investor Sentiment and the Closed- End Fund Puzzle." *Journal of Finance* 46, no. 1 (March): 76–110.

Lehman Bros., Inc. 2005. "Collateralized Mortgage Obligations." In *The Handbook of Fixed-Income Securities*, 7th ed., ed. Frank J. Fabozzi. New York: McGraw-Hill.

Lehmann, Bruce N., and David M. Modest. 1988. "The Empirical Foundations of the Arbitrage Pricing Theory." *Journal of Financial Economics* 21, no. 3 (September).

Leibowitz, Martin L. 1986a. "The Dedicated Bond Portfolio in Pension Funds—Part I: Motivations and Basics." *Financial Analysts Journal* 42, no. 1 (January–February): 68–75.

Leibowitz, Martin L. 1986b. "The Dedicated Bond Portfolio in Pension Funds—Part II: Immunization, Horizon Matching, and Contingent Procedures." *Financial Analysts Journal* 42, no. 2 (March–April): 47–57.

Leibowitz, Martin L. 1987. *New Perspectives on Asset Allocation*. Charlottesville, VA: Research Foundation of the Institute of Chartered Financial Analysts.

Leibowitz, Martin L. 1997. *Sales Driven Franchise Value*. Charlottesville, VA: Research Foundation of the Institute of Chartered Financial Analysts.

Leibowitz, Martin L., Thomas E. Klaffky, Steven Mandel, and Alfred Weinberger. 1983. *Horizon Matching: A New Generalized Approach for Developing Minimum-Cost Dedicated Portfolios*. New York: Salomon Brothers.

Leibowitz, Martin L., and Stanley Kogelman. 1990. "Inside the P/E Ratio: The Franchise Factor." *Financial Analysts Journal* 46, no. 6 (November–December): 17–35.

Leibowitz, Martin L., and Stanley Kogelman. 1994. *Franchise Value and the Price-Earnings Ratio*. Charlottesville, VA: Research Foundation of the Institute of Chartered Financial Analysts.

Leibowitz, Martin L., William S. Krasker, and Ardavan Nozari. 1990. "Spread Duration: A New Tool for Bond Portfolio Management." *Journal of Portfolio Management* 16, no. 3 (Spring): 46–53.

Leibowitz, Martin L., and Alfred Weinberger. 1982. "Contingent Immunization—Part I: Risk Control Procedures." *Financial Analysts Journal* 38, no. 6 (November–December): 17–32.

Leibowitz, Martin L., and Alfred Weinberger. 1983. "Contingent Immunization—Part II: Problem Areas." *Financial Analysts Journal* 39, no. 1 (January–February): 35–50.

Leland, Hayne E. 1999. "Beyond Mean-Variance: Performance Measurement in a Nonsymmetrical World." *Financial Analysts Journal* 55, no. 1 (January–February): 27–36.

Lessard, Donald R. 1988. "International Diversification." In *The Financial Analyst's Handbook*, 2nd ed., ed. Sumner N. Levine. Homewood, IL: Dow Jones–Irwin.

Lev, Baruch. 1989. "On the Usefulness of Earnings and Earning Research: Lessons and Directions from Two Decades of Empirical Research." *Journal of Accounting Research* (Supplement).

Lev, Baruch, and S. Ramu Thiagarajan. 1993. "Fundamental Information Analysis." *Journal of Accounting Research* 37, no. 2 (Fall).

Levine, Sumner N., ed. 1988a. "Bond Ratings." In *The Financial Analyst's Handbook*, 2nd ed. Homewood, IL: Dow Jones–Irwin.

Levine, Sumner N., ed.1988b. *The Financial Analyst's Handbook*, 2nd ed. Homewood, IL: Dow Jones–Irwin.

Levy, Robert A. 1966. "Conceptual Foundations of Technical Analysis." *Financial Analysts Journal* 22, no. 4 (July–August): 83.

Lhabitant, Francois-Serge. 2002. *Hedge Funds: Myths and Limits*. Hoboken, NJ: Wiley.

Lim, Kian-Guan. 1989. "A New Test of the Three-Moment Capital Asset Pricing Model." *Journal of Financial and Quantitative Analysis* 24, no. 2 (June): 205–216.

Lintner, John. 1965. "Security Prices, Risk and Maximal Gains from Diversification." *Journal of Finance* 20, no. 4 (December): 587–615.

Litzenberger, Robert, and K. Ramaswamy. 1979. "The Effect of Personal Taxes and Dividends on Capital Asset Prices: Theory and Empirical Evidence." *Journal of Financial Economics* 7, no. 2 (June): 163–196.

Liu, Jun, Francis A. Longstaff, and Ravit E. Mandell. 2006. "The Market Price of Risk in Interest Rate Swaps: The Roles of Default Risk and Liquidity Risks." *Journal of Business* 79, no. 5 (September): pp. 2337-2359.

Liu, P., and W. T. Moore. 1987. "The Impact of Split Bond Ratings on Risk Premia." *The Financial Review* 22, no. 1 (February).

Livingston, Douglas G. 1993. *The Fixed-Income Almanac*. Chicago: Probus.

Livingston, Miles. 1977. "Industry Movements of Common Stocks." *Journal of Finance* 32, no. 2 (June): 861–874.

Lo, Andrew W. 2002. "The Statistics of Sharpe Ratios." *Financial Analysts Journal* 58, no. 4 (July–August): 36–52.

Lo, Andrew W., and A. Craig MacKinley. 1999. *A Non-Random Walk down Wall Street*. Princeton, NJ: Princeton University Press.

Lo, Andrew W., Harry Mamasky, and Jiang Wang. 2000. "Foundations of Technical Analysis: Computational Algorithms,

Statistical Inference, and Empirical Implementation." *Journal of Finance* 55, no. 4 (August): 1705–1765.

Loomis, Carol J. 1996. "Short Sellers and the Seamy Side of Wall Street." *Fortune,* July 22, pp. 66–72.

Lorie, James. 1975. "Diversification: Old and New." *Journal of Portfolio Management* 1, no. 2 (Winter): 25–28.

Loughran, Timothy, and Jay Ritter. 1995. "The New Issues Puzzle." *Journal of Finance* 50, no. 1 (March): 23–51.

Lowenstein, Roger. 1995. *Buffett: The Making of an American Capitalist.* New York: Random House.

Lucchetti, Aaron, and Deborah Solomon. 2004. "Better Data on Prices of Corporate Bonds Would Slash Costs." *Wall Street Journal,* September 30, p. C4.

Ludvigson, Sydney C., and Serena Ng, 2007, "The Empirical Risk-Return Relation: A Factor Analysis Approach." *Journal of Financial Economics* 83, no. 1 (January): 171–222.

Lummer, Scott L. 1994. "Public Perception of the Investment Industry: Trends and Counteractions." In *Good Ethics: The Essential Element of a Firm's Success,* ed. K. Baker. Charlottesville, VA: AIMR.

Lummer, Scott L., and Mark W. Riepe. 1993. "Convertible Bonds as an Asset Class: 1957–1992." *Journal of Fixed Income* 3, no. 2 (September): 47–56.

Lynch, Peter. 1989. *One Up on Wall Street.* New York: Simon & Schuster.

Lynch, Peter. 1993. *Beating the Street.* New York: Simon & Schuster.

Macaulay, Frederick R. 1938. *Some Theoretical Problems Suggested by the Movements of Interest Rates, Bond Yields, and Stock Prices in the United States since 1856.* New York: National Bureau of Economic Research.

MacBeth, James D., and Larry J. Merville. 1979. "An Empirical Examination of the Black-Scholes Call Option Pricing Model." *Journal of Finance* 34, no. 5 (December): 1173–1186.

Madhaven, Ananth. 1992. "Trading Mechanisms in Securities Markets." *Journal of Finance* 47, no. 2 (June): 607–641.

Madhaven, Ananth. 1995. "Consolidation, Fragmentation, and the Disclosure of Trading Information." *Review of Financial Studies* 8, no. 2 (June).

Madhaven, Ananth, and George Sofianos. 1998. "An Empirical Analysis of NYSE Specialist Trading." *Journal of Financial Economics* 48, no. 2 (May): 189–210.

Maginn, John L., Donald L. Tuttle, Jerald E. Pinto, and Dennis W. McLeavey., eds., 2007. *Managing Investment Portfolios: A Dynamic Process,* 3rd ed. Sponsored by CFA Institute. Hoboken, NJ: Wiley.

Malkiel, Burton G. 1962. "Expectations, Bond Prices, and the Term Structure of Interest Rates." *Quarterly Journal of Economics* 76, no. 2 (May): 197–218.

Malkiel, Burton G. 2007. *A Random Walk down Wall Street.* 9th ed. New York: Norton.

Malkiel, Burton G., and John G. Cragg. 1970. "Expectations and the Structure of Share Prices." *American Economic Review* 60, no. 4 (September): 601–617.

Malvey, Jack. 2005. "Global Credit Bond Portfolio Management." In *The Handbook of Fixed-Income Securities,* 7th ed., ed. Frank J. Fabozzi. New York: McGraw-Hill.

Margrabe, William. 1978. "The Value of an Option to Exchange One Asset for Another." *Journal of Finance* 33, no. 1 (March): 177–186.

Markowitz, Harry. 1952. "Portfolio Selection." *Journal of Finance* 7, no. 1 (March): 77–91.

Markowitz, Harry. 1959. *Portfolio Selection—Efficient Diversification of Investments.* New York: Wiley.

Marshall, William, and Jess B. Yawitz. 1980. "Optimal Terms of the Call Provision on a Corporate Bond." *Journal of Financial Research* 3, no. 3 (Fall): 203–211.

McConnell, John J., and Gary Sanger. 1989. "A Trading Strategy for New Listings on the NYSE." *Financial Analysts Journal* 40, no. 1 (January–February): 38–39.

McCulloch, J. Huston. 1975. "An Estimate of the Liquidity Premium." *Journal of Political Economy* 83, no. 1 (January–February): 95–119.

McCulloch, Robert, and Peter Rossi. 1990. "Posterior, Predictive, and Utility-Based Approaches to Testing the Arbitrage Pricing Theory." *Journal of Financial Economics* 28, nos. 1 and 2 (November–December): 7–38.

McDonald, Robert L. 2003. *Derivatives Markets.* Boston, MA: Pearson Education.

McElravey, John N. 2005. "Securities Backed by Credit Card Receivables." In *The Handbook of Fixed-Income Securities,* 7th ed., ed. Frank J. Fabozzi. New York: McGraw-Hill.

McGee, Suzanna. 1998. "'$2 Brokers' Worried about Notoriety from Charges of Illegal Trading Scheme." *Wall Street Journal,* March 5, pp. C1, C22.

McGrath, Rita G., and Ian C. MacMillan. 2005. *Marketbusters: 40 Strategic Moves that Drive Exceptional Business Growth.* Cambridge, MA: Harvard Business School Press.

McGuire, S. R. 1991. *The Handbook of Convertibles.* New York: Simon & Schuster.

Merjos, Anne. 1990. "How's the Market Doing?" *Barron's,* August 20, 18–20, 27, 28.

Merton, Robert C. 1973a. "The Relationship between Put and Call Option Prices: Comment." *Journal of Finance* 28, no. 1 (March): 183–184.

Merton, Robert C. 1973b. "Theory of Rational Option Pricing." *Bell Journal of Economics and Management* 4, no. 1 (Spring): 141–183.

Merton, Robert C. 1981. "On Market Timing and Investment Performance: An Equilibrium Theory of Value for Market Forecasts." *Journal of Business* 54, no. 3 (July): 363–406.

Meyers, Stephen L. 1973. "A Reexamination of Market and Industry Factors in Stock Price Behavior." *Journal of Finance* 28, no. 3 (June): 695–705.

Meyers, Thomas A. 1989. *The Technical Analysis Course.* Chicago: Probus.

Milevsky, Mosha A., and Chris Robinson. 2005. "A Sustainable Spending Rate without Simulation," *Financial Analysts Journal* 61, no. 6 (November–December).

Miller, Janet T., ed. 2001. *Investment Counseling for Private Clients, III.* Charlottesville, VA: AIMR.

Miller, Merton H. 1991. *Financial Innovations and Market Volatility.* Cambridge, MA: Blackwell.

Miller, Merton H., and Franco Modigliani. 1961. "Dividend Policy, Growth, and the Valuation of Shares." *Journal of Business* 34, no. 4 (October): 411–433.

Miller, Merton H., and Myron Scholes. 1982. "Dividends and Taxes: Some Empirical Evidence." *Journal of Political Economy* 90, no. 4 (December): 1118–1141.

Miller, Robert E., and Frank K. Reilly. 1987. "Examination of Mispricing, Returns, and Uncertainty for Initial Public Offerings." *Financial Management* 16, no. 2 (January): 33–38.

Milligan, John W. 1990. "Two Cheers for 144A." *Institutional Investor* 24, no. 9 (July): 117–119.

Minton, Bernadette A. 1997. "An Empirical Examination of Basic Valuation Models for Plain Vanilla U.S. Interest Rate Swaps." *Journal of Financial Economics* 44, no. 2 (May): 251–277.

Mitchell, Roger S., ed. 2000. *Investment Counseling for Private Clients, II.* Charlottesville, VA: AIMR.

Modigliani, Franco, and Leah Modigliani. 1997. "Risk-Adjusted Performance." *Journal of Portfolio Management* 23, no. 2 (Winter): 45–54.

Mody, Ashoka, and Mark P. Taylor. 2003. "The High-Yield Spread as a Predictor of Real Economic Activity: Evidence of a Financial Accelerator for the United States." *IMF Staff Papers* 50, no. 3: 373–402.

Moore, Geoffrey. 1983. "An Introduction to International Economic Indicators." *Business Cycles, Inflation, and Forecasting,* 2nd ed. Studies in Business Cycles, No. 24. New York: National Bureau of Economic Research.

Moore, Geoffrey, and John P. Cullity. 1988. "Security Markets and Business Cycles." In *The Financial Analyst's Handbook,* 2nd ed., ed. Sumner N. Levine. Homewood, IL: Dow Jones–Irwin.

Moriarty, Eugene, Susan Phillips, and Paula Tosini. 1981. "A Comparison of Options and Futures in the Management of Portfolio Risk." *Financial Analysts Journal* 37, no. 1 (January–February): 61–67.

Mossavar-Rahmani, Sharmin. 1988. "Customized Benchmarks in Structured Management." *Journal of Portfolio Management* 13, no. 4 (Summer): 65–68.

Mossavar-Rahmani, Sharmin. 1991. *Bond Index Funds.* Chicago: Probus.

Mossavar-Rahmani, Sharmin. 2001. "Indexing Fixed-Income Assets." In *The Handbook of Fixed-Income Securities,* 6th ed., ed. Frank J. Fabozzi. New York: McGraw-Hill.

Mossavar-Rahmani, Sharmin. 2005. "Indexing Fixed-Income Assets." In *The Handbook of Fixed-Income Securities,* 7th ed., ed. Frank J. Fabozzi. New York: McGraw-Hill.

Mossin, J. 1966. "Equilibrium in a Capital Asset Market." *Econometrica* 34, no. 4 (October): 768–783.

Mozina, Dave, ed. 2001. "Size and Structure of the World Bond Market: 2001." International Fixed Income Research, Merrill Lynch, April.

Mull, S. R., and L. A. Socnen. 1997. "U.S. REITs as an Asset Class in International Investment Portfolios." *Financial Analysts Journal* 53, no. 2 (March–April): 55–61.

Munves, David. 2005. "The Eurobond Market." In *The Handbook of Fixed-Income Securities,* 7th ed. ed. Frank J. Fabozzi. New York: McGraw-Hill.

Myer, C. F., and James Webb. 1993. "Return Properties of Equity REITs, Common Stocks, and Commercial Real Estate: A Comparison." *Journal of Real Estate Research* 8, no. 1: 87–106.

Nasdaq Fact Book. Washington, DC: National Association of Securities Dealers, published annually.

Neal, Robert. 1992. "A Comparison of Transaction Cost between Competitive Market Maker and Specialist Market Structures." *Journal of Business* 65, no. 3 (July).

Nederlof, Maarten L. 1993. "The Comparison of Strategies Using Derivatives." In *Derivative Strategies for Managing Portfolio Risk,* ed. K. Brown. Charlottesville, VA: AIMR.

"New Ways to Play the Indexing Game." 1988. *Institutional Investor* 22, no. 13 (November): 92–98.

Nicholas, Joseph G. 1999. *Investing in Hedge Funds: Strategies for the New Marketplace.* Princeton, NJ: Bloomberg Press.

Norton, Joseph, and Paul Spellman, eds. 1991. *Asset Securitization.* Cambridge, MA: Basil Blackwell.

NYSE Fact Book. New York: New York Stock Exchange, published annually.

O'Shaughnessy, James P. 1997. *What Works on Wall Street.* New York: McGraw-Hill.

Odean, Terrance. 1998. "Are Investors Reluctant to Realize Their Losses?" *Journal of Finance* 53, no. 5 (October): 1775–1798.

Odean, Terrance. 1999. "Do Investors Trade Too Much?" *American Economic Review* 89 (December): 1279–1298.

Ohlson, J. A. 1980. "Financial Ratios and the Probabilistic Prediction of Bankruptcy." *Journal of Accounting Research* 18, no. 2 (Spring).

Olsen, Robert A. 1998. "Behavioral Finance and Its Implications for Stock-Price Volatility." *Financial Analysts Journal* 54, no. 2 (March/April): 10–18.

Ou, J., and S. Penman. 1989. "Financial Statement Analysis and the Prediction of Stock Returns." *Journal of Accounting and Economics,* no. 4 (November).

Pagano, M. 1989. "Trading Volume and Asset Liquidity." *Quarterly Journal of Economics* 104, no. 2.

Palepu, Krishna, Victor Bernard, and Paul Healy. 2004. *Business Analysis and Valuation.* Cincinnati, OH: South-Western.

Pardee, Scott E. 1987. "Internationalization of Financial Markets." Federal Reserve Bank of Kansas City *Economic Review* (February): 3–7.

Park, H. Y., and Andrew H. Chen. 1985. "Differences between Forward and Futures Prices: A Further Investigation of Marking to Market Effects." *Journal of Futures Markets* 5, no. 7 (February): 77–88.

Patelis, Alex D. 1997. "Stock Returns Predictability and the Role of Monetary Policy." *Journal of Finance* 52, no. 5 (December): 1951–1972.

Peavy, John. 1990. *Cases in Portfolio Management.* Charlottesville, VA: AIMR.

Peavy, John W., III, and David A. Goodman. 1983. "The Significance of P/Es for Portfolio Returns." *Journal of Portfolio Management* 9, no. 2 (Winter).

Penman, S. H. 1996. "The Articulation of Price-Earnings Ratios and Market-to-Book Ratios and the Evaluation of Growth." *Journal of Accounting Research* 34, no. 2 (Spring).

Performance Reporting for Investment Managers. 1991. Charlottesville, VA: AIMR.

Perry, Kevin J., and Robert A. Taggart, Jr. 1988. "The Growing Role of Junk Bonds in Corporate Finance." *Journal of Applied Corporate Finance* 1, no. 1 (Spring): 37–45.

Peters, Donald J. 1991. "Valuing a Growth Stock." *Journal of Portfolio Management* 17, no. 3 (Spring): 49–51.

Peterson, Pamela P., and David Peterson. 1996. "Company Performance Measures of Value Added." Charlottesville, VA: Research Foundation of the Institute of Chartered Financial Analysis.

Petrie, Thomas A., ed. 1993. *The Oil and Gas Industries.* Proceedings from the fourth AIMR Industry seminar, November 12–13, 1992, in Houston, Texas. Charlottesville, VA: AIMR.

Pettengill, Glenn, Sridhar Dundaram, and Ike Matthur. 1995. "The Conditional Relation between Beta and Returns." *Journal of Financial and Quantitative Analysis* 30, no. 1 (March): 101–115.

Pettit, R. R., and P. C. Venkatesh. 1995. "Insider Trading and Long-Run Return Performance." *Financial Management* 24, no. 2 (Summer): 88–103.

Pierce, Douglas, and Vance Roley. 1985. "Stock Prices and Economic News." *Journal of Business* 59, no. 1 (Summer).

Pierce, Phyllis S., ed. *The Business One Irwin Investor's Handbook.* Burr Ridge, IL: Dow Jones Books, published annually.

Porter, Michael E. 1980a. *Competitive Strategy: Techniques for Analyzing Industries and Competitors.* New York: Free Press.

Porter, Michael E. 1980b. "Industry Structure and Competitive Strategy: Keys to Profitability." *Financial Analysts Journal* 36, no. 4 (July–August).

Porter, Michael E. 1985. *Competitive Advantage: Creating and Sustaining Superior Performance.* New York: Free Press.

Porter, Michael E. 1988. "How to Conduct an Industry Analysis." In *The Financial Analysts Handbook,* 2nd ed., ed. Sumner N. Levine. Homewood, IL: Dow Jones–Irwin.

Power, William. 1992. "Big Board, at Age 200, Scrambles to Protect Grip on Stock Market." *Wall Street Journal,* May 13, pp. A1, A8.

Power, William. 1993. "Short Sellers Set to Catch Tumbling Overhead Stocks." *Wall Street Journal,* December 28, pp. C1, C2.

Pozen, Robert C. 2001. *The Mutual Fund Business,* 2nd ed. Boston, MA: Houghton Mifflin.

Prentice, Robert A. 2007. "Ethical Decision Making: More Needed Than Good Intentions." *Financial Analysts Journal* 63, no. 6 (November/December), pp. 17-30.

Pring, Martin J. 1991. *Technical Analysis Explained,* 3rd ed. New York: McGraw-Hill.

Pruitt, Stephen, and Robert White. 1988. "The CRISMA Trading System: Who Says Technical Analysis Can't Beat the Market?" *Journal of Portfolio Management* 14, no. 3 (Spring): 55–58.

Ptak, Jeffrey, "Morningstar's Tax Cost Ratio Tool." 2002. Working Paper, November 21.

Quan, D. C., and S. Titman. 1997. "Commercial Real Estate Prices and Stock Market Returns: An International Analysis." *Financial Analysts Journal* 53, no. 3 (May–June): 21–34.

Rappaport, Liz. 2004a. "Electronic Platforms See Surge in Trading of Corporate Bonds." *Wall Street Journal,* November 3, p. C5.

Rappaport, Liz. 2004b. "Transparency Increases for Price Data." *Wall Street Journal,* October 6, p. C4.

Redington, F. M. 1952. "Review of the Principles of Life—Office Valuations." *Journal of the Institute of Actuaries* 78: 286–340.

Reichenstein, William. 2006. "Trends and Issues: Tax-Efficient Saving and Investing," TIAA-CREF Institute Monograph, February.

Reichenstein, William, and Steven P. Rich. 1993. "The Market Risk Premium and Long-Term Stock Returns." *Journal of Portfolio Management* 19, no. 4 (Summer): 63–72.

Reilly, Frank K. 1975. "Companies and Common Stocks as Inflation Hedges." New York University, Center for the Study of Financial Institutions, *Bulletin* (April).

Reilly, Frank K. 1987. "Risk and Return on Art and Antiques: The Sotheby's Indexes." Paper presented at Eastern Finance Association Meeting, Baltimore, MD, May.

Reilly, Frank K., ed. 1990. *High-Yield Bonds: Analysis and Risk Assessment.* Charlottesville, VA: Institute of Chartered Financial Analysts.

Reilly, Frank K. 1991. "Using Cash Flows and Financial Ratios to Predict Bankruptcies." In *Analyzing Investment Opportunities in Distressed and Bankrupt Companies,* ed. Thomas A. Bowman. Charlottesville, VA: Institute of Chartered Financial Analysts.

Reilly, Frank K. 1997. "The Impact of Inflation on ROE, Growth, and Stock Prices." *Financial Services Review* 6, no. 1: 1–17.

Reilly, Frank K., and Rashid A. Akhtar. 1995. "The Benchmark Error Problem with Global Capital Markets." *Journal of Portfolio Management* 22, no. 1 (Fall): 33–52.

Reilly, Frank K., and James A. Gentry. 2004. "The Growing Importance of Credit Analysis." Working paper, University of Notre Dame.

Reilly, Frank K., Frank T. Griggs, and Wenchi Wong. 1983. "Determinants of the Aggregate Stock Market Earnings Multiple." *Journal of Portfolio Management* 10, no. 1 (Fall): 36–45.

Reilly, Frank K., and Michael D. Joehnk. 1976. "The Association between Market-Determined Risk Measures for Bonds and Bond Ratings." *Journal of Finance* 31, no. 5 (December): 1387–1403.

Reilly, Frank K., Wenchi Kao, and David J. Wright. 1992. "Alternative Bond Market Indexes." *Financial Analysts Journal* 48, no. 3 (May–June): 44–58.

Reilly, Frank K., and Dominic R. Marshall. 1999. "Using P/E/Growth Ratios to Select Stocks." Paper presented at Financial Management Association Meeting, Seattle, October.

Reilly, Frank K., and Rupinder Sidhu. 1980. "The Many Uses of Bond Duration." *Financial Analysts Journal* 36, no. 4 (July–August): 58–72.

Reilly, Frank K., and David J. Wright. 1984. "Block Trades and Aggregate Stock Price Volatility." *Financial Analysts Journal* 40, no. 2 (March–April): 54–60.

Reilly, Frank K., and David J. Wright. 1988. "A Comparison of Published Betas." *Journal of Portfolio Management* 14, no. 3 (Spring): 64–69.

Reilly, Frank K., and David J. Wright. 1994. "An Analysis of High-Yield Bond Benchmarks." *Journal of Fixed Income* 3, no. 4 (March): 6–25.

Reilly, Frank K., and David J. Wright. 1995. "Global Bond Markets: An Analysis of Alternative Benchmarks and Risk-Return Performance." Paper presented at Midwest Finance Association Meeting, Chicago, March.

Reilly, Frank K., and David J. Wright. 1997. "Introducing a Comprehensive U.S. Treasury Bond Market Benchmark." In *Yield Curve Dynamics,* ed. Ronald J. Ryan. Chicago: Glen Lake.

Reilly, Frank K., and David J. Wright. 1999. "An Analysis of High-Yield Bond Indices." In *High-Yield Bonds,* ed. Theodore M. Barnhill, Jr., William F. Maxwell, and Mark R. Shenkman. New York: McGraw-Hill.

Reilly, Frank K., and David J. Wright. 2001b. "Unique Risk-Return Characteristics of High-Yield Bonds." *Journal of Fixed Income* 11, no. 2 (September): 65–82.

Reilly, Frank K., and David J. Wright. 2002a. "Alternative Small-Cap Stock Benchmarks." *The Journal of Portfolio Management* 28, no. 3 (Spring): 82–95.

Reilly, Frank K., and David J. Wright. 2004. "Analysis of Risk-Adjusted Performance for Global Market Assets." *Journal of Portfolio Management* 30, no. 3 (Spring): 63–77.

Reilly, Frank K., and David J. Wright. 2005. "Bond Market Indexes." In *The Handbook of Fixed-Income Securities,* 7th ed., ed. Frank J. Fabozzi. New York: McGraw-Hill.

Reilly, Frank K., David J. Wright, and Edward I. Altman. 1998. "Including Defaulted Bonds in the Capital Markets Asset Spectrum." *Journal of Fixed Income* 8, no. 3 (December): 33–48.

Reilly, Frank K., David J. Wright, and Kam C. Chan. 2000. "Bond Market Volatility Compared to Stock Market Volatility." *Journal of Portfolio Management* 27, no. 1 (Fall): 82–92.

Reilly, Frank K., David J. Wright, and Robert R. Johnson. 2005. "An Analysis of the Interest Rate Sensitivity of Common Stocks." Paper presented at Financial Management Association European Meeting June 6, Siena, Italy.

Reilly, Frank K., and Thomas Zeller. 1974. "An Analysis of Relative Industry Price–Earnings Ratios." *Financial Review,* 17–33.

Reinganum, Marc R. 1981. "The Arbitrage Pricing Theory: Some Empirical Results." *Journal of Finance* 36, no. 2 (May): 313–321.

Reinganum, Marc R. 1983. "Portfolio Strategies Based on Market Capitalization." *Journal of Portfolio Management* 9, no. 2 (Winter).

Reinganum, Marc R. 1992. "A Revival of the Small-Firm Effect." *Journal of Portfolio Management* 18, no. 3 (Spring): 55–62.

Rendleman, Richard J., Jr., and Brit J. Bartter. 1979. "Two-State Option Pricing." *Journal of Finance* 34, no. 5 (December): 1093–1110.

Rendleman, Richard J., Jr., Charles P. Jones, and Henry A. Latané. 1982. "Empirical Anomalies Based on Unexpected Earnings and the Importance of Risk Adjustments." *Journal of Financial Economics* 10, no. 3 (November): 269–287.

Rhoads, Christopher. 2001. "Germany Is Poised for a Pension Overhaul." *Wall Street Journal,* May 10.

Ritter, Jay R. 1991. "The Long-Run Performance of Initial Public Offerings." *Journal of Finance* 46, no. 1 (March): 3–27.

Roenfeldt, Rodney L., Gary L. Griepentrog, and Christopher C. Pflamm. 1978. "Further Evidence on the Stationarity of Beta Coefficients." *Journal of Financial and Quantitative Analysis* 13, no. 1 (March): 117–121.

Roever, W. Alexander, John McElravey, and Glenn Schultz. 2005. "Securities Backed by Automobile Loans." In *The Handbook of Fixed-Income Securities,* 7th ed., ed. Frank J. Fabozzi. New York: McGraw-Hill.

Rogalski, Richard J., and James K. Seward. 1991. "Corporate Issues of Foreign Currency Warrants." *Journal of Financial Economics* 30, no. 2 (December): 347–366.

Rogowski, Robert J., and Eric H. Sorensen. 1985. "Deregulation in Investment Banking: Shelf Registration, Structure and Performance." *Financial Management* 14, no. 1 (Spring): 5–15.

Roll, Richard. 1977a. "A Critique of the Asset Pricing Theory's Tests." *Journal of Financial Economics* 4, no. 4 (March): 129–176.

Roll, Richard. 1977b. "An Analytic Valuation Formula for Unprotected American Call Options on Stocks with Known Dividends." *Journal of Financial Economics* 5, no. 2 (November): 251–258.

Roll, Richard. 1978. "Ambiguity When Performance Is Measured by the Securities Market Line." *Journal of Finance* 33. no. 4 (September): 1051–1069.

Roll, Richard. 1980. "Performance Evaluation and Benchmark Error I." *Journal of Portfolio Management* 6, no. 4 (Summer): 5–12.

Roll, Richard. 1981. "Performance Evaluation and Benchmark Error II." *Journal of Portfolio Management* 7, no. 2 (Winter): 17–22.

Roll, Richard. 1988. "The International Crash of October 1987." *Financial Analysts Journal* 44, no. 5 (September–October): 19–35.

Roll, Richard. 2004. "Empirical TIPS." *Financial Analysts Journal* 60, no. 1 (January/February): 31–53.

Roll, Richard, and Stephen A. Ross. 1980. "An Empirical Investigation of the Arbitrage Pricing Theory." *Journal of Finance* 35, no. 5 (December): 1073–1103.

Roll, Richard, and Stephen A. Ross. 1984. "A Critical Re-examination of the Empirical Evidence on the Arbitrage Pricing Theory." *Journal of Finance* 39, no. 2 (June): 347–350.

Roll, Richard, and Stephen A. Ross. 1995. "The Arbitrage Pricing Theory Approach to Strategic Portfolio Planning." *Financial Analysts Journal* 51, no. 1 (January/February): 122–131.

Rosenberg, Barr. 1984. "Prediction of Common Stock Investment Risk." *Journal of Portfolio Management* 11, no. 1 (Fall): 44–53.

Rosenberg, Barr. 1985. "Prediction of Common Stock Betas." *Journal of Portfolio Management* 11, no. 2 (Winter): 5–14.

Rosenberg, Barr, Kenneth Reid, and Ronald Lanstein. 1985. "Persuasive Evidence of Market Inefficiency." *Journal of Portfolio Management* 11, no. 3 (Spring): 9–17.

Ross, Stephen. 1976. "The Arbitrage Theory of Capital Asset Pricing." *Journal of Economic Theory* 13, no. 2 (December): 341–360.

Ross, Stephen. 1977. "Return, Risk, and Arbitrage." In *Risk and Return in Finance,* ed. I. Friend and J. Bicksler, pp. 189–218. Cambridge, MA: Ballinger.

Ross, Stephen, and Randall Zisler. 1991. "Risk and Return in Real Estate." *Journal of Real Estate Financial Economics* 4, no. 2: 175–190.

Rozeff, M. S. 1974. "Money and Stock Prices: Market Efficiency and the Lag Effect of Monetary Policy." *Journal of Financial Economics* 1, no. 3 (September): 245–302.

Rozeff, Michael. 1984. "Dividend Yields Are Equity Risk Premiums." *Journal of Portfolio Management* 11, no. 1 (Fall): 68–75.

Rubinstein, Mark. 1985a. "Alternative Paths to Portfolio Insurance." *Financial Analysts Journal* 41, no. 4 (July–August): 42–52.

Rubinstein, Mark. 1985b. "Nonparametric Tests of Alternative Options Pricing Models Using All Reported Trades and Quotes on the 30 Most Active CBOE Options Classes from August 23, 1976, through August 31, 1978." *Journal of Finance* 40, no. 2 (June): 455–480.

Rubinstein, Mark. 1992. "Options for the Undecided." In *From Black-Scholes to Black Holes.* London: Risk Magazine, 1992.

Rubinstein, Mark. 1994. "Implied Binomial Trees." *Journal of Finance* 49, no. 3 (July): 771–818.

Rueschhoff, Norlin, and David Strupeck. 2000. "Equity Returns: Local GAAP versus US GAAP for Foreign Issuers from Developing Countries." *Journal of International Accounting* 33, no. 3 (Spring).

Ruffenach, Glenn. 2001. "Fewer Americans Save for Their Retirement." *Wall Street Journal,* May 10, p. A2.

Salomon, Ezra. 1963. *The Theory of Financial Management.* New York: Columbia University Press.

Saudagaran, Shakrokh. 2001. *International Accounting: A User Perspective.* Cincinnati, OH: South-Western.

Schmid, Frank A. 1999. "Extracting Inflation Expectations from Bond Yields." Federal Reserve Bank of St. Louis *Monetary Trends* (April).

Schmidt, Klaus M. 2003. "Convertible Securities and Venture Capital Finance." *Journal of Finance* 58, no. 3 (June): pp. 1139–1166.

Schulz, Ellen R. 1996. "Workers Put Too Much in Their Employer's Stock." *Wall Street Journal,* September 13, pp. C1, C25.

Schwert, G. William. 1989. "Why Does Stock Market Volatility Change over Time?" *Journal of Finance* 44, no. 5 (December): 1115–1153.

Scott, J., M. Stumpp, and P. Xu. 1999. "Behavioral Bias Valuation and Active Management." *Financial Analysts Journal* 55, no. 4 (July–August): 49–57.

Sears, R. Stephen, and John Wei. 1988. "The Structure of Skewness Preferences in Asset Pricing Models with Higher Moments." *Financial Review* 23, no. 1 (February): 25–38.

Selling, Thomas, and Clyde P. Stickney. 1989. "The Effects of Business Environment and Strategy on a Firm's Rate of Return on Assets." *Financial Analysts Journal* 45, no.1 (January–February): 43–52.

Senchak, A. J., Jr., and John D. Martin. 1987. "The Relative Performance of the PSR and PER Investment Strategies." *Financial Analysts Journal* 43, no. 2 (March–April): 46–56.

Seyhun, H. Nejat. 1986. "Insider Profits, Costs of Trading, and Market Efficiency." *Journal of Financial Economics* 16, no. 2 (June): 189–212.

Shackalford, Aaron L., ed. 1997. *Economic Analysis for Investment Professionals.* Charlottesville, VA: AIMR.

Shakla, Ravi, and Charles Trzcinka. 1990. "Sequential Tests of the Arbitrage Pricing Theory: A Comparison of Principle Components and Maximum Likelihood Factors." *Journal of Finance* 45, no. 5 (December): 1542–1564.

Shanken, Jay. 1982. "The Arbitrage Pricing Theory: Is It Testable?" *Journal of Finance* 37, no. 5 (December): 1129–1140.

Shanken, Jay. 1985a. "Multi-Beta CAPM or Equilibrium APT? A Reply." *Journal of Finance* 40, no. 4 (September): 1189–1196.

Shanken, Jay. 1985b. "Multivariate Tests of the Zero Beta CAPM." *Journal of Financial Economics* 14, no. 3 (September): 327–348.

Sharpe, William F. 1964. "Capital Asset Prices: A Theory of Market Equilibrium under Conditions of Risk." *Journal of Finance* 19, no. 3 (September): 425–442.

Sharpe, William F. 1966. "Mutual Fund Performance." *Journal of Business* 39, no. 1, part 2 (January): 119–138.

Sharpe, William F. 1984. "Factor Models, CAPMs, and the APT." *Journal of Portfolio Management* 11, no. 1 (Fall): 21–25.

Sharpe, William F. 1987. "Integrated Asset Allocation." *Financial Analysts Journal* 43, no. 5 (September/ October): 25–32.

Sharpe, William F. 1990. "Asset Allocation." In *Managing Investment Portfolios: A Dynamic Process,* 2nd ed., eds. John L. Maginn and Donald L. Tuttle. Boston: Warren, Gorham, & Lamont.

Sharpe, William. 1991. "The Arithmetic of Active Management." *Financial Analysts Journal* 47, no. 1 (January-February): 7-9.

Sharpe, William F. 1992. "Asset Allocation: Management Style and Performance Measurement." *Journal of Portfolio Management* 18, no. 2 (Winter): 7–19.

Sharpe, William F. 1994. "The Sharpe Ratio." *Journal of Portfolio Management* 21, no. 1 (Fall): 49–59.

Sharpe, William F. 2007. "Expected Utility Asset Allocation," *Financial Analysts Journal* 63, no. 5 (September-October): 18-30.

Sharpe, William F. 2007. *Investors and Markets: Portfolio Choices, Asset Prices, and Investment Advice.* Princeton, NJ: Princeton University Press.

Sharpe, William F., and Guy M. Cooper. 1972a. "Risk-Return Classes of New York Stock Exchange Common Stocks." *Financial Analysts Journal* 28, no. 2 (March–April): 35–43.

Sharpe, William F., and Guy M. Cooper. 1972b. "Risk-Return Classes of New York Stock Exchange Common Stocks: 1931–1967." *Financial Analysts Journal* 28, no. 2 (March–April): 46–54.

Sharpe, William F., and Katrina Sherrerd, eds. 1989. *Quantifying the Market Risk Premium Phenomenon for Investment Decision Making: September 26–27, 1989, New York, New York.* Charlottesville, VA: AIMR.

Shasta, Theodore, ed. 1994. *The Automotive Industry: January 25–26, 1994, Chicago, Illinois.* Charlottesville, VA: AIMR.

Shaw, Alan R. 1988. "Market Timing and Technical Analysis." In *The Financial Analyst's Handbook,* 2nd ed., ed. Sumner N. Levine. Homewood, IL: Dow Jones–Irwin.

Shefrin, Hersh. 1999. *Beyond Greed and Fear: Understanding Behavioral Finance and the Psychology of Investing.* Boston: Harvard Business School Press.

Shefrin, Hersh. 2001. "Behavioral Corporate Finance." *Journal of Applied Corporate Finance* 14, no. 3 (Fall): 113–124.

Shefrin, Hersh. 2005. *A Behavioral Approach to Asset Pricing Theory.* Amsterdam: Elsevier-North Holland.

Shefrin, Hersh, and Meir Statman. 1995a. "Behavioral Capital Asset Pricing Theory." *Journal of Financial and Quantitative Analysis* 30, no. 3 (September).

Shefrin, Hersh, and Meir Statman. 1995b. "Making Sense of Beta, Size, and Book-to-Market." *Journal of Portfolio Management* 21, no. 2 (Winter): 26–34.

Shen, Pu. 1998. "Features and Risks of Treasury Inflation Protection Securities." Federal Reserve Bank of Kansas City *Economic Review* (First Quarter): 23–38.

Sherrerd, Katrina F., ed. 2001. *Benchmarks and Attribution Analysis.* Charlottesville, VA: AIMR.

Shiller, Robert J. 1984. "Stock Prices and Social Dynamics." *Brookings Papers on Economic Activity,* 2:457–498. Washington, DC: Brookings Institute.

Shiller, Robert J., and John Campbell. 1988. "Stock Prices, Earnings, and Expected Dividends." *Journal of Finance* 43, no. 3 (July): 661–676.

Shiskin, Julius. 1963. "Business Cycle Indicators: The Known and the Unknown." *Review of the International Statistical Institute* 31, no. 3: 361–383.

Siegel, Jeremy J. 1991. "Does It Pay Stock Investors to Forecast the Business Cycle?" *Journal of Portfolio Management* 18, no. 1 (Fall): 27–34.

Siegel, Laurence B., and Paul D. Kaplan. 1990. "Stocks, Bonds, Bills, and Inflation around the World." In *Managing Institutional Assets,* ed. Frank J. Fabozzi. New York: Harper & Row.

Singer, Brian. 1996. "Valuation of Portfolio Performance: Aggregate Return and Risk Analysis." *Journal of Performance Measurement* 1, no. 1 (Fall): 6–16.

Singer, Brian D., Renato Staub, and Kevin Terhaar. 2002. "Determining the Appropriate Allocation to Alternative Investments." In *Hedge Fund Management,* Charlottesville, VA: AIMR.

Smith, Clifford W., Jr. 1986. "Investment Banking and the Capital Acquisition Process." *Journal of Financial Economics* 15, no. 1–2 (January–February): 3–29.

Smith, Donald J. 1989a. "The Arithmetic of Financial Engineering." *Journal of Applied Corporate Finance* 1, no. 4 (Winter): 49–58.

Smith, Donald J. 1989b. "The Calculation and Use of Money Market Implied Forward Rates." *Journal of Cash Management* 98, no. 5 (September/October): 46–49.

Smithson, Charles W., and Clifford W. Smith, Jr. 1998. *Managing Financial Risk,* 3rd ed. New York: McGraw-Hill.

Solnik, Bruno. 1993. *Predictable Time-Varying Components of International Asset Returns.* Charlottesville, VA: AIMR.

Solnik, Bruno, and Dennis McLeavey. 2004. *International Investments,* 5th ed. Reading, MA: Addison-Wesley.

Solomon, Deborah, and Kate Kelly. 2003. "Wide SEC Review May Revamp Structure of U.S. Stock markets." *Wall Street Journal,* September 19, pp. A1, A2.

Solt, Michael, and Meir Statman. 1989. "Good Companies, Bad Stocks." *Journal of Portfolio Management* 15, no. 4 (Summer): 39–44.

Sondhi, Ashwinpaul C., ed. 1995. *Credit Analysis of Nontraditional Debt Securities.* Charlottesville, VA: AIMR.

Sorensen, Eric H., and Thierry F. Bollier. 1994. "Pricing Interest Rate Swap Default Risk." *Financial Analysts Journal* 50, no. 3 (May–June): 23–33.

Sorensen, Eric H., Keith L. Miller, and Vele Samak. 1998. "Allocating between Active and Passive Management." *Financial Analysts Journal* 54, no. 4 (September/ October): 18–31.

Sortino, Frank A., and Lee N. Price. 1994. "Performance Measurement in a Downside Risk Framework." *Journal of Investing* 3, no. 3 (Fall): pp. 59-65.

Sprinkel, Beryl W. 1971. *Money and Markets: A Monetarist View.* Homewood, IL: Irwin.

Squires, Jan R., ed. 1995. *Performance Evaluation, Benchmarks, and Attribution Analysis.* Charlottesville, VA: AIMR.

Squires, Jan R., ed. 1996. *Global Portfolio Management.* Charlottesville, VA: AIMR.

Squires, Jan R., ed. 1997a. *Global Bond Management.* Charlottesville, VA: AIMR.

Squires, Jan R., ed. 1997b. *Managing Currency Risk.* Charlottesville, VA: AIMR.

Squires, Jan R., ed. 1998a. *Asset Allocation in a Changing World.* Charlottesville, VA: AIMR.

Squires, Jan R., ed. 1998b. *Credit Analysis around the World.* Charlottesville, VA: AIMR.

Squires, Jan R., ed. 2000a. *Global Bond Management II: The Search for Alpha.* Charlottesville, VA: AIMR.

Squires, Jan R., ed. 2000b. *Practical Issues in Equity Analysis.* Charlottesville, VA: AIMR.

Stambaugh, Robert. 1982. "On the Exclusion of Assets from Tests of the Two-Parameter Model: A Sensitivity Analysis." *Journal of Financial Economics* 10, no. 4 (November): 237–268.

Standard and Poor's Corporation. 2000. *Corporate Ratings Criteria.* New York: Standard & Poor's.

Stanhouse, Bryan, and Duane Stock. 1999. "How Changes in Bond Call Features Affect Coupon Rates." *Journal of Applied Corporate Finance* 12, no. 1 (Spring): 92–99.

Starkman, Dean, and Patrick McGeehan. 1998. "Floor Brokers on Big Board Charged in Scheme." *Wall Street Journal,* February 26, pp. C1, C21.

Statman, Meir. 1987. "How Many Stocks Make a Diversified Portfolio?" *Journal of Financial and Quantitative Analysis* 22, no. 3 (September): 353–363.

Statman, Meir, and Neal L. Ushman. 1987. "Bonds versus Stocks: Another Look." *Journal of Portfolio Management* 13, no. 3 (Winter): 33–38.

Steidtmann, Carl E. 1993. "General Trends in Retailing." In *The Retail Industry—General Merchandisers and Discounters,* ed. Charles Ingene. Charlottesville, VA: AIMR, pp. 6–9.

Stein, Jerome L. 1961. "The Simultaneous Determination of Spot and Futures Prices." *American Economic Review* 51, no. 5 (December): 1012–1025.

Steward, Christopher. 2005. "International Bond Markets and Instruments." In *The Handbook of Fixed-Income Securities,* 7th ed., ed. Frank J. Fabozzi. New York: McGraw-Hill.

Steward, Christopher, J. Hank Lynch, and Frank J. Fabozzi. 2005. "International Bond Portfolio Management." In *The Handbook of Fixed-Income Securities,* 7th ed., ed. Frank J. Fabozzi. New York: McGraw-Hill.

Stewart, G. Bennett, III. 1991. *The Quest for Value.* New York: Harper Business.

Stewart, Samuel S. 1988. "Forecasting Corporate Earnings." In *The Financial Analyst's Handbook,* 2nd ed., ed. Sumner N. Levine. Homewood, IL: Dow Jones–Irwin.

Stickney, Clyde P., Paul Brown, and James Wahlen. 2004. *Financial Reporting and Statement Analysis,* 5th ed. Mason, OH: South-Western.

Stoll, Hans R. 1969. "The Relationship between Put and Call Option Prices." *Journal of Finance* 24, no. 5 (December): 801–824.

Stoll, Hans R. 1993. "Organization of the Stock Market: Competition or Fragmentation?" *Journal of Applied Corporate Finance* 5, no. 4 (Winter): 89–93.

Stoll, Hans R., and Robert E. Whaley. 1983. "Transaction Costs and the Small Firm Effect." *Journal of Financial Economics* 12 no. 1: 57–79.

Stoll, Hans R., and Robert E. Whaley. 1990. "Stock Market Structure and Volatility." *Review of Financial Studies* 3, no. 1.

Stulz, Rene M. 2003. *Risk Management and Derivatives.* Mason, OH: South-Western.

Sullivan, Rodney N., ed. 2003. *Equity Analysis Issues, Lessons and Techniques.* Charlottesville, VA: AIMR.

Sun, Tong-sheng, Suresh Sundaresan, and Ching Wang. 1993. "Interest Rate Swaps: An Empirical Investigation." *Journal of Financial Economics* 34, no. 1 (August): 77–99.

Sundaresan, Suresh. 2002. *Fixed-Income Markets and Their Derivatives,* 2nd ed. Cincinnati, OH: South-Western.

Swales, George S., Jr., and Young Yoon. 1992. "Applying Artificial Neural Networks to Investment Analysis." *Financial Analysts Journal* 48, no. 4 (September/ October): 78–80.

Sweeney, Richard J. 1988. "Some New Filter Rule Tests: Methods and Results." *Journal of Financial and Quantitative Analysis* 23, no. 3 (September): 285–300.

Szakmary, Andrew, Evren Ors, Jin Kyoung Kim, and Wallace N. Davidson. 2003. "The Predictive Power of Implied Volatility: Evidence From 35 Futures Markets." *Journal of Banking and Finance* 27, no. 11 (November): pp. 2151-2175.

Telser, Lester G. 1958. "Futures Trading and the Storage of Cotton and Wheat." *Journal of Political Economy* 66 (June).

Terhaar, Kevin. 2001. "Return, Risk, and Performance Attribution." In *Benchmarks and Attribution Analysis,* ed. Katrina Sherrerd. Charlottesville, VA: AIMR.

Thaler, Richard, and Schlomo Benartzi. 2004. "Save More Tomorrow; Using Behavioral Economics to Increase Employee Savings," *Journal of Political Economy,* 112, no. 1 (February).

Thoenes, Sander. 1998. "Economy Hit as Jakarta Is Paralysed." *Financial Times,* May 15, p. 17.

Thompson, Donald J., II. 1976. "Sources of Systematic Risk in Common Stocks." *Journal of Business* 49, no. 2 (April): 173–188.

Thorbecke, Willem. 1997. "On Stock Market Returns and Monetary Policy." *Journal of Finance* 52, no. 2 (June): 635–654.

Thornhill, John. 1998. "Russian Stocks Fall 10% over Lack of Support from IMF." *Financial Times,* June 2, p. 1.

Tito, Dennis A., and Wayne H. Wagner. 1977. "Is Your Bond Manager Skillful?" *Pension World* (June): 10–16.

Tobin, James. 1958. "Liquidity Preference as Behavior Towards Risk." *Review of Economic Studies* 25, no. 2 (February): 65–85.

Tokyo Stock Exchange Fact Book. Tokyo: TSE, published annually.

Tole, Thomas. 1982. "You Can't Diversify without Diversifying." *Journal of Portfolio Management* 8, no. 2 (Winter): 5–11.

Torres, Craig. 1990. "Third Market Trading Crowds Stock Exchanges." *Wall Street Journal,* March 8, pp. C1, C9.

Treynor, Jack L. 1965. "How to Rate Management of Investment Funds." *Harvard Business Review* 43, no. 1 (January–February): 63–75.

Treynor, Jack L., and Fischer Black. 1973. "How to Use Security Analysis to Improve Security Selection." *Journal of Business* 46, no. 1 (January): 66–86.

Tuckman, Bruce. 1995. *Fixed-Income Securities.* New York: Wiley.

Tully, S. 1993. "The Real Key to Creating Wealth." *Fortune* (September).

van der Does, Rein W. 1988. "Investing in Foreign Securities." In *The Financial Analyst's Handbook,* 2nd ed., ed. Sumner N. Levine. Homewood, IL: Dow Jones–Irwin.

Van Horne, James C. 2001. *Financial Market Rates and Flows,* 6th ed. Englewood Cliffs, NJ: Prentice Hall.

Vine, Allen A. 2001. "High-Yield Analysis of Emerging Markets Debt." In *The Handbook of Fixed-Income Securities,* 6th ed., ed. Frank J. Fabozzi. New York: McGraw-Hill.

Viner, Aron. 1988. *Inside Japanese Financial Markets.* Homewood, IL: Dow Jones–Irwin.

Volpert, Kenneth E. 2001. "Managing Indexed and Enhanced Indexed Bond Portfolios." In *The Handbook of Fixed-Income Securities,* 6th ed., ed. Frank J. Fabozzi. New York: McGraw-Hill.

Wagner, Wayne H., and Dennis A. Tito. 1977. "Definitive New Measures of Bond Performance and Risk." *Pension World* (May): 17–26.

Wahab, Mahmoud, and Amit Khandwala. 1993. "Why Not Diversify Internationally with ADRs?" *Journal of Portfolio Management* 19, no. 2 (Winter): 75–82.

Walmsley, Julian. 1998. *The New Financial Instruments,* 2nd ed. New York: Wiley.

Walter, John R. 1989. "Monetary Aggregates: A User's Guide." Federal Reserve Bank of Richmond *Economic Review* (January/ February): 53–61.

Ward, David J., and Gary L. Griepentrog. 1993. "Risk and Return in Defaulted Bonds." *Financial Analysts Journal* 49, no. 3 (May–June): 61–65.

Ware, James W. 2000. "Drawing the Line in a Gray Area." In *Ethical Issues for Today's Firm.* Charlottesville, VA: AIMR.

Waymire, G. 1984. "Additional Evidence on the Information Content of Management Earnings Forecasts." *Journal of Accounting Research* 22, no. 3 (Autumn).

Weigel, Eric J. 1991. "The Performance of Tactical Asset Allocation." *Financial Analysts Journal* 47, no. 5 (September–October): 63–70.

Weiss, Gary. 1996. "The Secret World of Short Sellers." *BusinessWeek,* August 5, pp. 62–68.

Wermers, Russ. 2000. "Mutual Fund Performance: An Empirical Decomposition into Stock-Picking Talent, Style, Transaction Costs, and Expenses." *Journal of Finance* 55, no. 4 (August): 1655–1695.

Whaley, Robert E. 1981. "On the Valuation of American Call Options on Stocks with Known Dividends." *Journal of Financial Economics* 9, no. 2 (June): 207–212.

Whaley, Robert E. 1993. "Derivatives on Market Volatility: Hedging Tools Long Overdue." *Journal of Derivatives* 1 (Fall): pp. 71-84.

White, Gerald I., Ashwinpaul C. Sondhi, and Dov Fried. 2001. *The Analysis and Use of Financial Statements,* 3rd ed. New York: Wiley.

White, James A. 1991. "The Index Boom: It's No Longer Just the S&P 500 Stock Index." *Wall Street Journal,* May 19, pp. C1, C3.

Widder, Pat. 1992. "Nasdaq Has Its Eyes Set on the Next 100 Years." *Chicago Tribune,* May 17, Section 7, pp. 1, 4.

Wilcox, Jarrod W. 1984. "The P/B-ROE Valuation Model." *Financial Analysts Journal* 40, no. 1 (January–February): 58–66.

Williams, J. B. 1938. *The Theory of Investment Value.* Cambridge, MA: Harvard University Press.

Wilson, Richard S. 2001. "Domestic Floating-Rate and Adjustable-Rate Debt Securities." In *The Handbook of Fixed-Income Securities,* 6th ed., ed. Frank J. Fabozzi. New York: McGraw-Hill.

Winkelmann, Kurt. 1989. "Uses and Abuses of Duration and Convexity." *Financial Analysts Journal* 45, no. 5 (September–October): 72–75.

Witschi, Daniel. 1998. "European Pension Funds: Turning More Aggressive?" In *Asset Allocation in a Changing World.* Charlottesville, VA: AIMR, pp. 72–84.

Womack, Kent L. 1996. "Do Brokerage Analysts' Recommendations Have Investment Value?" *Journal of Finance* 51, no. 1 (March): 137–167.

Wood, Arnold S., ed. 1995. *Behavioral Finance and Decision Theory in Investment Management.* Charlottesville, VA: AIMR.

Woolridge, Randall. 1995. "Do Stock Prices Reflect Fundamental Values?" *Journal of Applied Corporate Finance* 8, no. 1 (Spring): 64–69.

Working, Holbrook. 1977. "Economic Functions of Futures Markets." In *Selected Writings of Holbrook Working.* Chicago: Chicago Board of Trade.

Yaksick, Rudy. 1992. "Swaps, Caps, and Floors: Some Parity and Price Identities." *Journal of Financial Engineering* 1, no. 1: 105–115.

Yates, Jr., James W., and Robert W. Kopprasch, Jr. 1980. "Writing Covered Call Options: Profits and Risks." *Journal of Portfolio Management* 7 (Fall).

Zhon, Chunsheng. 2001. "Credit Rating and Corporate Defaults." *Journal of Fixed Income* 11, no. 3 (December): 30–40.

Zweig, Martin E. 1986. *Winning on Wall Street.* New York: Warner Books.

Zweig, Martin E. 1987. *Understanding Technical Forecasting.* New York: Dow Jones.

Zweig, Martin E. 2000. "You Get the Clients You Deserve." In *Ethical Issues for Today's Firm.* Charlottesville, VA: AIMR.

GLOSSARY

A

Abnormal rate of return The amount by which a security's actual return differs from its expected rate of return, which is based on the market's rate of return and the security's relationship with the market.

Accumulation phase Phase in the investment life cycle during which individuals in the early-to-middle years of their working career attempt to accumulate assets to satisfy short-term needs and longer-term goals.

Actuarial rate of return The discount rate used to find the present value of a defined benefit pension plan's future obligations and thus determine the size of the firm's annual contribution to the plan.

Agency conflict An ethical problem that can arise any time one person (i.e., agent) is hired to perform a service or act in the interest of another (i.e., principal).

Alpha A term commonly used to describe a manager's abnormal rate of return, which is the difference between the return the portfolio actually produced and the expected return given its risk level.

Alternative asset A nontraditional (i.e., not common stocks or bonds) asset class investment, including hedge funds, private equity, real estate, and commodities.

Alternative trading system (ATS) A nontraditional, computerized trading system that competes with or supplements dealer markets and traditional stock exchanges. While they facilitate trading in shares, they do not provide listing services.

American Depository Receipts (ADRs) Certificates of ownership issued by a U.S. bank that represent indirect ownership of a certain number of shares of a specific foreign firm. Shares are held on deposit in a bank in the firm's home country.

American option An option contract that can be exercised at any time until its expiration date.

Analysis effect The difference in performance of a security portfolio from that of a chosen index due to acquisition of temporarily mispriced issues that then move to their correct prices.

Anomalies Security price relationships that appear to contradict a well-regarded hypothesis; in this case, the efficient market hypothesis.

Arbitrage A trading strategy designed to generate a guaranteed profit from a transaction that requires no capital commitment or risk bearing on the part of the trader. A simple example of an arbitrage trade would be the simultaneous purchase and sale of the same security in different markets at different prices.

Arbitrage pricing theory (APT) A theory that posits that the expected return to a financial asset can be described by its relationship with several common risk factors. The multifactor APT can be contrasted with the single-factor CAPM.

Arithmetic mean (AM) A measure of mean annual rates of return equal to the sum of annual holding period rates of return divided by the number of years.

Asset allocation The process of deciding how to distribute an investor's wealth among different asset classes for investment purposes.

Asset-backed securities (ABS) Securitized debt that can be backed by a range of assets beyond the traditional mortgage assets. The other assets include car loans, credit card debt, student loans, or home equity loans.

Asset class Securities that have similar characteristics, attributes, and risk/return relationships.

Asset-liability management A matched-funding approach to portfolio management where the characteristics (e.g., cash flow amount, duration) of the assets are coordinated with those of the liabilities that the investor faces.

Assets under management (AUM) The total market value of the assets managed by an investment firm.

At the money A special case of an option where the exercise price and the price of the underlying asset are identical.

Attribution analysis An assessment technique designed to establish whether a manager's performance relative to a benchmark resulted from market timing or security selection skills.

Auction-rate securities (ARS) Securities issued by municipalities, hospitals, and museums in an attempt to pay short-term rates for long-term capital. Specifically, these securities have long-term maturities (20–30 years), but they act like short-term securities in terms of required yield because the coupon is constantly being reset during frequent auctions every week to 35 days. The risk (that became reality in 2007–2008) is that the auctions can "fail" when there are not enough bids to sell all the bonds available (i.e., for various reasons holders do not want to renew their positions).

Autocorrelation test A test of the efficient market hypothesis that compares security price changes over time to check for predictable correlation patterns.

Average tax rate A person's total tax payment divided by his or her total income.

B

Backtest A method of testing a quantitative model in which computers are used to examine the composition and returns of portfolios based on historical data to determine if the selected strategy would have worked in the past.

Backwardated A situation in a futures market where the current contract price is less than the current spot price for the underlying asset.

Balance sheet A financial statement that shows what assets the firm controls at a fixed point in time and how it has financed these assets.

Balanced fund A mutual fund with, generally, a three-part investment objective: (1) to conserve the investor's principal, (2) to pay current income, and (3) to increase both principal and income. The fund aims to achieve this by owning a mixture of bonds, preferred stocks, and common stocks.

Basis The difference between the spot price of the underlying asset and the futures contract price at any point in time (e.g., the *initial* basis at the time of contract origination, the *cover* basis at the time of contract termination).

Basis of an asset For tax purposes, the cost of an asset.

Basis risk The residual exposure to the price volatility of an underlying asset that results from a cross hedge transaction.

Bearer bond An unregistered bond for which ownership is determined by possession. The holder receives interest payments by clipping coupons attached to the security and sending them to the issuer for payment.

Behavioral finance Involves the analysis of various psychological traits of individuals and how these traits affect how they act as investors, analysts, and portfolio managers.

Benchmark error Situation where an inappropriate or incorrect benchmark is used to compare and assess portfolio returns and management.

Benchmark portfolio A comparison standard of risk and assets included in the policy statement and similar to the investor's risk preference and investment needs, which can be used to evaluate the investment performance of the portfolio manager.

Beta A standardized measure of systematic risk based upon an asset's covariance with the market portfolio.

Binomial option pricing model A valuation equation that assumes the price of the underlying asset changes through a series of discrete upward or downward movements.

Black-Scholes option pricing model A valuation equation that assumes the price of the underlying asset changes continuously through the option's expiration date by a statistical process known as *geometric Brownian motion*.

Bond insurance Insurance policies written by commercial insurance companies wherein the insurance company agrees to pay the bondholder principal and/or coupon interest that is due on a bond that is not paid by the issuer. These policies were originally issued only on municipal bonds, but have subsequently been written for corporate bonds and collateralized issues. Insured bond issues generally receive the bond rating equal to that held by the insurance company.

Bond ladder A strategy for managing a fixed-income portfolio where the investment funds are divided evenly among bonds that mature at regular intervals surrounding the desired time horizon.

Bond price volatility The percentage changes in bond prices over time.

Bond swap An active bond portfolio management strategy that exchanges one position for another to take advantage of some difference between them.

Business risk The variability of operating income arising from the characteristics of the firm's industry. Two sources of business risk are sales variability and operating leverage.

Buy-and-hold strategy A passive portfolio management strategy in which securities (bonds or stocks) are bought and held to maturity.

C

Call market A market in which trading for individual stocks only takes place at specified times. All the bids and asks available at the time are combined and the market administrators specify a single price that will possibly clear the market at that time.

Call option Option to buy an asset within a certain period at a specified price called the *exercise price*.

Call premium Amount above par that an issuer must pay to a bondholder for retiring the bond before its stated maturity.

Call provisions Specifies when and how a firm can issue a call for bonds outstanding prior to their maturity.

Cap agreement A contract that on each settlement date pays the holder the greater of the difference between the reference rate and the cap rate or zero; it is equivalent to a series of call options at the reference rate.

Capital appreciation A return objective in which the investor seeks to increase the portfolio value, primarily through capital gains, over time to meet a future need rather than dividend yield.

Capital asset pricing model (CAPM) A theory concerned with deriving the expected or required rates of return on risky assets based on the assets' systematic risk relative to a market portfolio.

Capital market instruments Fixed-income or equity investments that trade in the secondary market.

Capital market line (CML) The line from the intercept point that represents the risk-free rate tangent to the original efficient frontier; it becomes the new efficient frontier since investments on this line dominate all the portfolios on the original Markowitz efficient frontier.

Capital preservation A return objective in which the investor seeks to minimize the risk of loss; generally a goal of the risk-averse investor.

Certificates of deposit (CDs) Instruments issued by banks and S&Ls that require minimum deposits for specified terms and that pay higher rates of interest than deposit accounts.

Characteristic line Regression line that indicates the systematic risk (beta) of a risky asset.

Closed-end investment company An investment company that issues only a limited number of shares, which it does not redeem (buy back). Instead, shares of a closed-end fund are traded in securities markets at prices determined by supply and demand.

Coefficient of variation (CV) A measure of relative variability that indicates risk per unit of return. It is equal to: standard deviation divided by the mean value. When used in investments, it is equal to: standard deviation of returns divided by the expected rate of return.

Coincident indicators A set of economic variables whose values reach peaks and troughs at about the same time as the aggregate economy.

Collar agreement A hedging arrangement where an underlying asset is protected against decreases in value by the simultaneous purchase of a put option and sale of a call option.

Collateral trust bonds A mortgage bond wherein the assets backing the bond are financial assets like stocks and bonds.

Collateralized debt obligations (CDOs) Considered part of the asset-backed securities (ABSs) market because they are backed by the cash flows from a portfolio of securities. In contrast to the specific securities such as mortgages, credit card debt, and auto loans, CDOs are unique because they will generally include a variety of debt with a diversity of credit ratings. Finally, there are typically several tranches with different credit ratings from AAA to non-investment grade.

Collateralized mortgage obligation (CMO) A debt security based on a pool of mortgage loans that provides a relatively predictable term by paying of tranches in specified order.

Commission brokers Employees of a member firm who buy or sell securities for the customers of the firm.

Common stock An equity investment that represents ownership of a firm, with full participation in its success or failure. The firm's directors must approve dividend payments.

Common-size statements The normalization of balance sheet and income statement items to allow for more meaningful comparison of different-size firms. Balance sheet items are divided by total assets; income statement items are divided by total sales.

Competitive bid An underwriting alternative wherein an issuing entity (governmental body or a corporation) specifies the type of security to be offered (bonds or stocks) and the general characteristics of the issue, and the issuer solicits bids from competing investment banking firms with the understanding that the issuer will accept the highest bid from the bankers.

Competitive environment The level of intensity of competition among firms in an industry, determined by an examination of five competitive forces.

Competitive strategy The search by a firm for a favorable competitive position within an industry within the known competitive environment.

Completely diversified portfolio A portfolio in which all unsystematic risk has been eliminated by diversification.

Completeness fund A specialized index used to form the basis of a passive portfolio whose purpose is to provide diversification to a client's total portfolio by excluding those segments in which the client's active managers invest.

Composite measure An investment performance statistic that considers both the return and risk associated with a portfolio (e.g., Sharpe measure, Treynor measure, Jensen measure).

Computer-Assisted Execution System (CAES) A service created by Nasdaq that automates order routing and execution for securities listed on domestic stock exchanges and involved on the Intermarket Trading System (ITS).

Consolidated Quotation Sytem (CQS) An electronic quotation service for issues listed on the NYSE, the AMEX, or regional exchanges and traded on the Nasdaq InterMarket.

Consolidation phase Phase in the investment life cycle during which individuals who are typically past the midpoint of their career have earnings that exceed expenses and invest them for future retirement or estate planning needs.

Construct the portfolio Given the strategy and economic outlook, what specific stocks and/or bonds will be put into the portfolio at the present time that are consistent with the client's policy statement.

Contango A situation in a futures market where the current contract price is greater than the current spot price for the underlying asset.

Contingent deferred sales load A mutual fund that imposes a sales charge when the investor sells or redeems shares. Also referred to as *rear-end loads* or *redemption charges*.

Continual monitoring The constant evaluation of the economic environment, the policy statement, and the portfolio to ensure that it is consistent with the policy statement. Also involves evaluating performance to determine if changes are required in the portfolio, the strategy, or the policy statement.

Continuous market A market where stocks are priced and traded continuously by an auction process or by dealers when the market is open.

Contract price The transaction price specified in a forward or futures contract.

Contrarian An investment strategy that attempts to buy (sell) securities on which the majority of other investors are bearish (bullish).

Convenience yield An adjustment made to the theoretical forward or futures contract delivery price to account for the preference that consumers have for holding spot positions in the underlying asset.

Conversion factors The adjustments made to Treasury bond futures contract terms to allow for the delivery of an instrument other than the standardized underlying asset.

Conversion parity price The price at which common stock can be obtained by surrendering the convertible instrument at par value.

Conversion premium The excess of the market value of the convertible security over its equity value if immediately converted into common stock. Typically expressed as a percentage of the equity value.

Conversion ratio The number of shares of common stock for which a convertible security may be exchanged.

Conversion value The value of the convertible security if converted into common stock at the stock's current market price.

Convertible bonds A bond with the added feature that the bondholder has the option to turn the bond back to the firm in exchange for a specified number of common shares of the firm.

Convexity A measure of the degree to which a bond's price-yield curve departs from a straight line. This characteristic affects estimates of a bond's price volatility for a given change in yields.

Core-plus bond portfolio management This is a combination approach to bond portfolio management wherein a significant (core) part of the portfolio (e.g., 70–75 percent) of the portfolio is managed passively in a widely recognized sector of the bond market, such as an aggregate bond index or a U.S. Government/corporate sector. The rest of the portfolio would be actively managed in one or several "plus" sectors that are less efficient than the core component—for example, high-yield bonds, foreign bonds, or emerging market debt.

Correlation coefficient A standardized measure of the relationship between two variables that ranges from –1.00 to +1.00.

Cost of carry The net amount that would be required to store a commodity or security for future delivery, usually calculated as physical storage costs plus financial capital costs less dividends paid to the underlying asset.

Counterparty A participant to a derivative transaction.

Country risk Uncertainty due to the possibility of major political or economic change in the country where an investment is located. Also called *political risk.*

Coupon Indicates the interest payment on a debt security. It is the coupon rate times the par value that indicates the interest payments on a debt security.

Coupon reinvestment risk The component of interest rate risk due to the uncertainty of the rate at which coupon payments will be reinvested.

Covariance A measure of the degree to which two variables, such as rates of return for investment assets, move together over time relative to their individual mean returns.

Covered call A trading strategy in which a call option is sold as a supplement to a long position in an underlying asset or portfolio of assets.

Covered interest arbitrage A trading strategy involving borrowing money in one country and lending it to another designed to exploit price deviations from the interest rate parity model.

Credit analysis An active bond portfolio management strategy designed to identify bonds that are expected to experience changes in rating. This strategy is critical when investing in high-yield bonds.

Credit default swap An agreement in which the protection buyer makes periodic premium payments in exchange for the protection seller's obligation to make a settlement payment that is contingent on the occurrence of a credit-related event to a predetermined reference entity, usually a specific bond or bond index.

Cross hedge A trading strategy in which the price volatility of a commodity or security position is hedged with a forward or futures contract based on a different underlying asset or different settlement terms.

Crossover price The price at which the yield to maturity equals the yield to call. Above this price, yield to call is the appropriate yield measure; below this price, yield to maturity is the appropriate yield measure.

Cross-sectional analysis An examination of a firm's performance in comparison to other firms in the industry with similar characteristics to the firm being studied.

Cross-sectional return studies Studies wherein investigators look for public information that can be used to predict the cross-sectional distribution of risk-adjusted returns—e.g., is there an inverse relationship between market-value size of a firm and future risk-adjusted rates of return for its stock?

Current income A return objective in which the investor seeks to generate income rather than capital gains; generally a goal of an investor who wants to supplement earnings with income to meet living expenses.

Current yield A bond's yield as measured by its current income (coupon) as a percentage of its market price.

Cyclical change An economic trend arising from the ups and downs of the business cycle.

Cyclical company A firm whose earnings rise and fall with general economic activity.

Cyclical stock A stock with a high beta; its gains typically exceed those of a rising market and its losses typically exceed those of a falling market.

D

Debentures Bonds that promise payments of interest and principal but pledge no specific assets. Holders have first claim on the issuer's income and unpledged assets. Also known as *unsecured bonds.*

Declining trend channel The range defined by security prices as they move progressively lower.

Dedication A portfolio management technique in which the portfolio's cash flows are used to retire a set of liabilities over time.

Dedication with reinvestment A dedication strategy in which portfolio cash flows may precede their corresponding liabilities. Such cash flows can be reinvested to earn a return until the date the liability is due to be paid.

Defensive company Firms whose future earnings are likely to withstand an economic downturn.

Defensive competitive strategy Positioning the firm so that its capabilities provide the best means to deflect the effect of the competitive forces in the industry.

Defensive stock A stock whose return is not expected to decline as much as that of the overall market during a bear market (a beta less than one).

Defined benefit pension plan A pension plan to which the company contributes a certain amount each year and promises to pay employees a specified income after they retire. The benefit size is based on factors such as workers' salary and time of employment.

Defined contribution pension plan A pension plan in which worker benefits are determined by the size of employees' contributions to the plan and the returns earned on the fund's investments.

Delta The change in the price of the option with respect to a one dollar change in the price of the underlying asset; this is the option's *hedge ratio,* or the number of units of the underlying asset that can be hedged by a single option contract.

Derivative security An instrument whose market value ultimately depends upon, or derives from, the value of a more fundamental investment vehicle called the underlying asset or security.

Diffusion index for stocks An indicator of the number of stocks rising during a specified period of time relative to the number of stocks declining and not changing price.

Discount A bond selling at a price below par value due to capital market conditions.

Dividend discount model (DDM) A technique for estimating the value of a stock issue as the present value of all future dividends.

Downside risk The volatility in a portfolio based on returns that fall below a minimum acceptable threshold level, which is specified by the investor.

DuPont system A method of examining *ROE* by breaking it down into three component parts: (1) profit margin, (2) total asset turnover, and (3) financial leverage.

Duration A measure of the interest rate sensitivity of a bond's market price taking into consideration its coupon and term to maturity. The percent change in price for 100 basis point change in yield.

Duration strategy A portfolio management strategy employed to reduce the interest rate risk of a bond portfolio by matching the modified duration of the portfolio with its investment horizon. For example, if the investment horizon is 10 years, the portfolio manager would construct a portfolio that has a modified duration of 10 years. This strategy is referred to as *immunization of the portfolio.*

E

Earnings momentum A strategy in which portfolios are constructed of stocks of firms with rising earnings.

Earnings multiplier model A technique for estimating the value of a stock issue as a multiple of its future earnings per share.

Earnings surprise A company announcement of earnings that differ from analysts' prevailing expectations.

EBITDA Earnings before interest, taxes, depreciation, and amortization.

Economic value added (EVA) Internal management performance measure that compares net operating profit to total cost of capital. Indicates how profitable company projects are as a sign of management performance.

Effective duration Direct measure of the interest rate sensitivity of a bond (or any financial instrument) based upon price changes derived from a pricing model.

Efficient capital market A market in which security prices rapidly reflect all information about securities.

Efficient frontier The set of portfolios that has the maximum rate of return for every given level of risk, or the minimum risk for every potential rate of return.

Electronic Communication Network (ECN) A computerized trading system that matches buy and sell orders, usually for retail and small institutional trading. ECNs act for customers as a broker—they do not buy or sell from their own accounts.

Electronic Crossing System (ECS) An electronic trading system that matches large buy and sell orders.

Empirical duration Measures directly the interest rate sensitivity of an asset by examining the percentage price change for an asset in response to a change in yield during a specified period of time.

Ending-wealth value The total amount of money derived from investment in a bond until maturity, including principal, coupon payments, and income from reinvestment of coupon payments.

Enhanced indexing A portfolio management strategy that attempts to outperform a designated benchmark on a risk-adjusted basis by combining passive (i.e., indexed) and active management approaches.

Equipment trust certificates Mortgage bonds that are secured by specific pieces of transportation equipment like boxcars and planes.

Equity collar An option-based hedging strategy that protects a stock position from price declines by purchasing a put option that is paid for by the sale of a call option.

Equity swap A swap transaction in which one cash flow is tied to the return to an equity portfolio position, often an index such as the Standard and Poor's 500, while the other is based on a floating-rate index.

Estimated rate of return The rate of return an investor anticipates earning from a specific investment over a particular future holding period.

Eurobonds Bonds denominated in a currency not native to the country in which they are issued.

European option An option contract that can only be exercised on its expiration date.

Event study Research that examines the reaction of a security's price to a specific company, world event, or news announcement.

Exchange clearinghouse The functional unit attached to a futures exchange that guarantees contract performance, oversees delivery, serves as a bookkeeper, and calculates settlement transactions.

Exchange rate risk Uncertainty due to the denomination of an investment in a currency other than that of the investor's own country.

Exchange-traded fund (ETF) A tradable depository receipt that gives investors a pro rata claim to the returns associated with a portfolio of securities (often designed to mimic an index, such as the Standard & Poor's 500) held in trust by a financial institution.

Exercise price The transaction price specified in an option contract; also known as the *strike price.*

Expected rate of return The return that analysts' calculations suggest a security should provide, based on the market's rate of return during the period and the security's relationship to the market.

Expense ratio The percentage of a fund's assets deducted annually for expenses, including management fees, administrative fees, and operating costs, but not including security trading fees.

Expiry The expiration date of a derivative security.

Extended DuPont System A method of examming *ROE* by breaking it down into five component parts.

External efficiency A market in which prices adjust quickly to new information regarding supply or demand. Also referred to as *informational efficiency.*

F

Fiduciary A person who supervises or oversees the investment portfolio of a third party, such as in a trust account, and makes investment decisions in accordance with the owner's wishes.

Filter rule A trading rule that recommends security transactions when price changes exceed a previously determined percentage.

Financial risk The variability of future income arising from the firm's fixed financing costs, for example, interest payments. The effect of fixed financial costs is to magnify the effect of changes in operating profit on net income or earnings per share.

Fixed-income investments Loans with contractually mandated payment schedules from firms or governments to investors.

Flat trend channel The range defined by security prices as they maintain a relatively steady level.

Flexible portfolio fund Mutual fund that allows managers to shift assets between stocks, bonds, and cash acccording to changing market conditions; also known as *asset allocation* fund.

Floating-rate note (FRN) Short- to intermediate-term bonds with regularly scheduled coupon payments linked to a variable interest rate, most often LIBOR.

Floor agreement A contract that on each settlement date pays the holder the greater of the difference between the floor rate and the reference rate or zero; it is equivalent to a series of put options on the reference rate.

Floor brokers Independent members of an exchange who act as brokers for other members.

Forward contract An agreement between two counterparties that requires the exchange of a commodity or security at a fixed time in the future at a predetermined price.

Forward discount A situation where, from the perspective of the domestic country, the spot exchange rate is smaller than the forward exchange rate with a foreign country.

Forward premium A situation where, from the perspective of the domestic country, the spot exchange rate is larger than the forward exchange rate with a foreign country.

Forward rate A short-term yield for a future holding period implied by the spot rates of two securities with different maturities.

Forward rate agreement (FRA) A transaction in which two counterparties agree to a single exchange of cash flows based on a fixed and floating rate, respectively.

Franchise factor A firm's unique competitive advantage that makes it possible for a firm to earn excess returns (rates of return above a firm's cost of capital) on its capital projects. In turn, these excess returns and the franchise factor cause the firm's stock price to have a *P/E* ratio above its base *P/E* ratio that is equal to $1/k$.

Free cash flow to equity This cash flow measure equals cash flow from operations minus capital expenditures and debt payments.

Full replication A technique for constructing a passive index portfolio in which all securities in an index are purchased in proportion to their weights in the index.

Fully taxable equivalent yield (FTEY) A yield on a tax-exempt bond that adjusts for its tax benefits to allow comparisons with taxable bonds.

Futures contract An agreement that provides for the future exchange of a particular asset at a specified delivery date in exchange for a specified payment at the time of delivery.

G

General obligation bond (GO) A municipal issue serviced from and guaranteed by the issuer's full taxing authority.

Generally accepted accounting principles (GAAP) Accounting principles formulated by the Financial Accounting Standards Board and used to construct financial statements.

Geometric mean (GM) The *n*th root of the product of the annual holding period returns for *n* years minus 1.

Gifting phase Phase in the investment life cycle during which individuals use excess assets to financially assist relatives or friends, establish charitable trusts, or construct trusts to minimize estate taxes.

Government sponsored enterprises (GSEs) Entities set up by the government to provide support for specific segments of the economy considered important by the government. Prime examples are the Federal National Mortgage Association (referred to as Fannie Mae) and Federal Home Loan Corporation (Freddie Mac) that were set up to reduce the cost of borrowing by home owners. They issue securities directly in the market at rates that are generally higher than Treasuries because they are not backed by the full credit of the government, but lower than corporations. Funds from the sale of securities are used to acquire mortgages that are securitized and sold to institutions and individual investors.

Growth company A company that consistently has the opportunities and ability to invest in projects that provide rates of return that exceed the firm's cost of capital. Because of these investment opportunities, it retains a high proportion of earnings, and its earnings grow faster than those of average firms.

Growth stock A stock issue that generates a higher rate of return than other stocks in the market with similar risk characteristics.

H

Hedge A trading strategy in which derivative securities are used to reduce or completely offset a counterparty's risk exposure to an underlying asset.

Hedge fund An investment vehicle designed to manage a private, unregistered portfolio of assets according to any of several strategies. The investment strategy often employs arbitrage trading and significant financial leverage (e.g., short selling, borrowing, derivatives) while the compensation arrangement for the manager typically specifies considerable profit participation.

Hedge ratio The number of derivative contracts that must be transacted to offset the price volatility of an underlying commodity or security position.

High-yield bond A bond rated below investment grade. Also referred to as *speculative-grade bonds* or *junk bonds.*

Holdings-base measure A performance measure based on how a manager changes the portfolio's security holdings over time, often in comparison to a benchmark portfolio.

Holding period return (HPR) The total return from an investment, including all sources of income, for a given period of time. A value of 1.0 indicates no gain or loss. Equal to ending wealth/beginning wealth.

Holding period yield (HPY) The total return from an investment for a given period of time stated as a percentage. Equal to HPR-1.

I

Immunization A bond portfolio management technique of matching modified duration to the investment horizon of the portfolio to eliminate interest rate risk.

Implied volatility The standard deviation of changes in the price of the underlying asset that can be inferred from an option's market price in relation to a specific valuation model.

In the money An option that has positive intrinsic value.

Incentive compensations A scheme for paying investment managers according to the performance of the portfolio, often based on the level of assets under management.

Income bonds Debentures that stipulate interest payments only if the issuer earns the income to make the payments by specified dates.

Income statement A financial statement that shows the flow of the firm's sales, expenses, and earnings over a period of time.

Indenture The legal agreement that lists the obligations of the issuer of a bond to the bondholder, including payment schedules, call provisions, and sinking funds.

Indexing A passive bond portfolio management strategy that seeks to match the composition, and therefore the performance, of a selected market index.

Industry life cycle analysis An analysis that focuses on the industry's stage of development.

Information An attribute of a good market that includes providing buyers and sellers with timely, accurate information on the volume and prices of past transactions and on all currently outstanding bids and offers.

Information ratio Statistic used to measure a portfolio's average return in excess of a comparison, benchmark portfolio divided by the standard deviation of this excess return.

Informationally efficient market A more technical term for an efficient capital market that emphasizes the role of information in setting the market price.

Initial public offering (IPO) A new issue by a firm that has no existing public market.

Interest rate anticipation An active bond portfolio management strategy designed to preserve capital or take advantage of capital gains opportunities by predicting interest rates and their effects on bond prices.

Interest rate collar The combination of a long position in a cap agreement and a short position in a floor agreement, or vice versa; it is equivalent to a series of range forward positions.

Interest rate parity The relationship that must exist in an efficient market between the spot and forward foreign exchange rates between two countries and the interest rates in those countries.

Interest rate risk The uncertainty of returns on an investment due to possible changes in interest rates over time.

Interest rate swap An agreement calling for the periodic exchange of cash flows, one based on an interest rate that remains fixed for the life of the contract and the other that is linked to a variable-rate index.

Interest-on-interest Bond income from reinvestment of coupon payments.

Intermarket Trading System (ITS) A computerized system that connects competing exchanges and dealers who trade stocks listed on an exchange. Its purpose is to help customers find the best market for these stocks at a point in time.

Internal liquidity (solvency) ratios Financial ratios that measure the ability of the firm to meet future short-term financial obligations.

Internal rate of return (IRR) The discount rate at which cash outflows of an investment equal cash inflows.

International domestic bonds Bonds issued by a foreign firm, denominated in the firm's native currency, and sold within its own country.

Intrinsic value The portion of a call option's total value equal to the greater of either zero or the difference between the current value of the underlying asset and the exercise price; for a put option, intrinsic value is the greater of either zero or the exercise price less the underlying asset price. For a stock, it is the value derived from fundamental analysis of the stock's expected returns or cash flows.

Investment The current commitment of dollars for a period of time in order to derive future payments that will compensate the investor for the time the funds are committed, the expected rate of inflation, and the uncertainty of future payments.

Investment company A firm that sells shares of the company and uses the proceeds to buy portfolios of stock, bonds, or other financial instruments.

Investment decision process Estimation of intrinsic value for comparison with market price to determine whether or not to invest.

Investment horizon The time period used for planning and forecasting purposes or the future time at which the investor requires the invested funds.

Investment management company A company separate from the investment company that manages the portfolio and performs administrative functions.

Investment strategy A decision by a portfolio manager regarding how he or she will manage the portfolio to meet the goals and objectives of the client. This will include either active or passive management and, if active, what style in terms of top-down or buttom-up or fundamental versus technical.

J

January effect A frequent empirical anomaly where risk-adjusted stock returns in the month of January are significantly larger than those occurring in any other month of the year.

J-curve effect The tendency for the returns to private equity funds to be negative initially and then positive in later years as the more profitable investments are realized.

Jensen measure An absolute measure of a portfolio's risk-adjusted performance, computed as the intercept in a regression equation where the excess returns to a manager's portfolio and the market index are, respectively, the dependent and independent variables.

L

Lagging indicators A set of economic variables whose values reach peaks and troughs after the aggregate economy.

Leading indicators A set of economic variables whose values reach peaks and troughs in advance of the aggregate economy.

Limit order An order that lasts for a specified time to buy or sell a security when and if it trades at a specified price.

Limited partnership A business organization with one or more general partners, who manage the business and assume legal debts and obligations, and one or more limited partners, who are liable only to the extent of their investments.

Liquid Term used to describe an asset that can be quickly converted to cash at a price close to fair market value.

Liquidity The ability to buy or sell an asset quickly and at a reasonable price based on information.

Liquidity preference hypothesis One of the alternative explanations for the different shapes of the term structure of interest rates. This hypothesis holds that long-term securities should provide higher promised yields than short-term securities because of the higher price volatility of long-maturity (high duration) bonds.

Liquidity risk Uncertainty due to the ability to buy or sell an investment in the secondary market.

Long hedge A long position in a forward or futures contract used to offset the price volatility of a short position in the underlying asset.

Long position The buyer of a commodity or security or, for a forward contract, the counterparty who will be the eventual buyer of the underlying asset.

Long-term, high-priority goal A long-term financial investment goal of personal importance that typically includes achieving financial independence, such as being able to retire at a certain age.

Lower-priority goal A financial investment goal of lesser personal importance, such as taking a luxurious vacation or buying a car every few years.

Low-load fund A mutual fund that imposes a moderate front-end sales charge when the investor buys the fund, typically about 3 to 4 percent.

M

Macaulay duration A measure of the time flow of cash from a bond where cash flows are weighted by present values discounted by the yield to maturity.

Maintenance margin The required proportion that the investor's equity value must be to the total market value of the stock. If the proportion drops below this percent, the investor will receive a margin call.

Management and advisory firm A firm that provides a range of services from standard banking transactions (savings accounts, personal loans) to advising individual and institutional investors on structuring their portfolios and managing investment funds.

Management effect A combination of the interest rate anticipation effect, the analysis effect, and the trading effect.

Management fee The compensation an investment company pays to the investment management company for its services. The average annual fee is about 0.5 percent of fund assets.

Margin The percent of cost a buyer pays in cash for a security, borrowing the balance from the broker. This introduces leverage, which increases the risk of the transaction.

Margin account The collateral posted with the futures exchange clearinghouse by an outside counterparty to insure its eventual performance; the *initial* margin is the deposit required at contract origination while the *maintenance* margin is the minimum collateral necessary at all times.

Margin call A request by an investor's broker for additional capital for a security bought on margin if the investor's equity value declines below the required maintenance margin.

Marginal tax rate The part of each additional dollar in income that is paid as tax.

Marked to market The settlement process used to adjust the margin account of a futures contract for daily changes in the price of the underlying asset.

Market The means through which buyers and sellers are brought together to aid in the transfer of goods and/or services.

Market order An order to buy or sell a security immediately at the best price available.

Market portfolio The portfolio that includes all risky assets with relative weights equal to their proportional market values.

Market risk premium The amount of return above the risk-free rate that investors expect from the market in general as compensation for systematic risk.

Market value added (MVA) External management performance measure to compare the market value of the company's debt and equity with the total capital invested in the firm.

Maturity strategy A portfolio management strategy employed to reduce the interest rate risk of a bond portfolio by matching the maturity of the portfolio with its investment horizon. For example, if the investment horizon is 10 years, the portfolio manager would construct a portfolio that will mature in 10 years.

Mean rates of return The average of an investment's returns over an extended period of time.

Modified duration A measure of Macaulay duration divided by one plus the bond's periodic yield used to approximate the bond's price volatility.

Money market The market for short-term debt securities with maturities of less than one year.

Money market fund A fund that invests in short-term securities sold in the money market. (Large companies, banks, and other institutions also invest their surplus cash in the money market for short periods of time.) In the entire investment spectrum, these are generally the safest, most stable securities available. They include Treasury bills, certificates of deposit of large banks, and commercial paper (short-term IOUs of large corporations).

Money-weighted return The discount rate that sets the present value of a future set of cash flows equal to the investment's current value; also known as the *internal rate of return.*

Mortgage bonds Bonds that pledge specific assets such as buildings and equipment. The proceeds from the sale of these assets are used to pay off bondholders in case of bankruptcy.

Moving average The continually recalculating average of security prices for a period, often 200 days, to serve as an indication of the general trend of prices and also as a benchmark price.

Multifactor model An empirical version of the APT where the investor chooses the exact number and identity of the common risk factors used to describe an asset's risk-return relationship. Risk factors are often designated as *macroeconomic* variables (e.g., inflation, changes in gross domestic product) or *microeconomic* variables (e.g., security-specific characteristics like firm size or book-to-market ratios).

Municipal bond insurance *See* Bond insurance.

Mutual fund An investment company that pools money from shareholders and invests in a variety of securities, including stocks, bonds, and money market securities. A mutual fund ordinarily stands ready to buy back (redeem) its shares at their current net asset value, which depends on the market value of the fund's portfolio of securities at the time. Mutual funds generally continuously offer new shares to investors.

N

Nasdaq InterMarket A trading system that includes Nasdaq market makers and ECNs that quote and trade stocks listed on the NYSE and the AMEX. It involves dealers from the Nasdaq market and the Intermarket Trading System (ITS). In many ways, this has become what had been labeled the third market.

National Association of Securities Dealers Automated Quotation (Nasdaq) system An electronic system for providing bid-ask quotes on OTC securities.

Near-term, high-priority goal A short-term financial investment goal of personal importance, such as accumulating funds for making a house down payment or buying a car.

Negotiated sales An underwriting arrangement wherein the sale of a security issue by an issuing entity (governmental body or a corporation) is done using an investment banking firm that maintains an ongoing relationship with the issuer. The characteristics of the security issue are determined by the issuer in consultation with the investment banker.

Net asset value (NAV) per share The market value of an investment company's assets (securities, cash, and any accrued earnings) after deducting liabilities, divided by the number of shares outstanding.

Net present value (NPV) A measure of the excess cash flows expected from an investment proposal. It is equal to the present value of the cash *inflows* from an investment proposal, discounted at the required rate of return for the investment, minus the present value of the cash *outflows* required by the investment, also discounted at the investment's required rate of return. If the derived net present value is a positive value (i.e., there is an excess net present value), the investment should be acquired since it will provide a rate of return above its required returns.

New issue Common stocks or bonds offered by companies for public sale.

No-load fund A mutual fund that sells its shares at net asset value without adding sales charges.

Nominal yield A bond's yield as measured by its coupon rate.

Normal portfolio A specialized or customized benchmark constructed to evaluate a specific manager's investment style or philosophy.

Notes Intermediate-term debt securities with maturities longer than 1 year but less than 10 years.

Notional principal The principal value of a swap transaction, which is not exchanged but is used as a scale factor to translate interest rate differentials into cash settlement payments.

O

Objectives The investor's goals expressed in terms of risk and return and included in the policy statement.

Offensive competitive strategy A strategy whereby a firm attempts to use its strengths to affect the competitive forces in the industry and, in so doing, improves the firm's relative position in the industry.

130/30 strategy An active equity portfolio management approach that allows short positions up to a certain percentage (e.g., 30) of capital and an equal percentage of leveraged long positions.

Open-end investment company The more formal name for a mutual fund, which derives from the fact that it continuously offers new shares to investors and redeems them (buys them back) on demand.

Operating efficiency ratios Financial ratios intended to indicate how efficiently management is utilizing the firm's assets in terms of dollar sales generated per dollar of assets. Primary examples would be: total asset turnover, fixed asset turnover, or equity turnover.

Operating leverage The use of fixed-production costs in the firm's operating cost structure. The effect of fixed costs is to magnify the effect of a change in sales on operating profits.

Operating profitability ratios Financial ratios intended to indicate how profitable the firm is in terms of the percent of profit generated from sales. Alternative measures would include: operating profit (EBIT)/net sales; pretax profit (EBT)/net sales; and net profit/sales.

Optimal portfolio The portfolio on the efficient frontier that has the highest utility for a given investor. It lies at the point of tangency between the efficient frontier and the curve with the investor's highest possible utility.

Option-adjusted duration An estimate of the duration of a bond that specifically adjusts for the existence of an embedded put and/or call option in the bond. It can be envisioned as the duration of a noncallable bond minus the duration of an embedded call option or plus the duration of an embedded put option.

Options Clearing Corporation (OCC) A company designed to guarantee, monitor margin accounts, and settle exchange-traded option transactions.

Option contract An agreement that grants the owner the right, but not the obligation, to make a future transaction in an underlying commodity or security at a fixed price and within a predetermined time in the future.

Option premium The initial price that the option buyer must pay to the option seller to acquire the contract.

Option-adjusted spread A type of yield spread that considers changes in the term structure and alternative estimates of the volatility of interest rates. It is spread after adjusting for embedded options.

OTC Electronic Bulletin Board (OTCBB) A regulated quotation service that displays real-time quotes, last-sale prices, and volume information for a specified set of over-the-counter (OTC) securities that are not traded on the formal Nasdaq market.

Out of the money An option that has no intrinsic value.

Overfunded plan A defined benefit pension plan in which the present value of the pension liabilities is less than market value of the plan's assets.

Overweighted A condition in which a portfolio, for whatever reason, includes more of a class of securities than the relative market value alone would justify.

P

Par value *See* Principal.

Payback The time required for the added income from the convertible security relative to the stock to offset the conversion premium.

Peak The culmination of a bull market when prices stop rising and begin declining.

Peer group comparison A method of measuring portfolio performance by collecting the returns produced by a representative universe of investors over a specific period of time.

Performance presentation standards (PPS) A comprehensive set of reporting guidelines created by the Association for Investment Management and Research (AIMR) (now the CFA Institute), in an effort to fulfill the call for uniform, accurate, and consistent performance reporting.

Perpetuity An investment without any maturity date. It provides returns to its owner indefinitely.

Personal trust An amount of money set aside by a grantor and often managed by a third party, the trustee. Often constructed so one party receives income from the trust's investments and another party receives the residual value of the trust after the income beneficiaries' death.

Policy effect The difference in performance of a bond portfolio from that of a chosen index due to differences in duration, which result from a fund's investment policy.

Policy statement A statement in which the investor specifies investment goals, constraints, and risk preferences.

Portfolio A group of investments. Ideally, the investments should have different patterns of returns over time.

Portfolio turnover The total dollar value of securities sold from a portfolio in a year divided by the average assets under management for the fund during the same period.

Preferred stock An equity investment that stipulates the dividend payment either as a coupon or a stated dollar amount. The firm's directors may withhold dividend payments.

Premium A bond selling at a price above par value due to capital market conditions.

Price continuity A feature of a liquid market in which there are small price changes from one transaction to the next due to the depth of the market.

Price momentum A portfolio strategy in which you acquire stocks that have enjoyed above-market stock price increases.

Price risk The component of interest rate risk due to the uncertainty of the market price of a bond caused by changes in market interest rates.

Price/earnings (P/E) ratio The number by which expected earnings per share is multiplied to estimate a stock's value; also called the *earnings multiplier*.

Price-weighted index An index calculated as an arithmetic mean of the current prices of the sampled securities.

Price-yield curve Created by plotting the set of computed prices for a specific bond against an alternative set of potential yields. It generally shows the convexity of the curve.

Primary market The market in which newly issued securities are sold by their issuers, who receive the proceeds.

Principal (par value) The original value of the debt underlying a bond that is payable at maturity.

Private equity An ownership interest in a company or collection of assets that is not publicly traded on an exchange or in the over-the-counter market.

Private placement A new issue sold directly to a small group of investors, usually institutions.

Promised yield to call (YTC) A bond's yield if held until the first available call date, with reinvestment of all coupon payments at the yield-to-call rate.

Promised yield to maturity (YTM) The most widely used measure of a bond's yield that states the fully compounded rate of return on a bond bought at market price and held to maturity with reinvestment of all coupon payments at the yield to maturity rate.

Protective put A trading strategy in which a put option is purchased as a supplement to a long position in an underlying asset or portfolio of assets; the most straightforward form of *portfolio insurance*.

Public bond A long-term, fixed-obligation debt security in a convenient, affordable denomination for sale to individuals and financial institutions.

Pure cash-matched dedicated portfolio A conservative dedicated portfolio management technique aimed at developing a bond portfolio that will provide cash payments that exactly match the specified liability schedules.

Put options Options to sell a security (stock or bond) within a certain period at a specified price.

Put-call parity The relationship that must exist in an efficient market between the prices for put and call options having the same underlying asset, exercise price, and expiration date.

Q

Quadratic optimization A technique that relies on historical correlations in order to construct a portfolio that seeks to minimize tracking error with an index.

Quality financial statements Financial statements that most knowledgeable observers (analysts, portfolio managers) would consider conservatively prepared in terms of sales, expenses, earnings, and asset valuations. The results reported would reflect reasonable estimates and indicate what truly happened during the period and the legitimate value of assets and liabilities on the balance sheet.

R

Range forward A trading strategy based on a variation of the put-call parity model where, for the same underlying asset but different exercise prices, a call option is purchased and a put option is sold (or vice versa).

Rate anticipation effect The difference in return because of changing the duration of the portfolio during a period as compared with the portfolio's long-term policy duration.

Real estate investment trusts (REITs) Investment funds that hold portfolios of real estate investments.

Real options Options embedded in a firm's real assets that give managers valuable decision-making flexibility, such as the right to either undertake or abandon an investment project.

Real risk-free rate (RRFR) The basic interest rate with no accommodation for inflation or uncertainty. The pure time value of money.

Realized capital gains Capital gains that result when an appreciated asset is sold; realized capital gains are taxable.

Realized yield The expected compounded yield on a bond that is sold before it matures assuming the reinvestment of all cash flows at an explicit rate. Also called *horizon yield* for the yield realized during an investment horizon period.

Refunding issue Bonds that provide funds to prematurely retire another bond issue. These bonds can be either a junior or senior issue.

Registered bond A bond for which ownership is registered with the issuer. The holder receives interest payments by check directly from the issuer.

Registered competitive market makers (RCMMs) Members of an exchange who are allowed to use their memberships to buy or sell for their own account within the specific trading obligations set down by the exchange.

Registered traders Members of the stock exchange who are allowed to use their memberships to buy and sell for their own account, which means they save commissions on their trading but they provide liquidity to the market, and they abide by exchange regulations on how they can trade.

Relative-strength (RS) ratio The ratio of a stock price or an industry index value to a market indicator series, indicating the stock's or the industry's performance relative to the overall market.

Required rate of return The return that compensates investors for their time, the expected rate of inflation, and the uncertainty of the return.

Resistance level A price at which a technician would expect a substantial increase in the supply of a stock to reverse a rising trend.

Return prediction studies Studies wherein investigations attempt to predict the time series of future rates of return using public information. An example would be predicting above-average returns for the stock market based on the aggregate dividend yield—e.g., high dividend yield indicates above average future market returns.

Revenue bond A bond that is serviced by the income generated from specific revenue-producing projects of the municipality such as toll roads or athletic stadiums.

Rising trend channel The range defined by security prices as they move progressively higher.

Risk The uncertainty that an investment will earn its expected rate of return.

Risk averse The assumption about investors that they will choose the least risky alternative, all else being equal.

Risk premium (RP) The increase over the nominal risk-free rate that investors demand as compensation for an investment's uncertainty.

Risk-free asset An asset with returns that exhibit zero variance.

Risky asset An asset with uncertain future returns.

Runs test A test of the weak-form efficient market hypothesis that checks for trends that persist longer in terms of positive or negative price changes than one would expect for a random series.

S

Sampling A technique for constructing a passive index portfolio in which the portfolio manager buys a representative sample of stocks that comprise the benchmark index.

Seasoned equity issues New equity shares offered by firms that already have stock outstanding.

Secondary market The market in which outstanding securities are bought and sold by owners other than the issuers. Purpose is to provide liquidity for investors.

Sector rotation strategy An active strategy that involves purchasing stocks in specific industries or stocks with specific characteristics (low *P/E,* growth, value) that are anticipated to rise in value more than the overall market.

Secured (senior) bond A bond backed by a legal claim on specified assets of the issuer.

Security market index An index created as a statistical measure of the performance of an entire market or segment of a market based on a sample of securities from the market or segment of a market.

Security market indicator series An index created as a statistical measure of the performance of an entire market or segment of a market based on a sample of securities from the market or segment of a market.

Security market line (SML) The line that reflects the combination of risk and return of alternative investments. In CAPM, risk is measured by systematic risk (beta).

SelectNet An order-routing and trade-execution system for institutional investors (brokers and dealers) that allows communication through the Nasdaq system rather than by phone.

Semistrong-form efficient market hypothesis The belief that security prices fully reflect all publicly available information, including information from security transactions and company, economic, and political news.

Separation theorem The proposition that the investment decision, which involves investing in the market portfolio on the capital market line, is separate from the financing decision, which targets a specific point on the CML based on the investor's risk preference.

Serial obligation bond A bond issue that has a series of maturity dates. Typical for municipal bonds.

Settlement price The price determined by the exchange clearinghouse with which futures contract margin accounts are marked to market.

Sharpe measure A relative measure of a portfolio's benefit-to-risk ratio, calculated as its average return in excess of the risk-free rate divided by the standard deviation of portfolio returns.

Short hedge A short position in a forward or futures contract used to offset the price volatility of a long position in the underlying asset.

Short position The seller of a commodity or security or, for a forward contract, the counterparty who will be the eventual seller of the underlying asset.

Short sale The sale of borrowed securities with the intention of repurchasing them later at a lower price and earning the difference.

Sinking fund Bond provision that requires the issuer to redeem some or all of the bond systematically over the term of the bond rather than in full at maturity.

Small-firm effect A frequent empirical anomaly where risk-adjusted stock returns for companies with low market capitalization (i.e., share price multiplied by number of outstanding shares) are significantly larger than those generated by high market capitalization (large cap) firms.

Small-Order Execution System (SOES) A quotation and execution system for retail (nonprofessional) investors who place orders with brokers who must honor their prevailing bid–ask for automatic excution up to 1,000 shares.

Soft dollars A form of compensation to a money manager generated when the manager commits the investor to paying higher brokerage fees in exchange for the manager receiving additional services (e.g., stock research) from the broker.

Sortino measure A relative measure of a portfolio's performance, calculated as its average return in excess of minimum acceptable return threshold, divided by its downside risk coefficient.

Specialist The major market maker on U.S. stock exchanges who acts as a broker or dealer to ensure the liquidity and smooth functions of the secondary stock market.

Speculative company A firm with a great degree of business and/or financial risk, with commensurate high earnings potential.

Speculative stock A stock that appears to be highly overpriced compared to its intrinsic valuation.

Spending phase Phase in the investment life cycle during which individuals' earning years end as they retire. They pay for expenses with income from social security and returns from prior investments and invest to protect against inflation.

Spot rate The required yield for a cash flow to be received at some specific date in the future—for example, the spot rate for a flow to be received in one year, for a cash flow in two years, and so on.

Spread A trading strategy where long and short positions in two call (or two put) option contracts having the same underlying asset but different exercise prices or expiration dates are combined to create a customized return distribution.

Standard deviation A measure of variability equal to the square root of the variance.

Statement of cash flows A financial statement that shows the effects on the firm's cash flow of income flows and changes in its balance sheet.

Static yield spread Yield spreads over the total term structure.

Stock index arbitrage A trading strategy involving a long position in a stock portfolio and a short position in a stock index futures contract (or vice versa) designed to exploit a mispricing in the futures contract relative to the underlying index.

Straddle A trading strategy requiring the simultaneous purchase of a call option and a put option having the same exercise price, underlying asset, and expiration date. Variations of this theme include *strips, straps, strangles,* and *chooser options.*

Strong-form efficient market hypothesis The belief that security prices fully reflect all information from both public and private sources.

Structural change Economic trend occurring when the economy is undergoing a major change in organization or in how it functions.

Structured note A bond with an embedded derivative designed to create a payoff distribution that satisfies the needs of a specific investor clientele.

Style analysis An attempt to explain the variability in the observed returns to a security portfolio in terms of the movements in the returns to a series of benchmark portfolios designed to capture the essence of a particular security characteristic such as size, value, and growth.

Style grid A graph used to classify and display the investment style that best defines the nature of a security portfolio.

Subordinate (junior) bonds Debentures that, in case of default, entitle holders to claims on the issuer's assets only after the claims of holders of senior debentures and mortgage bonds are satisfied.

Support level A price at which a technician would expect a substantial increase in price and volume for a stock to reverse a declining trend that was due to profit taking.

Sustainable growth rate A measure of how fast a firm can grow using internal equity and debt financing and a constant capital structure. Equal to retention rate × *ROE.*

Swap spread A measure of the risk premium for an interest rate swap, calculated as the difference between the agreement's fixed rate and the yield on a Treasury bond with the same maturity.

SWOT analysis An examination of a firm's *Strengths, Weaknesses, Opportunities,* and *Threats.* This analysis helps an analyst evaluate a firm's strategies to exploit its competitive advantages or defend against its weaknesses.

Systematic risk The variability of returns that is due to macroeconomic factors that affect all risky assets. Because it affects all risky assets, it cannot be eliminated by diversification.

T

Tactical asset allocation An investment strategy that adjusts the investor's mix of stocks and bonds by increasing the allocation to the asset class that is relatively undervalued.

Tax cost ratio Based on the ratio of the portfolio's tax-adjusted and pretax returns, the measure indicates the average annual percentage of a taxable investor's assets that have been consumed by taxes over the measurement period.

Tax efficiency The extent to which the investor controls the tax consequences of the security trades in a portfolio by balancing capital gains and capital losses.

Technical analysis Estimation of future security price movements based on past price and volume movements.

Term bond A bond that has a single maturity date.

Term premium See *Liquidity preference hypothesis*.

Term structure of interest rates The relationship between term to maturity and yield to maturity for a sample of comparable bonds at a given time. Popularly known as the *yield curve*.

Term to maturity Specifies the date or the number of years before a bond matures or expires.

Third market Over-the-counter trading of securities listed on an exchange.

Tick The minimum price movement for the asset underlying a forward or futures contract; for Treasury bonds, one tick equals 1/32 of 1 percent of par value.

Time premium The difference between an option's total market value and its intrinsic value.

Time-series analysis An examination of a firm's performance data over a period of time.

Time-weighted return The geometric average of (one plus) the *holding period yields* to an investment portfolio.

Total return A return objective in which the investor wants to increase the portfolio value to meet a future need by both capital gains and current income reinvestment.

Total return swap An agreement providing for the periodic exchange of cash flows based on a floating-rate index and the total return (i.e., interest plus capital gain or loss) to a predetermined reference entity, usually a specific bond or bond index.

Tracking error The standard deviation of the difference in returns between an active investment portfolio and its benchmark portfolio; also called *tracking error volatility*.

Trading effect The difference in performance of a bond portfolio from that of a chosen index due to short-run changes in the composition of the portfolio.

Trading rule A formula for deciding on current transactions based on historical data.

Trading turnover The percentage of outstanding shares traded during a period of time.

Transaction cost The cost of executing a trade. Low costs characterize an operationally efficient market.

Treasury bill A negotiable U.S. government security with a maturity of less than one year that pays no periodic interest but yields the difference between its par value and its discounted purchase price.

Treasury bond A U.S. government security with a maturity of more than 10 years that pays interest periodically.

Treasury inflation-protected securities (TIPS) Treasury bonds backed by the faith and credit of the Treasury that provide a promised yield in real terms—i.e., the principal and interest payments are indexed to the consumer price index (CPI) published by the Bureau of Labor statistics.

Treasury note A U.S. government security with maturities of 1 to 10 years that pays interest periodically.

Treynor measure A relative measure of a portfolio's performance calculated as its average return in excess of the risk-free rate divided by its beta coefficient.

Trough The culmination of a bear market at which prices stop declining and begin rising.

12b-1 plan A fee charged by some funds, named after the SEC rule that permits it. Such fees pay for distribution costs, such as advertising, or for brokers' commissions. The fund's prospectus details any 12b-1 charges that apply.

U

Underfunded plan A defined benefit pension plan in which the present value of the fund's liabilities to employees exceeds the value of the fund's assets.

Underweighted A condition in which a portfolio, for whatever reason, includes less of a class of securities than the relative market value alone would justify.

Unrealized capital gains Capital gains that reflect the price appreciation of currently held unsold assets.

Unsecured bonds Bonds that promise payments of interest and principal but pledge no specific assets. Holders have first claim on the issuer's income and unpledged assets. Also known as *debentures*.

Unsystematic risk Risk that is unique to an asset, derived from its particular characteristics. It can be eliminated in a diversified portfolio.

Unweighted index An indicator series affected equally by the performance of each security in the sample regardless of price or market value. Also referred to as an *equal-weighted series*.

Unwind The negotiated termination of a forward or futures position before contract maturity.

V

Valuation analysis An active bond portfolio management strategy designed to capitalize on expected price increases in temporarily undervalued issues.

Valuation process Part of the investment decision process in which you estimate the value of a security.

Value stocks Stocks that appear to be undervalued for reasons besides earnings growth potential. These stocks are usually identified based on high dividend yields, low *P/E* ratios, or low price-to-book ratios.

Value-weighted index An index calculated as the total market value of the securities in the sample. Market value is equal to the number of shares or bonds outstanding times the market price of the security.

Variable-rate note A debt security for which the interest rate changes to follow some specified short-term rate, for example, the T-bill rate; see *Floating rate note*.

Variable principal redemption (VPR) A class of debt securities whose principal redemption at maturity is not fixed but tied to changes in the value of another economic entity, such as a stock index or commodity price.

Variance A measure of variability equal to the sum of the squares of a return's deviation from the mean, divided by the total number of returns.

Volatility index (VIX) A measure of investor expectations of near-term volatility in the stock market calculated as a weighted average of the implied volatilities estimated from Standard & Poor's 500 option contracts.

W

Warrant An instrument that allows the holder to purchase a specified number of shares of the firm's common stock from the firm at a specified price for a given period of time.

Weak-form efficient market hypothesis The belief that security prices fully reflect all security market information.

Y

Yankee bonds Bonds sold in the United States and denominated in U.S. dollars but issued by a foreign firm or government.

Yield The promised rate of return on an investment under certain assumptions.

Yield illusion The erroneous expectation that a bond will provide its stated yield to maturity without recognizing the implicit reinvestment assumption related to coupon payments.

Yield spread The difference between the promised yields of alternative bond issues or market segments at a given time relative to yields on Treasury issues of equal maturity.

Yield to worst Given a bond with multiple potential maturity dates and prices due to embedded call options, the practice is to calculate a yield to maturity for each of the call dates and prices and select the lowest yield (the most conservative possible yield) as yield to worst.

Z

Zero coupon bond A bond that pays its par value at maturity but no periodic interest payments. Its yield is determined by the difference between its par value and its discounted purchase price. Also called *original issue discount (OID) bonds.*

A

Accounting change announcements, semistrong-form EMH, 165–166
Accrued interest, bonds, 621
Accumulation phase, investor life cycle, 33–34
Active equity portfolio management. *See* Equity portfolio management; Portfolio management
Actuarial rate of return, 56
Aggregate market analysis, with efficient capital markets, 173
Aggregate profit margin, estimation of, 382–385
Alternative asset classes, 906–924
Alternative bonds, 14
Alternative industries, structural economic changes and, 413–415
Alternative investments, historical risk-returns, 80–85
Alternative trading systems (ATSs), 107–108
Altman Z-score model, credit analysis, 687–688
American Depository Receipts (ADRs), 74
American options, 733, 875–876
American Research and Development Corporation (ARD), 919
American shares, 74
American Stock Exchange (AMX), 78, 102–103
  information on bond prices, 601–602
AMEX. *See* American Stock Exchange (AMX)
Analysis effect, portfolio return, 1020
Anchoring bias, 170
Antiques, 79, 82–84
Arbitrage, 728
  stock index, 782, 783–787
Arbitrage pricing theory (APT), 238–246. *See also* Multifactor models
  alternative test techniques, 245–246
  comparing CAPM, 240
  empirical tests, 243–246
  security valuation with, 241–243
  using, 240–241
Arithmetic mean (AM), 7–9
Art, 79, 82–84
Asset allocation
  cultural differences, 52–54
  importance in the policy statement, 48–54
  insured, 572
  integrated, 568–570
  investment company portfolio objectives, 902

selecting an active method, 572
  strategic, 570
  strategies, 568–572
  tactical, 570–572
Asset-backed securities (ABSs), 595–596
Asset-liability management, 697
Asset management
  alternative asset classes, 906–924
  breakdown by fund characteristics, 904–905
  ethical conflicts, 928–929
  ethics and regulation, 924–929
    incentive compensation schemes, 928
    marketing investment management services, 928–929
    soft dollar arrangements, 928
  hedge fund investing, 910–911
  industry
    regulation, 924–926
    structure and evolution, 892–894
  principal securities laws, 925
  private management and advisory firms, 894–897
    investment strategy, 896–897
  standards for ethical behavior, 926–928
Asset manager, professional functions, 929–930
Asset pricing models. *See* Arbitrage pricing theory (APT); Capital asset pricing model (CAPM)
Assets
  correlations between returns, 82
  different classes, 51–52
  return and systematic risk, 81–82
  return and total risk, 80–81
Assets under management (AUM), 892–893
Auction-rate securities, 596
Autocorrelation tests, of independence in EHM, 154
Automatic adjustment, value-weighted index, 131
Automobile insurance, 32

B

Backwardated, 772
Balanced funds, 77, 902
Balance sheet, 266–267
  common size, 273
  high-quality, 302
  proportion of debt ratios, 291–293
Bankruptcy, prediction of, 305
Banks, 58–59
Bar charting, 530
Barclay's Global Investors (BGI), 78

BARRA, characteristic-based risk factor models, 250–252
Basis, 43
  defining, 768
  hedging and, 767–768
Basis risk, 768–769
Bearer bond, 580
Behavioral finance, 170–171
  explaining biases, 170–171
  fusion investing, 171
  insights, 176
Belief perseverance bias, 170
Benchmark error, 229, 1015
Benchmark portfolio, 37, 994
Benchmarks
  aggregate stock- or bond-market index, 128
  bond, 99
Best-effort basis, 96
Best Execution and Portfolio Performance (Jost), 92
Biases, 170–171
Binomial option pricing model, 865
  forecasting price changes, 865–866
  generalizing the model, 866–867
Black-Scholes valuation model, 867–870
  other extensions of, 876–878
  problems, 872–873
  properties, 868–870
The Blue List of Current Municipal Offerings, 606
Bond funds, 77
Bond ladder, 680
Bond market line, 1019–1021
Bond markets
  indexes, 137–139
    correlations with monthly, 142–143
  secondary, 97–98
  secondary corporate, 98
  technical analysis, 534–535
Bond portfolio management, 677–723
  active, 682–695
    credit analysis, 685–689
    global bond investing, 693–695
    implementing an active bond transaction, 690–693
    interest rate anticipation, 683–685
    valuation analysis, 685
    yield spread analysis, 689–690
  contingent and structured management strategies, contingent immunization, 708–714
  core-plus management strategies, 695–697
  matched-funding management strategies, 697–708

Bond portfolio management (*Continued*)
  dedicated portfolios, 698–699
  horizon matching, 707–708
  immunization techniques, 699–707
  passive, 680–682
    bond indexing in practice, 681–682
    buy-and-hold strategy, 680–681
    indexing strategy, 681
  performance, style, and strategy, 677–680
  rebalancing, 722–723
Bond ratings, estimating, 304
Bonds. *See also* specific bonds
  alternative, 14
  alternative issues, 587
  basic features, 579–582
  calculating future prices, 618–622
  callable, duration and convexity for, 652–655
  characteristics, 580–582
    impact on interest rate, 627–628
  collateral trust, 71
  commodity-linked bull and bear, 925–926
  computing yields, 613–618
  convertible, 72, 916–920
  convexity, 647–652
  corporate, 71–72, 94–95
  dual currency, 921–922
  features affecting maturity, 581–582
  general obligation (GOs), 70–71
  government, 94
  government agency issues, 589–592
  high-yield, 77
  income, 72
  indenture provisions, 581
  interest rate determination, 623–632
  international, 73, 601
  international domestic, 73
  interpreting quotes, 602–607
  intrinsic features, 580
  junk, 77
  mortgage, 71
  municipal, 70–71, 94, 592–593
  obtaining information on prices, 601–607
  participating investors, 585
  price and yield determination on
    noninterest dates, 620–621
  price volatility for, 640–663
    modified duration and, 643, 646–647
  promised yield to maturity, 614–616
  putable, 659
  rates of return on, 582
  ratings, 585–587
  secured, 71
  subordinated, 71
  tax-exempt, 621
  term-structure theories, 635–639
  treasury, 94
  types of issues, 580–581
  valuation of, 324–325
  yield books, 621–622
Bond swaps
  pure yield pickup, 690–691
  substitution, 691–692

Bond valuation. *See also* Valuation
  calculating future bond prices, 618–622
  fundamentals, 610–613
  present value model, 610–611
  using spot rates, 622–623
Book value (BV), 162
Book value/market value (BV/MV) ratio, 162
Borrowing rates, CML, 222–223
Breadth of market measures, 525–526
Brinson Partner Global Security Market
  Index (GSMI), 142
Broker, 96
Buffett, Warren, tenets, 460–461
Business cycle
  consumer sentiment and, 413
  industry sectors and, 411–413
  inflation and, 412
  interest rates and, 413
  international economics and, 413
  risk, 248
  stock market and, 411–412
Business risk, 17, 286–287, 419
  relationship to financial risk, 288–289
Buy-and-hold strategy, bond portfolio
  management, 680–681
Buyouts, private equity transaction, 919–920

C

Calendar effects, return prediction studies,
  159–160
Call markets, 99–100
Call option, 75, 732, 740–742, 881
Call premium, 581
Call provisions, 71
Candlestick charts, 530
Capacity utilization rate, effect on aggregate
  profit margin, 384
Cap agreements, 905–906
Capital appreciation, 39
Capital asset pricing model (CAPM), 205,
  214–222. *See also* Arbitrage pricing
  theory (APT); Capital market theory
  additional empirical tests, 226–228
  calculating systematic risk, 219–221
  comparing arbitrage pricing theory (APT),
    240
  conceptual development, 215–216
  multifactor models of risk and return,
    237–262
  security market line, 216–222
  summary of risk-return empirical results,
    228
Capital gain component, determination of,
  494–495
Capital gains
  realized, 43
  unrealized, 43
Capital market instruments, 70–72
Capital market line (CML), 208–210
  differential borrowing and lending rates,
    222–223

hedge fund performance, 916–918
heterogeneous expectations and planning
  periods, 225–226
investing with, 213–214
risk measure for, 212–213
risk-return possibilities with leverage,
  209–210
separation theorem and, 212
transaction costs, 224
zero-beta model, 223–224
Capital markets
  alternative efficient market hypotheses,
    153–154
  changes in conditions, 23–24
  conditions in, 16
  efficient, 151–179
Capital market theory, 205–214. *See also*
  Capital asset pricing model (CAPM)
  background, 206–207
  development, 207–210
  risk, diversification and the market
    portfolio, 210–213
Capital preservation, 39
Cash flow
  alternative measures, 295–296
  coverage ratios, 293–295
  financing activities, 268–269
  free, 270
  investing activities, 268
  measures of, 269
  operating activities, 268
  operating free, 467–470
  outstanding debt ratios, 295–296
  statement of, 267–268
  traditional, 270
  valuation theory, 323
Cash ratio, liquidity measure, 275–276
Cash reserves, 32
CDs. *See* Certificates of deposit
Center for International Business Conditions
  Research (CIBCR), 362
Center for Research in Security Prices
  (CRSP), 247
Certificates for automobile receivables
  (CARs), 596
Certificates of deposit (CDs), as a fixed-
  income investment, 70
Change in wealth, 5
Character-based risk factor models,
  extensions of, 250–251
Characteristic line
  calculating systematic risk, 219
  computing of, 221–222
Characteristic selectivity (CS) performance
  measure, 1010–1011
Chartered Financial Analysis (CFA)
  Institute, 926
Chicago Board of Trade (CBOT), 76
Chicago Board Options Exchange (CBOE),
  put-call ratio, 524
Chicago Mercantile Exchange (CME), 76
Chooser options, 884–885

Closed-end investment companies, 898–900

Coefficient of variation, 13, 29

Coincident indicators, 359

Coins and stamps, 79–80

Collar agreement, 755, 906–908

Collateralized debt obligations (CDOs), 597

Collateralized mortgage obligations (CMOs), 595

Collateral trust bonds, 594

Combined country investments, 64–69

Commingling of investment capital, 893

Commingled Real Estate Funds (CREFs), 84

Commission brokers, 108

Commodity-linked bull and bear bonds, 925–926

Common effect, 17

Common size income statement, 281

Common size statements, 273–274

Common stock, 73–74
    approaches to valuation, 326–327
    classifications, 73–74
    empirical duration for, 662–663
    funds, 77

Company analysis
    analyst conflicts of interest, 505
    economic, industry, and structural links, 456–457
    estimating earnings per share, 470–475
    estimating intrinsic value, 461–470, 486
    firm competitive strategies, 457–458
    focusing a strategy, 458–459
    global company and stock analysis, 505–506
    influences on analysts, 504–505
    internal performance, 476–477
    lessons from Peter Lynch, 460
    quarterly estimates, 478
    site visits and interviewing, 503
    versus stock valuation, 454–456
    SWOT analysis, 459–460
    tenets of Warren Buffett, 460–461
    value-added measures, 496–503
    when to sell, 503–504

Company earnings multiplier
    macroanalysis, 480
    microanalysis, 480
    Walgreen Co.'s, 481

Comparative analysis
    internal liquidity, 299
    ratios, 299–301

Competition, in industry analysis, 416–418

Competitive bid sales, 94

Competitive environment, 417

Competitive strategy, 417
    company analysis and, 457–458
    Walgreen Co.'s, 475–478

Completely diversified portfolio, 211

Completeness funds, portfolio construction technique, 542

Composite leading indicator index, 360–361

Composite stock-bond indexes, 139–142

Computer-Assisted Execution System (CAES), 117

Confidence index, 525

Confidence risk, 248

Confirmation bias, 171

Consistent investor actions, 637

Consolidated Quotation System (CQS), 116

Consolidation phase, investor life cycle, 34

Construction and development trusts, 78

Consumer Price Index for All Urban Consumers (CPI-U), 587

Consumer sentiment, business cycle and, 413

Contango, 772

Contingent, deferred sales loads, 901

Continuous market, 99–101

Contract price, forward, 729

Contrarian investment, 552

Contrary opinion rules, 522–524

Convenience yield, 772

Conversion factors, 774

Conversion parity price, bonds, 917

Conversion premium, preferred stock, 916

Conversion ratio
    bonds, 917
    preferred stock, 916

Conversion value, preferred stock, 916

Convertible bonds, 916–920

Convertible preferred stock, 916

Convertible securities, 915

Convexity, 647–652
    callable bonds, 652–655
    computation of, 651–651
    desirability, 649–650
    determinants, 650–651
    modified-duration-convexity effects, 651
    8 percent five-year bond selling to yield 6 percent, 675
    price-yield relationship for bonds, 647–649

Core-plus management strategies, bond portfolio management, 695–697

Corporate bonds, 584, 593–600
    interpreting quotes, 602–604

Corporate events, semistrong-form EMH, 166

Corporate insider trading, strong-form EMH, 166–167

Corporate profits, alternative estimates, 382

Corporate stocks, 95–96

Correlation coefficient, 89–90

Cost of carry, relationship between spot and forward prices, 771–772

Cost of equity, 327, 491

Counterparties, 729

Country (political) risk, 19, 420, 506

Coupon, bond price volatility determination, 640–641

Coupon reinvestment risk, bond portfolio management, 699

Covariance, definition, 89

Covariance and correlation, portfolio analysis, 187–189

Covariance of returns, portfolio analysis, 185–187

Covered interest arbitrage, 789–792

Credit analysis, 685–689
    high-yield (junk) bonds, 686–687
    investing in defaulted debt, 687
    models, 687–689

Credit balances, brokerage accounts, 523

Credit card receivables, 596

Credit default swap, 912

Credit-related swaps, 910–913

Crossover price, 616

Cross-sectional returns, semistrong-form EMH, 160–162

Currency, differences, 506

Currency forwards, 787–793

Currency futures, 787–793
    calculating an application, 792–793

Currency transactions
    interest rate parity and covered interest arbitrage, 789–792
    mechanics of, 787–789

Current consumption, 4

Current income, 39

Current ratio, liquidity measure, 275

Current yield, 613

Cushion bond, 684

Cushion spread, 709

Cyclical changes, 411

Cyclical companies, 455

Cyclical stocks, 455

Cyclic indicator approach, 359–363
    analytical measures of performance, 362
    categories, 359–360
    comparison with previous cycles, 362
    composite series and ratio of series, 360–361
    leading employment index, 363
    limitations, 362
    other leading indicator series, 362–363
    surveys of sentiment and expectations, 363

D

Dealer market (quote-driven market), 98, 116

Debentures, 71, 580

Debit balances, brokerage accounts, 525

Decimal pricing, 93

Declining trend channel, 521

Dedication, bond portfolio management, 698–699

Dedication with reinvestment, 698

Deep discount bonds, zero coupon bonds and, 597–598

Defensive companies, 455

Defensive competitive strategy, 457

Defensive stocks, 455

Deferred call provision, bond maturity, 581

Defined benefit pension plans, 56

Defined contribution pension plans, 56–57

Depreciation expense
  estimation of, 386–388
  industry, 433–434
Derivative investing
  adjusting put-call-spot parity for
      dividends, 749–750
  basic nature of, 736–738
  basic payoff and profit diagrams for call
      and put options, 740–742
  basic payoff and profit diagrams for
      forward contracts, 738–739
  creating synthetic securities using put-call
      parity, 748–749
  option profit diagrams, 743–745
  put-call-forward parity, 750–751
Derivative markets, 727, 728–736. *See also*
      Forward contracts; Futures contracts
  futures price quotations, 730–732
  interpreting option price quotations,
      734–735
  investing with, 735–745
  language and structure of forward and
      futures markets, 729–730
  language and structure of option markets,
      732–734
Derivatives
  embedded, 920–928
    commodity-linked bull and bear bonds,
        925–926
    dual currency bonds, 921–922
    equity-index linked notes, 922–925
    swap-linked notes, 927–928
  in portfolio management, 751–756
    alternative way to pay for protective put,
        755–756
    protecting portfolio value with put
        options, 753–755
    restructuring asset portfolios with
        forward contracts, 752–753
Designated market maker (DMM), 113
  specialist, 113–114
Developed markets around the world, 121–125
Diamonds, 80
Differentiation strategy, company analysis
      and, 458
Diffusion indexes, 362
Direction of change approach, earnings
      multiplier, 396
Display Book, NYSE, 115
Diversification
  elimination of unsystematic risk and, 211–212
  market portfolio, 210–213
  measurement of, 211
Dividend-bearing securities, valuing options
      on, 874–875
Dividend discount model (DDM), 327–329
  devaluation of, 352–353
  infinite period, 332–333
  present value of dividends, 461–466
  valuation model, 368–374
    reduced form, 419
Dividend growth rate, 371–374

Dividend-payout ratio
  earnings multiplier, 480
  estimation of, 394–395
  industry multiplier, 439
Dividends
  discount calculations, 425
  estimating growth for foreign stock, 348–349
  estimating growth rate, 393
  growth rate estimates, 463–464
  measure of cash flow, 327
  present value of, 461–465
Domestic diversification, 67
Dow Jones Industrial Average (DJIA), 36
  industry groups, 409
  price-weighted index, 129–131
Dow Jones World Stock Index, 136
Dow Theory, 526–527
Dreyfus Appreciation Fund (DGAGX),
      907–908
Dual currency bonds, 921–922
DuPont System, 282–284
  extended, 284–285
Duration
  for callable bonds, 652–655
  closed-form equation for calculation,
      798–799
  effective, 643, 656–659
  empirical, 643, 659–663
  Macaulay, 643–645, 655–663
  measures, 642–645
  modified, 643, 646–647, 655–663
  option-adjusted or call-adjusted, 654
  8 percent five-year bond selling to yield
      6 percent, 675
Dynamic true growth model, 495

E

EAFE index, 77, 250
Earnings momentum, 553–554, 556
Earnings multiplier, 336–339, 377–378
  comparing dividend payout rates, 480
  computation of, 486
  determinants of, 393
  estimation of, 395–398, 478–486
  expected growth rate, 484
  industry analysis, 428–440
  required rate of return, 480
  retail industry, 422
Earnings per share, 378–392
  estimating, 428, 470–475
  forecasting, 432
Earnings retention rate, 421
EBITDA (earnings before interest, taxes,
      depreciation, and amortization),
      270–271, 922
Economic news, semistrong-form EMH, 165
Economic series, stock prices and, 359
Economic value added (EVA), 496–498
  MVA relationship, 498
Economy
  company analysis and, 456

cyclical indicator approach, 359–363
  effects on interest rates, 626–627
  inflation, interest rates, and security
      prices, 364–367
  monetary policy, 364
  monetary variables, 363
  money supply and, 363–364
  security markets and, 358–359
Effective duration, 643, 656–659
  greater than maturity, 659
  putable bonds, 659
Efficient frontier, 197–198
  investor utility and, 199
Efficient market hypothesis (EMH), 151
  alternative, 153–154
  company analysis, 504
  fundamental analysis and, 172–174
  implications of, 172–176
  index funds and exchange-traded funds, 176
  portfolio management and, 174–176
  semistrong-form, 153
  strong-form, 153–154
  technical analysis, 520
  technical analysis and, 172
  tests and results, 154–170
  weak-form, 153
Electronic Communication Networks
      (ECNs), 107–108
Electronic Crossing Systems (ECSs), 108
Embedded option, bonds with, 652
Empirical duration, 643, 659–663
  common stock, 662–663
Employees Retirement Income Security Act
      of 1974 (ERISA), 925–926
Ending-wealth value, 614
Endowment funds, 57
Equipment trust certificates, 71, 594
Equity collars, 752. *See also* Collar agreement
Equity-index linked notes, 922–925
Equity instruments, 73–75
  special, 75–76
Equity-market indexes, price change
      correlations, 142
Equity options, 853–855
Equity portfolio management, 539–576.
      See also Portfolio management
  active, 548–559
    anomalies and attributes, 553–556
    fundamental strategies, 549–551
    momentum-based stock portfolios,
        556–558
    tax efficiency and active equity manage-
        ment, 558–559
    technical strategies, 552–553
  asset allocation strategies, 568–572
  passive, 541–548
    index portfolio construction techniques,
        542–543
    methods of index portfolio investing,
        545–548
    tracking error and index portfolio con-
        struction, 543–545

passive *versus* active, 540–541
    style analysis, 562–568
    value *versus* growth investing, 559–562
Equity risk premium, 369–370
    current estimate, 370–371
Equity swaps, 908–910
Equity trusts, 78
Equity turnover, 279–280
ERISA. *See* Employee Retirement and
    Income Security Act
Escalation bias, 171
Eurobond, 73
Eurodollar futures contract, mechanics, 778–779
European options, 733
Eurozone
    corporate bond market, 600–601
    government agency bonds, 592
    international bonds, 601
    sovereign bond market, 589
Event studies, semistrong-form EMH, 157,
    162–163
Excess (pure) profits, 491
Excess return form, 246
Exchange clearinghouse, 764
Exchange listing, semistrong-form EMH, 165
Exchange market makers, 113–115
Exchange markets, 108–119
    future trading techniques and exchange
        mergers, 117–119
    innovations for competition, 116–117
    membership, 108
    new trading systems, 115
    types of orders, 108–113
Exchange rate risk, 18, 420
Exchange-traded funds (ETFs), 75, 78, 128,
    545–548
    rational use in efficient capital markets,
        176
Expansion model, 494
Expectations hypothesis, 635–637
Expected earnings per share, 378–392
Expected growth rate, 345–348
    based on history, 347–348
    breakdown of ROE, 346–347
    calculation of, 389–392
    dividends for foreign stocks, 348–349
    earnings multiplier, 484
    estimation of, 421
    fundamentals, 345–346
Expected rate of inflation, 341–342
Expected rates of return
    calculating, 9–11
    estimation, 5
    individual investment, 183
    industry estimates, 439
    measuring the risk, 12–13
    portfolio of investments, 183–184
    relative measure of risk, 13
    risk-free asset plus risky portfolio, 207
    risky asset, 216
    standard deviation, 13
    variance for, 12

Expense ratio, 559
External (informational) efficiency, in a good
    market, 93

F

Fair game model, 153
Fama-French model, four-factor, 250
Fama performance measure, example of, 1005
Federal Home Loan Bank (FHLB), 70
Federal Home Loan Mortgage Corporation
    (Freddie Mac), 591
Federal Housing Administration (FHA), 70
Federal Land Banks (FLBs), 70
Federal National Mortgage Association
    (FNMA or Fannie Mae), 70
Fidelity's Magellan Fund (FMAGX), 254–255,
    257
Financial Accounting Standards Board
    (FASB), 266
Financial forwards, 773–793
Financial futures, 76, 98, 524, 773–793
Financial markets, U. S., relative size, 63
Financial ratios. *See also* specific ratio
    analysis of, 271–272
    computation of, 272–274
    limitations, 305
    relative, 271–272
    specific uses, 303–305
Financial risk, 18, 288–291, 419
Financial statements
    major, 266–271
    non-U.S., 301
    purpose of analysis, 271
    quality of, 301–302
    value of analysis, 302–303
Fixed exchange (FX) rate, 856
Fixed-income investments, 69–73
    style grid, 679
Flat trend channel, 521
Flexible portfolio (asset allocation) funds, 902
Floating-rate note (FRN), 900
Floor agreements, 905–906
Floor brokers, 108
FNMA. *See* Federal National Mortgage
    Association
Foreign competition, effect on aggregate
    profit margin, 385
Foreign currency options, 856–857. *See also*
    Currency
    Black-Scholes model, 877–878
Foreign equities, 74–75
Foreign exchange (FX) transactions, 787–788
Foreign exchange rates. *See also* Exchange
    rate risk
    technical analysis, 533–534
Foreign markets, technical analysis, 533–534
Foreign securities
    estimating dividend growth, 348–349
    expected growth rates for, 345–348
    expected required return for, 343–345
Foreign shares, 74–75

Forward contracts, 729
    basic payoff and profit diagrams, 738–739
    basic valuation concepts, 770–772
    comparing futures contracts, 767
    futures contracts and, 764–767
    option contract relationship, 745–751
    range (flexible), 887–889
    restructuring with asset portfolios,
        752–753
    unwind values, 770–771
Forward discount, 788
Forward market
    applications and strategies, 773–793
    currency in, 787–793
    currency quotations, 789
    futures markets and, 729–730
    spot markets and, 729
Forward premium, 788
Forward prices, spot price relationship,
    771–772
Forward rate agreements (FRA), 898–900
Forward rates
    calculating from spot rate, 633–635
    defined, 633
    implied, 800
401(k) plans, 45-46
Franchise factor, 498–499
Free cash flow to equity (FCFE), 327,
    374–377, 426–427
    constant growth model, 375–376
    two-stage growth model, 376–377
Free cash flow to the firm (FCFF), 467–470
Freely callable provision, bond
    maturity, 581
FT/S&P-Actuaries World Indexes, 134
Full replication, portfolio construction
    technique, 542
Fundamental analysis. *See also* Technical
    analysis
    EMH, 172–174
Fundamental risk, *versus* systematic
    risk, 20
Fusion investing, 171
Future consumption, 4
Futures contracts, 76, 730–731
    basic valuation concepts, 770–772
    comparing forward contracts, 767
    Eurodollar contract mechanics, 778–779
    forward contracts and, 764–767
    long-term interest rate, 773–778
    market to market, 763
    mechanics, 765–767
    options on, 858–859, 878
    short-term interest rate, 778–781
    stock index fundamentals, 782–783
    Treasury applications, 776–778
    unwind values, 770–771
Futures market
    applications and strategies, 773–793
    currency in, 787–793
    forward markets and, 729–730
Futures price quotations, 730–732

G

Generally accepted accounting principles (GAAP), 266
General obligation bonds (GOs), 592
Geometric mean (GM), 7–9
Gifting phase, investor life cycle, 34
Global bond market
  active investing: example, 693–695
  portfolio risk, 65–67
  returns, 64
  structure, 582–587
    participating issuers, 583–585
Global capital market, total investable assets in, 63
Global equity indexes, 133–137
Global equity market
  portfolio risk, 67–68
  returns, 64
Global funds, 905
Global government bond indexes, 139
Global industry analysis, 444–445
Global investments
  case for, 62–69
  choices, 69–80
Global mutual funds, 75
GM. See Geometric mean
GNMA. See Government National Mortgage Association
GOs. See General obligations bonds
Government associated organizations, Japanese bonds, 591–592
Government bonds, 94
Government National Mortgage Association (GNMA or Ginnie Mae), 70
Grinblatt-Titman performance measure, 1007–1010
Gross domestic product, estimation of, 380
Gross profit margin, 280
Growth companies
  actual returns above required returns, 491–492
  alternative growth models, 492
  analysis, 491–496
  definition, 491
  growth stocks and, 454–455, 492
  infinite period DDM and, 332–333
  long-run growth models, 493–495
  no-growth firm, 492–493
  in the real world, 495–496
Growth duration model, 499–503
Growth potential analysis, 297–299
  comparative, 301
  determinants, 297–298
  importance, 297
Growth stocks, 454–455
  growth companies and, 492

H

Harbor Capital Appreciation (HACAX) mutual fund, 561–562
Health insurance, 32

Hedge funds, 910–914
  characteristics, 911–912
  performance, 916–918
  risk arbitrage investing, 914–916
  strategies, 912–913
Hedge ratio, 763
  calculation of, 769–770
Hedge transaction, 728
Hedging
  basis and, 767–768
  calculating the optimal hedge ratio, 769–770
  duration-based approach to, 775–776
  forwards and futures, 767–770
  future funding commitment, 776
  understanding basis risk, 768–769
Hedging pressure theory, 638
High-yield bonds, 598–600
  credit analysis, 686–687
  indexes, 139
High yield/emerging market bonds, 584–585
Historical rates of return, 5–7
  realized, 9
  risk measures for, 13–14
HML (high minus low), 248
Holding period, 5
Holding period return (HPR), 5
Holding period yield (HPY), 6
  computation of, 9
Home or rental insurance, 32
Horizon matching, 707–708
Horizon (realized) yield, 617–618
  differential reinvestment rates, 619–620

I

IMF World Economic Outlook, 343
Immunization
  another view, 703–705
  bond portfolio management, 699–707
  classical, 705–707, 709
  contingent, 708–714
  interest rate risk and, 700
  mechanics, 700–703
  monitoring the immunized portfolio, 712–713
  portfolio rebalancing and, 722–723
Income bonds, 72
Income statement, 267
  common size, 273
  high-quality earnings, 302
Income taxes. See Taxes
Indenture, 71
Indenture provisions, bonds, 581
Index, definition, 128
Index funds, 77, 128
  rational use in efficient capital markets, 176
Indexing strategy
  bond portfolio management, 681
  enhanced, 695
Index mutual funds, 545–548

Indicator series, definition, 128
Individual Retirement Account (IRA), regular *versus* Roth, 46
Industry
  definition, 450
  influence on company analysis, 456
Industry analysis, 408–452
  characteristics to study, 450
  competition, 416–418
  cross-sectional performance, 408–409
  demographics, 413
  differences in risk, 410
  earnings estimate example, 436–437
  earnings multiple technique, 428–440
  with efficient capital markets, 173–174
  factors in, 450–451
  global, 444–445
  insights on industry ROAs, 451–452
  life cycle, 415–416
  lifestyles, 414
  performance of companies within an industry, 409–410
  performance over time, 409
  politics and regulations in, 414–415
  preparation of, 450–451
  process, 410–411
  rates of return, 418–427
    valuation with free cash flow to equity (FCFE) model, 426–427
    valuation with reduced form DDM, 419–425
  relative valuation approach, 428–440
  research, 410
  sources of information, 451
  technology, 414
Industry-economy relations, 428–429
Industry multiplier, 436–437
  comparing dividend payout rates, 439
  comparing expected growth rate, 439
  comparing required rates of return, 439
  macroanalysis, 436–437
  versus market multiplier, 439
  microanalysis, 437–438
  value and rate of return, 439–440
Inflation
  business cycle and, 412
  effect on aggregate profit margin, 384–385
  effects on investments, 50–51
  expected, 23
  expected rate, 16–17
  interest rates and, 364–366
Inflation rate, foreign securities, 344
Inflation risk, 248
Informationally efficient market, 152
Initial public offerings (IPOs), 95
  semistrong-form EMH, 163–165
Input-output analysis, industry, 428
Insolvency, prediction of, 305
The Institutional Investor, 407
Institutional investors, 55–59
Institutional theory, 638

Insurance, 32
Insurance companies, 57
Insured asset allocation, 572
Integrated asset allocation, 568–570
Interest coverage ratio, 293–294
Interest expense
    estimation of, 388, 434
    industry, 434
Interest-on-interest, 614
Interest rate anticipation, active bond
        management, 683–685
Interest rate collar, 906–908
Interest rate forwards, 773
Interest rate futures, 773–781
Interest rates
    business cycle and, 413
    determination of, 623–632
    duration measures, 642–645
    forecasting, 624–625
    fundamental determinants, 625–628
    impact of bond characteristics,
        627–628
    inflation and, 364–366
    parity in FX transactions, 789–792
    risk, 699–700
    stock prices and, 366–367
    swaps, 900–905
    term structure of, 628–632
    trading strategies and, 642
Intermarket Trading System (ITS),
        116–117
Internal liquidity (solvency) ratios,
        275–277
    cash ratio, 275–276
    comparative analysis, 299
    current ratio, 275
    quick ratio, 275
    receivables turnover, 276
Internal rate of return (IRR), pricing bonds,
        613
International bonds, 588, 600–601
    domestic, 73
    Eurozone, 600–601
    Japan, 601
    United Kingdom, 600
    United States, 601
International economics, business cycle and,
        413
International funds, 905
International leading indicator series, 363
Intrinsic value, definition, 733
Inventory turnover, cash conversion cycle,
        277–278
Investment, advisory opinions, 523
Investment Advisers Act of 1940, 925
Investment bankers, relationships, 96
Investment companies, 76–78, 892–935.
        See also Asset management
    breakdown by fund characteristics,
        904–905
    closed-end *versus* open-end, 898–901
    fund management fees, 902
    global, 905

organization and management, 897–906
    portfolio objectives, 902–904
    valuing shares, 898
Investment Company Act of 1940, 925
Investment-grade bond indexes,
        U. S., 139
Investment-grade securities, 587
Investment(s)
    alternative, 80–85
    constraints, 42–47
    decision process, 318
    defined, 4–5
    effects of taxes and inflation, 50–51
    legal and regulatory factors, 46–47
    low-liquidity, 79–80
    objectives, 39–42
    risk, 4
    unique needs and preferences, 47
Investment strategy
    bond portfolio, 679
    portfolio management, 36
Investor life cycle
    accumulation phase, 33–34
    benefits of investing early, 33
    consolidation phase, 34
    gifting phase, 34
    goals, 34–35
    insurance, 32
    long-term, high-priority goals, 35
    lower-priority goals, 35
    near-term, high-priority goals, 34–35
    spending phase, 34
Investors, 4
    individual life cycle, 32–35
    institutional, 55–59
    strategies over a lifetime, 32–34

J

January anomaly
    APT tests, 245
    return prediction studies, 159
Japan
    bank bonds, 600
    benchmark issue bonds, 589
    corporate bond market, 600
    government agency bonds, 591–592
    government bonds, 588
    international bonds, 601
Jensen Portfolio Performance Measure,
        992–994
Junk bonds, 77

K

k. *See* Required rate of return

L

Lagging indicators, 359–360
Land development, 78–79
Large-cap growth category, 133
Large cap value style category, 133

Leading employment index, 363
Leading indicators, 359
Leases
    capitalizing, 289–290
    consideration of, 289
    implied depreciation for assets, 291
    implied interest for assets, 290
Lehman Brothers U. S. Aggregate Bond
        (LBA), 677
Lehman Brothers U. S. Corporate Bond
        (LBC), 677
Lehman Brothers U. S. Government Bond
        (LBG), 677
Lending rates, CML, 222–223
Leveraged buyout (LBO), 919–920
Life-cycle phases, 33
Life insurance, 32
Life insurance companies, 57–58
Limited partnership, alternative asset classes,
        909
Limit-order processing, NYSE, 115
Limit orders, 109
Liquidity
    in a good market, 92
    needs, 42
    transaction costs and, 506
Liquidity preference (term premium)
        hypothesis, 637–638
Liquidity risk, 18, 419
    external market, 296–297
Long hedge, 767
Long-leading index, 363
Long position, 729
Long-run real growth rate of the
        economy, 15
Long-term, high-priority goals, 35
Long-term debt-cash flow ratio, 295
Long-term debt-total capital ratios, 292
Long-Term Equity Anticipation Securities
        (LEAPS), 855
Low-cost strategy, company analysis
        and, 458
Lower-priority goals, 35
Low-liquidity investments, 79–80
Low-load fund, 901
Low positive correlation, 65
Lynch, Peter, favorable attributes of firms,
        460

M

Macaulay duration, 643–645
    limitations of, 655–663
Macroeconomic-based risk factor models,
        247–248
Macromarket analysis, 358–367
Maintenance margin, 111
Management and advisory firm, 892
Management effect, portfolio return, 1020
Management fees, investment firms, 902
Margin, 76
Margin account, 765
Margin call, 111

Margin transactions, 109–112
Market
  characteristics, 92–93
  decimal pricing, 93
  definition, 92
  informationally efficient, 152
  securities, 93–94
Market-order processing, NYSE, 115
Market orders, 108–109
Market portfolio, 228–231
Market risk premium, in CAPM, 215–216
Market-timing risk, 248
Market value added (MVA), 496–498
  EVA relationship, 498
Markowitz Portfolio Theory, 182–199
  alternative measures of risk, 183
  efficient frontier, 197–198
  efficient frontier and investor utility, 199
  estimation issues, 197
  expected rates of return, 183–184
  standard deviation of a portfolio, 189–196
  three-asset portfolio, 196–197
  variance (standard deviation) of returns
    for a portfolio, 185–189
  variance (standard deviation) of returns
    for individual investment, 184
Matched-funding management strategies,
  697–708
Mean rates of return
  computing, 7–9
  dollar-weighted, 9
  portfolio of investments, 9
  single investment, 7–8
  value-weighted, 9
Mean reverting, 552
Merrill Lynch-Wilshire Capital Markets
  Index (ML-WCMI), 139, 142
Microeconomic-based risk factor models,
  248–250
Microvaluation analysis, 367–377
  world markets, 401–402
Midcap growth style category, 133
Midcap value style category, 133
Modified duration
  bond price volatility and, 643, 646–647
  limitations, 655–663
Modified-duration-convexity effects, 651
Money market funds, 76–77, 902
  calculating implied forward rates, 800
Money supply, 363–364
Money-weighted returns, 1022–1023
Morgan Stanley Capital International
  (MSCI) Indexes, 78, 134–135
Mortgage bonds, 71, 594
Mortgage pass-through securities, 594–595
Mortgage trusts, 78
Moving average, 526
  lines, 528–530
Multifactor models, 237–262
  estimating risk, 251–257
  in practice, 247–251
  risk estimation and, 246–257

Multiple discriminant analysis, credit
  analysis, 687
Multiple-indicator charts, 530–531
Multiplier effect, government spending, 320
Municipal bonds, 70–71, 94
  insurance, 593
  quotes, 606–607
  secondary markets for, 97–98
Mutual funds, 56, 76
  cash positions, 522–523
  comparing risk exposures, 254–257
  fund characteristics, 904–905
  global or international, 905
  objectives, 902–903
  open-ended investment company, 898
  organization and strategy, 905–906

N

NASDAQ market, 104
  information on bond prices, 601–602
  listing requirements, 105
  new trading systems, 115
  versus NYSE volume, 523–524
NASDAQ OTC Electronic Bulletin Board
  (OTCBB), 106
NASDAQ Quotation system, 104–106
NASDAQ Small Cap Market, 106
National Association of Insurance
  Commissioners (NAIC), 57–58
National Association of Securities Dealers
  Automated Quotation. *See* NASDAQ
National Association of Securities (NASD),
  602
National Bureau of Economic Research
  (NBER), 358
National Quotation Bureau (NQB) pink
  sheets, 106–107
National Securities Markets Improvement
  Act of 1996, 926
Near-term, high-priority goals, 34–35
Negative correlation, 65
Negative growth model, 494
Neglected firms, trading activity and, 161–162
Negotiated sales, 94
Net asset value (NAV), 898
Net fixed asset turnover, 279
Net present value (NPV), pricing bonds, 612
Net profit margin, 281
  estimate for company analysis, 475
  foreign stocks, 348
New issues, 95–96
New York Mercantile Exchange (NYM),
  Commodity Exchange (CMX), 765
New York Stock Exchange (NYSE), 101–102
  ADRs, 74
  changes, 118–119
  information on bond prices, 601–602
  versus NASDAQ, 523–524
  new trading systems, 115
Nikkei-Dow Jones Average, price-weighted
  index, 131

No-growth firm, 492–493
Noise traders, 171
No-load fund, 901
Nominal risk-free rate (NRFR), 15–17,
  368–369
Nominal yield, 613
Noncallable provision, bond maturity, 581
Nonlife insurance companies, 58
Nonrated bonds, 585
Nonrefunding provision, bond maturity, 581
Normal portfolio. *See* Benchmark portfolio
Notional principal, 898
NYSE. *See* New York Stock Exchange

O

Offensive competitive strategy, 457
130/30 strategy, 550
Open Automated Report Service (OARS),
  NYSE, 115
Open-end funds, load *versus* no-load, 901
Open-end investment companies, 898, 900
Operating efficiency ratios, 278–280
  equity turnover, 279–280
  net fixed asset turnover, 279
  total asset turnover, 278–279
Operating free cash flow, 327
Operating leverage, 288
Operating performance, comparative
  analysis, 299, 301
Operating profitability ratios, 280–286
  common size income statement, 281
  DuPont system, 282–283
  extended DuPont System, 284–286
  gross profit margin, 280
  net profit margin, 281
  operating profit margin, 280–281
  return on owner's equity, 282
  return on total invested capital, 281–282
Operating profit margin, 280–281
  industry forecast, 432
Optimum portfolio, 181, 199
Option-adjusted (call-adjusted) duration, 654
Option-adjusted spreads, 664–665
Option-based interest rate contracts,
  905–908
Option contracts, 851–895
  chooser options, 884–885
  covered call options, 881
  forward contract relationship, 745–751
  price quotations, 734–735
  profit diagrams, 743–745
  protective put options, 879–881
  put-call parity, 743, 747–749
  put-call-spot parity, 745–747
  range forwards, 887–889
  spreads, 885–887
  straddles, strips, and straps, 881–883
  strangles, 888–884
  terms, 732–733
  trading markets, 733–734
  valuation, 733, 859–873

American-style options, 875–876
basic approach, 859–860
binomial option pricing model, 865–867
Black-Scholes valuation model, 867–870, 872–873, 876–878
dividend-bearing securities, 874–875
estimating volatility, 871–872
European-style put options, 873–874
improving forecast accuracy, 860–864
Option markets, 732–734
conventions, 852–859
exchange-traded, price quotations for, 853–859
Option premium, 733
Options, 75
leverage and, 744–745
real, 928–931
trading strategies, 878–889
Options Clearing Corporation (OCC), 852–853
Order-driven market (pure auction market), 98, 116
Organization for Economic Cooperation and Development (OECD), 53
Overconfidence bias, 170–171
Overfunded plans, 56
Overreaction hypothesis, 552
Over-the-counter (OTC) market, interest rate agreements, 898–908
forward-based interest rate contracts, 898–905
option-based interest rate contracts, 905–908

P

Payback (break-even time), bonds, 917–919
Peer group comparison, evaluation of portfolio managers, 987–988
Pension funds, 56–57
Pension Protection Act of 2007, 925–926
Perpetuity, 325
Personal net worth, 33
Point-and-figure charts, 531–532
Point estimate, 9
Policy effect, portfolio return, 1020
Policy statement
asset allocation importance, 48–54
benchmark portfolio, 37
construction of, 47–48
evaluating portfolio performance, 36–38
input to, 38–47
investment constraints, 42–47
investment objectives, 39–42
investor goals, 36–37
need for, 36–38
other benefits, 38
portfolio management, 35
Politics and regulations, industry analysis and, 414–415
Portfolio, 5
benchmark, 37

characteristic line, 246
completely diversified, 211
construction, 36
continual monitoring, 36
optimum, 181, 199
risky, 207–208
standards for evaluating performance, 36–38
three-asset, 196–197
turnover, 558
Portfolio management. *See also* Equity portfolio management
definition of risk, 182
derivatives in, 751–756
efficient markets and, 174–176
equity, 539–576
flexible funds (asset allocation), 902
introduction, 181–204
minimum variance, 203–204
process, 35–36
requirements of portfolio manager, 986
risk aversion in, 182
with superior analysis, 174–175
without superior analysis, 175
Portfolio performance
attribution analysis, 1011–1014
example, 1011–1013
extensions, 1013–1014
bonds, 1018–1021
performance attribution, 1019–1021
returns-based measurement, 1018–1019
components, 1004–1005
composite measures, 987–998
application of, 998
comparison, 995–998
Information Portfolio Performance Measure, 994–995
Jensen Portfolio Performance Measure, 992–994
multiple risk factors, 1002–1003
potential bias for one-parameter measures, 1001
Sharpe Portfolio Performance Measure, 991–992
total sample results, 998–1001
Treynor's Composite Measure, 989
evaluating selectivity, 1004–1005
diversification, 1005
Fama performance measure, 1005
evaluation before 1960, 987
factors affecting performance measures, 1015–1018
global benchmark problem, 1016–1017
implications, 1017
required characteristics, 1017–1018
holdings-based, 1007–1011
characteristic selectivity (CS) measure, 1010–1011
Grinblatt-Titman performance measure, 1007–1010
market timing skills, 1014–1015
measures with downside risk, 1005–1007

Sortino and Sharpe comparison, 1006–1007
Sortino measure, 1005–1006
peer group comparisons, 987–988
relationship among performance measures, 1003
reporting investment performance, 1021–1025
performance presentation standards, 1023–1025
time-weighted and dollar-weighted returns, 1022–1023
requirements of portfolio manager, 986
Potential return, 711–713
Preferred habitat theory, 638
Preferred stock, 72–73
convertible, 916
valuation of, 325–326
Present consumption, 4
Present value of free cash flow to equity, 336, 461, 466–467
Present value of operating free cash flow, 467–470
Price/book value ratio, 339–340, 440, 487
Price/cash flow ratio, 339, 440, 487–488
Price continuity, in a good market, 92
Price/earnings/growth rate (PEG) ratio, 160–161
Price/earnings (P/E) ratio, 160, 337
Price for loanable funds, interest rate, 624
Price momentum strategy, 552, 556
Price risk, bond portfolio management, 699
Price/sales ratio, 340, 443, 488–489
Price-weighted index, 129–131
Price-yield curve, 611
Primary capital markets, 94–97
Principal (par value), bond, 580
Private equity investment, 918–924
development and organization, 919–920
investment process, 920–923
returns to, 923–924
Private placements, 94
Rule 144A and, 96–97
Professional money managers, strong-form EMH, 168–169
Promised yield to call (YTC), 616–617
computation, 617
Promised yield to maturity (YTM), 614–616
computation of, 615–616
Prospect theory, 170
Protective puts, 752
alternative way to pay, 755–756
Prudent Capital Management (PCM), 895–897
Pure auction market (order-driven market), 98, 116
Pure cash-matched dedicated portfolio, 698
Pure (excess) profits, 491
Pure rate of interest, 4
Pure time value of money, 4, 15
Pure yield pickup swap, 690–691
Putable bonds, 659

Put-call-forward parity, 750–751
Put-call parity, 743, 747–749
Put-call-spot parity, 745–747, 749–750
Put option, 75–76, 524, 732, 740–742
   European style, 873–874
   protecting portfolio value with, 753–755
   protective, 879–881

Q

Quadratic optimization, portfolio
   construction technique, 542
Quality (credit) spread, 627
Quarterly earnings reports, return prediction
   studies, 158–159
Quasi government and foreign government
   bonds, 583
Quick ratio, liquidity measure, 275
Quote-driven market (dealer market),
   98, 116

R

Range forwards, 887–889
Range of returns, measure of risk, 183
Rate anticipation effect, portfolio return,
   1020
Rates of change, 362
Rates of return
   abnormal, 157
   bonds, 582
   expected, 5, 157
   historical, 5–7, 13–14
   industry, estimation of, 418–427
   required. See Required rates of return
   risk-free, 206
Raw land, 78
Real estate, 78–79, 84–85
   direct investment, 78
Real estate investment trusts (REITs), 78
Realized (horizon) yield, 617–618
   differential reinvestment rates,
      619–620
Real options, 928–931
   company valuation with, 929–931
   defined, 929
Real risk-free rate (RRFR), 15, 341
   foreign, 343
   interest, 626–627
Receivables turnover, liquidity measure,
   276
Refunding issues, 581
Regional stock exchanges, 107
Registered competitive market makers
   (RCMMs), 108
Registered traders, 108
Regulation Fair Disclosure (REGFD), 168
Relative strength (RS) ratios, 530
Relative valuation ratio, 398–401, 428–440
Relative valuation techniques, 470–472
Relative variability, 13
Rental property, 79
Representativeness bias, 171

Required rates of return, 4, 14–25, 323, 343
   actual returns above, 491–492
   earnings multiplier, 480
   estimate, 464–465
   foreign securities, 343–345
   industry multiplier, 439
   relation of earnings multiplier, 393
   summary, 20
   summary of changes, 23–24
   valuation process, 341–350
Resistance levels, 528
Retention rates, foreign stocks, 348
Return on equity, 421
Return on owner's equity, 282
Return on total invested capital, 281–282
Return prediction studies, semistrong-form
   EMH, 157, 158–160
Returns. See Rates of return
Revenue bonds, 581
Reverse floating-rate contract, 927
Rising trend channel, 521
Risk. See also specific risk
   business, 17
   country (political), 19, 506
   different asset classes, 51–52
   exchange rate, 18
   financial, 18
   industry differences, 410
   market portfolio, 210–213
   in multifactor setting, 251–257
   in portfolio management, 181–182
   relative measure of, 13
   returns relationship, 20–24
   systematic, 19, 211
   unsystematic, 211
Risk analysis, 39–40, 286–297
   business risk, 286–287
   comparative, 301
   financial risk, 288–291
Risk arbitrage investing, 914–916
Risk aversion, 11, 181
   portfolio theory, 182
Risk-free asset, 206
   combining with a risky portfolio,
      207–208
   covariance with, 207
Risk-free investment, probability
   distribution, 10
Risk premium (RP), 4, 17
   foreign securities, 344–345
   portfolio theory and, 19
   proxies, return prediction
      studies, 158
   valuation theory and, 342–343
Risk-returns
   alternative investments, 80–85
   risk-free asset plus risky portfolio, 208
Risky asset, 207, 216–217
Risky investment, probability distribution,
   11, 12
Ross and Ross study
   empirical test of APT, 243–244
   extensions, 244

Rule 390, 117
Rule 415, 96
Rule 144A, private placements and, 96–97
Runs test, of independence in EHM,
   154–155
Russell 1000 Growth and Value Index, 563

S

Sales forecast, 429–432
   company, 473–475
Sales per share, forecasting, 428
Sales per share for a market series,
   estimation of, 380–382
Sales variability, 287
Sampling, portfolio construction technique,
   542
Savings account, as a fixed-income
   investment, 70
Seasoned equity issues, 95
Secondary equity markets, 100–108
Secondary financial markets, 97–101
   bonds, 97
   importance of, 97
Sector rotation strategy, 550
Secured bonds, 71
Secured (senior) bonds, 580
Securities
   convertible, 915
   foreign, rates of return, 64
   U. S., rates of return, 64–
Securities Act of 1933, 925
Securities Exchange Act of 1934, 925
Securities Industry and Financial Markets
   Association (SIFMA), 582
Securities markets
   global consolidation, 119
   organization of, 93–94
   world, 119
Securities valuation. See Valuation
Securitized/collateralized bonds, 583–584
Security analysts, strong-form EMH,
   167–168
Security-market indexes, 127–148
   comparison over time, 142–143
   computational procedure, 129
   factors in constructing, 128–129
   returns and risk, 143
   sample, 128–129
   weighing sample members, 129
Security-market line (SML), 21
   in CAPM, 216–222
   changes in the slope, 21–23
   estimated rates of return, 217
   heterogeneous expectations and planning
      periods, 225–226
   movement along, 21–24
   transaction costs, 224
   undervalued and overvalued assets,
      217–219
Segmented market hypothesis, 638
SelectNet, NASDAQ, 115
Self-attribution bias, 171

Semistrong-form efficient market hypothesis, 153
  adjustment for market effects, 156–158
  predicting cross-sectional returns, 160–162
  results of event studies, 162–166
  results of return prediction studies, 158–160
  summary, 166
Semivariance, measure of risk, 183
Separation theorem, CML and, 212
Serial obligation bond, 580
Sharpe Portfolio Performance Measure, 991–992
  comparative measures, 992
Short hedge, 767
Short sales, 112–113
Simple growth model, 493–494
Single-index market model, 246
Sinking fund, 581
Size effect, 161
Small Business Investment Companies (SBIC), 919
Small-cap growth style category, 133
Small-cap value style category, 133
Small-firm effect, 244–245
Small-Order Execution System (SOES), NASDAQ, 115
SMB (small minus big), 248
Socially responsible investment (SRI) funds, 133
Soft dollars, 928
Sortino measure, 1005–1006
Sovereign bonds, 583
Specialists, 113–115
  functions, 114
  income, 114–115
  U. S. markets, 113–114
Special orders, 109
Special situations, private equity transaction, 920
Specific estimate approach, earnings multiplier, 396–397
Speculative bonds, 587
Speculative companies, 455
Speculative stocks, 455
Spending phase, investor life cycle, 34
Split bond rating, 586
Spot market, currency quotations, 789
Spot prices, forward price relationship, 771–772
Spot rate, 629–632
  calculating forward rates from, 633–635
Spreads, 885–887
S&P (Standard & Poor's) 500, 76
Standard deviation. See also Variance, computation
  computation, 28–29
  expected rate of return, 13
  for a portfolio, 189–196
  risk-free asset plus risky portfolio, 207–208
Standard deviation of expected returns
  measure of risk, 183
  returns for a portfolio, 185–189
  returns for individual investment, 184

Static yield spreads, 663–665
Stock exchange specialists, strong-form EMH, 167
Stock index arbitrage, 782
  futures valuation and, 783–787
  implementing a strategy, 784–787
  program trading, 785
Stock index futures, 781–787
  application, 787
  fundamentals, 782–783
  valuation and index arbitrage, 783–784
Stock index options, 855–856
  Black-Scholes model, 876–877
  quotations, 856
Stock market analysis, 357–358
Stock market anomalies, APT and, 244–245
Stock market earnings multiplier
  estimation of, 392–401
  industry multiplier versus, 439
Stock-market indexes, 129–137, 146–148
  foreign, 533
Stock option, quotations, 854
Stock price tree
  creating, 861–862
  expanding, 863–864
  valuing in other subintervals, 862–863
Stocks. See also specific type
  cyclical, 455
  defensive, 455
  growth, 454–455
  speculative, 455
  value, 456
Stock split studies, semistrong-form EMH, 163
Stock valuation, versus company analysis, 454–456
Stock valuation models, 303–304
Stop buy order, 109
Stop loss order, 109
Straddles, 881–883
Strangles, 883–884
Strap, 883
Strategic asset allocation, 570
Striking price, 75
Strip, 883
Strong-form efficient market hypothesis (EMH), 153–154
  conclusions, 169–170
  corporate insider trading, 166–167
  professional money managers, 168–169
  security analysts, 167–168
  stock exchange specialists, 167
Structural changes, influence on company analysis, 456–457
Structural economic changes, 411
  alternative industries and, 413–415
Style analysis
  grid, 563, 565
  overview, 562–568
  two mutual funds, 566
  value and growth portfolios, 563564

Style indexes, 133
Subordinated bonds, 71
Subordinate (junior) debentures, 580
Substitution swap, 691–692
Super Dot, NYSE, 115
Support levels, 528
Sustainable growth potential, 297
Swap contracting extensions, 908–913
Swap-linked notes, 927–928
Swaps
  credit-related, 910–913
  equity index-linked, 908–910
Swap spreads, interest rates, 901–904
SWOT analysis, in company analysis, 459–460
Synthetic fixed-rate funding with Eurodollar strip, 779–780
Synthetic risk-free portfolio, 859
Synthetic securities, 748–749
Systematic risk, 19, 81–82, 128, 420
  versus fundamental risk, 20
  return and, 226–228
  stability, 226

T

Tactical asset allocation, 550, 570–572
Tax efficiency, 558
Taxes
  average rate, 43
  effects on investments, 50–51
  investment planning concerns, 43
  marginal rate, 43–44
Tax-exempt bonds, yield adjustments for, 621
Tax rate
  estimation of, 389
  industry, 434, 436
Tax swap, 692–693
T-bill-Eurodollar yield spread, 525
T-bills. See Treasury bills
Technical analysis. See also Fundamental analysis
  advantages, 519–520
  bond markets, 534–535
  challenges to, 520–521
  challenges to trading rules, 521
  contrary opinion rules, 522–524
  EMH, 172
  foreign markets, 533–534
  industry analysis and, 414
  momentum indicators, 525–526
  stock price and volume techniques, 526–533
  underlying assumptions, 518–519
Term bond, 580
Term to maturity, 610
  bonds, 580
Third market, 107
Thomas J. Herzfeld Advisors, closed-end funds, 900
Three-asset portfolio, 196–197

Time horizon, 42–43
Time horizon risk, 248
Time premium, definition, 733
Time-series analysis
 estimating future performance, 272
 return prediction studies, 158–160
Time-series plots, retail industries, 423–424,
 428, 443–444
Time-weighted returns, 1022–1023
Tokyo Stock Exchange, Nikkei Average, 76
Total asset/equity ratio, foreign stocks,
 348–349
Total asset turnover, 278
 foreign stocks, 348
Total debt-total capital ratios, 293
Total return, 39
Total return swap, 910
Tracking error
 indexing strategy, 681
 index portfolio construction and, 543–545
 in information ratio measure, 994
Trade Reporting and Compliance Engine
 (TRACE), 602
Trade-through rule, 117
Trading effect, portfolio return, 1020
Trading implications, term structure,
 638–639
Trading regulations, changes, 117–118
Trading rules, technical
 challenges to, 521
 indicators, 521–522
Trading systems, 98
 new, 115
 strategies for interest rates, 642
Trading turnover, 296
Transaction cost
 in a good market, 93
 liquidity and, 19, 506
Treasury bills (T-bills), 76–77, 94, 587
 Eurodollar yield spread, 525, 780–781
 three-month, 16
Treasury bonds, 94
 contract mechanics, 773–775
 futures applications, 776–778
 quotes, 604–606
 secondary markets for, 97–98
Treasury inflation-protected securities
 (TIPS), 587–588, 604–606
Treasury notes, 94, 773–775
 futures applications, 776–778
Treasury securities, 70
Treynor Composite Performance Measure,
 989–991
 comparative measures, 989–991
T. Rowe Price, private advisory services and
 publicly traded funds, 893–894
T. Rowe Price's Mid-Cap Value Fund
 (TRMCX), 254, 256–257
T. Rowe Price Value (TRVLX) mutual fund,
 561–562
12b-1 plan, 901
Two-state option pricing model, 865

U

Underfunded plans, 56
Underwriting, organization structure, 95
United Kingdom
 government agency bonds, 592
 government bonds, 589
 international bonds, 601
 pound sterling corporate bond market, 600
United States
 corporate bond market, 594
 government agency bonds, 589–591
 government agency securities, 70
 government bonds, 587–589
 international bonds, 601
 Treasury and agency bond quotes,
  604–606
 Treasury securities, 70
Unit labor cost, effect on aggregate profit
 margin, 384
Unlisted trading privileges (UTP), 107
Unsecured bonds (debentures), 580
Unweighted index, 131–132

V

Valuation
 alternative instruments, 324–336
 bonds, 324–325
 common stock, 326–327
 differences, 506
 discounted cash flow approach, 327
 discounted cash flow techniques,
  328–332
 dividend discount model, 328–329
 earnings multiplier approach, 377–378
 estimating expected earnings per share,
  378–392
 estimating stock market earnings
  multiplier, 392–401
 expected growth rates, 345
 flexibility, 928–931
 forward and futures contracts, 770–772
 free cash flows to equity, 336
 infinite period model, 331–332
 multiple-year holding period, 330–331
 one-year holding period, 329–330
 operating free cash flows, 335
 options contracts, 859–878
 preferred stock, 325–326
 price/book value ratio, 440, 487
 price/cash flow ratio, 440, 487–488
 price/sales ratio, 443, 488–489
 relative techniques, 327–328, 336–341, 461,
  470, 490–491
 sales, 473–475
 stock index futures, 783–784
 summary of industry/market ratios, 443
 temporary supernormal growth with,
  333–335
Valuation analysis, active bond management,
 685

Valuation process, 318–322
 overview, 318–319
 three-step, 319–320, 322
  company analysis, 321–322
  industry influences, 321
Valuation theory, 322–324
 investment decision process, 323–324,
  486
 required rate of return, 323, 341–343
 stream of expected returns, 323
Value-added measures, 496–503
 economic value added (EVA), 496–498
 franchise factor, 498–499
 growth duration model, 499–503
 market value added (MVA), 496–498
Value Line Index, 76
Value Line (VL), enigma, 167–168
Value stocks, *versus* growth stocks, 456
Value-weighted index, 131
Variable principal redemption (VPR)
 securities, 922–925
Variable-rate notes, 597
Variance
 computation, 28–29
 expected rate of return, 12
 measure of risk, 183
 returns for a portfolio, 185–189
 returns for individual investment, 184
Venture capital, private equity transaction,
 919
Volatility
 adjusting measures for growth, 287–288,
  313
 in options contracts, 871–872
Volatility Index (VIX), 872
Volume changes, 527–528

W

Walgreen Co.
 alternative present value of cash flow
  models, 462
 balance sheet, 267
 common size statements, 273–274
 competitive strategies, 475–478
 components of growth, 299
 consolidated statement of income, 479
 earnings multiplier for, 481
 estimates of intrinsic value, 486
 expected growth rate, 485
 extended DuPont system analysis, 286
 financial risk ratios, 483
 internal performance, 476–477
 mean price/earnings ratio, 480
 net profit margin, 478
 operating lease obligations, 312
 operating leverage, 316
 price/book value ratios, 487–488
 price/cash flow ratios, 489
 price/sales ratios, 490
 profit margins and component expenses,
  477